TRANS BODIES, TRANS SELVES

TRANS BODIES, TRANS SELVES | A RESOURCE FOR THE TRANSGENDER COMMUNITY

Edited by

Laura Erickson-Schroth

Purchased With Funds From
The Bequest Of
Paul O. Blanchette

OXFORD
UNIVERSITY PRESS

OXFORD

UNIVERSITY PRESS

Oxford University Press is a department of the University of
Oxford. It furthers the University's objective of excellence in research,
scholarship, and education by publishing worldwide.

Oxford   New York
Auckland   Cape Town   Dar es Salaam   Hong Kong   Karachi
Kuala Lumpur   Madrid   Melbourne   Mexico City   Nairobi
New Delhi   Shanghai   Taipei   Toronto

With offices in
Argentina   Austria   Brazil   Chile   Czech Republic   France   Greece
Guatemala   Hungary   Italy   Japan   Poland   Portugal   Singapore
South Korea   Switzerland   Thailand   Turkey   Ukraine   Vietnam

Oxford is a registered trademark of Oxford University Press
in the UK and certain other countries.

Published in the United States of America by
Oxford University Press
198 Madison Avenue, New York, NY 10016

Library of Congress Cataloging-in-Publication Data
Trans bodies, trans selves : a resource for the transgender community / edited by Laura Erickson-Schroth.
pages cm
ISBN 978-0-19-932535-1 (paperback)
1. Transgender people.   2. Transgenderism.   3. Gender identity.   I. Erickson-Schroth, Laura.
HQ77.9.T714 2014
306.76'8—dc23
2014007921

9 8 7 6 5 4 3
Printed in the United States of America
on acid-free paper

CONTENTS

SECTION 1
WHO WE ARE

SECTION 2
LIVING AS OURSELVES

ACKNOWLEDGMENTS

This project would not have been possible without our professional editor, Celeste LeCompte, who agreed to work on this book practically as a probono project because she believed so strongly in it. Jonah A. Siegel and A. Robin Williams were core organizers for this project when it was in its infancy. We also received assistance very early on from Scott Edelstein, who helped to shape our proposal to publishers. One of the most enthusiastic responses to our inquiries came from Dana Bliss of Oxford, who continued to send excited e-mails almost weekly throughout the process of putting together this book. Probono legal advice came from Maura Wogan (Frankfurt, Kurnit, Klein, and Selz) and Victoria S. Belyavsky, Jesse M. Brush, Adam E. Fleisher, Jennifer Kroman, Garth Spencer, and Stephanie Atwood (Cleary, Gottlieb, Steen, and Hamilton). On a personal note, the editor would like to thank her partner, Amanda Rosenblum, for her extensive work on the editing and shaping of this book, as well as organization of book-related events and the creation of the book's nonprofit entity. In addition to participating in this process, she was patient through times when the work did not stop at home.

I was 12 years old when I first opened my mother's copy of *Our Bodies, Ourselves (OBOS)*. I was fascinated by just about everything I read. I flipped through for interesting photos and pored over diagrams. Among my favorite parts were the quotes that appeared on nearly every page, representing the voices of hundreds of women. In some cases, I yearned to have their experiences; in others, I hoped I would never have to face them. I was comforted by all of the stories, knowing that they came from real people.

A few years ago, I bought a copy of an early edition of *OBOS* in a used bookstore. It was older than the one my mother owned. (Though she had seen this edition, she had been good at updating her collection.) Published in 1973, it was yellowing and thinner than the newer editions I was used to. On the cover was a photo of an older woman and a younger woman holding up a sign together that read, "Women Unite."

The 1973 edition of *OBOS* was billed as "by and for women"—a strikingly radical proposition then. At a time when over 90% of physicians were men, and only a small number of states allowed legal abortions, it was an extremely daring and exciting thing to publish a book in which women taught other women about their bodies, their sexuality, and their rights. This wasn't the stuff of polite conversation. It was about abortion rights, rape, intimate partner violence, and lesbian and bisexual identity. From the very beginning, *OBOS* questioned the medical establishment. If male doctors would not allow women access to information about their bodies, they would get that information, and they would share it with other women. Childbirth, once clouded in secrecy, would be a two-page photo spread, so that women could see just what they were in for if they decided to make that choice. To the writers of *OBOS*, it was clearly a choice. They believed that no one had the right to tell women whether or when to have children.

Trans Bodies, Trans Selves (TBTS) is written by and for transgender and gender nonconforming people (although we hope that many allies will read it as well!). We have endeavored to make it as radical as its predecessor. Where *OBOS* challenged the medical establishment's monopoly on knowledge about women's bodies, *TBTS* shares trans health information and implores medical providers to educate themselves about trans bodies. Where the original questioned psychiatry's condemnation of lesbian identity, we fight the similar treatment of transgender identity. As a psychiatrist, one of my personal goals for activism is to help lead the fight against pathologization of trans identities.

Not all feminists are trans allies, but I believe they should be. I wasn't sure what to expect when I first reached out to Judy Norsigian and Wendy Sanford, current board members of *OBOS*. Immediately I received mountains of enthusiasm for our new book, as well as indication that they were working hard to update the latest edition of theirs to include information on transgender and genderqueer identities. They even printed a story about our project in their most recent book. It was invigorating to see that they understood that all of our fates are linked.

In 1973, the cover price of *OBOS* was $2.95. Our book is more expensive, but we have fought to keep it affordable by today's standards. As we began writing this book, we also started a nonprofit organization with the immediate goal of disseminating the book to as many people and organizations as possible, regardless of ability to pay. All author proceeds from the book will go toward Trans Bodies, Trans Selves, Inc. Our hope is that we will publish, with your help, many more editions of this book, in many countries and in many languages, and the work of our organization will expand to include additional education around transgender issues.

In the lower right corner of the back cover of the 1973 edition of *OBOS*—the place where the reader finds, literally, the book's last words—there is a simple sentence: "Please share this book with others." After 40 years, this is still the most important message I can send. Please share this book with others.

Laura Erickson-Schroth, MD, MA

ABOUT THIS BOOK

This book does not need to be read from cover to cover. It is meant to be flipped through, referenced, picked up, and put down. Chapter 1, "Our Many Selves," provides an overview of terminology and concepts that may be useful before delving into other chapters. When terms are introduced for the first time, they appear in **bold** and are defined in the glossary.

One of the main goals of this book is to provide as many viewpoints as possible. Our authors come from varied backgrounds, with expertise in law, health, culture, and policy. They wrote text for their chapters collaboratively and worked with multiple knowledgeable advisors. Most chapters appear in sequence within the book. There are, however, two chapters (Media and Global Leaders) that instead appear as series of spotlights throughout the book.

Short pieces by hundreds of contributors add personal experiences and opinions to each chapter, demonstrating the diversity of our communities. Quotes in italics are taken from an online survey where over 3,000 people across the globe participated in answering questions about their lives. We also held forums in cities across the United States and Canada, to gather information on the kinds of resources community members wanted. The book is heavily illustrated, as pictures can often say more than words. We have taken liberties with English grammar at times, especially when it is gendered. For example, parts of the book use the third-person "they" where other books might use the phrase "he or she."

An effort was made to select short pieces, quotes, and art that represent the diversity of trans communities. We have inevitably failed at this goal. Most of the authors live in the United States or Canada. Many are middle or upper class, and many are white. There are stories that are not told here—voices that are not heard. If one of these voices is yours, please consider completing our online survey or sending your suggestions for the next edition of this book to info@transbodies.com.

This book is the beginning. We hope it will spark interest, enthusiasm, and debate. We will continue to seek out the perspectives of those most marginalized as we approach the production of future editions. More stories can only enrich our lives.

THROWING OUR VOICES

AN INTRODUCTION

Jennifer Finney Boylan

ONE EVENING IN JUNE OF 2006, I unexpectedly found myself stranded at a Kentucky hotel that was, at that same moment, hosting something called the National Ventriloquists' Association Convention. As I settled into the hotel bar after supper, the place was erupting with puppeteers, marionettists, and voice-throwers of every stripe. Many of the conventioneers were gathered at a long table eating pizza, wooden figures at their sides. Others swayed to the music of Elvis Presley on the dance floor, arms draped around their dummies.

Later, a dude at the bar tried to pick me up, using something he called "the muffle voice." It was, I admit, vaguely flattering. But I declined my suitor's generous offer, being married then, as now, to the woman who had wed me as a man in 1988 and to whom I had stayed married, even as I emerged as trans and became female 12 years later. Had he—or anyone that night—asked me about the particulars of my marriage, demanding an explanation for its seemingly unfathomable mysteries, I might have said, *It's because we love each other.* And I would have said this in my own voice.

But no one asked. Instead, I lingered happily over that pint of Guinness and observed the world around me, a world that you must admit contains no shortage of miracles and wonder.

Just shy of midnight, there was a bar brawl. Cartoon voices were raised in anger; a dummy flew through the air. The fellow at my side (the same one who had tried to pick me up using his muffle voice) summarized the trouble for me in a single phrase. "It's always the same story," he said. "A couple of comedians in a room is a conversation. But a couple of ventriloquists is an argument."

Since 2003, I've been an itinerant author, devoted, in my own awkward fashion, to shining a light on civil rights for transgender people using the medium of story. I've spoken to groups of stunned people who apparently had never laid eyes upon a trans person before; I've also addressed young scholars so sophisticated about gender issues that my homely little stories and fables were greeted with exhausted eye-rolling and a chorus of disappointed, audible groans. I've listened to what must be more than 5,000 different trans people by now, as well as the sons and daughters, fathers and mothers, and the many others that love them. In listening to them, I've often been put in mind of a phrase my mother liked to say: "It is impossible to hate anyone whose story you know." There are lots of different stories out there, told by so many different people, each of them trying, sometimes against long odds, to find their voices.

The more trans people I talk to, in fact, the clearer it is to me that we are all being guided by different stars. And some of us aren't being guided at all; we're just walking forward, one foot after another, trying to survive each day the best we can. I keep returning to the expression I heard at that Kentucky bar: a group of comedians is a conversation; a group of ventriloquists is an argument. In my head, I rewrite it this way: a group of gay people is a conversation; a group of trans people is an argument.

At the heart of our disagreements are the many differences in our experiences. Among transgender folks, our experiences vary wildly from each other not least because of differences in class, race, education, sexuality, marital status, politics, and social privilege. It can truly be disheartening, sometimes, to encounter a person who feels some of the things that you have felt, only to discover, at that same moment, that the two of you hardly agree on anything at all, and that the subject about which you most disagree is the one thing you supposedly have in common.

If ours is an occasionally contentious community, it's also a community that is filled with breathtaking courage and compassion. The fact that many trans people are among the most disenfranchised and at-risk individuals in the world also means that we are frequently called upon to watch each other's backs, to exhibit a kind of loyalty and solidarity and courage that can only leave one stunned and amazed at the resilience of the human spirit.

In preparation for writing this introduction, I interviewed the youngest trans person I know—15-year-old Nicole Maines—and her father, Wayne, a man who at one time was about as conservative as an American man can be, and who has now become one of the country's leading advocates for trans youth. "You have to love your child," Wayne Maines said to me. "Everybody wants the same thing. They want to be loved, they want to be respected, they want to have a bright future like everybody else. Just let people be who they need to be."

"I think I see the dark corners of the world a lot easier now," Nicole said, concerning the trouble she'd experienced at her middle school. "But at the same time, I've been exposed to this whole network of allies and supporters. And so, for every dark corner, there is a wall that the sun is shining on."

"If I'm on a mission for anything," Wayne said, "it's to make sure my daughter has the same rights and the same opportunities as her classmates." His eyes welled up, and tears rolled down his cheek. "I get emotional. But we have to let go of what we think we're supposed to be. That's why we're here on earth. You adjust."

The wide range of opinions and insights on trans experience can also be seen as a sign of health, the mark of a gender culture that is flourishing, abounding in a variety of ways of being. If I've met over 5,000 trans people, I've probably heard 5,000 different explanations of what it means to be trans, and what our defining experiences are.

It's worth reviewing what some of our disagreements are, here, at the outset of a volume that we hope will celebrate the many, many different ways there are of being trans. But as a first principle, it might be worth suggesting that the single most important element for understanding gender variance—or anything, for that matter—is love.

I came out to my own mother in 2002. At the time, she was well into her eighties—a conservative, deeply religious Republican woman from the Main Line of Philadelphia, whose name, incredibly, was Hildegarde. In coming out to Mom, at the age of 43, I feared I would be rejected, that I would have to proceed in the world without her.

Instead, in response to my confession, she took me in her arms and wiped the tears from my cheeks. "Love will prevail," she said, and then quoted First Corinthians. "Faith, hope, and love abideth these three. But the greatest of these is love."

Mom didn't know what it meant to be transgender—a term that wasn't even coined until she was in her seventies. But she knew that the thing I needed at that moment, both as her child and as a human, was love, and she did not pause in embracing me, even before she came—as she did, in the years that followed—to more intimately understand the issues.

Let's take a look at some of the different ways there are of being trans.

Some of us see ourselves as people born with a unique birth defect, one that can be "cured" by the intervention of the medical profession, and think of that journey in terms of physical transition.

Some of us see ourselves as people who want to celebrate the fantasy aspects of gender, who want to enjoy the sense of escape and joy and eros that embracing an alter ego sometimes provides.

Some of us see ourselves as people who reject the medical community and who are less interested in winding up at one gender destination or another than in the journey itself, a voyage that may or may not have a clear end point.

Some of us hope to free ourselves from the binary poles of gender, want a personal and political liberation from the tyranny of culturally defined gender markers, and wish to express ourselves as we please, anywhere along the wide spectrum.

Some of us go through medical transition and then assume a new identity, and in so doing—to use the word trans people use—"go stealth," meshing as seamlessly as possible with society post transition. Sometimes post-op stealth-goers no longer even identify as trans and look back at their days in their former sex in the same way a naturalized citizen might look back at a country in which they were born and then fled.

Some of us see our experience as being best understood through scholarly theory. For some of us, gender theory not only provides us with language for thinking about ourselves; it places our quest for self within the long tradition of philosophical inquiry.

Some of us are still seeking for the right words to describe ourselves, and for the best way to frame the discourse regarding our people. Some of us are not even particularly comfortable with the term "transgender."

Some of us have found that our sense of self has changed over time. Some of us, to be sure, "always knew" what we needed and who we needed to be. For others, that sense of identity has emerged only slowly, or morphed over time, or even fluctuated daily like the tides. Some of us don't have a single word for what we are, for what we feel, or what we need, and view the lack of a single label for our gendered selves as a fortune, not a curse.

With all this wide range of opinion, it's no wonder men and women who wish to be our allies—not to mention members of the trans community themselves—can find themselves perplexed.

There are so many, many ways of being us.

If we know anything, it's that trans identity and trans experience are a work in progress, a domain in which the discourse itself is still in a state of evolution and growth.

Which is why, when people ask me, "How can we help?" I sometimes think the most useful answer may be the one my mother suggested: Let love prevail.

Or, to put it another way: Open your heart, and see what happens.

In this book you'll find a set of resources for, and an archive of testimony about, the many different kinds of experiences that happen in the lives of transgender people and the people that love them. You will likely find the wide range of those experiences, cultural and medical and political, staggering. There will be plenty of stories and reflections that seem contradictory, which seem to belie the thought that any set of human aspirations so divergent from each other could all be thought of as part of a single phenomenon.

And yet, it is this abundance that is the strength of our movement. How could we ever expect that a community as rich and diverse as our own would ever have a single truth?

It is only in speaking our truth—and in learning the truth of others—that we can ever hope to be free.

Early in my own transition, back in 2000, I used to make what I called "milk runs" en femme to towns where I did not know anyone, to see how well I could pass in the world as a woman. It was a frightening prospect, at a time when no one at my place of work—Colby College, in Waterville, Maine, where I was a professor of English—knew I was emerging as trans. I was an awkward, frightened soul back then, wearing too much makeup, teetering in heels I did not know how to walk in, crowned by a wig that could have doubled, in its spare time, as a sparrow's nest. How I found the courage to drive from my home down to Freeport, Maine, to try on corduroy skirts at L.L. Bean, I cannot tell you. I remember the mantra I used to have back then, though. I used to whisper it to myself as I walked through the world: *Be brave. You are trying to learn something.*

One day, I found myself trying on jeans in The Gap. It was clear from the expression on the saleswoman's face that I was not "passing"—nowhere near it. I told myself to be brave, but it wasn't much help. The thing I was learning—and not, as it turned out, for the last time—was how hard all of this was going to be, and how very difficult it was going to be for me to find my voice in the world that now lay before me.

As I exited the store, I passed a woman and her daughter, who were on their way in. The little girl looked at me, with my curious makeup and my unfortunate wig, and she turned to her mother.

"Momma," she said, in a voice of astonishment. "Who was *that*?"

"That, honey," the woman replied to her daughter. "That was a human being."

Belgrade Lakes, Maine
January 1, 2013

INTRODUCTION TO MEDIA SPOTLIGHT SERIES

In a series of spotlights throughout the book, Dallas Denny and Jamison Green introduce us to some of their favorite books and films with gender nonconforming characters, and discuss the ways in which trans communities are portrayed in the media.

DALLAS

When I was in my early teens, I could find absolutely nothing about transgender issues. Nada. Zip. There were no zines, blogs, vlogs, Web sites, or radio shows. There was no Internet—in fact, the only computers were housed in special air-conditioned rooms in businesses and universities. Libraries and bookstores offered no help. I was alone.

The first two books I identified (in 1964, at age 14) were in the public library in Murfreesboro, Tennessee. One was in the reference section, which meant I would have to ask the librarian for it—AND THEN SHE WOULD KNOW AND MY LIFE WOULD BE OVER! The other was in general collections but wasn't on the shelves. I checked periodically all through high school, and it never appeared. I suspect it was stolen either by someone very much like me or by someone who wanted to eradicate people like me.

I was in my twenties when I chanced across two books about transsexualism. One was *The Man-Maid Doll*, an autobiography by a transsexual prostitute. The second was *Gender: An Ethnomethodological Approach* by sociologists Suzanna Kessler and Wendy McKenna. I can't imagine two books more different! I read them many times.

A few years later I found myself in the medical library at Vanderbilt University, searching *Index Medicus* and the card catalog (there were no computer databases) for anything that might help me to figure myself out. What I found was a psychological and medical literature that painted transsexual people as mentally disordered, psychologically and socioeconomically unstable, manipulative, and histrionic. Heavens, was that me?

Ten more years would pass before I finally found others like me—and, through them, the literature I had been looking for all those many years. Soon I had put together a large collection, which I donated to the American Educational Gender Information Service, the 501(c)(3) nonprofit I founded in 1990. That material is housed today in the Labadie Collection at the University of Michigan in Ann Arbor, where it's available to students, researchers, and the general public.

It's little wonder I'm excited by any well-presented media that relates to transsexualism. I was deprived for so many years!

JAMISON

I have always been fascinated by how gender is reflected in the mainstream media. I was born in 1948, so I grew up in the 1950s, when gender roles were prescribed pretty heavily and little deviation was tolerated. Artists, writers, and musicians were the daring ones, pushing gender boundaries in ways beyond the feminist movement, taking pieces of culture and rearranging them to make new ideas that were sometimes provocative, sometimes hilarious, and sometimes simply mystifying.

I knew from a very young age that I could not be what the adults around me told me I was going to grow up to be. I was somewhat safe, from a gender expression perspective, in the writer/rock musician world of the late 1960s, but there was horrible sexism there, too, and sexism, when it barrels into any room, makes its assumptions and renders gender moot. Trying to find a place for myself, and my particular difference, was not easy. Like Dallas, I had no idea that others like me existed until the mid-1970s, and I was unable to find reliable information that was reassuring—rather than pathologizing and insulting—until the late 1980s.

The media has such a strangle hold on the mainstream's cultural imagination, but paradoxically, the media is the most powerful tool we, on the fringes, are able to use to make our own messages clear and to increase our own safety. The struggle for power in the media is a very real one. I hope that the spotlights we shine on media messages—as well as entertainment—in these pages will provide perspective that readers can use to further the cause of freedom of gender expression, and transgender and transsexual health and rights.

INTRODUCTION TO TRANS POLITICAL LEADERS SERIES

Jamie Roberts and Anneliese Singh highlight a few of the many trans political leaders making change all over the world through a series of spotlights in this book.

Jamie Roberts (left) and Anneliese Singh (right)

As civil rights for trans people advance all over the world, the number of trans people elected to public office grows. Throughout the book, we'll be spotlighting some of their accomplishments. These are stories of adversity, struggle, victory, and the expected and unexpected complications that come along with it. As trans people move from the margins of their societies to increased visibility and participation in civil life, these stories show that we often become sources of discussion and inspiration for our neighbors, as well as lightning rods for controversy.

This topic is important to us because any achievement made anywhere in the world for trans folks is an achievement for every trans person, who now has the knowledge that there are people like them in this world who are confidently, proudly, and courageously standing up for themselves and demanding their rights not only to exist but to thrive. Every breakthrough we can report, everyone who is given leadership, everyone who contributes to the culture, is pushing us forward to a future where our humanity and our place in society are givens. We believe there is wisdom to learn from the experiences of our fellow trans folk in other cultures that can inform our own struggles in our own context.

SECTION 1
WHO WE ARE

OUR MANY SELVES

Holiday Simmons and Fresh! White

THERE IS NO ONE WAY TO BE TRANSGENDER. We are teachers, scientists, business leaders, ranchers, firefighters, sex workers, weight lifters, students, activists, and artists. We are young and old, rich and poor, gay, straight, bisexual, and queer. We are every different race and we live in every country in the world. We have families and friends who listen to us and who work to understand our stories and our lives. We have allies who stand up for us and our communities and work with us to make the world a more accepting place. We appreciate their help immensely.

As **transgender** and **gender nonconforming** people (or **trans** people, for short), we have many different ways of understanding our **gender identity**—our inner sense of being male, female, both, or neither. Some of us were born knowing that something was different about us. Others of us slowly, over time, began to feel that we were not our full selves in the **gender roles** we had been given. Our many different ways of identifying and describing ourselves differ based on our backgrounds, where we live, who we spend time with, and even media influences.

We find ourselves frequently creating and changing the terminology that best fits or describes who we are. These changes can, at times, create complications inside and outside our communities. Factors such as culture, location, and class sometimes mean we do not all agree. But our communities work to honor and respect everyone's self-identification.

> *"I use the terms trans guy, trans-masculine, queer, dyke. In the past I used the terms FTM and transgender in talking to others, as these were the terms available to me. I thought that using these more familiar and linear terms would make it easier for others to understand 'what I am.' I used to feel more of a need and pressure to fit a familiar and simple narrative of going from one point to another."* *

> *"I am an ally of minority communities within the transgender community: two of my friends are disabled and transgender identified. I have developed an awareness of people's intersecting identities, and the privileges I hold compared to others."*

SEX AND GENDER

Sex and **gender** have only recently begun to be thought of as separate concepts. Our sex is generally considered to be based on the physical characteristics of our body at birth and has traditionally been thought of as biological. In comparison, gender is thought of as related to our social interactions and the roles we take on. It is an oversimplification to think of sex as biological and gender as social, but these terms can help us to communicate about what our bodies look like in comparison to how we feel.

> *"I don't like to use terms like 'Bio-Female/Male' or 'Female/Male-Bodied' because I don't think they account for Intersex folks. They also refer to the bogus medicalization of the gender binary, which I think gives the binary more power. I want to use words that refer to the social construction of the gender binary, like 'Read as Female' and 'Female Assigned at Birth' because it makes it clear that these are descriptions forced upon me and they don't have any real standing."*

For a fun, interactive way to spend time thinking about your gender, find a copy of *My Gender Workbook: How to Become a Real Man, a Real Woman, or Something Else Entirely* by Kate Bornstein.

---

* Quotes in this book, unless otherwise specified, are taken from an online survey of transgender and gender nonconforming people on the *Trans Bodies, Trans Selves* website.

Cover of *The Gender Book*, a colorful short book made to educate and entertain.

Identity, orientation, and sex (kd diamond).

"Genderqueer, genderbender, boi. I don't really see myself as one sex over the other. I am biologically female, although I have had FTM top surgery. I am not on testosterone, as I don't feel like being labeled male would make me feel closer to what I feel I am. And what am I? Something in between."

Most of the time, a person's sex and gender are congruent. However, those of us who identify as trans generally experience **gender dissonance** or **gender incongruence**. We find that our **affirmed gender** doesn't match our **assigned sex** or societal expectations.

HOW COMMON IS TRANS IDENTITY?

Colt Keo-Meier, PhD, is a clinical psychologist, researcher, educator, and out trans man in Texas.

Many people have tried to count the number of transgender people worldwide. Unfortunately, all of our methods have flaws. Gender clinics may only count people who have received hormones and multiple surgical treatments. Some people choose not to be counted in research, for instance, if they have a transgender history but do not identify as transgender (Meier & Labuski, 2013).

However, it is still important to attempt to determine the numbers because basic demographic information on minority populations informs public policy, health care, legal discourse, and education (Winters & Conway, 2011). Many important and influential decisions are made based on how many of us there are. The government could spend more money on grants that benefit our community, and insurance companies could decide to cover trans-related medical care if we were able to show that there are large numbers of trans people. The best estimates we have right now identify 15 million trans people worldwide (Winter & Conway, 2011) and 700,000 in the United States (Gates, 2011). This translates to 0.3% of the US population, or about 1 in every 333 people. Historically, estimates have generally stated that there are many more trans women than trans men, and some theories have suggested that people who are assigned female at birth transition less because there is greater social acceptance for maneuvering with more masculine expression. More recently, experts have estimated that there are probably about the same number of trans men and women.

REFERENCES AND FURTHER READING

Gates, G. (2011). *How many people are lesbian, gay, bisexual, and transgender?* The Williams Institute, UCLA School of Law. Retrieved January 2013, from http://williamsinstitute.law.ucla.edu/wp-content/uploads/Gates-How-Many-People-LGBT-Apr-2011.pdf

Meier, S. C., & Labuski, C. (2013). The demographics of the transgender population. In A. Baumle (Eds.), *The international handbook on the demography of sexuality* (pp. 289–327). New York, NY: Springer Press.

Winters, S., & Conway, L. (2011). How many trans* people are there? A 2011 update incorporating new data. Retrieved December 2013, from http://web.hku.hk/~sjwinter/TransgenderASIA/paper-how-many-trans-people-are-there.htm

We choose our **gender expression** or **gender presentation** through our clothing, our hairstyles, and our behaviors, which help us present ourselves to the world as we want to be seen.

Transgender and trans are often referred to as umbrella terms because they can include many different identities. More recently, the terms **trans*** read as "trans star" and **TGNC**, an acronym for **trans and gender nonconforming**, are being used more broadly to signify that there are numerous identities within transgender communities. Some people who others refer to as transgender do not identify with the term *transgender* at all.

> *"I tend to prefer MTF. I do not consider 'transgendered' to be a natural state. It's more a bridge to cross as soon as possible in order to be female."*

> *"I'm a man, so I'd like people to refer to me as one. I find it offensive to be described as 'transgender,' first because I'm not sure what the word means or that anyone knows what it means; second, because there's nothing particularly transgressive or edgy or revolutionary about my gender. I'm a dude. That I was assigned female at birth is inconvenient for me, but has no greater social import."*

There are many ways we may choose to identify ourselves within trans communities. We may call ourselves **trans men** or **female-to-male (FTM/F2M)** transgender people if we were **assigned female at birth (AFAB)** and view ourselves as male. We may see ourselves as **trans women** or **male-to-female (MTF/M2F)** transgender people if we

Dallas Denny and Jamison Green comment on the use of *transgender* as a noun: "Transgender is increasingly used as a noun to describe individuals generically—such as 'Samantha is a transgender,' not 'a transgender woman' or 'a transgender person'—as though their variance from gender norms was their most significant feature. Though some of the main journalism guides support this, we feel the word *transgender* should modify a noun rather than becoming one. Giving it some grammatical context and variability as an adjective helps ensure this. When trans people are described only as 'transgenders,' we feel the term easily dehumanizes us."

TRANS REALITY IN CHILE

Andrés Ignacio Rivera Duarte, 42 años, Profesor, Transexual, Activista Defensor de los Derechos Humanos, un hombre con vagina.

Transsexual men have some advantages in belonging to a "machista" society like the one in Chile, because that society values masculinity. Being a lesbian woman is not criticized much or discriminated against, because we are more accepted as "marimachos" or "mujeres amachadas," and that allows some of us to study and finish school. There is some discrimination, but it is not as aggressive and also not as violent or life-threatening as violence toward feminine people.

The reality for transsexual women is much more difficult. They are treated as "maricones." In school they are discriminated against, and face physical aggression and mocking. Often, trans women quit or are forced out of school which limits their options to qualify for jobs. Then, many of them turn to prostitution as the only way to make a living. This leaves them exposed to the cruelty of the streets and extremely vulnerable to HIV, alcoholism, and drug addiction.

The realities for transsexual men and transsexual women are very different. In the eyes of mainstream Chilean society, there is a strong belief that transsexual women are "putas" and "maricones vestidos de mujer." Transsexual men are much more likely to be viewed as successful and to be considered people with basic or equal rights.

Check out these Web sites for trans men: transguys. com, trans-man.org, thetransitionalmale.com.

were **assigned male at birth (AMAB)** and see ourselves as female. Those of us who are younger may identify as **trans guys/boys** or **trans girls** instead of trans men or women.

> *"Trans, transgender, transsexual, MTF, girl, woman. I use those terms because they are more empowering than any of the other terms. When I use them I feel that I've had enough shame in my life. These do not impart shame."*

> *"I don't like transman written all as one word; this to me suggests a transman is something different from a man, which is not how I identify. I prefer trans man as simply descriptive, and no more emasculating than describing someone as a Jewish man or a gay man. I'm also not keen on when people refer to FTMs as female-bodied (or MTFs as male-bodied) since I feel the process of transition makes that very inaccurate very quickly (ridiculous to refer to someone with a t-pumped body and a beard as 'female-bodied')."*

The project *I AM: Trans People Speak* is designed to show the diversity of backgrounds and experiences that exist within trans communities. Check out the Web site for stories, photos, and videos from transgender people across the United States.

Those people whose sex and gender identity match may be referred to as **cisgender**, as *cis* in Latin means "on the same side," while *trans* means "on the opposite side." As trans people, we have many cisgender **allies**—those who show their support for the concerns, needs, and rights of trans people, even though they may not personally face the same issues. Many of us prefer the term *cisgender* to other terms like *biological male/female* or *natural male/female* because those terms make it sound as if there is something more real about being cisgender than transgender. Others of us do not mind these terms and use shorthand versions like **bio girl** or **genetic girl (g-girl)** to refer to cisgender women, and **t-girl** to refer to trans women.

WHAT IS FEMININE? WHAT IS MASCULINE?

Misster Raju Rage is a community organizer, artist, and writer who prefers to be undefined.

What is feminine? What is masculine? I field these questions a lot. I often refuse to answer, which tends to force people to consider gender as a fluid, rather than as a fixed, state. It also encourages them to question more deeply than they have before—which in turn pushes them beyond what they have been told and beyond the answers they expect.

People also ask this question of me to derive my gender status, in order to pin it down. I am ambiguous as male or as female, even though I do not consider myself strictly either and would define myself as transgender. I have taken to just saying I am "undefined" or that "I don't know or care" when people ask me my gender.

I have felt comfortable with both masculinity and femininity and uncomfortable with both at different times. I allow myself both expressions and in different combinations depending on many factors, such as environment, mood, or safety. I don't restrict my behavior or activities based on whether they are considered "masculine" or "feminine," so I generally do not get caught up in the distinction. I often cannot differentiate between them—both are enmeshed, and both are in me.

When I "drag up" as my alter ego "Lola," it is an expression of both my femininity and masculinity—my femme masculinity. "Lola" is a statement of the fact that I do not see myself as a solely masculine trans guy but that I am femme, even though I consider myself male and use male pronouns. When I dress up as Lola, I feel I possess a strength that I find truly feminine; and that is also a culturally Indian femininity, rather than a Western femininity.

My family cannot fully accept that I am transgender. They have been socialized in the dominant Western world. More dominant cultures tend to dictate what is acceptable in terms of defining gender, so my family does not understand that I want to be considered male, with masculine pronouns, because they see my femininity (which I do not conceal).

But in my culture, and in many others, many men are effeminate. In my culture, it is common for gender variation (with *hijras* and *kothis*, for example) to exist within and alongside broader cultures. If we open our eyes, we see that people are comprised of many different shapes and sizes.

For this reason I make a political statement to not define what is masculine or feminine. That can only be answered personally by each and every individual. For *me*, being feminine is looking into my heritage of strong Indian female role models who are not afraid to express who they are. For me, masculinity means being different from the negative male role models I have had in my life, making a stand to reject misogyny and introduce feminism, and embracing the idea of brother/sisterhood.

Sex is as variable as gender. Some of us are born with bodies that do not fit neatly into what we expect of male and female bodies, and we may refer to ourselves as **intersex** or may identify with the idea that we have a **disorder of sex development (DSD),** although for many people, the idea of being labeled with a disorder or condition is disparaging. An older term for intersex people is **hermaphrodite**, but few people find this respectful. Many of us understand intersexuality as a normal variation of human existence.

While many intersex people do not consider themselves part of trans communities, some do. Intersex is sometimes represented as the "I" in LBGTQI. Some intersex people take hormones or have surgeries, either to see themselves as more fully male or female, or to correct childhood surgeries.

> "I am post-op MTF. . . From a medical stand point I am FTMTF due to the fact I was born intersex. . . I was not born with a proper penis so one was constructed when I was younger. . . The penis was never finished and I told [my doctor] I didn't want him to finish it."

Some trans people identify as intersex or find that this can be a way to explain ourselves to others. However, it is important to respect the identities and experiences of intersex people when using this word. Over time, we have built many alliances between trans and intersex people. However, the needs and struggles of the two groups can often be different and they should not be generalized.

TRANSITIONING

When we begin to identify with a particular gender, we often go through a process of **coming out**, when we acknowledge to ourselves and our communities that we wish to live our lives as a gender different than the one we were assigned at birth.

As trans people, many of us choose to **transition**, to physically alter our bodies and our behaviors to align our gender identity with our gender presentation. Some of us take hormones or have surgeries. Some of us wish we could afford surgeries. Others of us do not want to take hormones or have surgeries, but we dress and act in ways that affirm our gender identity.

Those of us who have surgeries may want **top surgery**, which changes our chests, or **bottom surgery**, which changes our genitals. There are also numerous other types of surgery that have the potential to change our gender appearance, including facial surgery and tracheal surgery (to remove the Adam's apple).

Online guides to all things transgender include Transsexual Road Map (tsroadmap.com), The Transgender Guide (tgguide.com), T-Vox (t-vox.org), TG Forum (tgforum.com), Susan's Place (susans.org), Lynn's Place (tglynnsplace.com), and Laura's Playground (lauras-playground.com).

> "The incongruence between my mental self image and physical body has become increasingly distressful for me, so last year, after three years of therapy and two of binding my breasts, I decided to undergo a double mastectomy and male chest reconstruction surgery. I feel much better now that I no longer have breasts. I walk taller, I feel more comfortable going about my daily activities, and I can take my shirt off in front of my lover without feeling awkward now.

Since deciding on surgically altering my body to masculinize it, I've begun to identify as transsexual."

Some of us identify as **transsexual**, or **TS**. For many of us, identifying as transsexual means that we would like to or have had some variation of **sex reassignment surgery (SRS)** or **gender-affirming surgery (GAS)**, although this is not true of everyone who identifies as transsexual.

"Transsexual. I'm taking hormones now. That's what I'm called because of the hormones. There are stages I've been going through."

"I hate transsexual. The word really seems too closely linked to sexual behavior and completely misses the concept of gender identity."

The distinction between various trans people is not whether we have had certain kinds of body modifications but how we identify. Some of us have not had chest reconstruction surgery, hormones, or genital surgery, either for financial reasons or because we are at peace with our bodies as they are, but still identify as women or men. Some of us may choose to undergo medical or surgical interventions, without seeing ourselves as exclusively male or female.

Sometimes trans community members make judgments about other community members regarding whether they are authentically trans.

"Nobody in the lesbian community ever said I wasn't 'lesbian enough' whereas I was told early in my coming out that I wasn't 'trans-enough.'"

"I'd prefer if I was just called by my name, in whatever fashion they choose, the feminine or the androgynous version. For me, the way someone may believe I am is not necessarily how I see myself. And as a Black female, the identity I encompass as of present is so out of the box that this community doesn't know how to categorize me. So I've learned to accept that the only opinion of who I am that I care about is my own and the people I trust."

Some trans people use the term **transgendered**, while others find it offensive.

Some people believe that the term *transgender* should be used to describe only those who are legally or medically transitioning. This stance may come from the idea that those who transition in these ways face more discrimination and harassment, and have therefore earned their status as trans or proved that they are dedicated to the identity. However, those of us who have not transitioned in these ways may still face very difficult situations. **Gender policing** can be harmful and divisive.

"I really prefer 'transgendered'. . . as a descriptor, because it implies movement and fluidity."

"I hate when people say 'transgendered,' because it sounds like a disease, and it's dated."

While some of us may continue to live our lives as openly trans, some of us who "**pass**," or have our male or female gender presentation correctly **read** by others around us, choose to live **stealth**. This means that few, if any, of those around us know that we are transgender. Living stealth may be a matter of safety or privacy for some of us; for others, it is a matter of what feels natural and makes us happy. For most of us, our lives are combinations of living openly, passing, and being stealth depending on the context or situation.

"I live full stealth, I do not advertise my medical history or genital configuration. I am one of the fortunate few that is able to blend in well with other women. It works for me and that's how I live my life. Where I live, there are a LOT of ignorant bigots and it's not at all safe to be out and open about such things as this. I have a few cisgendered friends that know of my past but they treat me as 100% female and nothing less. So I do not like the tags because

Transgender Versus Transgendered

"Many people discourage use of the term *transgendered*. However, a number of well-known writers of transgender or transsexual experience use both *transgender* and *transgendered*, notably Kate Bornstein, Matt Kailey, and Susan Stryker.

Being transgendered is commonly compared to being 'deafed'—but it is not the same. All people are 'gendered' by our own or others' perception of us in relation to the binary assumptions about sex and gender that surround us. We have gender, and we are gendered by the world around us; and therefore, we can be transgendered. Deaf people, who have deafness, may have been deafened. We realize that no one person or group can control the evolution of language, and we think that's good!" *Dallas Denny and Jamison Green*

when the general public hears those tags they think pervert, freak, sicko, etc.
Those tags are all heavy, negative labels the people use to separate, isolate,
insult and harm us with."

"I strongly prefer simple female pronouns/references. I don't believe in
'stealth' (for myself) and I don't hide from my past, but I look at my gender
history the way someone would look at having spent their childhood in Poland
or Madagascar or on Army bases or something—an important part of my
development, sure—something that may make me a bit of a stranger to these
shores sometimes, but not the defining experience of my life."

Some of us do not identify as trans at all. Instead, we may identify as simply male or female. We may refer to ourselves as women or men **of trans experience**, or as **affirmed males** or **affirmed females**.

"Gay man of trans experience. I use this because being trans describes an
experience I've had, not an identity."

"I usually just call myself a man. In appropriate contexts, I call myself a trans
or transsexual man, or a man of trans experience. I used to call myself 'FTM,'
but it doesn't feel right anymore—maybe I grew out of it. I also call myself
queer, nelly, bear, and fag."

SEXUALITY

A common misconception about trans people is that we are all gay or lesbian. While we often form coalitions of **lesbian, gay, bisexual, and transgender (LGBT)** people, gender and sexuality are two separate things. Our gender identity is our own sense of whether we understand ourselves as men, women, or something else. The phrase **sexual orientation** is used to describe the gender or genders of the people to whom we are attracted. As trans people, we may be gay, straight, bisexual (attracted to both men and women), pansexual (attracted to all genders), or asexual (not sexually attracted to anyone). Our sexual preferences may depend on many factors other than the genders of the people we are attracted to. Like everyone, we may consider class, education, spiritual practices, body shape or size, and dominant or submissive attributes in picking partners.

"My preference is for people to use the same terms they would use for
cissexual men. I particularly don't like it when people assume that my
being transexual is what makes me queer. I'm queer because I'm a man
who is attracted to men and because I am a part of queer communities, not
because I was assigned the wrong sex at birth, or because my brain sex was
incongruent with my body sex."

"I have used, in various contexts, the terms trans, transgender, transsexual
and MTF to describe myself. Over time I tend to just use transgender or trans
simply because it's easier for people who don't understand the difference to
understand. I also found that the use of transsexual often led to the wrong
impression that somehow what I'm going through is sexually related."

LGBT is an acronym that is expanding considerably and has many current permutations. LGBTQ adds either questioning or queer to the end. Questioning refers to those people who are not yet sure about their sexuality or gender identity. Another permutation of LGBT is LGBTQIA (Lesbian, Gay, Bisexual, Transgender, Queer, Intersex, and Allies). These acronyms can become very long. For example, LGBTT2QQAAIIP stands for Lesbian, Gay, Bisexual, Transgender, Transexual, Two-Spirit, Queer, Questioning, Asexual, Allies, Intersex, Intergender, and Pansexual.

TRANS LIBERATION IS FOR EVERYBODY: TRANS ALLYSHIP AND THE TRANS CONTINUUM

Peter Cava is the Lynn-Wold-Schmidt Peace Studies Fellow at Florida Atlantic University, Boca Raton.

As trans politics have gained greater visibility, many people who do not self-identify as trans have been wondering if and how they have a stake in these politics. In a 2013 column, Dan Solomon addressed this question. He began by drawing a clear line between himself and trans people: "I'm not transgender....I am a dude who is straight and cisgender (that is, someone whose gender identity matches their biology)." He recognized that this difference afforded him privilege: "Everyone else seems to treat us [cis people] pretty well." Nevertheless, he believed that cis people should care about trans politics for two reasons. The first is compassion: "The fact that transgender people live under a constant threat of violence should stir you." The second is self-interest: Solomon imagined that if trans people were to remain preoccupied with "defending their right to exist," then a trans person would miss an opportunity to invent a "fucking flying car" that cis people could enjoy. Therefore, cis people could benefit from trans rights.

By appealing to both compassion and self-interest, Solomon made a valuable contribution to a conversation about trans allyship. We can take this conversation further by rethinking the cis-trans distinction. What would make a person's gender identity match their biology? For example, by this definition, could a cis woman have a dapper moustache, or a cis man, dainty ears? And what about gender *expression?* Is someone with a male identity, male biology (whatever that means), and a flirty cocktail dress, cis? No—no one is cis in all ways always (Enke, 2012). Rather, everyone is on the blurry and beautiful rainbow of diversity that gender theorists C. L. Cole and Shannon L. C. Cate have called *the transgender continuum.*

The trans continuum can inform the conversation about trans allyship in several ways. First, what does the trans continuum mean for cis identity? The "cis" identity label, like all such labels, is provisional. It can serve as a help or a hindrance, depending on the context. Second, what does the trans continuum mean for cis privilege? Cis privilege is not the exclusive property of a cis majority; rather, all people experience cis privilege when our gendered embodiments and expressions are perceived as more congruous than someone else's (see Enke, 2012, pp. 67–68, 76). Therefore, all of us can practice trans allyship by dismantling our cis privilege. Third, what does the trans continuum mean for trans allies? Allies have a stake in trans politics not only because allies have compassion, and not only because allies want fucking flying cars, but also because allies are part of the rainbow. And finally, what does the trans continuum mean for trans politics? If *trans* means more than a minority, then trans politics do not end at minority rights; rather, as trans activist Leslie Feinberg has emphasized, trans politics call for universal liberation. When we achieve that goal, it will be a cause (that is, a reason) for celebration. Until then, it is a cause (that is, an activist initiative) worthy of everyone's participation.

REFERENCES

Enke, A. (2012). Enke. A. F. (2012). The education of little cis: Cisgender and the discipline of opposing bodies. In Enke, A. (Ed.), *Transfeminist perspectives in and beyond transgender and gender studies* (pp. 60–77). Philadelphia, PA: Temple University Press.

Solomon, D. (2013, January 18). Guy talk: Why a straight man like me cares about transgender rights. *The Frisky.* Retrieved March 2014, from http://www.thefrisky.com/2013-01-18/guy-talk-why-a-straight-man-like-me-cares-about-transgender-rights/

Some people prefer to use the term **queer** to describe the many groups that make up the LGBTQ spectrum. Queer is a term that has been reclaimed by many LGBT people, and it is often used as an umbrella term for anyone who is not cisgender and heterosexual. Others of us use it as a political term that implies being radical and transgressive, separating ourselves from other LGBT groups that seek more traditional forms of acceptance. However, there are many of us who also find it difficult to use this term because it can carry negative connotations. Like any controversial term, it is best to allow each person to identify themselves with the term rather than using it to talk about someone else.

> *"I am a queer, pansexual, polyamorous, kinky, femme genderqueer faggot. 'Queer' is ambiguous and fluid. Like 'genderqueer,' it critiques the binary system and creates a space for me to live outside the binary confines. But the term 'queer' is also important to me because of its politics. Obviously not all queers think alike but, to me, 'queer' is about questioning and/or rejecting normative views. Some of my own beliefs include dismantling capitalism and*

working on wealth re-distribution; ending the prison system; and eliminating the gender binary. Bisexual assumes there are only two genders, which is inaccurate. I am attracted to queers and fags of all genders, so 'pansexual' is how I identify. I'm femme, though for the meantime I restrain myself from dressing or appearing how I would like to because most people perceive me to be female and I want to be perceived as a femme genderfucker, not female."

"I would find it offensive if someone called me a fag or queer, but only because those are hateful words."

For some of us, our sexuality is very important to our self-identity and it interacts with our gender identity. Some trans women who identify as queer or lesbian refer to ourselves as **trans dykes**. Like many cisgender lesbians, we have reclaimed the derogatory term *dyke* and use it in positive ways. Some of us who are transmasculine identify as **trans fags**, and reclaim the word *fag* in the same way.

"Some of the terms I use to identify myself are trans, trans man, trans guy, guy, boy, queer, boy with a vag, genderqueer, gender bender, aspiring femme, trans fag, and transgender. I like the term trans because it acts as an umbrella term for all kinds of gender variant people, so even though I would be called a transsexual by the medical establishment, trans unites lots of different people under one flag, and we need unity in our community if we're going to get anything done. I like queer for the same reason, because it unites lots of non-normative sexualities under one term, and also because I like how it sounds and its secondary definition of 'strange.' The terms I use for myself have changed as I've become more confident with my transition and my identity in general."

"I currently describe myself as a girl, lesbian, a trans woman, or a trans dyke. Girl is the term I most heavily identify with, and it simply feels right which is more than I can say for most terms. I occasionally use the terms trans woman or trans dyke which I mildly identify with but do not give the same comforting sense of simple correctness that I feel when I use the term girl."

Within North America, **people of color (POC)** have created numerous terms to better define ourselves and explain how we feel about our gender and sexuality. **Same-gender loving (SGL)** is often used to replace terms like gay or lesbian. **Masculine of center (MOC)**, a term coined by B. Cole, provides an opportunity for people of any sex and across the gender spectrum to identify as masculine without denying our feminine qualities. Similarly, the terms **transmasculine**, often used by trans men, and **trans-feminine**, often used by trans women, can convey that we fall generally to one side of a gender binary, but that we are not limited by the binary. The term **boi** is sometimes used by young trans men or by cisgender lesbians who see themselves as somewhat masculine.

Some of us use specific terms like **translatin@** that combine our culture and gender identity. Numerous other terms have come out of communities of people of color. For example, some of us who were assigned female at birth and have masculine identities do not necessarily identify as trans. We may use words such as **aggressives** or **AGs**, **playas**, **studs**, **G3 (gender gifted guy)** and **boys like us** to describe our identity and gender presentation.

Online Toronto-based *Stud Magazine* offers crisp images of masculine-of-center people along with spotlights on health, education, and employment.

The Aggressives (2005) is a movie directed by Daniel Peddle about six young people of color in New York City who were assigned female and identify in different ways as masculine.

"Queer, Pansexual, Transfeminine womyn of color. I am politically Queer. I don't like the term 'bisexual' because it assumes there's only 2 genders when there are so many more. I like 'transfeminine' because it relates to my journey of being born male and living in a body producing testosterone while transitioning into a feminine identity. Womyn of color, because I am."

Trans Bodies, Trans Selves New York City Forum (photo by Katia Ruiz).

> *"I am a transgender Latina woman. I chose to identify as a transLatina because I crossed the gender binary and I am of Mexican descendence."*

The term **tranny** is very controversial. Coming from the outside world, it is often experienced as rude, demeaning, and harassing. However, some of us use this term to talk about ourselves, especially when we are in circles of friends, and feel that we are reclaiming it for ourselves.

> *"I have a love/hate relationship with the word 'tranny'. . . it can be really misleading, and it has the potential to be really derogatory, and that's certainly not my intention. I use it precisely because it's a rubbish word. It's completely useless. I use it to show how useless it is."*

> *"I like other trans people who are my friends calling me a tranny. But I don't like it when anyone else does."*

> *"I'm not keen on 'tranny' at all, but it's in general use (typically by people who think it's completely harmless, and/or by people in the drag community). . . the problem with it is that it is THE go-to joke for drunken frat-boy humor (e.g. 'that chick Steve was macking on last night was a huge tranny,' etc), and by using it ourselves we only legitimize it for more cruel and hateful uses."*

Even within the trans community, *who* can reclaim the word can also be a controversial issue. The term has more often been used in a context of violence and hate toward transfeminine people. Some trans men feel that we should not use the term, because it has not been used against us in the same ways.

> *"I feel like the term 'tranny' is too scary a word for folks with MTF trans experiences, and [as a transmasculine person] it's not mine to reclaim."*

Depending on where we live, other terms may be used to describe our experience and identity in negative ways.

> *"Terms I find offensive would be the usual derogatory terms. Particularly in my country (South East Asian context), it would be transvestite. The media and government generally use this term for transsexuals with GID and make us look like freaks in dresses. So I am pretty offended by this term. Oh and there's Mak Nyah (Malay language), it means transvestite too and it is a very crude term."*

> *" 'She-male,' 'he-she,' that kind of thing is hate speech."*

NONBINARY IDENTITIES

Some of us do not feel we fit in the **gender binary**. Under the gender binary, there are only two genders and everyone has to be either male or female. We may understand our identities as falling along a **gender spectrum**.

> *"I despise labels and know who I am. I do not feel I need to label myself and narrow myself and narrow myself in order to make a binary society more comfortable in their dealings with me."*

> *"First I came out as bi. Then a lesbian. Then a dyke. Now as gender fucked up. The first were so much easier: I was saying something about myself. This is harder: I'm telling people what I'm not. It's a lot easier to say, 'I think women are sexy' than it is to say, 'I don't know what a woman is anymore, but I know it isn't me, and no I'm not a man, and I really can't explain it.'"*

We may identify as **gender variant, genderqueer, pangender**, or **gender fluid**, terms used by those of us who feel we are both male and female, neither male nor female, in between genders, on a continuum, or outside the binary gender system altogether. We may consider ourselves **androgynous,** having both male and female characteristics, or being somewhere in between. We may not feel we have a gender or that we want to choose a gender, and may define ourselves as **nongendered** or **genderneutral.** Those of us who consider ourselves genderless and also desire gender-neutral bodies may identify as **neutrois.**

> *"I consider myself genderqueer because I feel uncomfortable with the gender binary, and I am unhappy when I feel pressured to conform to the binary gender role expectations of women or men. I think a lot of cisgender people feel the same way to a degree."*

> *"I specifically consider myself MTF TS, but right at this moment I would describe myself as genderqueer—not as a goal or a political statement but a recognition of just how between/both I am right now."*

> *"Transgender, transsexual, transman, queer, FTM, femmy boi, androgynous, pangendered, tranny, transfabulous. I use 'pangendered' rather than 'bigendered' because 'bi' implies that I think that there are only two genders, when my mere existence proves that there aren't. 'Pangendered' fits pretty much everything. . . 'Transfabulous' is my own word. I think it's fantastic."*

Some of us understand ourselves as **Two-Spirit**, a category that exists in some Native American cultures. For many groups, being Two-Spirit carries with it both great respect and additional commitments and responsibilities to one's community, including acting as healers or providing spiritual guidance. The term can apply to people with nonheterosexual identities, in addition to people who are gender nonconforming. It is important to note that *Two-Spirit* is a term that comes out of specific cultures, and it may not be appropriate to use as a self-definition if we are not part of these cultures.

> *"I like FtM, trans*, transman, two-spirit (yes, I am First Nations), queer. . . all based on context or situation."*

> *"Two-Spirit is the best word to describe myself. I hate the words transgender, queer, gay, fag(got), trans man, boi, gender-bender, gender variant and gender queer. Those words belong in white culture and I don't like their oppression and colonization to extend to my identity because they don't own that."*

> *"I've started identifying with the term two-spirit, but I'm not sure about it yet. I am part Native American but I look much more like my European ancestors, so I fear that if I used the word it would be seen as co-optation."*

Gender Outlaws: The Next Generation, edited by Kate Bornstein and S. Bear Bergman, features essays and comic strips from radical trans and genderqueer voices.

Trans Bodies, Trans Selves Seattle Forum (photo by Ish Ishmael).

Hijras dancing (copyright Glenn Losack, MD/Glosack Flickr).

The Genderqueer Identities Web site (genderqueerid.com) provides resources and answers to all kinds of questions about genderqueer identity.

Outside of North America, there are many communities across the globe that incorporate **third gender** or **third sex** categories, allowing for gender nonconforming people to create new spaces to express their gender identities. Examples include the Fa'afafine in Samoa, Kathoey or Ladyboys in Thailand, and Hijras in India and Pakistan. Some people in the United States, especially in communities of color, are using the term *third gender* to self-identify.

TRANS POLITICAL LEADERS: SHABNAM BASO

Jamie Roberts and Anneliese Singh

Shabnam Baso was the first transgender woman to be elected to the State Legislative Assembly of Madhya Pradesh, India, in 1998. Baso's nickname was Mausi (or *auntie*)—which is a common term of endearment and familiarity in South Asian culture. Baso famously took up the mantle for Hijra rights, encouraging the Hijra community to take a more active role in everyday Indian society. The result of British colonization for the Hijras in India has been a specific loss of status and significant public health struggles. The British government created a statute, which they inserted into the Indian Penal Code in 1872 (Section 377), criminalizing sexual activity that was "against the order of nature." This penal code affected much of the way the Hijras were viewed in society. While the Hijras once held sacred status and prescribed roles in religious rites pertaining to births and marriages, in modern times the community struggles with issues of HIV/AIDS and homelessness.

Although the Hijras experienced significant destruction of their sacred rites, they continue to engage in activism. India granted suffrage rights to Hijras in 1994. In 2008, Bangalore police arrested several Hijras on charges of public begging. Unfairly targeted, these same Hijras were mistreated in jail, and a group of up to 150 activists from community-based organizations and women's groups worked toward their release. Many of these activists were part of Sangama, a human rights organization dedicated to furthering LGBTQ rights in India, in addition to engaging in social services and political advocacy.

We Happy Trans (wehappytrans. com) is a place for sharing positive perspectives about trans people from around the world.

GENDER CAN BE FUN

Many of us like to play with gender, even if we identify as male or female. Some of us enjoy dressing up and performing. We may live most of our lives as men but perform as **drag queens** in shows or live as women and perform as **drag kings** (formally known as

female or male impersonators). As drag queens and drag kings, our costumes are often outlandish and over the top. Trans people, not just cis people, can perform in drag shows. Trans men can perform as either drag kings or drag queens and trans women can do the same. Drag is about having fun with gender.

> *"I am a drag king who performs a great deal and spend a fair percentage of my life impersonating a man. I am very masculine, but still hold onto my femininity as it is a part of me."*

> *"I perform as a masculine persona or bind/pack/draw facial hair on for fun and to express myself butch."*

Whether or not we cross-dress or perform in drag, we may engage in **genderbending** or **genderf*cking**, where we purposefully play with gender, wearing clothes we are not sup-posed to wear or acting in ways that people do not expect.

> *"Genderqueer, androgynous, trans, transgender, genderf*ck (every so often), gender-variant. I like the openness of these. They never box me in and have a lot of flexibility."*

But not everyone embraces this idea. For many of us, our gender presentation does not feel like something we are experimenting or playing with.

> *"I don't like it when people use words like 'genderf*ck' to describe me, as I don't see what I'm doing as play. It's who I am."*

Those of us who live most of our lives in our **birth-assigned gender** but like to wear the clothes typically worn by another gender may refer to ourselves as **cross-dressers**, or more simply **dressers**. In English, an older term for cross-dresser is **transvestite**. Many people today find it offensive, although words similar to transvestite are in common use and not necessarily considered offensive in some other languages. During other periods in history, there were many female cross-dressers. However, today, since women in Western countries are typically given more leeway in their wardrobes than men, most of us who identify as cross-dressers were assigned male at birth.

The Drag King Book, by J. Jack Halberstam and Del LaGrace Volcano, is a collection of essays, interviews, and photographs.

Venus Boyz is a 2002 film directed by Gabrielle Baur that explores drag king culture.

Drag King Murray Hill, New York City Dyke March, 2007 (copyright Boss Tweed).

"Cross-dresser. I'm just starting out on my journey, so at the moment, I'm just dressing, but I want and fully intend to go much further."

"I am comfortable with transgender, transsexual, genderqueer, trans woman, femme, MTF, cross-dresser, transvestite, tgirl. I picked them because they are pretty much the only terms I don't find degrading."

Sometimes, we **cross-dress** only in our own homes, or as part of sexual play, and sometimes at public functions. For some of us, it may be an early part of our transition process, and for others, it may be our chosen gender expression.

PRONOUNS

Pronouns are one type of word that we use to talk about people. We often call someone "he" or "she" instead of using a name. Many of us want people to continue using these words to describe us when we transition, though our **preferred (gender) pronouns (PGPs)** may change from "he," "him," and "his" to "she," "her," and "hers," or vice versa. When we are not sure which pronouns someone prefers, it is polite to ask, "What pronouns do you use?"

"Personally, I find it charming when people use the appropriate name and pronouns, and go so far as to ask when they're unsure."

"I feel really relaxed and natural when people switch up their pronouns for me. They can use him, her, hir, zi, shi. . . Anything. . . I do enjoy being called 'male' pronouns more often, though. If you aren't sure what to call me right then, listen to how I refer to myself, and take it from there. If I sense your uncertainty (and I probably will), I'll help you out. Or you could just ask. I really don't mind."

In some languages, pronouns are gender-neutral. For example, when speaking Mandarin, there is no distinction between male and female pronouns. In other languages, people are developing gender-neutral pronouns as we are in English. In Swedish, the gender-neutral pronoun *hen* is starting to be used by some people in place of *han* (he) or *hon* (she).

Others of us prefer to have people refer to us using **gender-neutral pronouns.** One way to do this is to use the word "**they**," which is traditionally a plural pronoun, and apply it to just one person rather than multiple people. With some adjustment to the way we are accustomed to speaking, we can become used to phrases like "What are they doing today?" or "What's their favorite restaurant?" and know that both we and the others we are talking to understand that we are speaking about just one person, who was named earlier in the conversation. Other gender-neutral pronouns did not exist in English until recently and were invented in order to find new ways of talking about people in nongendered ways. These include **zhe** or **ze** (pronounced "zee") as a replacement for s/he, and **hir** (pronounced "here") as a replacement for him/her. Gender-neutral titles (replacements for Mr. or Ms.) include **Mx.** (pronounced "mix" or "mixter"), **Misc.** (pronounced "misk"), and **Mre.** (pronounced like the word "mystery").

"I prefer that people use gender neutral pronouns but that rarely happens because I do look quite femme (but don't present as such). Even when I talk about this with people, they still use feminine pronouns."

"I would prefer it if people referred to me using gender neutral pronouns (I use sie and hir) and possibly gender neutral salutations (Mre.)."

For the past few years, some teenagers in Baltimore have been using the gender-neutral pronoun "yo" when talking about people. For example, they might say, "look at yo," or "yo's wearing a new jacket."

Some languages employ only gender-neutral pronouns. Others, like English, make it difficult to talk about people without using gendered terms.

"I appreciate it when other people recognize my gender expression and take that in consideration when referring to me, as there are gender-neutral alternatives as well. Luckily, in the Finnish language we have a gender-neutral personal pronoun. Referring to me simply as a female based on my biological body makes me feel really uneasy, as it surpasses my sense of self and how I see my gender."

"Gender neutral/third gender pronouns aren't available in German. In English, however, I prefer ze/hir, if I'm in a suitable setting (either online or real life). I can't stand being called 'it'."

At times, people **mispronoun** us, calling us by incorrect pronouns, or **misgender** us, assuming incorrect genders. **Mispronouning** and **misgendering** can be intentional or unintentional. When it is intentional, it can be used as a form of harassment. Using our chosen pronouns, or substituting gender-neutral pronouns when it is unclear which pronouns we use, is a way others can treat us respectfully.

"Unfortunately, in too many situations there are people who can reluctantly recognize that I am a woman, but upon discovering that I'm genderqueer they insist that they cannot help but mispronoun me and think of me as a man."

DISCRIMINATION AND INTERSECTIONALITY

As trans people, we often face discrimination. Many people intentionally harass or bully those of us who do not fit into their visions for a gendered society. However, there are also many people who are potential allies to us who do not yet understand our identities or the struggles we face. They may unintentionally use offensive language or misinterpret our gender expressions. Meeting others and connecting through individual interactions is one of the most effective ways of creating allies to our communities. However, we all have our own sense of how much time and effort we want to spend educating others.

As trans people, we experience different types of discrimination based on our identities and presentations. **Transphobia** is discrimination based on our status as transgender or gender nonconforming people. Transphobia overlaps with **homophobia** (discrimination against gay, lesbian, and bisexual people), **sexism** (discrimination based on our perceived sex), and **misogyny** (hatred or dislike of women). For example, gay men who are seen as especially feminine are more likely to be harassed than those who are seen as more masculine. Young gender nonconforming people, who may be trans but may also be gay, lesbian, bisexual, or sometimes straight and cisgender, are bullied every day in schools across the world. **Trans-misogyny**, a term coined by trans writer and activist Julia Serano, is a form of misogyny directed at trans women.

"They," Portraits of a Noun (Hill Wolfe).

Unlearn transphobia (copyright Gustavo Thomas).

"There is no innocence nor insignificance to the mistake of 'she' for 'he' when referring to a person who has chosen to take on a 'wrong' pronoun, even if it is done thoughtlessly; that thoughtlessness comes from and supports the two cardinal rules of gender: that all people must look like the gender (one out of a possible two) they are called by, and that gender is fixed and cannot be changed. Each time this burden shifting occurs, the non-trans person affirms these gender rules, playing by them and letting me know that they will not do the work to see the world outside of these rules."—*Dean Spade, founder of the Sylvia Rivera Law Project*

Julia Serano is the author of Whipping Girl: A Transsexual Woman on Sexism and the Scapegoating of Femininity.

While all people who fall under the "transgender" umbrella potentially face social stigma for transgressing cultural gender norms, those on the male-to-female or trans female/feminine spectrum generally receive the overwhelming majority of society's fascination and demonization. This disparity in attention suggests that individuals on the trans female/feminine spectrum are targeted, not for failing to conform to gender norms per se, but because of the specific direction of their gender transgression. Thus, the marginalization of trans female/feminine spectrum people is not merely a result of transphobia but is better described as **trans-misogyny**, which appears in numerous ways in our society. For a few examples:

-Feminine boys are viewed far more negatively, and brought in for psychotherapy far more often, than masculine girls. Psychiatric diagnoses directed against the transgender population often either focus solely on trans female/feminine individuals or are written in such a way that trans female/feminine people are more easily and frequently pathologized than their trans male/masculine counterparts.
-The majority of violence committed against gender-variant individuals targets individuals on the trans female/feminine spectrum. In the media, jokes and demeaning depictions of gender-variant people primarily focus on trans female/feminine spectrum people.
-Perhaps the most visible example of trans-misogyny is the way in which trans women and others on the trans female/feminine spectrum are routinely sexualized. The common (but mistaken) presumption that trans women (but not trans men) are sexually motivated in their transitions comes from a broader cultural assumption that a woman's power and worth stems primarily from her ability to be sexualized by others.

Discrimination is not always (or even often) the result of an active bias against or hatred of a certain group. Our cultures are made up of established practices and systems that assume certain identities are the "default." For example, **cissexism** and **cisnormativity** describe a systemic bias in favor of cisgender people that may ignore or exclude transgender people, and **heterosexism** and **heteronormativity** describe a systemic bias in favor of heterosexual relationships.

> *"I have met heterosexual transgender people who are actually homophobic. It kind of blows my mind because they had a sex change and have the same chromosomes as their partner. That doesn't mean they're gay but I just think that would open their minds a little."*

Victor Mukasa, an LGBTQ rights activist from Uganda (copyright Linda Dawn Hammond/Indyfoto.com).

"Some people, even within the trans community, seem to think that because we're attracted to guys then we're not really trans, and that it would be easier for us to 'stay girls.' I've heard that from people and it's really disappointing that people are still that close minded."

Many of us fit into at least one of the "default" categories of our society; this gives us **privilege** in certain ways. Privilege refers to advantages conferred by society to certain groups, not seized by individuals. It can be difficult sometimes to see our own privilege, especially when we face discrimination because of our transgender status or other parts of our identity. Trans people reflect the diversity of our society and, in addition to our transgender status, we also have multiple identifications based on other factors, including our race, ethnicity, culture, class, age, immigrant status, disabilities, size, and numerous other characteristics.

The multiple identities and spaces we occupy can be interpreted through the idea of **intersectionality**, a concept coined by legal scholar Kimberlé Crenshaw (1991) and widely used among feminists of color. Intersectionality is the concept that our identities are complicated—our experiences as people of a specific gender, race, sexuality, ability, and ethnicity are interconnected and cannot be separated. Intersectionality allows us to approach trans discrimination as an interlocking system of oppressions rather than as one solely based on gender.

Facing discrimination based on any of these factors, along with transphobia, can be devastating, especially for those who have been cast from families or have little community, financial, or psychological support.

"I think a lot of times the wider community forgets that being trans doesn't automatically make you white and able bodied. My trans men friends who are not white have a harder time finding a packer that could believably be their skin tone. I, and my other trans friends who have different bodily ability, are sometimes glossed over by other trans people when looking at bathroom access and other needs. From what I have seen, the result is that our smaller groups bond even more tightly and instantly than the trans community more broadly. To a certain extent we are taking on the world over our gender and then, because of intersection of identity, we are taking on some sections of the trans community as well who may be racist or clueless as to how their bodies are actually a benefit to them."

"I am a fat, low-income trans person with a non-visible disability. While I am not involved in any official subgroups within the trans community I'm currently in, I do tend to gravitate toward people who are aware of their privileges and the intersectionality of multiple aspects of people's identity."

"As a formerly homeless and currently low-income trans woman, I sometimes have very little in common with middle class trans guys who are college students. The issues that affect me are different. I'm worried about whether the unemployment office is going to respect my identity."

Some of us have disabilities, impairments, or are members of the Deaf community. This can influence our ability to participate in community activities, and change our relationship with other members of the trans community.

"I am disabled and trans, so I know other disabled transfolk, just by being involved in both communities. We talk about issues that relate to how they intersect: how do you get health care for important things like hearing aids, wheelchairs, medication, when you present as a gender different from the ones on the form? My neurological disability is affected by hormones, which makes me scared to even bring it up to my doctors. It's something that's not discussed in the larger trans community."

A TRANS FATTIE TELLS ALL

Joelle Ruby Ryan is a lecturer in women's studies at the University of New Hampshire, the founder of TransGender New Hampshire (TG-NH), as well as a writer, speaker, and long-term social justice activist.

I am a genderqueer, trans woman. I also weigh over 400 pounds. These two realities have shaped my life in ways I never imagined, for both better and worse.

When I was a young, fat, feminine boy, my teacher was concerned that I was both out of shape and not behaving like the other boys when it came to recess and athletics. This is just one instance when my fatness and my transness came to be inextricably linked.

While I came out as trans at age 20, I didn't start peeking my head out of the "fat closet" until my mid-thirties. As I grew much fatter, I started to notice the discrimination and stigma from my family, my doctors, and the "caring" friends who expressed their worries. I became much more aware of the constant fat-shaming in the media, and the push by the medical establishment to forward the notion of the "obesity epidemic" and the need for dangerous gastric bypass surgeries.

But when I came out as queer and trans back in the early 1990s, I made a promise to myself: never to allow others to make me feel bad about who I am. I was sick and tired of others hating on me in a misguided attempt to puff up their own sagging self-esteem. And I also decided, after reading the fabulous book *Fat!so?* by Marilyn Wann, that I really didn't have to apologize for my size, and that fatness is a benign characteristic much like being blond, or left-handed, or tall, or flat-footed. It was not being fat that was the problem, but the prejudiced society in which the fat person lives.

As people who are marginalized due to our bodies and our identities, the trans community should be natural allies to the fat community. Sadly, I have witnessed a lot of fatphobia in the trans community. Some trans folks seem to think that by conforming to other hegemonic bodily standards (thin, nautilized, "passing," traditionally attractive, etc.) they will become more palatable to the mainstream. But we can never throw enough people overboard to win approval from our enemies.

We have learned the value of affirmative slogans over the years: Black is Beautiful! Gay is Good! Trans is Terrific! And the latest: Fat is Fabulous! In order to be a whole, healthy community, we must celebrate the dazzling diversity of everyone and stop the fat-hate once and for all.

NOLOSE* (nolose.org) is a community of fat queers and our allies with a shared commitment to feminist, antioppression ideology and action.

"I have some medical issues and have been involved in groups for people with disabilities but at those groups I'm normally the only person who is gender diverse except for one project that was for people who have disabilities to discuss issues of sexuality as a performance piece. I know a few people who have disabilities and are somehow queer."

Similarly, many of us come from working-class and poor communities and our experiences of gender and ability are profoundly affected by our experiences of classism and access to class privilege. Financial status may limit our ability to transition in many ways. We may not be able to afford the cost of name or gender change, to buy clothes that match our gender, or to have procedures such as surgeries or electrolysis that can affect the way we present our gender to the world.

"I'm working class and have a minor physical disability. The class issue comes up in ability to get medical care for trans issues."

"I've contemplated surgery, but the cost is a bit of a detriment to that particular dream."

"I grew up middle class, was lucky and privileged enough to receive an upper class education, and currently work in a service/lower income job. So my class experience is a mixed bag. Transitioning has been really difficult for me mostly because of the lack of money—there are times when I have been off and on T because of it for months at a time. So I am pretty resentful when I see people who have access to that kind of monetary privilege transition and get surgery in 6 months and then become an authority figure on 'trans issues,' when I don't think we have the same experience or care about the same things. Intersections with other social justice issues like racism and classism are really integral to

*a good trans politic, and I think that is missing from the narratives of a lot of
the spokespeople in the FTM movement. I would love to see a non-white or
gay-identified or low-income (or any combination) trans masculine person
be a highly visible person in the movement, but I don't see that right now and
I think it's disheartening for a lot of younger trans folks."*

Where we live can also affect our experiences as trans people. In rural areas we may have less access to trans-specific resources and may find unique ways of creating places of comfort and safety for ourselves. Sometimes the assumption is that those of us who live in small towns have to deal with more bigotry and transphobia. This can be true, but it is not always the case.

> *"Defining myself has never been an easy task. . . growing up in small town
> Indiana in a roman catholic family, I was never exposed to the various terms,
> let alone 'transgender' or 'transsexual.' I had only seen the word 'shemale'
> online (but I didn't think much of it, I'm just a normal girl born with a penis)."*

> *"I am in a small town with strong conservative views. The fact that we have a
> handful of transpeople surprises me."*

> *"Since I am generally seen as female, I tend to say I am. This is particularly the
> case since I live in a remote rural area. It parallels the fact that my partner, who is
> genetically female, and I are both fairly butch. We don't say to people that we are
> dykes, but we don't say we aren't. We aren't closeted, we just don't push the point."*

> *"For a variety of reasons I chose to not move as I transitioned, which means by
> virtue of shifting appearance, name, and pronouns, my personal life was public. . .
> Staying in my home town was more important for mainly familial reasons."*

The ways in which we each experience discrimination may change as we transition. Trans women may contend with sexism and misogyny in the workplace for the first time. Trans men, who often look younger than cisgender men their age, may face ageism and be seen as less knowledgeable or capable than others. Trans men of color often find themselves in the position of being suspected criminals much more often than when others viewed them as masculine women.

> *"Being perceived as a Black man is different than being perceived as a Black
> woman in a lot of ways, not to mention if you're neither perceivably man OR
> woman. I think that it's important for us to have those conversations since
> conversations about race, ethnicity, and their social connotations are rarely had
> in the LGBTQ community."*

> *"I was recently told that no matter how masculine I 'tried to be,' I was always
> a cute little Asian girl with a cute little face and body. In fact, this person
> told me she considered me to be 'femme.' This was a strong reminder that my
> gender presentation is inextricably linked to my race. There are notions about
> Asian masculinity at play here—that Asian men are not as manly as men of
> other races. There are also notions of Asian femininity—that Asian women are
> weak, that Asian women are hyper-feminine and hyper-sexualized. There is no
> room here for folks who were Female Assigned at Birth to be androgynous or
> masculine or strong."*

> *"I am discovering what it is to be Chican@ and trans on the day to day, how
> those identities intersect and relate to each other. As someone who can never
> fully identify as American or Mexican, but as hybrid of the two, I've learned
> to take the lessons from that liminality and use them in regards to my gender
> identity. Sometimes it's okay to occupy and exist in those gray, in between
> areas."*

The Gay, Lesbian & Straight Education Network (GLSEN) did a survey of LGBT youth in rural areas called "Strengths and Silences: The Experiences of Lesbian, Gay, Bisexual and Transgender Students in Rural and Small Town Schools."

SHARING THE BLACK TRANS PERSPECTIVE

Fredrikka Maxwell is happily retired and spends time with her partner Connie Goforth. She sits on the board of the Tennessee Vols, co-chairs the Dignity USA trans caucus, and gives seminars at varied trans- and church-related conferences.

I am a black transsexual. Like the Tooth Fairy or Santa Claus, a lot of people simply don't believe we exist. There was a time when I didn't believe we existed, either—but by the middle of my high school career, I had a very strong suspicion.

As an adult, at the Foundation for Gender Education convention in Philadelphia, I noticed that I was the only black person in attendance save for the hotel employees. That's another dirty little secret of the trans community: It's not as integrated as it likes to bill itself. I knew then that I was going to share a black perspective at the conference, because unless I did, it wasn't going to get done.

I started where I was familiar: my own story.

I was born in Savannah, Georgia. My dad jumped out of airplanes and helicopters for a living, which meant that my three brothers, my sister, and I went wherever the Army assigned Dad. I have a wonderful sister who has been a frequent companion at events like the Philly Trans Health Conference and Call to Action, a liberal Catholic group where I live. She was the first family member I came out to and she professed unconditional love from the start. My brother has accepted me with much love at his house near Atlanta—I have warm fuzzy memories of hot chicken wings and ice-cold Rolling Rock beer at his house before the Southern Comfort conference.

But it wasn't always that way. My brother once said that he didn't want his wife and kid exposed to me; I later told him we were talking about my life, not anthrax. It took my mom 10 years to reach the point where she concluded that I was hers, no matter what. My church family was divided about my transition, and some were clearly unhappy about it. I lost friends at work and outside. It wasn't easy.

I earned my BA from the University of Tennessee at Martin, but I couldn't get hired by any journalistic outlets. Maybe I wasn't white enough, maybe I wasn't bright enough, maybe I wasn't *something* enough. I eventually found a job in an unlikely place—the Metro Police Department in Nashville, a job I held for 25 years before coming out in 2001 to live as the woman I knew myself to be.

In Atlanta, at Southern Comfort, I ran my first seminar, appropriately named *Sharing the Black Perspective*. Southern Comfort and Call to Action, which do not have much black presence, know me now. I am not a rookie anymore, and I feel inspired to do more seminars as time goes by. The mission ahead, to share the black trans perspective, is one I've embraced wholeheartedly.

CONCLUSION

We each have unique ways of understanding and relating to our genders. The ways we talk about and explain these identities are important, and they are always changing. Ultimately, we recognize that many people have intersecting identities and many of us have claimed or reclaimed new terms or labels that have meaning for us specifically. Respect for the self-identity and changing nature of our identities is the glue that binds our communities together. The best way to make change is to assume less and ask more. We do not always agree on terminology and definitions. We define and redefine ourselves, and continually debate within our communities. This conflict can birth understanding, which in turn can encourage healthy dialogue. During all of this, we continue to strive for wholeness while being our many selves.

REFERENCES AND FURTHER READING

Brown, M. L., & Rounsley, C. A. (2003). *True selves: Understanding transsexualism—for families, friends, coworkers, and helping professionals.* San Francisco, CA: Jossey-Bass.

Crenshaw, K. W. (1991). Mapping the margins: Intersectionality, identity politics, and violence against women of color. *Stanford Law Review, 43*(6), 1241–1299.

Currah, P., Moore, L-J., & Stryker, S. (Eds.). (2008). Trans-. *Women's Studies Quarterly, Fall/Winter, 36*(3–4).

Herman, J. (2009). *Transgender explained for those who are not.* Authorhouse.

Hines, S., & Sanger, T. (Eds.). (2010). *Transgender identities: Towards a social analysis of gender diversity.* New York, NY: Routledge.

Nanda, S. (1999). *Gender diversity: Crosscultural variations.* Long Grove, IL: Waveland Press.

Nestle, J., Howell, C., & Wilchins, R. (Eds.). (2002). *GenderQueer: Voices from beyond the sexual binary.* Los Angeles, CA: Alyson.

Serano, J. (2007). *Whipping girl: A transsexual woman on sexism and the scapegoating of femininity.* Berkeley, CA: Seal Press.

Stryker, S., & Aizura, A. Z. (Eds.). (2013). *The transgender studies reader 2.* New York, NY: Routledge.

Stryker, S., & Whittle, S. (Eds.). (2006). *The transgender studies reader.* New York, NY: Routledge.

Sycamore, M. B. (Ed.). (2006). *Nobody passes: Rejecting the rules of gender and conformity.* Berkeley, CA: Seal Press.

Teich, N. M. (2012). *Transgender 101: A simple guide to a complex issue.* New York, NY: Columbia University Press.

Valentine, D. (2007). *Imagining transgender: An ethnography of a category.* Durham, NC: Duke University Press.

2

RACE, ETHNICITY, AND CULTURE
Kortney Ryan Ziegler and Naim Rasul

AS TRANSGENDER PEOPLE, we come from many different racial and ethnic backgrounds. Race and ethnicity are often difficult to define because they are complex and encompass both biological and sociological factors. Race generally refers to a group of people with shared biological or genetic traits, which may include common physical characteristics such as skin, eye, and hair color. Ethnicity on the other hand, refers to a person's culture, and it can encompass nationality, ancestry, language, and beliefs. An ethnic group may be made up of people who identify with each other based on a common genealogy or ancestry, shared cultural traits, group history, or religion. Race and ethnicity are important and dynamic factors in the lives of trans and gender nonconforming people. In our increasingly global world, many of us have diverse backgrounds that cut across and combine different racial and ethnic histories. These identities play a powerful role in shaping our experiences.

There are numerous social forces that affect how we define race and ethnicity. In different areas of the world, there are different racial categories, and the meanings of these categories depend on many historical and sociological factors. Many of us from the same racial backgrounds identify with different ethnicities. For instance, those of us who are Latin@ may identify with our Cuban, Venezuelan, Mexican, or Puerto Rican roots. Those of us who are white may identify with our Italian, Russian, or Irish roots. Many people from various ethnic backgrounds may identify as Jewish.

Our race or ethnicity, as well as other traits, such as our sex or gender, sexuality, wealth, immigrant status, or social class, may provide us with privilege over others. Privilege is certain sets of unearned or earned benefits that allow us to acquire resources and access to power. Privilege is divided along class, race, gender, ability, and sexuality lines. Privilege is not something that we, as individuals, claim. Instead, it is attached to groups of people based on our characteristics. One of the ways in which privilege works is that it is not always obvious or visible to those with privilege, and they often do not recognize that they have it. For example, in the United States, many of us who are white have the privilege of not thinking about our race as a characteristic of ourselves, and not worrying about the way people will react to us based on our race—because the system gives white people advantages over people of other races and ethnicities. Acknowledging privilege is not a moral condemnation. Rather, it is a call to action that requires collective work in order to more evenly distribute access to power and to resources so that human agency can be reclaimed and claimed by all.

Most people are privileged in some ways, but not in others. A poor white cisgender lesbian may benefit from cisgender and white privilege, while being vulnerable to discrimination based on her status as a woman, a lesbian, and a poor person. A wealthy straight transgender black man may benefit from male, heterosexual, and financial privilege, while being vulnerable to discrimination based on his status as a transgender person and a black person. Our privilege and the discrimination we face may also be intersectional, based not just on one characteristic of our identity or who we are, but on the combination of traits we possess. The type of discrimination faced by a black woman is different than discrimination faced by a black man. Characteristics about us can also provide us with either privilege or make us vulnerable to discrimination depending on the situation.

Looking for a trans or LGBTQ racial or ethnic group to attend? Some national organizations have created directories to make finding local groups easier. The National Confederacy of Two-Spirit Organizations and the NorthEast Two-Spirit Society have an online "Two-Spirit Resource Directory." The National Queer Asian Pacific Islander Alliance created "Queer Asian Compass: A Descriptive Directory of LGBTQ Asian American, South Asian, and Pacific Islander Organizations."

"Shades of Men" (Saterius Roberts of SiR Arts and Tattoos).

RAR@: CHICAN@, MIXED-RACE, GENDERQUEER, IN/VISIBLE

Lee Naught is a radical, genderqueer, chican@ organizer and sex educator. They spend most of their time working as a collective member at Bluestockings Bookstore in NYC, playing in the riot grrrl band Titfit, and educating with Fuckin' (A), the sex positivity collective they cofounded. You can find more of their writing in Mixed Up! A Zine About Mixed Race Queer & Feminist Experience.

It is difficult to describe being mixed-race, chican@, and genderqueer. On one hand, that's simply what I am; on the other hand, it feels almost impossible to be recognized as Mexican American while I present as genderqueer.

I was born in So Cal and raised by four latinas on my maternal side: my mom, my grandma, my tía, and my older sister. None of them had male partners for the majority of my childhood, and they stuck together to navigate a world that oppresses women, people of non-European descent, and people of color. I grew up refusing to be limited by gendered or racist social norms. I would buzz my light brown hair off completely or grow it out long and dye it jet black. I challenged myself to excel at pursuits that "girls" weren't supposed to do.

During those girl-identified years, I never had to insist on being recognized as latina. Presenting as a young woman, with dyed black hair, red lipstick, dresses or skirts, and sometimes embroidered tops en el estilo de Oaxaca o Michoacán, if I said that I was latina or chicana, it was not hard for folks to accept that I am a lighter-skinned Mexican.

Years later, I am the same person, with the same skin and face. I have some different ideas about how power and identity work, and I have an always-evolving gender. I keep my hair

"Until we are all able to accept the interlocking, interdependent nature of systems of domination and recognize specific ways each system is maintained, we will continue to act in ways that undermine our individual quest for freedom and collective liberation struggle."—bell hooks, *Outlaw Culture*

Laverne Cox, an African American trans woman, made history by becoming the first trans woman of color in reality television by appearing on the first season of VH1's *Who Wants to Work for Diddy?* designed to find an assistant for rapper icon P. Diddy. After her popular run on the show, Ms. Cox went on to produce the VH1 makeover spot *TRANSForm*, making her the first African American trans woman to create and star in her own television show. Most recently, she has portrayed a trans woman on the Netflix series *Orange Is the New Black.*

Ethnic FTM is a Yahoo Group that acts as a network for trans men from various racial, ethnic, and religious backgrounds.

Queer Women of Color Media Wire provides a space for art, music, film, books, and media created for and by queer women of color and gender nonconforming people of color.

cropped short, sometimes bleached blond with dark roots, sometimes natural medium brown. I do what I can to make my body's presentation read on the masculine end of its spectrum of possibilities, without medical intervention thus far. In this current gender, when I tell folks that I'm chican@, the most common response is along the lines of "Really? I would never have guessed! You don't look Mexican at all." I've often shifted my presentation in subtle ways, hoping that I'll discover the right combination of variables to be read as chican@ while staying true to my gender. But I've found that if I change my clothes or hair color, if I switch from English to Spanish, if I move to or visit another city, the reactions remain largely the same.

I'm not white; I also often don't feel comfortable claiming the label POC (person of color) because I move through the world with a lot of white privilege. But histories of colonialism and oppression created me—racism experienced by my family, manipulation and militarization of borders, codified government discrimination called immigration law, genocide and violence enacted against the indigenous Chichimeca and Purepecha, and more. A part of me is injured every time someone is shocked to hear that I am Mexican American. For people like me who are queer and not white, the conflation of queerness with whiteness is frustrating.

Being mixed-race feels a lot like being genderqueer; I have a pretty clear understanding of my own identities, but the world around me struggles to identify me and comes to different conclusions about what they believe I am. Maybe my experiences would be easier to explain if I could declare myself to be a member of a better defined, stable category, like woman or transgender man, 100% Mexican or plain gring@. But I live in a space of gray, which is what queerness is all about to me: defining oneself rather than being trapped within unchangeable categories.

PEOPLE OF COLOR

Some of us identify as **people of color (POC).** The phrase "people of color" was introduced to replace terms like "non-white" and "minority" because non-white defines us in terms of what we are not, and minority implies that a group is smaller or less important than another. In the United States today, whites no longer make up the majority of the population in many places, and the US Census predicts that whites will become a numerical minority before 2050. At times, we as people of color may use the acronym POC in conversation to stand for people of color. This term, however, is shorthand and may not be appropriate for those who do not identify as people of color to use.

Some of us who identify as people of color do so because we feel this phrase reflects the common experiences of racism that we share and points out that race is one of the most prevalent ways we make judgments about people. Some of us prefer to avoid this term, as we feel that by using just one phrase to describe us all, we lose our individuality.

Trans People of Color Coalition (TPOCC) is a national social justice organization that promotes the interest of trans people of color. Founded by Kylar Broadus, an attorney and activist, TPOCC sponsors lobby days, runs campaigns, presents at conferences, and produces a newsletter to follow national issues that affect trans people of color.

The Brown Boi Project is a community of masculine of center womyn, men, Two-Spirit people, trans men, and allies committed to transforming the privileges of masculinity, gender, and race into tools for achieving racial and gender justice by building the leadership, health, and economic self-sufficiency of young masculine of center people (photo by Miki Vargas).

BORN BAD

Wes

I was born in the Bronx, New York, into a family of Puerto Rican immigrants. I identify strongly as Nuyorican, and I think that—as for most queer diasporic peoples—in-between-ness is my life. I identify as queer and also identify very strongly with the trans community. I currently go to Oberlin College, a private college where finding my place as a low-income queer person of color is difficult to say the least. These opportunities separate me from my communities while simultaneously providing me with laboratory knowledge. But I guess sometimes struggle and knowledge go hand in hand.

My sister says I'll get out of this place one day, and I even pray sometimes that I will. My mother prays too, for me and for my people. Half of "getting out" is smarts and the other half is luck.

The 174th street station. Chipped paint on the pillars holding up the tracks. Dirty, full of clanking metal, a picture of the urban hell in the movies, which has eaten me up and threatens to swallow me if I don't thrash hard enough to keep myself afloat.

But the station sits within a vibrant community of perpetual resistance, of tired brown faces, the sidewalks as broken as their hearts. The brown faces, the brown resistance, the subway station, and cracked sidewalks. We still hold our heads high. My people are survivors.

It is hard to imagine these people as they once were—full of energy, hopeful, driven, not angry like the abandoned masses forgotten in the war, not drowning in discouraged hearts and ignored intelligence.

I don't know who decides who stays and who goes. One day I was crossing the street to go to school, the next I was walking to the 174th street station, getting on a train and riding far, far away from the Bronx. There's nothing that I did to "get out"; I was born bad. One stroke of luck here, one there.

Maybe I wasn't meant to get out. Maybe it was a fluke. Maybe someone else's name was called out and I accidentally wandered into their place. Or maybe someone thought that if I would have stayed, I would've contaminated the whole neighborhood with my deviance.

It might've been all the times I wanted to tell Cristal I thought she was beautiful in fourth grade, but didn't because I didn't want to get beat up by her boyfriend. It might've been the times I saw a white person walking in our neighborhood and got scared that we'd get kicked out of our homes so they could move in. It might have been the days when I looked into the mirror, surprised each time to see someone I didn't know, filled with rage and sadness.

I was the kid who wanted to be a kid instead of hating his body since as long as he could remember, instead of keeping secrets no one else ever had to keep.

It could've been anyone else, someone stronger than I am, to go off into this strange world where I'm even more invisible than I am at home. But fate has no eyes. It throws fishing hooks out of subway cars and drags the first thing it catches.

If you are ignored for long enough, in enough places, it starts feeling like you shouldn't even be there. Or anywhere. Sometimes you get used to the loneliness.

I go home to the tired brown faces and we're all alone, waiting in the 174th street station. We face each other on the subway trains as if we were looking past mirrors.

EXPERIENCES OF RACISM

For many of us, our lives are affected on a daily basis by racism. Discrimination against us may be intersectional and depend on multiple characteristics, such as our race, gender, and trans identity. (See Chapter 1 for an introduction to intersectionality.) Many of us are affected by gendered racism, in which we are discriminated against based not just on our race or gender presentation but the combination of these. Our experiences of racism and oppression are often demonization, scapegoating, police brutality, housing segregation, and lack of access to certain jobs and employment. We often struggle to acquire and maintain the equality afforded to our white trans counterparts.

"She Thinks She's a He" (Saterius Roberts of SiR Arts and Tattoos).

"Trans people of color have different experiences and at times have different issues that need solutions such as additional oppression because of intersections of identity involving race, class, AND gender."

Those of us who are trans people of color navigate a world in which institutionalized racism—racism that is part of our culture and systems of government—affects our lives on every level and severely limits our access to health care and educational resources, as well as our capacity for economic advancement. This reality, along with our transgender status, marks trans people of color as the most vulnerable members of the extended trans community, leaving us to experience high levels of discrimination and unemployment, and multiple instances of physical and sexual violence. Trans women of color continue to top the list of murdered individuals that are recognized every year on Transgender Day of Remembrance.

According to the annual Hate Violence Report by the National Coalition of Anti-Violence Programs, in 2012, 53% of anti-LGBTQ homicides in the United States were against transgender women, and 73% were against people of color.

"Lots of times when I'm with white people (not everyone, of course), they think everything works just fine and there is no awareness of how different life in These United States can be for different folks."

"I am Puerto Rican and Egyptian. I try to bring out the voice of the Latinos and Middle Easterners but it's quite complicated."

Unfortunately, our transgender communities are not immune to the racist attitudes and behaviors that pervade our society. It can feel isolating to be one of the only people of color in transgender and LGBT groups. We may feel silenced or invisible. We can also feel burdened by the responsibility of representing the experiences, diversity, and needs of trans people of color.

"Most of the genderqueer/trans people I roll with are people of color. It's totally different. We have a lot of other bullshit to deal with. I can be in a room full of beautiful white trans people, but still feel like my cultural background and skin color make me sort of invisible. Mainstream queer activism is so white-centric these days. We spend a lot of time talking shit about that and working constructively within our communities to address this."

"The common elements of mistrust, anger, fear, racism, etc. that exist in the straight world are just as prevalent in the trans world."

"I live in a medium sized city . . . or a huge suburb. There is only one PFLAG group and it's pretty white. People of Color come to PFLAG once and they don't come back. The very nice, generous, and accepting PFLAG folks don't have any understanding of how uncomfortable it can be to be the only Person of Color in a room full of white people . . . or that it just gets plain OLD. And sometimes I get tired of explaining that or of being disliked for explaining that or always being the one at the table 'making trouble.'"

REVELING IN OUR AUTHENTICITY

Willy Wilkinson, MPH, (www.willywilkinson.com) is an award-winning writer and public health consultant whose book, Born on the Edge of Race and Gender, *is forthcoming.*

It was a sunny summer day when I took my wife out to brunch for her birthday at an outdoor café. Our sandy blond waitress presented our respective plates of food, then freeze framed in a piercing stare, and in the absence of any finesse one would presumably adopt for tipping customers, demanded, "Are you part Asian? The Asian always takes over!" She then turned to my wife and proceeded to complain about how her half Filipino kids didn't look anything like her. As my food began to cool, it occurred to me that holding my Asian face responsible for her issues with her family was not a strategic way to get a decent tip.

I am *hapa*. My mother is Chinese from a little town in Hawaii, and my father is Caucasian from Oakland. Our family language was English peppered with Cantonese and Hawaiian, and everything tasted better with soy sauce. As a family we celebrated our multiculturalism. And yet throughout my life my features have been picked through, my cultural knowledge evaluated based on my looks or last name. "I didn't think you would know how to use chopsticks because you have brown hair." My loyalties have been decided, and my membership questioned. It hasn't just been "What are you?" but also "What are you doing here?"

Similarly, as a trans person, I embrace and celebrate my unique gender journey. And yet for most of my life people were equally confused about my gender and struggled with their need to categorize me. You know the drill. Their eyes bug; their mouth wrangles in an awkward attempt at gendered salutations. Pronouns fail them. They pause in midair without realizing it. "Sir? Ma'am? Uhh. . ."

Like many trans folks, many people of mixed heritage are not easily defined or fathomed. People who are mixed are assessed on their facial features, body type, skin tone, cultural knowledge and mannerisms, values, language, communities, and loyalties. And not just from white folks, but from every direction. There's an authenticity check, just making sure you are who you say you are.

Ah, authenticity. That beautiful thing that we as trans people continually strive for. The right to not just live but to unquestionably revel in our own unique authenticity, even when that expression makes people uncomfortable, curious, and confused. Our masculinity and femininity are measured for realness content. Our ability to be perceived as the gender we identify with is evaluated. We are resisted even when we assert our true selves repeatedly.

As trans people, we have experienced the world in different shoes, different realities, different bathrooms. We speak a different language, about T and getting clocked and transfeminism. We use gender-transgressive pronouns and in-house words. We've stepped beyond the expectations of our families, communities, and societies. Many of us know what it's like to live as both female and male at different times in our lives, or at the same time. Some of us are perceived in different ways from moment to moment. Some of us are perceived as clearly one gender or the other yet locate ourselves in the gender galaxy beyond, whether in the present or past. And even if our identity or presentation is not ambiguous, our truths, and those of our loved ones, are layered. It may be something we are keenly aware of every minute of the day, or it may fade from our daily thoughts, but these complexities are there, behind our eyes and under our skin.

That, to me, is where trans experience and mixed heritage experience intersect: the ambiguities and complexities, the layers of cultural experience that don't meet the eye, and the difficulties that people have acknowledging and accepting them. It's the opportunity to put a unique lens on the world, to see the views that others don't have eyes for. It's a cross-cultural experience, an adventure outside of easy categorizations. It's more than one reality at the same time, code-switching into different languages and norms of behavior, cranking up the brightness and color. And it's the confidence and courage to defy exclusion and revel in our bold authenticity.

A few good Web sites to check out: API Queer Women & Transgender Community (apiqwtc.org), BKLYN Boihood (bklynboihood.com), Black Transmen (blacktransmen.org), Black Transwomen (blacktranswomen.org).

Community, Kinship, Life (CK Life) is an organization based in the Bronx, New York, started by trans people of color, with a focus on family and community. CK Life runs support groups, trainings, and has a surgery scholarship fund.

BUILDING COMMUNITY

Trans people of color often face discrimination or silencing within trans and LGBTQ communities. Our own racial and ethnic groups can at times be very supportive of us as trans people, but they can also be some of our fiercest critics. Our communities can also impose expectations on how we should define ourselves and walk through the world. It can be challenging to feel like an outsider within our own communities as we struggle to deal with discrimination and invisibility that we face from society.

> *"I'm mostly involved with Black transmen, being that I am Black myself. I can't really say how different it is, besides other communities having privileges due to race and gender that we may not. I believe we definitely feel a lot more pressure as black males to be masculine in appearance and behavior, and I believe there to be more pressure to conform to heterosexual ideologies."*

Because trans people of color face loneliness and discrimination, many have built or joined communities of trans and queer people of color.

> *"The minute I started college I joined the QPOCC Queer People of Color Club."*

> *"I am involved in the black male community. I believe there is a greater sense of brotherhood in this community because we are members of two oppressed groups."*

> *"I have been attending the local Two-spirit group here in this part of Kansas."*

> *"I'm active in a Transmen of color greek organization."*

"We know each other out in the community, we have occasionally had a black butch brunch. I can't over emphasize how much these events have meant to us, as we rarely have queer of color only time, we love being together and feeling that solidarity and power."

"As an African American transgender female, I strongly believe that the experiences that me and other AA trans females have are at times very different than those of other trans people and therefore feel the need to meet, socialize and discuss the issues and experiences that are more relevant to us. I've been a part of more mainstream trans communities and although I have made friends and had positive experiences there was still a strong need to connect with those who look like me and share the dual difficulties of being both African American and transgender."

The issues that come up for trans people of color are somewhat different from those of the larger trans community.

"I have been involved in groups for Black transmen. The concerns for these groups tend to differ from larger FTM groups because they're more about community-identity, financial, and family issues."

*"I was at a Queer Youth conference at a university and there was a workshop called 'Queer As Folk—White As F***' The students there really were enjoying being young, Queer, and People of Color. . . and they were like—'White culture is a drag and why aren't WE represented except in token fashion on this Queer television show?!'"*

"Over time I've tapped into a loose network of other transgender jews. The core difference is that we can talk frankly as trans people about matters of interest to other jews, which is something that rarely comes up in general trans spaces. It is relaxing to (1) not have to teach constantly (2) not have to worry people are going to be prejudiced or harassing against me. While there's no guarantee of that in any group of people, having a critical mass of shared experience allows us to take a certain amount of common ground for granted (less teaching!) and a certain mutual appreciation for where we're coming from (less bigotry!). I find such communities very refreshing and stimulating."

bklyn boihood is a collective that champions healthy masculinity, intersectionality of identities, and antimisogyny for bois* of color all over the world.

Gun Hill Road, a film directed by Rashaad Ernesto Green, is the story of a trans Latina teen's relationship with her father after his return from prison to their home in the Bronx.

WORKING FOR LGBTQ YOUTH OF COLOR

Tiffany D. Wilkins was awarded graduate and teaching assistantships to pursue doctoral study in the inaugural cohort of the Professional Doctorate in Educational Leadership (ProDEL) program at Duquesne University, was recently named a Barbara L. Jackson Scholar at Duquesne, and currently conducts data collection for RAND Corporation while also an adjunct English professor at the Community College of Allegheny County.

I have faced numerous structural inequalities as an African American woman who is also part of the Lesbian, Gay, Bisexual, Transgender, and Questioning (LGBTQ) community, particularly with regard to accessing higher education. African Americans are raised and grow up learning a particular epistemology in the United States; at birth, the Mis-Education of the [American] Negro begins, reinforcing the assumption that college is not a goal for many students of color.

As an awkward, dark-skinned, "nappy-headed," athletic tomboy, I was a mediocre student. I fought for permission to attend one honors course, and lacking support for college prep, I had poor SAT scores. The guidance, support, and tenacity of my basketball coach/school counselor made my dream to attend college a reality.

Despite my access to college, as a young person of color, "questioning" my sexuality and gender expression became a part of learning my place and potential for success in a racist society. I struggled to see beauty in myself despite prevalent images and observations of white and black folks alike expressing otherwise. No longer a "sistah," my membership in the African American community—often at odds with my sexual orientation and gender identification/presentation—has become unhinged. On paper I am a fascinating, accomplished, exemplar of diversity; in person on a largely white, Catholic, heterosexual campus, I am a source of discomfort and embarrassment in the African American community.

My work focuses on higher education access for LGBTQ youth of color as a matter of social justice. My research examines how homophobia in the African American community creates barriers for LGBTQ youth of color who are forced to choose one identity over another, risking ostracism and hoping for acceptance. I hope to use my experience as a gender nonconforming African American butch lesbian to understand racism on college campuses and in the LGBTQ community, and to increase opportunities for LGBTQ professionals of color in literacy education.

In some places, especially in rural areas, it can be difficult for us to find communities of trans people of color. For various other reasons, many of us are not very involved in these communities. Often times, we are dependent upon the Internet and various online resources and social networking sites in order to connect and find the support of other trans people of color when we feel isolated in rural areas and small towns.

> "I'm not involved in any minority transgender groups, though I would love to live in a place with enough trans* people for there to be a minority within the minority. I'm multicultural, so that would be an invaluable resource for me."

> "I have only met two other black transsexual womyn."

> "I did go to a group for asian transgenders, but it was a small group that is a bit too far for me to drive and now that I got a job it makes going to these events hard."

> "I'm sort of adjacent to the Two-Spirit community, because I'm Alaska Native, but I haven't really gotten involved."

> "Ha! In Oklahoma? There aren't enough of us out in the open to segregate ourselves into races/cultures."

> "Although I am a person of color, I'm not really involved with minority GLBT* activism much. I am aware of it, especially online, and I definitely see the need for more activism—the intersection of racial and gender minority puts transwomen of color in more danger on a daily basis than most groups of any minority, and it's chilling—but I'm not personally very active in these communities. That's partly because despite being a person of color I don't feel like a lot of 'person of color' activism is targeted at people like me; I don't have a lot of the same experiences or worldviews and sometimes don't even agree with some of their concepts or methods. I'd like to help but I don't always feel like I have a place in their community."

> "I'm part of the Jewish genderqueer community. . . I don't know that many other Jewish genderqueers. I do know a few though, and one of them lives close enough to me that we can see each other during the holidays. It's hard to find minority groups within minority groups—like, there are so many different interpretations of genderqueer and so many different ways of being Jewish, so when you try to combine them and find people you really connect with and have similar beliefs to, it gets hard. . . It's different from the larger transgender community because of the beliefs and customs that people have. Growing up Jewish, I always felt really different from my non-Jewish friends. I think that growing up as part of one minority and then coming into another minority community is different than when people grow up as part of the majority in terms of the rest of their life and then only have one minority community."

LIVING ON THE OUTSIDE: BLACK WOMAN? BLACK MAN? NEITHER? OR BOTH?

Toi Scott is a visionary, community organizer, artivist, blogger, and author of Notes from an Afro-Genderqueer, as well as radical, brown, gender/queer plays Genderqueer Files:La Qolectiv@ and Resistencia: Sangre, who is an ordinary superhero working toward racial and gender justice and the eradication of oppression and disparities within the economic, food, and health systems.

The concept of gender is entrenched in the black community, if not the pillar of it. As I've come out as genderqueer, I have found it difficult to imagine disassociating myself from black womanhood. So much is tied to a black woman's identity. Slowly but surely, I have come to own and appreciate the struggle of a black woman, the burden on her back, the solidarity in calling each other "my sister."

In taking on the identity of trans and calling myself genderqueer, I felt that I was betraying my sisters in some way, and rejecting the women's spaces in which I felt so comfortable for years. At first I felt that I'd become an outsider to the community of women of color that I fought so hard to understand, be a part of, and protect.

As I began accepting the fact that I am genderqueer, that I am transmasculine, I began to panic. Does this mean I am a black man? Should I choose to transition and present myself as male? Will I have to routinely see white women clutch their purses and turn up their noses, and white men feel threatened or disgusted by my very existence? I did not—do not—want to be a black man. But unfortunately, I do not have much choice in the matter.

I am not a woman. I have the body of a woman, but anyone who gets to know me quickly finds out that, well, I'm not. I was not exactly socialized as a girl as a kid. My mother climbed the rungs of the police department slowly and steadily and was a warrior who did not revel in her femininity.

I always saw myself as a boy. By the time I was six or seven, and it was socially unacceptable to do "boy things," I started keeping my feelings to myself. I let people call me "she" and "her," but it never really fit. My stepfather and mother tried to make me dress like a little girl, but I felt disconnected from other girls, and like I was in drag when I wore dresses.

In high school, though, I started wearing flannel, plaid, corduroy, and boy shoes. After coming out in college I let people tell me that I was a lesbian, but I never owned that label, though I found solidarity with female-bodied people whose partners were women.

In the banking industry where I worked for six years, men accepted me as a mixture of male and female and thought of me as one of the "boys." When straight men hit on me, I wondered what their deal was. When straight women would flirt with me and then say "but I don't date girls," this did not compute. I wasn't a *girl*, I was a handsome young *boi*!

In my lesbian relationships, I did not take on a butch role. I do not identify as a stud or an AG. I wear my masculinity much differently. As I was coming out as genderqueer, I made the conscious decision not to take hormones or get chest surgery, in part because I don't particularly identify with the label FTM. I don't trust or identify with the social construct that is the gender binary.

As a person who identifies with some feminist ideals, concepts of power and privilege tied to maleness were an issue for me. Deep down, did I hate being female? I think of all of the women of color I know, and all my friends who are women healers, curanderas, homeopaths, naturopaths, herbalists, and shamans, who use their feminine power to heal. I love this! And that is what has made me sad—I don't want to leave those women's healing circles. I don't want to be an outsider or give up the power inherent in being a woman.

Skating the ice between the two genders is a struggle. Trans men want to know why I still have breasts and why I don't take hormones. Feminists want to know why I pack and bind, why I consider myself transmasculine. Men want to know why I hang out with women if I'm male. Though I have always understood men's thinking patterns better, I can also understand the actions of their girlfriends, wives, and sisters.

At the end of the day I'm not male or female. There is no label for who I am, except Toi. And maybe I feel guilty for being an unlabeled entity moving fluidly through all of these circles. I feel guilty because they all want me to take up allegiance to them—but I belong to all and none at the same time.

I will purge this guilt in my heart. I will try my best to explain to everyone who asks or is confused. I will try to keep an open heart and be full of compassion when people think that I am an anomaly, a freak, and not one of "them" any longer.

This is all I can offer: Dialogue. Compassion. Authenticity.

For some trans people of color, community building happens within religious and spiritual groups. Dealing with trauma, violence, and the stresses of everyday life often leads us to look for outlets centered on self-care. The organization TransFaith in Color puts on conferences, meetups, and other types of cultural events that draw diverse members of the community. Community members build alliances and help to combat

Monica Roberts, an African American trans woman, started the blog TransGriot in response to the lack of trans visibility in the blogosphere. She writes extensively on underexplored issues such as black trans icons and policy changes that will affect trans people of color. She is a vocal critic of homophobia and transphobia within racial communities.

The Audre Lorde Project (ALP) is a Lesbian, Gay, Bisexual, Two-Spirit, Trans, and Gender Nonconforming People of Color center for community organizing, focusing on the New York City area. ALP's antiviolence program, Safe OUTside the System, led by LGBTQ people of color living in Bed-Stuy and surrounding neighborhoods in Brooklyn, organizes and educates local businesses and community organizations on how to stop violence without relying on law enforcement. TransJustice is a political group of ALP created by and for trans and gender nonconforming people of color that works to mobilize communities and allies into action on political issues such as gaining access to jobs, housing, and education; the need for trans-sensitive health care, HIV-related services, and job-training programs; and resisting police, government, and anti-immigrant violence.

the misleading stereotype that people of color, especially those who are religious, are homophobic and transphobic.

ORGANIZING BY TRANS PEOPLE OF COLOR

Trans people of color are more often victims of violence, more often subject to targeting by police and other law enforcement agencies, and more often labeled as criminals. Many of our organizations led by trans people of color invest energy into fighting against police harassment and discrimination. Many of us also see law enforcement as a poor way to decrease crime and violence. For example, legislation aimed at lengthening prison sentences for crimes that are considered hate crimes perpetuates the use of law enforcement, rather than restorative justice, to solve problems. It means that more people spend more time in jail. Groups such as Communities United Against Violence (CUAV) and the Audre Lorde Project (ALP) create strategies for shifting discussions about hate crimes to discussions about community empowerment.

Trans people of color are also disproportionately affected by poverty. Instead of treating racial and wealth privilege as completely separate concepts, many groups led by transgender people of color make links between racism and poverty, and stand up for poor people by working against discriminatory institutions and systems that can include but are not limited to welfare/public assistance programs, educational systems, and health care systems.

Trans people of color have a rich history of activism. Two key players in this history are Sylvia Rivera and Marsha P. Johnson, whose visibility during the 1960s and early 1970s helped to shift the civil rights movement of the time, which focused on racial equality, to include members of trans and queer communities. Rivera, a Latina trans woman raised in New York City, and Johnson, a black trans woman from New Jersey, began their activism within gay movements, where they pushed the groups they were involved with to combat transphobia, sometimes succeeding and sometimes coming up against overwhelming resistance. They also worked collectively with the Young Lords and the Black Panthers. They were an integral part of the Stonewall Riots. Together they founded the first shelter in the United States designed to house homeless queer and trans youth sex workers, S.T.A.R. House, the name of which came from their activist group, Street Transvestite Action Revolutionaries.

Grassroots activism is not the only place in which trans people of color have effected change. In the past decade, we have seen growing representation in the political realm. In 2008, Latino trans man Diego Sanchez became the first transgender individual to be part of the Democratic National Committee (DNC). One of Sanchez's most important acts was his testimony before the US House of Representatives on discrimination toward transgender people in the workplace. In this speech, he shared his personal experience with discriminatory practices as a trans man of color. It was Sanchez's hard work with the DNC that propelled Rep. Barney Frank to solicit his services as a legislative aide, ultimately making Sanchez the first openly trans person to hold a congressional staff position. Diego Sanchez's precedent-setting speech helped to open the doors for other trans people of color to use their personal stories in the fight for gender justice on Capitol Hill. In 2012, African American lawyer Kylar Broadus became the first transgender person to testify before the Senate, publicly sharing his experiences of discrimination as Sanchez had.

THIS YA HISTORY

Micah Domingo is a rapper who utilizes hip-hop to narrate his existence living, struggling, and loving as a queer person of color. As a queer trans man born to South African immigrants, he speaks about the physical and the metaphysical, contemplating the gray areas of his life as well as the life around him.

Micah Domingo (photo by Alexander Rose).

This the life of a family boy
life of a tranny boy
stuck in the nooks and crannies, boy
i'll get you try to understand me,
but no promises, cuz i ain't that fancy
grew up in a world where my skin stuck out
didn't take after my brother, who took the
rough route
rode out my high school days, in a daze
thank god my adolescence was just a phase
working a shit job, getting paid
gotta get that wrist rocked,
heart ablaze
gotta get outta that cow town
before it sucked me in and made me bow down
fled the scene as soon as they found out
now i reside where the summers are humid
and the winters are brutal
my resistance is futile
but i move through
make my way from dirt to concrete
from green to gray in a heartbeat
trade the chains for a cotton long leash
chuck taylors and some skinny blue jeans
for those that knew me
and continue to be part of my history
through the chaos and misery, you're a part of me
like muscles and arteries
like plato and socrates
it's my history that elucidates me
an energy that moves me from point A to point B
with all that mess it can get a bit noisy
they say it started with a riot
but i don't buy it
humble beginnings from the times of pyramids and pirates
just more vocal, and a lot less local
now more photos, a lot more global
deeply buried stories coming to the surface
the arch of history bends with a purpose
toward victory and liberty
solidly toward equality and dignity
say it with me
we are a force to be reckoned with
we are a force to be reckoned with
our identities and rights are not tentative
not satisfied with the rights you pretend to give
exchange pleasantries for your own benefit
abuse those you got re-elected with
From Cal I forn-ia to Connecticut
We're put on this earth cuz we were meant to live

Trans people of color are active in performing all over the world. Catch one of these acts:
-D'Lo is a queer Tamil Sri L.A. nkan-American, political theatre artist/writer, director, comedian, and music producer.
-Ryka Aoki is a writer, performer, and professor at Santa Monica College.
-Wordz the poet emcee is a conscious HipHop artist of Jamaican descent from Philadelphia, Pennsylvania, who has dedicated his life to creating art for social change.

"Being allies to people of color in the struggle to end racism is one of the most important things that white people can do. There is no correct way to be an ally. Each of us is different. We have different relationships to social organizations, political processes, and economic structures. We are more or less powerful because of such factors as our gender class, work situation, family, and community participation."—Paul Kivel, *Uprooting Racism: How White People Can Work for Racial Justice.*

ALLIES

What does it mean to be an ally? Being an ally can mean different things to different people. People who identify as allies can come from various races, ethnicities, cultures, and socioeconomic backgrounds. Some of us who consider ourselves allies identify as white trans people, while some of us who are people of color can be allies who support the needs of trans people of different backgrounds. It is not easy to be an ally and it can be challenging to understand the ways in which we can effectively support the needs of trans people of color who have diverse ethnic, racial, and class backgrounds. Being an ally as a white trans person is difficult and necessary if we are to make society a better place for trans people of color.

> "I figure it's better to be a little quieter in my support than to invade safe-spaces that aren't mine, so I err on the side of caution there. My privilege means my involvement in a group could not be anything but problematic."

> "I think it would oppressive and appropriative of me to get involved in such groups. I do my best to be an ally to these folks."

Those of us who are people of color but do not consider ourselves of trans experience, can work to understand what it means to embody different gender identities, to transition, and to be subjected to the harsh realities of a world that often violently controls and suppresses the freedoms of trans people of color. Cisgender people of color who are or want to be allies to trans people of color are important in creating and challenging individuals and groups that oppresses trans people of color, often while residing within the same neighborhoods and communities.

Some of us who are allies have found ways to support people of color in ways that are helpful. There are also many ways to learn more about antiracist work we can do as allies.

> "I don't feel it's my place to be a part of these communities. However, I try to be the best ally I can in listening to these groups and helping them however I can when I am asked."

> "I am a white ally of FIERCE, the Audre Lorde Project, TransJustice, and a part of other multiracial projects like Third Root, Generation Five, SRLP."

> "I try to be the best ally that I can be, educating myself about my privilege as a white person and about how I can work with the larger trans community to better serve those who are more disenfranchised. We are too demonized by social conservatism already, and it horrifies me to see racism and ableism in our community. White trans folks can't allow themselves to forget that they still operate under racial privilege."

BOI

Megan Benton, also known as Emotions The P.O.E.T., has a master's degree (MA) in clinical psychology from Antioch University, with an emphasis in LGBTQ studies. Megan is an MFT Intern and one of the cofounders of Theta Xi Theta, Fraternity, Inc. Megan provides a healing space for clients to develop healthy identities in regard to the intersection of race, culture, sex, gender, lifestyle, and spirituality, and a brave space to explore life challenges (www.meandmybois.com).

New Orleans
Black in the middle of spring

Brass players congregating
As they prepare for the second line
My gown covering internal agony
What's next?
Success, failure, endless possibilities
Love covering my skin
Sweat drenching from my locs
Grass beneath my feet
I walk in violation
The leaders of the elite institution said:
All women must wear black dresses to commencement
No professor ever gave a lesson on gender expression
Why must womanhood be wrapped in expectation?
So I wear black
Black button down, slacks and loafers
All designed for male
Partially following directions
But why must I be directed by gender
I've always fallen somewhere in between
Restroom doors swinging off of filthy hinges
With signs dangling
Reading male or female
There is no third entrance
The world gender phobic
I gender fucked
Piss runs down my leg in disbelief
Who knew that dumping waste could be so complicated?
I was taught to act like a lady
Institutionalized to be feminine
Somewhere in between learning to put on lip gloss
I fell in love with masculinity
Hiding my body from the hyper sexual fantasies of men twice my age
Joe boxers painted against these curvy hips
Like graffiti paints a glow on cold brick in Los Angeles
I hid myself behind graphic tees that said: Fuck you pay me
Pay me attention
It takes a lot of courage to be vulnerable
Walking in violence
Men afraid of losing privilege
Women afraid of difference
Dapper, clean cut
Locs twisted to the scalp
Tappers, line of precision
See I make masculinity look pretty
We make masculinity look pretty
Me&MyBois
Brown Boi
Theta Boi
Queer Boi
Boi
B-O-I
Born obviously incredible
Wear that Bowtie with pride
Folded into perspective
Difference is not taught but learn to be subordinate

In elementary school
Perspective felt meaningless
Abnormality fractured faces on the play ground
Potential was written on the wall with chalk
I was a masterpiece easily erased
Blood covering skin
Knuckles tearing my beauty
Feet folding and stomping my insides out
Bullied for being a he she
I guess they thought they could beat the man out of me
Who am I safe to be?
Resiliency made me a success
I am BOI
B-O-I
Beaten outwardly and internally
Difference holds so much potential
Boi
Born obviously incredible
Especially when you wear it pretty

It is important to keep in mind that being an ally takes commitment and perseverance. Being an ally is not something that ever ends. Trans people of color will continue to struggle for the same rights and freedoms as white transgender and cisgender people. Some strategies for being a good ally include the following:

- *Actively listen.* When you find yourself thinking about what *you* are going to say before another person has finished speaking, take a pause and listen. You may be missing important information.
- *Acknowledge privilege.* Recognize your privilege, and understand the ways in which privilege contributes to how you walk through the world and the experiences that you have.
- *Center the experiences of people of color.* You may know the statistics or have friends who are people of color and be aware of their stories. Reporting these facts and stories can be helpful, but look around the room first to see if there is someone with a firsthand experience they are willing to share.
- *Be curious.* You may know a lot, but you can always learn more. Chances are that there is someone present who has an experience that will be new to you.
- *Empower people of color.* When there are important tasks to be done or leadership roles to be filled, nominate people you think would be strong leaders and who represent the faces of their communities. Be aware of how you can use power and privilege to help give others a voice, not silence voices.
- *Support the strategies of those affected.* It can be tempting to hear about someone's problems and feel as though you know how to solve them. Sometimes lending an ear is just as helpful as trying to solve another person's problems. Community-driven solutions are often the most successful.
- *Learn about other allies.* Look for role models who are solid allies working to foster equality and justice within social movements.
- *Move beyond guilt.* Empower holistic ally and community building by accepting and then moving beyond your own shame.

CONCLUSION

Our race and ethnicity contribute to the ways we see ourselves and are seen by others. Some of us experience oppression on a daily basis due to our status as people of color.

Many of us also benefit from privilege. As transgender people from many different racial and ethnic backgrounds, we are responsible for identifying our privilege and working toward changing systems that oppress us and the people we love in order to create a better world for ourselves and for future generations.

REFERENCES AND FURTHER READING

Cole, B., & Han, L. (Eds.). (2011). *Freeing ourselves: A guide to health and self-love for Brown Bois.* Oakland, CA: Brown Boi Project.

Driskill, Q-L., Justice, D. H., Miranda, D., & Tatonetti, L. (Eds.). (2011). *Sovereign erotics: A collection of two-spirit literature.* Tucson: University of Arizona Press.

Herdt, G. (Ed.). (1996). *Third sex, third gender: Beyond sexual dimorphism in culture and history.* Cambridge, MA: MIT Press.

Jacobs, S. E., Thomas, W., & Lang, S. (Eds.). (1997). *Two-spirit people: Native American gender identity, sexuality, and spirituality.* Champaign: University of Illinois Press.

Kivel, P. (2011). *Uprooting racism: How white people can work for racial justice.* Gabriola Island, BC: New Society.

League of United Latin American Citizens, National Center for Transgender Equality, and National Gay and Lesbian Task Force. (2011). *Injustice at every turn: A look at Latino/a respondents in the national transgender discrimination survey.* Retrieved September 2013, from http://www.transequality.org/Resources/Injustice_Latino_englishversion.pdf

Mock, J. (2014). *Redefining realness: My path to womanhood, identity, love & so much more.* New York, NY: Atria Books.

National Black Justice Coalition, National Center for Transgender Equality, and National Gay and Lesbian Task Force. (2011). *Injustice at every turn: A look at black respondents in the national transgender discrimination survey.* Retrieved September 2013, from http://www.transequality.org/PDFs/BlackTransFactsheetFINAL_090811.pdf

National Queer Asian Pacific Islander Alliance, National Center for Transgender Equality, and National Gay and Lesbian Task Force. (2012). *Injustice at every turn: A look at Asian American, South Asian, Southeast Asian, and Pacific Islander respondents in the national transgender discrimination survey.* Retrieved September 2013, from http://www.transequality.org/Resources/ntds_asianamerican_english.pdf

Newman, T. (2011). *I rise: The transformation of Toni Newman.* Seattle, WA: Amazon Digital Services/CreateSpace.

Snorton, C. R., & Haritaworn, J. (2013). Trans necropolitics: A transnational reflection on violence, death, and the trans of color afterlife. In S. Stryker and A. Z. Aizura (Eds.), *The transgender studies reader 2* (pp. 66–76). New York, NY: Routledge.

Valerio, M. W. (2006). *The testosterone files: My hormonal and social transformation from female to male.* Emeryville, CA: Seal Press.

3

IMMIGRATION
Kate Kourbatova and Elana Redfield

THE LIVES OF TRANS IMMIGRANTS ARE VARIED. We come from a broad range of cultural backgrounds, with many different religious experiences, economic situations, and racial backgrounds. The way we understand gender roles and the reasons that we migrated from one place to another can be quite different. Many of our experiences are very specific to a particular culture or transition from one place to another, and they may not be true for all trans immigrants. Nevertheless, there are threads that tie our experiences together and make the idea of a "trans immigrant experience" more than just an abstraction.

Immigrant is an umbrella term for anyone who moves from one country or culture to live in another. A multitude of factors contribute to the diversity of trans immigrant experiences. One of the biggest sources of difference is the reason each of us moves from our home country in the first place. Sociologist Everett S. Lee (1966) describes these motivations as either a "push" or a "pull."

We can be drawn to ("pulled" toward) a new country by something like a job opportunity, cheaper education or housing, or a desire to experience a new culture. We can also be "pushed" from our home countries by hostile conditions. This could be anything from unlivable social conditions, like war or drought, to more personally targeted forces such as a political climate that is transphobic or homophobic, or violently repressive toward political opposition. The terms *refugee* or *asylee* are sometimes used to describe immigrants who were "pushed" from their home countries.

The Web site Queer Immigration collects resources and information for LGBTQ immigrants.

PARALLEL WORLDS

Micah, 27, lives in San Francisco and blogs at www.neutrois.me.

When my life began on April 23, 1986, in Mexico City, I was a girl. The doctor peeked between my legs and proclaimed it so. Nobody questioned it much, except me; silently, of course. I grew up devouring Amelia Bedelia and Roald Dahl and singing along to the latest Disney hits. Fifteen years of an American education branded me as an outcast in the greater Mexican culture. My failure to identify with fellow estrogen-bearing beings further accentuated my alienation. By the time I was seven years old, I decided I'd be going to Harvard and maintained the secretly harbored wish that, like Pinocchio, I would someday turn into a real boy. The decision to leave my home and my country for a prestigious American university was a simple one—at least it was the only lifelong dream that still had a chance of becoming reality.

"But you don't look Mexican."
"Are your parents Mexican?"
And my favorite: "I have a friend in Albuquerque."

At first unexpected, these responses soon became the norm whenever an American asked where I was from. With my white skin and blue eyes, I float by inconspicuously; nobody ever gives me a second glance when I order coffee with my flawless American English that I've been perfecting since I was three. However, the US government loves to remind me that, although I've lived my entire adult life in this country, I'm still just a temporary visitor. Begrudgingly welcome, I pay taxes for services I'm not even entitled to.

Yet I could never return to Mexico without feeling handicapped. I don't even know how to say "friend request" in Spanish, let alone navigate a cultural terrain I haven't set foot on in 10 years. Not to mention the friends I've made, the career I've built, and the home my partner and I have nourished. I grew up in Mexico, but I came of age in the United States.

After graduating from college, my significant other and I prepared for our cross-country move from Philadelphia to San Francisco. As we packed up our house, my gender was also being stuffed into boxes whose contents would shift the course of my identity when unwrapped. Figuring out that I wasn't really a girl—and that I could do something about it—was just the first hurdle in an infinite race against the gender binary. My gender is best described as not female and not male—a true exercise in logic. It's a rainbow: a refraction of light you're certain you see yet sure you can't ever touch. It exists without form. I've had to create something out of nothing.

Surgery has had irreversible effects on my body; it is now physically impossible to go back to the sex I once was. Not to mention it has socially cemented my identity as being part of the other side: I've stood in front of a judge declaring M is the correct initial for my driver's license. Yet no matter how many times my coworkers refer to me as "he," I'll still look like my father's 16-year old son, and never like my father, because I refuse to grow up to be a man.

Nowadays people don't look between my legs, yet they still proclaim I'm a girl. Or a boy. Their confidence has been shaken, to say the least. I'm comfortable where I am, finally happy to just be me. But the evidence of where I'm from will always remain, even though I don't belong there anymore. Stranger in a home land; home in a strange land. My birth certificate will forever brand me as Mexican, regardless of the distance. But when I obtain a US passport, it will never say that I was female. Someday, I'll be a real American man.

Some of us may be trans immigrants but not consider this label to be definitive to our experiences or identities. For instance, a person may have immigrated to the United States from Australia, but rather than considering "immigrant" to be an important part of their identity, they may just think of themselves as being Australian.

> *"Technically I am an immigrant, but I have been living in the U.S. for 31 years so I do not feel like an immigrant. Other than having to notify the Immigration Service of my upcoming name change, I don't think there has been any impact between my immigration status and my transgender status."*

> *"I'm an American expatriate in Japan, but I don't feel that that experience overlaps much with the transsexual experience. I'm an expat, with everything that entails—language barriers, being visibly alien everywhere I go, employment and visa issues, cultural incongruence. I'm also part of the gay community here, which is very partitioned off from the mainstream in its own little gay ghetto (Shinjuku ni-choume). And then once every two weeks I make a trip down to my clinic and get stuck with 50 cc of testosterone. My life in Japan is much more about the gay experience than the trans experience."*

IMMIGRATION AND IDENTITY

Where we come from, geographically, socially, and economically, can lead to vastly different lived experiences and affect the degree to which being trans complicates the immigration process and our identity as immigrants. These factors also affect the degree to which our experiences with immigration impact our ability to find a supportive community as trans people.

Economic class affects, among other things, how mobile we may be after we move and what kind of health care options we will have. For those of us who know we want to transition physically, class can influence many aspects of our transition. Some of us may be able to attend regular provider visits, participate in long-term therapy, and afford expensive gender-confirming surgeries. Others of us may procure hormones from potentially unsafe sources and use unreliable discount surgeons or industrial silicone without medical supervision in order to transition our bodies.

WE ARE THE INTERSECTIONS

micha cárdenas, MFA, MA, is an artist, hacktivist, poet,
performer, student, educator, mixed-race trans femme Latina
survivor who works at the intersection of movement, technology,
and politics, and a PhD student in media arts and practice at the
University of Southern California.

[32' 53 6.4608 // -117 14 20.4282]
Working on the Transborder Immigrant Tool was a given for me.
After years of creating electronic disturbance online, Ricardo
and Brett came to me with a plan
to create border disturbance, at the intersection of recycled
electronics and networked gps satellites
to direct people attempting to survive the desert of the Mexico/US border to water.
[25.684486, -80.441216]
My father fled the violence of the drug war in Colombia, and ended up in Miami,
Kendall Drive and 152nd avenue.
My birth was a result of the neocolonial policies sending weapons and neoliberalism to
Colombia,
and a result of the endless hunger of the US for illegal drugs,
the same drug war causing massive nonviolent uprisings across Mexico now.
[32.71215, -117.142478]
Five years ago, I finally found a queer community and an activist life that
supported me in being the trans girl I've wanted to be for so long,
after another activist community couldn't handle my transition
and wanted me to go to the men's group.
3,000 miles away from Miami's anti-Castro anti-gay anti-communism
away from my parents' catholicism, both Irish and Colombian.
This year,
thanks to
spironolactone,
prometrium,
estradiol,
thanks to the femme wisdom of my lovers and friends,
the femme science we are developing,
I started passing as female, passing enough to get harassed on the street.
[32' 50 26.4402 // -117 15 31.6542]
Walking around as a femme in most places,
feels like walking around being hunted.
I am conscious every day that I live in a country, the US,
that silences victims of sexual violence and often provides more
safety for rapists than for their survivors,
every night as we walk home from wherever we can find parking,
often in dark alleys or poorly lit streets,
since we can't afford housing that includes parking.
Fearing for our physical safety,
constantly avoiding the men who stare at us, leering,
is perhaps a nanoscale molecule of the feeling of being hunted by the
Border Patrol that migrant people feel when they cross borders.
Hungry eyes like hollow circles of night vision goggles.
The year that I finally felt that people saw me as a woman,
was also the year I joined so many women I've been close to
who were survivors of sexual violence of some kind.
In January, I learned I was a survivor of sexual violence I could not remember,
committed by a family member, incest.

First came the numbness, then came the paralyzing fear of telling anyone,
the fear of being wrapped up and written off in a narrative of pathology.
I was reminded of the words of Professor K Wayne Yang to his students:
You may not choose to be in this war, but you were born into it.
Perhaps, again like how people born in the global south feel,
in countries like Colombia and Mexico, terrorized by war and poverty,
do they feel that they were born into it,
that through no fault of their own they are survivors of violence, like me?
Violence of colonial steel walls, corrugated and mesh,
akin to the force of sexual- and gender-based violence,
We are constantly navigating the violence of borders of all kinds,
skittering across earth pinging satellites that never correctly know our exact locations,
for they never know how many kinds of thirst we feel.
[34.088705, -118.281894]
Now this fierce mixed race transgender incest survivor femme lesbian pornoterrorista
is even more unraveled, bare,
stronger,
even more pissed, behind her eyeliner, in her too red lipstick, leather V heels and
her black miniskirt dress,
even more ready to fight and burn and
create and dream new worlds into existence,
where the logic of western reason isn't used to uphold some false
image of nations and laws that
masks the absolute violence faced by so many who step outside of the borders,
or who are born outside of them, or who choose to cross them.
and I am here to fight and fuck and give birth
to border disturbances,
to queer and mayan technologies that can reveal national borders for the fictions they are,
to technologies of survival and femme disturbance.
I am the intersection, of too many coordinate systems to name.
We are the intersections, and we exceed the borders placed upon us.

We may also have unique cultural expectations of gender depending on our racial or ethnic backgrounds. Racism among other immigrants or the citizens of our new country can also hinder our connection to the broader community. The scope of our social networks largely determines our economic opportunities.

> *"I'm an immigrant from Vietnam and it just adds onto all of the pressure. Being a minority within a minority."*

Because our cultural expectations of gender roles are shaped by the place we are from and the religion or culture we were raised in, the way we express gender in our home country may not be consistent with the culture of our new country. Many cultures have gendered expectations related to occupations, clothing, raising children, and family structure. These expectations are pervasive and often reach into the details of daily life, from who grows which crops to who is expected to wear which colors. As trans immigrants, we become particularly aware of these culturally determined gender roles, since moving from one country to another also forces us to transition to a new gender system.

> *"As a Brazilian immigrant in the United States, I feel that perhaps the up-bringing of the individuals in such minority groups was different and affects the way they view and express gender identity. I know from personal experience as a Latino(a) person, I was taught that the differences between the sexes are much more dramatic than they really are, meaning I had a particularly difficult time accepting my genderqueer identity."*

The languages we speak and how accented our speech is in the language of a new country affect both our economic opportunities and the degree of isolation we may feel in our new community. Moreover, some languages may be better suited for expressing nonbinary genders than others. This can affect the ease with which we are able to come out and communicate our identities to our families and communities.

GENDER ACROSS OUR CULTURES

Describing our journey as trans immigrants is a bit like trying to describe movement in multiple dimensions. There is the actual geographic movement from one place to another and the personal migration through which we come to redefine our social, cultural, and political context. Added to that is the dimension of gender expectations that comes with every society, which means that even without transitioning in some way, the way our gender is read and interpreted by others varies from place to place. Finally, there is the metaphorical "journey" of transition—shifting our gender expression or physical body. As trans immigrants, we can move in all of these dimensions at once, or one by one, in different orders and combinations.

As immigrants, we are raised, either in our home country or by our immigrant parents, to navigate gender using the compass provided by the culture we come from. Different cultures have different ideas about gender roles and responsibilities, and the experience of immigration can impact our feelings about our assigned and affirmed gender roles in a variety of ways. Moving into the context of another culture will likely change which parts of the gender norms "fit" our identity and which ones do not. This transition can be somewhat uncomfortable, even for cisgender people.

For trans immigrants, this can impact our family relationships, too. For example, younger generations are often more integrated than older generations into the mainstream society of the new country. A trans person who emigrated as a child, or is born to immigrant parents, may use the gender roles of the country of residence for reference as they figure out their gender identity, while their parents may still largely be operating on the gender ideals of the culture they came from, resulting in an extra source of misunderstanding and separation.

Our experiences as trans immigrants highlight the uncomfortable instability of gender norms, which can make even an otherwise constant gender identity look or feel

The documentary *Crossing Over* (2013), directed by Isabel Castro, tells the story of three transgender immigrants from Mexico who are seeking political asylum in the United States due to emotional, physical, and sexual abuses inflicted upon them in their home country.

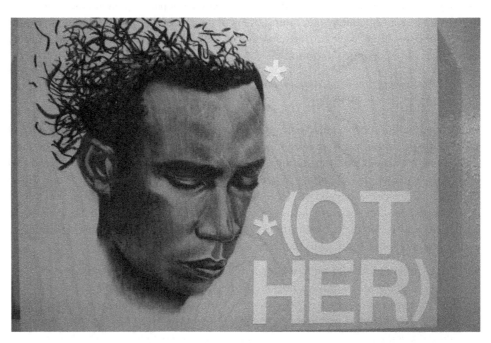

"Other," Portraits of a Noun (Hill Wolfe).

fluid. We either adapt to the new culture by adjusting our gender presentation to end up in a similar place on the gender spectrum as before, or we maintain the same gender presentation but have to deal with being seen differently.

OF MIGRATING AND LOCKETS

Elias Krell is a musician, scholar, performer, creative writer, and actor based in the Chicago area.

When I was younger, I was obsessed with lockets. I loved the idea of having an object around my neck that concealed something of significance, whose presence others were barely aware of, that I knew was there, and that I could show (or not show) to whomever I chose. For me, the locket works as an affirming and exciting metaphor for my trans identity—it is powerful, erotic, and it protects me.

After living in Europe, Honduras, and Mexico as a young person, I emigrated to the United States with my family when I was eight. A large part of my identity is in Honduras; the land, the people, the political, economic, and social issues there, and, of course, with my family, whom I love deeply and who love me. One aspect of trans experience that is often starkly absent in discussions in the US is the effect of being "out" on immigrants who migrate from non-US contexts, especially from neocolonized countries. I often field questions from within and without the trans community: When are you going to start T? Why can't you be "out" at that wedding you're going to?

But the idea of being "in" or "out" to my Latin American family and extended community is complicated by specific factors that have deep historic colonial roots. Medically transitioning involves contending with deeply entrenched religious and conservative ideals. That said, I don't support the inaccurate notion that the Global South is more homo- and trans-phobic than the US; these ideals have arisen in large part as a result of colonialism, and also in response to racism and xenophobia. In the US, immigrants and our families have much higher stakes in medically transitioning. We and our families experience xenophobia, racism, classism, and hegemony in the US on a daily basis. Trans identity, as well as sexuality, look and feel very different when you have to juggle two different national, cultural, and linguistic worlds.

Accessing Latino/a queer and trans communities within the States has been a crucial form of support, but it is not the same as being in the place that formed my soft palate, how I think (in Spanish first, then English), how I interact with others, and how my body reacts to the sun, humidity, and the passing breeze. To travel to Honduras, I depend on being accepted into cars and homes, without which I could not be safe.

The locket can work as an alternate framework for thinking about trans identity—one that doesn't come with the loaded connotations of being "in" or "out" (of the closet) but views trans identity as something special to share when/where we choose. A locket can be a source of strength and affirmation. I continue to walk in my Latino/a and non-Latino/a trans and queer communities, finding affirmation in the fact that part of me will always be more at home where I am least seen: in the warm, sunny places of my childhood.

These experiences can present a challenge to the idea that gender identity is constant and reflects an internal truth. Instead, the trans immigrant experience of having our gender suddenly read differently brings to light the dual nature of gender as a combination of identity or self-expression and the need to be correctly understood and seen by others.

IMMIGRATION STATUS

The institutions that immigrants deal with as we navigate a new country or culture are frequently indifferent to the complicated nature of our identities. For those of us who are both trans and immigrants, we confront unique issues as we live and work in society.

Whether we immigrate for work, to be with family members, or because we are unsafe in our home country due to our identities or political beliefs, most of us would prefer to have some form of legal immigration status. Temporary legal immigrant statuses in the United States can include business, student, or family visas; asylum applications; and withholding of removal; as well as others. Permanent resident statuses include permanent residency (i.e., green card) and citizenship.

Some legal immigration statuses mean we can travel freely, work with the benefit of labor protections and without fear of getting raided, and remain in our chosen country with some degree of security. Those with the most secure forms of status, such as green card holders, can access government support such as health care, welfare, and social security.

"I lived in Canada as an undocumented immigrant for a few years. It was hard to get a job without paperwork, and being visibly trans (this was pre-hormones) didn't help me get work either. I moved back to the States because I couldn't get status in Canada and it's so much easier for me to get jobs and access health care here. I knew that I needed to transition and that I could never do it without money and insurance, and since there was no way I could get those things in Canada, I resigned myself to moving back to the States even though my chosen family and all my close friends (except my wife) are still in Canada. So basically, being trans made being an immigrant impossible for me. And that is speaking as a relatively privileged American citizen who passes as white. I'm close with a lot of trans Mexican and Central American immigrants here in DC, and they have a lot of the same issues but it's much harder for them. And they mostly don't have the option of returning to their previous country, like I did."

Many immigrants face challenges to obtaining legal status, such as caps on the number of people eligible each year, lack of qualifying family or job relationships, language barriers, and financial barriers. Trans immigrants are likely to confront all of these, and we may have our own specialized issues as well.

IDENTITY DOCUMENTS

Immigrants seeking status may rely on documents from our home countries that are hard to obtain or contain old names, pictures, and gender markers that do not conform to our gender expression. Once we obtain immigration IDs, such as a green card or a work permit, updating that information can be a challenge due to many factors, including cost, complicated filing requirements, and long processing delays.

"A large part of my reluctance to go through various changes has to do with my fear for my papers. I need all my pictures and all my documents to match, and I can't afford to cause trouble right now."

"I was stopped at Immigration and questioned about my Visa photo as it was recent and very feminine, whereas my passport photo is a few years before I started transition. I came in 'boy mode' (the last time I did any such thing) because we thought it would be easier. [The immigration officer] told me never ever do that again. It's not fair on me and no one is going to treat me with disrespect. If any of the Immigration Staff tried that one on they'd have the entire colleague's team kicking their asses. I cried at the counter. She gave me a tissue and said 'Live the life you should' and stamped my Visa."

The Queer Undocumented Immigrant Project (QUIP) empowers queer undocumented youth by providing leadership development, establishing spaces for healing and support, creating a curriculum to educate our communities about the intersection between the immigrant and LGBTQ rights movements, and documenting the struggles of queer undocumented youth.

There is some progress being made in the US immigration system regarding identity documents. In 2012, The US Citizenship and Immigration Services (USCIS) issued a policy memorandum specifying the requirements for updating the gender marker on immigration identity documents. The USCIS policies allow us to correct the gender on our documents by presenting an amended birth certificate, passport, or court order recognizing our corrected gender or a medical certification from a licensed physician who has treated us or reviewed our medical history. This letter must say that we have had the appropriate clinical treatment for gender transition. Proof of gender-affirming surgery is not required.

FAMILY RELATIONSHIPS

Many forms of immigration status require a family member who already has status to file the application for the person who will receive it. The family member who files may also be required to show a willingness to financially support the recipient. As trans people, we may not have that kind of family support.

"I am a second-generation immigrant from Russia. It's very difficult for me to talk to my mother (dad is an American) about this. She is still stuck in the

mindset that even being gay is a mental imbalance, and so with any discussion of my identity I quickly become too tearful and disgusted to continue talking. I wish there was a way to approach it with her, but until I have become a bit more self-sufficient financially, that probably isn't going to be an option."

As trans people, we are disproportionately likely to be alienated from our families, have strained relationships, or be unwilling or unable to maintain the kind of relationships that non-trans people can rely on for emotional support, financial support, or help with immigration status. The National Transgender Discrimination Survey (Grant et al., 2011) found that 57% of trans people interviewed had experienced significant family rejection because of their trans status.

If we are alienated from our families or they do not accept our gender expression, we may have a hard time going through this process with them. Furthermore, family-based applications can last for years—sometimes more than a decade. These many complications suggest that trans people may be disproportionately unable to obtain legal immigration status through a family member.

For those of us who rely on our family's sponsorship in order to apply for legal immigration status, we may have difficult choices to make. Sometimes we may have to compromise about our gender presentation or behavior, at least around our families, in order for them to continue their sponsorship. This can potentially lead us to feel isolated from those who might understand and approve of our identities more readily. Sometimes our families learn, over time, to accept us for who we are, but some will not, and some of us may end up making sacrifices to protect our legal status.

UndocuQueer: Stories From the Intersection of the Undocumented and Queer Movements is a book project that shares the stories of undocumented queer people.

THE CAGE

Tommy, 31, is originally from Poland and now lives in California. He proudly attends UC Berkeley under California law AB540 (qualified undocumented students pay in-state tuition).

I live with the reality of an unsteady immigration status and transgender identity. I often visualize myself as a caged bird; each time I have encountered a demoralizing challenge, it was as if my flight feathers were being pulled out. I was scared that once my birdcage door was opened, I would not recognize freedom. Would I leave the cage? Could I still fly?

I lived with my mom and stepdad for a year after they married, before my stepdad kicked me out of their house for being queer. I was 19 and undocumented. At first I was homeless and lived out of my car or stayed with friends. I eventually began to earn a living cleaning houses and doing other odd jobs while attending community college. Seven years after being kicked out of my parents' house and living in fear, the reality of deportation materialized. After much distress, my two identities came together; it was because of my transgender identity that I was permitted to remain in the United States.

My cage door was open, but I did not fly right away.

Acknowledging that I am transgender challenged my inner strength. I lost loved ones when I began transitioning about 3 years ago, but I would have lost me had I not taken the chance to trust in myself. I have peeked my head out of the cage; I have even flown a few times. I like who I am becoming as a result of my humbling experiences.

EMPLOYMENT AND IMMIGRATION

Some trans immigrants may be able to get status through jobs. However, employment-based immigration status requires an employer to file on behalf of the immigrant, and most of the time the employer must file extensive paperwork showing the need and desire for the particular worker. This process requires a strong relationship between the worker and the employer.

The National Transgender Discrimination survey (Grant et al., 2011) demonstrated that transgender people face workplace discrimination at alarming rates and are disproportionately likely to be unemployed or on bad terms with employers. Twenty-six percent of respondents had been fired and as many as 47% had had some kind of negative job outcome simply because they were trans. Not only that, but 97% of those surveyed had experienced harassment or discrimination on the job. This is especially likely in low-wage jobs, where both immigrants and trans people are likely to find work.

HEALTH CARE

Unfortunately, most undocumented people and even many documented immigrants are ineligible for health care coverage, so many of us who are trans immigrants may not be able to meet our transition-related health needs, such as hormonal or surgical interventions. Unfortunately, sometimes those same treatments are required for official recognition of our gender identity, such as with the USCIS.

TRANSITION NARRATIVES

Many trans people seeking immigration status will at some point or another need to tell their story to an immigration officer. Whether we are seeking status based on discrimination or violence in our home country, or whether we simply need to make sure our new green card shows the right gender, the issue of our transition is likely to come up. The extent to which the immigration officer is familiar with trans issues will play a role in whether the transition narrative satisfies the officer.

The common narratives about gender transition come into play in the questions that we are asked by immigration officials. We will likely be asked when we transitioned, what medical treatments we had, and whether we have updated all of our other documents and changed our name legally. Often, the extent to which our stories fit into common narratives affects whether they will be successful.

For those who are still in transition, or whose gender identity is more fluid than simply male or female, the common narratives about trans people may hurt rather than help us in telling our stories. Additionally, gender transition in one country or culture may look very different in another country or culture. Generally, it is best to use as straightforward a narrative as possible with government officials, as many are unfamiliar with the concepts around transgender identities.

POLITICAL ASYLUM

Asylum is granted when a USCIS or immigration judge determines that a person is likely to face persecution in their home country on account of a particular characteristic. Some of the most common characteristics include race, ethnic group, religion, political belief, or membership in a particular social group. As trans people, many of us have been able to gain asylum status by showing that we faced persecution in our home countries due to our gender expression, sexual orientation, or political views. Gender expression and sexual orientation are generally felt to make us part of particular social groups that face persecution. In order to get political asylum, applicants have to be able to prove that they experienced persecution, and that it was either at the hands of their prior government's officials or that the prior government did nothing to stop persecution by nongovernment persecutors.

Sometimes we experience forms of violence that are easy to recognize and document, such as getting a death threat when speaking in public about trans issues. However, as trans people, we often face specific forms of abuse and discrimination that may be harder to document or that exist in countries that are not otherwise considered unsafe by immigration officials. For example, we may face violence from police when we go out dressed in clothes that affirm our gender, whereas people who fall more neatly within the accepted gender norms are less likely to experience this violence. We may not be able to open a business or go to work in our home country simply because we are trans. Sometimes we may experience persecution simply because our gender expression goes against cultural norms and expectations, even if we do not identify as trans. The fact that persecution is so unique and personalized for many trans people means that we can have a harder time making a case for asylum.

Immigration Equality is a national organization fighting for LGBTQ immigrants, especially asylum seekers. They have a pro bono asylum project in which they match low-income asylum seekers with volunteer attorneys.

The deadline for applying for asylum is one year from our most recent arrival in the United States. Even if we can make a convincing claim for asylum, we still may not be able to get asylum status if we do not file on time. Countless cases are denied on these grounds every year. Many transgender immigrants have come to the United States without any kind of status. We may be unaware that we could get asylum, or afraid that the case would be denied and we would be forced to return to our home country against our will. Some of us have been in the country for years before we apply. We may not apply until we are picked up by police or immigration officers and placed in removal proceedings, which can complicate the process further.

Sometimes we may be excused from the one-year rule because circumstances related to our gender transition made it impossible or extraordinarily difficult to file for asylum in a timely fashion. Our transition narratives can play a significant role in determining whether we are able to seek asylum after the one-year deadline. We may have been harassed and attacked in our home country throughout our lives for our gender expression. On the other hand, we might have come to the United States and transitioned here because we finally had a space where we could do this in relative safety.

Some of us experienced so much violence in our home countries because of our gender expression that we were traumatized and unable to begin the asylum process in time to make the one-year deadline. People who are diagnosed with posttraumatic stress disorder (PTSD), a condition where experiences of trauma or violence cause long-term damage to a person's mental health, often fall into this category (see Mukamusoni v. Ashcroft, 2004). Whether or not a person is able to obtain asylum is heavily dependent on the individual facts of the case.

Those of us not eligible for asylum may be able to obtain a status called "withholding of removal." Withholding of removal is exactly what it sounds like—the immigration judge can stop removal of a person who is in removal proceedings if the judge believes they are more likely than not to be persecuted. Unlike asylum, a person with withholding of removal cannot ever obtain a green card and therefore cannot obtain citizenship. It is a permanent "limbo" status. The United States has also signed on to an international agreement called the Convention Against Torture that forbids the government from deporting someone to a country where they are certain the person will experience torture.

MARRIAGE-BASED IMMIGRATION STATUS

Marriage is one of the most common ways that immigrants obtain lawful status. Immigration officials look extremely closely at marriages to make sure they are not fraudulent. The length of the marriage, whether finances are mingled together or separated, whether the couple lives together, photographs of the couple doing things together at various stages of the relationship—these are just some of the things immigration officers use to decide whether they think a marriage is "bona fide." However, if a couple can prove the marriage is bona fide, marriage can be a fantastic way to obtain status. A recognized spouse can often obtain what is called a "conditional" green card, which is a two-year green card, even if they were previously undocumented, and can then get a regular green card and become eligible for citizenship three years later (Monger & Yankey, 2011).

Unfortunately, the question of "bona fide" marriage, or legitimate marriage, is more complicated for transgender people. USCIS is concerned with the public policy implications of trans marriage. In many ways, the issue turns on whether a trans marriage is considered to be a heterosexual marriage or homosexual marriage under state law. Until 2013, the Defense of Marriage Act (DOMA) prohibited the federal government from recognizing gay marriage. Up until then, USCIS chose to dodge the bullet by using a simple rule: If the marriage was considered a valid heterosexual marriage in the state where it took place, then USCIS recognized it. If the marriage was not considered valid or was considered a

The National Immigrant Justice Center in Chicago offers consultations for LGBTQ asylum seekers and their attorneys, as well as collecting data and documenting persecutory conditions in different countries that can then be used by asylum seekers as evidence in cases.

Intimate partner violence (IPV) is physical, sexual, or emotional abuse that occurs between intimate partners. Studies have shown that trans people are particularly vulnerable to IPV situations. The same conditions that make transgender immigrants particularly vulnerable to IPV often prevent transgender immigrants from accessing social services for safety planning and mental health. Similarly, domestic violence shelters and legal services often refuse to provide support to trans people, leaving transgender and gender nonconforming immigrants without options. Finally, even when IPV services are trans inclusive, shame, fear, and not wanting to out oneself often prevent transgender immigrants from seeking necessary assistance. As a result, many transgender immigrants find themselves stuck in abusive or unhealthy relationships. For this reason, it is important to recognize these challenges and provide trans-affirming support services. —*Pooja Gehi, an attorney who works on intimate partner violence issues in transgender immigrant communities.*

homosexual marriage or civil union, then USCIS did not recognize it. The overturning of DOMA in 2013 opened many legal questions about the possibility of couples considered "same-sex" petitioning for legal immigration status. This question will likely be addressed in forthcoming lawsuits.

IMMIGRATION ENFORCEMENT AND DEPORTATION

We live in a time when immigration issues are treated similarly to criminal issues. Since the events of September 11, 2001, US immigration policy (as well as immigration in Europe) has become closely regulated. US states, such as Arizona, began passing laws allowing police and immigration officers to arrest anyone they suspected of breaking immigration laws. In 2012, the Secure Communities Initiative increased cooperation between government agencies, in order to close loopholes in immigration law countrywide. The result is that all immigrants—even people who have become US citizens—are vulnerable to being stopped and questioned about their immigration status. Undocumented people have fewer options than ever for obtaining immigration status or finding work or health care. More people than ever are being deported to their home countries against their will (Slevin, 2010).

Trans immigrants are more likely to be arrested and more likely to be stopped and questioned, because we are already facing scrutiny due to our gender expression. Any person who is arrested and convicted of a crime, or who serves time in prison, is at risk of losing immigration status or being unable to get it. Transgender people are sometimes arrested for doing things we need to do to survive. We are also sometimes targets for wrongful arrests because of discrimination (Mogul, Ritchie, & Whitlock, 2011). For example, it is not uncommon for a trans person to be charged with "loitering for purposes of prostitution" when we are simply waiting at a bus stop wearing clothes of our preferred gender. Any kind of arrest, wrongful or not, can jeopardize our ability to obtain lawful immigration status or keep it if we already have it.

We are also more likely to experience sexual harassment, isolation, and abuse than other people are while we are detained for immigration reasons (Harmon, 2012). Having ID cards that do not match our gender expression can cause us to face immigration consequences. Therefore, as trans immigrants we may be more likely to find ourselves placed in removal proceedings.

SAFETY AND COMMUNITY

As a response to the specific needs and challenges within our communities, trans immigrants and our allies are working together to provide support, address issues of health and safety, and participate in activism to challenge existing institutional problems.

Some examples of organizing by and for transgender immigrants include the following:

- Translatin@ in Los Angeles
- GLOBE Project at Make The Road NY in New York City
- TransgenerosLatinas NY in New York City

Many organizations provide services and advocacy for trans immigrants, including the following:

- Sylvia Rivera Law Project, based in New York City
- Asian/Pacific Islander Coalition on HIV & Aids (APICHA) Trans* Health Clinic, based in New York City
- Transgender Law Center, based in San Francisco, California

Often, trans immigrants turn to local LGBTQ centers and broader LGBTQ organizations for support. These organizations vary widely in scope. Some organizations are specifically concerned with immigration issues experienced by LGBTQ people. A few examples are as follows:

- Organization for Refuge, Asylum & Migration (ORAM), based out of San Francisco
- The LGBTI Refugee Advocacy program at PASSOP (People Against Suffering Oppression and Poverty) in Wynberg, Cape Town, South Africa
- Rainbow Refugee Association of Nova Scotia, based in Halifax, Nova Scotia, Canada

Some groups are specifically for LGBT people of a certain cultural background, such as Entre Hermanos, Seattle's Latino LGBT organization.

SERVING THE TRANSLATINA IMMIGRANT COMMUNITY IN QUEENS, NEW YORK

Cristina Herrera, BA, is a community organizer working with LGBT people in New York City, program coordinator for the Gender Identity Project (GIP) of the NYC LGBT Center, founder of the Translatina Network, and a board member of the Lorena Borjas Community Fund.

Over the past 13 years, the transgender Latina immigrant community of Western Queens has witnessed an evolution. Our Translatina group was first established in Queens in 2000 by the Hispanic AIDS Forum of New York City (HAF NYC). At that time, the Translatina community had very little support, and they often had to travel into Manhattan, hoping to find services. The HAF NYC Translatina group was started to address HIV/AIDS, trauma, transition, immigration, financial hardship, substance abuse, and discrimination.

As a group member, I remember learning that many participants bought hormones on the black market because they weren't able to connect with a doctor. Eventually the Callen-Lorde Community Health Center and HAF NYC came together and parked a mobile medical unit in front of HAF's office.

The Translatina Network enlisted the help of several NYC agencies with police harassment and unlawful arrest. At that time, Western Queens had become an epicenter for violence and hate crimes targeting transgender women, including incidents of profiling by law enforcement. Many women were subjected to Stop & Frisk and profiled as sex workers, especially when they had two or more condoms in their possession. The choice became clear: Don't carry condoms, or be at risk for arrest and deportation.

On Riker's Island, transgender women, who are usually housed in the men's unit, were being put directly into deportation if arrested without legal documentation. This led to the creation of the first-ever LGBT Bail Fund in NYC, which assists LGBT immigrants who are at risk of incarceration and deportation for misdemeanor offenses. It was amazing to see how much pride participants took in organizing and hosting the Ribbon Cutting Celebration for this initiative, named the Lorena Borjas Community Fund (LBCF) in appreciation of her work.

Perhaps our proudest achievement thus far has been training more than 17 group participants at the NYC Department of Health. They each earned certifications in HIV pre- and post-test counseling, group facilitation, and social networking. Currently many of our peer counselors work in prevention programs throughout the city, where they are helping other members of the community and providing unique insight.

Outside of larger urban areas, community groups explicitly supporting and advocating for trans immigrants are less common, partially because there are few places where there are enough of us to get such a group off the ground. Depending on where we are, it may be easiest to find an LGBTQ group or community center that is more general.

Some groups are trans-inclusive mostly in name, and a trans immigrant who joins such a group may have to do the work of creating a supportive space and guiding the group toward more inclusive organizing. The good news is, in recent years many community groups and activist collectives have been moving toward doing more intersectional and

The Bellevue/NYU Program for Survivors of Torture (PSOT) in New York City provides medical and mental health care, social and legal services to survivors of torture, and runs an LGBTQ therapy group.

inclusive work. More and more people are aware of the need for accessibility, gender-neutral facilities, sliding-scale fees, bilingual services, and are making other efforts to accommodate communities such as trans immigrants.

However, even with these new trends toward inclusiveness, some areas simply do not have these kinds of organizations. Luckily, we can turn to the Internet to help find people who are dealing with similar issues. Blogs, message boards, and social media can provide information and a sense of community when one is otherwise isolated. Groups such as Immigration Equality, the National Center for Transgender Equality, and the Transgender Law Center have Web sites that are informative on trans immigrant issues. Social media platforms like Facebook are providing space for very specifically targeted grassroots groups to spring up, such as Nigerian LGBTIs in Diaspora Against Anti-Same Sex Laws.

CONCLUSION

As trans immigrants, we often have the feeling of occupying two spaces, both with regard to our gender and the place where we belong. Our experiences are varied and complicated, and can often be difficult both emotionally and practically. However, our unique forms of knowledge as trans immigrants also provide us with the tools to understand the complexity of both gender and national identity. We live in a time when both trans and immigration issues frequently appear in the mainstream spotlight, paving the way for more understanding and acceptance both in LGBTQ spaces and with the general public. The political and social climate in many countries is warming up to the idea of trans rights as human rights. As we become more welcome in mainstream society, and our struggles become more visible, there are more opportunities than ever to find places where we belong.

REFERENCES AND FURTHER READING

Arizona State Senate Bill 1070, Forty Ninth Legislature, Second Regular Session, 2010.

Cotten, T. (Ed.). (2012). *Transgender migrations: The bodies, borders, and politics of transition.* New York, NY and London, UK: Routledge.

Danelius, H. (1984). *Convention against torture and other cruel, inhuman, or degrading treatment or punishment.* United Nations. Retrieved December 2013, from http://untreaty.un.org/cod/avl/ha/catcidtp/catcidtp.html

Gawaya, R. (2008). Investing in women farmers to eliminate food insecurity in southern Africa: Policy-related research from Mozambique. *Gender and Development, 16*(1), 147–159.

Grant, J. M., Mottet, L. A., Tanis, J., Harrison, J., Herman, J. L., & Keisling, M. (2011). *Injustice at every turn: A report of the national transgender discrimination survey.* Washington, DC: National Center for Transgender Equality and National Gay and Lesbian Task Force.

Harmon, A. (2012, May 7). Eight months in solitary: Is a government turf war over immigration putting transgender lives at risk. *The Advocate.* Retrieved December 2013, from http://www.advocate.com/news/news-features/2012/05/07/transgender-detainees-face-challenges-broken-immigration-system

Lee, E. S. (1966). A theory of migration. *Demography, 3*(1), 37–47.

Luibhéid, E., & Cantú, L., Jr., (Eds.). (2005). *Queer migrations: Sexuality, U.S. citizenship, and border crossings.* Minneapolis and London, UK: University of Minnesota Press.

Maglaty, J. (2011, April 8). When did girls start wearing pink? *Smithsonian.com.* Retrieved December 2013, from http://www.smithsonianmag.com/arts-culture/When-Did-Girls-Start-Wearing-Pink.html

Monger, R., & Yankey, J. (2011). *U.S. legal permanent residents: 2011. DHS Annual Flow Report.* Retrieved December 2013, from http://www.dhs.gov/xlibrary/assets/statistics/publications/lpr_fr_2011.pdf

Mukamusoni v. Ashcroft, 390 F.3d 110 (1st Cir. 2004).

Slevin, P. (2010, July 26). Deportation of illegal immigrants increases under Obama. *Washington Post.* Retrieved December 2013, from http://www.washingtonpost.com/wp-dyn/content/article/2010/07/25/AR2010072501790.html

Thomas, W. (1997). Navajo cultural constructions of gender and sexuality. In S-E. Jacobs, W. Thomas, & S. Lang (Eds.), *Two-spirit people: Native American gender identity, sexuality, and spirituality* (pp. 156–173). Urbana and Chicago: University of Illinois Press.

US Citizenship and Immigration Services. (2012). *Adjudication of immigration benefits for transgender individuals; Addition of adjudicator's field manual (AFM) subchapter 10.22 and revisions to AFM subchapter 21.3 (AFM Update AD12-02).* Policy Memorandum, PM-602-0061. Retrieved December 2013, from http://www.uscis.gov/USCIS/Outreach/ Feedback%20Opportunities/Interim%20Guidance%20for%20Comment/Transgender_ FINAL.pdf

US Citizenship and Immigration Services. (2013, February). *Immigration and Nationality Act.* Retrieved December 2013, from http://www.uscis.gov/portal/site/uscis/menuitem.f6da51a23 42135be7e9d7a10e0dc91a0/?vgnextoid=fa7e539dc4bed010VgnVCM1000000ecd190aRCRD &vgnextchannel=fa7e539dc4bed010VgnVCM1000000ecd190aRCRD&CH=act

US Citizenship and Immigration Services. (n.d.a). *I-90, application to replace permanent resident card.* Retrieved December 2013, from http://www.uscis.gov/portal/site/uscis/menuitem. 5af9bb95919f35e66f614176543f6d1a/?vgnextoid=b3f7ab0a43b5d010VgnVCM10000048f3d 6a1RCRD&vgnextchannel=db029c7755cb9010VgnVCM10000045f3d6a1RCRD

US Citizenship and Immigration Services. (n.d.b). *RAIO combined training course, guidance for adjudicating lesbian, gay, bisexual, transgender, and intersex refugee and asylum claims.* Retrieved December 2013, from http://www.uscis.gov/USCIS/Humanitarian/Refugees%20 &%20Asylum/Asylum/AOBTC%20Lesson%20Plans%20and%20Training%20Programs/ RAIO-Training-March-2012.pdf

US Citizenship and Immigration Services. (n.d.c). Rights and responsibilities of a green card holder. Retrieved December 2013, from http://www.uscis.gov/portal/site/uscis/menuitem. eb1d4c2a3e5b9ac89243c6a7543f6d1a/?vgnextoid=f3f43a4107083210VgnVCM100000082ca 60aRCRD&vgnextchannel=f3f43a4107083210VgnVCM100000082ca60aRCRD

US Department of State. (n.d.a). *Types of visas for immigrants: Employment-based immigrant visas.* Retrieved December 2013, from http://travel.state.gov/visa/immigrants/types/ types_1323.html

US Department of State. (n.d.b). *Visa bulletin.* Retrieved December 2013, from http://travel.state. gov/visa/bulletin/bulletin_1360.html

US Department of State. (n.d.c). *Types of visas for immigrants: Family-based immigrant visas.* Retrieved December 2013, from http://travel.state.gov/visa/immigrants/types/types_1306. html

Valentine, D. (2007). *Imagining transgender: An ethnography of a category.* Durham, NC and London, UK: Duke University Press.

The violation of the rights of lesbian, gay, bisexual, and transgender persons in Mexico: A shadow report. (March 2010). Global Rights, International Gay and Lesbian Human Rights Commission (IGLHRC), International Human Rights Clinic, Human Rights Program of Harvard Law School, & Colectivo Binni Laanu A.C. Retrieved from: http://www.globalrights. org/site/DocServer/LGBT_ICCPR_Shadow_Report_Mexico.pdf

Visas for spouses: Retrieved from http://travel.state.gov/visa/immigrants/types/types_2991. html#10

Whitlock, K., Mogul, J., & Ritchie, A. (2011). *Queer (in)justice: The criminalization of LGBT people in the United States.* Boston, MA: South End Press.

4

DISABILITIES AND DEAF CULTURE
Syrus Marcus Ware and Zack Marshall

WHEN YOU CONSIDER THE WORD *DISABILITY,* what comes to mind? Do you immediately think about someone using a wheelchair or another form of physical disability? Or maybe you think about other disabilities that affect the body? The meaning of the word *disability* can be very broad. For many people, disability is about a sense of difference. But it is also about the diversity of human experience.

There are links between trans identities, disabilities, and Deafness. There are many ways that people experience disability and gender. These experiences can overlap and interconnect through our identities, experiences of oppression, and community building. Instead of difference being perceived as negative, what would it be like if all human bodies, minds, and ways of thinking were celebrated as part of human experience? Regardless of how we define or understand the concept of "disability," trans people with disabilities are an integral part of LGBTQ communities.

DEFINING DISABILITY

Most often, disabilities are formally identified and labeled by professionals such as medical doctors and psychologists. These professionals have been trained within a specific medical model that frames disability as a medical condition or diagnosis. Using standardized assessment tools, they decide who fits the criteria and assign labels according to this system. Being assigned a medical label may or may not feel like a true reflection of how you think about yourself.

The Yahoo group QueerDisability connects LGBTQ people with disabilities.

Professionals do not always agree on what they consider disabilities. Individuals with disabilities have also contributed to an understanding of disability through disability scholarship and activism to change laws. There are over 40 definitions of disability within federal law alone (Ballan et al., 2011).

In the United States, the main tool for diagnosing mental illness (and therefore also for determining what conditions are labeled as psychiatric disabilities) is the *Diagnostic and Statistical Manual of Mental Disorders* (*DSM*), currently in its fifth edition (*DSM-5*). Diagnoses in the *DSM* include major depressive disorder, generalized anxiety disorder, learning disabilities, posttraumatic stress disorder, and gender dysphoria.

IS BEING TRANS A DISABILITY?

The Federal Americans with Disabilities Act (ADA) specifically excludes transgender people from its discrimination protections. Different groups of trans activists disagree on whether it makes sense to challenge this exclusion.

Gender dysphoria is a diagnosis in the *DSM*. For many trans people, in order to obtain access to medical transition, it is necessary to be diagnosed with gender dysphoria (GD) (formerly gender identity disorder [GID]). Similar to other diagnoses, gender dysphoria is a mental health diagnosis created by the American Psychiatric Association. Within this way of thinking, people labeled with gender dysphoria have a mental health "problem." In this model, people with GD are also disabled.

Labeling all trans people with gender dysphoria pathologizes trans identities. It suggests that being trans is a psychiatric condition, despite multiple experiences and expressions of gender throughout human history. It also suggests that being trans is a problem, one that is outside of the norm of human experience.

RESISTING PATHOLOGIZATION

Similar to trans identities, disability identities can be imposed, rejected, accepted, or embraced and there is no "right" way to live as a person with a disability. People may or

CJ Fung from *Our Compass*, a documentary co-written by LGBTQ youth labeled with intellectual disabilities (photo by Patrick Struys).

may not identify with the label, and this may shift over time. There are many who proudly call themselves disabled people, or people with disabilities.

How we relate to being labeled with a disability has a lot to do with what we have been taught about disabilities, oppression, and how our identities intersect. Within society, disability is often seen as an individual problem with disabled people's bodies or minds needing to be cured, fixed, or managed (Oliver, 1996). There is a global movement of people who disagree that difference should be diagnosed, labeled, and treated. As part of this movement, trans activism since the early 1980s has challenged the classification of transsexuality as a psychiatric diagnosis.

When people begin to question medical and psychiatric labels, they may also realize that disability has a lot to do with the world around us, meaning that it is created and reinforced by society. Societies limit access to people, locations, and activities by creating barriers. For example, we build buildings that have stairs at the entrances, limiting who can and cannot enter; we schedule long meetings that require a particular kind of brain work that limits who can participate; and we show movies in the classroom that do not have captioning and thus limit who can understand the information.

Rather than thinking about disability as an individual problem, there are other options. The *social model of disability* recognizes societal barriers and the impact of broader systems as the problem, rather than focusing on individuals in isolation.

"Disability is thus not just a health problem. It is a complex phenomenon, reflecting the interaction between features of a person's body and features of the society in which he or she lives. Overcoming the difficulties faced by people with disabilities requires interventions to remove environmental and social barriers."—World Health Organization

QUEER AND DIAGNOSTICALLY CHALLENGED

Rosalyn Forrester is a queer, pagan woman of color who was born with transsexualsim and lives with chronic pain. She's fought to create changes in family law and in how police treat people in the greater trans* communities. She's also involved in the Trans Forming Families project.

Many queer-identified and trans-identified people living with a variety of abilities face challenges while intermingling within the greater queer-identified and temporarily able-bodied (TAB) community. I expected to feel included and safe within my own queer community, but in fact it is a place where a person born with transsexualism who is also living with ability issues can actually be made to feel even worse and more left out. A marginalized group, marginalizing others. Go figure.

Queer community events often take place in nonaccessible spaces. When it is brought to the organizer's attention, the response they give is usually something like "This space was all we could find" or "We never thought about access since no one has brought it to our attention before." This makes it feel like it is our fault for not doing the hard work of teaching them beforehand.

Being queer, of color, born with transsexualism, and having a disability, it is hard to know where I am welcome sometimes. Sometimes I walk into a support group for women with disabilities and learn that to them I'm not equally female. I was not born as they were. Seeing signs that separate my identities like "women and trans* people welcome" or "queer and trans* people welcome" have me still feeling as if I am some sort of other species.

The greater queer community has to understand that we are human, we are women, we are men, we want to belong, and we do belong. We want and deserve a chance to not feel like outsiders looking in all the time.

ABLEISM IS A SYSTEM

The term *ableism* is used to describe prejudice or discrimination against people with disabilities. Ableism manifests in systemic exclusion of disabled communities from access to the right to self-determination and in daily individual micro aggressions and violence. *Audism* is the systemic exclusion of Deaf communities from access to self-determination in similar ways and the prioritizing of hearing ability and the use of verbal language. Similarly, cisnormativity reinforces the notion that there are only two genders/sexes and that these are mutually exclusive and set for life. This suggests an "ideal body," positioning trans bodies as outside of the preconceived norm. Ableism, audism, and cisnormativity are interconnected systems that combine in specific ways for trans people with disabilities.

want is a film by queer femme Loree Erickson that explores sex and disability by using sexually explicit images to show people with disabilities as sexy and to challenge the desexualization and devaluation of people with disabilities.

ACTIVISM: LINKS BETWEEN DISABILITY AND TRANS COMMUNITIES

People labeled with disabilities have a long history of organizing for social change. Some disabilities activists have worked for laws that recognize differences and provide for ways that all people can have access to the same opportunities. Like trans activists, disabilities activists have also led movements for depathologization and self-determination.

It is important to recognize that activism to remove GD from the *DSM* can come across as inherently ableist.

The International Stop Trans Pathologization (STP) Campaign is an activist initiative that works for the depathologization of trans expressions, trajectories, and identities, and hosts the International Day of Action for Trans Depathologization.

> *"I feel there's a very negative tension between mental health and trans issues at times. I worry that trans activists are trying a bit too enthusiastically to flee the 'stigma' of mental illness with regards to issues like GID ('gender identity disorder') or GD ('gender dysphoria') being in the DSM, and that this exacerbates the stigma on mental illness. What's SO bad about being mentally ill? Surely the problem is the stigma attached to all the various conditions in the DSM more than GID or GD being in there."*

By working to remove GD from the *DSM*, are we inadvertently saying that the guide remains a valid tool for pathologizing other mental states and mental difference? This suggests there are those whose identities do need to be in the *DSM*. This does not challenge the underlying power of the psychiatric system itself. While mental health providers may feel it is important to categorize people's experiences, there may be other approaches that are less stigmatizing.

When trans people say that they do not want to be labeled with mental health diagnoses, this reinforces the idea that there is such a thing as "mental health" and "mental illness." These are socially constructed diagnoses. In fact, there are many different ways that people feel, think, and process information. It is important to question why any of these experiences are pathologized. All of our lived experiences could simply be recognized and supported.

> *"In the transgender community, I'm also involved with the disabled—mainly the mentally ill, mentally disabled, etc.—community. I generally tend to find much more understanding of ableism and classism issues within this segment of the*

Activism (Elenore Toczynski).

trans community, as well as much more acceptance of less binary identities, less adherence to gender norms, etc. I also tend to see more caring about intersectionality. And of course I tend to relate much more to trans people who also struggle with mental illness."

By suggesting that trans identity does not belong in the *DSM* but that other identities do, we need to be careful not to further marginalize trans people who identify as disabled, whether they identify as having gender dysphoria or another disability altogether. Are there ways of developing a trans activism that is supportive of those of us diagnosed with psychiatric disabilities (i.e., labeled with a mental health diagnosis)? How do we fight for trans identity outside of ableist discourse?

FORMING COMMUNITY

There are thriving communities of Deaf and disabled people all over the world. In these communities, both online and out in society, people often find safety, support, and connection in experiences of difference. Sometimes people find connection about the experience of disability but do not find a similar sense of support when sharing other parts of their lives, such as being trans or people of color. Similarly, some may be active members of LGBTQ communities and feel like outsiders within those communities because of a lack of awareness about disabilities or trans identities.

"*Sins Invalid: An Unashamed Claim to Beauty in the Face of Invisibility" is a performance project that celebrates artists with disabilities, centralizing artists of color and queer and gender-variant artists as communities that have been historically marginalized. Normative paradigms of "normal" and "sexy" are challenged, offering instead a vision of beauty and sexuality inclusive of all individuals and communities.

> *"I am disabled and genderqueer, but I seem to be the only visible one in my neighborhood."*

> *"I'm an autistic trans person, but I'm not part of any specific group which addresses both of those concerns. I've come across a lot of people who are both online, and I have a couple of good friends who are also both. It's been very fulfilling to discover which experiences I have in common with them."*

> *"I am deaf, and know a few other deaf trans people online (two of whom I have met in person)."*

> *"While I do live in a major city with a fairly sizable Deaf population, and a fairly sizable trans population, there are very few (if any) other deaf trans people around, and I think this is true of most other cities as well. Everyone else who is*

The Ontario Rainbow Alliance of the Deaf hosts social events and provides educational workshops that are geared toward providing a safe space for the Deaf and Queer community and increasing Deaf Queer visibility within the larger community.

Participants from Compass, a social group for LGBTQ youth labeled with intellectual disabilities, at Griffin Centre in Toronto (photo by Patrick Struys).

deaf and trans I communicate with online via e-mail, instant messaging, or video chat. I think being deaf and trans binds us together a little bit closer, because we have two common experiences being part of two minority groups."

QUESTIONS FROM THE PUBLIC

Josh Smith is a creative and tenacious artist who identifies as a genderqueer no-op trans guy with a physical disability.

What is wrong with you
When will you die
Can they fix you
Can you have sex
Why are you in a wheelchair
Are your legs broken
Can you cum
How long do you have to live
Are you a Girl or a Boy
Why don't you just Transition
What's wrong with your voice
How do you have sex

Audrey Lorde was a black lesbian poet, scholar, and activist who experienced disability. Lorde (1984) wrote about the importance of bringing an integrated analysis to any academic or activist project, explaining: "[M]y fullest concentration of energy is available to me only when I integrate all the parts of who I am, openly, allowing power from particular sources of my living to flow back and forth freely through all my different selves, without the restrictions of externally imposed definition. Only then can I bring myself and my energies as a whole to the service of those struggles which I embrace as part of my living" (p. 121).

Many of us are part of racialized and Indigenous communities and experience trans, disability, and Deaf cultures in unique ways because of overlapping experiences of colonization and racism. Similarly, we may come from working-class and poor communities where experiences of gender and ability are profoundly affected by experiences of classism and access to class privilege. Ultimately, we have intersecting identities and many of us have claimed or reclaimed new terms or labels that have personal and specific meaning. Acknowledging these differences is important. Writing that portrays all disabled people as white, straight, and non-trans/cissexual is limiting, implying that all racialized people are nondisabled, and that all disabled people are white/nonracialized (Ejiogu & Ware, 2008).

DIVERSITY, DISABILITY, AND DEAFNESS

Deaf trans people represent another aspect of the diversity in LGBTQ communities. Deafness is typically recognized as separate from disability. Although Deaf culture intersects with disability, it is also distinct. Deaf culture is part of a unique linguistic and cultural community where being a Deaf person is considered a trait, not a disability (Jones, 2002). For this reason we also capitalize the D in Deaf, taking the lead from Deaf communities (Mog & Swarr, 2008).

DEAF AND DISABILITY IDENTITIES: AN INTERVIEW WITH TARA BIRL AND EMILY SORS

Trans Bodies, Trans Selves (TBTS): *How do you identify?*

Tara Birl (TB): Personally, I identify as female with genderqueer sparkles. I don't really like the trans labels. Probably the most accurate of the trans labels would be transsexual, but I like to just identify female with genderqueer sparkles!

Emily Sors (ES): Hmmm…how I identify is really complex. In terms of queer, well, I'm trans, queer, poly, pansexual, and kinky. I identify as a woman, gender-wise (and I'm not genderqueer, either). There's a lot of other stuff attached as well, mostly relating to my medical conditions (I have way too many of them). Being hard of hearing is one of them. I don't really know that I identify with the Deaf community, though—I've never really been a part of it, and my hearing impairment isn't really enough to affect me too much. I can usually get by even without my hearing aid. I am starting to learn ASL now, though, as my partner is also hearing impaired and we decided it would probably be a good thing for us to be able to sign to each other.

TBTS: *Is there anything you would like readers to know about your experience of gender and Deaf culture?*

ES: The only thing I've really noticed is that, back when I was a guy, people assumed more often that I just wasn't listening to them. Now, people understand more readily that I have a hearing loss. I would assume it has something to do with the stereotype that women are good listeners.

TB: Well, I'm personally pretty new to the Deaf community. I've been out as trans since 2005. I have only been in the Deaf community since 2009. I think there are lots of cross-cultural differences. For instance, in the Deaf community, it's expected to be very straightforward and direct with questions, so you get a lot of very direct questions about your gender, surgery/legal status, etc. These things in the trans community (and even in the larger LGBTIQQA community or even the hearing world) would be downright rude. Of course, you do get these types of questions in the Hearing world, but they usually are much more subtle, and rarely on very first meeting a stranger. In the Deaf world, those questions are much more common when you meet strangers for the first time. It's in some ways very refreshing.

I imagine someone deaf all their lives (or even most of their lives) would have fairly different experiences. I can't speak for them. I do have a few friends that were deaf at/near birth and came out trans later in life, but it would be wrong for me to speak about their experiences.

I think one GREAT advantage to being deaf and trans versus being trans and hearing is not having to hear the taunts, the verbal abuse, and hatred that come your way when you are discovered as being trans. I remember when I was hearing and would walk down the street, verbal abuse was a very daily activity in my life, regardless of where in the United States I happened to be that day. Now I never hear it!

TBTS: *What do you think are some of the ways that trans activism and Deaf culture overlap, or possibly disconnect?*

TB: I think there are similarities. Both groups of people face oppression in their everyday lives. A lot of that oppression is simply because of ignorance. People don't understand either one. In other ways, I think the Deaf community is WAY ahead of the trans communities here in the United States. I'm not saying there isn't work to do, but in the trans communities, the laws protecting us are barely happening at the state level. California being mostly complete (law wise), but pretty much every other state WAY behind. The trans community is still battling the medicalization process of us, like we are a disease. We have a LOT of work to do to get out of the *DSM*. I like to think the Deaf community has pretty much gotten past that, and our language of ASL is finally accepted as a language. Again, I think it all is oppression, and that both communities (and ALL communities of people that face oppression) have to come and work together, and find all of our commonalities and work toward ending ALL oppression, not just the ones that affect "my" communities.

ES: To me, Deaf activism seems so well established, though I don't know much about the history of it. Trans activism is relatively new, and still putting down roots. We're making incremental steps, but it's been slow, and there's a lot of backlash and hate.

TRANS PEOPLE AS DISABILITY ALLIES

Planet DeafQueer (planet. deafqueer.com) is a community Web site devoted to empowering the DeafQueer community and Allies.

There are many ways that people with disabilities are excluded from services, supports, and social and community events as a result of inaccessible physical spaces and environments which fail to accommodate disabled and Deaf people.

> *"I'm a cripple (I have arthritis) but I'm not really active in the disabled community. It just means I will only go to queer community events that aren't physically demanding: I can sit down and talk, but I won't dance all night or go on long walks."*

> *"I'm disabled but don't have a disabled community. My larger trans community is mostly abled, and they're working on their ableism and that's definitely hard! It's hard to go out to gay bars when they have strobe lights that give me seizures. I feel like being trans and disabled are important experiences that can't really be untied from each other. And it's frustrating that at the end of the day when I want to relax from all the transphobia I have to deal with out in the world I come home to my community only to deal with ableism."*

> *"I'm involved with a group called crazyqueers on Livejournal which is aimed at those who are queer/trans who have mental health issues or things like Aspergers/autism. I think it's a lot more tight-knit and more relaxed because of the various things we talk about and we don't talk about gender theory so much. We worry more about mental health issues than gender ones."*

"The stolen body, the reclaimed body, the body that knows itself and the world, the stone and the heat which warms it: my body has never been singular. Disability snarls into gender. Class wraps around race. Sexuality strains against abuse. This is how to reach beneath the skin." —Eli Clare (2009), *Exile and Pride: Disability, Queerness, and Liberation* (Boston, MA: South End Press).

> *"As a disabled mixed-race woman, I'm talking to everyone equally. I have friends among every race and creed and religion, but again I leave the activism to healthier people. I just have my friends and they matter to me more than analyzing whose oppression is easier or harder or whatever. All oppression is bad, period."*

The next time you are planning a trans community event consider how you could make it more open to people with intellectual disabilities. Set aside funds for American Sign Language (ASL) interpreters. Provide audio description of visual images and video/DVDs, and/or open or closed captioning of films and video clips. Hold your event in a physically accessible location and consider how cost, transportation, the organization of the room, and the activities you have planned may or may not be welcoming to people with differing abilities than your own. Work in solidarity and in collaboration with trans disability communities and help support their work and the fight for self-determination.

LIBERATION DOESN'T LEAVE PEOPLE BEHIND: ABLEISM, TRANSPHOBIA, CLASSISM, AND RACISM

A Campus Pride Hot List artist, 2013 Trans Justice Funding Project Panelist, and 2013 Trans 100 Honoree whose work has been featured in anthologies and on stages globally, Kay Ulanday Barrett (www.kaybarrett.net) is a poet, performer, and educator, navigating life as a disabled pin@y-amerikan transgender queer in the United States with struggle and laughter.

Life as a brown, trans, physically disabled crip person leaves me judged by all systems—the government systems that give harsh pity in public "assistance," the police who use more than billy clubs to enforce their brutality, the employers, the public transportation officials, the doctors who steal our agency of our own experiences and have no idea what to do with genderqueer people. All of these at once feel like an open wound, with multiple stings.

 Meetings, bedrooms, protests—these can be able-bodied supremacist spaces. The way crip and sick disabled people are treated in ableist settings is informed by gender binaries and unrealistic expectations. A trans disabled person like myself is not a strong leader if he's not in the march. A trans woman crip is seen as less effective if she's not at all of the pivotal events. Our everyday ways of love and movement are polluted with ableism.

A person's limitations and body are not the problem. It is a strength to know your own magic. If one cannot walk far or moves a certain way and that makes YOU uncomfortable, then that is your problem. It is a problem with how you have been taught to see humanity.

It is not only about ramps, interpreters, holding a bag or bringing medication; it's about meeting people where they are and moving with us, struggling with us without shaming, belittling, abusing, and resenting us. We will make mistakes on our way to being whole. Not whole as in unbroken, but whole as in complete—with our flaws, our hard truths, our complexities. We want a world that is whole and complex!

For us to move with one another, we must realize that able-bodied supremacy breeds racism, classism, and cissexism. The way we love, organize, make decisions, socialize, invite, give support, desire, and the way we see our gendered and raced bodies, all connect. Moving with one another is how we will transform not just the systems that harm us, but the systems that we allow to harm and invade our hearts and spirits. Liberation doesn't leave people behind. Liberation tries and transforms. Liberation shows up.

CONCLUSION

Human bodies and minds come in a variety of forms and manifestations. The ways our identities intersect and overlap with other experiences of racialization, class, gender, body size, and other forms of difference are opportunities for celebration. As disabled and Deaf trans people, our experiences of gender and disability have been medicalized and pathologized; and yet we resist, fight back, redefine, reclaim, and re-remember. Society's construction of disability and gender intersects in our experiences of oppression and it is from this place that we are at our most powerful to fight back and resist marginalization.

REFERENCES AND FURTHER READING

Baderoon, G. (2011). "Gender within gender": Zanele Muholi's images of trans being and becoming. *Feminist Studies, 37*(2), 390–416.

Ballan, M. S., Romanelli, M., & Harper, J. N. (2011). The social model: A lens for counseling transgender individuals with disabilities. *Journal of Gay and Lesbian Mental Health, 15*(3), 260–280.

Courvant, D. (1999). Coming out disabled: A transsexual woman considers queer contributions to living with disability. *Journal of Gay, Lesbian, and Bisexual Identity, 4*(1), 97–105.

Ejiogu, N., & Ware, S. M. (2008). *How disability studies stays white and what kind of white it stays.* Presentation at Society for Disability Studies Conference, Conference, CUNY, New York.

Hoff, D. (2001). *Access for all: A resource manual for meeting the needs of one-stop customers with disabilities.* Boston, MA: Institute for Community Inclusion. Retrieved December 2013, from http://www.communityinclusion.org/article.php?article_id=119

Jones, M. A. (2002). Deafness as culture: A psychosocial perspective. *Disability Studies Quarterly, 22*(2), 51–60.

Koyama, E. (2006). *From "intersex" to "DSD": Toward a queer disability politics of gender.* Retrieved December 2013, from http://www.intersexinitiative.org/articles/intersextodsd.html

Lorde, A. (1984). Age, race, class, and sex: Women redefining difference. In *Sister outsider: Essays and speeches* (pp. 121–123). Freedom, CA: The Crossing Press.

Marshall, Z., Burnette, M., Lowton, S., Skittles, R. S., Smith, R. T. S., Tiamo, J.,...Vo, T. (in press). An interview with trans and genderqueer people labelled with intellectual disabilities about art and activism. In R. Raj & D. Irving (Eds.), *Trans activism: A reader.* Toronto, ON: Canadian Scholars Press.

Mog, A., & Swarr, A. L. (2008). Threads of commonality in transgender and disability studies. *Disability Studies Quarterly, 28*(4). Retrieved December 2013, from http://dsq-sds.org/article/view/152/152

Oliver, M. (1996). *Understanding disability, from theory to practice.* London, UK: Macmillan.

Spade, D. (2003). Resisting medicine, re/modeling gender. *Berkeley Women's Law Journal, 18*(15), 15–37.

5

RELIGION AND SPIRITUALITY

delfin bautista and Quince Mountain with Heath Mackenzie Reynolds

HUMANS ARE CREATURES THAT SEEK CONNECTION TO OTHER BEINGS AND PLACES. We try to understand our worlds, both material and spiritual. Religious and spiritual practice may offer us an outlet for these needs.

Some of us are wary of religion, having been brought up within religious communities and institutions that may not have accepted us. But for many of us, religion has been a source of connection, meaning, and purpose. Our places and communities of worship may be our places of public celebration, social support, and even of childhood education. For others of us, religious or spiritual practice may be a private, personal way of recentering or reconnecting with ourselves, away from the noisy world. Religion can also be a kind of framework upon which, or around which, we sculpt our lives. Those of us with deep faith are likely to consider the values and beliefs associated with our religion before determining a course of action in our transition.

For some of us, our sacred practices are not connected to a higher power or divine creator. Many of us adhere to humanist doctrines of human agency or core principles that honor innate goodness and human rights. Many of us are atheists who do not believe in God. Others who are not atheists may be agnostic, unconcerned, or simply unsure about God.

Even for those of us not currently engaged in religious practice, habits of our childhood religions can strongly influence our feelings and actions. Our surrounding cultural norms—in which religion is often deeply embedded—can also affect our approaches to life.

FAITH IS MY MIDDLE NAME

Miles Rutendo Tanhira is a Zimbabwean LGBT rights activist, a journalist, feminist, and pacifist.

Faith is my middle name (*Rutendo shona*). I got this name when I was baptized as an infant in The Salvation Army Church. Having grown up in a Christian family, I was constantly reminded that I should follow the teachings of the Bible, and that attending church was as important as the air I breathe. As was expected of any junior soldier, I memorized Bible verses and sang Sunday school hymns, but there was one problem: the uniform. It made me feel uncomfortable in the house of God. It made me miserable. Then puberty hit me. I began to feel more and more like a stranger in the church I had grown up in. Teachings on "womanhood" and wearing skirts and blouses were harsh reminders of the internal conflict I was going through. I was drifting from the church and becoming a "rebel."

Although my cousins graduated to senior soldiers in the church, I did not. I felt I had let my mum down. I needed to make it up to her. I then resorted to the scripture union group at school. At least I could wear trousers to the Doonamies scripture union church group. The worst two years of my life. I had the liberty to wear what I wanted, but I still felt an emptiness. I had a horrid time, and the more I attended church service, the more I felt dirty, exposed, and uncomfortable with myself. I had a girlfriend, and I used to break up with her after every church service. I hated myself for not repenting and for failing to resist this temptation.

It was not until my mom passed on when I was 22 that I was reminded of the need to sort out my spirituality. I started going back to my family church, wore her skirts, attended services, and soon graduated as a senior soldier. I wanted to make my mum proud. Slowly during this process I began to rebuild my spirituality. Then a conference on religion and sexuality in 2009 changed my life. I met other LGBT religious people. There I began a process to self-discovery. I became comfortable with identifying as a transgender person. I began to approach the scriptures with an open mind. I certainly didn't need to be in a skirt to have a relationship with God.

Looking at my life, I know now my middle name was not a coincidence. I am hoping to become a theologian and one day serve as a pastor to preach love that heals broken souls.

RELIGION AND TRANS IDENTITY

Just as *transgender* is an umbrella term used to describe a continuum of identities, so too are *religion* and *spirituality* umbrella terms covering all manner of relationships with that which is greater than one's self. For some of us, there is a connection or intersection of faith and spirituality with our trans identities; for others, the two do not interact in any way.

> *"I'm an agnostic who attends Quaker meetings regularly. I began to identify as agnostic rather than atheist just about when I started to think seriously about transitioning. I see these two changes as connected: in both cases, I had to acknowledge that there was more to truth than logical necessity. Transitioning and admitting the possibility of religious faith both require the possibility of an internal reality that contradicts or transcends the truths proffered by external authorities. And to the extent that I identify with Quakerism, its focus on the sanctity of the individual's connection with God or whatever else you call the source of truth fits very well with the imperative for a trans individual to define themself in their own terms."*

The umbrella of religion and spirituality includes people who belong to traditional faith communities, people who belong to nontraditional (or "alternative") faith communities, and those who neither belong to institutionalized or organized religious groups nor believe in God but have reverence for some kind of higher power.

There are a plethora of ways trans people relate or do not relate to religion. We range from devout Christians to Reform Jews to practicing Wiccans or pagans to meditating Buddhists to agnostics who acknowledge varying ideas of spiritual goodness to atheists who believe in neither God nor in religion as a whole.

God means many different things to different people and takes a variety of shapes and forms. While there are compelling themes we may find shared between religions, we must also honor that there are vital differences in beliefs and values between faith groups. As trans people, we recognize the importance of the language people use to identify themselves. Similar to the language we use to describe our gender and sexual identity, the language of religion reflects a genuine diversity of practices, rituals, and deities worshipped around the world.

Transfaith (transfaithonline. org) is a national nonprofit led by transgender people and focused on issues of faith and spirituality.

HOW RELIGIOUS COMMUNITIES ENGAGE TRANS IDENTITIES

Many religious communities have barely begun the process of affirming gay, lesbian, and bisexual individuals, much less trans people. We are often not even blips on the radar of most congregations, and our needs and concerns are often overlooked. Many of us struggle to reconcile our faith within religious institutions that do not recognize nonbinary understandings of gender or do not acknowledge transgender as an identity in their religious community, theology, or practice. Some religious communities are even involved in practicing reparative therapy, which can be harmful to our identities and spiritual selves. As a result, it can be difficult to reconcile our religious identity with our trans and queer identity.

The Yes! Coalition, an interfaith and multidenominational organizing initiative based out of Philadelphia, records and publishes a guide to religious communities in the United States that are welcoming to trans people.

> *"I have always been a spiritually oriented person. My Christianity was a source of shame and self-loathing when I was a teen."*

> *"When I was still identifying as Christian, the LGBT community was a bit cold toward that aspect. It seems that Christianity and queer are mutually exclusive, but I don't think they need to be."*

> *"Religious ideas and a genderqueer identity are at times hard to reconcile, especially within religious communities. They believe there's something wrong with you—they accept you. . . but they think there's something wrong."*

"I am quite religious. In fact, I am an ordained minister. Fortunately, my denomination is very accepting so I have absolutely no issues there. There are many people of faith I have encountered in the trans community. Unfortunately, many have been driven from religion by lack of acceptance in their own churches or vile demagoguery from groups like Focus on the Family."

CREATING A WELCOMING RELIGIOUS COMMUNITY

Whether we belong to a religious community or are searching for one, there are a number of ways that a congregation or fellowship can be more inclusive of people of all genders.

Official Business

Do registration or documentation forms within the community include ways for an individual who chooses to identify as transgender to be able to do so? Does the congregation or denomination have a nondiscrimination policy?

Physical Space

Is the physical space in which a group gathers trans-friendly? One indication of this is the availability of gender-neutral or family bathrooms. Do you open your doors an hour before attendees are expected to arrive to give trans people an opportunity to change their clothing and be more comfortable than they may be out in the world? If spaces of worship are divided by gender, do trans people have access to the space designated for their affirmed gender?

Public Advocacy

Are members of the congregation or fellowship involved in advocacy efforts for trans equality? Advocacy efforts and public witness demonstrate concretely a community's commitment to equality for all. Religious groups may participate in Transgender Day of Celebration or Transgender Day of Visibility to commemorate and honor the lives of transgender individuals within the ritual, liturgical, or worship life of the community.

Education and Activism

Does the community or group have access to resources to engage trans issues? Organizations with trans curricula and workshops include the Institute for Welcoming Resources, the Human Rights Campaign, the Religious Institute, the Center for Lesbian and Gay Studies in Religion and Ministry (CLGS), Trans-Faith, Trans-Torah, and the LGBT Religious Archives Network.

Religious Practice

During liturgies, rituals, or cultic practices that honor women or men, specifically, are trans individuals included? In studies of scriptural and sacred texts, are trans-positive and trans-affirming interpretations part of the conversation? If we desire to do so, are we welcome to openly acknowledge and discuss our identity from the pulpit or altar? Are there opportunities to celebrate renaming or gender transition within the faith community? Are phrases such as "people of all genders" used in worship, sermons, bulletins, or other parts of the community?

Religious Leadership and Participation

Are trans individuals welcome to take on leadership roles within the congregation or group? Doing so allows us to contribute to the community based on our gifts and talents—to be seen as more than our trans identity.

Many of us have left our religious communities altogether, whether by choice or by force. Choosing to walk away from these communities as a response to injustice or bias can be empowering. However, it can also be isolating and traumatic, especially for people for whom participation in religious communities is important.

"I am religious and spiritual, but not in [my city]. The way they teach faith is wrong and hurtful towards people who are GLBT. . . One church I went to, the First Assembly of God, was progressive but then changed to a conservative Old Testament approach, and I stopped going."

"I am a religious person but have been afraid to go back to my church. I sometimes wish to contact the church and find out what their reaction would be. It would be nice to have communion again sometime."

"It has been traumatic to experience the rejection of the religious community. . . I have been hesitant to participate in that community as a man. . . But I have participated as male a few times (especially while traveling and going to synagogues where nobody knows I'm trans) and that was very meaningful to me."

As trans people, we are not alone in moving away from religion. Many people, both trans and cis, have found themselves leaving their faith communities in the last decade.

For those of us who feel a connection to our religion but have been unable to find a welcoming community, we may seek out new ways of worship or communities that accept and affirm our identities. A growing number of traditions now have specific organizations or communities for trans and LGBTQ people.

> *"I've been an evangelical Christian since I was 15 years old. Thanks to my grandma's support, I've been able to hold on to my faith through discrimination and hateful misuse of Scripture and belief by others."*

> *"After I changed my name and started my RLE (real life experience), I was asked to resign from a volunteer position at my church, and so my wife and I left that parish, one we had attended for 10 years, for one closer to home that was more accepting of LGBT individuals and couples."*

> *"The first thing that happened when I transitioned was that I lost my connection to my church. I've recently started attending an LGBT friendly church and like it."*

While many faith communities have begun to actively reach out to gay and lesbian participants, the specific concerns and experiences of trans communities are often missing.

"It is high time for congregations to study gender issues, to wake up to the importance of noticing and embracing their transgender members and to reach out in ministry with the transgender community as a whole."—Dr. Virginia Ramey Mollenkott, author, theologian, and activist

---

TRANS POLITICAL LEADERS: VLADIMIR LUXURIA

Jamie Roberts and Anneliese Singh

Vladimir Luxuria was elected to office in Italy in 2006 as the first trans person in a national parliament in Europe. She immediately attracted heat from conservative politicians and other figures in the heavily Roman Catholic country. Alessandra Mussolini, granddaughter of Benito Mussolini, the infamous dictator of Italy, went on TV and said of Luxuria: "Better to be fascist than a faggot." Some of the conservatives in Parliament, both before and after the election, publicly fretted about which restroom Luxuria would use. Subsequently, members of the center-right party called for the creation of separate trans restrooms. Thankfully, deputies of the ruling coalition came to Luxuria's defense. Luxuria was not shy about running on her desire to win more rights for LGBTQ Italians, advocating for civil unions for same-sex and heterosexual couples alike, as well as reform of prostitution laws. She was also not alone, as several other lesbians and gays were elected to Parliament that year.

Vladimir Luxuria at Rome Gay Pride, June 7, 2008 (photo by Stefano Bolognini).

CHRISTIANITY

Christianity is the most common religion in the United States. Most major Christian denominations have organizations that support LGBTQ Christians. Some examples are Dignity (Catholic), the Association of Welcoming and Affirming Baptists, Evangelicals Concerned (Evangelical/Pentecostal), AXIOS (Eastern Orthodox), and Kinship (Seventh Day Adventists).

Some LGBTQ Christian groups, such as Affirmation (Mormon) have specific groups or projects for trans members. Others, like the Unity Fellowship, strive to create congregations that are nonhierarchical and nonoppressive, and include people of a range of gender and sexual identities.

> *"I am Catholic. In spite of the attitude of the Church hierarchy towards LGBT people, I have actually been practicing more since my transition, thanks to the Dignity organization for LGBT Catholics."*

> *"I am a Christian and quite spiritual. This actually kept me in the closet for a long time. When I finally studied the bible as an adult, I found that the bible does NOT condemn the LGBT community at all. That is a great crime perpetrated by the corrupt church institutions. I now attend MCC church and know of several fully accepting churches."*

The Transgender Faith and Action Network offers expanded opportunities for trans people of faith and allies to vision, build, grow, heal, and shift culture within faith communities and the world through conferences, workshops, cultural events, networking, advocacy efforts, and the building of trusted networks.

"Spirit of the Season" (Brakie Singleton, visual artist).

BEING A TRANS MONK

A Franciscan friar

I'm a Roman Catholic monk. And I'm transgendered. I've come to decide that I'm not a monk *despite* being trans, but rather *because* I'm trans. That's the really funny part. I no longer buy the binary m/f routine. I'm not one or the other—I'm both and neither. Of course, it cramps my style. I can't be fully the monk I want to be and advocate for the TG community—nor can I fully be the woman I could be because of the monastery.

One definition of spirituality—the approach to the Divine—is that it's the process of self-revelation. We learn and say who we are, fully and without fear. If fear is the opposite of love, then we grow in love when we take off our masks. A major mask I have worn is that of being a man.

I started by rifling through my mother's underwear drawer *without a shred of self-awareness.* She must have known but never said anything. This became one of my patterns for many years. I've purged and shorn my soul and my closet too many times.

One thing that held me back is that the transgendered dimension has to do with sexuality. Clothes and the gender line are erotic for me. And, though the erotic is recognized by many/most cultures as an aspect of the Divine and as a source of revelation, the dominant thread of Christianity came to insist that love is spiritual and emotional, not physical or erotic. In the culture I grew up in, sex was covered over in toxic shame. My cross-dressing was infected by toxic shame.

A major source of self-knowledge is through categories. "Gender" is a phenomenally deep category. Religion is a large avenue of categorization, especially "good" versus "evil." With full authority, they say that there are two genders only and that the one we're "born into" is ordained by God. They're wrong.

A thread of early Christianity was egalitarian. St. Paul says that in Christianity, there is no slave or free, Easterner or Westerner, or *male or female.* But why I am a Roman Catholic monk goes further than egalitarianism. In addition to historical accident, one short answer is the Sacrament of Eucharist, in its insistence on the physical body and on community.

Beyond the psychological, transgender leads to true religion in its insistence on making space for the other; for the other as they are, not as I say they are. But above all, our transgender selves are turned toward a deep and abiding peace. Currently, the fundamental means of conflict resolution in our world is violence. For me, our insistence on self-revelation is a radical act of nonviolence. We are helping create a safe place for self-revelation.

We who are transgendered are making ourselves incredibly vulnerable when we take off our masks. This vulnerability will eventually result in a safe place. For me, the function of church is to create that safe place—and ultimately to prevent war. This is why I remain a monk. I'm not a man. I'm not a woman either. And I'm a monk. This makes me laugh and sing and dance.

While denominations vary widely on whether they ordain LGB and trans-identified people, there are increasing numbers of out trans-identified people both in congregations and in positions of religious leadership. There are also a number of community-, issue-, and region-specific LGBTQ Christian organizations, including TRUUST, a network of trans Unitarians who have professional careers within the Unitarian Universalist Association of Congregations.

> *"I'm a Unitarian Universalist. I'm lucky it's a very open and accepting church, and really tries hard to be that way. There's even a trans support group at my church so I've never felt my being trans to be at odds with my religious views at all."*

While many resources for trans Christians fall under the larger rubric of LGBTQ, there are some organizations and projects that more specifically target working with trans people within their denominations and congregations.

Born out of the spiritual needs of lesbian and gay communities in the United States, the Metropolitan Community Church is an international Christian movement, multidimensional in scope, that provides support to the fellowship and its local churches, not only through its Trans/GNC Advisory Council but also through the work of its trans and gender nonconforming clergy and lay leaders.

ISLAM

Though there are no publicly known LGBTQ-specific mosques in North America at this time, there are a few options available for trans Muslims who are seeking a welcoming environment for religious practice, including El-Tawhid Juma Circle in Toronto and local affiliates for Muslims for Progressive Values in Los Angeles, Atlanta, Philadelphia, New York City, Washington D.C., and Ottowa. Imaan is a similar group operating out of the United Kingdom, and the Safra Project is a group for lesbian, bisexual, and trans women in the United Kingdom. The Safra Project also includes some textual analysis regarding sexuality, gender, and Islam.

Transgender Muslims can meet on the Yahoo group TransMuslims.

> *"I pray, fast and give zakat. Unfortunately it is not easy for me to do Hajj both for financial reasons and because I have a very female body. . ... Sometimes I feel bad praying as a man and sometimes as a woman. It's something I'm still working on."*

Cultural organizations also allow members to come together in a religious context. These include the Iranian Railroad for Queer Refugees, Taqaseem (a Chicago-based group that supports LGBTQ people from the Middle East and North Africa), Trikone (a group for LGBTQ South Asians in San Francisco), and the South Asian Lesbian and Gay Association in New York.

There are a number of Web sites and email groups for LGBTQ Muslims, and a few that focus on trans Muslim experiences. Queer Jihad and Starjack both offer useful resources for LGBTQ Muslims, including specifics for trans people.

Many Muslims and Islamic supporters have expressed excitement over the announcement of the newly formed Muslim Alliance for Sexual and Gender Diversity founded at

The Al-Fatiha Foundation, an organization devoted to LGBTQ Muslims, was active for a decade starting in 1998. It was founded by a gay Pakistani American man named Faisal Alam, who began with an email group and now hosts a Web site called Hidden Voices: The Lives of LGBT Muslims.

the 2013 Creating Change Conference hosted by the National Gay and Lesbian Taskforce. The "Queer Muslim Working Group," made up of Muslim sexual and gender justice advocates and professionals, shared that the new Alliance will create dialogue and develop resources in support of women and the LGBTQ community, which have traditionally been excluded or marginalized from the practice and leadership of Islam.

JUDAISM

There are a number of organizations and projects that pay particular attention to the needs and concerns of trans Jews, ranging from organizations like Nehirim and Keshet, which both aim to support LGBTQ Jews in their communities, to specific projects like TransTorah, a Web site that provides essays, prayers, liturgies, and educational resources that focus on the experience of trans Jews. Another project called TransTexts specifically examines Jewish textual resources to see what they have to say about gender in general and about transgender and gender nonconforming people specifically.

> "I am a Reform Jew, and I have become more religious slowly with transition. My aunt, a rabbi, even performed a mikveh ceremony—a ritual cleansing bath used to mark all kinds of life transitions—for me."

> "I am Jewish. It is against the Jewish religion to permanently alter your body, and it is something with which I struggle. I have to weigh my beliefs and dedication to god with wanting to feel more comfortable in my own skin."

The Dina List (starways.net/ beth/dina.html) connects transgender Orthodox Jews.

> "I am not religious or spiritual, but I try to have a cultural connection with my Jewishness. I have to actively seek out trans-friendly congregations (such as the Society for Humanistic Judaism)."

There are increasing numbers of Jewish communities that have visible trans congregants and members, as well as increasing numbers of trans religious leaders. The rise of LGBTQ-specific congregations, such as Congregations Beth Simchat Torah (New York City) and Sha'ar Zahav (San Francisco), has been very important in opening up space for trans Jews in congregations. There are also congregations, minyans, and communities of Jews outside of LGBTQ-focused shuls that actively welcome and work on being accessible to trans people. In 2004, Mayyim Hayyim, a Boston-area mikveh, was created as an accessible and affirming place for trans people to seek spiritual renewal through Jewish ritual practices such as individual prayer and ritual baths, which is an indication of both possibility and shifting ideology within traditional Jewish practices. Mayyim Hayyim's founder, author Anita Diamant, has described her goal as creating a place for gay, lesbian, and transgender Jews to take part in physical rituals without judgment from conservative mikveh attendants.

Joy Ladin, Gottesman Professor of English at Yeshiva University, is the first openly transgender employee of an Orthodox Jewish institution. She is the author of a memoir, *Through the Door of Life: A Jewish Journey Between Genders*, and six books of poetry (photo by Lisa Ross).

> "My family is Reconstructionist Jewish, and they attend an extremely liberal synagogue. I'm not out to the people there, but one day I'll have to be. When that time comes, I don't anticipate anything other than acceptance."

> "I had one very very uncomfortable experience where I was helping to make a men's-only prayer quorum in my synagogue and was asked, point-blank, if I was male or not. I no longer pray with that community, and it was very alienating for a long time."

> "I am a liberal Jew. I've found a Jewish community that is very supportive of BTLG folks in general, and is pleasantly egalitarian in a lot of ways. I plan to have a mikvah ritual to religiously formalize my name change, but I haven't done that yet."

WHO WE ARE

MY TRANSGENDER PASSOVER

Julian Barlow is a preservice elementary school teacher, living and working in Brooklyn, New York.

Passover has always been my favorite holiday. I never truly understood why until recently. There are the obvious explanations that cannot go unmentioned—my Grandma Edie's mouthwatering matzo ball soup, the balance of seriousness and hilarity that my friends and family bring to our seders, my mom's richly flavored flourless chocolate cake—it's an endless list. Just on the surface, the food is delish and the company is phenomenal.

While doing some basic research to brush up on my Passover knowledge, I found a video on the PBS Web site in which Rabbi Sharon Brous from Los Angeles speaks of the importance of Passover themes and how they translate to the present and to the future. She says, "the symbols on the seder plate are some of the most powerful ways of communicating what the essence of the Passover experience really is about."

The symbology behind each item on the seder plate helped me negotiate my emotions during this recent time that I came out to my immediate family.

Let's begin with the *beitzah*—roasted egg. It's representative of the possibility of something new, or rebirth. Big changes are coming for everyone and I think this should remind us to embrace the new parts of our lives.

Dipping the *karpas* into the salt water evokes the memory of tears shed during our suffering. But from those hard times, something new and beautiful has emerged. We did, and we will again, overcome adversity.

Charoset represents the brick and mortar. Rabbi Brous adds that it signifies the ironic sweetness of being stuck in a life that you know you don't want to stay in, but it's comfortable because you've been there for a long time. In some ways it seems easier not to transition, but this is my identity and making this change will result in something far sweeter—living my life authentically and ultimately with much deeper happiness.

Bitter herbs remind us that even though we have attained a level of freedom, there is a bitterness that accompanies all that is unknown about our futures. Transition is something I have never experienced before and there is a bitterness and unease about what this new life holds for me.

Rabbi Brous ends her video by mentioning the significance of the *zeroah*—shank bone. Freedom only came to the Israelites after the night that they put the blood on the doorposts of their homes and said—and I am saying this now as a transgender person as well—"I'm ready to take part in my own liberation right now."

Three thousand years ago we, as a people, made the decision to become untethered. Right now, we can once again liberate ourselves from our own personal captivities and become free with the support and strength from our friends, from our families, and from within.

EXPERIENCES FROM OTHER SPIRITUAL COMMUNITIES IN THE UNITED STATES

How we are accepted and the roles we are able to play in our spiritual and religious traditions vary. Trans people are represented in Buddhist, Hindu, pagan and neopagan communities, Santeria, and various Native American religious practices, as well as secular humanism and many other religious and spiritual groups.

There are organizations such as The Queer East, for LGB and trans people of Asian descent, and NativeOut, for Two-Spirit Native Americans, which compile cultural and religious resources for their communities.

The LGBT Humanist Web site provides a forum for discussing life-cycle events and issues specific to life as an LGBTQ Humanist.

WHAT IS IT LIKE TO BE A QUEER INDIAN?

Cassidy Anne Medicine Horse, MA, is a university instructor, invited lecturer, film director, LGBT political activist, transgender scholar, and researcher working in Bozeman, Montana, and a member of the American Indigenous Research Association, American Association of University Women (AAUW), and the Montana State University LGBT Advisory Committee (AIRA).

On numerous occasions, I have been asked what it is like to be a queer Indian. Unfortunately, I am not at all sure that a definitive answer is possible, as both the words *queer* and *Indian* leave much room for individual interpretation and incorporate aspects of life that may be unfamiliar to some.

The concept of crossing genders was well understood in Native culture prior to the period of colonization that began in North America 500 years ago. Rather than being stigmatized, some tribes saw the presence of a cross-gendered individual as good luck and as a vital thread in the social, spiritual, and cultural web—a gift from a creative power.

A gender-crossing individual serves as a critical link in the balance of nature. As indigenous people, our traditionally innate understanding of our universal position is that we are connected directly to nature, not removed from it. We are at once both the essence of nature, as well as an aspect of it. To "see" with the experience and heart of both a man and a woman is our gift from the universe and our responsibility to our people.

Colonial mentality brought with it Christianity and, unfortunately, much of the associated baggage of an agenda-driven Europe. The disruption of thousands of years of indigenous spiritual understanding ensued and in its place was offered a pale concept of religious conformity.

Two Spirit Society, Washington, D.C., September 21, 2004. One of the many Indian organizations marching to celebrate the opening of the National Museum of the American Indian (NMAI) (FEMA NewsPhoto/Bill Koplitz).

Today, in the opening decades of the 21st century, we as Native people, and more significantly as gender-crossing individuals, are emerging from a long sleep of enforced compliance and entering an age in which it is necessary to look deeper.

My spirituality does not demand shame, dehumanization, or anonymity for being a woman, but rather encourages me to embrace the strength of my femininity as a gift and an affirmation of my place in the universe. Further, my spirituality tells me to have ceremony, even if it is private, as it honors our ancestors and our traditions. Finally, my spirituality tells me to seek out the elders and to ask their advice and to use the understanding of my womanhood to always "come a good way."

Perhaps, after all else has been said and I am again asked, at some future date, what it is like to be a queer Indian, I may have an answer.

Within Hinduism, the Gay and Lesbian Vaishnava Association provides educational resources about the "third sex" of Vedic literature.

> "In Hinduism there is a manifestation of Shiva who is half man, half woman. This figure, Ardhanarishvana, is very important to me as a transgender person. It's affirming to know one of the greater gods is at times partially a woman. My ishta-deva (personal god) is Ganesha, the remover of obstacles. I also direct prayers to Kali and Durga, goddesses of great power and strength. Hinduism is very important to me because it has such powerful feminine entities. The feminine presented in Hinduism has helped me to better understand and accept the feminine parts of myself. Femininity is placed on equal grounds with masculinity, and they aren't concepts separate or dichotomous from one another."

There are a number of LGBTQ Buddhist Sanghas throughout the United States, as well as the International Transgender Buddhist Sangha. In Buddhist traditions, the image of Mother Quan Yin or Kwan Yin has been claimed by many as a trans deity. Quan Yin, who is the bodhisattva for justice, mercy, and compassion, is honored in some places in East Asia as female and in other places as male, with both representations respected as equals.

> "As a Buddhist, I find that in my struggle with being transgender I am accepting things as they are and not struggling with big existential questions of why. In a way my spirituality isn't muddying the waters of my transition with other issues, it's clarifying it."

There are also a number of spiritual and activist communities throughout the United States, such as Cauldron Farm and various Radical Faerie communities, that are either run by trans people or have trans people as active parts of their communities and histories.

Statue of the androgynous Hindu god Ardhanarishvara (Anant Shivaji Desai, Ravi Varma Press, early 20th century).

Quan Yin, a Buddhist deity venerated as male and female.

"I think my spirituality (Paganism) has helped me to discover and embrace my sexuality and my gender identity, since it encourages free thinking and self-examination. Most Pagans I've met are very accepting of difference, and it's generally thought that there isn't any one 'right' way to live one's life—therefore everyone has to find their own specific path in each lifetime."

"I am Wiccan. . ... I pray to Aphrodite, Cybele and the Hearth Mother regularly for the day when all I can see in the mirror is a woman."

FAERIE DESTINY

Chelsea Goodwin, who with her partner Rusty Mae Moore, ran Transy House in Park Slope, Brooklyn, is currently the manager of Pine Hill Books and the hostess of In Goth We Trust on WIOX Radio Roxbury, 91.3 FM.

My involvement with the current generation of Radical Faeries began in 2010, when Jamie Roberts and I were involved in creating The Theatre of Transgression. It was through this endeavor that I met Blaise and Mila Roo. Blaise Bonfire (his Faerie name) is a brilliant costume designer, actor, ftm, and kink activist, and extremely active with Camp Destiny. Located on the side of a mountain near Chester, Vermont, Camp Destiny is a Radical Faerie space with a beautiful kitchen, a solar-powered shower, and some of the most picturesque countryside in New England. Mila Roo (also known simply as Roo) is a trans woman who among other things is a brilliant physicist, actress, and former stage tech for Goth/Steampunk musical legend Voltaire.

Blaise and Milla encouraged me to come to Camp Destiny for Llamas (a midsummer festival and one of the major pagan holidays cel-ebrated by Radical Faeries). Llamas for the Radical Faeries culminates with the burning of a Wicker Man named "Cornholio." Another highlight of Llamas in that year (2010) was a production of *Pinnochio* performed out in the woods with scenery draped over trees, light provided by candles and a bonfire, and elaborate glittery costumes.

That year Milla and I were the only trans women at Llamas, unless one counts the brilliant drag performers Verucca la'Pirannha and Miles DeNiro. There were several trans men besides Blaise in attendance. The wonderful thing about that weekend was the extreme kind-ness with which everyone treated me, with no awkwardness whatsoever. I became known as a bit of a Tarot reader and made some very, very good friends.

This past summer, Blaise and his "master" Scout organized a Radical Faerie kink weekend at Camp Destiny. It was the first event in which trans identified people outnumbered people who identify as gay men. While I understand that there was a lot of discussion behind the scenes, the event went very smoothly and was very, very warm and friendly (in a black leather whips and chains sort of way, of course).

For whatever reason, Radical Faeries have come to a place of openness to multiple genders and sexualities and multiple ways of being that is a refreshing contrast to the angst and battle that have gone on with womyn's music festivals and similar events. Founded origi-nally by Harry Hay as a space for gay identified men with an interest in the back to the land aspect of the hippie movement, as well as Wiccan-based paganism, Radical Faeries always had an element of pagan spirituality, a spirit of openness and tolerance, and a sex-positive attitude. With their multicolored beards, elaborate makeup, frilly dresses, and brightly painted butterfly wings, the Faeries have also always been gender transgressive, emphasizing the need for men in general to develop their softer, more nurturing side. Since then, the opening up to people of all genders and to diverse approaches to sexuality has served only to deepen Faerie spirituality.

In the book *A Queer and Pleasant Danger*, Kate Bornstein tells "the true story of a nice Jewish boy who joins the Church of Scientology, and leaves twelve years later to become the lovely lady she is today" (Boston, MA: Beacon Press, 2012).

SPIRITUAL BUT NOT RELIGIOUS

Many of us experience a disconnect with the institutional, corporate, or political struc-tures of our traditions and choose to connect only with their spiritual aspects—the deeper truths and practices that open the door for more personal or mystical experiences of the divine—identifying as "spiritual but not religious." For many of us, religious institutions are too confining or limiting. We desire to ask questions and find alternative ways to con-nect with the divine or that which is greater than ourselves.

"I am spiritual. I believe in the Earth. I believe in natural variation. I believe in humanity. I believe in a universally binding force of good and evil. I do not be-lieve in a higher god. Maybe an architect. But not a man. My religious view has been shaped alongside my gender identity."

"I am extremely spiritual, and it is that spiritual aspect of myself that is the more important identity for me. I feel that my gender presentation is a reflection of my spiritual self, which is non-gendered."

"I'm very spiritual, but I was always of the belief that we basically have no idea what's true, and all sorts of things could be and we just don't know. I don't

think any religion has the answers, really. I just base things off my experiences and understanding. Spirituality is the one area that really hasn't given me issues with being trans."

Because many mainstream religious groups uphold heterosexuality and cisgender identity as ideal or as the only "acceptable" or "normal" way of living and being, many of us have reconciled our gender identity and religious identity by adopting beliefs and practices that may be grounded in a particular tradition but free of regulatory "do's and don'ts." For some of us, it is the experience of the divine or sacred that is central, not strict doctrines that confine the holy to just one thing. Spiritual practitioners are often open to many different traditions or belief systems, adopting a universal approach to the sacred that affirms both/and rather than either/or. A both/and approach may be grounded in our trans experiences of gender identity and expression.

By not focusing on rules and regulations as central to our faith, we are free to connect with our spirits, with our essential or core truths, and with rituals that are life-giving rather than marginalizing or restricting. Some of us find that this can help in healing after experiences of judgment or condemnation we have experienced in mainstream religious groups. For some, this journey away from tradition results from a hurtful experience, while for others it is a personal decision that reflects our interests, comfort, idea of divinity, or desire to be part of a community that holds us in our brokenness and wholeness.

> *"I went spiritual when I transitioned! Before life felt meaningless, but now I feel life can be whatever I want it to be."*

> *"I was raised in a religious household, but we believed as strongly in doing good as in a god. That's pretty much how I still feel. I celebrate seasonal holidays, but not too religiously. I love hymn singing and wish my voice was at least an alto instead of tenor, and am going to try voice therapy to be able to sing as myself. Despite being a scientist and an atheist, I think of myself as spiritual in that there is more than the material world to life."*

RITUALS

As human beings, we create rituals or practices to celebrate and commemorate different aspects or moments of our journey through life. Through these practices we are able to meet others, carry out social activities, and celebrate life's happenings. Rituals allow us to set apart as special a particular moment or rite of passage.

Some rituals are held within a communal gathering at a temple, church, or synagogue, while others take place within the private sanctuary of our bedrooms, an outdoor hike, or even our office cubicle. Creating and performing rituals allows us to invite the sacred and divine into our space and our life. For some people these practices are reminders of how to uphold values or moral principles throughout the day. For others they are opportunities to connect with another person or people in a deeper and more intimate way. Rituals create opportunities to lift up, support, protect, celebrate, mourn, and claim both divine and communal affirmations.

Transition can be expanded beyond its clinical, medical, or social understandings in order to engage and describe our spiritual journeys of living as our authentic selves. To transition is more than surgery or medical treatment—it is the ongoing journey of honoring and expressing our gender integrity and wholeness. As we transition, there are rituals that can be practiced, either individually or in communities, to mark specific events or rites of passage.

Renaming or Rebaptism

For many individuals and within various traditions, naming is a significant and powerful event. Naming sets someone or something apart from everyone or everything else. For many of us, it is an important step to have a ceremony of renaming to affirm our personhood by uniting our bodies with our minds and spirits.

"One of the most amazing and exciting moments in the path of a transgender person's life is choosing, proclaiming, and christening a new name. This is an opportunity for many to name one's true self, one's core being, the person God created them to be. Whether one is Jennifer becoming Steve or James becoming Amanda, there is nothing quite like the experience of naming the person one has always been." —Melanie Martinez and Angel Collie, Metropolitan Community Churches Trans-Etiquette (p. 4).

Examples of renaming and rebaptism rituals can be found in the books *Courage to Love: Liturgies for the Lesbian, Gay, Bisexual, and Transgender Community*, by Geoffrey Duncan, and in *Equal Rites: Lesbian and Gay Worship, Ceremonies, and Celebrations*, by Kittredge Cherry and Zalmon Sherwood.

Naming ceremonies can be as simple as writing our name down on a piece of paper or as formal as an official baptism or rebaptism. Naming marks the letting go of what *was* in order to embrace who we *are* (and who we have always been). Naming ceremonies serve as an opportunity for us to be welcomed as a member of a group and have our personhood in its wholeness affirmed and celebrated. For many trans people, communal rituals may be one of the few places of safety and acceptance in our lives. Witnessing and being present at a baptism or name-changing ceremony is one way a community can demonstrate their solidarity with a trans person and their family.

"I had a naming ceremony when I came out as transgender."

"I plan on being baptized with my chosen name after it becomes 'official.'"

"My partner came out to her rabbi, the assistant rabbi, the president of the congregation, and our cantor. . . The cantor said, 'She's going to need us to do a naming ceremony!' [My partner] said, 'But she has never converted,' to which the cantor said, 'She can do more than one transition.'"

CONNECTING TO MY ANCESTORS

Tebogo Calvin Nkoana is a South African trans man.

When I reached puberty and was around boys more than girls, I realized that my body was developing differently from boys. I wanted to look strong and have my lovely flat chest forever, but my body started developing in a feminine way. That just destroyed me. My parents were aware of my feelings, but they never acknowledged it. Instead, they prepared me for my adolescent stage as a girl. They warned me about the things that could affect my future as a girl. They started teaching me all the things that women are supposed to do, and the roles of women. Some of these expectations were to wear women's clothing, to take responsibility for the home, to gather with women to discuss community matters (and to be excluded from gatherings of men), to walk and talk in feminine ways, and to defer to men's wishes.

I hated that period, as I strongly looked at myself as a young man who should be prepared for manhood. At about 14, I started getting sick and spent most of my time in hospitals, but no doctor could tell me what was wrong with me. My family then decided to consult a traditional healer (known as a "sangoma") to find out what the problem was. According to the traditional consultant, my sickness was a warning that my Ancestors were calling me to practice traditional herbal healing. When my parents investigated more, they discovered that the Ancestor who was calling me was a male person. They were very shocked to hear this, since most often the Calling comes to a male from a male Ancestor and to a female from a female Ancestor. They were surprised since I was still so young. It is believed that being Called by the Ancestors means that the one who is Called continues that Ancestor's life. My parents started to accept and respect my desire to represent myself as male. Since that day they have respected and supported me. Neighbors became very curious to know how my family dealt with my gender identity, because it was surprising to them to see me and my family getting along well.

My mother told them: "He inherited it from his great grandfather." The people in my area became convinced when they heard the Ancestor stories my mother shared. They started to understand my situation and started to respect me without any hesitation. Since then, I've been living freely and I've been able to express my masculinity. I've also been treated like any other man in our community. African culture helped me to escape the stereotypes and the discrimination in my community. My treatment was different from other FTM transgendered people, thanks to my having a Calling by a male Ancestor.

Everyday Rituals

Everyday practices such as taking a hormone regimen, binding our chests, or putting on makeup can become profound acts of self-care, affirmation, and resilience. Though to some these may seem mundane or secular, these simple everyday acts can become powerful rituals commemorating our ownership of our own lives, bodies, and souls. With them, we are taking pride in ourselves and embracing the journey we have embarked on, with its ups and downs. From the perspective of ritualization, everyday life becomes a journey of co-creation with the universe or God, upholding the idea that creation is a dynamic, ongoing process we are invited to be in solidarity with as signs of our inner and outer resilience.

"The rituals I have involve getting in drag . . . The strapping of my breasts. . . Lighting a cigarette once I come on stage . . . Applying a layer of foundation (I *never* wear foundation as a girl)."

"I am very much an atheist, but I've found the process of binding my chest has become almost spiritual. . . It's like a healing process and even though I'm physically hurting my body, I know I'm getting a step closer to becoming the real me, and it's a great feeling."

"I'm not religious or spiritual at all—the closest thing to ritual is getting ready for a drag show and getting 'all the way' into a 'fully masculine' persona for the stage."

"Every Friday night, I take a bubble bath, light a candle, and shave those parts I wasn't taught to shave as a boy. As I soak, I remember who I am and where I have come from and that I have been true to myself."

Prayers, Mantras, and Self-Affirmations

Sadly, many of us have suffered discrimination and marginalization within church and social circles that do not affirm or recognize our dignity, worth, or personhood. To counter these harmful narratives, some of us find power in regularly and actively reminding ourselves of our self-worth, beauty, significance to others, and amazing uniqueness.

Some of us make self-affirming statements facing a mirror, while others recite mantras and prayers shared through the use of malas, rosaries, or communal creeds that affirm the worth and dignity of all people. These practices can be ways of reconnecting with ourselves and connecting ourselves to a greater, shared community. They are all acts of remembering and honoring the complex, quirky, and wonderful beings we are.

"I am a lifelong atheist, with no belief in anything that does not really exist in a way that can be at least detected in people's minds. . . Still, once knowing that I was trans felt real to me, I've been affirming to myself in the mirror that I am a beautiful woman, even as my face grows hair."

EMBRACING OUR SPIRITUAL SELVES DURING TRANSITION

Ja'briel Walthour is a transgender advocate, community organizer, and author residing in Hinesville, Georgia. She currently works with special needs students and has penned a children's book series which is loosely based on her experience growing up black and transgender in the South. She was included on the inaugural "Trans 100 List" and has also written for Ebony.com, Elixher.com, GLAAD, and the Huffington Post.

Transitioning is often a scary and sometimes frightening experience. While charting the waters of change, many of us may become overwhelmed with the challenges of embracing our authentic selves. Furthermore, the constraints of organized religion may lead some to abandon and disregard a personal desire to feed our spiritual being. Too often, our spirit is left malnourished, starved for manna and sustenance. Nevertheless, there are several ways we can stave off apathy of the deprived soul. Here are a few tips to support the foundation of your spirit:

1. *Meditate.* Never underestimate the power of being alone with your thoughts while transitioning. Ten or fifteen minutes of daily relaxation, void of television, cell phones, and the Internet can rejuvenate your soul and replenish lost energy.

2. *Seek purpose.* It is imperative to find your passion(s) during transition. One of the most unnerving experiences of transitioning is the lack of belonging and the fear of the unknown.

3. *Actively pray.* Sincere communication with a sovereign and divine source of inspiration can transform a dull, empty religious experience into a rich and fulfilling spiritual life. Open and honest prayer allows you to express gratitude, vent frustrations, and release your cares to the Universe.

4. *Foster faith.* A vital step to securing a healthy, spiritual existence upon transition includes the act of believing in your mission and also remaining optimistic during every aspect of your journey. Faith-building takes work, which may include adopting a clear and positive vision, utilizing resources such as daily devotionals or self-help manuals, and simply consulting a trusted friend or confidant for support.

5. *Receive the promise.* Along the way, you will find that transitioning requires mustering courage and resilience. However, you should keep in mind the ultimate goal and reward of nurturing your soul. Your peace, happiness, and well-being are just a few of the benefits you will receive on your quest for spiritual enlightenment.

Meditation

Many of us have meditative or mindfulness practices that ground us in our everyday lives and provide us with a sense of connection to ourselves and to the world. These may be as simple as exercises that focus our breathing or that encourage us to pay attention to the details of the spaces around us. Some of us have extensive experience with meditation and spend time at retreats or put aside time each day to meditate.

> *"As part of the process to arrive at my gender and my current definition of my state, I have used meditation and visualization so that I may find the strength within me to do what must be done to be true to myself."*

> *"My gender identity and sexed body-mind relation feels even more natural and authentic when I do yoga or meditate."*

The Eastbay Meditation Center's Alphabet Sagha page lists LGBTQ meditation groups across the United States and Canada and parts of Europe.

TRANSFORMATIVE THEOLOGY: CONTRIBUTIONS FROM THE TRANS COMMUNITY

Many religious communities do not recognize or respect a dynamic, expansive approach to gender identity and expression, but trans activists have begun to challenge these barriers. Theologians and religious professionals have started to develop, redefine, and deconstruct religious traditions, practices, teachings, and devotions in ways that are affirming and celebratory not only for trans people but for all people.

Many of us have received religious messages that claim that our understanding of body and gender is wrong, that we are inherently disordered and no procedure can cure us. Trans religious approaches can undo the false beliefs and erroneous messages that our bodies are evil or not good enough. These approaches offer an invitation and challenge to embrace who we are as beings living in wholeness and integrity.

> *"I was able to reconcile [my spirituality] with my identity by really digging down and finding out what my religion and my gender each really meant deep down, and I think I came out stronger in both regards as a result. . ."*

"Our faith traditions have a role to play in the expansion of society that will create a world in which everyone's multifaceted and complicated gender identity can develop without the threat of violence or humiliation. . . religion grounds and contextualizes human experience, congregational life offers individuals concrete sustenance and support."—Rabbi Elliot Rose Kukla, HRC's "Gender Identity and Our Faith Communities."

By reclaiming our rights, body, and spirit, a trans religious voice is emerging that proclaims that our lives, experiences, joys, and challenges are sacred texts in which the divine speaks—trans people theologizing about the trans experience on our own terms and with our own voices.

Reimagining God

Many people of Judeo-Christian faith wrestle with questions about the image of God. What does it mean to be created in the image of God if the images shared by the dominant culture do not look like me? Does this mean that my body and who I am as a person are somehow less than or inherently defective? Not having spaces or images in which our personhood and body are affirmed can lead to feelings of isolation, self-hatred, and destructive behaviors. Due to the efforts of feminist and LGBTQ religious leaders as well as religious leaders of color, many spiritual movements have rediscovered the divine feminine and images of the sacred of various genders—inclusive representations that reflect a multicultural, multigendered, and multibodied God and world.

As trans theologian Justin Tanis explains in his book *Trans-Gendered: Theology, Ministry, and Communities of Faith*, "Transgender people. . . have a unique opportunity to witness to the gender of God. . . We who embody more than one gender within our lifetimes have learned something about our ability to hold both of these spaces within one body. . . If we, as human beings, can do it, surely God can do it" (pp. 134–135). By being able to engage an image of the sacred that transcends gender or inhabits a space in-between, many of us have been able to find ourselves in the divine and embrace the divine within ourselves.

> *"I find incredible peace from my spiritual beliefs and the knowledge that God loves me and made me just as I am—a trans woman."*

A broader understanding of the gender of God and the divine does not threaten or diminish masculinity or femininity as conservative religious scholars fear. Rather, it opens up our ability to approach the divine and the holy as a lover, comforter, mother, creator, grandparent, or protector. Honoring these aspects or images of the sacred is not new—they are upheld within certain sects of Christianity and Judaism as well as pagan and goddess-centered traditions.

In his book, Tanis cites Jann Aldredge-Clanton, who states that "men, as well as women, benefit from gender inclusive images of God. . . equality of male and female, in heaven and on earth, does not lower the self-esteem of men [or women]. . . in fact, males [and females] can feel new kinds of power through androgynous concepts of God and humanity" (Tanis, 2003, p. 135). This opening up of gender and of the divine recognizes that just as human beings cannot be reduced to just one aspect of who they are, the sacred cannot be limited or boxed in to a single aspect, image, trait, or manifestation.

The trans experience of religion is a prophetic and poignant reminder that, if faith communities uphold the belief that the divine is so awesome that our ability to comprehend

"It's a low kick in the nuts when you put so much into looking like a woman and people still call you 'Mister' or by your real name, or *faggot*—just because they don't know who they are or can't see you for you. It is because they don't know themselves and think of you as less. Just from a look sometimes, I ask myself, am I a human? What is wrong with me? Are they human? What's wrong with them? It would kill me if I did not know God—but I know He is here, and I was made this way and no one can take this from me. I am a trans woman—once a lil' boy, now a woman. And I love it." *Tanay Smith, the queen of Guyana, is a 23-year-old fabulous young lady living in the Bronx.*

Sixteenth-century Italian reliquary bust of St Marinus the Martyr, who was born female and lived as a male monk (courtesy of Mary Harrsch).

"I defied the gender binary. I challenged the first pronouncement ever made about me. I questioned the evidence my body presented to me, and I took issue with the guidance of my parents, who assumed, and nudged my life down one path without even asking me if that's where I wanted to go. I confounded my society and my culture, and I ignored what I was told was the norm. I lived on the edges and I defied definitions. I am far more than the names I have been called. I have done many things and lived many lives. I am the rule-breaker, the exception, the trickster, the one who divides and multiplies the gender binary until it becomes a string of infinite possibilities. In ancient times I was celebrated as one who walked in many worlds. I was revered as the one who embodied transformation and who showed the world we can change. But ancient wisdom has long been forgotten and now I pay the price for our forgetfulness. We tend to behave badly toward that which we do not understand, and therein lies the pain. Like all of creation, I am a mystery. I don't seek to be understood. I just seek to be accepted."—I AM by Emma Lee Chattin (from the Metropolitan Community Churche's Holy Conversations Workshop)

it fully is limited, then representations of the sacred are beyond our limited categories of gender and identity. The trans faith experience is an invitation to engage and grapple with multiple, diverse, inclusive images and aspects of the sacred. By doing this, we, as individuals and communities, are able to affirm that our complex selves and bodies are also holy and cannot be limited by traditional understandings of gender, identity, and expression. We are reminders of human diversity, inviting and challenging others to realize the need for language and imagery of the holy that is as diverse as we are. To put it simply, "don't box God in and don't box me in!"

Sacred Texts and Holy Heroes

More and more religious scholarship by trans and trans-affirming scholars is revisiting sacred texts—such as the Hebrew Bible, the New Testament, and the Holy Qu'ran—in order to discover, and often rediscover, narratives that affirm the lives of trans people.

Our understanding of gender in the 21st century is very different from concepts of gender and sexuality that existed thousands of years ago when many of these documents were written. While honoring these differences, many theologians and religious scholars have interpreted texts in a trans-positive light, balancing historical context with messages of liberation and transformation. Some scholars, such as Professor Patrick Cheng (2011), describe their work as "queering" religious studies—in other words, interpreting and studying these texts in ways that push us to embrace transgressive or challenging ideas, beyond society's limited or traditional expectations of sexuality and gender.

For example, Judeo-Christian readers might ask: If God created both male and female in God's image, does this mean that God is a transgender or intersex entity? Though concrete answers are perhaps not possible, these questions open the door for healing and holistic interpretations and conversations with ourselves, with the sacred, and with others.

By taking this kind of approach to sacred texts, we can find characters whose lives transgressed or challenged the gender expectations of their time, without needing to know their gender self-identification. It is not possible to know how prophets, saints, ancestors, or deities identify. But we can find liberating meaning in their actions and words.

For many religious and spiritual traditions, importance is given to the presence of ancestors, saints, intercessors, and intermediaries—figures we look to for inspiration and as examples to be followed. By revisiting histories, sacred stories, and traditions, we can lift up individuals who were radical transgressors of social and gender norms—individuals who disrupted gender and offered alternative ways to express our faith and relationship with the divine. We can rediscover a trans presence that is often not foreign to a tradition but is very much integral to a religion's teachings, devotions, experiences of God, and even critical to the initial establishment or formation of a religious community.

How did the Buddha, Deborah in the Book of Judges, or Jesus in the Gospels transgress gender norms in ways that are affirming of trans people today? Often the religious figures we venerate were countercultural revolutionaries who strove to be in solidarity with the oppressed and marginalized peoples of their day, preaching and living inclusive and alternative ways of viewing religion and community—a spirit which can be tapped into today to affirm trans people.

We do not have to look far for trans-affirming messages—often we just have to take another look at tradition and uncover a presence that has always been there but for various reasons has been neglected or hidden. By reclaiming and remembering the past, trans religious people have been able to make sure that traditions, stories, and history are inclusive and complete—a practice that honors the prophetic voices and radical lives of *all* those from yesterday and better helps us to celebrate diversity today, tomorrow, and always.

Trans Religious Leaders

Though many religious traditions bar trans people from pursuing ordination or consecration as spiritual leaders, there are several groups that are beginning to affirm those of us who are called to ministry. Religious leaders who identify as trans reflect a diversity of traditions and callings. Such prophetic voices include Rev. Malcolm Himschoot (United Church of Christ), Rev. Dr. Justin Edward Tanis (Metropolitan Community Church/Unitarian Universalist Association), Rev. Moshay Moses (Metropolitan Community Church), Rev. Cameron Partridge (Episcopal Church USA), Rabbi Elliot Rose Kukla, Rabbi Reuben Zellman, Patricia Kevena Fili (Wiccan/Pagan), Rev. Louis Mitchell, Angel Collie (Metropolitan Community Church), Rev. Shannon "Shay" T. L. Kearn (North American Old Catholic Church), and Dr. Virginia Ramey Mollenkott (Trans-Religious Christian). Their ministries are as diverse as they are and include university chaplaincy, pastoral work within hospices, serving congregations as pastors, developing social policy within nonprofits, and university research (and for some, combinations of more than one of these). Trans people in ministry are not only ministering to other trans people and their families but are serving whole communities.

CONCLUSION

Our bodies, experiences, and lives as trans people reveal a richness and diversity of religious expression—an expression that also reflects the diversity of our human experience of journeying and transitioning into wholeness. A trans religious approach invites us to take another look at practices within our traditions in order to embrace concepts, convictions, definitions, redefinitions, and ways of being that are outside the norm—not with fear, but with excitement and awe.

Faith and spirituality grounded in trans experiences and narratives boldly proclaim that all people have the human and sacred right to choose how we care for, dress, decorate, cover and uncover, craft, and tweak our bodies as we seek to be at home with ourselves and within ourselves.

REFERENCES AND FURTHER READING

Chattin, E. L. (2012). I AM: A journey into the realm of gender variance: A poem written for the 11th annual transgender day of remembrance (remembering our dead), November 20, 2009. In V. Miller (Ed.) *Reflections (MCC theologies: Trans)*. Retrieved December 2013, from http://www.opendoormcc.com/pastor_files/12_0520_reflections.pdf

Cheng, P. (2011). *Radical love: An introduction to queer theology*. New York, NY: Seabury Books.

Glaser, C. (Ed.). (2008). Gender identity & our faith communities: A congregational guide for transgender advocacy. *Human Rights Campaign Foundation*. Retrieved December 2013, from http://www.hrc.org/files/assets/resources/Gender-Identity-and-our-Faith-Communities_2008-12.pdf

Martinez, M., & Collie, A. (UFMCC Transgender Resource Team). (2005). Trans etiquette: Welcoming transgender communities to MCC. *Universal Fellowship of Metropolitan Community Churches*. Retrieved December 2013, from http://www.presbyterianwelcome.org/wp-content/uploads/2011/03/transetiquette.pdf

Mollenkott, V. R. (2001). *Omnigender: A trans-religious approach*. Cleveland, OH: Pilgrim Press.

Tanis, J. E. (2003). *Trans-gendered: Theology, ministry, and communities of faith*. Cleveland, OH: Pilgrim Press.

Chris Paige is the founder of TransFaith Online, a nonprofit that affirms, empowers, and engages transgender and gender nonconforming people and their communities.

"I am convinced that one reason that people become enraged by and frightened of us is because we have had the courage to change something fundamental about ourselves in order to become more fully realized human beings, more joyful people. . . that freedom and courage scares people, and pushes buttons for many, but that path is the road to liberation. . . we who have changed our own lives and fulfilled our own dreams have much to offer a world in need of both transformation and greater dreams of its own."—Justin Tanis, *Trans-Gendered: Theology, Ministry, and Communities of Faith*

6

SEX AND GENDER DEVELOPMENT

Laura Erickson-Schroth, Miqqi Alicia Gilbert, and T. Evan Smith

MOST PEOPLE ASSUME THAT THERE ARE TWO GENDERS, male and female, and that both our sex and gender depend on our genitals—whether we were born with a vagina or a penis. However, research in a variety of fields, including psychology, genetics, sociology, and anthropology, suggests that sex and gender are not the same thing. Today, our "sex" typically describes our anatomical and biological characteristics. Usually, this means our genitals and our genetics. "Gender" is most often used to refer to our social roles and behaviors. But sex and gender are not completely separate concepts, and social and biological factors play an important role in defining both our sex and our gender.

CURIOSITY ABOUT OUR ORIGINS

Some of us are extremely interested in how we come to develop our identity as transgender or gender nonconforming people.

> "I admit that I am curious about why I am the way that I am."

> "That is exactly what I hope to study as a doctoral student of psychology. I hope to attend graduate school next year and investigate this question, so ask me again in five or six years."

For others of us, the hows and whys are less important.

> "I don't think knowing a 'cause' will make one bit of difference in my life. I am who I am. That's good enough for me."

> "I don't know what causes people to be transgender, and I honestly don't think it matters. . . Does it matter if gay people were born that way? They are now, and their identity should be respected. Same for transgender people."

> "The great diversity of creation 'causes' individuals to 'be' transgender. . . What causes a person to be cisgender?"

Some of us believe that being transgender or gender nonconforming is something we have a say in, while others of us believe it is out of our control.

> "I believe it's something innate, brought on by something that happens during fetal development. I don't believe in any of the 'nurture' theories, for I was brought up in a very masculine, blue-collar environment. I still enjoy the outdoors and machines and all that, but I know I'm a girl, and nothing in my upbringing either caused it to happen or made it go away. It just was, and it just is."

> "It doesn't matter what causes it, the only important thing is that it's not a choice."

For some of us, the idea of our choosing our gender identity is powerful.

> "I get really sick of this never-ending debate about 'what causes someone to be trans,' because these debates invariably revolve around whether people 'choose' to be trans or whether they 'can't help it because they were born that way.' There

is an underlying assumption within the very framing of this debate that trans people are somehow more legitimate if they do not claim any autonomy over their own gender identity, which I find a completely absurd position. I am really proud of who I am, and I want to take credit for my autonomy in that process! I think that what causes people to be transgender is having an enlightened view of the world. Trans people are people who can imagine different possibilities, who can question the things that others simply accept as being unquestionably true, and who have the strength of character to act on their convictions even without support from other people."

"CHOICE" OF GENDER IDENTITY

Jaimie Veale, PhD, is a trans woman currently working on a postdoctoral research fellowship in trans people's health at the University of British Columbia.

There is a lot of disagreement and debate about biology versus "choice" in all kinds of LGBTQ communities. The overwhelming majority of trans and queer people report that they don't find their sexual orientation or gender identity to be a choice—the only choice that we believe we have is whether and how to express these. All but the most vocal opponents of trans and queer rights agree that sexual orientation and gender identity aren't characteristics people have a choice about.

While some people find that their gender identity and/or sexual orientation stay the same throughout their life, others report that they change. For example, trans people may have a significant change in social context when they see themselves and are seen by other people as a different gender to what they had previously. As part of this "transition" process, it is not uncommon for people to report changes in the types of people we are sexually attracted to. There is very little evidence that conscious efforts to change someone's gender identity or sexual orientation, such as "reparative therapy," have any effect.

If being trans isn't a choice, is it all about biology, then? People often think that they have a choice about things as long as they are not "biological." This isn't necessarily true, though—it is possible for something to be caused by factors other than biology and to also not feel like it is under our control. If I am a very punctual person because of growing up in an environment where there were serious consequences for being late, this is an example of something about me that I feel I don't have a choice about, that is the result of a nonbiological factor.

Many people are suspicious of studies that look for reasons why people are or are not trans. They may believe that these studies are inherently prejudiced because it seems that trans people need to legitimize our identities whereas non-trans people do not. Some believe these studies are inherently pathologizing to us because they may bring about questions of whether being trans can be "cured."

On the other hand, biological studies have been used to argue that our variant identities are not our "fault," and we may have gained some rights based on this idea. We should be cautious of this way of thinking though—it is too simplistic and it disregards the many real and legitimate reasons for our identities. We should also be aware that biological explanations have been used not only to protect groups of people but also to take away their rights. For example, in Nazi-led Germany, gay people were murdered because it was believed that being gay was genetic.

While gender identity is not usually something people feel that they have a choice about, it is something that may differ for people across different social environments and time periods. Trans identities not being experienced as a "choice" does not tell us much about whether gender identity is formed by "nature," "nurture," or both, and it certainly does not change the need for equal rights for trans people.

Regardless of our own questions or beliefs about why we are trans or gender nonconforming, many of us worry about the ramifications of searching for a "cause."

"I don't feel like it's productive to ask the question what causes people to be transgender in the sense that the question itself presumes that something went wrong, that it's abnormal."

"I'm scared that if people started to identify causes they would follow that with suggesting cures."

"Why would I want a test or a found discovery that would define why I am this way? I would then be required to further prove, as if it isn't already difficult enough, to outsiders and legitimize my feelings to find the peace I now have."

OUR GENDERED WORLD

How do we see ourselves? What kinds of people do we feel similar to? What do we feel comfortable being called? All these things make up our gender identity, our inner sense of being male, female, something in-between, or something entirely different. There are as many ways of identifying as there are people. Unlike gender identity, gender roles are not determined by our inner sense of ourselves. Instead, they are defined and enforced by society. Gender roles give us rules about how we are supposed to behave and what kinds of opportunities and responsibilities are available to us.

Gender roles may also help shape our ideas about what "feminine" and "masculine" characteristics are. Often, feminine or masculine traits are thought of as natural or innate to people with certain types of bodies and therefore taboo or off limits to people with other kinds of bodies. These are **gender stereotypes**, which describe how men and women look, behave, and feel. Gender stereotypes may differ among cultures, but in many cases, submissive or supportive behaviors are seen as "feminine," while aggressive, achievement-oriented, and independent individuals are seen as "masculine."

INTRODUCTION TO QUEER THEORY

Reese C. Kelly was born and raised in the suburbs of Detroit, Michigan. He received a PhD in sociology from the University at Albany, SUNY, and is at Dartmouth College.

What we now call queer theory began with a set of texts written during the late 1970s into the mid-1990s by scholars including Gloria Anzaldua, Judith Butler, Cathy Cohen, Michel Foucault, C. Jacob Hale, Gayle Rubin, Eve Kosofsky Sedgwick, and Michael Warner, which presented new ways to conceptualize sex, gender, and sexuality.

Although the phrase "coming out of the closet" is widely used in LGBTQ politics and popular culture, scholars argue that the heyday of the closet era was from the 1950s to the 1980s. During this time period, people were sent to psychiatric hospitals, imprisoned, and fired from their jobs merely for their sexuality or perceived sexuality. Because of this extreme homosexual oppression, some LGBTQ people felt tremendous pressure to lead outwardly appearing heterosexual, cisgender lifestyles. As gay liberationist and feminist movements began to blossom in the late 1960s, gays and lesbians were encouraged to be "Out and Proud!" as opposed to being ashamed or scared.

The collective action of LGBTQ individuals and allies led to significant civil rights advancements such as nondiscrimination policies in housing and work, the removal of homosexuality from the American Psychiatric Association's *Diagnostic and Statistical Manual of Mental Disorders*, and procedures for legal sex reclassification. Within the current legal and political system of the United States, adopting a shared label of "lesbian," "transgender," "bisexual," or "gay" provides an effective way to identify inequities and advocate for the needs of marginalized people.

However, the unintended consequence of "coming out" is that sexual fluidities, inconsistencies, and variances are silenced, ignored, or rewritten. People mold their bodies, life histories, relationships, and behaviors to fit the definitions of gay, lesbian, bisexual, or straight, while excluding a range of other possible desires and acts. As an example: A woman comes out as a lesbian and decides to cut her hair in order to "look" more "like a lesbian." This example highlights that "coming out" is not a solitary or individualized act.

The notion that all lesbians, gays, and bisexuals share a set of universal experiences, practices, and political goals is at the heart of many contemporary LGBTQ organizations and politics. It is also under heavy criticism from queer theorists for two primary reasons. First, sexual practices, desires, and relationships are shaped by many factors, including race, ethnicity, disability, nationality, class status, gender, sex, and size; therefore, even when individuals share the same sexual identity, their experiences, expressions of self, and politics may vary drastically. Second, the paradigm of the closet can exacerbate rather than alleviate social pressure because, as queer theorists argue, "coming out of the closet" and adopting a restrictive label often results in an individual feeling pressure to conform to behavior widely expected from someone who identifies that way.

In the United States now, we have antidiscrimination laws protecting gays and lesbians from employment and housing discrimination; there are gays and lesbians in political office, the military, and serving as religious leaders; and sodomy laws were rendered unconstitutional in the 2003 Supreme Court decision *Lawrence v. Texas*. But this does not mean that there is sexual equality, merely that the challenges facing LGBTQ people have shifted.

Queer theorists claim that current US culture is characterized by *heteronormativity,* in which it is not just homosexuality that is seen as bad, unnatural, or immoral, but a range of sexual behaviors, relationships, and identities other than "normal" heterosexuality. Behaviors that boost the status of reproductive heterosexuality—monogamy, sex during marriage, and sex in private spaces—are given higher social status and material benefits (like tax deductions for married couples) while behaviors that threaten or challenge reproductive heterosexuality are socially degraded and deemed sick or undesirable.

Queer theorists insist that sexual desires and practices are cultural concepts and not biological facts that can be confined to isolated identity categories. They claim that people are *not* "Born this way!" but that identities are mapped onto us based on what our society prescribes.

We learn about gender by watching other people, by imitating what they do, and by identifying with them and mimicking their behavior. The feminist philosopher Judith Butler calls gender a **performance** (Butler, 1990). However, this performance is not the same thing as acting. We learn and repeat others' behaviors, internalizing them and interpreting them as a sense of self. We also repeat gendered behaviors over generations, solidifying our culture's understanding of gender. While not everyone would agree that gender is completely created by us, rather than having some biological components, there is significant evidence that our gender identities are influenced by social factors.

Due to sexism, the treatment of women as inferior to men, many of the traits that are perceived as "feminine" are devalued, compared to "masculine" traits. Fighting sexism means allowing people to act in ways that are masculine or feminine, regardless of their bodies, as well as recognizing value in all kinds of behaviors. Regardless of our sex or gender, we all have a wide array of characteristics that might be considered feminine or masculine.

Queer Theory, Gender Theory: An Instant Primer by Riki Wilchins (Los Angeles, CA: Alyson Books, 2004) combines personal stories with accessible language to describe the history and ideas that are part of queer and gender theory.

Creating and Learning Gender

Characteristics of femininity and masculinity do not "naturally" belong to women or men. Scholars call this the **social construction** of gender, meaning that we construct, or create, gender by telling men and women how to act. Judith Butler wrote that "gender is a kind of imitation for which there is no original; in fact, it is a kind of imitation that produces the very notion of the original as an effect and consequence of the imitation itself" (Butler, 1993, p. 313). This statement refers to the idea that gender does not come from a biological or otherwise essential starting point. Butler argues that gender is a product of culture, and its meaning is created by people.

> *"I don't think anything causes people to be transgender. I think dichotomous socialization makes people M or F."*

> *"I think patriarchy and the societal construction of the gender binary are what cause people to be trans. The only reason people are 'gender non-conforming' or trans is because we as a society create gendered expectation in the first place. If we viewed the spectrum of human characteristics and emotions as simply attributes that anyone can possess instead of assigning them to one gender or the other, there would not be any kind of gender archetype to strive for."*

Learning Trans is a web project designed to create and highlight trans community-produced knowledge as part of a living history. It includes videos, presentations, fact sheets, and course materials.

Transgender Studies Quarterly (TSQ) is a journal edited by Paisley Currah and Susan Stryker that hopes to push trans theory forward.

INTRODUCTION TO TRANS THEORY

Kai Kohlsdorf is finishing his PhD at the University of Washington, where he focuses on trans* moments of sexual disclosure through the lenses of cultural studies, queer theory, and trans theories.

Trans theory emerged from a realization that trans people have long been used in research to prove various theories but were not given a voice within that research. Even queer theory has been a prime perpetrator in the invisibilizing of trans people. One of the major contributions of trans studies involves the "politics of naming": particular identity groups can reclaim agency by taking back words that have been used against us.

Historically speaking, feminism, gender studies, and sexuality studies have had a difficult relationship with trans identities. The feminist sex wars of the late 1970s and 1980s are infamous in both sexuality scholarship and feminist history, with debates that centered around pornography, pro-sex ideology, sadomasochism, and the role of trans women in the lesbian community (Duggan & Hunter, 1995). At times, second-wave feminists wrote disparagingly about transgender people and identities (Raymond, 1979).

The legacy from this time period has not entirely disappeared. Some more recent academic works use these same kind of dated and transphobic ways of thinking. Sheila Jeffreys, a well-known feminist theorist, continues to argue that trans women's identities are "obviously about men's sexual rights" and that lesbians are disappearing because young butches are becoming men. Her arguments rely on the misconception that all trans identities uphold the gender binary and are opposed to true feminist thought (Jeffreys, 2011).

Trans studies is often credited as being launched into academia in 1991 by Sandy Stone. Stone's piece "The Empire Strikes Back: A Posttranssexual Manifesto" strikes back against anti-trans feminism and describes a need for us to speak for ourselves in trans research (Stryker & Whittle, 2006). While many trans academics and activists have combated the misuse of trans bodies by paying attention to trans lived experiences, we have also begun to think beyond the limits of these experiences.

Early trans studies came under critique for being US focused and lacking racial analysis. *The Transgender Studies Reader*, edited by Susan Stryker and Stephen Whittle (2006), was the first anthology of its kind and provided articles that spanned trans studies in the first decade of its academic life. The text traces how trans people were viewed and described through more than a century of published work. Only two of its fifty articles incorporate a central analysis of race—so some critics have argued that the book paints an overall picture of trans people and trans studies as white, US focused, and mostly uninterested in sexuality (Noble, 2011).

Increasing attention is now being paid to the multitude of trans experiences globally, as well as issues of national borders, race, and class. Trans studies has also continued to grow in conversation with both feminist theories and queer theories. More feminist and non-trans queer writers are using trans voices in their research. The list of major players in trans theory is growing all the time.

REFERENCES

Duggan, L., & Hunter, N. D. (1995). *Sex wars: Sexual dissent and political culture.* New York, NY: Routledge.

Jeffreys, S. (2011). *Where have all the radicals gone? When feminism gets moderate.* Interview. Retrieved December 2013, from http://rabble.ca/podcasts/shows/f-word/2011/04/where-have-all-radicals-gone-when-feminism-gets-moderate.

Noble, B. (2011). My own set of keys: meditations on transgender, scholarship, belonging. *Feminist Studies, 37*(2).

Raymond, J. G. (1979). *The transsexual empire: The making of the she-male.* Boston, MA: Beacon Press.

Stone, S. (2006). The empire strikes back: A posttranssexual manifesto. In S. Stryker & S. Whittle (Eds.), *The transgender studies reader* (pp. 221–235). New York, NY: Routledge.

Stryker, S., & Whittle, S. (Eds.). (2006). *The transgender studies reader.* New York, NY: Routledge.

Labeling Bodies

When the earliest cells that will one day become a human being begin to grow, they have the potential to develop in many different ways. They may grow into a uterus, a vagina, a penis, testes, breasts, or other characteristics health providers use to classify sex. Our early cells depend on signals created by genes and hormones to determine how our bodies will look. But these are not the only factors that shape our bodies and identities. Throughout our lives, medical decisions, social expectations, cultural norms, and environmental factors play a role as well. Biology continues to play a role, too, as hormones move throughout our bodies during puberty and adulthood.

Our bodies have certain characteristics that are often used to label us as male or female. These may include a vagina, penis, breasts, facial hair, or a number of other physical traits. We assign meaning to these body parts by deciding that there are two sexes—male and female—and that certain body parts are found on men and others on women. We make these physical characteristics significant by dividing the world into two categories and requiring people to adhere to the expectations that come with each of those categories.

In reality, there is a great deal of variation in our bodies, and social influences determine what our bodies mean to us and to others. In addition to the diverse range of bodies that are defined as male and female, some of us have bodies that do not conform to these accepted categories. We may be intersex, born with bodies that others perceived as neither male nor female, or transgender, and we may have altered our bodies later in life so that they no longer fit these categories exclusively. How we are perceived and how we identify may not match our anatomy in the expected ways.

The social meaning of having particular physical traits has come into being over time, and it differs among cultures. Different cultures have different meaning attached to male and female bodies that is not always consistent with male and female gender roles. In some cultures, individuals may have a gender identity that is consistent with their physical sex but for economic or political reasons may be assigned (or choose) a different gender role. We do not *have to* divide the world according to whether we have certain types of genitals.

On the other hand, we may miss important information if we assume that gender is completely social. Our genetic makeup and the hormones that we are exposed to as fetuses have the potential to affect our gender identities. Though gender is thought of as a social concept, there is some evidence that biological components may contribute to our gender identities.

Women Who Become Men: Albanian Sworn Virgins by Antonia Young (New York: Berg Press, 2000) tells the stories of people assigned female at birth who take on the roles of men for familial reasons as an accepted part of Albanian culture.

BIOLOGICAL ORIGINS

Over the years, researchers have identified two principal biological factors that may be involved in establishing our gender identity: the genes that we inherit and the hormone levels we are exposed to in the womb.

RESEARCH ON THE BIOLOGY OF TRANS* IDENTITY

Rachel Levin is an associate professor of biology and neuroscience at Pomona College. She studies the origins and evolution of gender identity and reproductive behavior of humans and other wild animals.

If you were to read in tomorrow's newspaper that scientists had found a trans* gene, how would you react? Would you be concerned that the motivation might be to find the gene and excise it prior to birth? Would you be less legitimate as a trans* or cis person depending on the presence or absence of the gene? Our relationship with science is complex and fraught with tension, especially when it comes to issues of identity or sexuality.

Scientific research is based on the art of asking a well-worded question and testing the possible answers to it. Questions about a trans* gene could be asked in many different ways, ranging from "what controls the formation of gender identity?" to "what *goes wrong* that leads to trans* identity?" The lens through which scientists see the world is colored by the same cultural biases that affect everyone. Scientific research is often used as the platform for policies and treatment plans, so it is critical to tackle these issues.

Many studies of transgender identity have their origin in the work of Ray Blanchard. In a series of widely cited studies in the 1980s, Blanchard interviewed adult trans women at gender clinics and reported that his subjects seemed to fall into two types—those who knew early in their lives that they were gender dysphoric and who were attracted only to men (i.e., "androphilic") and those who realized their dysphoria later in life and who were not solely attracted to men. One of the indirect implications of this practice is that androphilic trans women are treated as the "true transsexuals," and the second group is suggested to be less legitimate.

As a result of this, the single group most often studied in research on trans* identity is androphilic trans women. Thus, the group selected to represent the entire trans* population makes up substantially less than half of those who identify as trans women, and, of course, only a tiny percentage of the greater trans* community. Trans men are sometimes included in research studies but are only recently becoming a research focus. People who identify *outside* of the gender binary—as genderqueer, bigendered, or other identities—are almost always excluded.

Cultural bias also plays a role in how data are analyzed. Typically, data from androphilic trans women are compared to data collected from heterosexual cis men, which suggests that researchers are assuming an inherent similarity between all people who are designated male at birth. Imagine the difference if, instead, scientists automatically compared data collected from trans women to results from cis women, or if subjects were allowed to place their identities along one or more continua instead of choosing among a very limited set of options.

We live in a new era, and the science on gender identity needs to catch up. Terminology used needs to be more inclusive and respectful, so we can free ourselves from the legacy of past cultural biases that influence or limit our experimental approaches and color the ways that we interpret our data. Several research groups, including my own, are taking new approaches to consider the full diversity of human experience.

If some day we read about the discovery of a trans* gene, we must remember how elements of both nature and nurture determine who we are. We should ask questions of the science, form our own opinions about its claims, and remember that—regardless of what is found—we are always the experts on our own identities.

Genetics

Chromosomes are long strings made up of thousands of genes, small pieces of genetic material, which are in turn made up of billions of molecules. Chromosomes are located in the nucleus (the main organizing center) of each cell in the body.

Most people have two copies of each of 23 different chromosomes, making a total of 46 chromosomes, although some individuals who are intersex have more or fewer than 46 chromosomes. Our first 22 pairs of chromosomes are numbered 1–22, but the last pair—the so-called sex chromosomes—are named for their shapes, X and Y. The X chromosome is much larger, containing about 2,000 genes, while the Y chromosome has only 78 genes. The total human genome is estimated to have about 20,000 genes.

Most people have two sex chromosomes. When someone is born with two X chromosomes (XX), the person typically develops as female. When someone is born with one X and one Y chromosome (XY), the person typically develops as male. Scientists are still discovering why these combinations usually lead to female and male development.

Most transgender people have the chromosomes that are expected based on their birth-assigned sex, although there may be slightly higher rates of chromosomal differences in transgender compared to cisgender people.

There have been some early studies of specific genes that could be connected to transgender identity. Some of these genes may be related to the way our bodies develop, and others may be related to how we see ourselves. These studies have been designed to take a guess at the types of genes that might be involved in transgender identity and then to analyze those genes in a group of transgender people and a group of cisgender people and compare them. Some "candidate" genes scientists have investigated are genes for hormones, hormone receptors, and enzymes, molecules that help convert one substance to another. A few small studies have shown average differences in some of these genes between cisgender people and people who identify as transsexual or are diagnosed with gender dysphoria, but there is considerable overlap between the groups.

GENETICS OF TRANS* IDENTITY

Lewis A. Raynor, PhD, MPH, MS, is a genetic epidemiologist with a passion for social justice.

The Human Genome Project finished mapping the human genome in 2003, and for the last decade the media has seemed preoccupied with reporting the discovery of a gene for everything—including a trans* gene.

Most phenotypes (the observable property of a person) are complex and are influenced by both our genes (plural) and our environments. The first thing researchers do to determine whether genes are contributing to an outcome is look at the family of an individual, to see if there is a family history of the outcome. Twin studies are very good for determining whether genes contribute to an outcome (i.e., if something is heritable) because identical twins share nearly 100% of their genes, fraternal twins share 50% of their genes, and both have family environments that are likely to be the same.

Once researchers know that genes contribute to an outcome, they try to identify the specific genes that are associated with the outcome in either a group of related or unrelated individuals. Candidate genes are genes that geneticists have some biological reason to suspect are associated with the outcome of interest. Most trans* studies have focused on sex hormone genes. These studies compare the occurrence of a genetic variant in the group with the outcome (cases) to those without the outcome (controls).

An important point to make about all genetic research is that the definition of the observable property being tested influences the statistical results. If we say that trans* identity is heritable, we have to know the way the researchers define trans*. This is often based on an individual being diagnosed with gender dysphoria and is rarely based on an individual self-identifying as transgender or gender nonconforming. So the research would not say that being transgender is heritable; it would say that having gender dysphoria is heritable. The definitions of trans* used are very specific and so are the results. So we can't say that a variant of the androgen receptor gene causes one to be transgender, but we can say that the variant of the androgen receptor gene is associated with being transsexual, specifically a transsexual man.

At this point, none of the genes found to be associated with being transsexual or having gender dysphoria have been replicated in additional studies. Future genetic studies will likely focus on epigenetics, which is a newer area in genetic research. Epigenetics, put simply, are changes in gene activity that do not change our DNA but are still heritable. Oftentimes the gene activity is changing because of environmental factors like diet, stress, or prenatal nutrition. To date, there has been only one, unreplicated study (Dorner et al., 2001) that suggested that endocrine system disrupters, like the chemical insecticide DDT, could contribute to epigenetic changes associated with transsexualism.

Much like the search for the "gay gene" in the 1990s, results from genetic studies of being trans* have been both limited and inconclusive. Furthermore, the definitions used fail to capture the diversity of experiences within the trans* community.

REFERENCE

Dorner, G., Gotz, F., Rohde, W., Plagemann, A., Lindner, R., Peters, H., & Ghanaati, Z. (2001). Genetic and epigenetic effects on sexual brain organization mediated by sex hormones. *Neuroendocrinology Letters*, *22*(6), 403–409.

Another way to indirectly research genes is to perform studies on families. Most research studies of families of trans people look exclusively at transsexual people or those diagnosed with gender dysphoria. The results, therefore, may not apply to all of us. This is true of many studies of our communities. Findings from family studies reveal that trans participants are more likely to have a sibling who is transgender than other people are. The chance is still very low, and most siblings of transgender people are cisgender. The increased chance of being transgender if you have a transgender sibling could be due to genetics, hormones, or even to the way we are raised. Identical twins may both be transgender, but there are also many identical twin pairs where one person is transgender and the other is not, suggesting there are factors other than genes that influence our gender identity.

For more on research about sex and gender, check out Rebecca Jordan Young's book *Brainstorm: The Flaws in the Science of Sex Differences* (Cambridge, MA: Harvard University Press, 2010).

> "I do not know what causes people to be transgender but my uncle came out shortly after I did and he/she is now my aunt. My family thinks it's genetic since there are rumors that my great aunt also struggled with her gender identity growing up."

Epigenetics is a new field of research where scientists look at the way our genes can change without the underlying structure of our DNA shifting. These changes can sometimes occur during our lifetimes, so that our genes are actually changing while we are alive. Future studies on epigenetics and other areas of genetics may shed light on the ways in which our unique genetic makeup plays a role in our gender identity.

Hormones and Development in the Uterus

The environment in the uterus is important for sex development. In the uterus, we are exposed to different conditions depending on characteristics of our parent, the environment

Identical Twins Aidan Key and Brenda Bowers (copyright Stewart Cook).

around our parent, whether we are one of a twin pair, and many other factors. Some hormones we are exposed to in the uterus come from our own developing bodies.

Genes help to guide the body's cells to create internal and external organs that we think of as male and female. All fetuses have the potential to develop a number of different sexual characteristics. Up until about 8 weeks into development, each of us has gender-neutral gonads (early versions of ovaries or testes) accompanied by two pairs of tubes called Mullerian ducts, which have the potential to become a uterus and fallopian tubes, and Wolffian ducts, which have the potential to develop into the structures that produce sperm.

At 8–10 weeks into development, the body begins to form structures that will become the testes and ovaries. A gene called SRY, typically (but not always) found on the Y chromosome, produces a protein called Testis Determining Factor (TDF) that tells the neutral gonads to develop into testes. When there is no TDF, the neutral gonads develop into ovaries.

One of the ways we know that the SRY gene is responsible for turning the neutral gonads into testes is that some people born with XX chromosomes have testes due to an SRY gene on one of their X chromosomes. There are also people with XY chromosomes who do not have an SRY gene, and these people have ovaries rather than testes.

The testes produce a hormone called Mullerian Inhibiting Factor (MIF), which causes the Mullerian ducts to recede, and testosterone, which supports the Wolffian ducts and causes other masculinizing changes in the body. Ovaries do not produce significant levels of hormones before birth, and in the absence of MIF and testosterone, the Wolffian ducts recede.

All of these structures are formed inside the body. The testicles descend later, outside the body, into the scrotum. The external genitalia (clitoris, labia, penis, scrotum) are formed somewhat differently than the internal sexual organs.

Like our internal anatomy, we all start off with similar external anatomy—with parts that will eventually develop into the labia or scrotum and the clitoris or penis. The formation of male-appearing genitals depends on androgens, a group of hormones that includes testosterone and are secreted by the testes. When there is a uterus and ovaries, and little or no androgens, the genitals develop to look female. When the testes of the fetus produce testosterone, the genitals begin to appear more male.

THE SCIENCE OF SEXUALITY VERSUS GENDER IDENTITY

Starting in the 1950s, researchers began experimenting with animals to see the effects of changing the levels of hormones animals were exposed to before they were born. They removed the testicles of male animal fetuses and injected testosterone into female animal fetuses. Male animals that had been castrated before birth were more likely to position themselves to be mounted than to attempt to mount others.

The scientists running these experiments believed that they had done something to change the sexual orientation of the animals. They believed that the male animals that positioned themselves to be mounted were similar to gay men, and they hypothesized that gay men were exposed to different levels of hormones as fetuses than straight men were. Of course, sexual behavior is much more complicated in humans. A man may identify as gay but prefer to "top" his partners. A woman may identify as lesbian and always be the "bottom" partner. People can be bisexual, or like bondage, or be able to orgasm only if a particular object is nearby.

As complex as sexual behavior is, gender identity is probably even more complicated. Prenatal hormone theories are used to explain both sexual orientation and gender identity, despite these concepts being very different. There is also a considerable amount of overlap in the studies done with gay men and transsexual women. As an example, in studies of both gay men and transsexual women, an area of the brain called the third nucleus of the interstitial nucleus of the hypothalamus (INAH-3) is hypothesized to be different from that of straight cisgender men. If INAH-3 is similar in trans women and gay men, then it is more likely to be related to sexual orientation than gender identity—in part because most of the trans women recruited to participate in these studies are attracted to men.

As humans, our sexual and gender identities are extremely complicated. Can animals provide a model for why people are transgender? Do animals have gender identities? If hormones affect both sexual orientation and gender identity, they do so in more complicated ways than we currently understand.

The Brain and Gender

One way that some scientists understand gender development is the theory that our brains themselves can be gendered, an idea that is called **brain organization theory**. This theory suggests that the same hormones that cause changes in internal sexual organs and external genitalia also cause permanent changes in the brain that lead people to think in certain ways about their gender as adults.

Critics of brain organization theory argue that gender is not something that can exist before birth because it is created by society. They argue that while we might have predispositions to think and behave in certain ways because of our genes or hormones, we would not feel male or female without society to tell us what male and female are.

Critics of brain organization theory point out that it matches some people's experiences of their gender, but not other people's experiences. Some people, for instance, do not see themselves as having any gender at all. Others feel comfortable shifting between genders.

> *"I very adamantly DO NOT believe that [being trans] is a birth defect, and I don't believe there is such a thing as a male brain or a female brain (so I don't believe a person can have the wrong body for their brain)."*

THE "TRANSGENDER BRAIN"

Are our brains different from the brains of cisgender people? Some scientists seem to think so, and they argue that when we develop as fetuses, hormones affect our brains and lead us to identify differently from the sex we are assigned. Others remain skeptical.

The area of the brain that most researchers focus on is the hypothalamus, which helps to control hunger, thirst, sleep, and temperature, and secretes a number of hormones (see The Hypothalamus illustration). The hypothalamus is a target of research into gender identity because there are parts of the hypothalamus that are different in cisgender men and cisgender women.

Most scientists in this field study trans women and not trans men. The goal of the majority of research into the "transgender brain" is to show that trans women have brains like cis women, rather than cis men.

The first studies of the "transgender brain" were direct studies of brains donated to science after people died. The scientists doing these studies looked at three areas of the hypothalamus—the bed nucleus of the stria terminalis (BSTc), nucleus 1 of the interstitial nucleus of the anterior hypothalamus (INAH-1), and nucleus 3 of the interstitial nucleus of the anterior hypothalamus (INAH-3). In all three studies, the brains of trans women were found to have similar numbers of brain cells as those of cis women, or to be somewhere in between cis women and cis men.

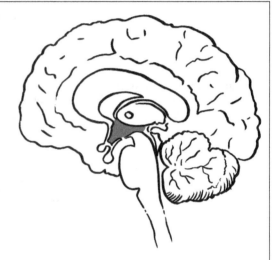

The Hypothalamus (kd diamond).

However, there were a number of problems with these studies. For one, they used very small sample sizes (as few as six trans women's brains). In addition, all of the studies shared brains, so they were not really independent studies. All of the trans women in these studies had taken estrogen before their deaths, so it is possible that this affected their brain structure. In fact, in a follow-up study, researchers found that the BSTc is similar in cisgender men and women until puberty, when it is possible that hormones or other factors affect its size.

As new technologies develop, we no longer need to wait until we have physical brains because we can place live people into magnetic resonance imaging (MRI) machines. While some individual imaging studies have found differences in the size of parts of the brain, such as the putamen and corpus callosum, the findings seem to be inconsistent from study to study.

In addition to looking at structural differences in our brains, some scientists are focusing on functional differences—differences in the way our brains work. The main problem with studying functional as opposed to purely structural differences is that our environments have a large impact on the way we think and feel, so even if differences are found, they are not necessarily caused by biological factors. In fact, our social environments can make measurable changes in the anatomy and function of our bodies, including our hormone levels and even the way our genes work.

There have been a number of studies of both trans women and trans men related to their spatial abilities, because this is an area in which cisgender men and women tend to perform differently. However, most studies of spatial ability in trans people have shown that we have similar abilities to those of our assigned sex and not our gender identities.

One area of brain functioning where trans people do seem to be different is in whether we are left or right handed. Most people do not think of this as a brain function, but our brains control which hand we feel more comfortable using. Most people are right handed, but more cisgender men than women are left handed. Some researchers believe this is because hormones affect handedness in utero. However, there are lots of other theories for why people are left handed, including genetics and something called "developmental instability." Still, multiple studies show that both trans men and trans women are more likely to be left handed than cisgender people are. We do not yet have good theories about why this might be the case.

Intersexuality

One way that researchers have studied the biological origins of sex and gender identity is by studying intersex people, who are born with anatomy that is not considered standard male or female development.

The organization Bodies Like Ours (bodieslikeours.org) seeks to end the shame and secrecy that surrounds people born intersexed and/or with atypical genitals through community and peer support.

Intersex people have been the subjects of research into gender and sexuality for some time, and they have not always had a voice to speak up for themselves. Some intersex people consider themselves to be part of transgender communities. Others do not. Some feel they are a part of our communities because, similarly to us, their bodies are different from what is typical. Others "transition" the same way some transgender people do when they find that the gender they were assigned does not fit them.

While understanding the biology of intersex people may provide some insights into biological factors in transgender experience, we should be cautious about using intersex research to explore our experience. The Intersex Society of North America (ISNA), an advocacy group for intersex people, wrote that "people with intersex conditions ought to be treated with the same basic ethical principles as everyone else—respect for their autonomy and self-determination, truth about their bodies and their lives, and freedom from discrimination. Physicians, researchers, and gender theorists should stop using people with intersex conditions in 'nature/nurture' experiments or debates," (isna.org).

The Intersex Society of North America is no longer active, but an organization called Accord Alliance gathers information and makes recommendations on health care for intersex people.

There are a number of different ways that our bodies can develop. It is difficult to estimate the prevalence of intersex conditions because there are many different definitions of intersex. A small number of infants are born with visibly ambiguous genitalia. If we include the many conditions that differ from typical male or female development, however, it has been estimated that as high as one in sixty infants may be born intersex (Fausto-Sterling, 2000).

Parents whose children are identified as intersex in infancy or at a young age may feel strong social pressure to choose a gender for their child. The sex of their baby is often one of the first questions new parents are asked. It can be hard or embarrassing for many parents who do not have a simple answer. Parents may also worry that if they do not choose quickly, their child will be teased or ostracized for being different.

A MEANS TO AN END: ADDRESSING MEDICALIZED SEXUAL ABUSE OF INTERSEX INFANTS AND CHILDREN

Sean Saifa M. Wall is an intersex man of African descent, who is also a researcher, lover of freedom and equity, and certified rabble rouser. He thanks Generation Five and Advocates for Informed Choice (AIC) for the inspiration and information in this article.

As an intersex man raised as a woman, I have firsthand experience with the sexual abuse under the guise of medical care that too often characterizes the treatment of intersex infants and children.

Child sexual abuse (CSA) is an intimate form of violence that takes place with people whom we love or trust. Parents of intersex children often trust doctors with their children's bodies because of their expertise, and as a result, they subject their children to unnecessary treatments that often include genital surgeries. The medical community perpetuates secrecy and stigma around these conditions, which in turn creates an environment that is conducive to the sexual abuse of intersex children in medical settings.

In *As Nature Made Him: The Boy Who Was Raised as a Girl* (New York: HarperCollins, 2000), author John Colapinto details the life of David Reimer. Although he was not born intersex, Reimer was subjected to similar treatment as intersex infants after a circumcision accident left him without a penis. Desperate to help their son, his parents brought him to Dr. John Money at Hopkins Hospital in Maryland, who suggested that David be raised as "Brenda." Under the care of Dr. Money, David and his brother were reportedly sexually abused through rituals that involved viewing pornography, and Money observing sexual play between the two children. Money proposed that children could be raised as either gender regardless of their sex assigned at birth, and his ideas would lay the foundation for the management of intersex children. As a result, David was raised as female, but later through this own volition and defiance, reaffirmed his gender as male.

Many people with "normal" genitals describe uncomfortable experiences at the doctor's office, and this discomfort is only exacerbated for people with "abnormal" bodies. Like many intersex people, the medical community reduced my humanity to what is between my legs. I was born with partial androgen insensitivity syndrome (PAIS), which, until recently, was referred to as testicular feminization syndrome. Although I was not subjected to any genital surgeries, my presence with the genitals that I have has created alarm and curiosity among many doctors that I have visited.

As a young woman, doctors stared and made objectifying comments about my "enlarged clitoris" while awkwardly grabbing and touching me as I stared at the ceiling, either leaving my body or dreading the entire experience. Sometimes doctors would also insert their fingers into my rectum, which I later learned was a prostate exam—but they would not tell me what they were doing. Since doctors told me that my anatomy was "weird" or "not normal," I became estranged from how beautiful, complex, and pleasurable my body is. In addition to shame, years of objectification at the hands of physicians brought about disassociation whenever lovers touched my body. For years I lived with the shame and secrecy that was nurtured between doctors and my family of origin that dictated, "No one needs to know what happened." I wish mine were an isolated experience, but the issue is endemic.

When I began to learn about the impact of CSA through an organization called Generation Five, I saw direct parallels between CSA and my experience as a person living with PAIS. I realized that CSA doesn't have to involve direct physical contact but can include sexual exposure/voyeurism, shaming, and creating silence about the violation. I have heard countless stories from other intersex people about how as young children, their bodies were on display for attending doctors and residents. When these cases have shown up in medical literature, their naked bodies are exploitatively displayed with a black bar over their eyes.

Medically sanctioned sexual abuse of intersex children is not a closed chapter in history. Recent examples of medicalized sexual violence include a surgeon at Cornell University who freely performed clitorectomies on young girls and afterwards masturbated them with a vibrator to see if the children retained sensitivity in their genitals (Battan, 2010). A grown man using a vibrator on a young girl is molestation and using his power as a doctor to exact this violence is an example of institutionalized child sexual abuse. In a reflection of the pervasive homophobia and transphobia in the medical community, a doctor prescribed large doses of estrogens to a pregnant woman suspected of carrying a female child with Congenital Adrenal Hyperplasia (CAH) (Elton, 2010), an experiment intended to prevent the fetus from developing into a "tomboy" or lesbian (Dreger, Feder, & Tamar-Mattis, 2010). This kind of thinking is pervasive and widespread. Many of the surgeries done on infants assigned as female promote heterosexual relationships. Young girls are often urged to have vaginal construction surgeries or vaginal lengthening procedures to accommodate their "future spouse's penis." There is not a second thought as to whether this woman could be queer or gender nonconforming, or not want a vagina.

Our bodies display the intricacies and nuances of nature. Similar to other forms of gender variance, we must celebrate the complexity of bodies illustrated by intersex individuals. We must speak out against practices that seek to erase the complexity of human bodies, reinforce the gender binary system, and exact violence.

REFERENCES

Battan, C. (2010). Leading Cornell doctor performing genital cutting. The Nation blog. Retrieved March 2014, from http://www.thenation.com/blog/36481/leading-cornell-doctor-performing-genital-cutting#

Dreger, A., Feder, E. K., & Tamar-Mattis, A. (2010). Preventing homosexuality (and uppity women) in the womb? The Hastings Center Report Bioethics Forum. Retrieved March 2014, from http://www.thehastingscenter.org/Bioethicsforum/Post.aspx?id=4754

Elton, C. (2010). A prenatal treatment raises questions of medical ethics. Time. Retrieved March 2014, from http://content.time.com/time/health/article/0,8599,1996453,00.html

While "choosing" a gender for an intersex child can mean many different things depending on the condition, parents are often encouraged to consider surgery that will make the child's genitals appear more masculine or feminine. These early surgeries have many potential risks, including loss or reduction of sensation, change in sexual or reproductive functions, and psychological effects. There is controversy over whether parents and health care providers should make these kinds of decisions early or wait until people are old enough to make their own decisions. Although surgery in infancy has become less common, it still occurs.

Heidi picketing Columbia-Presbyterian Babies' Hospital (photo by Mariette Pathy Allen).

XXY is a Spanish film directed by Lucia Puenzo about an intersex teenager exploring gender identity and sexuality.

Cultural pressures can have a profound influence on whether intersex children are assigned male or female at birth. For example, in many Western cultures, when an XY baby is born with no penis, or a penis shorter than 1 centimeter (known as a "micropenis"), the child is brought up as a girl because of the presumed stigma of living as a man without a typical penis. These children often undergo multiple surgeries to appear female and are then unable to have their own biological children. In contrast, in some non-Western cultures, the desire for a son is so high that XX babies born with slightly masculinized genitals are typically raised as boys.

For many types of intersexuality, researchers have attempted to determine the most likely gender to fit the child. There is wide variation in the eventual gender identities of intersex people depending on their bodies and the way they are raised. However, overall, the gender that parents choose seems to be the best predictor of the eventual gender identity of people as adults. This may indicate that social forces in childhood and beyond have a strong impact on our gender identities.

TYPES OF INTERSEXUALITY

There are so many ways in which people can be classified as intersex that it is not possible to describe all bodily configurations here. However, knowing about some common body types that fall outside of the male-female binary can help us understand a little more about the diversity of human life.

Klinefelter's syndrome is a variation in which an individual is born with XXY chromosomes, rather than XX or XY. Most people with Klinefelter's syndrome appear male and identify as male, and often do not discover the presence of this condition until later in life, if ever. They may have problems with infertility or signs of decreased testosterone, such as small penises, more breast tissue, and decreased body hair or muscle mass compared to other men. As many as one in five hundred men may have Klinefelter's syndrome. There are cases of people with Klinefelter's identifying as transgender, but there is little evidence that rates of transgender identity are increased.

Congenital adrenal hyperplasia (CAH) occurs when the adrenal glands produce hormones differently due to blockages in enzyme pathways. In one type of CAH, people with XX chromosomes are born with genitals that look more masculine than is typical for girls. The degree of difference in their genitals from the typical XX person depends on the amount of androgens their adrenal glands produce in utero. A person with CAH may have a large clitoris or labia that are fused together and look more like scrotum, although they have the same internal organs as other XX people, including a uterus and ovaries. Most people born XX with CAH are raised as girls, although they are sometimes raised as boys if their genitals appear very masculine.

Many researchers who study brain organization theory are interested in people with CAH and XX chromosomes (often called "CAH girls"), and there have been numerous studies of CAH girls and their interests, abilities, and play habits, for the expressed purpose of testing whether they are more "masculine" than other girls. Most CAH girls raised as girls grow up to identify as cisgender. A little over 5% show serious concerns about their gender identity. This is higher than the percentage of transgender people in the general population, which may provide some evidence that hormones in utero can affect later gender identity.

When someone with XY chromosomes has *androgen insensitivity syndrome (AIS)*, the body produces androgens (such as testosterone), but the androgen receptors in the body's cells cannot recognize the hormones, so they cannot have an effect on the body. In complete androgen insensitivity syndrome (CAIS), the body's receptors do not respond at all to androgens, and the person's body appears female, including their genitals. Babies born with CAIS are typically pronounced female at birth. Girls with CAIS often do not learn of their condition until they fail to menstruate at puberty. The majority of those with CAIS identify as women. In partial androgen insensitivity syndrome (PAIS), the body's receptors may respond somewhat, but not completely, to androgens. People with PAIS have a wide variety of bodies and gender identities.

In *5-alpha reductase deficiency (5-ARD)*, the body cannot convert testosterone into another androgen called dihydrotestosterone (DHT) because the enzyme that performs this conversion, 5-alpha-reductase, does not function properly. DHT typically masculinizes the genitals while the fetus is developing. An XY baby with 5-ARD may have mostly female-appearing genitals, and those with this variation are often raised as girls. At puberty, testosterone in the body increases, and their bodies begin to masculinize in a way similar to typical male puberty, with facial hair growth, deepening of their voices, and enlargement of their genitals. Some people with 5-ARD continue to live as women, but more than half transition to men when they go through puberty.

CHILDHOOD

Once we are born, our social environment begins to shape our identity, through social norms and personal relationships with our parents and friends. Many researchers have studied the ways in which children develop a sense of gender, both personally and in the world around them. There are multiple theories about how this process happens, but it is likely that both biology (nature) and culture (nurture) play a role.

> "Babies are not born with a gender identity: gender is something that is taught to us as we grow up. However, it is not a choice. People cannot choose their gender any more than they can choose their sexual orientation. . . I think that it has to do with being taught about gender and how everyone has to fit into one of these two boxes with no exceptions, and subconsciously knowing that it's bullshit."

Cognitive Developmental Theory

The cognitive developmental theory of gender identity, introduced by American psychologist Lawrence Kohlberg (1966), proposes that children's understanding of gender progresses through three stages: gender labeling, gender stability, and gender constancy.

Gender labeling occurs around two to three years of age, when children are building their vocabularies very quickly. During this stage, they become good at giving names to things—including gender. Children are often very insistent about using labels, even before they completely know what these labels really mean. For example, a toddler might label a person a woman because the person has long hair, not knowing that some people with long hair are men.

Cognitive developmental theory proposes that around four to five years of age children begin to develop the notion that gender typically does not change. This helps the child develop *gender stability*—in other words, the notion that an individual's gender is stable over time. Very young children do not understand gender as an inherent trait of a person and often think that people can be one gender one day and another gender the next day.

According to cognitive developmental theory, around six to seven years of age, children begin to develop a sense of *gender constancy*. They start to understand that gender is not just about surface appearance and will stay the same even if someone's clothing, hairstyle, or activities change. Gender constancy is just one example of how children learn that surface appearances are not always the same as underlying characteristics.

(For example, kids often find Halloween a lot less scary at this stage, because they realize that people do not actually become monsters when they put on a Frankenstein mask!)

Cognitive developmental theory demonstrates that children do not automatically understand the role of gender in society but instead have to be taught the rules of gender. This suggests that these rules may be created by society. As an example, young children may be able to tell you that people are different colors, but they do not yet understand the very complicated ways that we divide people into races, because race is a concept created by society.

Cognitive developmental theory explains that the process by which children learn about gender is consistent with how they learn about their world in general. How children come to understand gender depends on their individual experience and what they have learned about gender from their family, community, peers, and others.

Gender Schema Theory

Like cognitive developmental theory, gender schema theory also focuses on the way children learn about gender as a concept. Jean Piaget, a Swiss developmental psychologist, introduced the term *schema* to describe a framework that helps us understand one specific aspect of the world.

For example, we all have a schema for a bird. We have an idea of what birds look like, sound like, and what they do. When we see a bird we have never seen before, our schema for birds is automatically activated and helps us understand and remember this new information about a bird that we are seeing for the first time. If the new bird is similar to our current schema for birds, we will simply assimilate the new information, leaving the schema rather unchanged. If the new bird is dramatically different (for example, a penguin), we might accommodate the new information into our schema (we might include the information that "some birds do not fly"), or we might leave our schema unchanged but consider penguins to be exceptions. In the face of a new example that contradicts our schema, we are much more likely to ignore the new information and maintain our schema, unchanged. Gender schema theory suggests that children learn to understand gender through this process as well.

According to gender schema theory, children develop schemas for gender that link certain behaviors and traits together under the schemas for male (or "boy") and female (or "girl"). Parents and teachers, as well as other people who spend time around children, can influence the way that these gender schemas develop. Children's schemas then, in turn, influence how they experience events and how they interact with the world. This can have an impact on shaping future behavior, preferences, and skills.

> "For me, I think it was a series of cognitive errors in childhood. Like the idea that girls didn't play on any of my teams, therefore they didn't like sports. I wasn't good at sports, therefore I should've been a girl."

Imagine that a sister and a brother are living in an apartment with their family and are home when a repair person comes over to replace a broken cabinet door. If these children have learned over time to identify physical tasks with their schema for "male" behavior, the boy will be more likely both to pay attention to the steps that the repair person is following to replace the door and to try and tackle similar projects on his own in the future.

Of course, children must be able to identify themselves as boys or girls in order to apply their schemas to themselves. They must learn to label themselves, likely through a process similar to cognitive developmental theory, which was described earlier. Even without yet being able to label themselves, they may still be able to start forming gender schemas.

Researchers have found that people have a much more specific and deep schema about their own gender group (known as the own-sex schema) as compared to their schema about the other sex (other-sex schema). This may be because they pay more attention to those things they see as relevant to their gender.

Most people do not follow the "rules" of gender exactly. People vary in terms of how gender schematic they are, likely based on how much their brains need to fit things into categories and how rigidly they were taught to think about gender as children. Those who are highly gender-schematic focus strongly on the gendered nature of the people, behaviors, and characteristics of those around them. For these people, gender strongly influences the way that they see the world. Other people have much weaker gender schemas, meaning that gender is not as key a factor in the way they see the world.

Social Theories of Gender Development

Social theories of gender development focus on how we learn gender from our social interactions. There is a great deal of evidence showing that girls and boys are positively reinforced or rewarded (by parents, peers, teachers, and even strangers) when they engage in behavior that is considered typical for their sex (gender-typed behavior). There is also a great deal of evidence showing that girls and boys may experience negative consequences (or punishments) when they engage in behaviors that are considered typical for the other sex and not for their own sex (cross-gender-typed behavior).

Social learning theory, developed by American psychologist Albert Bandura (1977), emphasized the importance of observation for people's learning of social behaviors. Social cognitive theory, also developed by Bandura (2001), suggests that three basic processes are important to gender development: children model the gender-related behavior of others, experience consequences for their gender-related behaviors or characteristics, and are directly taught information about gender roles.

> "I identify as a trans man because I see forms of masculinity I relate to and connect to more than I do to any forms of femininity I see. But if I were in a culture with entirely different constructions of gender would I be biologically compelled to bind my breasts? I'd doubt it. The way our culture presents options for gender and the context of people's negotiations with those terms matters just as much, if not more, than the way your body is expressing sex."

> "As I have grown up I have noticed the usual male model is a very violent or aggressive being. I don't like it at all. I find that male role models are war heroes or sports stars. Very rarely is it an artist, except in music. Men are usually made to hide their bodies under shapeless or baggy clothing. Women, on the other hand, are nurturing, caring, and beautiful. Women are able to express themselves in a far broader way than men can."

Despite the fact that we learn childhood behaviors through reinforcement and punishment, it is worth noting that **reparative therapy** or **conversion therapy**, in which a mental

Gender Development by Judith Owen Blakemore, Sheri Berenbaum, and Lynn Liben (New York, NY: Psychology Press, 2009) is a comprehensive textbook that explores biological, psychological, and social theories of gender development.

SOCIAL THEORIES OF GENDER DEVELOPMENT

MODELED BEHAVIOR

INNATE PERSON

LEARNING ENVIRONMENT

Social theories of gender development (kd diamond).

health practitioner uses behavioral techniques to reward and punish patients for their behaviors, has not been found effective in changing either sexual orientation or gender identity, and it can be emotionally damaging. Practicing these types of therapy is discouraged by the American Psychological Association, American Psychiatric Association, American Academy of Pediatrics, and numerous other organizations.

Psychosocial Environmental Influences on Gender Development

Children learn about gender from the many environments in which they participate. Families, peers, and the media impact children's gender development. Each of these groups has the potential to affect the ways that we label gender, understand gender constancy, form gender schemas, and model our behavior after others. In other words, we can apply many of the gender development theories discussed earlier to the environments in which we are raised.

FAMILY INFLUENCES

The family is the first context of children's development, and parents' ideas about their child are influenced by the child's sex even before the child is born. Studies have asked couples that knew the sex of their fetus to view an ultrasound image and rate the characteristics of the fetus. On average, they rate female fetuses as smaller, softer, weaker, and more beautiful than male fetuses. After birth, parents perceive male infants to be bigger, stronger, and better coordinated, and female infants to be softer and more delicate.

These differences in perception can have long-term effects on how children develop. When parents believe that boy babies are tough and strong, they are more likely to be physically rough with them. Likewise, when parents believe that girl babies are delicate and emotional, they are more likely to hold them close and talk softly to them. Through these early interactions with parents, boys may get used to being handled roughly and learn to interact with others roughly, whereas girls may get used to being held closely and learn to interact with others in a gentle way.

Fortunately, research shows that in the United States most parents provide a similar amount of warmth, discipline, interaction, and encouragement of achievement to their children regardless of their sex. However, sex does play a major role in the types of activities that parents encourage. Parents provide different types of clothing and toys to their daughters and sons, and they encourage them to participate in different activities at home and at school. Research also suggests that male parents are more likely to treat children differently based on their sex than female parents are.

By providing children with different opportunities and expectations based on their sex, parents influence their children's perception of what sorts of behaviors and activities are appropriate for girls and boys. The effects help shape individuals' attitudes and lives, as well as reinforcing larger cultural expectations and assumptions about gender.

How do parents treat children who do not conform to societal norms of gender? In general, in a Western context, parents are more accepting of daughters who do not adhere to norms of femininity than of sons who do not adhere to norms of masculinity.

Particular gender nonconforming behaviors may be more or less accepted, and there are differences in tendencies of female parents versus male parents to accept gender nonconforming behaviors. Research shows that female parents often support boys' interest in domestic chores, such as cooking, and their displays of nurturance or empathy.

However, many female parents do not support their sons' interest in feminine clothing or icons such as Barbie. Male parents, as a whole, typically respond more negatively to gender nonconformity displayed by their sons, and they are particularly concerned with their sons' displays of passivity or emotion, such as crying. Of course, there are many male parents who are extremely accepting of their sons' gender nonconforming behaviors and many female parents who are not. Research can only give us averages.

ON NOT JUDGING A BOOK BY ITS COVER

Mx. Nathan Tamar Pautz, of The Villages, Florida, is a culturally Jewish, mixed-gender, free-dressing person with a passionate interest in genderqueer spirituality and a special devotion to the goddesses of the ancient Near East.

I sat, as a toddler, by the sandbox. My mother asked if I wanted to play with the little boy "over there." I vaguely recall saying, "I'm a boy." She replied, "No, you're a girl." I took her word for it. I dream of a world in which I might have been left to figure this out for myself.

In kindergarten, my teacher asked us to form two lines, one for the boys and one for the girls. I don't remember whether I tried to get into the boys' line or went straight to the girls' line, but either way, I felt sad to be in the girls' line. I remember a vague, queasy feeling that this might just be how it was always going to be, a feeling that I now recognize as gender dysphoria.

My relatives socialized in two separate rooms, men in one and women in another. As a child, I would move back and forth between rooms to listen. I couldn't decide which room I preferred and realized that I could fit into either. I expected this social flexibility to last forever.

On the rare and brief occasions when I got to play with a male cousin or talk with a male schoolmate, I dreaded the end of those moments. On the playground, a boy who played with girls risked being called a "girl." I dream of a world in which children can socialize based on interests rather than on designated birth sex, of a world in which "girl" is no longer an epithet.

I never dated in high school or college. If a male friend saw me as a potential date, I would cruelly vanish without explanation or make myself unattractive. My lifelong interest in spirituality drew me toward celibate men, priests and seminarians whom I deemed safe. I wanted to relate as a brother but was generally treated as "other." I began dating at age 31. My first relationship was with a fellow student from a class I was taking at a Catholic seminary. I felt like a fellow seminarian, but he saw me as female. I knew nothing about men's bodies and sexuality, not even about my own. Terrified of committing a mortal sin, even in thought or desire, I kept myself rigidly locked up in a moral fortress, trying to offer only affectionate, nonerotic touch.

As a 35-year-old virgin, working in the "real world" after my previous job where I worked with nuns, my body made me a target for married men. I deemed them "safe," bound by vows and satisfied by their wives. I was shocked to learn otherwise. I was starving for male company, and I was beginning to feel that if I could find that in the context of a sexual relationship, it might actually be worth changing my moral standards. So, after months of inner conflict, I entered into a sexual relationship with a married man in which I exchanged sex for companionship. This resulted in an abusive relationship, and I was devastated when my "friend" left me friendless.

I had one good relationship for a few years with a man from work. I struggled with disabilities and admitted that I did not feel like a woman and that I was anorgasmic with men. My friend eventually married someone else, but he was still the most significant person in my life. Later, I realized that I really wanted a buddy. Around 1995 I attended my first transgender conference and began reading voraciously on transgenderism. I spoke about it with my friend, wondering whether, if I became male, people would allow us to be friends without judgment.

Had I been able to simply identify myself as "not female," and to have been treated by others as such, I would not have needed to alter my body. I had gender role dysphoria, a social phenomenon, not body dysphoria. Unlike some transgender persons, I had no problem with my body per se, but rather I had a problem with what it signified to others. To me, my body was just there, signifying nothing of a sexual nature. It is possible that I have an asexual orientation.

In 2007, after my friend's death, I began to physically transition along the FTM spectrum. I currently identify as mixed gender or polygender. I see it as a gift, like being bilingual, where I speak the "languages" of more than one gender. I dream of a world where pronouns are self-chosen, where every person's gender identity is acknowledged without necessitating physical transition, where fashion is not defined by gender, and where a book is not judged by its cover.

PEER INFLUENCES

Elementary-aged children spend approximately 40% of their waking hours with their peers. While the immediate family may be the primary social influence during infancy, toddlerhood, and the preschool years, some developmental researchers believe that peers have a greater impact on children than do their parents once they reach school age.

Children as young as two and three years old show a preference for playing with same-sex peers, and this preference gets stronger as they move toward the school years. By the age of six, they may spend up to 10 times as much time with same-sex peers as they do with other-sex peers. There are probably many reasons that this segregation takes

In the book *Sexing the Body: Gender Politics and the Construction of Sexuality*, Anne Fausto-Sterling reveals how our knowledge of sex and gender is shaped by culture.

place, and much of it may have to do with social learning and modeling, which can shape our ideas about ourselves, but also about whom we are supposed to spend time with.

Segregation by gender is strongest during the early elementary school years and declines as children move toward adolescence. Some researchers argue that girls' and boys' peer groups are so different that they really represent two distinct cultures. Other researchers, however, believe that the two-cultures idea overlooks the many similarities between girls' and boys' peer groups. Regardless, studies indicate that girls and boys do, on average, engage in different types of activities, have different styles of play, and have peer groups of different sizes and with different leadership styles. Boys, more than girls, tend to enforce these groupings by gender, and they are more likely not to allow girls to enter their groups than vice versa. In elementary school, both boys and girls tease their peers about contact with those outside of their gender group.

What happens when a child does not want to play with the children that everyone expects them to be playing with? Or what if children prefer to play the games that children of the other sex typically play? Children can be cruel to those who are different, and intolerant of children who do not conform to expected gender roles. Research generally shows that peers, like parents, tend to respond more negatively to boys who do not conform to norms of masculinity than to girls who do not conform to norms of femininity. Children respond most negatively to boys' violations of gender norms when they relate to appearance—boys are judged harshly for having clothing or hairstyles that are perceived as feminine. This is likely because masculinity is a more valued trait in society than femininity, so boys who enjoy feminine activities or display feminine behavior are considered weak.

PUBERTY AND ADULTHOOD

Puberty is a time of change, when our bodies develop from being relatively gender-neutral (aside from our genitals) to looking much more typically male or female. During puberty, testosterone levels increase in both sexes, but they increase more in people assigned male. Estrogen and progesterone levels begin to cycle monthly in people assigned female. The changes that happen due to hormones during puberty, such as increased body hair, changes in voice pitch, and breast development are typically called **secondary sex characteristics**. For many transgender people, puberty is a difficult time because secondary sex characteristics begin to make us look less and less like the gender with which we identify.

As we go through puberty and enter adulthood, the hormones surging through our bodies every day have powerful effects on our thoughts and mood. Popular media sources such as magazines and television often lead us to believe that testosterone is a male hormone and estrogen is a female hormone, and they may link these hormones to masculine or feminine behaviors. The truth is that both men and women have testosterone and estrogen in their bodies, and the levels of these hormones vary considerably between people of the same sex. Most cisgender men, however, have higher levels of testosterone than most cisgender women, and most cisgender women have higher levels of estrogen than most cisgender men.

Until the 1970s, many scientists thought that differences in adult hormone levels could be responsible for our feelings about our gender identities. They even thought that homosexuality might be caused by differences in hormone levels—specifically, that gay men and trans women might have lower levels of testosterone than cis men. These early notions have been shown to be untrue. Some groups also believed that lesbians and trans men might have higher levels of testosterone than cis women. There is no evidence of this for lesbians, but there is ongoing debate about testosterone levels in trans men.

Today most researchers believe that adult hormone levels have very little effect on gender identity. One exception is that recent studies have looked at trans men and a condition called polycystic ovary syndrome (PCOS). In PCOS, people assigned female at birth have higher than typical levels of testosterone, increased body hair, acne, irregular periods, and problems with fertility. PCOS is associated with obesity, high cholesterol, and diabetes. The name comes from the cystic appearance of the ovaries when an ultrasound is done. Some studies suggest that trans men seem to have higher rates of PCOS than cis women. However, most people with PCOS are not trans. In fact, PCOS is relatively common, affecting 5%–10% of those assigned female. It is possible that PCOS could affect the way we understand our gender identity, but it probably does not explain why most of us are trans. If you have PCOS, or symptoms of PCOS, you should talk about it with your health care provider. Some of the effects, such as increased body hair and irregular periods, may be desirable, but others, like acne, decreased fertility, and a tendency toward diabetes, are not.

BIOPSYCHOSOCIAL THEORIES OF GENDER DEVELOPMENT

Historically, gender development researchers emphasized the differences between biological and social theories—known as the "nature versus nurture" debate. But biological, psychological, and sociological stances on gender development are all simply different perspectives. Understanding that biology influences us does not mean rejecting the concept of social influences. Each perspective prioritizes different things—and none has the full picture.

Many people now believe that gender is influenced by many factors, including biology, psychological experiences, and social interactions. Theories that incorporate all of these factors are called biopsychosocial theories.

An example of a biopsychosocial theory is Milton Diamond's biased-interaction theory of gender development. According to this theory, early biological factors (possibly including genetics or fetal hormones) set us up to interact with our environments in certain ways. They give us temperaments or predispositions. Although these early biological factors do not decide our gender identities, they influence our preferences and aversions. We then compare ourselves to others to decide whether we are like them or different from them, and this helps us to form our gender identities. Whether our gender identities come about in exactly this way or not, it is likely that they are influenced in some way by biology as well as our social environments.

> "I think everything is a result of the combination of nature and nurture. People may be hardwired for certain things, but it requires a life experience to activate the feelings. An easy example is alcoholism. Many believe it runs in families, but if a person never has a sip of alcohol in their life, they will never trigger that gene. It just so happens with transgenderism that normal social conditioning is the trigger. If the world weren't so black and white in terms of gender, there would not be as much dysphoria. As soon as a child is made to wear a dress (or refused the chance to wear one), they realize there are two genders and that they are embodied in the wrong one."

A transgender psychologist, Jaimie Veale (2010), proposes the identity-defense model of gender variance, in which biological factors and early childhood influences determine whether, and to what degree, a gender-variant identity develops, and then personality and environmental factors determine whether defense mechanisms are used to repress the gender variance. Veale argues that our biological factors, as well as our defense mechanisms or coping strategies, determine whether we are going to identify as transsexual, transgender, cross-dressers, or drag artists.

> "I think people all identify in different ways. I don't think there is a simple explanation. There are probably many different causes of transgender experience resulting in the broad spectrum of transgender, transsexual, and gender diverse people we see. Biologically there are probably a range of different causes that all add together to lead to the phenomenon–I doubt it's anything simple. It's also quite likely that the genes and other effects involved in male to female transgender people are totally different from those in female to male

transgender people. More abstractly I think for someone to be transgender takes a combination of an intense innate gender identity and a 'mismatched' body. I think only a minority of non-trans people feel their gender identity as strongly as people who need to transition (though I could have an unusually queer group of friends). I think some cis people genuinely derive their identity from their body and the way they are treated by their culture, with nothing internal or innate to match this. There's probably a full range from a total blank slate to a very intense and unchanging innate gender identity. This isn't very visible in non-trans people, but it shows up as the queer, transgender, transsexual spectrum in people where the gender identity is incongruous with their body."

CONCLUSION

As trans people, we have a wide range of experiences and thoughts related to how our gender identities develop. We often disagree about the influences of biology versus culture. Some of us spend a considerable amount of time thinking about these issues, while others of us find them less important to our sense of who we are. There is no one right way to understand the many influences on our gender identities. In addition, no matter how far science advances toward isolating influential factors, we will always be a community rooted in our own experiences—and no one will be able to tell us who we are except ourselves.

REFERENCES AND FURTHER READING

Bandura, A. (1977). *Social learning theory.* Englewood Cliffs, NJ: Prentice Hall.

Bandura, A. (2001). Social cognitive theory: An agentic perspective. *Annual Review of Psychology, 52,* 1–26.

Bettcher, T. M. (2007). Evil deceivers and make-believers: On transphobic violence and the politics of illusion. *Hypatia, 22*(3), 43–65.

Blakemore, J. E. O., Berenbaum, S. A., & Liben, L. S. (2009). *Gender development.* New York, NY: Psychology Press.

Butler, J. (1990). *Gender trouble: Feminism and the subversion of identity.* New York, NY: Routledge.

Butler, J. (1993). Imitation and gender insubordination. In H. Abelove, M. A. Barale and D. M. Halperin (Eds.). *The lesbian and gay studies reader* (pp. 307–320). New York, NY: Routledge.

Diamond, M. (2006). Biased-interaction theory of psychosexual development: How does one know if one is male or female? *Sex Roles, 55,* 589–600.

Ducat, S. (2004). *The wimp factor: Gender gaps, holy wars, and the politics of anxious masculinity.* Boston, MA: Beacon Press.

Erickson-Schroth, L. (2013). A review of the biology of transgender identity. *Journal of Gay and Lesbian Mental Health, 17,* 150–174.

Fausto-Sterling, A. (1992). *Myths of gender: Biological theories about women and men.* New York, NY: Basic Books.

Fausto-Sterling, A. (2000). *Sexing the body: Gender politics and the construction of sexuality.* New York, NY: Basic Books.

Garfinkel, H. (1967). Passing and the managed achievement of sex status in an "intersexed" person. In H. Garfinkel (Ed.), *Studies in ethnomethodology* (pp. 166–185). Englewood Cliffs, NJ: Prentice-Hall.

Gilbert, M. A. (2009). Defeating bigenderism: Changing gender assumptions in the 21st century. *Hypatia, 24*(3), 93–112.

Gilbert, M. A. (2011). Esse es interagere: To exist is to interact, or, there is no life in the closet. In *American Philosophical Association Central Meeting* (March 30-April 2). Minneapolis, MN.

Hopkins, P. (1998). Gender treachery: Homophobia, masculinity, and threatened identities. In N. Zack, L. Shrage, & C. Sartwell (Eds.), *Race class, gender, and sexuality: The big questions* (pp. 168–186). Oxford, UK: Blackwell.

Kessler, S. J., and McKenna, W. (1978). *Gender: An ethnomethodological approach.* Chicago, IL: University of Chicago Press.

Kimmel, M. (1994). Masculinity as homophobia: Fear, shame and violence in the construction of gender identity. In H. Brod & M. Kaufman (Eds.), *Theorizing masculinities* (pp. 119–142). Thousand Oaks, CA: Sage.

Kohlberg, L. (1966). A cognitive-developmental analysis of children's sex- role concepts and attitudes. In E. E. Maccody (Ed.), *The development of sex differences* (pp. 82–173). Stanford, CA: Stanford University Press.

Serano, J. (2007). *Whipping girl: A transsexual woman on sexism and the scapegoating of femininity.* Emeryville, CA: Seal Press.

Stryker, S. (1994). My words to Victor Frankenstein above the village of Chamounix: Performing transgender rage. *GLQ: A Journal of Lesbian and Gay Studies, 1*(3), 227–254.

Veale, J. F., Lomax, T. C., & Clarke, D. E. (2010). The identity-defence model of gender-variance development. *International Journal of Transgenderism, 12,* 125–138.

West, C., & Zimmerman, D. H. (1987). Doing gender. *Gender and Society, 1*(2), 125–151.

SECTION 2
LIVING AS OURSELVES

COMING OUT
Reid Vanderburgh

7

Coming out is a process of acknowledging to oneself or disclosing to others something that is not readily apparent or understood about who we are. For those of us who are trans or gender nonconforming, that something is our gender identity or expression. Coming out as trans or gender nonconforming is a lengthy, individual process, often messy and sometimes traumatic, but it can also be affirming, liberating, and positive.

Growing up as we do in a world that does not often honor and respect trans identities, it can be hard to see anything to celebrate in coming out as trans. However, living as our authentic selves, whatever that might mean for each of us, *is* something to celebrate.

> *"Since coming out I have made many more friends. It was like a weight lifted off of my shoulders. For the first time in my life I felt authentic and real."*

THE COMING-OUT PROCESS

Our first coming-out process is to ourselves. Coming out might lead to changes in our self-understanding, different ways of presenting ourselves, name or pronoun changes, or modification of our bodies, but if and when we choose to undertake these changes is up to each of us. We might be able to find aspects of others' stories that resonate with our own journey, but we still undertake the process in our own way, in our own time.

In the context of family and friends, coming out touches our closest relationships. At work and in our social and religious communities, coming out may have socioeconomic or political aspects. Our friends and family members have their own coming-out processes, too, especially when others ask them about changes in our gender presentation.

Coming out can be proactive—telling others as we begin our process, on our own timeline. It can also be reactive—answering questions raised by new behaviors, a new appearance, or information shared unexpectedly by someone who already knows. For most of us, coming out is some combination of all these experiences.

COMING OUT TO OURSELVES

Most of us grow up without role models and with little experience of other trans people. Many of us begin our process wondering, "Am I really trans? Is this what it feels like to be trans?"

> *"The model that was out there was that trans people feel that they are trapped in the wrong body and have always known they were actually a different gender. I didn't fit that model and I didn't know anyone who identified as neither man nor woman, both butch and femme. I was afraid of being judged for claiming a label that wasn't mine to claim; I was afraid of appropriating a culture that wasn't mine: trans culture. It took years to feel confident in my gender and in my ability to name it and claim the labels that felt right. It took meeting other people with fluid genders and being seen and validated by close friends and lovers."*

Some of us say we have always known, since we were children. Others say that we always knew there was something different about ourselves but did not understand why. Still others never realized anything felt different until adulthood.

Therapists who work with trans people are starting to develop models for identity development specific to trans communities. Aaron Devor (2004) has developed a 14-stage model based on witnessing and mirroring. In her book *Transgender Emergence* Arlene Istar Lev (2004) discusses six distinct developmental stages.

Some of us knew who we were at a very young age.

"On the first day of kindergarten, our class went out to the playground and the teachers told the boys to go over here and the girls over there. I dutifully went with the girls. There was much giggling. The teacher tried to gently correct me, but I insisted I was a girl and refused to go with the boys. This led to a lot of trouble; finally I ran off by myself rather than go with the boys."

Not all of us were able to express these feelings, and some of us felt we had to hide our identity from friends and family. Some of us felt a great pressure to conform and fit in to mainstream gender norms as a young person—to "act like a lady" or to not be a "sissy." As a result, some of us worked very hard to adopt the gender role expected of us.

BORN ON THE DAY OF THE GODDESS

Ranjita Sinha is proud of her status in between the two worlds of male and female as transgender.

I am Ranjita, originally named Ranjit by my parents. My mother gave birth to me on the auspicious day of Laxmi puja—the day when people in West Bengal worship the goddess of wealth. My mother understood that my father could be disappointed that I was not a girl, so she dressed me up as a baby girl when my father saw me for the first time. However, the truth needed to be unveiled sooner or later, and so my mother slowly disclosed my identity to my father.

From my childhood I was different from any other normal boys, though the realization came much later. Where the other boys of my age would have played cricket or football, I was more comfortable staying back at home and playing with my dolls. Then I developed an inclination toward Indian dance and music, which was initially strongly protested by my paternal uncles—but my mother stepped in and encouraged me to pursue the curricular activities of my choice.

My father passed away when I was very young, and my mother raised me and my elder brother, who also opposed my effeminate behavior. However, as I grew up, I became exposed to more people like me, and I realized I was transgender. It was a long transformation to become Ranjita, but today I am happy and satisfied to establish myself as what I am.

There were moments in my past life where some people around me extended a friendly hand and understood me; some others have pushed me away. In my school days, I was lucky to find three friends in the same class who shared a similar identity, and this made us strong to fight against some other classmates. We were also lucky to have some of our teachers who accepted us as we were. As we crossed into college life, we came in touch with a cosmopolitan crowd where acceptance was low. For the first time, I felt suffocated and forced to keep a low profile.

After completing a hotel management course at Chandigrah, I returned to Kolkata and got in touch with organizations doing work on social issues. Those days the MSM (men who have sex with men) were dominant. Most of the projects were targeted to cover the MSM population and there was very little space for transgender people. Since then, I have run organizations and projects for the well-being of my community, and I started a network called Association of Transgender/Hijra in Bengal (ATHB) along with some of my other transgender partners. ATHB is the first registered network in India working with people like us and also with the Hijra community. Even those MSM community members who in the past discriminated against us are now showing interest in the transgender projects.

For some of us, recognizing our trans identity catches us by surprise. Often, some incident or reference to trans identity comes our way at just the right time or with just the right language, and we have a sudden deep feeling of identification, resulting in an "Aha!" moment. This realization may raise conflicting feelings, everything from euphoria to denial.

Some of us have grown into a new self-understanding as an adult. We may have always felt different, though we could not explain it. For some of us, our feelings may have changed over time; transitioning may be less about realizing some old truth about ourselves and more about recognizing new possibilities.

No matter when or how we begin to recognize ourselves as trans, coming out is not a static process. Our understanding of ourselves is always changing and maturing. Coming out as trans does not mean we are committing irrevocably to a specific process. Some of us desire a social transition path that does not involve physical body modification. Some of us choose to undertake medical or surgical procedures that affirm our gender identity. Some of us choose not to undertake any changes to our daily lives or appearance, because of existing relationships, economic barriers, or other factors.

A Deepening Process of Self-Understanding

Many of us change course on our transition paths as we come to have a deeper understanding of ourselves.

> *"The self-discovery of my gender was basically the same as that of my sexuality. I started out with the assumption that I matched the 'norm' simply because it was the 'norm.' When I discovered there were other options, I began to try on labels as I discovered them, each more accurate than the last."*

Some of us come out as genderqueer and later decide that a physical transition toward living as men or women is right for us. Conversely, some of us start down the path of physical transition toward "woman" or "man," thinking that is "the way" to transition, only to discover we feel more comfortable with genderqueer or gender nonconforming identities.

> *"I was a big butch dykey Carhartt-wearing, Indigo Girls-listening, Subaru-driving lesbian before transitioning. I never really transitioned into being a dyke. I just always was one. I never remember being attracted to men or being girly at all. I came bursting out of the womb wearing rainbow suspenders while Melissa Etheridge played 'Come to My Window' in the background. Interestingly, I have turned into a very feminine boy. I am much more girly now than I ever was when I was female bodied. I am also attracted to men now. Go figure."*

GENDERQUEER: "C. NONE OF THE ABOVE."

Shannon E. Wyss lives outside of Washington, D.C., with hir life partner, volunteers with a group of gender nonconforming children and with the DC Trans Coalition, and works at AIDS United.

"Are you a boy or a girl?" This is a sincere question i get sometimes but always from children or young teens. It's not that adults don't wonder, too; they've just learned that such questions are inappropriate. And the answer is "i'm neither."

The term "genderqueer" first appeared in the mid- to late 1990s and describes a wide range of identities. If there is any commonality among us, it is that we reject the "binary sex/gender system." Some genderqueers see themselves as a combination of feminine and masculine. Others (like me) see themselves as neither masculine nor feminine. Some genderqueers consider themselves trans and others (including me) do not.

There are probably also as many reasons for being genderqueer as there are genderqueers. For me, it was a combination of factors, including my increasingly-androgynous gender expression, a growing exposure to the trans community, my intellectual and political development, and rethinking my own gender socialization (how i was taught to be a girl).

How do i live as neither a man nor a woman? That is probably the most challenging aspect of being genderqueer. I'm fortunate to be surrounded by friends and coworkers who are, for the most part, politically progressive. My life partner is pansexual, so being with a genderqueer is easy for her. My parents had a harder time with my identity. And while my father has since died, my mother supports and loves me unconditionally, even though she still doesn't fully understand.

Dealing with institutions is another matter entirely. Everywhere we are faced with "M" and "F" choices. If possible, i will add a "Genderqueer" option on forms. Other times, however, i cannot put in my own box. In those instances, i have to choose between not completing the questionnaire or marking "F," my assigned sex. With sex-segregated bathrooms, i use the women's room because i don't fear physical or sexual assault there—although that is hardly a comfortable place and I sometimes find myself stared at.

Remember, it is your life to understand and define. Figuring out who we are can be a bit like peeling an onion—as we remove layers, we get ever closer to the heart. Give your life permission to emerge in its own time, without self-condemnation.

SELF-CARE

Finding support for ourselves is key to helping us stay centered as we come out to ourselves and to all the various people in our lives. There are many techniques and practices that may help with this, from yoga and meditation to exercise to counseling and therapy. Educating ourselves and finding social support systems can also be an important part of self-care during our coming-out and transition process.

Online Resources

In this day and age, many of us find our first support systems online. We are able to find information about hormones, surgery, body modification, name change, pronoun usage, and more.

The Internet can also connect us to thriving online communities where we can learn from others' experiences, and read, hear, or see stories from others who have gone before us. Reading or hearing other people's stories can help us clarify for ourselves how we conceptualize our identities, which in turn helps us develop the language we use to come out to the people in our lives.

As you connect with online communities, do not forget to listen to yourself. Your experience is unique, and what works for someone else online might not be the right fit for you.

Face-to-Face Support Groups

Unlike many online resources, face-to-face support groups can provide two-way communication about the issues we face as we struggle to understand our own identity, communicate that identity to others, or begin transition processes.

Many of these groups are peer led, while others are therapist moderated. Peer support groups tend to focus on the real-world aspects of transition, such as transition in the workplace and which health providers are best for access to hormones. These groups may have a set fee, a sliding scale, or simply a donation jar by the door.

Therapist-moderated groups are often more focused on the emotional aspects of transition such as how our families are reacting, how we are coping with the day-to-day stresses of transition, and what we are noticing about our relationships and identities. These groups usually have a set fee for coming each week but often go deeper into emotional content than peer-led groups. Therapist-moderated groups may also be scheduled for specific eight- to ten-week periods.

There are pros and cons to both styles. Go to more than one group and go more than one time to help decide whether a group is a good fit for you. The best of all possible worlds would be to have both kinds of groups available, as they enable us to focus on our transition from different perspectives.

Difficulties Finding Support

In some places and situations, it may be hard to find a supportive group that works for you. Small towns may have limited or no options, or there may be privacy concerns—especially for those of us who are just beginning to explore our gender identities. For those of us who come from tight-knit communities, perhaps held together by racial, ethnic, or religious ties, more general groups may not offer the kinds of support we need.

Find a way to plug into as many forms of support as you can. Find support groups outside your physical or social communities, where you may have more privacy. Find online resources and communities or attend conferences (many of which offer scholarship programs to help offset costs of attendance) and talk to people when you are there. There are many events specific to trans issues in different communities where we can connect with others who share our experiences. Forming relationships and friendships through these avenues can help as we move forward.

COMING OUT TO OTHERS

As we come out to others, each of us has very different life circumstances to consider. For some, unsafe situations, job loss, loss of family security, and loss of housing are realistic possibilities. For others, our fears are rooted in shame or guilt. Prior to coming out to anyone, many of us live in fear of others' reactions. However, as we begin telling people our stories, we often find the result is not as dreadful as we feared.

> *"Coming out was extremely frightening until I said it, and then it was extremely relieving."*

> *"It doesn't matter as much what others think about me when I come out to them. They will either accept me, or they will not. I have faced the fear of losing everything and I now know that not all will be lost. The fear of the unknown decreases the more I speak my own truth."*

It may be hard to start these conversations, but to begin taking control over our own lives, coming out to others is an important first step. If we choose to live our lives full time in a new gender role, it is inevitable that the people in our lives will find out, whether we have talked about it or not. For some of us, we may wish to have these conversations, even if we have no plans to pursue a physical transition.

WHERE DO I STAND?

Hannah J. is a full-time student, part-time activist, and just trying to figure stuff out.

I stand at the cusp of a new life. A new self. A woman's identity, in theory. But where do I stand? I don't know.

I hear people are going to treat me differently, but the "how" of it all remains elusive.

I hear it's going to be a great adventure, starting to fit into my body, growth, change, things will happen that I never expected—and what I expected will never happen.

But it's all like sand through my fingers. I can hold a few of the grains; I can hold just enough to start imagining, but nowhere near enough to comprehend, to actually build a sandcastle out of it, to build a self. What is my self going to be?

I've spent my entire life wearing clothing chosen to hide my figure and who I am, clothing comfortable by virtue of it interacting with my body as little as possible and hiding the maximum amount of me.

I've spent my life apart from guys, but not quite "in" with girls (at least not in recent memory), and I'm figuring out where I fit.

Where do I stand? I don't know. My life is like sand through my fingers. A cusp of everything where nothing will ever be the same and who I am is up for grabs, uncertain. I am far more lost than I ever imagined.

Coming out to others means letting them get to know us better and taking control of our own lives. Doing so will allow us to live more full and complete lives. When we are living the life we have chosen, we will be happier—and that can benefit everyone in our lives. The way that we frame our coming-out process to others will affect the way they see it. If we have expectations of loss or assume that we will be a burden, others may see it this way, too. On the other hand, if we approach coming out as a positive change in our lives, our families and friends may follow our lead.

What to Expect

Coming out is a deeply personal, often complicated process, and it can be difficult and painful. There is a range of reactions people will have to us coming out, from complete hostility and rejection on through varying levels of tolerance and acceptance, to full support. Even if someone seems to reject the idea at first, they may come around over time. Trans identity can be a hard thing for many people to understand.

> *"Telling people I was male was like telling them that there is no such thing as gravity: my experience is that people generally take gender to be immutable."*

For those of us with nonbinary identities, it can be especially difficult to explain how we see ourselves. For many of our friends and family, nonbinary identities are far outside their realm of experience and worldview.

No matter how we identify, it is not easy to talk about feelings we have felt we had to hide for years. It takes practice, but it will help us and those closest to us make the journey together. What we do and say can help the people in our lives understand how to respond to us.

Some people we tell may have a lot of resistance to the idea and may continue to use our old name and pronoun. On the other hand, they may be a bit too enthusiastic and start telling others before we are ready for our whole world to know who we are.

As we start sharing our process with the people in our lives, we may find some retreating from us and others approaching us with more openness. If we list our friends prior to transition in order of who we feel closest to, many of the names will stay on the list, but the order may change as we move forward.

It is likely that some of our friends and family members will not support our transition. Fortunately, most of us do not lose our entire family, but many of us do lose a few people as we move forward into living as our authentic selves. It is hard to let go, but if we have a friend or family member who refuses to transition with us, who continues to use an inappropriate pronoun or name, or is hostile every time they use our new name or pronoun, we may feel we have to back away from the relationship. However, it is possible to do so in such a way that the door is open if they have a change of heart down the road. It may be that at some point, perhaps with the help of more supportive friends or family members, they come around.

In these cases, it is all too easy to take a self-righteous stance of being hurt by their lack of support and to lash out at them in anger. It is harder, but in the long run better for our psyche, if we can step back and see that they are reacting from their own socialization of gender as fixed reality. Holding a place of sympathy for their plight may help us keep the door open for a future relationship while creating a self-protective boundary for the present. We can track their progress through other friends or family members.

Many of us discover that the people we thought would take it the worst took it the best, and the people we thought would take it the best took it the worst. We may find support in unexpected places.

> "I found out when I came out that some people who said they would be with me
> through my coming out and early transition, quickly left me. I experienced that some
> of the people who I suspected would disapprove, shunned me. I also had people who
> I barely knew at work and such come up to me and say things like 'I know we haven't
> been friends, but I just wanted to let you know that my brother is gay,' or they'd say
> 'my daughter is bisexual, and you can come talk to me anytime you want.'"

Many of us find that if we can stay centered in knowing the truth of our identity, we can approach most situations with grace and courage, allowing others the space to acknowledge the enormity of our journey and honor us for it. Certainly, there will be times when we will be met with hostility or derision rather than honor, but this is the time to remember how sad it is for some people that they feel that way.

Creating a Coming-Out Plan

It can be hard to figure out how to come out to friends and family who are part of a close-knit group. If everyone is not informed at the same time, is there a possibility someone may find out through others in the group? This can be a scary experience. Will we lose control of our coming-out process? Will someone be hurt because they were not told personally?

There are steps we can take to address these issues. It may help to make a list of friends and acquaintances, grouping them by levels of intimacy, and then make a disclosure plan based on factors such as the following:

- Which friends/family members know each other?
- Are any friends/family members likely to gossip or pass on sensitive information without permission?
- Is coming out via e-mail or letter the best way, or should it be done in person or on the phone?

Coming out to family (Elenore Toczynski).

Consider why you are having the conversation with each person and what you would like the outcome to be. We come out to different people at different points in our process, so the information we have, and the information we are willing to share, will change over time.

"Coming out is never a past-tense thing."

With all coming-out experiences, it can be helpful to share our experience, our feelings, and help set expectations with our friends and family about what we need from them. We may want to discuss what name we would like them to use, what pronouns, if any, we would like them to use, and how we would like them to talk about us with other people. There may be other, specific changes we want to make in our lives where they can show their support by providing assistance or positive feedback.

It may help to remember that when people we know slip up (and it will be "when," not "if"), they are not always doing it to hurt us. Our identities are often outside their framework, and it may be hard for them to make the adjustment. Be patient and focus on making the changes that are most important to you.

Educating Others

Many people are not going to understand on their own precisely what it means to be trans. We will need to tell them more about who we are and help them understand more about what we go through. We may need to help people understand how to address us and how to talk about us with others.

The Internet is a useful tool for educating friends and family members. Keep track of Web sites that you find useful or that you think could help your friends and family understand you better. These can then be forwarded to people when the time seems right. Connecting these resources with face-to-face conversations can be helpful. Consider sharing a Web site, article, or book with a friend or family member—then invite them to talk about it with you over lunch.

In-person meetings can also be good places to begin to educate our family members and friends. Local LGBTQ community centers often have support groups, sometimes separated into trans people and their **significant others, friends, family, and allies (SOFFAs).** These groups may even meet at the same time in different rooms, allowing us to travel to the center with our friend or family member and meet up with them again afterward. LGBT centers also often have pamphlets about transgender identity that we can pick up and give to our friends and families to read. Another thing we can do to educate our friends and families is to introduce them to other trans people, so that they see some of the diversity of trans experiences.

Though the coming-out process provides many opportunities to help educate the people around us, it is essential to remember that it is not always our responsibility. As we begin to share our stories, we must be prepared to answer hard questions. We may not have

Colorado therapist Karen Scarpella suggests a "good news" approach when coming out as trans. If we can help our families and friends understand that our coming out is a gift, they may feel closer to us and less distressed.

all the answers, and we will not want to answer all of the questions we are asked—even if we know the answers. As you come out to others, consider with whom you feel comfortable keeping the door open for further questions and discussion.

> *"I'm tired of feeling like I have to give a lesson about gender before I can have a meaningful conversation with my best friend."*

Be sure to check in with yourself about your energy level. Do what takes care of you. Do not educate other people for their sake, if you do not have the energy to do so. Educate them to the extent that it helps you feel you are treated better.

Just as many cities have some form of trans support group these days, many also offer support groups for spouses, partners, or family members. Those who are close to us will need to let go of parts of our old identities before they can be expected to embrace the new, but that is not a process we will always be happy watching or participating in. Our families may not be able to be our major support, and we may need to help them see that we cannot be their primary source of support, either. All of us have transitions to undertake, and each can benefit from an additional source of support.

More Than Just Personal Relationships

Each of us has a unique ethnic, cultural, and religious background, with its own norms and beliefs about gender, gender roles, and sexuality. This context is an important piece of how we view our own identity, and it may influence how our friends and family respond to our coming-out process.

For example, some cultures value family connection over individuality, which can make our decisions to come out or to transition difficult if our family is (or is likely to be) unsupportive. Some of us have decided to put our transitions on hold until the older generation of our family has died, not wishing to create a family schism. Many people may encourage us to pursue a transition path, despite these concerns. This idea of self-actualization is a highly Western concept, and it may not fit with the way we see our role in our communities. Our cultural backgrounds can influence the ways in which we choose to come out or present our gender identity to others.

Religious communities are also an important factor in coming out for many of us. Many religious traditions extend far beyond the actual worship service and are rooted in daily home life. We may form our closest social ties with other church members, and sometimes we have no friends outside the church.

Many of us lived our adult lives within lesbian or gay communities, before coming out as trans. What we may find is that our worldview has been shaped by our participation in lesbian or gay communities such that we can hardly see ourselves as "straight" after transition, even if others perceive us that way based on who we form relationships with. We may gravitate toward language such as "queer" to define our sexual orientation. Many of us find that we do not lose our individual gay or lesbian friends. What we may lose is our place within that community, as some of us feel that the gay and lesbian community is not where we belong any longer. Others of us may have connected with a queer community to begin with and find that our gender transition is understood and accepted within these circles.

Those of us who come from close-knit communities—whether defined by geography, race, sexuality, or religion—may feel quite lonely during our coming-out process, especially if we are excluded from familiar religious or cultural practices. In many communities and cultures, gender plays a significant role in the rights, roles, and responsibilities we have. Even when we are accepted in our affirmed gender, it can be painful to lose access to the traditions and extended communities with which we have grown up.

Some of us find that our communities have opened up and found ways to accommodate our new identity.

> *"Even my uber-Christian family members have in subsequent years relayed to me that now they've come to believe that god has answered prayers about me and my well-being with testosterone, name change, and medical technology."*

Parents, Families, Friends, and Allies of Lesbians and Gays (PFLAG) has over 350 chapters in all 50 states and provides group settings for our loved ones to discuss their journeys.

Many of us feel "stuck" between two communities—one defined by our background and one by our trans identity. Moving between these communities can be a lonely feeling, perhaps not feeling fully "seen" in either one. It may help to find others, through conferences and online forums, who share our same two communities. Though our experiences will have differences, we will at least have a common ground with which to understand each other.

Negotiating Transition

In some cases, we may find that coming out to our families and partners changes our plans for transition. We may choose to delay making some kinds of social or physical transitions to ease relationships with our school-age children, to avoid confrontation with aging relatives, or out of a desire to accommodate our intimate partners' needs.

Some of us have faced criticism for choosing to prioritize such relationships over our own desire. However, our culture, relationships, and sexuality are a core part of our identity, and sometimes we navigate our needs alongside those of our family and partners.

Many people (trans or otherwise) may judge us harshly for transitioning while our children are young, feeling we should do what is best for them and put our own needs and desires on hold until they are on their own. However, there is no evidence that transitioning while our children are young makes things harder for them. In fact, having a parent who is happier and more secure in their identity can have a very positive influence on a parent–child relationship.

Close Friends

Our closest friends are often among the first people we come out to. They can also be the hardest. Many of us are afraid of losing the relationships that we have had for many years, of not being accepted by those with whom we have shared so much.

> "I wasn't really afraid of being completely rejected by them so much as having my identity rejected. I didn't think that they would cut me out of their lives, but I was afraid they would simply laugh it off or just refuse to accept it. Some did laugh it off. I don't maintain much contact with them anymore."

However, friendships always change over time, and the friends we make and keep may have changed, shifted, or stayed constant through any number of other life changes. The same is true for a transition.

In many cases, it is our friends who know us best, and they may have an intuitive feeling that our news makes sense.

Coming out to friends (Elenore Toczynski).

"Coming out to friends and my sisters, I frequently got the response, 'Oh! NOW that makes sense. That fits.' It had always been clear something was going on with me, and no one really knew what."

"My parents hate it, my fianceé is coming to terms with it, and most of my friends wonder what took so long."

Coming out is not quite like other life changes. When we announce a change in our gender, this often changes the nature of our friendship, because of the different ways in which we socialize, based on gender. The ways in which people relate to us will likely change based on their perception of our gender. They may talk to us about different things, touch us differently, relate to us in new ways, and even invite us to participate in different activities. These changes may feel affirming, but we may also grieve the loss of our former friendships.

"The best coming out experience was a male friend I came out to, who shortly thereafter asked me out on a date, it made me feel absolutely wonderful and I felt so bad that I couldn't accept since I'm just not attracted to men."

We may find as we proceed that the close friendships we had previously do not follow us through transition. But we are also rewriting our own script for our lives, and many of us may drift away or choose to distance ourselves from people we once thought indispensable to our lives.

When we give ourselves the freedom to reimagine our lives as we wish to live them, we may discover new interests and hobbies, change careers, and become interested in new kinds of friendships. Perhaps it becomes important to us to develop friendships with people who never knew us in our previous identity. Perhaps our worldview and style of relating to people change sufficiently that we do not feel as much of a common bond as we did with close friends prior to transition.

Sometimes our closest friends are still our closest friends years later.

"I was surprised how much of a non issue it was. True friends will always be true friends no matter what."

Family

Coming out to our families is often more complicated than coming out to our friends. Our relationships have deeper roots and may be tied to many matters of daily life, such as economic stability, housing, marriage, or parenting. Some members of our family have known us our entire lives—or their entire lives—and coming out to them may destabilize their understanding of themselves, our family, and their own relationships with us and others in our family.

MY GRANDFATHER

Juliet Meggs, MS, is a doctoral student in counseling psychology at the University of Tennessee.

If there's one thing my life has taught me again and again, it's that saying and doing are two significantly different things. It can often be easy for someone to *say* they love you. But authentically embracing you for who you are, regardless of the trappings of your life, is much more difficult.

So it was when I came out as transgender. On many different occasions, I had a very common experience coming out to my extended family. They would tell me they would "love and support me no matter what." But they would then proceed to thoroughly question and undermine my decision to transition, as though I were asking their permission or soliciting their advice. They framed it as concern, but it felt more condescending and invalidating, saying "I was young and wanted to make a change once too, and I don't want you to make a mistake you'll regret." They acted as though I had woken up that morning, decided I needed a different life, and flipped a coin to choose between becoming a woman and joining the Peace Corps.

But coming out to my grandfather was different. We had always had a special bond; I was his first grandchild, and he wanted nothing more in his life than to see me happy. Still, I feared coming out to him. An 88-year-old man, born and raised in rural Tennessee with little secondary education, who spent most of his old age in his La-Z-Boy watching Fox News for hours, he fit the profile of a man who would never understand—much less tolerate—having the grandson he'd known for 24 years now be a woman. And it's true, he certainly did not understand. But whereas everyone else had questioned me, he said, "I'm sure you wouldn't be doing this if you didn't have a good reason." Whereas everyone else had pushed their discomforts upon me, he said, "I may not understand, but I just want you to be happy. And I really hope you'll keep visiting."

It wasn't easy. He had a really difficult time remembering my gender and chosen name, and it was often hard to tell how much of this was the gradual onset of his mild dementia and how much of it was him just not wanting to accept I was female. But I still visited and brought sandwiches and old movies when I could. There were, of course, awkward moments when he introduced and referenced his "grandson" to visitors and, later, nurses. Yet it was so clear that he really valued having me in his life. And just as I was worth it to him, he was more than worth it to me.

He passed away last year, on my birthday and one week from his 90th. I'd missed a celebration with the family the evening before he died because I knew they'd all be uncomfortable if I was there, and I still wish I'd been there to take part in what became goodbye. But we didn't really need it. I knew he loved me, through his words and his actions. And now even though he's gone, I hope that I can honor his memory by not just extolling his strong spirit of acceptance and love, but, like my Boppo, by living it too.

Even if members of our family have trans friends or acquaintances, it is still quite an adjustment for them to call *us* a different name and pronoun. In many languages, our immediate family relationship words are gendered—mother, father, sister, brother, son, daughter—with certain roles associated with the words. Asking our family to stop seeing us as a "daughter," or "father," becomes part of their process.

> *"My mom had some initial trouble. . . but then my grandma put her right on it. Told her that most women don't get to have a son and a daughter in one lifetime without having to give birth twice, so she needed to get over herself. I love my grandma a lot."*

It may be difficult for family members who have known us closely to believe our new identity is real, because they have not recognized it themselves, despite years of closeness or proximity. It may be hard for close family to accept that we have had something this big going on inside us and they never knew. Sometimes they will express guilt for not "seeing" it at earlier times in our lives, though in reality, we may have been doing all we could to hide our true selves.

For some of us, our families think we are making a snap decision that we have not thought through. While we may have been contemplating this transition for quite a while, our families are just beginning their process.

> *"Everyone said that I went too fast. But the question is: 'too fast for what, for who?' I'd been 36 years in the wrong sex, I'd like to say it wasn't that fast."*

Not all families want, or need, to have extensive discussions about our new identity. This may not reflect lack of support—simply a family dynamic. If your family has had a history of quiet, understated discussions (or notable silence) about important changes in the past, you may experience a similar quiet kind of response.

As you prepare to talk to your family, you may want to consider how they have reacted to other important news in the past, to help gauge their response.

In some cases, families and friends may change their reactions once we begin to make our transition, recognizing the positive effects of us living in our affirmed gender.

> *"All my family but my sister took it well, she took some time away from me and didn't see me for a few months. I had at that point started hormones. The family got together for a funeral and she told my mom there was no way she could be against it anymore because she had never seen me so happy. Since then I have had 110% support from my family."*

Unfortunately, sometimes it does not get better.

> *"I came home for Christmas one year and my mom refused to go out in public with me because she was embarrassed by me. She said the coat I was wearing made me look 'like a woman.' I said, 'That's because I am a woman,' and she literally screamed. I locked myself in a room and cried for hours until I drove myself into a panic attack. My mom told me I was sick, possessed by Satan, and was going to hell and then didn't speak to me for hours. Then she decided she didn't want me to 'ruin Christmas' so we pretended like nothing happened, but I wasn't allowed to tell my dad or siblings to maintain the status quo. For months after that, my mom would call me and pretend like nothing ever happened. I finally wrote them a letter saying basically look, this isn't a phase. . . I'm on hormones, etc. They wrote back and told me I was never allowed to come home again because I was a threat to their 'remaining children.' This hurt me more badly than all the transphobes who ever bashed me, because I love my siblings more than anything in the whole world."*

Turning to our other support systems, practicing good self-care, and creating new, chosen families can be helpful as we grieve our losses.

In some cases, transition fractures our families, with some family members adamantly refusing to support our process and others completely on board. We may feel guilty—feeling responsible for causing such upheaval. If your family is reacting like this, it helps to hold onto the knowledge that you did not sign up for this any more than your family members did.

PARTNERS AND SPOUSES

Regardless of the type of transition you are considering, or the length of your relationship, there is no right time, easy way, or simple explanation that will make coming out to an intimate partner easy. The exact content of the emotional process will differ from relationship to relationship, but partners often experience an overwhelming set of conflicting feelings as they sort through their reactions to a possible transition. Explore Chapter 16 for more information on coming out to partners.

CREATING CHOSEN FAMILIES

Many people with LGBTQ identities find that as they come out they begin to form close friendships that sometimes become like families. Because many of us develop rifts with our biological family members, our "chosen families" can become places of much needed love and support. Families do not need to be tied by blood—and often some of the most successful family relationships are not.

CHILDREN

Coming out to children can be a scary prospect, but talking to our children or the children of family members and friends about gender can be a positive and empowering opportunity. Many children are more open-minded about gender than adults and may accept our new identities more easily than other family members. It is a myth that talking to a child about gender will change the child's gender identity.

The most important consideration in how to talk with children about our gender identity is the child's developmental age.

Young Children

Children learn about different aspects of gender at different times, and how children will understand and accept gender transitions differs over time. See Chapter 6 for more information on the ways that children of different ages understand gender.

Young children are often concerned about loss of consistency, loss of continuity, and loss of love. As with other members of the family, children's concerns are often linked to what our new identity means for them and the family. They may have questions like:

"Can I still call you 'mommy' (or 'daddy')?"
"Are you going away?" "Are you getting a divorce?"
"Where are you going to live?" "Where am I going to live?"

If they ask whether this means they will grow up to be a different gender themselves, most will be reassured by the explanation that our gender identity is not going to affect theirs. Let them know that they can continue to feel about themselves however they do.

"ARE YOU A BOY OR A GIRL?"

Nick Moore-Hunley is a young trans man currently attending Sonoma State University to pursue a degree in sociology with a minor in queer studies; he aspires to hold a career in rights advocacy and mental health for queer people.

The question seems to come up fairly often, but not usually within my own family. This time it comes from my little brother, Ethan. Ethan is many things; he's cute, he's funny, he's great at video games, he's a proud third grader, he's a Godzilla fanatic, but above all in this situation, Ethan is autistic.

The disorder makes it difficult to communicate with him, even about basic things, so it's no surprise that my gender transition would be incredibly confusing for him. I had spoken with my mom about how we could best explain the fact that his sister was actually his brother. We decided that I should talk to him alone, and that she would begin introducing me as "your sibling Nick" rather than sister or brother.

Every once in a while, I would walk into his Lego- and action figure–covered room and ask if he wanted to talk. If he was in a good mood and had a minimally stressful day at school, he usually seemed open to listening. We'd sit down on his bed, I'd pull him into my lap, and then we'd just talk. We talked about all sorts of things, but it would usually end with talking about my transition. At first, it was subtle.

"Hey buddy, do you think I'd look cool if I cut my hair even shorter and made it spiky like Sonic the Hedgehog?" I'd ask.

"That's so silly 'Kolie!" He'd laugh but approve of the suggestion, and the next day I took him to the salon with me so he would recognize that it was still me after the haircut. (He seems to have some difficulty with facial recognition.) After the hairdresser removed the cape and dusted the excess hair off, Ethan exclaimed, "Wow 'Kolie, you look like a cool dude!"

"Hey bud. Do you think I'm more like a brother or more like a sister?" He'd frown a little bit, deep in thought, and tell me that I was "kinda like both."

Then Mom started doing things that suggested the use of male pronouns: calling us "the boys" to her friends in front of him, or calling us out for meals with "Boys, dinner!" Ethan never comments on it, but he also never tries to correct her, so we hope that the message is getting through.

In the last few years, I can say with confidence that Ethan has come a long way in his understanding of my transition from sister to brother. When asked, he usually says things along the lines of "Well, I had a sister, but now 'Kolie's kinda like a brother." It's certainly a childish understanding, but it's more than I could have ever asked for.

Once word gets out that we are transitioning, children who spend time in day care, school, church, or community groups may hear gossip and unkind remarks about us. At younger ages, children do not have a large enough worldview to understand history and the transmission of misinformation and prejudice through generations. They will take things personally that are in no way personal to them or their family. Reassure them that there is nothing wrong with them or with you. Give them space to talk through the experiences they are having, even if the information they report hearing is painful for you. As children mature, it may become helpful to provide them with more historical education, placing discrimination in a cultural context.

Children develop at different rates, and even in the same family, one child may be ready for the larger cultural perspective at 9, while a sibling may not be ready for that level of discussion even at eleven.

Lamar OK, an elementary school teacher, is a self-identified queer "fighting for my liberation and liberation of my people."

I am afraid to invite my students into that part of my life. I tried last year, and I failed. I think about it every day: The day that I lost courage, the day I'd never get back. But at the time, I was afraid it would have been the day when I lost the respect and love of my 23 students. I can openly talk about race, class, the absence of my father, the neglect of my mother, the endless days when I starved and lived in a car, the mistakes I made as a kid, but for some reason, I can't seem to talk about who I really am, the piece that truly makes me happy about myself. It kills me every day. The more intimate I become in the lives of my students, the more guilt I feel. The way they defend me, advocate for me, cry with me, laugh with me, makes it so hard for me to invite them in. They are my everything. I don't want to lose them the way I lost my black mother when I invited her in. I don't want to feel again the pain I felt - and still feel - when she walked away and never turned back to see that I was drowning in my own tears and only wanted her to love me for me. Not again. Not with these beautiful, impressionable, strong, very conscious loving students of mine. I ask myself every morning: "Is today the day?" I then go to bed every night and tell myself, "Next time. Maybe tomorrow."

Adolescents

Adolescents value honesty and straightforward information. They have developed the capacity for abstract thinking, and they may be more engaged with the idea (in both positive and negative ways) of our transition. When coming out to adolescents, it is often helpful to explain our experiences, as well as the nature of the process, as we understand it. In essence, teens need the explanation given to adults *and* the reassurance given to children, as they are in a bridge period in their lives.

As with younger children, reassurance of stability and continuity can go a long way toward reconciling the adolescent toward the idea of a parent or close adult in their life transitioning. Reinforce that your identity does not reflect on the adolescent's emerging gender and sexual identity.

Adolescence is the time when the need for peer acceptance and approval is at its highest. It is important to reassure adolescents that as much as possible, it is their choice whether to tell their friends and teachers about our transition, and that we will do what we can to make them comfortable among their peers. The school milieu belongs to the adolescent, and we can help teens weather our transition by keeping our distance from the school setting until they are ready for our presence there.

While some teens may see our transition as embarrassing, or shameful, at first, others may feel that having a trans parent or close adult friend somehow gains them "cool points" with their friends. Talk with them about your own goals and timeline for coming out and make sure they understand when and with whom you are comfortable sharing this information.

Adolescence is also a time of coming to understand social issues on a broader scale than is possible for younger children. Adolescents begin to form a worldview at this point in their lives, adopting political opinions and taking stances on various issues. Their views are often polarized, with "black and white" or "right or wrong" judgments about issues.

Some adolescents may see the social discrimination against trans individuals as a civil rights issue and be appalled at the pariah status of trans people. Others may continue to see gender as polarized; the "black and white" thinking that characterizes adolescence dovetails unfortunately well with the gender binary concept. Sometimes adolescents withdraw from a transitioning parent on this basis, only to come around later in their lives, when their worldviews have evolved.

Adult Children

Many of us who transition midlife may have had full lives in our birth-assigned sex, including marrying and having children, who are now adults with their own lives. They may be more or less dependent on us and more or less involved in our lives today, and coming out to our adult children may be similar to the conversations we have had with other adults in our lives.

However, while some of us may have been happy in our roles at the time we were raising our children, not all of us felt comfortable in the lives we were leading. Some of us struggled with depression, anxiety, or other mental health issues, and in some cases, we self-medicated with drugs or alcohol. In these cases, our family may need to address these issues before grappling with our new identity.

Children who struggled with feelings of neglect or helplessness, or felt responsible for our health and well-being, may feel a great deal of anger and bitterness. Having lived through their entire childhood with an unhappy parent, it can be difficult for the adult child to forgive the parent, and we may find ourselves having to make amends for quite some time.

In many other cases, our children may be delighted to see us taking control of our lives, even if we did not struggle with these issues during their childhood.

> *"I anguished a long time, fearing what would happen when I came out to my daughters. I knew that if they accepted me, from there on out it would be much easier. Although I thought I would be coming out to my oldest daughter first, it turned out to be the youngest who guessed I was Transgender from all the clues I'd been giving for so long. When I came out, trembling, she walked over, embraced me, and said 'I LOVE YOU UNCONDITIONALLY!!!' At that moment, I knew that even if the rest of the world despised me, I was going to be OK."*

Even with this level of acceptance, the adjustment is still a process, as for all family relationships. We may transition to living as female, but our children may still see us as "dad." They will (probably) over time change the way they refer to us, wanting to respect our transition, but may also experience a certain natural grief over this level of change.

No matter what our past relationship with them, or their initial reaction, coming out can be an opportunity to establish a *new* relationship with our adult children.

ON THE JOB

Work is an unusual environment, because it is a place where we are known and visible to those around us but may not have deep personal relationships. The workplace is the most challenging milieu in most people's attempts at maintaining privacy. Workplace relationships are professional in nature, but coworkers often socialize outside the work environment. See Chapter 9 for more information on coming out at work or in the job search process.

Stuck in the Middle With You: A Memoir of Parenting in Three Genders by Jennifer Finney Boylan (New York, NY: Crown Publishers, 2013) combines Boylan's personal narrative with interviews of others.

Coming out at work (Elenore Toczynski).

TRANSITIONING AS A TEACHER

Jake Loren is a teacher and current employee of the New York City Department of Education.

I began teaching English at a Title I middle school in Brooklyn right after college as visibly gender nonconforming "Ms." I never had to worry about "coming out" as queer because it was never a question—or an option. Students at my school, even kids I didn't know, came out of the woodwork to solicit advice and support. My students asked incessant questions: Were my parents okay with me? When did I first kiss a girl?

At the end of my second year of teaching, I brought two colleagues whom I trusted with me when I announced to our volatile principal that I would return the following fall as "Mr." We pressured her to offer a brief whole-staff "LGBT 101" focused on the needs of LGBT youth. For the next two years, my principal attempted to threaten my job or place unsatisfactory notes in my file on several occasions without supporting evidence—and despite the academic gains my students were making.

Adult colleagues, especially self-identified liberal adults on staff, loved to talk to me about their gay friend as though we were the same. These colleagues tended to feel authorized by their good intentions to ask lots of questions about my body and how I have sex. During work, I fielded questions like "So do gay guys hit on you now?" and "What kind of underwear do you wear?" and "You don't have a dick, right?" and "Do you still menstruate?" (a colleague asked me this last one in front of students).

In my everyday life as I transitioned, I began to experience very different treatment than I had as a butch woman. As "Mr." with sixth graders who were new to the school and did not learn my history as "Ms." until much later in the school year, I noticed this immediately as well. All of a sudden, my "personal life" seemed to be off the table until I brought it up. Classroom management techniques that always came naturally to me immediately began to work far better than they had in the past—the silent "teacher stare," the refusal to raise my voice, the pausing to wait for attention. Male students actively approached me just to talk about their lives, to "bond" with me—something my male students, except boys struggling with sexuality or masculinity, actively avoided the prior two years.

This was my first experience not feeling "out" and experiencing the privilege that came along with being a white, straight man; and because I'd associated being "out" with "doing the right thing" for so long in a queer context, at first I experienced a tremendous guilt for not disclosing to my classes. Over time, however, I realized that it's quite different to disclose a trans history (especially in a work environment) than it is to come out as queer—not just in terms of legal protections but in terms of the body monitoring and scrutiny that most people impulsively do the moment I tell them I'm trans.

When my students began to "get the memo" about me and ask me questions, I would readily disclose. One student approached me to ask about the trans woman he saw on *The Real World: Brooklyn*. "Is that a real thing?" he asked. I said, "Yes, it is a real thing, and I know because I'm trans myself." He thought for a moment and then asked, "So in middle school, you were a girl?" The next day, he put a Post-It on my desk with three questions written on it: "Was it hard to change?" "How did you know you needed to change?" and "Do you feel better now that you are yourself?"

That is why I teach, and why we need even more LGBTQ educators and allies who will proactively incorporate LGBTQ issues into our classrooms and who, when we feel safe and able, can be out and disclose our histories.

A WIDENING CIRCLE

When we begin the process of coming out, most of us experience a period in which the information has spread beyond those who we have told ourselves. Our friends and family may have reached out to their support networks and disclosed some of our information, and news may have traveled through our informal community networks as rumor or gossip. Once this happens, we do not always know who knows and who does not, and we may worry about what information people have been given.

Some of us have the choice to come out taken away from us when we are outed by others, sometimes in ways that dictate the course of our transition and family adjustment process.

"I came out to my parents in 1985. My mom immediately rejected the idea and instructed me to not tell my father. When I changed my name, I had to publish the name change in the paper for three weeks. A local radio personality read the announcement on the air to be funny. My cousin heard it and called her mother (my aunt), who called her mother-in-law (my grandmother), who called her daughter-in-law (my mother), who called me and told me I was destroying my family. It was years before I reconciled with my parents, but by the time I went for surgery, my parents and one of my brothers drove me to the airport."

When we have come out to certain people and not others, group settings can be awkward. We may not know who in the situation knows and who does not. Those who do know may feel awkward about using new pronouns or a new name for us, unsure whether the others in the group know. If the group is tightly knit, it is often easiest for all concerned if we tell everyone as quickly as possible. If we are not able to tell everyone in a group at once, it can sometimes be confusing for those we have told to navigate their roles. They may be unsure what to say to others, particularly if we have begun a visible social or physical transition—changing our way of dressing, our hairstyle, taking hormones, or undergoing surgeries. The best thing we can do is to talk through with them how we would like them to interact with others during our transition.

The desire for privacy may not be realistic if we are early in transition. Some of us may choose not to come out yet, but we may use interactions with others to gauge the "progress" of our transition.

> *"To complete strangers I may not meet again, I usually just go with whatever their first impression is. It is a good gauge of how I'm perceived by others."*

Some of us want our friends or family members to help us spread the word, feeling overwhelmed by the numbers of people who need to know and wanting to be able to focus more on our own internal processes. If this seems like the right course for you, you may want to help them identify the kinds of questions they are likely to be asked and craft standard answers together. In some cases, even if we are ready for others to begin sharing our information, they may still be in the middle of their own transition process. Be prepared to help them navigate these difficult conversations.

And what about friends or family members who find out before we have had a chance to tell them? If someone feels they are the last to find out and is hurt to hear about our transition through other people, it can help to tell them, "It is not because you do not matter—it is because you matter so much." We often think our close friends and family members know this automatically, but this is not always true.

Casual Acquaintances

Interacting with casual acquaintances can be very awkward and uncomfortable when we are early in our transition. Casual acquaintances are not close enough friends to have earned our trust. They are the people we sit next to in the office or the fellow student we study with occasionally. Those who fall into the casual acquaintance category may not feel close enough to us to ask questions, or even acknowledge, our transition.

Sometimes these relationships become close friendships over time, but while the person is still in the category "casual acquaintance," we might wish they did not have to know something this personal about us. It can feel awkward to the casual acquaintance to have this level of intimate knowledge about someone they are not close to. Many of us who transition find ourselves avoiding casual acquaintances for a while, if we can, to ease the tension.

Some of us come out to a casual acquaintance and are pleasantly surprised to receive great support and admiration. Sometimes the person ends up in the category "close friend" as a result of the disclosure. Perhaps the relationship would have blossomed into close friendship anyway, but it was catapulted forward by the depth of intimacy involved in coming out.

> *"The best reaction was from a woman who I had known casually for years as a man. When she saw me en femme with a long streaked salt and pepper wig on, she asked if my hair had always been streaked."*

Reconnecting With Our Past

Throughout our lives, we often lose touch with people we were once close to or with whom we shared jobs, schools, sports teams, or housing arrangements. As we begin our transition, we may re-encounter these people in new social settings, at planned reunions, or professional events. In these settings, honesty and humor can go a long way.

"I attended my 40th college reunion in my new identity. After the banquet, we each were invited to tell the class what we had been doing personally and professionally. I began with the words 'Well, there have been a few changes. . .' which immediately got me a big laugh followed by a standing ovation."

"I've had a good response from my Naval Academy classmates and will attend our 50th class reunion in October 2010. I out myself now and then to people we meet. It is often the Naval Academy connection which provokes the 'I didn't know that women. . .' question. 'Well, actually, they didn't. I was a man back then.'"

DISCLOSURE

When we are just beginning our coming-out process, it may seem impossible that we could reach a point in our transition when we can live in our affirmed gender without needing to explain ourselves to the people in our lives. But for many of us, a time comes when we start to be seen, at least by some people, as the gender that matches our identity. We may no longer be frequently "read" as our birth-assigned gender, or "clocked," while in public.

When we are perceived as the gender with which we identify, we may "disclose" information about our gender history or experience. For some of us, disclosing our trans status becomes a choice. Many of us find unique ways of relating to our gender and our personal history in which we disclose under certain circumstances and not others. Some people choose to integrate their personal history into their lives, being out when it feels safe and relevant, and other times choosing to address the world only on the terms of their current identity. The most important part of this decision, however, goes back to feeling grounded in who you are.

Who we choose to discuss our gender with varies widely within our community, and when we choose to tell people is a matter of fierce debate. How you choose to navigate these decisions is, ultimately, up to you. All of the options have benefits and consequences that should be carefully considered.

The biggest concern in any situation is our own safety and comfort. Is choosing to share about ourselves going to make a situation safer or more dangerous? Is it going to make us more or less comfortable?

The "Need to Know" Category

Regardless of how much privacy we might desire, there are some situations in which we should disclose our history if at all possible. It can be very helpful for our primary care provider to know that we once transitioned, in order to fully understand our physiology and medical needs.

"I wouldn't have the faintest idea what its like to be 'out.' I live in deep stealth, which means my GP (general practitioner) is the ONLY person who knows of my medical history, and I intend upon keeping it that way! I was raised with the idea of social decorum. To me this is a VERY personal issue and in the words of my mother 'no one's damned business but my own!'"

It may also be wise to fully inform certain professionals, such as attorneys, caseworkers, therapists, and accountants, who are providing us with legal or medical services. We may not be able to foresee in advance a way in which our transition might prove relevant, but it may, in fact, be important down the line. As an example, transition-related medical care is often tax deductible, and an accountant knowledgeable about our trans status can help us use this to our advantage.

For those of us who live in states that will only respect our identities if we have had certain forms of gender-affirming surgery, we may need to come out to our attorney, our tax preparer, and our health provider. These are the people who can best advise us of all our rights and what is available to us—but only if they know exactly what our status is under state law. And they can only know that if they know we are trans.

CONCLUSION

Coming out is a complicated process that involves exploring our identities and sharing them with others. The nature of our relationships determines the ways in which we individually choose to come out or are outed by others. Though sometimes difficult, coming out can be an exciting and self-affirming journey.

REFERENCES AND FURTHER READING

Boenke, M. (Ed.). (2008). *Trans forming families: Real stories about transgendered loved ones.* Hardy, VA: Oak Knoll.

Devor, A. H. (2004). Witnessing and mirroring: A fourteen stage model of transsexual identity formation. *Journal of Gay and Lesbian Psychotherapy, 8,* 41–67.

Green, J. (2004). *Becoming a visible man.* Nashville, TN: Vanderbilt University Press.

Haskell, M. (2013). *My brother, my sister: Story of a transformation.* New York, NY: Penguin Group.

Hubbard, E. A., & Whitley, C. T. (2012). *Trans-kin: A guide for family & friends of transgender people.* Boulder, CO: Boulder Press.

Keig, Z., & Rohrer, M. (Eds.). (2010). *Letters for my brothers: Transitional wisdom in retrospect.* United States: Wilgefortis.

Lev, A. I. (2004). *Transgender emergence: Therapeutic guidelines for working with gender variant people and their families.* Binghamton, NY: The Haworth Press.

Rudacille, D. (2005). *The riddle of gender: Science, activism, and transgender rights.* New York, NY: Random House.

Saltzburg, N. L. (2010). *Developing a model of transmasculine identity.* Retrieved December 2013, from Open Access Disserations, http://scholarlyrepository.miami.edu/cgi/viewcontent.cgi?article=1431&context=oa_dissertations

Vanderburgh, R. (2011). *Transition and beyond: Observations on gender identity.* Portland, OR: Odin Ink.

8

SOCIAL TRANSITION
Heath Mackenzie Reynolds and Zil Garner Goldstein

FIGURING OUT WHO WE ARE AND WHO WE WANT TO BECOME IS A UNIVERSAL HUMAN EXPERIENCE. For many people, this process becomes less active over time, as we settle into our sense of self and build a community and a life around that identity. But not for everyone—many people find the process of defining who they are to be lifelong and full of changing directions, shifting goals, new communities, and new identities. As trans people, we may find that we are plunged back into a more active phase of self-discovery than we had been before coming out. Once we make a decision to begin making changes that will better reflect our identity, there are numerous ways to start. Some of us spend a considerable amount of time thinking about how we would like to be addressed and whether we want to change our name or pronouns.

CHOOSING A NAME

The process of picking a new name can be one place to start thinking about how we want to integrate the different parts of our lives. The most important part of coming up with a name is feeling like it fits. There are many different strategies for coming up with a name.

> *"Changing my name was a very important aspect of re-creating myself in the form that I want to be—of becoming myself, as my own ongoing creation process."*

Many people find a name that feels good by looking into their own family or cultural background, or examining the parts of their identity and history that have played the biggest role in shaping their sense of self. Talking with trusted friends and family can help. It can also be useful to try out the new name with a few people before telling lots of people about the change.

There is, however, such a thing as too much advice. It is important to feel confident in the name we are choosing but also to avoid thinking about it for too long. You do not want to repeat your new name so many times that it loses meaning before you have even settled on a decision.

When we ask other people about possible names, we have to be prepared for all kinds of answers. We may not hear what we want, and we certainly might not hear what we are expecting to hear. It can be hard to ask a friend or family member about a name, or some other aspect of our transition, and hear an answer that is not supportive. Figuring out who to ask can be a challenge, and we can often be surprised by the people around us when we bring up aspects of ourselves related to trans identities.

Sometimes it can be tempting to use names that come from cultures other than our own. When thinking about these names, consider that some of us who come from those cultures may be offended by an outsider's use of our community's names. Even if you think a name has a nice sound to it, try to think about whether it is an appropriate choice, given your own background.

Some of us take more time than others to settle on a name. We may even use one name for a year or two and then decide that it does not quite fit. This can be a natural part of our process.

PRONOUNS

Pronouns are the part of speech we use to refer to someone without using their name. Most commonly, people use "he" and "him" or "she" and "her." Gender-neutral pronouns such

Questions to Consider When Picking a Name

1. What do I like about my current name? Is there a part of it I want to keep?
2. What do I like about other people's names?
3. What is important to me about who I am?
4. What is important to me about who I want to be?
5. Do I want my name to reflect my heritage?
6. Is there a family name I want to use? How would my family react to this?
7. What name would I feel good saying to everyone I meet?
8. Do I like this name? Does it feel like it fits?
9. Do I feel proud telling people that this is my name?
10. How many other people have this name?

as "ze" (pronounced "zee") and "hir" (pronounced "here") reflect a gender identity that is neither male nor female. "They" and "them" can also be used to speak about an individual without referencing their gender.

Deciding when to start using new pronouns is often harder than deciding when to start using a new name. Much of the same process we use to choose our names applies to choosing our pronouns. Our use of pronouns may shift over time as our gender presentation changes or as our gender identity shifts.

> *"When people use my preferred pronoun, I feel like a worthwhile and real human being."*

Some of us begin by using new pronouns with close friends or family, and gradually expand to different friend groups or social communities. Many of us end up using different pronouns in different parts of our life, at least for a while. It may be hard to use gender-neutral pronouns at work, for example, where most people may be unaware of their existence. Some of us have not yet come out at work and use our old pronouns with colleagues.

Over time, we may figure out how to manage having multiple pronouns and even like it, or we may switch to using a more consistent set of pronouns in all contexts. For some of us, pronouns are not important at all, or we might grow tired from using different pronouns in different spaces, so we use whatever seems to be most "default" for those we interact with. Everyone has different strategies for dealing with gender, pronouns, and the world around us.

Gender-neutral pronouns can be a useful tool for those of us who are gender nonconforming, either because we are in the midst of a physical transition process or because we identify as nonbinary in some way. "They," "them," "ze," and "hir" are common choices. If you were using these in a sentence, you might say: "Avi went to the store. They went to get us some ice cream." Or "Morgan forgot hir sweater." Or "That's Riley, ze is new in town." The Gender Neutral Pronoun Blog (genderneutralpronoun.wordpress.com) provides information about such pronouns, trends in their use, and communities who use them.

People Make Mistakes

When we are changing our name and pronouns, it is very common for people in our lives to use the wrong pronouns when referring to us ("misprounoun" us). When someone messes up a pronoun, it often makes us upset, angry, or sad. It can upset the person who made the mistake as well, especially if they care about us. If we decide to correct the person who made the mistake, it is often helpful to say something like "he not she" or "ze not he," instead of simply stating the correct pronoun. Keep in mind that using gender-neutral pronouns can be harder for people to adopt, and they will likely need more time to adjust.

> *"At first I delighted in getting folks to use a mix of pronouns—to switch it up. Now I use she/her almost exclusively. It is comfortable for me. When I made that switch, I was very self-conscious when anyone messed it up. I got embarrassed and annoyed. To this day I still flinch when I hear someone mess it up, but I am much more graceful about correcting them if needed."*

TRANS ETIQUETTE

Peter Cava

Following are some of the most important principles for respectfully communicating to, and about, trans people. I have learned these principles from writings by Jacob Hale, Matt Kailey, and Riki Wilchins; videos by Calpernia Addams and Ethan Suniewick; and my participation in trans communities.

- *Remember* that you're not the expert on others' experiences. Everyone experiences gender differently. Exercise humility. Practice good listening skills.
- *Honor* others' self-definitions. For example, use others' chosen names and pronouns. If you don't know someone's pronouns, avoid pronouns or ask. If you make a mistake, don't turn it into a scene, and don't be too hard on yourself; discreetly apologize or just move on. If you're in a situation where it would be appropriate to speak about someone's genitals, use their chosen language.

- *Don't expect* others to serve as spokespeople or educators. No one can speak for every member of their group or community. Many trans people are happy to share their experiences. However, no one can be "on" as an educator 24/7. Take advantage of published resources. If you want to talk with a trans person about their experiences, wait until the topic comes up, or ask consent.
- *Don't "out"* others as trans. Even if someone is out to you, they may not be out in all areas of their life, such as family, work, and social media. Outing someone can have negative, even devastating, consequences.
- *Don't assume* that others' gender expressions tell you something about their bodies, identities, or sexualities. For example, if someone looks to you like a woman, don't assume that the person was assigned female at birth, self-identifies as a woman, or is sexually oriented toward men. If you proposition someone for sex and they do not have the genital shape that you were expecting, they were not necessarily deceiving you; rather, you were making an assumption. If you want to have sex with someone who has a particular genital shape, say so. If imagining these scenarios makes you feel uncomfortable, that's okay. Consider exploring those feelings as a way of learning more about yourself, and consider waiting to have sex until you feel more comfortable.
- *Don't ask* invasive questions about others' bodies, identities, or sexualities. Often the first question that trans people are asked is, "Have you had the surgery?" Other common questions are, "Are you a man or a woman?" and "Do you want to be with a man or a woman?" (As if "a man or a woman" were the only options.) A rule of thumb is that in a situation where it would be considered rude to ask a cis person a particular question, it is rude to ask a trans person.
- *Don't criticize* others' bodies, expressions, or sexualities for not aligning with their identities in a socially expected way. For example, if a trans man does not go on testosterone, don't make him feel like he is "not trans enough." Conversely, don't critique others' bodies, expressions, or sexualities for *aligning* with their identities in a socially expected way. For example, if a trans man has sex with women only, don't make him feel like he is "not queer enough." We are all enough. At its best, trans-ing gender is not about transitioning from a confining *cis* box to an equally confining *trans* box. Rather, it's about transcending all of the boxes that keep us from being fully ourselves.

Most people do not know what to do when they are corrected on someone's pronouns. It is not something that is commonly talked about. Letting someone know that it hurts our feelings when they say the wrong thing can help them learn that it is important to us that they not do it again. Try to communicate these issues in a calm and reasonable way, even if you are very upset. Reacting in highly emotional, angry ways can often exacerbate the situation. It can be difficult to strike the right balance, and it definitely takes some practice.

Even if we believe that someone is using the incorrect pronouns on purpose or hurtfully, it is more productive to communicate our needs in a clear, firm way than to appear angry. Set limits, and let the other person know what the consequences of mispronouning you are, including how it makes you feel and how you will respond if they continue to act that way.

CHANGING OUR APPEARANCE

There are many different ways we can make our bodies feel like a better fit with our gender identities. Each of us has different goals as we begin to make changes to our appearance. Some of us make changes to be seen by others as the gender with which we identify. Some of us make changes that result in us looking more androgynous in appearance, which makes it harder for others to label us with a gender.

Some of us choose highly masculine or feminine styles that make our gender clear, while others are drawn toward more casual looks that do not highlight gender differences. Our preference may shift over time.

> *"When I was younger, I cared about that—and I am a makeup artist so I can do good face, but nowadays I do not wear makeup or even worry about how I look or if I pass. I do glam up for public speaking and presentations, but other than that it is a ponytail and bare face."*

As we begin to change our appearance, we also have the opportunity to express other things about ourselves or to embrace new parts of our personality and choose colors and styles that we may have felt were off limits. Over time, we may shift our ideas about how we want to dress to reflect our personality, more than our gender presentation.

Clothing, hairstyles, and accessories are easy places to start changing the way our gender is perceived by others. Some of us find that these changes give us a sense of feeling at home in our bodies, while for others they are ways of experimenting with how we want to look before making more permanent changes. We can always start dressing a different way, or do something for a little while and then stop. As we begin exploring our gender identity and becoming more comfortable, temporary changes in our appearance can help us decide how we will feel most at home in our bodies and the world.

"When I move, I plan to live like a woman in professional settings and dress and act like a man in casual settings. Even now, as I start to admit to myself that I'm trans, I realize how much acting I do on a daily basis. I change my voice and my mannerisms to present as a female. Before, I thought that this was just how life was, but now I realize that I am acting and I'm acting all the time and that is exhausting. I wish I could change my name, records, get top surgery, and dress like a guy all at once because I would love to stop acting most of the time, but I understand that transition must be a long process. I think living in the gray zone will be confusing and frustrating, but if it helps me sort out what I really want for my body and my gender presentation, then I hope I can get through it without getting called out for it."

For a forum on transition-related voice issues, check out the Yahoo group voicets.

GENDER AND THE VOICE

Lal Zimman, PhD, is a visiting assistant professor of linguistics at Reed College, where he teaches a variety of courses on language and society and conducts research on the relationships between language, gender, and sexuality in transgender and LGBQ communities.

The voice is an important cue in the process of categorizing people by gender, and many trans people shift their speech during transition. These changes may be brought about through individual experimentation, speech therapy, the unconscious process of language socialization, or theatrical or musical training, but many trans men and their providers put greater emphasis on the changes in vocal pitch testosterone therapy may bring about. However, biology cannot explain all of the gender differences found in the voice, and there is tremendous linguistic diversity among people of the same sex or gender.

Anatomy puts some limits on our voices, and exposure to testosterone is known to enlarge the larynx (or voicebox), which generally lowers vocal pitch. But even pitch, which is strongly linked to biology, is also influenced by social factors. Speakers of some languages show much more dramatic differences between women's and men's pitch than speakers of others. Most children learn to sound male or female before sex differences in the vocal anatomy develop at puberty.

In addition to pitch, the shape of the vocal tract determines which frequencies will resonate most strongly, and women's vocal tracts tend to be shorter than men's. Smiling causes the vocal tract to shorten, while rounding the lips makes it slightly longer. There is also the option of raising or lowering the larynx within the throat, which is something children begin to do early in life.

There are also significant gender differences in the pronunciation of particular sounds. Among American English speakers, women tend to pronounce [s] at a higher frequency than men by placing their tongue closer to the upper teeth while making this sound. The other ways that women's and men's voices have been shown to differ tend to relate to the notion of clarity, with women generally speaking with greater precision than men—"mumbling is macho," as one linguist puts it.

Some trans people may wish to change their speaking styles as part of a shift in gender expression, and the fact that many gender differences are learned rather than innate suggests that kind of change is possible, if challenging. Others may prefer a nonnormative voice, in order to signal a queer or distinctly trans identity.

FINDING OUR VOICES, LITERALLY

Christie Block, MA, MS, CCC-SLP, is a clinical speech-language pathologist who specializes in voice communication training and rehabilitation for transgender people at her private practice, New York Speech & Voice Lab, in New York City.

How exactly is gender conveyed when we talk? Pitch is usually what we first think of. However, many other aspects of speech come into play, including intonation, resonance, articulation, vocal quality, stress, loudness, and speech rate. A combination of some or all of these elements can result in a more feminine voice that sounds higher, smaller, lighter, and/or more expressive, compared to a more masculine voice that sounds lower, bigger, heavier, and/or more matter of fact.

In addition to how we sound, other aspects of communication can display gender. These include word choice, the number of words used, conversation topics, and conversation style (such as the degree of politeness or directness). Gender can also be expressed in nonverbal communication or body language, such as eye contact, facial expression, hand gestures, or head movements.

Some of these aspects of communication are based on biological sex differences of the vocal mechanism, for example, the length of the vocal folds. Many other aspects are based on sociolinguistic norms that we have learned since childhood and that depend on language, dialect, region, socioeconomic class, and other factors.

To explore and learn authentic and effective communication skills, a person can seek help from a qualified specialist in transgender voice and communication, typically a speech-language pathologist. Feedback is an essential benefit of working with a specialist, as new skills are practiced, employed in real life, and established over time. Voice and communication change requires patience, like learning a new language or adjusting to other aspects of transition.

For transgender people who choose HRT or voice surgery, pitch change can occur is certain cases. Transmasculine people who take testosterone almost always experience a welcome effect of lower pitch within the first year of treatment, with an eventual permanent drop of up to an octave or more. Hoarseness sometimes occurs in the initial months of therapy or with each dose. In contrast, feminizing HRT has no known effect on the adult voice. Pitch-raising voice surgery has resulted in widely varying degrees of satisfaction and long-term improvement; pitch-lowering surgery is rare and results are not generally observed at this time with or without these treatments. Voice and communication training remains a recommended form of intervention for feminization or masculinization to address not only nonpitch aspects of speaking but also vocal health issues.

Our communication skills are a fundamental part of us, and we can intentionally change them if we desire. Here are a few tips to get started: (1) Think seriously about the way you talk, focusing on aspects you like and ones you would like to change; (2) mimic people who speak in a way that you like; (3) when talking, use your intuition and try your best—intuition can go a long way; and (4) practice healthy voice habits, such as avoiding excessively high or low pitch. Consult a doctor or speech-language pathologist if you experience hoarseness, vocal strain, or throat discomfort.

Clothing

The simplest way to change how our gender is perceived is through what we wear. Finding our new style can take some time. When searching for ways to dress, the best thing to do is look around. Do you see an outfit you like? Is the person wearing it a coworker, someone you see on the street, or a model in a fashion magazine? We can find good looks anywhere or piece them together from multiple things we see. Finding the different pieces can be tricky, though.

Many of us have specific ideas in mind about the kinds of clothing we would like to wear, and we may have gradually collected a small wardrobe—an item here, an item there. We may have tried on these new garments in the comfort and privacy of our homes, at first, or strutted our stuff on the stage as a drag performer.

For some of us, shopping for what we want can be a challenge. We may be nervous about other people's reactions or simply uncertain about where and how to begin. In most places, clothes shopping is a highly gendered activity, with physical separation between men's and women's departments, different sizing conventions, and style choices and details that we may not fully understand. There are many ways to educate ourselves before we head into a retail store. Arming ourselves with information can help

A transgender person strikes a pose, during celebration of LGBT rights in Guatemala City, Guatemala. June, 2012 (photo by Duffboy).

give us the confidence we need to approach staff, try on apparel, and make successful purchases.

Shopping for items online can be a way to build a new wardrobe from the privacy of our own home. Most online stores offer sizing charts with advice on how to take our own measurements and choose the right size. Many retailers also offer online-only sales, special offers for free shipping and returns, and may carry a broader range of sizes than their brick-and-mortar shops. For example, many retail stores do not carry extra-small sizes in men's clothing or larger sizes in women's items—these items are often available online, however, providing us with more flexibility to find the right fit in the styles we like.

Trans Bodies, Trans Selves New York City Forum (photo by Katia Ruiz).

Thrift stores and secondhand shops can also be a good place to start when we begin shopping. They typically have a large selection of items, often in a range of sizes, at a low price, and can help us figure out what styles and sizes suit our bodies. The staff at such

Recently, some specialty shops have begun to market clothing to people who are masculine of center. They include Marimacho, Tomboy Tailors, Saint Harridan, Fourteen, The Butch Clothing Company, and others.

dapperQ (dapperq.com) is a visibility project that, through a focus on fashion, celebrates the inner and outer beauty of masculine-presenting lesbians, gender nonconformists and genderqueers, and transmasculine individuals of all colors, shapes, and sizes.

places are also unlikely to interact with us as we browse the selection, and many people use thrift stores to procure clothing items for a range of unconventional purposes—such as theater, crafts, and costume parties—which can put us more at ease with making our purchases. Thrift shops can also be an important source for clothing and accessories if we cannot afford to shop in retail outlets or boutiques. It may take more work, but there are often great finds waiting to be discovered.

Many of us find shopping in mainstream retail outlets to be daunting, but it does not have to be. As in many public settings, acting with confidence can diffuse awkwardness and prevent questions from others that make us feel defensive. It can be helpful to remember that even cisgender people may feel anxious shopping for new clothing. Some of us prefer to take along a trusted friend who can be a second set of eyes to help us figure out whether something looks good, what could be changed to make it better, and to help quell some of the anxiety we feel in new situations.

Many of us have trouble finding appropriate shoes in the right size. There are often specialty stores and online deals available, and sales people are often happy to special order shoes in different sizes. Many discount shoe stores have shoes organized by size, which can also help us from falling in love with shoes that are not made to fit our feet. Transmasculine people may find that there are lines of children's shoes that look professional enough for work.

Remember that cisgender people come in all shapes and sizes, too. There are tall cis women and short cis men. Some cis women have large feet and some cis men have small feet. Each store's brand tends to fit taller or shorter, thinner or heavier people, and we simply have to find our match.

Hair

Choosing a hairstyle is another way many of us change our appearance. We may focus on growing, cutting, or styling our natural hair in different ways, or we may use wigs. We may want to choose androgynous hairstyles that allow us to present our gender differently based on different contexts or choose strongly feminine or masculine styles that help others read our gender correctly.

When making a radical change in our hairstyle, communicating with the person cutting our hair is important. Many hairdressers are accustomed to people bringing in pictures and saying, "This is how I want my hair to look." Take pictures, look for styles online, or cut out pictures from magazines to find something you like, and do not be afraid to tell the person cutting your hair exactly what it is that you want. Let them know how much time you want to spend styling your hair and consider whether you will be able to maintain a look that requires lots of styling product, blow drying, or frequent return visits to the stylist.

Trans Bodies, Trans Selves New York City Forum (photo by Katia Ruiz).

If going for a shorter cut, some stylists may be concerned about cutting too much. Worried we will be unhappy with the results, they may leave more length than we want or provide a more feminine shape than many trans men would like. Do not be afraid to ask for the stylist to continue cutting, go shorter, or give the cut a more masculine shape.

If you are growing your hair out, getting intermediate cuts to give your new locks a better style can help make you feel more confident and attractive, and can help the hair stay healthy as it grows. Frequent trims can help avoid split ends that can give hair a ragged look. Sometimes we have to cut some parts shorter while we wait for other parts to grow longer.

SCALP HAIR REPLACEMENT

Hair loss is a source of great stress for both trans women and trans men. In trans women, once we begin taking hormones our hair loss should stop and, to some extent, reverse. The degree to which our hair loss may reverse depends mostly on how much loss we had to begin with. Testosterone-blocking medicine is the most important component in our regimen to combat hair loss and assist in hair regrowth. It is unclear whether using a medication like finasteride or dutasteride when we are already on a testosterone blocker like spironolactone will have any added benefit. Some of us have used minoxidil (Rogaine) with mixed results. Remember that many cisgender women have thinning or receding hairlines as well.

Managing hair loss can involve using wigs, hairpieces, head wraps, bands, or hats, or it can involve any one of a number of procedures. Hair systems usually involve a wig made of real human hair, which is bonded to the scalp using a special adhesive. These systems need to be periodically adjusted and refastened. Surgeries can include scalp advance, where the scalp is incised and stretched forward with an island of skin being removed, or it can involve transplants of individual hairs or blocks of hair. Hair transplants generally involve taking a strip-like graft from the back of the head, stretching the two open ends together and sewing them in place, and then using the graft hair for a strand-by-strand replacement. As with facial hair removal, scalp hair procedures require that they be done correctly. Be wary of discounted procedures or cutting corners to avoid unfavorable results.

Trans men may notice the onset of male pattern baldness when starting testosterone. For some of us, this can be quite dramatic, and we may lose most of our hair very quickly. For others, it may happen after a number of years on testosterone. In general, the older we are when we start taking testosterone, the more likely we are to see balding more quickly, because we are closer to the normal age that other men start to go bald. Trans men have similar options to cis men for dealing with undesired scalp hair loss. Medications like finasteride or dutasteride can help to block the conversion of testosterone to dihydrotestosterone (DHT) in the hair follicles, and therefore decrease hair loss. Minoxidil (Rogaine) is also helpful for some of us. Acceptance can be key to dealing with hair loss. Many cisgender men experience scalp hair loss and find ways to cut their hair (or shave their heads) that make them feel attractive.

Makeup

Many trans women begin using makeup with transition. We may do this to enhance our feminine appearance or to play around with colors and shades. For some of us, this is a very new experience and can be daunting at first if we have not seen others apply makeup up close. This is the case for many cisgender women as well if they did not grow up in households where makeup was used and would like to start using it.

Trans community members often share makeup tips and even create video tutorials online. Mistakes we often make when first starting to use makeup include putting on too much or choosing bright colors, rather than those that match our skin, eyelashes, and lips.

Nonmedical Body Modification

There are many ways that we can change the presentation of our bodies to make them look more or less masculine or feminine without medical or surgical interventions.

We can modify the appearance of our chest and genitals by using a range of wearable accessories.

PACKING

Packing refers to putting things in the crotch of our pants to create the outward appearance of a penis and testicles. This look can be achieved in a variety of ways. A folded pair of socks or a condom filled with hair gel (or a similar substance), can create the profile we are looking for, and there are also products specifically made for this purpose. Packers or packeys are made out of silicone or other materials that simulate the look and feel of a nonerect penis and testicles. Packers can be worn with tight-fitting underwear, a jock strap, or a special harness made for them, which is different from a harness used to hold a dildo in place during sex ("strap on.")

The Web site Transguys publishes in-depth discussions of different types of packers, binders, and stand-to-pee devices.

There are two types of packing: hard packing and soft packing. Soft packing is meant to give the impression of flaccid genitals, and soft packers are typically not suitable for penetration. Hard packers, on the other hand, are erect and capable of penetration. We may choose hard packers for visual eroticism or if we intend to have sex later. There are a growing number of "dual-use" packers that offer both wearability and function.

To wash packers, many people just use soap and water. If a packer is used for sex, it should be cleaned appropriately according to what material it is made from. See Chapter 17 for more information on cleaning sex toys.

STAND-TO-PEE DEVICES

A stand-to-pee (STP) device is a tube with an upturned curved opening that can be placed against or underneath the urethra. Urinating into the opening directs fluid away from the body and out the other end of the STP device in front of us.

Some packers are designed, or can be modified, to allow the wearer to urinate through them while standing, and function as STPs. If you are choosing a packer that you wish to modify, look for an option that has a wide base through which a hole can be cut.

There are also many other, nonwearable STP options that can be used in settings where standing to pee, not visual presentation of a functional penis, is all that is desired. Many camping and outdoor supply stores—as well as vendors at many music festivals—sell STP devices that are easy to clean and carry. Some are disposable. STPs may be used by a variety of people for a number of reasons, such as dirty bathrooms, lack of privacy, or no available bathrooms.

It can take some practice to get the hang of using an STP device. Be sure to spend some time practicing at home before taking your new accessory out into the world, especially if you are planning to use it in a public men's room. Also consider how to transport and clean your device on the go if it is not part of a wearable packer.

TUCKING

Tucking is a practice that helps create a more feminine-appearing profile. This is most often done by curving the penis between the legs toward the anus, and pushing the testicles up into the inguinal canals, the cavities through which the testicles descend from the abdomen to the outside of the body. To find your inguinal canals, start with one side of your body. Take a finger and push your testicle aside while lifting the finger up toward your body. You should hit an area of skin where your finger can push into your body just slightly. That is the entrance to your inguinal canal on that side.

To share information on tucking, check out the Yahoo Group theartoftucking.

When tucking, once everything is in its tucked position, some of us use medical tape to keep things in place. Duct tape can cause skin reactions and irritation. Most of us choose to shave the area where tape is used, as this makes the tape stick better and makes

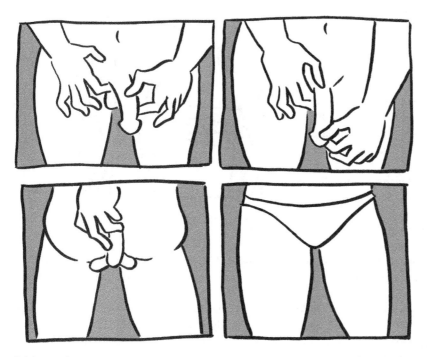

Tucking (kd diamond).

it more comfortable to remove the tape. Snug-fitting underwear adds an extra layer of security and creates a smoother profile. Special undergarments, known as gaffs and dance belts, can also be used to keep everything in place when tucking. Gaffs are specifically designed for this purpose, and more easily obtained online, while dance belts—designed to provide comfort and reduce the visibility of external genitalia for cisgender men—are available from many theater and dance shops.

NONSURGICAL BREAST ENHANCEMENT

By wearing a bra and stuffing the cups, many of us are able to create the appearance of larger breasts. Some of us use easily obtainable household materials such as socks or tissue, or fill water balloons with birdseed, hair gel, or similar materials. Padded bras are available at most stores that sell bras, and they can help provide a smoother shape under clothing. Breast forms, also called cutlets or jellies, are different materials molded into the shape of breasts. These are often used to fill out bras, but some are designed to be attached to the skin with adhesive and may be worn without a bra. Breast forms are available in costume, theatre, and dance supply shops, through online retailers, and at lingerie and underwear shops catering to cisgender women.

BINDING

Binding is a method of compressing breast tissue to achieve a flatter chest profile. Depending on the size of our chest, there are several options that we can use to achieve this. Athletic gear such as sports bras or compression shirts can often be effective. Some people use elastic bandages (commonly known as ACE bandages), although these can sometimes cut off circulation if they are too tight. While it is tempting to bind as tightly as possible to create as flat a chest as possible, it is important to make sure you can still comfortably breathe when binding to avoid health problems.

There are also special garments, called binders, made for both trans and cisgender men with unwanted breast tissue. These binders are very effective, even for those of us with large breasts. They can be purchased online and from some medical supply shops.

Because binders can be expensive, programs such as the Big Brothers Used Binder Program and In a Bind collect and then give away new and gently used binders.

BINDING

Hudson is the author of ftmguide.org, a comprehensive information site for trans men and their loved ones, established in 2004.

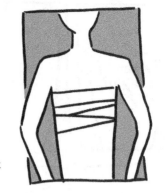

Binding (kd diamond).

The term "binding" refers to the process of flattening one's breast tissue in order to create a male-appearing chest. There is no "one-size-fits all" binding method because everyone is shaped differently, and we all have different levels of comfort with our bodies. Some trans guys don't bind at all. Some slump or hunch over to hide their chests (which can be very effective but can also cause posture problems over time). Some use different methods of layering clothing to help hide their chests. Some bind only on certain occasions; others bind all the time.

A few binding methods you might consider: layering of shirts; Neoprene waist/abdominal trimmers or back support devices; athletic compression shirts; chest binders/medical compression shirts; or new products designed specifically for FTM binding. Perhaps ironically, it can sometimes be helpful to know your bra and cup size when comparing notes with other trans men on binding solutions. For information about how to calculate this, see ftmguide.org.

Use caution and common sense when binding—if it hurts, cuts your skin, or prevents you from breathing, it is too tight. In the past, trans guys relied on do-it-yourself (DIY) binding solutions because there weren't any ready-made products available to suit the purpose. Some of these DIY binding methods (like wrapping yourself in Ace bandages or duct tape) are easily accessible, but they aren't very good for your body, and can even cause serious injury. If you can avoid it, don't use tape to bind, especially directly on your skin, as it may cut you, cause painful rashes, and pull off layers of skin and hair when removed. It also tends to be too rigid, making it difficult to breathe and move.

Buy the size binder that correlates to your physical measurements. Binders are already designed to be very tight when they fit properly—buying a size too small will be so tight that it may cause severe discomfort or injury. Give yourself a break from binding! The compression on your skin and body from a binder is a lot to take, so don't bind all day and all night. And when you begin binding, start with just a few hours at a time to let your body get used to it. If a binder's material doesn't breathe or wick away sweat, you can end up with sores or rashes on your skin. One way to minimize this risk is to apply a nonirritating body powder to your skin before binding. Another is to wear a thin undershirt beneath your binder that is made of fabric that wicks away sweat. Keep your binders clean.

You might find that the binder you choose tends to roll up in certain areas, particularly around the waist. If this is a problem for you, try sewing an extra length of fabric all the way around the bottom of the binder, and tuck that extra material snugly into your pants. If you find that you have areas of chafing or bulging around the armpit area, you might want to try trimming or otherwise altering that area with a needle and thread. You can often find inexpensive solutions, such as Spandex, Lycra, Velcro, and other materials at your local fabric store, using trial and error to make alterations that suit your specific frame. If you are not handy with a needle and thread, check your local community for a friendly tailor or costume maker who might be able to help you custom fit your binder, or even make a binder from scratch to fit you perfectly.

Finally, if a binder doesn't work well for you, consider donating it or selling it to another trans man who might have better luck with it.

FACIAL AND BODY HAIR REMOVAL

Facial hair removal can be one of the most difficult components of physical transition. A minority of transgender women have sparse facial hair. However, many of us desire some degree of hair removal. Facial hair will slow with estrogen treatment and testosterone blockade. For some it will be slow and thin enough that we are able to avoid extensive hair removal procedures and perhaps need to shave only every couple of days. Plenty of cisgender women have to deal with unwanted facial hair, and many cisgender women have to regularly shave. Like most things in transition, it is important to consider that all women face internal and external pressures on their bodies and physical appearances.

Most creams, depilatories, and other methods of facial hair removal designed for cisgender women will not work for transgender women. These products are designed to remove the "peach fuzz" (known as villous hair) on cisgender women's faces. Removing the thicker (terminal) hair on trans women's faces requires a different approach. Using a method designed for villous hair can even cause injury. Most trans women will either seek electrolysis, laser hair removal, or some combination of the two.

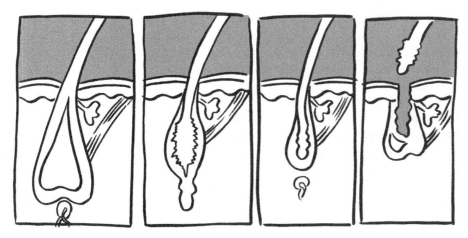

Electrolysis (kd diamond).

Electrolysis involves inserting a needle-shaped probe into the hair follicle and then using electricity or heat to permanently kill the hair root. The process is slow and painful, but it is permanent. Because of multiple follicles, individual hairs may require several passes until they are gone. We may need as little as 20 or as many as 200 hours of electrolysis to clear our face and be free of shaving. It is a good idea to ask a provider to prescribe an oral pain medicine containing a narcotic as well as a topical anesthetic cream when going through electrolysis. In some cases we may be able to find a hair removal facility where an on-site provider gives anesthetic injections into the face to numb certain areas before electrolysis is performed.

> *"I have done about 75 hours of facial electrolysis, resulting in the removal of about two-thirds of my beard. The cost so far is almost US$4,000."*

> *"I am currently doing electrolysis in the genital area to prepare for GRS. I am also doing electrolysis on my face to remove a few new dark hairs. I expect to spend $2,000 on electrolysis."*

Another option for removing facial hair is laser hair reduction. It has not been approved by the FDA as a method of permanent hair removal, but it does cause hair reduction. Laser therapy involves using a focused beam of high-energy light whose frequency is "tuned" to the color of the pigments in hair. Because of this, only the pigments receive the light and the surrounding skin and tissues are not affected. When the pigment receives this high-energy light, it rapidly heats and then explodes. Because the laser probe covers more area than an electrolysis probe (about one-half square inch), laser sessions are quicker than electrolysis. Laser can also bring about dramatic results, though there will be some regrowth within a few weeks and many people require ongoing maintenance treatments. Because laser is "tuned" to the colors of dark hairs, people with dark skin or light facial hair are not good laser candidates. Luckily, many people with blonde or red facial hair may not require facial hair removal if they do not mind shaving regularly because they will not develop a "shadow."

> *"Am most of the way through [laser] on my face, chest and stomach. Now have very little 5 o'clock shadow and don't need to cake myself in foundation to feel comfortable passing. Have currently had 7 or 8 sessions at NZ$600 per session. I expect to have another 2 to 3 sessions."*

> *"At my advanced age, most of the hair was too white to adequately kill off with a laser, so electrolysis was my only option. The results have generally been good, but I am still working on a few stubborn areas. The total cost has been several thousand dollars."*

Electrolysis and laser can both leave our face red and swollen, and sometimes there may be small areas of mild bleeding and crusting or scabs. Ice will help minimize these symptoms, as will tea tree oil applied liberally after the procedure. While laser can be done on someone who is clean-shaven, electrolysis requires a couple of days' worth of growth so that the tip of the hair can be grasped with forceps. As such, many of us go for electrolysis on Saturday so we can grow our hair for a day before it becomes noticeable, and then have a day for recovery before returning to work Monday morning.

When considering electrolysis or laser hair reduction, make sure to research who will be doing this work. You have only one face and one chance to do it properly. Home systems and excessive discounts should raise suspicion. Proper laser removal centers include a physician medical director who oversees care, and they typically hire registered nurses to operate the equipment. A growing number of LGBTQ health and social centers are beginning to offer such services at a reduced cost. For example, the Mazzoni Center in Philadelphia, Pennsylvania, offers laser hair removal. Primary care providers may also have resources for inexpensive, local trans-friendly hair removal specialists.

PRIVACY

At some point during our transition, many of us begin to desire more privacy around our gender identity, history, or transition. Many of us have an experience of feeling like we have spent so much time focusing on our gender that it has, in some way, taken over our lives. Sometimes we feel tired or bored of talking about gender, or we discover that it is no longer as important to highlight as it had once been. Some of us also shift from feeling like it is important to talk about or disclose our trans identity, status, or experience to feeling like it is not important to highlight. Privacy for some people may include passing or living stealth, while for others it may mean being out in certain contexts and not others.

Being Read Correctly

Most of us would like to be seen in a way that is congruent with our internal identity. This is sometimes called "passing," being "read the right way," or not being "clocked." Many trans people take issue with the concept of "passing," because it puts the onus on the trans person to prove their legitimacy (Bergman, 2009). Some of us are not read correctly on a consistent basis and wish we were. Others of us take pleasure in looking a little different.

> "By nature, I can't pass. There's nothing to pass as. So I just dress outrageously and attempt to look as androgynous as possible. My hair is short, my clothes are a punk rock mess, but I'm short and small and my face is feminine, so I'm consistently read as female."

> "I'm not transitioning to another gender, but rather embracing a queered gender identity that defies categories. I am lucky that I have an uncommon name which doesn't carry a clear gender identity with it, and depending on which culture it is located in, can denote different genders. I've not changed that name, but rather happily embraced its ambiguity. In fact, I've often wondered how much my name is connected to my gender dysphoria. I certainly hope it is connected, as it is a great name and I much like where I am with my own identity."

Many of us go through some combination of social, medical, and surgical transitions, changing the way we look, how we behave, and how we interact with others. When we are read correctly, it can make life much easier. Being read correctly is not necessarily the same thing as being stealth. Those of us who are read correctly may be open with many people about our transition history, but we have the option not to talk about it until it comes up naturally, over the course of a conversation or friendship.

Living Stealth

"Stealth" is a common term used to describe the experience of living privately post-transition. Some of us prefer the word "private," feeling that "stealth" has a quality of sneaking around, or getting away with doing something wrong.

The decision to live privately as a trans person is different for each of us. For most of us, every use of the right pronoun and name is an affirmation of our identity. If we choose not to tell people how we got there, that does not necessarily mean we are ashamed of being trans. It may simply mean that we are living our lives the way we have chosen.

"I no longer feel the need to tell everyone about my past. If they figure it out, I really don't care, but I'm more concerned with the present."

For some of us, living stealth may be motivated by the desire for privacy, job or family security, or physical safety. It may be an opportunity to recharge our batteries and live without needing to constantly explain ourselves. Many of us get tired of giving the same answers to the same questions, over and over, as time goes by.

Others of us reach the opposite conclusion, wanting to help bridge the gulf of understanding. Mainstream cultural beliefs about "transness" are so far off the mark that some of us want to be out and visible everywhere we go, to put a face on what "trans" does and does not mean.

"I'm through with addressing the subject in subtle, hushed tones. Give me a damn megaphone and a soapbox, and I'll parade through the streets screaming it."

Some of us want to be out, while others desire privacy. Those of us who were activists at the beginning of our transitions may desire more privacy over time. Some of us who desire privacy find that over time we want to focus on activism again. We may come to realize that we just needed a "breather," to regain our peace of mind and inner resources after spending so much energy on our early transition processes. Many of us donate our time or money to community organizations and choose not to use our own workplace or personal life as an arena for trans activism.

THE SHOWER

Nyah Harwood is a queer trans woman. She lives in Cairns, Australia. She is currently engaged in her honors year in cultural studies at Southern Cross University. Her research examines the biopolitics of administrative classifications of sex and gender in Australia. Her interests are strongly focused on critical trans politics and trans feminism, as well as antioppression, harm reduction, and sex work politics.

My housemates don't know that I am trans. At least, I haven't "come out" to them. I make a point of raising my voice just that little bit higher when I'm talking to them. I walk around the house with my chest poked just that little bit further out. I hold my head up high, but low enough to hide my Adam's apple. As much as I pride myself on gender fucking and confusing people, I am constrained by my need to protect myself.

I am standing naked in the bathroom of my house, waiting for the shower to warm up. The doorknob turns, and the door opens. I realize I forgot to lock the door. I can see my housemate standing in the doorway and she can see me. I don't think anything of it at first, but then, suddenly, internalized cissexism kick-starts my shame and I realize once again not just that I am naked but also what my body *means*. In this moment, as all around the world gender wreaks violent havoc on unknowing, unwilling bodies, my trans body materializes that violence in my bathroom for my housemate to see. "Welcome to the world of nonnormative gender!"

I am situated in a space between knowing and feeling—I feel shame, though I know I shouldn't. It's a familiar feeling, once again— the tensing of my muscles, the flushing of my face, the nervousness. I panic. As if through instinct, my arms tense and my hands move together down toward my crotch to hide my penis, leaving only my estrogenated breasts visible. That's right, I remember now: I am a liability.

My housemate and I say an awkward "oops." The door shuts as quickly as it was opened, and we go back to our business. But I can't simply return. I feel illegitimate. I want to explain myself to others. To warn them even: "My body is a fucking weapon." I keep telling myself how fucking transgressive I am; but a moment later I am crying from the shame I feel. I am the embodiment of a constant tension between legitimacy and illegitimacy, invisibility and transgression, and the potential ridicule, violence, or death that comes with being "seen," or not being seen at all.

Challenges to Keeping Our Privacy

There are practical reasons that living completely privately may not be a realistic goal. The power of the Internet, coupled with post-9/11 security laws, makes it impossible to live with certainty that our old legal identity is permanently inaccessible to others.

Even for those of us who are long into a physical transition and living privately, events such as looking for a new job can lead others to discover our gender histories. A background check, listing references on a resume, listing schools we attended—any of these may lead a prospective employer to our old identity. We can ask references to respect our transition and use our new name and preferred pronoun, choosing to drop from our resume those who refuse or are unreliable, and we may be able to get our school transcripts changed to reflect our new identity. However, none of these strategies is foolproof.

When someone misreads our gender, or identifies us as trans, it can be easy to beat ourselves up, thinking that we should be better at being who we are, or to feel anxious about what that misreading means. Knowing where those judgments are coming from and balancing what it takes to feel good while avoiding putting too much pressure on ourselves can be tricky. It is easy to set up an unattainable goal of passing all of the time.

Online Privacy

It can be challenging to completely eliminate our online presence. Any information about our past that appears online—from news stories that identify us as a particular gender to public records of our name changes to blog posts and social media sites—is archived somewhere and may be accessible to others. Our digital footprints are increasingly difficult to erase, and the dense connections between friends, family, and colleagues online can blur the boundaries between these groups, providing opportunities for accidental disclosure to those we would prefer not to tell. There are a few things we can do to secure our online privacy as much as possible:

- *Consider using a pseudonym, nickname, or other unofficial name online.* While those who know us in real life may have access to these sites, this will ensure that we are not "searchable" by potential employers, colleagues, or college admission officers with whom we do not choose to share this information. There are many examples of successful individuals who have built strong online communities, brands, and careers using a name that is not their own. However, be aware that once you have built a community or presence with a pseudonym, it is possible that it may be difficult to reconcile this with your real name later on. For example, some important contacts may not recognize your real name.
- *Understand and use the privacy settings on social networks.* Most social networks allow us to restrict access to our accounts, entirely, to the general public, or to specific groups of people who can see certain types of information. Know what you are sharing, who can see it, and consider the potential risks if all of the information were to become public. Once information is put online, it can be easily shared with others, either intentionally or accidentally.
- *Monitor your online reputation.* Conduct online searches for your name(s) on a regular basis. It is unlikely that you will be able to have everyone remove information you do not like, but knowing what is out there can be helpful in knowing how to discuss the information with others who are likely to look you up.

As trans people, we take many different approaches to privacy in our lives. Some of us live completely stealth, while others of us are open as much as possible about our identities. Most of us fall somewhere in between. Whether we choose to live more private or more open lives, we all struggle with making sure that we have as much control as possible over how we do this.

Transitioning as a Public Process

The people we see on the street every day and at work and school are going to notice over time if we begin living in a new gender role. For those of us who choose to transition to live full-time in a new gender, our transition becomes a public process unless we leave everything we know behind.

Many of us who physically transition desire privacy but are remaining in the same communities. This can lead to a longing to just "be," to find groups and spaces where the transition is not an automatic focus.

> *"So many people already know that I think most people that I meet are likely to find out rather quickly. It has made me long for a masculine space where no one knows. A separate group of guy friends I can be stealth with."*

People are going to have different reactions to our transition. Some may be confused or even hostile, while others may be accepting but afraid to bring it up. We may try out living in our new gender by dressing in it at first only when going on trips out of town or to places where we are not known.

Most of us go through gradual changes and live in a gray area for some time, where sometimes we are recognized in our affirmed gender and sometimes we are not. If we remain in our communities, we often have to deal with them knowing our past. However, we also have the benefit of being near people who (hopefully) love, support, and nurture us.

LEARNING NEW GENDER RULES

One area of transitioning that can be particularly bewildering for many of us is dealing with the new stereotypes and expectations that come with living in our affirmed gender. Some of us welcome the changes. However, these changes can also be confusing and surprising. Acting the same way we have always acted may be read very differently now than it was when we were living as our birth-assigned gender.

Some arenas in which we may run into gendered expectations include social situations with colleagues or friend groups and dating situations. Rules govern how men and women interact in public spaces. Some are more obvious, such as rules about holding doors and shaking hands. Others are more subtle. Men are typically expected to be more aggressive and women less so. It is easier for women to come off as pushy than it is for men. Women are expected to smile more. Women can generally smile at or wave at young children, while men may be suspect for this behavior.

Groups of men and groups of women may act differently when they are alone. We are sometimes surprised or shocked to find out what happens in groups that we had not been a part of until now.

> *"Man talk was a very strange discovery. Men do not talk the same way if there are any female people in the room, but as soon as women leave the room there is a strange shift in the tone, the body language, the subject of conversation."*

> *"Men act different when they are in a group without women around. Men also tend to 'give each other a hard time' and it is seen as affection. I had to learn to not take verbal jokes to me so seriously and instead of getting my feelings hurt just make sure I laughed it off and had a good comeback."*

> *"It's been a lot easier than I thought making friends with other women and being more socially active with them."*

"I attended a Men's only recovery group and I was amazed at how much these men talked about their feelings. They also talked about feeling oppressed by society by being told they had to be a good provider financially, be good with tools, and that they should not show fear. Outside of that very emotional group they went right back to 'being guys.' Talking about cars, women, hunting, etc."

There are often things people expect us to know by virtue of being a man or a woman.

"When I was female, and throughout the gray area, I always had friends cut my hair, because if I went somewhere and got it cut it was always too girly. I went to a barbershop as a guy for the first time a few months ago and they asked me, 'How do you usually tell the barber to cut it?' I had no idea. I didn't even know the kind of language I was supposed to use, and I felt even more awkward because I knew that most men have this as part of their cultural knowledge from very early on."

"As a single mother, nothing I did was ever good enough and I was treated like shit for having bred at such a young age. As a single dad, I'm a hero and it's so awesome that I'm there for the kid."

"It is often frustrating being pigeon-holed and misunderstood because everyone in our culture expects certain traits from women that I am hard-pressed to exhibit. I realize this speaks more to culture than to my transgenderedness but still, it constrains. Perhaps it is more of a plain feminist issue."

"Being seen socially as male is strange occasionally because I am now viewed as an automatic expert in certain areas based on my age and gender, and all of a sudden no longer an assumed expert in matching colors of rooms to curtains or advising about fashion. Yet somehow in all this gender changing I kept my knowledge of proper color combinations and cooking and didn't get the manual on cars, electronics, small appliances, and plumbing. Is there someone I can trade with? Someone out there who desperately wants the book on cooking and fashion and can trade for the car/electronics/repair manual I seem to have lost?"

The way we flirt with others and they flirt with us may change.

"The unforeseen was to have men open doors for me or stare at my breasts while talking to me. That took a little to get used to."

Our sexuality is sometimes perceived differently by others depending on our gender presentation. Trans men are often perceived as gay because they may have more stereotypically feminine hand gestures or vocal inflections.

"Social interactions as a guy are strange. Generally I think I am accepted as a gay guy within straight male spaces—straight bars, bathrooms, etc.—which is fine with me and makes being different a little easier."

The existence of stereotypical gender roles does not mean that we need to fulfill all those expectations. In fact, very few people do. As trans people, we have many different ideas about gender roles, how we want to be treated as gendered beings, and what gender justice looks like to us. Identify for yourself your sense of what people are projecting onto you about your gender and how they expect you to act because of it. Evaluate your values and ethics around gender equality and try on different ways of being in your new gender. Figure out how to be your best self in your gender and how to be yourself in a way that is in line with your values and visions for how the world should treat people of all genders. Find other people who are wrestling with similar questions, challenge expectations of your gender that you do not accept, and celebrate the aspects of your gender presentation and experience that you love most.

Colby Lenz, a volunteer organizer for the California Coalition for Women Prisoners (CCWP), provides an introduction to incarceration in trans communities.

Colby (second from the right, holding microphone).

Who is in prison? People whose genders do not conform to fixed gender categories are targeted by police and state violence and overly represented in jails, prisons, detention centers, mental health lock-ups, and all kinds of youth lock-ups. I use the term "lock-ups" here to describe this range of systems that cage people.

Why are so many transgender and gender-variant people locked up? Transgender, gender-variant, and intersex people, especially poor people and people of color, face discrimination from early on in life and have significantly decreased chances of avoiding cycles of poverty and incarceration. Facing discrimination, transgender people are pushed out of legal economies. In the United States, criminal punishment systems masquerade as solutions to violence, poverty, addiction, and illness but only add violence, addiction, poverty, and illness. Many gender nonconforming youth are pushed onto the streets or into out-of-home care or youth lock-ups because of discrimination, violence, and a lack of family support.

What is the impact on people's lives inside and outside of these lock-ups? Transgender and gender-variant people trying to survive in lock-ups face increased violence and severe neglect. Because most of these systems are sex segregated, transgender people whose genders don't match their birth sex are often denied access to services or do get access—only to face more harassment and violence. Transgender and gender-variant people in lock-ups face more time in segregation, whether by outright discrimination or as a violent form of "protection." Transgender people in lock-ups face early illness and death because they lack access to health care or are outright denied health care. People in lock-ups continue to fight for access to hormones and other transgender health care needs. People struggle for access to clothes that fit their gender and permission to wear them (i.e., boxers, bras). Transgender people are also made more vulnerable to harm and death because of the lack of protection from violence in lock-ups, including sexual violence. Official protections do little to increase safety for transgender people since guards often commit or instigate the violence.

How can we fight against lock-ups? For those living outside of lock-ups, we see our community members constantly ripped away from our communities. Because transgender people are so heavily policed and incarcerated, organizing against this policing and incarceration is all the more complicated. Despite these challenges (and many more), our communities continue to rise and survive! We don't need more cages; we need real resources and opportunities—to heal and to thrive, and to build power together to end poverty, violence, and all kinds of incarceration. For examples of organizations led by people who have survived time locked-up and fighting for collective liberation, see the Transgender Gender Variant Intersex Justice Project (TGIJP), the Sylvia Rivera Law Project (SRLP), Black & Pink, CCWP, and BreakOUT!

WHEN OUR IDENTITIES CHANGE

Not all trans identities are static. Some are, of course—when some of us transition, that is it: We settle into our gender identity, and it remains fairly stable throughout our lives. For many people, though, gender is more of a constant, evolving identity. We might find that, even after what we thought was a "complete" transition, there are parts of our identity that are still shifting. Perhaps these are small things—changes in the range of appearance, style, or activities we feel comfortable embracing as part of our gender expression. Or perhaps they are larger, more substantive changes in our gender identity itself. If you find your gender identity shifting, allow yourself the space and freedom you need to try to understand your evolving gender identity.

When gender identities shift after an initial transition, many of us begin to question why we feel the way we do. We may echo the negative feedback we have received from others, asking ourselves whether others were right all along, or whether we are just confused. However, there is no limit on the number of times we are allowed to reevaluate our identities, rethink how we would like to be perceived, or reinvent ourselves.

It may also be the case that our particular gender identity just shifts over time. This is OK. Recognizing these shifts and nuances will help us to more authentically be ourselves.

It can be helpful to look at other people in our lives to see how their gender identities or presentations change over time. Many cisgender people shift their gender presentation over time—it is a normal part of growing into being who we are. Remember that gender is only one piece of our whole selves—our community, our economic situation, our relationships, and our family can also play a role in shaping the range of identities, opportunities, and expressions we choose.

People who transition multiple times might use different words to describe their experiences. Some might identify as transgender, gender-variant, or gender nonconforming. Others will not. Some of us use words like "detransition," "peel," "retransition," or "transition again" to describe our experiences.

If you are a person who has transitioned and are now having new and complicated questions and thoughts about your gender identity, try to find a supportive person in your community who can help you work through these questions.

If you have someone in your life who is facing these questions, find ways to support and understand them. Sometimes people want to ask us questions about our medical status, like "Do you regret going on hormones or having surgery?" Trans people have many different identities, needs, experiences, and body configurations. A change in our gender identity or expression does not necessarily mean we are unhappy with the changes we have made so far. Regret is not the only (or even the main) reason we may continue to question or change our identity after transitioning.

The yahoo group No Going Back provides support to those of us who transition multiple times.

INTERVIEW WITH KRYS SHELLEY

Krys Shelley is 30 years old and lives in Los Angeles, California.

Colby Lenz: What was your experience in a women's prison as someone who doesn't fit gender stereotypes?

Krys Shelley: Well, the first thing they do when you get to prison is strip search you and force you to wear a dress that's like a gown your grandma might wear. I found that so humiliating and discriminating. You have to get naked and then wear that dress for hours. Then later, if your room got seriously searched, even if you weren't the main focus, they forced you back into a dress and cuffed you. And if you weren't in compliance by wearing that dress, they would attack you more. Even if you meant no disrespect, you were just so uncomfortable.

We were fighting to change this before I left Valley State Prison for Women, but the fight ended when they crowded everyone from that prison into the women's prison across the street. They would

Krys (front center, holding banner) leading the march.

also make us wear women's underwear and cone bras. We were fighting to be able to wear boxers and sports bras, because they don't accommodate people who are different, only who they decide a "woman" is or should be.

Colby: How did the guards and other staff in prison treat you?

Krys: I definitely faced more discrimination because I look different. I was seen as a man and so they treated me like a man in terms of how aggressive they were. Basically the guards would get away with whatever they could, like saying something stupid about my gender to try to get me to react. The harassment I faced was more verbal than physical, but it did get physical more than once. The guards attacked me because they read me as aggressive because I look masculine, and I think they were threatened by me. They messed with me because of the way I dress, my physical appearance, because of the way I choose to be. Just like the real world, they mess with you out there and in prison; it's just more intense in there because they can legally do it.

Colby: How did you and other gender nonconforming people you know support each other in prison?

Krys: People definitely organized and supported each other, but of course we weren't always united. One thing we did was file complaints about harassment. We tried to file those as class actions, but the prison system changed the policy to block us from doing this. We also had a Two-Spirit Circle for people with nonconforming gender or people who identified as male or having a lot of masculinity. We would get together and talk about problems we were having. People were equal in the circle but one person organized and united us. We all respected each other and talked with each other and not at each other. It helped us survive in there.

SELF-CARE AND SELF-EFFICACY

As we struggle to keep up in our daily lives, it is easy to forget to take care of ourselves. This is an important part of life, and during a transition, it can be particularly vital to make a habit of practicing good self-care. Even in the best of circumstances, a transition means a lot of upheaval and change in our lives. Remember to spend time doing things that make you feel good, and that are good for you. See Chapters 5 and 14 for more information on self-care.

The flip side of self-care is self-efficacy. This term means remembering that we are able to affect the world around us. It can be easy for some of us to develop a sense of victimhood or carrying a burden that we did not ask for. The world can be a hard place for us to navigate, and while self-focused habits and routines are an important part of a healthy life, it can be incredibly powerful to take control of other parts of our lives as well. We can make good things happen, for ourselves and others.

Nurturing Our Interests and Passions

As trans people, we often spend much of our time, especially while actively transitioning, thinking about transition and focusing on gender. However, we all have other parts of ourselves that are not directly related to our gender identity or experience.

Some communities we are involved in include artistic communities such as visual art, dance, music, performance art, DJ-ing, and filmmaking; political and activist communities that pursue social change; cultural communities based on our cultural experiences; professional associations and networks; and activity groups, like reading or knitting groups. We may be interested in assisting with our local senatorial race campaign, doing HIV and STI prevention work in our community, or joining an area coalition of feminists who support women's rights. We may be interested in silent films, spoken word, or our local music scene. Whatever our interests are, nurturing them can offer potential for meeting caring and supportive people.

> "My community life is not as rich as it has been at other times in my life, because I'm a middle-aged college professor with two kids, one a babe in arms, and I don't get out at night as much as I would like. Still I have a number of sustaining friendships that fill a community function for me. Many of these have academic origins, oddly—people I've met through queer theoretical networks, or at my local LGBT historical society. And many of these people are busy middle-aged professionals like me. When I see them, it's at work-related events more often than not, and the rest of the time my contact with them is online or on the phone. Earlier in my life I was a very active member of an SM/leather community in San Francisco that overlapped with a genderqueer/trans community. That scene was very different! It couldn't have been more embodied and fleshy—it was fabulous, challenging, scintillating with the excitement of self-creation and the joy of discovering expansive possibilities."

For some people, being out as transgender or gender nonconforming is essential to their participation in other communities, while for others, their trans status may not feel connected or relevant. There is no "right" way to be trans, and there are no rules about whether, or how, to disclose our gender identity. Making the decision that is right for us in building the types of relationships we want to build is most important.

Finding Trans Community

The past decade has seen an explosion in the number and variety of resources that are available for trans people in the United States, both regionally and nationally. While it is certainly true that our access to other trans people varies widely based on where we live—it might be a few stops on the train or hundreds of miles by bus or car—there are more options out there than there have ever been for connecting with other trans people.

Eli Conley (copyright Portraits to the People).

The Transgender Housing Network (transhousingnet-work.com) is a temporary housing network intended to connect trans people in need with safe and supportive places to crash.

Trans groups in the Midwest include the Bloomington TG Group, Central Illinois Gender Society, City of the Lakes Crossgender Community, FORGE, Genderqueer Chicago, Genderwork Chicago, Illinois Gender Advocates, K-Step, Midwest Trans* & Queer Wellness Initiative, Minnesota Transgender Health Coalition, Sienna—Louisville Transgender Social Outreach & Support, Southern Illinois Transgender, St. Louis Transgender, The Twofold Group, TransCollaborations, Transgender Michigan, and TransOhio.

Trans social groups offer support in transition and in the day-to-day issues that come up as a trans person. They may also give us a chance to engage in activism to address transphobia and advocacy to get the kinds of care and resources that we need. Support groups may allow us to channel our creativity through balls, parties, pageants, and art shows. Finding a group that fits our particular needs may take a little time, but it can also be a rewarding experience that helps us build a community that includes people with shared experiences. Some people find this to be an indispensable part of their trans experience, while it is less meaningful to others. As with everything else, it is important to spend time figuring out what types of social support we need so that we are more able to find the best resources.

Trans groups and organizations take many forms. Some are gender-specific (trans women, trans men, gender-variant/genderqueer people); some are for specific identities or experiences (trans people of color, Two-Spirit people, trans people with disabilities,

Trans Bodies, Trans Selves Seattle Forum (photo by Ish Ishmael).

Friends (copyright Portraits to the People).

Some NorthEast trans groups are the Audre Lorde Project, Compass, Connecticut TransAdvocacy, DC Area Transmasculine Society, Delaware Renaissance, Gender Identity Project at the NYC LGBT Center, Innvestments Cape Cod, Metro Area Gender Identity Connection, Maine TransNet, Massachussettes Transgender Political Coalition, New Jersey Support Group, North East Two Spirit Society, Northeast Trans Women's Alliance, Pittsburgh Transsexual Support Group, Spectrum Transgender Group of Western New York, Trans Maryland, TransCentral PA, TransGender Education Association of Greater Washington, D.C., Transgender, Gender-variant, and Intersex (TGI) Network of Rhode Island, and TransPitt.

trans parents); and some are a mix of everything. There are also many groups specifically for young people, such as Queer Youth Seattle, the Transgender Youth Drop-In Center (Chicago), and the Attic Youth Center (Philadelphia). There are online support groups, like Laura's place; local and regional groups, like Tri-Ess chapters around the United States, TransGuyzPDX in Portland, Oregon, TransJustice at the Audre Lorde Project in New York City, Trans & Friends Transitionz by Feminist Outlawz in Atlanta, Georgia; state-wide organizing groups, like the Connecticut Trans Advocacy Coalition; national groups like the National Center for Transgender Equality; and annual events and conferences, like Gender Odyssey in Seattle and the Philadelphia Trans Health Conference.

There are also many groups and organizations that serve specific communities within the larger trans community. Groups like the Transgender Justice in Prison Group and Hearts on a Wire provide support for trans people who are currently or formerly incarcerated, through letter-writing, advocacy, and policy work. Organizations like Southerners on New Ground (SONG) in the South and GenderJustice in Los Angeles offer space for multiissue community organizing. Many HIV/AIDS service organizations throughout the country have specific programs for transgender and gender nonconforming people that address HIV prevention, as well as related social and political issues.

Finding a group that is right for you might take a couple of tries. Perhaps the discussion is not quite what you thought it would be, or the other participants are not exactly who you were anticipating. Challenging yourself to continue to put yourself out there can be a rewarding experience. If the group you attend is simply not right for you, ask someone there if they have other ideas of places to go in your area. Try not to be discouraged if your first visits are not exactly what you are looking for—relationships can take some time to build. Meeting just one person you connect with is a huge success, because it will give you a place to grow from. You might find that your supportive community comes out of that one connection.

"I've found it's really hard to form a cohesive transgender community from nothing. If these things don't coalesce on their own, they tend to fall victim to infighting and anger, possibly because trans phenomena cut across so many other identities and intersect with so many privileges and marginalizations. That said, I find the trans and genderqueer people with whom I am acquainted to be wonderful folks. They're fun to hang around with and talk

Southern trans groups include Alabama Gender Alliance, Arkansas Transgender Support, Atlanta Gender Explorations, Carolina Transgender Society, Coalition for Transgender Rights in Virginia, James River Transgender Society, Louisiana Trans Advocates, Mississippi Transgender Alliance, North Carolina Transgender Unity, Northwest Arkansas Transgender, Palmetto Transgender Association, Someone Cares of Atlanta, Southern Association for Gender Education, Southerners on New Ground (SONG), TEA TIME (Transpeople Empowerment in Action) at AIDS Action in Baltimore, Tennessee Transgender Political Coalition, The Tennessee Vals, T-House Florida, Trans*Action Florida, Transgender Center of Houston, Transgender Education Network of Texas, TransGeorgia, and the Virginia Transgender Resource and Referral List.

In the West, check out trans groups like Gender Alliance of the South Sound, Gender Identity Center of Colorado, GenderJustice LA, Identity LGBT Center of Alaska, Inland Northwest LGBT Center, Kulia Na Mamo, Montana Gender Alliance, Northwest Gender Alliance, Southern Arizona Gender Alliance, TEA: Transgender Education Advocates of Utah, Transgender Resource Center of New Mexico, Transgender San Francisco, and TransOregon.

CenterLink is an online directory of LGBTQ Community Centers that can help you locate the Center nearest to you.

to and don't generally freak out when I get radically counter-cultural in the middle of a McDonald's. Of course, there's the issue: The people with whom I am acquainted are not the only trans people out there, and often a specific trans-centered support group draws in an older crowd with a different view of trans issues informed by the communities of the '70s and '80s. That view is often incompatible with the views of trans people who came to understand themselves in a post-queer-revolution world."

Online social networks like Facebook, Tumblr, and Twitter offer trans people a wide range of opportunities to connect with one another. Email lists and Yahoo/Google groups similarly offer various ways for trans people connect with one another and share resources and personal stories. For example, the Dina List is an email list made up of Orthodox Jewish transgender people.

Online resource lists are useful first steps in finding current groups in our city, state, or region. One word about online resource lists is that the Web sites they are found on are not always kept up to date, and there is not currently one comprehensive list of all trans support resources available in the United States.

All About Trans members with BBC Executives at the London Aquarium. All About Trans is a project in the United Kingdom that brings media professionals and trans people together in informal settings, building relationships and leading toward better understanding and representation.

Sports

Sports and athletics are often an important part of our lives. They can have a hugely positive effect on us, including the health and mental health benefits of exercise; providing social community among our teammates, competitors, and fans; developing leadership and collaboration skills through teamwork; and giving us opportunities to build skills through practice, hard work, and perseverance. Because of these broad benefits, the growth of opportunities for cisgender women to participate in sports has been linked to their growing achievements in the workplace and society, in general. As trans people become a more visible and vocal part of communities, we are asserting our right to access sports as well.

Activism on this issue has been led by a coalition of gay, lesbian, and trans organizations, as well as by women's athletic groups, who have experience helping create opportunities for female-assigned individuals within male-dominated athletics.

INCLUSION POLICIES

Many sports teams and organizations are beginning to develop policies around the inclusion of trans athletes. These policies vary widely, based on context, age of participants, and other factors.

Many of these policies focus on testosterone and the perceived advantages it confers on athletes. Testosterone has been used by cisgender athletes to enhance performance. Concerns about the long-term effects of testosterone on physical development are often used to limit the ability of male-assigned trans individuals to participate in women's athletics. Typically, participation in women's athletics requires antiandrogen treatments. Concerns about female-assigned individuals using testosterone revolve around its possible use as a performance-enhancing drug. As a result, many inclusion policies incorporate guidelines for hormone use.

INTERNATIONAL SPORTS

The International Olympic Committee is the most recognizable international sports body in the world. Its Medical Commission developed guidelines in 2003 to allow trans people who have undergone physical gender transition to compete in the Olympic Games under the following conditions:

1. They must have undergone gender reassignment surgery.
2. They must have legal recognition of their gender by their country of citizenship.
3. They must have at least two years of hormone therapy administered by medical personnel prior to competition.

Athletes are tested only if someone calls their gender into question, and the specific results of the test are kept confidential, beyond a confirmation or rejection of the athlete's ability to participate. These guidelines came into full effect at the 2004 Olympic Games and are known as the "Stockholm Consensus."

The Stockholm Consensus is a controversial method for determining inclusion, as it excludes individuals who have not undergone surgical transition, which many of us do not require or desire. It also sets the bar for hormone therapy higher than some guidelines that have been adopted by other athletic organizations.

COLLEGE ATHLETICS

The National Collegiate Athletic Association (NCAA) adopted a policy for inclusion of transgender student-athletes in 2011. The policy states:

- A trans male student-athlete who has received a medical exception for treatment with testosterone for gender transition may compete on a men's team but is no longer eligible to compete on a women's team without changing the team status to a mixed team. A mixed team is eligible only for men's championships.
- A trans female student-athlete being treated with testosterone suppression medication for gender transition may continue to compete on a men's team but may not compete on a women's team without changing it to a mixed team status until completing one calendar year of documented testosterone-suppression treatment.

Individual schools have also adopted their own policies. For example, Eastern Kentucky University adopted an inclusion policy that follows the guidelines laid out by the IOC's Stockholm Consensus—a policy many people find imperfect. However, the policy also stipulates that name and pronoun choices are to be respected, regardless of what gender the athlete competes in; that gender identity should be considered when making locker room and hotel room assignments; and that team dress code policies should be gender-neutral.

Transgender conferences are exciting ways to meet other people and talk about issues important to our communities. See if you can attend one of these: Black Transmen Advocacy Conference, Butch Voices, Be-All, Circles Transgender Conference & Retreat, Colorado Gold Rush, Creating Change, Diva Las Vegas, Empire Conference, Espirit, Fantasia Fair, Femme Conference, First Event Boston, Gender Odyssey, Gender Spectrum Family Conference, Just You Week, NOLOSE, Philadelphia Trans Health, Southern Comfort Conference, Texas Transgender Nondiscrimination Summit, The Keystone Conference, Trans Ohio Transgender & Ally Symposium, Trans Youth Summit, Transcending Boundaries, Transgender Leadership Summit, Transgender Lives: The Intersection of Health & Law, Transgender Religious Leaders Summit, Translating Identity Conference.

Michelle Dumaresq from Vancouver, Canada, is a trans downhill mountain bike competitor who became licensed to compete in the Professional Women's category of her sport in 2002 after winning her first race as a beginner the previous year. Despite some negative reaction from some of her competitors early in her career, she was allowed to keep competing by the licensing body of her sport. She quickly won the Canada Cup and later qualified for the Canadian National Downhill Women's Team, attracting sponsors like Santa Cruz Bicycles.

The traditionally hypermasculine Australian surfing scene was recently hit with a wave of media attention regarding Westerly Windina, formerly known as junior surfing champion Peter Drouyn. Windina, who went on to become a lawyer in addition to a legendary surfer, was one of the individuals involved in founding the competitive surfing world of today, establishing a well-known tournament called the Stubbies Classic and a style of competition known as "man on man."

Keelin Godsey is an open trans man who attempted to qualify for competition in the Olympics as a member of the Women's Track and Field Team in 2012. He decided not to pursue hormone treatment for the sake of competition on the collegiate and international level. While he placed fifth at the qualifying trials and ultimately did not make the Olympic team, he enjoyed a record-breaking collegiate career and became a 16-time All-American athlete. His story of struggling to compete as an open trans man landed in national headlines, including an article in Sports Illustrated (www.gophertrackshots.com).

GAY AND LESBIAN ATHLETICS

Gay and lesbian communities often intersect with recreational sports teams, and many national and international organizations have formed to allow gay- and lesbian-focused teams to compete in organized competitions. Many of these organizations have adopted policies regarding the participation of trans athletes. For example, the Federation of Gay Games states that the gender in which an athlete competes will be dictated by their legal documents. If our legal documents do not match our affirmed gender, we may provide proof that we have been living as our affirmed gender for at least two years, such as a letter from a medical doctor stating that we have been undergoing hormone treatment. However, these policies continue to evolve, and they vary widely among different organizations.

TRANS-SPORTING OURSELVES

Christopher Henry Hinesley, EdD, is an instructor in the women's and gender studies program and coordinates operations in the GLBT Center at the Rochester Institute of Technology in Rochester, New York. He is also a guest instructor in the Wilson School of Education executive leadership doctoral program at St. John Fisher College.

As an athlete, it is hard to imagine life without sports. But as a trans man, it has been a surprising challenge to reimagine sports during and after transition. Even with a gym across from my office, it has felt a great distance from me. It's not the inconvenience of foul smells or inappropriate behavior in the men's locker room that I am concerned with. I need a private or curtained shower for safety and privacy reasons. What I have noticed while using the locker room is that most guys are self-conscious, and that they are unconsciously performing for other guys. The locker room is the tip of the spear of masculinity, as far as I can tell.

The years I spent in women's locker rooms were not comfortable either, but I never felt afraid. The smells and behaviors on that side of the court were an inconvenience, but the feeling that I should not be there was constant. Keeping my head down or eyes away from the bodies was easy enough. Tuning out the personal, for-women's-ears-only conversations was more difficult.

Competing in basketball as a woman, with men, presented an unwanted challenge to them. Many women have written about the frustrating mix of competition and caretaking that goes on when women compete against men. You want them to do their best. You want them to continue to compete with you. But you have to be aware that they are on the edge of losing it if and when you beat them. All things considered, they are faster, stronger, and bigger because they have higher levels of testosterone in their bodies. If, as a woman on the basketball court, I was keeping up with and sometimes beating my male counterpart, it was satisfying. It was also risky. Regardless of the hours spent grinding it out in the weight room, I broke my arm blocking a pass thrown by a man, felt the length of my spine crack taking hits from men, and did not have the body strength or size to take a charge without wondering about my health insurance annual maximum coverage.

As a man, playing against men means being just another guy to pound on. The addition of the "power hormone" takes you further than you could ever go before, and you are with people who have had access to it much longer than you. Their puberty was many years ago, while yours is still unfolding. But you have the benefit of being hyperaware that you are "in" and that you can expect the workout to make you stronger. You can relax into the sense of belonging, of just being one more guy that makes mistakes and scores and goes back to work when it's over. But it sure would be nice to have that private shower. Even nicer if the water would get hot.

BATHROOMS

One of the trickiest public places to be a trans person is a public restroom. Whether at work, in school, in public places like libraries, or in social settings, navigating bathrooms can be difficult.

Many of us are concerned with the lack of privacy in a communal setting such as a multistall bathroom. Not all bathrooms are created equal. For example, door locks may be unreliable or absent. Some of us are nervous about being perceived as weird if we pee while sitting down in a men's bathroom. Others of us are worried about being profiled and harassed in women's bathrooms. Some of us fear physical violence or denial of access if we are not read as the gender we are presenting as.

There are, typically, cultural and structural differences between men's and women's bathrooms. Most men's rooms have urinals and at least one stall, while women's rooms generally only include stalls. Women's bathrooms may be more social than men's bathrooms.

"Male bathrooms are generally areas where men simply don't make a lot of eye contact or linger very long, unless they're cruising. And if they're cruising, they are looking for someone else who meets their eyes and also lingers. Using the stalls instead of the urinals is really not a big deal, and no one else in the restroom is really watching if you sit to pee."

"Women talk to each other in public toilets! It's going to take me a while to get used to that—and first I have to stop being nervous about being caught in the ladies' room. I'm a 'lady' now, nobody minds me being there."

If you are concerned about your safety or unsure which bathroom will be most comfortable, look for a private, single-occupancy bathroom. In urban areas, many smaller restaurants and coffee shops have single-occupancy bathrooms. Suburban grocery chain stores also frequently have family restrooms that offer privacy. Starbucks coffee shops typically have gender-neutral bathrooms and do not require that people buy something to use them.

Bathroom Best Practices

How do we as trans and gender nonconforming people work through the anxieties that can arise in these spaces? Different people have different "fixes." Some trans men choose to use a stand-to-pee (STP) device or have had surgery that allows us to pee in a urinal. Some of us who do not pass on a regular basis, or are not feeling confident or safe about using men's or women's rooms, do our best to find alternative bathroom arrangements.

"I have tried to switch to using the mixed gender (often handicap) bathroom as a way to deal with my discomfort with going into either gendered bathroom. I love our local queer clubs that have mixed bathrooms for everyone. That makes the most sense to me."

"I always use gender-neutral bathrooms if they're available. Otherwise, I use female ones just because, I guess, it's easier and causes less of a stir. I use male bathrooms sometimes if there aren't too many people around, or if there are long lines for the girls' room."

"I really would like to see more unisex bathrooms to avoid the whole silly issue."

"Bathrooms ended up being easier than I thought; however, I do strive for those with less traffic."

Some of us have developed strategies to feel more comfortable in public, communal bathrooms.

> "In locker rooms. . . I change in the shower stall and get in and out as fast as I can."

> "Bathrooms are ok now. I just use the stalls in the men's room, and that is never an issue. Locker rooms are more difficult—I change my underwear in the bathroom stall."

> "Bathrooms are always scary. . . But a stiff upper lip and acting like you belong there always helps."

> "I tend to avoid public bathrooms usually, but if I have to go, I don't use the urinals. One thing I've found with men. . . If you're scared, they'll know and suspect you and look twice. If you walk in like you do this every day and don't really care, they won't even notice."

> "On my campus I have scoped out every bathroom at different times during the day to see when they are occupied the most."

Arizona bathroom laws (copyright 2013, Kevin Moore, www.mooretoons.com).

Some trans people rely on allies, friends, and partners to help us navigate bathrooms.

> "I still use the women's restroom in my everyday life, and because of how I look I won't use a bathroom unless someone (friend, partner) is going in with me."

> "Using restrooms was awkward, but I'd go with my girlfriend. . . and she'd stare down the women who would be gawkers or intimidating."

> "Early in my transition from female to male, I asked a friend to accompany me into any gendered public restroom I used."

In addition to accompanying us when appropriate or requested, allies and friends can be sensitive to this issue by holding events and meeting friends in public places where bathrooms are single stalls and have functionally locking doors. It is nice to have friends who are sensitive to the nervousness and feelings of unsafety that can arise for us when encountering a new bathroom or using a crowded communal bathroom such as at rest stops or airports.

Restrooms at Work

Although many employers are adopting good nondiscrimination policies, many others are still entirely uninformed about transgender issues. When we transition or are out as trans on the job, it is important for us to know our legal rights and also to know how we want things to be handled. We may need to negotiate with our employer or manager, and we should know what we want when we go to have that conversation. If an announcement needs to be made about something, that announcement should come from a place of authority so there is no room to question it. A discussion may not be necessary when we just come into a job, or if we start our job after we have transitioned. Regardless, we have the right to use whatever bathroom matches our gender identity.

Many workplaces have single-occupancy restrooms, which can simplify the issue of which bathroom we should use by eliminating potential concern about the feelings of other employees or the exposure we may feel as trans people in a multistall bathroom. In some places, such as Washington, D.C., all single-occupancy restrooms are required to be gender-neutral. The best practice is to ensure that single-occupancy or gender-neutral restrooms are available for any employees who wish to use them, while also permitting us to use the sex-segregated restrooms appropriate for our gender identities if we so choose.

The Transgender Law Center's "Peeing in Peace" guide is a good personal reference and can also be used to help educate employers.

Employers may wrongly assume that we must have genital reconstructive surgery before being permitted to use the restroom that corresponds to our gender identity. However, there is no justification for limiting bathroom access on this basis; any such rule violates our medical privacy. Employers do not require non-trans employees to verify that they have "typical" genitals, so it is discriminatory to apply such a rule only to transgender employees. The current medical standards of care require a trans person to live fully as a man or woman, including at work, in order to qualify for genital surgery, so preventing us from using the appropriate restroom unless we have had genital surgery also undermines our medical treatment and is directly contrary to medical standards of care.

Though many of us agree that bathrooms can feel harrowing and even dangerous at times, many of us have also had very positive bathroom experiences.

> *"Going to the men's bathroom was a really big deal to me initially, but it was incredibly easy to get used to the experience of not getting thrown out, stared at, questioned, or challenged."*

> *"Bathrooms were an issue for me when I first came out. But these days I have no issue chatting with women or feeling comfortable in ladies' rooms."*

> *"It sounds corny, but I love going into the men's bathroom! My life pre-transition found me always having to justify why I was using the ladies bathroom."*

> *"When I was in the bathroom at the Denver International Airport after having returned from Thailand and my sex reassignment surgery, some lady next to me at the sink commented on the ring I got in Thailand. I knew then that I was accepted as a woman in female spaces."*

IDENTIFICATION DOCUMENTS

When we are just beginning our transition process, most of us lack official identification documents like driver's licenses, passports, and social security cards with gender markers that match our gender identity and presentation. Chapter 10 includes information on how to go about changing different identity documents, but we are often required to live as our affirmed gender for defined periods of time before we are eligible to change these documents.

This can be a challenging position as we are often asked to present identification in a wide range of situations for a variety of essential and nonessential services such as:

- Purchasing alcohol, tobacco, or other controlled substances
- Entering a bar, music venue, or other age-limited space
- Checking in for and boarding many forms of transportation
- Cashing checks
- Accessing public benefits
- Purchasing some over-the-counter medications, such as emergency contraception or decongestants containing pseudoephedrine

One thing that can be helpful is to keep our identification document photos as up to date as possible, even if we are not yet pursuing legal changes to the name or gender marker. For example, we may be able to get our photo retaken for a driver's license, school identification, bank card, work identification badge, or other forms of photo identification that we use regularly, even if we are not able to change our gender marker yet. This can help provide a bridge between our appearance and our documents. Having multiple forms of up-to-date photo identification can help persuade skeptical store and bar owners that our documents are authentic.

Once we begin the legal paperwork process, we may have multiple forms of documentation with different names, gender markers, and photos. Managing this situation can get complicated. Many of us have found that having a solid paper trail for the changes that we have made can be very helpful. This usually means keeping a copy of our name-change paperwork handy when traveling or accessing benefits.

Some of us also find it helpful to obtain a "carry letter" from our health care provider. Carry letters can be used to explain our transgender status to officials. They typically include information about our birth-assigned name and gender and our affirmed named and gender, along with a brief explanation that we are undergoing some form of medically supervised transition. A carry letter can be used to "validate" our identity and explain any discrepancy between our presentation and our documentation, or between different types of documentation. Carry letters are not legally binding. However, in many situations, having official documentation is all that is needed to convince someone to accept our identification documents. If you do get a carry letter, make sure it is on official letterhead. See Chapter 12 for a sample carry letter.

When we are interacting with people who need to review our documents (such as Transportation Security Administration [TSA] officials or police officers), the best thing we can do is show our paper trail and patiently explain why our identification documents look the way they do. If we do not have a paper trail, then explaining how we got different documents changed helps as well.

TRAVEL

Travel is an important part of many of our lives, whether for work or for pleasure, and as trans people we have some unique concerns about how to navigate an increasingly regulated environment for travel, in which our bodies, identity documents, and baggage are scrutinized by officials.

Many of us worry that we cannot safely travel until we are consistently read as our correct gender or our identity documents are all correct. While both of these things may ease travel and moving through checkpoints, we should not feel like we cannot go anywhere until either of these conditions is fulfilled. Many gender nonconforming people travel frequently, and travel can be a wonderful way to experience our new gender outside of the expectations and history we have with our friends, family, and local community. Travel can also open our eyes to the diversity of gender presentations and expectations in the world. Sometimes those expectations are different just a few miles down the road.

Ticketed Travel

Most ticketed travel in the United States and internationally now requires travelers to show identification that includes a photograph, name, and gender. Be sure to know what identity documents are required to obtain a ticket and prepare for any questions about discrepancies between your documents and your appearance. Some of us make exceptions to our usual wardrobe when traveling and dress to be read as whatever is indicated on our identity documents. Other options include correcting identity documents or bringing a carry letter with us. If you are asked to complete forms, such as customs or immigration forms, during your travel, use the name and gender marker information that is on your ID.

Some public transportation passes, especially those for special-fare passes (elders or people living with disabilities), require a gender marker. Often, tickets for longer range travel, such as air travel, must have the gender marker that is on our identity documentation. Even if we do not plan to travel internationally, it can be helpful to have a new passport issued. Even though it can be difficult to change our gender marker on identification documents in some states, federal regulations now allow many of us to obtain corrected passports and social security cards.

Airport Security

Full-body scanners are now in use in many airports. The TSA is switching to a visual report from these scanners that shows only general areas of the body, and not specifics about our bodies. This is a huge benefit for trans people, as many of us fear being outed by these scans. You can still opt out of the full-body scan and instead be physically searched. According to policy, security personnel of the "same sex" should screen travelers. This can pose problems for trans people. There have been a number of incidents already reported regarding the invasion of privacy by TSA personnel. The National Center for Transgender Equality (NCTE) is working with the TSA to develop procedures and policies for airport security in screening trans people.

When traveling, we have the right to wear the clothes that are most comfortable for us. Decide what clothing will put you at the most ease as you travel, and also know that materials with metal or bone and piercings may set off security scanners. If you are trying to avoid scrutiny, consider whether to wear binders, corsets, bras, or other clothing with metal or bone, and remove jewelry, shoes, and belts before going through airport security.

Some of us travel with packers, binders, or breast forms. Most do not contain metal and so are unlikely to set off a metal detector, but they may confuse the operator of a body scanner if they give us an appearance that does not match other gender markers such as our hairstyle or clothing.

Be up front and honest with TSA representatives. They are likely to be more responsive if they feel they are being told the whole story. If you are selected for pat-down or strip searches, you should be searched by someone of the same gender. Decide for yourself what you believe will be the best for you if you are required to go through such a search. If you have any concerns about your treatment during security screening, you can request to speak with the screening supervisor.

Traveling With Injectable Hormones

One other point of consideration during travel is how to best carry medication. Having our medications in an easily accessible separate pouch will assist with screening. For those of us currently taking hormones and traveling with hormones or syringes, it can be useful to have a specific medication carry letter from our provider that explains why we are carrying syringes. Make sure the letter is on official letterhead. Many other people who take medications that require syringes carry such letters.

CONCLUSION

Living our daily lives can be complicated and at times challenging due to our trans identities. We often run into difficulties in a number of areas, such as shopping for clothes,

The National Center for Transgender Equality (NCTE) has an online guide on airport security that offers tips for travel and contact information for the TSA should you experience difficulties and want to file complaints.

Sample Medication Carry Letter

[Date]

To Whom It May Concern:
[Name on your prescription and travel documentation] is a patient under my care. It is medically necessary for [him/her] to carry the following hormonal medications:

- Injectable hormones [name and dosage]
- Syringes for injection
- Additional needles

If you have any questions regarding the treatment of this patient, please feel free to contact me at [phone].

Sincerely,
[Provider name and credentials]

using bathrooms, and traveling. Navigating new social worlds and learning about what is expected of us in terms of our gendered behavior and expression as we transition can be daunting or exciting. Balancing our privacy with our impulse to be ourselves in the world is one of our most complicated tasks. In the end, we each figure out unique ways to approach our worlds and find community.

REFERENCES AND FURTHER READING

Beck, K., & Speckhard, A. (2013). *Warrior princess: A U.S. Navy SEAL's journey to coming out transgender.* McLean, VA: Advances Press.

Bergman, S. B. (2009). *The nearest exit may be behind you.* Vancouver, BC: Arsenal Pulp Press.

Boedecker, A. L. (2011). *The transgender guidebook: Keys to a successful transition.* Seattle, WA: Amazon/CreateSpace.

Cromwell, J. (1999). *Transmen and FTMs: Identities, bodies, genders, and sexualities.* Champaign: University of Illinois Press.

Green, J. (2004). *Becoming a visible man.* Nashville, TN: Vanderbilt University Press.

Kailey, M. (2005). *Just add hormones: An insider's guide to the transsexual experience.* Boston, MA: Beacon Press.

National Center for Transgender Equality. (2012). *Airport security and transgender people.* Retrieved December 2013, from http://www.transequality.org/Resources/AirportSecurity_November2012.pdf

EMPLOYMENT

Jessica Lina Stirba, Zil Garner Goldstein, and Cecilia Gentili, with Heath Mackenzie Reynolds, Tobi Hill-Meyer, and Dean Scarborough

9

ECONOMIC SECURITY IS AN IMPORTANT PART OF OUR LIVES. In our culture, employment is also often an important aspect of our identity. We may seek work that feels meaningful, see ourselves as the breadwinner for our families, or find value in being a productive member of society. In all cases, work is central to how we view ourselves and our place in our communities.

Trans and gender nonconforming people have a wide array of careers and jobs. We are lawyers, artists, dancers, scientists, members of law enforcement, administrators, nurses, social workers, sex workers, doctors, tech professionals, nonprofit workers, teachers, movie directors, county clerks, and every other profession.

In a culture where employment can be seen as a very large part of personal identity, it is important to acknowledge the challenges that trans and gender nonconforming people face in the job world, as well as the opportunities we have to build successful careers.

LOOKING FOR A JOB

As we begin the process of re-creating our lives, we may seek out new jobs or careers for a variety of reasons. We may be looking for a job that reflects new confidence or a sense of possibility about how we live our lives. We may seek out a new career to separate ourselves from our former identity or life. Or we may be forced to seek out new work because our previous profession is no longer open to us in our new life for any number of reasons, including discrimination or harassment. We may be joining the workforce for the first time, either as a young adult or after separating from our family, spouse, or partner as a result of our transition.

> *"Being at a new job, my work colleagues don't know me as any different than I am currently."*

> *"I am employed. I transitioned on a job I was at for 5 years. I have since left that job and was able to find another job as a female. One of the measures I had for myself for me to say that I had transitioned successfully was to be able to find, interview, and be offered a job in my new gender role."*

Networking

Networking—or building relationships with others who share our professional skills, interests, or background—is a valuable skill in any industry. By building a community, we may be able to find out about job openings before they are posted, benefit from personal introductions to hiring managers, or otherwise have allies who will vouch for us when we are applying for work.

Attending "networking events" can be challenging for anyone who is not a natural extrovert, but there are plenty of other ways to build our professional networks and reputations. We may get involved in volunteer work or a community cause—often we meet people there who are tied in to their own employment hubs, and it gives us an opportunity to show our strengths in context.

The Human Rights Campaign's (HRC) Corporate Equality Index (CEI) is one place to find companies that identify themselves as trans-friendly. To get a perfect score on the CEI, a company must offer comprehensive benefits for transgender health care, including surgeries. Some of the companies listed there are parent companies of companies that might have a range of jobs available in our area of expertise.

In a competitive job market, networking can be especially important, because it helps give us an "in" when applying for a job. This can be particularly helpful if we are concerned that our gender presentation is making it harder for us to get jobs. By having allies in our job search, we may feel less isolated and find out about more potential work opportunities.

EMPLOYMENT TIPS FOR TRANSGENDER AND GENDER NONCONFORMING PEOPLE

Clair Farley is the Manager of Employment Services and a trans* advocate at the San Francisco LGBT Community Center, and head of the nation's first Transgender Employment Program (TEEI) (employmentservices@sfcenter.org). She answers some common questions and provides tips for trans job seekers.

Q. What name should I use on my resume?
It depends; you can use the name that you currently go by, whether or not it's the same as the name on your ID documents. A resume is not a legal document, so you have the right to use your preferred name, stage name, or legal name.

Q. I am in early transition and afraid that my resume will out me to future employers. What do you recommend?
Using the name that matches your current gender identity and expression can help prime an employer to see you the way you want to be seen. A resume is usually the first image of you that an employer will have. If you are very early in your transition, are genderqueer, or are afraid you won't "pass" as the gender expression that you identify with, using your new name can "out" you. If you're not sure about the trans-friendliness of the employer, it may be safer to go with your old name. After you are offered the job, you can explain the situation if you prefer. Coming out after the job offering can provide you with further legal recourse if discrimination takes place.

Q. Can I include a job I held under a different name and/or before my transition?
Yes! Transitioning doesn't have to mean "starting over" professionally. Including a job on your resume does not give employers permission to contact your former employer. You can include a job on your resume without giving the new employer permission to contact them. Do not include past employers' contact information, address, or supervisors' names on your resume. If you are asked to share this information on a paper or online application, you can check that you prefer they not contact your past employer. Or you can provide contact info for someone other than your supervisor, such as a supportive coworker who knows your history and can confirm that you worked there.

Q. How do I account for time I was out of work because of transition and/or due to discrimination or other barriers to employment?
The same way you would account for any other gap in employment. You can use your cover letter to explain longer gaps (over a year). I do not recommend going into depth or coming out in your letter, just mentioning it in passing should be fine. For example, "After being out of the workforce for two years due to personal obligations, I am ready and eager to return to work for a dynamic company like XYZ." For shorter gaps on your resume, include only the year and not the month when listing dates of your past jobs. You can also minimize gaps by adding professionally relevant activities to your resume (such as volunteering, consulting, temp or part-time work, or taking classes). If you choose to leave a position or opportunity off your resume, make sure that the skills and experience you acquired at the organization are addressed in your cover letter and summary of qualifications.

Q. What if my references don't know I'm trans*? Or what if my references do know I'm trans*, but I don't want my new employer to know?
In either case, you have three basic options. You may choose one of these strategies or decide on a plan that meets your unique needs.

---

1. Tell your references that you're applying for jobs and you'd like to continue to list them as a reference, but that it's very important they refer to you by the name and pronoun you use now. It can be helpful to have a friend call your references and pretend to be an employer to double-check that your references get it right.
2. Talk to potential employers. Explain in confidence, if the employer is trans-friendly, that even though you go by a particular name and pronoun now, people from your past may not be aware of this and may refer to you by another name. It is an employer's responsibility to maintain your privacy, so this does not mean that you have to be out to your coworkers once you start the job.
3. Get new references! This can often be the best or easiest alternative if coming out is not an option for you. Some ways to get new references are volunteering, working in unpaid internships, and taking classes where your teachers can serve as professional references.

Applying for Jobs

Many of us worry about the job application and interview process. We may have faced discrimination in the past, or we may be overwhelmed by the very idea of it.

"I am not employed. That is mainly because my kid is disabled and I'm taking care of her, but my transition is also a factor. I have no idea how to deal with references or background checks. It makes me very tired to think about having to come out to any and all potential employers."

"I am employed, but I spent some time this year unemployed and found it difficult to get a job, despite being well qualified. I am not sure whether this was due to the economic climate or because, at interview, I present as transgender."

However, many of us have found that there are clear steps we can take to ease the process of finding and applying for new work.

RESUMES AND CURRICULA VITAE

Resumes or curricula vitae (CVs) are often the first pieces of information an employer has about us. A resume is a short, one- or two-page description of our work history and skills. A curriculum vitae is a longer document used in some employment fields that lists more details about us, such as presentations we have done or articles we have published.

Whether the types of work we are applying for require a cover letter and resume, a standardized job application, or other documentation, there are a number of categories of information we may need to update depending on where we are in our transition process.

On a resume or CV, our personal information should generally be updated to the name that we currently use, even if it is not yet a legal name. For those of us who have transitioned and do not intend to be "out" on the job, it is preferable to update our legal name before we need to complete employee paperwork for payroll or benefits. Establish an e-mail address for professional use with your current name to include on your resume.

EDUCATION AND SKILLS

Most schools and professional certifications have a mechanism for changing the name on our documentation to reflect any legal changes we have made. Consider taking the time to change your name on school records, professional licensing, professional organization membership, certifications, and professional licenses as you prepare your resume. Depending on our profession, many of these do not include a gender marker that needs to be changed.

A cover letter is a letter written by the job applicant to the employer to go along with their resume or CV. Cover letters generally focus on skills, the position we are applying for, and the reason we are a good fit for the job. Unless our experience as a trans person has helped make us uniquely prepared for the position, it is not necessary to disclose any information about our history in a cover letter.

WORK HISTORY

Many companies do background checks to verify self-reported work history. They are simply verifying the fact that we were employed at the job listed on our resume or application during the dates given. To ensure that our prior employers can confirm this information, we may want to call and inform them of our new name and information. Typically, this can be handled by the Human Resources or administrative staff, and there is no requirement to have a discussion about the changes or provide any more information than is necessary.

For us as trans people, making these changes can be deeply personal, but at many companies updating our records is likely to be a bureaucratic process that simply requires adding information to a file. This is often true for those checking our references as well; particularly in larger companies, the individuals who check references are often far removed from the actual interview and employee relationship-building process.

For some of us, there are jobs we have had that we just cannot imagine going back to with this information. If that is the case, it may make sense to leave some jobs off our resume or application. Keep in mind, however, that employers may request information on up to the last 10 years of our employment, and we may have to explain gaps in our work history.

REFERENCES

References often play a critical role in our success landing a new job. Plan to provide three references, distributed across your employment history, for any job you apply to. You do not have to use a direct supervisor as a reference, and there is no requirement to have references from all past jobs.

References should be able to speak to our work, not just our personality. If we do not already have three references who can speak about us with our new name and pronouns, we may need to approach others from our past and speak with them about acting as our reference. Coming out to people from our past can be scary, but the people we ask for references should be people who are ready to say positive things about our work ethic, skills, and qualifications.

APPLICATION FORMS

In many cases, we are required to fill out a standard form application for jobs, either as part of submitting an application or as a formality during the interview process. As part of legal background checks, we may be asked to disclose our legal name and any other names we have been known by in the past. This may out us with the hiring manager, the person responsible for conducting our background check, or others in the hiring process. There is no one right way to handle this experience, but it helps if we are prepared for responding to questions about why we changed our name.

Interviewing

Interviews are all about presenting a version of ourselves that seems like the best fit for the job—regardless of our gender status. The job interview is the time we have to convince the people across the table that they want to hire us. There are many books and workshops devoted to the art of the interview. Employers want to feel that they like us, that they want to spend more time with us, and that we are the most capable person for the job at hand. We need to show that we are good workers, and that we will be productive and also flexible in the workplace. These qualities are relayed in diverse ways, but the most important thing is always that we feel comfortable talking about our professional selves.

Have confidence in your skills and abilities, and be able to talk about what will make you the best candidate for the jobs you are applying for. If you do not have a resume, have never had an interview before, or are having difficulties applying for jobs, public libraries and local workforce centers offer many resources.

OUT for Work is an organization that runs a national career conference and travels to college campuses to help LGBTQ students prepare for the workforce.

Val (Arthur Robin Williams, MD, www.MyRightSelf.org).

Make sure you are as comfortable as possible physically during an interview. Take some time to consider what kind of interview outfit you might feel best in. If you are interviewing for a position that requires professional dress, that might mean a skirt or pants and a blouse or a suit jacket. What matters most is that we are "dressed the part" for the job we are trying to get, and that we are comfortable. If walking in heels is new, consider wearing flats instead. If you are not comfortable wearing suits yet, consider coordinating dress slacks and a vest or blazer, or wearing a button-up shirt, tie, and sweater. For genderqueer and other gender nonconforming people, decide what combination of wardrobe elements might make you feel most confident. We want our interviewers to be focusing on what we are saying, not on what we are wearing.

Here are some tips to consider as an interview approaches:

- *Prepare for the interview.* Do some role playing with friends. Practice fielding tricky questions and turning inappropriate questions into opportunities to talk about your work experience.
- *Practice gender-specific mannerisms.* You may be nervous in an interview, and you need to be comfortable presenting as you want to be seen.
- *Use open, engaging body language*—such as leaning forward in your chair and making eye contact—not closed body language. Practice your handshake and your eye contact.
- *Dress as professionally as possible.* Interviews are all about presentation of self, and this is your first impression. Even if it is a casual office environment, dress up for the interview. Regardless of your gender, it is important to stand when someone enters the room and have a good handshake.
- *Be prepared to out yourself to the appropriate person.* If you have an interview with a person from Human Resources and you need to tell them that you have previously gone by a different name, prepare for that to happen.

INAPPROPRIATE QUESTIONS

It is not appropriate for a potential employer, a boss or coworker, a colleague, or clients or patrons to ask about our medical care or gender history. However, in reality, this often happens anyway. Employers have been known to ask, "Has that always been your name?" or comment, "You have such a low voice." If a potential employer does ask an inappropriate question, it is fair to tell the person that we would like to keep that private, or that we do not feel comfortable discussing our personal medical information. If you are not comfortable telling someone directly to mind their own business, it can help to use light humor to deflect such questions. For example, we may say something like "Oh, I have to keep *some* secrets."

Even though there is pressure in a job interview to put ourselves out there, that does not mean that we should, or need to, tell stories about our lives as trans or gender non-conforming people. In interviews, potential employers need to know information that is relevant to our skills for the job we are applying for only, and personal matters, including our gender identity and experience, should be set aside. If we choose to disclose later, that is completely up to us.

Difficulty Finding Employment

According to the National Transgender Discrimination Survey (Grant et al., 2011), unemployment in the trans community is double the national average, and the rate for trans people of color is four times as high. According to the same survey, trans people reported very high levels of workplace harassment, employment discrimination, and job loss due to their gender identity.

Despite these potentially daunting numbers, it is important to remember: You are not unemployable! You may feel that you have more challenges, or that things are more unfair for you. This may be true, sometimes—but even if the process is harder or takes longer, it is not fundamentally different from others' journeys toward employment.

If you are passionate about something, do whatever you can in your power to get there. Volunteer, attend events, get training, or go back to school.

ON THE JOB

For those of us who already have jobs, or find jobs during our transition, there are a number of work-specific issues that can come up, including when and how to disclose or come out to employers or coworkers, how to interact with colleagues, how to dress, and which restrooms to use.

Disclosure

No one *needs* to know about our status as trans people. However, we may want Human Resources, or whoever is responsible for reference checks, benefits, or insurance, to know, especially if there is a discrepancy between our IDs and the way we present. Sharing with a supervisor can help to build trust, but it is not required if it makes us uncomfortable.

Many of us choose not to disclose our trans status to our coworkers. For some of us, it can be helpful to have mental and emotional space from talking about our transition. For others, we simply live our lives in our affirmed gender, and talking about our transition history does not feel appropriate or necessary. However, some of us feel that setting aside parts of our identity and lives as off-limits in the office can create its own challenges.

> "I accepted a new job 8 months ago and moved to a new state for the job. Only my direct boss knows of my transgender status. As far as I know, no one else at work suspects anything. I am hesitant to come out, mostly because I never thought I would be able to be stealth. I figured that no matter what, people would always be able to just tell. This isn't the case though, and I feel in some ways like I am living a lie allowing them to believe a certain 'truth' about my life."

The types of jobs we have, and our workplace culture, can also influence how we handle disclosure. If we are in a culture where we do not spend much time talking with our coworkers, or where sharing things about ourselves is not a part of our days, then it may be inappropriate to share intimate parts of our lives.

Whether or not we decide to talk about our gender identity with coworkers is completely up to us. We should be prepared for questions and how we want to answer them

The Web site TJobBank.com allows members of trans communities to search for jobs posted by trans-friendly employers.

Internships are one way to gain experience and get to know a potential employer. Many people are able to convert internships into full-time paid employment. However, many internships are unpaid or paid very poorly, and there is no guarantee that a job will result. Before starting an internship, talk to others who have done so, and ask about the skills you will learn, as well as the possibility of later employment.

(or not answer them). People we work with might also feel as though they can ask us more questions at any time once the subject is broached. Whether or not you decide to talk about your trans identity, work to maintain boundaries that help you feel safe.

When we are working in service-industry jobs like retail, food service, or maintenance, it may be important to get support from our coworkers when dealing with customers. An ally at work can help us remain professional if a customer becomes inappropriate, asks personal questions about us, or tries to cause trouble because of how they see us.

> *"I was employed as a social worker and had a problem only once, when I 'came out' in support of a client. One woman was not nice about me being different and told the whole rest of my team. I found this out after the fact, because they told her to leave me alone and they never even let me know they knew. They just kept being friendly and respectful. I actually did go to Human Resources for the company about this and was supported at the time."*

Whether or not we feel comfortable being out at work, we may want to advocate for trans issues to be included and discussed as a part of any diversity training that our workplace offers. Sometimes efforts like this can transform the entire culture of a workplace.

MEDIA SPOTLIGHT: PUTTING A FACE ON TRANS EMPLOYMENT ISSUES

Dallas Denny and Jamison Green

Transgender employment issues caught the spotlight in February 2007, when an article in the *St. Petersburg Times* announced that Steve Stanton, who had been the city manager of Largo, Florida, for 14 years, was undergoing sex reassignment. Under media scrutiny, Stanton confirmed the story long before she was ready to do so, revealing publicly that she would soon become Susan. Even though the city had enacted an employment nondiscrimination ordinance, Stanton was fired from her post within days of the announcement, following a heated protest at a City Council meeting. Litigators thought Stanton would have a good chance of prevailing if she sued to retain her job under the provisions of the nondiscrimination ordinance, but Susan visibly surprised her attorney when she announced on *Larry King Live* that she would not sue. This was a national story, and CNN began following her around, making a documentary about her that aired later in the year.

Later that same year, the proposed Employment Non-Discrimination Act (ENDA) was gutted of a provision that would have protected workers from discrimination based on gender identity or expression. In the media, however, this issue was soon overtaken by the global economic downturn. Trans employment issues took a backseat to general unemployment; we didn't hear much about trans people in the workplace, unless it was Susan Stanton applying for another city manager job in yet another city, Susan Stanton being hired, Susan Stanton leaving or being let go and looking for work again. While Stanton has sought to keep a low profile, the media has capitalized on the sensational aspects of her late-in-life transition, the slight sadness that often seemed to spill out from within her, and the admirable strength of a person who didn't want the spotlight.

Meanwhile, little mainstream media attention was paid to the landmark case of Mia Macy, a trans woman who was dismissed from a government job and took her employer to court. In 2012, the Equal Employment Opportunity Commission (EEOC) ruled in favor of Macy, determining that Title VII of the 1964 Civil Rights Act covers discrimination against transgender people under the provisions concerning discrimination on the basis of sex. This ruling was ratified in July 2013 when the Department of Justice investigation of the EEOC ruling confirmed the original decision.

In August 2013 the Movement Advancement Project, in collaboration with the National Center for Transgender Equality, two prominent national LGBT advocacy organizations, a labor organization, a progressive think tank, and a major labor union, released a report on workplace discrimination against trans people, *A Broken Bargain for Transgender Workers*. So far, the media has been fairly low key in covering this report. We hope that the media picture is changing as more positive images and profiles of successful trans people begin to circulate to ever-wider audiences.

Office Politics and Social Situations

Building social relationships in the workplace builds opportunity. There are many mini-environments in the workplace, including departmental lunches and lunch break times. How private we keep our lives may determine (or limit) our ability to connect with others in those situations. However, there are many things we can share about our lives that have nothing to do with gender—we should not feel like we have to keep entirely to ourselves. If we do keep to ourselves, we may have fewer connections to coworkers, be more easily overlooked for a new position, or otherwise limit our professional development.

Many of us are reclusive because we are worried about calling attention to our transition. We may think some aspects of our appearance are obvious when no one else notices. We tend to be highly aware of things we would like to change about ourselves, and we can be our own worst critics.

We may face additional conflict in highly gender-segregated industries. A trans woman who works in construction might face discrimination or harassment based on the conflict between her identity and the way the work she is doing is considered to be masculine. Similarly, a trans man working in education or nursing might face barriers because those types of employment are generally associated with feminine traits. While we can all work toward a society in which these stereotypes and assumptions no longer affect us, it is important to be aware that these are challenges we might have to face if the industry in which we work is a "gendered" one.

Communication Styles

On the job, coworkers sometimes ask each other inappropriate questions, and this is especially common for us as trans people. If it is in keeping with your personality, one option is to punt unwelcome questions using a lighthearted approach. There are also ways to deflect uncomfortable topics and questions.

> *"My favorite answer to the 'Have you had your surgery yet?' question is, 'What do you mean? I've had my wisdom teeth out.'"*

As we get to know our coworkers better, they may start to feel more comfortable asking us more personal questions. No matter who asks, we never have to answer questions that make us feel uncomfortable. If we start sharing personal information with people—particularly about our bodies—they may feel it is OK to ask additional questions that we are not comfortable answering. Take the time outside of work to think about what your limits are and stick to them.

Dressing for Work

Picking clothing for work can be a challenge for many of us, especially if we are new to the gendered clothing that we are currently wearing. As we transition, many of us inform our employers before we start wearing new gender-specific clothing. Some people change their clothing styles at transitional moments, such as after a holiday or at the beginning of a new semester if working at or near a school. Others change the next day. For some of us, transitioning our clothing style more slowly, and having a period of wearing more gender-neutral clothing, helps us and others at work to ease into a new phase.

Many workplaces have dress codes, including sales environments, money and finance, and food service. Certain retail stores require that every sales person wear at least some of their products each day. In some places, dress codes are legal, and we need to navigate gender-specific requirements. Dress codes can be different for women and men, and not allow for dressing "in-between" the two options.

In some work environments, there are unspoken dress codes that are not strictly enforced or required but are generally followed. These are not legally binding, but they can affect the way we are perceived by our coworkers and bosses. In general, look as clean and professional as possible. If there is a choice to dress up or dress down, dress up as long as the clothes make you feel comfortable.

Restroom Access

Federal law requires employers to provide all employees with reasonable access to restrooms. However, what it means to provide reasonable access is still being established in states, cities, and counties around the country. Some states and localities also prohibit discrimination against transgender employees with respect to bathrooms. Local laws in your area may provide additional protections or guidance on this issue. It may be helpful to keep in mind that there are other, nonlegal tools at your disposal for resolving conflicts over bathroom use. For ideas, check out the section on bathrooms in Chapter 8.

JOB PROTECTIONS

We have a number of avenues for protection from workplace discrimination, including both laws and company policies. In some places, state and local laws prohibit employers from discriminating based on gender identity. Federal, state, and local laws that prohibit sex discrimination may also protect us, as well as some state laws that prohibit disability discrimination.

LGBTQ groups have spent many years working to pass a federal bill called the Employment Non-Discrimination Act (ENDA), which would prohibit private employers across the country from discriminating based on sexual orientation or gender identity. If ENDA passes with gender identity protections, it will be illegal to discriminate against trans employees anywhere in the United States. In the meantime, there is no federal law that expressly protects trans employees, although more courts are holding that trans people are protected under federal laws that prohibit sex discrimination. See Chapter 10 for more information on legal protections in applying for jobs and in the workplace.

Internal Workplace Protections

Many workplaces have their own internal nondiscrimination policies that protect trans workers from discrimination. This will most likely be found in an employee handbook, if there is one. If not, ask your Human Resources representative for a copy of the company's nondiscrimination policy. If your employer has such a policy and it prohibits gender identity discrimination, make sure you follow the rules and procedures it describes for reporting discrimination. Internal policies typically have a protocol you must follow in order to make a complaint about discrimination.

> *"I transitioned at my last job and it was handled reasonably well, although to be honest, it seemed more like they were scared of doing it wrong and getting sued than they were of just not being an asshole to an employee."*

In addition to specific protections based on gender identity, many companies have in place procedures to prevent employees from being fired for unlawful reasons. This benefits us, as employees, while also protecting employers from legal action. Usually, such policies require the employer to document specific problems and ensure that employees are given

Allie (Arthur Robin Williams, MD, www.MyRightSelf.org).

warnings and opportunities to address the issue before they are eligible for termination. Unfortunately, in some cases, employers go out of their way to target and write up trans employees, making internal systems less useful.

Getting Help for Problems at Work

When anything goes wrong at work, the first step is always to talk to a supervisor. If we are having problems with a client or customer, it is good to get our boss on our side as soon as possible. They may have helpful tips for dealing with troublesome customers, and also need to know if there is an issue before someone else brings it to their attention. The most important thing we can do is to remain professional when we are having problems with a customer. If we do not escalate the situation, we are more likely to get help from our bosses and coworkers and resolve the problem quickly and easily.

Pride at Work is a labor organization through AFL-CIO that organizes mutual support between the organized Labor Movement and the LGBTQ Community for social and economic justice.

If the supervisor is not able to resolve the problem, it never hurts to call someone in the Human Resources department and talk to them. Most organizations have procedures to address complaints, and they often lay out the best way to address problems in the workplace. Human Resources should be an ally and resource, and interpret the rules in order to ensure everyone adheres to them. There are a lot of ineffective or unqualified Human Resources employees, and it can be difficult or frustrating working with someone who has not helped companies or organizations work with their trans employees before. However, there are also many people who want to do the right thing and create a positive environment for everyone.

If internal processes do not help to resolve the problem, it is time to get some outside help. Many LGBTQ community centers can help people find resources for dealing with harassment at work. The process varies from area to area. See Chapter 10 for more information on trans-supportive legal resources.

TODAY I AM A WHOLE HUMAN BEING

Stacy Soria is an ordinary girl with intriguing experiences who has victoriously climbed her mountain.

I was born in Brooklyn and raised in North Carolina. Due to homelessness caused by my mother's battle with drug addiction and domestic abuse, we had to relocate before the state stepped in. My single-parent family moved into a small town adjacent to Camp Lejeune Marine base where my uncle served in the US Marine Corps. I was raised within the church community—a diverse setting that was built on love and positive regard for human life.

I have always known that I did not think or feel the same way other boys felt. I remember wanting to express myself in more effeminate ways, which came naturally to me. These expressions led to being shunned and ostracized, resulting in isolation. I had two choices—fight or flight. I chose to leave at the tender age of 15 and start a new life in New York City.

Transitioning was difficult because I did not know how to navigate the systems to obtain health coverage for hormone therapy. Instead, for many years I obtained black-market hormones and self-medicated. High school was strenuous because I had to keep my identity a "secret"—only the principal knew. I ultimately dropped out of high school after being outed by a male classmate and threatened by other students.

Lack of support and resources led me to homelessness. I remember walking the streets of Manhattan at three o'clock in the morning and being fed a chocolate and a peanut butter sandwich from a mobile unit that came out every night to feed homeless youth. Going into a youth shelter was scary and proved to be dangerous, as I was met with aggressive sexual advances and hostility.

I began to abuse substances to cope with the colossal issues in my life. My first attempt at drug treatment was unsuccessful because I was told that I had to wear men's attire and cut my hair short in order to be admitted. This incident sent me back out to the streets, where I continued the cycle of abuse. I began to get arrested for petty crimes and accumulated a rap sheet full of justifications to further discriminate and isolate me, a minority transgendered Hispanic.

After many failed attempts at treatment and years of recidivating, I obtained my G.E.D. on Rikers Island after months of rigorous studying. This was the first time I felt like I had accomplished something that no one could take away from me. However, this stint did not help me heal or understand the patterns of my life or what it was to become. I was released from Rikers with no identification, money, or place to stay, and went back out into the streets. Years passed with a multitude of employment and recovery attempts but nothing sustainable enough for long-term stability.

Six years had passed by and my friends were becoming extinct. They were young and dying from AIDS-related complications and violence in the streets. There were many days I wanted to give up. I did not feel I was born to cheat, steal, and lie for a living, but I had tried to do things the right way with very little opportunity and ongoing rejection.

Eventually I was arrested and sent to state prison and sentenced to four years. After battling the case for a year on Rikers Island I was angrily addressed by a frustrated lawyer who told me, "You have no way of winning this case. You are a transsexual drug addict and no one is going to believe you on the stand. Whether you believe you are innocent or not, you need help. Four years is what we're offering. Take it or leave it. Your life is already over." His statement cut deep into my soul as I sat feeling invisible, as if I did not even matter within this bigger community called society.

In prison I was exposed to all types of harassment and discrimination from both inmates and officers alike. I was isolated and harassed daily for being different. I was strip-searched in front of laughing officers who would take Polaroid pictures of me, passing them around to colleagues for "laughs." I was often met with rude and hostile remarks from the medical staff who told me that they were not going to give me the hormonal treatment I was receiving before incarceration. They made me shave my face even though I did not have facial hair, which caused me pain and mental stress. A prisoner attacked me and the incident was met with accusations that I brought the attack on myself by being a "freak."

These experiences led me to find refuge within the church in the prison. I began to set personal goals and learn as much as I could throughout my incarceration. I had taken an interest in HIV education, counseling, psychology, and developing workshops. After several months of studying for a general business certification, I was given a job within the prison facility as a program facilitator. I was coached and mentored by a veteran inmate and correctional counselor who became invested in my safety and development.

Four years had passed and I was ready to be released with only a plan and $40. I was physically and emotionally withdrawn. I had no place to stay and was facing homelessness. One day before my release, I attended a presentation by The Doe Fund's Ready, Willing, and Able program. I spoke with the recruiter and signed up for the program. I was afraid that going into this program would expose me to the same settings I had grown accustomed to in prison. Contrary to my fears, I was welcomed and provided with a safe space and staff who assisted me with reintegration into the community.

After just a few months, I was accepted into the Occupational Training Program, where I learned clerical skills. On my day off, I went to a school for counseling to inquire about tuition and met with their director, who, after hearing my story, invited me to begin classes in the evenings and weekends with a full scholarship. This training lasted six months and allowed me to work toward the nationally recognized Certification for Alcohol and Substance Abuse Counselors (CASAC). I was very grateful for the opportunity and asked the director why she chose me. She said, "Stacy, there are not too many people like you in the field. We have a lot to learn from you. The transgender population is not a new population, but we have a lot to learn."

Today, I manage a 138-bed Veterans Program alongside a staff of 6 dedicated social services professionals. I became a first generation college student and obtained a master's degree in Public Affairs and Administration and graduated with honors. I have passed the Alcohol and Drug Counseling state exam and obtained a Certificate of Good Conduct. I am a mentor, advocate and employable law abiding citizen who is actively contributing to her city.

I am a whole human being. My story is not uncommon. It is a testimony to what is possible when each of us is able to access the support, love, resources, and recognition we need to be live as whole human beings.

Transitioning on the Job

Some of us are already employed when we come out, but many of us transition while we are employed. At what point during our transition process we choose to come out at work is entirely up to us, but it can be helpful to make a plan for raising the issue with your employer before you begin making a full social or physical transition. Some employers have preexisting policies for managing an on-the-job transition, but more often than not, we will need to establish a plan for our own personal transition in conjunction with our supervisor or Human Resources.

Transitioning on the job is, usually, an unavoidably visible process. Unless we have a very close friend at work, it may be helpful to talk to a supervisor or Human Resources manager, first, to help ensure that our rights are protected during our transition.

Many of us have found that it helps to approach our employer with a clear expectation and desired course of action when we first come out.

"I am in full-time employment with a British software company. I have worked for them for about 25 years and only came out at work two years ago! It was my very last step. I had all sorts of assumptions about how that would go—many of which were not that optimistic. But in the event, they handled it magnificently. It was almost immediately not an issue and the sole conversation was about how to handle logistics (how/when to make the announcement, changing my details, etc.)."

Having clear expectations and a plan we would like to see implemented helps to ensure that we are in control of the process. Whatever initial meeting we have with our supervisor or Human Resources, we should come prepared with legal information in case someone is not supportive.

DEVELOPING AN ACTION PLAN

Developing an action plan eases communication and can help make transitioning on the job a less overwhelming prospect. Some questions to consider when developing an action plan include the following:

- Will I be going by a different name and/or pronouns?
- Will I be wearing different clothing? Are there gender-specific dress codes?
- Which bathroom, locker room, or other gender-segregated facilities do I intend to use?
- What would I like to communicate to other employees? Do I want to "come out" to all staff, or only to people I work with directly?

In addition to *what* we want to change, it is important to consider *when* we would like the changes to happen. The timeline we choose is up to us, but it can be helpful to be flexible. If your company asks for a reasonable period of time to make any necessary adjustments, it may make sense to going along with them, as long as the adjustments and timeline are clearly defined.

In addition to social aspects of transition, there are administrative tasks to be completed. Ensure that your name is updated on all public-facing documentation and correspondence, such as name tags or badges, employee ID cards, e-mail addresses, mail, employee lists, company Web sites, and business cards. One way to make this process easier is to make a list of all the required changes and ask for assistance from a manager.

Wait to update your name with payroll until you have added your new name to your bank account. For those of us without bank accounts, checks should be made out to the name that is on the ID required to cash our paychecks.

When updating your name on your bank account, make sure you leave your previous name(s) on the account; you may need to use them to access funds from a savings bond you were given as a child, a dividend or gift check written out to your former name, or a 401(k) cash-out from a previous chapter of your life.

If you wish to change your name or gender marker on employee benefits, you will need to provide documentation. Some of us may be able to make these changes through our Human Resources department, while others may be able to manage our own benefits accounts online—in that case, our employer might not even need to know. Open enrollment periods can also ease the documentation requirements for many insurance changes. For example, if we add a spouse or partner to our benefits plan outside of open enrollment, we typically have to provide a marriage license; during open enrollment, we simply provide our spouse's information. Some companies have a supportive benefits administrator, but even if they do not, they are required to provide information about available benefits, eligibility, and open enrollment to all employees. This documentation should have information and contact numbers for finding answers to our questions. Keep in mind that the wheels of bureaucracy can sometimes turn very slowly, so it helps to have some patience as you clear any administrative hurdles.

SOME THOUGHTS ON BEING A TRANS PROFESSOR

Dr. Rachel McKinnon is an assistant professor at the College of Charleston.

I am an out trans woman in academia who transitioned on the job with the full support of my department at the University of Waterloo. Having management express complete support helps set the right tone for a less bumpy transition. It was relatively smooth, although there were some significant problems with some people continuing to use the wrong pronouns many months after my transition.

Thankfully, I even found support from my students. In May 2012, I came out to both of my classes at the beginning of the semester. I had to, as I was visibly trans at that point. I wanted them to know what to expect from me over the term. I also wanted them to see an out trans person as someone who's successful and completely normal. More than a few students immediately commended my courage to be open about the process, and some felt honored to be in my class.

I was worried, legitimately I think, about how students would react on their end-of-term evaluations. These matter a great deal to professors but especially lecturers like me who are contract workers from term to term. In almost every example of a trans professor that I came across in my research prior to transitioning, the professor transitioned after obtaining the job security of tenure. However, my fears came to naught: I received some of my best evaluations ever. I also received some very heartwarming comments from students.

Early in my transition, while teaching, I conjectured that I might receive higher evaluations merely because I felt that I was now a better teacher. Open to be myself, I was certainly happier, and this translated into my teaching. I was warmer, friendlier, and more connected to my students; and I think that they picked up on this. Some departments may fear hiring or supporting a transitioning professor because of fears of how students may react, but I hope that my case provides some evidence that students can surprise us.

I was also on the job market, aiming for the elusive tenure-track position, which would be at a different institution. This creates some potential worries. First, I'm out about my trans status. While I don't widely advertise this fact, and I generally prefer people to view me as a woman first, and a trans person second (if ever), I have written about being trans, and about being out. While my publications are evaluated anonymously—without any knowledge about who I am—this isn't true for job searches.

The climate for women in philosophy can sometimes be frosty; the climate for trans women can be worse. However, I know that I'm not alone, and my social and professional networks are stronger than ever. I now have to be cautious about which jobs I apply to, since I have to be concerned about new features of department climates. Even if I land a good job, will the students, my colleagues, the administration, and the community be welcoming? These are some of the realities of being an out trans professor without tenure, and they're concerns that I didn't have prior to transitioning. Hopefully, I will find a job where I can build a life with welcoming colleagues. (At the time of publication, I can report that my job search has been successful, and I've accepted a tenure-track position at the College of Charleston.)

COMMUNICATING CHANGES TO COLLEAGUES

When transitioning at work, no matter what type of communication we decide is best, there should be a point person. Ideally, the point person is not the person who is transitioning, and preferably he or she is affiliated with Human Resources. If your organization does not have a Human Resources department, pick your best ally—an office manager, supervisor, or supervisor's supervisor. If there is no obvious person you feel comfortable with, then there may not be an obvious choice for who will be the strongest ally. Figuring out who will be the most supportive may take some time.

There are various ways of communicating information about our transition—via e-mail or in person, through an announcement from us or sent by Human Resources (and sometimes written/edited by us). A letter from Human Resources acknowledging the company's support for our transition can go a long way toward improving the climate at work. Whatever type of communication you choose, feel no pressure to share information about surgeries or background—these are private areas of our lives that are not relevant to our jobs.

When transitioning, it is a good idea to be consistent with whatever set of pronouns we choose. Figure out what is best for you in your line of work. Some gender nonconforming people work in places where colleagues are more easily able to switch to gender-neutral pronouns. We may want to choose ahead of time which gendered pronouns we are more willing to be called if our job is not the kind of place where coworkers will understand the concept of gender-neutral pronouns.

Chances are good that we will have to support others through their experiences of our transition, too. Prepare yourself for this and have standard answers for common questions. Humor can be a useful tool to address inappropriate conversations or questions; alternately, we may simply point out that certain questions are inappropriate or ignore them. Try play-acting these conversations with friends, just as you would do to prepare for a job interview.

We might be asked to educate our new employer or coworkers on trans issues. It is not generally considered good practice for an employer to ask the affected employee to do this. Employers can bring in outside trainers to teach cultural competency with LGBTQ communities. However, despite the availability of trainers, employers often ask us to help, and the role we take in educating our colleagues and employer is up to us. Many of us work with our supervisors or Human Resource representatives to make a plan for how to direct questions about our trans experiences. Working in a team can help things run smoothly. Some of us wish to be addressed directly by coworkers with these questions. Others of us do not want to have to deal with these questions, and prefer them to be directed to Human Resources or to a supervisor, who can respond with something that we and they come up with together. Having clarity about what is best for us will help support us in doing the job we were hired to do.

CORRECTING MISTAKES AND FINDING STRONG ALLIES

No matter where we work, there will be uncomfortable or awkward moments. Even if people are supportive, they will make mistakes. Some people may forget our proper pronouns. If we go by gender-neutral pronouns, it may take time for our coworkers to get them right.

Pronoun use in group settings can be an issue, and you should point this out. In particular, it is important for bosses to use the correct pronoun, to avoid undermining the success of a trans or gender nonconforming employee's transition. When mistakes happen in a public setting, it is often more effective to approach the person after the fact. You want them to be on your side, and not to feel defensive or embarrassed. You are asking for basic respect—but you are still asking for something. When someone makes a mistake, you can pull the person aside in a confidential space. One example of what you could say is: "It would mean a lot to me if you could use this name. A lot of people here respect you, and if you use this name and pronoun for me, it will help others respect me, too." Many people will love to be your champion.

To find strong allies, look for some of these traits:

People who want to be leaders. Who will want to set an example and demonstrate open-minded leadership?
People who want to be caretakers. Who brings brownies to the office, for instance?
People who are more open to new ideas. Who are the out-of-the-box thinkers on the job and in the office? They may be less likely to fear change.
People who clearly value work and skill. Who are the people that seem to care more about the job you are doing than what you wear to work?

OUTSIDE THE 9-TO-5

Many of us do not have a 9-to-5 job. We may work in bartending, food service, or retail; take on odd jobs; drive a cab; or engage in sex work. There can be some real benefits and challenges for trans individuals in these spaces. For example, some of these jobs pay "under the table," meaning that less documentation is required. Some jobs rely more heavily on an "audition" process rather than deep background checks, which can have its advantages—or it may mean that whether we have a job is at the whim of our employer or supervisor.

In some of these jobs, the environment around job history and gender presentation may be more relaxed—or there may be stricter gender-specific dress codes. There may

Jamie Roberts and Anneliese Singh

In New Zealand, Georgina Beyer made history as the first trans person ever elected to a national parliament. Her transition in her mid-twenties included roles as both nightclub singer and sex worker, the latter occupation on one occasion landing her in jail for solicitation. During her first term, her experience as a sex worker informed her advocacy for reforms to New Zealand's prostitution laws. Another one of her aims in parliament was to introduce a bill that would outlaw discrimination on the basis of gender identity. Before the bill passed, however, New Zealand's Solicitor-General wrote an opinion that the current Human Rights Act protected trans New Zealanders from discrimination as part of the class of people protected from "sex discrimination," so she withdrew it. Beyer, who is Maori (the people indigenous to New Zealand), left Parliament at the end of her second term in 2007. Her life story was compelling enough to inspire a documentary, *Georgie Girl*, which was released in 2002.

Georgina Beyer with the Rt. Hon John Key, Prime Minister, and Wellesley College Principal, Warren Owen (photo courtesy of Mark Tantrum/Wellesley College, New Zealand).

also be less built-in protection against discrimination. Some employers may demonstrate disregard for legal rules. With nighttime work in particular, we may have concerns for our personal safety.

Underground jobs fall into many different categories. Some industries may connect to alternative lifestyles that welcome our participation as trans people. For instance, in kitchen culture in the food service industry, we may benefit from being perceived as different or "weird." In some settings, there may be more blurred lines between work relationships and friendships.

Sex Work

Sex work tends to come up often in trans communities. Many of us have been kicked out of our homes or have trouble finding employment, and sex work can become an important means of survival. Some of us may experience shame or sadness about engaging in this kind of work but feel that we lack other alternatives. Some of us come to this country to transition, or are escaping from bad conditions in other countries, and do not necessarily have legal immigration status or speak English comfortably, and sex work may be one of our only options economically. Others of us, regardless of other employment opportunities, may choose to engage in sex work. It can be a lucrative profession in which we make a lot of money very quickly. For this reason, it can be hard to stop doing sex work, because finding an alternative job making a similar wage can be tough. Sex work may also be a form of employment in which our trans identity is seen as an asset. Many of us find the attention to be validating—being seen as sexually desirable can be a great compliment.

INTERVIEW WITH MONIQUE FONTAINE, 26, A TRANS WOMAN LIVING IN NEW YORK CITY

How do you identify? When and where did you begin your transition?
I identify as a heterosexual trans female—I date both genetic and trans men. I was always a girl, it was awkward to be a boy growing up—even the "flamboyant gay boy"—but it was more socially acceptable so I lived with it for a while. I figured once I was 17 I could do what I wanted, so I came out as trans and transitioned a little in high school. People knew me by my boy name, but close friends knew me by my girl name. I was "Monique" full-time by the time I was 18, but I didn't transition hormonally until 22, when I moved to New York City.

What community did you find in New York City? What is your relationship like with the gay men's scene?
Finding your niche in New York City is hard enough, so starting a new job and starting hormones, too—it all came at me at once. It was rough. I was living with two gay boys at the time, and I became known in the gay men's scene. So at first I had my gay male friends, and I had my straight friends at my day job. I knew a couple of trans girls, but I was new and naïve and didn't really speak to them. I didn't

get along with other trans girls—I found them catty, and I thought they were all two-faced. I was friends mostly with gay boys and drag queens until I realized that wasn't working out for me.

Why was it difficult for you to get along with other trans women? Has that changed over time?
I think trans women are always trying to be better than each other. It's always about who's more passable, who's better looking, who can get along in the real world without being noticed. Over time, I started venturing out of the gay men's scene because I realized I wasn't finding the right guys to date, and the guys I was dating didn't really want to be in the gay community. It was a reality check, so I started meeting other trans girls. The first support groups I went to were weird, with all these older trans women who weren't passable. I couldn't relate to them. But then I met this girl Brooke out one night, and she became my first sister. I was also working at Lucky Cheng's at the time, and though some of the girls there were negative, they taught me how to pick friends and choose people to be around. Now I have some close trans friends, and we all want the best for each other.

How does dating come into play? Does it connect to this competition?
The challenge with dating is finding someone that's willing to sacrifice part of himself to make you happy—because for most people it is a sacrifice. Being trans female, the guys that we date have to be very secure, especially if we're not passable, because they may have to deal with family issues and friends. The guy I'm dating right now is very open-minded and we always talk about it, and I'm very lucky because I've gotten to meet his family and his friends.

Dating is hard no matter who you are. But with us, you have girls who are passable, girls who are semipassable, and girls who aren't passable at all. You'll think a girl is your friend, but she'll be talking to your boyfriend behind your back, saying, "I'm way more passable." Competition happens everywhere, but I think it happens more in the trans and gay scene. We're pitted against each other, and everyone is trying to be the best of a very small community. It may sound really shallow, but it makes me feel better about myself to see someone who is less passable than me. I can be a bitch, to an extent.

You mentioned that you "work," and that it's "not your typical 9-to-5." Do you find community among others who do the same kind of work?
Yes. Some of my girlfriends "work." There are a lot of trans women who "work." It's a form of sisterhood, all about making money. I get along with some girls I work with really well—in this line of work it's not so much of a dog-eat-dog world because there's always someone who wants a different girl. It's about capitalizing on how trans women are hypersexualized. For example, a girl I knew was murdered last year, and the first thing the newspapers talked about was how curvaceous she was and how she used to be a man. The first thing people notice about trans women are looks and sexual persona—and a lot of girls capitalize on that. A lot of trans women feel like unless you have a certain look you're not going to get very far, and I think that's mainstream for all women (both genetic and trans) but it is amplified being a trans woman because you have to strive harder to get that image.

How do you stay positive and hopeful despite challenges that come along with being trans?
A lot of trans people become negative and jaded, because we don't have a support system or positive role models. Many trans people can't make a connection with someone who's been through things that they're going through. Counselors and therapists can really help, but we also individually have to focus on the positive and believe that if we work hard and grow from the negative, we can get what we want.

What would you like everyone to understand about trans bodies?
You can't judge a book by its cover. Trans people deal with more scrutiny and confusion than cis people because whenever anything is out of the ordinary, people judge. People make assumptions based on what they look at—but you have to ask questions to get answers. I hate saying that because I hate when random people ask me questions, but I'd rather people ask questions than assume.

TYPES OF SEX WORK

There are many different kinds of sex work. Many types of work that are more physically risky leave less of a permanent record, and many types of work that are less physically risky leave a paper or electronic trail that can be found later on.

Some of us act or pose for pornographic films. In this type of work, models do not typically have ownership of the end product. Not only does this mean that someone else is making more money than we are off of our work, but it means that even if we become opposed to the use of our image, we do not have a right to say "no" to its use. Some models have started their own Web sites to get around these issues, but like any small business there is no guarantee of success.

Many pornographers seek out transgender talent, which can make us feel both loved and welcomed. However, we are still being hired as wage laborers. While we may be able to make money as trans people in pornography, it is ultimately the producers and production companies that are profiting the most from the work that we do.

Keep in mind that anything we put online—whether photos, video, or live camera work—can potentially be used by someone else, and it could be used against us for blackmail purposes. Also, for those of us who are undocumented, if it is discovered that we did this work, it could undermine a case for asylum or visa.

Another type of sex work is exotic dancing, or stripping. Exotic dancing is usually an in-person transaction in which we dance for tips, typically in little or no clothing. It can be very lucrative, but like any tipping profession there is variability in how much money we take in based on where we work. While this form of work is not without its risks, dance clubs are usually staffed with security personnel for our protection.

Professional BDSM work is sometimes criminalized, depending on the state and on the nature of the physical contact between a worker and a client. The closer the conduct to traditional concepts of sex, the more we expose ourselves to the law. As a general rule of thumb, it is physically safer to do professional dominatrix (pro-domme) work than it is to do professional submission (pro-sub) work, due to the power dynamics inherent to BDSM.

THINGS I WISH I KNEW BEFORE I BECAME THE ONLY TRANS BOY ESCORT IN TOWN . . .

Anonymous

Starting testosterone meant I only faked half my orgasms with paid dates. This was unexpected and occasionally disturbing. Sometimes it was good, but it started out confusing. Sometimes my dates would be really great guys who taught me how to shoot a gun, tie a tie, and swagger through hotel lobbies. Sometimes it seemed like they researched FTM on Google only to find the most hurtful things to say. Everyone paid up front, and I always showered afterwards.

The right binder for dates is not the one that looks best; it's the one that you can get in and out of fastest. Save your good binder for yourself and your sweetie(s).

It is possible to hear the word "pussy" and not get pissed off.

It is possible to feel like a miserable freak and still get a tip.

Gay truckers give phenomenal blowjobs and tip better than businessmen. Try to not judge a date by his hotel.

It is possible to advertise even on the most dysphoric day. Pretend it is opposite day, be objective, and never, ever, take it personally when no one wants a date.

It is possible, but not a good idea, to advertise for casual sex and escort dates at the same time.

My previous years as a girl escort didn't help much. Old habits tripped me up, and it took weeks to get over my pride and advertise gay boy rates. Having a goal and a plan kept me on track.

Find other sex workers and make the best of those friendships—but be cautious of unsolicited advice.

Returning dates always trump new dates, and neither trumps plans with friends.

No matter what, no matter how safe you feel, always have a phone check-in with someone who knows who you are and where you are. No excuses.

Respect your security person's time and concern; this is your lifeline. You don't have to start a blog, be a career sex worker, or work long term, but working in complete secrecy is a recipe for unsafe and crazy-making dates. Always have a back-up plan. There's no such thing as being tough enough to handle it alone.

Having sex in exchange for money or gifts is criminalized in most parts of the United States. There are many different ways to engage in this type of work. *Indoor calls* take place in an apartment or hotel room and the exchange is usually determined before the meeting. Indoor calls can be safer from legal repercussions, as the transaction is conducted in a private space. However, it is easy for personal information to become public if the meeting takes place in the sex worker's home or a hotel room rented under the worker's name. If the indoor call is taken at the home of a client, or at a place determined by the client, the worker is potentially exposed to greater risk of physical or legal harm. *Outdoor calls* are generally the least safe type of sex work because it is harder to screen clients, and workers are more likely to be stopped by a patrol officer or an undercover officer specifically looking to arrest sex workers. It can also be dangerous to be carrying large sums of money in public.

STAYING SAFE

When interacting with law enforcement, our rights vary depending on where we live. Many cities have Web sites where people have gathered information and advice on how to interact with police in that city. These are often called "Know Your Rights" bulletins. Look for one that talks about where you live.

There are a number of ways that sex workers stay safe. Practice safer sex, if possible. Sometimes this can create other risks, such as risk of incarceration in jurisdictions in which condoms are considered evidence of prostitution, or risk of injury if a client resists or refuses our efforts. Some people employ harm reduction techniques, such as using condoms for those sexual acts that are most likely to transmit infections. Do not lie to clients. If you do not have or cannot do something they want, do not promise it to them. It can be very dangerous if they find out. Remember to get the money before starting to work. Work in pairs or groups when possible. Make sure that anytime you meet a client in private or go to a private location with a stranger, someone you trust has your client's information, whether that is a phone number, address, or just the license plate numbers of the client's car. Do not carry valuables or all of your IDs when working, and avoid wearing necklaces or scarves that could be used to choke you. Make safety arrangements with a friend, such as a set check-in time when the friend will call you and a plan for what to do if you are in trouble. If you are working by yourself, pretend to give identifying information to a friend over the phone. Some cities also have "bad date" services that allow you to report and check records of clients known to harm sex workers.

If you are taking indoor calls, use the Internet to help screen potential clients. This can be as simple as looking them up on a social networking site. This can help avoid undercover police officers (who do not have an obligation to say that they are law enforcement before having sex), as well as avoid dangerous individuals. Set limits and be firm about them. This often includes barrier use and safer sex, what types of sex you are willing to have, your rates, and where you will work. It is always OK to have boundaries, even when doing sex work. Asserting boundaries firmly will help you stay in control of your work. Do not trust clients—they will tell you what they know you want to hear.

Those of us who are sex workers may have certain expectations placed on us by others. People around us may expect us to be more willing to have sex with them or share our personal sexual experiences. Clients may also push boundaries by asking for longer sessions or additional services without paying an extra fee. If we are working for someone else, we may be promised one type of work, and then told to do another when we show up. If someone is pushing your boundaries, you often have the power to refuse. There will always be consequences to that decision, whether it is not getting a repeat client or losing a job at a strip club, but there is usually middle ground between giving in to something that makes you uncomfortable and walking away completely.

COMMON ISSUES IN SEX WORK

Transition-related decisions can be impacted by our participation in sex work. In some cases, client preferences—which drive our ability to seek out and retain clients—may lead us to reduce or delay our use of hormones, or defer gender-affirming surgeries, to preserve sexual function. The intense focus on our genitals, which we may have ambivalent or negative feelings about, may trigger dysphoria.

Sexual assault is common in sex work. Learn the location of sympathetic medical clinics and the procedure for reporting a perpetrator before it happens. Clinics often stock postexposure prophylaxis (PEP) that helps prevent HIV infection if taken soon after unprotected sex. Medical facilities can also help by taking a rape kit that will compile evidence from the perpetrator (potentially including DNA, hair and skin samples, and fiber evidence). Engaging in sex work does not mean that we have any lesser right to live free from sexual assault.

Law enforcement officers, in general, have wildly varying standards of practice and acceptable conduct when it comes to the policing of sex workers. It is not uncommon for officers to sexually assault sex workers they catch engaging in illegal conduct, and it is hard to get those officers to face legal repercussions. Know your rights where you live with regard to interacting with police.

Drugs (including alcohol) are common in sex work. Many of us prefer to be on some sort of drug when performing this work. With drugs or alcohol, there is a risk of addiction. Addiction takes away our control over our lives and can lead us to engage in unsafe behavior. If you find yourself addicted to a substance and want to quit, there are numerous LGBTQ-specific mental health resources. See Chapter 15 for more information.

Isolation can be a problem in sex work. Stigma over sex work can disrupt the connections we have with members of our community, friends, or even family. For this reason, many sex workers form communities with one another for mutual support and protection. There are sex work communities where we are sometimes exploited, but there are also many communities where we look out for each other and keep each other safe.

CONCLUSION

While trans and gender nonconforming people may face challenges with employment, there are overwhelming examples of how fulfilling our employment experiences can be and what fantastic employees we can be. Though it should go without saying, work should not determine or undermine our value as human beings. For some of us, our work is a calling, but for others it is a means to an end. Neither one of these perspectives is more valid than the other. Go after the jobs you would like, work hard to attain them, and focus on what is within your control. Whatever challenges you may face, do not lose hope. We must be able to believe that things will get better before they actually can. Work hard, get your documents and stories in order for your job search process, and have confidence in yourself as a potential employee. It takes hard work to succeed. Though options can be limited at times, that is no reason not to pursue whatever career you desire.

REFERENCES AND FURTHER READING

Bender-Baird, K. (2011). *Transgender employment experiences: Gendered perceptions and the law.* Albany: State University of New York Press.

Grant, J. M., Mottet, L. A., Tanis, J., Harrison, J., Herman, J. L., & Keisling, M. (2011). *Injustice at every turn: A report of the national transgender discrimination survey.* Washington, DC: National Center for Transgender Equality and National Gay and Lesbian Task Force.

Maggie's Toronto Sex Workers Action Project. (n.d.). *Resources for sex workers.* Retrieved December 2013, from http://maggiestoronto.ca/legal_updates

Schilt, K. (2011). *Just one of the guys?: Transgender men and the persistence of gender inequality.* Chicago, IL: University of Chicago Press.

Sheridan, V. (2009). *The complete guide to transgender in the workplace.* Santa Barbara, CA: ABC-CLIO.

The Sex Workers Project at the Urban Justice Center. (2012). *Know your rights!* Retrieved December 2013, from http://sexworkersproject.org/downloads/2012/2012-know-your-rights.pdf

Weiss, J. T. (2007). *Transgender workplace diversity: Policy tools, training issues, and communication strategies for HR and legal professionals.* North Charleston, SC: BookSurge.

10

LEGAL ISSUES
Kylar W. Broadus and Shannon Price Minter

This chapter provides an over-view of key legal issues for trans people in the United States, along with some practical advice on how best to protect ourselves and our loved ones. The information provided in this chapter is necessarily general and cannot take into account each individual's circumstances or changes in the law. The information in this chapter should not be construed as legal advice. If you need legal help or advice, consult with an attorney or legal organization that can provide you with specific, detailed guidance based on your individual situation and the laws where you live.

The National Transgender Discrimination Survey (Grant et al., 2011) found that as many as 40% of transgender respondents who presented ID that did not match their gender identity or expression experienced harassment as a result.

THE LAW PLAYS A UNIQUE ROLE IN THE LIVES OF TRANS PEOPLE. Many of us face legal challenges related to our gender identity. Navigating those challenges may sometimes be a lot of work, but in most cases, with persistence and accurate information, we can protect ourselves and our families. One of the most common challenges is obtaining identity documents that accurately reflect our gender. In almost every arena of life, including our ability to marry and parent, work, and even to enter a restaurant or use a public restroom, having legal recognition of our gender identity and legal protections against discrimination is essential.

For those of us who are homeless or poor, legal recognition may be necessary to get shelter, participate in job training programs, or even access basic health care resources. For trans youth, legal protections in school districts may mean the difference between living safely as ourselves, or being subjected to daily harassment, being forced to repress our identities, or having to leave school.

We are still fighting for equality under the law in many ways, and we will continue to push legal institutions to recognize and counteract the forces that threaten our health, our ability to support ourselves, and, in some cases, even our lives. We are making progress every day.

One way to empower ourselves is to understand the law and the rights that we do have, and to work together and with our allies to win further legal protections. The best we can do is to be prepared, stand up for ourselves, and be strong advocates for our communities.

IDENTITY DOCUMENTS

Having identity documents (IDs) that match our gender identity and the way we live in the world is an important part of being able to participate in society safely and with dignity and privacy. Having ID that matches our gender is validating and helps many of us feel recognized and supported, which then empowers us to stand up for ourselves in other ways. Not having accurate documents may discourage us from taking part in everyday life. Furthermore, having to "come out" or be identified as transgender every time we need to show a piece of identification—whether to enter a bar or to apply for a job—can expose us to unnecessary personal and financial risks. Therefore, many of us take steps to change our legal name and gender marker on our identity documents.

Legal Name Changes

In the past, if a person started using a new name and became known by it, the person could use that new name legally. However, in part due to increased concerns over identity theft, most states have tightened the legal requirements for changing your name. Most states now require anyone wishing to legally change their name to obtain a court order. The court order enables us to change our name on other forms of documentation, such as driver's licenses and bank accounts.

> *"I legally changed my name by court order. I was supported by a lawyer who worked pro-bono for trans people. He filed most of the paperwork and got the judge to waive most of the fees and the requirement to place an ad in a paper about my name change."*

US law governing name changes is very flexible, and anyone can legally change their name in every state. The process for getting a legal name change varies slightly from state to state, but the basic requirements and process are similar in most places. Typically, a person

San Francisco Trans March, 2011 (copyright Rick Gerharter, rickgerharterphotos.com).

starts the process by filing a short petition that states the person's current legal name, the name the person wishes to use, and a very short explanation of the reason for the change. Every state has preprinted forms for these name-change petitions that you can pick up at your local courthouse or print online.

BLURRING GENDER ACROSS STATE LINES

Christian, JD, is the president of operations for a frozen yogurt franchise on the East Coast and a law school graduate with a concentration in gender and sexuality studies, utilizing his legal training as a public speaker, community activist, and educator on trans issues.

I was born in California on November 14, 1985. I was reborn in Massachusetts on September 22, 2009. These two states, on opposite ends of the country, aided in my gender transition from female to male. I was accepted into law school on the East Coast in 2008. I had no idea when leaving sunny California for snowy Massachusetts that my life would change in ways I could not have possibly imagined.

The decision to physically transition depended on logistics as much as it did intention. Each area of the country varies in the methods and requirements for trans people to obtain hormone therapy, some clinics and providers being more stringent than others. Locating a therapist who could understand, treat, and provide the appropriate gender identity diagnosis (at the time) in my geographic area was the first step. The area of Massachusetts in which I reside has fortunately been blessed with many trained individuals to provide support for the trans community. My endocrinologist worked 20 minutes from my therapist's office and 10 minutes from my law school.

For some trans people, this journey can be much harder. Massachusetts turned out by chance to be a great choice for my physical transition. My therapist and endocrinologist knew each other, had past trans clients, and have been available to ease my anxiety over the years. For others, the nearest trans-aware therapist may be hours or even a state away from where they reside. So, unless finances become a nonissue, access to the first steps of transgender psychological and medical care can seem impossible and prompt some to fall into states of depression, isolation, and/or self-harm, including suicide.

The state where I was born has played the largest role in terms of changing my identity documents. California's laws are some of the more relaxed as far as obtaining new forms of identification goes. My court-ordered name change mirrored most states' policies. I published my intent to change my name in a newspaper, paid the necessary fees, and then went before a judge swearing my name change was not for fraudulent purposes. My name change was granted, and I proceeded to the DMV to update my license. In California, all that is required to change your name on your license is the court order. All that is required for the gender marker change on your license is a letter from a doctor—whether that is from a psychiatrist or general doctor makes no difference. One year into seeing my therapist, I was on hormones and held a court-ordered name change, as well as a driver's license reflecting a new picture, new name, and new gender. I was very lucky. Others did not and do not share in that luxury.

The next steps in my transition also pertain to updating identity documents, namely my birth certificate. Changing one's gender in their birth state can be difficult or, in states such as Ohio and Tennessee, forbidden. California fortunately allows for a completely new birth certificate to be issued. This means my name and gender will accurately reflect my identity, once I provide a copy of my court orders. For trans people who happen to have been born in states that deny gender changes on birth certificates, one thing that can be done is to obtain a court-ordered gender change, which must be recognized from state to state. While I am incredibly grateful for the somewhat simple logistical steps in my transition, my heart is heavy for those with little or no options. The work is far from over.

Most people handle their own name changes without the help of a lawyer. In every state, there are self-help legal books in libraries or bookstores that explain how to go about seeking a legal name change. State court systems often have helpful information online about how to represent yourself in a legal name change hearing as well. There may also be good information available through local or state transgender peer support or advocacy groups. Those of us who are low income may qualify for assistance from a legal aid organization.

In California, the Transgender Law Center helps many people with legal name changes, as does the Sylvia Rivera Law Project in New York City.

"I had to go to court to get my name changed. This was a very important step in my transition. I was nervous but it was so exciting. I just wish I would have had someone like a mentor to explain all the paperwork."

Most states require people seeking a name change to publish a short statement that they are changing their name from "x" to "y" in one or more local newspapers for a specified period of time (often six weeks). The purpose of this requirement is to help ensure that the person is not seeking to change their name for a criminal or fraudulent purpose. Then, once the publication period is over, the person appears before a judge in court, who grants the name change and gives the person an order stating that their name has been legally changed. Having that legal document may be important in case you ever need to prove that you have obtained a legal name change, so be sure to hang onto it and keep it in a safe place. You may also want to make copies.

"I live in New Jersey. It was very easy. I did it without a lawyer by filling out required forms. I had to post public notice. Reading about my name change in the paper made me feel very proud."

Most states allow a name change for just about any reason, as long as the purpose is not to commit a crime or engage in fraud. For example, a person cannot legally change their name to evade creditors or to make money by pretending to be a famous movie star. Apart from these broad restrictions, most states permit individuals to change their names freely, without any additional limitations or requirements. (As a side note, this is not true in many European countries, which tend to impose very strict limitations on name changes.) In the United States, anyone can apply for a name change in the state where they currently live—they do not have to have been born in that state to legally change their name there.

Important to note is that there is no requirement that we must undergo any medical treatment or surgery to legally change our name in any state. Despite this, some courts may try to impose medical requirements or force us to disclose details about our medical treatment.

"My name was changed prior to going full time. I had an attorney and she was very helpful and it was accomplished easily. I had tried to change it on my own and the judge said he would not do so unless I had the reassignment surgery completed. When I found my attorney, she simply said 'he can't do that.' She was right."

If a judge asks you to produce medical records or testify about your medical treatment, or is otherwise expressing resistance to granting your name change, the best thing to do is to ask for a continuance, which will postpone the court proceedings, so that you can seek legal help. An attorney can submit a memo explaining to the court that the law does not require a transgender person to undergo medical treatment or pass any other special test in order to change their name. In most cases, that will be sufficient.

If a court still denies your name-change petition, you can appeal the order. Contact an attorney or reach out to an LGBTQ legal organization for help.

> *"I legally changed my name. The lady judge gave me a big grin and said, 'Welcome to the sensible half of humanity.'"*

Legal Gender Changes

As with changing our names, changing our legal gender often begins at the state court level. This is often called a court-ordered Declaration of Legal Gender, Declaration of Gender Designation Change, or simply Declaration of Gender Change. Each state has its own rules and terminology. In some cases, a legal gender change may also amend your birth certificate, while in other cases, it will not.

We can apply for a court-ordered gender change in the state where we live, even if that is not where we were born. In most states, this happens as a routine matter, though there are some jurisdictions where it may not be possible. In practice, you may run into a particular judge who is unfamiliar with this process, and who will require some extra education. If you have trouble finding an attorney who knows how to file this type of petition, or if you run into resistance from a judge, reach out to an LGBTQ legal organization.

In order to get a legal gender change, most states require us to submit a petition providing some basic information about ourselves, along with documentation from a medical provider and a filing fee. If you cannot afford the fee, many states allow you to request a fee waiver.

The medical standards vary somewhat from state to state. Most courts and administrative agencies require a physician's letter documenting that some type of gender-affirming surgery has been obtained, although the exact requirements vary from state to state. Some states, such as California, Vermont, and Washington, have updated their policies to be consistent with current medical knowledge and the World Professional Association for Transgender Health (WPATH) Standards of Care. In these states, rather than requiring proof of surgery, the laws or regulations require submission of a letter from a medical provider stating that the person requesting the gender change has had "appropriate clinical treatment." A number of other states are also in the process of updating their laws and policies to adopt similar standards.

In the meantime, however, many states still require some type of surgery (although not necessarily genital surgery). Requiring surgery excludes trans people who cannot afford surgery, who cannot have surgery, or who do not require surgery to live comfortably. This may leave some of us without legal documentation that matches our lived gender and puts us at greater risk for discrimination and harassment.

> *"I had to testify that I have altered my body permanently through taking hormones and growing breasts that can only be removed surgically. I had to come up with the money for court cost fees, an office visit to a 'friendly' physician, and a graduated fee structuring therapist. It took me over a year to save up and prepare for all this, but it was well worth it!!"*

Important to note is that all states are legally required to recognize a court order from other states—even those that currently do not grant court-ordered legal gender changes for transgender people, such as Ohio and Tennessee. Therefore, it is advisable to obtain a court order declaring that your legal gender is male or female. Even if you are not required to do so by the law in your state, having a court order provides powerful protection if anyone ever questions your legal gender. Additionally, having a court order stating that you have legally changed your gender generally must be accepted and respected by third parties such as insurance companies and employers.

Jamie Roberts and Anneliese Singh

Anna Grodzka was the second trans person to be elected to a national parliament in Europe, winning office as an MP in Poland in 2011. She ran as a member of the Palikot movement, a left-leaning party and the third largest. Grodzka faces discrimination within the parliament. Krystyna Pawlowicz from the conservative Law and Justice Party refuses to address Grodzka with correct pronouns and makes outrageous personal attacks based on Grodzka's trans status. Poland is noted for having a highly medicalized and technical process for legal recognition of one's gender identity, which is applied unevenly across the country. In 2012, Grodzka, working with other trans activists, endorsed a bill called the Gender Accordance Act, which would modernize Poland's approach to transition-related laws and procedures.

Polish MP Anna Grodzka interviewed in the Sejm.

Driver's Licenses and State Identification Cards

Within the United States, the most commonly used form of identification is a state driver's license or state identification card (state ID). Having a driver's license or state ID that matches our name and gender identity is important for us in our daily lives. When we do not have a correct state ID, we may be unable to apply for jobs, travel, cash a check, or engage in many other routine activities of everyday life.

Each state has its own rules for changing the name and gender marker on a driver's license or state ID. In general, to receive a state ID or driver's license, a person has to provide proof of identity, which, depending on your state's requirements, may include a birth certificate, passport, Social Security card, utility bill, official tax return, W2 forms from an employer, or other forms of identification (and, of course, a written and/or behind-the-wheel driving test). If you have already changed your name on these documents, that should suffice to obtain a driver's license or state ID with your new name. In some instances, however, you may have to produce a court-ordered name change.

The standards for changing a gender marker on a driver's license or state ID card vary quite a bit from state to state. In some states, you must first obtain a new birth certificate or court-ordered gender change. In others, a gender marker can be changed based on a declaration from a doctor. In some places, the doctor must disclose what forms of medical treatment the person has undergone. Increasingly, however, states are updating their policies simply to require verification by a doctor or other health care provider that the person is transgender and is living as a man or a woman. This approach allows individuals, in conjunction with their health care providers, to determine what medical treatments are best for them.

If you need help figuring out what your state requires to change the gender marker on your state driver's license or state ID, many states now post their policies online. You can also try calling ahead or reaching out to an LGBTQ legal organization.

The National Center for Transgender Equality (NCTE) has an online map called Driver's License Policies by State that provides information on the necessary steps for changing our name or gender designation on our driver's license.

Passports

As of 2010, the State Department has clear guidelines on how to change the gender marker on a passport that are in line with accepted medical guidelines and standards of care. The new passport guidelines allow us to change the gender marker on our passport if any licensed physician, including a primary care physician or specialist, writes a supporting letter, on official letterhead, with the following information:

• Physician's full name
• Medical license or certificate number
• Issuing state or other jurisdiction of medical license/certificate
• Drug Enforcement Administration (DEA) registration number
• Address and telephone number of the physician

- Language stating that the physician is your attending physician and that the physician has a doctor–patient relationship with you
- Language stating you have had appropriate clinical treatment for gender transition to the new gender
- Language stating "I declare under penalty of perjury under the laws of the United States that the forgoing is true and correct"

The letter should be submitted along with all other documents required for a passport application. If the doctor's letter states that the transition is "in process," a 2-year temporary passport will be issued and can be extended at the end of that term.

Birth Certificates

Many of us change the name and gender marker on our drivers' licenses and passports. Some of us also obtain corrected birth certificates, though this is a more challenging process, and in some states it is not permitted. As a practical matter, there are not many situations in which a person has to produce a birth certificate. However, some states require one to get a new driver's license, and people from other countries often need to produce one in various immigration-related contexts.

> "I live in a state where I can't legally change the sex on my birth certificate, but I will be able to change my sex on my driver's license. My state actually made that process easier."

While it is fairly easy to change the name on a birth certificate, it can be more difficult or, in some instances, impossible to change the gender marker. The majority of states require a court order to obtain a new or amended birth certificate with a corrected gender marker. Some other states will issue a new or amended birth certificate through an administrative process. Three states (Ohio, Idaho, and Tennessee) will not issue new or amended birth certificates with gender changes unless presented with a court order from another state, and even with such an order, you may run into resistance in these states.

Those states that do grant changes to the gender marker on birth certificates vary on whether they issue a new or amended birth certificate. Many provide a new birth certificate with a new gender marker that cannot be distinguished from the original document. This provides a trans person with maximum privacy and legal protection. Others, however, provide a certificate that is visibly amended and shows that the gender has been changed.

> "I submitted the needed forms to the state of Illinois, where I was born, and they issued a brand new birth certificate that says 'boy.'"

Why should we obtain a new legal birth certificate? In some cases, doing so is necessary to get a driver's license or state ID that matches our correct gender. But even if we live in a state that does not require a new birth certificate before providing us with state ID, having a new birth certificate provides a lot of legal protection in the event that our legal gender is ever questioned—especially if we have a court order saying that we are entitled to a new birth certificate because we have legally changed our gender.

> "I was not married at the time of transition, and have married since then. I transitioned from female to male, and then eventually married a woman. By the time I got married, my transition was complete and all my paperwork read with my correct name and male gender. We were legally married with no issues."

Note that there is a significant difference between getting a new birth certificate and getting a court order stating that you have legally changed your gender. For example, a state is not necessarily required to recognize a corrected birth certificate from another state, although many do. However, all states are required to recognize a court order from other states.

Social Security

Those of us who change our name, gender, or both will also need to update our information with the Social Security Administration (SSA). This prevents delays in our tax refunds and ensures that our wages are correctly attributed to our Social Security record. To change your name on your Social Security card, you will be required to fill out an SS-5 form, available online.

If you changed your name though a court order, when you go to the SSA, you will be required to bring:

- The court order showing your new name
- One identity document in your old name (may be current or expired)
- One identity document in your new legal name (must be current)

Even though Social Security cards do not have the gender of a person printed on them, the SSA does track the gender of each cardholder. As of 2013, the SSA requires only government-issued documentation reflecting a gender change, or a certification from a physician confirming that we have undergone appropriate clinical treatment for gender transition, in order to update our gender marker.

The letter requirements are the same as those required to update the gender marker on a passport—the letter must come from a licensed physician with whom you have a patient–doctor relationship and who is familiar with your transition-related treatment. This may be any physician who is familiar with your treatment, including a primary care physician or a specialist. All certifications must be on the physician's office letterhead and include all of the same information needed in the case of a letter for a passport gender change.

It is important to note that changing the gender marker on your SSA records does not necessarily mean that the federal government will recognize your gender when determining whether you are in a valid marriage under federal law—for example, when deciding whether you or your spouse is eligible for Social Security survivor benefits when one spouse dies. Whether your marriage is valid under federal law generally depends on whether the state in which you got married recognizes your marriage as valid (see Sidebar on the Defense of Marriage Act).

HEALTH CARE

Trans people do not yet have specific legal protections against health care discrimination in most states or under federal law, but that is changing for the better every day as more states and localities are enacting such laws. In the meantime, there are many ways we can advocate for ourselves, support other trans people seeking care, and fight back against the denial of care or discriminatory care.

Laws Prohibiting Discrimination in Health Care

Trans people and allies are working hard to pass laws that specifically protect trans people in the health care system. A growing number of states are passing or considering such laws, although we have a long way to go. In the meantime, even in places where no specific antidiscrimination laws exist, trans people who are denied care or discriminated against are not powerless. In almost every situation, there are ways we can stand up for ourselves and each other, either through the law or other kinds of advocacy.

FEDERAL PROTECTIONS

In the United States, there are no federal laws that specifically protect trans people against discrimination in the health care system. There is a federal law, the Americans with Disabilities Act, that prohibits discrimination against people with a wide variety of medical conditions, but transgender people are specifically excluded from protection under it.

However, the Patient Protection and Affordable Care Act (ACA), which was signed into law in 2010 and has begun to go into effect in various stages, prohibits sex discrimination. The federal Department of Health and Human Services (HHS) has clarified that discrimination based on transgender status is sex discrimination. Under the ACA, there are protections against sex discrimination in insurance and by service providers that receive federal financial assistance, which includes most hospitals. This new law may be an important source of legal protection for transgender people in the health care arena, but much work remains to be done to ensure that individual states understand and implement the ACA's nondiscrimination requirements.

THE DISABILITY RIGHTS MOVEMENT

Sadie Baker is an activist, an advocate for homeless and street-based LGBTQ youth (currently working with Chicago's Broadway Youth Center), and a former core member of the DC Trans Coalition.

Like trans communities, people with disabilities face a world that is not built to accommodate us. Just as trans people are forced to navigate gendered spaces and bureaucratic forms that cannot make sense of our minds and bodies, people with disabilities must move through a world full of constructed barriers that make their lives needlessly difficult. From the way we build sidewalks to the way that schools measure intelligence, people with physical and mental disabilities must contend with a world that privileges some bodies and minds while marginalizing others. Similar to transphobia, ableism (the oppression faced by people with disabilities) creates societal ignorance and hostility toward certain individuals, while treating others as "normal."

These similar experiences of exclusion and cultural stereotyping make disability rights and trans rights go hand in hand. Both movements are seeking to change the way society treats people that are deemed "different." There is some tension here as well. "Disability" is a protected legal status in the United States, and in some cases, trans people have been able to fight discrimination under this category (where "gender identity and expression" are not already explicitly protected).

This strategy has proven to be contentious on all sides. Many trans people do not believe that being trans is a medical condition and thus disagree with this approach. At the same time, some people with disabilities resent trans people using this category to claim rights.

Despite this, there are still many opportunities for trans communities and the disability rights movement to work together. In Washington, D.C., the DC Trans Coalition (DCTC) worked with disability advocates to advance the human rights of prisoners. When the D.C. Department of Corrections (DOC) attempted to create a special exemption for itself so that it would not have to follow the D.C. Human Rights Act mandate to house trans people according to their gender identity, DCTC worked with disability rights groups to fight back. If the DOC had been able to set a legal precedent that it did not have to respect the human rights of trans prisoners, this would have meant that it might try to exempt itself from human rights provisions that required it to provide special housing and medication for people with physical and mental disabilities. This is just one example of how disability rights and trans rights can intersect.

STATE AND LOCAL NONDISCRIMINATION LAWS

Many cities and counties and some states have enacted laws that prohibit discrimination against trans people in "public accommodations," which is a legal term that refers to businesses and other establishments that are open to the general public. These laws generally include hospitals, doctors, and other medical providers. However, depending on the law in your city or state, these laws may not apply to private clinics, religious hospitals, or single-sex facilities.

Thirteen states and the District of Columbia have enacted local laws that specifically protect trans people from discrimination in public accommodations: California, Colorado, Hawaii, Illinois, Iowa, Maine, Minnesota, New Jersey, New Mexico, Oregon, Rhode Island, Vermont, and Washington. Many cities and counties have as well. State and local laws that prohibit discrimination on the basis of sex or, in fewer cases, on the basis of disability may also protect trans people depending on how they are interpreted in the courts.

OTHER POSSIBLE SOURCES OF LEGAL PROTECTION AGAINST HEALTH CARE DISCRIMINATION

Those of us who live in places where no specific antidiscrimination laws exist may still have a legal claim if we are denied emergency medical care by a doctor, hospital, or first responder simply because we are trans. Medical providers generally have a duty to provide emergency care and cannot refuse to treat someone simply because they disapprove of their gender identity.

We may also be able to bring malpractice or personal injury claims against a provider who fails to provide medical care for a problem or condition that is not related to treatment for gender transition. For example, a doctor should not refuse to treat a transgender person for high blood pressure, diabetes, a heart condition, a broken bone, cancer, or any other medical problem simply because the person is transgender. We may also be able to bring a complaint against the provider with their professional medical association or licensing agency.

Private Health Insurance Plans

In the United States, companies that sell private health insurance are generally free to exclude coverage for any condition state law does not require them to include. For example, many private health insurance plans used to exclude coverage for illnesses related to HIV until states responded by enacting laws prohibiting those exclusions. Similarly, some states require insurance plans to cover pregnancy and contraception, while others do not. Most states also prohibit insurance companies from discriminating based on race, sex, religion, and other specified characteristics.

California, Oregon, Vermont, and the District of Columbia are the only states/districts that prohibit private insurance plans from excluding coverage for treatments for gender transition, although other states are considering similar measures. In addition, more labor unions are negotiating contracts that require employers to cover transition-related care.

Many private insurance plans still have provisions that exclude treatments relating to gender transition. These exclusions are often based on the classification of gender transition treatments as "cosmetic" or "experimental." Today, doctors and other health care providers with expertise in trans issues recognize that treatments for gender transition are medically necessary and effective. Nonetheless, many insurance companies continue to exclude them from coverage.

The good news is that more employers are demanding the ability to buy insurance plans that do not exclude their trans employees. As a result, many insurance companies are getting rid of those exclusions and making nondiscriminatory plans available. The Human Rights Campaign (HRC) now requires employers to make significant efforts to obtain equal health care benefits for trans employees in order to get a perfect rating from their Corporate Equality Index. Many employers care deeply about demonstrating their commitment to equality for LGBTQ employees, so this can be a powerful tool.

In addition, a growing number of municipalities and universities are starting to change their health care plans to include coverage for transition-related care. For example, San Francisco has provided equal health care benefits to city and county employees for several years, which has supplied helpful data showing the very low cost of doing so. Because the City and County of San Francisco have paved the way for other municipalities, like the City of Portland and Multnomah County, some private employers have been willing to provide nondiscriminatory benefit plans as well. If you live in a city or town that might consider changing its policy to provide equal health benefits to trans city employees, that can be a powerful way to lay a foundation for greater health coverage for all trans people in your state.

In addition to denying coverage for transition-related care, some insurance companies exploit their exclusions for treatments related to sex-reassignment or gender transition to deny all sorts of unrelated medical care. For example, an insurance company may deny reimbursement to a trans man for a hysterectomy, even if the hysterectomy was necessary because of cancer or a risk of cancer rather than for the purpose of gender transition. Similarly, an insurance company may deny reimbursement for treatment of a blood clot to a trans woman, on the theory that the blood clot may have been caused by or related to the estrogen she was taking for her gender transition.

Some of us may also experience problems related to how our gender is coded in our insurance plan. For example, a trans woman may be denied coverage for a prostate exam because she is designated as female on her insurance plan. A trans man may be denied coverage for testosterone because he is coded as female on his plan, or may be denied coverage for a pap smear because he is coded as male.

These denials of coverage are unlawful and wrong. If you are experiencing this type of discrimination, appeal the denial and reach out to an attorney or an LGBTQ or trans legal group for help.

WHAT YOU CAN DO ABOUT HEALTH CARE DISCRIMINATION

If you are discriminated against or harassed by a hospital, clinic, counselor, doctor, or other health care provider, reach out to an LGBTQ or trans legal organization to find out if you may have some legal recourse. Even if you are not protected by a specific law, you may be able to file an ethics complaint. Our stories can help advocates document the extent of this problem, so we can educate providers, legislators, and policy makers about the need for more specific protections and training. If you experience discrimination, make sure to take detailed accurate notes about what happened, including the names of the individual health care providers involved.

Those of us who face denials of coverage for transition-related care may have a variety of legal options. First, check to see whether your policy has an exclusion for transition-related treatment. Some do not. If you are fortunate enough to have such a policy, then there is no basis for a company to deny reimbursement for medically necessary care such as counseling, hormone therapy, or gender-affirming surgery. Every plan has an internal administrative process for appealing a denial of coverage. Follow that appeal process, and be sure to get documentation from your therapist, hormone provider, or surgeon that the care provided is medically necessary. If possible, have an attorney or legal organization help guide you through the appeal process. Dealing with insurance companies can be stressful and tedious, but persistence can really pay off. Many of us who appeal denials of coverage are successful.

If your policy does have an exclusion, look closely at the exact wording. In some cases, the wording may exclude only sex-reassignment surgery, but not counseling or hormone therapy. If so, the company may have to pay for medically necessary counseling and hormone therapy. In addition, for some surgeries, there may be a medical reason other than gender transition that would require the company to pay. For example, a trans man with abdominal pain from fibroids or endometriosis may be eligible for a hysterectomy. Similarly, a trans man who knows he is at high risk of breast cancer due to his genetic heritage may be eligible for a double mastectomy.

In other cases, a policy may say that it excludes certain treatments related to gender transition because they are "cosmetic." In such a case, you may be able to challenge the denial of coverage for transition-related care by showing that in your particular case, the treatment is medically necessary. Similarly, if a policy says that it excludes treatments related to gender transition because they are "experimental," it may be possible to challenge that exclusion by showing that the treatment at issue has been proven to be effective and is accepted as a standard, nonexperimental treatment by experts in the field.

Some policies include a provision excluding treatments relating to gender transition, while also including another provision stating that medically necessary care will be covered. In such cases, we may be able to argue that a reasonable person would interpret the policy to cover medically necessary treatments for gender transition. This argument has proven successful in many cases—especially if the company has paid for any treatments related to transition, such as counseling or hormone therapy, but is now balking at paying for surgery.

Many of us who are persistent and keep pushing back will meet with at least some success in getting reimbursed for some or all of our transition-related care, even including some surgeries.

Publicly Funded Health Programs

Many of us use publicly funded health programs, like Medicare and Medicaid, to pay for our health care. These can be helpful in covering basic health care costs, but it can be very difficult to obtain transition-related care under them. However, because these programs are operated by administrative agencies, it may sometimes be possible to appeal such decisions to sympathetic officials or even advocate for change on the regulatory level.

MEDICAID

Medicaid is a federal-state assistance program that provides health care benefits to low-income people and families. Each state sets its own eligibility requirements and scope of services provided, within limits set by the federal government. The Medicaid statute does not specifically exclude treatments related to gender transition. However, almost every state makes it difficult or impossible to access transition-related treatments from coverage under Medicaid.

California is one state that does not bar transition-related treatments from its Medicaid program, Medi-Cal. In other states, advocates are fighting hard to turn the tide against these discriminatory bans. If you are on Medicaid and have been denied access to transition-related care or to other care simply because you are trans, consider reaching out to an LGBTQ or trans legal group to report your experience. In order to change the law, we need to show examples of the harm caused when people in our community cannot access treatments related to gender transition.

MEDICARE

Medicare is a federal insurance program for seniors and people with disabilities. The Medicare regulations currently exclude coverage of gender affirming surgery, but they do not exclude coverage for other treatments related to gender transition such as counseling and hormone therapy. Medicare also has good policies about providing care to trans men who still need gynecological care and to trans women who still need care related to their prostate, penis, or testicles. Many trans advocates and supportive public officials are working to change Medicare's surgical exclusions, and a legal challenge to the exclusion is currently pending.

If you are on Medicare and have been denied reimbursement for counseling or hormone therapy, you should appeal the denial. Reach out to an attorney or legal organization to help you appeal and share your story with other advocates.

Impact of Federal Health Care Reform

In 2010, Congress enacted and President Obama signed the Patient Protection and Affordable Care Act (ACA), a far-reaching federal health care reform law that affects many aspects of our health care system. It is not yet entirely clear how the new law will affect trans people in particular, although there are some indications that it will have some positive impacts. A few of the expected positive changes include the following:

Nondiscrimination provision: The ACA prohibits insurance plans and any health program that receives federal dollars from discriminating based on a number of factors, including race, ethnicity, sex, age, and disability. While gender identity is not specifically listed, the Department of Health and Human Services (HHS) has issued a policy clarifying that "sex" protections prohibit discrimination on the basis of gender identity and sex stereotyping. HHS has also proposed a regulation prohibiting gender identity discrimination by insurance exchanges and plans offered on them. While it is not clear whether plans will be prohibited from denying coverage of transition-related care, they are not permitted to discriminate against transgender people in enrollment, marketing, administration, and customer service.

Requirement that insurance companies cannot discriminate based on preexisting conditions: Currently, many health insurance companies deny coverage to us because we are deemed to have a "preexisting condition"—simply because we are trans or have received transition-related care. Under the ACA, insurance companies will no longer be able to exclude anyone because of preexisting conditions.

Establishment of essential health benefits available to all: The ACA's essential health benefit standards specify items and services that all health insurance plans must cover, including hospitalization, prescription drugs, mental health services, and preventive care. The standards also prohibit discrimination on the basis of sexual orientation, gender identity, or health condition in benefits, making it more difficult for insurance companies to exclude transition-related care from coverage.

Increased access to health insurance for low-income people: The ACA greatly expands the number of people who are covered by Medicaid, the federal-state program that provides health care benefits to low-income people as well as those with disabilities who are not eligible for Social Security Disability (SSD) benefits but qualify for Supplemental Security Income (SSI). Under the ACA, Medicaid will cover individuals with income below 133% of the federal poverty line, including single adults who have not typically been eligible for Medicaid benefits in the past.

The ACA also provides tax subsidies to help low- and middle-income people buy insurance plans from new state health insurance exchanges and expands the services covered by Medicare, the federal program for seniors who receive Social Security Retirement benefits and people with disabilities who receive SSD benefits. While these changes are not targeted at trans people specifically, they will help many people in our communities who would otherwise not be able to afford any health insurance at all.

Many of us do not have jobs that provide health insurance and cannot afford to purchase individual health insurance. Rates of poverty among trans people are extremely high. The ACA will enable many of us to get health insurance by increasing access to health insurance for more poor and low-income people.

AKRAM FROM KYRGYZSTAN

My name is Akram. I will soon turn 23. I am a transgender man, and I am hoping to become simply a man in the future. I was raised in a regular traditional Kyrgyz family. Before I was 14, I was raised as a girl, although I had my [male] self-consciousness since I was 5, probably.

When I was diagnosed (as transgender) in August 2007, I realized I would need to change my passport. In March 2008, I applied to change my birth certificate. To do so, I made an arrangement with a woman from the Chui Legal Department. She said that "people changed their documents in Soviet times. Before you, there were very many people who changed their passports for the same reason. About the birth certificate, tell them that I consulted you, and if they have any questions let them phone me."

With a sense of confidence, I went to the office in Yssyk-Kul (a rural area in a different region of Kyrgyzstan), where I live and am registered. I collected the documents I was told to collect. They treated me all right there—they looked at me and agreed to change it. They said that it would be confidential but that I would need to ask the Yssyk-Kul Oblast Department, the Juridical Department, for permission from its head.

I went to Germany, then when I came back I was told they could not reach me by phone. A week before the permission was given, they issued everything, changed, and informed me to come receive my new birth certificate. I wanted to shout for joy, I was so glad. I could not believe that within a week the documents were changed. Was it really possible?

After that, I submitted the documents as necessary. I paid the state fees, and when I was given the birth certificate, I did not pay any extra money—even when I was given the passport, I only paid the state fees. And the woman from earlier—a major, I think, the head of the Passport Office—admitted me herself because she said it was confidential and she alone would process my case.

Now I could find a job, no one would ask anything, and no more problems would arise. Before, when I saw police officers, I was afraid they would ask me to show my ID card. Once I was taken to GOM [City Police Department], and they had thought I was carrying my sister's passport. I got a passport registered at Jety-Oguz district of Yssyk-Kul Oblast. I consider this activism, because employees of ZAGS, the Passport Office, and Juridical Department told me that they will be more aware of this. It turns out I was the first case in our region, and now they know which forms need to be filled out.

Later, our LGBT organization, Labrys, wrote a letter to the Minister of Healthcare, citing the Law about Civil Status Acts regarding gender changes issued by medical organizations. The Ministry of Healthcare is the highest level medical establishment, and we wanted them to develop a document "in accordance with given templates." Per their request, we created a working group consisting of specific people to create that document: Ministry of Healthcare officials, nongovernmental organization representatives, and a lawyer. We also developed a procedure for diagnosis at the National Center of Mental Health, because the working group decided that transgender people can change passports only after getting the diagnosis. In the beginning, I went to Labrys simply as a "beneficiary" or client—but Labrys turned into my second home. I did what I could.

Federal Tax Deduction Issues

Many of us have to pay for transition-related medical care out of our own pockets, so being able to claim a medical deduction for federal tax purposes can be very important. The US Tax Court has ruled that treatment for gender dysphoria qualifies as medical care under Section 213 of the Internal Revenue Code.

The US Tax Court's ruling relied heavily on the Standards of Care established by the World Professional Association for Transgender Health (WPATH) to determine whether specific treatments were appropriate. Some examples of potentially tax-deductible expenses include the following:

- Psychological counseling for initial diagnosis, for guidance through transition, and to obtain letters required for surgery
- Hormone therapy, including office visits and lab work
- Permanent facial hair removal for trans women, including laser treatment or electrolysis on the face and neck, and sometimes on the body
- Breast augmentation or prosthesis for trans women
- Bilateral mastectomy and chest reconstruction for trans men
- Hysterectomy for trans men
- Genital reconstruction for both trans men and women
- Skin flap hair removal
- Penile and testicular prostheses for trans men
- Certain facial plastic and reconstructive surgeries

These treatments are not automatically deductible. Medical deductions can always be audited, so having strong medical documentation is important. In case this happens, you must be able to show that your medical care providers documented that your deduction was for an appropriate and necessary treatment of gender dysphoria in your individual situation.

For example, in the tax court ruling that established the new policy, the court found that the plaintiff, a trans woman, was not entitled to take a deduction for breast augmentation because she had adequate breast growth from hormone therapy. This does not mean that breast augmentation can never be a deduction—just that every treatment has to be justified based on the person's individual medical situation and needs.

The IRS allows you to file an amended tax return within three years of your original filing. If you have spent money on medical treatments in the past three years but have not claimed medical deductions, you may still be able to file an amended return. Likewise, if you claim a medical deduction and it is denied, you have the right to appeal. This book cannot give you specific tax advice. You should consult a tax professional to discuss whether claiming a medical deduction makes sense for you.

TRANS SURVIVAL AND THE LIMITS OF LAW REFORM

Dean Spade is an associate professor at the Seattle University School of Law. In 2002 he founded the Sylvia Rivera Law Project, a nonprofit collective that provides free legal help to low income people and people of color who are trans, intersex and/or gender nonconforming and works to build trans resistance rooted in racial and economic justice. He is the author of Normal Life: Administrative Violence, Critical Trans Politics and the Limits of Law.

For many people, the concept of winning "trans rights" mainly means passing antidiscrimination laws and hate crime laws that cover gender identity and expression. Many people advocate for antidiscrimination and hate crime laws because they see that similar laws exist that explicitly name discrimination and violence on the basis of race, sex, disability, national origin, and sometimes other categories like sexual orientation, and they want the violence and discrimination experienced by trans people to be seen as important and included in the laws.

There is no doubt that trans people experience enormous harm and violence and that our lives are shortened because of it. Trans people are often poor and homeless because of employment discrimination, family rejection, and exclusion from social services. Trans immigrants face high rates of immigration imprisonment and deportation. Trans people tend to be placed in social services spaces based on birth-assigned gender and to face high rates of sexual assault and other violence because we "break the rules" of gender. This is especially true for trans people of color, trans people with disabilities, and trans immigrants, who are more likely to be poor, to be targeted by the police, and to be underserved or excluded from social services, or face heightened violence in sex-segregated spaces.

The problem is that antidiscrimination laws and hate crime laws do not address the horrible conditions of poverty and violence that trans people are experiencing. They have not solved the problems of racism, sexism, or ableism that we are told they exist to address. Worse than that, they are part of a national myth that these problems have been solved, which prevents a realistic understanding of them or meaningful solutions to them. According to this myth, we live in a country that used to be racist, and used to have slavery and Jim Crow segregation, but the laws were changed, everyone was made equal, and any remaining racism is just a problem of a few bad people with bad ideas. This story suggests that groups that are facing harm and violence should focus on changing the law to say good things about us so that the government will become our protector.

But declarations of equality in law have not brought the improvement of material conditions that people want and need. During the last 40–50 years in the United States, when the law has supposedly started treating people equally and protecting against racism, sexism, and other harmful systems, inequality has actually *increased.* Attacks on labor and social welfare systems have helped fuel growing economic inequality. People work more but are less likely to have health insurance or pensions through their jobs and are more likely to work as temps. The criminal and immigration systems have drastically expanded—the United States now imprisons more people than any country in the world and more than any country that has ever existed. We have 5% of the world's people and 25% of the world's prisoners. Government is run by the wealthiest people and corporations for the benefit of a small elite.

Given this, our trans resistance strategy has to be thoughtful about the role of law reform in our efforts. We have to be careful that we don't get tricked into supporting systems that actually target us. Hate crime laws, for example, do nothing to prevent our deaths, but they do expand funding for and the punishing power of the criminal punishment system. We have to make sure we do not assume that getting the law to "say good things about us" will save or improve our lives. We need strategies that actually help trans people survive and be protected from the brutal forces of state violence like criminal and immigration systems.

So what does this mean we should do? If hate crimes laws and antidiscrimination laws will not solve our problems, what will? We have to focus on supporting people trying to survive harmful systems, dismantling those systems, and building alternatives. Supporting people trying to survive means taking up local work to address the poverty and violence trans people are experiencing. That can mean things like starting prisoner pen-pal projects for trans prisoners, working to make the homeless shelters in our towns safer for trans people, making sure trans people getting out of prison have housing and other resources in place, making various health care systems include gender-confirming health care for trans people, and making sure trans immigrants facing deportation have free legal help.

Dismantling violent systems means identifying places where we are getting caught up and building campaigns to take them apart. For example, in many cities people are trying to decriminalize sex work or stop the police from relentlessly arresting trans people in the sex trade. In some places people are trying to get rid of mandatory minimum sentences for drug possession, which funnel many people into prison. In other places, people are fighting to get their local criminal law enforcement systems to stop collaborating with immigration enforcement. In some cities and states, activists have won battles to stop the building of a new jail, prison, or juvenile punishment facility. Dismantling is extremely important, and one way to tell if legal work we are doing might be a trap for us is to ask whether it expands or dismantles violent systems of law enforcement.

Building alternatives means thinking about how we actually want our needs to be met in the world we are trying to build and starting to make that happen now. One example is that a lot of people around the United States and beyond are building projects that try to offer alternatives to using the police or prison system to address harm and violence. Calling the cops or going to court often escalates or multiplies violence for people and communities that are targeted for criminalization, but we need ways of dealing with harm that happens. Developing strategies for communities to address and resolve harm and work toward preventing it from happening again is essential for our well-being.

In all of our survival and resistance work, we should prioritize the experiences of people facing the worst manifestations of transphobia rather than being tempted to try to solve problems for those who are least vulnerable. Social justice does not trickle down. If we solve problems only for trans people who are white, high-paid professionals, it will not solve them for people who are poor, who are locked up, and/or who are facing racism and transphobia and ableism all at once. When people try to make change through the law, they often end up focusing on those from the group who are most likeable in the eyes of judges and legislators and who fit normative standards of what "American" is supposed to look like. When we choose that path, we reproduce harmful divisions among trans people and we undermine the opportunity to get to the root problems that make trans people's lives so dangerous and short. Putting the most dangerous experiences of transphobia at the center can help us make sure we are directing resources to the most urgent conditions, supporting those most in need, and building solutions that will remedy the worst harms.

EMPLOYMENT PROTECTIONS

As trans people, we work in a wide variety of environments. We have a number of ways to come together with our colleagues and employers to make our transition and day-to-day life on the job comfortable and safe. However, there are also local, state, and federal laws that can help ensure that our rights are protected in the workplace.

Employment Nondiscrimination Laws

A number of companies have internal workplace policies that afford some protection against employment discrimination. When these fail to meet our needs, we may look to federal, state, or local laws prohibiting employment discrimination based on gender identity, sex, or disability.

The Movement Advancement Project has online maps of the United States showing the current status of each state with regard to LGBTQ legislation, including employment nondiscrimination laws.

In a 2012 ruling, the EEOC held that the Library of Congress discriminated against a trans woman when it withdrew a job offer to her after learning that she was transitioning from male to female. The commission explained: *"Imagine that an employee is fired because she converts from Christianity to Judaism. Imagine too that her employer testifies that he harbors no bias toward either Christians or Jews but only 'converts.' That would be a clear case of discrimination 'because of religion.' No court would take seriously the notion that 'converts' are not covered by the statute. Discrimination 'because of religion' easily encompasses discrimination because of a change of religion."*

PROTECTION UNDER LAWS PROHIBITING GENDER IDENTITY DISCRIMINATION

No federal law currently protects against discrimination in employment based on gender identity or sexual orientation, although the Employment Non-Discrimination Act (ENDA) has been proposed during past congressional terms.

Over 15 states (California, Colorado, Connecticut, Delaware, District of Columbia, Hawaii, Illinois, Iowa, Massachusetts, Maine, Minnesota, New Jersey, New Mexico, Nevada, Oregon, Rhode Island, Vermont, and Washington) and over a hundred cities have enacted laws that protect people from discrimination based on gender identity. If you work in one of the states or local areas that have passed such a law, it is illegal for you to be harassed or discriminated against because of your gender identity at work. Even if your state has not passed a law prohibiting discrimination against trans employees, you may still be protected if your county or city has passed a local law prohibiting discrimination.

Sometimes an employer will have an office in one state, but its headquarters will be located in another state. For example, you may live and work in Pennsylvania, which does not have a state law prohibiting gender identity discrimination, but your employer's main office may be located in New Jersey, which does prohibit discrimination. There are no guarantees, but it may be possible to argue that the employer is actually bound by the law of New Jersey and, so, is prohibited from discrimination based on gender identity.

PROTECTION UNDER LAWS PROHIBITING SEX DISCRIMINATION

Under federal law, Title VII of the Civil Rights Act of 1964 prohibits employers from discriminating against employees based on sex. Several federal and state courts across the country have ruled that Title VII and other federal sex discrimination laws protect us as transgender people.

Sex discrimination laws prohibit employers from discriminating based on gender stereotypes. Discrimination against us often fits within this definition because we may be seen as "too masculine" for a woman or "too feminine" for a man. For example, in one case, a court used sex discrimination laws to protect a firefighter, who was transitioning from male to female, because she was fired for using nail polish, wearing makeup, and generally being seen as "too feminine."

In 2012, the Equal Employment Opportunity Commission (EEOC), the federal agency responsible for enforcing nondiscrimination laws, also ruled that Title VII prohibits discrimination on the basis of gender identity. This means that a trans person who is discriminated against at work can file an EEOC complaint in every state.

TRANSGENDER RIGHTS AS HUMAN RIGHTS

Daniela Jauk, PhD, graduated in sociology from the University of Akron in 2013 with a dissertation on the social construction of global (trans)gender policy in the context of the UN, before she returned to her home country, Austria, where she currently works as a gender studies and sociology lecturer at the University of Graz.

The Yogyakarta Principles and the United Nations (UN) Resolution on the Rights of LGBT people are two human rights instruments that have been used to address transgender rights.

The Yogyakarta Principles are a compilation of 29 principles drawn up in 2006 from existing international human rights laws in order to explain how to apply these laws to LGBT populations. The Yogyakarta Principles are being used by activists on a daily basis all over the world. The Web site "YP In Action" tracks the implementation of the principles into laws in different countries. Other Web sites connect activists in various countries and offer free educational materials on the Yogyakarta Principles.

In 2011, the Human Rights Council (HRC) of the UN (formerly the United Nations Commission on Human Rights) passed the first-ever UN resolution on the human rights of LGBT people (A/HRC/17/L.9/Rev.1). The same year, the HRC published a report on "discriminatory laws and practices and acts of violence against individuals based on their sexual orientation and gender identity" (A/HRC/19/41 2011). The report summarized forms of interpersonal and structural violence on the basis of sexual orientation and gender identity in all regions of the world and recommended comprehensive antidiscrimination legislation, legal recognition of preferred gender, free right of assembly, and training for law enforcement personnel in all member states.

The Yogyakarta principles and the UN resolution are not law per se. Their success depends on how many people know about them, use them locally to pressure for recognition of trans violence and trans discrimination, and identify appropriate counterstrategies.

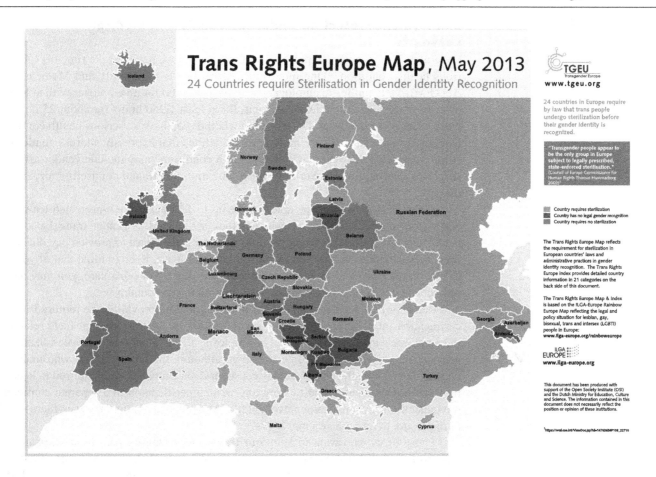

Trans Rights Europe Map and Index (2013). Based on the ILGA-Europe Rainbow Europe Map (May, 2013). (copyright Transgender Europe www.tgeu.org.)

The commission went on to rule that the same logic applies under sex discrimination laws when an employer discriminates against a transgender person because of a change of sex.

PROTECTION UNDER LAWS PROHIBITING DISABILITY DISCRIMINATION

Most areas of federal disability law specifically exclude trans people from protection. However, not all state and local disability laws include such exceptions. In those jurisdictions, trans employees may be protected from employment discrimination under local statutes.

The purpose of disability discrimination laws is to acknowledge that many people are born with or at some time in their lives acquire serious medical conditions that do not affect their ability to work or contribute to society, but that may require some accommodation. That is, disability discrimination laws recognize that the "disability" does not reside in the individual but in biased attitudes and assumptions.

Whether a particular person feels comfortable relying on disability laws to challenge transgender discrimination is a personal decision. Some of us may be uncomfortable with our trans status being labeled as a disability. Others feel that there is nothing stigmatizing about viewing it as a medical condition and see this as a powerful source of legal protection. Some of us who have experienced discrimination at work or in schools have won major victories by relying on disability discrimination laws. For example, one court in Massachusetts held that a high school's refusal to permit a trans girl to dress as a girl in school was no different than refusing to let a student with diabetes use insulin.

Employment Protection Under the Family and Medical Leave Act

Federal and state laws also protect employees when we need to take time off for a "serious health condition." One important federal law is the Family and Medical Leave Act (FMLA). It applies to employees who have worked for an employer with at least 50 or more employees, for at least one year, for at least 1,250 hours (or about 25 hours per week) during the past year. Determining whether you have a "serious health condition" is fact specific, and there are no federal guidelines that expressly address gender transition treatments. However, a "serious health condition" may include gender-affirming surgeries that require an overnight hospitalization, continued counseling, or hormone therapy.

Under FMLA, we may be able to take up to 12 weeks of job-protected leave to recover from medical treatments, whether they are related to gender transition or other health concerns. While an employer does not necessarily have to provide pay during this time, they cannot terminate you while you take this leave. Keep in mind that, if you wish to rely on the FMLA to take an unpaid leave for surgery or other care, you may need to provide documentation of your medical condition to your employer.

Under FMLA regulations adopted in 2008, doctors providing the required medical certification must list their areas of specialization as well as medical facts relating to the employee's medical condition. The employer may contact the employee's health care provider to verify the medical certification, although the representative who makes the contact must not be the employee's direct supervisor. Employers are required to keep this information confidential and to store any written certification in a separate confidential file rather than in your general personnel file. As a practical matter, however, there is a risk of disclosure to immediate supervisors.

Those of us who want to keep our transgender identity private at work may not wish to use the FMLA because of concerns about disclosure. If you specifically decline to provide such documentation, you cannot later claim protection under FMLA regulations. This has been tested in the courts. In one case, an employee declined to use the FMLA to take a leave for sex-reassignment surgery because she did not want to provide medical certification for confidentiality reasons. The employee took a personal leave instead. The employer fired her shortly after she returned to work, and she filed a lawsuit arguing that she should be protected under the FMLA. The Eighth Circuit Court of Appeals held that she was not protected, because she had specifically declined to ask for leave under the FMLA. The court explained that, while an employee does not have to mention FMLA by name to be protected, the employee cannot specifically state that she does not want to rely on the FMLA and then later ask to be protected under it.

Some of us may also be protected under state laws that are similar to the FMLA—some of which may even provide for paid leave under certain circumstances. To find out about the law in your state and whether it might cover taking time off for surgery or other transition-related treatments, contact a legal organization or attorney who is knowledgeable about trans legal issues.

Under FMLA, a spouse, parent, or child may also be able take up to 12 weeks off of work to care for a trans spouse, parent, or child who is undergoing gender transition-related medical care. Some states, like California, have similar medical leave laws that may also allow employees to use this job-protected leave to care for a domestic partner undergoing gender transition-related medical care.

Protections for Federal Employees

Federal employees (and applicants for federal jobs) are protected under the Civil Service Reform Act, which prohibits discrimination based on gender identity. The Office of Personnel Management (OPM)—a federal agency that manages civil service of the federal government—has issued guidance on how to treat trans employees with dignity and respect:

- An employer must treat a trans employee's transition as confidential and sensitive medical information.
- Agency dress codes should be applied equally to trans employees as to their affirmed gender—that is, a trans woman should be allowed to dress according to the women's dress codes.
- Federal managers, supervisors, and coworkers should use the name and pronouns appropriate to the employee's affirmed gender.
- Federal agencies should allow trans employees to use bathrooms and locker rooms that reflect the employee's gender identity, and proof of a particular medical procedure is not necessary to access these facilities.
- Federal agencies should change employee records to reflect name and gender changes.

LEGAL ISSUES IN MILITARY SERVICE

While the "Don't Ask, Don't Tell" military ban on lesbian, gay, and bisexual service members has been repealed, trans people are still barred from military service. The exclusion of trans people from the military is typically justified in three ways:

1. Medical regulations exclude people who have had genital surgeries.
2. Individuals who have been diagnosed with mental illnesses, including psychosexual disorders, are often excluded from service. Gender dysphoria and other gender identity–related designations fall into this category.
3. Gender nonconforming behavior, including "cross-dressing," is considered grounds for exclusion or dismissal based on conduct.

In addition to trans people being barred entrance into the military, beginning to transition while already serving in the military may result in being disqualified from further service.

Even if you pursue transition-related treatments in a civilian setting, outside active duty service and with civilian health care providers, you may still be disqualified from service. If you are in the armed services and need more information, contact the Servicemembers Legal Defense Network (SLDN) or another LGBTQ or trans legal group.

TRICARE and Other Military Health Insurance Plans

TRICARE is the insurance plan provided to current and retired members of the armed services and their families. The US Department of Veterans Affairs administers it, as well as the Civilian Health and Medical Program of the Department of Veterans Affairs (CHAMPVA), for spouses and children of disabled or deceased veterans, and the Veterans Health Administration (VHA), for veterans. Like its predecessor, CHAMPUS, TRICARE excludes coverage for transition-related surgery, although it may cover some surgeries for intersex people.

TRICARE allows us to change our name and gender marker on our medical records, and it has been clarified that if our record indicates our transgender status, TRICARE will provide coverage, even for care that appears to conflict with the current gender marker in our records—for example, a trans man who needs gynecological care or a trans woman who needs a prostate exam. TRICARE adopted formal procedures for its insurance claims processing to ensure that this coverage is not denied. If you are denied coverage, you can and should appeal the decision.

TRICARE has also reiterated that medical information about care received is considered private. However, transgender people are excluded from active service, and annual medical exams of active duty military personnel may result in disclosure of our transgender status, resulting in discharge.

Veterans Health Administration

The Veterans Health Administration (VHA), which is responsible for providing health care to current and former service members, has issued a directive instructing all of its facilities and staff to prevent harassment and discrimination, protect privacy, provide nonsurgical transition-related care, and generally respect patients' gender identities. This directive applies to all Veterans Administration (VA) hospitals and medical facilities. On the local level, some VA bureaus have been very supportive of trans people. For example, in 2007, the Veteran Affairs Boston Healthcare System issued a landmark patient care memorandum to its staff, providing detailed guidelines for how to provide supportive care to trans patients.

However, trans veterans have had mixed experiences with VA facilities. A 2008 study released by the Palm Center at the University of California, Santa Barbara, and conducted by the Transgender American Veterans Association found that 10% of trans veterans surveyed reported being turned away from VA hospitals because of their gender identity, and 22% reported being disrespected by VA doctors. Others reported being denied gender-specific care such as Pap smears, mammograms, prostate exams, and hormone treatments.

TRICARE and CHAMPVA both specifically exclude transition-related services and supplies, but VHA excludes only surgery. If you are having problems getting counseling or hormone therapy covered, you should appeal the denial and reach out to an LGBTQ or trans legal organization for help.

DISCRIMINATION IN HOUSING, CREDIT, AND OTHER PUBLIC ACCOMMODATIONS

Current federal law does not explicitly protect transgender people from discrimination in housing, credit, or public accommodations (a legal term referring to government facilities such as courts, as well as businesses such as restaurants, hotels, and doctors' offices that are open to the public). As a result, we are vulnerable to discrimination in many areas of public life.

In the National Transgender Discrimination Survey conducted by the National Center for Transgender Equality and the National Gay and Lesbian Task Force, 19% of trans people reported having been refused a home or apartment, and 11% reported being evicted because of their gender identity or expression. Home ownership in the trans community is 32%, less than half the national rate, and one in five respondents reported experiencing homelessness as a result of discrimination or mistreatment because of their gender identity or expression. Forty-four percent of trans people surveyed reported being denied equal treatment or service at least once at one type of public accommodation.

While we continue to push for federal laws that protect us in these areas, there are two main ways we may currently be protected from discrimination. Many states and localities have passed their own laws prohibiting this discrimination. In addition, the Department of Housing and Urban Development (HUD) has adopted policies that can provide significant protection in housing.

CISNORMATIVITY AND HOUSING PROGRAMS

Jama Shelton, PhD, LMSW, is the director of the True Colors Fund's Forty to None Project, a national organization dedicated to ending homelessness among LGBTQ youth.

Trans and gender nonconforming (TGNC) people may face discrimination when trying to access shelter services and housing programs. The concept of cisnormativity can explain why this discrimination occurs. Cisnormativity describes the assumption that all people will identify with and live as the sex they were assigned at birth, and that two distinct options exist for this identification—male or female. Cisnormativity shapes our entire social context, from the individual practices of human interaction to the establishment of organizations and the procedures of institutions. Unlike the idea of transphobia, cisnormativity refers to a prejudicial ideology that is systemic in nature. Conversely, transphobia refers to an individual attitude or behavior.

Thinking about access to shelters and housing programs through the lens of cisnormativity broadens the analysis of the harassment and discrimination experiences of TGNC people from the micro level of interpersonal interactions (transphobia) to the macro level of institutional structures that produce and maintain marginalization. Because most programs are unaware of the idea of cisnormativity and do not recognize that their policies and programs are organized for cisgender people, when a TGNC person shows up, program staff often experience it as a crisis which they are ill prepared to handle. The common solution when this happens is for program staff to either send the TGNC person elsewhere or to figure out how to navigate this single, special case. The problem here is viewing the TGNC person as a "single, special case" instead of seeing it as a problem with the way programs are designed. Rather than coming up with temporary answers that attempt to resolve the present situation, programs can re-examine the ways they are designed. Individuals and institutions that refocus their attention on cisnormativity in their interactions with others and in their institutionalized policies may begin to recognize that the setup of the system—the assumptions we make as individuals, institutions, and society—is actually the problem, *not* the individual who doesn't fit within that restrictive system. Can a program be designed with more than only two sex-designated wings or floors? There are other options. The shelter or housing program could (1) not be segregated by gender, (2) be divided into three (or more) gender designations, or (3) be composed of single living arrangements.

The practice of broadening the analysis in this way is not new. The same type of shift occurred when people traded the concept of homophobia for words like heteronormativity and heterosexism. Heteronormativity and heterosexism enable an understanding of the systemic marginalization of LGB people and the structural favoring of heterosexual people over LGB people. The same shift should occur—from transphobia to cisnormativity and cisgenderism. It is necessary for people to grasp this concept if they are to make real change for people experiencing harassment and discrimination based on gender identity or expression.

State and Local Laws

Many states and localities have passed laws that prohibit discrimination based on gender identity in housing, credit, public accommodations, or some combination of these.

For example, many states, including California, Colorado, Connecticut, Delaware, Hawaii, Illinois, Iowa, Maine, Minnesota, New Jersey, New Mexico, Oregon, Rhode Island, Vermont, Washington, and the District of Columbia, protect us from discrimination in public accommodations.

Others, including California, Colorado, Connecticut, Delaware, the District of Columbia, Hawaii, Illinois, Iowa, Maine, Massachusetts, Minnesota, New Jersey, New Mexico, Oregon,

Rhode Island, Vermont, and Washington, protect us from discrimination in housing and real estate, which means that a tenant or homebuyer's transgender status cannot be used as a basis for refusing—or offering less favorable terms in—leases, mortgages, homeowner's insurance, and home sales.

Some states—including Connecticut, Hawaii, Illinois, Iowa, Maine, Massachusetts, Minnesota, New Jersey, New Mexico, Oregon, Rhode Island, Vermont, and Washington—also protect us from discrimination in the extension of credit. This means that lenders cannot refuse or offer less favorable terms of credit to a person because of their transgender status, which can help us in purchasing a car or obtaining store credit.

HUD Policy

The Department of Housing and Urban Development (HUD) is a federal agency that oversees many federal housing policies and programs and enforces many fair housing laws. HUD oversees public housing, assists first-time homebuyers in obtaining mortgages and loan insurance, and helps low-income individuals with rental assistance. In July 2010, HUD announced that it would treat "gender identity discrimination, most often faced by transgender persons, as gender discrimination under the Fair Housing Act." This means that HUD will prohibit discrimination against us in all of the areas it oversees.

Access to Homeless Shelters

Being able to access homeless shelters and being protected from discrimination at those shelters are important issues for the community. According to the National Transgender Discrimination Survey, nearly one in three trans people (29%) who tried to access a shelter was turned away outright, and that rate was even higher for trans people of color. A majority of respondents (55%) who did access a shelter reported being harassed by staff or other residents there, and 42% said they had been forced to live as the wrong gender to be allowed to stay. One quarter (25%) reported being physically assaulted in a shelter, and nearly as many (22%) reported being sexually assaulted by either another resident or a shelter staff member.

HUD has taken a strong stand against transgender discrimination in all federally funded facilities, and more cities such as Boston, New York City, San Francisco, and others have adopted strong nondiscrimination policies that require shelters to provide access to trans people and to respect our identities.

SEX-SEGREGATED SHELTERS

Most shelters are overseen by HUD, which has issued guidance to all federally funded shelters explaining that the Fair Housing Act protects transgender people from discrimination in all aspects of public housing, including public shelters. In addition, HUD has issued a rule that sex-segregated shelters may only segregate people based on their gender identity, without regard to sex assigned at birth. This means that in most shelters, we have a right to be housed in the facility that matches our gender identity. We may not be asked to prove private information about our medical or surgical history in order to be housed in the appropriate facility. In the past, many shelters adopted policies that required trans people to disclose information about their medical and surgical history and only permitted trans people who had undergone genital surgery to be housed according to their gender identity. This created a discriminatory and unsafe environment for many trans people—and it is now prohibited by federal law.

In addition to federal protections for any federally funded shelters, some jurisdictions have their own laws against sex discrimination in housing that include gender identity, requiring shelters with gender-based rules to provide equal access to trans people. States like New Jersey, Colorado, and Iowa, plus the District of Columbia, do this across the board. Some cities, including Boston, New York, and San Francisco, also have local ordinances or regulations designed to ensure trans people have equal access to shelters.

If you believe you have been discriminated against in the housing context, or in any transactions relating to obtaining financing for housing, you can call HUD (800-669-9777) and explain that you are facing discrimination based on your gender identity or file a formal complaint online.

Transitioning Our Shelters: A Guide to Making Homeless Shelters Safe for Transgender People, by Lisa Mottet and John M. Ohle (2003) of the National Gay and Lesbian Task Force Policy Institute and National Coalition for the Homeless, can be downloaded and used in local shelters.

We have a right to be free from violence and harassment while in shelters. If you are harassed, assaulted, or attacked while staying in a homeless shelter, either by staff or other residents, you can report it to law enforcement officials. If you are targeted for an attack based on your gender identity, it may be classified as a hate crime based on a federal law. If you think you have been a victim of a hate crime while at a homeless shelter, one thing you can do is notify law enforcement officials immediately, or as soon as it is safe to do so.

CONFIDENTIALITY AND PRIVACY IN SHELTERS

In most shelters, you have a right to have your gender identity respected and kept confidential. In some cases, it can be considered discrimination or harassment if shelter staff give information about your gender identity to others. If you disclose your gender identity during an intake process at a shelter, make sure you tell the staff member you speak with if you want that information kept private. If any arrangements must be made concerning your privacy (for example, if you are at a shelter that does not have single-occupancy showers and you wish to shower alone), others working in the shelter may need to be notified. In practice, however, shelter staff in many places may not know the law and may not protect our privacy. Communicate your need for privacy clearly and regularly, if needed. If you or someone you know is mistreated in a shelter, reach out to a local, state, or national advocacy group for help.

YOUTH SHELTERS

Although more families are accepting their trans youth, too many trans youth still face family rejection and may be forced to rely on shelters. Some states, like Connecticut and Illinois, have established policies for state child welfare agencies specifically addressing the needs of LGBTQ youth in an effort to channel them into the foster care system rather than onto the streets. However, for those who do end up without homes, many shelters cater specifically to young people, which can be especially important for trans youth.

Under federal law, we have a right to be housed in the facility that corresponds with our gender identity. Often youth facilities have policies designed to reduce the risk that residents will engage in sexual activity with each other. Unfortunately, many facilities use this concern as a reason to place trans youth living in these facilities in the incorrect facility based on their gender identity. Trans youth have a right to be housed based on their gender identity and should not be asked any information about their medical or surgical history with respect to their transition. If a shelter has a desire to reduce risk that residents will engage in sexual activity, its policies should prohibit *that* activity. Youth who face any discrimination, harassment, or violence in shelters should report their experience immediately.

MARRIAGE

Many of us choose to marry, both before and after our gender transitions. In the United States, states are able to make their own laws governing who can legally marry, as long as their laws do not violate the Constitution. Different states limit who is eligible for marriage based on characteristics such as the age, sex, and relationship between the parties (for example, a parent and a child are not eligible for marriage in any state). The US Supreme Court has not yet decided whether state laws that bar same-sex couples from marriage are unconstitutional.

The most important factor affecting couples in which one or more partners is trans is the legal gender (or legal sex) of both spouses. At the time of last editing, 17 states (California, Connecticut, Delaware, Hawaii, Illinois, Iowa, Maine, Maryland, Massachusetts, Minnesota, New Hampshire, New Jersey, New Mexico, New York, Rhode Island, Vermont, and Washington) plus the District of Columbia and at least eight tribal nations permit same-sex couples to marry. In all other states, we must be a different legal gender than our partner in order to legally marry. While several states have passed laws barring same-sex couples from marriage, no state has passed a law prohibiting (or specifically permitting) trans people from marrying.

THE SUPREME COURT'S DOMA CASE: WHAT DID IT SAY AND WHAT HAPPENS NOW?

Nancy S. Erickson, Esq., JD, LLM, MA in forensic psychology, is an attorney specializing in domestic violence and custody evaluations in cases involving child or intimate partner abuse.

The recent Supreme Court decision regarding the Defense of Marriage Act (DOMA) brought up a number of new questions for gay and lesbian couples. Because many trans people are gay or lesbian, and even those who are not are sometimes considered by their states to be in same-sex relationships, the DOMA ruling will have implications for transgender communities.

Congress and the federal government have generally taken a hands off approach to marriages by recognizing any marriage that was valid in the state where it was contracted. The general rule with regard to recognition of marriages performed in other jurisdictions is that if a marriage is valid in the place where it took place (even a foreign country), every state will recognize it as valid. The major exception is that if a court in another state finds that the marriage violates a strong public policy of its own state, then that state may hold it invalid. This exception is almost never applied in situations where the spouses got validly married in their home state and then moved to another state that would not have allowed them to marry there. In such situations, the second state usually recognizes the marriage even if the second state would not have allowed it.

The way a public policy exception issue usually arises is when a couple leaves their home state in order to evade their state's prohibition on their marital union, gets married in a state that permits their marriage, and returns to their home state. Then the courts of their home state might need to determine whether the state's prohibition on such marriages evidences a strong public policy so that the marriage should be held invalid or only a weak public policy so that the marriage should be recognized. All states have strong public policies against marrying more than one person, but aside from such cases, courts have rarely held that a marriage violated a strong public policy of the state. Many years ago, some states used the "violation of a strong public policy" reasoning to refuse to recognize interracial marriages, but the Supreme Court's 1967 decision in *Loving v. Virginia* required all states to recognize interracial marriages.

Congress' hands-off approach to marriage laws was changed in 1996 when Congress passed the Defense of Marriage Act (DOMA). Section 3 of DOMA defined marriage for purposes of federal law as a union of one man and one woman. In 2013, Section 3 of DOMA was held unconstitutional in *United States v. Windsor*, 570 US 12, but all other sections of DOMA still stand. Other sections of DOMA permit any state to refuse to recognize same-sex marriages contracted under the laws of other states, just as states are usually free to refuse to recognize out-of-state marriages that violate a strong public policy of their own states.

Federal recognition of same-sex marriage is very important, because many federal statutes, such as Social Security, immigration, and military benefits laws, depend on whether the federal government recognizes the marriage. After Section 3 of DOMA was overturned, most federal agencies declared they will recognize same-sex marriages. However, this does not change the power of each state to decide whether to permit same-sex marriages in its own state or to recognize same-sex marriages performed elsewhere. Only another decision by the Supreme Court could change that.

Obtaining a Marriage License

When obtaining a marriage license, there are two main considerations: (1) what forms of identification are required to get a marriage license in your state and what gender marker is on your required documents, and (2) whether same-sex marriage is allowed in the state where you wish to be married.

When you apply for a marriage license, you are typically required to present one or more forms of identification that confirm your identity, age, and sex. These may include a birth certificate, passport, driver's license, or social security card. The gender marker displayed on these documents is the sex that will be used for deciding whether you are legally permitted to marry your spouse in that state.

As a general rule, a trans person who has taken all the steps necessary to legally change their gender in the state where they marry should be able to legally marry a person of the other legal gender.

Those of us who marry a partner of another gender after undergoing a gender transition typically do not face any legal issues. However, there have been a few cases (in Florida, Kansas, New York, Ohio, and Texas) where courts have decided that chromosomal or birth-assigned sex determines eligibility for marriage—not current documentation. Typically, these marriages are contested well after the fact, often because of claims brought by a third party.

If you and your partner have the same gender markers on your identification at the time of your marriage, your marriage will be considered valid only if the state where you marry permits same-sex couples to legally marry. If you marry a same-sex partner in a state that has marriage equality, your marriage may not be valid in states that do not permit same-sex couples to marry. You should also be aware that while the federal government provides federal benefits to most married couples regardless of whether your marriage is legal in your home state, as long as it was legal in the place you married, there are some federal benefits that depend on whether your home state recognizes your marriage.

> *"I am married to another trans woman. Gay marriage is legal in DC, so people can get married regardless of what was on their birth certificate. So luckily, we have had no problems at all!"*

Transitioning Within a Marriage

Many of us transition while we are married. Sometimes, during or after the transition, we divorce. But often, we stay together. If we were in a different-sex marriage before our transition, we may worry that our marriage is no longer legally valid in our state, especially if we live in a state that does not permit same-sex couples to marry. However, this is unlikely; in general, a marriage is recognized as legal if it was legal at the time and in the place where it was performed.

Many of us who transition within an unmarried same-sex relationship find that we are now eligible for legal marriage in our home state as a different-sex couple. If you decide to marry in your home state and that state does not permit same-sex couples to marry, obtain a legal gender and name change and change the gender marker on as many official documents as you can before you get married.

Divorce and Dissolution of Marriage

If legally married, and one or both spouses want to end a marriage, a divorce is necessary in order for postdivorce rights, such as alimony and division of the marital property, to be recognized.

In the past, a non-transgender person married to a transgender person could often have the marriage declared invalid in order to get out of having any financial responsibilities to the transgender spouse.

Sometimes the non-trans spouse claimed the marriage should be annulled because of fraud, alleging that the trans spouse fraudulently failed to reveal their biological sex. These annulments were often successful if the non-trans spouse disavowed the marriage as soon as possible after discovering the "fraud." If the non-trans spouse "ratified" the marriage by continuing to live as a couple, the fraud ground would not be successful. An annulment action based on fraud may be brought only by one of the spouses. However, cases in which these annulments are granted are increasingly rare. More commonly, spouses will need to seek a divorce in order to end their marriage.

> *"I had a formal divorce, but my ex-wife is now petitioning the courts years later to have our original marriage voided on the grounds that we defrauded the Colorado courts. Luckily, the courts have thus far upheld both our marriage and divorce."*

In other cases, the non-trans spouse would ask a court to declare that the marriage was void, based on the argument that a trans man is not "really" a man or that a trans woman is not "really" a woman. In such an action, the non-trans spouse would claim that the marriage was void and always had been totally invalid from the beginning because the state recognized marriage only when contracted between a man and a woman. This claim can also be brought by family members of the non-trans spouse after the trans person's death, to contest inheritance claims.

Spousal Benefits and Legal Protections

In some cases, a third party such as an insurance company may challenge the legal validity of a marriage. For example, you or your spouse may be denied benefits—such as health

Legal Gender

"This expression gets thrown around a lot, but there is no such magical wand to make you 'legally' male or female when it comes to gender transition. Laws vary from state to state concerning the requirements for changing gender markers on birth certificates and other identity documents. Laws also vary concerning whether a state will accept such identity documents as conclusive with respect to your gender identity. Finally, context also can make a difference with respect to whether your gender identity will receive respect. For example, a court might recognize your gender identity or the sex designation on your birth certificate as your 'legal gender' in one marriage-related context, but a government agency in the same state might deny you respect in another marriage-related context despite the change to your gender marker."—*"Transgender People and Marriage Laws," Lambda Legal*

Tony Amrich at his wedding (copyright Portraits to the People).

insurance, life insurance benefits, inheritance, spousal pension benefits, or alimony—that depend on the validity of the marriage.

The issues raised by these cases may be complex. For example, the Social Security Administration determines whether you are legally married based on your gender under state law and your state's marriage laws—it is not based solely on the gender marker on your Social Security record. As with all legal issues, the law at the time the issue arises should be consulted, as laws change.

To maximize the chances that your marriage will be recognized as legal, there are a few steps you can take:

- Have your spouse sign a prenuptial agreement stating that the person knows you are transgender and will not seek to challenge the marriage on that basis.
- Have a will and a relationship agreement that spells out how you will divide your property with your spouse if you were to separate. That way, you will have some legal protection even if your marriage is challenged and found to be invalid.
- Those of us who are nonbiological parents should also be sure to go through a second parent adoption or get a court order stating that we are a legal parent.

If you are married and considering transition, or planning to get married after transitioning, consider seeking help from an LGBTQ or trans legal organization. Many times, getting some initial advice and advocacy can head off bigger problems down the road.

PARENTING AND CHILD CUSTODY

We create families and become parents in many different ways—including through sexual relationships, assisted reproduction, and adoption. Our families also take many different forms. We may be raising children in married or unmarried relationships, as adoptive parents or stepparents, in blended or extended families, or in chosen families that include more than two parents.

Regardless of the particular circumstances and choices about parenting, trans parents often face unique legal challenges. It can be empowering to know that we have taken all the steps possible to protect our relationships with our children.

Becoming a Legal Parent

Every state has laws that define who will be recognized as a child's legal parent or parents. If you are parenting a child, it is important to know whether you qualify as a legal parent under your state's family law. If you gave birth to the child, then you are a legal parent except under very unusual circumstances such as certain surrogacy situations. However, if you did not give birth to the child, then being a biological parent to the child does not necessarily make you the legal parent to your child, especially if you and your partner are not legally married.

If you meet the criteria for being a legal parent in your state, it is often advisable to get a court order confirming that you are a legal parent. Having a court order gives you the maximum legal protection, because once a court has declared that a person is a legal parent, other states and third parties (such as insurance companies) have to respect that order.

If you do not qualify as a legal parent, there may be steps you can take—such as adoption—that will enable you to become a legal parent. In almost all cases, a person who is not a biological parent has to take affirmative legal steps to be recognized as a child's legal parent. This means getting either a court order of parentage or an adoption. Which one of those two options makes the most sense for you depends on the law in your state. To ensure that your relationship with your child is legally protected, a nonbiological parent should get a court order of parentage or an adoption as soon as possible. Having your name listed as a parent on a child's birth certificate does not necessarily mean that your status as a legal parent cannot be challenged. The only way to be sure that you are a legal parent is to get a court order of parentage or adoption.

Having a court order of parentage or adoption will protect your relationship with your child in the event that a third party—such as an extended family member or an insurance company—challenges your parental status. A court order of parentage or adoption is also advisable because it has to be recognized in every state. This means that even if you move to a state that does not legally protect transgender parents, that state will have to recognize that you are a legal parent because you have a court order saying so from another state.

Getting a court order of parentage or adoption generally requires help from a family law attorney. It may be possible to do it on your own if you have no other option, but reach out to an organization focusing on transgender parents' legal rights before beginning. Unlike a name or gender change, which many people can handle for themselves, protecting your legal rights as a parent is more complex, and it can be easy to make a mistake that may cause you and your family serious harm at some point in the future.

It is also important to be sure that your attorney knows how to protect you. Many family law attorneys and legal service organizations do not have experience advising trans parents, so be sure that you find an attorney who knows how the law applies to trans people and has experience representing other trans parents. It is always a good idea to contact one of the national LGBTQ or trans legal organizations for free information and guidance about the parentage laws in your state. Even if you can afford a private family law attorney, it is highly advisable to contact one of these legal groups to be sure your attorney's advice is up to date.

ADOPTION

Adoption is the most common way for a person who is not a biological parent to establish a legally recognized parent–child relationship. The procedures and requirements for completing an adoption vary from state to state. They also depend on the type of adoption you are seeking. For example, the process for adopting a child from a state child welfare agency will be different—and sometimes more expensive and complicated—than the process for adopting your partner's child.

One common requirement in most types of adoption is a "home study" in which a trained professional such as social worker or psychologist evaluates your home and family to determine whether you have created an appropriate and safe environment for the child and are capable of handling the responsibility of being a parent. Many states, however, do not require a home study for a stepparent adoption.

You may—understandably—feel that you should not have to legally adopt your own child, such as a child your partner had after years of planning together. While that is an entirely valid feeling, the legal reality may be that adoption is the only way to ensure that you are recognized as your child's legal parent in every state and by the federal government.

Second-Parent or Stepparent Adoption

"Second-parent adoption" is the term used when an unmarried partner or co-parent adopts a child as a way to ensure that the child has a legal relationship with both parents. In most cases, one person has given birth to the child or adopted the child as a single parent, and then that person's partner becomes the child's second legal parent through a second-parent adoption. This type of adoption is available in about half of US states. Other states do not permit second-parent adoptions because they will only permit a second person to adopt if that person is legally married to the child's parent.

Those of us who are married to a child's legal parent can obtain a stepparent adoption. A stepparent adoption is similar to a second-parent adoption, but it is available only to people who are legally married to a child's parent. A stepparent adoption may cost less and require fewer legal steps than a second-parent adoption, depending on what state you are in. If you have any questions about whether your marriage is legally valid, you may want to consider obtaining a second-parent adoption that is not based on your marriage.

The benefit of obtaining a second-parent adoption rather than a stepparent adoption is that even if someone were to challenge the validity of your marriage, your adoption would not be in question. If your marriage is determined not to be valid, it does not necessarily void a stepparent adoption—however, a second-parent adoption is more secure.

Other Forms of Adoption

A trans person may also become a parent by means of an independent adoption (i.e., an adoption arranged not by an adoption agency but by another intermediary, such as a lawyer or a physician or even the biological parent(s) themselves) or by adopting through foster care, an adoption agency, or internationally, either as a single parent or with a partner. No state legally bars transgender people from adopting, although we may encounter informal discrimination.

One question that often arises is whether we should tell the adoption agency, social worker, or judge that we are transgender. Ultimately, the decision about whether to disclose our transgender status is personal and only we can make that decision for ourselves. As a practical matter, however, it may be difficult or impossible to keep that information private if the application asks us to disclosure prior names used or any prior medical diagnoses or treatment. In the worst case, it is possible that someone might later challenge the adoption on the ground that the adoptive parent's transgender status was not disclosed.

If you are considering adopting through an adoption agency, be aware that you may face bias from social workers or other agency staff who are unfamiliar with transgender issues and may harbor inaccurate stereotypes about transgender people. To increase the chances of success, contact adoption agencies that are open to lesbian, gay, and bisexual parents, which are more likely to be open to transgender parents as well. To overcome these false stereotypes, it may be necessary to have a supportive therapist or other health provider who is knowledgeable about transgender issues and can be a resource for social workers, adoption agency staff, or judges who may have questions or concerns.

Advice for Nonlegal Parents

In some states, there may be no way to become a legal parent, and the best you will be able to do is to take other steps, such as having the legal parent nominate you as a guardian of the child in his or her will, to provide some limited protection to your child.

It is important to know that even if the law in your state gives some limited recognition to people who function as parents but are not legal parents, your ability to protect and care for your child may be limited if you are not a full legal parent. For example, in most cases, a person who is not a legal parent cannot provide health insurance or other benefits for a child or make religious, medical, or legal decisions for a child. The child may not be eligible for survivor's benefits from Social Security if you die, and, in most cases, the child will not have a right to inherit from you if you die without a will.

Some states also recognize that a person who is not a legal parent, but who has functioned as a child's parent, should have at least some parental rights and responsibilities. For example, in Pennsylvania, if a partner lives with a person who has a child and functions as the child's second parent, even if the partner is not a legal parent, the partner can seek visitation with the child and may also be responsible for child support if the couple separates. A number of other states also give similar limited parental rights and responsibilities to people who have formed a parent–child relationship with a child but who do not meet the criteria to be recognized as a full legal parent.

In other states, however, the law is much more restrictive: If you are not a full legal parent, then you have *no* legal rights or responsibilities with respect to a child, even if you have parented the child for years and have a close parent–child bond. In these states, a person who is not a legal parent can be cut off from any contact with a child if that person is no longer in a relationship with the child's legal parent or if the legal parent becomes incapacitated or dies.

Assisted Reproduction

There are many ways that assisted reproduction can play a role in creating our families. We may use techniques that allow us to have children that are genetically related to us and our partners, or we may use donors and surrogates to bring children into our lives. Some of us preserve our gametes—sperm and eggs—for later use with a partner or surrogate. Examples of ways we may use assisted reproduction techniques include the following:

- A trans woman uses her sperm to impregnate her female partner.
- A trans woman wishes to become a parent with a male partner or as a single parent, and her sperm is used to impregnate a surrogate.
- A trans man who has a male partner after transitioning may wish to fertilize his eggs with his partner's sperm and then implant the fertilized egg or eggs in a surrogate.
- A trans man who has a female partner after transitioning may wish to use donated sperm to fertilize his eggs, which could then be implanted in his female partner.
- Anyone with a partner who is capable of giving birth may wish to use donor sperm to impregnate the partner.

Our parental rights in these cases vary from situation to situation, but there are a few basic assumptions. In most states, there is a legal presumption that a child born to a married couple is the legal child of both spouses. However, that presumption is rebuttable in virtually all states, so it cannot be relied upon.

Those of us who use our stored gametes for reproduction will likely be recognized as a legal parent in many states, based either on having a genetic connection to the child or on having consented to the procreation of a child through assisted reproduction. A court order of parentage or adoption is still advisable, unless we also give birth to the child.

Those of us who do not have a partner to carry a pregnancy typically require a surrogate. If the surrogate carries a child conceived using genetic material from you and your partner, both of you are likely to be considered the child's legal parents, depending on the laws governing surrogacy in the state where you live. If only one parent is genetically related to the child, the other parent will probably need to seek an adoption or court order of parentage. Couples who are in this situation should be sure they understand their state's laws governing transgender people and surrogacy.

State laws with respect to surrogacy vary widely, ranging from states that outlaw it altogether to states that actively facilitate and encourage the use of surrogacy. A growing number of states provide that intended parents may use gestational surrogacy to have a child, and that when they do so following state law requirements, the intended parent or parents are recognized. Some of these states require the intended parents to be married. Because these laws vary, it is vital that you speak with an attorney with expertise in assisted reproduction before taking any steps involving alternative insemination or surrogacy.

If you are having a child through assisted reproduction, it is important to get expert legal advice before conceiving. How the child is conceived and whether you have the right written documents and agreements can make the difference between whether you are recognized as a legal parent or not. For example, contrary to what many people falsely believe, simply having a written agreement with a known donor that the donor will not be a parent is not enough to prevent the donor from being a legal parent in any state. You must meet all the requirements under your state's law, and if you do not meet them, a known donor may be the child's legal parent, even if that is completely contrary to everyone's intentions and written agreements. In addition, in some states, it is impossible to use a known donor without the donor being the child's legal parent.

Trans Men Who Give Birth

In some cases, a trans man who has not had a hysterectomy may decide to stop taking hormones, permit his ovulation and menstrual cycle to recommence, and become pregnant in order to have a child who is biologically related to him. As a legal matter, a trans man who gives birth under these circumstances should be recognized as a legal parent. If he has a partner who is the other genetic parent to the child, both parents should be legally recognized.

There may be questions about how he should be identified on the child's birth certificate. While he may prefer to be identified as the child's father, some states may resist that and may list him as the child's mother. It is advisable that trans men who are contemplating giving birth seek out legal advice in their home state to ensure that they understand how they are likely to be treated and can anticipate any legal complications that may arise.

Child Custody

A trans parent who is considering divorce or separation and may end up in a custody battle should seek out legal advice from a family law attorney with experience representing transgender parents as soon as possible. Consulting with an attorney can help to prevent decisions that can later impact your rights as a parent. For example, a parent who leaves the family home and permits the other parent to have temporary custody of the children may be at a disadvantage in any subsequent custody proceeding.

Trans parents should also be aware that they are likely to be under extra scrutiny by courts and may also face considerable bias and stereotyping by judges and custody evaluators. To mitigate the impact of that bias, a trans parent may need to retain experts who can testify that being transgender has no impact on a person's ability to be a good parent.

Trans parents who are in the process of transitioning must be especially careful to seek out expert advice about the best way to talk about the transition with the children and to discuss the decision to inform the children with the other parent before doing so. Judges may be particularly critical of parents who disclose this information in what the judge views as an insensitive or inappropriate way or without consultation with a child therapist. To avoid this danger, and to ensure that your children are best equipped to hear this information from you, it is critical to document that you are putting the best interests of your children first by seeking out and following the advice of experienced professionals with expertise in child welfare and child development. You should also inform the other parent of your plan and, if possible, involve them in the process.

Termination of Parental Rights

Tragically, a few courts have terminated a person's parental rights simply because the parent underwent gender transition. Courts doing this usually base their rulings on unsupported fears that being "exposed" to a transgender parent would be harmful to the child. But, even in those cases, someone had to file a court case. Simply changing gender does not have an automatic effect on our status as a legal parent. As we become more visible and accepted, and as we gain more legal protections, this type of discrimination and bias will become less prevalent.

INTIMATE PARTNER VIOLENCE AND ABUSE

Intimate partner violence (IPV) happens in all communities, but it is often underreported or minimized when it affects the trans community. Police officers, judges, and even domestic violence advocates often operate based on stereotypes that make it hard for them to see or understand violence against a trans person. For example, they may believe that men are not vulnerable to abuse or that abuse of a trans partner is not as serious as other types of IPV. In addition, LGBTQ people may fear that reporting IPV will reflect badly on the community as a whole. Abusers often try to convince their partners that no one will believe them if they come forward, for instance, or that no one will care. With respect to trans people in particular, abusers claim that people will not believe them because of their trans status. Abusers may also try to convince their victims that coming forward will "air dirty laundry" in the community and will be harmful for trans people generally. These claims are false.

Trans people who report IPV or seek help from shelters or domestic violence advocates may face discrimination and a lack of sensitivity. This can be devastating for a person who is already facing serious abuse. But increasingly, there are programs and services that are sensitive to the needs of trans people, and more police departments are getting training and protocols on how to deal with trans people who are the victims of IPV. If you are in an abusive situation, there may be a supportive program or advocate in your community who can help you. If you encounter discrimination by police officers, shelter workers, or others, reach out for help to a local, state, or national LGBTQ or trans organization.

Identifying Intimate Partner Violence

Trans people are especially vulnerable to sexual or physical abuse because we are socially and legally stigmatized. As a result, abusers may believe they can get away with abusing a trans person without being held accountable by society or the law. There is a direct connection between the lack of legal rights and protections for trans people and high rates of IPV targeting trans people.

One reason IPV in the trans community is minimized is because it happens in ways that are not always obvious. Violence and physical abuse are common forms of IPV, but there are other ways abuse happens as well. If an intimate partner threatens to "out" you to other people such as friends, coworkers, a boss, or family members in order to control your actions, that is IPV. If an intimate partner threatens to take your children away if you leave the relationship, and threatens to use your gender identity against you, that is IPV. For trans people, these types of threats create a fear that is just as powerful as a threat of physical violence.

If you or someone you know is in a violent or abusive relationship, contact the National Domestic Violence Hotline page at 1-800-799-SAFE. That number can be called toll-free from anywhere in the United States. Calls are answered in English and Spanish, with interpreters available for an additional 139 languages. They can refer you to the intimate partner violence services closest to you.

Reporting

Trans people tend to underreport IPV for a number of reasons. Many trans people have faced discrimination, harassment, and even abuse at the hands of law enforcement officers. Trans people who are homeless or who are sex workers are at high risk of abuse, but we may be afraid to report it because we fear we will be harassed or arrested by the police or that no one will believe us. People with children face additional barriers to reporting violence and leaving an abusive relationship. Many trans people fear that if we get involved in a custody dispute with a partner, the court will be biased against us. Trans men may be reluctant to report abuse, especially at the hands of a female partner, because they believe that being abused will cause others to question their male gender identity. Other trans people may be reluctant to report IPV because they fear their identity will not be respected and the prospect of facing discrimination is too overwhelming.

The good news is that more agencies that provide services for people who have experienced IPV are educating themselves about trans people, and more courts that hear IPV cases are being educated as well.

LEGAL ISSUES AFFECTING TRANSGENDER CHILDREN AND YOUTH

Because of increased visibility and support, children are realizing and understanding their gender identity at earlier ages. A parent's decision to accept a child's gender identity can be literally lifesaving. Studies have shown that children who grow up with parents who accept and celebrate their identity as transgender are significantly less likely to experience negative mental health outcomes such as depression, substance abuse, and suicidal thoughts and attempts. Parental acceptance is critical and directly linked to a child's self-esteem and healthy development.

Custody Disputes Over Trans Children

Thanks to positive changes in cultural acceptance and visibility, transgender children and youth are more likely to come out and their parents are more likely to be supportive. Generally, parents do not run into any legal obstacles in supporting their trans children or seeking out medical treatment for their children so long as both parents agree. But legal problems can arise if a child's parents are divorced or separated and do not agree on how to parent their trans child. As in any custody dispute, it is best for everyone involved that the parents try to work out their differences before going to court. In some circumstances, that is not possible, leading to bitter custody battles.

When one parent does not support a child's transgender identity, the supportive parent can best protect against a loss of custody by getting help from professionals who know about transgender children. Where possible, a parent should seek advice from mental health and medical professionals with expertise in gender identity issues. The parent should document these steps, including showing attempts to include the other parent in the process. The parent should carefully follow the advice of those professionals. If a supportive parent ends up in a custody battle, the court is likely to scrutinize everything that parent has done. It is important to be able to show that the parent was following expert medical advice, not acting on their own.

If you have a trans child and the child's other parent is not supportive, it is important to seek out legal advice early on so that you can take steps to protect yourself. If you do not have access to a local attorney with experience advising other parents of transgender children, contact an LGBTQ or trans legal group. Those groups can provide you with free information and guidance.

Safe Schools

Schools have a legal duty to keep children safe. Federal laws may help to protect against bullying and harassment, although they do not specifically address the concerns of trans youth.

Bullying and harassment can take many forms. In addition to violence, taunting, and cyber-bullying, refusing to use a child's correct name and pronouns is a type of harassment. Teachers and school officials also sometimes mistreat trans students, and this is particularly damaging. The school can be liable for failing to discipline or remove teachers or officials who mistreat students based on gender identity. Refusing to permit a trans student to use the appropriate restroom or locker facilities or to play on a sports team that corresponds to the child's gender identity are other types of discrimination. Gender nonconforming youth may be able to make a legal claim that discrimination, bullying, and harassment are sex discrimination, which is against federal law.

Recognizing the needs of transgender students, a growing number of states and local school districts have adopted laws or policies protecting trans students from discrimination. Currently, 10 states (California, Colorado, Illinois, Iowa, Maine, Minnesota, New Jersey, Oregon, Vermont, and Washington) and the District of Columbia have laws specifically prohibiting gender identity discrimination in public schools. In some cases, these laws may also apply to private schools that receive state funding. In addition, many states and school districts are providing that trans students be allowed to use restrooms and locker rooms and participate in sports in accordance with their gender identity.

LEGAL ISSUES FOR TRANSGENDER ELDERS

Legal issues facing transgender elders are becoming increasingly visible. This is due to many factors, including more advocacy on this issue and the fact that more trans people who were able to take advantage of modern medical treatments relating to gender transition are aging. For the first time, all of the systems that are set up to deal with elders in our society—such as hospitals, nursing facilities, hospices, retirement communities, public guardian offices, adult protective services, elder law attorneys, and others—are being confronted with significant numbers of trans elders. For the most part, these systems are not prepared to deal with trans elders and often fail to treat us appropriately or with the respect we deserve—although every day, trans elders and advocates are working to change these conditions so that trans elders can receive safe and competent care.

Hospitals and Nursing Facilities

When transgender elders require care in a hospital or nursing home, discrimination and disrespect are serious concerns. Doctors and nursing home staff wield enormous power to try to force a transgender person to go back to living in their birth-assigned sex, either through denying hormone therapy or refusing to allow someone to wear clothes that express their gender. In some cases, nursing home officials will refuse to admit a senior because the person is transgender.

Fifteen states, the District of Columbia, and over 100 cities have nondiscrimination laws that protect transgender people against discrimination in public accommodations. These laws generally apply to nursing homes. Other states are considering LGBTQ-inclusive laws to protect elders in nursing homes, and many nursing homes are developing policies that will help ensure proper care and respect for transgender elders.

The Nursing Home Reform Act also protects trans elders by granting nursing home residents specific rights, including (1) the right to dignity; (2) the right to be free from mental and physical abuse; (3) the right to be free from involuntary seclusion; (4) the right to receive visitors; (5) the right to receive adequate and appropriate care; (6) the right to make independent personal decisions such as what to wear; (7) the right to privacy and confidentiality; (8) the right to complain; (9) the right to self-determination; and (10) the right to participate in community activities both inside and outside the nursing home.

The federal housing agency, HUD, also protects transgender elders from discrimination in housing based on gender identity. Additionally, some states, like California, have passed laws mandating that nursing home staff must receive training about how to address the needs of transgender residents.

While there is no law explicitly requiring long-term care facilities to house transgender elders according to our affirmed gender, most legal advocacy groups agree that the laws that prohibit sex discrimination and gender identity discrimination in housing

The Department of Justice's online Community Relations Service is a free, confidential resource that offers mediation, conciliation, technical assistance, and training for schools that are experiencing problems with harassment based on conflicts around any number of factors, including gender, gender identity, sexual orientation, religion, disability, race, color, and national origin.

require this. There is a lot of work being done to make sure facilities are following this important practice and to create more explicit laws on this issue.

There are a number of ways in which we, as trans elders, can protect ourselves, by ensuring that people we trust will be empowered to make medical and financial decisions for us if we become ill or incapacitated. We should all have wills, advance directives regarding our health care—which should include specifying that we want to continue hormone therapy and to be treated consistently with our gender identity—and powers of attorney for finances and medical decision making.

The Importance of Wills and Advance Directives for Health Care

All trans people should protect themselves and their children, family members, and friends by making sure to have wills and advance directives for health care. Because our marriages are not always legally respected, and because no states automatically respect unmarried relationships, our assets may go either to our blood relatives or to the state if we die without a will. Even if you have few assets, having a will is worthwhile to save your partner, children, or friends from the pain and stress of being treated as legal strangers to you or having unsupportive relatives or state officials disposing of your personal belongings and taking any assets that you may have. For those who have significant assets (such as a home, property, money, cars, or other valuable belongings), having a will is crucial to ensure that your assets will go to the people you want to have them.

When making a will, you must be sure to comply with all of the legal requirements for making a valid will in your state. If you do not comply with the legal requirements, your will may not be accepted, or it may be vulnerable to being challenged. To find out what those requirements are where you live, contact a transgender or LGBTQ legal organization. In some places, there may be free legal services that can help you make out a will. If you can afford an attorney, hiring a knowledgeable attorney who has experience representing transgender people to help you create a will is highly advisable. It is also a good idea to review and update your will every year or so, or when the circumstances in your life change.

Your will can also include a provision saying who has the authority to make your funeral arrangements. In some states, a person can fill out a separate form to designate who can make their funeral arrangements. This is important because if you do not designate a person to do this before you die, unless you are legally married and your marriage is respected where you died, the law will give the authority to make your funeral arrangements to blood relatives or the state. If your family of origin or the state is not supportive, this may mean that your gender identity will not be respected at your funeral.

Every trans person should also have an advance directive for health care, which is a document that identifies who you want to make legal decisions if you are injured or too ill to make decisions for yourself. If you do not have an advance directive, most state laws provide that your legal spouse or, if you are not married, your blood relatives, have the power to make medical decisions for you. Even if you are legally married, a hospital or health care provider may challenge the validity of your marriage and refuse to let your spouse make decisions for you, so it is important to have an advance directive regardless of your marital status. For unmarried people in relationships, or who would like to designate a friend to make health care decisions, having an advance directive is essential.

An advance directive can also specify what medical treatments a person does or does not want to undergo if they are no longer able to make decisions due to illness or incapacity. This is sometimes referred to as a living will. For trans people, it may be important to specify in your advance directive that you want to be maintained on hormone therapy and you want to be treated consistently with your gender identity if you are ill or incapacitated, including issues such as the use of gender-appropriate clothing, names, pronouns, and grooming. Every state provides free forms for advance directives. Different states have different laws about health care directives, so be sure to update your directive if you move to a new state.

For more information about how to protect ourselves as we age, see *Lifelines: Documents to Protect You and Your Family*, published by the National Center for Lesbian Rights and available online.

PRISONS, JAILS, DETENTION FACILITIES, AND LOCK-UPS

Unfortunately, as trans people we are disproportionately represented in criminal justice system facilities due to discrimination and targeting. There, we face difficulties related to abuse and mistreatment, as well as denial of access to medical services and gender-appropriate housing.

Housing Issues in Lock-ups

Current federal regulations require every jail or prison receiving federal dollars to make a case-by-case determination of whether a transgender inmate would be safer housed in a men's or women's prison. These regulations enforce a federal law called the Prison Rape Elimination Act. Some places such as Denver, Colorado; Chicago, Illinois; Portland, Maine; and the District of Columbia have adopted this approach.

In practice, however, most federal and state prisons and local jails are not yet following these regulations. Instead, most prisons and jails house transgender inmates according to their birth sex. That means that trans women are housed in men's facilities, and trans men are housed in women's facilities. This system can especially put transgender women at serious risk for physical and sexual assault.

Some jails and prisons also routinely separate trans prisoners from other prisoners either by putting them in cells by themselves or by creating a separate wing or unit for trans prisoners. Many trans prisoners do not want to be separated from other inmates since that means they are denied access to many recreational, social, work, and educational activities. When someone is placed alone in a cell, he or she can also experience serious mental health problems like depression, anxiety, or even suicidal thoughts.

Community members can help change these dangerous and outdated policies by becoming involved with local and state groups that advocate for prisoners and work with those groups to make sure that prison officials in your state know about the new federal regulations—and that transgender inmates in your state know about them as well. There are groups that advocate for prisoners in every state and in most towns and cities. To find a group that helps prisoners where you live, contact the American Civil Liberties Union's National Prison Project or Just Detention International.

TRANSGENDER WOMEN AND PRISON

Miss Major is 70 years old and lives in Oakland, California. She is affiliated with the Transgender, Gender Variant & Intersex Justice Project.

When I went to prison, it was the most frightening thing that ever happened to me because I was a target of so much violence. It is hard to avoid harassment and abuse by guards and other prisoners, and the guards like to set up abusive situations between prisoners. They try to strip you of your dignity, and it's hard when the rest of the world has already been trying. They strip away your privacy, humiliate you—anything to make sure you know you are worth nothing and while you're there, you don't exist. This is degrading for everyone and just makes the trauma deeper for transgender people who are dehumanized all the time.

At the Transgender, Gender Variant & Intersex Justice Project (TGI Justice), the transgender girls we're in touch with are trying to fight the isolation and dangers inside. They're fighting to make sure their humanness is seen. We send them information about changes in laws and any victories transgender people in prison or jail win. The problem is the guards don't read the laws, or enforce them, so usually things don't change. We also send materials for transgender people going into prison on how to deal with all the harassment.

We hear from transgender women inside California prisons who have a sense of pride that's new. They say it's because they know that we're on the outside supporting their fight. We fight this together to build our pride and help us all survive. Sometimes it's hard when the hatred is so real and the problems so big, but at least we're trying. We're in touch with over 700 transgender people in California prisons. At TGI Justice we want to train and hire more transgender people coming out of prison to organize against this system and support each other.

We are survivors because we have survived with nothing. This is especially true for transgender women of color. We know how to live in the hole (solitary confinement) for years and still muster enough respect for ourselves and decency for others. We will survive!

Protection From Violence and Assault

Prison officials have a legal duty to protect prisoners from violence at the hands of other prisoners or prison staff. Prison officials who show a "deliberate indifference" to this duty can be held legally liable under the Eighth Amendment, which bars cruel and unusual punishment. In the 1994 US Supreme Court case *Farmer v. Brennan*, a transgender prisoner who was beaten and raped by her male cellmate sued prison officials for failing to protect her. Unfortunately, the Supreme Court held that prison officials are liable for violence inflicted on a transgender prisoner by other prisoners only when the officials have actual, specific knowledge that a particular transgender prisoner is at risk and deliberately fail to take any steps to stop the violence from happening. That Supreme Court decision has made it hard for transgender prisoners to sue when they are raped or assaulted because it is often hard to prove that officials had actual knowledge of a specific risk. Despite this difficulty, however, many transgender prisoners who are assaulted continue to bring cases, and some courts are beginning to be more sympathetic to these claims.

In addition to litigation, another way to help prevent violence against transgender inmates is for community members to become pen pals with transgender inmates and to visit them. When prison officials know that an inmate has friends and supporters in the outside world, the officials may be less likely to let that inmate be abused or mistreated. Community members can also help by bringing the issue of violence against transgender prisoners to the attention of legislators and public officials and urging them to adopt better policies to protect transgender prisoners and to keep transgender people out of prison in the first place.

Unfortunately, one way that some jails and prisons deal with the problem of violence against transgender inmates is to separate them from other prisoners by putting them in their own cells. This is referred to as "administrative segregation." While that kind of segregation may provide temporary protection for some individuals, many trans prisoners report that it puts them at greater risk because they are separated from their support networks. Administrative segregation also excludes transgender inmates from recreational, educational, and occupational activities, and it may violate their constitutional right to be free from cruel and unusual punishment. Being held in isolation for extended periods of time—even when it is supposedly for your own "protection"—has an extremely negative impact on a person's mental health and has been condemned as a serious human rights abuse by international human rights organizations. The fact that so many transgender prisoners are held in isolation in the United States is one of the worst forms of abuse and discrimination suffered by our community.

Access to Transition-Related Medical Care

Courts have ruled that transgender people in prison have a constitutional right to at least some kinds of medically necessary transition-related medical care. In 2011, for instance, a federal appeals court ruled that a Wisconsin law forbidding prisons from providing medical treatment to transgender prisoners was unconstitutional. Other courts have also ordered prisons to provide transgender prisoners with hormone therapy. In 2012, a federal judge in Massachusetts ordered prison officials to provide gender-affirming surgery to a transgender inmate.

Under the Obama administration, the federal Bureau of Prisons adopted a policy that trans prisoners must be given all medically necessary care related to gender transition. The new policy requires medical and mental health staff in federal prisons to meet with transgender prisoners to determine what types of counseling and medical care they need, based on their individual circumstances. In practice, however, this policy is often not followed. Many transgender federal prisoners are denied any sort of care related to transition or to being transgender.

In state prisons and county jails, the medical treatment available to transgender people varies widely. For instance, in California, trans people in state prisons are supposed to be provided with supportive counseling and hormone therapy. But that is not

LIVING AS OURSELVES

true in many other states. And even in California, many county jails do not provide transition-related care.

Transition-related care also includes being able to use a person's preferred name and pronouns and to dress consistently with the person's gender. These aspects of a trans person's medical care and human dignity are routinely violated in prisons and jails. Guards and prison officials often refer to trans prisoners by their birth names and genders, which are on their badges, medical records, and other documents. Prison staff may also make fun of trans prisoners and call them degrading names. The federal prison system and some state prison systems have policies that should prevent this abuse, but they are not always enforced.

Preventing trans prisoners from wearing clothing or accessories that match the person's gender is one of the most common ways that prison staffers humiliate and harass trans prisoners. Trans prisoners are often denied access to clothing that matches their gender identity. Trans women may be deprived of bras, even when they are obviously needed. In some prisons and jails, merely having a bra in a male facility may be grounds for punishment. Trans women are also routinely denied access to makeup and other cosmetics. Trans men housed in women's facilities are often forced to wear feminine clothing. Some trans male prisoners report being forced to wear dresses, even when other female prisoners are not, solely in order to humiliate them. Trans prisoners of both genders are often denied the ability to groom their hair and fingernails consistently with their gender identity.

In theory, transgender people in prison should be able to change their names legally to reflect their gender identity. In practice, however, prisons often create rules that make it difficult for trans prisoners to file name-change petitions, or courts may wrongly deny the petition simply because the person is in prison. Despite these obstacles, some trans prisoners do succeed in filing successful name changes while incarcerated.

Treatment of Trans Youth in Juvenile Facilities and Foster Care

Trans youth are more likely to end up in juvenile detention or foster care due to family rejection, harassment at school, and bias and discrimination in the legal system. According to a 2005 Amnesty International report, "police regularly profile LGBTQ youth as criminals, and selectively enforce laws . . . such as loitering, public drunkenness, public urination, and littering" (Majd et al., 2009).

Once trans youth are in a juvenile facility or group home, they are very likely to experience harassment and even physical and sexual abuse at the hands of other youth or facility staff. In many facilities, trans youth are not permitted to use the right pronouns or names or to wear clothing that corresponds to their gender identity. They may be segregated from other youth or treated as sex offenders, and they are often housed based on their birth sex. California has passed state laws prohibiting discrimination against trans youth in foster care and state juvenile facilities, and some other states have similar policies.

GETTING HELP FOR LEGAL ISSUES

If you need legal information or advice, it is a good idea to seek out a lawyer. Do not be afraid to interview potential lawyers to see whether they have prior experience representing trans clients and to ask questions that will help you decide if you feel comfortable working with a particular attorney or firm.

An ethical lawyer will not mind answering your questions or providing you with the information necessary to assure you that they are qualified to represent you. If an attorney is not respectful of your identity, that is a sign that the person does not understand trans issues and likely will not do a good job representing you.

Keep in mind that few lawyers are knowledgeable about how the law affects trans people or about how to represent trans people, but many of them enter the legal profession as a way to help others. Lawyers who are experts in the area of law where you need

Because trans youth experience so much discrimination and mistreatment in state care, child welfare advocates have developed model policies and practice guidelines on how to provide appropriate services and care for trans youth in juvenile facilities and group homes. For more information about these policies and practice guidelines, see Jody Marksamer's *A Place of Respect: Serving Transgender and Gender Non-Conforming Youth in Group Care Facilities* (National Center for Lesbian Rights 2011) and Katayoon Majd, Jody Marksamer, and Carolyn Reyes's *Hidden Injustice: Lesbian, Gay, Bisexual, and Transgender Youth in Juvenile Courts* (Equity Project, 2009). Both handbooks are available online.

help—such as employment law or family law—may be able to help you find ways to work through challenges specific to your situation, even if they are unfamiliar with the law as it applies to trans people specifically.

There are also a growing number of national, state, and local nonprofit legal organizations that specialize in LGBTQ or trans law. These organizations are a treasure trove of information. In many cases, they may be able to provide you or your lawyer with the information you need to avoid problems or at least to find additional legal resources in your area.

Working with lawyers can be a new and confusing experience for many of us. Come prepared to discuss your situation in detail. To better serve you, lawyers may need to know information about your transition and personal history that you would not disclose to many others. If you feel uncomfortable answering a question that your lawyer asks, let the lawyer know, and find out why they are asking that particular question. You can determine, together, whether it is needed information or if it is information that you can provide in a different way that preserves your privacy and peace of mind. Although every state requires attorneys to protect the confidentiality of communication with clients, you may want to discuss this with the attorney to make sure the attorney understands your need to be certain that your confidential information will be protected.

ORGANIZATIONS PROVIDING TRANSGENDER LEGAL RESOURCES

The American Civil Liberties Union (aclu.org) has an LGBT rights project.

Equality Advocates (center4civilrights.org) is an LGBT legal organization in Pennsylvania.

Gay and Lesbian Advocates and Defenders (glad.org) is an LGBT rights organization in New England.

Lambda Legal (lambdalegal.org) is a national organization dedicated to LGBT civil rights.

The Massachusetts Transgender Political Coalition (masstpc.org) is an advocacy, education, and community-building organization that works to end discrimination on the basis of gender identity and expression.

National Center for Lesbian Rights (nclrights.org) is a national organization dedicated to LGBT, not just lesbian, rights.

The National Center for Transgender Equality (transequality.org) is a social justice organization dedicated to advancing the equality of transgender people.

The National Gay and Lesbian Task Force (ngltf.org) trains activists and organizes pro-LGBT legislation.

The Southern Poverty Law Center (splcenter.org) is a nonprofit civil rights organization dedicated to fighting hate and bigotry, and to seeking justice for the most vulnerable members of society, including transgender people.

The Sylvia Rivera Law Project (srlp.org) in New York City works to guarantee that all people are free to self-determine gender identity and expression, regardless of income or race, and without facing harassment, discrimination, or violence.

The Transgender Law and Policy Institute (transgenderlaw.org) works on law and policy initiatives that benefit transgender people.

The Transgender Law Center (transgenderlawcenter.org) is an organization that provides legal resources for transgender people.

The Transgender Legal Defense and Education Fund (transgenderlegal.org) focuses on education, legal services, and public policy efforts.

CONCLUSION

The law affects us all in different ways. As trans people, we often have increased contact with the law and law enforcement because of a need for legal ID changes and protection against discrimination, as well as targeting by law enforcement officials. Legal changes that have the potential to improve our lives are, in some ways, coming very quickly, and in other ways, moving at a snail's pace. We can affect the pace and direction of these changes by working together for justice both inside and outside of legal systems.

REFERENCES AND FURTHER READING

Coleman, E., Bockting, W., Botzer, M., Cohen-Kettenis, P., DeCuypere, G., Feldman, J.,…Zucker, K. (2011). Standards of care for the health of transsexual, transgender, and gender-nonconforming people, version 7. *International Journal of Transgenderism*, *13*, 165–232.

Currah, P., Juang, R. M., & Minter, S. P. (2006). *Transgender rights*. Minneapolis: University of Minnesota Press.

Grant, J. M., Mottet, L. A., Tanis, J., Harrison, J., Herman, J. L., & Keisling, M. (2011). *Injustice at every turn: A report of the national transgender discrimination survey.* Washington, D.C.: National Center for Transgender Equality and National Gay and Lesbian Task Force.

Levi, J. L. (2012). *Transgender family law: A guide to effective advocacy.* AuthorHouse.

Majd, K., Marksamer, J., & Reyes, C. (2009). Hidden injustice: Lesbian, gay, bisexual, and transgender youth in juvenile courts. *Equity Project: National Juvenile Defender Center, National Center for Lesbian Rights, and Legal Services for Children.* Retrieved December 2013, from http://www.equityproject.org/pdfs/hidden_injustice.pdf

Mogul, J., Ritchie, A., & Whitlock, K. (2011). *Queer injustice: The criminalization of LGBT people in the United States.* Boston, MA: Beacon Press.

Spade, D. (2011). *Normal life: Administrative violence, critical trans politics, and the limits of the law.* Boston, MA: South End Press.

Stanley, E. A., & Smith, N. (2011). *Captive genders: Trans embodiment and the prison industrial complex.* Oakland, CA: AK Press.

American Civil Liberties Union Lesbian, Gay, Bisexual, Transgender, and AIDS Project. (n.d.). *Transgender people and the law: Frequently asked questions.* Retrieved December 2013, from https://www.aclu.org/sites/default/files/images/asset_upload_file781_33764.pdf

National Center for Transgender Equality. (2013). *Transgender people and the Social Security Administration.* Retrieved December 2013, from http://www.transequality.org/Resources/SSAResource_June2013.pdf

US Department of Veterans Affairs. (2013). *Providing health care for transgender and intersex veterans.* Retrieved December 2013, from http://www.va.gov/vhapublications/ViewPublication.asp?pub_ID=2863

US Office of Personnel Management. (n.d.). Guidance regarding the employment of transgender individuals in the federal workplace. Retrieved December 2013, from http://www.opm.gov/policy-data-oversight/diversity-and-inclusion/reference-materials/gender-identity-guidance/

SECTION 3
HEALTH AND WELLNESS

GENERAL, SEXUAL, AND REPRODUCTIVE HEALTH

11

Nick Gorton and Hilary Maia Grubb

WHEN TALKING ABOUT COMMUNITIES WITH LIMITED ACCESS TO HEALTH CARE, the focus is often on illnesses and diseases that are more common or more severe in those communities. Discussions about transgender health often concentrate on our higher rates of HIV, lack of access to primary care providers, vulnerability to interpersonal violence, and silicone injection. It is critical to address these conditions that threaten our health and welfare. However, it is also important to understand transgender health in terms of physical, mental, and social well-being. Health represents a positive state of wellness, strength, and stability; not simply the absence of illness.

Our health is impacted by our environments and communities. These include where we grow up, live, work, and seek health care services. Many health care providers, researchers, and educators have focused on these areas, also called the "social determinants of health." If we cannot find a find job due to being trans, we may be unable to afford food or safe housing. We might then need to access underground methods of survival and engage in sex work in order to have money to eat and pay rent. Doing this exposes us to increased risk of violence, HIV, and other sexually transmitted infections (STIs), and mental health issues such as depression and suicidality. We might have no choice but to live with an abusive partner because we cannot afford to move out. We may not be able to afford to see a health provider who knows how to prescribe and manage hormone therapy, so we might buy hormones on the street. Without a provider monitoring hormone therapy, we could have complications that go unnoticed, such as diabetes or a blood clot in the leg. Social determinants of health are linked to stable employment, a safe home and environment, access to transgender-sensitive and competent health care, healthy food choices, and opportunities to exercise.

Some social determinants of health are unique to trans people. One of the most important is access to health care that is safe and does not discriminate against us because we are trans. This includes hormone therapy and surgical procedures, but we have needs similar to cisgender people too, such as vaccines, treatment of high blood pressure and asthma, and screening for diseases like colon cancer. Unfortunately, transgender people are less likely than cisgender people to have these needs met, and we face many barriers to maintaining good health.

Many of us have delayed or avoided health care and health maintenance screenings because of negative interactions with the health care system. We have been denied care because our providers refused to see us or because our insurance company would not pay. We have waited disproportionately longer. We have been asked to fill out forms with boxes that do not describe us. We have been called names or pronouns that are accidentally or deliberately incorrect. We have heard biased and harassing comments from clinicians and staff. We have had unnecessary or prolonged physical exams. We have been denied access to safe and appropriate bathrooms. We have been assigned to inappropriate hospital rooms. And the list goes on.

> *"I avoid health care providers due to my gender identity. I experienced severe discrimination when I identified myself as queer in terms of sexual orientation, and I realize that gender is even less understood."*

Bias and discrimination in health care settings are not only unethical but also violate law and policy in many areas. It is critical that health care providers respect us; have a

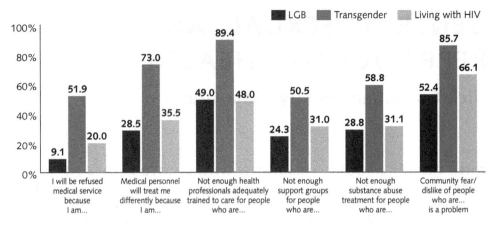

Fears and concerns about accessing health care (reprinted from "When Health Care Isn't Caring: Lambda Legal's Survey of Discrimination Against LGBT People and People Living With HIV" [New York, Lambda Legal, 2010]).

basic knowledge of social, medical, and surgical transition; and be aware of the specific health concerns of our communities. To improve our general health, it is important to focus not only on hormones and surgery: we must also address our environment and community. We need transgender-focused job fairs, transgender-friendly homeless and domestic violence shelters, transgender cultural competency education for police departments, and access to appropriate identity documents. One of the meanings of "to heal" is "to make whole." Making our homes, jobs, streets, hospitals, grocery stores, doctors' offices, and neighborhoods safer—free of discrimination and bias—will be one step in the right direction.

HISTORY OF TRANSGENDER HEALTH CARE

Transgender and gender nonconforming people have existed throughout history, but only in the past century has the medical profession been able to provide help to change our bodies to match our gender identities. In 1917 in the United States, Dr. Alan Hart underwent a hysterectomy and eventually a mastectomy to help him live his life as a man. In 1930, Lily Elbe had the first of five surgeries in Germany to transition from male to female. Almost as soon as synthetic sex hormones were available, physicians provided them (or transgender people obtained them) to transition medically.

Christine Jorgensen's public transition in the early 1950s increased general awareness about transgender people. From that time until the 1980s, transgender care became more available at academic medical centers. However, in the early 1980s, dozens of academic medical centers in the United States closed their doors to transgender people seeking transition-related care. This was set in motion by the closure of the first and most well-known gender identity center at Johns Hopkins University School of Medicine in Baltimore.

The program at Hopkins Gender Identity Clinic closed under the direction of then-chairman Dr. Paul McHugh. Dr. McHugh argued that transgender women were "caricatures of women. They wore high heels, copious makeup, and flamboyant clothing;

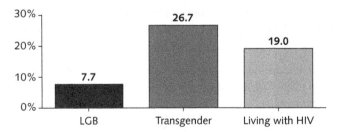

I was refused needed health care (reprinted from "When Health Care Isn't Caring: Lambda Legal's Survey of Discrimination Against LGBT People and People Living With HIV" [New York, Lambda Legal, 2010]).

they spoke about how they found themselves able to give vent to their natural inclinations for peace, domesticity, and gentleness—but their large hands, prominent Adam's apples, and thick facial features were incongruous (and would become more so as they aged)." Dr. McHugh set out to study trans women and to discredit what he viewed as a "misdirection of psychiatry" that allowed some of us to access hormones and surgery (McHugh, 2004, p. 34). In his later writings, he explicitly stated his perspective on the gender identity program at Hopkins: "It was part of my intention, when I arrived in Baltimore in 1975, to help end it" (McHugh, 1992, p. 501).

Indeed, an influential research study conducted by psychiatrist Jon Meyer and coinvestigator Donna Reter under McHugh's direction (Meyer & Reter, 1979) resulted in the closure of many academic medical center transgender care programs. This study compared transgender women who were offered surgery to those who were not (Lombardi, 2010). There were serious problems with the methodology of this study, and subsequent criticisms suggested that its conclusions were motivated more by politics than good science (Lothstein, 1982; Pfafflin & Jung, 1998). In addition, the paper did not conclude that transgender women had poorer outcomes with surgery; in fact, they had the same or better outcomes in each area measured in the study, and they experienced a better overall sense of well-being. However, the amount of improvement did not reach statistical significance, so the paper concluded that surgery was of no benefit.

This conclusion is at odds with the vast majority of research on transgender people who are offered gender-affirming surgical treatments. However, because this study came from the first and biggest US academic medical center that provided transgender care, it had tremendous influence and was reported in the popular press at the time (Brody, 1979). Furthermore, the study was used to justify the closure of every other gender program at US academic medical centers (except for the University of Minnesota Program in Human Sexuality, which has operated continuously since 1970 and provided patient care since 1973). After the closure of these gender programs, almost all care for transgender people in the United States was provided outside of mainstream academic medicine.

Around the same time, most insurance coverage for transgender care was eliminated if it existed. While, over the last decade, this has begun to change due to the efforts of countless advocates and activists, to this day most insurance policies expressly exclude transgender care (Transgender Law Center, 2012). Part of the justification for these exclusions was based on Meyer and Reter's conclusions that transgender care is experimental and has not been proven to improve health outcomes (Meyer & Reter, 1979).

Fortunately, as a result of transgender care leaving academic medical centers and being provided in community settings, the development of a more patient-centered model of transgender medicine is happening in many places. Activists in the United States are working to expand insurance coverage of transgender care. Ultimately (though he did not intend it) Dr. McHugh's schemes at Hopkins may have inadvertently made positive change in transgender medicine possible. His closure of the Hopkins program may have pushed us further toward the goal of culturally sensitive and affordable transgender care.

CARE AND CLASSIFICATION: HOW WELL DOES "TRANSGENDER" TAKE CARE OF US?

Christoph Hanssmann, MPH, is a doctoral student in sociology at UC San Francisco, where he is conducting research on classification, care, and citizenship as they pertain to trans health.

"Transgender" is a name and a category for which many gender nonconforming people have fought. It hasn't come easily, and we're still called by a lot of other names. For some of us, the term "transgender" is too broad. For others, it's too restrictive. It is important to pay attention to what it makes possible and what it limits in its use as a category.

When it comes to "transgender" (or other similar categories, like "trans" or "trans*"), it is important to consider its emergence over time. Nineteenth- and twentieth-century US and European sexologists were very keen on classification, generating cascades of names and descriptions of "deviant" bodies, genders, and sexual desires. It was through the acts of *naming* and *expert classification* that "pathologization" emerged.

One of the ways gender nonconforming people fight pathologization is by *naming ourselves*. But because much of our scrutiny has focused on how *other people* have categorized us, we have failed to truly analyze what has gone into these processes of self-categorization. Within any group, some voices are inevitably granted more credibility than others. This begs the question: Who, within a community, determines "who we are" and how we should be defined?

Trans health is an important place to consider the *effects* of categories on different people—whether these are categories that "we" claim, or whether they are thrust upon us (or a combination of the two). "Transgender," as a category, collectivizes us. But it can sometimes offer a false sense of the "us" that makes up that collective. If trans health is *exclusively* concerned with gender-confirming surgeries, for example, it overlooks the health needs of those who do not pursue these. This narrow version of trans health also solidifies the idea of "transgender" as only being *possible as a category* through bodily modification—even though we are well aware that there are many more ways to be trans. Conceptualizing trans health broadly allows for a much more expansive reach and focus. In the broad sense, trans health can center anything—from ending police violence and homelessness to ensuring access to all forms of health care.

Trans health and care entails focusing most scrupulously on those for whom chances for survival are most severely compromised. We can see patterns in what happens to those of us who are viewed as diverging from the norm. For example, CeCe McDonald—a black trans woman who defended herself against a life-threatening attack—was criminalized by the same system that has also criminalized non-trans black women resisting violence.

Fostering health and survival for all "transgender" people requires paying close attention to how differences along lines of race, class, geographic location, age, sexuality, and disability make a difference in individuals' experiences. Thinking inclusively about trans health means thinking not just about whether a person experiences medical neglect, or whether surgeries, hormones, or electrolysis are reimbursable—it also means fighting violence and profiling, abolishing prisons where medical neglect is the norm, expanding welfare benefits and Medicaid access, redistributing wealth, fighting forced sterilization in the United States and abroad, and many more intersecting issues.

By no means must we dispose of "transgender," "trans," or "trans*" as categories—indeed, they have been quite useful, and for some of us they feel like home. But we must keep asking whether they *take good care* of us, and who the "us" is that gets the most tender care within its embrace (Mol, 2008).

REFERENCE

Mol, A. (2008). *The logic of care: Health and the problem of patient choice*. New York, NY: Routledge.

Medicaid is a public insurance for some low-income people. In most states, Medicaid programs do not cover any transgender care despite federal laws requiring they do so (Title XIX, 440.230(c)). Individuals in some states have challenged their state Medicaid offices and won treatment for their specific cases by proving medical necessity. Currently, only California's state program explicitly covers a comprehensive range of treatment options, including surgery. In states with coverage of transition-related care, it can be very difficult to find a surgeon because payment rates are often so low that after the bills are paid a surgeon can lose money. —*Ronica Mukerjee FNP, LAc*

ACCESSING HEALTH CARE

Although many people in the general US population are uninsured, transgender people are less likely to have insurance than cisgender people. There are many reasons for this, but the most significant is that transgender people are less likely to be employed than cisgender people, and most people are insured through an employer. In addition, because transgender people have more difficulty obtaining identity documents with the appropriate name and gender, we may have more difficulty applying for public insurance, even if we qualify.

For those of us who have insurance through an employer, the majority of us have policies that exclude transgender care. This is steadily changing, with more and more employers offering inclusive insurance. According to the Human Rights Campaign's (HRC) Corporate Equality Index, 340 private companies currently offer at least one transgender-inclusive health care plan. Furthermore, 28% of Fortune 500 companies cover comprehensive transgender care for employees (Human Rights Campaign, 2013). In addition, California, Colorado, Oregon, Vermont, and the District of Columbia now outlaw insurance plans from excluding medically necessary care for transgender people. However, even when an employer offers insurance that covers transgender medical care, it may be difficult for us to find a provider who both provides the care we need and also takes our insurance. In addition, because of co-payments or travel expenses to see specialists, there can still be a considerable cost associated with accessing necessary care.

Fearing denial of care, many of us choose not to inform our insurance providers of our transgender identity. This can be risky because if insurers subsequently discover our transgender status they may retroactively deny care and seek repayment. It can also be difficult to sustain because insurers receive a great deal of information about us from different sources in order to pay for care. Information comes from health care providers, pharmacies, labs, and others.

> *"Until my nurse practitioner wrote me a letter to change all of my legal paperwork to say female, they would not cover my estrogen. But now my insurance covers it because my gender marker matches the hormone I am being prescribed."*

Since insurers use gender designations on insurance forms to determine what care is needed, transgender people are faced with choosing which designation is most appropriate. For example, if a transgender woman lists "F" (for "female") on her insurance forms, she may be able to obtain coverage for estrogen prescriptions and mammograms, but she may be denied care for prostate issues. Likewise, if a transgender man selects "M" (for "male"), his insurance may cover testosterone prescriptions, but it may reject claims for a Pap smear. Even in the best case where an insurance company covers transgender-related care, obtaining authorization overrides for care specific to the sex assigned at birth may delay care and payments.

> *"I have insurance that has an exclusion on trans-related care. None of my transition-related care has been covered. I also pay out of pocket for gynecological care because I am listed as male on my insurance. This can be expensive. For example, I paid $1,000 for an ultrasound to screen for ovarian cancer because I was experiencing severe pelvic pain. I will pay out of pocket for my hysterectomy and oophorectomy. My wife and I make a good living, but these costs put a strain on our budget. We are giving up the money we have saved on a down payment for a house to pay for my hysterectomy and oophorectomy."*

With the full provisions of the US Patient Protection and Affordable Care Act (ACA), many of us may be able to obtain public or private insurance. Each state under the ACA can determine the minimum necessary benefits (in addition to the federal standard) that must be included on policies available on the exchanges in that state. This means that some states may include transgender care while others may not. The ACA does include language that protects against discrimination based on sex, which has been interpreted as covering gender identity. However, how this will affect inclusion of transgender-specific benefits in insurance exchanges remains to be seen. The US Department of Health and Human Services (HHS) has issued a clarification that this does not mean that insurance will be required to cover transition-related surgery, but they have not clarified what this means with respect to other treatments. It is likely that this provision will be argued in court—possibly multiple times in multiple states.

In addition to the ACA providing more access to private insurance, it will increase the number of people eligible for Medicaid, public health insurance for those of us with low income levels. Included in the ACA is a Medicaid expansion that will encourage states to cover more people. In states that participate in the expansion, Medicaid will cover everyone with incomes up to 133% of the federal poverty level. Since transgender people are more likely to live at or below the poverty level, many more transgender people will be newly eligible for Medicaid.

> *"I was on charity care at one particular hospital and on sliding scale at Country Doctor for many years. Because I've been extremely low income for the past 10 years (with the exception of one 8 month stint), my health care has always been a patchwork job based largely on where I could get free or cheap trans friendly care."*

Medicare is public insurance for those over 65 years old. Unlike Medicaid, there is no provision in Medicare that can be interpreted to require coverage for transgender care. The coverage determination written in 1981 states that treatment is experimental but is being reviewed. —*Ronica Mukerjee FNP, LAc*

Many of us have commercial insurance like Aetna or Blue Cross/Blue Shield, which we purchase ourselves or is provided by our employers. Commercial insurance policies most often have a specific exclusion for coverage of transition-related surgeries. Some have a prohibition for any kind of transition-related treatment altogether. However, in recent years, there has been a growing trend among large employers to cover treatment. Some states, including California, Oregon, Colorado, and the District of Columbia, have issued regulations or guidelines that bar exclusions for trans care.

The Veterans Health Administration (VHA) provides medical care for veterans. The VHA issued a directive in 2013 that trans veterans are entitled to all necessary preventive care, hormone therapy, mental health services, preoperative evaluations, and postoperative care. The VHA does not currently provide for transition-related surgeries.

TRICARE is government insurance for military service members and their families. TRICARE is unlikely to pay for any trans-related health care. Transgender identity remains a reason for discharge from the military.

Many students have health care insurance through their universities. A growing number of colleges cover transgender medical and surgical treatments for their students.

Transgender people and allies who wish to work on furthering positive change for insurance coverage can seek more information in the Transgender Law Center's online guide *Organizing for Transgender Health Care.*

The San Francisco Experience
In 2001, the City of San Francisco decided to offer transgender medical and surgical coverage in all of its contracted health plans covering city employees. It was estimated by insurance professionals that the monthly cost would increase by $1.70 per employee, a total monthly cost of $170,000 given the 100,000 employees of the city. As you might imagine, paranoia set in and people were concerned that San Francisco, already a transgender mecca, would attract every transgender person in the country and bankrupt the system. Instead, over the years 2001–2006, the monthly cost was gradually reduced due to low claims costs. In 2006 it was determined that a total of $386,417 had been spent over the past 5 years on all transgender-related claims, while $5.6 million had been collected. At this point, the additional monthly cost was eliminated completely, and transgender health care is now packaged with other routine health care services such as blood pressure management or gallbladder surgery. If the cost was this low in a city like San Francisco, it is likely even lower in other places with smaller transgender communities.— *Maddie Deutsch, MD*

In California and Oregon, laws mandate nondiscrimination in provision of health insurance regarding gender identity and expression. Recently in both states, these laws have been interpreted to mean that insurers may not deny transgender people care that is provided for cisgender people for different diagnoses. For example, if an insurer pays for hysterectomy to treat cervical cancer in cisgender women (or in transgender men, for that matter), the insurer must also pay for hysterectomy in transgender men to treat gender dysphoria. In California, Medi-Cal (the California Medicaid program) covers medically necessary transition-related care according to guidelines from the World Professional Association for Transgender Health (WPATH). In other states, some individuals have succeeded in getting transition-related care covered by Medicaid. However, even in cases where Medicaid does cover care, finding providers skilled at providing this care that will accept the very low Medicaid rates can be difficult.

ESTABLISHING A PRIMARY CARE PROVIDER

Primary care is our first stop in the health care system. Primary care providers (PCPs) are trained to diagnose and treat almost any health care problem regardless of the cause, the diagnosis, or the system of the body involved. They also provide ongoing care for chronic problems, offer services to prevent or screen illness, coordinate specialized care, advocate for patients in the health care system, and focus on treating the whole person.

> *"[A comfortable health care environment] includes referring to me with my chosen pronoun (he, him, their); being friendly and accepting; taking time to answer questions; having literature about LGBT organizations or having progressive magazines. [An uncomfortable environment can result from] not having a box on the medical form for Transgender identity; being cold and aloof; intentionally calling me with female pronouns; attempting to hurry through the visit; no knowledge of the WPATH standards of care."*

For transgender people, having a PCP is especially important. While increasingly more providers are sensitive to and knowledgeable about transgender patients' needs, many remain uneducated about our health. Because of this, advocacy and care coordination roles for PCPs are even more important. For example, if we need referral to a cardiologist, a PCP can speak with that provider before referral to ensure the specialist feels comfortable with transgender patients and can encourage sensitivity among staff. Additionally, because some transgender patients avoid health care as much as possible due to negative past experiences or fear of negative encounters, a PCP who provides comprehensive care can decrease the care we have to obtain outside of familiar safe spaces. For example, a PCP trained in some gynecologic procedures can provide gynecologic care for transgender men without requiring referral to a gynecologist.

> *"I have a wonderful primary care physician who I found strictly by accident. She turned out to not only be LGBT friendly but also had an interest in transgender health care. At first she didn't really know much about transgender health, but when she didn't know, she contacted colleagues to find the answers. She has had such an interest in transgender care that she asked me to participate in resident round table discussions with family medicine residents to better find out how to meet our health care needs."*

> *"I found a trans* positive doctor (who is actually trans* herself). She is incredibly respectful and knowledgeable."*

> *"When I turned 18, I needed to find an adult provider, so I picked somebody whose name I liked, called his secretary, and asked if he had experience with*

people with my medical issues (yes) and whether he had experience with transgender people (no) and whether he was open to seeing a transgender patient (he's open to all kinds of people). He has been great about respecting my identity. He put down my sex as male even before I was on testosterone, and referred to me by male pronouns and with my given name before I had my name change finalized, despite the fact that my mother was there and using the wrong name and pronoun at the first two visits I had with him. I had initially hoped that he would be willing to put me on testosterone, but he says I'm the only transgender patient he's aware of having, and he'd rather I saw somebody with experience in that area, so I see another doctor as well."

PREVENTIVE HEALTH CARE

Preventive care is proactive health care to prevent and diagnose disease as well as to identify harmful health-related behaviors early enough that poor outcomes can be prevented. Some of the leading causes of preventable death in the United States include poor diet and physical inactivity, tobacco smoking, alcohol and drug use, and STIs, including HIV. Like many groups experiencing discrimination, transgender people have elevated rates of harmful health-related behaviors compared to the general population. The greater prevalence of these behaviors in our communities is partly a reflection of the stress arising from bias, discrimination, harassment, and violence.

NUTRITION AND PHYSICAL ACTIVITY

In our body-obsessed culture in which "you can never be too rich or too thin," size can be something that we use against each other and against ourselves. Medical providers are often trained to prioritize the body mass index (BMI)—used to categorize people as "underweight," "healthy weight," "overweight," or "obese"—as a measure of health. However, many people with BMIs above the "normal" range are perfectly healthy. Fat-positive activists seek to challenge fatphobia in our society just as we might challenge transphobia, cissexism, racism, classism, and other forms of personal and institutionalized bias. Part of our general health is connected to our capacity to determine a healthy size for ourselves as individuals, rather than being driven by media portrayals of a feminine or masculine ideal.

Although there is evidence that lesbian-identified women are at increased risk of obesity compared to their heterosexual peers, there are limited data regarding obesity risk in trans people. Taking either estrogen or testosterone is correlated with weight gain and can be associated with increased risk of developing certain health problems like diabetes and heart disease (Gooren et al., 2007). Therefore, when starting hormone replacement therapy it is especially important to embrace balanced nutrition and healthy exercise regimens. For some of us, the process of initiating gender-affirming treatments helps us value our bodies more and feel motivated to stay as healthy as possible.

Many guidelines recommend moderate-intensity exercise for 30 minutes, 5 days per week. "Moderate intensity" can mean we are able to carry on a conversation while exercising, but not able to sing a song. Walking briskly is an easy, inexpensive way to engage in moderate-intensity exercise. For those of us with busy schedules, we may feel like we do not have 30 minutes per day to devote to exercise. However, evidence shows that walking for 10 minutes, three times per day has similar benefits for weight loss and cardiovascular health as walking for 30 minutes continuously. Taking the stairs really can make a difference.

Some of us feel such intense pressure to appear thin that we develop restrictive eating patterns or force ourselves to throw up. There is also evidence that cisgender

In California, clinics providing transgender care include the LA Gay & Lesbian Center and the San Francisco clinics Tom Waddell, Lyon-Martin, Dimensions, and Castro-Mission Health Center.

In the Northeast, clinics with a specialty in transgender health care include the Hartford Gay & Lesbian Health Collective, Fenway Health (Boston), Tapestry Health (Northampton), and Green Mountain Gender Clinic (Vermont).

New York has a number of clinics with trans health care providers: APICHA Community Health Center, Callen-Lorde Community Health Center, Gay Men's Health Crisis, Beth Israel LGBT Health Services Center, and William F. Ryan Community Health Center.

In Chicago, the Center on Halsted and Howard Brown Health Center both have transgender health programs.

The Whitman-Walker Clinic in Washington, D.C., and Chase Brexton Health Services in Baltimore have a focus on LGBT health.

In Texas, Legacy Community Health Services in Houston and The Resource Center in Dallas provide trans health care.

In the Midwest, the University of Michigan Comprehensive Gender Services Program (Ann Arbor), the University of Minnesota Program in Human Sexuality (Minneapolis), and MetroHealth Pride Clinic (Cleveland) provide trans health care.

The Mazzoni Center in Philadelphia and the Persad Center in Pittsburgh provide trans health services to Pennsylvanians.

In Canada, Vancouver Coastal Health (B.C.), Nine Circles Community Health Centre (Winnipeg, Manitoba), Sherbourne Health Centre (Toronto), Sandy Hill Community Health Centre (Ottawa), and Rainbow Health Ontario provide trans health care.

Ryan K. Sallan's memoir *Second Son: Transitioning Toward My Destiny, Love, and Life* tells the story of a trans man who battles anorexia (Greenbay, WI: TitleTown, 2012).

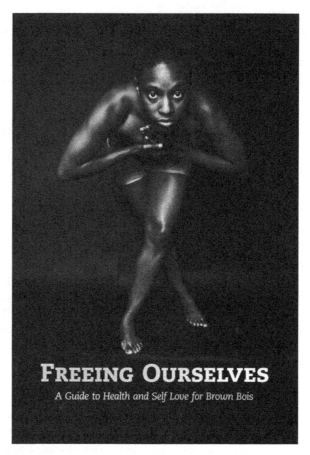

Cover of *Freeing Ourselves: A Guide to Health and Self-Love for Brown Bois* (art by Rebecca Emmanuelle Photography/Micah Bazant Designs).

gay-identified men are at greater risk for developing eating disorders such as anorexia and bulimia. However, there are limited data regarding eating disorders in trans people. Unfortunately, most eating disorder treatment programs are segregated by gender, and few eating disorder programs currently address the specific needs of our communities. For those of us looking for help with eating disorders, we may want to start with our PCP. Trans-knowledgeable PCPs can sometimes point us toward a provider or clinic that they believe will be especially trans-friendly.

One additional factor to consider in constructing our diets and exercise plans is our bone health. There are a number of ways to improve our bone health and prevent osteoporosis (decreased bone density that can lead to fractures), including taking in enough calcium and vitamin D, as well as doing weight-bearing exercise. As trans people, our bone health can be affected by surgeries that remove our gonads (ovaries or testicles) or our hormone treatments. Estrogen is known to be protective for our bones, and taking either estrogen or testosterone may help to protect our bones because some testosterone is converted to estrogen in our bodies. Trans women who have had orchiectomies (removal of the testicles) who are not taking estrogen, and trans men who have had oopherectomies (removal of the ovaries) who are not taking testosterone may be particularly at risk because their bodies do not have the protection of estrogen. Talk to your health care provider about whether you should undergo a screening test (DEXA scan) or should be changing your diet, exercise, or taking medication to prevent osteoporosis.

OUR BODIES, OURSELVES

Arlene (Ari) Istar Lev is a social and family therapist who specializes in working with LGBT families in Albany, New York.

My original copy of *Our Bodies, Ourselves* is tattered and torn, yellow with age. I read the original in my late teens or early twenties, and the chapter called "In America They Call Us Dykes" astonished and titillated me. I stared at the picture of the strong, brazen dyke at the opening of the chapter. She represented everything that liberation held possible.

The other part of *Our Bodies, Ourselves* that I vividly remember is a story of a mother in the bathtub with her young daughter. The daughter asks why Mommy doesn't have a penis like daddy does. Mommy says, "Because I have a clitoris." The girl asks can you show me, and her mom does just that. I have often contemplated how different my life would've been, how different the lives of so many women would've been, with this simple event happening early in our lives.

I joined the Berkeley Women's Health Collective in the late 1970s because I saw myself as part of this great women's health movement that was exemplified in *Our Bodies, Ourselves*. I taught self-breast and self-speculum exams. We started the first lesbian health clinic in the country.

Fast forward 15 years, and I am a therapist specializing in working with LGBT people and their families. Some of my clients are middle-aged transgender women who are seeking gender confirmation surgery after spending much of their lives fantasizing and desiring to live as women. I realize as I'm listening to their struggles for authenticity that some of them know very little about women's bodies, particularly about how women's genitalia look or function. Struggling to reconcile my early feminist worldview with my growing trans-positive queer sensibility, I often stumble. I find myself more than a bit shocked that someone could be so driven to be a woman that they are willing to spend a small fortune on life-threatening surgeries to have women's genitalia, but yet they are not exactly sure how cisgender women's bodies actually look.

In these moments, I put down my feminist ruminations and pull my worn copy of *Our Bodies, Ourselves* off the shelf. I show them pictures of women's bodies, images of a diversity of vulvas and clitorises. Sitting there with the book between us, sister to sister, I realize that *Our Bodies, Ourselves* has been a text that wears incredibly well with time. I realize that in some ways transsexual women's ignorance about their own bodies and desires is no different from my own once upon a time, and no different from the experience of most cisgender women. I confess I never thought 30 years ago that I would—or could—use *Our Bodies, Ourselves* as a resource for transsexual women, yet my 1970s feminism has laid the foundation for the queer health activism I still practice over 30 years later.

SUBSTANCE USE

Because most studies of alcohol and other drug use have not included questions about gender identity, data about substance use in trans communities are limited. Some recent studies of transgender people in several large urban areas across the United States have identified substance abuse as a substantial concern.

Tobacco Use

Evidence indicates that rates of tobacco use among transgender people significantly exceed those of the general population. Since the mid-1990s, tobacco companies have made themselves highly visible in our communities via advertising, sponsorships, and promotions. In 1995, R. J. Reynolds actually created a campaign, internally named "Project SCUM" (an acronym for "Project Sub-Culture Urban Marketing"), that targeted LGBTQ and homeless people.

Tobacco use is a major risk factor for heart attacks, strokes, chronic obstructive pulmonary disease (COPD), and cancer. Studies have shown that smokers lose about a decade of life expectancy on average as a result of tobacco. Fortunately, quitting smoking can significantly reduce the number of years of life expectancy lost. For transgender women on hormone replacement therapy, smoking is an even greater risk. Smoking while on estrogen may increase the risk of developing a blood clot—otherwise known as a deep venous thrombosis (DVT)—in the legs or elsewhere in the body—that can migrate to the lungs and cause difficulty breathing or even death.

For those of us who want to quit, there are medical treatments available, including nicotine replacement therapy (NRT) such as the nicotine patch, gum, and lozenge; nicotine-free medications such as buproprion (Zyban) and varenicline (Chantix); and integrative treatments such as acupuncture and hypnotherapy. Health care providers can be excellent resources for information about local programs that support smoking cessation free of charge.

TRANS SMOKING

Scout, PhD, is the director of the Network for LGBT Health Equity.

There is a consistent pattern among available transgender smoking data, demonstrating that our population shares a profound smoking disparity with the intertwined LGB communities. The National Transgender Discrimination Survey provides our best information to date, showing transgender people smoke at rates that are 50% higher than the general population.

In the study, Black transgender people smoked at the highest rates, 150% higher than the general population. Undocumented people also smoked more than other groups, as did trans people with lower socioeconomic status. Transgender people who have been involved in street economies smoked at the highest rate of any subset in the survey. Gender spectrum also affects smoking rates, with female-to-male (FTM) spectrum people smoking at slightly higher rates than male-to-female spectrum (MTF) people.

Interestingly, the study also provided some insight into the relationship between stress and smoking. As would be hypothesized, people who experience less stress "passing" smoke at lower rates (27% versus 37% of those who do not pass). Congruent identity documents also improve smoking rates (25% versus 34% for those with no congruent documents). When researchers stratified Oregon counties by levels of acceptance of LGBT people, they found a positive correlation between acceptance and lower smoking rates.

Smoking is a pediatric epidemic; the average LGBT person begins by age 12. Current research and hypotheses directly connect the stigma and stress of growing up as "other" to youth turning to cigarettes for stress relief, and as a way to fit in with peers. In addition, when youth seek their adult trans or LGBT community role models, the higher smoking rate among the adults also lures the youth toward smoking.

The tobacco industry has proven very adept at using micro-targeting campaigns to engage specific population subgroups, including LGBT people.

Smoking is a broad-scale health depressant, specifically hindering circulation and the normal healing process. While rigorous research is lacking, there are numerous reports of doctors who will not attempt gender confirmation surgery for patients who smoke. At the extreme end of the spectrum, this author witnessed one doctor from Belgium attribute the failure of a phalloplasty surgery directly to the patient's continued smoking.

For transgender smokers, the best current options for cessation are to do *all* of the following: (1) talk to your health provider about health impacts and medication options; (2) explore if cessation groups are available through your employer, insurance, or community center; and (3) call your state run quitline at 1-800-QUITNOW. If any of the above entities do not treat you in a respectful manner, contact the Network for LGBT Health Equity.

Alcohol and Drug Abuse

Abuse of alcohol and drugs like methamphetamine and heroin are significant problems in our communities. In addition to the risks of the drugs themselves, injecting drugs with shared needles carries an increased risk of contracting infections like HIV and hepatitis B and C. Another issue for transgender people who use drugs is the risk of arrest and prosecution. Prisons and jails are dangerous places for anyone, but especially for gender nonconforming people. In addition to the dangers associated with being housed in a jail based on our sex assigned at birth, we may be deprived of hormone therapy, thereby risking emotional trauma and, in some cases, regression of the effects of hormones on our bodies.

These concerns are complicated by the fact that recovery programs and rehab facilities may require strict binary male/female segregation based on our sex assigned at birth. Some may also require discontinuation of hormone replacement therapy. However, 12-Step Programs like Alcoholics Anonymous have meetings for transgender and gender nonconforming people in recovery, especially in urban areas.

Syringe exchange programs ("needle exchange") exist in most states in the United States. Needle exchange programs are based on a philosophy of harm reduction and embrace the belief that all individuals who use drugs should have free access to clean supplies that will decrease their risk of contracting blood-borne diseases. These programs provide free sterile syringes and collect used syringes from people who inject drugs to reduce transmission of blood-borne pathogens, including HIV and hepatitis B and C. There is evidence that these programs reduce needle sharing and the use of dirty needles, as well as the transmission of HIV.

In addition to syringe access, many programs provide other equipment such as safer smoking supplies for people who smoke crystal meth and crack cocaine, safe sex supplies, and overdose prevention medications like naloxone injections (Narcan), which reverses an opiate (e.g. heroin, oxycontin) overdose and can be kept on hand by friends and family of people at risk. They also often offer HIV and hepatitis C testing and referrals, STI screenings, vaccinations for hepatitis A and B, and referrals for people who want to get sober.

SAFETY, VIOLENCE, AND TRAUMA

Staying healthy also means staying safe. Unfortunately, because of discrimination and antitransgender bias in society, it is not always possible for us to be in safe environments. We are more frequently the victims of sexual assault than cisgender people (Balsam, Rothblum, & Beauchaine, 2005), and we are often the targets of hate-based crimes. However, many members of our communities distrust law enforcement and the criminal justice system due to decades of bias and discrimination. As a result, the majority of assaults against transgender people are never reported to the police.

Lifetime prevalence of intimate partner violence among transgender individuals is 35% (Ard & Makadon, 2011), which is more than double the prevalence for gay- or lesbian-identified individuals, and significantly higher than the 25% among cisgender women (Tjaden & Thoennes, 2000). A link between these experiences and post-traumatic stress disorder (PTSD) is widely suspected, but it has not been adequately documented.

We are less likely to be employed and financially independent than cisgender people, and we may need to stay with our abusive partners in order to have food and shelter, especially if we have children. Financial dependence can make it more difficult to leave an abusive relationship. Many domestic violence programs and shelters do not offer services to transgender people—some offer services only to cisgender women. Many of us worry about finding other partners because we have experienced discrimination and rejection from potential partners in the past—we therefore may be more inclined to stay in an unhealthy relationship. Since transgender people experience mistreatment and even violence from police, we may be much less likely to call 911 for help.

It is critical that our health care providers screen us for intimate partner violence just as they would screen other patients. In addition, a growing number of intimate partner violence agencies are receiving education in the needs of transgender (and LGB) individuals. In areas lacking trained agencies, we may seek support from a national LGBT antiviolence organization, such as the National Coalition of Anti-Violence Programs.

The National Domestic Violence Hotline is available 24/7 at 1-800-799-SAFE or TTY 1-800-787-3224.

HIV AND OTHER SEXUALLY TRANSMITTED INFECTIONS

As trans people, we can face more barriers getting tested for STIs, including HIV, than our cisgender peers. A sensitive sexual health assessment should identify our actual risk of STI exposure, which is based on sexual behaviors and the body parts involved, not on our sexual or gender identities. STI screening is guided by our actual risk level: high-risk sexual practices include receptive anal sex without a condom ("barebacking"), sex with multiple partners, sex with anonymous partners, and sex in conjunction with substance use. If we engage in these behaviors, we should receive STI screening every three to six months. If we engage in lower risk behavior, it might be OK to be screened annually. A good reason to get tested is that bacterial infections like chlamydia, gonorrhea, and syphilis are harmful but can be treated with antibiotics if they are found.

Our sexual behavior may change over time, and we might shift from high-risk to low-risk categories and vice-versa. It is important to remember that although providers will ask us whether we are experiencing any symptoms consistent with STIs, many STIs do not show symptoms so it is good to be honest about our behaviors, so we can be screened appropriately.

Hepatitis

Although there are limited data about STIs in transgender people, there is good evidence of higher risk of STIs—including syphilis, gonorrhea, chlamydia, human papilloma virus (HPV), hepatitis A (HAV), and hepatitis B (HBV)—among cisgender men who have sex with men (MSM), and it may be possible to make a guess from these data that anyone practicing penile-anal sex would be at a similar risk. Transgender men and women who have sex with cisgender men (TMSM, TWSM) may be at higher risk than the general population for contracting both HAV and HBV, viruses that attack the liver. HAV can be transmitted by unprotected fecal-oral contact during sex ("rimming"), and HBV can be transmitted through exposure to infectious blood or bodily fluids such as semen and vaginal fluids. The Centers for Disease Control and Prevention (CDC) and other professional groups have long recommended that all cisgender MSM be vaccinated against HAV and HBV, yet many clinicians are unaware of this recommendation. Although no vaccination protocol exists for transgender people, we may speak with our health care providers for more information about our risk level, and whether this preventive step may be appropriate. Hepatitis C is another virus that attacks our liver, and it is spread when there is blood-to-blood transmission, such as blood transfusions, sharing needles for injections, unclean tattoo or piercing instruments, or certain types of sexual practices such as fisting or rough anal sex where blood is exchanged.

Pelvic Inflammatory Disease

There is also evidence of underrecognition of STIs—including chlamydia, gonorrhea, herpes simplex virus, HPV, and trichomonas ("trich")—in cisgender women who have sex with women (WSW), and it may be possible to assume from this that anyone sharing sex toys, oral-vaginal sex, or vaginal-vaginal sex/rubbing could transmit these infections as well. Chlamydia, gonorrhea, and trich are especially important to know about for individuals who have an upper reproductive tract (i.e., uterus and fallopian tubes). These infections are easily treated with antibiotics, but if left untreated may lead to pelvic inflammatory disease, which is dangerous and has long-term consequences such as pelvic pain and infertility. These STIs may be asymptomatic, which is why sexual risk assessment and screening are important, with follow-up screening and treatment as appropriate.

Human Papilloma Virus

It is important to remember that *health care screening is based on the organs present!* In other words, *if you've got it, check it!* Transgender people with a cervix have gynecologic health needs, but our gynecologic health may suffer because of avoided, delayed, or substandard care. Our gynecologic health is also endangered by the common misconception among clinicians that transgender men do not require Pap smears or STI screening. Those of us with a cervix need Pap smears according to the same screening criteria for cisgender women.

THE PELVIC EXAM AND PAP SMEAR

Lauren Abern, MD, is an Ob/Gyn at the University of Miami Miller School of Medicine.

For those of us assigned female at birth, including trans men, the pelvic exam is an important part of preventive health. The pelvic exam can detect sexually transmitted infections and precancerous lesions, as well as help a health care provider to evaluate pain and abnormal bleeding.

The pelvic exam is sometimes difficult for cisgender women, and it can be even more so for trans men. Trans men may feel frustrated about having to do something medical that is so gendered, or worry that the provider will not be sensitive to their needs or how to talk about their bodies. The pelvic exam can also potentially be more physically uncomfortable for trans men because the vagina may have thinner lining and produce less lubrication. The best way to be prepared is to be educated about the components of the exam.

The pelvic exam has three parts. The first is inspection of the outside of the body, including the vulva and anus. This is done once you are on the exam table and your feet are up in stirrups.

The second part of the pelvic exam is the speculum exam. This consists of placing a speculum (a device that looks like a duckbill) into the vagina so that the provider can see the cervix and vaginal walls. A very small q-tip can be placed into the hole in the cervix, called the cervical os, in order to test for gonorrhea and chlamydia. A Pap smear is done by inserting a brush the size of a q-tip into the cervical os and swirling it around, then rubbing a small broom-shaped brush inside and around the os to pick up more cells. These procedures are followed in order to gather cells from the cervix so that they can be looked at under the microscope to determine whether they are cancerous. Those trans men who have had their cervix removed (this is sometimes done with a hysterectomy and sometimes not) do not require a Pap smear.

The third part of the pelvic exam is called the bimanual exam. This is where an examiner places a gloved hand into the vagina and another hand on your stomach. The hand inside the vagina will push the uterus up so the hand on the abdomen can feel the shape and size of the uterus. The provider will then push down on the sides of your abdomen to feel the ovaries. This is the part of the exam where any masses may be identified. The examiner is also checking to see whether any tenderness is present.

The pelvic exam can be uncomfortable for some people and not for others. It is important to discuss your needs during the pelvic exam with your provider so that they can work with you to make the exam more tolerable. There are also a few tricks to making it a little easier. First, ask your provider to start with the smallest sized speculum. Lubricant can be put on the speculum so it is not as painful during insertion. Pulling your knees apart as far as possible can make it a little more tolerable. A friend or a chaperone from the office can be brought into the room with you for support or distraction. The provider can also start up a conversation to get your mind off of the exam. There are people that feel a little more comfortable if they know what is going on during the exam. If this is the case, let your provider know so that they can talk you through it. The most important thing is finding a provider who you feel comfortable with and trust. For trans men, that may mean finding someone who has worked with other trans men, but it could also mean finding a supportive person without as much experience who is willing to learn.

Trans women who have had vaginoplasty do not need Pap smears because these are only necessary to screen for cervical cancer. However, they may benefit from speculum exams so that a provider can identify any visible lesions or infections. Trans women may want to request lubrication and the smallest available speculum, since the vaginal opening is often small. In addition, trans women should be sure to see their primary care providers for prostate care.

Many of us may have heard about the relationship between HPV and cervical cancer, but it is important to know that not all HPV causes cervical cancer. HPV is the most common STI, and there are over 100 different strains of the virus. Some of the strains are responsible for causing genital and anal warts, and some strains lead to the changes in the cervical cells or the cells inside the anus that can cause cervical or anal cancer. HPV infections occur through sexual or even intimate genital skin-to-skin contact with a person who is already infected, and unfortunately, barriers do not protect against HPV transmission as well as they do against other STIs.

Cervical cancer prevention is a good example of how powerful preventive health care is. Before Georgios Papanikolaou discovered that cervical cytology (the "Pap smear" or "Pap test") could detect early changes that lead to cervical cancer, cervical cancer was the number-one cause of cancer death in cisgender women. Since then, in places where this testing is routinely available, deaths caused by cervical cancer have been reduced by 98% (DeMay, 2007). We also now have a vaccine to protect against HPV infection available to anyone age 9–26 years. Pap tests need only be done every three years once they are normal for three years in a row. The recommendations changed because research showed that in most people, doing the test every three years is as effective as doing it every year.

People of all sexual orientations and gender identities who have a cervix are at risk of contracting HPV and developing cervical cancer if we are or have been sexually active, regardless of the sexual orientations or gender identities of our partners. It is a misconception among patients and providers that HPV can only be transmitted via penis-vagina sex among cisgender men and women. In fact, HPV infection on the cervix can occur in people with a cervix, of all gender identities, who have *never* had sex with cisgender men. Prevention of cervical cancer includes both immunizing young people against HPV and performing screening Pap tests to find early cervical changes so they can be treated before becoming cancerous. It should also be noted that cervical cancer is more likely to

Ads from Check it Out Guys (Creative: The Publicstudio.CA).

be diagnosed in individuals who smoke, those with compromised immune systems, and those who have not had regular Pap tests.

HPV in the anus can cause changes to the cells, and in some at-risk individuals, if it is not detected and treated early, the changes can develop into anal cancer. Anal cancer is more common in people who have HIV, anyone who has had precancerous changes on their cervix, and anyone who practices receptive anal intercourse. Recent data show that anal cancer is up to 80 times more common in cisgender MSM than in the general population. While little data exist regarding the incidence of anal cancer in transgender populations, it is important for people of all gender identities who have had receptive anal sex, have had anal warts, who are HIV positive, or have any condition that weakens their immune system, or had precancerous lesions of the cervix or vulva to speak with a health care provider about whether anal Paps are an appropriate part of preventive health care. The CDC has expanded its recommendations for the HPV vaccine Gardasil to include prevention of anal cancer, so if we are under the age of 26 we can ask our provider about the vaccine for protection against anal cancer in addition to cervical cancer (Huyett, 2011).

HIV

In our communities, the rate of HIV infection is four times higher than the national average (Grant et al., 2011). In transgender women, the rate is six times higher. If we are homeless, the rate is eight times higher, and if we are engaged in commercial sex work, it is 25 times higher. Although these statistics are worrisome, it is important to remember that they stem from social determinants of health. If we are unable to obtain gainful employment, we may be more likely to engage in commercial sex work with its accompanying risk of infection with HIV and other STIs. Furthermore, due to many factors, including internalized reactions to transphobia, we are more likely to abuse alcohol and drugs, which can lead to increased sexual risk-taking. Current guidelines indicate that routine HIV screening is recommended for all people between the ages of 13 and 64 years.

"Some transgender clients (and even some providers) worry about the effect of hormones on antiretroviral medicines. The good news is that there are almost no worrisome drug-drug interactions and we can continue hormone therapy, although small adjustments may occasionally be made in the dose. An antiretroviral drug called fosamprenavir could possibly be affected by estrogen, so we should let our providers know we are taking hormones if this is prescribed." —*Anita Radix, MD*

CANCER RISK AND SCREENING

In addition to obtaining Pap tests to decrease our risk of developing cervical or anal cancer, there are other cancer screening tests that are important for us. There are limited data on the cancer risks we may face as a result of hormone replacement therapy, although several providers and organizations (including the Vancouver Transgender Health Program and the UCSF Center of Excellence for Transgender Health) have examined the data that are available and have developed screening recommendations.

Breast Cancer

Screening for breast cancer is recommended for trans and gender nonconforming masculine-spectrum people regardless of medical or surgical history. Those of us who have had top surgery—even bilateral mastectomy—will have some residual breast tissue that is susceptible to breast cancer. Therefore, an annual clinical breast exam by a health care provider is recommended. Trans men who have not had top surgery require breast cancer screenings based on guidelines for cisgender women, including annual mammograms starting at age 50. Those of us with a family history of breast cancer may need to start screening mammograms earlier, and speaking to our health care providers can help us determine what is right for us. In theory, cross-gender hormone therapy in trans and gender nonconforming masculine-spectrum people could potentially increase breast cancer risk, due to the conversion of excess testosterone to estrogen, although there are limited data on this.

Trans and gender nonconforming feminine-spectrum people over age 50 with additional risk factors also require screening mammograms. Additional risk factors include estrogen and progestin use over five years, positive family history, and BMI greater than 35.

Ovarian Cancer

Those of us with ovaries, depending on family history, may require screening for ovarian cancer, particularly if we have a first-degree relative with ovarian cancer, or a known history of one of the genes that increases risk of ovarian cancer (BRCA1 or BRCA2). There are no data to suggest that ovarian cancer risk is increased, decreased, or unchanged in trans and gender nonconforming masculine-spectrum people who still have their ovaries. This does not mean that there is not a difference. However, because of the size of the transgender community, limits of statistics and medical research, and the infrequency of this cancer, it is not possible to answer this question. When thinking about risks and benefits of surgery to remove the ovaries, it is still reasonable to consider the average risk that cisgender women have.

Uterine Cancer

The most common initial symptom of endometrial cancer is vaginal bleeding. Most bleeding in transgender men is not from cancer. However, if you have bleeding after a period of a year on testosterone without bleeding or after the age of natural menopause if you are not on testosterone, see your provider to have this evaluated. The provider may order an ultrasound or perform a biopsy in the office or refer you to a gynecologist for this office procedure. If you have difficulty with exams, the provider may be able to arrange for sedation.

Prostate and Testicular Cancer

Screening for prostate and testicular cancers is unfortunately not very effective in individuals of average risk. The United States Preventative Services Taskforce (USPSTF) recommends against routine testicular cancer screening in people assigned male at birth (US Preventive Services, 2004). The reasoning is that this cancer is rare, generally found by patients without performing an actual exam, and even when it has spread from the testicles it is usually very treatable. Therefore, screening has not been shown to prevent death from this cancer. However, screening might find noncancerous lesions, thereby causing the patient undue stress and potentially leading to unnecessary additional testing and surgery that could be harmful. Because the risks outweigh the benefits, the USPSTF recommends against routine screening.

Screening for prostate cancer is also not strongly recommended even for people of the age most likely to benefit from this screening (Fifty to Seventy five years old). In those who are not at higher risk, the harms of screening may outweigh the benefits. This is because the tests for prostate cancer, including the prostate-specific antigen (PSA) blood test and the digital rectal exam (feeling the prostate by inserting a finger into the rectum), may not detect cancer early, and they may be positive even if no cancer exists. Even if the tests were more accurate, not all prostate cancer is life-threatening: Some prostate cancers grow so slowly that most people die *with* them rather than *from* them.

Estrogen therapy can falsely lower PSA even if cancer is present, so the PSA screening test performs even more poorly in trans women than in cis men (Makadon et al., 2007). Those of us who have a high risk of prostate cancer (people of African descent or those of us with a family or personal history, for example) may benefit from screening, but this is a decision that we should make in partnership with our health care providers. In other words, our providers might recommend this screening even though it is an imperfect test, and we can always ask our providers why they believe this test is appropriate.

In almost all cases, vaginoplasty does not involve removal of the prostate. This is because removal can be a more dangerous surgery and could result in chronic problems with incontinence (leaking of urine). It is therefore important that our health care providers know about the presence of the prostate, regardless of whether we pursue vaginoplasty or other surgical procedures. Even if the physician performing an examination cannot tell whether we are cisgender or transgender, it is important to disclose this information so that our medical care is most effective. Screenings and guidelines are based on body parts and internal organs present, not on gender identity.

If a prostate exam is performed on a trans woman who has had vaginoplasty, a finger inserted into the vagina may offer a better exam than a finger inserted into the rectum because the prostate sits on top of the vagina instead of directly on top of the rectum. Providers may perform this exam in a manner similar to a gynecologic exam for cisgender women: lying with stomach facing up, with feet in adjustable brackets ("stirrups"), and knees spread slightly apart.

UNPLANNED CARE

In addition to the care that is provided at a primary care office, we may need care at other locations such as a hospital, radiology center, emergency department (ER), or at a specialist's office. There are several things we can do to help ensure we get the care we need without worrying about meeting unfriendly people or being in an unsafe space. An important first step is to enlist our primary care provider's help: A call from a PCP to a specialist or the staff can smooth the process. If treatment like surgery or a planned hospitalization is involved, it is often possible to tour the facility in advance. If a tour would be helpful, calling the facility well ahead of the planned care is a good idea.

Unscheduled health care can be provided in a PCP's office, but it is sometimes provided in ERs or urgent care settings where we may not know any of the health care providers. This can be scary for anyone whose status could potentially subject them to discrimination and harassment. This is especially true for us as transgender people because our bodies and identities do not necessarily fit within the typical medical binary of sex and gender (Polly & Nicole, 2011; Schaffer, 2005). However, it is important to take our health care needs seriously even if that means a trip to the local ER. While this may seem daunting, there are things we can do that will help us have a safe and comfortable visit.

One of the most important things we can do when we go to the ER is bring a friend who can advocate for us. (This is true for everyone, not just transgender people.) It is important to choose this friend wisely: This should be someone we trust to be with us in vulnerable situations such as after taking medicines that may have a sedating effect. This person should also be someone level-headed enough to be a good advocate if the situation escalates and becomes challenging. Finally, this person should ideally be someone who is able to drive us home after the visit or escort us in a train, bus, or taxi.

Many health providers in ERs genuinely want to help everyone who comes in. However, it is sometimes hard to do this when crucial pieces of information are missing. So it is important that we make sure we either have the following written down or are able to state it reliably and completely:

1. All medications we take as well as doses and frequency, including over-the-counter medicines and supplements
2. Any allergies we have (to medications, foods, latex, etc.), including the reactions we have had
3. Our complete medical and surgical histories, including hospitalizations and any important tests performed relating to current or past medical problems
4. A copy of our insurance information, if we have insurance
5. Names and contact information for our emergency contacts (who we would like contacted in case of emergency), our primary care provider, and our health care proxy (surrogate medical decision maker), if we have one
6. If our emergency concern is related to a surgical issue, the treating surgeon's contact information

7. A copy of an advanced health care directive or durable health care power of attorney, if we have one
8. If the emergency concern is related to transgender care, a few resources to provide in case the treatment provider has not had experience with such care

When we first arrive in the ER, we will be triaged by a nurse who determines chief concerns and does a brief history and exam, including checking vital signs, such as heart rate and blood pressure. *Triage* means "to sort," so the nurse is sorting us into a category based on level of illness. Generally ERs see people in the order in which they come, but people who are sicker (or who have a higher potential to deteriorate quickly) are bumped to the front of the line. This can mean that if we have a less serious or more stable issue, we may be passed over for other people. This can sometimes seem arbitrary, but often people do not look as sick as they are found to be in triage.

If a problem arises in the ER, we can talk to someone to see whether it can be addressed. However, it is important to realize that while some problems may be resolved, some may not. We can start by asking the nurse caring for us (or the triage nurse if we are in a waiting room). Our advocate can help with this. If the new problem is not an emergency, we may need to wait a short time before the nurse can talk with us; that is, a triage nurse may have to triage a new patient before they can address our issue. If the nurse is unable to resolve the problem, we can ask to speak to a patient advocate or a nursing supervisor. Be prepared to wait because these people may have to be called to the ER from another part of the hospital.

When we see the emergency physician, physician's assistant, or nurse practitioner who will provide care, we should be prepared to answer many questions. These may be questions we do not expect but are important for our care. For example, if a transgender man comes to the ER with a possible concussion, it may not immediately be clear why it is important to know whether he has had a hysterectomy. However, the provider may be asking that to determine whether a pregnancy test is required before performing a head computed tomography, or CT (a scan that detects acute changes in the skull and brain, such as bleeding, swelling, or bone trauma), due to risk of radiation exposure to a fetus. In addition, the question "Have you had any surgeries?" is asked of everyone when taking a complete history. However, this question does not just refer to gender-affirming surgeries, but all surgeries, for example, whether a person has had an appendectomy. Residents (physicians in training) and medical students also frequently ask more questions than more senior physicians, because as part of their training they are expected to gather more information about patients. If we think a question may not be appropriate, it is always OK to ask why it is relevant to our care.

> *"In 1997, two years after [male-to-female] SRS, I had to have a serious kidney operation at [a major academic medical center in New York City]. They put me in a private room (when I was covered for semi-private) and gave me a wristband that said 'M.' The doctor was great. . . but he had a coterie of students who followed him around taking notes and asking questions. I was asked to sit up with my legs spread and a bunch of tubes going up my vaginal area to bladder and kidneys while the students discussed 'his' condition and referred to me as 'Mr.' There must have been some cognitive dissonance about this because after about 3 days a nurse came in and cut the bracelet off and put on a new bracelet which said 'F.' It was one of the few times in my life I was glad to get an 'F' on something. The operation was a success, so pronouns were really not critical, but the medical obliviousness made me uncomfortable."*

In general, while we may be apprehensive about unscheduled care in an ER, assuming the best but being prepared for problems is a good plan. Unpleasant experiences may be due to discrimination, but they may also be due to lack of knowledge, poor communication,

The Philadelphia Transgender Health Conference takes place every June and welcomes everyone. There are special professional tracks for lawyers, general health providers, and mental health providers.

or simply a busy ER. Being prepared for people to succeed when given a second chance makes it more likely we will have a positive experience in the end.

SEXUAL HEALTH

Our sexual health is a crucial aspect of our overall health. Sexual health includes prevention and early diagnosis of STIs, as well as contraception when needed. It also includes screening for conditions that might impair sexual function.

Just like general health, sexual health is a positive state of soundness, strength, and stability, not simply a lack of illness. Sexual health includes physical, emotional, mental, and social well-being with respect to sexuality. Good sexual health requires an approach to sexuality and sexual relationships that is respectful of ourselves and our partners. One implication of this approach is that we try to ensure a safe sexual experience for everyone involved, without coercion, discrimination, or violence.

Although we emphasize the positive components of sexual health, is important to remember that sexual health is also connected to freedom from disease and dysfunction, including STIs and impairment of body parts involved in our sexual experiences. Consider these examples:

1. A transgender man who wants to enjoy vaginal penetration but has pain that prevents him from doing so
2. A transgender woman who wants to maintain an erection but is unable to as a side effect of hormone therapy
3. A transgender man who wants to enjoy stimulation of his nipples but has lost erotic sensation as a complication of chest surgery
4. A genderqueer person who has less interest in sex because of side effects of a medicine they take

When we have issues such as these with our sexual health, it can be important to seek out help. This can come from our primary health care providers, but sex therapists, mental health providers, and members of our communities who have experienced similar issues can also be valuable resources.

Safer Sex

Sometimes we may have more difficulty communicating about and negotiating for safer sex than cisgender people. We may feel less empowered to assert boundaries around our sexual safety, or be more invested in engaging in certain sexual activities as gender-affirming behaviors (Sevelius, 2010). Bias and stigma are also associated with an increased risk of engaging in unsafe sex practices (Herbst et al., 2008; Nemoto et al., 2004).

Communication about safer sex helps to reduce the chances of acquiring and transmitting an STI. Just as gender can exist on a spectrum, safer sex can, too. Some activities are very safe, some are very risky, and some are in between.

The relative safety of an activity depends on the activity but also what things we do to decrease risk. For example, with respect to HIV transmission, anal sex *without a condom* is about three times riskier for the receptive partner ("bottom") as it is for the insertive partner ("top"). However, anal sex *with proper condom use* is three times *less* risky for the receptive partner than anal sex *without a condom* is for the insertive partner (NAM, 2013).

To decrease our risk, we may use barriers, avoid use of alcohol or drugs during sex, engage in open and honest communication, and possibly take antiretroviral medicines before or after sex to prevent transmission of HIV (called pre-exposure prophylaxis [PrEP] or post-exposure prophylaxis [PEP]) (CDC, 2012). Barriers can include latex condoms, so-called female condoms, and latex dental dams. The female condom currently available (FC-2) has that name because it can be used by cisgender women during vaginal penetration. However, the FC-2 can also be used by anyone who is having vaginal or anal intercourse regardless of gender identity (Planned Parenthood, 2013). One advantage is that it can be inserted prior to sex, giving the receptive partner control over protecting their health.

Condoms and other barriers are one of the most important ways to protect ourselves from STIs. When using latex condoms (or any other latex barrier), it is very important to use only water-based lubricants. Oil-based lubricants or vaseline can break down latex and make them ineffective against the transmission of HIV and STIs.

Sexual health is a positive state of balance and includes physical, emotional, mental, and social wellness. A pleasurable and healthy sex life, however we conceptualize it, starts with sexual health. The bottom line is that sex and sexuality can be pleasurable, fun, and important parts of our well-being.

TRANS COMMUNITIES AND REPRODUCTIVE JUSTICE

Rye Young is the Director of the Third Wave Fund, an activist youth-led gender justice organization. He is dedicated to social justice philanthropy, gender liberation, and challenging white supremacy and classism.

When I was working at Third Wave Foundation, a gender justice foundation that gives grants to youth-led organizations, one of our grant partners was a group led by people involved in the sex trade. Many of their community members were trans* women of color who were working in the sex trade for economic survival. They reported that when community members tried to access STI and HIV testing at hospitals, they were routinely turned away with no explanation, and sometimes they would be arrested because the hospital staff called the police. In this example, basic reproductive health care was denied because of barriers such as racism, transphobia, and classism.

Reproductive justice means that we cannot separate the struggle for reproductive rights—such as contraception, safe abortion, and comprehensive sex education—from other struggles. Trans* people, like all people, have reproductive health needs, and though the reproductive health needs of trans* people are vast, we are often left out of reproductive health services and rights movements.

While reproductive justice teaches us to look at oppression as a barrier to access, it also means we must look at the flip side of how privilege increases our access to reproductive health and rights. For example, if I sought out HIV and STI testing in the same hospital that turned away trans women, even though I am trans and queer, the fact that I am white, class privileged, and male would make it more likely that I'd receive care. If denied care, I would be safer filing a discrimination complaint, the complaint would be more likely to be taken seriously, and I would not have to wonder whether my complaint would result in my arrest.

It is important for trans* people to fight for reproductive justice because we cannot assume that anyone is going to fight for our liberation and rights if we don't. Part of being a trans* activist for reproductive justice is making sure that our issues are present in women's spaces, and that we stand with trans* women if they are pushed out of or treated as inferior within feminist and women's spaces. We must also make sure that reproductive justice is on the agenda within LGBT movement spaces, and if people ask why, it is because being queer and trans impacts our access to reproductive health care. This work is important because we are important!

REPRODUCTIVE HEALTH

Reproductive health care includes the ability to make informed choices about whether and when we would like to have children. This includes two different types of decisions. The first ensures that if we do not want to be pregnant, we can choose from contraceptive options that suit our needs. The second type connects individuals with assistive reproductive techniques and technologies that can improve chances of a successful pregnancy. Every technique or method of assisting people with reproductive health has benefits, risks, and varying success rates.

In some ways these techniques are not very different for transgender people than for cisgender people. Condoms are condoms regardless of gender identity. However, the special needs of transgender people and the effect of cross-sex hormone therapy can make certain techniques preferable. As technology advances, even more options for fertility and contraception may become available for transgender people.

Contraception in Masculine-Spectrum People

One of the most important things to remember is that *testosterone is NOT birth control.* In some transgender men, testosterone may diminish fertility, but this is not reliable and has not been tested clinically. This is important because testosterone is a United States FDA "Pregnancy Category X" drug. In pregnancy, drugs are classified as A, B, C, D, or X. Drugs in class A and B are commonly used in pregnancy and are generally regarded as reasonably safe. Drugs in class C and D are known or suspected to cause harm to the fetus, but in some circumstances their use may be justified because the condition they treat may be more dangerous than the drug. Category X is reserved for drugs that are known to cause harm and whose use is never justified in pregnancy. In addition to testosterone, finasteride, another drug sometimes used by transgender men to treat balding, is also Category X. Therefore, good contraception is important in transgender men who have sex with cisgender men (TMSM) who choose to have receptive vaginal sex. Contraception in TMSM is also complicated by the fact that unlike cisgender women, transgender men on testosterone often do not menstruate, so pregnancy may be detected later in trans men than it would be in cis women because there is no missed period.

There are many options for cisgender women to prevent pregnancy, and many of these are very reasonable options for transgender men. Barrier methods like the male or female condom are effective at preventing both pregnancy and sexually transmitted infections. If used correctly every time, out of 100 sexually active cisgender women, after one year, two will become pregnant. However, in typical use, this number can be as high as 15 pregnancies. Traditional hormonal contraceptive methods ("the pill") have not been studied in transgender men, so recommendations for their use are uncertain. However, some reasonable options for transgender men include treatment with progestins like DepoProvera or Implanon. These can be used in trans men who are on testosterone as well as those who are not. In trans men who are not on testosterone, these methods may decrease or eliminate menstruation, which can be a welcome side effect for some people. In addition, intrauterine devices (IUDs) are a highly effective and safe method. Options for IUDs include those with and without hormones. The progesterone in the Mirena IUD decreases ovulation and significantly decreases vaginal bleeding. For trans men who sleep with cis men and need good contraception and who also have residual vaginal bleeding on testosterone, the Mirena IUD may both provide highly effective contraception and help decrease bleeding.

Emergency contraception (the "morning-after pill") may also be effective, although it has not been tested in transgender men. This medication is now available over the counter to people of all ages and can be taken for up to 72–120 hours after sex (depending on which medicine is used). If you are a trans man and think you may be pregnant, stop taking testosterone (and finasteride) immediately until you have contacted your primary care provider or gynecologist for advice and testing. These medicines should not be restarted until advised by a provider, as they can cause serious harm to a fetus.

PRECONCEIVED NOTIONS

Jack Hixson-Vulpe is often very busy and unsure of what he is doing.

As a boy, someone who identifies as not female—I never thought I would have to pee on a stick. The summer of 2010 proved otherwise.

In May 2010, I traveled on a plane to see my partner, and that same month I returned with more luggage than I came with. When I peed on the stick, it took less than two minutes to come out positive; it took me even less time to get my partner on the phone. I cried. He was very supportive. I got off the phone with him and made a phone call to schedule my abortion.

I scheduled an appointment at a "women's clinic." The clinic's materials talked about the busy lives of women who might need to schedule abortions and all the help they were willing to provide for women. This sent the message that in order to go through this process, I needed to be a woman. What would this abortion clinic do if someone called and wanted to make an appointment for a pregnant person named Jack? A boy couldn't walk into this women's clinic. I felt I had no option but to become a woman for that two-hour stretch; so I used my legal name, the name that was given to me as a little girl, to book the appointment.

I got off the phone realizing that there was no possible way I could go through this and be a boy. How are boys supposed to get abortions? I wasn't supposed to be able to get pregnant.

I sat in a waiting room littered with fashion and gossip magazines. A woman sat down next to me and flipped through a magazine. I started a conversation; my hairy legs and short hair made me feel conspicuous, and I needed to get out of my own head. She talked to me about how she had done this before. I am pretty sure she could tell how nervous I was, and she told me that everything was going to be okay. At the time I didn't know how to respond to her words. I wish I could say thank you.

I was called in to see the clinic doctor. They referred to me by my legal name and used female pronouns. They asked when I conceived and how I knew I was pregnant, and they gave me a quick breakdown of the entire procedure. I was handed a light blue nightie with pink pigs all over it, and an overwashed flannel that looked like it should have belonged to a 70-year-old grandmother. Not something that I, as a boy with a baby, should be wearing.

It did end up okay. One of the nurses doing the procedure thought to ask me why I was on T. I told her that I was transitioning, and from that point she never used my name or a single pronoun. Instead, she referred to me as "honey." I wish I could go back to say thank you.

After the procedure, I lay on a chair completely out of sorts, my stomach aching, feeling nauseous, and watching multiple women slowly walk by me. I had performed my role; I had passed as a woman. I was no longer pregnant. I left the clinic.

I wanted to be okay with the process, but talking to my partner revealed otherwise. I started to look for support material. It was a difficult process, as I had to sift through the pro-life material that masked itself as wishing to help "women" who have gone through abortions. I came across material that wasn't pro-life and instead talked about some of the feelings I was experiencing, but it was all geared toward women. None of what I read spoke to my experience.

I searched for some reflection of what I had gone through, but all the information I could find pertained to issues that were not important to me. My experience was outside of the "trans experience" and outside of the standard "abortion experience." I was a boy who got an abortion, and it still sounds like a contradiction to me.

In transgender men who do not desire to retain the ability to produce offspring, surgical sterilization is also a permanent method of birth control. In a tubal ligation (having your "tubes tied"), the fallopian tubes are clamped or blocked, preventing eggs from reaching the uterus. Other options for trans men include a hysterectomy (removal of the uterus) or a hysterosalpingo-oopherectomy (removal of the uterus, fallopian tubes, and ovaries). This may be a part of gender-affirming surgery for some transgender men. Typical methods of surgical sterilization now include laparoscopic procedures, in which instruments and a camera are introduced into the abdomen through a small surgical incision. There are also methods in which the sterilization is performed by entering through the vagina into the uterus and inserting the sterilization device into the fallopian tubes.

Contraception in Feminine-Spectrum People

Transgender women who retain testicles can potentially produce a pregnancy in a cisgender female or transgender male partner who is fertile. Estrogens and spironolactone may decrease sperm counts and the viability of sperm, but enough may remain to result in a pregnancy. The best nonpermanent contraceptive option currently available for people born with a penis (and who still have a penis and wish to use it during sexual activities) is condoms. In addition to decreasing the risk of impregnating a partner, condoms also decrease the transmission of STIs.

If pregnancy in a partner does occur while a transgender woman is on estrogens and spironolactone, there is no risk of harm to the fetus. However, if you are using finasteride to decrease hair loss, it is very important to keep the drug away from a pregnant partner. Pregnant people should not even touch this medicine during pregnancy.

For transgender women with no desire to produce offspring, there are permanent contraception options. Cisgender men typically have a vasectomy for this purpose, which is a procedure where the vas deferens, the ducts that carry sperm, are cut to prevent sperm from leaving the body. In addition to the typical vasectomy, transgender women can also have an orchiectomy (removal of the testes) even if they do not need or wish to have a vaginoplasty. While this option is not used in cisgender men for contraception, it is a viable option for transgender women and may not be that much more expensive than a vasectomy. There are added benefits to this, including simplifying hormonal regimens and improving the ability to "tuck," as well as benefits in legal recognition, as this is considered a type of sex-reassignment surgery.

Fertility Options for Masculine-Spectrum People

Transgender men may actively seek fertility, either by carrying a baby themselves or donating an egg to be fertilized and implanted in a partner or surrogate. In addition, trans men who are undergoing gender-affirming surgery that involves hysterectomy (removal of the uterus) or oophorectomy (removal of the ovaries) may wish to preserve future options for fertility.

Pregnancy in transgender men who retain the uterus and ovaries is possible. However, transgender men may face issues with fertility. The effect of testosterone on future fertility is not certain, but it is possible that testosterone can reduce or eliminate fertility even after treatment is stopped. If transgender men want to become pregnant, they must be off testosterone for a sufficient period of time for hormone levels to return to a typical female range. In trans men who use topical testosterone, this process may take a relatively short time (days), whereas in trans men who are using injected testosterone, it may take weeks to months. Even after menstruation has restarted, testosterone levels may be too high to become pregnant safely. Transgender men who wish to become pregnant should therefore have testosterone levels tested before attempting fertilization. In addition, a visit to a primary care provider or gynecologist before pregnancy allows for certain prenatal tests and treatments to be performed. Finally, transgender men who are considering pregnancy should start 0.8 mg of folic acid daily, which is recommended by the US Preventative Services Taskforce for people who may become pregnant in order to prevent birth defects (US PSTP, 2009).

There are options for transgender men who wish to preserve fertility for the future, but they can be expensive and are not always successful. The standard technique for decades has been to harvest oocytes (egg cells) after patients are given hormones that induce increased ovulation. These eggs are then fertilized with sperm either from a known or anonymous donor to produce embryos that are subsequently frozen. Over the past decade, freezing unfertilized eggs without sperm (rather than fertilized eggs) has become a more viable option, although it is still considered experimental because eggs alone are harder to freeze and then use for fertilization than they would be if they were part of an embryo (Noyes, Boldt, & Nagy, 2010). Both freezing fertilized embryos and freezing unfertilized eggs generally costs over $10,000 as well as a yearly fee for as long as the embryos or eggs are preserved. Given this cost, many transgender men opt to preserve their fertility by delaying or avoiding hysterectomy.

FIVE TIPS FOR "WOMEN'S HEALTH" PROVIDERS WORKING WITH GENDER-VARIANT CLIENTS

Simon Adriane Ellis is a genderqueer certified nurse midwife.

1. Focus on your skills and biases. You are compassionate and dexterous at meeting people where they are at. Keep doing what you do best. And keep an eye on your biases. What if your patient doesn't identify as a woman? Does that make their experience less authentic?

2. Build trust and offer accommodations. Fear of discrimination presents a huge barrier to care; it is your job to make care accessible by creating trust. Some patients will desire

anonymity, in which case you can offer appointments at the beginning or end of the clinic day. If you refer the patient to another provider, make it an LGBTQ-friendly one and offer to call ahead and provide the patient's background.

3. Keep your wording inclusive and honor patient preferences. Changing the way you speak may seem hard at first, but it can be as easy as simply replacing the word "women" with the word "people." Include fields on your intake forms for preferred name and pronoun, then make sure your staff respect the patient's wishes. If you slip up and say the wrong thing, just acknowledge your mistake and move on.

4. Don't let curiosity get the best of you. Gender-variant people are constantly asked to justify our existence. This is stressful. Maintain your professional integrity and ask only what you need to know in order to provide excellent care.

5. Don't pass the buck. The urge to refer patients to "someone who has more experience" than you do is strong; often, it is grounded in sincere concern for the client's well-being. But the truth is that, with very few exceptions, there is no one with more experience. Using compassion and clinical/professional acumen as your guide, you will do an awesome job.

Fertility Options for Feminine-Spectrum People

Fertility preservation in transgender women is easier and less expensive compared to transgender men. The process of obtaining semen for preservation is simple and the cost for the initial process and preservation for up to five years is in the range of \$2,000–\$3,000. Sperm can be frozen for longer periods of time, but additional annual costs do apply. For those of us who wish to use this technique, it is extremely important to think about preserving sperm before starting hormonal treatments, as we may become less fertile or theoretically even permanently sterile on hormones.

For those of us who are already on hormones, cessation of hormones for long enough for sperm counts to rise to viable levels is an option in many cases and likely increases the chances of successful insemination of a partner. However, hormone use may reduce fertility, and this may be permanent even if hormones are discontinued. Estrogen may also have the effect of reducing libido, erectile function, and ejaculation.

CONCLUSION

Health is a positive state of wellness, and includes physical, emotional, mental, spiritual, and social well-being. Despite a history of bias, discrimination, and stigma in our interactions with health care systems, we now have the potential to seek out competent and sensitive providers that support us in all aspects of our health. We can take responsibility for our own general, sexual, and reproductive health, as well as the health of our partners, families, and communities. We still have a long way to go, but the future of transgender health care is bright.

REFERENCES AND FURTHER READING

Ard, K. L., & Makadon, H. J. (2011). Addressing intimate partner violence in lesbian, gay, bisexual and transgender patients. *Journal of General Internal Medicine, 26*(8), 930–933. doi: 10.1007/s11606-011-1697-6.

Balsam, K. F., Rothblum, E. D., & Beauchaine, T. P. (2005). Victimization over the life span: A comparison of lesbian, gay, bisexual, and heterosexual siblings. *Journal of Consulting and Clinical Psychology, 73,* 477–487.

Brody, J. E. (1979, October 2). Benefits of transsexual surgery disputed as leading hospital halts the procedure. *New York Times.*

Centers for Disease Control and Prevention. (2012). *Pre-exposure prophylaxis (PrEP).* Retrieved January 2014, from http://www.cdc.gov/hiv/prep/

DeMay, M. (2007). *Practical principles of cytopathology* (Rev. ed.). Chicago, IL: American Society for Clinical Pathology Press.

Gooren, L. J., Giltay, E. J., & Bunck, M. C. (2007). Long-term treatment of transsexuals with cross-sex hormones: Extensive personal experience. *Journal of Clinical Endocrinology and Metabolism, 93*(1), 19.

Grant, J. M., Mottet, L. A., Tanis, J., Harrison, J., Herman, J. L., & Keisling, M. (2011). Injustice at every turn: A report of the national transgender discrimination survey. *National Center for Transgender Equality and National Gay and Lesbian Task Force.* Retrieved January 2014, from http://www.thetaskforce.org/reports_and_research/ntds

Herbst, J. H., Jacobs, E. D., Finlayson, T. J., McKleroy, V. S., Neumann, M. S., & Crepaz, N. (2008). Estimating HIV prevalence and risk behaviors of transgender persons in the United States: A systematic review. *Aids and Behavior, 12*(1), 1–17.

Human Rights Campaign. (2013). Corporate Equality Index 2014. Human Rights Campaign. Retrieved February 2014, from http://www.hrc.org/files/assets/resources/cei_2014_full_report_rev7.pdf

Huyett, J. (2011). Love your hole: An ass manifesto. *Radical Faerie Digest, Winter,* 148.

Lombardi, E. (2010). Pittsburgh Transgender Health Research Summer Institute. Transgender health: A review and guidance for future research—Proceedings from the Summer Institute at the Center for Research on Health and Sexual Orientation, University of Pittsburgh. *International Journal of Transgenderism, 12*(4), 211–229.

Lothstein, L. M. (1982). Sex reassignment surgery: Historical, bioethical, and theoretical issues. *American Journal of Psychiatry, 139,* 417–426.

Makadon, H., Mayer, K., Potter, J., & Goldhammer, H. (Eds.). (2007). *The Fenway guide to lesbian, bisexual and transgender health.* Philadelphia, PA: American College of Physicians.

McHugh, P. (2004). Surgical sex. *First things: A monthly journal of religion and public life, 147,* 34–38. Retrieved January 2014, from http://www.firstthings.com/article/2009/02/surgical-sex

McHugh, P. R. (1992). Psychiatric misadventures. *American Scholar, 61*(4), 497.

Meyer, J. K. & Reter, D. J. (1979). Sex reassignment follow-up. *Archives of General Psychiatry, 36*(9), 1010–1015. doi: 01780090096010.

NAM. (2013). *HIV transmission and testing.* Retrieved January 2014, from http://www.aidsmap.com/Estimated-risk-per-exposure/page/1324038/

Nemoto, T., Operario, D., Keatley, J., Han, L., & Soma, T. (2004). HIV risk behaviors among male-to-female transgender persons of color in San Francisco. *American Journal of Public Health, 94*(7), 1193–1199.

Noyes, N., Boldt, J., & Nagy, Z. P. (2010). Oocyte cryopreservation: Is it time to remove its experimental label? *Journal of Assisted Reproduction and Genetics, 27*(2–3), 69–74.

Perrone, A. M., Cerpolini, S., Maria Salfi, N. C., Ceccarelli, C., De Giorgi, L. B., Formelli, G., & Casadio College of Physicians. (2007). *Program in human sexuality.* Retrieved January 2014, from http://www.phs.umn.edu/about/home.html

Planned Parenthood. (2013). *Birth control.* Retrieved January 2014, from http://www.plannedparenthood.org/health-topics/birth-control/female-condom-4223.htm and http://www.plannedparenthood.org/health-topics/birth-control/condom-10187.htm

Pfafflin, F., & Junge, A. (1998). *Sex reassignment: Thirty years of international follow-up studies SRS: A comprehensive review, 1961–1991.* Retrieved January 2014, from http://web.archive.org/web/20070503090247/http://www.symposion.com/ijt/pfaefflin/1000.htm

Polly, R., & Nicole, J. (2011). Understanding the transsexual patient: Culturally sensitive care in emergency nursing practice. *Advanced Emergency Nursing Journal, 33*(1), 55–64. doi: 10.1097/TME.0b013e3182080ef4

Schaffer, N. (2005). Transgender patients: Implications for emergency department policy and practice. *Journal of Emergency Nursing, 31*(4), 405–407.

Sevelius, J. (2010). There's no pamphlet for the kind of sex I have: HIV-related risk factors and protective behaviors among transgender men who have sex with non-transgender men. *Journal of the Association of Nurses in Aids Care, 20*(5), 398–410. doi:10.106/j.jana.2009.06.001

Tjaden, P., & Thoennes, N. (2000). *Full report of the prevalence, incidence, and consequences of violence against women: Findings from the national violence against women survey.* Retrieved January 2014, from https://www.ncjrs.gov/pdffiles1/nij/183781.pdf

Transgender Law Center. (2012). Organizing for transgender health care. *Transgender Law Center.* Retrieved January 2014, from http://transgenderlawcenter.org/issues/health/orgguide

US Preventive Services Task Force. (2004). *Screening for testicular cancer.* Retrieved January 2014, from http://www.uspreventiveservicestaskforce.org/3rduspstf/testicular/testiculrs.htm

US Preventative Services Task Force. (2009). Folic acid to prevent neural tube defects. Retrieved January 2014, from http://www.uspreventiveservicestaskforce.org/uspstf/uspsnrfol.htm

MEDICAL TRANSITION

Maddie Deutsch

12

MANY OF US SEEK OUT HORMONE THERAPY to help our bodies feminize or masculinize. Hormone therapy (sometimes called cross-sex hormone therapy or hormone replacement therapy) involves taking medications that will cause our bodies to develop secondary sex characteristics, such as hair growth or breast development. Understanding our bodies and how hormones will affect us is an important step in having a safe and healthy transition. Some of us may not choose to take hormones. In the end, what is most important to know is that taking hormones can be done in a safe and healthy way, when we work with a trained medical provider and understand all of the ways hormones will change us, including the possible risks.

HOW HORMONES WORK

Hormones are chemical messengers that deliver instructions to various tissues and organs in the body. Many hormonal functions have nothing to do with sex or gender. Hormones are produced in glands all over the body, including the thyroid (metabolism), parathyroid (bones), pineal gland (secretes melatonin, which controls sleep/wake "circadian rhythms"), adrenal gland (secretes cortisol and other stress-related hormones), and pancreas (insulin for sugar control). There are many other glands and hormones, some of whose function is still unknown, and probably many that have yet to be discovered.

Hormones work through a system of receptors. A receptor is an area on the outside of a cell (or sometimes in its center or "nucleus") that is specially designed to "fit" one specific hormone. We can think of hormones as keys and receptors as locks. If, for example, an estrogen molecule tries to attach to a testosterone receptor, nothing will happen. When an estrogen molecule finds an estrogen receptor, it is able to deliver its message to the cell. This message might be to tell breast tissue to grow, skin to become softer, or a brain cell to "feel" a certain way. Hormones are floating around in our bodies in a complex soup of messages that all work in balance and opposition to each other and make us who we are.

Hormones are controlled through feedback. The pituitary gland is the master gland of the body, in the brain just behind the eyes and the nose. The pituitary sends messages out to the gonads (testicles and ovaries), telling them when and how much estrogen or testosterone to make. When the levels of estrogen or testosterone reach a certain point, the pituitary receives feedback about how successful it has been, and shuts off its messages to the gonads, so that hormone levels gradually fall until they get low enough to trigger the pituitary to turn on again.

The hormones we typically take as trans people—estrogen, testosterone, and progestogens—are considered sex hormones because they affect our sexual and reproductive drives and capacity. All people, male, female, or otherwise, have all of the sex hormones swimming in their bloodstream. It is the amounts of each of these hormones in relationship to one another that give us the physical characteristics we have. Sex hormones have multiple functions, not all of which are related to sex or gender.

Although estrogen is traditionally thought of as the "female hormone," all males have a certain amount of estrogen. The normal range of estrogen levels for cisgender males has a small amount of overlap with the normal range of levels for cisgender females. Everyone, including males, needs estrogen. Estrogen is very important for bone health, and males who have problems with their estrogen receptor develop osteoporosis at a young age.

Testosterone is also present in everyone. Cisgender men typically have higher levels than cisgender women, but cisgender women produce testosterone, too, and it helps them with building muscle and maintaining sex drive.

241

Hormones and hormone receptors (kd diamond).

Hormones do not exist in a vacuum; they interact with each other. If you develop uncomfortable symptoms while on hormone therapy, it is important for both you and your provider to keep an open mind about possible causes, including other hormone systems, such as the thyroid, which may have been set off balance when starting hormone therapy.

BASICS OF HORMONE THERAPY

To explain the effects of hormones, we will categorize them into masculinizing or feminizing. The intention is not to further perpetuate the gender binary or create rigid gender divides. The truth is that there are two ends of the spectrum, and we will choose a certain hormone regimen depending on which direction we want to move.

In general, there has been little (if any) research comparing one regimen to another, or testing the safety or effectiveness of any particular regimen. Current recommendations are based on a combination of expert opinions as well as information based on other ways that hormones are used, such as in menopause, contraception, and testosterone deficiency.

Many people are eager for hormonal changes to take place rapidly. It is important to remember that how much and how fast our bodies change depends on many factors, including genetics, the age we are when we start taking hormones, and our overall state of health. How fast and how much our bodies change is more influenced by these things than by how high of a dose we are taking. Consider the effects of hormone therapy as a second puberty. Puberty normally takes several years for the full effects to be seen. Taking higher doses of hormones will not necessarily bring about faster changes, but it could endanger our health. Because everyone is different, one person's medicines or dosages may vary widely from that of their friends, or what is in books or online.

We can maximize our health and minimize risks and side effects while on hormones by doing a few important things. Eating a healthy and balanced diet with plenty of vegetables and whole grains, and avoiding processed and junk foods, including foods with added sweeteners, provides our bodies with the building blocks they need. In addition to

Hormone Protocols for Prescribers
- Endocrine Society Guidelines for Endocrine Treatment of Transsexual Persons
- Tom Waddell Health Center Protocols for Hormonal Reassignment of Gender
- TransLine Medical Consultation Service Transgender Lab and Medication Protocol
- UCSF Center of Excellence for Transgender Health Primary Care Protocol
- Vancouver Coastal Health Guidelines for Endocrine Therapy for Transgender Adults
- World Professional Association for Transgender Health (WPATH) Standards of Care

eating well, our bodies benefit from engaging in frequent exercise (even brisk walking) several times a week and cutting down or quitting smoking. We have been through a lot to get our bodies where we want them to be. Why not do our best to keep them healthy so we can enjoy them for a long time?

GENDERQUEER IDENTITY AND HORMONES

Some of us identify as genderqueer. This may mean different things to different people. Some of us want to start on hormones and only take them for a little while, to develop just a little bit of the secondary sex characteristics that will result. It is important to remember that we cannot pick or choose which parts of our body will be affected by hormones. For example, if we wanted to have some facial hair development, but not have any change in the pitch of our voice, and we try to do this by taking just a little bit of testosterone, there is no guarantee that just a little bit of testosterone will not change the pitch of our voice. Despite this, many of us do choose to start hormones at lower doses, and then stop once we like the effect they have on our bodies. There are some medical providers who tell us that we have to fit into the gender binary, and unless we want to be a "full" man or a "full" woman, they will not prescribe hormones for us. This is changing, and a growing number of professionals have begun to be open to prescribing lower doses. We will want to understand exactly what the effects of lower doses might be, though. Talking with our medical providers openly and honestly about what we are looking for is very important.

WHY TO SEE A PROVIDER FOR HORMONES

Why should we see a medical provider for hormones? After all, for some of us, hormones are readily available without a prescription from overseas mail-order companies or from street sellers or friends. Why should a trans person decide to access a provider with the associated cost, inconvenience, and possible trauma of going to a medical office?

Monitoring of Hormones and Potential Risks

Hormone therapy can be dangerous if not administered properly. Anything we put into our body can have a possible risk. Many of us have heard of the really scary things that are associated with hormone therapy, such as blood clots in the leg or lung in trans women or high hemoglobin (thick blood) causing a stroke in trans men. Even though they are some-what rare, these risks can be life threatening, and these risks are not the whole story—they are only the tip of the iceberg.

More commonly, a transgender person on hormone therapy will have less serious but still significant side effects that are often overlooked when thinking about risks, because everyone tends to focus on blood clots or thick blood. More common and equally concerning risks that your medical provider should talk with you about include high blood pressure, high cholesterol, weight changes, diabetes, and possible increases in the risk for certain types of cancer as well as benign (noncancerous) tumors.

> "I reverted to internet research and got estrogen from another country. While I exercise, watch what I eat, do not smoke and live a healthy lifestyle, it was discovered during a routine physical that I had had a silent heart attack. That was a huge awakening. I got off the do-it-yourself meds and put myself in the hands of a trusted physician. That was the best move I ever made. All systems are now 'go' and my state of mind is the best ever."

The Web site for *GLMA: Health Professionals Advancing LGBT Equality* provides a list of health care providers all over the country.

Ensuring We Are Taking the Proper Amounts

Like anyone seeking any kind of changes to one's body, we may be drawn to treatments that promise to deliver amazing results, such as high doses of hormones or free silicone injections. In many cases, these treatments are dangerous and can be life threatening. Many of us want to maximally feminize or masculinize our bodies and are willing to do this at almost any cost. However, the cost can be steep.

Harm reduction models of treatment are more frequently used with clients who are already using hormones, regardless of the source of those hormones. For example, if a client is seeking medical care and has been taking street hormones for a period of time, the provider who follows a harm reduction model is not likely to prevent the trans person from continued access to hormones. The provider recognizes that it may be in the best interest of the client to continue taking hormones, and that in reality, having access to hormones from a provider may be safer than the use of street hormones.

—lore m. dickey, PhD

One important myth to dispel is that taking higher than prescribed doses of hormones will increase the speed of physical transition. This has not been shown to be true. Instead, taking more than normal prescription doses adds nothing to the speed of transition and causes unwanted side effects.

Taking high doses of hormones has a number of risks. Estrogen in high doses can cause blood clots, anxiety, migraines, weight gain, constipation and bloating, and immune system disorders ranging from severe allergies to autoimmune conditions such as lupus or rheumatoid arthritis, where the body's defenses attack itself. There are injectable street hormones that contain a month's worth of estrogen and progesterone. Some of us inject this as often as every day and suffer from migraines, muscle aches, nervousness, and insomnia. There are myths that all estrogen leaves the body after ejaculation or orgasm, but this is not true.

Testosterone in high doses increases the risk of developing dangerously high cholesterol levels or dangerously thick blood (also known as a high hemoglobin or hematocrit). Either of these conditions can lead to strokes, heart attacks, and kidney or eye damage. In addition, testosterone in excess is converted to estrogen in the body, which may cause menstrual cramping or a return of periods.

We work so hard to become the people we are and to have our bodies match our identities. At the same time, many of us abuse those same bodies and put those bodies at risk.

INFORMED CONSENT

Laura A. Jacobs, LCSW, is a psychotherapist, activist, and presenter in the New York City area focusing on LGBTQ and sexual/gender minority communities, on the board of directors for Callen-Lorde, and is completing and pursuing publication of her own book, Many Paths: The Choice of Gender.

Informed Consent is about empowerment. The prior Standards of Care, as established by the World Professional Association for Transgender Health (WPATH), required we adhere to a very specific definition of trans identity: an individual was expected to assert that they had always identified as the "other" gender, to be willing to live as the "other" gender before commencing medical interventions, to present in ways that were conventional for the "other" gender, and to be heterosexual as the "other" gender to receive medical care.

Informed Consent arose to combat these authoritarian forces. Developed first at the Tom Waddell health clinic in San Francisco, and spreading in the early 2000s to LGBTQ Health Centers like Callen-Lorde in New York City, Fenway Health in Boston, and the Mazzoni Center in Philadelphia, Informed Consent is a model of care that redefines the relationship of provider and client as one of equals where the individual becomes a partner in determining the course of their own treatment, aware of the benefits and risks.

The development of Informed Consent represents a major piece of trans activism. The effectiveness of this movement is made clear when we see that many of the basic principles of Informed Consent have been incorporated into the most recent version of the WPATH Standards of Care.

PAYING FOR HORMONES

The cost of obtaining hormones includes both the cost of seeing a health care provider and also the cost of the hormones themselves. Affording hormones can be very difficult for those of us who barely get by.

> "When I first started using hormone replacement therapy, they did not pay for my prescriptions or for the blood work related to them. I was paying entirely out of pocket, and cut down on my food expenses by dumpster diving and stealing food in order to afford transition-related expenses."

Depending on whether we have insurance and what kind of insurance we have, the amount we are personally required to pay may be very high or very low. Some insurance plans do not cover prescriptions of any kind, whether they are for hormones or other medications. Some companies will pay for hormones knowing that we are transgender and that the hormones are being prescribed for that reason. Other companies specifically exclude any

Trans Healthcare Now (San Francisco Pride March, June 24, 2012). Photo by Liz Highleyman.

kind of transgender care but will pay for hormone prescriptions if the hormones could be used for other purposes than transitioning.

For those of us who have insurance that covers hormones, we often still have to pay part of the cost ourselves. This is called the copay. There may also be a deductible, which is an amount of money that we have to pay ourselves in that particular year before the insurance company will start paying any portion of our prescriptions.

> *"I have medical insurance, but transition is out of pocket and covering treatment has been a challenge financially, but I'll make it."*

> *"I have medical insurance through my place of employment. So far, at least, my gender-related care has been treated like any other medical condition by my insurance company. I pay deductibles and a copay, and they cover quite a bit of the rest of it. I am just barely able to afford my part of all this."*

> *"I have insurance but it has not covered most transition-related expenses. It explicitly covers gender reassignment surgery, so it was forced to pay for my top surgery but other expenses like doctors' visits, hormones, and blood work are more of a gray area and my insurance is allowed to reject claims at their discretion. So far I have had trouble getting them to cover visits to the psychiatrist to be cleared for surgery, hormones, needles, and blood work."*

Hormones can vary significantly in cost depending on where we buy them. With a prescription from a health care provider, we may go to a local pharmacy, discount pharmacy, or compounding pharmacy, or send the prescription away to a mail-order pharmacy. Some insurance companies even have their own mail-order pharmacies.

> *"Currently I pay $10 per month for all three of my medications using a discounted mail-order pharmacy that has a partnership with my insurance company. If I were to purchase these medications at another pharmacy, it would cost about $30 per month."*

In many cases, large pharmacy and big-box warehouse-type chains offer deep discounts on generic medications. However, transgender people sometimes take higher doses of certain medications than the standard dose used in cisgender people for other issues, and the pharmacy may only offer the reduced rate for the standard dose.

Compounding pharmacies make their own medicines in house. Many compounding pharmacies offer products similar to commercial pharmaceuticals at a lower cost. Because compounding pharmacies make their own blends, they are not standardized from one pharmacy to another. A dose of 1 mg at one pharmacy may be equivalent to 2 mg at another pharmacy. Be sure both you and your provider are informed about compounding pharmacies and their products before filling your prescriptions with them.

Some of us attempt to save costs by obtaining our prescriptions from overseas, Canadian, or Mexican pharmacies. In some cases, there may be significant savings. In other cases, the savings are minimal and not worth the hassle of waiting months at times for our medicines to clear customs. Laws may govern how much or what kind of medicine can be imported. Some of these pharmacies are in countries where a prescription is not needed for medicines like hormones.

"Insurance doesn't cover my meds. So even though I have legitimate prescriptions, I buy my meds overseas (online) from the same sources that are frequently used by trans women and men lacking prescriptions."

"Having private insurance disqualified me from both the sliding-scale discount and from Medicaid. During that time, it was cheaper for me to order my hormones from the Internet rather than pay full price at the clinic. I paid roughly $50-75 per month for estradiol, spironolactone, and medroxyprogesterone (Provera) combined."

The US government is cracking down on prescription medicines ordered from abroad without a prescription. For this reason, many people still obtain written prescriptions from a provider, even if using an international pharmacy. A written prescription makes sure we order the correct prescription, helps the medicine clear customs more easily, and protects us if we are ever asked to provide a prescription for any medication we take that is a controlled substance, such as testosterone. If you do choose to order from an international pharmacy, be sure to do your homework. Ask around and learn about what pharmacies other transgender people have used. Do your best to be sure you are getting medicine that is not mislabeled, expired, tainted, or falsified.

MEDICAID AND TRANS BODIES

Pooja Gehi and Gabriel Arkles are affiliated with the Sylvia Rivera Law Project.

As the wealth divide between rich and poor grows, trans people are especially likely to be poor because of the discrimination they experience. Because they are less likely to be able to get health insurance through a job, school, spouse, or partner, and because they often can't afford to buy health insurance on their own, many trans people don't have any health insurance. When they do have health insurance, it's often Medicaid.

One big problem for a lot of trans people who get Medicaid is that they usually can't get gender-affirming health care covered. Some state Medicaid programs have rules that specifically exclude this care from coverage, even though federal law forbids discrimination. Other Medicaid programs don't have rules like that, but administrators still deny gender-affirming care. Sometimes trans people get wrongly denied Medicaid or programs put the wrong name and gender on trans people's Medicaid cards. The media doesn't help. It seems like any time there is a rumor that a trans person got Medicaid to pay for any sort of gender-affirming care, some news story runs decrying tax payer money going to "sex changes."

People across the nation are doing amazing work to fight back against discrimination that trans people face when trying to access Medicaid and the health care they need. For example, in New York City a group called the Welfare Warriors—made up of transgender Medicaid recipients and members of the Audre Lorde Project, The Sylvia Rivera Law Project, Housing Works, and Queers for Economic Justice— negotiated with the New York City welfare department to create a new nondiscrimination policy. A lot of different groups of people have problems with getting access to health care they need through Medicaid. If groups dedicated to reproductive justice, immigrant justice, economic justice, disability justice, and trans justice all work together, we can make a lot more change.

GETTING HORMONES FROM A REPUTABLE SOURCE

Hormones that are not received and packaged by a pharmacy are not regulated, so they can contain substances other than what someone says they contain. However, some of us seek out alternative sources for our hormones, over concerns about cost or privacy.

Ordering hormones over the Internet can be problematic. These hormones may be counterfeit, expired, or may contain other medications or substances. They may be delayed for months at customs or even be confiscated. Availability may fluctuate, so that a hormone which was available 3 months ago is now out of stock, requiring frequent changes of regimens or dosing, which can cause unpleasant side effects.

Getting hormones off the street can offer the same dangers, and in many public clinics, the cost of seeing the provider, obtaining labs, and purchasing the hormones from the pharmacy is less than the local cost of street or black-market hormones. Not only is it safer to use provider-prescribed hormones, it can often be cheaper.

Getting hormones from a reputable source can also come with other benefits. A prescription for hormones means that we have a written, official document that explains why we are carrying medicine or needles. Should we require medical care for an unrelated condition, such as a car accident, heart attack, or psychiatric visit, having a prescription for our hormones will help legitimize our treatment in the eyes of other providers. Many providers will also write a care (also known as "carry") letter for us. This can be used in numerous situations, including if we have to deal with law enforcement or are arrested.

SAMPLE CARE/CARRY LETTER

Month and Day, Year

To Whom It May Concern,

John Doe (formerly known as Jane Doe), D.O.B. 3/5/1970 is a patient with whom I have a provider–patient relationship and who is under my care. I am a Licensed Physician in the state of _____, License #X12345, DEA# ZZ1234567.

Mr. Doe is a female-to-male transsexual and has undergone all medically necessary treatments for transition from female to male; his transition is complete. *(Note to letter writer: Transgender identities and the transition process are poorly understood by many people. It is best to not confuse them and simply always state that the transition is complete.)* He should be referred to using his preferred name of Joe and male pronouns such as He and Him. He should be allowed access to male facilities such as bathrooms, changing rooms, and airport screening. His documents, such as driver's license and US passport, should be amended to the male gender.

The process of changing one's sex both medically and legally is complex and may sometimes take up to several years to complete fully. Because of this, Mr. Doe may currently have some identity documents that do not reflect his gender identity or name. Thank you in advance for giving Mr. Doe assistance and understanding. Please feel free to contact me directly should you have any questions or concerns. Sworn as correct under penalty of perjury on Month and Day, Year in City, State.

Sincerely,

Name of Doctor, M.D./D.O.

123 X St, City, State, Zip Code

Phone number

TRANSMASCULINE HORMONE THERAPY

The primary aim of transmasculine hormone therapy is to add testosterone (T) to the body. No blocking of estrogen is needed because testosterone causes changes that override many of estrogen's mechanisms. There are numerous temporary and more permanent changes that occur with testosterone. These include changes in strength and body fat distribution, as well as alterations in libido and sexual functioning. Some may be desired and some may not be.

Testosterone Regimens

Testosterone comes in several forms. Most transgender men use an injectable form to start. Some choose to begin on a lower dose and increase slowly, while others choose to begin at a regular dose. Both approaches have their pros and cons. Testosterone levels tend

For those of us who do end up obtaining hormones outside of the care of a medication provider, there are ways we can protect ourselves from further risks. Never share hormones with anyone else or use anyone else's hormones, especially injectable hormones. Diseases such as HIV and hepatitis can be spread this way (even if clean needles are used) if the hormone in the vial has not been properly stored or prepared.

to be most even over time when injections are given weekly, but some of us use injections
every two weeks or even every month.

> "I use testosterone enanthate (Primoteston) 250. With the pharmacy I get it from
> now it costs me $31 for a 9 week supply. . . Though I get the needles, sharps
> containers, and medicated swabs for free from a needle exchange. The syringes
> come with needles to use but they're too big so I change them to a 21g needle."

There are different techniques for injection, and we should always talk explicitly with our
health care provider about the one that is recommended for our medication. Intramuscular
(IM) injection is giving a shot into the muscle. Subcutaneous (SQ) injection is done
directly under the skin.

In addition to injections, there are also transdermal forms of testosterone, including
patches, gels, and creams. These methods can be beneficial in those of us who do not like
needles. They may also provide a more even amount of testosterone in our blood over
time. In some men, these forms cause changes to progress at a slower pace. Be sure to keep
these medications away from children and also away from any adults who do not wish to
masculinize their appearance.

> "Testosterone patches and gels are much more expensive, and with insurance
> coverage were costing me $30 a month, five years ago. I used them only for a
> short time due to the increased expense."

> "Right now I am using testosterone cream but I am about to switch to injec-
> tions. I have a huge phobia of needles, but once my health insurance ends next
> month, the cream will be prohibitively expensive. I need to learn to self-inject,
> but I am so nervous."

> "I prefer the injections to the cream for a few reasons. I don't have to remember
> to take my medications every day on the injectable and there is less mess with
> injectable. Plus I have seen changes faster on the injectable."

Regardless of the type of testosterone we are taking, adding more will not make changes
progress more quickly, but it could cause serious health complications. There is no such
thing as a full, half, or quarter dose. Each person has their own dosing needs and care
should be taken to avoid making comparisons to the doses our friends are taking. Excess
testosterone can be converted to estrogen, which may increase our risks of unwanted side
effects and possibly even cancer. High doses can make us feel anxious or agitated, and
they can cause our cholesterol or blood count to get too high.

The best way to monitor a testosterone dose to make sure it is correct is to take note of the changes it causes and any side effects. Health care providers may not follow testosterone levels, but instead they use what clients tell them about how they are doing to make changes to prescriptions. This is because the goal of treatment with testosterone is not to have a certain testosterone level, but to look and feel differently. Cisgender men have testosterone levels that vary significantly from person to person. Testosterone levels often cost more than other labs because they are not considered routine. There are a few instances in which a health provider may check a testosterone level. For example, if someone is taking a regular dose of testosterone, but not seeing any changes to their body, the provider may want to see whether testosterone blood levels are within a normal male range. They may also want to check a testosterone level if someone is having unpleasant symptoms or ongoing vaginal bleeding.

Physical Changes on Testosterone

Physical changes with testosterone can be exciting for many of us. For most of us, there will be some that are welcome and some that are less welcome. Some of the effects of hormone therapy are reversible if we decide to stop taking testosterone, but there are a number of changes that are more permanent. The degree to which they can be reversed depends on how long we have been taking testosterone. Clitoral growth, facial hair growth, voice changes, and male-pattern baldness are not reversible.

The first noticeable change with testosterone is usually that the skin becomes thicker and oilier. The pores become larger and there is more oil production. We may develop acne. The amount of acne depends on a number of factors, and some people are more prone to acne than others—some of us had acne during our first puberty and others of us did not. In some cases the acne caused by testosterone can be bothersome or severe, but it can usually be managed with good skin care practices and common acne treatments. We may also notice that the odors of our sweat and urine change and we may sweat more overall. Some of us notice that when we touch things they seem to feel somewhat different, and we may perceive pain and temperature differently.

> "I've got increased muscle mass, and my skin is a lot more oily. Also, I'm a lot hungrier."

> "I take weekly T shots. They've shifted my body fat, my voice changed (thankfully), and I got facial and chest hair!"

> "My voice has lowered and changed tone. I cannot make it high anymore. I've grown hair in places I expected (i.e., face) and places I didn't expect (i.e., knees). I vary between having a lot of acne and not so much."

The chest does not typically change a lot during transition, though there is sometimes some breast pain or a slight decrease in size. There is no evidence that starting testosterone therapy before having chest reconstructive surgery changes the outcome of surgery.

On testosterone, our body weight begins to distribute differently. Fat diminishes somewhat around the hips and thighs. Our arms and legs develop more muscle definition, and a slightly rougher appearance, as the fat just beneath the skin becomes a bit thinner. Some of us also gain fat around our abdomen, the beginnings of the development of a "gut." Some trans men on testosterone notice minor changes in shoe size or height. This is not due to bony changes but to changes in the ligaments and muscles of our feet and spinal column.

There are some facial changes on testosterone. Our eyes and face will begin to develop a more angular appearance as facial fat decreases and shifts. It is not likely that our underlying bone structure will change, though some people in their late teens or early twenties may see some subtle bone changes. It may take two or more years to see the final result of facial changes on testosterone.

Whether we gain or lose weight on testosterone depends on a number of factors. Muscle mass will increase, as will strength, but weight is also affected by diet, exercise, and genetics. Some of us may find that our appetite increases. Some trans men will need more calories and protein—especially those who are vegan or vegetarian.

> *"I gained a lot of weight then lost a lot. Now I'm thinner than I was before. My muscles and veins are more prominent. My butt is flatter."*

> *"Since I am a triathlete, I have noticed that my running is much faster as are my cycling and swimming times."*

> *"I have more muscle mass now, and my muscles have been stiff lately, I think because they're growing."*

Testosterone causes a thickening of the vocal cords, which will result in a deeper voice. Not all trans men will experience a full deepening of their voice with testosterone, and some men may find that practicing various vocal techniques or working with a speech therapist helps to develop a voice that feels more comfortable and fitting. Voice changes may begin within just a few weeks of starting testosterone, first with a scratchy sensation in the throat or feeling like you are hoarse. Next, your voice may break a bit as it finds its new tone and quality. Voice deepening on testosterone is a permanent change, and thus it is something to consider when deciding to take testosterone.

On testosterone, the hair on our bodies, including our chest, back, and arms, will increase in thickness, become darker, and will grow at a faster rate. We can probably expect to develop a pattern of body hair similar to other men in our family, but everyone is different. It can take five or more years to see the final results for hair growth.

> *"I have been taking testosterone for exactly 646 days now. My voice has dropped considerably. Facial hair has come in to a considerable extent. My hairline has changed to a more typical male pattern. I have begun growing some chest hair and I have a formidable happy trail. My whole body's features have altered slightly as fat distribution has changed and I have become stronger and somewhat more muscular."*

> *"When I began taking T, my voice dropped an octave (over time), and it was great. I've also developed more muscles, have less 'softness' and less 'flab' in general, and I am actually an inch taller, and I wear a lot larger shoes than I used to. I had to throw out all my old shoes, in fact, even though most of them were men's already. I've also developed a male hairline, and jaw line, and my facial features in general have become more square and masculine, which is great. I'm a lot hairier all over, in fact."*

Regarding the hair on our heads, most trans men notice some degree of frontal scalp balding, especially in the area of the temples. Depending on our age and family history, we may develop thinning hair, male pattern baldness, or even complete hair loss. If we are older when we start testosterone, we are more likely to begin balding right away when we start testosterone. Beards vary from person to person. Some people develop a thick beard quite rapidly and others take several years, while some never develop a full and thick beard. This is a result of genetics and the age at which we start testosterone therapy.

> *"I inject 'T' every week and have for about 8 years now. Even after all this time I am still experiencing changes. My facial features have changed. I have some facial hair, but that is because of my genetics. I am half bald (able to do the comb-over if I let it grow out). I have hair under my arms and on my legs but not a lot on my arms, again genetics. My muscles have changed shape and I went through what I called growing pains through those changes."*

> *"I have taken T for over 6 years. I can grow a full beard, my voice is lower, I have a more male body shape, and I am losing my hair."*

Dane and Erin in the nursery (Arthur Robin Williams MD, www.MyRightSelf.org).

Emotional Changes on Testosterone

Puberty is a roller coaster of emotions and the second puberty we experience during our transition is no exception. We may find that we have access to a narrower range of emotions or feelings; have different interests, tastes, or pastimes; or behave differently in relationships with people.

Some people describe feeling more amped up or angry on testosterone. While this may be a reality for some of us, many of us say that we feel calmer. Popular media tells us that testosterone is a "male" hormone and should therefore make us more stereotypically male, often meaning more aggressive. In the same way, we are taught that estrogen, as a "female" hormone, causes us to be more emotional. However, some trans men say that they have more connection to their feelings after starting testosterone. Emotions are extremely complicated and depend on all sorts of factors—including how comfortable we feel as ourselves.

> *"The only emotional change I've noticed is that things like Hallmark commercials evoke a strong emotional response immediately. I tear up a bit, or feel like I'm going to. This happens over weird things, too. I've described it as tearing up over 'the slightest hint of conviction.' I was a little like that before testosterone, but it's increased a lot."*

> *"I am happier. I used to have a feeling of walking through molasses which is associated with depression; that feeling is gone and I have more energy and confidence."*

> *"My mental changes have come drastically in such a short time. I already feel much more confident, and much more in tune with my body, like a missing piece has finally been put back in its place."*

For some of us, hormones have a strong effect on our emotions and how we relate to others. Psychotherapy is not for everyone, but most of us have the potential to benefit from counseling that helps us to explore our new thoughts and feelings.

Sexual and Reproductive Changes on Testosterone

Many trans men report that one of the earliest effects of testosterone is a significant increase in sex drive (also known as libido). Some say that sexual arousal can come unexpectedly and more frequently. Sometimes our sexual preferences broaden to include people we may not have been attracted to before. Some of us use erotic images (pornography) more than we did before. This is all healthy—as long as it feels healthy to us.

It is important to take time to give ourselves sexual pleasure, whether through masturbation or through sex or mutual masturbation with a partner. It can be helpful to talk openly with our partners about changes in our libido or attractions. If we find that we are sexually aroused several times a day but our partners are not interested in sex this frequently, discussing the effects that testosterone has on libido may help everyone feel reassured. We may need to take time for private masturbation. Our partners can also benefit, too. If our sexual attractions expand, we may be interested in trying something our partners have wanted that we were not interested in before. The most important thing is open communication.

If libido changes are concerning or uncomfortable, there are things we can do to address them. Talking to our health care provider is a good first step. The provider may recommend changing how we take testosterone and how much we take. Taking a lower dose overall may help. For trans men injecting testosterone, taking a smaller dose at more frequent intervals can decrease fluctuations in testosterone levels, thereby evening out sex drive. In addition, there are some medicines that decrease sexual arousal (as a side effect), and it may be possible to take a low dose of one of these medicines to temper libido.

As we begin taking testosterone, our clitoris/phallus enlarges. The increase in size is different for different men, but research has shown that those of us who start hormones at a younger age have more growth (Gooren et al., 2008). However, the differences in growth between trans men who start testosterone earlier and later are small. For many of us it is exciting to see phallic growth. However, it can be a new sensation to have something protruding that rubs against our clothes and becomes large and erect. For some of us, this takes getting used to.

> *"My clitoris has enlarged quite a bit, my voice has become scratchy and unstable. I now have a visible adam's apple protruding from my throat. I am more easily aroused, and I have very bad acne on my face and back."*

> *"Over the past eight weeks, my voice has started to change and my dick has started to grow, along with my inner labia."*

NONSURGICAL TECHNIQUES USED TO ENLARGE THE PHALLUS

Nick Gorton, MD

Testosterone increases the size of the clitoris/phallus. Some of us look for other ways to continue to increase our phallus size. There are no research studies that suggest ways to accomplish this. Two commonly used methods are the application of testosterone creams and the use of genital pumps. If properly done, there is little risk and there *may* be a small benefit.

In the United States the only available cream is testosterone. In other countries, cream containing dihydrotestosterone (DHT), a stronger hormone than testosterone, is available. Research in cisgender men with genetic conditions that result in an unusually small penis suggests that topical treatments can be somewhat effective. However, this does not mean that the same is true in transgender men. It is important to remember that testosterone (or DHT) applied to the phallus is absorbed into the body, so any topical dose needs to be calculated into the total dose of testosterone. In addition, DHT is the hormone most responsible for male pattern baldness. In fact, a popular medicine to treat baldness—finasteride (Propecia)—works by decreasing the amount of DHT in the body. Just as medicines like finasteride could theoretically decrease the amount of DHT in the phallic area and decrease enlargement, DHT absorbed from the phallus could theoretically increase the chance of baldness.

Some surgeons recommend their patients use pumping techniques. Some trans men report that they have an increase in the size of their phallus after pumping for some time. There is no evidence as to whether this method is effective. It is important to follow the suggestions of the surgeon about frequency and duration of pumping. If any pain or numbness is experienced, pumping should be stopped and not resumed until advised it is safe by a health care provider.

Many trans men develop heavier genital hair after starting hormones. Testosterone affects all the hair on our bodies, not just the hair on our heads. We may also develop hair on our buttocks and lower abdomen that meets the top of the pubic hair. For many of us this is welcome, but if it is not welcome for you, hair removal (both temporary and permanent) is possible.

Some trans men have increased or decreased vaginal fluid production. Increased fluid production is usually associated with increased libido. Dryness can happen because estrogen levels may fall when starting testosterone. Vaginal dryness and itching often occur in postmenopausal cisgender women and can occur in some transgender men as well. If this happens, using over-the-counter lubrication can help. If dryness or itching persists, our health care providers will have information about additional treatments available.

Testosterone typically causes menstruation to stop within two or three cycles. A few trans men report that starting testosterone stops menstruation immediately. Some of us have persistent occasional bleeding or may not stop menstruating at all. Stopping menstruation is important to some of us, but not to all. Even after bleeding stops for over a year, it can sometimes recur. If we stop taking testosterone (or miss a dose or take a lower dose), bleeding can occur. Even after starting testosterone it is a good idea to have supplies like tampons or pads at home in case of irregular bleeding.

"I've taken testosterone for three years. The changes I have seen and felt included a dramatic reduction in menstrual bleeding. I have had three episodes of peeing pink for a week in three years, versus bleeding heavily for about two weeks per month."

"I inject testosterone enanthate once a week. The cost is $10-15 a month. Changes so far include a higher libido, growth of clitoris, more muscle mass, more appetite, increased strength, coarser skin, more and coarser facial hair, weight gain (mostly in the belly area), and end of my menstrual cycle."

If you have trouble getting bleeding to stop once on testosterone, talk to a health care provider. This may be due to low levels of testosterone or occasionally may happen even with typical male levels. If levels are low and it is appropriate to increase your dose, your provider may do so. Another possible way to stop bleeding is by adding a dose of a progestogen either by taking a daily pill or by using progestogen-containing birth control methods like injected medroxyprogesterone (Depo-Provera) or etonogestrel implant (Nexplanon). Medications like these have the added benefit of good contraception for those of us who choose to have receptive vaginal sex, though they do not protect against sexually transmitted infections (STIs). Another option is a progestogen-containing intrauterine device (IUD), which is also effective for contraception.

If you experience unusual bleeding despite taking your usual dose of testosterone, see a provider right away to evaluate for the presence of precancerous or cancerous changes in the uterus.

Pelvic pain is a common problem in those of us assigned female at birth. Trans men can have pelvic pain before, during, or after initiation of hormone therapy. Some report that pelvic pain improves after starting testosterone. However, a frequent complaint is a cramping pelvic pain that occurs during or after orgasm. This can be mild to severe, and it can happen occasionally or frequently. This may be similar to the postorgasmic pain that some cisgender women experience during and after menopause, and it may be related to decreased estrogen levels from taking testosterone. Trans men who have this pain frequently may need to see their health care provider about this, although for most this is an occasional or mild problem. Some people take an anti-inflammatory medicine (such as ibuprofen or naproxen) one to two hours before sex.

Taking testosterone greatly reduces our ability to become pregnant, but it does not completely eliminate the possibility. Transgender men can become pregnant while on testosterone, so for those of us who remain sexually active and have penile-vaginal sex, we should always use a method of birth control to prevent unwanted pregnancy. If you suspect you may have become pregnant, discontinue testosterone treatment and see your provider as soon as possible, as testosterone can endanger the fetus.

Depending on how long we have been on testosterone therapy, it may become difficult for our ovaries to release eggs, and we may need to use fertility drugs or expensive techniques such as in vitro fertilization to become pregnant. It is also possible for testosterone therapy to cause us to completely lose the ability to become pregnant.

Risks and Side Effects of Taking Testosterone

Some of the physical, emotional, and sexual changes brought on by testosterone may be unwanted for some of us. What is considered a side effect depends on the person. In addition to the predictable changes, there are also some medical risks that come with taking testosterone. Testosterone can affect our red blood cells, cholesterol, liver, and possibly increase our risk for certain types of cancer.

Testosterone increases the production of red blood cells, which is measured as hemoglobin or hematocrit. Cisgender men generally have higher hemoglobin levels on labs than cisgender women do because testosterone affects hormones that stimulate the bone marrow to produce our blood cells, and also because cisgender men do not menstruate. When we start taking testosterone, there is usually an increase in hemoglobin/hematocrit, putting us in the normal male range. It is important that medical providers know that once we start taking testosterone, all of our labs should be compared to normal male levels. Hemoglobin is an important lab to monitor because of the risk that taking testosterone could increase the hemoglobin level too much, causing our blood to become too thick, and leading to strokes or heart attacks. This can be a problem if we are taking a dose that is too high. It can also be related to the frequency of doses. Those of us taking testosterone every two to four weeks instead of every week will have more peaks in our testosterone levels, which can cause more red blood cells to be made.

Cholesterol is another lab value that can change on testosterone. Like high hemoglobin, high cholesterol can be a "silent killer," as it causes few symptoms, and by the time we develop serious conditions such as coronary artery disease (narrowing of the arteries in the heart), heart attack, or stroke, the damage has already been done. Testosterone frequently raises our "bad" (LDL) cholesterol and lowers our "good" (HDL) cholesterol. A provider will be able to monitor cholesterol with a simple blood test obtained after an eight-hour fast. This test is generally done in the morning before breakfast. In addition to making sure we are on the correct dosage of hormones, a provider will be able to help us control our cholesterol, either through diet, exercise, supplements, or medication if needed.

> *"Right from the beginning my doctor diagnosed me with high cholesterol and started prescribing meds to keep that down."*

In addition to hemoglobin and cholesterol levels, our providers will also run periodic tests of our kidney and liver function, as well as a diabetes screening test. All steroid hormones, including testosterone, can affect our liver because that is where our body breaks them down. Testosterone can also cause shifts in our body weight and fat distribution, and it can sometimes affect our likelihood of developing diabetes.

As a result of testosterone treatment, our overall health risk profile can change. Our risk of heart disease, diabetes, high blood pressure, and high cholesterol may go up, though these risks may still be less than a cisgender man's risks. However, there are no data to suggest that trans men live any shorter lives than cis women.

TransLine (www.project-health.org/transline) is a free national online transgender medical consultation service that offers health care providers up-to-date clinical information on trans health and individualized case consultation across a broad range of clinical issues.

The risk of certain types of cancer may be increased by taking testosterone, although we know very little about the risk at this point. Uterine, cervical, ovarian, and breast cancer are all possible in those of us who still have these organs, whether we take testosterone or not.

Endometrial (uterine) cancer typically develops after a thickening of the uterine walls called endometrial hyperplasia. The lining of the uterus grows very thick, and ultimately so thick that some of it begins to slough off and there is spotting or what may seem like a period. This highlights the importance of talking to a provider if you develop any spotting or bleeding after a time without any menstruation. While there is often another explanation, such as changing testosterone dose, the provider may want to order an ultrasound of the uterus, a biopsy of the uterus, or both. A biopsy of the uterus is similar to a Pap smear, using a speculum. During the procedure, the provider will pass a small tube that looks like a coffee-stir straw through the cervix and into the uterus to extract some uterine tissue. The procedure can cause some cramping or a little bleeding. For an ultrasound, a probe may be inserted into the vagina to allow the provider to get a detailed look at the uterus. While both of these procedures are unpleasant, and may dredge up a flurry of emotions relating to our gendered organs and anatomy, they can be lifesavers. Endometrial cancer has been linked to increased levels of estrogen. Because testosterone is converted to estrogen by the ovaries and by fat cells, excess testosterone will be converted to estrogen. This makes it theoretically possible that testosterone increases our risk of endometrial cancer. However, very little research exists on the risks of endometrial cancer in those of us taking testosterone.

It is unclear whether testosterone treatment causes an increased risk of ovarian cancer. Ovarian cancer is a vicious illness and most cases of ovarian cancer, whether is transgender or cisgender people, are discovered after it is too late to be treated. There is no simple blood or imaging test to screen for this condition. A periodic pelvic exam, where the provider uses a gloved hand to examine the vagina, uterus, and ovaries, may be useful to help detect this condition. There are not sufficient data to make inferences about whether trans men taking testosterone have increased, decreased, or similar levels of risk to cisgender women. At present the only way to screen for ovarian cancer is by taking a detailed family history to learn about any breast or ovarian cancer history in the family.

Our risk of cervical cancer relates to our past and current sexual practices because it is caused by the sexually transmitted infection human papilloma virus (HPV). There are many ways to be exposed to HPV, and we can still acquire it even if we have never had penile-vaginal sex. There is no known link between taking testosterone and developing cervical cancer, but testosterone does have a tendency to cause decreased lubrication and vaginal wall thinning, which could potentially lead to more breaks in the tissue, allowing HPV to be transmitted more easily. Pap smears are used to screen for cervical cancer and for precancerous conditions caused by HPV.

Some experts recommend a full hysterectomy and bilateral salpingo-oopherectomy—which would include removal of the uterus (hysterectomy), ovaries (oopherectomy), and fallopian tubes (salpingectomy)—5–10 years after beginning testosterone treatment to minimize the risk of cancer and eliminate the need for screening. This is not a general recommendation at this time. For those of us who have our ovaries removed, it is important to remain on at least a low dose of hormones until we are 50, and perhaps older, to prevent a weakening of the bones, otherwise known as osteoporosis.

Testosterone treatment does not seem to significantly increase the risk of breast cancer, but there are not enough data to be certain. Recent research shows that testosterone does not seem to change the risk of breast cancer from where it was for us before testosterone. In other words, if before starting testosterone we had a 16% lifetime risk of developing breast cancer based on our overall risk factors, taking testosterone will not increase (but also might not lower) our risk. It is important to receive periodic mammograms or other screening procedures as recommended by a provider. After chest reconstruction surgery, there is still a small amount of breast tissue left behind. It may be difficult to screen this small amount of tissue for breast cancer, but it should be attempted.

TRANSFEMININE HORMONE THERAPY

The primary focus of transfeminine hormone therapy is to reduce the testosterone levels into the female range using a testosterone blocker, while providing a relatively low dose of estrogen to bring estrogen levels into the female range. Changes that occur on these medications can be temporary or permanent. One important permanent change to be aware of is that our ability to have biological children after taking transfeminine hormones can potentially be taken away. Other changes include decrease in strength and shifting in body fat distribution. We may desire certain changes and not others.

Transfeminine Hormone Regimens

Hormone therapy for trans women may include three different kinds of medicines: estrogen, testosterone blockers, and progesterone.

Estrogen is the hormone responsible for most female characteristics. It causes the physical changes of transition and many of the emotional changes. Estrogen may be given as a pill, by injection, or in a number of skin preparations such as a cream, gel, spray, or patch.

Pills are convenient, cheap, and effective, but they are less safe for those of us who smoke or are older than 35. They are more likely than other methods to lead to blood clots. Patches can be very effective and safe, but they need to be worn at all times. They can also irritate the skin.

"I use a generic estradiol patch. It costs about $60 for a month's worth."

Many trans women are interested in estrogen through injection. Estrogen injections tend to cause very high and fluctuating estrogen levels, which can cause mood swings, weight gain, hot flashes, anxiety, or migraines. Of note, these side effects can be seen with any regimen—not just injections, and especially if the dose is high. Little is known about the effects of the peak levels caused by injections over the long term. If injections are used, it should be at a low dose with an understanding that there may be uncomfortable side effects, and that switching off of injections to other forms of estrogen may cause mood swings or hot flashes.

Ashley at the breakfast table (Arthur Robin Williams MD, www.MyRightSelf.org).

> "I began transition by using estrogen patches and spironolactone. . . I also use [estradiol] (Estrace) cream to soften and lubricate my vagina for dilation."

> "I inject estradiol valerate intramuscularly every two weeks (about $50 for a six month supply including equipment). . . I have some modest breast development."

Maximum transitional effects can be achieved with relatively small doses of estrogen. Taking high doses does not make changes happen more quickly. It can, however, endanger our health. For those of us who have genital surgery or orchiectomy (removal of the testicles), our estrogen dose can be lowered even further. Without our testicles we need less estrogen to reach normal female blood levels and maintain our feminine characteristics and overall health.

While taking estrogen and testosterone blockers, our providers may check our estrogen and testosterone levels if we are progressing slowly or having side effects such as migraines or mood swings. However, levels are not always accurate, and what works for one person may not work for another. The most important way to judge whether hormones are effective is by looking at how they affect us physically and emotionally.

> "I was prescribed spironolactone, medroxyprogesterone (Provera), and estradiol. So far, my skin has become softer, my body hair has thinned immensely, I have developed breasts, and my hips have widened."

> "I am currently taking both oral estrogen and spironolactone for HRT. Supposedly, I am producing less testosterone and I have developed small breasts."

There are a number of medicines, known as antiandrogens, that can block testosterone. Most testosterone blockers are very safe, but they can have side effects. The blocker most commonly used, spironolactone (spiro), can cause us to urinate excessively and feel dizzy or lightheaded, especially when we first start taking it. It is important to drink plenty of fluids with this medication. Because spironolactone can be dangerous for people with kidney problems and because it interacts with some blood pressure medicines, it is essential we share our full medical histories with our providers. A rare but potentially dangerous side effect of spironolactone is a large increase in the blood levels of potassium, which could cause our heart to stop. Therefore, while taking this medication we should have our potassium levels checked periodically.

> *"In my 20s I added spironolactone to that mix. The spironolactone helped with redistribution of my bodily fat."*

Finasteride and dutasteride are medicines that prevent the production of dihydrotestosterone (DHT), a specific form of testosterone that has action on the skin, hair, and prostate. These medicines are weaker testosterone blockers than spironolactone but have few side effects, and they are useful for those who cannot tolerate spironolactone. It is unclear whether there is any added benefit of taking one of these medicines at the same time as spironolactone.

Progesterone is a source of constant debate among both trans women and providers. Though it is commonly believed to have a number of benefits, including improved mood and libido, enhanced energy, and better breast development and body fat redistribution, there is very little scientific evidence to support these claims. Nevertheless, some trans women say they experience some or all of these benefits from progesterone. Progesterone (as a class of medications referred to as "progestogens") may be taken as a pill or applied as a cream. There are both bioidentical (micronized progesterone) and synthetic (medroxyprogesterone acetate, cyproterone acetate) forms of this medication. There is not enough evidence to recommend one form versus the other. Some experts argue that progesterone can increase our risk of depression, weight gain, mood swings, or breast cancer. These arguments are rooted in research on cisgender women. It is unclear whether these risks and side effects translate to transgender women.

Progesterone can serve as a testosterone blocker in women who cannot tolerate other blockers or who are having difficulty lowering their testosterone levels while taking blockers. Cyproterone is widely used outside the United States as the primary testosterone blocker in transgender women. Cyproterone, however, is not authorized for sale in the United States for any condition and has been associated with liver problems.

> *"When I first started transition, I took cyproterone acetate to totally shut down testicular testosterone production and finasteride to block processing of testosterone already in my system, along with estradiol sublingually."*

Physical Changes on Transfeminine Hormones

There are many physical, emotional, and sexual changes that result from taking estrogen and testosterone blockers. Many of the effects of hormone therapy are reversible. The degree to which they can be reversed depends on how long we have been taking hormones. Two permanent changes are breast growth and possibly sterility.

The first noticeable changes with transfeminine hormones are often that our skin becomes a bit drier and thinner. Our pores become smaller and there is less oil production. We may become more prone to bruising or cuts, and in the first few weeks we may notice that we sweat less and that the odors of our sweat and urine change. Things may feel different to the touch.

> *"The biggest changes have been in my skin and the development of breasts. My skin, while still oily, is not as acne prone as it was before. In fact, ever since*

adolescence, my back was always like reading Braille. Since being on HRT, it has cleared up. My nose no longer gets blackheads as it did before. It is almost as if my body had been 'allergic' to the testosterone."

"Other than my breasts, the most significant changes for me were psychological. My senses of smell and taste have grown somewhat more acute, and my sense of touch has changed immensely. We don't have much language to describe these changes, but I feel far, far more in touch with my body, connected, with a much clearer, sharper sense of touch. It's kind of analogous to wearing gauze over my ears for twenty years and suddenly having it removed. I also hadn't heard about and wasn't anticipating changes to my senses, so that took me by surprise, though they're very welcome!"

Within a few weeks, many of us begin to develop small "buds" beneath our nipples. These may be slightly painful, especially to the touch, and the right and left side may be uneven. This is the normal course of breast development and the pain typically diminishes significantly over the course of several months.

Breast development varies from person to person. Not everyone develops at the same rate and most of us, even after many years of hormone therapy, can only expect to develop an "A" cup or perhaps a small "B" cup. Like all other women, the breasts of transgender women vary in size and shape and will sometimes be uneven with each other. It is best to wait until 18–24 months on hormones before considering breast augmentation surgery in order to have a good idea of what our natural breast contour will look like.

"Physically I got most of the usual results. Breast development was a disappointment so I later had an augmentation at the same time as my SRS."

"I am very happy with my breasts, they are not super big, but they fit my body image very well. I have not had implants and do not plan to."

"All the women in my family are big girls, and I am totally my mother's daughter. Thankfully my breasts STOPPED at 'C' cups. My sister had TWO reductions, and I think if she'd been able, been allowed to, my Mom would have had a reduction done herself. So my breasts are at a size that I'm happy with."

On transfeminine hormones, our bodies will begin to redistribute weight. Fat will begin to collect around our hips and thighs and the muscles in our arms and legs will become less defined and have a smoother appearance as the fat just below our skin becomes a bit thicker. Hormones do not tend to have a significant effect on the fat in our abdomen or "gut." We can expect our muscle mass and strength to decrease significantly. To maintain muscle tone, and for our general health, exercise is recommended—even just 30 minutes of brisk walking most days of the week. What we eat is also important—the best way to stay healthy is to eat a balanced diet with plenty of vegetables and whole grains, and avoid processed and junk foods, including foods with added sweeteners. Overall, we may gain or lose weight once we begin hormone therapy, depending on our diet, lifestyle, genetics, and muscle mass. What will not change is our bone structure, including our hips, arms, hands, legs, and feet. Some people may notice minor changes in shoe size or height.

"I have had a substantial amount of fat redistribution, have lost a lot of upper body muscle mass, and had a large amount of breast growth."

"I take estrogen daily. I have developed very nice breasts and am seeing other appropriate shifts in bodily form."

"Probably the most amazing change was being able to lift a box of heavy books at first and three months later I could barely push it across the floor."

Our eyes and face will begin to develop a more female appearance as the fat under the skin increases and shifts. Because it can take two or more years for these changes to fully develop, it is probably a good idea to wait at least that long before considering any facial feminization procedures.

> *"Within a few months my face looked different. It was subtle, but significant. I began to see a woman looking back at me in the mirror."*

The hair on our body, including our chest, back, and arms, will decrease in thickness and grow at a slower rate. However, it may not go away all together. Many trans women consider electrolysis or laser treatment. Remember that all women have some body hair and that this is normal. On transfeminine hormones, facial hair may thin a bit and grow slower, but it will rarely go away entirely without electrolysis or laser treatments. For those of us with scalp balding, hormone therapy should slow or stop it, but how much of it will grow back is unknown.

> *"I have only been on the hormones 18 months, and I have seen some great reduction in bodily hair everywhere except the face. On the face, however, it does grow slower."*

> *"My breasts are tender from growth, body fat is shifting around, eyes twinkle more, acne has gone away, skin has softened, and receded hair has regrown."*

Emotional Changes on Transfeminine Hormones

Our overall emotional state may or may not change when we begin taking estrogen or blockers—this varies from person to person. By taking hormones, we are putting our body through a second puberty, which can be an emotional time. Some of us find that we process emotions differently or relate to others in new ways.

> *"Everyone says I look younger. My libido has decreased dramatically, and I am much happier and nicer to others."*

> *"I cry way more than I used to. I'm generally more prone to rapid changes in mood, but I became more content in and at peace with my body. I gained self-confidence."*

Estrogen is typically considered a "female" hormone, and we learn to expect that we will act stereotypically female once we start taking it. However, cisgender women are not universally more emotional than cisgender men, and when they do act differently from cisgender men, the reasons may be more social than physical.

It may be challenging for many of us to experience new hormones coursing through our bodies at the same time that we are making large social changes in our lives. This can be a good time to start seeing a therapist, who may be able to help us explore our new thoughts and feelings, and help us to get to know our new bodies.

Sexual and Reproductive Changes on Transfeminine Hormones

Soon after beginning hormone treatment, we typically experience a decrease in the number of erections we have. When we do have erections, we may lose the ability to penetrate, because our erections will not be as firm or last as long. We should, however, still have erotic sensations and be able to orgasm.

> *"I never have spontaneous erections anymore."*

> *"My semen became clear, and reduced greatly in volume."*

Some of us find that we get erotic pleasure from different sex acts and different parts of our bodies. We may find different images and activities more or less arousing than we did before. Orgasms may last longer, and feel like more of a whole-body experience, but with less peak intensity. We may experience ejaculation of a small amount of clear or white fluid, or perhaps no fluid. This is all healthy—as long as it feels healthy to you. Do not be afraid to explore and experiment with your new sexuality through masturbation and with sex toys such as dildos and vibrators.

If any of the sexual changes on hormones are concerning, there are ways to address this. Changing our doses of testosterone blockers can sometimes help. As always, it is important to talk to a provider before changing medication doses. In addition, there are other things that we can do to retain erectile function independently of hormones. Medications like sildenafil (Viagra) or tadalafil (Cialis) that improve erectile function in cisgender men with erectile dysfunction can be beneficial for those of us who wish to retain erections while on hormones. We may also benefit from other treatments for erectile dysfunction, such as suction pumps.

Hormone therapy can cause a decrease in the size of the testicles. For some of us, they shrink to less than half their original size. Most experts agree that the amount of scrotal skin available for future genital surgery is not affected.

Within a few months of beginning hormone therapy, we must assume that we will become permanently and irreversibly sterile. Some people may maintain a sperm count on hormone therapy, or have their sperm count return after stopping hormone therapy, but many do not.

If there is any chance you may want to parent a child from your own sperm, you should speak to your provider about preserving your sperm in a sperm bank. This process generally takes two to four weeks and costs roughly $2,000–$3,000. The sperm should be stored before beginning hormone therapy. All too often, we decide later in life that we would like to parent a child using our own sperm but we are unable to do so because we did not take the steps to preserve sperm before beginning hormone treatment.

Mel and Allie (Arthur Robin Williams MD, www.MyRightSelf.org).

For those of us on hormones but remaining sexually active with someone who could become pregnant, we should always continue to use a birth control method to prevent unwanted pregnancy. As always, safe sex and testing for sexually transmitted infections and HIV as appropriate are very important.

Risks and Side Effects of Taking Transfeminine Hormone Regimens

One well-known risk of taking estrogen is an increase is the likelihood of blood clots, which can move to our lungs and cause us to stop breathing. If we are taking a safe and appropriately monitored regimen, as well as avoiding cigarette smoking, the risk of blood clots is minimal. The type of estrogen we take may impact our risk for blood clots. There are different forms of estrogen. 17-beta estradiol is also known as bio-identical estrogen. This estrogen is identical to the estrogen created in a human ovary. Research on this form of estrogen is reassuring with respect to risk of blood clots. Other forms of estrogen include ethinyl estradiol, which is a synthetic estrogen found in birth control pills, and conjugated equine estrogens ("CEE," Premarin), a form of estrogen obtained by keeping horses pregnant, collecting their urine, and isolating the estrogen in the urine in order to make it into pill form. There is evidence that synthetic estrogen may increase risk of blood clots or other side effects such as stroke.

TRANSNATURAL: HOLISTIC SUPPORT FOR TRANS BODIES AND SPIRITS

Dori Midnight is a community-based healer and educator who teaches workshops on community healing and queer magic and maintains a local and distance healing practice in western Massachusetts. Jacoby Ballard is a genderqueer trans guy and cofounder of Third Root Community Health Center in Brooklyn, where he teaches yoga (including queer and trans yoga) and Third Root's Herbal

Dori Midnight   Jacoby Ballard

Education Program. Together, Dori and Jacoby are available to come to your school, community center, or gathering to teach workshops on herbal support for trans health.

Herbal medicine has always been a people's medicine. All over the world, people use plants for their health in daily ways. Herbal medicine is accessible, affordable, empowering, and grassroots; it is also powerful because it allows us to take care of ourselves and each other and puts our wellness in our own hands.

There are many ways to bring more herbal and holistic medicine into our lives as transgender or gender nonconforming people. Herbs and nutrition can be used to support our bodies before and after surgery, to support our mental and emotional well-being, and to maintain health for the rest of our lives.

Herbs, like people, are unique, and there is no one herb for everyone. We recommend finding an herbalist, acupuncturist, or other holistic practitioner in your area if you're interested in using more natural ways to support your health.

"Transition" means something different to every trans person. However, the medical path that is offered to us can often be linear in a way that our transitions are not. Holistic medicine, which supports and encourages people to be wherever they are at, is particularly well suited to meet the varied paths we each may take. There are many herbs that can help increase the effects of hormones. There are also many that can mitigate side effects, including anxiety, acne, hair loss, and heart disease.

Herbs, nutrition, and some nutritional supplements can also greatly support the body's natural healing process from surgery. You can use herbs for the nausea, sleep difficulties, and pain that you may experience. If you are taking both herbs and pharmaceutical medications, make sure to let your providers and pharmacists know, in order to avoid "drug-drug" or "herb-drug" interactions. Well before surgery, let your surgeon know what herbs you are taking because many surgeons will want you to stop taking certain herbs (especially those that can increase bleeding) for a period of time before surgery.

For more information on holistic approaches to health for trans folks, look for the yahoogroup "transnatural."

In addition to increasing the risk of blood clots, estrogen can also raise our blood pressure. High blood pressure can lead to problems, including vision trouble and blindness, kidney disease requiring dialysis, strokes, heart attacks, and heart failure. High blood pressure causes few symptoms at first, so we may not recognize that we have it.

> "I also have concerns about the long-term health effects of estrogens on everything from cholesterol profiles and heart disease to cancer risk to liver function and beyond."

High cholesterol is also a condition with few initial symptoms. By the time we develop problems from high cholesterol, such as heart attacks or strokes, the damage has been done. Progestogens (especially the synthetic ones found in medications like medroxyprogesterone, as well as "street" hormone products such as Perluetal and Progravidinona) may raise "bad" (LDL) cholesterol as well as triglycerides. High triglycerides can lead to a dangerous inflammation of the pancreas called pancreatitis. Estrogen tends to lower bad cholesterol, but certain synthetic forms may cause it to rise. Whether this rise ends up changing our risk for heart disease and strokes is not known. A provider can monitor cholesterol with a simple blood test obtained after an eight-hour fast, usually performed in the morning before breakfast. In addition to making sure we are on the correct dosage of hormones, a provider will also be able to help us control our cholesterol through diet, exercise, vitamins, or prescription medications if needed.

In addition to monitoring our blood pressure and cholesterol, our providers will also run lab tests to monitor our kidney and liver function, as well as a diabetes screening test. Estrogen, like other hormones, can affect our liver because that is where our body breaks down hormones. For some of us, estrogen can lead to changes in our body weight and fat distribution, and it can affect our likelihood of developing diabetes.

While we are taking estrogen, we are thought to have some protection from developing osteoporosis—weakened bones that can lead to fractures as we age. For those of us who have an orchiectomy (removal of the testicles) or vaginoplasty (in which the testicles are typically also removed), we can often take a lower dose of hormones. However, we should remain on at least a low dose of estrogen until we are 50, or perhaps older, to prevent weakening of our bones.

There is not much scientific evidence regarding the risks of cancer in transgender women. It is likely that our risk of prostate cancer decreases when we start taking hormones. In fact, in many cases of prostate cancer, the treatment is testosterone blockage, and in some cases also the administration of estrogen. However, recent research suggests that estrogen may play a role of its own in certain prostate cancers. The prostate-specific antigen (PSA) test used sometimes for cisgender men for prostate cancer screening may not be as useful when taking estrogen. It is best to continue to follow the current recommendations for prostate cancer screening.

Risk of breast cancer in transgender women is not well understood. From what knowledge we do have, it seems that taking hormones may slightly increase our risk of breast cancer. However, we are still at lower risk than cisgender women. When we have been on hormones for at least two to three years, we should begin regular breast cancer screenings based on our age and other risk factors, such as family history.

Medical providers taking care of transgender women are typically aware of another risk of estrogen—a prolactinoma, a benign (noncancerous) tumor of the pituitary gland. The pituitary gland controls many of the hormone systems in our body. It is about the size of a pea and rests inside the skull behind our eyes. Parts of the pituitary gland can grow in response to estrogen therapy. If a benign tumor grows large enough, it can press on the nerves coming from our eyes into our brain and cause visual problems. Pituitary tumors can be treated by surgery or medication.

There are limited and conflicting data on the risk of prolactinoma from taking hormones. Some providers recommend periodic checks of the level of the hormone prolactin.

Others disagree and instead just watch for vision complaints. One argument against testing prolactin is that it is elevated in many people who are taking estrogen, including those of us who have no tumor. If you are found to have a high prolactin level, your provider should lower or stop your estrogen dosing for several weeks, and then recheck the level. If it has gone down, then you do not likely have a tumor and may resume taking estrogen. Checking estrogen and testosterone levels at this point is also a good idea, because the high prolactin level might have been because your estrogen dose was too high. If prolactin levels do not go down when estrogen is lowered or stopped, the provider may send you for a computed tomography (CT) scan or magnetic resonance image (MRI) to evaluate for prolactinoma.

CONCLUSION

Starting hormones can be exciting. Try to be patient and remember that all of the changes associated with the puberty you are about to experience can take years to develop. We may not always like every change, but many of them come together, and we have to accept the positive with the negative if we want to continue taking hormones. Finally, our hormonal treatment does not exist in a vacuum. Our health, diet, lifestyle, stress management, sleep, and other factors are even more important when we are making changes to our bodies.

REFERENCES AND FURTHER READING

Alegria, C. A. (2011). Transgender identity and health care: Implications for psychosocial and physical evaluation. *Journal of the American Academy of Nurse Practitioners, 23*(4), 175–182.

Byne, W., Bradley, S. J., Coleman, E., Eyler, A. E., Green, R., Menvielle, E. J.,...Tomkins, D. A. (2012). Report of the American Psychiatric Association Task Force on treatment of gender identity disorder. *Archives of Sexual Behavior, 41*(4), 759–796.

Ettner, R., Monstrey, S., & Eyler, A. E. (Eds.). (2007). *Principles of transgender medicine and surgery.* New York, NY: Haworth Press.

Gooren, L. J. (2011). Clinical practice. Care of transsexual persons. *New England Journal of Medicine, 364*(13), 1251–1257.

Gooren, L. J., & Giltay, E. J. (2008). Review of studies of androgen treatment of female-to-male transsexuals: Effects and risks of administration of androgens to females. *Journal of Sexual Medicine, 5*(4), 765–776.

Hembree, W. C., Cohen-Kettenis, P., Delemarre-van de Waal, H. A., Gooren, L. J., Meyer, W. J., III, Spack, N. P.,...Montori, V. M. (2009). Endocrine treatment of transsexual persons: An Endocrine Society clinical practice guideline. *Journal of Clinical Endocrinology and Metabolism, 94*(9), 3132–3154.

Vancouver Coastal Health, Transcend Transgender Support and Education Society, & Canadian Rainbow Health. (2006). *Endocrine therapy for transgender adults in British Columbia: Suggested guidelines.* Retrieved January 2014, from: http://transhealth.vch.ca/resources/library/tcpdocs/guidelines-endocrine.pdf

Williamson, C. (2010). Providing care to transgender persons: A clinical approach to primary care, hormones, and HIV management. *Journal of the Association of Nurses in AIDS Care, 21*(3), 221–229.

World Professional Association for Transgender Health. (2008). *WPATH clarification on medical necessity of treatment, sex reassignment, and insurance coverage for transgender and transsexual people worldwide.* Retrieved January 2014, from http://www.wpath.org/site_page.cfm?pk_association_webpage_menu=1352&pk_association_webpage=3947

World Professional Association for Transgender Health. (2011). *Standards of care for the health of transsexual, transgender, and gender nonconforming people, seventh version.* Retrieved January 2014, from http://www.wpath.org/uploaded_files/140/files/IJT%20SOC,%20V7.pdf

Xavier, J., & Bradford, J. (2005). Transgender health access in Virginia: Focus group report. *Virginia Department of Health.* Retrieved January 2014, from http://www.vdh.state.va.us/epidemiology/DiseasePrevention/documents/THIFocusGroupReport.pdf

SURGICAL TRANSITION

Jules Chyten-Brennan

13

FOR SOME OF US, SURGERY is a natural step in our process. For others, it is never part of the plan. No matter what we ultimately decide, most of us at least grapple with the question of surgery because of our own or others' curiosities about it. It is often assumed that every trans person desires surgery, and that without constraints it would be a matter simply of when, not if. Truthfully, however, each of us relates to our body differently and makes individual choices to best suit our needs. We may have many surgeries or no surgeries, and it is important to recognize that each decision is just as right as the next.

For some of us, surgery may be extremely important to our sense of self, while others of us never wish to have surgery. For many more of us, our feelings lie somewhere in between, and we must evaluate personal desires and logistical supports and constraints.

> "I didn't so much decide to have this surgery as I felt I could not go on living without it."

> "I have no desire to surgically modify my body because I would like to find a way to become comfortable with my body as it is."

> "I've known even since before I started identifying as genderqueer that I didn't like my breasts. They were big and didn't look good, and were of no use to me. I wanted to be able to wear clothes that didn't hide my body, and to be able to take my clothes off without my body sending false signals about who I was."

There are a variety of terms used to describe transgender-related surgeries. Some of these include gender-affirming surgery (GAS), gender reassignment surgery (GRS), sex reassignment surgery (SRS), and gender-confirming surgery (GCS). These terms are often used interchangeably as umbrella terms that encompass all possible procedures undertaken in the process of surgical transition. In some contexts they are used specifically in reference to genital surgeries.

THE SOCIAL MEANING OF SURGERIES

As trans people, we are often asked whether we have had "the surgery." This question implies (falsely) that there is one single surgery to get and we all desire it. In most contexts, this question of "the surgery" refers to "bottom," or genital surgery. Our surgical status as "pre-op" or pre-operative versus "post-op" or post-operative is also often used to judge whether we have "completed" transition.

Within our own communities, we also sometimes make judgments about other trans people based on the kinds of surgeries they have or have not gotten. We may believe that someone is not committed enough to being trans if they have not had particular types of surgeries.

How anyone's gender is perceived on a daily basis is not related to our genitals at all—we never see, or even think about, most people's genitals, and yet we manage to relate to people as a certain gender without knowing this information. However, when our trans identity is revealed, our surgical status becomes crucial to others to place us in a new box.

The curiosity and expectation about having genital surgeries also has to do with the belief that we need to be able to fulfill particular sexual roles, with either insertive or receptive sexual acts. The assumption here is that we are transitioning with the goal of becoming more heterosexual as opposed to more ourselves. This is made more explicit when trans people openly engage in same-sex or queer relationships. Confused outsiders frequently ask, "Well, why didn't you just stay a (boy/girl)?"

Why then is it so important to know the status of a trans person's genitals—or if we have had "the surgery?" Perhaps when the world can consider that sexual orientation and gender identity exist as natural healthy spectrums, we will not hear this question quite so often.

FACTORS AFFECTING OUR DECISIONS ABOUT SURGERY

There are numerous factors affecting our decisions about surgery, and they are different for each of us. We may desire surgery but not be able to afford it. Some of us may be able to afford it but might not feel the likely results will meet our expectations. Many of

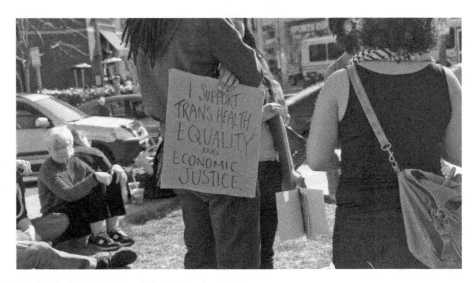

2013 rally (photo by Ted Eytan, MD, Washington, D.C.).

Yahoo groups for learning more about surgery include ftmsurgeryinfo, MTF-SRS-FTM, ftmphalloplastyinfo, FFS-support, Finances_SurgeryFTM, TheDecidingline, and ftmmetoidioplasty.

Because of the social associations between gender and specific body parts, many of us feel uncomfortable with the standard anatomical names used to describe our bodies. Some of us choose alternate names for our body parts. Others of us separate the individual parts from their gendered associations and refer to "people with ovaries," for example, instead of "people with female parts." In this chapter, we largely use this second approach for the purposes of clarity. However, feel free to cross out and replace any words you do not like with your own. See Chapter 17 for more about naming our own body parts.

us postpone surgery, even if we could have it earlier, because we want to make sure that other things in our life are taken care of, such as mending relationships with our partners or preserving our fertility.

Cost

The majority of gender-affirming surgeries are not covered by insurance, and so many of us have to pay for them out of pocket. Cost, therefore, is one of the most common considerations we have to take into account. For an idea of the range of prices for different types of surgeries, see the sections on each procedure later in this chapter. On top of surgical expenses, additional funds are required for medical clearance, travel, hotels, aftercare, and time off from work. For most people these are sizeable expenditures. As trans people, we are disproportionately in lower socioeconomic brackets, making the financial burden even more prohibitive.

> "I. . . have no job and have had fruitless searches for a part-time job ever since I transitioned. The thought of future medical bills and how I'll ever pay for my vagina scares and depresses me."

> "I can't afford surgery, and the lottery hasn't helped me any."

If the cost is not out of reach, the question becomes whether surgery is worth the expense, or if other priorities take precedence.

> "At this time I do not anticipate having SRS. It's not that I would mind having a fully female body (where's that magic wand when you need it?), but I don't feel that I want it bad enough to justify the cost and risk/discomfort of major surgery."

Others of us feel that surgery is a necessary step toward gaining financial security. The ability to "pass" may mean more confidence in the job market and more comfort in the workplace.

> "I had a thyroid cartilage reduction, partly to increase passability last year while I was looking for a new job. I didn't want part of my appearance to be out of the ordinary and cost me a chance to work, although that surgery hadn't previously been a big priority. I am glad that I had it done and I feel much more confident now that it's all healed up and while I hadn't thought it was so important, it turned out to have a really big impact on how I see myself and I wish I had considered it sooner."

HEALTH AND WELLNESS

ON TOP SURGERY, CHESTS AND RACE/CLASS PRIVILEGE

Kay Ulanday Barrett

I have always been at the cusp of different cultures. I went to a liberal university but felt surrounded by white, affluent people. This translated into the queer and transgender community. We carved queer and trans people of color (QTPOC) space, but having spaces for trans people of color was seen as too militant or as snobby, and it was dubbed as separatism or as a "gang approach."

The mostly white, affluent people around me in school tended to have insurance, and benevolently liberal families. So much of the FTM community ushered themselves into liberal white, male, able-bodied privilege that I didn't want to affiliate my manhood or boihood with them. I was at the cusp; in my own neighborhood I could be a kuya, butch, AG, stud, or brown boi, but out of place with my upwardly mobile language and not having to do manual labor or struggle with language barriers the way much of my blood family has.

I attended a "top/chest surgery for FTMs" workshop held at an Asian and Pacific Islander health clinic, but more than half of the attendees were white and hadn't considered any of the negative cultural implications of white people taking up space at an LGBTQ POC organization that serves immigrant communities. That community also had a troubling, evident financial privilege. Several mentioned their insurance, or their families who could pay for top surgery, without even considering that the clinic served low-income and working-class Asians, migrant workers, and queer, trans, and HIV-positive immigrants.

This is a trend in many liberal and mainstream Asian and Pacific Islander spaces, sometimes carried out in our internalized racism. Queer, trans, and gender nonconforming people of color and low-income people in the United States have issues accessing surgery, but they also deal with concerns related to housing, the medical industrial complex, foster care, homelessness, police brutality, and more.

I am in a different place than I was five years ago, or eight years ago. When I was younger, growing up Midwestern and in a segregated Chicagoan space, forging queer, gender nonconforming, and trans person of color joy was hard, but happened on a daily basis, whether it's your homey going with you to the Medicaid office or you asking someone to help you process your late food stamps.

When I "was" a woman of color dyke/butch/AG, white feminist womyn would call me their "sister." That word *sister* rotted in me, for so many reasons. I do not feel at home with whiteness. I can no longer open my heart up to it, unless it is about redistribution of resources and not taking up space. I now see how my brotherhood, my boihood, is developed and building. I am not your little brown brother, white people. We are not starting at the same line or "in this together," as you may say.

My body and existence—as I grow, evolve, and become—cannot be bogged down by white expectations, but must be of brown/mixed/black/of color creation and preexisting cultures. I am excited to call my homeys and hear their stories, how they felt when their Nigerian, Filipin@, Latin@, Chinese, upsouth Black boi manhoods came up.

White trans and queer people specifically, when you are taking up space in brown, person of color, mixed trans and queer communities, know that I see you. Our brown and mixed lives are not to be toured through like a vacation getaway. Just because we might hold the transgender or queer or masculine or male banner together, we are not the same.

Relationships

Our loved ones have emotional investments in our bodies and life choices. The decision to have surgery may cause an emotional response in those closest to us. Even within relatively supportive relationships, there may be some apprehension caused by concern for our physical safety, fear of potential regret, or grief over a perceived loss of who we "were." The impact on our relationships can be an important part of our decision-making process. We may grapple with the possible outcomes of our decisions and work with our loved ones to develop understanding before we take action. Some of us may wait a period of time until we have worked through some of these issues with our partners.

> *"Decided against top surgery due to potential loss of nipple sensation and potential impact on my current relationship."*

> *"My partner doesn't seem to care if I keep it or not, and I don't ever intend to have sex with a guy (gay or straight), so having a vagina isn't as critical. And to be honest, at age 56, I don't look at the issue of having the right plumbing with as much anxiety as younger trans people."*

Reproductive Capacity

Some transition-related surgeries alter our reproductive organs, which can affect our fertility. For some of us, knowing that we have reproductive organs that belong to a sex with which we do not identify becomes a strong source of discord. Hence, surgical removal is a high priority. Others of us choose to hold off on surgery until after we have children or store our sperm or eggs for reproductive purposes before we have surgery. Chapters 11 and 18 provide more information on fertility options for us as trans people.

> "I have not had gender-related surgery except getting my tubes tied. I insisted on that because it was all my insurance would cover and simply being fertile as a 'woman' was humiliating."

> "Preserving my fertility is a big reason I ruled out transition (at least in the near future). I know trans men can sometimes give birth, but I'm not willing to risk it. . . I wish I could make sperm, but transition won't give me that. I'm becoming a bit less scared of the womb and birth side of things."

Safety

Violence against trans communities is a real threat that we are all aware of, and it affects some of us more directly than others. Therefore, some of us seek out surgery in order to be read correctly and, hence, feel safer.

> "I have had MtF genital revision surgery. . . including bilateral orchiectomy, vaginoplasty by penile inversion technique and labiaplasty. . . When I began transition, the ultimate goal was always to have surgery. Because of where I live, remaining in a transitory state—living full time without surgery—was just too dangerous. . . I have been very satisfied by the results."

> "I would have had facial feminization surgery as well had it been on offer and if I could have afforded it. When I have been read in public, it has always been my facial structure that made people suspicious. Regardless of any vanity concerns, I would have been much safer with that surgery."

Some of us, however, also avoid surgery for similar reasons, and instead we want to retain the ability to be read as our gender assigned at birth.

> "I must present as a male in my career, so I have deferred any decision on surgery."

Surgical Fears and Knowledge of Realistic Outcomes

Some of us fear surgery itself or the surgical process. Previous surgical experiences, good or bad, may influence how enthusiastic we are about "going under the knife" again.

> "I have not had any gender-related surgery. I like my body as is, and I've had non-gender-related surgery and that experience was miserable. . ."

> "I doubt I'd go through with it. . . if only because I have a strong aversion to having to see medical professionals for anything. Surgery is generally not something I'd want to go through ever again."

Some of us fear potential surgical complications or do not think the results will be satisfying. For example, although we may desire a certain procedure, we may fear disappointment because of poor cosmetic outcomes, loss of sensation, loss of orgasmic ability, or urinary complications. We may want a newly contoured chest but fear scars. Some of us doubt that available surgical procedures will live up to our expectations for our imagined selves.

> "I have thought about SRS for a long time, literally even before I identified as trans/genderqueer. But now that I know more about it, I really am not interested in going under the knife and risking my life for something that's not going to work so well."

> "I was scared of surgery for the longest time, but I really wanted to be able to experience my sexuality the way it worked in my head. The results are still pending. It's beginning to look like you'd expect, but things are still sore and there are still bits that are very red. Sensation is just beginning to return, but

I don't yet know how much sensation I'm going to have, or whether I can have an orgasm."

SILICONE INJECTIONS

As an alternative to surgery, some trans people use injection of free silicone or "pumping" to enhance their hips, buttocks, breasts, lips, cheekbones, and other body parts. The practice has gained increasing coverage in the news and has been a source of friction between some trans communities and the greater medical community due to the importance it holds for those who use it and the associated health risks the practice poses.

Why do some trans people use silicone injections? Cost is often the major determining factor in whether we are able to get the surgical procedures we need. Silicone injection may cost up to 90% less than traditional surgeries, making it more widely accessible. Many of us also prefer to avoid contact with medical providers due to previous negative experiences or fears of maltreatment.

What is silicone? Silicones are a family of chemical substances that are used for different purposes—from medical equipment and implants to industrial engineering. The specific makeup of different types of silicone varies based on what it is used for. Medical silicone, for example, is a much purer form of silicone than that used for other purposes.

How is silicone used medically? In medical contexts, silicone implants are enclosed in pouches designed to prevent the silicone from leaking out. Use of free silicone is not considered safe by the Food and Drug Administration outside of very specific eye surgeries. Certain medical providers—plastic surgeons and dermatologists—have developed "off-label" techniques (not approved by the FDA) in which free silicone injections are given in certain circumstances such as to counter the facial lipoatrophy (wasting) that sometimes happens in people with HIV. These procedures involve very small amounts of silicone—a couple of milliliters (less than half of a teaspoon)—injected into the face over multiple visits.

How are free silicone injections different than silicone implants? Injection of "free silicone" means that the silicone is not encased but instead injected directly into muscles and fat. This means it may move from the spot it is originally injected into or interact with the tissue surrounding it.

How are silicone injections different when performed outside of a medical context? Outside of a medical context, free silicone injections are often given in the quantity of liters (picture a 2-liter bottle of soda), which is up to a thousand times more than that used in medical contexts. Also, free silicone—unless specifically labeled as such—may not be medically graded, and it could be another form of silicone not designed for use in humans. It may therefore have additional toxic effects on the body or have substances other than silicone added to it.

Why are free silicone injections considered dangerous? There is consensus in the medical community that use of free silicone injections poses significant health risks. The degree of risk may increase based on the specific techniques and sanitation used for injection, the amount and quality of silicone injected, the site of placement, and the training of the person doing the injections. Many medical providers have seen their patients suffer greatly, or even die, because of infections, inflammation, necrosis (death to the tissue), or other serious and dangerous outcomes of having injected free silicone.

Examples of specific risks associated with silicone injections include the following:

- *Migration.* Free silicone injected at one spot may move through the body to end up in another, causing painful and disfiguring lumps. For example, silicone injected into the hips may end up behind the knees.
- *Infections.* These can occur at the site of the injections and can also spread throughout the body when they reach the bloodstream. Infections can cause damage and scarring at injection sites, and they can become life threatening when more widespread.

- *Pulmonary embolism.* Bits of silicone can migrate into the bloodstream (they are then known as emboli) and block blood vessels in the lungs. There, they can damage the lungs and cause a sudden and life-threatening condition.
- *Damage to other organs.* Bits of silicone can also become lodged in blood vessels leading to other organs, such as the brain, the heart, or the kidneys, and cause strokes, heart attacks, or kidney damage.

The potential dangerous effects of silicone can occur within minutes, weeks, or even years after injection. Because some of the harmful outcomes can happen very suddenly, it is important to know what to watch out for. Many symptoms that can result from silicone injection are not specific and could have another medical cause. However, any of the following symptoms after injection of silicone should prompt an immediate trip to the nearest emergency department:

- Shortness of breath
- Worsening warmth, redness, and swelling around the injection site
- Fever
- Dizziness
- A racing heartbeat
- Chest pain
- Nausea or vomiting
- Confusion

On arriving, it is critical to tell the health care providers there that silicone was injected so that they can provide the correct treatments. For example, the body's immune response to silicone may appear the same as an infection but require a completely different treatment. It is also important not to delay seeking treatment or to withhold information for any period of time. The most serious complications from silicone injection are very time sensitive. The faster the proper treatment is applied, the better the chances for survival.

SILICONE USE IN THE TRANSGENDER COMMUNITY

Aamina Morrison is a specialist and co-coordinator at the Trans-health Information Project (TIP).

Free-flowing silicone is a commonly known option for body modification among transgender women of color. With all of the crazy stories floating around about silicone usage, it is understandable that there are fears.

Many sites that are in support of professional cosmetic surgery procedures have demonized those who use silicone for a few decades now, magnifying the toxicity of its usage in free-flowing form, and characterizing individuals (especially transwomen of color) as lazy, poorly educated, and undesirable. With all of the horror stories and warnings that are given, we must examine the reasons why individuals, especially a community as disenfranchised and marginalized as the trans community of color, resort to these options for furthering their transition. It's very simple: Money.

The economy only makes it harder for us to obtain employment, and even then we may not have medical coverage for basic primary care. When we factor in discrimination, societal exile, and the desperate need to further one's transition at any cost, we have the formula for why our community is in such turmoil.

Imagine everyone—your peers, your friends, the media—recommending these professional options without trying to fix the far larger problems at hand. The blatant discrimination against trans individuals as a whole prevents sex reassignment surgery from being included in medical coverage, and the very old argument that the transgender experience is a disorder is still prevalent. Until these larger issues are addressed, silicone injections are not going anywhere.

It is important to make sure that our primary care providers know our history of silicone pumping for the same reasons that they should know our other surgical history. In addition, if we ever have complications at the sites where silicone was injected, any provider we see about this should be made aware. For example, if months or years later we get redness, warmth, and swelling over a site where we had silicone injected, this can look very much like a skin infection called cellulitis. However, it is more likely to be an immune reaction to the silicone. A provider who knows about our silicone use can provide us with the appropriate treatment, which may include a short course of steroid medications like prednisone instead of antibiotics, which will not help the problem.

Stories exist about people administering silicone as opportunists in order to exploit trans people. There are also many people who perform silicone injection and may be doing so as a service to friends or community members rather than as an attempt to exploit us.

It is important for trans people using free silicone and for medical providers to be able to have honest and open dialogue about this issue. Many of us have felt judged and ridiculed by our providers who tell us not to do it, and many medical providers feel frustrated by a practice they see harming their patients. More work needs to be done to bridge this gap in communication.

THE SURGICAL PROCESS

Going for surgery, gender related or not, can be a daunting process for anyone. For many trans people, fear of discrimination, the need to find highly specific surgeons, and the added steps necessary for approval can make the process especially difficult. The best way to embark on the journey of getting surgery is to first equip ourselves with knowledge about what to expect.

Choosing a Surgeon

Doctors designated as appropriate to perform trans surgeries are trained in the fields of Plastic Surgery, General Surgery, Urologic Surgery, or Gynecologic Surgery, as specified by the World Professional Association for Transgender Health (WPATH). Generally, these surgeons are board certified, meaning they have passed additional examinations of competency within their respective specialty. However, most surgeons obtain their transgender surgical experience through a combination of specialization skills and apprenticeship with another surgeon or surgeons already performing these procedures. Specific fellowships in transgender surgery, done after residency, are not currently available in the United States.

Because of this lack of ability to credential surgeons, there have been cases in which surgeons without proper training in these procedures performed them, and this may remain a problem until a certifiable fellowship is established. Dr. Stanley Biber, who is considered by some to be the father of American gender-affirming surgery, performed his first surgery on a transgender woman in 1969 after adapting his surgical technique from drawings obtained from Johns Hopkins.

Choosing a surgeon requires consumer savvy in weighing personal needs, the intimacy needs of one's partner, surgical offerings, and price and location of surgery, in combination with the surgeon's reputation (person-to-person and online), potential complications and complication rates, functional and aesthetic surgical outcomes, recovery times, accessibility, waiting list, postsurgery care, and good old-fashioned "bedside manner."

Here are some questions to consider:

- If you have a specific surgery in mind (and assuming you are eligible for that surgery), does your chosen surgeon perform and feel comfortable with that surgery? For example, you would prefer periareolar (keyhole) top surgery. Is your chosen surgeon comfortable with this surgery, and are you an appropriate anatomical candidate?
- Are aesthetic outcomes a top priority? Functional outcomes? Complication rates? What is the surgeon's track record for results with the type of procedure you desire?
- Where is the surgeon located, and what would it mean to travel there? Is it important to be close for possible follow-up needs, or is there another local provider who could manage follow-up care? What about having surgery abroad?

- How much does the surgeon charge for a given procedure? There is no standardized list of costs for trans surgeries. This means prices may vary greatly from one surgeon to another, so it may be worth it to comparison shop a bit if this is a concern. What will be the other prices involved in the surgery (for example, anesthesiologist and hospital or surgical center payments)? If you have insurance, does the surgeon accept your insurance and will they help you preauthorize the care or do you have to pay in full and then appeal for reimbursement? What type of copay will you have?
- What type of reputation does the surgeon have for "bedside manner?" Some people are entirely focused on results, while for others the process plays a role in their decision making. Surgeons are people, too, and come with personalities of their own. If this matters, finding out more about others' experiences might be important before getting rolling with your own. Many trans surgeons have patients that are willing to talk about their experiences, so it is worth it to ask the surgeon's office for contacts or to look online for reviews.

As with many other resources for us, we may rely on personal referrals by friends and extended community networks as the first line of investigation. Being able to hear about the experience firsthand from someone we know will help prepare us for the process, and it may be an opportunity to see the results of a surgeon's work firsthand. Many surgeons also have Web sites with pictures of their results.

TransBucket is an online resource for comparing and sharing surgical outcomes.

We can also ask trans-friendly medical providers or mental health providers for recommendations or referrals. LGBT-specialized medical clinics collectively see large numbers of trans people before and after surgery and may also refer us to a proper surgeon. Some have even assembled information packets, which explain surgical options and outline the surgical process. These providers see relatively high numbers of different surgeons' results while providing follow-up medical care. They may have information on how satisfied patients were with their particular surgeons, and they may help us set realistic expectations. They are also likely familiar with the presurgical requirements for local surgeons.

If traveling is a possibility, a number of conferences around the world offer gathering places for trans people, where there are sometimes surgery workshops. These

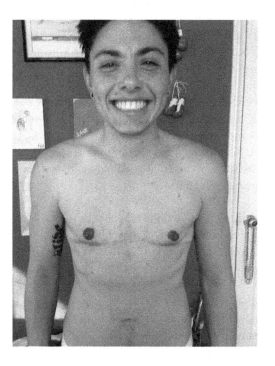

Franco.

include the True Spirit Conference, the Philadelphia Trans Health Conference, Seattle's Gender Odyssey, California's Transgender Leadership Summit, and Canada's CPATH Conference, among others. There, we can meet other trans people, talk about the experience of getting surgery, and get information about trans surgeons. Some surgeons attend these conferences themselves and give presentations on their surgical techniques. Some conferences also have "show and tell" events for trans people considering surgery. Willing trans people who have previously undergone surgery show their results and talk about their experiences.

Preparing for Surgery

Before being approved for surgery, there are a number of steps we must go through to satisfy surgeons' preoperative criteria. Some of the requirements are standard for most types of nonemergency surgeries, while others are specific to the particular surgeons and the surgeries they perform.

To start the process, most of us set up an initial consultation with a potential surgeon or surgeons. At this first visit, we have an opportunity to discuss our goals and ask questions. We may also get a feel for what it is like to interact with the surgeon and the surgical team. The surgeon may perform a physical exam and discuss different surgical options and what they believe are realistic surgical expectations. They should explain the different procedures in detail and inform us of possible risks and complications. If we have a specific surgical technique in mind, it is important to bring this up at the consultation and ask whether the surgeon feels comfortable with that technique in our case. Some surgeons provide free initial consultations, but most charge $100–$300 for the appointment.

Before the initial consultation, it is a good idea to think about and write down any questions. Whether we are excited, or nervous, or neither, the experience can be disorienting. Having questions ready can help make sure we get them all out there. For that reason and others, it is also a good idea to bring someone we trust with us to help gather and retain information. Here are some things to consider addressing:

- The different surgical techniques that particular surgeon has to offer
- The advantages, disadvantages, and limitations of each type of surgery
- Any before and after pictures available of prior patients
- The inherent and patient-specific risks of each surgical procedure
- Expectations about the appearance (scars, etc.) and function of that part of the body after surgery

Once we decide to pursue surgery with a particular surgeon, there are several other providers we may need to see first. The primary care provider who sees us prior to surgery helps us to determine whether we are physically healthy enough for surgery. A mental health provider may also be required to recommend us to have surgery. Many of us have strong feelings about the requirements imposed for hormones and surgery. Some of us as trans people are involved in organizations like WPATH so that we can be a part of helping to establish fair guidelines.

When we are seen by a primary care provider prior to surgery, the first step will be to examine us and assess our medical history and risk factors for undergoing surgery. This is sometimes referred to as "surgical clearance." For young and healthy people, this may involve a single office visit and a few lab tests. If we have certain medical conditions or are older than 40, additional tests such as a chest X-ray or electrocardiogram (EKG) may be required. Infrequently, if we have significant medical problems such as heart disease, our primary care provider may require that we have a consultation with a specialist like a cardiologist before clearance can be given. If chest reconstruction is being performed, we may also need to have a mammogram done before surgery if we are older than a certain age or have a family history of breast cancer. All of this is standard for any planned

Gatekeeping

Historically, the relationships between trans people and the medical and mental health fields have been rocky. Providers have often been perceived as playing the role of gatekeepers, holding us back from our ability to transition. For this reason, many of us have felt forced to convey a textbook story of having been born one gender trapped in the body of the other in order to satisfy providers and to secure the necessary approval for transition. Others have chosen to avoid medical and mental health care altogether. While this aversion may be understandable, it is important to recognize the potential benefits of working with trans-friendly providers, many of whom strive to be *gate openers* in helping us access care. No matter how we feel about our surgical decisions and process, it can be an emotionally tumultuous time, and having a skilled mental health professional on our support team can be invaluable. Likewise, medical providers can be valuable advocates and guides through the various medical processes. See Chapters 14 and 15 for more information on this topic.

surgery to make sure our bodies are healthy enough to undergo the stress of surgery and appropriately recover afterward.

Some preexisting medical conditions can make surgery more risky. For example, surgery may be more dangerous or have a greater risk of complications if we have heart or lung problems. Even something as simple as high blood pressure may put us at increased risk if it is not well controlled. Very rarely do a person's medical conditions exclude them from surgery altogether. However, surgeons generally require that any serious health problems be well controlled before they operate. Many surgeons will also ask us to modify risk factors within our control, such as smoking, or temporarily discontinue specific medications that increase bleeding potential. Others may also require us to be within certain weight parameters to make surgery more successful.

Throughout the clearance process, it is extremely important to be completely honest with our surgeon and the other providers involved. To provide us with the best care possible, they need as much accurate and complete information as possible.

Along with surgical clearance, most surgeons will also require us to acquire one or two recommendations from mental health providers. Many surgeons rely on the WPATH Standards of Care (SOC), to identify patients for whom a specific surgery is appropriate. For chest/breast surgery, the SOC advise obtaining one letter of reference from a mental health professional confirming the presence of "persistent, well-documented gender dysphoria," the "capacity to make a fully informed decision and consent for treatment," legal adulthood, and if present, any significant mental health concerns be "reasonably well controlled." For removal of the ovaries or testicles, the guidelines additionally suggest the above and two such letters, along with "12 months of hormone therapy appropriate for a person's gender goals." For vaginoplasty, metoidioplasty, or phalloplasty the above and "12 continuous months of living in a gender role that is congruent with their gender identity" are recommended. Some surgeons may follow a different set of guidelines or may have their own specific requirements in addition to those set out by WPATH.

In many cases we will need to see a therapist or psychologist to have an assessment and acquire a letter. However, the SOC also recognize that primary care physicians may have adequate expertise to assess patients, especially if they provide our care in a multidisciplinary environment (where medical and behavioral health providers work together to provide care in the same location). If our primary care provider has such competency and experience, generally their letter is sufficient for chest/breast surgery and as one of the two letters required for bottom surgery.

Paying for Surgery

Cost is often the biggest logistical barrier between trans people and surgery. In the United States, the majority of gender-affirming surgeries are paid for out of pocket by patients. However, this is changing. Recently, California, Oregon, Vermont, and the District of Columbia have started enforcing law and policy that insurers cannot exclude transgender health care services from insurance policies. In addition, an increasing number of corporations, universities, local governments, and large unions like CalPERS in California are providing health insurance that covers transgender medical and surgical treatments.

Despite these promising advances, for most of us, the amount of money needed for surgery is not easily accessible, and for many of us it takes years to raise the funds, if we are ever able to do so. There are a number of different ways we may pay for surgery.

PAYMENT PLANS

Some surgeons work with lenders to provide payment plans. If paying little by little is a possibility, this might be an option to at least expedite the actual surgery. Different surgeons work differently in this regard, but if it is an appealing alternative, it is worth asking.

INSURANCE COVERAGE

Despite the fact that many insurance companies specifically exclude coverage of transgender surgeries, and that trans people are less likely to have employer-sponsored or privately purchased health insurance, in an increasing number of instances, insurance may be useful to cover gender-related surgeries.

A growing number of employers and schools have independently negotiated for coverage of transgender care in their plans. If you are thinking about going to or working for a college, this might be something to consider when applying. A list of universities with trans-inclusive insurance plans can be found on the Web site for the TONI (Transgender On-Campus Non-Discrimination Information) Project.

Having an anatomically related health issue that is not considered connected to our trans status may open the door for insurance to pay for the surgery. For example, if you would like breast tissue removed, a family history of breast cancer might make insurance funding possible.

> *"I had medical insurance when I had chest surgery and was able to get it covered as a breast reduction. My insurance company was not aware that it was a transgender related surgery, otherwise, they would not have covered it."*

One potentially major drawback of dealing with insurance companies is that they may obligate us to go to a specific surgeon within their network of providers. If we have our heart set on a particular surgeon, it might not be possible through insurance coverage. However, we may be able to argue that there is no one in-network with the appropriate skills and experience.

COMMUNITY FUNDRAISING

Another strategy many of us utilize to help afford surgery is to call on family, friends, and community members for support by requesting individual donations or holding fundraisers. Different people organize these events differently based on personal taste, talents, and community, but some example ideas include the following:

- *Benefit events*: dance parties, concerts, comedy nights, dinner parties with an entrance fee, paid food or drinks, or a donation bucket
- *Donations via the Internet*: donation sites with a written request posted on a private Web site or circulated via social media

Right Before Surgery

Many of us have to travel to another town or city for surgery. Before setting off, it is a good idea to make sure all necessary logistical arrangements are taken care of. These may include travel plans (flights, trains, someone to drive us, etc.), staying arrangements (depending on the surgery and our general level of health, this may require staying overnight one or more nights in a hospital), and who will be accompanying us. Some surgeons have developed relationships with nearby hotels, which may provide deals for medically based stays or assistance with transportation to and from the surgical site. They will provide this information at the time of the initial consultation, but if it is important to know beforehand, it is worth asking when you call. If you need to stay around for follow-up care, make sure you know in advance how long this is likely to be.

TYPES OF SURGERY

There are numerous surgical options that have the potential to alter our gendered appearances. We may have "top" surgery to increase the size of our breasts (breast augmentation) or to create a more male-contoured chest. "Bottom" surgeries refer to procedures performed on our genitals or reproductive organs. There are also a number of other surgeries that can be performed to change our gendered appearance, such as facial or tracheal surgeries.

A relatively new resource for funding transition-related surgeries is the Jim Collins Foundation, a unique non-profit organization that has the explicit mission of providing financial assistance to transgender people for gender-affirming surgeries. The organization accepts applications between April 1 and August 1, and the number of grantees varies per year based on the success of fundraising efforts. Their grantees are selected based on financial need and level of preparedness, according to their Web site. Visit their Web site for more information on the application process or to make a contribution to the organization.

The information in this chapter has been compiled to give a general overview of the types of surgical procedures that many of us choose from. Before choosing a surgery, it is very important to fully understand the specific risks and complications associated with it—every surgery will have the possibility of complications and some of them can be serious. The list of possible complications in this section is not comprehensive or complete, and it should not replace a detailed conversation with the surgeon performing the procedure(s).

There is no one-size-fits-all approach. Each of us must identify our own particular goals. We may ask ourselves which, if any, body parts feel inconsistent with our gender identity or cause us distress. We may consider which situations (public spaces, intimate partnerships, looking in the mirror) cause us to feel these discrepancies most acutely. We may also think about what would help alleviate our distress—being able to urinate while standing up, seeing a different reflection in the mirror, being more physically comfortable by not having to tuck or bind anymore, or requiring a lower dose of hormones.

Top Surgeries

Top surgery refers to surgeries performed on our chests. These include breast augmentation, as well as reconstructive chest surgery to create a male-contoured chest. Top surgery is more common than bottom surgery for those of us on the transmasculine spectrum because it costs less and has a greater impact on our outward appearance.

RECONSTRUCTIVE CHEST SURGERY

Reconstructive chest surgery, commonly referred to as "top surgery," involves removal of breast tissue and formation of a male-contoured chest.

Approximate Cost
$5,000–$10,000

Procedure
There are a number of different techniques for reconstructive chest surgery, with the two most common types being double-incision procedures and periareolar (keyhole) procedures. The type of surgery we get depends both on our preferences and the recommendation of the surgeon, who will suggest a particular procedure based on the size, shape, and skin elasticity of our original chests. Each surgeon has particular standards for size and elasticity that guide which surgery they feel most comfortable with for a given patient.

DOUBLE INCISION (DOUBLE MASTECTOMY) WITH NIPPLE GRAFTING

In this procedure, incisions are made at the base of each breast, and breast tissue and excess skin are removed. The nipples and areola are taken off, resized, and grafted back into the appropriate position. This procedure can be used with any chest size and shape, but it is often reserved for those with larger chests or minimal elasticity. The procedure leaves sizeable scars on both sides of the chest.

Because the nipple and areola are removed and replaced, there will be loss of erotic sensation to the nipple, though generally nonerotic sensation will return but may take months to years. In some cases, the nipple and areola are completely removed and a subsequent

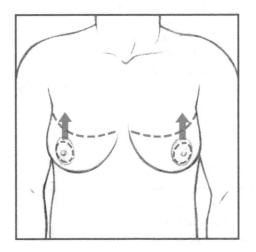 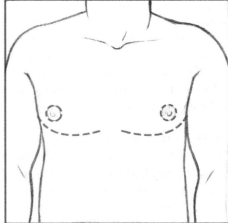

Double-incision (Ron Burton).

surgery or tattooing is performed to re-create the appearance of nipples. This may be necessary if you are a carrier of gene mutations that increase your risk for breast cancer.

PERIAREOLAR (KEYHOLE) PROCEDURE

In this method, incisions are made around the borders between the areolas and the surrounding skin, and breast tissue is removed through these incisions. Some skin may be removed, and the remaining skin is reattached at the border of the areola, which leaves minimal scarring. This procedure is typically reserved for smaller chest sizes or a smaller amount of loose skin, and is associated with faster healing times. Usually, erotic sensation of the nipples is preserved with this procedure.

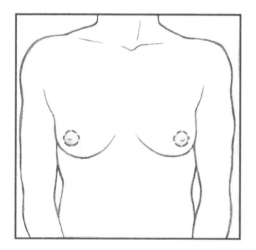 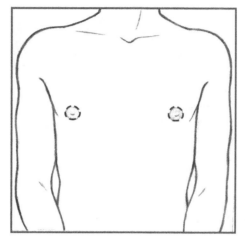

Keyhole incision (Ron Burton).

LIPOSUCTION

A minority of patients with very small presurgical chest sizes may choose to have liposuction only. Erotic sensation is usually preserved, but since the breast tissue remains there is a greater risk for breast cancer and need for screening. In addition, if you have this procedure and later become pregnant, there is a good chance that the breast tissue will become more prominent again during pregnancy.

Recovery

Reconstructive chest surgeries are generally performed without an overnight stay in the hospital. However, it may be necessary to stay locally for a period of time. Drains—pieces of long thin tubing with plastic bulbs on the end—are typically placed under the armpits to allow fluid to leave the body, and are removed a few days to a week after surgery. Time for return to regularly scheduled (nonstrenuous) activities varies by surgical type and the individual, but upper body weight bearing is typically not advised for six weeks.

After the procedure, it is common for some people to feel numbness in the chest and nipples. Some people also experience tingling, burning, or other sensations. For many, these feelings resolve and normal sensation returns over a period of months to a year as inflammation decreases and nerves regrow. However, many also experience some permanent loss of sensation.

It is also important to note that some breast tissue will remain with any technique, so we should make sure to discuss routine screening for breast cancer with our primary care provider. This usually involves a simple chest exam in the office.

BREAST AUGMENTATION

Breast augmentation involves increasing the size of the breasts. It is a common procedure in cisgender women.

Approximate Cost

$6,000–$8,000

Procedure

In breast augmentation, implants made of either enclosed silicone or saline are used to enhance the size of the breasts. Incisions are made around the areola (circumareolar), near the armpit (axillary), or just below the breast (inframammary). The implants are introduced through the incision and situated either in front of or behind the pectoral muscles. Other alternative methods involve the transplant of fat, muscles, or tissue from other parts of the body into the breast.

It is important to note that use of estrogen will stimulate breast growth. Many people are satisfied with hormonally induced growth alone. While it is not a criterion for referral for surgery, the WPATH Standards of Care recommend that at least 12 months of continuous hormone treatment is done before surgery to see the outcome of natural breast growth. Some surgeons even recommend this be as long as 18 months.

Recovery

Breast augmentation is often done in an outpatient setting (i.e., not in a hospital), and it may not require an overnight hospital stay. However, we may need someone to accompany us after the surgery, and the surgeon may require us to stay locally for an additional few days.

COMPLICATIONS OF BREAST AUGMENTATION

Maddie Deutsch, MD

Different breast augmentation techniques require different aftercare. Silicone implants can leak or rupture, or a capsule of scar tissue called a capsular contracture can form around them. Silicone implants that are leaking may cause no symptoms, or they may cause lumps, pain, or a firm or immobile implant. Silicone leaking out of an implant may travel to places near and far in the body, and cause pain, lumps, and inflammation. Research shows that by 10 years, most silicone implants have leaked to some extent.

Once a silicone implant has leaked, there are a few approaches to take. If there is no pain, we may simply do nothing. If the implant is firm or painful, the surgeon may suggest removing or replacing the implants. Each time an implant is replaced (including to gain a larger size), there is an increased risk of scarring or contractures, as well as infection. If the implant becomes infected or is scarred to the point that it cannot be replaced, it might leave breasts that appear saggy.

Saline implants also run the risk of contracture or infection, but the risk is less than with silicone. Since saline implants are filled with salt water, when they leak, they leak quickly. A sudden and rapid loss of breast fullness and shape will result—this will be quite obvious. The salt water is absorbed into the body without any harmful effects.

Bottom Surgeries

Bottom surgeries are those procedures performed to alter our genitals or internal reproductive organs. These surgeries are generally among the most expensive of surgical options, often costing upward of $30,000 or more. Many of us delay or do not have bottom surgery due to the prohibitive cost, or because we choose to prioritize more publically visible aspects of appearance. Some of us also experience pleasure from our genitals and do not wish to chance compromising function or satisfaction. Others wish to maintain fertility. For those of us who do prioritize bottom surgeries, however, they can be deeply meaningful and provide a profound sense of relief.

> *"I had a vaginoplasty, which I decided to have as soon as I realized that I was a transsexual. . . Due to poverty and cultural disapproval, I had to wait over nine years for the procedure. When I awoke from surgery, I looked out my clinic bedroom window. . . At last I felt like me."*

ORCHIECTOMY

Approximate Cost

$3,000–$5,000.

Procedure

An orchiectomy is the removal of the testicles. The testicles produce sperm, as well as the hormone testosterone, so an orchiectomy may eliminate the need for testosterone blockers, such as spironolactone, and reduce the amount of estrogen required to achieve and maintain the desired effects. The procedure can be done under local anesthetic or general anesthesia, and it is generally far less expensive than vaginoplasty—the creation of a vagina. Rarely, scarring from the procedure can affect the results of a vaginoplasty in the future. Most surgeons do not have a problem with this, but we should consider talking with our surgeon about whether this might impact future surgical options.

Recovery

Orchiectomies are typically done on an outpatient basis, which means we do not have to stay in the hospital overnight. Most surgeons, however, will require that we have someone to accompany us out after the procedure, and some require that we stay locally for up to three to five days. After this time, we should be able to return to regularly scheduled activities, if they are not too strenuous, and be back to most activities within two weeks.

Once the testicles are removed, we may be able to stop testosterone blockers, but it is important to stay on some form of estrogen so our bodies have hormones to keep our bones and other parts of our bodies healthy. Removal of the testicles will result in complete and permanent inability to have biological children. If children may be desired in the future, we should consider preservation of sperm.

PENECTOMY

A penectomy is the removal of the penis with or without reconstructive efforts. In the United States, penectomies are rarely performed, having been mostly replaced by vaginoplasties.

VAGINOPLASTY

Approximate Cost

$15,000–$30,000

Procedure

Vaginoplasty is the creation of a vagina. Tissue from the shaft of the penis is used to construct a vaginal canal. The glans (head) of the penis and the nerves that supply it are used to create a clitoris (clitoroplasty) and scrotal tissue is used to create the labia (labiaplasty). Alternative techniques may involve taking skin from another area of the body or tissue from the colon to create the vagina, although this is less commonly used and often leads to more complications, such as constant discharge. A labiaplasty to improve the aesthetics of the labia and to create a clitoral hood may also be performed in a second surgery, although today most vaginoplasties include labiaplasties.

Generally, overnight stays in the hospital are necessary after vaginoplasty. When first out of the surgery, we will have a catheter, a long thin plastic tube, coming out of the urethra, which we will urinate through. This is usually removed one to two days after surgery. We may not be able to safely travel home for a week or more.

Electrolysis or laser hair removal of the penile and scrotal areas is generally recommended before vaginoplasty to provide hair-free tissue for the procedure. This process may take several months. Surgeons have different opinions about presurgical hair removal, so it is a good idea to gather as much information as possible from your surgeon well in advance of the surgical date.

The prostate is not removed at the time of vaginoplasty. This is because removal of the prostate is not needed to get good results and removal risks greater complications, including blood loss, infection, and loss of control over urinary function.

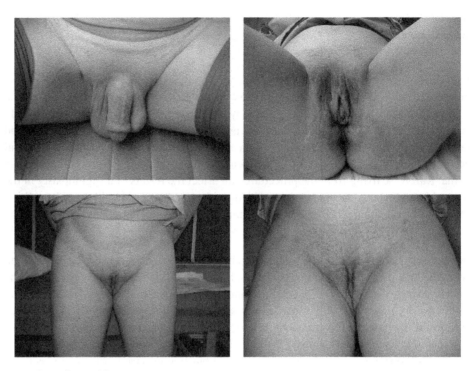

SRS results (Pichet Rodchareon, MD).

Recovery and Follow-up Care

Recovery time can range from one to two months. It is important to follow the surgeon's instructions carefully as per the length of time to wait before engaging in sexual activity with the new vagina. The surgeon will also provide a set of vaginal dilators, used to maintain, lengthen, and stretch the size of the vagina. Dilators of increasing size are regularly inserted into the vagina at time intervals according to the surgeon's instructions. Dilation is required less often over time, but it may be recommended indefinitely.

Complications of vaginoplasty can include infection, fistula (a small tunnel that develops between the rectum and the vagina), and slow healing (also called granulation tissue) that can be painful or bleed. Although the procedure also comes with a degree of risk in terms of loss of sensation or interference with urinary function, long-term outcomes for sensation, orgasmic ability, sexual satisfaction, and urinary function are much improved. Despite possible complications, various studies have shown that after vaginoplasty, there is an improvement in our quality of life, body satisfaction, and psychosocial function. The WPATH Standards of Care Version 7 includes an appendix, which discusses all of the studies we have so far about the outcomes of surgeries, including vaginoplasty.

METOIDIOPLASTY

In metoidioplasty, the clitoris/phallus length is increased without grafting tissue from other parts of the body.

Approximate Cost

Depending on the type of procedure and the surgeon, metoidioplasties may cost less than $5,000 without, and more than $15,000 with urethral lengthening.

Procedure

During this procedure, the clitoris/phallus is freed from its attachments to the labia minora and a suspensory ligament (which holds the clitoris/phallus close to the body). The overall effect is to lengthen and straighten the clitoris/phallus. Greater girth is also achieved by bringing the undersurface of the clitoris/phallus and added bulk from the labia to the midline. An additional procedure known as a "urethral hookup" can be done at the same time, which allows for standing urination. In a urethral hookup, the urethra is extended through the released clitoris/phallus using a graft traditionally taken from the lining of the mouth. A newer variation of the metoidioplasty called the ring metoidioplasty is performed with a urethral hookup consisting of lining derived from the inner labial skin and a flap from the vagina, eliminating the need to take tissue from the mouth.

Metoidioplasty typically results in an unstimulated phallic length of between 3 and 8 cm. Full sensation and erectile and orgasmic functions are generally retained. The procedure may also be converted to a phalloplasty—creation of a penis—at a later time if desired.

Many people take testosterone to enlarge the clitoris/phallus prior to metoidioplasty. Some surgeons recommend the use of topical testosterone creams or pumping, although there is no research yet as to whether these techniques increase phallic size. If we do use pumping, it is important to avoid anything that causes pain or numbness. Pain and numbness can signal tissue damage, which could ultimately make our surgical results worse.

Surgery to permanently close or (less often) remove the vagina is not required for a metoidioplasty. Penetration and Pap smears may not be possible following a metoidioplasty. Some surgeons recommend removing the uterus, cervix, and ovaries at the same time as the metoidioplasty, while others do not. Scrotoplasties (creation of scrotum) are also sometimes done along with metoidioplasties.

Recovery

Depending on the type of metoidioplasty, when we first come out of the surgery, we may have to remain in the hospital for a short time and may have a catheter, a long thin plastic tube, coming out of the urethra, which we will urinate through. This is usually removed 1–2 days after surgery. Recovery time for metoidioplasties may be up to two weeks, and may require remaining close to the surgeon for at least a few days.

PHALLOPLASTY

Phalloplasty is the creation of a penis. Phalloplasties are relatively rare in the United States due to high cost, the need for multiple procedures, scarring at skin donation sites, and variable results.

Approximate Cost
$30,000–$100,000

Procedure

Donor skin with which to construct the new penis is taken from another area of the body, typically the forearm, lateral thigh, calf, lower abdomen, or flank. The skin is then rolled into the shape of a phallus, and is anchored in the normal position for the penis. Phalloplasties require a large amount of donor skin, and the graft sites often heal with significant scarring or disfigurement. Most surgeons situate the clitoris/phallus within the base of the new phallus in an attempt to retain erogenous stimulation. Generally, this is at least somewhat successful but it is possible to permanently lose erotic sensation.

The procedure is often broken up into multiple steps, with up to three scheduled surgeries. Urethral lengthening to allow for urination through the tip of the penis is considered a difficult addition to the procedure, but can be done. Variations may also include grafting of nerves and blood vessels to provide sensation to the new penis, however this is considered a much more complex procedure, with a higher likelihood of complication and is not frequently done. A glansoplasty may also be performed as a separate procedure

For more information on bottom surgeries for trans men, check out Trystan Theosophus Cotton's book *Hung Juries: Testimonies of Genital Surgery by Transsexual Men* (Oakland, CA: Transgress Press, 2012).

to sculpt the head of penis. Medical tattooing may also be used to create a distinction between the head and shaft.

Silicone rods or pumps are sometimes inserted into the penis to allow it to become erect. These rods or pumps may allow for desired sexual practices, but may be uncomfortable, and there have been reports of them becoming infected or eroding through the skin.

Recovery

When emerging from surgery, there will be a catheter, a long thin plastic tube, coming out of the urethra, to urinate through. Depending on the type of surgery, it may take some time for this to be removed. After phalloplasty, we will have to stay in the hospital for at least a few days. Phalloplasties have relatively high rates of postoperative complications and may require multiple follow-up surgeries. Recovery rate is largely variable, from about four to twelve weeks depending on the individual and the exact procedure.

SCROTOPLASTY

A scrotoplasty is the creation of a scrotum. In a scrotoplasty, testicular implants are inserted into the labia, which are sealed around them.

Approximate Cost

$3,000–$5,000

Procedure

In this procedure, egg-shaped silicone implants are placed into the labia majora through small incisions. In preparation for permanent prostheses, expanders may be placed under the skin to encourage the expansion or growth of new skin. This is done by gradually filling the expanders with more saline through an external port over a period of months. Once the skin is adequately expanded, the permanent implants are inserted.

Recovery

Each expansion procedure is generally performed in an outpatient visit, and so does not require an overnight stay at a hospital. The surgeon will likely require a local stay for a few days, and because the expansion procedure is gradual, it is necessary to return several times before placement of the permanent prosthesis. A common complaint is that the implants are uncomfortable. Less frequently, they have the potential to wear through the surrounding tissue or to become infected.

HYSTERECTOMY AND SALPINGO-OOPHERECTOMY

Hysterectomy is removal of the uterus, and may or may not include the cervix and upper part of the vagina. If one of the surgical goals is to eliminate the need for ongoing Pap smears, it may be best to ask the surgeon to remove the cervix as well. A hysterosalpingo-oophorectomy (HSO) includes removal of the uterus, fallopian tubes, and ovaries.

Approximate Cost

The procedure typically costs between $6,000 and $8,000, but it may be less if combined with other procedures. Hysterectomy/HSO is also covered by insurance more frequently than many of the other described surgeries because it can often be argued that it could help with non-gender-related issues such as menstrual pain.

Procedure

There are several methods for performing a hysterectomy:

1. *Laparoscopic (robot-assisted) approach.* Small incisions are made in the abdomen through which a tiny camera and specially designed surgical tools

are inserted to perform the procedure. Unless there are specific reasons to do otherwise, a laparoscopic approach is generally preferred due to minimized scarring and shortened healing times. Recovery time for this type of procedure is typically one to two weeks before return to daily function, and no more than a two-day hospital stay.

2. *Vaginal approach.* This procedure is similar to that described above, but entry is through the vagina rather than abdominal incisions.

3. *Open (abdominal) approach.* In this procedure, a larger incision is made in the lower abdomen above the pubic bones through which the uterus and ovaries are removed, usually resulting in a larger scar. Recovery time is typically longer for this procedure and can be up to six weeks. Generally, this is done when the uterus or ovaries are too large to be removed through the small incisions with laparoscopy. Recovery time is typically longer for this procedure and can take up to six weeks before complete healing is achieved.

When making a decision about whether to have an HSO, we may want to consider whether testosterone changes the risk of gynecologic cancers (cervical, ovarian, or endometrial). As a baseline, we should assume our risk is at least that of a cis woman. Removal of the ovaries significantly reduces that risk. There is not enough information in the medical literature to give any reliable advice on whether ovarian cancer risk is increased, decreased, or unchanged when taking testosterone. The risk of cervical cancer appears to be no different from that of cis women as long as we follow recommended screening tests. There is debate about whether the risk of endometrial (uterine) cancer is higher. If we get appropriate screening tests and make sure to report any abnormal bleeding to our providers, most uterine cancer, if it develops, will be found early enough to treat.

Overall, there is a need for more research in this area to arrive at a more definitive answer for these questions. Currently there are no guidelines to suggest that HSO is necessary at any specific point after beginning testosterone, but some of us choose to have this surgery. It is reasonable to consider a reduction in the risk of cancer and need for fewer screening tests as one of the benefits we weigh when deciding to have surgery.

HEAD AND NECK PROCEDURES

Gender-related head and neck procedures include facial feminization surgery (FFS), tracheal shave, and hair transplantation. Some of us find that these procedures have been crucial in our transition, often above all others, because they impact those parts most readily seen by others.

Many surgeries not performed on the chest or genitals are referred to as *cosmetic*. It is important to distinguish between *cosmetic* and *elective*. Cosmetic surgery includes procedures done to alter the physical appearance. Elective generally means that the surgery is not necessary to treat a health problem. There are cosmetic surgeries that are elective, such as a face lift to appear more youthful. However, not all cosmetic surgeries are elective. For example, if a child has burns to the face with noticeable scarring, he might have medically necessary cosmetic surgery. Trans women often undergo medically necessary cosmetic surgeries to the face in order to feminize their features. Gender-affirming surgeries, including facial feminization surgeries, are medically necessary cosmetic procedures whose benefits include improved ability to be read consistently as female, as well as to avoid harassment and discrimination.

> *"Man, I hate it when people refer to procedures like electrolysis or Adam's apple reduction surgery as cosmetic. For some people, they're a necessary step toward alleviating gender dysphoria. The medical community shouldn't be able to decide when individual trans people should be 'finished' or satisfied with*

their transition. Moreover, for some people such 'cosmetic' procedures as elec-
trolysis or Adam's apple reduction surgery are a matter of safety. If you don't
pass completely successfully 100% of the time in society, you may be physically
or sexually assaulted or killed. There's nothing 'cosmetic' about that."

"I consider Facial feminization surgery one of my highest priorities alongside
getting my voice right. . . People don't look at your genitals. Your voice and
your face are how people judge you in face-to-face conversation and are what
you look at every day in a mirror."

FACIAL FEMINIZATION SURGERY

FFS represents a diverse set of plastic surgery techniques in which alterations are made to the jaw, chin, cheeks, forehead, nose, and areas surrounding the eyes, ears, or lips to create a more feminine facial appearance. The hairline may be adjusted to create a smaller forehead, cheekbones and lips can be augmented to become more prominent, and the jaw and chin can be reshaped and resized to resemble more classic feminine facial features. In the process, significant amounts of bone may be reduced, or prosthetic implants may be inserted. Reduction in bone mass may potentially lead to excess skin, and some people choose to have additional skin tightening surgeries as well.

Approximate Cost

Cost can vary greatly depending on the number of procedures desired.

Procedure

The techniques used in FFS can be highly varied between different surgeons, and it is a good idea to understand those employed by a potential surgeon, as different techniques come with different risks.

Recovery

Most facial feminization surgeries are performed on an outpatient basis, with no hospital stay required. However, complete recovery time may vary depending on the number of FFS procedures combined. Most procedures require about 2 weeks recovery time, but adjustments to the jaw may result in significantly longer recovery.

TRACHEAL SHAVE (ALSO KNOWN AS ADAM'S APPLE REDUCTION, THYROID CARTILAGE REDUCTION, CHONDROLARYNGOPLASTY)

This procedure minimizes the thyroid cartilage (also known as Adam's apple), a traditionally gendered feature.

Approximate Cost

$3,000–$5,000

Procedure

In a tracheal shave, a 3–4 cm incision is made under the chin, in the shadow of the neck, or in an existing skin fold, to conceal the resulting scar. The cartilage is then reduced and reshaped. The surgery is sometimes performed at the same time as others elsewhere on the body.

Recovery

Tracheal shave is generally performed in an outpatient setting, which means it will likely not require an overnight stay. However, there is usually a requirement to have someone to accompany us when we leave.

Hair Reconstruction/Transplantation

In this procedure, hair follicles from the back and side of the head are removed and transplanted to balding areas of the head. Costs vary greatly based on surgeon and size of scalp to be grafted, but they generally range from $4,000 to $15,000.

RECOVERING AFTER SURGERY

Postoperative care greatly depends on the type of surgery we have. Recovery time may be anywhere from a few days to over a month. Planning ahead can help us to make sure we have everything we need during our recovery period.

Recovery Time

One thing we should find out before surgery is what the expected length of recovery time will be for our surgery so that we can make accommodations to give ourselves adequate time off from any activities that might slow down the healing process. Numerous people have shared experiences of pushing their recovery time by going back to work too soon, exercising to build up their newly contoured (yet unhealed) chest, or prematurely using their new sexual equipment. Time off, particularly from work, will be more challenging for some people than others based on financial resources. However, it is important to keep in mind that complications in the healing process may compromise our long-term outcomes and, depending on the complication, may require additional surgery or lengthen our overall healing process even further.

Support Team

Having a well-planned support team in place to welcome us home can make the healing process smoother, both physically and emotionally. We may require assistance with some of our basic daily activities, such as cooking, bathing (we may not be able to shower for up to a period of weeks), using the bathroom, getting around, and performing basic household tasks. Our support people should include whoever makes most sense for us—friends, family, partners, community members—and ideally people who we would feel comfortable having help from in vulnerable situations (i.e., using the bathroom, sponge baths, etc.). Some people choose to preplan caretaking shifts to ensure that help is always available and that primary caretakers have added support as well. Support people can also provide us with the invaluable resources of love and affirmation, which are just as critical in the healing process.

Setting Ourselves Up for Success

Before surgery, some people choose to "surgery proof" their living space. Depending on the type of surgery we plan to have, we may have limited mobility or range of motion of particular body parts for a period of time. For example, after top surgery, lifting the arms up overhead or bearing weight with them may not be possible. Placing necessary items at a level easily reachable for our postsurgery selves may increase our independence and physical comfort. Many people also choose to invest in or borrow pillows to prop themselves up while resting. Something else to consider is how we might occupy our time while letting our body recuperate. We may or may not have a lot of mental capacity in the days after surgery, so movies, easy reading material, and good company are good investments.

Medical Follow-Up Care

After surgery is complete, and we have been cleared by the surgeon to go home, we will require follow-up medical care. The particular surgeries, surgeon, and any complications that arise will determine the specifics of this care. If our surgeon happens to be within reasonable travel distance, they may be the one to continue caring for us. For many people, however, their surgeons of choice are in another state or country, and accommodations must be made to have access to another provider. If we had not previously found a trans-friendly and knowledgeable medical provider prior to surgery, it is imperative that we find someone who can monitor our progress and help distinguish between a normal healing process and complications.

We may also require follow-up procedures. For example, some surgeries require the placement of drains to collect blood and other fluid that our body naturally produces as a response to the trauma of surgery. Excess fluid collections can cause hematomas (collections of blood) and seromas (collections of plasma without the presence of blood cells). A portion of the drain is placed inside the body, which connects to collecting bulbs outside the body that are secured with stitches. The drains will remain in place until a time specified by the surgeon and then must be removed by a medical professional. It is a good idea to know before surgery who will be removing the drains. Leaving them in for too long can open the door to additional complications, and medical providers unfamiliar with the procedure or surgeon may hesitate to touch the work of a surgeon unfamiliar to them.

To receive the best follow-up care possible, it is also beneficial to be informed about the type of surgical procedure we had. The more information we can provide, the more our medical providers will know what kind of care we require. We may even choose to bring copies of our medical records to show new medical providers.

Knowing the details of our surgery will also ensure that we get the best preventive medical care, even after we have healed. For example, after a vaginoplasty, we likely still have a prostate and will need appropriate cancer screening. Or, if we have had our uterus removed, it is important to know whether we still have a cervix, which may also require proper cancer screenings with Pap smears.

In addition to finding a competent local medical provider to oversee our follow-up care, we should not hesitate to contact our surgeon if we have any questions at all regarding the recovery process. Ideally, the surgeon and their staff should be available for questions. Because they were the ones who performed our surgeries (and likely hundreds or even thousands like them before), they will be most familiar with what was done and with any potential complications.

Before leaving the surgeon's office after surgery, we should also be given a written set of postsurgical instructions. This might include a timeline for removal of bandages or drains, when we may start activities again, how to use our dilators (if applicable), possible complications, and signs/symptoms that should prompt us to seek medical attention. It is important to read, completely understand, and follow these instructions. It is the surgeon's responsibility to make sure we have all the information we need for as successful a recovery as possible, and it is our job to ask for clarification if we need it.

Additional Aftercare
In addition to following up with an appropriate medical provider, it is a good idea to keep ourselves as healthy as possible throughout the healing process to boost our body's natural ability to repair itself. This means getting enough sleep, staying well hydrated, and having the proper nutritional intake. Healing after any type of surgery requires additional energy and nutrients. In particular, adequate protein, vitamin A, vitamin C, B vitamins, and zinc are known to be important in healing. It is also important to refrain from activities that will actively slow down healing, such as smoking cigarettes.

Some people also choose to use "complementary" health modalities to assist in the healing process, such as acupuncture. Massage therapy has also been shown to decrease inflammatory chemicals in the body, and it has been used successfully to improve the appearance and functional movement of scar tissue. Consult your surgeon about when in the healing process it is appropriate to utilize massage or other modalities involving direct contact with the postsurgical areas of the body.

GETTING TO KNOW OUR BODIES AGAIN

After we have healed enough to begin reentering our daily lives, we may have to readjust to living in our new body and to using our bodies in everyday circumstances. This process will mean something different for everyone, but it may include the clothes we wear (or don't wear), the way we have sex, the way we feel when we look in mirror, and how we feel about our surgical results in comparison to our expectations.

Scars

The process of surgery inherently causes scarring. The location and size of scars will depend in part on the type of surgery we have. For example, a tracheal shave may leave a small scar line just under the chin or in a fold of neck skin. A perioareolar reconstructive chest surgery might leave fewer visible scars around the areolas of the nipple, while double-incision reconstructive chest surgery might leave large scars across both sides of the chest. Even among people undergoing the same procedure, there is natural variability in scar formation from person to person in terms of color, texture, and size of the scars.

One important example is keloid scars. Keloids are larger, more raised, and can often be more painful than other scars. Keloids form when the body reacts by overproducing an altered form of scar tissue. They can occur with any break in the skin, including piercings, severe acne, or surgery. Keloids are most common on the ears, neck, jaw, chest, shoulders, and upper back.

The exact cause of keloid formation is not known. However, we do know there can be a genetic predisposition, so if someone has previously gotten keloid scars, or has family members who get them, keloid scar formation after surgery is more likely. If we know or suspect we are prone to keloids, we should tell the surgeon before surgery. Although the surgeon may not be able to stop keloid formation, they may be able to take steps to partially prevent or minimize it.

With any potential for scarring, it is advisable to keep newly healing incisions out of the sun. Various creams and massaging newly forming scars at the appropriate stage of healing may also help reduce them. Be sure to consult your surgeon about the details of how to best manage scarring, if this is a concern.

Just as with every other aspect of surgery, trans people have widely varied feelings toward our surgery-related scars.

> *"I have had chest reconstruction surgery, double-incision with nipple grafts. . .. I desperately needed this surgery to feel comfortable in my body, present as male, and survive the summer heat. Binding in the summer is a special kind of hell! I think my results are perfect and my scars are kinda badass."*

> *"I'm satisfied by the results but have pretty major scars that can be embarrassing for others to see. I am paranoid that my scars will out me or that people will want me to put a shirt on if I go without a shirt at the pool, but that hasn't happened yet."*

> *"I feel positively about having scars on my chest as a reminder to myself that I have a trans body."*

Regardless of how we feel, or anticipate we will feel about our surgical scars, we should discuss scarring with the surgeon before surgery to have as realistic an idea as possible about what to expect.

Sexuality

For many people, having surgery changes how we experience sex. Some surgeries physically alter our sexual sensations. For example, vaginoplasty directly alters an area with a concentrated set of nerves for erogenous sensation. Although many people report being able to orgasm after having had this surgery, doing so may require relearning how to experience pleasure from our parts. Other surgeries, such as reconstructive chest surgery, may result in a permanent loss of sensation in areas we once found highly sensitive.

Our surgeries may also affect the emotional and social aspects of our sexuality. Some of us feel more sexually inclined after having surgery because we feel more at home in our bodies. Others may feel more sexual, or differently sexual, when they feel recognized by others as their self-identified gender. See Chapter 17 for more information about sexuality after surgery.

CONCLUSION

Surgery means something different to every trans person, whether it is the most important step in our transition or something we never want. We make our decisions based on our personal feelings about our bodies, our safety, our jobs, our relationships, money, and countless other factors. For some, it is a straightforward decision. For others, it is a complex decision that takes years to make.

For those of us who do desire surgery, the planning process requires careful consideration at every step: choosing a surgeon and surgeries, getting the necessary clearances, making logistical arrangements, funding the process, and ensuring proper aftercare. The more planning and support we can have, the better prepared we are for successful surgical experiences.

REFERENCES AND FURTHER READING

Bockting, W. O., & Goldberg, J. M. (2006). *Guidelines for transgender care.* New York: Haworth Press.

Bowers, M. (2011). *Genital reassignment surgery.* Retrieved January 2014, from http://www.marcibowers.com/grs/gender.html

Bowman, C., & Goldberg, J. M. (2006). Care of the patient undergoing sex reassignment surgery. International Journal of Transgenderism, 9(3-4), 135–165.

Clark, R. F., Cantrell, F. L., Pacal, A., Chen, W., & Betten, D. P. (2008). Subcutaneous silicone injection leading to multisystem organ failure. Clinical Toxicology, 46, 834–837.

Coleman, E., Bockting, W., Botzer, M., Cohen-Kettenis, P., DeCuypere, G., Feldman, J., ... Zucker, K. (2012). Standards of care for the health of transsexual, transgender, and gender-nonconforming people, version 7. International Journal of Transgenderism, 13, 165–232.

De Cuypere, G., & Vercruysse, H., Jr. (2009). Eligibility and readiness criteria for sex reassignment surgery: Recommendations for revision of the WPATH Standards of Care. International Journal of Transgenderism, 11(3), 194–205.

De Sutter, P. (2009). Reproductive options for transpeople: Recommendations for revision of the WPATH's standards of care. International Journal of Transgenderism, 11(3), 183–185.

Djordjevic, M. L., Stanojevic, D., Bizic, M., Kojovic, V., Majstorovic, M., Vujovic, S., ... Perovic, S. V. (2009). Metoidioplasty as a single stage sex reassignment surgery in female transsexuals: Belgrade experience. Journal of Sexual Medicine, 6(5), 1306–1313.

Djordjevic, M. L. (2013). MTF surgery, FTM surgery. Retrieved March 2013, from http://www.genitalsurgerybelgrade.com/index.php

Feldman, J. L., & Goldberg, J. M. (2006). Transgender primary medical care. International Journal of Transgenderism, 9(3/4), 3–34.

FTM Surgery Network. Metoidioplasty procedures. Retrieved March 2013, from http://www.metoidioplasty.net/procedures/

Gender Outlaw. (2008, December 6). Dr. Miroslav Djordjevic—FTM metoidioplasty surgeons, Part 4—Dr. Miro, Serbia. Message posted to http://genderoutlaw.wordpress.com/2008/12/06/metoidioplasty-scrotoplasty-surgeons-djordjevic/

Human Rights Campaign. (2011). Corporate equality index. Human Rights Campaign. Retrieved from http://www.hrc.org/corporate-equality-index/#.URMdjRLd7i8

Jim Collins Foundation. (2013). Application information. Retrieved April 2013, from http://jimcollinsfoundation.org/

Jones, D. H., Carruthers, A., Orentreich, D., Brody, H. J., Lai, M., Azen, S., & Van Dyke, G. S. (2004). Highly purified 1000-cSt silicone oil for treatment of human immunodeficiency virus-associated facial lipoatrophy: An open pilot trial. Dermatologic Surgery, 30, 1279–1286.

Laura's Playground. (2013). Transgender. Retrieved January 2014, from http://www.lauras-playground.com/index.htm

Meltzer, T. (2013). MTF surgeries and procedures, FTM surgeries and procedures. Retrieved January 2014, from http://www.ftmtransition.com/transition/transition.html

McGuin, C. (2010). Gender confirmation surgery. Retrieved January 2014, from http://www.drchristinemcginn.com/services/srs/

Perovic, S. V., Stanojevic, D. S., & Djordjevic, M. L. (2005). Vaginoplasty in male to female transsexuals using penile skin and urethral flap. International Journal of Transgenderism, 8(1), 43–64.

Prather, C. L., & Jones, D. H. (2006). Liquid injectable silicone for soft tissue augmentation. Dermatologic Therapy, 19, 159–168.

Rachlin, K., Hansbury, G., & Pardo, S. T. (2010). Hysterectomy and oophorectomy experiences of female-to-male transgender individuals. International Journal of Transgenderism, 12(3), 155–166.

Spade, D. (2011). About purportedly gendered body parts. Retrieved November 2012, from http://www.deanspade.net/wp-content/uploads/2011/02/Purportedly-Gendered-Body-Parts.pdf

Spehr, C. (2007). Male-to-female sex reassignment surgery in transsexuals. International Journal of Transgenderism, 10(1), 25–37.

Styperek, A., Bayers, S., Beer, M., & Beer, K. (2013). Nonmedical-grade injections of permanent fillers: Medical and medicolegal considerations. Journal of Clinical Aesthetic Dermatology, 6(4), 22–29.

Transexual Roadmap. (2012). Physical modifications for trans women. Retrieved January 2014, from http://www.tsroadmap.com/physical/index.html

van Trotsenburg, M. A. (2009). Gynecological aspects of transgender healthcare. *International Journal of Transgenderism*, *11*(4), 238–246.

World Professional Association for Transgender Health. (2011). *Standards of care for the health of transsexual, transgender, and gender nonconforming people, seventh version.* Retrieved January 2014, from http://www.wpath.org/uploaded_files/140/files/IJT%20SOC,%20V7.pdf

MENTAL HEALTH SERVICES AND SUPPORT

14

Ruben Hopwood and lore m. dickey

IN ADDITION TO OUR PHYSICAL HEALTH, we also need to pay attention to our mental and emotional health and well-being. As trans people, we have many reasons to look for support from our friends and family and from mental health professionals. We may feel distressed in some aspect of our lives, or we may wish to have more information about ourselves to make choices about how to express and affirm our gender identities.

When we have good mental health, we may experience relative comfort functioning in society and experience minimal emotional and behavioral problems. We are able to think clearly, access and control our emotions, cope with daily life, meet responsibilities and challenges, and maintain mutual and supportive relationships with others.

While most of us function at a good level of mental health (Dean et al., 2000; Shipherd, Green, & Abramovitz, 2010; Sperber, Landers, & Lawrence, 2005), when there are interruptions or difficulties in our lives, we may begin to feel significantly distressed. Cultural differences can affect how we handle stress. We may be in a state of good mental health at some points in our lives and not at others. It is also possible to have some areas of life that are going well while other areas seem to be falling apart. In many instances, it is possible to regain mental health when it has become unbalanced. At moments when it seems there are more areas of life falling to pieces than operating smoothly, we may seek the services of mental health professionals to help to put things back together again.

For many trans or gender nonconforming people, our first experience with a mental health professional may be when we decide to begin a gender affirmation or transition process and discover that we need someone to help locate providers and write introduction letters to get the services we want or need.

> "I'm just starting the actual transition, after more than a decade of yearning. . . I spent my grade[school] and college years burying my feelings, but could not keep doing so when I finally struck out on my own. I spent weeks in soul-searching introspection, then decided to at least give therapy a shot. At that point it was as though the balance of my life had shifted, and I went from a conflicted, confused cisgendered man to a happy, certain woman-to-be (internally, of course) in less than a month."

Deciding who to see and then finding a knowledgeable professional may be the most challenging aspect of getting support. We may seek the care of a gender specialist, an expert in trans issues, in order to explore our gender or talk about issues in our relationships. Or we may look for a more general mental health provider to talk with about anxiety or depression. Some of us seek out mental health providers because we need an evaluation in order to be referred for gender affirmation treatments (Bockting, Knudson, & Goldberg, 2007; Lev, 2004, 2009; Rachlin, 2002). For those of us seeking gender affirmation, we may not have a choice about whether to see someone but may have some choice about whom to see (Bockting et al., 2007; Ehrbar & Gorton, 2010).

> "I didn't see a gender specialist until I was 20, but I'd gone to therapists and psychiatrists before that for other reasons. When I went to see that therapist when I was 20, it was strange because I felt like I was finally talking about real matters with a therapist. I was only able to see her twice until 7 years later—I have started seeing her again."

(BEYOND) SUFFERING AS A MEASURING TOOL

Xander (Sly) Sarkisova is a queer and trans person who has been working in mental health and addictions counseling for the past 13 years in Vancouver, British Columbia (occupied Musqueam, Tsleil-Waututh, and Squamish Territories) and Toronto, Ontario (Mississauga and Anishnaabe).

In Ontario, you are required to go to your nearest mental health institution to receive a diagnosis of gender dysphoria in order to get funding for surgeries. Many trans folks experience serious mental health issues and have histories of trauma due to transphobia. Yet if you disclose your trauma history and mental health status, you may be refused access to surgery. Paradoxically, you are required to present your trans narrative as if it is an unbearable burden and admit that your gender identity is a mental illness. It is not simply enough for you to know that you are trans and that access to care would be beneficial to you; in order to qualify for treatment, you are expected to meet a certain subjective threshold of dysphoria, as defined and assessed by cisgender and Eurocentric medical gatekeepers. Trans women of color have spoken out about this idea of the "tragic trans narrative" as the only possible narrative applied to them by mainstream society.

Using suffering as a measurement of "transness" while withholding health care is simply a means by which the state regulates and controls our bodies. If trans people were reared to explore and accept themselves from a young age, many of the sources of their suffering would be absent. The stigma and restricted access to decision making in trans health and trans embodiment is a major *cause* of suffering for many trans folks. Having trans people measured for degree of suffering is a systemic multiplication of transphobia under the guise of psychiatry.

Trans folks who resist the "tragic trans narrative" or who do not have a definitive "endpoint" of gender in mind, but who nonetheless seek masculinization or feminization, can challenge medical service providers to see us in our full complexity. We do this by authentically presenting our own stories in the manner that fits us, using terms that we choose for ourselves, not altering our histories and understanding of our genders, and by seeking out and demanding medical practitioners and surgeons who will listen to us.

SELF-CARE AND WELLNESS

Not every problem requires the help of a therapist or mental health professional. Sometimes we can feel better after doing positive things for ourselves, like reading a book, exercising, taking hot baths, or engaging in creative activities. When going through difficult times, emotional issues, or personal struggles, many of us benefit from talking to someone we trust, such as a friend, relative, or spouse. Sometimes talking, laughing, or crying with friends can be therapeutic. There are many ways we can take care of ourselves and improve our mental health in addition to seeing professionals.

Some of the possibilities include the following:

Self-care. This includes getting enough sleep and sunshine, eating well, exercising, and finding time for personal relaxation. Some of us allot time for ourselves to participate in activities we enjoy like jogging, yoga, getting massages, playing video games, painting, gardening, or listening to music.

Using creative outlets. Many of us sing, play instruments, draw, dance, or write poetry or stories in order to express our inner selves and find ways to channel how we are feeling. For example, keeping a journal can be a very good way to put our thoughts onto paper and process stress.

Religious or spiritual work. Some of us find solace in our spirituality, faith, or faith communities. We may meditate, pray, talk to trans-friendly religious leaders, or get involved in a trans-affirming religious or spiritual community. However, some religious communities may be unfriendly and can be a source of additional stress, so we may want to weigh the pros and cons of being involved in them.

Community service. In order to take our minds off of personal stress and to give back to the community, we may spend our time volunteering at soup kitchens, homeless shelters, community centers, or LGBTQ organizations. Some of us focus on creating social change, especially if it has potential to improve the issues that are causing our stress to begin with.

Building community and support groups. Depending on where we live, it can be hard for us as trans and gender nonconforming individuals to find people who understand what we are going through. Some of us have never met another person who identifies as trans or gender nonconforming and feel alone in the world. For this reason, it can be especially helpful to seek support groups or create one of your own. Some community or LGBTQ centers have existing support groups. Some are geared specifically for people of color, youth, the elderly, or other groups. There are also social scenes that are traditionally more trans-friendly. The Ball scene and drag communities are both great places to find trans-friendly spaces. For those of us who live in rural areas that do not have local trans-friendly community centers, we may have to look online.

ACCESSING PROFESSIONAL SUPPORTS AND SERVICES

Should we decide we would like to find a mental health provider, there are resources at our disposal. Many of us go to a local county or community mental health agency. The staff at state or local agencies may include psychologists, counselors, social workers, and psychiatrists. One advantage to a county or community mental health agency is that it is usually possible to get most of our mental health needs addressed at the same agency. Be aware, though, that gender identity support and services may not be available at such agencies. Another feature of some county or community agencies is that they are likely to have sliding fee scales that are based on income. While figuring out if you qualify for services on a sliding scale may be time consuming, it can be worthwhile for those of us who are underinsured or uninsured and have little to no extra income to pay out-of-pocket expenses for mental health support.

For college students, a good source for short-term mental health services is the counseling center that is affiliated with your college or university. Typically, these services are covered through student fees, though there may be a small copayment depending on the school you attend.

Another resource, not just for college students, is university-based clinics that provide therapist training programs. For example, a university psychology or social work department may provide low-cost counseling and testing services in a clinic where the therapists are student trainees who are closely supervised by licensed providers. A disadvantage to this type of counseling center is that the trainees are likely to have less experience working with clients than a licensed mental health provider. Advantages to these clinics are that they typically have appointments outside "normal business hours" (i.e., after 5:00 p.m.) and may offer very low-cost services.

Some major cities have LGBTQ-focused medical and mental health centers. While these centers can be good sources for counselors with experience with LGB-related issues, there is no guarantee that these providers have experience with concerns within trans or gender nonconforming communities. Even so, we may have a better chance at finding a trans-friendly provider at one of these centers than we would at a general mental health agency or private practitioner's office.

Many of the mental health professionals who specialize in LGBTQ or trans care have private practices outside of clinics. In a clinic, a provider typically sees whoever comes through the door, while in private practice, the provider may specialize in a certain area. Private practice providers may be harder to locate, but finding them can be rewarding.

Locating Care

Overall, there are usually more resources for trans and gender nonconforming people in larger urban areas than in rural and sparsely populated areas. Additionally, it is common in many geographic areas for there to be mental health professionals, but no medical providers, who treat trans people. Some of us find that we need to travel to a nearby larger city for trans-specific, competent care. This may increase the burden on some of us who do not live in or near a large city while seeking support or gender affirmation treatments.

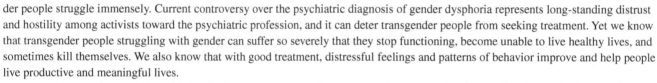

WHY WE NEED MENTAL HEALTH CARE

Jack Pula, MD, is a psychiatrist and therapist in New York City on faculty in the Department of Psychiatry at the Columbia University New York Presbyterian Hospital. He is chairperson of the transgender committee of the Association of Gay and Lesbian Psychiatrists (AGLP) and is himself a transgender male.

Transgender people have not always benefited from mental health "treatment." Due to misunderstanding by professionals and the creation of a gateway system, an unhealthy relationship developed between the transgender community and the psychiatric profession. Unfortunately, the tension of these controversies has raised doubts about the role of mental health professionals in the lives of transgender people.

When someone decides to transition using hormonal and surgical treatment, standard protocols in the medical community have dictated that the person first undergo psychotherapy treatment. Over the years, clinical consensus about psychotherapy has evolved, taking into consideration criticisms by transgender people who were harmed by rigid standards that made them wait too long, obtain expensive therapy they could not afford, or jump through unnecessary hoops.

Today, many transgender people go to mental health providers to understand their gender identity, seek transition, and explore how to live comfortably in their body and gender. Some transgender people struggle immensely. Current controversy over the psychiatric diagnosis of gender dysphoria represents long-standing distrust and hostility among activists toward the psychiatric profession, and it can deter transgender people from seeking treatment. Yet we know that transgender people struggling with gender can suffer so severely that they stop functioning, become unable to live healthy lives, and sometimes kill themselves. We also know that with good treatment, distressful feelings and patterns of behavior improve and help people live productive and meaningful lives.

Transgender people struggling with dysphoria may or may not choose to transition. There is evidence that those who do transition have better outcomes if they have undergone psychotherapy in preparation for their transition. In the best-case scenarios those who transition experience resolution of their dysphoria. However, this is not always the case. Even those who transition remain at higher risk for depression, anxiety, substance abuse, and suicidality than the general population.

Many transgender people need no psychiatric care. They have embraced their gender identity and navigated their lives with success and few symptoms. Some of these folks may see a therapist to help with the process of transitioning and integrating life goals. Some feel offended at the suggestion of seeing a mental health professional, feel no conflict, are certain about their path, and fully understand the risks and benefits of transition.

Some transgender people suffer from serious mental illness such as schizophrenia, bipolar disorder, major depression, or major personality disorders that lead to self-injury. To struggle with a major mental illness in addition to the strain of being transgender can be daunting. In this case, quality psychiatric treatment competent in dealing with both major mental illness and the unique aspects of being transgender is necessary.

Despite the unfortunate reality that some practitioners are not knowledgeable about transgender issues and express a transphobic bias, there is now a community of competent psychiatric providers who enjoy working with transgender people and are devoted to improving care. We can take care of our mental and emotional lives with help from skilled professionals when we need it. We deserve nothing less.

The best resources for finding local services and supports are usually other trans and gender nonconforming people who live in or near our region. Many regions have online trans community support and information groups. Online trans resource directories often list therapists and medical providers by city or state. There are even a few gender specialists who will work with people online for some aspects of their gender care (Fraser, 2009). It is always important to check any listings or referrals for accuracy. Call to verify that the person is still in practice, is licensed as a mental health professional (or is under the supervision of a licensed professional and working toward obtaining the appropriate clinical license), and that they see people with your specific needs—particularly if you are seeking someone who is experienced working with other trans people.

> *"I mentioned my gender variance to my psychologist when I was being treated for depression as a young teenager. We didn't talk about it because I didn't find it particularly important at the time. As I transitioned in my teens, there got to be a point where that was important. Very important. I sought out therapists specifically for that issue then."*

Affording Mental Health Services

For those of us who are fortunate to have health insurance that covers mental health treatment, the use of that insurance for mental health services can be a complicated decision. Many insurance companies in the United States have a standard exclusion for care related to gender identity and transition-related services, including mental health care.

> "I have faced discrimination with my insurance carrier which was covering all my psychotherapies until they found out it was gender related. After that they became non-covered medical care."

At times, people work around insurance concerns by paying for mental health care out of pocket. If you choose to self-pay for mental health services, you may find that you are able to negotiate a rate that works for your financial situation. Providers and clinics may offer discounted rates based on income (sliding scale). Most agencies have strict requirements to determine who qualifies for a reduced fee. They may also have time limits for services at that lower fee to enable as many people as possible to have access to less expensive services. Talk with the provider about your financial situation or any changes in it, and discuss available options. These options may include referral to a different, more affordable provider or agency, reduction in frequency of visits, or ending treatment until a later time when you are able to afford it.

Even if you have insurance and want to use it, your insurance may or may not cover mental health services. If it does, you may want to contact your insurance company directly to find the names of providers who are "in network" for your coverage, meaning that the insurance company has agreed to pay for those providers' services, though you may still be responsible for any copayments and deductibles. You may also use what is called "out-of-network" providers if there is no in-network provider with the correct expertise. Many mental health care providers are not affiliated with any insurance companies because some insurance companies have a poor track record of paying for mental health care. If this is the case with the provider you want to see, you may end up paying out of pocket and submitting claims for reimbursements, or you may negotiate a self-pay rate you can manage. At times, insurance companies may cover out-of-network services it there are no in-network providers who offer the specialized treatment or service you need.

In seeking a mental health professional for support with gender-related issues, some people specifically choose to use an out-of-network therapist for complex reasons. These reasons may include privacy or concerns about what might be reported to the insurance company or to our family members if they receive our insurance statements. Additionally, some people do not wish to let insurance companies have access to details of their mental health care, or they may work in jobs where accessing some mental health treatments may be reason to be terminated. Some people are also reluctant to utilize insurance for fear that they will not be able to access other services or benefits in the future if the reason they needed care is revealed or recorded in insurance records as gender related.

Advocating for Ourselves in Accessing Care

Each person who accesses mental health care has a different reason for doing so. There is no one perfect process to follow to assure that you are able to find a provider who meets your needs. However, there are some things to consider that might help in the process. In some ways, finding a therapist is similar to interviewing and hiring an employee. It is not uncommon to have a phone interview with a therapist before arranging an appointment to meet that person. When interviewing a therapist, ask about the professional qualifications of the provider, type of licensure (e.g., psychologist, psychiatrist, clinical social worker, counselor, etc.), and type of services provided. Mental health professionals work from a number of theoretical models to address the same client concerns.

If you are looking for someone who can prescribe psychiatric medications, the Association of Gay and Lesbian Psychiatrists (AGLP) Web site has a member directory where you can search for providers in your city or state.

Trans-friendly mental health centers in California include Dimensions, LA Gay & Lesbian Center, LA Gender Center, Lyon-Martin, Michael's House, Morningside Recovery, South Coast Recovery, Stepping Stone, Tenderloin AIDS Resource Center, Tom Waddell, Transgender Counseling Program of the San Diego LGBT Community Center, and Van Ness Recovery House.

Northeast LGBTQ-friendly mental health centers include Brattleboro Retreat, Green Mountain Gender Clinic, Gender Identity Clinic of New England (Hartford), Hartford Gay & Lesbian Collective, Fenway Community Health (Boston), and Triangle Program at Arbour Health System (Brookline).

In the Midwest, LGBTQ mental health services are provided at Center on Halstead (Chicago), Howard Brown Health Center (Chicago), Valeo LGBT Program at Chicago Lakeshore Hospital, Pride Institute (Minnesota), and Gender Dysphoria Program of Central Ohio (Columbus).

Talk with trusted friends and members of the trans community in your area about who they recommend as a mental health provider. There may not be official lists to refer to, but it is common for community members to have unofficial lists that include the names of people with both good and not-so-good reputations for their work with trans communities. There are also growing numbers of online lists of therapists who are competent in working with trans communities. Be aware that simply having one's name listed on a Web site, even a reputable or prominent Web site, does not necessarily mean that the person is professionally licensed as a mental health provider. It is okay to ask about and check out a person's licensure before scheduling a visit. Being listed on a site or being a trans or trans-friendly therapist also does not mean that you will work well with that person, that the therapist will know everything about all the variety of gender expressions and identities in the community, or that the therapist will have the same goals and objectives you have. Always check out a mental health provider before committing yourself.

Types of Mental Health Professionals

Mental health professionals may include psychiatrists, psychologists, social workers, counselors, therapists, psychotherapists, coaches, and others. Nonprescribing mental health professionals use talk and behavioral activities to treat difficulties in mental, emotional, and behavioral functioning. A small set of professionals (e.g., psychiatrists, psychiatric nurse practitioners, and prescribing psychologists in Louisiana and New Mexico) may also prescribe specific medications to help treat conditions causing significant mental, emotional, and life distress.

Some providers have areas in which they specialize and areas in which they have little to no training. Some providers are considered generalists. A generalist has basic training and experience in a variety of mental health concerns. It is important to ask providers whether they have training or experience in treating the type of issue you would like to address. Most professionals will admit when they do not have enough experience in the area you need assistance with and may be able to help direct you to another colleague who might be more qualified to help. People may change types of providers or individual therapists during their treatment and may engage in more than one style of therapy at once or over time. For example, one person may have an individual therapist and psychiatrist as well as being part of a group therapy program. Over time, individual therapy may shift from one modality of treatment to another.

General Mental Health Professionals

Most mental health professionals provide face-to-face counseling or talk therapy services that focus on thoughts, feelings, behaviors, and systems (e.g., family, culture) in order to improve a person's development, health, and wellness. It is common for a mental health professional to see a client for a set time on a recurrent schedule (i.e., 45 minutes once weekly). Some providers offer time-limited treatment, meaning they may see a client for a preset number of visits. This is especially true with some agencies and with some specific types of treatment. It is also possible to find a provider who will work with people on an open-ended basis, meaning there is no preset or expected time limit to how many visits you will need for your particular situation or before stopping care. Generally, mental health professionals will stop seeing a client when the initial reason for treatment is resolved, the person's goals have been reached, or because the client is not benefitting from services.

As clients, it is up to each of us to choose to participate in therapy. Like everyone, mental health professionals are unique, with their own values and goals shaped by training and life experience. It can be helpful to speak to potential providers on the phone before scheduling any appointments. When seeking care, it can be hard to know whether we will click with a therapist until we meet for one or more sessions. Therapy may feel awkward or uncomfortable at first because it is new or you have never spoken about some things with another person before. It takes time to know and experience feelings of comfort and safety in therapy.

"I still see the therapist I started going to when I was about 16 or 17. He's helped tremendously and nobody else has ever made me feel as normal, as

loved, and as whole as he has. I mean this platonically, of course, he's just good at making you understand that you are important even if the things you do don't make sense to the majority of people."

It is important, when and where possible, to find someone who fits reasonably well with you, can meet your needs for treatment, and supports your goals. Many of us meet with more than one therapist before deciding on which is the best fit. A word of caution, however, is that changing therapists repeatedly or after only one or two visits may prove to be more problematic than helpful in receiving support and relief from distress.

In addition to face-to-face therapy services provided in office settings, a few counselors may provide therapy over the Internet, telephone, e-mail, or in real-time online visual and talk programs. This is called e-therapy or tele-mental health. The difference between face-to-face and e-therapy is in the method of delivery, not in the therapy that is provided or in the credentials of the therapist (Fraser, 2009). There may be problems with payment or reimbursement for treatment through insurance if the mental health clinician is not licensed in the state the client is in. Some advantages to e-therapy are the ability to keep our mental health treatment relatively anonymous in our local communities, and the ability to find care while living in isolated locations where there may be no other resources available (Fraser, 2009; Israel & Tarver, 1997).

Gender Specialists

Some mental health professionals specifically focus on gender issues or work primarily with gender nonconforming clients. These gender specialists or gender therapists may assist people who are experiencing questions or confusion about their gender, write letters recommending hormones or surgery, or assist people in mental health issues unrelated to their gender. There is no specific training required for therapists to call themselves gender specialists, so their backgrounds and experience vary.

"I as of this writing have gone to see a therapist who specializes in transgender issues. The best part of that experience was the therapist has a wealth of knowledge and was extremely easy to talk to. I think one of the big issues that transgender people face is just being able to find someone to talk to. I found the experience to be very uplifting and plan on seeing her again soon."

In New York, find mental health providers at Callen Lorde, Gay and Lesbian Affirmative Psychotherapy, Gender Identity Project at the LGBT Center, Identity House, Rainbow Heights Club, Realization Center, and William F. Ryan Community Health Center.

Pennsylvania has a number of LGBTQ-affirmative mental health clinics at Mazzoni Center (Philadelphia), Persad (Pittsburgh), Pink & Blues (Philadelphia), and Prevention Point Philadelphia.

Adam (No Regrets tattoo, right) and friends at start of Trans March, Toronto Pride 2009 (copyright Linda Dawn Hammond/IndyFoto.com).

We may seek mental health services to get into gender transition services or to process the changes or difficulties that result from transitioning. Gender therapists can help us to find a place of comfort in whatever gender or body fits best. This complex process encourages us to make informed choices about our care while reducing the potential for nonproductive or harmful coping behaviors, along with attending to and treating other mental health needs, if present (Lev, 2009).

BOOKS FOR THERAPISTS TREATING TRANSGENDER CLIENTS

True Selves: Understanding Transsexualism—For Families, Friends, Coworkers, and Helping Professionals *by Mildred L. Brown*

Casebook for Counseling Lesbian, Gay, Bisexual, and Transgender Clients and Their Families *by Sari H. Dworkin and Mark Pope*

Counseling LGBTI Clients *by Kevin G. Alderson*

Counseling Sexual and Gender Minorities *by Lynne Carroll*

Handbook of Counseling and Psychotherapy for Lesbian, Gay, Bisexual, and Transgender Clients *by Kathleen J. Bieschke, Ruperto M. Perez, and Kurt A. DeBord*

Handbook of LGBT-Affirmative Couple and Family Therapy *by Jerry J. Bigner and Joseph J. Wetchler*

The LGBT Casebook edited *by Petros Levounis, Jack Drescher, and Mary E. Barber*

Transgender Emergence: Therapeutic Guidelines for Working With Gender-Variant People and Their Families *by Arlene Istar Lev*

Transition & Beyond: Observations of Gender Identity *by Reid Vanderburgh*

Conferences That Provide Training for Mental Health Professionals

- Behavioral Health Providers Training, Philadelphia Transgender Health Conference
- GLMA: Health Professionals Advancing LGBT Equality
- Gender Odyssey Professional Seminar
- Gender Spectrum Professional's Workshop
- Mental Health Track, National Transgender Health Summit
- Provider Track, Minnesota Trans Health and Wellness Conference
- Providers Training Day, The Empire Conference
- World Professional Association for Transgender Health (WPATH) Symposium

In the past, gender therapists were charged with assessing our eligibility and readiness to successfully make use of gender-affirming treatments such as hormones and surgery, and with evaluating whether there were other mental health issues masking as gender dysphoria (Coleman et al., 2011). At times, this is still a necessary step. However, this gatekeeper model, or withholding of treatments until the provider deems it is appropriate, is gradually falling to the wayside, especially in light of the new transgender treatment guidelines, published by the World Professional Association for Transgender Health (WPATH). WPATH is an international group of mental health, medical, and other professionals who work with trans people and who utilize research and accepted clinical practice to develop guidelines for the treatment and care of mental and physical health needs of the trans community. Generally, surgeons require a referral letter from a mental health professional that is based on the WPATH *Standards of Care*. Letters are sometimes also required for hormone treatment, although this practice is decreasing as many medical providers now prescribe hormones based on an informed consent model.

Mental health professionals who work with trans communities listen to, support, and make suggestions or offer feedback, while helping us explore our inner conflicts, ideas, fears, coping skills, strengths, and resilience. Gender specialists work with us to create realistic treatment goals for any mental health issues and help to support and enable any plans we may have for gender transition. Each person's transition experience and path is unique. It is important to recognize that a gender specialist's role is not to mold people to a gender binary or make everyone follow the same path. Instead, they collaborate with us to foster expression of our gender identities in the most accurate and authentic way possible for each of us (Rachlin, 2002). As part of therapy, gender specialists will focus on how we feel about our current experience of ourselves physically and emotionally, and explore what supports are in place in our lives to meet our future goals. They may review with us our gender identity development and expression, level of distress, current gender presentation, safety, and plans.

Throughout transition, gender therapists can help us to assess our safety and living situation. They may assist us in exploring options that we might not have been aware of or may have had unrealistic expectations about, such as living cross-gendered without hormonal or surgical body alterations (Rachlin, 2002). For those of us working toward physically changing our bodies with hormone treatments or surgery, a gender specialist may discuss our plans for affording hormones or surgeries, expectations around the physical changes, and anticipated and unanticipated outcomes.

HOW TO WRITE A LETTER FOR HORMONES OR SURGERY

Kit Rachlin, PhD, a clinical psychologist and gender specialist in private practice in New York City, provides tools for mental health providers asked to write letters recommending clients for hormones or surgery.

Medical providers may ask a mental health professional for an evaluation of an individual who is requesting gender-affirming hormones or surgery. The evaluation includes information which the medical provider may not have the time or training to obtain. The letter is a statement that the client is ready and able to give informed consent, and it is also intended to give the treating provider a sense of the client as a person, to help support the client's individualized care.

SECTION I. INTRODUCTION AND OPENING SUMMARY

The client's general identifying characteristics, age, affirmed identity, and preferred pronoun. The nature of the letter writer's contact with the client, the name of the person writing the second opinion (if any), and a statement that the letter writers are in agreement. If certain criteria must be met (such as a diagnosis for insurance reimbursement), put it right up here. The statement that the individual is ready and able to consent to treatment can be made in this first paragraph, and the rest of the letter provides support for the statement.

SECTION II. PERSONAL HISTORY

This section contains information standard in any psychosocial evaluation and gives the medical provider a picture of the patient as an individual. A holistic approach calls for the provider to attend to all aspects of the person—physically, emotionally, professionally, and socially. A discussion of gender history includes the client's history of identity exploration and expression, future goals for expression, and explains why this medical treatment makes sense for this person in the context of their life.

SECTION III. MENTAL HEALTH ASSESSMENT AND ABILITY TO CONSENT TO TREATMENT

The client's history of psychotherapy, history of mental illness, emotional distress, and current mental status. History of physical or sexual abuse, suicide attempts, and substance use, as relevant to the current treatment. If the client has ongoing mental and emotional problems, make a statement about how these other diagnoses will impact the treatment requested.

SECTION IV. SUMMARY

A statement that the individual is prepared, ready, and able to give informed consent to the requested medical treatment. A statement that the mental health professional welcomes a phone call to discuss the case further.

Letter writers should be familiar with the WPATH Standards of Care (Coleman, E., Bockting, W., Botzer, M., Cohen-Kettenis, P., DeCuypere, G., Feldman, J., ... Zucker, K. (2011). Standards of Care for the Health of Transsexual, Transgender, and Gender-Nonconforming People, Version 7. International Journal of Transgenderism. *13*(4),165–232.)

DIAGNOSES AND BILLING

During work with a mental health professional, it is typically necessary to use a formal mental health diagnosis for treatment, billing, and referral purposes. The idea of diagnosis is controversial. A diagnosis of a gender-related disorder may cause problems with an insurer that has treatment exclusions for trans care, or at other times, gender-related services may be covered only if there is a gender diagnosis given. Whether a diagnosis is needed, and what diagnosis is appropriate for the care being provided, can and should be a topic of discussion with your provider. See Chapter 15 for more information on diagnoses.

> *"I do not think there is anything bad or disordered about being trans, but I have no problem with it being categorized as a mental health condition. I feel that those who are outraged by this may need to check their privilege as regards*

mental health issues. There is also nothing bad about having the brain condition that produces clinical depression—except the distress it causes, much like that often caused by being trans. Much like trans people, those who deal with depression require treatments ranging from positive thinking and healthy habits to therapy and medication in order to live well. As long as trans people experience distress and require medical help as a result of being trans, I think the categorization of transgender feelings as a mental health issue makes sense. When it comes to the specifics of the diagnosis, its section in the DSM, etc., I have some disagreements—but that's a different question."

APPROACHES TO GENDER AFFIRMATION TREATMENT

Clinics and providers use different approaches to gender affirmative treatments. Many clinics create their own internal protocols based on research and evidence-based guidelines or standards of care. Having guidelines for ethical care serves to protect trans people from unscrupulous or uninformed providers. These standards of care are usually created and published by groups of medical or mental health providers with experience in research or providing care to trans people. These approaches all follow varying degrees of harm-reduction or client-centered approaches to care that focus on the needs of the trans person over the needs of the provider, and on providing the services that will most quickly help reduce risks of physical and mental health problems. Three of the more prominent formal guidelines for mental health care of gender nonconforming people commonly used in North America are the World Professional Association for Transgender Health's *Standards of Care, Version 7*; the Endocrine Society's *Endocrine Treatment of Transsexual Persons*; and Vancouver Coastal Health's *Clinical Protocol Guidelines for Transgender Care*.

Application of Guidelines and Standards of Care

There have been times in which guidelines and standards of care served as roadblocks for transition-related care with mental health and medical providers as the gatekeepers.

Bowtie (copyright Portraits to the People).

Historically, formal standards and guidelines placed mental health professionals in a position of determining access to medical care (Bockting et al., 2007). Today, a growing understanding of the role of the therapist in gender affirmation is moving more toward seeing gender specialists as expert trans health advocates—invaluable assistants who open doors and make introductions to key people who will make a gender transition possible and safer (Bockting et al., 2007; Lev, 2009; Rachlin, 2002).

Ideally, mental health and medical providers work together to empower us to move toward our goals and visions for our lives. Client-centered care, however, does not mean that mental health or medical providers withhold recommendations for additional care and support services that they have assessed and recognize that the individual may need. This approach also does not mean that everyone who presents to a clinic using this model is guaranteed gender-affirming medical treatments (sometimes called "on-demand" care). Situations remain in which a medical transition may be dangerous or life threatening to a person, and health care professionals are obligated to treat the person in their care and help them understand and cope with this situation, or in other words to first and foremost "do no harm."

Under any model of care and following any of the formal standards and guidelines, client-centered support and services operate from the belief that most of us are well adjusted and need only realistic information and direction on where to find appropriate care. Client-centered gender specialists emphasize our self-determination in choices. The role of the mental health provider is based on support and guidance with an emphasis on our autonomy. Client-centered care emphasizes the vast differences among people who are gender nonconforming and recognizes that not all of us wish to follow the same pathway to self-expression, move from one end of a gender binary to the other, or medically transition at all. Client-centered approaches recognize at the start that not all gender nonconforming people are dealing with mental health concerns or life situations that require mental health treatment.

FAMILY SERVICES AND COMMON FAMILY CONCERNS

Prior to coming out to partners and families, it may be helpful for us as gender nonconforming and trans people to get support from a mental health professional to help think about how to best come out, set realistic goals and timelines, and prepare for potential reactions and responses. A central issue often revolves around deciding when we disclose our identities or histories to others.

> "After much therapy over the years for my depression and getting to a point where it was either come out to my spouse about being trans or die, I came out to her. Fully prepared to lose everything, even my marriage and child and vocation, I told her and, while she didn't understand it, she did accept that this is who I am. (As an aside, she was actually relieved because she thought I was gay all these years. Funny thing is, I actually do consider myself to be a lesbian. . . it's complicated.) I also came out to my daughter and she has accepted me without any reservation. I'm in the process now of coming out to other family members. I am still very much 'stealth' because of both my (and my spouse's) vocation. We're both ordained priests working in the church. Did I mention that it's ummm. . . complicated?"

Delaying talking to a partner may result in our partner feeling betrayed, lied to, or not trusted. It is common for us to be nervous about coming out. It is also common for our partners to have questions about their own gender or sexual orientation based on our gender nonconformity or gender transition plans and process. Some of us may be concerned that our disclosure or plans to affirm our gender will end the relationship—a realistic fear, yet there are examples of relationships that endure the gender transition of one or both partners. Being trans does not mean that we will lose our partner or never be able to find a partner. Honesty, effective communication, and respect can help relationships survive

In Washington, D.C., Us Helping Us and Whitman-Walker provide trans mental health services, and in Baltimore, Chase Brexton.

Houston and Dallas, Texas have LGBT-affirmative mental health services at Legacy Community Health Services, Montrose Center, and the Resource Center of Dallas.

In the West, find mental health providers knowledgeable about trans people at the Glow Counseling Center (Denver), Wingspan and Southern Arizona Gender Alliance (Tucson), Ingersoll Gender Center (Seattle), or Seattle Counseling Service for Sexual Minorities.

Florida's LGBT-affirmative mental health centers include the Pride Institute (Fort Lauderdale) and Freedom Rings Rehab Program (Jacksonville).

Canadian mental health centers specializing in LGBTQ clientele include Transgender Health Program (Vancouver), Rainbow Resource Centre (Winnipeg), Village Clinic/Nine Circles Community Health Centre (Winnipeg), Central Toronto Youth Services: Pride and Prejudice, Centre for Addiction and Mental Health (Toronto), Counseling Program at the 519 (Toronto), Family Service Toronto: David Kelley Services, and Rainbow Health Ontario.

and thrive during the transition period. Chapter 16 provides more information on mental health in relationships.

Just as some of us who are trans-identified or gender nonconforming travel paths of gender affirmation, or transition, so must our partners and family members, which can be difficult for both our loved ones and for us. Our families' reactions may include shock and confusion, and they may range from acceptance and celebration to rejection and sometimes violence (Lev, 2004; Xavier, 2000). However, there are increasing numbers of partners and families who accept the revelation with minimal difficulty.

In the past, therapists and medical providers required trans people to leave their families in order to access medical gender affirmation treatments. Though leaving one's family may still be a common practice in some cultures, it is not recommended. Unfortunately it is still something that a few trans people believe they must do in order to live their lives as their authentic selves. Seek out a mental health professional to talk with before making such a significant life decision.

A mental health professional may be able to assist us and our families in navigating difficult life situations and relationships before, during, and after transition. Some partners and families may be accepting of one type of gender expression or treatment, but not another. For instance, a partner or family member may feel comfortable with a trans loved one's dressing and grooming themselves as their affirmed gender but may struggle with the idea of gender-affirming hormones or surgeries. These partner and family concerns are issues with which a mental health professional might be able to assist, and they would likely include partners and family members in some of the therapeutic sessions. Partners and families are beginning a sort of gender transition of their own and may also need their own support and counseling to understand what this will mean for their lives and identities, and how to deal with possible changes ahead. Partners and families must also wrestle with the consequences of coming out to other people, just as the trans person does. For instance, some partners may have their sexual identities questioned or made invisible as a partner transitions.

> *"I used to love going to gay pride parades and events, but after my partner transitioned from female to male and we later had a child, we were no longer welcome at most LGBT events. We were often asked why we were there or told to leave. People won't talk to us and they stare. No one seemed willing to think we might be a part of that community, because we looked like an average straight couple with a child. It was very hurtful because I still am a lesbian, and my partner identifies as bisexual, but to be welcome now, we have to go alone or wear shirts that say 'nobody knows I'm a lesbian,' 'trans parent,' or something like that. I think it's sad."*

Some partners, family members, friends, and chosen family may say they suspected or knew about their loved one's trans identity for a long time and were just waiting for the individual to disclose their gender identity in their own time and on their own terms. Yet whether loved ones are supportive from the start or not, it is common for people to change how they feel over time. When our partners and families are accepting and supportive from the start, there still may be days, months, or even years of challenging conversations and movement forward as everyone transitions together. Some families and their trans or gender nonconforming members may at times withdraw from one another, while others do the exact opposite, turning inward into the family system and withdrawing from others outside the family. Some families may go into denial, trying to forget that the gender identity or transition information was ever shared and pretend everything is as it was before. Others, unfortunately, completely sever ties.

Our partners' and families' reactions are impossible to predict. Many of us fear complete familial and social rejection, and then are extremely surprised when these dire predictions turn out to be false. As trans and gender nonconforming people, we may find ways to balance our own needs with the demands and needs of our partners and families.

Some of us find it easier to appease uncomfortable partners or family members by limiting the amount of time we dress in our affirmed gender or delaying certain aspects of transition. Others of us gain the acceptance of partners and families and will continue to have support from our loved ones as we express ourselves more fully and authentically.

Mental health professionals experienced in working with trans or gender nonconforming clients may be able to assist in working with families. It is helpful for all the people affected directly by a gender transition to have support whenever possible. We should have separate individual therapists from our partners and family members whenever possible, because working individually and as a family with the same therapist may make it very hard for everyone to feel equally supported.

GROUP SUPPORT AND COUNSELING

Besides individual, couples, and family counseling, we may find support groups helpful. Support groups generally come in three types: peer led, therapist led, and online. In peer-led support groups, a member of the trans community leads a face-to-face group at a community location. It is not uncommon for these locations to be undisclosed for the purpose of ensuring privacy of the group members. These groups might meet weekly, every other week, or monthly. There is usually a small, suggested donation for the meeting that is used to cover the cost of the space. Many of these meetings recognize that trans people are often struggling to make ends meet so will offer a reduced fee or no cost until you are able to help support the meeting. Usually the leaders of these groups have been trained or have skills in group management. Additionally, these groups may be open only to certain people in the trans community, such as cross-dressers, trans men, trans women, or people of color. In some cases, the meetings are open to anyone, including friends, family, and loved ones.

Other groups are therapist-led groups, as known as "group therapy." In these cases, there is usually a screening process for the group to determine whether you are a good group candidate. This is done for a variety of reasons, including the need to assure a sense of balance in the group as well as to be certain that group members will benefit from the experience. Therapist-led groups can be in an open or a closed format. In an open format, group members can come and go. This might be used in a group that is designed to help you understand the transition process and to benefit from the experience of others. In a closed group format, a set number of group members agree to participate in a group experience for a certain number of sessions. Usually, these group experiences last at least six weeks and may go as long as twelve or more weeks. When signing up for a closed group, you are expected to be in attendance at each of the group sessions. In fact, this commitment is often part of the screening process. Closed groups focus on a specific area of concern, such as coming-out experiences, preparing for medical transition, or work or career concerns. It is common for two therapists to lead group sessions together. Unlike peer-led groups, these group sessions almost always have a cost associated with them, although the fee may be negotiable.

The final type of groups is online support groups, such as Yahoo, Google, or Facebook groups. While these groups can be useful for accessing support, they do not take the place of face-to-face meetings. However, for those of us who are unable to access in-person meetings, they can be a great substitute. Online, we can be sure that we will be able to find a group for just about any interest or identity we might have.

CONCLUSION

By taking action and responsibility for locating our own supports and services, we can help to improve our therapeutic relationships and mental health outcomes. We have the right to be treated with dignity and respect in therapy. There are supports and services to assist us in our journeys of self-discovery and expression. Knowledgeable therapists are available in many regions across the country and are becoming trained in working with gender nonconforming and trans populations in increasing numbers. Competent mental health treatment is attainable and can be highly effective in helping us to reach our goals and relieve distress.

REFERENCES AND FURTHER READING

American Counseling Association. (2010). Competencies for counseling with transgender clients. *Journal of LGBT Issues in Counseling, 4*, 135–159.

Bockting, W. O., Knudson, G., & Goldberg, J. M. (2007). Counseling and mental health care for trans adults and loved ones. *International Journal of Transgenderism, 9*, 35–82.

Coleman, E., Bockting, W., Botzer, M., Cohen-Kittenis, P., DeCuypere, G., Feldman, J., ... Zucker, K. (2011). Standards of care for the health of transsexual, transgender, and gender-non-conforming people, Version 7. *International Journal of Transgenderism, 13*(4), 165–232.

Dean, L., Meyer, I. H., Robinson, K., Sell, R. L., Sember, R., Silenzio, V. M. B., ... White, J. (2000). Lesbian, gay, bisexual, and transgender health: Findings and concerns. *Journal of the Gay and Lesbian Medical Association, 4*(3), 102–151.

Devor, A. H. (2004). Witnessing and mirroring: A fourteen stage model of transsexual identity formation. *Journal of Gay and Lesbian Psychotherapy, 8*(1/2), 41–67.

Ehrbar, R., & Gorton, R. N. (2010). Exploring provider treatment models in interpreting the standards of care. *International Journal of Transgenderism, 12*(4), 198–210.

The Endocrine Society. (2009). Endocrine treatment of transsexual persons: An endocrine society clinical practice guideline. *Journal of Clinical Endocrinology and Metabolism, 94*(9), 3132–3154.

Fraser, L. (2009). Etherapy: Ethical and clinical considerations for version 7 of the world professional association for trans health's standards of care. *International Journal of Transgenderism, 11*(4), 247–263.

Hembree, W. C., Cohen-Kettenis, P., Delemarre-van de Waal, H. A., Gooren, L. J., Meyer, W. J., III, Spack, N. P., ... Montori, V. M. (2009). Endocrine treatment of transsexual persons: An endocrine society clinical practice guideline. *Journal of Clinical Endocrinology and Metabolism, 94*(9), 3132–3154.

Hendricks, M. L., & Testa, R. J. (2012). A conceptual framework for clinical work with transgender and gender non-conforming clients: An adaptation of the Minority Stress Model. *Professional Psychology: Research and Practice, 43*(5), 460–467.

Israel, G. E., & Tarver, D. E., II. (1997). *Trans care: Recommended guidelines, practical information, and personal accounts.* Philadelphia, PA: Temple University Press.

Lev, A. I. (2009). The ten tasks of the mental health provider: Recommendations for revision of the world professional association for trans health's standards of care. *International Journal of Transgenderism, 11*(2), 74–99.

Lev, A. I. (2004). *Trans emergence: Therapeutic guidelines for working with gender-variant people and their families.* Binghamton, NY: Haworth Press.

Mizock, L., & Fleming, M. Z. (2011). Trans and gender variant populations with mental illness: Implications for clinical care. *Professional Psychology: Research and Practice, 42*(2), 208–213.

Rachlin, K. (2002). Transgender individuals' experiences of psychotherapy. *International Journal of Transgenderism, 6*(1), n. pag.

Shipherd, J., Green, K., & Abramovitz, S. (2010). Trans clients: Identifying and minimizing barriers to mental health treatment. *Journal of Gay and Lesbian Mental Health, 14*(2), 94–108.

Sperber, J., Landers, S., & Lawrence, S. (2005). Access to health care for transgender persons: Results of a needs assessment in Boston. *International Journal of Transgenderism, 8*(2-3), 75–91.

Xavier, J. M. (2000). The Washington Transgender Needs Assessment Survey. *Us Helping Us, People Into Living.* Retrieved January 2014, from http://www.glaa.org/archive/2000/tgneedsassessment1112.shtml

MENTAL HEALTH CONCERNS

Tamar Carmel, Ruben Hopwood, and lore m. dickey

15

SOME OF US SEEK MENTAL HEALTH CARE to assist in the process of transition or to understand ourselves more fully. Others of us have concerns about problems like depression or anxiety that are interfering with our ability to lead fulfilling lives. We may feel sad or down much of the time, easily become frustrated or angry, or have anxiety attacks that prevent us from feeling safe. Some of us have problems with alcohol or drugs and are not sure where to go or who will be able to understand or help us.

As trans people, many of these problems happen to us more commonly than they do to other groups because of what we have been through in our lives. Many of us have been teased, rejected by our families, threatened with violence, or even physically or sexually abused. We may have also spent years uncomfortable in our bodies or our roles in life. There was a time when it was almost impossible to find a mental health provider who could see us as whole people and not as having a mental illness just by being transgender. However, it is increasingly more common to be able to find trans-friendly mental health providers who listen to our stories and understand that we have many of the same struggles as everyone else. Some of us are even going into mental health fields as our careers.

Seeing a therapist or other mental health provider for the first time may be a daunting or scary experience. They ask a lot of questions, some of which we are unsure why they are asking. They may talk with us about a diagnosis, and it can be difficult to hear someone label us. Some of us may have had bad experiences with therapists in the past and may be afraid to open up again. Others may worry about a power dynamic developing between us and the clinician. However, our first priority should always be our health and wellness. Many of us have successfully navigated mental health services and found valuable support systems.

CONFIDENTIALITY

During the first session with a mental health provider, most providers will bring up the topic of confidentiality. This is an agreement that the clinician makes with us to keep the information we share with them private. Mental health professionals are trained to keep information confidential. Be aware, though, that his may not include some people we typically think of as mental health providers, such as certain types of counselors at school or work. It also does not always apply to those of us under 18, as our therapist is permitted to talk with our guardians about us. If in doubt, ask. There are a few instances where confidentiality may be broken. If the provider thinks we are in danger of hurting ourselves or other people, the provider is obligated to try to prevent that from happening. Providers are also required to report suspected abuse of a child or vulnerable adult. In addition, providers may, at times, share some information about us with colleagues or supervisors in order to get help with our case. Your provider should clearly tell you the limits of confidentiality.

DIAGNOSIS

Many mental health providers structure their first few interviews with us by asking many different questions in order to arrive at a diagnosis. A diagnosis involves analyzing clinical information and drawing conclusions about the nature or cause of an issue. For some of us, it is scary to be burdened with a diagnosis. For others, it can be comforting to find a term that describes what we are going through. Providers generally use diagnoses to help guide their care. They may recommend certain medications or types of therapy that are known to be effective based on the diagnosis they give us. For example, they may say that in people with our diagnosis, individual therapy has been found to be helpful, and they may explain the type of therapy they think would be most effective, such as supportive therapy, cognitive behavioral therapy, or dialectical behavior therapy. They may recommend a group therapy setting or couples therapy. They may tell us about antidepressant, antianxiety, mood-stabilizing, or antipsychotic medications.

During a first visit, mental health professionals will most likely perform a comprehensive assessment, where they will ask us many questions. Most of the questions are standard and are asked regardless of our gender identities. Some of these questions may include the following:

- What brings you here today? What kinds of issues are you having? How long have they lasted for you?
- Have you had any problems with sleep? Appetite? Mood? Concentration?
- Have you heard voices or seen things that other people do not?
- Have you seen a mental health professional before? Were you diagnosed with any mental illnesses in the past? Have you needed to be hospitalized for a psychiatric illness?
- Do you have any medical illnesses? Are you taking any medications (psychiatric or otherwise)? Do you have any allergies?
- Where did you grow up? What was your family like? What are your sources of social support? Are you in a relationship?
- How much alcohol do you drink? Do you use (or have you used) any other drugs? Have you had a problem with alcohol or drug abuse?
- Do you have any family members who have been diagnosed with a mental illness?
- Has there ever been a time when you have considered ending your life? Have you had a suicide attempt before?
- Do you have insurance? Does it cover mental health care?

Some questions may be related to our gender identities.

- When did you first discover that your gender identity or expression was not what others expected or wished it would be?
- Do others know? To whom have you come out? What are your fears about coming out as trans?
- Have you experienced discrimination or stress because of your gender identity? How has that affected you?

While many of these questions are standard, some may seem invasive or make us feel uncomfortable or embarrassed. Most of the time, mental health professionals have good reasons for asking the questions they do. If we are unsure why a question is important for them to ask us, we can always bring this up. There are some clinicians who are unfamiliar with trans people. They may ask ignorant questions, and we may need to decide whether we feel comfortable (gently) educating them, or we may decide we want to seek out care from someone else. There are even some clinicians who will ask probing questions on purpose, out of curiosity, or because they see our trans identity as a disorder. Many of us seek mental health care for reasons unrelated to our gender, and someone who focuses solely on our gender when we are trying to communicate other issues may not be a good fit. If we feel we are being targeted or victimized by a mental health provider, it is OK to leave. We go to mental health providers to find help and should never feel attacked.

> *"I was deathly scared of therapists. I remember one time, my mother and father took me to see a therapist because my brother and I were fighting a lot. I deliberately lied to the therapist. I remember feeling sort of proud of myself for lying to him, but what I didn't remember until very recently is why I lied. . . I lied*

*because I was one-hundred-percent, absolutely, positively certain that if I told
the truth, I would be locked away in an insane asylum for the rest of my life."*

During the initial assessment, a clinician may start to consider whether our psychological or emotional concerns warrant a diagnosis. The clinician may give us a diagnosis during the initial assessment or may wait until the second or third visit. In some cases, we may not receive a diagnosis at all and may work out a treatment plan that focuses on resolving our individual issues.

Some of us do not like the idea of being labeled with a diagnosis. Because there is still a lot of stigma associated with mental illness, the idea of having a diagnosis can be intimidating, insulting, or scary. We may feel we do not like having a label attached to our individual and personal experiences. We may wonder why a clinician needs a diagnosis, instead of simply helping each individual with their specific issues. Some clinicians, in fact, do follow this method of helping their clients. Some clinicians use a diagnosis solely for billing or referral purposes. Most insurance companies will not pay for mental health care without a diagnosis. If we have any concerns about the diagnosis being used, it is appropriate to ask the provider about it and have a discussion. It may be important to us that a gender-related diagnosis is used, or we may be adamantly against it. A collaborative mental health provider will work with us on these issues.

Many clinicians rely on a diagnosis to help them (and us) understand the nature of our issues, identify possible causes, determine potential treatment options, and predict potential outcomes. For example, if we are seeking the help of a therapist because of overwhelming feelings of sadness and hopelessness, the clinician may be trying to figure out if what we are going through can be classified as major depression, grief, or adjustment to changing life circumstances. If our symptoms sound similar to the experiences of others who have major depression, it can help us determine how long those feelings may last and what kinds of therapy or medications may be helpful. In addition, receiving a diagnosis may also be a source of relief for some of us who feel alone in our emotional suffering. It may validate our experiences and assure us that we are not the only people who have had this type of experience.

To diagnose and treat mental conditions, most mental health professionals in the United States use the *Diagnostic and Statistical Manual of Mental Disorders (DSM)* (APA, 1980; APA, 1987; APA, 1994; APA, 2000; APA, 2013), which is a diagnostic tool created by the American Psychiatric Association (APA). It is designed to provide clinicians with a framework for understanding mental health issues and diagnoses. The book is currently in its fifth edition and changes every decade or so, as our understanding of mental health changes through research and clinical observation. Like all scientific work, the *DSM* is a product of the society in which it is created, so it has the biases that American society does. The majority of its committee members are white and cisgender, and for many years they were almost completely male. This certainly affects the way it is organized. It is up to each clinician to determine how the *DSM* does or does not benefit their work; and it is up to each of us, as people, to determine how we will or will not use any diagnoses we are given.

> *"I am not familiar with medical classifications. I think it should be something
> people are able to struggle with themselves (or with medical assistance should
> they wish it), but that they should not have medical intervention forced on them.
> I think they should have access to whatever forms of care they need, within the
> confines of medical codes of ethics and appropriate guidelines (as long as those
> guidelines are constructive rather than paternalistic and confining)."*

GENDER DYSPHORIA AS A DIAGNOSIS

Dysphoria involves feeling a sense of discontent or discomfort with our lives or a part of our lives. We may feel dysphoria about our jobs, our relationships, where we live, with our bodies, or with our assigned gender. It may cause us to feel overwhelming stress, discomfort, or anxiety. Gender dysphoria can be defined as having unhappy feelings about the sex we were assigned at birth or the gender roles that come with that.

"Dysphoria can cause a lot of anguish and should be treated as part of the process in becoming comfortable with oneself, however that may be managed (hormones, surgery, nonphysical modification, and so on)."

A gender identity that varies from what is expected has been considered to be a disorder in the *DSM*, which has sparked tension between trans activists and mental health professionals. It can feel degrading and invalidating for us to have our gender identity, expression, or feelings of dysphoria labeled as a disorder by clinicians.

Transgender identities first appeared in the *DSM* in 1980 as "gender identity disorder of childhood" and "transsexualism." Transsexualism eventually became "gender identity disorder" (GID). These diagnoses did not change much until the fifth edition of the *DSM* came out in 2013 and GID became gender dysphoria (GD). Some people compare the evolution of trans identity as a diagnosis to that of homosexuality, which was included in the *DSM* as a mental illness until 1973. If GD follows the same path, it may eventually be removed completely from the *DSM*. Some speculate that the removal of homosexuality and addition of GID to the *DSM* at the same time was not a coincidence (Drescher, 2009).

"I think transgenderism is not inherently a mental disorder at all, regardless of the type. However, I think the gender dysphoria that usually accompanies it *is* something that could and I think should be described as a mental condition. It's distressing and otherwise meets all of the criteria for a mental disorder; it's a temporary state that can be treated and can go away (unlike transgenderism), so it's not like it's something that is permanently bound to us; and it provides a straightforward way for us to request coverage for sex reassignment from medical insurance companies."

"I don't feel it needs to be categorized at all. Nobody benefits when we're crammed into boxes that we don't necessarily fit into. It's these boxes that cause a lot of the problems."

"I think there is a problem with transsexual people being dismissed as 'crazy,' but I don't think the categorization as a psychological/psychiatric issue is the problem, I think the stigma we attach to all mental illness is the problem."

In the fourth edition of the *DSM* (APA, 1994), GID was defined as a "strong and persistent cross-gender identification" with "persistent discomfort with his/her sex or sense of inappropriateness in the gender role of that sex," causing "clinically significant impairment in social, occupational, or other important areas of functioning." Classification of trans identity as a disorder aggravated many trans activists who felt it was degrading for us to be told that we have a disease or disorder for being who we are.

Diagnosing Difference is a film directed by Annalise Ophelian that explores the impact and implications of gender identity issues being classified in the *DSM* through interviews with trans scholars, artists, and activists.

For more information on the history of transgender identity in the *DSM*, read Jack Drescher's paper "Queer Diagnoses: Parallels and Contrasts in the History of Homosexuality, Gender Variance, and the Diagnostic and Statistical Manual" published in the *Archives of Sexual Behavior*, April 2010, 39(2), 427–460.

TRANS PATHOLOGIZATION

Pau Crego Walters

Mainstream culture often depicts trans people as wanting to take hormones or have surgeries because most people think that our core desire is to change our bodies. Even though this is not true for all of us, organizing for trans rights has generally developed in parallel with trying to access trans-specific health care.

We have been studied by the medical community for many years, but the most prominent scientist in relation to trans people is Harry Benjamin. Based on Benjamin's recommendations, in 1980 "gender identity disorder" was included in the *Diagnostics and Statistical Manual of Mental Disorders* (*DSM*). Since then, gender identity disorder (most recently renamed as gender dysphoria) has been the label that medical and mental health professionals use to talk about trans people.

Regardless of the intentions that health providers had in creating these protocols, it is important to be aware of the responsibility that comes with having the power and credibility to frame certain identities as medical issues. The medical labels of "transsexual" and "gender identity disorder/gender dysphoria" are not the first to be created for folks who are different from the social norm. For example, psychiatrist Benjamin Rush believed that slaves during colonial times suffered from a disease that he called "negritude," thought of as a form of leprosy, and for which the only cure was to become white. At around the same time, physician Samuel Cartwright identified the mental disorder of "drapetomia," a disease that supposedly made slaves of African descent try to escape the violent situations they lived in. Also, homosexuality was considered a mental illness until 1973.

Some of us feel comfortable with the idea of trans identities stemming from a biological or mental health disease, and others don't. Many trans people fear removing current trans-related labels from the *DSM* because it will make it seem as though the desire for hormones or surgeries is not an important health need and will not be covered by insurance plans and public funding. Activists have worked on various strategies to address this complex question: maintain the situation as is, use these labels as just a tool to getting our health needs met, defend the right to be free of these imposed labels, fight for everyone's right to health care, and more.

We need to think about how this relationship affects how the world sees us and how we see ourselves. Why are we expected to be a certain way in order to access trans-specific care? Why must we tell the same stories of ourselves, say we experience our bodies in the same ways, claim that we want the same things? And why is suitable health care so scarce and unattainable? Indeed, perhaps we need to look beyond how trans and gender nonconforming people are affected by this, and notice that satisfactory health care is inaccessible to most people (especially in the United States). This provides a great opportunity to build coalitions with other communities.

With the development of the *DSM-5*, significant changes were made to the diagnostic name and definition of GID. Some people feel that the new term, gender dysphoria, is less stigmatizing because it does not include the word "disorder." Others feel that this name change does not matter if the diagnosis is still included in a manual of mental disorders. One of the most notable changes is that GD no longer specifically designates our trans identities as pathological unless we are disturbed by them. The GD classification instead characterizes a discrete period of dysphoria or discomfort with one's body, and it does not apply to those of us who feel at ease with our bodies, either with or without medical intervention. GD also allows for more fluid identities than GID did, recognizing those of us who have identities that are not male or female. These changes recognize the diversity of our identities and question the notion that our trans identity itself is a mental illness. However, there remains much dissatisfaction within trans communities and among trans-affirmative mental health providers with the GD diagnosis.

> *"I prefer not to see it as some terrible disease. It's just how I choose to live my life. I understand that a recent trend in psychiatry is to define disorders such that a trait isn't a disorder unless it has a negative impact on your life. If I can successfully live as a woman as I set out to do, then it isn't a disorder, but rather a personal triumph."*

> *"I believe that a mental health professional should be the one to diagnose a person with gender identity disorder. This would be to eliminate other possibilities. But since this is a treatable disorder . . . I believe it should be categorized as a medical condition that is treatable."*

HAVING AN OPPRESSED IDENTITY

There are a number of mental health issues known or suspected to affect transgender people more than cisgender people. Very little research has been done on how being transgender or gender nonconforming can put us at greater risk of mental illness. However, we can make inferences about mental health issues in trans or gender nonconforming communities based on existing LGBTQ research and the Minority Stress Model, which says that LGBTQ people living in societies that stigmatize them are under increased stress (DiPlacido, 1998; Hendricks & Testa, 2012; Meyer, 1995).

GID Reform Advocates is a group of medical professionals, caregivers, scholars, researchers, students, human rights advocates, and members of the transgender, bisexual, lesbian, and gay communities and their allies who advocate for reform of the psychiatric classification of gender diversity as a mental disorder.

Outside the United States, and in some places in the United States, a different system than the *DSM* is used to diagnose mental illness. *The International Classification of Diseases* (*ICD*) is currently in its 10th edition. With the 11th edition, the internal working group is recommending that gender identity diagnoses be removed from the section on mental and behavioral disorders.

Some professionals use the minority stress theory to explain why many of us are at greater risk of mental health issues. The theory suggests that minority, oppressed, or marginalized groups are more likely than privileged groups to experience mental health issues because of the negative way they are treated by society. This applies not only to transgender and gender nonconforming individuals but also to those of us who are oppressed because of our race, gender, sex, religion, nationality, disability, or socioeconomic status.

As trans people, we face discrimination both within the LGB community and society as a whole. For example, we are at greater risk of experiencing family rejection, peer rejection, bullying, threats of violence, abuse, assault, homelessness, job prejudice, lower socioeconomic status, internalized transphobia (the view that one's own trans identity is abnormal or bad), societal stigma, negative media attention, lack of governmental and legal protections, and religious bigotry. People who experience this kind of discrimination in their lives are at heightened risk of emotional distress, transgender or not.

> "Transphobia is one of the most 'allowed' forms of abuse left in our society. You hear the trans world being made fun of in movies, TV shows, and in print. It's a sad commentary that the gender binary is still being held up as 'natural' when there is so much research showing the opposite. Due to the lack of understanding, it's easy for people to actively persecute us without fear of reprisal."

In addition to our being trans or gender nonconforming, some of us may also belong to other oppressed groups. Our identities do not exist in separate bubbles but interact with each other and affect how we are treated by our society as a whole. Belonging to more than one minority, oppressed, or marginalized group can further subject us to more stress and increase our risk for mental illness. Also, as we change how we express our gender, we may notice a change in how we are treated. For example, a transgender woman who starts transition and presents as a woman after presenting as a man for the majority of her life may experience a loss of male privilege for the first time and become subject to the stressors that women experience as a marginalized group in our society. This added stress can also put us at risk for mental health issues and may warrant the help of a mental health professional.

VIOLENCE, VICTIMIZATION, AND TRAUMA IN OUR COMMUNITIES

As members of the trans community, we may experience high levels of violence, victimization, and trauma, which puts us at an increased risk of mental health issues. The violence and trauma many of us experience includes emotional, psychological, verbal, physical, and sexual abuse. It can occur at home, at school, or in the community, and it can come from family members, friends, peers, or strangers.

Several studies in the United States (Clements-Nolle, Marx, & Katz 2006; Kenagy, 2005; Lombardi, Wilchins, Priesing, & Malouf, 2001) have assessed our communities' experiences of verbal, physical, and sexual abuse, with greater than 50% (and in some studies as high as 80%) of us reporting having been victims of harassment, discrimination, violence, or forced sex. Extreme examples of victimization and violence against our community have been increasingly portrayed in the media over the last couple of decades.

> "I have been seriously mistreated, especially as a child. Those experiences were awful, humiliating, denigrating, and painful. My tormentors were motivated by hate, religious intolerance, and ignorance."

> "I have lost my job and have since been unable to find a position that suits my work experience and education. I am living where I am because of the goodness of a friend who is helping financially. I have been called names, laughed at, and mocked out in public and I have been threatened."

"So far, I've had a handful of coworkers stop looking at or speaking with me, and it's a dehumanizing experience. I cannot guess as to their motivation."

There is not much research available on how violence, victimization, and trauma specifically affect trans communities. However, what minimal research is available on trans populations, combined with the more prevalent research done on lesbian, gay, and bisexual youth, has shown that trauma can increase the risk of developing substance use disorders, depression, anxiety, suicide, and risky sexual behaviors such as unprotected sex and the transmission of sexually transmitted infections (Breslau, Davis, & Schultz, 2003; Clements-Nolle et al., 2006; D'Augelli et al., 2005; Garofalo, Wolf, Wissow, Woods, & Goodman, 1999; Herek, Gillis, & Cogan, 1999; Hendricks & Testa, 2012; Hershberger & D'Augelli, 1997; Marshal et al., 2011; Mays & Cochran, 2001; Reisner, Mimiaga, Safren, & Mayer, 2009; Remafedi, Farrow, & Deisher, 1991). We as transgender people are likely affected in the same ways.

"I have been part of groups of trans women bashed on the streets. Usually by a bunch of young bucks, sometimes even uniformed cops, shouting epithets on the streets, and sometimes throwing long-range bottles at us. My response to small scale face to face bashing has always been to say that 'yes I am a woman of transsexual experience, let me explain to you what that means,' looking them directly in the eye. It has always worked so far, although I must say that being a septuagenarian reduces the street scrutiny applied to a person."

"As a kid, I was physically and verbally attacked on a pretty regular basis, especially in high school. I didn't identify as anything in particular back then, but I've looked flamingly genderqueer basically since preschool, so others' perceptions of me had more to do with harassment than how I saw myself. High school was a nightmare, between regular death threats and being pelted with rocks and garbage. I never came up with a coherent answer to what motivated this harassment, and really, there didn't seem to be much thought or intention behind it. As a general rule, taking care of my own safety was more important than psychoanalyzing my enemies."

Unfortunately, discrimination, victimization, and violence are realities for many of us. Luckily, more and more attention is being paid to this epidemic. Our communities, families, friends, and allies are advocating for more acceptance and protections. Cultural stances and legal policies continue to change. More and more, we are finding supportive communities and seeing gender identity and gender expression added to nondiscrimination policies in schools, organizations, workplaces, and even the government.

Even though many of us have experienced discrimination and violence, we may not experience mental illness because of it. This suggests that we have resiliency factors that protect us from negative mental health outcomes. Hopefully researchers will start to identify these factors so that we can continue to improve our community's quality of life and mental health. Those of us who have experienced violence are not alone. There are many ways to connect with others within our community for support and to find empathic, caring, trans-friendly mental health providers.

INTERNALIZED TRANSPHOBIA

Ami B. Kaplan, LCSW, is a psychotherapist in New York City working with transgender clients. She sits on the Policy and Procedures Committee of the World Professional Association for Transgender Health.

Internalized transphobia refers to hatred and shame some people have inside about their being trans. This happens primarily because of discrimination, ignorance, and stigma in society. Growing up in a culture where this attitude is common, you take it in and part of you believes it whether you want to or not. We learn that a certain group of people should be mocked before we know that we are *in* that group—and then we are stuck in the position of hating something about ourselves.

Feelings of hate and shame for yourself, of which you might not even be aware, can result in low self-esteem and depression. They can make you not want to be around people, to withdraw, or to be a loner. Some people take a long time to come out as trans because they have so much internalized transphobia. It can hold you back in many areas of your life such as forming deep and satisfying connections to others. Sometimes internalized transphobia can keep you from connecting with other trans folks. When one has a deep hatred of the genderqueer inside, it can get confusing to be around other trans people. You may see them in the way you learned early on—as freaky or not good enough in some way.

The first thing to do to try to address internalized transphobia is to be aware of it. This is hard to do, because we usually automatically try to avoid things about ourselves that we are embarrassed about. One can feel ashamed of being ashamed! It gets complicated, so it really helps to have a therapist who is knowledgeable about gender issues to do this work with, but a supportive friend or a support group can work, too. It takes time to "undo" deep-down beliefs about gender-variant people—just like it took time to acquire those beliefs.

Depression

Depression is a serious, yet common, mental illness that affects people worldwide of all races, ethnicities, genders, and incomes. It can severely impact our day-to-day functioning, work, relationships, and physical health. According to the World Health Organization, depression affects over 350 million people worldwide and is the leading cause of disability around the globe (World Health Organization, n.d.).

People experience depression in different ways. Some of us may have more severe depression than others, which can make diagnosing depression difficult. Most people who experience depression feel sad or down for an extended period of time. While feeling sad or blue from time to time is normal, the feeling of sadness or despair for someone who has depression tends to be much more persistent, drawn-out, and profound. We may feel extremely blue—even when good things are happening around us.

In addition to feeling down, depression carries other symptoms as well. We may feel more irritable. We may feel more tired or have difficulty falling asleep. We may lose interest in activities that once gave us pleasure or joy, like hobbies or spending time with friends. We may experience decreased motivation, excessive guilt, low energy or fatigue, or have difficulty concentrating. We may also notice changes in our appetite. Depressed people may either lose or gain weight. A few of us hear things or see things that are not real. Unfortunately, at its worst, depression can lead some people to contemplate or attempt self-injury or suicide.

> *"Because I was shy and depressed, my parents sent me to a psychologist several times when I was a kid and teenager. I knew that the transgender topic was something people were not supposed to mention. Also I never trusted them. So I never talked about it."*

Trans communities experience higher rates of depression compared to the general population and the non-trans LGB community. Lifetime prevalence of depression in our community may be as high as 50%–67%, compared to 9.1% in the United States overall (Bockting Miner, Swinburne Romine, Hamilton, & Coleman, 2013; CDC, 2010; Clements-Nolle, Marx, Guzman, & Katz., 2001; Kim et al., 2006; Nuttbrock et al., 2010; Rotondi et al., 2011). This increased risk is related to our experiences of gender discrimination, transphobia, abuse, and victimization.

> *"I went to therapy at various times growing up, starting when I was about seven or eight for depression and ADHD or something, but I never discussed my gender identity issues."*

The intersection between transition and mental health is quite complicated. Many of us have feelings of sadness related to body dysphoria or feeling out of place. This may not rise to the level of clinical depression. The Ontario Trans PULSE research study found that some of us who plan to medically transition but have not yet started are at high risk of depression (Rotondi et al., 2011). There is some suggestion that our anxiety and depression may lessen with hormone treatment (Gomez-Gil, 2012), although this theory has not been substantiated with evidence from other studies (Mergeri & Khoosal, 2007; Udeze, Abdelmawla, Khoosal, & Terry, 2008). Many of us expect our mental health problems to be solved by medical or surgical transition, but that does not seem to be realistic. We may have preexisting depression or unrealistic transition expectations that worsen our mood and functioning. Many of us hope that completion of our gender transition will resolve all of our problems, but it may not. Even with hormone therapy, depression can lower our quality of life (Gorin-Lazard, 2012). It is important that we approach our transition and everyday lives with realistic expectations, and that we actively work on improving our lives.

Treatment for depression should be sought out as soon as possible. If left untreated, depression can be devastating because it affects all areas of our lives as well as the lives of our loved ones. This is where trans-friendly mental health providers can help. Counselors, therapists, and psychiatrists can not only help us navigate the amazing and sometimes overwhelming journey of transition, but they can also help us work on improving our mood, everyday functioning, relationships, and any other speed bumps that appear down the road. Together with a mental health professional, we can problem solve any number of issues, including how to cope with depression or anxiety, how to work through thoughts of self-harm, disclosure to family and friends, coming out on the job, and productive ways to address real or perceived discrimination.

An important and empowering advocacy campaign is Dan Savage's "It Gets Better Project," which collects videos from adults directed at LGBTQ youth.

> *"During my transition, I had several clients who fired me from their projects. I thought I was prepared for this eventuality, but I was not. Looking back, I don't think it was possible to adequately prepare for being told that I am no longer a good consultant because I am trans*. I was devastated by these firings. I thought these firings were the end of my career; several times I began wailing uncontrollably on the way home from work, and I am lucky I didn't wreck my car."*

Depression can be treated with therapy or antidepressant medication to improve our mood, functioning, and quality of life. Therapy and medications can be used together, and the combination often has the best success rates. Before starting an antidepressant medication, make sure to discuss your medical history (especially other medications you are taking) with your prescriber, because it will help guide your clinician in choosing the right medication for you.

James Darling "It Gets Better" (copyright Amos Mac).

When you encounter a transgender individual struggling with depression, it is important to acknowledge and accept the individual's true identity, gender-related or otherwise, because not doing so can be emotionally damaging, not to mention disrupt the therapeutic alliance. Do not assume that the mental health concerns that trans clients face are solely related to their gender identity. On inpatient units, it is important to treat every patient with dignity and respect. For your transgender patients, this means making sure all staff respect the individual's transgender identity by using the patient's preferred name and pronoun, making appropriate rooming and bathroom adjustments, and ensuring the patient is protected from violence or discrimination from other patients or staff. This is an area where advocacy for peer education and proper patient treatment is essential.

"I have had severe depression for a good portion of my life—that's a psychiatric disorder. It has greatly influenced my life experiences, but it doesn't define who I am—how I deal with my depression defines me."

When discussing treatments with your clinician, make sure to ask about lifestyle changes that can also help with depression. Many of us benefit from regular exercise, a balanced diet, a daily routine, a regular sleep schedule, positive social supports, writing and journaling, and Eastern medicine practices such as meditation and acupuncture. Self-care is very important when recovering from depression.

SELF-INJURIOUS BEHAVIOR

Some of us, for many different reasons, may cut, hit, burn, or injure parts of our bodies without the intention of ending our lives. Mental health professionals call this nonsuicidal self-injurious behavior. We may cut ourselves to obtain a physical release of our emotional pain, as a cry for help, or due to discomfort or discontent with our physical bodies. Some of us do it to cope with overwhelming feelings or stress. Those of us who do it may also have depression, a history of personal trauma, or another mental health diagnosis.

Research suggests that as trans and gender nonconforming people we are at greater risk of self-harm than others (Hoshiai et al., 2010; Walls, Laser, Nickels, & Wisneski, 2010). However, those of us with strong support networks are less likely to harm ourselves. Trans and gender nonconforming youth have a self-injury rate that is at least twice as high as the general population (Hoshiai et al., 2010). We appear to be at particularly high risk of self-injury because we are more likely to be bullied or victimized (Liu & Mustanski, 2012). One study of LGBTQ youth (Walls, Laser, Nickels, & Wisneski, 2010) found that trans youth had increased rates of cutting behaviors, even when compared with lesbian, gay, and bisexual youth.

There are dangers to cutting ourselves, even if we do not intend to cause serious harm. Sometimes people die from their self-injuries or from infections of their wounds. Self-injury can be an indication of unresolved mental health issues or stress and should definitely be cause for concern. Many of us feel shame or embarrassment and keep it a secret. We are not alone and help is out there. If you or someone you know engages in self-injurious behaviors, please seek help from a mental health provider. Talk therapy can be particularly helpful to channel our injurious thoughts or behaviors into more positive and productive outlets. Therapy can also help us address the underlying causes of these thoughts. Some of us have found it helpful to join in-person or online support groups.

SUICIDE

Unfortunately, suicidal thoughts and suicide attempts have become all too common in our trans community. Lifetime rates of suicidal thoughts for trans people in various studies have ranged from 48% to 79% (Hoshiai et al., 2010; Kenagy, 2005; Krehely, 2009; Nuttbrock et al., 2010; Terada, 2011; Xavier, Honnold, & Bradford, 2007). Between 21% and 41% of trans people report a history of suicide attempts (Clements-Nolle, Marx, & Katz, 2006; Grant et al., 2010; Kenagy, 2005; Nuttbrock et al., 2010; Xavier, Honnold, & Bradford, 2007).

"I saw psychologists starting from when I was about 10 and was having suicidal thoughts that I could never really explain. I don't know if gender variance had to do with that or not."

The reasons we may consider or attempt suicide are often related to our experiences of rejection, discrimination, and victimization (Clements-Nolle et al., 2006; Grossman & D'Augelli 2007). In general, suicide attempts occur more often in those of us with a history of low self-esteem, depression, substance use disorders (such as alcohol or drug abuse), discrimination, victimization, abuse, and inadequate or very limited social supports (Clements-Nolle et al., 2006; Grant et al., 2010; Grossman & D'Augelli 2007; Kenagy, 2005; Liu & Mustanski, 2012; Risser et al., 2011). In one study of LGBTQ young adults, those who experienced victimization at school during adolescence were 5.6 times more likely to report having attempted suicide (Russel et al., 2011). Other studies confirm that younger age is a risk factor for suicidality in our community (Clements-Nolle et al., 2006; Terada, 2011). The reasons for increased suicidality in our community are not entirely clear, but gender nonconformity and early traumatic experiences definitely play a role (Fitzpatrick, 2005; Liu & Mustanski, 2012). In any population, a previous suicide attempt is a risk factor for future attempts.

> "Well I self identified as a girl at age 4, and had my family promptly freak out. . . I then went into the closet and spent the next 12 years pretending to be 'normal' until a series of back to back suicide attempts caused me to realize that the closet was made to kill LGBT individuals."

Although the statistics are very troublesome, luckily, there are many valuable resources available for those of us who are suicidal. Therapy can help us to understand our thoughts and feelings, and channel suicidal thoughts into more positive and productive outlets. A therapist may help us to develop a suicide safety plan, which organizes our thoughts about helpful resources and encourages us to try to focus on positives when we feel suicidal. Medications can help treat underlying mental health concerns that may contribute to suicidal thoughts.

ANXIETY AND TRAUMA-RELATED DISORDERS

Experiencing high levels of violence, victimization, and trauma can put us at risk of having increased anxiety. Anxiety can take many different forms. It may range from a general sense of mild uneasiness or nervousness to a nearly constant distressing worry, nervousness, fear, or apprehension. Anxiety can be normal. It is necessary to have some level of anxiety in order to avoid harm in our daily lives, such as when crossing a busy street, going on a date, or driving in snow.

It is quite normal for us to experience anxiety. Some may even say that it is part of the process of accepting ourselves as transgender and gender nonconforming people (Devor, 2004) to experience anxiety before and during the transition process. We may worry about what it will be like to go through social and medical transition and whether transition will meet our expectations. We may have fears about how others' views of us will change, whether we will be rejected by our family and friends, and whether we will be physically safe. Whether medical transition itself helps alleviate our anxiety symptoms is debatable. Some studies say yes, and some studies say no (Gomez-Gil et al., 2012; Haraldsen & Dahl, 2000; Mergeri & Khoosal, 2007; Ubeze et al., 2008). In those of us who desire medical and surgical transition, changes we make to our bodies and being read more consistently as our affirmed gender may help alleviate some of our anxiety (Gomez-Gil et al., 2012).

> "Having to disclose who I was and my transition was traumatic for me because I knew and worked with so many people over the years. I really did not know how they would react. But after all was said and done, most everyone was very accepting or just didn't care. It was a huge weight off my shoulders. I no longer felt like I was deceiving everyone."

For some of us, our feelings of anxiety may reach a debilitating level, warranting the need for intensive therapy or medication. Some of us may feel constantly anxious. We may have panic attacks, where we have temporary but terrifying periods of paralyzing fear or the feeling of "impending doom." Some of us are so anxious that it keeps us from performing daily activities, like going to the store or to school.

In 2012, the trans magazine and Web site *Original Plumbing* began a campaign called "Talk About It," with videos and stories about our experiences feeling suicidal. The goal is to share solutions and end isolation.

The Massachusetts Transgender Political Coalition, Fenway Health, the Samaritans, and the Massachusetts Department of Health have created transgender-specific online suicide prevention training videos and brochures called *Saving Our Lives: Preventing Suicide in Transgender Communities*.

If you are thinking about hurting yourself or taking your own life, please seek out help immediately. You may need to go to a local hospital or emergency room or call 911. If possible, try bringing someone you trust for support. Most counties and cities have emergency psychiatric resources and crisis lines. There are also LGBTQ-specific helplines, including the following:

- The Samaritans: 1-877-870-HOPE (4673)
- The Trevor Project: 1-866-4-U-TREVOR (866-788-7386)
- The GLBT Helpline: 1-888-240-GLBT (4528)
- The Gay and Lesbian National Hotline: 1-888-843-4564

There are different types of anxiety disorders, and severity differs from person to person. Anxiety disorders are more common than we typically think. One in four people may develop an anxiety disorder across their life span. Anxiety disorders are often experienced alongside other mental health issues, including depression, bipolar disorder, substance use, and personality disorders. The rate of anxiety disorders in trans and gender nonconforming communities is higher than the general population (De Vries et al., 2011; Hepp, Kraemer, Schnyder, Miller, & Delsignore, 2005; Hoshiai et al., 2010).

> *"Being a man, in and of itself, even in a woman's body, doesn't make me mentally ill, but it does come with considerable mental stress to be in a body that doesn't fit you. The fear, dysphoria, depression, discomfort, confusion, etc, it all takes its toll."*

Common anxiety disorders include the following:

- Phobia—excessive fear about a situation or object, such as fear of flying or spiders
- Social anxiety—difficulties in social situations, such as being afraid of what others will think of us
- Generalized anxiety disorder (GAD)—frequent, excessive worry about many different things
- Obsessive-compulsive disorder (OCD)—intrusive repetitive thoughts or behaviors, such as turning on/off the lights multiple times, frequently checking locks, or washing our hands excessively
- Panic disorder—discrete episodes in which we may have a racing heart, fast breathing, profuse sweating, or a fear of dying, which may occur in particularly distressing circumstances or at random

Treatments for anxiety disorders can vary as widely as the anxiety symptoms themselves, and they depend on the type of anxiety disorder, severity, and our ability to function (or not) in our daily lives. Treatment can involve individual therapy, exposure therapy, group therapy, and medications to help decrease symptoms. Medications are particularly helpful in treating panic disorder and generalized anxiety disorder. Anxiety disorders are very common, so most mental health professionals are trained and comfortable working with those who struggle with these conditions. Some therapists and psychiatrists may also have expertise in specific areas of anxiety, such as OCD.

Posttraumatic stress disorder (PTSD), classified as an anxiety disorder until the *DSM-5*, can occur after someone experiences or witnesses significant trauma causing a hypersensitive emotional response. Trauma can be defined as any personal experience in which we fear for the safety or lives of ourselves or others. Traumatic events may include (but are not limited to) rape, violence, near-death experiences, natural disasters, or being in an abusive relationship. Those of us with PTSD may experience flashbacks, nightmares, or periods of dissociation (which is likened to "blacking out" or losing memory of a period of time). We may work really hard to avoid things that remind us of the traumatic incident.

> *"As a child, I was harassed constantly because I didn't fit in. I became somewhat of an expert in avoiding situations that would get me into trouble, that might include sneaking through backyards to avoid meeting people on the street. In high school my family moved to another state which allowed me to start over so to speak."*

Luckily, not everyone who experiences trauma gets PTSD—it affects less than 10% of the population as a whole. Factors that put people at greater risk of PTSD include having a lower socioeconomic status, having a family history of PTSD, and having combat exposure. Being trans or gender nonconforming likely also put us at higher risk of developing PTSD because we are more likely to experience violence, trauma, and victimization, and are therefore more likely to have an experience that can trigger symptoms of PTSD.

People who suffer from PTSD tend to deal with other mental health issues as well, such as depression, substance use disorders, or other anxiety disorders.

Treatments are available for PTSD, the mainstay of which is counseling/therapy. Medications may also be helpful to address specific symptoms such as panic attacks, depression, sleep problems, and nightmares. The majority of people who experience PTSD have a good recovery, although up to a quarter of those with PTSD may have chronic symptoms. When people experience PTSD, they need strong social support, and it is therefore essential for us to support others who experience PTSD within the trans community.

MY GENDER TIMELINE

Amy Roberts

The media likes to portray one "standard timeline" of transness, but in truth there is no one single way we come to know we are trans. My own narrative matches the mainstream narrative in a few superficial ways, but it differs from it greatly in others. Due to my posttraumatic stress disorder (PTSD), I often have vivid flashbacks of memories that are "frozen in time." I experience them as if they are happening in the present. I have relived many of my earliest memories this way. These early memories are from when I was a preverbal child, younger than two years old.

My first memories are of being female. I don't subscribe to the binary model of sex, so when I say "female," what I mean is that I experienced my body as having internal sexual anatomy. In my memories from this period I do not have a penis at all. In reality, I did—but I was not aware of it. Because I was operating on my internal sense of self, it is inaccurate to say I "believed" my body had female anatomy, or to say I felt my body "should" have female anatomy. My body was just female, period.

As I aged, I became aware of the physical reality of my body. Around age three I figured out I had a penis. I tried to explain this sudden change by saying "girls have penises too, they're just tucked inside." Around age four I became aware of the social concept of gender and the meaning others placed on my body. Around the same time, I was abused in explicitly corporeal ways. I rationalized this as external forces "changing me into a boy." It made me very angry. It felt like my body and my family had betrayed me. This marked the beginning of a period where people reinforced a damaging message: "What you experience isn't real." My abusers told me the rape wasn't abuse. The other people in my life told me indirectly, without even realizing it, that my self-perception as a girl was wrong. Everybody said they did these hurtful things because they loved me.

After this onslaught of invalidation, I doubted every thought in my head. Reality became fantasy; fantasy became reality. The part of me who knew she was female shrank and went into hiding. We fractured into several pieces, one of whom was a boy facade. The boy fronter served several purposes: One, he stopped relating to our rapists as a girl, which they found less attractive. Two, he remained separate from the crushing pain of dysphoria and others' disbelief about who I really was. Over time he learned how to "act like a boy." By the time we reached high school, he had completely forgotten about that little girl, and achieved complete denial about being female. Since it was primarily the female part of us that endured the abuse, he also forgot all about the rape.

This was an extreme alienation from the self, and it was inherently unstable. Cracks began to form. In the later years of high school, the boy fronter began to question his gender and his sexuality. A year out of high school, he reconnected with that crying little girl locked away in a bubble. A month or so later, "he" came out as a girl. The next decade was a painful, arduous process of re-remembering my own past. The boy fronter had one version of the past; our core had a very different version. There were countless other fragments who held onto repressed traumatic memories. My memories lacked a space or a time. After a lot of hard work, though, I have constructed a story that fits these memories together as a whole.

I was born a girl. Then something happened to turn me into a boy. I pretended to be a boy until I forgot I had ever been a girl. Then I remembered and went back to being a girl, except my body was stuck being a boy body. I have changed it to be more like it should be, but it's not quite there yet. This is my gender timeline.

SUBSTANCE USE DISORDERS

Substance use disorders (SUDs) refer to the use of drugs (legal or illegal) or alcohol in excess to the point of causing problems in our lives. SUDs are all too common around the world. Substances of abuse include cigarettes, alcohol, marijuana, crack/cocaine, heroin, prescription pain pills, and amphetamines. In our community, substance use may even include misuse of our prescribed hormones. SUDs can lead to emotional or physical health problems, deterioration of relationships with family and friends, loss of employment, or legal problems such as fines or arrests for disorderly conduct, assault, or driving under the influence (DUI).

Not all substance use is problematic. Many people are able to moderate their substance use and do not experience negative consequences. However, others do not have this luxury. Some subcultures within society may enable the use of illicit substances, like "club drugs" (e.g., crystal meth, special K, poppers), despite negative effects. LGBTQ communities have historically revolved around bars and bar culture for safety and community; from back-alley bars when homosexuality was illegal, to now commonplace circuit clubs and bars. Adolescents and young adults who frequent bars and party-like environments may have easier access to drugs and alcohol, and may be more prone to using them in excess. On the other end of the age spectrum, the elderly seem to be particularly susceptible to undiagnosed alcohol and drug problems for a variety of reasons, including poor access to health care and isolation (Briggs, 2011).

"For many years I thought that my cravings were erotically driven. Mostly when I was under the influence of mind-altering chemicals, pot and alcohol. The pot and alcohol always seemed to go together with the cross-dressing. Just a few years ago when I had accumulated a number of years clean and sober and found that I still had the cravings to dress and pretend that I was a woman, I realized that I was indeed a woman to me."

The reasons people use drugs are as varied as the drugs available. People often try drugs to feel relief from difficult situations, such as being harassed, coping with homelessness, feeling inadequate or uncomfortable, wanting to fit in, or to self-treat other mental health conditions. Chronic cigarette, alcohol, or drug use can lead to dependence. Dependence occurs when someone wishes to stop or cut down but is physically or mentally unable to do so. We may develop tolerance to substances, meaning that it takes more and more of the drug to feel the same effects we once felt with only a little. Alcohol commonly has this effect on people who drink regularly. People experience temporary physical and mental changes when using drugs or alcohol, ranging anywhere from a slight feeling of relaxation or increased energy, to experiences of hallucinations and disorientation. Some people enjoy these experiences of altered mental and mood states, which we may describe as feeling "high" or "strung-out."

What sets regular substance use apart from SUDs mostly depends on whether we experience negative consequences of our use, such as mental, medical, social, or financial problems. For instance, people who continue to drink alcohol even after they have lost any combination of health, job, home, or partner because of alcohol most certainly have an SUD. Another example is people who spend all of their income and sell their belongings to buy and use drugs. SUDs can lead to various types of self-harm, including medical problems, sexual risk taking, incarceration, cutting, suicide attempts, or accidental overdose. Some people suffer permanent mental health disorders because of their drug use.

"The drug use helped to quell my discomfort, but it quickly became an obsession. Benzoates, stimulants, marijuana, and alcohol. No time for food. No time for school, no time for work. I began living full time as male when I was 22 years old. I quit most of these things cold turkey, about 9 months into the binge. . . I have sought professional help at a gender and chemical dependency clinic. I will be starting testosterone within the next month or so."

SUDs appear to be more common in gender nonconforming communities (Grant et al., 2010; Leslie, Perina, & Maqueda, 2001; Lombardi, 2008; Risser, 2005). In the general US population SUDs are most common in the teens to early twenties. This puts our community at particular risk of SUDs and negative mental health outcomes because young trans people already have higher rates of depression, anxiety, self-injurious behaviors, and suicidality than other youth. Alcohol and drug use in any population, trans or not, further increases these risks.

As trans people, we may use substances for a variety of reasons, such as to cope with the difficulty of living in a society that discriminates against us, to alleviate discomfort in our bodies, to facilitate sex work, or to self-medicate underlying mental health issues (Scourfield, Katrin, & McDermott, 2008; Xavier et al., 2007). In our LGB peers, substance use is known to be related to sexual risk-taking behaviors, mental health issues, homelessness, sex work, and internalized homophobia, particularly among youth (Cochran et al., 2002; King et al., 2008; Marshal et al., 2008; Weber, 2008). This likely holds true for us as well—substances may provide a temporary escape from the challenges of being trans. Regardless of the reason for use, drugs and alcohol can have serious effects on our minds and bodies, and they can get in the way of transition for those of us desiring hormones or affirmation procedures. SUDs put us at significantly increased risk of medical problems (HIV, STIs) and mental health issues. This puts providers in a difficult position, particularly when deciding whether we are emotionally and physically able to undergo medical transition, as transitioning has its own risks.

> "It took me 29 years to come to terms with who I am. When I was very young (about 3 or 4) I would try and wear girl clothes and do typical female activities because that is what I liked. However, my parents did not think this was good. Every time they saw me doing something a boy should not do I would get beat. Out of survival I learned to hide. I hid things so well that no one had any clue I was trans. Eventually, I was not able to deal with the feelings of self hatred by myself, so I started to drink. . . a lot. Eventually it became a huge problem and I was forced to go into an inpatient rehab. After I got sober, it became clear that I either needed to transition, or end my life. Being that I am a parent to a wonderful 6 year old son, I decided to stay in his life and transition. It has been one of the best decisions of my life. My son and I are closer than ever, and I am finally happy with who I am."

In thinking about a plan to decrease or stop our substance use, it is also very important to consider the effects of cigarette smoking. Tobacco use is a major risk factor for heart disease, lung disease, and many different cancers. Smoking while on estrogen increases our risk of dangerous blood clots. Smoking also increases our risk of heart disease and impairs our body's ability to heal after surgery.

Making life-changing decisions while actively using substances can be very damaging to our overall well-being. While under the influence of drugs or alcohol, we may have difficulties making healthy choices, may act impulsively, or may make decisions without careful regard for the consequences. Mental health providers may be able to assist us in evaluating our choices. In some cases, it may be important to address the SUD before starting hormones or having surgery. For some of us, starting medical transition with hormones or surgery can help alleviate the discomfort that contributes to substance abuse. Of note, most surgeons would be reluctant to operate on someone with heavy substance use. It can sometimes feel like gatekeeping to be prevented from access to medical transition due to substance use or another health problem. We should have these challenging conversations with our providers. If we do have to wait for hormones or surgery, mental health providers can help us deal with the emotional struggle that entails.

> "I am in AA and I am part of a close-knit all-women's group. I am currently taking a break from this group. I feel conflicted about this as I care about the women in the group, but I no longer feel like I fit in given my gender exploration. So I'm not sure what to do. There are all-male groups in AA, but I do not necessary feel like I fit there either. So I focus my recovery on all-gender groups. Social interactions are pretty easy because I'm calm and centered in myself first and foremost."

SUD treatment is widely available. Regrettably, as trans people, we tend to enter SUD treatment with more severe substance use and mental health issues than cis people (Cochran & Cause, 2006). We need to seek out help sooner. Treatment can help minimize further bodily, emotional, and neurological harm caused by our substance use.

As trans people, we have higher rates of substance abuse. We are also more likely to experience violence and victimization, sometimes from our own family members and significant others, and often when they are drinking or using drugs. Al-Anon is a network of support groups for family and friends of people with alcohol and drug problems that provides a place for us to talk about what it is like to be close to someone who has a substance abuse problem.

The Yahoo group transobriety connects trans people in recovery.

SUD treatment providers may have specialized training in helping those of us with SUDs that general mental health providers may not have. Treatment for SUDs can vary depending on the type of drug used, the conditions of our dependence, and the available treatment methods in our community. A common approach to SUDs is harm reduction, which focuses on decreasing negative outcomes by minimizing risk and does not necessarily require us to stop using completely. SUD recovery treatment options include individual therapy, support groups, 12-step programs (i.e., Alcoholics Anonymous, Narcotics Anonymous), Eastern medicine practices (i.e., acupuncture, yoga), medications for substance use (i.e., Suboxone, Methadone) or other mental health problems, or residential treatment or hospitalization. Once we find a program that fits our needs, those of us in SUD recovery often choose to remain in our support groups for months, years, or even forever. We choose to do so to have the continued support of our peers with similar experiences, to help us remain sober. Many cities have LGBTQ-focused 12-step or recovery groups that are welcoming and supportive of our identities.

It is important to recognize that our unique stressors and experiences, such as societal stigma/transphobia, internalized transphobia, friend and family rejection, homelessness, legal issues, body image issues, sex work, and STI risks, have a strong impact on our recovery from substance use disorders. These issues may or may not be adequately addressed in mainstream SUD treatment programs. In general SUD treatment programs, we may fear or experience hostility, insensitivity, strict bathroom and rooming segregation, or lack of welcoming and gender-affirming recovery groups (Leslie et al., 2001; Lombardi & van Servellen, 2000). Our actual or perceived discrimination and lack of trans-specific provider education may prevent us from seeking out treatment and affect our other mental health issues. However, these fears should not stop us from looking for help. Fortunately, trans education and acceptance has been gaining traction over the years, particularly in mental health and substance use care, making these scary situations less and less common. Additionally, trans-affirming SUD resources exist to help us through the demanding process of recovery.

Collage (by Natasha Shapiro, www.natashart.com).

BODY IMAGE AND EATING DISORDERS

Body image refers to our perceptions of our bodies, as well as our comfort (or discomfort) and satisfaction (or dissatisfaction) with them. Many people, both trans and cis, are uncomfortable with some (or many) parts of their bodies or desire to change certain aspects of their bodies. These feelings of insecurity can be so severe that they distort how we see our bodies. We may think we are very overweight when we are actually very thin. This discomfort may compel some of us to refuse to eat, vomit food we recently ate, or exercise for several hours a day.

Such activities may indicate an eating disorder. However, body dysphoria is very common in trans communities, and most of us do not have eating disorders. Those of us with eating disorders like bulimia (binging and purging) and anorexia (restricted food intake and low body weight) may have unrealistic views of our body and size. Generally, people who struggle with eating disorders experience insecurity and concerns about their attractiveness. Many also obsess over food or calories. Many people with eating disorders suffer from physical exhaustion or may be unable to concentrate as their bodies struggle to keep up with a lack of proper nutrition.

We know very little about eating disorders in trans and gender nonconforming communities. The limited studies that exist do not seem to show differences in body image between trans and cis people (Wolfradt & Neumann, 2001). One study indicates that trans women may engage in more body-checking than other women (Vocks, Stahn, Loenser, & Legenbauer, 2009). Body checking refers to the actions we do in order to inspect or scrutinize (and sometimes obsess over) the appearance of our bodies. We may constantly ask others about our appearance. It can be normal to think about how we look, but if it causes extreme distress or compels us to harm or starve ourselves, we should consider seeking help to find more comfort in our own skin.

> *"I had a boatload of issues as a teenager, including eating disorders, self harm and dealing with an alcoholic and narcissistic mother. I have been in therapy for the last ten years dealing with it all and so [my gender] really has not been a priority. I think working on my self esteem has been an indirect way of addressing it."*

Body checking is important in transgender and gender nonconforming communities for various reasons other than staying slim. Body checking may be protective, helping us to be read as the correct gender and keeping us safe from unintentional outing and victimization. We may try to attain a certain body shape to help us in attempting to be read correctly. For example, a trans woman may choose to put on weight to appear more curvy or hide more traditionally masculine features. We have many reasons for wanting to shape our bodies. A trans man may work out or try to lose weight to appear less curvy or make his menstrual periods stop.

> *"I went through a lot of self-hatred, dieting, and eating disorders in school. In retrospect, I was trying to get my body so thin that my curves would go away. I was 126 pounds and could bench press 100 and still thought I was 'fat.' My body felt 'wrong' but I still didn't know why."*

Those of us with particular distress about our bodies may have improved self-image after taking hormones or having surgery (Kraemer, Delsignore, Schnyder, & Hepp, 2008). Although many of us choose the path of medical/surgical transition due to discomfort with our bodies, others of us are perfectly content in our bodies without such interventions, or we may engage in other activities, like changing our diets or doing targeted exercises, in order to change our appearances. Negative feelings about our bodies can be alienating, as our loved ones may not understand what we are going through. Luckily, we are not alone. We are creating more and more resources within our community to build connections and find camaraderie in our shared experiences. Whether we choose to alter our bodies or not, mental health providers can help us feel more at ease in our skin.

> *"I've started running in the hopes this will cut down my hips (although you have to run without a binder and I'm most comfortable doing this in the dead of night), and doing push-ups and sit-ups and what little exercise I can find the time and resources for."*

BIPOLAR DISORDER

Bipolar disorder is a mental illness with strong genetic links that affects less than 3% of the US adult population (Kessler et al., 2005). Those with bipolar disorder may go through periods of depression as well as periods of mania, which many describe to be the "opposite of depression." During a manic episode we generally have an elevated mood and very little need for sleep. Some do not sleep more than a few hours a night for several days or even weeks at a time. Two people with bipolar disorder may have very different symptoms. When we experience a manic episode, we may become irritable, experience racing thoughts, talk very fast, get distracted easily, feel like we are on top of the world, partake in risky or impulsive behaviors, or overwhelm ourselves with lots of different activities. In more severe forms of mania, some of us may experience psychotic symptoms, including hearing or seeing things that are not real. This can be very scary for us and our loved ones.

Currently, there is no research or anecdotal evidence to suggest that trans people are at any increased or decreased risk for bipolar disorder compared to the general population. It is, however, nonetheless important for our mental health providers to screen for bipolar disorder during their initial assessment. Most people develop bipolar disorder between the ages of 15 and 25, when many of us start to explore our gender identities. Stress that comes with exploring our gender, dealing with discrimination or oppression, or coming out as trans can coincide with, exacerbate, or trigger manifestations of underlying mental health issues, like bipolar disorder. However, experiencing symptoms of bipolar disorder is most likely unrelated to our gender identity.

If our clinician detects symptoms of bipolar disorder, treatment may help us avoid risky behaviors that can accompany manic or depressive episodes and have the potential to negatively impact our transition or transition-related decisions. During a severe manic episode, we tend to have impaired judgment and make impulsive, rash decisions. Hence, we may lack the true ability for full consent for gender treatments while in mania. However, having bipolar disorder itself does not exempt us from the informed consent model for gender affirmation treatment, nor does it prohibit our decision-making ability to take hormones or have gender-related surgery.

Treatment for bipolar disorder is widely available and should be sought out. Treatment may include talk therapy, group therapy, and mood-stabilizing medications. In severe or life-threatening episodes (i.e., suicidal thoughts, risk of harming others), an individual may require inpatient hospitalization for safety until stabilized on medications. Contrary to popular belief, taking hormones does not trigger mania or aggressive behaviors when taken at standard doses.

SCHIZOPHRENIA AND OTHER PSYCHOTIC CONDITIONS

Schizophrenia is a mental illness with strong genetic links, and it affects about 1% of individuals around the world. Schizophrenia can present with a wide range of different symptoms, but the characteristic ones include hallucinations (hearing or seeing things that are not real), delusions or false beliefs (such as paranoia; for example, someone may think the FBI is after them), problems with thought processes, memory, and planning, as well as what are known as negative symptoms (such as stoic appearance, absence of mood, and slowed movements). Although schizophrenia is passed on through genetics,

---

Note to Mental Health Providers

In individuals who are transgender and happen to struggle with bipolar disorder, denouncing or ignoring the patient's true identity can be emotionally damaging and will negatively affect the therapeutic relationship. Acute mania is a contraindication to starting hormone treatment, but not to continuing its use if the patient was on hormone treatment outside the hospital. If you are taking care of a transgender patient with bipolar disorder in the emergency room or on an inpatient unit, continue the patient's hormone treatments in the hospital. Contrary to popular belief, hormone use at standard doses does not trigger mania or aggressive behaviors. Stopping hormones abruptly or without cause can further worsen mood and interactions with providers.

there are certainly risk factors that influence the emergence of the illness in predisposed individuals. Studies show that early and chronic use of marijuana increases the likelihood of developing schizophrenia (Andreasson, Allebeck, Engström, & Rydberg, 1987; Arseneault et al., 2002; Henquet, Murray, Linszen, & van Os, 2005; Zammit, Allebeck, Andreasson, Lundberg, & Lewis, 2002) and ongoing marijuana use also predicts worse outcomes in schizophrenia (Henquet et al., 2005), although a link does not necessarily mean that one thing causes the other.

Currently there is no research or anecdotal evidence to suggest that as trans and gender nonconforming people we are at any increased or decreased risk for schizophrenia compared to the general population. Providers screen for this condition during initial interviews by asking whether we have had symptoms of psychosis, such as hearing voices or feeling paranoid. Most people express their first symptoms of schizophrenia in their early twenties, a time when many of us start to explore our gender identities and figure out who we are. It is a ripe age to explore ourselves, and the stress, discrimination, or oppression that comes with that exploration could coincide with, exacerbate, or trigger an underlying mental illness. Hence, it is important for providers to check for mental health issues, and schizophrenia in particular, so that we get optimal medical and mental health care as soon as possible.

Additionally, individuals experiencing severe psychotic symptoms may temporarily lack the ability for informed consent for gender-related medical or surgical treatment. However, having schizophrenia itself does not prevent us from making decisions about taking hormones, getting gender-related surgery, or having a gender nonconforming identity. A clinician may feel compelled to conduct a closer evaluation of our decision-making ability. Sometimes clinicians do see cisgender individuals who assert a cross-gender or gender nonconforming identity as a symptom of their psychotic illness; however, this is rare and usually resolves when the psychosis does.

Treatment for schizophrenia generally involves both therapy and antipsychotic medication. If we have underlying medical problems, such as liver disease, high cholesterol, or obesity, the psychiatrist may want to avoid prescribing certain medications that can exacerbate these issues, especially since hormones can also make these medical problems worse. Unfortunately, all antipsychotic medications have the potential side effects of weight gain, increasing cholesterol, and sugar intolerance (diabetes), but there are differences between the medications as to which are more likely to cause such side effects. It is important to talk about these issues with our prescribing psychiatrists. People with schizophrenia can and do live successful and fulfilling lives.

Note to Providers

When seeing a psychotic patient, it is important that providers not make the assumption that cross-gender identification is solely related to psychosis. This is an area that needs to be explored and evaluated over time. Transgender identity generally remains stable as psychosis waxes and wanes. If you are a provider and have this type of clinical situation and are unsure about whether it is appropriate for your patient to start transition, look for a psychiatrist experienced in working with transgender clients to help you. In individuals who are transgender and happen to struggle with schizophrenia, denouncing or ignoring the patient's true identity can be emotionally damaging and will negatively impact the therapeutic relationship, making treatment even more difficult. For staff in the emergency room or on inpatient units, continue the patient's hormone treatments if they have been on them as an outpatient and there is no contraindication to continued use. Contrary to popular belief, hormone use at standard doses does not trigger psychotic or aggressive behaviors.

THE RELATIONSHIP BETWEEN MENTAL HEALTH AND HIV RISKS IN OUR COMMUNITY

Sari L. Reisner, ScD, MA

Worldwide, trans communities are at high risk of HIV infection. Trans women have HIV rates as high as 25% and trans men as high as 3% (Baral et al., 2013; Herbst et al., 2008; Schulden et al., 2008; Stephens et al., 2011). Behaviors that put us at risk for HIV include having multiple partners or unprotected sex, doing sex work, having sex under the influence of alcohol or drugs, and sharing needles for hormones or IV drugs (Brennan et al., 2012; Chen et al., 2011; Clements-Nolle et al., 2001; Holton et al., 2013; Kosenko, 2011; Nemoto et al., 2004; Nuttbrock et al., 2013; Operario et al., 2008; Reisner et al., 2010; Rowniak et al., 2011; Sevelius, 2009).

Many different factors contribute to our increased risk of contracting HIV as trans people. These factors do not just add together but also interact and strengthen each other. Researchers call this interaction of factors "syndemic theory" (Singer & Clair, 2003). As part of the trans community, we are more likely to have mental health issues such as depression and anxiety. We are more likely to be socially isolated and be the victims of violence. These factors have been shown to contribute to HIV risk behaviors (e.g., Brennan et al., 2012; De Santis, 2009; Operario & Nemoto, 2010). Many times, mental health and psychosocial problems occur together and affect each other. For example, experiences of transphobic violence may lead to or worsen depression, and depression can drive us to have unprotected sex for emotional comfort or to validate our gender identity (e.g., Melendez & Pinto, 2007; Nuttbrock et al., 2013).

PERSONALITY DISORDERS

Personality disorders encompass a wide range of complex conditions that are hard to diagnose and are often missed or misdiagnosed. These diagnoses refer to deeply rooted personality characteristics that impair our functioning in many areas of our lives. Personality disorders often present as inappropriate or maladaptive ways of dealing with situations and other people, leading to increased distress and difficulties.

Depending on the personality disorder, we may have relationship/social difficulties, express dramatic behaviors, manipulate our friends, family, or strangers, have more intense or inappropriate emotional responses, or act more impulsively or in a more paranoid way than other people. Many of us who have a personality disorder tend to believe that our issues, problems, or struggles are not due to our own behaviors. Individuals with personality disorders are more likely to have other mental health issues, such as anxiety, depression, PTSD, self-harm, suicidality, and substance use. Having a personality disorder may make treating these other issues more difficult.

It is not clear whether being trans or gender nonconforming puts us at greater risk of developing a personality disorder. Most research done on the topic has shown conflicting results. Certain personality disorders, such as borderline personality disorder, are correlated with early life trauma or abuse. In theory, this would put us at heightened risk of personality disorders, since our community has a much higher rate of violence and victimization than the general population, especially at a young age (D'Augelli, Grossman, & Starks 2006; Ploderl & Fartacek, 2009; Roberts, Rosario, Corliss, Koenen, & Austin, 2012).

Personality disorders are treatable with specialized group and individual therapy, such as dialectical behavior therapy (DBT) (Linehan, 1987), which focuses on mindfulness, emotional stability, and avoidance of impulsive and self-harming behaviors. Medications can also be helpful, especially in people with personality disorders and other mental health issues such as depression, anxiety, or bipolar disorder.

THE AUTISM SPECTRUM

The term "autism spectrum" (also sometimes known as Asperger's) is used to categorize people who have certain experiences and see the world in ways that may be different from the mainstream. These differences are often linked to the way we relate to other people, communicate, experience sensations, or respond to change. Autism spectrum disorders are listed in the *DSM* as a mental illness, although some people on the autism spectrum, like many of us who are transgender, are involved in movements for depathologization of their experiences.

> "I came to the social model of disability through neurodiversity activism (I'm autistic) before I admitted to myself that I could be trans. Identifying transness as an illness strikes me as wrong and stigmatizing. . . Transness is part of natural human variation and should be treated like that; trans folk should get the services they need just like any other neurological or physiological setup of person."

Some of us are both trans and fall on the autism spectrum. There is little research about the number of trans people who are on the autism spectrum. Some research indicates that we may be more likely than cis people to be on the autism spectrum (de Vries et al.,

2010), although there are very little data to back up this assertion, and it is premature at this point to draw any conclusions (Jones et al., 2003). Some researchers are interested in why we might be more likely to be on the autism spectrum than other groups are, and hypothesize that it may be related to hormonal exposure before birth (Baron-Cohen et al., 2011; Ingudomnukul, Baron-Cohen, Wheelwright, & Knickmeyer, 2007; Knickmeyer et al., 2006, 2008). A good reason for all of us to learn about the autism spectrum is that those trans people who also fall on the spectrum may have more trouble than other trans people connecting to our communities, and they may need extra support and outreach.

> *"I have joined the internet forum Transgender PDD, a newsletter for people with autism who have gender identity issues. I was diagnosed with Asperger's about 2 years ago."*

RESILIENCE

As trans people, we face many challenges and barriers to stable mental health, but we also demonstrate tremendous amounts of resilience. Every day that we get up, go to school or work, and interact with others, we are moving our lives forward and making the world a better place for future generations. Some researchers have begun to look at what factors contribute to our mental health, not just those that cause problems and lead to mental illness.

A well-known research group called the Family Acceptance Project has found that having accepting parents increases general health and self-esteem and protects against depression, substance abuse, suicidal thoughts, and suicide attempts in LGBTQ youth (Ryan, Russell, Huebner, Diaz, & Sanchez, 2010). From interviews and focus groups, researchers have also learned that there are things we can do to improve our resilience (Singh, Hays, & Watson, 2011). Those of us who build connections to supportive communities do better. We also do better when we understand how oppression works—that we are not alone, but instead are oppressed by systems that affect many people. For many of us, it also helps to participate in social activism so that we can feel part of movements for social change. When we have opportunities to serve as role models for others, we also gain a sense of accomplishment and have improved resilience. Staying positive can be difficult, but it really does influence how we deal with life circumstances. When we are struggling

Trans Bodies, Trans Selves Seattle Forum (photo by Ish Ishmael).

to stay positive, turning to friends, family, and mental health providers can help steer us back in the right direction.

> *"I've been in counseling for several years on and off for my depression and mild bipolar disorder. I have always been the one to bring up my being transgender. I wasn't always comfortable or confident in revealing such a fundamental part of me, but because it was fundamental to my being I realized I HAD to reveal it so the psych could fully evaluate and advise me. I've never had a negative reaction; the only reactions I've had so far are ones of interest in learning more about 'my kind.' I think I've 'enlightened and inspired' at least 3 college counselors so far to learn more about transsexualism and transgenderism."*

> *"I have experienced nothing but acceptance and love to date, for which I am very grateful. I imagine it will be a bit more challenging in my work context as I am a consultant to the mining industry. I am trying to remain positive and set the tone and pace of my transition so that I feel safe and respected. I know that there may be a couple bumps in the road ahead, and it may have more serious professional implications, but I'd rather be true to myself than work in an industry that would have me be disingenuous. There are plenty of types of work that I could do. I am of the thinking: Where one door closes, another opens. I know the universe has a special plan for me. That may sound uber cheesy, but I know there is something greater at play, and I am open to the mystery of it all."*

CONCLUSION

Similar to many oppressed or marginalized populations, as trans people we are at increased risk of various mental health issues such as depression, anxiety, substance abuse, and suicidal thoughts. Our oppression and traumatic experiences lead to this discrepancy. Over time, the mental health field has evolved and there are now many sensitive providers available to help us improve our mental health issues. As a community, we can also work to take care of ourselves and each other by building methods of resilience into our daily lives.

REFERENCES AND FURTHER READING

American Psychiatric Association. (1980). *Diagnostic and statistical manual of mental disorders* (3rd ed.). Washington, DC: American Psychiatric Publishing.

American Psychiatric Association. (1987). *Diagnostic and statistical manual of mental disorders* (3rd ed., Rev.). Washington, DC: American Psychiatric Association.

American Psychiatric Association. (1994). *Diagnostic and statistical manual of mental disorders* (4th ed.). Washington, DC: American Psychiatric Association.

American Psychiatric Association. (2000). *Diagnostic and statistical manual of mental disorders* (4th ed., Text rev.). Washington, DC: American Psychiatric Association.

American Psychiatric Association. (2013). *Diagnostic and statistical manual of mental disorders* (5th ed.). Washington, DC: American Psychiatric Association.

Andreasson, S., Allebeck, P., Engström, A., & Rydberg, U. (1987). Cannabis and schizophrenia: A longitudinal study of Swedish conscripts. *The Lancet, 330*(8574), 1483–1486.

Arseneault, L., Cannon, M., Poulton, R., Murray, R., Caspi, A., & Moffitt, T. E. (2002). Cannabis use in adolescence and risk for adult psychosis: Longitudinal prospective study. *British Medical Journal, 325*(1212), 1212–1213.

Baral, S. D., Poteat, T., Stromdahl, S., Wirtz, A. L., Guadamuz, T. E., & Beyrer, C. (2013). Worldwide burden of HIV in transgender women: A systematic review and meta-analysis. *The Lancet, 13*(3), 214–222.

Baron-Cohen, S., Lombardo, M. V., Auyeung, B., Ashwin, E., Chakrabarti, B., & Knickmeyer, R. (2011). Why are autism spectrum conditions more prevalent in males? *PLoS Biology, 9*(6), e1001081.

Bockting, W. O., Miner, M. H., Swinburne Romine, R. E., Hamilton, A., Coleman, E., Bontempo, D. E., & D'Augelli, A. R. (2002). Effects of at-school victimization and sexual orientation on lesbian, gay, or bisexual youths' health risk behavior. *Journal of Adolescent Health, 30*(5), 364–374.

Bockting, W. O., Miner, M. H., Swinburne Romine, R. E., Hamilton, A., & Coleman, E. (2013). Stigma, mental health, and resilience in an online sample of the US transgender population. *American Journal of Public Health, 103*(5), 943–951.

Brennan, K., Kuhns, L. M., Johnson, A. K., Belzer, M., Wilson, E. C., & Garofalo, R.; Adolescent Medicine Trials Network for HIV/AIDS Interventions. (2012). Syndemic theory and HIV-related risk among young transgender women: The role of multiple co-occurring health problems and social marginalization. *American Journal of Public Health, 102*(9), 1751–1757.

Breslau, N., Davis, G. C., & Schultz, L. R. (2003). Post-traumatic stress disorder and the incidence of nicotine, alcohol, and other drug disorders in persons who have experienced trauma. *Archives of General Psychiatry, 60*(3), 289–294.

Briggs, W. P., et al. (2011). Substance use, misuse, and abuse among older adults: Implications for clinical mental health counselors. *Journal of Mental Health Counseling, 33*(2), 112–127.

Centers for Disease Control and Prevention. (2010). Current depression among adults—United States, 2006 and 2008. *Morbidity and Mortality Weekly Report, 59*(38), 1229–1235.

Chen, S., McFarland, W., Thompson, H. M., & Raymond, H. F. (2011). Transmen in San Francisco: What do we know from the HIV test site data? *AIDS Behavior, 15*(3), 659–662.

Clements-Nolle, K., Marx, R., & Katz, M. (2006). Attempted suicide among transgender persons: The influence of gender-based discrimination and victimization. *Journal of Homosexuality, 51*(3), 53–69.

Clements-Nolle, K., Marx, R., Guzman, R., & Katz, M. (2001). HIV prevalence, risk behaviors, health care use, and mental health status of transgender persons: Implications for public health intervention. *American Journal of Public Health, 91*, 915–921.

Cochran, B. N., & Cause, A. M. (2006). Characteristics of lesbian, gay, bisexual, and transgender individuals entering substance use treatment. *Journal of Substance Abuse Treatment, 30*(2), 135–146.

Cochran, B. N., et al. (2002). Challenges faced by homeless sexual minorities: Comparisons of gay, lesbian, bisexual, and transgender homeless adolescents with heterosexual peers. *American Journal of Public Health, 95*(5), 773–777.

Cochran, B. N., Peavy, K. M., & Robohm, J. S. (2007). Do specialized services exist for LGBT individuals seeking treatment for substance misuse? A study of available treatment programs. *Substance Use and Misuse, 42*(1), 161–176.

D'Augelli, A. R., Grossman, A. H., Salter, N. P., Vasey, J. J., Starks, M. T., & Sinclair, K. O. (2005). Predicting the suicide attempts of lesbian, gay, and bisexual youth. *Suicide and Life-Threatening Behavior, 35*(6), 646–660.

D'Augelli, A. R., Grossman, A. H., & Starks, M. T. (2006). Childhood gender atypicallity, victimization, and PTSD among lesbian, gay, and bisexual youth. *Journal of Interpersonal Violence, 21*(11), 1462–1482.

D'Augelli, A. R., Hershberger, S. L., & Pilkington, N. W. (2001). Suicidality patterns and sexual orientation-related factors among lesbian, gay, and bisexual youths. *Suicide and Life-Threatening Behavior, 31*(3), 250–264.

De Santis, J. P. (2009). HIV infection risk factors among male-to-female transgender persons: A review of the literature. *Journal of the Association of Nurses in AIDS Care, 20*, 362–372.

Devor, A. H. (2004). Witnessing and mirroring: A fourteen stage model of transsexual identity formation. *Journal of Gay and Lesbian Psychotherapy, 8*(1-2), 41–67.

de Vries A. L., Noens, I. L., Cohen-Kettenis, P. T., van Berckelaer-Onnes, I. A., & Doreleijers, T. A. (2010). Autism spectrum disorders in gender dysphoric children and adolescents. *Journal of Autism and Developmental Disorders, 40*(8), 930–936.

de Vries, A. L., Kreukels, B. P., Steensma, T. D., Doreleijers, T. A., & Cohen-Kettenis, P. T. (2011). Comparing adult and adolescent transsexuals: An MMPI-2 and MMPI-A study. *Psychiatry Research, 186*, 414–418.

de Vries, A. L., Doreleijers, T. A., Steensma, T. D., & Cohen-Kettenis, P. T. (2011). Psychiatric comorbidity in gender dysphoric adolescents. *Journal of Child Psychology and Psychiatry, 52*(11), 1195–1202.

DiPlacido, J. (1998). Minority stress among lesbians, gay men, and bisexuals: A consequence of heterosexism, homophobia, and stigmatization. *Stigma and Sexual Orientation*, *4*, 138–159.

Drescher, J. (2009). Queer diagnoses: Parallels and contrasts in the history of homosexuality, gender variance, and the Diagnostic and Statistical Manual. *American Psychiatric Association* (online version, 2009) and *Archives of Sexual Behavior*, *39*, 427–460.

Fitzpatrick, K. K. (2005). Gender role, sexual orientation, and suicidal risk. *Journal of Affective Disorders*, *87*(1), 35–42.

Garofalo, R., Wolf, R. C., Wissow, L. S., Woods, E. R., & Goodman, E. (1999). Sexual orientation and risk of suicide attempts among a representative sample of youth. *Archives of Pediatrics and Adolescent Medicine*, *153*(5), 487–493.

Garofalo, R., Deleon, J., Osmer, E., Doll, M., & Harper, G. W. (2006). Overlooked, misunderstood, and at-risk: Exploring the lives and HIV risk of ethnic minority male-to-female transgender youth. *Journal of Adolescent Health*, *38*(3), 230–236.

Gomez-Gil, E., Zubiaurre-Elorza, L., Esteva, I., Guillamon, A., Godás, T., Cruz Almaraz, M.,... Salamero, M. (2012). Hormone-treated transsexuals report less social distress, anxiety, and depression. *Psychoneuroendocrinology*, *37*, 662–670.

Gorin-Lazard, A. (2012). Is hormonal therapy associated with better quality of life in transsexuals? A cross-sectional study. *Journal of Sexual Medicine*, *9*(2), 531–541.

Grant, J. M., et al. (2010). Injustice at every turn: A report of the national transgender discrimination survey. *National Center for Transgender Equality and National Gay and Lesbian Task Force*. Retrieved January 4, 2014, from http://www.thetaskforce.org/reports_and_research/ntds

Grossman, A. H., & D'Augelli, A. R. (2006). Transgender youth: Invisible and vulnerable. *Journal of Homosexuality*, *51*, 111–128.

Grossman, A. H., & D'Augelli, A. R. (2007). Transgender youth and life threatening behavior. *Suicide and Life-Threatening Behavior*, *73*, 527–537.

Haraldsen, I. R., & Dahl, A. A. (2000). Symptom profiles of gender dysphoric patients of transsexual subtype compared to patients with personality disorders and healthy adults. *Acta Psychiatrica Scandinavia*, *102*(4), 276–281.

Henquet, C., Murray, R., Linszen, D., & van Os, J. (2005). The environment and schizophrenia: The role of cannabis use. *Schizophrenia Bulletin*, *31*(3), 608–612.

Hendricks, M. L., & Testa, R. J. (2012). A conceptual framework for clinical work with transgender and gender non-conforming clients: An adaptation of the minority stress model. *Professional Psychology: Research and Practice*, *43*(5), 460–467.

Hepp, U., Kraemer, B., Schnyder, U., Miller, N., & Delsignore, A. (2005). Psychiatric comorbidity in gender identity disorder. *Journal of Psychosomatic Research*, *58*(3), 259–261.

Herbst, J. H., Jacobs, E. D., Finlayson, T. J., McKleroy, V. S., Neumann, M. S., Crepaz, N; HIV/AIDS Prevention Research Synthesis Team. (2008). Estimating HIV prevalence and risk behaviors of transgender persons in the United States: A systematic review. *AIDS Behavior*, *12*(1), 1–17.

Herek, G. M., Gillis, J. R., & Cogan, J. C. (1999). Psychological sequelae of hate-crime victimization among lesbian, gay, and bisexual adults. *Journal of Consulting and Clinical Psychology*, *67*(6), 945–951.

Hershberger, S. L., & D'Augelli, A. R. (1997). The impact of victimization on the mental health and suicidality of lesbian, gay, and bisexual youth. *Journal of Adolescent Research*, *12*, 477–497.

Holton, A. L., Garofalo, R., Kuhns, L. M., & Johnson, A. K. (2013). Substance use as a mediator of the relationship between life stress and sexual risk among young transgender women. *AIDS Education and Prevention*, *25*(1), 72–71.

Hoshiai, M., Matsumoto, Y., Sato, T., Ohnishi, M., Okabe, N., Kishimoto, Y.,... Kuroda, S. (2010). Psychiatric comorbidity among patients with gender identity disorder. *Journal of Psychiatry and Clinical Neurosciences*, *64*(5), 514–519.

Ingudomnukul, E., Baron-Cohen, S., Wheelwright, S., & Knickmeyer, R. (2007). Elevated rates of testosterone-related disorders in women with autism spectrum conditions. *Hormones and Behavior*, *51*(5), 597–604.

Jones, R. M., Wheelwright, S., Farrell, K., Martin, E., Green, R., Di Ceglie, D., Baron-Cohen, S. (2011). Brief report: Female-to-male transsexual people and autistic traits. *Journal of Autism and Developmental Disorders*. Epub.

Kenagy, G. P. (2005). Transgender health: Findings from two needs assessment studies in Philadelphia. *Health and Social Work, 30*(1), 19–26.

Kessler, R. C., Chiu, W. T., Demler, O., & Walters, E. E. (2005). Prevalence, severity, and comorbidity of twelve month DSM-IV disorders in the national comorbidity survey replication. *Archives of General Psychiatry, 62*(6), 593–602.

Kim, T. S., Cheon, Y. H., Pae, C. U., Kim, J. J., Lee, C. U., Lee, S. J.,...Lee, C. (2006). Psychological burdens are associated with young male transsexuals in Korea. *Psychiatry and Clinical Neurosciences, 60*(4), 417–421.

King, M., Semlyen, J., Tai, S. S., Killaspy, H., Osborn, D., Popelyuk, D., & Nazareth, I. (2008). A systematic review of mental disorders, suicide, and deliberate self-harm in lesbian, gay, and bisexual people. *BMC Psychiatry, 8*, 70.

Knickmeyer, R. C., Baron-Cohen, S., Fane, B. A., Wheelwright, S., Mathews, G. A., Conway, G. S.,...Hines, M. (2006). Androgens and autistic traits: A study of individuals with congenital adrenal hyperplasia. *Hormones and Behavior, 50*(1), 148–153.

Knickmeyer, R. C., Wheelwright, S., & Baron-Coen, S. (2008). Sex-typical play: Masculinization/defeminization in girls with an autism spectrum condition. *Journal of Autism and Developmental Disorders, 38*(6), 1028–1035.

Kosenko, K. A. (2011). Contextual influences on sexual risk-taking in the transgender community. *Journal of Sex Research, 48*(2-3), 285–296.

Kraemer, B., Delsignore, A., Gundelfinger, R., Schnyder, U., & Hepp, U. (2005). Comorbidity of Asperger syndrome and gender identity disorder. *European Child and Adolescent Psychiatry, 14*(5), 292–296.

Kraemer, B., Delsignore, A., Schnyder, U., & Hepp, U. (2008). Body image and transsexualism. *Psychopathology, 41*, 96–100.

Krehely, J. (2009). *How to close the LGBT health disparities gap*. Center for American Progress. Retrieved March 2014, from http://www.americanprogress.org/issues/2009/12/pdf/lgbt_health_disparities.pdf

Krieger, M. J., McAninch, J. W., & Weimer, S. R. (1982). *Self-performed bilateral orchiectomy in transsexuals*. Journal of Clinical Psychiatry, 43(7), 292–293.

Kulkin, H. S., Chauvin, E. A., & Percle, G. A. (2000). Suicide among gay and lesbian adolescents and young adults: A review of literature. *Journal of Homosexuality, 40*(1), 1–29.

Landén, M., & Rasmussen, P. (1997). Gender identity disorder in a girl with autism: A case report. *European Child and Adolescent Psychiatry, 6*(3), 170–173.

Lee, A., & Hobson, R. P. (1998). On developing self-concepts: A controlled study of children and adolescents with autism. *Journal of Child Psychology and Psychiatry, 39*(8), 1131–1144.

Leslie, D., Perina, B., & Maqueda, M. (2001). *Clinical issues with transgender individuals. A provider's introduction to substance abuse treatment for lesbian, gay, bisexual and transgender individuals*. Rockville, MD: Center for Substance Abuse Treatment, Substance Abuse and Mental Health Services Administration, US Department of Health and Human Services.

Linehan, M. M. (1987). Dialectical behavior therapy for borderline personality disorder: Theory and method. *Bulletin of the Menninger Clinic, 51*(3), 261–276.

Liu, R. T., & Mustanski, B. (2012). Suicidal ideation and self-harm in lesbian, gay, bisexual, and transgender youth. *American Journal of Preventive Medicine, 42*(3), 221–228.

Lombardi, E. L. (2008). Substance use treatment experiences of transgender/transsexual men and women. *Journal of LGBT Health Research, 3*(2), 37–47.

Lombardi, E. L., Wilchins, R. A., Priesing, D., & Malouf, D. (2001). Gender violence: Transgender experiences with violence and discrimination. *Journal of Homosexuality, 42*(1), 89–101.

Lombardi, E. L., & van Servellen, G. (2000). Building culturally sensitive substance use prevention and treatment programs for transgendered populations. *Journal of Substance Abuse Treatment, 19*(3), 291–296.

Lowy, F. H., & Kollivakis, T. L. (1971). Autocastration by a male transsexual. *Canadian Psychiatric Association Journal, 16*(5), 399–405.

Lyles, C. M., Kay, L. S., Crepaz, N., Herbst, J. H., Passin, W. F., Kim, A. S.,...HIV/AIDS Prevention Research Synthesis Team. (2007). Best-evidence interventions: Findings from a systematic review of HIV behavioral interventions for US populations at high risk, 2000–2004. *American Journal of Public Health, 97*(1), 133–143.

Marshal, M. P., Friedman, M. S., Stall, R., King, K. M., Miles, J., Gold, M. A.,...Morse, J. Q. (2008). Sexual orientation and adolescent substance use: A meta-analysis and methodological review. *Addiction, 103*(4), 546–556.

Marshal, M. P., Dietz, L. J., Friedman, M. S., Stall, R., Smith, H. A., McGinley, J.,...Brent, D. A. (2011). Suicidality and depression disparities between sexual minority and heterosexual youth: A meta-analytic review. *Journal of Adolescent Health, 49*(2), 115–123.

Mays, V. M., & Cochran, S. D. (2001). Mental health correlates of perceived discrimination among lesbian, gay, and bisexual adults in the United States. *American Journal of Public Health, 91*(11), 1869–1876.

McGovern, S. J. (1995). Self castration in a transsexual. *Journal of Accident and Emergency Medicine, 12*(1), 57–58.

Meier, S. C., Pardo, S. T., Labuski, C., & Babcock, J. (2013). Measures of clinical health among female-to-male transgender persons as a function of sexual orientation. *Archives of Sexual Behavior, 42*(3), 463–474.

Melendez, R. M., & Pinto, R. (2007). 'It's a really hard life': Love, gender and HIV risk among male-to-female transgender persons. *Culture, Health, and Sexuality, 9*, 233–245.

Mergeri, D., & Khoosal, D. (2007). Anxiety and depression in males experiencing gender dysphoria. *Sexual and Relationship Therapy, 22*(1), 77–81.

Meyer, I. H. (1995). Minority stress and mental health in gay men. *Journal of Health and Social Behavior, 36*, 38–56.

Money, J., & De Priest, M. (1976). Three cases of genital self surgery and relationship to transsexualism. *Journal of Sex Research, 12*(4), 283–294.

Mukaddes, N. M. (2002). Gender identity problems in autistic children. *Child Care Health and Development, 28*(6), 529–532.

Nemoto, T., Operario, D., Keatley, J., Han, L., & Soma, T. (2004). HIV risk behaviors among male-to-female transgender persons of color in San Francisco. *American Journal of Public Health, 94*, 1193–1199.

Nuttbrock, L., Bockting, W., Rosenblum, A., Hwahng, S., Mason, M., Macro, M., & Becker, J. (2013). Gender abuse, depressive symptoms, and HIV and other sexually transmitted infections among male-to-female transgender persons: A three-year prospective study. *American Journal of Public Health, 103*(2), 300–307.

Nuttbrock, L., Hwahng, S., Bockting, W., Rosenblum, A., Mason, M., Macri, M., & Becker, J. (2010). Psychiatric impact of gender-related abuse across the life course of male-to-female transgender persons. *Journal of Sex Research, 47*(1), 12–23.

Operario, D., & Nemoto, T. (2010). HIV in transgender communities: Syndemic dynamics and a need for multicomponent interventions. *Journal of Acquired Immune Deficiency Syndrome, 55*(2s), s91–s93.

Operario, D., Soma, T., & Underhill, K. (2008). Sex work and HIV status among transgender women: Systematic review and meta-analysis. *Journal of Acquired Immune Deficiency Syndromes, 48*(1), 97–103.

Perera, H., Gadambanathan, T., & Weerasiri, S. (2003). Gender identity disorder presenting in a girl with Asperger's disorder and obsessive compulsive disorder. *Ceylon Medical Journal, 48*(2), 57–58.

Ploderl, M., & Fartacek, R. (2009). Childhood gender nonconformity and harassment as predictors of suicidality among gay, lesbian, bisexual, and heterosexual Austrians. *Archives of Sexual Behavior, 38*(3), 400–410.

Proctor, C. D., & Groze, V. K. (1994). Risk factors for suicide among gay, lesbian, and bisexual youths. *Social Work, 39*, 504–513.

Reisner, S. L., Mimiaga, M. J., Safren, S. A., & Mayer, K. H. (2009). Stressful or traumatic life events, PTSD symptoms, and HIV sexual risk taking among men who have sex with men. *AIDS Care, 21*(12), 1481–1489.

Reisner, S. L., Perkovich, B., & Mimiaga, M. J. (2010). A mixed methods study of the sexual health of New England transmen who have sex with nontransgender men. *AIDS Patient Care and STDs, 24*(8), 501–513.

Remafedi, G., Farrow, J. A., & Deisher, R. W. (1991). Risk factors for attempted suicide in gay and bisexual youth. *Pediatrics, 87*(6), 869–875.

Remafedi, G., French, S., Story, M., Resnick, M. D., & Blum, R. (1998). The relationship between suicide risk and sexual orientation: Results of a population-based study. *American Journal of Public Health, 88*(1), 57–60.

Risser, J., et al. (2005). Sex, drugs, violence, and HIV status among male-to-female transgender persons in Houston, Texas. *International Journal of Transgenderism, 8*(2–3), 67–74.

Roberts, A. L., Rosario, M., Corliss, H. L., Koenen, K. C., & Austin, S. B. (2012). Childhood gender nonconformity: A risk indicator for childhood abuse and post traumatic stress in touth. *Pediatrics, 129*(3), 410–417.

Rotondi, N. K., et al. (2011). Prevalence of and risk and protective factors for depression in female-to-male transgender Ontarians: Trans PULSE Project. *Canadian Journal of Community Mental Health, 30*, 135–155.

Rowniak, S., Chesla, C., Rose, C. D., & Holzemer, W. L. (2011). Transmen: The HIV risk of gay identity. *AIDS Education and Prevention, 23*(6), 508–520.

Russel, S. T., Ryan, C., Toomey, R. B., Diaz, R. M., & Sanchez, J. (2011). Lesbian, gay, bisexual, and transgender adolescent school victimization: Implications for youth adult health and adjustment. *Journal of School Health, 81*(5), 223–230.

Ryan, C., Russell, S. T., Huebner, D., Diaz, R., & Sanchez, J. (2010). Family acceptance in adolescence and the health of LGBT young adults. *Journal of Child and Adolescent Psychiatric Nursing, 23*(34), 205–213.

Safren, S. A., & Heimberg, R. G. (1999). Depression, hopelessness, suicidality, and related factors in sexual minority and heterosexual adolescents. *Journal of Consulting and Clinical Psychology, 67*(6), 859–866.

Schulden, J. D., Song, B., Barros, A., et al. (2008). Rapid HIV testing in transgender communities by community-based organizations in three cities. *Public Health Reports, 123*(s3), 101–114.

Scourfield, J., Katrin, R., & McDermott, L. (2008). Lesbian, gay, bisexual and transgender young people's experiences of distress: Resilience, ambivalence and self-destructive behavior. *Health and Social Care in the Community, 16*(3), 329–336.

Seikowski, K., Gollek, S., Harth, W., & Reinhardt, M. (2008). Borderline personality disorder and transsexualism. *Psychiatric Praxis, 35*(3), 135–141.

Sevelius, J. M. (2009). 'There's no pamphlet for the kind of sex I have': HIV-related risk factors and protective behaviors among transgender men who have sex with nontransgender men. *Journal of Association of Nurses in AIDS Care, 20*, 398–410.

Sevelius, J. M., Carrico, A., & Johnson, M. O. (2010). Antiretroviral therapy adherence among transgender women living with HIV. *Journal of Association of Nursing in AIDs Care, 21*(3), 256–264.

Sevelius, J. M., Keatley, J., & Guiterrez-Mock, L. (2011). HIV/AIDS programming in the United States: Considerations affecting transgender women and girls. *Women's Health Issues, 21*(6), 278–282.

Singer, M., & Clair, S. (2003). Syndemics and public health: Reconceptualizing disease in bio-social context. *Medical Anthropology Quarterly, 17*(4), 423–441.

Singh, A. A., Hays, D. G., & Watson, L. S. (2011). Strength in the face of adversity: Resilience strategies of transgender individuals. *Journal of Counseling and Development, 89*, 20–27.

Skidmore, W. C., Linsenmeier, J. A., & Bailey, J. M. (2006). Gender nonconformity and psychological distress in lesbians and gay men. *Archives of Sexual Behavior, 35*(6), 685–697.

Stephens, S. C., Bernstein, K. T., & Philip, S. S. (2011). Male to female and female to male transgender persons have different sexual risk behaviors yet similar rates of STDs and HIV. *AIDS and Behavior, 15*(3), 683–686.

Stieglitz, K. A. (2010). Development, risk, and resilience of transgender youth. *Journal of the Association of Nurses in AIDS Care, 21*(3), 192–206.

St. Peter, M., Trinidad, A., & Irwig, M. S. (2012). Self-castration by a transsexual woman: Financial and psychological costs: A case report. *Journal of Sexual Medicine, 9*(4), 1216–1219.

Substance Abuse and Mental Health Services Administration (SAMHSA). www.samhsa.gov

Tateno, M., Tateno, Y., & Saito, T. (2008). Comorbid childhood gender identity disorder in a boy with Asperger syndrome. *Psychiatry and Clinical Neuroscience, 62*(2), 238.

Terada, S. (2011). Suicidal ideation among patients with gender identity disorder. *Journal of Psychiatric Research, 190*(1), 159–162.

Udeze, B., Abdelmawla, N., Khoosal, D., & Terry T. (2008). Psychological functions in male-to-female transsexual people before and after surgery. *Sexual and Relationship Therapy, 23*(2), 141–145.

Vocks, S., Stahn, C., Loenser, K., & Legenbauer, T. (2009). Eating and body image disturbances in male-to-female and female-to-male transsexuals. *Archives of Sexual Behavior, 38*, 364–377.

Walls, N. E., Laser, J., Nickels, S. J., & Wisneski, H. (2010). Correlates of cutting behavior among sexual minority youths and young adults. *Social Work Research, 34*(4).

Weber, G. N. (2008). Using to numb the pain: Substance use and abuse among lesbian, gay, and bisexual individuals. *Journal of Mental Health Counseling, 30*(1), 31–48.

Williams, P. G., Allard, A. M., & Sears, L. (1996). Case study: Cross-gender preoccupations with two male children with autism. *Journal of Autism and Developmental Disorders, 26*(6), 635–642.

Wolfradt, U., & Neumann, K. (2001). Depersonalization, self-esteem, and body image in MTF transexuals compared to male and female controls. *Archives of Sexual Behavior, 30*(3), 301–310.

World Health Organization. (n.d.). Fact Sheet on Depression. Retrieved March 2014, from http://www.who.int/mediacentre/factsheets/fs369/en/

Xavier, J. M. (2000). *The Washington, DC Transgender Needs Assessment Survey.* Washington, DC: *Us Helping Us, People Into Living.* Retrieved March 2014, from http://www.glaa.org/archive/2000/tgneedsassessment1112.shtml

Xavier, J. M., Honnold, J. A., & Bradford, J. (2007). *The health, health-related needs, and life course experiences of transgender Virginians.* Virginia HIV Community Planning Committee. Retrieved March 2014, from http://www.vdh.virginia.gov/epidemiology/diseaseprevention/documents/pdf/THISFINALREPORTVol1.pdf

Zammit, S. G., Allebeck, P., Andreasson, S., Lundberg, I., & Lewis, G. (2002). Self-reported cannabis use as a risk factor for schizophrenia in Swedish transcripts of 1969: Historical cohort study. *British Medical Journal, 325*, 1199.

SECTION 4

OUR RELATIONSHIPS AND FAMILIES

INTIMATE RELATIONSHIPS

Sarah E. Belawski and Carey Jean Sojka

16

OUR RELATIONSHIPS COME IN ALL SHAPES AND SIZES. Some of us are interested in dating casually, while others of us have met a lifelong partner. We live and love like everyone else, but being trans can also add some unique joys and challenges to our relationships—and sometimes both at the same time.

We have an incredible amount of diversity in our relationships. We start relationships before, during, and after we come out as trans or start to transition. We have straight relationships, same-gender relationships, queer relationships, monogamous relationships, polyamorous relationships, and nonsexual relationships. Some of us are married or have domestic partnerships, while others of us do not want or cannot attain legal recognition of our relationships. There is no one model for our relationships. However, there are basic strategies we can use to ensure that our relationships are healthy for us and our partners.

DATING AND TRANS IDENTITY

For those of us who are dating or would like to be dating, there are many steps to finding the types of relationships we desire. For some of us, out trans identities may not really affect our dating relationships any more than other aspects of ourselves. Others of us may believe that we are unattractive or not worthy of our potential partners. We may wonder whether the people attracted to us are attracted for the right reasons. We may need to learn new ways of interacting in dating cultures as we transition and figure out with ourselves how to approach disclosing our trans status to potential partners.

Loving Our Bodies

One of the first issues we often confront as trans people is our self-esteem and sense of our own attractiveness. Having a trans body is not seen as the norm, and we sometimes internalize society's judgments about our bodies and see our trans identity as a negative aspect of ourselves. It can be difficult to allow ourselves to seek out the partners we desire if we do not see ourselves as attractive.

If we enter into a relationship without a healthy self-image, that relationship is starting at a disadvantage. Communicating to a partner that we are ashamed of ourselves or that we are not worthy of love can make those who are hoping to start healthy relationships with us feel uncertain about how to treat us.

We may spend a significant amount of time and effort working to build our self-esteem and still be faced with the fact that many people are not open to dating someone trans. This can be very hurtful, and it can lead us to feel alone and isolated.

Despite all the negative stereotypes about trans people, there are many people who are attracted to trans bodies, and many of us find loving, secure, and sexually fulfilling relationships. Even if we are not having good luck with romantic relationships, there are many ways we can build our self-esteem so that when we find the kind of person we are interested in dating, we will be ready to accept their affection. These include spending time with friends who value us and rewarding ourselves for the hard work it takes to spend every day being who we are.

Finding Potential Partners

As trans people, we may have a hard time meeting partners, as being trans can limit the spaces in which we can find people who will potentially be interested in us. We may not be able to meet potential partners as easily as others can through spaces where people share interests, beliefs, politics, or even sexual orientation.

"I love my trans boyfriend" (photo by Gustavo Thomas).

One way that we may look to meet partners is through traditional means such as going out to bars or getting to know people through work or school. This has the advantage of capturing a wide net of people who could potentially be a good fit for us. It also means that the people we meet may not be aware of our trans identity, and we may have to navigate when and how to disclose this information to them.

Others ways of finding potential partners include specifically seeking out trans-attracted people or dating within transgender or LGBTQ spaces. These also have their advantages and disadvantages.

Seyi Adebanjo & Ni'Ja Whitson (photo by Seyi Adebanjo).

TRANS-ATTRACTED PARTNERS

There are some people who are specifically attracted to trans people. Some call themselves transamorous or transensual, while others refer to themselves as trans-attracted people. Sometimes these people are dismissed as "tranny chasers." Particularly for transfeminine people, there is a history of fetishization of our bodies. Some transmasculine people question the interest of those who only date transgender men and not cisgender men, because they feel that these boundaries attempt to reinforce the negative image that trans men are not "real" men. Both of these situations carry negative consequences for the sexual and romantic autonomy of trans people, and the term "tranny chasers" is often used as a derogatory term that reflects these problematic histories.

A person with a particular attraction to a trans body should not necessarily be dismissed as someone with a fetish. We are often bombarded with messages that our bodies are less desirable than cis bodies, but trans bodies are just as good as other bodies—saying that there is something wrong with being attracted to trans bodies is the same as saying there is something wrong with having a trans body. In this light, it is not a problem to be attracted to trans people per se—it becomes negative when those attracted to us do not see us as whole people with unique desires or do not respect our own ways of defining and understanding ourselves.

> *"My partner was already in transition when we met. Although she first introduced herself to me as a man, she admitted within the first few minutes of our conversation that she was, in fact, trans. The idea excited me. I had wanted to have a sexual experience with a trans woman for a long time . . . My partner is a beautiful, loving person with a good head on her shoulders. The fact that she is trans, while making her more attractive to me initially, is largely irrelevant in our day to day lives."**

A person who is particularly attracted to our bodies, or even exclusively attracted to trans bodies, should be held to the same standards as someone particularly or exclusively attracted to other gendered bodies. A healthy relationship involves our partners loving us in a holistic way that values who we are and not just what we are.

FOR THE CIS PERSON WHO WANTS TO KNOW HOW TO BE MY FRIEND

Katka Showers-Curtis

(inspired by Pat Parker's "For the white person/
who wants to know/how to be my friend")
    The first thing you should do is forget that I'm
Trans*.
    Then, you must never forget that I'm Trans*.
    Get comfortable with the word
"cis."
    Remember that when the oppressor can name the
oppressed
but the oppressed cannot name the oppressor,
oppression wins.
    Read Trans* theory, and let's talk about it, but don't expect me
to teach you everything you need to know about being Trans*.

Katka Showers-Curtis (photo by Enrique Centeno).

---

* Quotes in this chapter come from both the general *Trans Bodies, Trans Selves* online survey and from a survey of partners of trans people, also located on the *Trans Bodies, Trans Selves* website.

You say Trans* identity is a "new concept,"
but I promise, you can find Thomas Beattie, S. Bear Bergman,
Kate Bornstein, Patrick Califia, Eli Clare, Leslie Feinberg,
Jamison Green, Jack Halberstam, Mara Keisling, Joy Ladin, Ashley Love,
Miss Major, Janet Mock, Pauline Park, Sylvia Rivera, Monica Roberts,
Julia Serano, Dean Spade, Sandy Stone, Susan Stryker,
and countless others
with a simple click of a mouse.
When you've done this,
ask what being Trans* means to me,
but know you must ask
every person who identifies as Trans*
what it means to them. Even then,
know that not everyone can give you a full answer,
and that that answer may change with time.
We are a community,
but none of us identifies exactly like another,
and shit changes.
And if some Trans* person
expects you
to be accountable for your actions,
reminds you
of the proper use of their pronouns,
scoffs
when you call them a "pronoun Nazi,"
or is just being an ass,
please,
do not tell me I am
"different"
or "better than" that person.
It makes me wonder if you see your own
cissexism
and transphobia,
and I will wonder if you really see me.
And even if you truly believe Trans* lovers are the "best
of both worlds," don't tell me.
Instead, learn to respect our bodies and minds.
In other words—
if you really want to be my friend—
take initiative to learn
what it might mean to be Trans*,
and ask what it means to me,
but don't go out of your way
to tell me what a great job you're doing.
I see it. Remember.

DATING OTHER TRANS PEOPLE

Partnering with someone who shares many of the same experiences of being trans and going through transition can reduce some of the stress associated with dating. Other trans people are more likely than cis people to have a reference point in understanding some of our potential insecurities. The increasing visibility of trans movements and the creation of trans-specific spaces, as well as the rise of the Internet, have greatly increased our ability to find and connect with other trans people. We cannot assume that other trans people will always understand our experiences, but finding and partnering with other trans people can create a greater likelihood that our partner "gets it."

"Well I'm bigendered, and she's mtf, and she's the only one I've come out to and that means the world to me. She's so supportive and we lean on each other. We understand each other."

"Now, my fiancé and I are together, and we're both trans. It's amazing in so many ways! I feel more relaxed, much safer emotionally, and more at home with her than I ever did 'dating out' with cisgender people. Some of that, I'm sure, has to do with emotional growth and personal changes I've made over the years. But there are things that just don't end up being an issue that needs to be navigated when your partner is also trans."

DATING WITHIN QUEER COMMUNITIES

Our relationships (Elenore Toczynski).

The Yahoo group Transcouplesmtfftm discusses relationships between people who are both transgender or genderqueer.

Some of us may never have dated in queer communities and may not be interested in doing so. However, others of us have participated in queer communities before, during, and after a transition, and we may continue to seek relationships in these spaces. While many queer spaces can be safe and welcoming for us as trans people, not all LGBQ spaces are trans-friendly—in fact, a lot of transphobia, trans exoticization, and trans invisibility can occur in these spaces and can potentially negatively influence our dating experiences.

"It seems as if many queer women's communities are accepting of trans guys in their communities, and are accepting of the women who date them. But the acceptance and welcoming that is there if I date a trans man largely vanishes if I date a cis man. So what is this really saying? It seems to me that it's saying that a trans man is not actually a man, and this is deeply problematic. Queer communities have a long way to go, still, in fully accepting, welcoming, and understanding bisexual and trans people, and not just paying lip service to it. Another example of this is how few trans women you'll see in queer women's communities, and how often trans women feel unwelcome and hurt by queer women. This is trans misogyny, and it is androcentrism, and we need to examine it in our lives and communities if we ever hope to truly make progress."

Despite some of these challenges, many queer spaces are trans inclusive. Many trans women find women partners and trans men find men partners in queer spaces. Sometimes we also find partners of other genders in queer spaces. For instance, some trans men prefer to date queer-identified or lesbian-identified women. This can be confusing for others to understand, but queer spaces can sometimes leave more room for these seeming contradictions.

COMMUNITIES LIKELY TO BE TRANS-FRIENDLY

There are some spaces that are not specifically trans or queer but that have an increased likelihood of trans inclusion. Multiple cultures exist that not only condone but encourage gender variance. An example of this is how femininity is valued in both men and women in goth culture. Many trans women have found that goth culture gives us a nonjudgmental space in which to experiment with our gender expression. Someone assigned male can feel comfortable entering such a space wearing makeup, skirts, and fishnets. In such a space where the rules of normative gender expression are suspended, we are less likely to encounter harassment. Other examples of subcultures that are not specifically queer, but where queer themes have been a long-existing influence, are punk culture and anime culture. In spaces like these, we may find increased inclusion and acceptance that can influence our dating experiences.

Effects of Gender Norms and Socialization on Dating

When we transition, we may notice that our transition to a different gender impacts how other people relate to us. This happens in casual but also intimate relationships. We may or may not change how we act during a transition, but people may change how they act toward us because of gendered norms and expectations. For instance, transmasculine people may start to find that our partners expect us to initiate more in the relationship, from being the one to ask someone else on a date to initiating sexual intimacy. Transfeminine people may notice that others expect us to take up less space in conversations or that other people may invade our personal space more often. These changes may be minor or more major. In either case, it can be important to be aware of how people may change in their interactions with us and how this influences our own dating experiences.

> "I guess that since transitioning, with women, I felt at first a lot of pressure to 'perform.' Be The Man. Always be hard and ready, always be the top. I think those expectations were largely in my head. A lot of this pressure would have probably resolved with more sincere and open communication, queer pride, and readiness to laugh at myself. My partners were great and probably weary of gender roles themselves. What I didn't understand was that as a guy, trans or cis, I'm almost always less vulnerable than she is when we're entering a new sexual dynamic, even if I feel insecure. It took a while for the privilege to kick in, like until I started doing what I was 'supposed' to do in my new gender. Women will flirt with me and I'd try to be a 'gentleman' and 'safe' by not being sexual at all. I was afraid to be a perpetrator. They'll have their boobs intentionally in my face, and I'd be like, 'I am looking in your eyes!!' Then when I finally did 'get the clue' and hook up with women, I realized, we'd reenact a power dynamic where I get to enjoy and benefit from both the high sexual desirability of queer guys and the lack of sensitive and safe masculine people to hook up with. Women still need to have such low expectations, and endurance, just to get laid. Like it's really outstanding if I'm not a complete jerk. And that is not quite the feminist sex we tried to have. We need to challenge sexual hierarchy to be able to share really good sex with each other."

Disclosing While Dating

For some of us, we are not necessarily read as trans in public, and we may not be in private either. When we are forming new relationships, we have to decide for ourselves when (or if) to disclose our trans status to potential partners.

"Cori and Max, reversed couple, Atlanta" (copyright Mariette Pathy Allen).

> *"I've had lots of sexual and intimate relationships. Some of them I don't disclose, some of them I do. . . it depends on what I'm looking for."*

For many of us, our identity as trans is just as large a part of our core being as our gender identity, and it may be very important to us that a potential partner understand our trans identity and experiences. We may be left feeling that a part of ourselves is missing from a relationship if we do not disclose.

The "if and when" of disclosure depends entirely on our personal comfort. We are not being dishonest about who we are if we do not choose to out ourselves as trans to everyone we date. The expectation that we must out ourselves to every potential partner or that we are otherwise being dishonest is problematic. If trans people are expected to disclose their trans status at the beginning of a relationship and no equivalent expectation exists for cis people, a cissexist power dynamic is created. If an individual self identifies as female and is seen by their prospective partner as female, then there is no incongruence between who they are and how they are perceived and therefore no act of dishonesty.

For some of us, our physical bodies are completely aligned with the typical external sex characteristics of our identified sex or gender. In such a case the choice not to disclose is entirely valid, even in a long-term relationship. However, if we engage in a relationship with an expectation of physical intimacy and our bodies differ from what may be assumed by a reading of our outward presentation, then disclosure of a trans identity can be important for our own safety. It is up to us to decide for ourselves whether it is right, when it is right, and how it is right for us to disclose our trans identity to our partners.

We must remember, though, that the longer we wait to disclose, the more deeply involved we might be in a relationship before learning how our partner handles our trans history. The timing can be tricky, and as a result, some of us develop clear guidelines for ourselves as we gain experience in the sphere of dating.

> "If I want to see someone a second time, I disclose on the first date. I've learned that the earlier, the better for my emotional well-being because the relationship is so new. And even if she responds very positively, I tend not to 'make a move' unless she does on the first date—because the reality of physical intimacy with a trans person for the first time can be overwhelming or intimidating even for supportive cisgender people. By the second date, she has gotten the chance to process on her own, and I have protected myself from being (unintentionally) dragged through her emotional process."

> "I generally don't tell people until I know we are going to sleep together. At that point, I've gotten a good sense for how they will likely react and don't allow relationships to develop if I think the person will react poorly. In 13 years, I've only had one bad reaction and he later apologized."

The "how" of disclosure can be challenging in the moment as well. It is helpful to keep in mind that many people, trans and cis alike, experience the burden of disclosure when they start getting to know a potential partner. We might not be the only one on the date who is worried about disclosing certain personal information, even information that pertains to physical intimacy such as fetishes, aspects of the body that are different than expected, or HIV status or other chronic illness. Some of us make our disclosure light hearted.

> "I've found that the more comfortable I am with my trans history when I'm disclosing, and the less nervous I seem, the more comfortable my date is. I say that it's shaped who I am in many ways, and I want the other person to know and ask me about it—but it's not a negative thing. I've had many dates where my disclosure has opened up an entirely new realm of conversation and has put my date at ease about sharing aspects of themselves with me."

Sometimes we are pleasantly surprised by dates who have already dated trans people, or who have a strong foundation of trans-awareness, or who are even trans themselves. Other times, we find ourselves having to teach Trans 101 to a date who has no reference point for or experience with trans identities. In these cases, we can engage however we feel most comfortable. Some of us are happy to answer a slew of questions, while others of us might share some basics but then suggest that deeper conversations about the topic wait until future dates. All we can really do is to approach a potential disclosure with a sense of what we want to communicate (and how) and be prepared for the various possible responses.

Safety should always be a top priority. While it can be difficult at times to work up the courage to disclose, it can be dangerous to keep this information from someone who might discover it while we are alone with them and vulnerable to being physically hurt. Leaving our trans status to a partner to discover in the heat of the moment can be awkward at best and dangerous at worst.

Having Multiple Partners

Our status as trans can constitute a significant factor in our relationships, but it is far from the only variable in effect. Our sexual orientation, attractions, kinks, and potential desires for multiple partners are among the aspects of ourselves that can affect our dating lives.

Many of us have spent a significant portion of our lives in an identity that does not suit us, and find that with a better understanding of ourselves, we are not ready to be with a

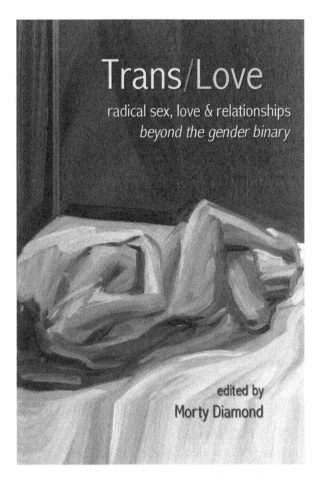

Trans/Love cover (copyright 2011, Manic D Press. Cover painting, "Embrace" by David Van Everen copyright 2009. All rights reserved. Reprinted with permission of publisher).

single person. We may have a desire to experience a variety of different types of relationships with a variety of people in order to find what is right for us. There are also some of us for whom having multiple partners is not an experimental period but a core part of our sexuality.

For some people, the process of transition opens up many new questions and interests in different kinds of partnerships. An open relationship may be a helpful way to maintain a loving partnership with someone we were with before transition, while allowing us to explore new parts of ourselves. Navigating opening up a monogamous relationship can be complicated, and it is important to work together to ensure that everyone's needs continue to be met through the process. We must also be able to recognize incompatibility with a partner if one member truly needs an open relationship while the other functions best in a closed monogamous partnership.

Polyamory—relationships that are consensually open to sexual and/or romantic relationships with others—can be even more complex and requires significant cooperation and communication. If you are interested in creating a healthy polyamorous life, you should seek out specific resources in order to do this, as it is beyond the scope of this book.

Start your exploration of nonmonogamous relationships with *The Ethical Slut: A Practical Guide to Polyamory, Open Relationships & Other Adventures* by Dossie Easton and Janet W. Hardy (Berkeley, CA: Celestial Arts, 1997, 2009).

Deciding Not to Be Sexual

Asexuality can have many varied definitions depending on who you ask, but it generally refers to those of us who do not have or are not interested in sexual relationships. Some of us prefer not to have sexual relationships in our lives. We may or may not desire romantic relationships. Some of us who are asexual may enjoy the benefits of intimate relationships without sex.

> *"I'm in a committed relationship with another trans* person now, and it's completely different from any other relationship I've ever been in. It was hard at first, because I'm used to playing by very traditional rules, and that's not appropriate for what we have. We both identify as asexual, so the physical component of our relationship is limited. It's also not a traditionally romantic relationship; any romantic aspect at all is more in the context of a romantic friendship. We're open to including other people in the relationship if that ever became a possibility, and to having a considerable amount of freedom in terms of being able to see other people individually. But we are committed to staying together, to supporting one another, and to working as an actual partnership. It's the healthiest relationship I've ever been in, and the most honest."*

Some of us who are not asexual temporarily opt out of sexual relationships while we are adjusting to our identity. We may wish to wait until after a physical transition to begin a relationship that could include sexual intimacy because we feel we will be more comfortable with our body then. Others of us may fear the reaction of a potential partner toward either our gender identity or our body.

> *"I don't see a relationship in my future anytime soon. Right now, I feel like I am going through puberty all over again. I have to get comfortable in my body and gender presentation before I can even think about involving someone else."*

COMMITTED RELATIONSHIPS

Some of us are in committed relationships. They may have begun before, during, or after our transition. They may be extremely healthy or may have problematic power dynamics. Many of our relationships have significant challenges, and we have to learn how to communicate well and respect our partners in order to have fulfilling and lasting partnerships.

Building Healthy Relationships

Healthy relationships are not always easy; they often take work. Healthy relationships are those in which we respect our partners and are respected by them. There are a number of ways to create respectful relationships.

Setting boundaries with our partners can contribute to healthy relationships. Our boundaries may relate to our own emotional health. For instance, we may want our partners to understand when and how we can talk about particular issues. We may have certain situations in which we are happy being out about our transgender identity, and others in which we want our partners to understand that we would prefer not to be. Boundary setting is a mutual process, as our partners may also have similar needs around their own boundaries. Boundaries can change from day to day, and respecting these changes is important for our relationships.

We can also nurture healthy relationships through constructive communication with our partners. If we approach our relationships with the intention of fostering open communication between ourselves and our partners, we are able to be more honest about what we want from a relationship, and we can also better respond to our partners' needs and desires. Fostering communication does not mean that we will never argue with our partners—disagreement can be a positive way to clarify our own needs in relation to those of our partners.

> *"I began a relationship with the person who is still my partner after socially transitioning but before physically transitioning. We've been able to maintain*

the relationship by being open, honest, and respectful of one another. My trans-sexuality has been less of an issue than other challenges."

BOUNDARIES: THE BEST RELATIONSHIP CURE

Allison Vogt, LBSW, advocates for LGBT victims and survivors of domestic violence, sexual assault, hate crimes, and human trafficking through direct services, advocacy, and education for the Montrose Center in Houston, Texas. Her blog, Ask Allie, is popular among teens requesting healthy relationship advice.

Boundaries help us feel good, and they keep us feeling good. Boundaries are simply what we say we are and are not willing to do. Trans people are often thought of as being not as valuable as cis folks. Trans folks mistakenly feel we should not or do not have as many boundaries as others and think our body is open season for questions, grabbing, and viewing. This should never be the case—even with our friends, family, and partners. We should never feel that a friend of ours won't be our friend if we don't do exactly what they want when they want it.

To set our boundaries, we have to be consistent. When something feels uncomfortable, we have to say it despite the real and perceived consequences—like embarrassment or losing a friend. If we allow people to make us feel uncomfortable and are afraid to say so, we are setting ourselves up to have them do it again. The more they do it, and the more we don't say what our feelings are, the harder it will be to set the boundary in the future.

To set your boundaries, know what they are. If you are uncomfortable with friends who expect you to go out every time they want to go out, that is your boundary; ask your friend to give you a day's heads up. If you are uncomfortable with your partner touching your chest, tell your partner you find that weird, but that you do like it when they touch your [fill in the blank with what you like]. Setting boundaries will keep us from resenting the people in our lives and will garner respect—and we all deserve that.

Intimate Partner Violence

Healthy relationships are a continuous process. There can be difficult times that we work through. We may sometimes find ourselves in relationships that are harmful to us or to our partners.

Intimate partner violence (IPV) involves abuse that occurs in our intimate, romantic, or sexual relationships. Abuse in a relationship can include verbal abuse such as put-downs, physical abuse such as hitting or shoving, financial abuse such as withholding or controlling finances, emotional abuse such as threatening or intimidating, and sexual abuse such as forcing or coercing sexual encounters. The term *intimate partner violence* is similar to domestic violence. However, it includes not only abuse between people who

Argument (Elenore Toczynski).

The center of the wheel reads: **POWER AND CONTROL**

COERCION AND THREATS: Making and/or carrying out threats to hurt you or people you care about. Threatening to 'out' you. Threatening you with exclusion from trans community. Threatening to leave or commit suicide. Threatening to tell others you're not 'trans enough' or that you're not a good ally.

INTIMIDATION: Making you afraid by using looks, actions, or gestures. Throwing or smashing things. Destroying your property. Abusing pets. Displaying weapons. Making you afraid of seeking help because you're transgender.

USING PRIVILEGE: Using privilege to justify abuse. Being the one to define the roles in the relationship. Using trans or cis status to define your worth. Using their privilege to discredit you.

EMOTIONAL ABUSE: Putting you down. Telling you you're not a 'real man' or a 'real woman'. Making you feel bad about yourself. Calling you names. Making you think you're crazy. Playing mind games. Reinforcing internalized transphobia. Humiliating you. Making you feel guilty.

ECONOMIC ABUSE: Preventing you from getting or keeping a job. Making you ask for money. Giving you an allowance. Taking your money. Not letting you know about or have access to income. Making you support your partner financially. Threatening to stop paying for hormones.

ISOLATION: Controlling who you contact, what you do, or where you go. Using jealousy to control you. Telling you that others couldn't love or accept you. Telling you no one will believe you about the abuse.

USING CHILDREN: Making you feel guilty about the children. Using children to relay messages. Threatening to take the children. Threatening to tell your ex-partner or authorities that you are transgender so they will take the children.

MINIMIZING, DENYING, AND BLAMING: Making light of the abuse. Justifying abuse because of the pressures of your own or your partner's transition. Saying the abuse isn't happening. Shifting responsibility for the abuse.

Outer ring: physical VIOLENCE sexual physical VIOLENCE sexual

Outermost ring: heterosexism transphobia cissexism trans misogyny racism ableism classism sexism heterosexism transphobia cissexism trans misogyny racism ableism classism sexism

Trans power and control wheel (adapted by Carey Jean Sojka from the Power and Control Wheel created by the Domestic Abuse Intervention Project in Duluth, Minnesota).

live together but also abuse that occurs between people in relationships who are not living in the same place.

The power and control wheel is a model that has been used to illustrate the ways that IPV can function. Power and control are at the center of abuse—the hub of the wheel of IPV is the idea that one person can and should have power and control over someone else. Within the spokes of the wheel, there are many aspects of abuse that support physical and sexual abuse and systematic oppressions. The spokes include things like intimidation, economic abuse, and emotional abuse. The outside of the wheel is what keeps the wheel rolling—the violence we experience in our society through transphobia and other forms of oppression such as racism, classism, and sexism, which also contribute to violence within our relationships.

Historically, there has been a backlash against discussing IPV in many marginalized groups. IPV is too often seen as something that contributes to negative stereotypes that are already oppressive. In many communities of color, there has been a backlash because of the fear that openly discussing violence, particularly violence against women in heterosexual relationships, will be used by others to perpetuate negative and false stereotypes about men of color as violent or sexually aggressive. These stereotypes have historically, and even today, been used to oppress communities of color. However, many women of color still speak out about violence in their attempts to end it and to provide support for those who experience it.

In lesbian, gay, and bisexual communities, we have seen a parallel pattern. While it stems from different causes, in the end, it has also led to silencing around issues of intimate partner violence. Many gay and bisexual men have been afraid to speak out about IPV because of the assumption that men cannot be the ones who are abused, and many lesbians and bisexual women have been afraid to speak out because a woman does not fit the typical profile of an abuser. On top of that, some lesbian, gay, and bisexual people fear that public acknowledgment of IPV in same-gender relationships will only perpetuate negative and false stereotypes that lesbian, gay, and bisexual people cannot form healthy, lasting relationships.

As trans people, we can be vulnerable to specific types of abuse. Something an abusive partner may threaten to do is stop paying for hormones or claim that we are not a "real man" or a "real woman." An abusive partner may threaten to out us to our friends, family, coworkers, or community. These tactics work over time to diminish our sense of self-worth.

Trans people can be abusers, too. Some people who are abusive partners and also trans will use emotional abuse to threaten a cis partner with exclusion from trans communities, or act out against a cis partner and then claim that if their partner were really a trans ally, they would understand how hard it is to be trans and excuse the abusive behavior. Our hormones and our transitions should never be an excuse for abuse—it can be easy to shift blame for abuse onto the stresses of transition.

If you are someone who is in an abusive relationship, there are a number of things you can do.

1. *Find help.* You may wish to speak with a therapist or contact an organization, such as a local organization that works against intimate partner violence or a national hotline. It can be helpful to have a list of organization phone numbers available in case you need them. Contacting these organizations can provide a place for you to discuss your experiences with someone who understands, and they can help you to figure out your options.
2. *Consider who your allies are.* Who are the people in your life, such as friends, family members, or neighbors, who you can trust and who will support you?
3. *Create a plan for what you would do if you need to get out, even if you are not currently planning on leaving the relationship.* Think about things such as where you would go, who could lend you money, what you would need to do about your children, and who would take care of your pets. You may also wish to have a packed bag with essential items handy and hidden so that you could leave at a moment's notice if necessary.

If you have a friend who you think might be in an abusive relationship, there are many ways you can help. First, never underestimate the power of listening. Having someone to listen in a nonjudgmental way can be very helpful for a person in an abusive relationship. Second, try to avoid giving advice about what they should do, even if your friend asks for it. A person in an abusive relationship may already be accustomed to not having choices, and one of the most empowering things can be for them to be able to make choices for themselves. Instead of giving advice, you can offer options and resources instead. Help them brainstorm about the possibilities they have. Do some research for your friend to find the contact information for a local, trans-friendly nonprofit working to end IPV or find the number of a 24-hour hotline. Even if your friend leaves their abusive relationship, be prepared for them to potentially return. Many people return to their abusive partner at least once after leaving, some many more times than that. The most important thing for you to do is to support your friend through their choices, and to be there to listen to and support them when they need it again. Each time someone leaves an abusive relationship, it can help to empower them to eventually leave for good.

Getting Help With Intimate Partner Violence
National Domestic Violence Hotline: 1–800–799–SAFE (7233)

Gay Men's Domestic Violence Hotline (for all LGBTQ people): 1-800-832-1901

GLBT National Hotline (can call about issues other than IPV as well): 1-888-843-4564

Intimate partner violence happens in our communities, too. Check out the book *The Revolution Starts at Home: Confronting Intimate Violence Within Activist Communities* by Ching-In Chen, Jal Dulani, and Leah Lakshmi Piepzna-Samarasinha (Brooklyn, NY: South End Press, 2011).

TAKING A RELATIONSHIP THROUGH A TRANSITION

For those of us in relationships prior to identifying as or coming out as trans, they may be strong relationships that we want to continue as we transition. Some of us may already be out to our partners in some way before we tell them everything we understand about our identities. For others of us, our partners may not be as prepared.

Justus and Johnnie (copyright Mariette Pathy Allen).

Coming Out to a Long-Term Partner

Will everyone you ever meet or love
Be just a relationship based on a false presumption?

—Laura Jane Grace of Against Me!

In general, our relationships are healthier if we are treated the way we identify. The stress associated with pretending to be something other than ourselves can be a hindrance to healthy communication and connection. There is a wide spectrum of how out we may be to a partner before transition. Some of us voice to our partners a discomfort with adhering to traditional gender roles, or we act in ways around our partners that communicate an androgynous or ambiguous style without voicing a trans identity. Others of us disclose our intent to transition to our partners even if we are not ready to do so yet or if barriers exist that prevent transition. Even if we are not able to fully transition, being out on some level to someone we are close to can have the potential to strengthen bonds and even help us move forward with transition.

> "I have just started transitioning and have been married for a year. My husband has been very supportive of me being whatever I feel I should be. He is fine with me being a male and even admitted to his own gender-fluid state when I came out to him. I know that I'm extremely lucky to have him. I have previously been in a relationship where I was afraid to ever disclose my trans identity because he couldn't accept me as I was. My husband has been a phenomenal source of support in me discovering myself and allowing me to express myself in whatever way works best for me as a person, not what society expects me to be."

Announcing to the people in our life our identity, our desire to transition, or that we have already begun the transition process is an act of bravery and honesty. Disclosing our status as trans, or communicating that our presentation is not aligned with our identity and we do not have a strong connection to our assigned birth sex, can potentially end a relationship, greatly strengthen the connection with our partner, or fall somewhere between.

PUTTING IT ON FAITH

Aja Worthy Davis is a bureaucrat and blogger based in Clinton Hill, Brooklyn. She has a degree from Pace University, a wonderful partner, and an obsession with high fantasy.

I wasn't supposed to be this person. Not yet. I wasn't supposed to be the one planning a wedding with their long-term partner, with a mortgage and two cats that are perpetually on the verge of murdering each other, and larger family responsibilities. Me, the *non-committal bisexual* (the stereotypes exist for a reason).

I was supposed to travel, and get a graduate degree in something ridiculous, and have overly emotional but hollow affairs with older men that didn't work out because I'm pretty romantically queer and politically black and other things that tend not to work in the long term with intellectual and crotchety white men. In all fairness, I *have* done some of those things. But here I am, a few years shy of 30, and a few months away from being the *wife* of a guy I've known and loved since I was 15. Back when he was a girl.

We are what happens when *Pariah*'s Alike and the flighty femme she fell for get older and try to make a go of it.

Are we still on for dinner? I text him. We had planned on meeting at my Downtown Brooklyn office, where I'd lug my newly altered wedding gown in order to meet him halfway between his Eastern Brooklyn workspace and whatever restaurant we're going to drive to. The reason I'm unsure of his commitment to the date is because we went to sleep last night after rehashing an argument that's become so routine it's at the top of the list of issues we'll be discussing in our upcoming premarital therapy sessions.

It basically goes like this—I am not sure I want kids. Which would be fine, because as a teacher and a child therapist, he's pretty emotionally spent dealing with other people's kids. But the reason I'm not sure is because of him. I'm afraid of raising a kid—a son especially—with a trans man. I fear how a parent's history of trauma and gender dysphoria will affect a kid. Even as I write that, I wish I weren't so sure of the absolute truth in that statement, in the same way I am absolutely sure that he and I are made for one another.

I wish I didn't know he'd make as great a father as he is a partner—other people's children have literally told him, "I wish you were my father." But most of all, I wish I wasn't still a little bit of the selfish, stupid girl who always imagined she'd get a buffer-life before he and I came together. That buffer-life would include a marriage to a biological man. One who was kind and made me smile and was a great dad. He would teach our kids to play sports and navigate traditional masculinity, and hopefully would be okay with being with a woman who wasn't in love with him. I wouldn't have to *think* about feminism or racism or any -ism. I wouldn't have to be me, which is so thoroughly fucking *exhausting* sometimes. We'd get divorced, of course, after the kids were adults. Then I'd go knocking on my Alike's door, hoping for the chance to begin my life.

I look at all the older femmes in our community, many fresh out of the heterosexual marriages they settled for, and I get a full appreciation of how messed up a plan that is to have at 15. But it was my plan, because spending my whole life with a girl (and that's what I saw my fiancé as at the time) actually seemed more terrifying a prospect than hoping to get a shot at happiness at 50.

I never know how to speak about his transition. It changed how the world sees us. But it didn't change us at all. I am a born realist who tries to meticulously plan out every decision in her life—even the unplannable shit—yet at the same time I am always waiting for the other shoe to drop. As the great Oprah would say, that constant waiting for something to go wrong or *be* incomplete is a self-fulfilling prophecy. I know that I'm incredibly lucky to get to be happy as *me* now, and not wait until I'm 50. I'm lucky to be healthy and alive and to be with *him*, who waited 10 years for me to be ready for *us*. And, obviously, I'm still a work in progress, on the kids issue and other things.

You know what's right for you almost immediately. What takes time—years of time in my case—is letting go of all your internalized expectations and fears. Relinquishing the sense of absolute control over your life and trusting that everything will be okay. My fiancé is home to me. I don't know if there's anyone I could be a better parent or *person* with, because being this happy makes you want to be the best version of yourself. I was never the kind of girl who thought about her wedding day, but here I am watching those horrible bridal shows, truly excited to become his wife. Everything else—I'm willing to put on faith.

Being Out as a Couple

When we are in long-term relationships, our relationships are often known to others in our lives. As such, every time we out ourselves, we also out our partners, and vice versa. We may need to discuss with our partners whether we are comfortable being out as trans in various situations. We may be comfortable being out with our partner's extended family but not with our work friends, and we need to be able to discuss and negotiate these differences.

We also need to consider whether or when our partners are comfortable being out, because every time we come out as trans, our partner is also outed as the partner of a trans person. At times our needs can conflict, with one partner wanting more or less visibility than the other. Our partners may even find themselves the targets of discrimination or violence. There is no simple answer when one person's needs or safety are in conflict with another's, but it is often possible to negotiate a comfortable and safe solution that will work for both people.

> *"I was married when I started my transition and I remained married. I think the most important thing that we did to maintain our relationship is talk about what was going on. I did not hide my questioning and my confusion over my gender from my partner. We talked, we shared reading materials, we wondered together what this all would mean for our relationship and our family. And we didn't make any promises. As my transition became more real, we agreed that we'd try to stay together, but we relieved ourselves of our wedding vow to stay together no matter what. She returned to school to enhance her earning capacity just in case we broke up. We tried to prepare ourselves the best we could for the experience. And we realized that my transition was just one of the many transitions that happened to our family: we transitioned from a straight couple to a queer couple; my boys now had two 'moms' and no 'dad'; my partner went from appearing straight to appearing gay. All of these things had to be explored and dealt with to move forward. And it's ongoing."*

In addition, there are always outside influences on our romantic relationships. Our friends and families matter in the support they give to our relationships. Our communities matter, too; religious communities, racial and ethnic communities, queer communities, and so on, can all play a part in shaping our relationships. The challenge is to seek out the people in our communities that will support us and help us to build healthy relationships.

LIFE AFTER TRANSITION

Helen Boyd, MA, is the author of My Husband Betty *and* She's Not the Man I Married. *She blogs at myhusbandbetty.com and teaches gender studies at Lawrence University.*

Betty transitioned. Apparently we've forgotten to announce that officially. I can't imagine anyone is surprised; looking back, I see chapter 5 of *My Husband Betty* as tea leaves neither of us wanted to read. But I wrote *My Husband Betty* seven years ago (and it's still in print!), and that old joke says it only takes two years, right? Maybe that's from cross-dresser to transsexual, because surely it takes more years than that to become a woman or a man. It certainly took me a few more than two to become a woman, and that was without any trans interference. (Sometimes, when someone asks me if I'm trans myself, I wonder if I ever did make it to "woman," but for me, that's a compliment, that all of my genders are showing.)

What we are, post transition, is more relaxed. That has something to do with our move from New York to Wisconsin, and something to do as well with us both having jobs we like. It may also have something to do with our being together for 12 years now. But hearing that other shoe drop, at long last, has brought us both relief as well.

We find it easier being perceived as a lesbian couple than as a trans couple. Granted, we "do" lesbian with our bizarre heterosexual privilege—by which I mean we are still federally recognized as legally married. I certainly don't mean to imply it's easier to be a lesbian couple; it's not. It's way harder than when we were seen as a somewhat eccentric het couple. But you do a lot less explaining at parties, and that's a nice break. People know what lesbians are, even if, as in our case, the label isn't wholly accurate. Mostly we don't prefer to tell people Betty is trans; if they know, and have questions, we answer them when we're in the appropriate time and place to do so, like in a private conversation and not at a party. But otherwise, I have no interest in outing her on a regular basis.

Often the question of whether or not to be out as trans rests upon the assumption that you're either out or stealth. Yay, another binary! The reality is that there is a significant gray area. What has surprised us most is that the old advice—to move clear across the country—has its reasons. We did, but not as part of her transition plan. We did, and so we've reaped the benefits of being in a place where no one knew her as male, where no one knew us as het, where no one knew us before at all. That is, when we meet people now, they need only know us as a same-sex couple. Unlike many if not most trans people, Betty is undeniably out. Once someone asks me what I do, for instance, it is only a few short stops to "She used to be a man?" To preserve some of our privacy—and yes, even memoirists like some privacy—I usually tell people I write gender theory which invariably leads to one of two responses: (1) "Oh," or (2) they actually want to know what I think of Lady Gaga's/Caster Semenya's gender, at which point the conversation turns away from me and onto cranky female athletes or Gaga's little monsters. That is, the titles of my books don't ever have to come up, which keeps me from outing Betty. One of the best parts of working in academia is having people assume they haven't read your work.

What we've found is that the guy at the local equivalent of the 7-11 doesn't need to know. We are often assumed to be friends, and not a couple, because of general LGBTQ invisibility, and I'm learning to live with that and all the heterocentric bullshit the world is steeped in. When someone's head is still getting used to the idea of homosexuality, you don't really want to hit them with The Trans, anyway. They're not ready.

A friend of mine, both lesbian and trans, was once asked to talk to a student about being out. My friend promptly explained her experiences being out as trans, to which the slack-jawed undergrad responded, "I thought you were just a lesbian."

So now we're "just lesbians." But is anyone "just a lesbian?" Every lesbian woman I know is a host of other things: parent, daughter, lawyer, trans, Asian, etc. We are not "just lesbians" either. We are something like post trans queers. Or I am, at least. I'm not really sure anymore.

The only sad thing for me is that I have lost my partner in crime. Betty is (quite frustratingly, some days) gender normative, trendy, and magazine feminine. I have to remind her not to flip her hair so much. I love her, but I still nurse a general dislike of normative femininity. I'm naturally suspicious of people who fit in. I assume I'll get over it. You don't really make it through transition as someone's partner without having an awful lot of flexibility.

What I will say to the partners: my resolve to be her friend first, and her lover/wife second, was tantamount. We still worry that our friendship has replaced or supplanted our marriage, but I suspect that's the kind of thing a lot of long-term relationships wrestle with. When it comes down to it, our journey, and my midwifery, has been an honor and a pleasure. It is a remarkable thing to watch someone go through gender transition and to help them do so. She has assisted me through a few life transitions, and we will, no doubt, see a few more in our lifetimes, and any and all of those changes can be a threat to a couple's permanence and happiness. Her gender transition's challenge to who we are as a couple was maybe more challenging than others, or maybe just more obvious in the ways it accessed axes of identity. But surely unhappiness, self-repression, and stagnation would destroy any relationship as easily and with far more bitterness and regret, and you know? Phooey to that.

Changing Sexuality Through Transition

Some people experience a shift in their sexual or romantic desires during a transition. Some of us experience changes in our libido, our interest in specific sexual practices, and even the types of people to whom we are attracted. It can be confusing to understand what our new desires mean for both our existing relationships and our future relationships.

For those of us who are in relationships, we may have many questions, such as: Can my partner help me fulfill my new sexual desires? What if they cannot or they are not interested? While there are no simple answers to these questions, one of the best things we can do is to be honest with ourselves and clearly communicate our feelings with our partners.

Many of our relationships thrive after disclosing our identity as trans or our intention to transition. However, not all of us find that our existing relationships are a good fit once we transition. Some of us find that our own desires change and no longer include our existing partner. For others of us, our partners' desires do not include the new us. A partner who identifies as strictly homosexual or heterosexual may consider a transition to be a relationship ender. Our sexual orientation can be much more than an indication of our attractions. It can also be a core part of our identity, representing not only how we see ourselves but also the community with which we find comfort and how we want to be seen by others.

"My wife and I have been married for 16 years. I began my transition in our fifteenth year of marriage. My partner had suspected for some time, but has recently fully embraced being bisexual. This I believe is the single largest factor in keeping our marriage together, as we transition together from living as a heterosexual couple to living as lesbians. Our love is very strong, but I believe if she was not attracted to my feminine body that would erode over years. I'm very optimistic now that we will continue to have a strong romantic relationship for the rest of our lives."

There is often an expectation that supportive partners will still desire those of us who are transitioning in the same way as before our transition, but this can be an unfair expectation. Many relationships change during transition, including those with our romantic and sexual partners. Our partners may find that their sexual desire or identity no longer aligns with our gender. Expecting someone to alter a core aspect of their identity in order to accommodate us would be just as unreasonable as expecting us to refrain from transitioning to preserve the relationship.

"I have not begun transitioning, yet. I am married to a wonderful woman and when I told her, she was very loving about it. She told me she hurts for me having to hide this my entire life, wants the best for me, but. . . she doesn't want to be around as she is not lesbian and does not want to be married to a woman. We are still together but I see our marriage ending sometime. That will hurt, thinking about that hurts my heart greatly."

Supporting Our Partners

While we struggle with being our authentic selves, our partners have their own challenges and concerns, and they may need our support. Their lives often change as ours do. They may now need to be out to others as the partner of a trans person. They may wonder about their own identity as we disclose ours. It is good to keep in mind that, as we transition, it can be a whirlwind experience for our partners. We can give them support in the same ways we would like to have support: by listening without judging, asking questions, and making an effort to understand our partners' perspectives and needs. It is also a great idea for partners to educate themselves about transitioning and what may be involved and seek support for themselves. There are many email lists, community groups, and resources where partners can share experiences, learn from one another, and discuss joys, fears, challenges, or frustrations.

Resources for Partners of Trans People
A list of online resources for partners of trans people can be found at T-Vox, a wiki that maintains a list of various types of online support, including email lists, groups, and forums for partners of trans people. Partners of trans people also recommend:

- TMatesFTM Youtube channel
- Engender Yahoo Group
- FTM UK
- Forge Forward
- Depend Partners MTF
- Trans Family Couples and Trans Family
- Partners of TG livejournal group

"I was in a very intimate relationship when I started mentally and openly transitioning. My boyfriend at the time was very open-minded, but unsure at first, about my transition. We had lots of long conversations talking about different scenarios and timelines for my transition and our future together. I spent a lot of time sharing new information that I found with him and including him in my discovery process, and the more he knew the less unsure and scared he was. In the end he completely accepted me and started to mentally prepare himself for me to eventually come out to his family, and it actually helped him to reveal a part of himself that he hadn't felt comfortable sharing with anyone before."

LEGAL PARTNERSHIPS

The legal recognition of trans relationships is sometimes very simple and other times incredibly complex. Some of us get married legally, and some of us have other legal

Timnah Steinman and Jay Williams (copyright Portraits to the People).

partnerships like domestic partnerships or civil unions. Some of us form partnerships without ever having the government recognize them—we make our commitments to each other public, whether this is with our friends, families, or religious communities.

Some of us do not prioritize public or legal recognition of our relationships. Whether or not we have legal recognition of our relationships, we may still want to consider additional legal protections such as health care visitation, second parent adoptions if we have children, or completing a will (see Chapter 10 for more information). Taking these extra steps can protect us not only from discrimination by people outside of our relationships but also from potential vulnerability if a relationship ends.

CONCLUSION

Relationships are about finding what fits for us and for our partners at any particular point in our lives. What we and our partners need and desire may change over time, even from one day to the next, but in the end, working toward mutual respect, open communication, and being true to ourselves can help us to create and maintain healthy, happy relationships of all kinds. No matter how we identify, our relationships have the possibility to contribute to our lives in meaningful and fulfilling ways. In all of our intimate relationships, we deserve to be valued and loved.

REFERENCES AND FURTHER READING

Bolus, S. (2002). "Loving Outside Simple Lines," in *GenderQueer: Voices from Beyond the Binary*, edited by Joan Nestle, Clare Howell, and Riki Wilchins, pp. 113–119. Los Angeles, CA: Alyson Publications.

Boyd, H. (2007). *She's not the man I married: My life with a transgender husband*. Emeryville, CA: Seal Press.

Califia, P. (2003). "The Invisible Gender Outlaws: The Partners of Transgender People," in *Sex Changes: The Politics of Transgenderism*, edited by Califia, P., pp. 196–220. San Francisco, CA: Cleis Press.

Cromwell, J. (1999). *Transmen and FTMs: Identities, Bodies, Genders, and Sexualities*. Urbana, IL: University of Illinois Press.

Diamond, M. (2011). *Trans/Love: Radical Sex, Love & Relationships Beyond the Gender Binary*. San Francisco, CA: Manic D Press.

Hardy, J. (2010). "The Old Folks at Home." In *Gender Outlaws: The Next Generation*, edited by Kate Bornstein and S. Bear Bergman, pp. 47–51. Berkeley, CA: Seal Press.

How to Be a Supportive Partner

As our partners, we may ask for support from you around our transition process. Support does not mean putting your own needs or desires aside for the sake of our transition. There are many other ways for our partners to support us. Supportive partners try to listen without judging, ask questions, and make an effort to understand our perspectives and our needs. Supportive partners validate our gender identities, whether it is as simple as using our chosen name and preferred pronouns, or as intimate as using our preferred words for bodies and sex acts during sexual moments. This does not mean that we expect you to always get it right, or even that you will still desire us in the same way as before our transition, but it does mean that we want you to show us that you value us for who we are. It can be supportive to accompany us to medical appointments or attend trans gatherings and conferences with us. We also understand that you may need to set boundaries for how much or in what ways you can support us, because a transition can sometimes be overwhelming for you, too.

"Without knowing that anyone like you existed, I searched for you. And now that I've found you, I feel such relief to know that you are real. Now I want to know the wealth of your mind, body, and soul, the hell of being you in this world, and the joy that also comes from living outside simple lines. You ask me to marry you. 'Yes' is my answer. And I say yes to life. I say yes with my eyes wide open. . . .. I marry you, and it is more than words or license or tax break, more than a church wedding or a white dress/tuxedo affair, more than a political statement, commitment ceremony, holy union. Marriage with you is life. You extend your hand to me. I step into your world and unite you to mine."

—Sonya Bolus

Hines, S. (2007). *TransForming Gender: Transgender Practices of Identity, Intimacy and Care*. Bristol, UK: Policy Press.

Hubbard, E. A., & Whitley, C. T. (2012). *Trans-kin: A guide for family and friends of transgender people*. Boulder, CO: Bolder Press.

O'Keefe, T., & Fox, K. (2008). *Trans People in Love*. New York, NY: Routledge.

Pratt, M. B. (1995). *S/HE*. Ithaca, NY: Firebrand Books.

Sanger, T. (2010). *Trans People's Partnerships: Towards an Ethics of Intimacy*. Palgrave Macmillan.

Valentine, D. (2006). "'I Went to Bed with my Own Kind Once': The Erasure of Desire in the Name of Identity," in *The Transgender Studies Reader*, edited by Susan Stryker and Stephen Whittle, pp. 407–19. New York, NY: Routledge.

Varian, F. (2010). "Daddy Gets the Big Piece of Chicken," in *Gender Outlaws: The Next Generation*, edited by Kate Bornstein and S. Bear Bergman, pp. 136–142. Berkeley, CA: Seal Press.

OUR RELATIONSHIPS AND FAMILIES

SEXUALITY

Tobi Hill-Meyer and Dean Scarborough

17

SEXUALITY IS A FUNDAMENTAL PART OF OUR EXPERIENCES AS PEOPLE. It encompasses feelings of desire and connection, intimacy and arousal, power and control, comfort and soothing, and much more. Most cultures and communities have their own ideas about the kinds of sex we should or should not be having. These can range widely, but they often include beliefs that the shape of our genitals or the gender of our partner determines what we can and should do. The truth is that there is no such thing as a *wrong way* to have sex. The kind of sex we enjoy is the kind of sex we should be having.

LOVING OUR BODIES

Sex can be a touchy concept for many trans people. We are taught to feel shame, fear, and guilt about our bodies and sexualities. Like many cisgender people, we may also have negative feelings that our bodies are too fat, too thin, or not muscular enough. But humans come in all shapes and sizes, and there are people attracted to every kind of body that exists.

Our ability to have fulfilling sex is linked to accepting our feelings and desires as valid, and paying attention to the things that make us feel good about ourselves, as well as the things that do not. When we show care for our bodies, we may find that we become more respectful to ourselves about our feelings and desires. There are many ways to do this, from practicing self-affirmations or engaging in therapy to getting regular exercise or beginning medical or surgical transitions.

For some of us, accepting and loving our bodies may seem counterintuitive. We may feel that being uncomfortable with some of our body parts is central to our identity as a trans person. We may be pursuing surgical and medical transitions that are intended to radically alter the appearance of our bodies. However, our bodies are much more than our gendered parts. Our bodies are our home in the world, and learning to love and care for our bodies, even when (or because) they are imperfect, can be a powerful way to reject the negative messages we have received from others.

Naming Our Bodies

One way many of us show our bodies love is by rewriting the language we use to describe them. Many of us have body parts that feel gendered in ways that do not match our sense of self. This can make it difficult for some of us to hear these body parts called by their standard names.

> *"I find any reference to my genitals by male terms, any proposed stimulation of them in male terms, or any mention of my taking on a male role in any way to be vehemently repulsive. I will not engage in conversation or consider dating anyone who does so. I also will not date men saying they want 'a girl with something extra,' want 'a special girl,' or want 'a chick with a dick.'"*

Many of us create our own names for our body parts. For example, some of us born with a vagina may prefer to call it a "front hole" because this term is less gendered. Some of us create new words that are just ours, or that we share with our sexual partners. Others may use terms, such as "cock," "clitoris," or "vagina," to refer to other parts of our bodies that we use or think about in these ways. For example, some of us who do not have a front

Choose Your Own Adventure
The kind of language that makes us feel good or bad about our genitals varies widely. This chapter has tried to balance the use of nontriggering language with the need for clear information about what body parts are being described. The goal is to help us and our partners be creative, find new ways to think about sex, and discover new ways of stimulating pleasure in our bodies, regardless of the anatomy that we have. If you do not like the words we have chosen, feel free to cross them out and replace them with the words that feel right for you.

Hayley (Courtney Trouble).

hole may call our anus our vagina. For others, using clinical language is most comfortable because we feel it describes the body part that we have, not the gender we are.

> *"Actually, I have a very good relationship with my vulva. I'm fond of it, I guess. It doesn't read as female to me—it reads as a body part that I happen to have, and that gives me a great deal of pleasure."*

Whatever we want to call our body parts is up to us. You might want to use different words in different contexts. Talking to medical providers and talking to lovers may call for different communication styles. We all approach naming our body parts in different ways. The words you choose are up to you. Find language that makes you feel good, use it, share it with partners, and have fun.

Embodiment: Managing Dysphoria and Dissociation

Dysphoria, or negative feelings, about our bodies can affect our sexuality and sexual practices. Social gender dysphoria describes the negative feelings we may experience when people mispronoun or misgender us through their behavior or language. Body dysphoria describes the negative feelings we may have when our body does not match up with our internal map of ourselves. Dysphoria of both kinds can be traumatic. It may cause us to isolate ourselves, become depressed, or feel frustrated and anxious in relationships.

> *"It's very uncomfortable when this ugly thing which is unfortunately still between my legs 'wakes up again.'"*

> *"Some things cross the 'sexual' line for me right now that I hope will not post-transition, like being shirtless. I would really really like to be comfortable taking my clothes off and not have to fight a combined dysphoria and sexual connotation."*

> *"Specific sexual acts that enforce my lack of penis and presence of breast tissue bother me. I get frustrated that I can't fuck my partner the way I want (with the body parts I want). I am trying to work through some of this in therapy."*

Many of us feel uncomfortable in sexual situations because we may feel pressured to use our genitals in ways that do not match our sense of our gender. We may even feel uncomfortable masturbating, because we do not like being reminded that we do not have the kind of genitals that we feel are appropriate for our gender.

For some people, engaging in certain types of sexual activity can trigger body dysphoria and lead us to dissociate. Dissociation is when we separate from, ignore, or minimize our feelings, experiences, and their importance. For some of us, dissociating makes us feel as if we have left our bodies. It can also be a more subtle experience. We may, for example, tell ourselves that what a partner is doing during sex *should* feel good, even when it does not.

Embodiment is the opposite of dissociation. Becoming embodied means accepting that our feelings are valid and that it is important that they be recognized, felt, and respected, including by us. If many of our feelings seem intolerable or if we believe we are wrong or bad for having them, learning to pay attention to and honor our feelings can be very difficult. In order to have safe, fulfilling sex, we have to learn to tolerate or cope with our feelings to some degree. With care, gentleness, and patience it is possible to learn to accept our feelings.

THE SEXUAL BODY

Ignacio Rivera, aka Papí Coxxx, is a 42-year-old, Two-Spirit, genderqueer, Black-Boricua Taíno. Ignacio lives in Brooklyn, New York.

As a sex educator, sex worker, and as a trans-identified person of color (POC), sex(uality) has been central in the examination of oppression and how it spills out into many aspects of our lives. How does a trans person of color experience desire within a body that has been regulated by society and the state?

Colored bodies have been probed, abducted, put on display, colonized, owned, sold, questioned, distrusted, abhorred, and feared. These bodies continue to suffer trauma from outside and within. The juxtaposing of POC and white bodies within slavery, colonialism, and current-day media representations feeds stereotypes and internalized hatred of skin color, full lips, curvy bodies, broad noses, and more. The trans body at one time was revered, seen as superior among POC tribes, communities, and societies. Forced religion and colonization refocused those ideals, and the impact has been devastating.

Positive or radical sexuality begins from within; the sexual body is what you make of it, however you define it within your body. It is the sexual place that allows you to feel comfort, have agency, ask for what you want, say no, communicate about sex, expose your desires, and much more. This is radical because it is reclaiming one's body that has been probed by society and the state. It is power, and that transcends into supporting mental health, healthy relationships, and self-esteem. It refocuses how the POC/trans body has been viewed.

Dominant culture's ideals have affected queer and trans people but have also had implications for poor people, women, and POC. The sterilization of poor women and poor women of color happens through, for example, government funding of abstinence-only-until-marriage programs that have existed for over 30 years. These programs, enforced via welfare reform, ignore harm-reduction approaches and provide monetary incentives for poor women on welfare to get and stay married. Laws and policies regulate who has sex, how one has sex, punishment for having sex, and the elimination of sex dialogue.

Even when movements and struggles have emerged to fight injustice, the color of the battles has maintained its whiteness. The feminist movement was a white woman's movement until women of color bonded together and named themselves Chicana, black, First Nations, Latina, and Women of Color (WOC) Feminists. The face of the LGB struggle was seen as white, although POC and trans people were at the forefront of the struggle. The trend has continued in the HIV/AIDS struggle, transgender liberation, and most recently, with the sexual liberation movement. The coloring of these movements has repeatedly shown the unique realities that POC and poor people face.

From welfare reform to sex education in public schools to women's health care, these issues are embedded in sex and in the body. They go beyond the simplistic definition or physical act of sex and seep into our livelihood, our relationships, our family structures, our mental health, and our pleasure. How does the POC/trans body experience sex when sex has been constructed in a heteronormative, cisgender, white framework? There has been no context in which to navigate sex, desire, fantasy, and lust as a poor person, a person of color, and a trans person outside of that structure.

It is a privilege to love, be in a relationship, and have sex in a way that the state deems normal, satisfactory, or American.

We must each journey to understand our sexual bodies. Coming out as a trans or LGB person of color in a homo/transphobic, classist, racist culture, we have been resilient. We have created language for ourselves, reclaimed our ancestry, and honored our past. We have discarded the ways dominant culture has force-fed us how to love and live. We have begun the process of questioning. We are going through the often painful process of unlearning information about our bodies, our histories, and our lives. We have and continue to do this work individually, in community, and systematically to gain our right to the sexual body and beyond.

For many of us, our response to strong emotions or intense physical sensation is to dissociate, distract ourselves, or use drugs or alcohol to limit our capacity to feel. These techniques make it harder for us to seek out positive sexual and interpersonal relationships and prevent us from setting clear boundaries around the kinds of sex we do and do not want to have. We may have a lot of unlearning to do as we work on feeling embodied and empowered during sex.

The first step we can take is to notice when we dissociate, what makes us dissociate, and in what ways we dissociate. Observe what feelings arise and when, as well as what you or your partner is doing. Paying attention to these things does not mean that we should feel bad, or guilty, for dissociating. Learning to listen to ourselves and our bodies can be a long process—take your time and tune in.

"[My girlfriend] has been one of my strongest and most amazing supporters in transitioning. She sees me as completely male, and she's never used the wrong pronouns. She's also helped me feel more comfortable sexually, in every way."

Many of us are used to having sex that is uncomfortable and frightening, and we may even be used to having our sexual boundaries and preferences violated either intentionally or through ignorance. If this is true for you, one option is to take a step back from sex until you are in a better headspace or with a partner who is safer and more understanding. Work on staying present and embodied during masturbation before you try partnered sex again. If you are unable to stay present during masturbation, it is unlikely you will be able to stay present enough to set safe boundaries during partnered sex. Be patient with yourself, learn how *you* work, and keep experimenting.

If you have a safe, supportive partner, discuss with them what triggers your dissociation. Many of our partners *want* to share mutually enjoyable sexual experiences with us. They may be unaware that there is a problem unless we talk with them. These can be hard conversations, especially if we are unfamiliar with talking about ourselves, our needs, and our feelings. But these conversations are usually rewarding, over time, and can help us discover ways to feel more at home in our bodies and our relationships.

"I am pretty comfortable with the body I've got and trust my partner totally."

Being treated as the correct gender regardless of our hormonal or surgical status is vital. This includes during sex, even if it is sex all by yourself. We will naturally be able to stay more present and self-aware during sex when the language and kind of touch used is right for us and our bodies.

Rethinking Our Sexual Bodies

As human beings, we are more alike than different. Sexual pleasure starts in the same place, no matter what our gender is or what genitals we have: the brain. Our brains interpret the signals we receive from the outside world and from our body parts, translating them into coherent messages for us. Our brains determine whether we are interested in sex and who we are attracted to. The brain regulates all of the systems that play a role in our sexual experience. It is what raises our heart rate and body temperature, and releases hormones that influence sexual feelings and response, such as testosterone, oxytocin, vasopressin, serotonin, and dopamine. The brain helps us process sensory information to decide if what we are experiencing is pleasurable, painful, ticklish, frightening, or otherwise.

Any part of the body can contribute to sexual pleasure, with the right cues and context. The entire surface of the skin contains nerves that can be thrilling or exciting when touched. Different parts of the body are typically more sensitive than others. Nipples, for example, have more nerve endings than kneecaps.

Keep in mind that our gender does not determine how sensitive parts of our body are. Many people who are either assigned female at birth or identify as female do not enjoy having their nipples touched, and many people who are either assigned male at birth or identify as male find nipple stimulation very arousing. What gives us pleasure is unique to us, not our gender.

One of the body's most nerve-dense areas is, of course, the genital region. Many of the sexual sensations in our genitals are related to the pudendal nerve, which is located at the bottom of the spinal cord. The pelvic nerve, the genitofemeral nerve, and the ilioinguinal nerve also play similar roles and exist in people with all kinds of genitals. Together, these nerves carry signals from our genitals and surrounding areas up to our brains. No matter what kind of genitals we have, or what we choose to call them, the nerves connecting them are nearly all the same—but there are many different ways to stimulate them.

All of our genitals are similar in position, structure, and origin. That includes both external and internal parts of our genitals, from the nerves and glands we have to the types of tissues they are made of. For example, we all have phallic structures (penis/clitoris) with areas on the tip and underside that are particularly sensitive to fine touch, and softer, looser skin (labial/scrotal tissue) that is more sensitive to pressure. The shape, size, and sensitivity of these parts vary widely among individuals, both cis and trans.

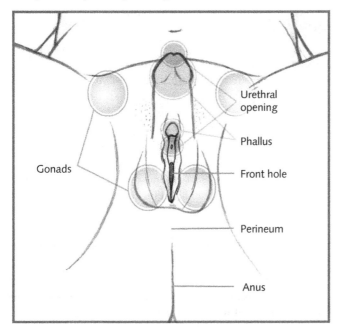

Possibilities for genital anatomy (Ron Burton).

Just because our genitals look a certain way does not mean we can only experience sexual pleasure in ways expected by mainstream society. There is no one way—and definitely no one *right* way—to use our genitals for sex. Many of us have found lots of ways to engage in sexual activities that we feel are appropriate to our affirmed gender.

EFFECTS OF TRANSITION ON SEXUALITY

Hormone therapy can cause many subtle changes in our bodies and minds, such as alterations in the scent of our armpits and genitals or how much we sweat. Many of us will experience changes in our sexual feelings with transition. For some of us, the kinds of stimulation we once used to prefer may no longer work for us, and new types of stimulation may start to be effective instead. We may find that we are turned on by different things as well—sometimes many more things, and in some cases, far fewer.

> *"My libido has really disappeared since starting on hormones, which I really don't miss much."*

A body that feels like it is our own is much more capable of receiving pleasure. Sometimes surgery or hormones can mean relearning our bodies, however, as we may no longer respond in the way we did before. Be patient, learn how you work, and keep experimenting. Whatever feels good is right for you. Try not to worry if you do not respond or feel the way that you may have heard others do.

The human experience of sexual arousal is a topic of ongoing discussion and research. In the most widely used model, proposed by William Masters and Virginia Johnson (1966), there are four stages of sexual response: excitement, plateau, orgasm, and resolution. In the excitement phase, Masters and Johnson noted that our heart rate, breathing, and blood pressure increase. Our genitals receive increased blood flow, which can make our bits (of all shapes and sizes) swell or become erect. During the plateau phase, our heart rate increases further, and our muscles tighten. Next, as we orgasm, we experience rhythmic muscle contractions, a sense of euphoria, and ejaculation may occur (in people of any sex or gender). After orgasm, we enter the resolution phase, where our blood pressure drops and our muscles relax.

This model, while descriptive of many people's experience, is not the only way that human sexual response has been described. Many researchers are beginning to suggest alternative ways of thinking about sexual desire and response. One area of research focuses on the role that social and cultural factors—such as intimacy, power relationships, and past experiences—play in determining sexual behavior and response. For example, research has shown that some people do not experience spontaneous desire at the beginning of sexual encounters. Instead, we may engage in sexual encounters for a variety of other reasons, such as wanting to share intimacy with a partner, and physical arousal may precede—or exist without—emotional or mental feelings of sexual desire.

Research also suggests that there are differences in the way that cisgender men and cisgender women experience sexual response. For example, cis men may become aroused more easily by visual stimulation and cis women by touch. Social and biological factors are both thought to play a role, and for those of us who pursue a physical transition, we may experience significant changes in our sex lives as a result of our transition process.

Possible Effects of Estrogen/Testosterone Blockers on Sexuality

Taking estrogen (with or without testosterone blockers) may stimulate breast and nipple growth and increase nipple sensitivity. During the growth process, our breast tissue may be hard to the touch and our breasts may even be painfully sensitive. Some people enjoy that sensitivity, while others will want to limit or restrict stimulation.

> *"I found that my breasts and nipples became really super sensitive once I was on hormones. Having my nipples sucked became one of my favorite things."*

For those of us who take estrogen or antiandrogens, our external genitals can shrink somewhat, and we may produce less semen or none at all. Erections may become less frequent or not happen anymore. These changes do not mean that we cannot enjoy many kinds of touch—and they definitely do not mean that we cannot achieve orgasm. Erections,

Vancouver (Courtney Trouble).

orgasm, and ejaculation are three separate events—they need not happen together, and many of us achieve orgasm without ever becoming erect.

After starting estrogen or testosterone blockers, some of us find that our orgasms feel different or that we require different kinds of pressure and stimulation. It is also possible that our refractory period, the time after orgasm when we cannot yet orgasm again, can decrease, resulting in the ability to have multiple orgasms.

> "Ejaculation and spontaneous erections are things of the past, and the orgasms themselves much more intense and lengthy."

Many trans people who were assigned male at birth experience a decreased sex drive from estrogen/antiandrogen hormone therapy. Individual experience varies and many factors are involved. Taking estrogen can certainly decrease sex drive in some people. However, some of us discover over time that what we first interpreted as a lower sex drive was a change in what it feels like to be aroused. How we experience desire may simply be different. For others, having the right hormones in our bodies and having a body that reflects our sense of self allows us to be more present and connected to ourselves and thus we experience increased sexual desire.

> "My libido decreased after I started estrogen. However, this did not affect my desire for intimacy."

> "My libido has changed, yes. Contrary to the popular wisdom, my sex drive is much more robust now than before estrogen."

Spironolactone, a common testosterone blocker, has libido-suppressing and erection-suppressing effects in addition to lowering testosterone.

> "My libido dropped precipitously once I started androgen blockers."

In some cases, after an orchiectomy or vaginoplasty, when we stop testosterone blockers, our sex drive improves again, even though our testosterone levels are still low. For some of us unhappy with our sex drives, taking a little bit of testosterone or progesterone can help boost our libido. Cisgender women have some testosterone in their bodies, too. Talk to a medical provider to learn more. Although there are some providers who do not understand that those of us who identify as female may wish to preserve our libido or erections, there are many who do.

Testosterone is often thought of as determining libido. Many of us who begin testosterone notice that we become sexually aroused more easily, and those of us who take testosterone blockers often notice a decrease in libido. Testosterone can certainly affect our sexuality. However, there are many other factors. Some people with high testosterone levels have low libido and some people with low testosterone levels have high libido. Trans women taking testosterone blockers, for instance, sometimes notice an increase in sexual arousal because they feel more content in their bodies and can now allow themselves to feel attractive and aroused. Sexuality is complicated, and it never comes down to just one thing.

Possible Effects of Testosterone on Sexuality

For many people, starting testosterone therapy can have quite dramatic effects. Growth of genital erectile tissue is stimulated by testosterone. This means that many people assigned female at birth who take testosterone experience major shifts in the size and shape of our external genitals. The bundle of tissue commonly referred to as the clitoris, which many trans men call our dick, cock, or dicklet, may double, triple, or quadruple in size from testosterone. As a result of the change in size, erections may become clearly visible for the first time. Some people notice that the external genitals become darker in color and are much more rigid when aroused.

With testosterone treatment, the mucus membranes on the inside of the front hole can thin and become more delicate. They may also produce much less lubrication than before. As a result, penetration of the front hole may cause bleeding and may feel a little rougher or more raw. This effect may be mitigated in some people by using lube or engaging in regular penetration of the front hole.

YOU AND ME

Anonymous, 22

You and I were always 10 minutes behind schedule. Sneaking you through the side-porch door so your parents could pretend not to hear. We listened to a lot of Bikini Kill, and used your electric flosser to get off.

The first time you slept over was after a Leftover Crack show, where you bravely held my hand in front of the boy who had raped me. You didn't know who he was at the time, but it made me pretty damn sure I was going to get naked with you later.

You were really sweet and acted like you knew exactly what you were doing. Afterwards I made you sleep on the couch, so my parents wouldn't think we were fucking, or maybe so they understood that we were. It's still unclear.

I texted the gayest friend I had at the time to tell them I had finally slept with a bulldagger. In the morning, I woke you up with coffee and a bowl of Cinnamon Toast Crunch.

The first time I touched you, I was shaking so hard I thought I was actually going to hurt you. Plus we had promised to be home by 6 p.m., and we were already 10 minutes behind schedule. Remember that time we spent all summer fucking in the back of my car? We were both so drenched in sweat afterwards we would take our shirts off before driving you home and literally wring the wetness out of our collars.

You asked me to tie you up. All I had with me was electrical tape and a lighter. We made do.

I knew you were trans the first time I sucked you off. Along with my spit, I must have swallowed something bitter and cruel, and as your body shook from cumming and crying I knew that all I had to do was make space for you.

You don't smell the same way you did when we were 18. The testosterone I watch you inject when you visit makes your sweat smell sweet and sickly, and it reminds me of cold medicine or some sort of poison. I hate it.

Tracing my tongue along your waistband feels like licking wounds. You're the sweetest boy south of the Mason Dixon line.

Once I dislocated your thumb while you had half your fist inside of me.

I told you exactly what you were getting yourself into. I probably made some joke about red wings, and then proceeded to cover my face in your cum and smear blood hearts on your shoulders. Legs slipping and hips grinding, I knew you were a force to be reckoned with.

We totally freaked out your neighbor who saw us dancing covered in each other's blood to the dorm showers.

I sure liked you a whole lot.

Two years later you would tell me you were not a feminist, I'd build your bed frame using only my Leatherman, and you would get into my bed and shatter me into a million pieces.

The way we fucked was desperate. It was sweet. It was self-discovery and shame lapped up and sucked off. It was 15-year-olds at a slumber party. It was superhero dance-athons. I never knew what to make of you. It was standing ovations in the hallways of dorms, it was Mario Kart high scores with me between your thighs, it was racing you home and the first one to the door got to kiss the other one any way they wanted to.

You would call me Harvey when I strapped on and then ask me when I was getting top surgery. And when Kevin told me I should just go by Abby because maybe then people would stop asking me if I were a boy or a girl, you didn't stick up for me.

Actually, you just slept with him.

Bright-eyed blue sparkle glitter bounce. Bike rides, beets, and BDSM. Knives, Saran wrap, coming home from practice to you crafting naked in a sunbeam. You sure do make me oatmeal a lot, Dreamgirl.

You're glaring at me from the seat next to mine. I know you are upset with me. I know you are pissed I licked her fluids and refused yours. I know you know that it has to do with you sleeping with men. I know you feel that I am ashamed of you.

Some days you come home to me covered in Cheerios and tempera paint. Some days you fall asleep on my lap, with my grasp wrapped around your pretty throat. Your half of the farm share is on my porch, and I love you.

Sparkle boy, glitter faggot, butch hunter. Tough take no shit crybaby cupcake. Perfect rough and tumble bruise prince.

Brown eyes that pierce my stone and a smart mouth to match. Kissing you tastes like iron, rage, survival, and every sweet thing. I spent my last semester at Smith licking your cum out from under my fingernails, and putting stars on your chore chart.

You hit me like the best brick wall I never saw coming.

When they call us "ladies" I can see the invisibility chill you down to your marrow. February feels like forever, and I want to suck the cold out. Transparent and vulnerable, I contract around your fingers and your voice is the only thing connecting me to my body. "I'm here. You're safe. I love you."

Many of us who begin testosterone therapy also find that it increases our sex drive. For some, this may mean a dramatic increase—we suddenly fantasize about everyone and everything we see, all the time, uncontrollably, and want sex almost nonstop—while for others, we might only want sex a little more often than before.

"Testosterone makes you want to f*ck every attractive thing out there."

"My libido has most definitely changed. I have higher sexual cravings than ever before."

The way in which sexual arousal occurs may also change with testosterone. Some people report needing visual stimuli to become aroused while on testosterone, meaning that they may grow more interested in pornography than before. Some report being able to become physically aroused without emotional engagement in the situation, where before emotional and physical arousal were inextricably linked. Some find casual sex easier to engage in as a result, because sex no longer feels as automatically emotional. These are, however, completely individual changes, and some people find themselves more emotional about sex than before or more emotional in general. Do not worry about how you are supposed to feel or how others feel. Everyone is different.

December (Courtney Trouble).

"I am easily aroused. I am more visually stimulated. I have always been pan-sexual, but I find men even more attractive now."

"I was unable to maintain my relationship, especially after testosterone. Testosterone made me very unemotional compared to what I used to be. My partner noticed that."

For some, orgasm becomes easier to achieve while taking testosterone, while others lose the ability to have multiple orgasms or find that orgasms are less intense. Sometimes the way in which people have multiple orgasms changes as a result of taking testosterone—where before some people were able to have multiple huge orgasms or have continuous orgasms for long periods of time, they may start to instead have a pattern of several small orgasms leading up to one larger one.

For some people assigned female at birth who start testosterone, the stimulation we need in order to achieve climax may also change. We may begin to prefer more external than internal stimulation, or to prefer anal sex to front-hole sex, or vice versa.

Effects of Surgery on Sexual Response

Those of us who have surgeries may notice that our bodies now respond in different ways. For those of us who have top surgeries, the sensitivity we retain in our chests can differ significantly depending on the type of surgery. For those of us who have bottom surgeries, we may have to relearn ways of stimulating ourselves or achieving orgasm. It may have been easy for us to become aroused or achieve orgasm before, or it may have been a long process of discovering what felt good and worked for us. It can be frustrating to feel like we are starting all over again.

For those of us who have had a phalloplasty (creation of a larger phallus), there are several different surgical techniques, some of which allow our phallus to become erect and others that do not. If you have had a vaginoplasty, keep in mind that your vagina might not be able to produce its own lubrication—different surgical techniques have different results, and some of us find that we produce some lubrication. Many of us find that store-bought lubrication is helpful or necessary for penetration. We may also have to maintain regular use of a dilator—a tool used to help create more flexibility in the muscles and tissues inside the vagina. This can allow for easier, more comfortable penetration.

It is normal for it to take some time after surgery to regain sexual function. After surgery, our nerves may be distributed slightly differently, so our bodies may respond somewhat differently. One of the best ways to start exploring our new bodies is by ourselves, where we can experiment in a safe and comfortable environment. For those of us with supportive partners, we may want to try new positions or ask them to stimulate us in new ways.

If it is taking longer than expected to recover sensation, speak to a medical provider. There are many different kinds of surgery, and techniques differ by surgeon. We may want to speak with our individual surgeon about the technique used and ask for any advice based on how our anatomical parts are now arranged.

Shifting Preferences

Most people's sexual preferences shift a little over time. Changes in sexual preference are especially common as a result of transition. Just because we used to have sex a certain way does not mean we should be expected to do it again now; and even if we once declared we would never do something, it is OK to change our minds. When we transition, the context in which we date and have sex naturally shifts, and the ways we approach dating and having sex may change. Having our gender recognized may mean that people—especially people we are dating or having sex with—respond and interact with us differently than before. What was uncomfortable before transition might become comfortable afterwards—or vice versa.

Some of us find that after we transition we are attracted to people of a gender we were not interested in before. For example, trans men who had been exclusively attracted to women before transition may be attracted exclusively to men, or to both men and women, after transition.

> "I was pretty sure that I was still going to prefer women post transition, but I'm now not so sure. I am starting to wonder what it would be like to be with guys post transition and I have started to notice them more. It's actually pretty confusing for me right now."

> "A few years after starting transitioning and testosterone, my sexual orientation shifted from women only, to both men and women, but I am now primarily attracted to men."

> "Since I started T, I have steadily become more interested in women. Pre-T, I was not interested in them at all. Now I consider myself bisexual."

Shifting preferences could be related to hormones, but it could also be about the way we see ourselves and what kinds of relationships we feel socially comfortable in. Being interpreted as a woman in a lesbian relationship is different than being interpreted as a man in a straight relationship. Being interpreted as a woman in a straight relationship is different than being interpreted as a man in a gay relationship. Similarly, being viewed as a trans person in a relationship can be different than being viewed as a cis person of any gender in a relationship.

The kinds of sex we are comfortable having and the people we want to have sex with may shift as the way we are perceived by other people shifts. For some people, this may look like a shift in sexual orientation. This can be challenging for many of us, particularly for those who have been deeply involved in gay, lesbian, or queer communities, where our social relationships may have been linked to our sexuality.

> "My sexual orientation does seem to have changed during my life. I was more attracted to other women in my teens than I am now."

Some of us know ourselves to be fundamentally oriented in certain ways. Prior to transition we may be attracted to women, and we may retain our attraction to women after transition. Those of us who identified strongly as straight before transition may still identify as straight afterward, despite the fact that the gender of the people we want to have sex with is different.

For many people, including cisgender people, sexual orientation can be fluid in the moment or over time. It is completely normal and healthy to follow our attractions, wherever they may lead us.

MASTURBATION AND SELF-EXPLORATION

Many of us find that masturbation is one of the most fulfilling ways for us to be sexual. We are often the people who know our bodies best. We can also fantasize about any number of things while masturbating, allowing ourselves to explore our desires in many different ways. Masturbation is also one of the best ways to get to know our bodies and learn how our responses may have changed during transition. It is a chance to explore, play, and learn what works for us.

Fantasy

For many of us, fantasy and imagination started off our transition, and they can be the way we move into having good sex during and after transition as well. Being trans requires that we rethink and question what is expected of us, and we can do this during sex as well as in our daily lives. Fantasy gives us the power to reimagine, reshape, and reclaim our bodies. When we fantasize, we can look and behave however we want. Our fantasies are for us and us alone, and they are thus allowed to be whatever we want or need them to be.

No matter what gender we are, we may have fantasies about ourselves as another gender, and we may have fantasies about sex with people of all different genders. There is no reason to feel ashamed about any sexual fantasy we have. Our sexual fantasies do not determine the validity of our gender identity. Historically, some mental health professionals used our fantasies to diagnose some of us designated as male at birth with "autogynephilia" (meaning sexual arousal at the thought of oneself as a woman). This diagnosis was often used to deny the validity of our gender identity and prohibit us from accessing medical transition. This is no longer considered an acceptable diagnosis. Our sexual fantasies do not dictate the validity of our gender identities. We do not have to feel ashamed of our desires, and it is wrong for others to tell us what our desires should look like.

Queer porn TV (Courtney Trouble).

"I could and can and do fantasize about myself as entirely female and cannot picture myself sexually in any other way."

"In recent times, I've started fantasizing about having a big, fleshy dick, or a dildo and performing as the soft, sensual, but strong top that lives in the back of my consciousness."

If we want, our fantasies can also be incorporated into our partnered sex life. Sharing them with a partner during or before sex can be a great way to get us both going. Role playing our fantasies as part of sex can help us stay in our bodies if dysphoria makes that difficult. Even if we do not want to act out our fantasies with a partner, it can be nice just to share what we like with someone else.

Touching Ourselves

Masturbation can be an extremely useful way to learn more about ourselves and the way our bodies respond. It is a good opportunity to explore by ourselves without fearing what anyone might think and without concern for anyone's needs but our own.

Even though most of us masturbate in private, we often wonder whether the way we masturbate is "normal." We all masturbate in many different ways, so there is no normal way to do it. We might actually be wondering not whether the way we masturbate is normal, but whether it is OK. When it comes to masturbation, the answer is almost universally "yes." It is OK to masturbate frequently, infrequently, or not at all. It is OK to use toys or to stimulate any part of our bodies that feels good. So long as what we are doing is not dangerous to ourselves or others, what we are doing is OK.

"I masturbate a lot with my underwear on. I'm not sure if that has anything to do with anything."

"My masturbation is more in line with the techniques of females and I now use a vibrator just as other women do. Touching my breasts, nipples, and other areas of my body is more sensual and comforting."

"Masturbating has become a lot more awkward. I used to do it a lot, but now that I'm out, I don't even want to touch myself. It feels weird and I don't know why. Maybe its subconscious."

Trans people may face many cissexist expectations around masturbation. For example, trans men may internalize messages that enjoying penetration in a front hole means that we are not "real men." Trans women may worry that stroking our bits is a "male" thing to do. Some of us fear that if we fantasize or masturbate in the "wrong" ways we are not really trans. This is completely incorrect. We can masturbate in any way we like, and this does not affect our gender identity.

Partnered Masturbation

Some people find masturbating with a partner to be very intimate. It can be a great way to show a partner what kinds of things we like and how they work for us, especially when first getting to know someone sexually. By taking turns and really paying attention to what our partner is doing, we can learn a lot. We may also want to let our partner masturbate us, perhaps while we masturbate them. For some people, it may be difficult to achieve orgasm, especially through someone else's touch. Masturbating together can be a way to share an orgasm with a partner if it would be difficult or impossible otherwise.

ASEXUALITY AND ABSTINENCE

Some of us identify as asexual, meaning we do not want to engage in sexual activity. Those of us who are asexual often desire intimate relationships with others, but we do not see sexual activity as a desirable component of our relationship. Many of us have long, fulfilling relationships with other asexual partners; have happy, healthy open relationships with long-term partners who desire sexual activity with other partners; or find a variety of other relationship styles that work for us. Asexuality is as valid a form of sexual expression as all others.

ON BEING ASEXUAL AND TRANSGENDER: NOTES ON IDENTITY, VISIBILITY, AND EMPOWERMENT

Joelle Ruby Ryan is a lecturer in women's studies at the University of New Hampshire, the founder of TransGender New Hampshire (TG-NH), as well as a writer, speaker, and long-term social justice activist.

I have "come out" in terms of my gender and sexual identity at least three times so far in my life. My first coming out was as a transgender woman in my late teens. This was followed by coming out as queer/lesbian and immersing myself in women's studies and feminist activism shortly thereafter. The third coming out is the most recent: I have come out as an asexual person.

From my early to mid-thirties, I was in a long-term relationship. Over time in the relationship, I became less and less interested in sex with my partner. At first I thought this was just because we had very different libidos. But then I started researching asexuality on the Internet and came across a group called the Asexual Visibility and Education Network (AVEN). I started to think about my own life, sexual journey, and lack of sexual attraction as well as lack of interest in sex and having sex. I realized my lack of desire to "do it" was not about a low libido but about an asexual identity.

When my relationship broke up, I started to peek my head out of the asexual closet and tell people about my newfound, asexy sense of self. Not all reaction was positive. Some in the queer community seemed hesitant to add another letter to the LGBTQ+ rainbow acronym. Others seemed skeptical about the very existence of asexuality or questioned whether I was "really" asexual or just going through a phase. Some sex-positive queers seemed threatened by asexuality because of their hard-fought battles to liberate queer sex from the closet of shame and negativity. Despite this resistance, coming out as asexual has been a liberating and exciting process in my life journey. I identify as a lesbo-romantic asexual, and thus hope to find a woman-identified partner that will accept my asexuality. (Some asexuals are aromantic but many of us hope to find romantic partners to share our lives with.)

I now give asexual workshops, screen the film *(A)sexual* with a postfilm discussion, and try to have conversations with my friends and colleagues about asexual identity and acephobia. There is great need for education and visibility, but there is also tremendous interest and curiosity about the subject. I am proud to be asexual and feel more empowered every day. I doubt that this will be my last coming out as I continue to explore my own complex personhood into the future. I welcome the next "coming out" and wherever it takes me on my journey.

Because our gender identity is separate from our sexuality, we may still want to make changes to our genitals through hormones or surgery, even if we do not want to use our bodies to have sex. As with many of the other ways that we care for and maintain our personal expression and appearance, we make changes to our bodies that feel right for us, not because of how others see us.

Asexuality is not the same as abstinence. Those of us who are abstinent refrain from having sex, even though we experience sexual desire and feelings. As trans people, many of us choose abstinence for a period of time before or after transition, for numerous reasons. Sometimes prior to transition we do not feel completely ourselves, and it is not pleasurable for us when others see or touch our bodies. Some of us engaged in sex before transition, but become less interested afterward. This could be due to the effects of hormones or surgery, or it could have to do with the way we see our bodies.

"I had relationships after SRS but without sex. Each was for a period of 8 years. People can't believe I had relationships without sex, I just laugh."

"Sex is uncomfortable now, physically and mentally, and so I avoid it."

We do not need to have sex in order to feel positive about sexuality. There are many behaviors that other people may or may not consider to be sex, such as making out, naked cuddling, or sensual touching. We can engage in activities like these without having to do anything else. These forms of physical intimacy can constitute our entire sex life, and that is a valid way to be sexual.

Even if we do not describe ourselves as asexual or abstinent, we may choose not to have sex in the way most people define it. Jumping straight to "sex," however we describe it, may not be what we want or need right now.

> *"I'm actually more comfortable with and interested in nongenital play that does not require nudity and may or may not culminate in orgasm."*

If we are not ready, we are not ready, and that is always OK. If it feels most natural to stick to kissing, hugging, cuddling, groping, or other forms of physical intimacy, no one has the right to make us do things that make us feel uncomfortable—or to make us feel guilty for not doing them.

SEXUAL PARTNERS

Although some of us prefer to be sexual when we are alone, many of us seek out partners with whom to share sexual experiences. For some of us, beginning a sexual relationship—whether for the first time, or every time—can be intimidating. Our bodies may not match our ideas of ourselves, and we may worry that other people will not understand us in the same way we understand ourselves or that they will desire us to use our bodies in ways that make us uncomfortable.

However, many of us find that we have wonderful, supportive partners who share exciting, fulfilling sexual experiences with us. Good partners can help us feel more comfortable in our bodies, help us explore new ways to enjoy sexual experiences, and by using the names, pronouns, and language that we prefer, may make our sexual experience a powerfully affirming part of our lives.

> *"I started a relationship right in the middle of my process of identification. He's being really supportive and helpful at this point, and he is the only person who treats me fully like a male."*

Privacy and Disclosure

Disclosure is one of the major issues facing trans people when we date or look for sex partners. When to disclose, how to disclose, and how much to disclose are very important decisions. These choices are completely individual, and all of us assess our comfort and risk level anytime we disclose.

Some trans people view delayed disclosure as very dangerous, and preempt this by disclosing immediately upon meeting someone new. Some of us want to be desired as a trans person and always disclose to potential partners to ensure this is the case. Others of us may choose to delay disclosure until trust is established because of concerns about the information getting out. Some of us may use delayed disclosure to ensure we are not fetishized or singled out for our trans status. Some trans people never disclose at all. When and if we disclose is up to us.

> *"I prefer to come out before I start a relationship, because I think it is better. My partner won't feel cheated. I found that nowadays, there are some people who love other people just the way they are. So, it's getting better, I think."*

> *"I do let everyone know that I am transgender up front, so if they have an issue with me, then they can leave right then."*

> *"I figured it was easiest to just be upfront and write 'I'm a tranny' on my online dating profile. Saves hassle later on. After all, I wouldn't want to date someone who doesn't want to date someone like me, would I? It worked, too. I met a lovely trans friendly dyke online and we've been together for a year."*

For those of us who have begun to date someone who does not yet know that we are trans, we can take different approaches to telling (or not telling) them. Deciding how and when to disclose our trans status to a partner is an individual decision. It is usually safer and more effective to have this conversation when neither person has been drinking or using drugs.

Even if a partner is supportive of trans identities and attracted to us, getting news that our body is different than they expected, or finding this out during a sexual encounter, can be a surprising and confusing experience. People have different reactions to finding out about our trans status in the middle of a sexual encounter. Some partners may have experience with other trans partners or feel otherwise unconcerned by potential differences in our anatomy or gender identity and be comfortable continuing. Others may want to slow things down and take time to process their feelings. In some cases, a partner who wants to be supportive may feel pressured to continue having sex so as not to hurt us or send a message that we are not attractive, even if they would rather take some time to think through things. In some cases, people who find out about our trans status in the middle of a sexual encounter become very angry that we did not tell them, and our physical safety may be at risk.

Some of us have bodies that are not recognizable to most people as trans bodies. For example, we may have had a breast augmentation and vaginoplasty, and feel we are at low risk of a partner finding out that we are trans without us telling them. When we choose to discuss our status with a partner is up to us—and many of us feel that we have no obligation to tell anyone about our history as long as it is safe to keep it from them. Especially if we have a series of short-term relationships or one-time sexual encounters, it can sometimes be more dangerous to disclose than to keep our trans status private.

If we are in a longer term relationship, however, there may come a point where we feel it is important to open up about our trans status. Disclosing our status to a long-term partner may be important to us as a way of demonstrating and building trust, or it may be relevant information to a partner who desires to have children in a traditional manner. Waiting to tell a long-term partner about our transition history can pose challenges, and we should prepare for some difficult conversations.

BOUNDARIES AND CONSENT

Many of us believe that if we talk to our partners about what we want before, during, or after sex, it means we are unsexy or bad lovers. Many people believe that we should be able to read body language so well that we never have to ask any questions. This is completely false. The more we are able to communicate with our partners before, during, and after sex, the better lovers we are able to be. Even if we are whizzes at reading body language, some needs are too subtle to be interpreted merely from squirming or moaning. Many people think that being open about our desires is embarrassing, so in a lot of cases there is no outward sign of what someone's sexual needs are. This is why we need communication.

> "I don't take off my clothes. Pretty much ever. No one touches me. No one is permitted to touch me. I perform any number of acts upon my boyfriends, all of which we all enjoy, but they know not to touch anything but my face and hands."

> "I love it when my breasts are petted."

> "I am comfortable with any sex act as long as my partner is."

Enthusiastic Consent

Sexual consent is often framed in a negative way. Our concepts of consent are frequently around one person attempting to do something (typically a cisgender man) and another person saying no (typically a cisgender woman). When both parties agree to a sexual act, they are not usually portrayed as talking about it. Silence is made to look sexy. Enthusiastic consent is the idea that taking charge of our own sexuality is hot. There are many ways to give and receive enthusiastic consent.

In porn and in mainstream movies, panting, gasping, or screaming during sex is portrayed as how to tell that we are giving consent. But we can also pant and gasp in discomfort, or be in a location where loud noise would get us in trouble. If we want to be clear about our enjoyment (or to know that our partner is experiencing pleasure), try actually saying "yes." Whether you whisper it, say it gently, or scream it, "yes" communicates consent well. Other explicit ways of saying that we are enjoying what is happening include "like that," "so good," "just right," and "I love this." We do not have to make speeches in praise of our partners' actions, but no matter what we are doing sexually, positive feedback tends to be appreciated.

FIRST KISS REVISITED

Giselle Renarde

I still smile when I think about my first kiss with Danielle. It was one in the morning. We were sitting on my balcony, teacups in hand, eating chocolate-covered digestive biscuits. She wore a green skirt, wedge heels, and no stockings—it was summertime, and the air was lovely and warm.

When I looked up into her face, I fell in love all over again. We hadn't been together long, but it was the first time I'd seen her presenting female. That night, I realized *why* I'd fallen in love with her. It hadn't made sense before, because Danielle presented male when we first met. Being primarily attracted to women, I didn't understand why I was so gaga for "him." But when I saw Danielle wearing clothes that made her comfortable and shimmering with a pronounced sense of joy, I knew I'd fallen for the woman behind that male facade.

I kissed her lips. Not a big, messy smooch, but more than just a peck. It was the sort of kiss where you press your lips against the other person's lips and then you breathe together for a moment, and then release. You gaze into each other's eyes, and you want to cry because you're so overwhelmed.

The next day, when we talked on the phone, Danielle said, "I felt uncomfortable."

It was the most emotional kiss I'd ever experienced, and it made her *uncomfortable*?

"I wasn't sure why you did it," she said, and explained that she had trouble seeing her female self as a sexual being. She hated that the word "transsexual" contained the word "sexual," because it made her feel like people would view her as some kind of deviant. She wondered if I fetishized her, or if I viewed her as a "guy in a dress" and I got off on that sort of thing.

She said it was okay that I kissed her, that maybe one day she'd let me kiss her again, but I needed to give her time. She wasn't sure what she wanted; it was all so confusing. We would never have sex—that was for certain. There were so many things we'd never do.

And now, after five years of building trust and understanding, Danielle and I have done *everything*. We took our time, and she came to realize that I loved her and desired her for who she was: my sweet, nerdy, gorgeous girlfriend.

Before Sex: Negotiation

Negotiation is a process of letting our partners know beforehand what our boundaries are and what kind of sex we would like to have. Negotiation can, for some people, be a lengthy process involving lots of discussion. For others it may be as simple as "Do you want me to touch you here?" and getting a response like "Yeah!" Getting clear verbal consent before we start can help everyone feel safer.

> *"For my body there are certain areas that need to be touched in certain ways— for instance, I love being sucked off but not eaten out, I cannot be penetrated in the front, only in the back, and my chest cannot be played with. These guidelines allow me to feel more comfortable in my body during sex."*

Given all the changes many of us experience during transition, we may need to experiment to know what we enjoy, which often results in trying sex we do not enjoy. There is nothing wrong with trying something and not liking it, or even retrying something we might not have liked the first time. However, no one has the right to do anything to us that we do not want to happen. We are allowed to say things like "I'd like to keep it above the waist for now," "I'm not in the mood this week," "I don't feel safe in this place," "Sucking my earlobes is what gets me hot, not genital petting," or "I need a condom to do that."

When a sexual partner is able and willing to hear our requests, boundaries, and sexual input, that is a very good sign. It is a serious warning sign if a partner takes boundaries or requests personally, gets angry at us for having sexual boundaries or needs, or tries to pressure us to do something we have already refused. Even if we are in love with the person doing this, attempts at sexual pressure, coercion, or shaming are a problem to take very seriously.

Sometimes it is not a matter of a partner crossing our boundaries, but of struggling to mesh seemingly incompatible desires. What if one person needs penetrative sex to get off, and the other does not feel comfortable having genital sex at all? If we are creative and motivated, we can usually find solutions that will work for everyone. If we are not willing or able to use our bits for penetration, we may use our hands or a dildo to satisfy our partner. If using a dildo with a harness triggers dysphoria, try a thigh harness or hold a dildo in your hands. If you do not want to receive oral sex, but your partner wants to perform it, negotiate other ways to satisfy your partner's interest; for instance, is there another part of your body that you like to have licked or sucked?

During Sex: Updates

Many people benefit from continued communication throughout their sexual encounters. Like negotiation, this can be anywhere from very brief to very involved. Everyone has unforeseen issues arise during sex sometimes, whether it is a full bladder or a flashback. Getting and giving updates during sex, even when everything is going great, can be very helpful. For some of us, dysphoria can make us unwilling or unable to speak. In such a situation, a partner who is used to getting updates during sex is likely to notice that something is wrong, long before a partner who is used to nonverbal sex.

Many of us find that using "safe words" can make it easier to communicate when something is wrong. Instead of saying "no" or "stop" to our partner, having a shared word that means "something is wrong" can make it easier to put on the brakes without worrying about hurting our partner's feelings. What words you use are up to you—just be sure that they are clear and easy to remember, so that you and your partner both know when they are being used. Some of us find it helpful to use "traffic signal" language (green, yellow, red) to check in with our partners during sex. Green may mean, "That's good!" while yellow may mean, "Slow down" or "Let's do something different," and red means, "Stop."

After Sex: Checking In

Sex can touch us deeply or bring up a lot of baggage. Whether it is trauma-related triggers, dysphoria, or new positive feelings about the person we had sex with, talking to each other after sex can be a good idea. Most of us are aware that consent is important and must be established before sex begins, but there is also a lot of important processing that happens after the sex is over. Many of us are too charged full of hormones to know what we are feeling right after sex, though, so talking about it a day or two later may give us a more complete picture and lead to better sex in the future.

It can be especially important for those of us with any history of abuse or feeling bad after sexual encounters to check in with ourselves after sex. What feels good in the moment may leave us miserable or panicked for days afterward. If we notice that after sex we are not sleeping well, having nightmares, losing our appetite, experiencing unexplained body pain, getting unusually intense depression or anxiety, or feeling the urge to isolate or harm ourselves, we should reach out to others. Having an established system of checking in after sex can really help.

SAFER SEX

Safer sex is sex that minimizes risks. There are a number of ways that we can reduce our risks. We each have to decide how much risk we are willing to take and that may be different depending on the partner and the situation. Being aware of health issues that come up around sex and making informed decisions to minimize our risk is an important part of taking care of ourselves and our partners. There are a number of different sexually transmitted infections (STIs) out there, many of which are treatable if identified. With some basic information we can significantly reduce our risk.

The risks associated with sex can sometimes seem far off and improbable. This is especially true for those of us who are living with a significant amount of day-to-day risk, such as the discrimination, harassment, and violence. When validation and support seem scarce, it can be difficult to insist on safer sex when it might mean rejection from a sexual partner. Support does not need to be scarce. Many of us have found partners, allies, and community organizations that affirm our needs and our identities.

Sexually Transmitted Infections

Infections spread when bodily fluids such as blood or semen pass from one person to another, through mucous membranes or cuts. Barriers such as condoms and gloves can be used to block these fluids. Mucus membranes include the eyes, nasal passages, mouth, throat, urethra, anus, and genital orifices. One of the best safer sex strategies is to engage in sexual activity that reduces or eliminates the exchange of bodily fluids. This might involve mutual masturbation, use of toys, engaging in nongenital sex, or using barrier methods such as condoms.

Some people choose to engage only in oral sex rather than penetrative sex because it is considered a lower risk activity. However, while the risk of HIV transmission is far lower, it is still possible to transmit HIV this way, and other STIs such as herpes, gonorrhea, chlamydia, and syphilis can be transmitted orally. Assess your own comfort and risk levels to make decisions about your sexual behavior. See Chapter 11 for more information on sexual health.

Barrier Methods

A barrier is something that we put in between one person's body and another person's body. Barriers come in many varieties: traditional condoms, receptive-partner condoms (aka "the female condom"), gloves, and dental dams (latex squares used for oral sex). They are most commonly made out of latex, but nonlatex options are available for people with latex allergies.

Making barriers work for us can sometimes be tricky. We are often told that condoms and dental dams are for cis people of particular genders, so it can feel invalidating or degendering to use them. More importantly, they often do not work with our bodies and the things we want to do. Condoms require our genitals to be able to get and stay hard at a certain size, for example.

Get creative, and remember the bottom line is to prevent exchanging bodily fluids. For example, a glove can be altered and used in a variety of different ways. By removing the fingers and cutting open the exterior side of the glove, you can create a wide latex sheet with a pouch (formerly the thumb) that can be placed over smaller bits. This may be used by those of us whose genitals have been enlarged by testosterone who wish to receive oral sex. Those of us with larger genitals can stretch the thumb open and put it over our bits, which might be especially useful if getting erect is difficult or condoms are too loose, or for those of us who want to experience our genitals being reshaped in a new way. Another technique for altering a glove can create a dental dam with finger holds. Dental dams and

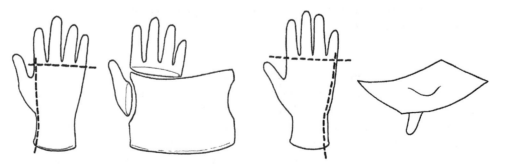

Two ways to cut a glove to use as protection for smaller bits (Dean Scarborough).

receptive partner condoms can also be used creatively. For those of us with long or rough fingernails, we can put cotton balls, tissue, or toilet paper in the fingers of a glove for added protection from scraping.

There is no one way to have safe sex that works for everyone. What is important is finding ways to reduce the risk to a level that feels reasonable to us. For some people that might mean using barriers for every single sex act. For others that does not fit with our desires or situation, and we have to decide what risks we are willing to take in different situations.

Fluid bonding

Some of us may also form "fluid bonds," where we choose to allow fluid exchange in one relationship but take precautions to make sure that neither person has any infections that could be sexually transmitted. Regular STI testing and sexual exclusivity or consistent use of barriers with other sexual partners is what makes this strategy effective.

If you and your partner are choosing to have unprotected sex together, but engaging in sex with other partners, you should share information about potential risk exposure with your fluid-bonded partner. If you are concerned about a potential infection, consider resuming use of protection methods with your fluid-bonded partner temporarily. If you are unable to tell your partner about the potential risk, consider engaging in lower risk activities, coming up with creative reasons (such as a minor health concern or a role-playing fantasy) for using barriers, or abstaining from sex until you can be tested (and, if necessary, treated).

Contraception

The heterosexist and cissexist way that pregnancy is typically talked about can make it easy to forget that many trans people are capable of becoming pregnant or getting someone else pregnant. It is also often assumed, even among trans people, that wishing to give birth or impregnate someone somehow makes us less trans. This is simply not true. It is just as valid for us to want to produce our own children as it is to want to avoid it.

Discussing the issue of pregnancy with a partner can be difficult, as it may remind us of sexual anatomy that does not represent our gender. However, not talking about the possibility of pregnancy when that possibility exists can result in us or our partners becoming unexpectedly pregnant. See Chapter 11 for more on contraception.

USING TOOLS FOR SEX

There are a number of tools that we can use to expand and improve our sexual experiences. We may incorporate tools or toys into our sex life for a number of reasons. For example, we may want to make some sexual practices more comfortable, affirm or reinforce our gender presentation, or help ourselves or our partners achieve orgasm.

Lubricants

Lubricant (lube), which helps reduce friction and irritation during sex, can be an important tool for making our sex lives safer and more fun. In addition to feeling unpleasant, friction can create small tears in the skin and cause condoms to break, increasing our risk of getting STIs.

Everyone can use lube, but as trans people, we often need lube even more than cis people. Taking testosterone can reduce the natural lubrication in a front hole, and in most cases, vaginoplasty does not create a self-lubricating vagina. The anus does not typically produce sufficient lubrication for penetration.

Lube can be purchased in many different places, from the grocery or drugstore to specialty sex shops and online retailers. There are many different kinds and brands of lube, and each one feels different depending on its type, thickness, and components. Whether you have many options, or just a few, know what is in the lube you choose:

- Oil-based lubes will break down latex and should be avoided when using condoms and other latex barriers.

- Water-based lubes are the most common sexual lubricants and are condom and barrier safe. However, they can dry out during sex. You can reactivate the lube with water—or just keep plenty around and reapply as needed.
- Silicone-based lube is also condom and barrier safe, but it may require soap to wash off. Some people prefer it because it is less likely to dry out.

Some people will have an allergic reaction to certain kinds of lube. Try spot testing the lube by rubbing a small amount on the inside of your wrist before using it on your genitals. All lubricants are different, and some people may have nonallergic, but still negative, reactions to a particular lube. For example, some lubes contain glycerin, which is added to many flavored lubes as a sweetener and to some unflavored lubes for texture. Because glycerin is a form of sugar, it can increase the likelihood of yeast infections. Applied anally, it can also act as a laxative, encouraging the user to have to use the bathroom. Other ingredients in some lubes may also cause changes in the pH balance of your genitals or disrupt the natural bacterial growth inside your body. Bacterial infections and yeast infections can affect anyone, regardless of gender. If you notice any bad odors, discharge, or discomfort (such as itching or burning) after using a new lubricant, stop using it. If the symptoms do not subside, consider seeing a health provider and getting tested for STIs.

Pumping and Extenders

Genital pumps are typically hand-operated and include a clear cylinder that is used to create suction to enlarge body parts and engorge them with blood. Pumps can be used on external genitals, nipples, genital openings, or the anus. Pumping can create increased sensitivity and an intense tugging sensation, which some of us find very pleasurable. Pulling blood into an area can help create erections and temporarily increase genital size. A cock ring, which keeps blood from flowing back out of the body part being pumped, can be used to help sustain erections.

When using a pump, try to get a good seal between the cylinder and your skin.

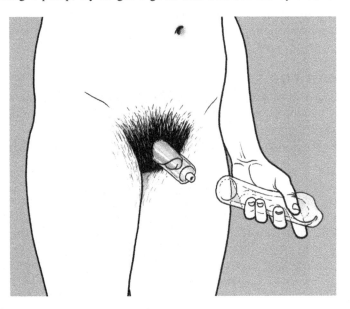

Using a pump for penetration (Dean Scarborough).

Warming the area and encouraging blood flow by being turned on can help. Body hair can prevent a good seal, so shaving or using a thick water-based lube can help. Pumps can be tested on a less sensitive area like the thigh in order to practice and become familiar with using them. There is typically a quick release valve. Be sure to go slowly and experiment when first getting used to a pump. Be sure you know how to release the pressure before using it on your genitals. If pumping is done too frequently or too strongly, it can desensitize the area or even cause burst capillaries. If you notice blue or purple marks or bumps under the skin where you have been pumping, remove the pump immediately and ice the area to decrease swelling. After removing the pump, the area will continue to be extra sensitive for a while.

With certain kinds of pumps, the tube and pump can be detached while leaving the cylinder suctioned on to play with. Some of us use a pump, remove the tube, and then slide an erection-enlarging sheath (extender) over the cylinder, which can be used for penetration and is also stimulating to the wearer. Extenders are marketed for cis men who want bigger endowments, but they can be used by other folks as well with a little creativity.

Sex Toys

Many people have the false belief that sex toys are only for cis women or are just for masturbation. This is not true. Toys are for anyone who enjoys them, whenever we want to use them. While not everyone enjoys or can achieve orgasm from vibration or penetration, many people do—regardless of their gender or the shape of their genitals.

> *"Since going on HRT, I have erectile dysfunction and so we have figured out other ways to have sex, including the use of toys, vibrators and strap-ons."*

Rodeoh (Courtney Trouble).

MATERIALS FOR SEX TOYS

Material is an important consideration when buying sex toys. Most commonly, sex toys are made with jelly rubber, hard plastic, or silicone. A sex toy should say on its packaging what it is made of. If it does not say what the materials are, chances are that it is jelly rubber or some form of plastic. Silicone toys tend to advertise themselves as such.

Jelly rubber toys can be good for first-time buyers, who are unsure what they want, since they are often much less expensive than their more lasting counterparts. The reason they are so cheap is that jelly rubber is a porous material, meaning that it absorbs fluids, bacteria, and fungi, and it cannot be sterilized. Some jelly rubber toys also leak toxic chemicals called phthalates, which may be carcinogenic and can cause irritation in contact with the delicate tissues of our genitals. Sex toys made from jelly rubber are thus best used with a condom.

Hard plastic is an excellent material for sex toys. Hard plastic can be cleaned with soap and water, bleach, alcohol, or other cleaning products, so long as the cleaning materials are rinsed off thoroughly before putting the toy near our genitals.

Silicone sex toys tend to be expensive, but they also usually last longer and are better made. Silicone is a nonporous material, which means that it is easily sterilized and can be used without condoms. (However, condoms are great when sharing toys or if you want to alternate between anal penetration and front-hole penetration.) Silicone comes in a variety of textures, from toys that are very soft and feel fleshy and realistic, to very hard toys that feel almost as firm as hard plastic.

Many sex toys on the market today are being made with thermal plastic, which has a very realistic feel but is very porous. Some sex toys are also made of natural materials like wood, steel, glass, or ceramic. Find out what material your sex toys are made of and how to best use and clean them.

SHOPPING FOR TOYS

Even people who have access to sex stores may not want to shop there. Many sex stores are directed at cis men, and they can seem like very hostile environments to anyone who is read as female or gender nonconforming. Other sex stores are directed solely at cis women, and they may police the genders of those who try to enter. Even sex stores that are not gender specific can feel unwelcoming to trans people, as they may separate their merchandise into "men's" and "women's" sections, implicitly meaning cis men and cis women. Check the store's Web site or call beforehand to find out more about whether they are trans friendly. Many stores in gay neighborhoods or ones that are identified as queer or feminist may be more likely to be trans friendly.

For those of us without nearby trans-friendly sex toy shops, Internet stores are a good option. Most reputable online sex toy vendors have review sections, in which customers comment on how intense a vibrator is, how many batteries it consumes, a toy's texture and materials, or if it is really as big or small as it looks. Most online stores will also send products in unmarked or generic packaging. There are plenty of ways we can safely and anonymously get what we want.

VIBRATORS

Vibrators are sex toys that vibrate. Vibrators today come in many shapes and sizes and can be used for a wide variety of erogenous zones. Some vibrators are shaped like a phallus and may be used for penetration. Some of these are specifically designed to reach the prostate. Others are designed to be used externally on the genitals, perineum, nipples, feet, or anywhere else we want. Vibrators can be especially good tools for those of us who want to experience genital stimulation but due to body dysphoria do not want to touch our genitals directly. For those of us who enjoy touching our genitals or having them touched, a vibrator can add additional stimulation. Some of us cannot orgasm from manual touch because it does not provide enough intensity, and we may require a vibrator to orgasm.

When shopping for a vibrator in a store with demo models, a good way to test vibrators is to touch them to the tip of the nose. Consider the power source for vibrators before buying them. Some vibrators plug into a wall socket, while others have removable batteries or rechargeable batteries. Check what kind of batteries are needed and how many before taking a new vibrator home. Battery vibrators are by far the most common type, though the market is changing very rapidly, and many of the newer products use charging cradles, USB connections, or other electronics to keep them charged for action.

There are not very many vibrators that run directly from plug-in power, but those that do tend to be especially intense. Consider first testing a plug-in vibrator with a towel between the vibrator and your body before using it directly on your genitals or other sensitive areas. Plug-in vibrators are often marketed as back massagers rather than sex toys, and they may be found in drug stores, health and body stores, and other mainstream outlets. This may make them more accessible to those of us who do not otherwise have access to sex toys.

When traveling with plug-in or plug-charged vibrators, remember that different countries have different standard voltages, so plugging a vibrator into a socket outside the country in which it was purchased could potentially destroy the motor. When traveling with vibrators that use battery power, one option is to tape them securely into the "off" position or remove the batteries to make sure our bags do not start vibrating while being inspected.

DILDOS, STRAP-ONS, AND PROSTHETIC COCKS

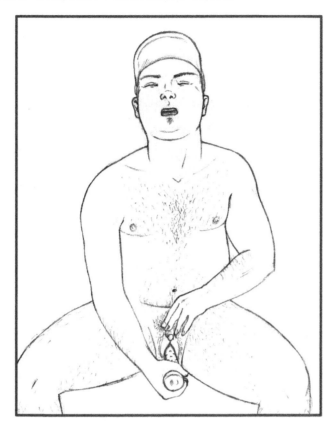

Self-pleasure with a dildo (Ron Burton).

Dildos are sex toys shaped like a phallus. Dildos can be used for masturbation. They can also be used by a partner who holds the dildo or straps it on with a harness. Dildos can be used for penetration, but they have many other uses. We may strap on a dildo, for instance, and have a partner perform oral sex on the dildo. Anyone can use a dildo for penetration, regardless of their gender identity, the gender they were designated at birth, or the shape of their genitals. For example, those of us who are trans women sometimes use strap-on dildos to penetrate our partners. Just as strap-ons can be used by anyone regardless of gender, no one is obligated to enjoy strap-ons. For some of us, wearing a strap-on can cause us to feel dysphoric. Trans men, for example, are not obligated to like wearing a strap-on just because they are men.

> "I like using strap-ons but sometimes the thought of it makes me very upset since I can't feel it."

> "I am not particularly interested in strapping on a dildo, but would do so if the occasion called for it if I really really liked the person."

> "Now that I'm more gender-queer I really love to wear a strap-on, and I particularly like to top males with it because I'm a fag."

Selecting the right dildo is important. Some of us have a very clear sense of what shape and size our external genitals should be, so finding a dildo that fits that mental image can be critical. Others of us specifically want to avoid the appearance of external genitals. Dildos come in all sorts of shapes, sizes, colors, and textures. Some are promoted as coming in "skin colors" with "realistic" shapes and textures. Others are manufactured in bright, unnatural colors with textures and shapes designed to feel good on specific parts of our bodies.

Like dildos, harnesses also come in many shapes and sizes. They are typically designed to have a dildo inserted into them so that the dildo is held in place on the front of the body when the harness is on properly. Some have adjustable straps and can be shared easily (once washed). Others fit like underwear and need to be bought in the appropriate size.

Sex with a strap-on (Ron Burton).

Prosthetic cocks are phallus-shaped dildos that can be worn over our other bits. They can be used or worn by people of all genders, sexes, and identities—and there are various types created for different bodies. They are also sometimes called "packers" or "packs." Packers can be hard or soft, and they can be worn throughout the day or put on before or during sex. Some of us identify more strongly with one cock or packer; some of us use multiple different packs to our liking. We may wear a soft packer during the day, or when out in public; we may put on a hard packer when expecting intimacy. Some packers allow the user to stand to pee. See Chapter 8 for more information on packers.

MASTURBATION SLEEVES
Many sex toy manufacturers produce what are called masturbation sleeves. They are designed to be pleasurable to penetrate, often with textured patterns on the inside. Some of them may have openings made to resemble genitals, anuses, or mouths, but others have plain, nondescript openings.

Sleeves may be made of silicone or jelly rubber like other sex toys. Those made of silicone can be more easily washed and sterilized, while those made from jelly rubber need more careful washing, cannot be sterilized, and as a result may wear out faster. Trans women and others assigned male might appreciate these toys. Difficulty with erections or dysphoria might become problems, but some sleeves are made in a small egg shape and may work more easily without erections or for anyone with smaller genitals.

For those who cannot tolerate penetration but want to please their partner by providing it, or who want to be penetrated in the front but cannot be, one option is to place a masturbation sleeve between our thighs and have our partner penetrate the sleeve.

WEAPONRY OF BODY RE/CON/FIGURATION

Aimee Herman disembowels the language of gender, body, sexual diversions, and scar tissue in her book of poetry: to go without blinking.

I am seven. I am eight.

David Achbar sits behind me in first grade. He taps me on the shoulder and gestures for me to look down. David's tiny dick is dangling between his gangly legs, shorts pulled past knees.

I say nothing, though I wonder how long I'll have to wait before what sits between *my* legs grows long like his.

I am thirteen. I am fourteen.

My mother stuffs my torso in buttons and lace and I wonder if boy and girl gender can be interrupted by a third called *tablecloth*, called ironed out and lovely and fit for Thanksgiving china placed over belly and smooth legs and I can check the box labeled "L" for *linen* as gender.

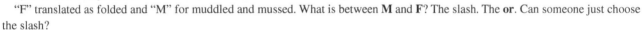

"F" translated as folded and "M" for muddled and mussed. What is between **M** and **F**? The slash. The **or**. Can someone just choose the slash?

My mother takes me to the mall where big-boned woman wearing lipstick on teeth finds a training bra with built-in drill sergeant. What if I am not ready to enlist in breast boot camp?

I am sixteen. I am seventeen.

I trade in my dresses for jeans, torn at the knees from running fast and falling without rhythm. My hair becomes the last part of me that is not mine anymore. It is my mother's, who brushed it on days when the knots screamed. It is my grandmother's, who always begged me not to cut it.

I grab scissors, gather my hair between my fingers, and begin to cut.

One inch for each twist of hair held by my mother, who left me when I was twelve when I needed her to tell me she'd love me, girl or boy or just the slash, without exchanging pills for potatoes as a side with my supper. Without sending me into rooms to be analyzed because I was lingering my looks at girls instead of boys. Being called a *tomboy* felt more complimentary than *pretty* or *girly*.

Two inches for my vagina, for feeling like I am mourning something that has remained but become something else, has begun to stand for something more than just a genital. It stands for something more than the **F** after the slash following the **M**. I feel a desire to fight it out of me, fight it off of me, somehow change its purpose or intended architectural reasoning.

Three inches for this time of my life where Queer Straight Alliances happened elsewhere, far enough that I had no idea what QSA stood for, that it meant alliance. That it meant bridge of communication. That it meant *help*.

Four inches for the boy in my high school who didn't make it, who decided to wrap his neck in knots made from Boy Scout training rather then ask for hands to hold him. When he hung away his life, they finally started to pay attention. They wrapped ribbons around their brand new sports cars' antennas and missed football-cheerleading-math club practice to attend his funeral. And for the other boy who gathered his lunch quickly into his mouth each Monday through Friday in crowded cafeteria where tater tots and ignorance arrived on the side of each plastic sectioned tray. I always wanted to tell him to slow down. He rushed each bite as though preparing for war, as though bombs were just below him and he just wanted to digest before the eruption and removal of limbs.

And one more inch for that time the whispers grew louder and I heard the word FAGGOT for the first time in my suburbia. And the way this boy's face changed from careful to cautious to deeply concerned, in search of the nearest exit sign. The way they spoke it as though it was his name like Charles or Greg. *Hey, Faggot, did you get the notes from last class? Hey, Faggot, I'll bring my extra Nintendo controller when I come over to your house today.*

In this inch, I cut away the shame. I take back words used as weaponry, but really just letters pressed together and I replace the bullets with blanks.

SEXUAL PRACTICES

There are as many ways to be sexual as there are people. How we have sex is not determined by our gender or sexual orientation. No matter how we identify, we choose the kinds of touch we enjoy, decide whether we enjoy penetrating or being penetrated (or both, or neither), and how we want to work and play with our partners to have satisfying, fulfilling sex lives.

One of the most challenging areas of sex that many of us face is penetration. Our culture sends us many messages about who enjoys penetration, and how. But these messages ignore the wide range of people who enjoy different kinds of sexual penetration. For some of us, giving or receiving penetration can be a way to affirm our gender, while for others, the opposite is true. For many of us, there are specific practices, positions, and toys that we enjoy, even if we are uncomfortable in other situations. Some of us enjoy penetration—just not with our genitals. When we leave behind cissexist, homophobic ideas about sex, we may discover that there are a fabulous variety of different ways to penetrate and be penetrated.

> "When I feel as though I am expected to act very 'macho,' that makes me uncomfortable, but I am comfortable with most sex acts. I don't think that for instance, penetrating my partner with my penis is an inherently 'macho' act (it's like an organic strap-on, I suppose). However, sometimes after sex (after I orgasm), that can make me feel very unpleasant. So I've thought about tucking and using a strap-on instead of using my penis."

> "I have always been uncomfortable with being penetrated anywhere unless I am extraordinarily comfortable with my partner. It is more about vulnerability and fear of being dominated than it is about my gender, however."

Penetration is far from the only way we can have sex. Touch, massage, licking, sucking, fantasy, and fetishes are all ways that many of us enjoy sex with our partners that do not involve penetration.

Touch and Massage

There are many types of sexual contact that do not focus on our genitals. As trans people, some of us may feel dysphoria around our genitals, and many of us choose to instead explore different ways to have sex. Erogenous zones exist all over the body. For some of us these may include the scalp, earlobes, armpits, inner thighs, feet, or neck. Sexual play may involve sensual kissing, touching, or massaging these areas, and it can be very intense even without any genital touching.

Licking and Sucking

For some of us, oral sex can feel like an up-close inspection of our genitals—which can be anxiety provoking, especially if our genitals feel wrong for our gender identity. But for those of us who do enjoy giving or receiving oral sex, the ways in which we enjoy doing so may also be very individual and include a lot of variation.

There are many different ways to use our mouths to lick, suck, or penetrate someone. Our tongues are muscular and can be made into a variety of different shapes. Being licked by the firm tip of a stiff tongue is different from being licked with the soft surface of a flat tongue. Try a variety of different tongue movements and shapes to see what your partner likes best. Trace shapes with your tongue and see what patterns they like.

Letting someone lick or suck on our bits can be very exciting for some of us, and too intense for others. Be sure to ask your partner what they like. Some people like the tongue to be wiggled back and forth, while others like an up-and-down stroke. Some enjoy stimulation with the lips. Some like to be nibbled or outright bitten with teeth. Always, always ask before using your teeth—and keep in mind that breaking the skin can also increase the risk of infections, such as HIV or hepatitis.

There also many places we like to be licked. Between our navels and our knees there are lots of very sensitive areas that feel wonderful when touched, licked, or sucked. The anus, the perineum (the strip of skin between the genitals and the anus), and our genitals are some of the most sensitive spots, and licking and sucking these areas is one way many of us experience orgasms.

No matter what kind of genitals we have, we can enjoy the kinds of oral stimulation that feel right for us. Big bits and small bits can both be sucked or licked.

Using a dental dam on a trans woman (Dean Scarborough).

Most of us have particularly sensitive areas on the tip and along the underside of our bits, large and small, that we may enjoy having licked during oral sex. For those of us with larger bits, our partners can use their hands or a dental dam to flatten our genitals onto our body to receive different kinds of stimulation and attention. A dental dam used this way can also act as a gender-affirming barrier for some of us.

For some of us, suction is our favorite type of oral stimulation. Some of us enjoy intense suction, while others prefer a gentle slurp. Again, ask to find out. When taking someone's genitals into your mouth, remember to cover your teeth. Do this by wrapping your lips over your front teeth to form a ring of soft tissue between your teeth and your partner's body.

> *"Wearing a cock and having it (or my own clit, which I often refer to as my dick) sucked is way more comfortable and pleasurable."*

Depending on our partner's anatomy, there may be lots of parts for us to suck. Anything that points away from or hangs down from the body can go in our mouths. If a partner has external gonads (which some people refer to as testicles), be careful about how you suck them. Most people get more pleasure from stimulating the loose, soft skin around the glands rather than from pressure to the glands themselves.

Hands can also be helpful to keep us from gagging or choking if our partner has larger genitals. Gauge how much length you can comfortably take in your mouth—for most people it's about 3 inches. Wrap one hand around your partner's genitals at or right below the maximum length you can take. By doing this, we can prevent ourselves from taking more than we can handle, while also manually stimulating the parts of a partner's genitals that are outside our mouth. This is especially helpful if a partner enjoys thrusting, since otherwise this might cause us to gag.

If a partner's genitals are larger, we may want to try deep throating them. Many of us have a gag reflex, however, and deep throating can trigger this. The gag reflex is a natural self-preservation response built into our bodies to prevent choking, so if you cannot manage to overcome it, there is no need to feel ashamed. Some people can either work around their gag reflex, train themselves out of it, or did not have a sensitive one to start with. Certain positions can also be helpful. Any position that aligns our mouth with our esophagus in a relatively straight line can make larger genitals easier to take. For example, lying on our back with our head over the edge of the bed, our mouth lines up with our throat. The key is to relax as much as we can. When we are nervous, our body's automatic self-defense responses, such as our gag reflex, tend to increase in sensitivity and intensity. As with any sexual activity, it may take some practice to learn how to deep throat.

Many people require consistent movement or suction to orgasm. When performing oral sex, it can sometimes take a long time for a partner to orgasm. Pace yourself, and use your hands when you need a break.

ANALINGUS

Analingus, also known as rimming, is performing oral sex on the anus. Lots of people enjoy it, and for some trans people it can be a pleasure to receive oral sex on a body part that is not seen as gender specific. For those of us assigned male who have not had vaginoplasties, analingus can be a great analog for cunnilingus in a way that is not currently possible for us.

Oral sex performed on the anus comes with health risks. In addition to all the usual STI concerns, rimming can also put us at risk for diseases specific to oral-fecal contact, such as *Giardia* and *E. coli*. While safer sex is always a good idea, analingus in particular is a great time to bring out the barriers.

Some people feel safe and comfortable rimming without protection. If you are going to do this, wash the anus with soap beforehand, including inside the first sphincter. Enemas, which insert liquid into the rectum, can be used as prep for any kind of anal sex. They are by no means necessary, and they do have their drawbacks. If you do use an enema, remember to perform it 2 hours in advance rather than right before, as enemas can cause us to need to use the bathroom and can also leave unexpected water in the rectum, which most people do not want to discover with their mouths. Rimming is otherwise straightforward. Licking, sucking, kissing, and penetrating can all be fun, so experiment and see what you and your partner enjoy.

Fisting and Fingering

Hands have dexterity and versatility that genitals do not have, and they have the added benefit of carrying less gender significance. Unlike genitals, however, fingers have fingernails, and these have to be trimmed down to the pink in order to be safely inserted into someone else. If you trim your nails right before using them inside someone's body, be sure to use a file or emery board to smooth out rough edges—better yet, trim them in advance to avoid sharp edges. For those of us who enjoy having long nails, we can insert cotton balls into the fingers of gloves to make our nails safer for penetration. Fingering—using our fingers to press, rub, stroke, and touch our partner's sexual spots—can be fun for people with almost any anatomical configuration.

Fisting is when the whole hand is inserted into the body. It can provide a very pleasurable sense of fullness and pressure in either the anus or a front hole. However, not everyone enjoys the sensation—and if it hurts, slow down. Fisting should be tried very carefully, slowly, and with lots of lube. It is a good idea to wear latex gloves when fisting, particularly for anal fisting, or if you have hangnails or other sores or cuts on your fingers.

The receptive partner should be relaxed and aroused to make fisting enjoyable. When you are ready to insert more than just a few fingers into your partner, press your fingertips together to form a "duckbill" and insert this slowly into either the front hole or the anus. Use lots of lube, and add more as you go. When you get the widest part of the knuckles past the pelvic muscles or sphincters, your hand will naturally curl into a fist. Once you get to this point, ask your partner how much or how little movement they want.

Using Bits for Penetration

People of any gender identity and birth designation may have smaller external genitals. What we are able to penetrate and how we go about doing it depends on both the size and firmness of our genitals. If our genitals do not become very erect, are relatively small, or located in such a way that achieving penetration can be difficult in most positions, there is a lot we can still do.

Experiment with positions to see what works best. Sometimes the position of our genitals on our body makes penetration difficult. Some of us can penetrate more easily if our partner is on top. Another way to increase our ability to penetrate someone if we have smaller genitals is to place a hand on the flesh of our pubic mound just above our external genitals and pull the flesh upwards so that our genitals slide further up on our pubic mound. This can move our external genitals into a more accessible position. Inserting a finger or fingers along with the external genitals can be another way of going deeper and increasing pleasure with penetration.

For many people, starting testosterone therapy can have quite dramatic effects. Growth of genital erectile tissue is stimulated by testosterone. This means that many female-assigned people who take testosterone experience major shifts in the size and shape of our external genitals.

> *"With the changes brought on by testosterone, both my girlfriend and I feel that I have an ordinary dick. We do all the old-fashioned vanilla stuff most straight folks do."*

For those of us with larger external genitals, we may wish to use them for penetration. Plenty of people engage in this type of sex, and it is fine for us as trans people to do so as well. Some of us who were assigned male at birth fear that engaging in this kind of sex will mean that we are "not really trans," but this is not true. People of all genders, trans and cis, choose to penetrate their partners.

Hormones affect our ability to achieve and maintain erections. Those of us on androgen blockers or estrogen therapy may need assistance to become erect or want to figure out ways to penetrate our partner without an erection. It may be helpful to try different types of stimulation or more stimulation to become erect. "Cock rings," which go around the base of our genitals, or pumps may be helpful. Some of us use medications like Viagra to produce erections. Viagra generally works even if we are taking androgen blockers and undergoing estrogen replacement therapy. For some of us, skipping an antiandrogen dose or reworking our estrogen schedule helps. If you feel comfortable, it can be useful to discuss this with a health provider to best balance your transition needs and ensure that you minimize risks of altering your hormone protocols.

It is possible for some of us to penetrate a partner with our nonerect genitals. Patience is key, as well as moving slowly to prevent ourselves from falling out during sex. It may be difficult to use a traditional condom on nonerect genitals, but a partner can wear a receptive condom ("female condom") as a barrier method.

Anal Penetration

Penetrative anal sex can be very enjoyable and comes with the added bonus that all of us have this part of our bodies.

> *"I love anal sex. Partly why I love it is because it can be performed with any-one, regardless of body parts."*

To have safe, pleasurable anal sex, lube is a necessary first step. The second step is relaxation. The anus has two sphincters. We can consciously control the outer layer of muscle but not the inner layer. This means we have to be very gentle with the inner ring. Its job is to keep tight at all times, so learning to relax it can take practice and patience. Start with smaller objects like fingers or small toys and work your way up.

Those of us who were assigned male at birth also have prostates. Stimulating this gland via anal penetration can be very sexually pleasurable. The prostate is located 1–3 inches inside the anus, on the side closest to the front of the body.

Be careful that anything you put into your anus is not capable of slipping completely inside—it should either be firmly attached to something or have a flared base. Otherwise insertables may get sucked in by the muscles inside us, which can result in a costly and embarrassing trip to the hospital.

Always use lube when inserting genitals, fingers, or toys in the anus. It is also a good idea to use a condom, especially if your partner produces ejaculatory fluid, to prevent HIV and other STIs. Condoms also make it easy to clean up genitals or toys after anal penetration. If you are using your fingers or hands, it is a great idea to wear gloves for the same reasons.

Front-Hole Penetration

Those of us who were assigned female at birth usually have a front hole, unless we have chosen to have it surgically removed via vaginectomy. Many of us have complicated feelings about using our front holes for penetrative sex. We may be turned off by it because front holes are gendered as female. On the other hand, there are many of us who enjoy front-hole sex a great deal. However we enjoy using our genitals is great, and it does not invalidate our genders.

Sometimes we enjoy front-hole penetration with hands or toys as part of other sexual acts, such as receiving a blow job. Some of us find that we are more comfortable enjoying front-hole penetration if our partners use hands or toys, instead of their genitals. Some of us choose sexual positions that are not as gendered as "missionary style" sex, such as being on top of the other person while we are being penetrated, or having the other person penetrate us from behind.

The front hole is very muscular, and while its own tissues have very few nerves of their own, it is connected to many other sensitive parts of our body—parts of the clitoris/cock can be stimulated through front-hole penetration, for example. The clitoris/cock has two "legs" which run down inside our bodies from the pubic bone on either side of the opening of the front hole where they end at the anus, and these are part of what is stimulated during penetration of either the anus or the front hole.

About one-third of the way inside the front hole, on the front side of the body (closest to the navel), is an area often called the G-spot. This area may include other glands that provide lubrication and parts of the clitoris. Stimulation of the G-spot can be extremely pleasurable for some, while others may find it uncomfortable or unpleasant. Pressure on it can make us feel like we have to pee, especially at first. During orgasm, many people experience fluid release from glands that are thought to be located in this area. This can be as subtle as a general increase in lubrication or as extreme as a high-pressure, high-volume squirt.

> "Sometimes I worry because I enjoy sexual acts that don't fit with my idea of myself as a dominant male. But by worrying about it, I know that I am just giving credit to useless stereotypes, so I tell myself to ignore it and carry on!"

> "Penetration of the front hole used to terrify and nauseate me. Post-T, I love it. I've fucked two guys with it. Damn, that statement is weird."

Some of us do not produce enough lubrication for comfortable penetration, or we stop being able to because of changes caused by testosterone. Lube is often necessary for front-hole sex. Choose lube carefully based on the type of sex and any allergies you may have. In general, water-based lubes can be used with most sex toys and barrier methods.

Those who have been on testosterone treatments may bleed after front-hole penetration, as testosterone can cause thinning of the mucus membranes. Sex where fingers are inserted into the front hole, in particular, may cause bleeding, as may the insertion of larger objects. Starting with smaller insertables and working slowly to larger ones can help prevent bleeding. Listen to your body's cues. If it feels good, keep doing it, but if you notice any discomfort or distress, you may want to slow down or stop and figure out whether you want to keep being penetrated.

Sex After Vaginoplasty

Surgically constructed genitals have qualities that others do not. Most vaginoplasty surgical techniques are not able to produce genitals that self-lubricate. As a result, many of us need plenty of lube for penetration to be comfortable. Genitals produced in this way may be limited to smaller objects for penetration, or they may require extra dilation to take larger objects.

> *"Over the years my libido has increased to the point where I enjoy sex thoroughly and unashamedly. I never knew if my vagina worked until I was 26 years post op. 'How bizarre is that,' everyone exclaims."*

Penetration of surgically constructed genitals is mostly similar to what we would expect for other orifices. That said, there are a few things to keep in mind. Many details of anatomy may vary depending on the surgeon and the surgical technique used—placement of the new vagina in relation to the prostate, for example. Because the G-spot is made up of erectile tissue around the urethra that everyone has, after vaginoplasty there will be both a G-spot and a prostate that can be stimulated from inside the vagina. Results vary based on a number of factors, but the internal tissues will not be as stretchy as they are in someone born with a front hole. Most people who have had vaginoplasty report not being able to be fisted, although in some cases it may be possible. Regular dilation will affect the size to which our vagina can comfortably stretch. For more information, see Chapter 13 and talk to your individual surgeon.

Bleeding during sex can be a special concern for those of us who have had vaginoplasties. We may bleed occasionally after penetration. Bleeding is not necessarily a concern, however, depending on how it occurs. It can be normal to go to the bathroom after sex and find pink smears on the toilet paper. However, if you bleed a lot, for extended periods of time, or start finding blood clots, seek medical attention immediately.

Muffing

Muffing is a slang term for penetration of the inguinal canal. The inguinal canal is the passage through which people's external gonads (what a health provider calls testicles) descend from the abdomen, and into which the gonads are typically pushed back up when tucking. (For more information on tucking, see Chapter 8.) The inguinal canal is also the place where doctors give hernia exams, which might include the instruction "Turn your head and cough." For those of us who have experienced penetration or stimulation of this body part only while in a provider's office, we may not be instantly excited to try it. However, there is a big difference between a medical exam done for diagnostic purposes and something done with the intention of sexual pleasure and self-exploration.

During muffing, because the skin covering the external gonads is loose, it simply moves into the canal along with the finger when pushed. The inguinal canal is a comparatively small cavity, but it can vary greatly in size from person to person. Experience playing in the area may increase its capacity over time. When first exploring, many of us find we can take only one finger up to about the first knuckle. Other people can receive a whole thumb or more.

Nerves in the area of the inguinal canal can be very sensitive, so it is important not to push ourselves and to begin exploration slowly. The sensation of muffing can be very different from other kinds of sexual stimulation, and there is little to which it can be compared. The intensity of the sensation may feel uncomfortable at first, but many people find

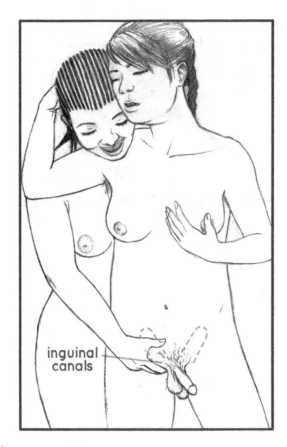

Muffing (Ron Burton).

it powerfully pleasurable and a good way to experience being penetrated in the front when they would not otherwise be able to.

Sounding

Sounding, or inserting objects into the urethra, is most commonly done by those of us whose urethral opening is located at the tip of our external genitals. Sounding can be a very pleasurable form of penetration and can be done on both erect and flaccid genitals.

The urethra is very sensitive to infection, so it requires very smooth objects and sterile lube (which is different than ordinary personal lubricants). Use stainless steel or hard plastic rods designed specifically for urethral insertion. Do not use household items such as pens, nails, or other similar objects. Rods designed for sounding can be purchased in a variety of gauges—start small and work your way up if you are interested in sounding. Sounding rods can be purchased in kits that have a range of sizes, and they often come with cleaning supplies.

While sounding is possible for those of us whose urethra is not located at the tip of external genitals, it is far more difficult and dangerous.

Kink

We do not have to like latex, leather, or whips to be kinky. There are many elements of kink that we use in our sex lives without realizing it. If you have ever given or received a hickey and liked it, then you enjoyed marking or biting your partner. If you have ever enjoyed consensually holding someone down or being held down yourself, then you have enjoyed a form of dominance/submission and power exchange. If you have ever used handcuffs or blindfolds, you have experimented with erotic restraint and sensory deprivation. "Kinky" people are often just those who have created names for certain types of intimacy and experimented with them more.

Fully expanded, the acronym BDSM means Bondage & Discipline, Dominance & Submission, and Sadomasochism. BDSM is also sometimes referred to as kink. What it boils down to is people enjoying a variety of different sensation types, consensual power dynamics, and sex fantasies.

> *"I think that getting involved in the kink/leather/BDSM community has really opened up my perspective on what are 'acceptable' sex acts for a man, and has helped me divorce gender from power, penetration, and dominance."*

> *"I was never into BDSM or leather or kink when I was married. My second lesbian partner introduced me to that."*

> *"Recently, I have begun to explore BDSM with my new partner. I am very interested in pursuing this, always have been, but was really waiting for someone to explore with whom I felt I could really trust."*

Many of us have had fantasies that involve power, domination, submission, or role dynamics, such as teacher/student or boss/employee. Many people think of these as "just fantasy" and never realize that such scenarios can be safely and responsibly acted out in real life without any real authority figures being involved.

For many people who do not desire genital sex, kink can be a great substitute. For those who do, it can be a fun addition to our repertoire. Giving and receiving consensual pain, for example, can create intense intimacy and give both parties the same kind of emotional "high" as orgasm. While kink may not always result in the specific kind of physical pleasure we call climax, kink can give some people feelings of intense euphoria, pleasure, connectedness, and passion in much the same way that genital sex might.

Certain types of play are more dangerous than others. If you are interested in experimenting with something comparatively risky, like needles, seek in-depth information from experienced sources. Everything that goes into making safe, consensual, and fulfilling sex is true of kink as well: Be careful about consent, negotiate before you play, have check-ins, and give each other aftercare. Practice good communication with your partners and negotiate safe words before beginning play.

Misgendering Fantasies and Nonconsent

Having fantasies about traumatic situations is a relatively common response in those of us who have either been traumatized by individuals or have been culturally traumatized by what has happened to people around us. In particular, some survivors of violence (sexual or not) may have rape fantasies or fantasies about other forms of brutality. Some trans people have fantasies of being misgendered, degendered, attacked, or oppressed. This is not because we enjoy being oppressed or violated in real life; rather, it is simply one way the brain tries to process such traumas.

In some of us, fantasies of this type can be a form of emotional self-harm. If these fantasies cause you to feel depressed or worthless, consider seeking emotional support for dealing with these destructive thoughts.

In other cases, fantasies of oppression or violence can be a useful tool in healing. We may not have had the power to keep ourselves safe in real life when we experienced trauma, but in fantasy we have the power to experience frightening or damaging events and come out safe and whole. In our fantasies we may be saved by our friends, beat up our attackers, scream until our rapist runs away, or do whatever we need that we could not do when the trauma occurred.

Involving a safe partner in our fantasies can be a way to process and heal the trauma. Acting out a misgendering scene with someone who cares about us and understands our gender as well as the importance of respectful communication, for example, can allow us to feel the feelings we were too overwhelmed to feel before. We can get a chance to be comforted afterward. Many of us wish that the people who have hurt or abandoned us would apologize and give us the care we need in order to heal, and role play of this type is one way to get some form of closure.

If you engage in this sort of role play, please be careful. Consent, check-ins, and a good support network are more important here than ever. Role playing in this way can bring up traumas we did not realize were still affecting us or cause unexpected emotions. Any slips in communication can be disastrous. If you try anything like this, be sure to have a good support network in place to help you cope with any unintended consequences.

SEX WORK

People enter sex work for a variety of reasons. For some of us, it might be something we feel good at or enjoy. It could be that it offers the best flexibility and freedom to accommodate our disabilities or childcare responsibilities. It could be that it allows for greater income than other jobs available to us. Or it could be because we have no other choice. Sex work can include a variety of kinds of jobs, such as street work, performing in porn, escorting, erotic massage, pro-dom/pro-sub, or Webcam work. It can include both legal and criminalized work, and laws about exactly what is criminalized vary from state to state and country to country. See Chapter 9 for more about sex work as a job.

Sex workers have friends, partners, and relationships just like everyone else. If you have a friend who is doing sex work or you are dating a sex worker, there are some useful things to keep in mind.

- *Respect their boundaries.* Do not pry for gossip if they do not seem interested in talking about it, and do not tell others about their work without their permission.
- *Do not project your judgments.* You might think that sex work is horrifying or that it is the coolest thing in the world, but they might not see it that way. It is important to let them define their experience for themselves.
- *. . . but don't hide your feelings.* If you have insecurities, fears, or other difficult feelings come up, find an appropriate time to discuss them.
- *Sex for work can be different.* A lot of sex workers make a strong distinction between sex for work and sex in their personal life. This can look different for different people, but for the most part clients and partners are not interchangeable, nor are they in competition.
- *Be willing to listen.* It is good not to have things feel like a secret. We all need to vent about work sometimes. If they talk about having a bad day at work, it does not mean things are horrible and they need to be rescued from their job.
- *Do not fall for the stereotypes.* Just because someone does sex work does not mean they are hypersexual. They might not be up for sex sometimes, and that is fine.
- *Learn the issues.* Sex worker organizations and advocacy groups are constantly dealing with political issues, support projects, or community building. From protesting condom confiscation by police to organizing storytelling and performance spaces, there are a lot of things that you can get involved with.

CONCLUSION

When it comes to sex, what feels right to us is what is right for us. Sex is about desire, pleasure, enjoying our bodies and others' bodies, spending time alone, or connecting with others. Sex can be a way for us to feel empowered in our bodies and in our gender. It has the potential to bring us great pleasure and joy.

REFERENCES AND FURTHER READING

Bellwether, M. (n.d.). *Fucking trans women: A zine about the sex lives of trans women.* Retrieved January 2014, from http://fuckingtranswomen.tumblr.com

Blank, H. (2011). *Big big love, revised: A sex and relationships guide for people of size (and those who love them).* New York, NY: Random House.

Corinna, H. (n.d.). With pleasure: A view of whole sexual anatomy for every body. *Scarleteen: Sex ed for the real world*. Retrieved January 2014, from http://www.scarleteen.com/article/body/with_pleasure_a_view_of_whole_sexual_anatomy_for_every_body

Diamond, M. (2011). *Trans/love: Radical sex beyond the binary*. San Francisco, CA: Manic D Press.

Dr. Nerdlove. (2013, March 29). Getting a yes (instead of avoiding a no): The standard of enthusiastic consent. *Paging Dr. Nerdlove*. Retrieved January 2014, from http://www.doctornerdlove.com/2013/03/enthusiastic-consent/

Easton, D., & Liszt, C. A. (1998). *How to get terrible things done to you by wonderful people*. Emeryville, CA: Greenery Press.

Easton, D., & Liszt, C. A. (1998). *The topping book: Or getting good at being bad*. Emeryville, CA: Greenery Press.

Haines, S. (2007). *Healing sex: A mind-body approach to healing sexual trauma*. San Francisco, CA: Cleis.

Kaufman, M., Silverberg, C., & Odette, F. (2007). *The ultimate guide to sex and disability: For all of us who live with disabilities, chronic pain and illness*. San Francisco, CA: Cleis.

Masters, W. H., & Johnson, V. E. (1966). *Human sexual response*. Boston, MA: Little, Brown.

Taormino, T. (2008). *Opening up: A guide to creating and sustaining open relationships*. San Francisco, CA: Cleis.

Winks, C., & Semans, A. (2002). *The good vibrations guide to sex: The most complete sex manual ever written*. San Francisco, CA: Cleis.

Yourlesbianfriend. (March 22, 2013). Un-memorizing the "silence is sexy" date script. *Queer Guess Code*. Retrieved January 2014, from http://queerguesscode.wordpress.com/2013/03/22/un-memorizing-the-silence-is-sexy-date-script/

18

PARENTING
Kel Polly and Ryan G. Polly

THOSE OF USE WITH CHILDREN EXPERIENCE UNIQUE JOYS THROUGH OUR CONNECTIONS TO THE LIVES WE SHAPE. Many of us do not have children of our own, but we are close with children who may be our relatives, students, or mentees. As transgender people, we have the potential to teach younger generations to value gender diversity and to respect the many ways in which people express themselves.

Parenting is one way that we can have an impact on future generations. Many of us dream of being parents, and at a certain point we feel we are ready to make it a reality. We may want to share our authentic selves and provide unconditional love and support to a child as a parent. Whatever the reasons, and whatever the stage in our life, there are many things that we, as trans individuals, may have to consider that are not likely to affect the general parenting population.

WORRIES ABOUT PARENTING AS TRANS PEOPLE

Due to the stigma of living as transgender people, many of us worry about how we will be received as trans parents, and how our children will manage the teasing and bullying they may face. We may have internalized negative stereotypes about ourselves, and we may wonder whether we are capable of being good parents. Some of us may have had parents who were not supportive of us, or who abused us, and question whether we have the skills to parent differently. We may also worry that we will not be able to provide financially for children. It can be difficult to find secure employment with benefits that will cover our families.

> "I don't know if I want children. I am very much ready to adopt, but sometimes I wonder if I will make a good parent being transgender. I never thought I needed to have children of my own. I think the bigger issue is that I don't ever want to be pregnant. I'm worried that all those hormones would change my personality and make me a woman. I really like my masculine side and I don't want to lose it. If I had children I think I would be more comfortable playing the dad roles than the mom roles. I'm worried how being trans will affect professional opportunities. If I don't have enough financial resources, I could not raise a child."

People become parents every day by accident. There are many people in the world who put little effort or planning into raising children. As trans people, many of us have experienced significant difficulty growing up, and we have the potential to be extraordinary parents, to be purposeful in the way we raise our children, and to teach them to be thoughtful and caring people.

OPTIONS FOR BECOMING A TRANS PARENT

When we reach the point in our lives when we begin to consider whether to become a parent (the timeline of which varies widely from one person to the next), one of the questions we must ask ourselves is how we will do so. Some of the most common answers to this question include the following: initiating a pregnancy, adopting a child, or becoming a parent by combining our lives with a partner or spouse who is already a parent themselves.

"Dite moi pourquoi" (Takeya Trayer).

PARENTING A PARTNER'S CHILD

Many of us begin relationships with people who have children. As we get to know our partners, we may also become part of their children's lives. We may unofficially begin to parent them, or we may officially take steps to adopt them. Becoming a parent to a partner's child can be a wonderful way to add a child to our lives. However, it can also pose challenges.

Many of the challenges of joining in raising a partner's child are not unique to being a trans parent. Unless we join our partners' families when their children are very young, it is difficult (but not impossible) for us to be involved in disciplining the children because the children may not know us well enough yet to trust that we are making good decisions for them. What we can do is support our partners' disciplinary decisions. If the child has another parent besides our partner, we should also be careful to support the child's relationship with that person and not put the child in the position of having to take sides with us or with the other parent.

In addition to the hurdles that many parents face when they begin to parent their partners' children, we also have concerns that are unique to us as trans people. We may wrestle with when it is appropriate to tell the children about our transgender identity. Likely, this will involve a long conversation with our partner about how they would like to approach the topic. There may also be legal concerns. If our partner is in a custody battle, for example, with the child's other parent, the child's other parent may want to use our transgender status in court to make our partner look like an unfit parent for exposing the child to living with a transgender person. While this may not be legal, in some areas it may be an effective means of gaining custody. If in doubt about any legal issues, it is always important to ask for legal advice.

ADOPTION AND FOSTERING

In the quest for parenthood, we may turn to adoption as an option that fits our lives and particular circumstances. When we make the choice to either foster or adopt a child, we will be put through a rigorous and extensive process of interviewing and investigation, just as are our cisgender counterparts. This process can be quite invasive as the agencies will look into our background for evidence to either support that we will be good parents or to prove that we would be in some way unfit. Our trans status should not exclude us from being able to adopt or foster a child. We may, however, encounter barriers unique to the trans community.

Kim and Cris with their adopted daugher (copyright Mariette Pathy Allen).

There are numerous people and entities that can potentially be involved in the adoption decision process, including the biological parents, the agency itself, staff within the agency, staff within the court system, and the judge deciding placement, and it is possible to encounter bias. Laws and guidelines vary from state to state, and from country to country, but there is the potential to encounter discrimination based on our gender or sexual orientation. Some states do explicitly ban same-sex couples from adopting, but it is unclear whether trans people would be excluded from adopting in those states.

At present there are no laws specifically addressing adoptions by trans people, and there are some agencies that openly pursue prospective transgender parents. These are usually agencies looking for trans people to foster openly LGBTQ youth and to serve as role models.

When deciding to adopt or foster a child, it is necessary to do preliminary homework to avoid any disheartening or potentially discriminatory treatment. Some suggestions include the following:

- Go through an agency that is specifically looking for trans people to foster.
- Reach out to agencies that are known to work with lesbian and gay prospective parents. Let them know up front that you are trans so that you avoid any trouble as you move through the process.
- Consider retaining an attorney who specializes in transgender law and adoptions. The adoption process can be complicated, but being represented by someone that understands adoption as well as trans rights can make it less so.
- Consider consulting with a qualified therapist who would be willing to speak on your behalf to the adoption agency.

It can be quite challenging to foster or adopt a child. It is not impossible, however, and armed with the right information, trans people have successfully fostered and adopted children into their lives.

PLANNING A BIOLOGICAL FAMILY

While conceiving and carrying a child is not an option for some, for others it is the preferred method by which to expand a family. Some of us may have the opportunity to conceive in the traditional manner, but for many of us this is not possible. In such situations, we face a number of considerations, many of which are similar to the choices faced by cisgender individuals or couples who wish to become pregnant but cannot do so on their own. At times, we have our own unique sets of concerns.

Fertility Considerations

One factor that affects potential trans parents is how our unique hormonal situations affect our fertility. For example, a person whose body could be capable of making sperm, and who is taking estrogen, should be aware that irreversible infertility is a possible outcome of hormone therapy, even after as little as three months. On the other hand, a person whose body could be capable of carrying a pregnancy may be able to do just that, even after many years of taking testosterone. If we know about our desire for children before beginning hormone therapy, we might consider preserving and storing sperm or eggs in a cryogenic bank for potential use later in our life.

> "I do not currently have children, but my desire to be a biological parent has caused me to delay my medical transition for many years. I am in the process of preserving my fertility via cryopreservation so I can move forward with my medical transition now, as living pre-medical transition has become increasingly untenable. I think all trans people should be given the option to preserve their reproductive capability. All too often it's not even brought up as a part of medical transition."

Adoption Resources
The American Civil Liberties Union (ACLU) offers maps and other resources related to adoption laws in the United States.

Families Like Ours provides resources for families and for professionals, with the end goal of overcoming barriers for LGBTQ families in adoption and fostering.

The Human Rights Campaign's (HRC) project "All Children—All Families" works with adoption agencies on LGBTQ competency. A list of participating agencies is available on their Web site.

PLANNING OUR FAMILY

Heather Davis is a writer and educator, and mother to two fabulous kids who are growing up to be creative, wonderful human beings.

I always loved the idea of having a known donor—a tangible person in our life that our child could know they came from biologically. For me, choosing that donor was a no-brainer. I had talked to my friend Chris for years about his being a donor before I was even ready to have kids. But when I met my husband, there was suddenly another person in the equation—and a pretty important person since he was going to be the real father of our child.

For both me and my husband, it was a loss for him to not be able to be the dad in the biological sense. We considered using his brother as a way of incorporating his genes, but there ended up being too many issues around it. In the end, though, we decided that choosing Chris felt best for us, so I asked him, and he said yes.

Chris and I spent a lot of time talking through this alone first, and in hindsight, I think it might have been better for all of us to talk from the start, including Chris's husband, David. In the end some of the following was made clear: Chris would not be known as the child's father

---

and would have no financial obligations or decision-making rights for the child's life but would be involved in some way. He wanted the kid to know who he was, be able to visit, and perhaps take vacations together as a group when he/she was older. Chris also wisely said that it was easy to talk about things hypothetically, but he knew he would probably have a completely different reaction when he first saw the child.

Then there were also the more mundane but equally important questions, ranging from STD testing, to sexual activity, to the winningly awkward discussion that it was "best" to not masturbate for 24–48 hours before your first inseminations so the sperm can build up—generally, fun things to discuss with a friend. It was helpful to share a book chapter on issues and logistics on using a known donor for at-home inseminations because it laid the groundwork for a lot of this conversation.

We did at-home inseminations with freshly donated sperm, where my husband got to "get me pregnant." And then we got pregnant and had a wonderful baby. After a year or so, we decided we wanted to have another child. I assumed we would use Chris again, but my husband suggested we use Chris's husband, David. My first reaction was, "No way." I thought it was important for our kids to be related and I was worried about what would happen if Chris and David broke up, and one of our kids ended up having a relationship with his donor and the other didn't. But my husband pushed a little, arguing that he thought it would be a great way to bring us all together, that David's heritage was actually closer to his own, and that he had really grown to like and respect David, too, and in the end, it just felt right.

It is a hard and highly emotional process, but I think struggling through it has made us all closer. We continue to learn to be more honest and respect other people's boundaries. It's like being in a polyamorous relationship, without the sex. There were both painful and uncomfortable moments, but honesty and listening got us through it, and in the end, I expect we will have a lifetime of conversations. But I am so deeply in love with how we created this family and wouldn't have it any other way.

LGBTQ-Friendly Cryobanks

Early in the development of cryobanks, many exclusively worked with heterosexual couples and would not treat single women or LGBTQ families. Since then, a number of cryobanks have begun to have much more open policies and some even cater to or recruit LGBTQ people as donors or recipients. Some cryobanks known to work with LGBTQ clients are Biogenics Corporation, California Cryobank, Cryobiology, Cryogenic Laboratories, Cryos New York, European Sperm Bank USA, Fairfax Cryobank, Idant Laboratories, Pacific Reproductive Services, Manhattan Cryobank, Rainbow Flag Health Services and Sperm Bank, Reprolab, Sperm Bank of California, Xytex Corporation, and Zygen Laboratory.

Harvesting Genetic Material

Harvesting genetic material such as sperm or eggs is the process by which it is taken out of the body. It may then be stored for later use. Harvesting sperm is generally a simple, nonintrusive process. It usually involves having a blood (and/or urine) test to identify any potential health problems that could affect the viability of the samples, and collecting ejaculate in a sterile container at a provider's office or sperm bank.

Harvesting eggs, on the other hand, is a complicated, costly, and physician-assisted process. As with harvesting sperm, the first step is often a set of lab tests. Additional initial steps include a pelvic exam, an ultrasound, and sometimes mandatory counseling. Once the decision is made to proceed, the next step is daily injections of hormones that stimulate the ovaries to increase the number of eggs available for harvest. For a few weeks, your provider will likely want you to come in for daily or every-other-day visits in order to monitor the effects of the hormones with blood work and ultrasounds. After several weeks of treatment, an appointment is scheduled for the actual collection of the eggs. The retrieval process usually takes about a half hour. You are put under sedation and the provider uses a long needle to remove eggs from the ovaries via the vagina. You will then want to go home to rest for the day. This entire process can cost anywhere from $5,000 to $15,000 per ovulation cycle and harvest.

Storing Genetic Material

Cryogenic banks may be found online, and they generally have storage rates that vary depending on the length of the storage contract. The cost of storage is comparable, regardless of whether we are storing eggs, sperm, or embryos (combinations of eggs and sperm). Depending on the facility, price and commitment range from about $100 per month with no commitment to $1,500 flat fee for a five-year commitment. Important to note is that most health providers encourage the storage of embryos, rather than eggs alone, because embryos are more likely to be successfully implanted this way. This may mean considering where sperm will come from long before the embryo is actually implanted.

Purchasing Genetic Material or Using a Donor

When one or more partner is unable to contribute genetic material to initiate a pregnancy, we may consider using donated sperm or eggs. These contributions can come from a friend or relative, can be arranged online through a donor matching service, or purchased from any of a number of cryogenic banks. The majority of these banks have catalogs to browse or search during the process of finding a donor that matches criteria we feel strongly about. Some facilities even provide a photo-matching service that allows us to choose donors whose features resemble our own. Some of these facilities will ship genetic material only to a provider's office. Others will ship sperm directly to a person's home. Many facilities also provide the option to specifically select between donors who wish to remain anonymous and those who are willing to be known. Typically, donors who are willing to be known can be contacted by a child when the child reaches the age of 18.

Even if a facility will ship sperm to an individual's home, they may require a letter from a provider in order to confirm our ability to purchase frozen sperm. Prices per specimen vary from bank to bank, and they can range anywhere from $350 to $700, plus shipping costs, and the cost of renting the cryogenic tank during the time it is away from the facility.

Because the act of harvesting eggs is more involved, the costs associated with using donated eggs are much higher, ranging anywhere from $7,000 to $20,000, for five or six eggs. Even if we choose to use the eggs of a friend or relative, the costs associated with harvesting them ($5,000–$15,000) should still be expected.

MY BROTHER AND I

Caleb Wolfson-Seeley is a graduate of Wellesley College and lives in Kensington, California with his wife and son.

My brother and I were never very close. More than two years his junior, I spent my childhood looking up to him, vying for his affection, and watching him slip into the angst of adolescence far earlier than I would. He didn't finish college and traveled the country doing odd jobs; I graduated from a top liberal arts college, got married, worked an office job, and saved for retirement. I love him, but sometimes I don't understand him, and I doubt he understands me. So when, after long conversations about how to start a family, my wife raised the possibility that my brother could be our sperm donor, my immediate reaction was negative. I told her it wasn't an option, and we resumed looking though databases at various spermbanks. But once mentioned, the thought wouldn't leave. It festered, invading my brain like a parasite. He became the ideal against which all other donors would be judged. The perfect donor had to be Jewish. He had to be shorter than 6 feet, have dark features, and be open to contact with our child. Why were we settling when we had what we were looking for right in front of us?

The call to ask my brother if he would father my child was a lot easier than I thought it would be. I built it up in my head, nearly making myself sick, but when the words flew out of my mouth, he just listened, paused, and said yes. This man I had never understood and to whom I was only connected because we were related had just agreed to give me the most precious gift one could give without a second thought. It was humbling, and it created a bond that had never been there through blood alone.

When two people create a child through procreation, they have the option to be insular, to not invite anyone else into their family unit. They are creating the illusion of control. By being forced to open our definition of a family, my wife and I are able to be honest about what it truly takes to raise a child. We, in the most physical of definitions, cannot do it alone. We are not threatened by outside forces having influence on our child; in fact, we welcome them in with open arms. Expanding my family to include my brother was natural, and it means that not only will my son gain a father, but I have gained a stronger relationship with my sibling.

PREGNANCY

For those of us interested in pregnancy, we face a number of choices and challenges that are unique to us as trans individuals. We may wonder whether we will be able to find a provider who is respectful of our situation, or how we will preserve our sense of self as a masculine person in such a feminine area as pregnancy.

If we want to carry a pregnancy, and natural conception is not an option, there are processes available to help initiate a pregnancy through the use of artificial insemination (AI) or in vitro fertilization (IVF), each of which involves different combinations of biological contributors, and level of health provider involvement.

Regardless of the method of artificial insemination used, the chances of success are greatly increased with ovulation predictor kits (available in drug stores) or careful monitoring of the menstrual cycle, body temperature, and cervical mucus. Beginning to track such data several cycles before attempting insemination will greatly aid in accurately predicting when to attempt insemination. Talking with a specialized health provider such as an obstetrician/gynecologist (OB/GYN) can help to clarify any questions that arise about the proper way to measure data and how the collected information can be useful in increasing the chances of a successful insemination.

Artificial Insemination

Artificial insemination techniques include the following:

- Intrauterine insemination (IUI), where sperm is introduced into the uterus by a health care professional.
- Intracervical insemination (ICI), where sperm is introduced into the cervix by a health care professional.
- Vaginal insemination, a less precise (and less reliably successful) technique, which is able to be performed outside of a provider's office (i.e., in your home) as it requires that sperm be introduced into the vagina, just outside of the cervix (colloquially called the "turkey baster" technique).

In any of these circumstances, the egg comes from the person carrying the pregnancy. The sperm, on the other hand, may come from a partner or from an anonymous or known donor.

In Vitro Fertilization

Another potential option for help with initiating a pregnancy is IVF. In IVF, the sperm and egg are introduced to one another in a laboratory setting, then transferred directly into the uterus as an embryo by a health care professional, or stored in a cryogenic bank for later use. The egg and sperm may come from the intended parents or from anonymous or known donors.

While IVF is considerably more expensive than AI techniques, it is a highly effective procedure that sometimes results in a pregnancy of multiples (twins, triplets, and sometimes even more) because more than one embryo is often inserted in order to ensure that one develops into a human being. Each person decides with their physician how many embryos to place into the uterus, depending on age and medical situation (both of which can affect the likelihood of an embryo developing into a fetus).

Carrying a Pregnancy

For those of us able to carry a child, do we want to? Along with all of the questions this might raise for a cisgender woman, we are likely to face questions that are unique to being trans. We may wonder whether we will be able to remain emotionally healthy through a year of intense female hormonal fluctuations or whether we will be able to handle the physical act of labor and delivery, something that could be argued to be the most female experience possible. Some of us can. Some of us do and say, "Never again," regardless of the immeasurable depth of love that we feel for our children.

> *"I gave birth to my daughter. It was. . . horrible. I never ever want to do that again! Thankfully, I will never ever have to as I no longer possess the necessary parts. . ."*

"I gave birth to both my sons. Despite identifying as male, biology doesn't change the fact that I am capable of giving birth and it was the only financially feasible way to have children since military medicine does not cover any kind of alternative parenting options like adoption or surrogacy. I did not start transitioning until recently, holding off until I was sure I didn't want any more children. Both pregnancies were extremely hard on me both physically and emotionally and my husband and I made the decision that two was more than enough for our time and resources."

For those of us who choose to carry our own child, we may be faced with challenging and potentially discriminatory situations. Wherever possible we should consider using an OB/GYN or midwife who specializes in queer or trans health. Having a health care provider who is an advocate can help us to navigate the biases associated with being a pregnant person who is not female identified. We may also wish to join a support group to help us handle the emotions associated with being trans and pregnant. While these support groups are limited, our local queer centers may be of assistance in finding a group or perhaps even starting one for us.

Surrogacy

When carrying a pregnancy is not possible, there are still ways for us to plan our families from the moment of conception. Either IUI or IVF can be used in a surrogacy—some carriers have a pregnancy conceived with their own eggs (often called surrogate carriers), and others have a pregnancy conceived with someone else's eggs (often called gestational carriers).

Choosing a carrier is a highly personal process. Sometimes a close friend or relative is willing to carry a pregnancy, while other times parents meet a prospective carrier through a Web site or agency and build a relationship with them before initiating pregnancy.

The Birthing Process

Unfortunately, the medical community is not always educated or equipped to handle patients who are, or express themselves as, outside of gendered expectations. Birthing rooms, for example, are often set up in light pastel colors and pink flowered gowns are often given to the birthing parent. Whether we are supporting our partner, giving birth ourselves, or intend to be present when our surrogate or gestational carrier goes into labor, we need to be prepared for the possibility that hospital staff may be ignorant, or even discriminatory, regardless of how supportive our obstetrician, midwife, or doula may be. Our chosen provider will likely not be present for 100% of the labor, prior to actual delivery.

The birthing process is a highly stressful time for everyone involved. In order to serve our best interests, we need to advocate for our needs well in advance of the big day. There are a few ways to plan for complications before they come up:

Many hospitals have patient advocacy departments. These departments are set up to advocate for their patients' best interests. By contacting this department in advance, we can be assured that the medical personnel in the birthing unit are aware of our pronoun and name preferences, as well as how we would like to be addressed throughout the hospital stay. The patient advocacy department can also assist with room placement for postbirthing recovery. Many of us prefer a private room so that we can recover in a comfortable environment away from other, potentially transphobic, new parents. Whatever the case, be sure to discuss this with patient advocacy or your health provider before labor begins.

Consider what you or your partner will want to wear during the delivery and after the baby is born. Most hospitals will allow the birthing parent to wear their own clothing (unless they need surgery), so discuss this in advance

Decide who will hold the baby when the baby is first born. Traditionally the baby is given to the birthing parent for an immediate bond. We need to discuss and advocate for our preferences with our health provider, patient advocacy, and the nursing staff.

Transparent is a 2006 documentary by Jules Rosscam that follows the lives of 19 trans men in 14 different states who gave birth to their children.

Decide whether the birthing (or nonbirthing) parent or carrier will breastfeed, or whether the baby will be bottle fed. We need to be prepared to advocate for our position before the baby is born so that we do not feel pressured by the medical staff to conform to their expectations. We should discuss our desires with our health care provider before labor begins and with the nursing staff early in the labor process.

Traditionally, the birthing parent is listed as the mother on the birth certificate. In most states, the parent who gives birth is automatically categorized as the mother regardless of that person's identification. Some states do have the choice of a parent/parent designation rather than the traditional mother/father designation. While this option is largely in response to same-sex couples wanting an accurate birth certificate for their children, trans parents may wish to use this as well. Unfortunately, this is only available in a few states at this time.

If the child was conceived using vaginal insemination in an at-home situation (in other words, without the involvement of a member of the medical community), discuss and decide ahead of time what information will be disclosed to whom and when. The nurse attending the delivery does not need to know this information, any more than they would need to know it if you and your partner were a cisgender heterosexual couple, for example. You might even decide not to disclose this information to your OB/GYN—this might be possible in the case of a couple whose gender presentation is perceived as fitting the male/female binary.

Protecting the Rights of Transgender Parents and Their Children: A Guide for Parents and Lawyers (2013) is available online for free download. It was produced by the American Civil Liberties Union (ACLU) and the National Center for Transgender Equality (NCTE).

Postnatal Considerations

As trans parents, we face many of the usual considerations about what will happen once a baby is born, such as where the baby will sleep, who will be the primary caregiver, and what supports are in place for us as new parents. However, we also find ourselves needing to consider things that might not be quite as complicated for non-trans parents.

BREASTFEEDING

Deciding whether to nurse a new infant is a highly personal decision under any circumstance. Trans parents deciding whether to nurse an infant face another level of questions, not generally applicable to cis parents. If a trans man is physically able to nurse his child, will this affect his sense of gender? If a trans woman is able to nurse her child, something that is possible for some trans women, is she prepared to defend her decision to friends and relatives?

Bonded (Takeya Trayer).

Sometimes we may want to nurse our child but are unable to produce the milk needed to meet our infant's needs in either the short or long term. Devices called lactation aids, or supplemental nursing systems, have been designed to help parents who are unable to produce enough milk or who need to artificially induce lactation (if they were not the person that carried the pregnancy, for example, but want their body to be able to produce milk). These devices allow a parent to nurse their child on their chest using formula and a length of flexible narrow tubing that ends on the chest where the baby can nurse. Supplemental nursing systems can be researched and purchased online. Your provider may also be able to help you to learn about the best nursing systems.

BEING A FATHER MADE ME MORE OF A MAN

Mitch D. is lucky to have a wonderful wife, two exceptional children, and a ragtag global assortment of loving and supportive chosen family—none of which he thought was possible for a very long time.

It's strange to put it that way, but I learned more about the man I wanted to be when I became a father. I don't know too many trans guys who have incredibly close, nurturing, and supportive relationships with their fathers. I had already reconciled myself to the fact that my dad was not going to be my role model for "how to be a man." He didn't want the responsibility and walked out when I was five. We saw him regularly, but he was on drugs and never paid child support. After several ups and downs we grew to have a decent adult relationship. When I came out and transitioned, he didn't really get it, but we were open and talked about it and things seemed to settle down for a while.

I called to tell him my wife was pregnant with our son. His response was to say, "I think I'm out of coffee." Then he wrote a very long e-mail about my transition, and how it was bad for my body and he worried about me, and how he didn't understand what his relationship to my child would be since they won't really be related. I told my dad that if he didn't treat my child with the same regard as my nephew, he didn't need a relationship with my family. Every single thing he did wrong as a father flashed before my eyes. I was very angry; every memory was a fresh stab wound with laser accuracy into my heart. That led me to question my own fitness for fatherhood. How could I be a father if the only healthy models I had were fictional characters? What *does* it mean to be a father?

But everything changed when my son was born. I need to work hard and provide him with a bountiful upbringing. I need to make sure he is safe crossing the street. I need to keep him away from scary people. It dawned on me. Being paternal can be good. Honest. Strong. And nurturing and sweet and tender. This is the kind of father and the kind of man that I want to be. It is important to me that my son grows up to be a caring and emotionally available man, so I will model what was not afforded me.

BEING A TRANS PARENT

Regardless of whether we become parents before or after we recognize our trans identity, who we are will have an impact on our children's lives in one way or another. If we bring children into our lives after establishing ourselves as who we are, we will need to evaluate if or when to have a conversation with them about what it means to be trans. The idea that our life was ever any different may be confusing, especially for particularly young children. Waiting until our children are older (in their teens, for example) may be appropriate in some families, but in others it may leave them feeling as though they have been lied to.

> *"Let your children come to terms with it, let them define how they want to relate to you. Be honest, be kind, and remember not to ask them to lie or try to buy into some contrived story to hide your history, it is their history too."*

The decision about when to talk with our children about our trans identity is highly personal. There is no single right answer about when is the right time or how old children need to be before they are able to understand what exactly it is that we are talking about. There is no way to predict how a preteen, teen, or even an adult child will react to learning that a parent is trans. Our children may react to the news the very same way that anyone else we come out to might react—with support, with confusion, with anger, with fear, or even with respectful matter-of-fact-ness. It is not uncommon for children of trans parents to go through a period of mourning for the parent's identity they may feel they are losing.

Books for Children About Trans Parents
Carly: She's Still My Daddy (2004) by Mary Boenke is a story from a child's point of view about his father's transition from Carl to Carly. It also introduces the reader to other trans people.

The Little Boy (2008) by E. Kelly and E. Webster is about a trans man's childhood, transition, and adult life as a married person with his own children. It is written to children, and it includes photographs of the main character as a little girl and talks about him going to a doctor to learn about transgender identity.

My Mommy Is a Boy (2008) by Jason Martinez is a short story about a little girl who is explaining to the reader why her trans male mommy looks like a boy.

My New Daddy and *My New Mommy* (2013) by Lilly Mossiano are two children's books which follow young children through their parents' transition process.

No Dumb Questions is a 2001 documentary by Melissa Regan that follows three sisters ages 6, 9, and 11, who are learning about their uncle's transition to female.

After we come out to our children, they will likely go through their own period of transition. This process can take months, years, or even a lifetime, although the general consensus is that the younger a child is when we come out, the less rigid the child will be with regard to their expectations about gender. Preschool children often have an easier time with the process than teenagers because their expectations of gender are not as rigid.

Some older children may decide that they are most comfortable not discussing their parents with their peers and find a way to navigate their way out of such conversations. Others feel the need to pretend that nothing has changed. Still others might find creative ways to tell half-truths, and only reveal the true nature of their trans family to chosen people they feel they can trust. When possible, it can be helpful to discuss our children's thought processes with them and to understand that we may need to let our children decide if and when they want to "come out" as the child of a person who is trans.

Regardless of the age of our children at the time of our transition, we need to offer them patience, understanding, and our unconditional love. Listen to them and make sure they feel they are being heard. Be open and honest with them and do not hide any important details from them. Hiding information can lead to mistrust and hurt feelings.

The Gervasi Family (photo by Jes Deis).

REFLECTIONS OF YEAR TWO

Dan Connor, PsyD, is a clinical psychologist.

I knew that I needed to become a parent. I didn't know what kind of dad I would be, just as I didn't know what kind of man I would be. After my experiences with femininity, which meant entrapment in a gender norm that negated my power, I had models of the don'ts of masculinity. When I heard that our first child would be male, I felt an even greater anxiety that perhaps I would not be able to teach him the ins and outs of manhood. My friends insisted he would have no greater a teacher than his father.

Currently, I have one toddler whom I parent with my female partner of 11 years. There are days when we both forget that we are queer-identified parents because we are so lost in our day-to-day life. I highlight this because I am convinced that my child's lived experience is that I am his dad, not a transgender parent. I limit his shenanigans, give great hugs, and am usually game for a quick wrestle. I don't believe that I am a stronger or weaker parent because I am trans*. I think I am a more informed parent because I am familiar with trans* narratives. On harder days, when I am all caught up in the gripping shame of not being enough, I ask myself what one thing my child needs to thrive. I relax again when I remember it has nothing to do with my body, and everything to do with my heart.

I live in a culture that presupposes my child and I are biologically linked. The foundation of this assumption lives within ableism, which is the compulsory belief that my body functions in absolute congruence with societal expectation. On account of being a white, educated person, I have access to privileges that could enhance the likeability of our family. In other political movements, such as the fight for gay marriage, our white faces are marketed as a redemptive code for normalcy. I believe this leads to disintegration of our diverse community and suggests a myopic view of family formation.

My family relies on intention, commitment, and creativity just to grow. One result is that my kid is much less likely to wonder if he was truly wanted in this world. It turned out that I need not carry around internalized transphobia which suggests I wouldn't have lessons to teach my son. And while I am saddened that I must teach my children to survive in a world that can be so unloving and so unkind, I am also tasked with the pleasure of teaching resiliency, compassion, and self-actualization. These too are trans* narratives, and they are just as important to witness and to honor.

Before we talk with our children, we should attempt to understand our own process as fully as possible so that we can properly share it with them and answer any questions they may have. We can prepare ourselves for talking with our children by considering the following questions:

- Am I changing my name? If so, how does that impact the name I want my children to call me?
- Will there be a physical transition—hormones or surgery?
- What should my children tell their friends, their friends' parents, and their teachers?
- What will I tell my children if they ask whether my personality will change?
- Will I still be their mother/father?

We should be sure to be as transparent as possible with our children and offer them age-appropriate support and understanding. Do not be afraid to mourn with them—they may be scared that they are losing us. Help them to understand that we are not going anywhere, that we are simply becoming more of who we are supposed to be, and that we will be happier and healthier as a result.

When divorce is a factor, the matter becomes even more complicated. We may find ourselves at the mercy of our child's other parent for everything from our ability to remain in contact with our child to the level of acceptance our child is able to express for our trans identity. Children can be highly susceptible to influence, and parents are high on the list of influential people in their lives. Unfortunately, this means that it is very possible for an unsupportive ex-partner to influence our child in a way that does not allow for a positive parent–child transition experience.

MEDIA SPOTLIGHT: TRANS LEGAL ISSUES IN THE MEDIA

Dallas Denny and Jamison Green

When trans people have legal problems, sometimes our personal matters end up being the subject of news reports simply because we are trans. Headlines like "Texas Judge Voids Transgender Widow's Marriage" (Fox News, May 2011) are often splattered all over various media sources, making the issue more about a person's trans status than about the problem they're facing or the crime that was committed.

The most intense continuous media exposure of a transgender legal case was Court TV's 2002 coverage of Michael Kantaras's Florida divorce and child custody case, which went through 3 weeks of 24-hour national coverage of the courtroom testimony. Michael had filed for divorce from Linda, his wife of 9 years, and sought joint custody of their two children, then ages 10 and 12 years. Six months into the divorce proceedings, Linda decided to announce that Michael was "a woman," completely surprising both attorneys and the judge. Suddenly, the case became less about the divorce and more about whether Michael, as a transsexual, was considered a man for the purpose of marriage. If he was instead "a woman" as Linda claimed, there couldn't be a marriage, and there couldn't be a divorce.

On the witness stand, on national television, Michael was asked how he urinated, how big his penis was, how he was able to have sex. He answered carefully and gracefully. Medical expert witnesses described the process of sex reassignment, various surgical procedures, and aspects of mental health. Michael's parents described his childhood and how they dealt with his transition. Friends of Michael's and Linda's testified that they had no idea that he was transsexual, and some stated they never wanted anything to do with either of them now that they knew his history.

Michael won the decision, issued a year later (in February 2003), but Linda won a 2004 appeal, when judges ruled that the trial court did not have the authority to declare Michael a male, saying it was a matter for the state legislature to determine. The Florida Supreme Court declined to hear Michael's appeal, but in 2005 a joint-custody settlement was brokered by television therapist Dr. Phil. Michael had very limited contact with his children until they were both over 18, when their mother couldn't control their lives so much, and they both sought to repair their relationships with him.

What Should Our Children Call Us?

The names children call their parents are generally very gendered. Sometimes these work—we may want to be called "dad" if we identify as male. But what if what our children should call us does not seem quite so black and white? For some trans parents, finding a term that works can be stressful.

Maybe our gender presentation does not quite match our gender identity, causing concern about what other people outside our family will think if our children use certain language when referring to us. Perhaps our child has another parent who has already laid claim to our preferred term. Sometimes our children are used to calling us something that does not feel comfortable anymore. We may find ourselves struggling internally to define our parental relationship with our child, as could be the case if we genetically contribute to a pregnancy in a way that does not reflect the traditional contribution of our gender identity. Whatever the challenge, sometimes it might seem like there is no easy answer. The truth is, often there is not. There is no one-size-fits-all solution because every family and every situation is different.

"I have a four year old daughter, so she is still pretty young and catches on quickly. My ex-wife handled explaining things to her. She asked what my daughter should call me, and I had to come up with something. I did not want to be called daddy, and mommy was taken. I remember reading how it was handled in the

Online Resources for Trans Parents

COLAGE (Children of Lesbians and Gays Everywhere): Hosts a Web site with great resources for LGBTQ parents, in-person events for parents and their children, and a Kids of Trans Program designed to assist kids in meeting other kids who have trans parents so that they do not feel alone. Also offers a *Transition Tips for Trans Parents* guide.

TransParentcy: Supports transgender parents and their advocates (including lawyers and mental health professionals) by providing information and resources to dispel the myths about any adverse impact being transgender might have on our children.

Yahoo Groups: Transsexual Parenting Group (TSParenting) and Genderqueer and Transgender Parenting Group (GQTGParenting).

The Talk (Tikva Adler, KimchiCuddles.com).

book 'She's Not There.' I like the use in her story of combining the two, so I settled on my daughter calling me maddy. When interacting with my daughter, I do my best to be myself, and show her that I love her always. I have not changed my parenting style. The only thing that has changed is my looks. I think that every situation is different, and would not know how to advise other trans parents."

Alternative parental pronouns that have been used in trans families include Maddy, Mada, Mapa, and Pama, as well as the more traditional labels of Mom, Mommy, Mama, Ma, and Dad, Daddy, Papa, and Pa. Some children refer to their parents by their first name, while others find a name that comes naturally as a child learns to speak, such as "Bo" or "Dee." Whatever feels the most comfortable to both us and our children is really all that matters.

GENDER-DIVERSE PARENTING

Arwyn Daemyir is a writer and massage therapist parenting with gender diversity in Portland, Oregon.

When it comes to parenting and gender, it can seem like there are very limited options. Pink princesses and blue puppy dogs or yellow onesies for all, excising any hint of gender? Or, a favorite among queer parents, full-out rainbows and gender-f*cking?

There can be another way. Start with this: What if, instead of believing our children come into this world needing to be shaped and molded, we accepted they come to us fully and perfectly themselves—needing only our help to figure out who they are and how to live in the world? What if, instead of believing we knew best, we started out admitting our ignorance? What if, instead of making trans* and gender creative kids come to us and tell us that they're not who we assumed they would be, we traveled with them, watching and waiting for their true selves to grow? It's possible, and it's called gender-diverse parenting. Here's how you can do it:

Assign gender provisionally. Rather than saying we know who's a boy and who's a girl based on genitals at birth, play the odds and make a guess—but let the kid and family know it's just a guess! Instead of "you're a girl," let your baby know that their identity is *theirs*, and you're waiting to hear directly from the source.

Show them a full spectrum of gender. In order for our children to figure out who they are, of course they need to know who it's possible to be—so show them. Introduce them to a wide array of gender possibilities, men and women and genderqueers and neutrois, femme and butch and manly and mixing, transgender and transsexual and cisgender and gender outlaws, flamboyant and calm, out and stealth, loving and strong. If your social circles aren't as diverse as you'd like, make sure your playtime characters, your books, and media attempt to represent a rainbow of gender.

Fill their gender tool box with as much diversity as possible. Rather than trying to eliminate all gender cues from your child's wardrobe, or keeping anything that aligns with stereotypes out of the toy box, put it *all* in.

Play with gender and encourage your children to play with gender. Play is the primary way kids come to know the world around them, so not letting them play with gender is doing them a significant disservice.

Accept them—whoever they are. It's easy enough to accept our children when they grow up to be like our image of them, whether we've always wanted a cis-heteronormative little dude to play baseball with, or a pansexual genderqueer to take over the anarchist family movement. But it's always the breaking of expectations that risks breaking our relationships, and too often breaks families apart—so let go of gendered expectations altogether.

To Disclose or Not: Providers, Schools, and Friends

In a perfect world, we would not have to disclose our trans status unless we wanted to. Unfortunately, when raising children, it can sometimes be difficult to control the information that becomes public. Kids say the darndest things, and they may "out" us unintentionally. It can certainly feel awkward when a child says something like "This is my dad, I was in his belly!" Either you come out then and there, or you let the other person think your child is extremely imaginative.

When determining whether to disclose to the outside world, we take into consideration not only our own needs but those of our families as well. When disclosing to the

Lorelei and Lee.

Our Children Talk About Us
Even Benestad, a Norwegian
filmmaker, produced the 2002
documentary *All About My
Father.*

Paul Hill, whose father is a
transgender woman, created
the 2001 documentary *Myth of
Father.*

Noelle Howey wrote
the 2003 memoir *Dress
Codes: Of Three Girlhoods—
My Mother's, My Father's,
and Mine.*

school system, for example, we may worry that we will create a situation where our child is mistreated. While there is no way to guarantee our or our children's emotional and physical safety, we can take certain steps regarding disclosure to minimize the negative impact.

We should talk with our children about their feelings surrounding our trans status and whether they wish to disclose to the school or to their friends. Younger children may not understand reasons that they should not disclose. They may need to have coaching around appropriate disclosure and when it is not appropriate (for example, if a situation is potentially unsafe, it might be better to keep the information private).

When situations arise where we cannot opt out of disclosure (having to provide a birth certificate to enroll our child in school, for example), we may need to become an educator, explaining why our child calls us "Bo" and requesting that the system honors and supports our child.

We should remember that our trans status impacts our family regardless of when we transitioned. While we can certainly request that they respect our privacy, we should also respect their process. For example, our partner may understand that we would rather not disclose our status publically, but they may need to discuss our trans status with their close friends. We should trust that our family will respect our needs, and we should honor their needs as well.

In some situations we may find that despite our best efforts to educate others, our disclosure creates unnecessary mistreatment for ourselves or our families. If this happens, there are services available to assist us. See Chapter 10 for more information and resources.

CONCLUSION

Even in the simplest of circumstances, being a parent is a difficult, complicated, and thoroughly exhausting job that continues long after our children have become adults and have children of their own. Couple this already tricky endeavor with possessing a marginal, not well-understood identity, and things can become even more challenging. However, there is no reason to deny ourselves the opportunity to become parents, if doing so is something we wish to experience. Through the scientific advancements of cryogenic preservation, artificial insemination, and in-vitro fertilization, we have reproductive opportunities available to us that simply did not exist for trans people, even in the recent past. In addition, while there are still barriers for us with regard to adoption, it is possible to find resources online or through our local queer community centers that can help connect us with a child desperately searching for a home as loving as our own. It need not be blood that defines our family.

Through talking with our children openly about gender, gender roles, and gender expression, we are empowering them with the tools they will need to navigate challenging conversations with peers about their trans family. This can only work to strengthen the bond between us and our children. We should take care to surround ourselves with friends, supporters, and allies—people we can rely on—and we should encourage our children to do the same.

REFERENCES AND FURTHER READING

Carpenter, L. R. (2011, Summer). We are not all women. *Squat Birth Journal*, 31–32. Retrieved January 2014, from http://www.magcloud.com/browse/issue/206528

Howey, N., & Samuels, E. (2000). *Out of the ordinary: Essays on growing up with gay, lesbian, and transgender parents*. New York, NY: St. Martin's Press.

Perez, M. Z. (2012). The radical doula guide. *Radical Doula*. Retrieved January 2014, from http://radicaldoula.com/the-radical-doula-guide/

Trevor. (2013, May 9). Trans women and breastfeeding: A personal interview. *Milk Junkies*. Retrieved January 2014, from http://www.milkjunkies.net/2013/05/trans-women-and-breastfeeding-personal.html

SECTION 5
LIFE STAGES

CHILDREN

Aidan Key

19

AS ADULTS WHO CARE FOR GENDER NONCONFORMING CHILDREN, we have enormous power to make a positive impact that will affect their lives and health. Children who are supported in exploring their gender identities from a young age learn to embrace their whole selves and develop skills to maintain self-esteem throughout their lives. It takes a village to raise a gender nonconforming child. As biological or foster parents, or other guardians of children, we can feel isolated and alone, unsure of how to approach certain topics or where to connect with others who are having similar experiences. As teachers, counselors, or other providers, we may be interested in learning more about the ways we can be helpful to children and their families. There is no right answer for every situation. Gender nonconforming children—like all children—are unique, and their needs are different. The most important task we have is to make all children feel loved and accepted for their whole selves.

TERMINOLOGY

There are many ways to talk about children whose gender identities and behaviors fall outside of societal norms. **Gender nonconforming (GNC)** is a broad term that can be used to describe children with varied interests and presentations. Some people prefer the term **gender variant (GV)**, while others feel that the word *variant* implies that something is wrong with the child. There are those who use the terms *gender creative, gender diverse*, or *gender fluid* because they have positive connotations related to children being original and imaginative.

Transgender is a word many adults use to describe themselves, and this term is sometimes applied to children as well. For adults, it is often used as an encompassing term to describe many forms of gender-diverse expressions and identities. However, many professionals and families use the term *transgender* to denote a child with a clear cross-gender identification (i.e., a child assigned male at birth who strongly and consistently identifies as female). For the sake of this chapter, we will primarily use the term *transgender* to describe those children with a solid cross-gender identity and the term *gender nonconforming* to describe those with more fluid or creative identities or means of expression.

Some families and youth programs refer to those who are assigned female at birth but identify as male as **trans boys,** and those who are assigned male at birth but identify as female as **trans girls**. Many youth centers and providers use the phrase **transgender/gender nonconforming (TGNC)** as an umbrella term to refer to groups of children and youth who fall into these categories.

RECOGNIZING TRANSGENDER AND GENDER NONCONFORMING CHILDREN

Many parents have an idea early on that their child is transgender or gender nonconforming based on the child's toy and clothes preferences, playmates, or specific statements. For others, it can be a shock to hear a child say something that indicates they do not necessarily see themselves as the gender they were assigned at birth.

There is no checklist to determine a child's gender identity. We can only do our best to put together available clues and to listen to children as closely as possible. Some

As adult trans people, many of us were gender nonconforming children growing up. This chapter provides tools and resources for those of us, including non-trans people raising gender nonconforming children, who are caring for the next generation.

It is often difficult to draw a line between children and youth. Puberty begins at vastly different times for different people. Cultural shifts occur in middle and high school to transform us from completely dependent to much more self-reliant. For the purposes of this book, this chapter is directed to adults caring for children up to approximately 12 years old, and the next chapter speaks to youth approximately 12 years old and up.

gender-diverse children make statements about their gender early on, many as soon as they learn to speak. They may say things like:

- *I'm not a boy, I'm a girl.*
- *God made a mistake. I am supposed to be a girl.*
- *When is my penis going to grow in?*
- *Why do they keep calling me a girl? I'm a boy.*
- *I don't want to be a mother—I want to be a father!*

If a child has articulated statements like these *consistently and over a long period of time*, chances are that the child has a sense that their gender identity is different from the one dictated by their sex assigned at birth.

Some families have observed certain behaviors from their children who later identify as transgender adults:

- Expressing anger at a parent for "correcting" someone who perceives the child to be a gender other than the gender assigned at birth
- Allowing or encouraging other children to believe they are a different gender
- Announcing to parents, family, and friends that they have a new name that is typically associated with another gender
- Adopting the identity of an animal such as a dog, bear, or kitten in order to have a nongendered identity and experience

These behaviors are not sole indicators of a child's gender identity but, if observable over an extended period of time, could point to a transgender identity.

Many times, none of the aforementioned examples are evident. Some parents feel blindsided when, seemingly out of nowhere, their child announces that they are transgender and that they wish to change gender. It is not uncommon for a parent to say that there were no signs at all.

WHAT WERE THE SIGNS?

Educator/activist/poet Lee has written a chapbook about her journey of raising a queer child in a straight world, entitled, Sawing a Lady in Half.

Every mother knows. It was all there. If I was willing to see beyond my expectations and dreams. As a little girl, Ricky (not real name) always loved baseball caps and uniforms. On Halloween he always picked the Fireman, Gorilla, or Bullwinkle costume. Never the make-up, lipstick, and press-on-nails. I missed playing dress-up in those girly ways.

In second grade, the teacher asked the class to present a person from history, in costume, and the class would guess: "Who Am I?" All the girls picked famous women such as Rosa Parks, Abigail Adams, and Marie Curie. Ricky dressed as Houdini complete with top hat and white gloves. I felt this flair for male attire was telling me my child was different. He was always comfortable in loose pants and sneakers and I got used to shopping in the boy's department.

As I write, I notice I keep writing *she* and then back spacing to correct. It is still hard. When the 2000 Winter Olympics aired and the Men's Hockey players slid out on the ice, Ricky cheered, "That's what I want to do." Ricky mostly played with boys, suited up in full protective gear with face mask and stick. He still had his long, curly chestnut pony tail hanging out of the back of his helmet. Sitting in the chilly stands, that's how Ricky's dad and I knew our child from the rest of the guys.

At 15, with a girlfriend, he came out as gay and at 18 he realized his true identity was transmasculine or gender-queer. Is the journey over? I don't know, but as a mom, I'm still looking for signposts to lead the way to his heart.

NONBINARY GENDER IDENTITIES

Supporting a child in a transition from one gender to another can feel like a huge decision for most adults. Many go through intense personal conflict and soul searching, but most ultimately come to a place of support and advocacy. For many of us, when facing a problem, we would like very much to be presented with an identifiable solution. While initially hard to accept, a transition appears to be such a solution. A transition from one gender to another offers a parent, therapist, or teacher a step-by-step process to "completion"—a definitive end point. This can provide comfort during an unstable time.

It can be even more difficult to consider that there may not be a definitive endpoint. A child's gender may simply be a blend of genders or that child may experience a gender fluidity that changes from time to time, even day to day. It can be extremely distressing for a parent, teacher, or provider to see a variable gender expression in a child or to hear a child state that sometimes they are a boy, sometimes they are a girl, or "it just depends."

Some important points to consider include the following:

1. Kids do the best they can with the available vocabulary. It is important to understand that binary language such as boy/girl, masculine/feminine, and pink/blue offer children restrictive words with which it may be difficult to describe the full spectrum of their experience.
2. Some children have a gender identity that is a bit of both, neither, or one in which they experience varying degrees of fluidity.
3. Gender, like life, can be a journey, not just a destination.
4. Gender does not exist in isolation. Two questions any trans person faces are "Who am I?" and then "Who am I in relation to the world?" While children may not be able to articulate this for themselves, they are certainly exploring these questions and attempting to find their best fit.

When a trans or gender nonconforming child does not make a definitive statement such as "I am really a boy," or "I am really a girl," it is difficult for many of us to know what to do. In some cases, parents cling to this fluidity as an indicator that the child is not really transgender. In other cases, they may ignore the child's statements that they feel themselves to be a blend of genders, and actually press the child onward to a gender transition before they are ready or when this is not the child's desire. Both scenarios are ways to relieve the adult's discomfort with uncertainty.

Providing support for a child's gender identity and exploration is not the same as insisting on a specific path from point A to point B. Pay attention to the truth a child offers and meet them there—daily, if need be. Delineate between your own discomfort, confusion, and need for certainty and the child's need for support, encouragement, and authenticity. The latter will serve the child best in the long run.

IS THIS A PHASE?

One of the questions most commonly asked by parents, teachers, and therapists is whether gender nonconformity could be a phase. The simplest answer is yes. The only way to really determine whether a child's interests are short term is to allow the passage of time. Whether a child, who may or may not be transgender, is going through a phase is not really the point. A nonjudgmental and supportive response to the child's exploration is the critical component. Letting a child know that they are loved and accepted unconditionally should always be the first course of action.

Creating an environment of support will allow for healthy exploration. Supporting a child's interests is supporting the child regardless of the outcome. Allowing a child's musical interest through piano lessons will not necessarily make them a professional

Books for Parents

- *The Transgender Child: A Handbook for Families and Professionals* by Stephanie Brill and Rachel Pepper
- *Transitions of the Heart: Stories of Love, Struggle and Acceptance by Mothers of Transgender and Gender Variant Children* by Rachel Pepper
- *Gender Born, Gender Made: Raising Healthy Gender Non-Conforming Children* by Diane Ehrensaft, PhD
- *On the Couch With Dr. Angello: A Guide to Raising and Supporting Transgender Youth* by Michelle Angello
- *Far From the Tree: Parents, Children and the Search for Identity* by Andrew Solomon
- *Coming Around: Parenting Lesbian, Gay, Bisexual and Transgender Kids* by Anne Dohrenwend

Books for Professionals

Treating Transgender Children and Adolescents: An Interdisciplinary Discussion by Jack Drescher and William Byne

Gender Variant Children and Transgender Adolescents, An Issue of Child and Adolescent Psychiatric Clinics of North America by Richard R. Pleak, MD

pianist. A great percentage of children experiment with gender, but only a small percentage are transgender. Supporting a child's gender exploration will not "make" them transgender. Providing love and support simply shows the child that the things in which they have an interest are OK, normal, and part of healthy self-discovery.

PERSONAL ACCOUNT BY A PARENT OF A TRANS GIRL (AGE 10)

Anonymous

The first time I realized that something was different about my child was when at about the age of 2, I referred to him as a boy and he said that he was a girl. I assumed that since he was so young he was confused about his gender so I corrected him. He said adamantly "no" and told me again he was a girl. I then started to observe him more closely and saw that he liked to play with dolls, wanted long hair, and sat on the bathroom seat to urinate. Since I have training in the mental health field, I immediately suspected that my child might be transgender and began to read more about this.

My initial reaction included feeling scared, alarmed, and anxious. However, this subsided as I love my child and knew that I needed to support him. I decided that I would allow my child to be who he is and let him know that he is loved unconditionally. I spoke to close family members and disclosed my child's interests and let everyone know that I was okay with this and supporting my child. Things have not been easy for him, but he is aware of the support he has at home and this has helped him to explore his gender identity at his own pace.

Although he identifies as a girl to me, he has chosen at this time not to refer to himself as female. He has chosen a female name that he likes and I have offered to call him this in private, but he is not ready to do this yet. Part of his hesitation has to do with enduring bullying in school, but he is resilient and slowly making friends. My child is the kindest, most gentle person I know, and he inspires me to be a better person every day.

It takes a huge amount of courage, persistence, and confidence for a child to communicate their gender identification to the grown-ups around them. It is most likely that a child's sense of their gender will remain fixed regardless of how adults respond. However, children may revise their gender label based on responses from adults.

Gender nonconforming children may change the way they express their gender identities over time for various reasons:

1. A child may identify as another gender early in life because they have not had the freedom to explore and express their gender. If a child is provided greater latitude to step outside of restrictive gender expectations, they may find their gender assigned at birth is not limiting.
2. A child may recognize the distress of others and take self-sacrificing steps to decrease or eliminate that distress even at their own expense. If a child feels that their parent will not love them, or that their parents might divorce over the issue, they may be scared enough to minimize the importance of their own needs.
3. Some transgender children have experienced daily bullying and violence and can see no other way to make it stop except to "go back." Others find that they are isolated or rejected by their peers at school or within their neighborhood and understand that, if they compromise their own identity, they may regain some of that acceptance and inclusion they so deeply desire.
4. Children who feel themselves to be more fluid in their gender identity may find difficulty "landing" on a single gender. Our current options of either "male" or "female" may feel inadequate or limiting. If a parent or therapist does not recognize a child's gender-fluid identity and a child is restricted by only two options, that child may feel like they have no choice but to "settle" for one over the other, finding neither one to be a perfect fit.

WHAT DOES THIS MEAN FOR THE CHILD AS AN ADULT?

The first question on many parents' minds is whether a gender nonconforming child will grow up to identify as transgender. In some cases, adults also wonder whether the child will identify as gay, lesbian, or bisexual. Outdated research has indicated that, for most children, a cross-gender identification disappears over time. In this research, however, there is usually no distinction made between a child's gender identity (who they say they are) and gender expression (what they prefer to wear and toys they like to play with). In other words, the children in these studies may have been challenging gender norms but may never have identified outside of their assigned gender. In these cases, the children did not have anything to "grow out of."

Gender nonconforming children grow up to identify their sexual orientation as lesbian, gay, bisexual, heterosexual, queer, asexual and so on. If they do identify as transgender as adults, there are many ways in which they might understand their gender identity, including as trans men or trans women, or as genderqueer, identifying with neither gender or both genders.

As those caring for gender nonconforming children, we have a strong desire to know exactly how they will identify as adults. However, in many cases there are too many variables to accurately predict how children will later see themselves. The best we can do is to be respectful, loving, and nonjudgmental, creating safe environments for children to use their most truthful voices.

WHERE DOES GENDER IDENTITY COME FROM?

Many parents ask themselves, "Have I somehow caused this?" A father may wonder whether he spent enough time with his son, and whether this affected his son's identification as a girl. Some parents wonder whether factors in pregnancy led to their child's gender nonconformity. Others feel guilty that they wished for a boy during pregnancy and that somehow they transferred that desire to their daughter, who ultimately decided to become a boy. Some parents blame themselves for parenting styles they believe led to their child's gender nonconformity.

The search for an answer is natural, but it can also be quite damaging. It can cause rifts between parents and cause parents extreme amounts of guilt and shame. While we do have some basic theories about gender identity development (explored in Chapter 6), no developmental theory has shown conclusively that any particular genetic, hormonal, or social influences lead to gender nonconformity. Parenting style has not been linked to later transgender identity. As far as we know, there is nothing we can do to influence our children's gender identities or sexual orientations. We cannot change whether they will be LGBTQ, but we can change *how* they will be LGBTQ—whether they will be proud of themselves, take care of their health and well-being, and retain close connections with their families.

GENDER IDENTITY VERSUS SEXUALITY

It is critical to make the distinction that sexuality—or to whom one is attracted—is different from gender identity—one's innate sense of their gender. While some boys with a more feminine nature or girls who are more masculine may grow up to have same-sex attractions, a child's gender identity is not the same as their sexual orientation. The reality is often that peers and even adults interacting with children conflate concepts of gender and sexuality. Peers may ridicule children for being "gay," but their teasing is often based on gender expression.

The difference between gender identity and sexual orientation is important to think about in relation to children for a number of reasons. Assuming that a child is dealing only with an issue of sexuality when it is their gender they are exploring can result in an adult caretaker missing a chance to connect with the child and support them. The best stance is always to be open and affirming of any gender expression that children seem to be exploring.

Talking about gender with children is different than talking about sexuality. Conversations about gender are appropriate for children of all ages. For the most part, issues of sexuality can be saved for the beginning of adolescence, but there are many nonsexual ways to talk with children of all ages about attraction. We can talk with children about same-sex and different-sex couples, and explain that some men love other men or women love other women, laying the groundwork for healthy conceptions of both gender and sexuality.

Some adults working or living with gender nonconforming children are confused when a child discloses a gender identity and sexuality that do not seem to "match." For example, a young person assigned male at birth may announce an attraction to women and a gender identity as a woman. This child's caretakers may have assumed that no matter the child's gender identity, the child would arrive at a heterosexual orientation, when the truth is that transgender people can have any sexual orientation.

MEDIA SPOTLIGHT: CHILDREN'S BOOKS

Dallas Denny and Jamison Green

Nancy Silverrod of the San Francisco Public Library has compiled an annotated bibliography of children's books dealing with gender transgression in all its forms. She points to Munro Leaf's 1936 *Ferdinand the Bull* as perhaps the first book for children that shows a character refusing to conform to gender norms. Ferdinand is expected to participate in bullfights, but he prefers to smell flowers. Two other early children's books identified by Silverrod are Charlotte Zolotow's 1972 *William's Doll* and Tomie de Paola's 1979 *Oliver Button Is a Sissy*. In all three instances, the conflict is resolved normatively. Ferdinand becomes properly bull-like when he is stung by a bee;

William's grandmother tells his father he requires exposure to a doll so he can learn to be a good father; and Oliver's tap dancing is OK'ed because "his father reluctantly decides it is a 'form of exercise.'"

Silverrod contrasts the aforementioned books with Harvey Fierstein's 2002 celebratory *The Sissy Duckling*, which ends when Elmer the Sissy Duckling's father accepts him. Before Fierstein, Ron Pejril, in his 1989 *Fluff the Bunny*, used a nonhuman character to explore gender transgression. Fluff is attracted to both pink (for girls) and blue (for boys). Expected to be blue, and losing friends because he can't bring himself to be only blue, Fluff goes into his closet to wear pink things and listen to pink songs. He eventually blends pink and blue and comes to accept himself as purple.

In this century, a new category of young adult books has arisen in which the protagonists are transgendered or transsexual or just ungendered. As examples, Silverrod lists Anne Peters's 2004 *Luna*, Ellen Wittlinger's 2007 *Parrotfish*, and Carol Plum-Ucci's 2002 *What Happened to Lani Garver*. A growing number of books about and for children—some authored by parents with trans kids—celebrate trans children, calling for the rights of children to express their gender without interference. These include Marcus Ewart's 2008 *10,000 Dresses* and Cheryl Kilodavis's 2010 *My Princess Boy*.

Many young trans people have found inspiration in manga like Takahashi Rumiko's *Ranma ½*, in American comic books (Superman's pal Jimmy Olsen had a real penchant for dressing up!), and in the magazines and books of science fiction and fantasy. Prior to the 1990s, material was scarce and hard to find, but trans people have always been skilled at ferreting out information—and sometimes they come across something memorable quite by happenstance. At age 13 one of us (Denny) chanced upon L. Frank Baum's *The Marvelous Land of Oz* in the Pack Library in Asheville, North Carolina. In this 1904 book of children's fiction, the boy Tip turns out to be none other than an enchanted Princess Ozma of Oz.

HOW CHILDREN UNDERSTAND GENDER

The ways in which children understand the concept of gender are closely linked to their age and developmental level as well as their exposure to information. As children, teens, and then as adults, we have learned many things about the world, including our current framework of gender. To understand the world in the same ways we do, children must learn these same concepts. For example, we, as adults, see (for the most part) two genders in the world. We then equate the genders of male and female with particular body parts. We also understand that (without hormones or surgeries) our bodies will remain the same with respect to those body parts. We then know that people have certain expectations placed on them because they have either "male" parts or "female" parts. Children do not come into the world knowing these things. See Chapter 6 for an exploration of how children at different ages understand gender.

A three-year-old child, assigned male at birth, would likely have difficulty understanding why he could not be a mother when he grows up. Some professionals tasked with assessing a child's gender identity will draw a distinction between a child who says, "I am a girl" and a child who says, "I wish I were a girl" with the former being a child with an identity issue (transgender girl) and the latter being a child who simply has feminine interests (gender nonconforming boy). However, consider that it might be much easier for a child who is four years old to say, "I am a girl" than it is for a ten-year-old. The more developmentally mature ten-year-old has had considerably more time to learn about gender, society, and the perceived limitations of their own physical body. The ten-year-old may have already lost considerable hope about ever being a girl and, in a resigned way, articulate their wish instead.

Some children may not have the language or the ability to articulate their distress regarding their gender. They may have at one point tried to communicate their thoughts but were dismissed or reprimanded, and thus discouraged from attempting any further discussion. There may have been one time a child said, "I wish I were a boy" and a well-meaning adult may have responded by saying, "Oh honey, it's so wonderful that you are a girl! You can do anything that boys can do." Even a "positive" message like that can be silencing and invalidating to a young child trying to articulate their internal feelings.

Many adults are hesitant to discuss gender diversity with children because they believe that it may cause or encourage them to become transgender. The truth is that a child's gender differences exist whether they are discussed openly or silently avoided. There is no evidence that anything we say to children increases their likelihood of being lesbian, gay, bisexual, or transgender as adults.

Books for Young Children Exploring Gender

- *10,000 Dresses*
  by Marcus Ewert
- *The Adventures of Tulip, Birthday Wish Fairy*
  by S. Bear Bergman
- *Backwards Day*
  by S. Bear Bergman
- *Be Who You Are*
  by Jennifer Carr
- *A Boy in a Bikini*
  by Russell Frank
- *A Different Kind of Life*
  by Katie Leone
- *My Princess Boy*
  by Cheryl Kilodavis

Cover of *Backwards Day* (copyright S. Bear Bergman, 2012. Illustration by kd diamond).

Movies About Gender Nonconforming Children
The film *Ma Vie on Rose* (1997), directed by Alain Berliner, tells the story of a young boy named Ludovic, who dreams of growing up to be a woman. In the movie *Tomboy* (2011), directed by Celine Sciamma, young Laure moves to a new neighborhood and introduces herself to the town children as a boy.

EXPLORING GENDER

Identity exploration is a natural part of childhood. This includes exploring bodies, language, clothing, games, and music. An exploration in clothing choices, where a child seemingly "crosses" gender lines, may not be about that child's gender identity. It might simply have to do with the child's color preferences or a tactile interest in fabric textures. Some children are very imaginative, while others are physically active; some are emotionally expressive, while others are introverted. These are not characteristics of gender but are qualities of being human. Exploring identity and how to express that identity is a natural part of the healthy development of any child. Gender expression is simply one aspect of that exploration.

Toys, colors, clothing, hairstyles, and activities do not have a gender of their own. They are given a gender designation by our society. A girl may have a preference for pants and a boy may enjoy wearing a dress. Neither outfit will "make" a child desire to change their gender. For a child, what is confusing are the arbitrary societal rules assigning gender to nongendered items.

> *"My dad said that boys don't belong in the kitchen. That makes me sad because I really love to cook with my grandma. She's sad, too."* —nine-year-old boy
> (Classroom training led by Aidan Key)

Cooking will not make a boy gay or transgender. Teasing him, belittling his interests, or preventing him from engaging in this activity will only show him that something he loves is somehow wrong, or that there is something wrong with him for wanting to do it. The reality is that children can learn to conform to society's rigid gendered expectations. No child wants to give up the toys, activities, or clothes they love—they simply recognize that life will be harder if they do not. Rejection by peers and disappointment or anger from parents inspire powerful motivation to conform. Children may simply give up as their words are either ignored or are dismissed as impossible. The price tag of this conformity is high and can be devastating.

Emotions do not belong to one gender over another. Our society values toughness and resiliency in boys, but these qualities are beneficial for girls as well. Sensitivity to others is encouraged in girls, but boys need to learn this, too. These emotions and qualities are attributes of a well-balanced child. For a child to develop strong mental health, it is important to allow that child to experience the full array of emotional expression.

It is important to talk with other adults and children who are part of your child's life about the accepting and affirming environment you are striving to create. Colors, toys,

Children (Elenore Toczynski).

activities, and friends should not have restrictive parameters assigned to them based on gender. Disparaging comments or actions toward a child, based on archaic gender norms, should not be tolerated. Wherever possible, make sure that any environments your child enters (such as schools, camps, or after-school programs) have inclusive policies and an antibullying commitment.

> *"I see my daughter's transition as one of the biggest gifts of my life. I see her as heroic, and only wish we could have helped her transition when she was 6 and spared her all the years of pain and secrecy."**

AN UNLIKELY ACTIVIST

Wayne is opening up a new dialogue aimed at addressing transgender children, fatherhood, family, school culture, and civil rights. His blue-collar roots, industrial background, and leadership abilities have prepared him well to relate concepts of diversity and transgender issues.

I never thought I would become an activist for any cause. I am a conservative man. I am a proud military veteran, hunter, and sports fan. But when you love someone, you do things beyond the norm. Until a few years ago, I had an average family. I had identical twins. They were born boys, but I would soon learn that I had a daughter.

When Nicole first expressed her feelings to me, I had trouble sharing my emotions and having the courage to tell the world about my daughter. When I finally accepted her, I thought that the world would too. In the fifth grade she put on a new dress and proudly

The Maines family.

---

* Quotes in this chapter, when not otherwise specified, come from an online survey of parents/guardians of gender nonconforming children that accompanies the general *Trans Bodies, Trans Selves* survey.

attended school as Nicole. Her classmates said it was about time, but adults did not respond the same way. A grandfather, the Maine Christian Civic League, and the children who followed them placed my daughter in harm's way. One day early that school year a male student followed Nicole into the bathroom and said, "My grandfather says we do not have to have any faggots in our school. If you can use the girl's bathroom, so can I." From that point on Nicole faced bullying, harassment, and discrimination.

I was angry, disappointed, and frustrated that people feared the unknown. But there also seemed to be people who stood by us—people like Dr. Norman Spack at the Boston Children's Hospital, who helped develop a plan for Nicole to grow and prosper; our friends at Gay and Lesbian Advocates and Defenders (GLAD), who are helping us protect her civil rights; and the Transgender Equality Youth Foundation in Portland, Maine, which has supported us every step of the way.

We thought the school would do the right things to protect our children. When they didn't, I found myself talking to people at the end of our driveway, at sporting events, and at school. This approach was not enough. Nicole continued to suffer and we thought we had failed her. No matter how hard we tried, the school would not allow her to use the girls' bathroom and Nicole continued to be separated from her classmates, every day reinforcing that she was different from her peers.

With our backs to the wall, we submitted a Maine Human Rights Commission complaint—and we have been on an emotional roller coaster ride ever since. One afternoon we learned that conservatives in Maine wanted to roll back transgender rights protections through a bill called LD1046. After much discussion, we agreed the stakes were too high and that failure was not an option—and we let our 12-year-old daughter join the public fight. The time Nicole spent at the state capital lobbying to defeat LD 1046 was a turning point for me. Speaking out gave Nicole a voice. I watched her begin to heal in the hallways of our State House. Throughout our legal battles, the negative press, and the legislative challenges, our children have been brave and suffered dearly. They had to leave their friends, had to live in hiding, and lost their love for school. But my children are stronger and more confident for having the chance to be heard.

The need for courage is sometimes forced upon you. When my daughter was placed in harm's way, I knew I had to do something. I find myself being described as an LGBT activist, but I see myself as a dad just trying to protect his children.

CARETAKERS' STAGES OF ACCEPTANCE

The Family Acceptance Project, directed by Caitlin Ryan at the Marian Wright Edelman Institute at San Francisco State University, includes significant research on families of LGBTQ youth. One of the most important findings in their studies is that family acceptance of LGBTQ youth protects against depression, suicide, and substance abuse, and improves health and self-esteem. Many parents inherently know this, and many with teens or young adults wish that they had provided a more accepting environment for their children early on.

Parents can experience a high degree of mixed emotions in relation to their children's gender differences. In families with two parents, one parent may experience hope and optimism, while the other parent is resistant, only to find that they switch experiences later on. Seeking out parent support groups or individual or family therapy can be extremely valuable in learning how to work together as a family to acknowledge everyone's needs.

Conflicting feelings can be readily present even within a willing, supportive parent. It is not easy, especially at the beginning, to support and advocate for a gender nonconforming child. It is quite common for parents, even as they seek support for their child, to have mixed feelings and experience internal resistance. Parents frequently say things like this to themselves and each other:

- *I didn't sign up for this!*
- *You're always letting her get away with stuff. Now look what happened!*
- *You're too hard on him. I wish you'd lighten up!*
- *I wish my child were "just gay."*
- *I'm a shy person; I can't even stick up for myself. How am I supposed to do this for my child?*
- *I hate to say this, but I wish my kid had diabetes or something. At least people know what that is!*
- *At first, I didn't want to be seen with my child. I felt like everyone was looking and judging. I was embarrassed.*

Parents of gender nonconforming kids come from all walks of life—liberal and conservative, religious and agnostic—from all class backgrounds, and all ethnicities. Expectations of gender and gender roles are intrinsic to these other aspects of identity, and it is rare to find parents who do not need to reexamine their own hearts and minds as they move into acceptance and support of their child.

Denial and Fear

Rarely will you encounter a family that, at least initially, considers it a blessing to have a gender nonconforming child. Part of being a good parent is keeping your child fed, warm, and safe from harm. While attitudes are changing, transgender people have historically experienced ridicule, ostracism, contempt, and violence. What parent wants to support their child's innate gender identity and expression when the repercussions of this "acceptance" can lead to such a marginalized life? It is no wonder that many parents, teachers, therapists, and others who are caring for these children are fearful.

Denying the presence of a gender identity issue is quite common. Many parents point to their child's level of femininity or masculinity as proof that their child is not really gender nonconforming. For example, if their child is active in Boy Scouts, on the basketball team, and has a girlfriend, they may insist that it is impossible for their child to be a girl. This parent has made the mistake of equating their child's gender expression with their gender identity. Of course, a child can like the Scouts (embrace group activities), play basketball (enjoy team sports), and like girls (have a lesbian orientation). Another form of denial can include hanging tightly to the belief that a child is going through a "phase."

Very common explanations for children's behaviors include the following:

- *She'll do anything for attention!*
- *He's very dramatic and will do anything simply for the shock value.*
- *This is just one more thing in a long list of things he's done to drive us crazy!*
- *This gender stuff isn't her issue—she is easily influenced by friends and always dives into new things without thought.*

Coming to terms with a child's identity can be heartbreaking for some parents and much easier for others. It is safe to assume that most parents want what is best for their children—to see them happy and to keep them safe. It takes a caring, brave parent to embrace and support a child when the fear of societal judgment and stigmatization can be so high.

Grief

Those who champion the cause of a child they know and love may be quite surprised to discover they have deep feelings of grief. On one hand, they recognize the value of support and may even see immediate improvements in both temperament and self-esteem of the child. On the other hand, this was a child they loved—deeply—for exactly who they perceived them to be. Many assume that the child will have no chance to be in a loving relationship, have a satisfying career, or a family of their own. Despite the living, breathing presence of their child, the loss is present and is important to acknowledge. Moving through grief allows for a person's sense of loss, and it also makes room for the rediscovery of hopes and dreams.

While everyone's experience is different, there can be an even deeper sense of grief for parents whose children are older. This may simply be because they have had a greater number of years raising their child, cultivating those ideas of grandchildren and someone to love their child. Switching names and pronouns, not to mention discarding any gender-influenced hopes and dreams for that child, is very painful. Additionally, older children may make demands like removing family photos from the walls or any other "evidence" of the gender that caused them so much anguish. It is not an exaggeration to say that, for some parents and other family members, it can feel like a death in the family.

I LOVE MY SON, BUT I MISS MY DAUGHTER. . . .

Francesca Terry is an elementary school teacher and the mother of three vibrant boys, the oldest of whom transitioned at age five.

My daughter socially transitioned into my son when he was five years old. This was done against the advice of "specialists" at the local children's hospital, based on my strong gut instinct and validated by members of Gender Diversity's parent support groups. I remember the day I finally got it—what he'd been trying to tell me since he was three—that he was a boy. That day was intensely bittersweet because, while relieved to finally have the "reason" for his angry and chaotic behavior, I was secretly devastated to lose my daughter.

When a child transitions, some have likened it to a death in the family. But, unlike the actual death of a child, we as parents of a transgendered child have to defend, advocate for, protect, and educate despite the grief we feel inside. We don't experience the empathy and understanding that, in another situation, would be immediately offered to alleviate the pain we feel inside and really need. Many days I hid my grief behind a veneer of confidence and acceptance.

For me, the grief felt shameful and was isolating. The few people in whom I did confide told me how lucky I was to have a child at all, or said how wonderful I was for accepting my child and doing the right thing. I realize now that I was grieving not the *actual* loss of my daughter but the *idea* of my daughter. I still wanted the hopes and dreams I had for her when she was born, you know—mother/daughter stuff: the prom dress, mani-pedi spa trips. This is where the shame set in—that grieving my daughter was wrong because I had a healthy happy son. I felt isolated from other parents of transgender children in my support group. They weren't voicing this grief.

Two years after he transitioned, I had nothing left to advocate. We had pared down our family and friends to only those who unconditionally supported us. The school and doctors were on board and life was settling down. I had been successful managing the "logical" parts of the transition. I could finally focus on me, but I had yet to address my hurting heart. I was an angry, sad, confused mess inside. I started confiding my guilty secret to a few other parents at the support group, and realized that they too were struggling with similar emotions! Here we were sitting in the same room with the same suffocating feelings, but no one was saying a word. When I opened up about my own feelings, it was almost as if we all finally had permission to talk about our grief. It was transformative to speak honestly, one parent to another. Acknowledging the grief—knowing we all felt the same way—allowed the logical part of my brain to meld with the feelings in my heart. I began to truly heal.

Guilt

In a culture that has not provided gender options beyond "male" and "female" and operates on the assumption that anatomy equals gender, most adults raising children take this for granted. Many parents feel guilty about not seeing their child's gender nonconformity earlier, and many judge themselves for not listening to their child earlier.

> *"My 5-year-old trans daughter is struggling with the fact that people keep telling her that she 'used to be a boy.' Her response is anger and frustration, and she says, 'No, I was ALWAYS a girl.' When I tried talking with her about this, explaining that we had 'made a mistake' when we assumed she was a boy, she got really angry. I realized how hard it is for her that we didn't understand earlier that she wasn't a boy. I told her that it was OK to be angry and apologized that I had been mistaken in her gender. She is obviously having a hard time with this, and clearly feeling betrayed and frustrated. I don't see how I could have known sooner, but really, should I have been able to see this? She certainly thinks so and the pain and hurt in her eyes is hard to see. I am feeling so guilty. It breaks my heart that I have unwittingly hurt her."*

Not every parent will experience all the emotions expressed here. There are as many ways for a parent to experience a child's gender nonconformity as there are parents. Feelings sometimes considered negative are an important part of a parent's process of acceptance. Parents and other family members often need time and space to express denial, anger, grief, and fear before they are able to step into acceptance, support and even advocacy for their children. A parent can be fully supportive while deeply wishing their child's gender "issues" would just disappear.

Acceptance and Willingness

Increased distress experienced by a gender nonconforming child is often what propels an adult to finally seek outside help. Pressure from peers, parental or teacher reprimands for gender-atypical behavior, reproachful looks and disapproving comments are occurrences that are readily perceived by a trans child and subsequently internalized. This can result in angry outbursts, elevated frustrations, increased anxiety, depression, withdrawal, violent behavior, and threats or actual self-harm. For many adults, this distressing behavior from a child can launch them from a place of resistance to one of acceptance (sometimes it starts as resignation). The bottom line is that we do not want to see our children in pain. Not all parents are resistant—some may have viewed their child's presentation as a phase, while others did not see it coming. Regardless, it is necessary to become willing to take the next step—accept the child as they are and identify the ways in which they need support.

Celebration/Gratitude

As parents roll up their sleeves to learn more and get past the early confusion and fear, they quite often come to a place of delight and gratitude for the positive changes in their child's life as well as their own. While agreeing that it is challenging, and sometimes painful, many parents ultimately declare they would not have had it any other way. They recognize their child as an amazing and beautiful gift—someone who teaches them about bravery, authenticity, and acceptance. Many name their child as the hero in their lives.

> *"If you had told me a year ago that I would be the proud parent of a trans boy, I would have told you you were crazy! Now I can honestly say that it's the best thing that ever happened to me!"*—Father of a 10-year-old trans boy at a Gender Diversity Parent Support Group

---

SUPPORTING MY CHILD'S AUTHENTIC JOURNEY

Carolyn MacGregor is a freelance editor who lives with her two daughters in Seattle, Washington, and has been active on the planning committee for the Gender Odyssey and Gender Odyssey Family Conferences since 2011.

My gender journey with my oldest child began the moment Ian was born, or perhaps even conceived, but it wasn't until he asked for a dress at the age of four that I really started to notice. Yes, there were signs—his preference for female playmates, his choice of female characters in role play, his interest in nail polish and "pretty" colors and clothes—but I attributed that to my parenting style; I bought bright-colored clothes for him, dolls *and* trucks, didn't cut his hair very short, and tried to avoid gender stereotyping. After several requests, I bought Ian a few skirts and dresses for Ian at Goodwill, thinking he intended them for play, but the moment we returned home he changed into them and headed out the door to play at the park. After that, the dresses joined his existing wardrobe, he asked to grow his hair long, and as he outgrew his "boy" clothes, we replaced them with "girl" apparel. Yet, all this time, Ian played happily with trucks and trains, was fascinated by construction vehicles, and enjoyed building things. Ian was Ian—a boy who liked girl things, and boy things, too. Before long, strangers started to identify Ian as a girl—a tomboyish girl but a girl nonetheless.

And so began the next five years of our journey; effectively, Ian lived as "she" but went by "he," for the most part quite assuredly. During this period of time, he would occasionally comment to me: "I wish I was a girl; it would just be easier." Would it have been easier for me? Undoubtedly! My job as the parent was to walk ahead and clear the obstacles from his path, so to speak. I talked with the schools, the camps, the babysitters, other parents, ensuring that anyone who might have any influence or authority over him would be respectful of his choices and my decision to support him.

At nine years old, Ian entered a head-heart process of several months during which he worked over the dilemma constantly. There might as well have been steam coming out of his ears, as he turned the question over and over—who am I? Boy or girl? Some percentage of each? Somewhere in the middle? Somewhere between the middle and girl? As I would tuck him in each night, he would present his current findings in a fraction or percentage split. And then it happened—one night he said to me: "Mom, I want to transition. Boy just isn't working anymore." And with that, she became Zoë. . . at home, school, and everywhere in between. But here's the rub—Zoë didn't change, her name and pronoun did, and, as one might expect, the way the world responds to her has changed as well. And yes, it does seem easier. At eleven, Zoë loves who she feels herself to be. But we both smile as we look at the adorable baby in the old photos, and the toddler in boy clothes, because that is who she *was*. In every moment, she was never asked to be anyone other than herself. The pride she has in her identity is fierce and I wouldn't have it any other way.

CONSISTENT PARENTING

It can be difficult to set clear boundaries and expectations for a child while working through the many different emotions a parent or guardian experiences. It is important to recognize that consistent, strong parenting, on all issues (gender related or otherwise) provides children with feelings of security and safety.

Ideas for maintaining consistent parenting in gender-related areas:

1. *Do not use gender-related care as a reward for good behavior or as punishment for bad behavior.* Acknowledgement, support, and transition-related care are not items to dangle in front of a child in order to encourage good behavior, nor are they things to withdraw in the case of bad behavior. A parent would not withhold medical or mental health treatment if a child brought home bad grades. Gender-related care should be no different.

2. *Do not use your child as the sounding board for your distress, grief, anger, or confusion.* Parents can have a hard time navigating their feelings regarding their child's gender identity or expression. This can be compounded by the fact that so many have to navigate their feelings in isolation. The lack of societal understanding, difficulty finding an experienced therapist, spousal conflicts, and loss of friendships and other bases of support can leave a parent with only one outlet for their feelings—their child. This is *not* the appropriate outlet. Children can and do internalize the challenging feelings expressed by their parents and feel guilty, responsible, shameful, anxious, and confused. A parent should find an adult with whom they can address their feelings. Keep looking until you find a supportive, caring person who can help you look after your own heavy heart, but do not burden your child with it.

3. *When confused about what to do, take gender out of the equation.* Because the "gender issue" can take center stage in a family's life, and sometimes for a lengthy period of time, it is easy for a parent, teacher, or therapist to assume gender is a factor in situations where it may not be. This can result in overexplaining, defensiveness when none is needed, and an inability to see solutions to problems. One way to address a situation where the solution is not clear is to frame a scenario where the gender component is removed. Imagine if the child of a friend were in a similar situation. What advice would you give to that parent? Replace the gender piece with another aspect of identity. Does that help develop a better perspective or solution?

WHEN PARENTING APPROACHES DIFFER

Parents and experts agree that having a consistent parenting approach to a child's upbringing is ideal. Parenting a gender nonconforming child is no exception. In the past, some gender experts said that insisting that a child conform to societal gendered expectations was the best way to keep them safe. Now experts are saying that the best way to keep children safe is to support a child's gender identity, develop their self-esteem and resiliency, and ultimately change society. It will come as no surprise that this less-than-definitive messaging from the professional world can serve to put parents at odds with each other. The question for parents ultimately comes to this: How do we keep our child safe today while we work to change the world around them?

Parenting is often divided into two basic roles. In families with two parents, one parent sometimes serves as nurturer and protector, while the other takes on the role of pragmatist and disciplinarian. In families with one parent or where parents have similar personality structures, these roles can occur within one person.

The nurturing part of a parent views the child as the center of the universe, while the pragmatic side of the parent focuses on the child's role as a member of a family, student within a school, and ultimately a member of society. Normally, these parental roles can be reasonable and complimentary. The nurturing side of a parent may lead them to be a frontline supporter of a gender nonconforming child, ready to buy the preferred gender clothing, accommodate hair length requests, do online research, read relevant books, and more quickly adopt name and pronoun changes. The pragmatic side of a parent may appear more resistant to allowing and supporting a child's gender preferences because their role is to protect their child. It can be difficult to imagine the hardships a child may encounter at school, within a neighborhood, or in relation to extended family, making a parent resistant to actions of support that feel too permissive, impractical, and potentially dangerous to a child's safety.

Following are some considerations for parents who are coming into conflict with themselves or each other about parenting styles:

1. If at all possible, it can be helpful to utilize a counselor skilled in negotiating parental conflict as well as one who is familiar with gender-diverse children.

2. Approach differences of opinion with mutual knowledge that each parent comes from the same foundation of wanting what is best for their child.

3. Recognize that each parent may have their own timeline for understanding all the issues, navigating personal barriers, and making determinations on the best course of action for their child. For example, one parent may need to move faster than they would like while the other could consider slowing their pace, ideally allowing everyone the ability to move forward as a family.

4. Consideration for the child's distress may trump any timetable or course of action that the parents decide. If you have a child considering self-harm, waste no time getting professional help and put the needs of your child first and foremost.

5. If your child has consistently asserted their gender presentation over time, do not try and convince the other parent (or yourself) that your child is going through a phase. Days, weeks, and even a few months may constitute a phase. A year or more is significant and should not be dismissed.

6. Do not leave the information seeking or knowledge gathering to one parent alone. Reading a book about transgender children does not make your child transgender, nor does consulting with a knowledgeable professional. If one parent has more knowledge on the issue than the other, it can create an even wider chasm when important decisions need to be made.

7. For parents who are divorced or separated, it is extremely wise to set aside relationship differences as much as possible. Bringing a child's gender issues into a courtroom can serve to prolong the proceedings as courts seek to educate themselves on what may be a very unfamiliar topic. Court cases can go on for years. The increased expense could be greater than a child's entire college education. The resulting damage to the child could permanently affect them and destroy their relationship with one or both parents. For parents involved in legal battles over custody and care for gender nonconforming children, it is important to seek out legal advice from someone knowledgeable about gender issues.

SEEKING SUPPORT

One of the first steps that many parents take when realizing their child is gender nonconforming is to search for others who are grappling with the same issues or service providers who have experience working with gender nonconforming children. It can be lonely and isolating to face these issues on our own, and many people make wonderful connections that enhance their ability to be the best caretakers possible.

Parent Support Groups and Children's Play Groups

There are several organizations that provide support for families through in-person groups for both parents and children. Ideally, a parent group occurs at the same time and place, in a separate room, from the children's group. Some children's groups have volunteers who engage children in imaginative play while guardians have time to express their fears, frustrations, and triumphs to understanding ears. Other parent groups have email lists and chat rooms that provide online connections for those who live far away from in-person groups. As children grow older, there are also online resources for them. In addition, annual conferences provide places for parents to connect with each other and for children to meet and play with other gender nonconforming children.

Making Early Connections With Providers

There are providers such as pediatricians, child psychiatrists and psychologists, and family therapists who have experience working with gender nonconforming children and their families. These people can be great resources in thinking about the many factors

Parent Support Groups
- Gender Diversity: genderdiversity.org
- Transforming Family: transformingfamily.org
- Trans Youth and Family Allies: imatyfa.org
- Gender Spectrum: genderspectrum.org
- TransActive: transactiveonline.org

contributing to an individual child's identity. Establishing relationships with providers early on can also be important as a child approaches the age at which some families begin to think about possible medical intervention related to gender. Families that do not have established relationships with providers before this stage may end up in more of a rush to connect with providers as puberty approaches.

Supporting Siblings

For many families raising a gender nonconforming child, the distress experienced by that child, coupled with societal challenges, can become a focal issue within that family. By the time a family seeks (or manages to find) any outside support, the urgency/conflict within the family can be quite high. The gender nonconforming child's needs understandably take center stage. Sometimes, however, this state of crisis continues for a prolonged period of time. A sibling can recognize the challenges experienced by the transgender child and subsequent higher demand on family resources and, at first, adapt to the decreased attention. They may make an effort not to bring any "extra" challenges into the family and, initially, deemphasize or minimize their own needs. This is neither ideal nor sustainable. Overwhelmed parents can inadvertently sideline a sibling's needs or experiences.

By the time a family has weathered much of the early gender-related crises or transition hurdles, they may realize that a sibling is suffering. Siblings of gender nonconforming children often experience greater teasing. Parents may see a decline in school performance, acting out, depression, or anxiety. What may be harder to notice is when a sibling overcompensates by being overly helpful or accommodating.

Sometimes a sibling will inadvertently disclose a child's gender status without realizing the potential repercussions. A sibling may also deliberately disclose in an effort to be a part of, or gain some ownership over, an issue that has taken center stage for the family. While this is a normal response, the repercussions can be life altering for the gender nonconforming child and the family as a whole. Siblings should be made aware of why privacy is important.

Parents should find dedicated time for each child regardless of the increased sense of urgency related to the gender nonconforming child. Create one-on-one opportunities where the focus is solely on the sibling. An ounce of prevention is far better than having two (or more) children in distress. If at all possible, it can be advantageous to find a therapist or group for the sibling. It is not always necessary to find supports that are well versed in transgender issues and can be more important to identify a therapist who has experience working with siblings of children with any kind of special need.

MENTAL HEALTH CARE FOR GENDER NONCONFORMING CHILDREN

There are many things we can do at home to assist children in developing good mental health. Often, for gender nonconforming children, it is also helpful to bring in an experienced therapist.

Emotional Resiliency

One of the greatest gifts we can give a child is to help them build their emotional resiliency. The world can be a tough place for a gender nonconforming child, even those children whose families are fully on board. It is critical to build healthy coping skills. It can mean the difference between a child who knows how to empower themselves and a child with poor self-esteem and greater likelihood of victimization. It is common for gender nonconforming children to experience varying degrees of anxiety and/or depression despite having identity-affirming support. Having an atypical gender in a narrowly gendered world can be a hefty burden. Studies have shown that the development of a strong emotional resilience can result in greater success in school, stronger friendships, and being less likely to experience depression. If a child is aware of how they feel and has tools to move through their intense emotions, they will have acquired a skill that will last a lifetime. In order to help children recognize their emotions, we, as adults, need to spend time thinking about the underlying causes for a child's emotions and talking to them about how to identify their feelings. Many times, an angry outburst actually comes from a place of fear or shame.

In addition to teaching children about their own emotions, we have to teach them about the emotions of others. Children who are taught that insensitive comments often result from ignorance can be sad and disappointed but also compassionate. As adults, we can model this kind of resiliency when dealing with comments from other adults in front of children. We should be ready to address or deflect comments in ways that show confidence and support for a child. If we are having difficulty doing this, it can be important for us to spend time talking with family members, friends, or our own mental health providers about the feelings we are having, while continuing to model appropriate responses for the child.

Body Awareness

Many, but not all, transgender or gender nonconforming children have negative relationships with their bodies, or specific parts of their bodies, feeling a sense of betrayal that their bodies are not in alignment with how they feel. These children may have an extremely difficult time developing an attuned body awareness. Efforts should be made from an early age to encourage gender nonconforming children to participate in dance and sports, activities that can put them in touch with their bodies and give them pride in their bodies' accomplishments.

Johnny Science in a King Arthur costume from Christmas morning in 1959. Johnny transitioned in the mid-1980s and died in 2007. He was an artist and musician and organizer of the trans community in New York City in the 1980s and 1990s. He hand-colored this childhood photo of himself (courtesy of Kit Rachlin).

Mental Health Providers

Mental health providers such as psychologists, psychiatrists, and social workers can be wonderful allies to gender nonconforming children and their families. Some of these providers have chosen to specialize in working with transgender children and can also be great resources to connect families with support groups and other services. They often work in conjunction with physicians, who manage children's general physical health as well as assist families with decisions about important gender-related medical care.

When selecting a mental health provider, look for one that is knowledgeable regarding gender nonconformity and transgender issues. This provider should be one who can distinguish between a child's gender expression (interests, clothing choices, etc.) and their gender identity. An optimal provider will be one who starts with a holistic assessment of the child and their family to ascertain all variables that impact that child's life. To adequately assess a child's gender identity and state of exploration may require several sessions and include discussions with the child, parents, and sometimes siblings. The ideal provider will simultaneously be paying attention to the child's gender concerns, determining familial comfort or distress, assessing supportive networks for all family members, and addressing issues of possible anxiety, depression, behavior, and any other concern regarding the child's health and well-being.

It can be extremely valuable to establish a relationship with a mental health provider early in a gender nonconforming child's life. Not only can providers be important resources and supports for both the child and their family, but they can also be strong advocates for the child's needs when the child approaches a time that the family is considering puberty blockers or other medical interventions. Most medical providers require a child to have a relationship with a mental health provider in order to start puberty-blocking medications, and families have found themselves rushing to establish relationships when puberty is starting.

Not all mental health providers are the same. Gender nonconformity is not a required part of most mental health curricula for those in training to work with children. Some providers believe that gender nonconforming behaviors should be suppressed or discouraged. Proximity to larger cities can make it easier to connect with knowledgeable providers; in more rural areas this can sometimes be extremely difficult. Some families have found that they do not mind educating their child's mental health provider about these issues as long as the provider is open and affirming. Others prefer to travel longer distances to see someone who is more extensively trained around gender nonconformity. We should always look for the best fit for our families, even if it takes seeing a few different providers for evaluations in order to find the person with whom we will work best.

Behavioral Issues

It is not uncommon for gender nonconforming children to be diagnosed with one or more behavioral conditions as a child's family seeks the source of their child's unhappiness. Considering the direct inquisitiveness or teasing of other children, the subtle or direct disapproval from some adults, and the rigid gender stereotypes presented by society, it is no wonder a gender nonconforming child may have behavioral challenges, including outbursts of anger, times of being withdrawn, feelings of anxiousness, sadness, despair, and depression. If children feel boxed in or trapped, their innate selves rendered invisible, it is quite likely that behavioral issues may manifest. Children may also feel they are under considerable pressure from family and peers—even society as a whole—to conform to rigid gender expectations.

It is important to recognize the possibility that a child's frustration, anger, or despair may originate with the fact that they are not being recognized or acknowledged for who they are. Many families have found that when they finally acknowledge and support their child's gender identity, other behavioral issues decrease or simply fade away. In some cases, there are other underlying issues such as depression or attention-deficit/hyperactivity disorder (ADHD) that could be contributing to a child's behavior. Thus, it is important to involve a knowledgeable, caring mental health provider to help sort this out.

Occasionally, even if gender is acknowledged as a factor in need of being addressed, it can be assigned a secondary "ranking" by a less knowledgeable provider, which can indefinitely postpone treatment or support for a gender nonconforming child. A therapist might suggest addressing gender issues once anger, anxiety, depression, or behavioral outbursts are under control. These issues should be considered alongside gender identity, but they are not more important.

Gender Diagnoses

Among transgender adults there is considerable debate over the categorization of transgender identity as a mental disorder. The latest version of the *Diagnostic and Statistical Manual of Mental Disorders* (*DSM-5*) renames gender identity disorder as gender dysphoria. Families who are raising a transgender child often grapple with the ramifications of a child being diagnosed with gender dysphoria.

Gender dysphoria in childhood is defined as a period of at least six months of a child experiencing a difference between their expressed and assigned gender, and which causes significant distress or impairment. While many parents recognize that there is nothing "wrong" with their child's mental health—only ignorance and bias in our society—the advice from medical, mental health, and legal professionals may be to obtain a gender-related mental health diagnosis. There are various reasons for doing so, which may include insurance coverage, access to hormone blockers, and even divorce or child custody issues. Arriving at a definitive diagnosis can also be comforting for many parents as it is concrete and paves the way for specific action such as ID and school records changes.

It is important to recognize that there are pros and cons to a child receiving a diagnosis of gender dysphoria. Diagnoses remain permanently in medical records. There are a number of opportunities, services, and situations where a mental disorder diagnosis could potentially prevent or greatly hinder someone's access—either now or later in life. Insisting on a label could potentially serve to silence a child and squelch any further attempts to find their authentic self, which may or may not be as a transgender adult. In an effort to decrease the discomfort of their parents and others, a child may make choices that are *not* aligned with how they actually feel. A diagnosis can also lead to a later situation where a child "changes their mind" or says they have "made a mistake" simply because they felt pressured to make a decision before they were ready. Each family should educate themselves as to the potential benefits and repercussions of obtaining a gender dysphoria diagnosis.

Steven, 10 years old.

CONSIDERING SOCIAL TRANSITION

Many families come to a point where they feel that the best thing for a gender nonconforming child will be to support the child in expressing their gender identity publicly.

Parents may have already spent considerable time allowing the child to try out different clothes, names, or pronouns at home, or with select groups of peers and other parents. For parents considering social transition for their children, there are a few concrete steps to affirm a young child's gender. These can include all or some of the following:

- Changes in hairstyle, clothing, preferred toys, or accessories
- Name change
- Pronoun change
- Identity document changes
- A reversible, medical delay of puberty

For some parents, these tasks seem quite daunting. For others, especially those parents who tend to cope by finding solutions and implementing them as quickly as possible, having tangible, concrete actions to focus on can provide a sense of relief. While these tasks often do need completing, some may not. Some may be premature or simply not applicable to every child.

It is easy to focus on this "checklist" of transition-related tasks. It can provide a parent with what feels like a step-by-step through unfamiliar territory. Moving quickly through these tasks may provide some comfort, or a sense of purpose, but it can also result in a bit of tunnel vision that can hamper a parent's ability to see other more immediate issues. It can also send a message that a child "needs" to transition fully when their gender identity is of a more fluid state and transition is premature or not necessary.

Even if all these tasks are necessary, it does not mean they are easy to accomplish. It is quite common to encounter barriers within systems (e.g., the rules dictating ID document changes can vary state by state). These barriers are often not insurmountable but can take an incredible amount of time and require legal assistance. It is important to pace ourselves in order to avoid burnout, financial hardship, or an overall drain on our day-to-day life experience.

For parents, teachers, and therapists ready to help children with social transitions, one of the biggest fears expressed is that we are moving too fast, and that the child may "change their mind." A decision to transition a child's gender can feel like an irreversible course of action. When a trans adult transitions, some steps, like hormones and surgeries, do change the body in permanent ways. This is not true for a child pursuing a transition. A child's transition primarily consists of a "social transition" where no permanent physical changes are made.

Many times, fears are larger than reality. It can be helpful to actually "play out" a scenario in which the child does change their mind. Say that a family supports their child in a social transition. The child takes on a different name, perhaps changes their hairstyle, is supported in their clothing preferences, uses the bathroom that aligns with their gender identity, and everyone works very hard to get the new pronoun to easily roll off their tongue. Then the child comes home one day and says, "I want to go back!"

If a child states that they made a mistake or that they want to go back to the gender they were before, simply work the aforementioned steps backwards. These steps are all reversible and it surely will not be as hard as it was the first time. This is not to say that it will be easy. A parent will still be placed in the position of explaining to others why "supporting" their child includes a gender transition and, if need be, a change "back." As those caring for gender nonconforming children, our fears about a child "changing back" may be more about our own shame at having been "wrong" than about concerns for the child's safety or well-being.

COMING OUT OR DISCLOSING

The first step for many families in social transition is to inform extended family members, parents of a child's friends, and school officials that the child is going to be transitioning gender. When disclosing a child's gender experience, keep in mind that it is impossible to accurately predict a person's reaction. Those who we think will be supportive right

Gender Odyssey Family Conference, the Gender Spectrum Conference, the Gender Infinity Conference, and Philly Trans Health Conference all offer programming for gender nonconforming children and their families.

away may not be, and those who we fear telling the most can sometimes be surprisingly supportive. It is best to proceed cautiously with each person. Positive outcomes are significantly higher when parents exhibit their own confidence, without hesitancy or shame.

There is no doubt that creating a network of support involves a fair amount of work. Most people, unless their lives have been touched by a transgender person, have had no opportunity to learn anything about this issue at all. Finding support from your extended family and your neighborhood may take time and patience, but expanding your network of support will provide a very worthwhile payoff. Families that take the time to sit and discuss this issue with others find that, while some people are unreceptive, many more are supportive. Do not spend a lot of time trying to reach people who are displaying a high degree of resistance. It can deplete your energy and sometimes serves to increase the resistance. Some may never come around. Some people may simply need some space and time to navigate their feelings before they are able to find some level of understanding.

> *"My sister was really angry when we discussed with her what was happening with our transgender son. She had strong opinions and was not willing to listen to me or read anything that I suggested. We mostly stopped seeing her for a while, which was really hard, especially on our son, as her children—his cousins—were really close. But, we kept going to family functions and everyone else came around, especially when they saw how happy he was. My sister's children started to push back and asked more questions about why we all weren't spending time together. They wanted to know what the 'big deal' was. After a little while, she just seemed to let go of all her resistance. Things are back to normal now—even better really—and I am so glad I didn't pressure her. She seemed to need the space."*

Statements that can be made to connect with people who are having trouble understanding your family's decision to support a gender nonconforming child:

- *At first, we too were really confused by this issue with our child.* This response can serve to validate someone's confusion. They may be too embarrassed to admit they know nothing about transgender issues.
- *I was angry at first, too. It seems so unfair—I didn't ask for this!* A response like this can work to validate and diffuse the unexplained anger or rage a person may be feeling.
- *I was scared for my child's safety and what this issue might mean for our family.* Expressing fears can validate the fears of another. Some people wonder whether their own children will be safe when around a trans child. While this is quite offensive to hear, it is the reality of what some people think.
- *We were unsure whether we were doing the right thing at first. There is so little information out there. But then our doctor gave us some good advice and resources.* This can help dispel the notion of overly lenient parenting while at the same time communicate that you have received professional guidance.

There can be situations when these steps do not work and things become quite volatile. These are dangerous. If you perceive a sudden or extreme negative response in another person, do whatever you can to remove yourself from the situation calmly and quickly.

SAMPLE LETTER TO FAMILY MEMBERS ABOUT A CHILD'S TRANSITION

Dear Family,

We have some big news to share, so we thought it best to write you personally. Our child, who you know as Lacey, has shared since she was two or three years old that she feels she is a boy. Not that she wants to act like a boy or play boy games, but she feels like she was born a boy. We have, in fact, learned we are not the parents of a little girl, but the parents of a little boy. Through long and careful exploration, discussion, prayer, therapy, family talks, and careful self-reflection, we have come to understand this new truth. We are proud and excited to introduce a new but old member of our family, Justin!

Justin, as he is now known by everyone in our neighborhood and school, is living full time as a boy. He is unbelievably happy and comfortable about this big change and so are we. As you are a very important part of our lives, we decided to also share this truth with you. We understand this may be confusing. In the beginning, we too felt confused. For years now Justin has told us how he feels inside with the words he knew.

There is plenty of information available about transgender children—we invite you to explore this information as we have. There is quite a bit of information on the Internet. There are also several good books on the subject. We recommend *The Transgender Child* and *Gender Born, Gender Made*.

We request you welcome Justin fully as part of our family. Please refer to Justin only with male pronouns (he, him) and by his name, Justin. Despite any personal reservations you may have, we expect and hope you will be fully welcoming, respectful, and kind to Justin. All the experts we have consulted on this subject agree this is the right approach for maintaining Justin's mental health and happiness long term. Transgender kids are much more prone to suicide, depression, and self-harm when they don't have the support and love of their family.

If you are no longer able to treat our child with complete respect, we will decline further contact until that changes. Regardless of religious belief, all of us as parents want our children happy and safe. Our friends, community, and Justin's school have been extremely helpful and supportive. Our love and support for Justin is complete. We hope yours will be also. We love you all so much and miss you.

The Johnsons

PREPARING CHILDREN FOR QUESTIONS

It is critical to prepare gender nonconforming children for questions, whether they come from an inquisitive child or an insensitive or unthinking adult. Some people will let their curiosity override their sense of what is appropriate to ask of a child. If you do not think an adult would ever ask a child if they are going to have a sex change operation, think again!

Children ask questions that are simple and address immediate curiosities. Simple answers are highly effective. Adults may have a different agenda. They are more likely to couch their questions in politeness and express their discomfort or disapproval in more subtle ways. A young child may sense an adult's inappropriate agenda but not be able to articulate what they perceive to others, including a parent or a therapist. This is where the attentiveness of the supportive adults in a child's life is critical. One option is to tell your child that they do not have to answer *any* gender-related questions from adults. Equipping a child with a response like "My mom says you shouldn't ask me questions but should come talk to her" can immediately relieve a child's pressure to respond. If the adult persists, tell the child to find their parent immediately.

It is ideal to talk with children about how to address questions from different types of people. Is the person a friend at school? A favorite cousin? How should the answer be different if the person is a stranger? Remember that siblings of transgender and gender nonconforming children have to navigate these waters as well. Discuss scenarios and questions that they may have already encountered. Some children have "outed" their trans siblings and need their own guidance and attention to negotiate whatever situations arise. Young children may not yet understand why respecting someone's privacy is so important. The desire to tell a "secret" can be high, so it is important to discuss with children the importance of privacy in anyone's life. Additionally, children should know that there are safety issues at hand.

Role Playing

One activity shown to be highly effective in building resiliency in children is role playing. This involves the creation of any number of potential situations where a child might need to think on their feet. The parent or other support person plays the role of one person and the child practices potential responses. This can be helpful in any number of situations.

A whole family can engage in role-playing exercises and the whole family can benefit. To start, brainstorm potential situations and list them on paper. These can include school scenarios and even be narrowed down to specific students who may be benignly persistent in their questions or others who are aggressively teasing and bullying. It might include an upcoming family reunion and seeing relatives for the first time since affirming a child's gender.

> *"My son who had socially transitioned at a young age was having a conversation recently with a friend who'd known him for a long time. His friend said, 'Hey, didn't you used to have a girl's name?' My child just shrugged, rolled his eyes, and said, 'Yeah, can you believe my parents named me that!' Both kids laughed at how silly adults can be and went on to something else. We've done a lot of role playing and it paid off. He really thought on his feet."*

Role playing should not be limited solely to the gender nonconforming child. Parents need to be prepared to address the gender question at any time and with any person. That is not to say that an in-depth explanation—or any explanation for that matter—is necessary. However, parents need to envision a number of scenarios and determine what, if any, explanation is needed depending on who the person is, what degree of relevance they have in the family's life, how much time they have at that moment, and their assessment of that person's receptivity.

Scenario: *You are in a grocery store with your eight-year-old trans daughter and you see someone you know from your neighborhood. They say hello, seem confused when you mention your daughter, and then inquire about your son. You are a little caught off guard and do not quite know how much to say, but end up providing an explanation about how your daughter used to be your son, that you became aware that he was transgender, and that now you support her in her true gender identity as a girl. Your neighbor has an uncomfortable smile on their face, comments on your bravery as a parent, says they wouldn't know what to do if they had a child like "that," and then moves on down the aisle. Your child seems to have been thoughtfully contemplating the cereal boxes the whole time and because your child says nothing, you say nothing.*

Inherently, this response to an unexpected situation was handled pretty well. A brief educational response may be just the thing for an unexpected supermarket interaction. But there is a really good chance that your child was listening to all that was said. She could have easily stolen a glance or two at both you and the neighbor as the conversation progressed, felt the discomfort of both adults, and registered how quickly the neighbor moved away. The child can internalize this discomfort and develop a sense of shame about themselves. Because this was not addressed by the parent afterward, it could cause a child to conclude that their parent's own discomfort comes from a sense of shame they have about her. This unintended consequence, instilling shame and silence, can be long lasting.

Here are two examples of responses to the above scenario that elevate family support and trust as the number-one priority.

Example Response 1: *You are in a grocery store with your eight-year-old trans daughter and you see someone you know from your neighborhood. They say hello, seem confused when you mention your daughter, and then inquire about your son. Because you have done your own preparation, you are not caught off guard. You say, "No, I only have a daughter" and that's it. You allow them their confusion as you excuse yourself and say, "Sorry I have to run. It was nice seeing you," leaving them with a quizzical look on their face and a very relieved child.*

Example Response 2: *Perhaps this is a family with whom you would like to discuss your family's journey but you recognize that the grocery store is not an ideal place. You take the lead in the conversation and say how nice it was to run into them. Then you mention that you have been meaning to stop by and visit them and ask whether they are going to be around tomorrow morning. If they ask a question about your child, you gracefully state that you would love to catch up with them soon and if tomorrow does not work, you will call them to find another time.*

Have fun with role playing. Try out silly responses along with your serious ones; shout out some one-liners, or speak them using your favorite accent. If a child is relaxed and having fun during the role playing, chances are they will be able to bring some of those feelings into real-life situations.

CHOOSING NEW NAMES

Many gender-diverse children are eager to shed their gendered names assigned at birth. This can be a difficult task for a parent who may have put careful consideration into selecting their child's name. It is normal to feel attachment to a child's name and grief at the thought of it changing. Many parents also worry that giving a child too much leeway in choosing their own name could result in a choice that the child is upset about later in life. Young children often choose silly names, such as those of Disney characters or other toys. The amount of influence the child has in decisions related to name changes depends greatly on the age and developmental level of the child.

Some parents feel it is important for their child to have a family name, or one that fits well within their culture. Many families have trial periods, where the child's new name is used at home or among family members to be sure it is a good fit. Some children may try multiple names before settling on one. Gender-neutral names can sometimes be good choices because they allow for children to explore their gender identity without making any big decisions.

Legal name changes take time and money. Taking legal steps can be very important in many cases in order to affirm a child's identity. However, holding off on a legal name change does not mean that a child needs to be addressed by their birth name at school or in a health provider's office, as these entities often have options for the use of a child's nickname or preferred name. Changing a child's legal name generally follows the same process as that for adults, but it requires the approval of a parent or guardian. See Chapter 10 for more information about how to make a legal name change.

PRONOUNS

While pronouns are among the smallest words in the English language, they are a highly structured part of our speech. Within a moment of meeting someone for the first time, we assess that person's gender and begin to use male or female pronouns to refer to them. In rare circumstances where we misgender someone, we often feel mortified—for them *and* for ourselves. We may stumble over our words and quickly apologize.

It is no wonder that there is so much resistance to considering a pronoun change for a child. Allowing a child to switch pronouns can, for many adults, feel as if they are, at best, aiding a child in an imaginary unreality or, at worst, assisting in an act of deception.

For adult trans people, changing a pronoun can feel like a monumental step. For a child, however, it can be a simple and straightforward validation of who they feel themselves to be. For children who strongly cross-identify as either male or female, the pronoun that aligns with their gender identity is the obvious choice. That being said, not many adults are adept at switching pronouns quickly. It takes practice, as well as acceptance of a child's innate gender identity, to make a new pronoun flow off the tongue with ease.

When a child's gender identity is less definitive, it can be harder to know which pronoun to use. The best place to start is to simply ask the child whether they want to be called he or she. The answer you get might be "neither," "both," I don't care," or even "I'm just me!" Older youth and adults are creating alternative pronouns like *zie, hir,* or even the plural *they.* These are options for children. Using no pronouns at all is also an option.

It is a little awkward at first, but most people can readily adjust to addressing a child without using pronouns (sometimes simply substituting their first name) or using pronouns interchangeably. Be assured, this act in and of itself will not change a child's gender—it is simply being respectful of what that child tells you. Additionally, it creates a little more breathing room for a child to explore gender in a less restrictive way.

Taking a Gender Vacation
While not an option readily available to all, there are some families who will opt for a trial "gender vacation." If your family has a trip out of town or to someplace where you are not likely to run into people you know, consider testing the waters by giving your child an opportunity to adopt their preferred gender clothing choices, pronoun, or even a different name while away from home. Many parents have been quite surprised at how happy and at ease their child is as well as how uneventful the temporary "social transition" is as they see how society readily receives their "new" daughter or son.

SCHOOLS

Outside of home, most children spend the majority of their time at school. Unfortunately, gender conforming expectations exist at most schools and at every age level. Pressure to conform can come from peers and teachers alike and in varying degrees. These expectations are present in school traditions and policy. Even the most progressive schools can have practices or policies that unintentionally marginalize or silence a transgender student.

For many teachers and administrators, the desire to be inclusive within the school community is strong, but the knowledge of *how* to do this is limited. Many schools and districts are willing to help but need a road map for creating a gender-inclusive environment. A school pursuing a healthy, inclusive, and safe community is well poised to incorporate the concept of gender diversity into its existing framework.

Many schools have the capacity to create an inclusive environment for trans students without any major overhaul. Administrators, teachers, and other staff can prepare to care for the needs of gender nonconforming children in a number of ways. Here are a few:

1. Gain familiarity with specific questions that may arise from students or parents and become confident in providing knowledgeable answers
2. Address classroom situations/questions in a manner consistent with other areas of diversity
3. Create and/or implement school policies that specifically name gender identity and gender expression

Some schools are excited to be on the cutting edge of trans student rights, but many are not, at least not at first. Many, however, are happy to ride on the coattails of schools that have successfully implemented trans-inclusive practices. Knowing that other schools have broken this ground with little controversy and to the benefit of all students can mean all the difference in the world. Fortunately, a number of schools have done this work and can provide other schools and districts with successful experiences and model policies.

MAKING CHANGE IN SEATTLE PUBLIC SCHOOLS

Lisa Love, MEd, works in Seattle schools overseeing LGBTQ programs, health education, and prevention efforts.

The Seattle Public Schools' Health Education Office has worked with students, staff, and families to address issues regarding sexual orientation and gender identity since roughly 1987. We already had inclusive policy language, which specifically identified gender identity and expression within its protected classes. What we did not have was a procedural guide for school administrators. Using our *Washington State Healthy Youth* data and our *Youth Risk Behavior Survey* data, as well as our estimates of numbers of students needing support in our schools, we made a strong case to district administrators and the legal office in support of needing a Superintendent Procedure. We convened a group of parents, community members, and staff to gather content input, and we also collected sample language from other states and school districts.

We reviewed language from a few other existing district policies and some national model policies. After much tweaking, wordsmithing, committee reviews, and meetings with students and families, we finally had a draft Superintendent Procedure for addressing the most common questions asked by school administrators and families. Our draft, *Superintendent Procedure 3210SP.C*, was in an almost-final version and slowly made its way through the vetting process within our school district. While Seattle is a progressive city, it was not always easy to move things forward. Many questions and concerns were raised by everyone from principals, to people in the enrollment office, to PE teachers, to folks who address the district technology systems. When we had nearly half of our approval signatures, the process was halted to gain even more input. Administrators expressed concern that we did not have enough buy-in from those in Operations. Another committee was convened. In the end, everyone was on board with moving forward and the document was signed by the Superintendent. Some of the key policies in the document include the following:

- Names/Pronouns: Students shall have the right to be addressed by a name and pronoun that correspond to their consistently asserted gender identity.
- Official Records: The District shall change a student's official records to reflect a change in legal name or gender upon receipt of documentation that such legal name and/or gender have been changed pursuant to Washington State Law.

- Restroom Accessibility: A student should be provided access to a restroom facility that corresponds to the gender identity the student consistently asserts at school.
- Locker Rooms: Schools may provide a student access to a locker room facility that corresponds to the gender identity the student consistently asserts at school.
- Sports/Physical Education (PE) Classes: Transgender and gender nonconforming students shall not be denied the opportunity to participate in PE or extracurricular activities.
- Dress Codes: Students shall have the right to dress in accordance with the gender identity they consistently assert at school, within the constraints of the dress codes adopted at their school site.
- Gender Segregation in Other Areas: As a general rule, in any other circumstances where students are separated by gender in school activities, students shall be permitted to participate in accordance with the gender identity they consistently assert at school.

State and Federal Laws Around Gender in Schools

Each state has a governing body that oversees education at a state level, with a set of guidelines governing discrimination against students. Contacting these officials or obtaining a copy of the guidelines can be good first steps for approaching a school district about the needs of a gender nonconforming child. Local school districts may also have their own policies. As recipients of federal financial assistance, school districts are obligated to follow federal civil rights laws and regulations, including Title IX of the Education Amendments of 1972, which prohibits discrimination in education on the basis of sex. A number of precedent-setting cases are making evident that discrimination based on a person's gender identity or transgender status does indeed constitute sex discrimination and falls under federal protections. Learning all you can about any existing policies and guidelines relevant to your school, municipality, and state will better equip you to advocate for your child within the legal expectations rather than being perceived to be requesting special considerations.

Working With School Officials

Discussing gender inclusivity with a person in a position to effect change on a school-wide basis is important. Think about who would be the strongest ally within your local school system and reach out to that person. It may be the principal, vice principal, a teacher, or school counselor. Tell them that you would like to hear about what practices they already have in place and how you can help them to create a safe, healthy learning environment for all children. Ask them whether they have had transgender students in the past. If so, was the student private about their gender history or was there open knowledge of the student's status? How did the school protect the student's privacy and protect the student from teasing or marginalization? What are the existing policies in relation to bathrooms, locker rooms, and other gender-separated spaces?

The head of the school is responsible for enforcing the legal requirements for both preventing discrimination and maintaining an optimal learning environment for all students. Administrators are often unaware of how to create this optimal environment and minimize/eliminate instances of teasing or bullying in relation to gender identity and expression. Many are appreciative when provided with educational or training resources. Sometimes an administrator is resistant or hesitant to learn from parents themselves. Training organizations or gender advocates can be very helpful in situations like this.

Implementing New Guidelines

A great starting place for any school is to examine the school's inclusion policy. It is important to update existing antidiscrimination language and any other guidelines. This serves to set the tone for the entire school community. Review the school's mission statement or school handbook. An ideal mission statement will include language that takes a stand against discrimination based on gender identity and gender expression. If this terminology already exists, it is likely that the school has already encountered gender-diverse students. It may not mean that the school has everything figured out with respect to the unique day-to-day situations related to gender nonconforming students, but it at least provides a place from which to launch your work. It is important to note that a broadly worded antidiscrimination policy is not enough. The most successful outcomes for gender nonconforming children and the entire school community come when gender identity and gender expression are clearly stated.

School Training

Once school administrators are ready to increase their knowledge and understanding, it is ideal for the full staff, parents, and students to receive training. While individual teachers who have direct, daily contact with a trans or gender nonconforming student are often ready and willing to address gender inclusivity within the classroom setting, it is extremely beneficial to have both the support of the administration and the participation of the whole school community. Other students, their parents, and teachers often have questions or concerns, especially at first, regarding the presence of a transgender student at a school. There are organizations, such as Gender Spectrum, Gender Diversity, and the Gay, Lesbian, and Straight Education Network (GLSEN), that offer specialized training in this area. While it involves the investment of time to educate the students, teachers, and support staff at the outset, the end result will benefit any existing students as well as the future trans and gender nonconforming students that will come.

STAFF TRAINING

It is important that all staff receive education on gender nonconformity and trans identity. Teasing and bullying can occur on the bus to school, in the classroom, in the lunchroom, in the gym, or during after-school programs. Every adult needs to have familiarity with issues that come up for trans and gender nonconforming children.

When seeking a qualified trainer, look for someone who can offer the following:

- An explanation of gender variance and the ways it is expressed in children of all ages
- Definitions and in-depth explanations of gender-related terminology
- An overview of current research regarding gender variance and children
- Information on legal issues, obligations, and best practices for schools in relation to trans students
- Basic strategies that allow all students to safely navigate classrooms, play areas, lunchrooms, bathrooms, and school trips
- Direct antibullying and harassment methods related to issues of gender diversity
- A safe environment for teachers to learn more about trans students and issues

Schools that have undertaken trainings have been delighted at the positive outcomes. Principles and concepts learned in a training can later be built into academic lesson plans, classroom conversations, and will also serve the purpose of enhancing the overall culture of acceptance at the school. Teachers and administrators alike who, at the outset, were cautiously optimistic, express great excitement and satisfaction when witnessing the ways young students engage in conversations about gender.

One first-grade teacher had this to say:

"Despite my increased understanding of gender [from the training], I was still nervous about how the kiddos might react. Would they accept that Sara was now JJ and that 'she' was now 'he?' And I was still really worried that the conversation about gender differences was too mature for them. Wow, when I saw the encouragement and support sent JJ's way, I was so moved. Then I heard how excited the kids were to talk about their own gender and how much they all felt the gender 'squeeze' restricting what they could do, and wear, and enjoy! I felt like I was a kid again and was reminded of the simplicity of gender at that age. Amazing!" —Teacher reporting on a classroom training led by Aidan Key

PARENT EDUCATION IN SCHOOLS

Parent education opportunities allow parents to gain an informed understanding of the training the school is undertaking as well as the education the students are receiving. Offering education for parents creates a way to increase parental awareness of this topic and answer any questions they might have. It can help to relieve parental concerns as to whether this topic is age appropriate for their children and culturally relevant. In trainings, parents are informed of the school's legal obligations with respect to local, state, and federal antidiscrimination policies as well as the school's own policies and approaches.

A qualified presenter can structure an evening of parent education as a stand-alone presentation or a facilitated presentation that includes a panel discussion. Panel members may include a gender identity therapist, teachers, parents of trans children, and trans teens and adults. One of the most valuable ways to shift those who may be fearful or resistant to discussions of gender diversity is for them to hear real-life stories of those who are walking this path.

Parents of other children often have lots of questions and feelings about gender-related discussions in school. These may include the following:

- Won't this confuse my child?
- This does not align with my faith.
- What will you say to the children in the classroom?
- Which child at the school is transgender? Don't we have the right to know?

These are questions worthy of response. Offering parents a chance to ask questions will greatly relieve their concerns and better equip them to continue the conversation with their own child in a more informed way.

Many parents express great delight when they hear how their own children respond to discussions of gender. One parent, who came to a parent education night, had this to say:

> "I pick up my third-grade daughter from school every day and I always ask how her day went. She always gives me a flat, 'Okay.' Today, I picked her up as usual, but this time she wouldn't stop talking! She said people came to her class today to talk about 'being different,' and that she got to share how she was different! I've never seen her so excited. She had no problem understanding how a person might feel like they were a different gender, even though she doesn't feel that way herself. But, she says, 'I know how it feels to be different and I get teased for that.' When class was over, she said all the other kids made an agreement to no longer tease or be mean to each other. Whatever you talked to those kids about today in class, I'd really encourage you to keep doing it!"

EDUCATION OF STUDENTS IN SCHOOLS

Children have different ways of understanding gender at different developmental stages. It is important to frame concepts in ways that children can understand at each of these stages. Parents and teachers can have age-appropriate conversations with children starting from very young ages about gender identity, gender roles, and the social expectations we have about people based on their gender assigned at birth.

A discussion about gender variance is a simple conversation and one that is quite exciting for most kids. Young children are eager to talk about gender and how it relates to the clothes they wear, the games they play, and how other children treat them. Children are able to easily challenge society's gendered expectations about the things we wear, the things we like, the things we want to do, and how these expectations are unfair and restricting. Children can readily articulate the inequities they experience as a result of their gender.

"It's not fair! Girls get to wear dresses, skirts, pants, and shorts—we just get pants and shorts. Girls get to wear any color they want! We get brown, blue, and black." —seven-year-old boy at a Gender Diversity classroom presentation

Children are also quite capable of understanding the parallels between diversity in gender and other aspects of a person's identity. When asked about the reasons for which any of them had ever been teased, second graders in a classroom presentation provided these kinds of answers:

- *Kids tease me because my family moved from Korea last year and I didn't know any English.*
- *People tease me because I'm adopted.*
- *I get teased because my skin is darker.*
- *I'm the tallest kid in the class and a girl. I get teased for that.*
- *I get teased because I have two dads.*
- *Kids tease me because I have a little skin tag by my ear.*

Children are naturally curious about new things and, of course, have questions. What is important to remember is to provide a direct answer to a direct question at the level the child can understand. When talking to children about gender nonconformity, we often worry that we are going to confuse them. There is no need to delve into mature or complex explanations beyond their developmental capacity. For example, a six-year-old child might make this comment about her friend: "Jason looks like a boy but says he's a girl!" A direct way to respond would be to say, "Yes, it may seem confusing at first but what Jason is saying is that, while he may have the body of a boy, he has the heart and mind of a girl. Some kids feel that way and perhaps you didn't know that."

Parents, as well as teachers and other providers, can use opportunities like these to talk with children about gender. Bringing these conversations directly to children of all ages can serve to dramatically lessen bullying between children. It provides children the opportunity to practice inclusion, respect, and compassion.

School Bathrooms

Bathroom transitions can be a source of intense debate among parents and school officials. There are a number of issues that emerge when families and schools begin talking about which bathroom a trans or gender nonconforming student will use.

The first step in deciding on the correct bathroom for a trans or gender nonconforming child is to spend time talking with the child about where they feel they belong. All children should use the restroom that best aligns with their gender identity. For trans boys, this is likely to be the boys' restroom and for trans girls, the girls' restroom. Children who have a more gender-fluid identity should use the restroom that provides them the greatest degree of comfort and safety.

Parents of gender nonconforming children often indicate that their main concern about which bathroom their child uses at school is where they are going to be the most safe. Parents may worry that their child will be teased or physically assaulted. Often the greatest fear is expressed by parents of trans boys who assume that the likelihood of violence is greater in the boys' bathroom. Parents of trans girls also express concern, not so much for physical assault in the bathroom, although that can occur, but for verbal harassment and ostracism.

Many adults are concerned with how children will react when a trans student changes bathrooms. The best way to predict how children will respond is to take a look at how the adults in the children's environment are responding. If the school leadership approaches the "bathroom question" with a matter-of-fact, respectful approach, this provides an excellent example for the children to emulate. Sometimes children are ready for a change even before adults come on board.

Occasionally there are students who are truly uncomfortable when sharing a bathroom with another student who is transgender. Or perhaps a trans or gender nonconforming student is not comfortable using either the boys' or the girls' bathroom. This can happen for a variety of reasons and may or may not be temporary. School districts are adopting policies to meet the needs of any student experiencing discomfort by offering the use of an alternative restroom such as the staff or nurse's bathroom. The important distinction to recognize is that this option is not being forced on the trans student and it is one available to any student desiring the need for increased privacy.

Many parents are unaware of what can occur when their child does not have a safe and accessible bathroom. Some gender nonconforming children avoid using the bathroom at all at school. Many parents are shocked to discover this and may only become aware of it when their child develops a urinary tract infection, kidney infection, or suffers from dehydration. Trans children will sometimes avoid drinking any fluids during the day to minimize the need to urinate. If a child is not provided with the appropriate restroom, they may simply make a choice to "hold it."

Some schools have felt like an acceptable "middle ground" means providing the youth with an alternative bathroom such as one in the nurse's office or in the teachers' lounge. This can work in some temporary situations, but a child may even avoid this option if it draws unwanted attention to them, so it is important to find out from the child if they feel comfortable using the new bathroom they have been assigned rather than assuming they will use it if they need to.

When a school begins to talk about a student transitioning bathrooms, parents of other children may have strong reactions. They may express concern that their children will not be safe when a transgender child is in the bathroom. This feeling is not exclusive to other parents and may even be felt by principals, teachers, or support staff. They may vocalize their fear or concern and yet be unable to articulate exactly why they are afraid. These vaguely defined concerns directly tie into our cultural fears and misperceptions of who trans people are—at least who we have been led to believe they are—and that includes imposters, sexual deviants, or people who are mentally ill. Many adults subconsciously project these misperceptions onto even very young children.

In a Gender Diversity training session, one elementary teacher expressed her concern for the safety of other girls in the restroom if a trans girl were to begin using the bathroom. When asked to expand on her concern, the teacher said she was fearful that the other students would somehow see the trans girl's penis. When the leader inquired as to how she thought that might happen, she said, *"Well, you know, girls might look over the walls of the stall."* The leader suggested that the trans girl in the stall would feel more frightened by this behavior than the other girls. The teacher nodded her head in agreement, as if by speaking her fears aloud, it was made evident which student would be traumatized by this scenario. She learned that this was not a gender issue; rather, this was an issue of bad behavior. Any student looking over the stall wall at another was violating the other child's privacy and deserving of some form of intervention or discipline. All in the room agreed.

Use of public restrooms in places like airports, malls, restaurants, and other highly trafficked areas are often concerning for parents of children who are of an age where they are expected to enter unaccompanied by their parent. The concern seems greatest for mothers of trans boys. Mothers can feel less confident at instructing their sons about male bathroom culture as well as have greater fear of predatory behavior from strangers.

Some suggestions to be restroom-ready:

1. Role-play different scenarios from the practical, the ridiculous, and the serious. Get on a trans parent email list and ask for some "bathroom stories." Likely, you will get so many varied responses that there will be no problem getting a child prepared for just about anything.

2. Trans children, teens, and adults are not the only ones who struggle with adapting to "bathroom culture." There are a surprising number of books that present many bathroom do's and don'ts and offer great tips for taking care of business.

3. Instruct your child on basic safety issues regarding any interaction with a stranger and what to do if they feel uneasy or scared.

4. Parents: Remember, bathrooms are *not* sacred territory! If your child is using a different restroom than you and it is taking longer than expected, do not hesitate to (1) give a shout into the restroom, (2) enlist the help of another person in that restroom, or (3) simply go right in to get your child. Nothing trumps the safety of your child.

Extracurricular Activities

Gender-separated activities are everywhere—not just schools. Parents can face a perplexing challenge when considering overnight camps, after-school programs, sports, and other group activities. The issue of whether to disclose a child's gender status or keep it private may have been settled some time ago at school only to find that it crops up all over again for each new situation. Joining a sports team or attending a new camp or after-school program can be like starting from square one. Inclusive policies may or may not exist, and they may or may not be enforced. A camp administrator may propose that a transgender child attend the weeklong camp but stay in a separate cabin or with the adult chaperones in their cabin. To a child, this arrangement is the complete antithesis of why they would like to attend a camp. An instructor or coach may feel like the other parents "have a right to know" the child's gender status and place different participation requirements on the transgender child.

Whatever the situation, know that an ounce of prevention is worth a pound of cure. Seek out any existing policy in advance. Provide examples of trans-inclusive school guidelines. Find out if any other trans children have ever attended/engaged in the activity and the pathway provided for their participation. There are situations across the country where various youth programs have had trans youth participation. Call them. Find out what they experienced and what they learned. If an entity has successful experience(s), see whether they have a policy that reflects that. Ask whether an administrator, coach, or other program head would be willing to discuss this with the camp or troop you are considering for your child. Unfortunately, there have been too many situations where a family is left with no alternative but to pursue legal assistance.

CAMP ARANU'TIQ: THE WORLD'S FIRST SUMMER CAMP FOR TRANSGENDER KIDS

Nicholas M. Teich is founder and president of Camp Aranu'tiq.

Nicholas M. Teich

Summer camp meant a great deal to me growing up, even before I was conscious of my transgender identity. I attended a traditional overnight camp in Maine, where I was a camper, counselor, and eventually a member of the camp's leadership. Later on, I began to volunteer at a separate nonprofit camp. In 2007, after several years volunteering and being involved in the nonprofit camp, I was abruptly told that I could not return because my impending gender transition would apparently be detrimental to the well-being of the kids. That hurt. A lot.

Once I dusted myself off and gained some perspective, I began to think: How do kids who identify as trans or gender-variant go to overnight camp? I believed they must face rejection in droves, and unfortunately I was correct. I set out to start a safe place for these youth. When I founded Camp Aranu'tiq in early 2009, I could never have dreamed of the impact the campers would have on me.

The locations of our camps remain undisclosed to the best of our ability. It's unfortunate that this has to be the case, but we live in a world where people fear difference. Our first summer week began in 2010, with 41 campers at a quaint Connecticut camp overlooking a stunning waterway. We grew in 2011 and again in

Campers hiking at Camp Aranu'tiq.

2012, expanding to another week at a location in California. In 2014, we will have 5 camps for ages 6–18, including a family camp, and we will serve over 300 campers.

Camp Aranu'tiq (a word that describes someone who transcends gender boundaries and is revered for it, in the Yu'pik language) was established with the express purpose of giving transgender and gender-variant kids a place where they could connect with one another and still have a typical overnight camp experience. In other words, Aranu'tiq would not be a place where we sat around in groups and talked about gender or what it was like to be seen as "different" in school or in our home communities. These children have to defend and talk about their gender enough outside of camp. Camp would just be camp.

Though we do not have formal talks about gender, the campers take it upon themselves to talk a lot about their shared experiences. This happens organically around the dinner table, while waiting in line for the restroom, or even while playing ball or crafting a skit in drama class. One of the funniest moments from our first summer was witnessing a group of teenage trans boys completing a low ropes course element where they had to come through a tunnel of ropes and out the other side. When they emerged, their friends shouted, "It's a boy!" and they deemed it their "rebirth."

I've learned a lot from our campers. They often don't feel beautiful, handsome, or confident in the outside world—but at camp, they do feel this way. It's the simplicity of being with others like them and being encouraged by adult role models, some of whom share their transgender or gender-variant identity, and some of whom do not. They occasionally complain, talk back, and cause unnecessary drama like any other kids. They prefer fried chicken and ice cream to baked salmon and fruit. They sometimes insist on wearing dresses and high heels to go canoeing. They might not get to wear these outfits at all outside of camp or the privacy of their own bedrooms, so they are going to make the most of it, common sense be damned.

In 2012, we had a preapproved visitor to camp who told me a few times that she was struck by how much like any other camp we were. That is all I ever wanted to show an outsider. Many people believe that transgender kids will look and act differently than non-trans kids in ways that I believe they cannot even picture in their minds. I am unsure if they are expecting a circus or a Jerry Springer episode or what, but those of us who know what a day in the life of Camp Aranu'tiq looks like know that they would be shocked and even bored by the mundaneness of kids running, playing, doing crafts, swimming, and laughing. That was the plan all along.

People always ask what happens after the camp week is over. For the past two years we have done a six-month postcamp survey and found that the vast majority—in fact almost all our campers—are in touch with others on a regular basis. Many of them have told me that they met their best friends at Camp Aranu'tiq. We encourage these bonds. After a tough day at school, it's wonderful for them to be able to call or connect with a camp friend who understands what they are going through. I consider myself incredibly lucky to be able to watch our campers grow and change from year to year, and I can't wait to see what amazing adults they grow to be.

Bullying

Even teachers who are completely on board in their support of a gender nonconforming child in their classroom may find themselves at a loss for words when another child says, "Why does Sam wear dresses to school? That's stupid!" How should they respond? What are the actual words?

If this comment were addressing a topic with which the teacher had familiarity, the response might feel like a no-brainer. But because many teachers often do not feel knowledgeable about issues related to gender, they are often caught off guard and end up saying nothing. Or they may not feel able to convert a child's off-the-cuff remark into a "teachable moment" for simple logistical reasons. For example, the comment could have been said on the way to the lunchroom. The teacher again does not respond, feeling as if the comment needs to be handled in a gentle, thoughtful manner that might inspire a deeper conversation for that particular student or for the whole classroom.

The reality is that the gender component of the conversation does not necessarily need to be addressed in depth if that is not realistic. However, no response at all can imply implicit approval. The critical part of the comment to address is the denigrating "That's stupid!" A reasonable and appropriate response could be something like "Sam likes to wear dresses and, at our school, we believe every student has the right to be exactly who they are. What we DON'T do at this school is make fun of anyone for any reason. It is not OK to call someone stupid, and I am asking you not to do that anymore." The gendered component of the initial comment was addressed simply—without ignoring or overexplaining it—but the more harmful element ("Sam is stupid") was handled swiftly. If there are any further denigrating comments, the teacher is easily positioned to follow up with any disciplinary action based solidly on school policy (no teasing or bullying).

A large percentage of children are teased and bullied because of atypical gender expression even in the earliest grades. Often teachers and other support staff feel helpless to intervene because femininity in a boy and masculinity in a girl are viewed as indicators of future gay or lesbian sexual orientation.

"Davey is a sissy!"

"Why does Keisha look like a boy?"

If a teacher's first thought is that Davey will grow up to be gay or that Keisha may eventually be a lesbian, they have just inadvertently categorized this situation as one that is about sexuality—and therefore off limits for discussion with younger age students. Because of this, the unwelcome comment or question goes unaddressed. But this situation is about gender, not sexuality, and can be addressed with children of any age. Silence on the part of the teacher allows the teasing to go unchecked and worsen. No response can offer implicit approval for continued teasing and bullying.

Switching Schools

Changing schools can be stressful but can also be an opportunity for a gender nonconforming or transgender child to have a fresh start. When efforts to address school problems at the administrative level have not been successful, some families consider a different school for a child. Other families consider a change of school at the point that a child begins to socially transition because it can provide an opportunity to "start fresh." This new start can sometimes be just what a child needed. On the other hand, it is important to consider that information spreads easily between parents, administrators, and students at different schools, so a new school may not mean a group of people who are unaware of a child's past.

Some families with means find that private schools are more welcoming than public schools. Others discover that homeschooling, online school, or other alternative educational options fit their children well. There are homeschooling groups where parents and children meet up to work on projects together, and many of these are supportive of gender nonconforming children. An argument that is sometimes presented against alternative schooling options is that the child misses out on important socialization opportunities. However, if a child is being teased, bullied, harassed, or assaulted at school, positive socialization opportunities are lost.

CONSIDERING MEDICAL INTERVENTIONS

The decision to pursue medical intervention with gender nonconforming youth can be complicated and is unique to each family. The possibility of medical intervention is important to talk about early, and with a supportive pediatrician or family doctor. Building relationships with experienced health care providers can be extremely rewarding, and doing this early can prevent feelings that a family is rushing at the last minute to explore options.

Finding Providers

In addition to mental health providers, many families of gender nonconforming children benefit from connecting early with a supportive pediatrician or family doctor. For some families, it is also important to see a pediatric endocrinologist, who specializes in hormones and children's bodies.

General pediatricians working in communities often have little training in working with gender nonconforming children. Some are eager to learn. Many families have established relationships with their pediatricians and want to continue working with them, while others feel more comfortable finding new pediatricians who have more experience working with gender nonconforming children. Children come into contact with other types of medical providers such as nurses and dentists on a regular basis, and it is appropriate to request and expect these providers to use the proper name and pronoun for a child during all interactions. If a pediatrician or other health care provider is not respectful of a family's wishes, it may be important to change providers.

Pediatric endocrinologists are pediatricians who specialize in hormonal disorders such as diabetes and growth problems. Many pediatric endocrinologists are not familiar with treatments for gender nonconforming children, although they use the same medications (puberty blockers) to treat growth disorders. Like many pediatricians, pediatric endocrinologists are often eager to learn about gender nonconforming children. There are a few who specialize in this area. Puberty blockers can be prescribed by a general pediatrician, family practitioner, or a pediatric endocrinologist. A number of providers find that, with adequate resources or consulting opportunities, the endocrine care of preadolescents falls well within their scope of practice.

WORKING WITH CURRENT PROVIDERS

Many of us feel comfortable with the providers our children are already seeing and would like to continue seeing them. If this is true, it can be important to schedule a special visit to talk about our child's gender identity. If the child has been assessed by a therapist, state that. If you are supportive of your child's identity and/or their gender exploration, state that as well. It is helpful for the doctor to have a snapshot of your family's process so they can best determine where their responsibility begins and ends. Determine your objective for the visit. Are you just updating them on the current state of events? Wanting continued care for your child, including medical interventions? Start with the former, regardless of later needs. Doctors are just like anyone else and may have unpredictable emotional reactions. If you have a doctor who expresses support and willingness to learn, that is great. They may look to you to point them to resources, connect them to providers with whom they can consult, or to answer their direct questions related to concepts of gender diversity.

FINDING NEW PROVIDERS

You may find that your child's current doctor is unwilling or lacks the confidence to care for your child. Or perhaps you prefer to not put yourself in the educator role. Selecting a new doctor then becomes the next step. Calling or e-mailing a doctor's office to assess their experience and willingness may not be enough. The front desk staff may insist the doctor does not provide this care when indeed they do. Or a scheduler may tell a new caller that the doctor's practice is full when the provider actually makes exceptions for new transgender patients. If at all possible, arrange for a direct conversation with the doctor.

Your local LGBTQ center may be able to refer you to experienced providers. You can also join an email list for parents of transgender children and ask for referrals. Other parents are one of your greatest resources for so many things related to this journey. If you make enough information-gathering inquiries, there may be a name or two that is mentioned again and again.

A Sampling of Medical Clinics for Transgender Children

- Center for Transyouth Health and Development, Children's Hospital of Los Angeles
- Child & Adolescent Gender Center Clinic, UCSF Benioff Children's Hospital
- Gender & Sexuality Psychosocial Programs, Children's National Medical Center, DC
- Gender & Sexuality Service, New York University
- Gender Management Service (GeMS), Boston Children's Hospital
- Gender, Sexuality and HIV Prevention Center, Lurie Children's Hospital of Chicago

MEDICAL INTERVENTION FOR TRANS CHILDREN

Johanna Olson, MD, is the medical director of the Center for Transyouth Health and Development at Children's Hospital Los Angeles. Her career is dedicated to clinical care and research promoting authentic living for all youth.

The Endocrine Guidelines, published in 2009, recommend that children who are identifying as transgender or gender nonconforming when puberty begins can be placed on "puberty blockers," a group of prescribed medications that suppress or inhibit a child's unwanted pubertal development. Ideally, this intervention should be used as early as Tanner Stage Two (the second stage of puberty) for several reasons:

1. *The effects of blockers are fully reversible.* This means that if the medication is stopped, puberty will progress as it would have. While the use of these medications for transgender children is relatively recent, blockers have been used for decades to halt early onset of puberty in young children (a condition known as central precocious puberty).

2. *Blockers can buy time for kids and parents.* Delaying puberty allows for an amount of added time so that a child can continue in their gender exploration, if needed. Perhaps even more important, it serves to alleviate fears that parents or other adults may experience. It simply allows the time needed for them to gain increased confidence and certainty.

3. *Blockers can optimize the development of preferred physical characteristics.* In trans girls, blockers initiated prior to the development of male secondary sexual characteristics will effectively prevent voice deepening, skeletal enlargement, and penile enlargement. In trans boys, these early medications can prevent characteristics such as breast development, hip widening, and starting menstruation.

Medications most commonly used for puberty delay are called gonadotropin-releasing hormone (GnRH) analogs. GnRH is a hormone released from the hypothalamus in the brain to trigger the pituitary gland in the brain to release leutinizing hormone (LH) and follicle-stimulating hormone (FSH). LH and FSH stimulate the ovaries or the testes to secrete estrogen or testosterone. The easiest way to understand the role of GnRH analogs is to imagine the medication as a way to "block" the release of LH and FSH and, subsequently, estrogen or testosterone.

The GnRH analog mimics the action of the body's natural GnRH. It bombards the pituitary, effectively shutting down the feedback loop. This is why occasionally, when adolescents are first started on blockers, they experience an actual increase in pubertal symptoms during the first month or so. This is temporary and usually recedes with time.

Puberty blockers come in two main forms: intramuscular injections or a surgically placed implant positioned in the upper arm. The injections happen either monthly or every three months. The implant (usually placed at an outpatient office visit) tends to last between 12 and 18 months, sometimes longer. Both forms of blockers are very expensive, although increasing numbers of insurance companies are starting to cover them. Pediatricians, family doctors, internists, gynecologists, and endocrinologists are all well suited to prescribe and deliver hormone blockers.

Trans girls (assigned male at birth) begin puberty on average between 11 and 13 years of age. The first sign of puberty is generally testicular enlargement. Trans girls should be advised to look out for these initial changes. This is important because, as trans children begin puberty, they are likely to be very unwilling to allow their parents to see their naked body, especially if they feel distress about their body. At Tanner Stage Two, a trans girl will have some testicular enlargement and some growth of adult-type pubic hair. This is the time to begin hormone blockers. Ideally, hormone blockers are initiated prior to any further development such as voice deepening, skeletal enlargement, or penile enlargement, as these characteristics are not reversible with feminizing hormones. Transgender girls who take puberty blockers are *not* going to be peer-concordant in their sexual development simply because the average male puberty begins two years later than the average female puberty. If a 12-year-old transgender girl begins puberty, goes on blockers, and gets on cross sex hormones even as early as 14, she will still be behind her female peer group in breast development. This may be a factor in deciding when to initiate cross sex hormones.

Trans boys (assigned female at birth) usually begin puberty between the ages of 9 and 11 years. Invariably, it almost always begins with the development of breast buds and, occasionally the development of a few adult-like pubic hairs, signaling Tanner Stage Two. Transgender boys need to be taught about the early signs of puberty so that they can alert their parents or caretakers that it is time for medical intervention. Transgender boys have a better chance of being peer concordant with regard to typical male sexual development, but they will likely be on blocking medication longer than transgender girls.

The most common concern regarding hormone blockers is that of diminished bone density. While there have been many studies examining the bone density of children who are prescribed hormone blockers for central precocious puberty, there has been only one small study considering this question in transgender youth. This study, undertaken in the Netherlands, showed that bone density was diminished during puberty suppression on GnRH analogs, but that it recovered with the addition of appropriate cross sex hormones, ultimately reaching appropriate levels. Any medical decision must weigh the benefits of use versus the risks (both known and unknown).

Cross sex hormones are used in those youth who persist in their transgender identity into adolescence and subsequently desire a physical body that matches their internal gender identity. Cross sex hormones are also used by adults who are beginning their gender transition.

Transgender young men may be treated with testosterone in order to suppress female physiologic traits and to enhance masculinization of the body. The primary goals of testosterone therapy are menstrual cessation, or primary amenorrhea (never starting menstruation), deepening of the voice, development of male pattern body hair, increased muscle mass, and clitoral enlargement. These processes occur at different stages of testosterone therapy, not unlike a typical male puberty. The timeline varies from person to person, and it usually takes years to be complete.

Transgender young women may take estrogen alone or in combination with testosterone blockers. Those on puberty blockers may not need to take testosterone blockers. The purpose of estrogen and testosterone blockers is to aid in the development of female physical characteristics while avoiding the development of the laryngeal prominence (Adam's apple), deepening of the voice, development of male pattern body hair, testicular and penile enlargement, and excessive height.

Suppression of one's naturally occurring puberty and the progression of the affirmed puberty will result in the inability of young people to have their own biological children. Additionally, trans girls who begin blockers at Tanner Stage Two and then proceed to cross sex hormones will not develop mature enough sperm to bank for future use. Trans youth should be made aware of their options with regard to fertility and the potential that they may not be able to have their own biological children if they start cross sex hormones. These are difficult discussions, but ones that should be had.

Puberty blockers and cross sex hormones are not for every youth or family. Puberty blockers can be prohibitively expensive for some, and not the right choice for others, but they are an option to be aware of and discuss.

Educating Health Care Providers

For some families, especially those living in larger metropolitan areas, knowledgeable health care providers may be close by. However, for many people, reaching someone with experience may involve a plane ride that is not necessarily affordable. For those with means who live in remote areas, one option is to travel to see a more experienced provider in a larger city a few times a year, and to work with a local pediatrician. For those who cannot afford to do this, there may be a local physician who is willing to learn what is necessary to help. In either case, families may spend a considerable amount of time and effort educating providers about working with gender nonconforming children.

Adult transgender people often find that they need to provide resources and support to their providers. There is little taught in nursing, medical, or physician assistant programs about transgender health. While it can be extremely frustrating to have to educate providers, it can also be rewarding to see that their new knowledge is helpful to other families struggling with similar issues.

It is important to be aware that there are providers who are not knowledgeable about gender nonconforming children but may present themselves as such because they do not want to appear ignorant. Some may have knowledge that is outdated or that is only relevant to adult transgender people. If this situation presents itself, seek out a second opinion or change providers. On the other hand, there are some care professionals who may not know much but will readily own this. They will seek out more experienced providers with whom they can consult; find up-to-date research to enhance their learning; and, if possible, refer a family or child to someone better suited to meet their needs. If no adequate referrals are available, this proactive provider could still be an excellent choice.

One therapist who was eager to learn had this to say:

> *"A parent came to my practice to talk about her newly trans-identified child. As a lesbian, I wasn't completely unfamiliar with transgender issues—I even had a trans man as a client—but, I had no idea how to help this parent regarding their trans child nor did I know anyone who could help. The next time I saw my adult client, I asked him if I could have 15 minutes of his time at the end of his session to discuss how I might best support this parent. I offered to give him a free session as well. He readily agreed and was so delighted in how I handled it! He said he'd already paid a number of therapists to find help for working on family-of-origin issues (not gender issues) and found that every one of them incessantly questioned him about his now years-old gender transition. He was so relieved by my approach that it not only was helpful to me and my other client but also deepened the trust that he and I had. Everyone benefited!"* (Conversation with Aidan Key)

CONCLUSION

Raising a transgender or gender nonconforming child can be both exciting and scary. Being open minded and supportive, as well as seeking out resources and community, are important to creating an optimal environment for exploration. Providing children with loving homes, acceptance, and emotional tools builds the resilience and self-esteem that all people need to have happy and fulfilling lives.

REFERENCES AND FURTHER READING

Adelson, S. L. (2012). Practice parameter on gay, lesbian, or bisexual sexual orientation, gender nonconformity, and gender discordance in children and adolescents. *Journal of the American Academy of Child and Adolescent Psychiatry, 51*(9), 957–974.

American Psychiatric Association. (2013). *Diagnostic and statistical manual of mental disorders* (5th ed.). Washington, DC: American Psychiatric Publishing.

Angello, M. (2013). *On the couch with Dr. Angello: A guide to raising and supporting transgender youth.* Philadelphia, PA: Author.

Boenke, M. (2008). *Trans forming families: Real stories about transgendered loved ones.* Hardy, VA: Oak Knoll Press.

Brill, S. A., & Pepper, R. (2008). *The transgender child: A handbook for families and professionals.* San Francisco, CA: Cleis Press.

Davenport, C. W. (1986). A follow-up study of 10 feminine boys. *Archives of Sexual Behavior, 15,* 511–517.

Drummond, K. D., Bradley, S. J., Peterson-Badali, M., & Zucker, K. J. (2008). A follow-up study of girls with gender identity disorder. *Developmental Psychology, 44*(1), 34–45.

Ehrensaft, D. (2011). *Gender born, gender made: Raising healthy gender- nonconforming children.* New York, NY: The Experiment.

Green, R. (1987). *The "sissy boy syndrome" and the development of homosexuality.* New Haven, CT: Yale University Press.

Hill, D. B., Menvielle, E., Sica, K. M., & Johnson, A. (2010). An affirmative intervention for families with gender variant children: Parental ratings of child mental health and gender. *Journal of Sex and Marital Therapy, 36*(1), 6–23.

Mallon, G. P. (2009). *Social work practice with transgender and gender variant youth.* New York, NY: Routledge.

Menvielle, E. (2012). A comprehensive program for children with gender variant behaviors and gender identity disorders. *Journal of Homosexuality, 59*(3), 357–368.

Pepper, R. (2012). *Transitions of the heart: Stories of love, struggle and acceptance by mothers of transgender and gender variant children.* Berkeley, CA: Cleis Press.

Pleak, R. R. (2011). Gender-variant children and transgender adolescents. *Child and Adolescent Psychiatric Clinics of North America, 20*(4), xv–xx.

Ryan, C., Russell, S. T., Huebner, D., Diaz, R., & Sanchez, J. (2010). Family acceptance in adolescence and the health of LGBT young adults. *Journal of Child and Adolescent Psychiatric Nursing, 23*(4), 205–213.

Simons, L., Schrager, S. M., Clark, L. F., Belzer, M., & Olson, J. (2013). Parental support and mental health among transgender adolescents. *Journal of Adolescent Health, 53*(6), 791–793.

Spack, N. P., Edwards-Leeper, L., Feldman, H. A., Leibowitz, S., Mandel, F., Diamond, D. A., & Vance, S. R. (2012). Children and adolescents with gender identity disorder referred to a pediatric medical center. *Pediatrics, 129*(3), 418–425.

Steensma, T. D., van der Ende, J., Verhulst, F. C., & Cohen-Kettenis, P. T. (2013). Gender variance in childhood and sexual orientation in adulthood: A prospective study. *Journal of Sexual Medicine, 10*(11), 2723–2733.

Wallien, M. S., & Cohen-Kettenis, P. T. (2008). Psychosexual outcome of gender-dysphoric children. *Journal of the American Academy of Child and Adolescent Psychiatry, 47,* 1413–1423.

Zuger, B. (1978). Effeminate behavior present in boys from childhood: Ten additional years of follow-up. *Comprehensive Psychiatry, 19,* 363–369.

20

YOUTH

Colt Keo-Meier and Lance Hicks

AS TRANS YOUTH, we deal with many of the same issues as trans adults, but at the same time we have our own unique set of concerns. Many of us are legally or financially dependent on adults. As youth, we are often told we are too young to know who we are and what our gender identities are. Like our cis peers, we may also face other challenges as people of color, poor or working-class people, people with disabilities, overweight people, or gay people. We all deal with a combination of struggles—gender is only one small piece.

SELF-EXPLORATION AND SELF-REALIZATION

Adolescence is a time when we are beginning to figure out who we are. During these years, we go through significant biological and social changes that usher us into adulthood. Puberty sets in and our bodies change—usually in ways that highlight sex differences. It is also when we experience increased gender segregation and more pressure to follow gendered social norms. For most people, adolescence is a time when we begin to explore our gender and sexual identities, and many of us begin to recognize ourselves as trans during these years.

Parents, teachers, and other authority figures already routinely set boundaries around the social and sexual behaviors of teenagers. When we begin to express our identities in ways that are different or challenging to their assumptions, it can be hard for them to know how to react. They may write off our trans identities as rebellion, confusion, "just a phase," or otherwise invalidate our experiences. But having freedom to explore our gender identities is an important part of becoming an adult. These are the years when we are learning what kind of adults we will be—and how we inhabit our social genders is a big part of that process.

Shifting Identities

As trans youth, we are brave. We challenge what the world has told us about choices related to our appearance, clothing, and activities. Some of us feel that we have "always known" exactly what gender we are and how we are most comfortable expressing that gender.

> *"I've felt different my entire life, as far as I am aware."* *

> *"I pretty much always knew I was different, but I just found a name for it this year."*

Others of us start out with only a vague idea, or end up changing our minds a few times (or even over and over again). Uncertainty is normal, and figuring out who we are is not a journey that happens overnight.

> *"Before identifying as male, I had a whole lot of labels—bigender, genderqueer, genderfluid, androgyne, dyke, etcetera, etcetera. Mostly this was to do with a sense of ambivalence more than outright hatred of my chest or genitals, although I did have my moments of dysphoria."*

The organization Gender Spectrum has begun an online forum called the "lounge" with communities specifically for trans teens.

---

* Although this is a youth-oriented chapter, quotes in this chapter and throughout the book are taken only from those who identified as 18 or older on the *Trans Bodies, Trans Selves* online survey.

"Unlike so many of the trans stories I hear, even from some of my friends, I didn't really 'know' at a young age. I had feelings, sure, but no framework in which to understand them, no language to describe them; I never, as a kid, consciously knew I was a girl, and certainly never would've said this."

Some of us identify as male or female, while others have nonbinary identities that do not fit neatly into the social categories of male or female. We may immediately recognize which of these labels fits us best, or we may develop a sense of our gender over time. There is no one "right" way to come to terms with our identity.

"I made friends with a trans* guy when I was 14. Up until this point, I wasn't aware that transgendered people even existed, except in the media's crude and inaccurate representation. I was intrigued and did a lot of online researching, because I felt like I did not identify wholly as a female. But I dismissed these feelings as I also didn't identify wholly as a guy. After I turned 15, I found out about non-binary genders and things clicked into place. I hadn't felt comfortable in my body, and having a label, even one I used very loosely, gave me a sense of security. I started binding my chest and feeling good about how I looked, but only in the privacy of my bedroom. At school, I cringed when we were told to divide into lines of boys and girls. I became aware very quickly how many things are gendered in this world, and grew to resent it. I eventually came out to my gay best friend, who completely supported me, and in fact had already been sensing, in his words, a 'genderless vibe' from me. I was more apprehensive coming out to my binary trans friend, but after I did, I felt a lot better having someone I could talk to. I am comfortable in my identity today, and have made it my mission to educate people about non-binary genders."

"I've always felt like I was a bit different than what everyone assumed I was (which was female). When I was younger, I was pretty seriously convinced I was a boy. For a year or so, I made people call me Mike, and I acted like a little boy. As the years went on, that behavior was curbed a bit, but not enough that I was really stifled. I was always a tomboy, and when I got older, I realized I was gay. I came out as a gay woman in high school, and identified that way for a few years. Then I began to identify as genderqueer, which made me much more comfortable with myself and my identity. Recently, within the last few months, I've come to realize that I still want to be the boy I was when I was four. He never went away, he just was hiding for a while. Now I'm the person he grew up to be. I came out very recently as trans, and it has been one of the best things I've ever done."

As we go through our discovery process, many people tell us "it's just a phase." This can be incredibly hurtful, and it may discourage us from openly communicating with those around us about our questions, thoughts, and feelings about our gender. But many parts of people's identities are fluid. The way we dress, speak, and relate to others is something that changes often as we grow up, and our gendered self-image is only one factor that plays a role in shaping our behavior. Even cisgender people, whose gender identity matches their birth-assigned sex, do not always express or view their genders in the same way throughout their lives.

So, how do we know if exploring our gender is "just a phase?" The simple answer is: It does not matter. Exploring our gender identity is part of the path to finding out who we are. As we allow ourselves to do this exploration, we are becoming more healthy, self-actualized, and whole people.

Jackson Radish is a teen librarian and writer living in Toronto, Ontario, whose writing on young adult literature for trans teens and other topics can be found at jackdoeslibraryschool.wordpress.com.

Have you ever encountered a character—in a movie or book or on TV—who "got" you? One reason television and movies are so popular is that they give us an opportunity to see ourselves in another character. When we are different—because of our gender, race, religion, dis/ability, or any other reason—the people we see on TV and in movies don't always look like us. This does not mean that no one has ever told our stories, though; it just means we have to look a little harder for characters like us.

Young adult (YA) literature for transgender youth is still a relatively new genre and there are as many bad books out there as good ones. That being said, there are a few solid fiction and non-fiction books available that talk about the kinds of things trans teens care about, and the genre is growing every year.

Some of us love to read for information and others for fun. Either way, most people are sure to fall in love with books by Kate Bornstein. *My Gender Workbook* reads like a teen magazine, complete with quizzes and juicy stories, but it is designed to help people of all ages and genders explore tough questions about gender and their identities, and have fun in the process. *Hello Cruel World: 101 Alternatives to Suicide for Teens, Freaks and Other Outlaws* reads like a "how-to" guide for overcoming bullying and depression.

Cris Beam's novel *I Am J* is great for trans teens. As a foster parent to a trans daughter, the author has special insight into the lives of trans teens and writes from a perspective that a lot of young people can relate to. *I Am J* tells the story of a teen trans boy in the early stages of his transition. The story is different from a lot of books out there because it isn't sugarcoated. J has a lot of fears about what will happen to him if he transitions and a lot of those fears come true. The characters are culturally diverse and complex, each having a whole life to deal with beyond simply being trans or having trans people in their lives. While the main character, J, is a teen trans boy, his close friend, Chanelle, a teen trans girl, is a prominent secondary character who is arguably the strongest character in the book.

Ten years ago, only a few YA trans books existed, so it's pretty exciting that trans characters are finding their way into the kinds of books teens like to read. That being said, there's still not that much out there. And a lot of the stuff that is out there is not actually very good. So while we are busy devouring everything we can find and wishing there was more to read and watch, let's keep in mind that we have stories to tell, too. A lot of the people who write the books we love are readers, just like us, who got sick of never finding the story they really wanted to read in the pages of someone else's book.

A few other books dealing with trans and gender nonconforming teen characters and issues to get your reading list started include the following:

Fiction
Parrotfish by Ellen Wittlinger
Being Emily by Rachel Gold
Brooklyn Burning by Stee Brezenoff
Choir Boy by Charlie Anders
Beauty Queens by Libba Bray
Beautiful Music for Ugly Children by Kristin Cronn-Mills
Please Don't Kill the Freshman by Zoe Trope
London Reign by A. C. Britt
The End by Nora Olsen
New Swimsuits by Eva Odland
The Trans-fer Student by Elise Himes

Comix/Manga
Wandering Son by Shimura Takako
Ranma 1/2 by Rumiko Takahashi
A + E 4ever by ilike merey

Nonfiction
Transparent: Love, Family and Living the T with Transgender Teenagers by Cris Beam
The Nearest Exit May Be Behind You by S. Bear Bergman
Kicked Out by Sassafras Lowrey

Self-Esteem and Body Image

We get messages about the "right" way to be from every angle—at school, from family, in our communities, and via the media. Our cultures shape our view of how our bodies should look, what we should wear, where our priorities ought to be, and how to be successful. For those of us who are trans, the challenges can be multiplied.

Of course, as youth, we all deal with a lot of social pressures. Our society's ideas about what girls and boys "should" be like make up a seemingly endless list dictating body shape and size, clothing, sexuality, career goals, and just about everything else. It is unfair that anyone should have to live up to such unreasonable standards in order to gain basic respect. Each of us is an individual, with our own unique perspectives and experiences—we are all different. Just like not all cis girls are interested in joining the cheerleading squad and not all cis guys play sports, we as trans people are not carbon copies of one another.

COMING OUT

Coming out is the process by which someone comes to terms with a sense of personal identity (in this case, trans identity). There are a lot of steps in coming out—it is a process rather than an event. Chapter 7 covers many aspects of this process. Trans people of all ages have their own coming-out experiences, and there are some special considerations for us as trans youth.

With an increasingly bright spotlight on trans issues, youth are coming out earlier and earlier. While visibility and validation are important, our safety and survival are more important. Unfortunately, for many of us, coming out can mean risking the loss of a good education, health care, social support, or housing.

If you are considering coming out to others for the first time, keep in mind that it should not be done without any preparation beforehand. Before deciding when, how, and to whom to come out, it is important to consider the possible risks that could come with disclosing a trans identity. The risks that we, as trans youth, take when coming out will vary, depending on our specific circumstances and who we choose to tell. For example, coming out to a parent who pays for things like food, housing, and clothing has different—and possibly more significant—risks than coming out to a friend at school.

We wish that we could expect everyone to celebrate our identities. And this does happen for some of us. However, many of us have the experience of hearing people who we thought cared about us say very hurtful things either to our face or over text or online. This can be disappointing, hurtful, or scary.

Other times, we may be met with acceptance. Acceptance does not necessarily mean that we will get a joyful, happy response. It may still take a long time for people to understand what it means for us to be trans or to use the names and pronouns we prefer.

Whether someone is shocked and angry or supportive but unsure, we may need to educate our friends and family on how to be there for us. Sometimes people need time and space in order to become our allies.

Choosing Someone Safe

Knowing we are trans can be a huge weight to carry around, and we may want to come out to have someone we can talk with. Picking a safe person to come out to first can help us find support for ourselves as we think about how we want to live our lives authentically. The first people that we choose to tell may not be our parents, guardians, or other people who ensure our access to housing, food, employment, health care, or education. Most of us choose a close friend, sibling, teacher, or counselor who we think will be safe to talk with.

> "My sister has been wonderful about my transition, I couldn't have asked for a better sister than her. She means the world to me."

We can usually figure out whether someone is safe by listening to how they talk about lesbian, gay, and bisexual (LGB) people. If they speak negatively about LGB people, there is a good chance that they will not be safe to come out to. However, even if they speak well of LGB people, they might not be affirming of trans people. If they do not bring it up, we might try bringing it into casual conversation by asking whether they have heard of well-known trans people or how they feel about laws that relate to trans people. Their response can tell us a lot about whether they are safe to come out to.

Sometimes we have to make compromises. If we are going to interview for a job that we really want, we may have to make some compromises with how we dress in order to get the job. Many of us have to dress a certain way to be allowed to stay in our parents' houses and have food to eat. Not getting to wear what we want is hard, but sometimes we have to concede for a little while to get our needs met. It may be helpful to remember that it is very likely that we will not always have to make these sacrifices and that we will be better off in the future if we get our basic needs met in the present. We do not want to risk our short-term safety or our long-term goals over something we can do without for the short term.

If we do not want someone we talk with to tell other people, it is good to make sure to say so before saying anything else. This especially goes for school counselors. Make sure to ask what the counselor's confidentiality policy is before disclosing. While private therapists cannot share most information about us with others, school counselors often are not held to the same strict standards. If we are currently supported by a parent or legal guardian, we should make sure the person we come out to realizes that keeping our information private may be a matter of survival.

Private Versus Secret

In some cases, we do not have to come out to people if we do not want to or if keeping our trans identity private will keep us safe. If we are not sure if we identify as trans or we are not sure what kind of trans identity fits best, telling everyone we know can add a lot of pressure we may not be ready to deal with. Also, if we find out that someone we thought was safe turns out not to be, we might feel discouraged and invalidated. Instead of isolating, be sure to continue to reach out to others if that person did not work out. If no one in your community seems safe to come out to, you might try reaching out to other trans people online.

For some of us, it is important to be "out" or to be open about being a trans person in all areas of life. On the other hand, some of us prefer to keep that part of ourselves more private. We get to determine the level of openness that is right for us. Most trans youth do, however, end up telling at least a select few trusted friends about their identity. Our trans identity is not a *secret*; it is our *private information*. Secrets are things that we might be ashamed about if others found out. We do not need to be ashamed of being trans. But we get to decide who gets to know that part of us.

Coming Out to Parents and Guardians

Coming out to our parents and guardians can be an exciting and scary prospect. We all have different relationships with the adults who are responsible for our care, and their reactions will vary widely.

> *"Just before college started, I went on a backpacking trip with others from the school. I came out to them there (to 'figure out whether I was really a guy'), and when I got back I came out to my parents. They felt like Sara had gone away on a trip and never come back. When I told them, for a minute no one said anything. My dad finally said that no matter what, they loved me. My mom was silent."*

> *"My parents were both really solidly in denial, and remain so. When I first came out, my mom insisted on taking me to a therapist, who rightly told her that I was healthy and wonderful, but not a girl. After being told that, my mom cried for two days and then told me that her life was falling apart. My dad has taken the stance that it's just a 'phase,' but he's been heard using male pronouns to refer to me."*

Flesh prison (Zarva Barroso).

While some of us are fortunate to have parents who embrace our gender identity immediately, many of us find that our parents need time to adjust. Even though parents may initially express fear, anger, guilt, sadness, or confusion, they can ultimately become our biggest supporters. If we can give them some time and space to experience their feelings, they may be more likely to come around. It is really difficult to be patient during these times, but a little patience may pay off in the long run. It may also be helpful to provide our parents with resources.

> "My mom has, I believe, finally accepted the news about me. She is unfortunately very religious and she was less than enthusiastic and told me I was going to hell, blah blah blah. Finally I had enough and e-mailed her this Christian lady's website. . . I guess she read the website because she has been a lot better lately."

Additional challenges may arise for those of us whose parents' first language is not English.

> "My mom is from Cambodia and she asked me if I was a 'lesbian-transgender.' I was not sure what she meant by that, so the whole conversation was really awkward. There is only one word for LGBT in Cambodian, so talking about the different identities is challenging!"

If we do not know where our family stands on being trans, we can try to test the waters before coming out. Casually bring up queer or trans issues with family members and gauge their reaction. Are they generally queer positive? Do they have personal or religious stances on queer issues? Remember to factor in the level of your current relationships. The closer we are with our family member(s) before coming out, the more likely it is (though not guaranteed) that things will be OK afterward. It may also be beneficial to come out to people individually rather than in a big group. We might choose to send some people a coming-out letter if we are uncomfortable telling them in person.

Providing our families with information and resources can help them understand our needs and concerns. Parents, Friends, and Families of Lesbians and Gays (PFLAG) has an online "Support Guide for Families and Friends of Transgender and Gender Non-conforming People" where we can refer our families.

ASYMMETRICAL WE (FICTION)

Nick Hadiwka Mwaluko, author of "The Blessing," is an American born in Tanzania who was raised in neighboring Kenya and other east African countries.

Twist the doorknob to the apartment, walk inside.

"I'm holding a doctor's letter saying my daughter wants a sex change operation into a man. That true?"

Letter in one hand, an angry five-foot-three Mom stands taller than any building I imagine.

"Do not look away from me. Is it true?"

No answer.

"Cause if it's true, watch me call the police right now. And you know what them cops'll do to a masculine butch woman behind bars the minute her single mother turns her back on her? They will rape you—that's how Authority turns a masculine butch bitch back into a lady. And Superiority couldn't give two shits 'cause black women, we don't get raped, not according to White America. We cannot, do not never-ever experience rape—ask Tawana Brawley, ask Naffisato Diallo, ask every slave woman from the beginning of time. You wanna go through that behind bars? Or—"

Mom takes a step so close, her voice dips into a shallow whisper.

"Or do what's easy. Wear a dress, some earrings, put on make-up, get a decent job, get a boyfriend, get married, get a house, get a car, get pregnant, get kids, get fat, he'll cheat, you'll separate, he'll lie, you'll divorce. It is that simple."

She's less than two steps away. Hit me, Mama. I don't give a damn what you do so long as you don't do what Daddy did, up 'n leave without a word one day 'cause if you abandon me Mom I won't know what'll happen.

"Dress or no dress? Decide."

"Mom," I say, "when I transition, is you afraid I'll leave you like Dad did?"

She's so small, her breath so even and still as she stands motionless for what adds up to time eternal. I continue.

"Why are you so scared of this, Mom? Tell me.

"Say 'Are you rejecting me as your mother? 'Cause it feels like I'm losing my baby. You're changing into someone else. I'm a single parent, you're my only child, what else I got left in this world besides you?'

"Ask, 'Will I get grandkids after you do this operation?'

"Say, 'I've had to take control to put food on the table, clothes on your back, change in your pocket. You do this, I won't know what to do and that scares me more than I care to admit, yeah, your calm cool collected controlled mother is terrified of the unknown.'

"Say, 'What will God make of this change?'

"Then we'll talk deep and real and honest, and it'll hurt like hell in the end. Mom, look me in the eye with every contradiction in your heart, knowing how hard it will be to forgive me for who I am.

"Ask me, Mom, 'How can I support you in this?'

"That's what I want you to say."

Mom is silent. In her silence everything she cannot say exists. How she blames herself because we can't afford to move out the ghetto. How she blames herself for making past choices she can't unmake. No amount of hard work or planning can change who we are, or what they see and say about us with our backs turned.

Bulldagger butch dyke daddy trans king tomboy faggot total transsexual pink tragedy—those are my labels, the ones I have to wear in the world.

But they stereotype my Mama even more: Welfare Queen, hoochy, African, homophobe, transphobe, limited, too black, not white enough, too poor, too ethnic, postracial, too urban, too ghetto, too southern, too country, too uppity, too proud, too empowered, too black and too free, dangerous.

Mom is silent.

"Please say you'll support me in this, Mom."

Mom shuts her eyes. I shut mine too, imagining my world bathed in sunshine yellow like in movie-mode when ideal families gather at the table during meals, laughter spilling skyward against a backdrop of artificially sweet sounds.

The movie I see in my head in the moment is called *My Life*, subtitled *XXXX*.

I emerge from a steamy hot shower radiant black, towel round my waist. Mom reaches for my chin, strokes my facial hair—beard, mustache, sideburns. She touches my chest, her fingers running clear across my scars. In this imaginary world, there's a place where my mother understands me.

"Son, I am so proud of you. You found your true self."

Mom caresses my flesh wounds, her fingers travel up, down, soft strikes across my chest.

Mama, let me teach you how to look at me.

Don't use your eyes.

Touch my body. Look with your hands.

Know how you say you can't trust a black man, Mama? Well, I'm that black man you can trust. Touch, Mama. Know how you say black men have no feminine side? Do you feel mine? Know how you say men think first with their penis? What would that make me in your eyes? I'm no woman; I'm no man. I could be in-between, or nothing.

You have pain, Mom. I have scars. Dig deep into them. There is power in a queer body that cannot conform to them labels but has healed, survived, lived beyond them. Why would I want to be normal?

I open my eyes. The movie ends.

Mom is still silent.

"Say it, Mom. Say you'll support my transition. Say you'll support me."

Her silence is eternal, to this day.

Mom?

An important step for trans youth when coming out to a parent or guardian is to identify the risks. The unfortunate truth is that coming out to family can mean losing family. Only we can decide if this is a possibility we are willing to chance. If you want to come out to your family, but are concerned about their reaction, it can be helpful to plan for "what if" scenarios. For example:

- *Find a short-term place to stay.* If you are concerned that you may not be welcome or safe in your home, it can be comforting to have planned ahead. Some of us may have friends, classmates, or relatives who we may be able to stay with over a short-term period. In some places, youth or LGBTQ focused shelters may be able to provide a safe place to sleep, as well as access to support services.
- *Plan a budget for the long term.* Find out how much money you could make at a job and how much it costs living in an apartment, getting furniture, having electricity and water, buying groceries to have three meals a day, doing laundry, using transportation, wearing decent clothes, and buying things like toothpaste and toilet paper. Keep in mind that as a young person, it may be challenging (or impossible) to rent an apartment without a co-signer for a lease, and you may be limited in the kinds or hours of work you can legally do.
- *Pack a bag.* Even if you are relatively sure things are going to be OK, it is never a bad idea to have a bag packed just in case. Include some clothes, a toothbrush, and anything you need for school. Make sure to bring important documents like IDs and birth certificates, and any medications you take on a regular basis.

Some of us choose to wait to come out to our parents until we are more socially and financially independent. For some of us, this may mean waiting until we no longer live with our parents, while for others, it may mean waiting until we have finished our education.

"I tried once to come out when I was 16 or 17, to my mom, but after her tearful reaction I guess I went back 'in.' I convinced her it was a phase. Once I was at college. . . I started hinting that I wanted to tell my mom about some identity issues when we saw each other next. She told me that some things are best kept to ourselves. . . and when I told her that wasn't my style, she outed me to her parents and to my father. My parents' reaction at that point was not so great. I was promptly disowned—but at this point, I suppose we've made up and I'm sort of 'un' disowned, or something."

If we choose to wait until we have more independence, we may be able to maintain better control over own transition process.

Thinking about talking to your parents about your gender identity? Check out the online guide "Considering Coming Out as Gender Variant or Transgender to Your Parents?" on the TransYouth Family Allies (TYFA) Web site.

"I really never came out as trans so much as I came out with the news that I was headed to a trans support group, putting in my paperwork, looking to go on testosterone, etc. It wasn't a 'guess what, I'm trans,' it was a 'by the way, I'm doing these trans things.'"

Each of us has a unique situation, and we must decide for ourselves what is the best, safest way to approach coming out to our families. While there are real risks, many of us find that we have allies within our families that we might not have expected.

"My grandparents and uncle and aunt have been completely supportive in a way that surprised even me. I came out to my 94-year-old grandfather by telling him I had been living as a young man, and he tried to comfort me by saying that it was natural and fine!"

Coming Out at School

The decision about when—or whether, or how—to come out at school is something that many of us spend a long time grappling with. Many of us want to share our identity so we can be seen as a complete person and live authentically. At the same time, we may be afraid of the challenges we will face. The decision to come out at school is very personal and should be based completely on our level of comfort, access to support networks, and safety.

Coming out at school is usually a long process. It is unlikely that our school will be willing to have a giant mandatory assembly where we can stand in front of everyone in the school and come out to all of them and then never have to do it again—nor would many of us want that. The reality for most of us is that we will find ourselves coming out to people one by one, in small groups, or in a class setting. We will have conversations with teachers and administrators, coaches and counselors.

When we are beginning our coming-out processes, something to think about is who we want to tell first and how, when, and where we want to go about telling them. There is no right or wrong way to come out to someone. For many students, considering beginning the process of a social transition involves coming out to teachers, guidance counselors, and in some cases, our principal or other administrators. When thinking about coming out to any of these adults at school, it can be useful to go into the conversation with some talking points prepared. Essentially this means thinking ahead of time about what we want to say to this person and what we hope to get out of the conversation.

School settings can be giant rumor mills. The more people we tell, the higher the chance that someone will tell someone else who we may not want to know. We can think through how we might deal with this with a supportive adult at the school or a close friend before disclosing to anyone. If we are out at school, it is also likely that our parents or guardians will find out. It can be helpful to have the support of a counselor or other ally when coming out to our families, but we may also risk losing control of when and how we come out to them. We should understand what confidentiality we are guaranteed when speaking with school staff and know that information can travel quickly through the community, even if we have only told a few friends.

SOCIAL TRANSITION

Social transition is the process of making nonmedical changes to how we look and live in order to feel more at ease with our gender role. Just like everything else about being trans, there is no one right way to approach social transition. Some common steps include making a name change, switching pronouns, wearing different types of clothing, wearing our hair differently, or making nonmedical physical alterations such as binding our chests or wearing a bra with breast forms.

These are changes that adult trans people make, but our transition process typically happens in a school setting, where we have different challenges and opportunities. We may encounter problems with peers or teachers, and with school rules, and administrators

Self-portrait (Darnell Davis).

may limit how we experiment with our gender presentation. As minors we have more "gatekeepers" who control our access to medical, mental health, and legal services, and are more likely to face economic constraints in our transition process.

Name and Pronoun Changes

Changing our name or pronouns can be fun. It can give us a chance to define ourselves in a very literal way—to reinvent ourselves in a way that feels authentic to us. But as empowering as choosing a new name or pronoun set can be, getting people who have known us for a long time to change the way they address us is likely to take a lot of work. We may have to correct them and remind them about our pronouns. Some people, especially those who have known us for a long time, may have trouble using our new pronouns or names consistently. They may be even slower to make the switch if the new pronouns are gender-neutral, since they will be learning to speak in a new way. Do not be afraid to be assertive if people do not use your name or pronouns correctly.

When our attempts at being assertive are not met with respect, we need to consider our safety and what we want to get out of the situation. If a person in a position of power over us (teacher, principal, parent, coach, pastor, etc.) is not respecting us, we need to decide what we are willing to compromise on and what we are not. For example, if we really want to play on the sports team and can play only under the wrong name and pronouns, we are faced with a decision. Some of us may feel comfortable using different pronouns in different contexts, while others may decide to take legal action or address the issue with the school board. We get to decide what is important to us. Not all of us will make the same decision.

Experimenting With Gender Expression

Some trans adolescents decide to play around with gender expression as a part of social transition. Trying out new clothes, wearing (or not wearing) makeup, shaving (or not shaving) our legs and/or our faces, learning to raise or lower our voice, or anything else that might affect the way others perceive our gender, can all be fair game.

Many of us have already been experimenting with our gender expression at home alone or with friends or in some social settings. Legally, we have the right to dress in gender-affirming clothes in public places. However, schools and employers are permitted to set standards for dress and can mandate that we conform to gender-specific dress codes. Typically, we are able

Streetwise and Safe is a project by and for youth of color in New York City that shares the "ins & outs, do's & don'ts, and street politics" of police encounters between LGBTQ youth of color and the police. Check out their online interactive "Map of the Criminal Injustice System" that talks about each step of the process if you are in an encounter with the police or are arrested or detained.

to choose which set of gendered appearance rules we follow, so long as we follow them consistently. For those of us with nonbinary, or otherwise fluid identities, we may have to choose whether we want to present as male or female in order to remain employed or enrolled.

Changing our gender expression causes us to be perceived differently by others. While that is often the explicit goal of the changes we make, we may also discover some unintended consequences. We may discover that we encounter new privileges or that new dangers appear when we alter our gender expression. People may make different assumptions about our interests, skills, and talents based on our gender presentation. We may also be seen differently—as more or less threatening, aggressive, sexual, vulnerable, or approachable. These perceptions can shape the way everyone from shopkeepers to police to passersby interact with us. Police may be more likely to stop us for suspected criminal activity, or different kinds of crimes, and we may face new kinds of street harassment.

As you learn to navigate these new social rules, there are ways to make your experience safer and more fun. One is to use a buddy system. If you are headed out to shop for clothes, consider asking a friend to tag along. When going to a party late at night, stick with a group. Know your rights. Interacting with law enforcement can be a frustrating or scary experience. Knowing what your rights are can help you know what is required or expected of you, making the interactions less emotional and less likely to end in arrest or punishment.

The Pressure to Pass

The ability to present our gender in such a way that we are consistently seen as our correct gender identity is frequently called "passing." Some of us take pride or pleasure in "passing," while some of us do not desire to do so. Many of us have rejected the term since it suggests that we are not *really* the gender we present as or that we are deceiving others. No matter how we, personally, feel about it, the pressure to "pass," or to blend in as cis, can be very real, especially for male- or female-identified trans youth. Society often imposes heavy expectations on us as trans people to live up to normative gender roles.

The pressure can be particularly strong during adolescence, when all of our peers are shaping their own gender identities as well. As a result, we receive many messages about the "right" way to express our gender. This pressure may come from both our cisgender family and friends, and from our trans peers.

Many trans youth feel astounding pressure to prove we can fit into preexisting gender categories in our society and to prove we can live up to the standard of a "real" man or woman, even among other trans youth.

> *"The only problem I have is that some [trans] guys are not as accepting of gender variance. They think you have to have this really typical trans narrative, want to do as much to transition as possible, and be really stereotypically masculine in order to fit in (and want to live stealth). They are always pointing out people who 'make the community look bad.' That makes me nervous, because I do some things that others think make the community look bad (I'm sometimes very feminine, I am dating a lesbian, I call myself a lesbian sometimes). I'm afraid that admitting that I go by female pronouns sometimes is going to get me kicked out of the core community. Although there are some people who are not like this, who support me 100% and that I trust to always support me no matter what. It is a toss-up, just like any community."*

Being read correctly is just one experience of living as our authentic selves. It is wrong for others to impose their ideas of gender on us, and we should work on unconditionally accepting and encouraging each other. There are as many ways to be trans as there are trans people in the world.

Gender-Segregated Spaces

When we are coming out at school, one issue we may want to discuss with school administrators is use of gendered spaces, such as sports teams, cheerleading, school clubs, hotel rooms when traveling, bathrooms, and locker rooms—points of anxiety for almost all transgender people. One of the most feared gender segregated places is the public bathroom. This can be especially problematic for transgender students because we spend eight hours a day in a school where it might not be safe for us to use the bathroom.

Choosing whether to use bathrooms, locker rooms, or other facilities that correspond to the gender we are transitioning into is a personal decision. We might come into conflict with peers who are uncomfortable or surprised to see us in those spaces and we might not get support from all teachers and school officials. There may be concerns raised about our right to be in those spaces and we may be put in a position of having to advocate for ourselves in order to access them. We might also have to make a compromise in order to show the school that we are willing to work with them. For example, while using the nurse's bathroom can be a real pain, it may be the safest possible option, at least for a short time.

How we respond to the school administration can influence whether they are more or less likely to continue to work with us. If we get upset and scream at the principal for being transphobic and not understanding (even if the principal deserves to hear this because it is true), our principal may be less likely to want to try to help us out. If we demonstrate patience, an ability to stay calm, and a willingness to compromise (as the *adolescent* in the situation!), we may find that adults are more willing to take steps to affirm us and keep us safe.

Gender is something that comes up in all sorts of ways. At school dances, there are typically a homecoming and prom king and queen, and our school might also have a policy on who we can go to a dance with. To find out more about our school's policies on gender, we might consider joining the Gay Straight Alliance (GSA). If the school does not have one, we can use resources at the Gay, Lesbian, and Straight Education Network (GLSEN) and The GSA Network to create one. Not just high schools, but some middle schools also have LGBTQ support groups. Even if we are the only trans student in the group, we can still learn a lot from other students as well as the adult mentor. At the same time, we might have to do more outside research, education, and networking than the non-trans LGB students. In the end, it is more important for us to be safe than to be right about the school's policies.

In the TV show *Degrassi: The Next Generation*, Adam Torres navigates school and relationships as a trans teen.

Building Community

One of the most helpful things we can do for ourselves when we first take on a trans identity is to find our own communities. As youth, we are often restricted by things like transportation, our families' rules, money, or other issues. We all do the best we can with what we have. If we have access to the Internet, we can try searching for blogs, forums, or chat rooms where we can connect with other trans youth.

> *"I'm mostly involved in the transgender YouTube community, which is really huge. I have a vlog where I talk about gender, and I'm subscribed to a ton of transguys and their partners. It is a nice community, very supportive."*

As youth, we live in a culture where we and our peers often post very personal material in public forums, and we may desire to document our transition process and share it with others online. Many of us appreciate and find community through others who do so, and being trans is not something to be ashamed of. However, cultural and legal practices around the privacy of online information are changing rapidly, and we want to spend some time thinking about our privacy limits. See Chapter 8 for more information on online privacy.

THE KIKI SCENE

Jonovia Chase, Evie Pucci, Tamara M. Williams, and Daphne Wynn from Hetrick Martin Institute (HMI) provide an introduction to the Kiki ballroom scene (with support from Leigh Tomppert, Elizabeth Glaeser, Laura Erickson-Schroth, Alli Javors, and Jermaine Ellis).

The word *Kiki*, which originated in the house and ballroom scene, is a loosely defined term that is often understood as "to have fun." The Kiki scene is a youth-oriented house and ballroom community that many would say began to form in New York City around 2005 as groups of young people, who were either in the mainstream ballroom scene or were interested in the scene, began to get together at the Gay Men's Health Crisis (GMHC) agency to practice and battle other young people in a less competitive and more affordable environment.

In order to capitalize on the popularity of the ballroom scene, agencies such as GMHC and the Hetrick-Martin Institute (HMI), which provide HIV/AIDS prevention, care, and advocacy, along with other direct services for LGBTQ youth, began to organize Kiki balls and sponsor functions with their young clients, using the opportunity to promote safer sex education, harm reduction, and prevention and testing for HIV and sexually transmitted infections (STIs).

Participants at a Kiki ball (photo by Jairo Alcantara).

Kiki houses also host their own events and balls. Many Kiki houses encourage participation in community service activities, and Kiki balls often revolve around messages to stay healthy or address issues that specifically affect LGBTQ youth of color, such as racial and gender profiling, police violence, and the police practice of Stop and Frisk.

"For me, being in the Kiki house of Old Navy is a lot like my second family because we hang out like one; we talk, fuss, fight, get angry, yell, but always find the time to come together whenever we need each other. I truly enjoy being an Old Navy, not only because of the balls we walk, but because of how much we love and respect each other and the fun we have when we come together. I'm truly grateful to have them in my life."—Daphne

The Kiki scene, while completely open and inclusive to youth of all races, ethnicities, and gender orientations, is mostly comprised of African American and Latin@ LGBTQ youth.

"It's also a socioeconomic thing, you have kids who come from nothing, or you have kids who can't afford to go to dance classes, or kids who have the potential to do something but don't have the resources. The ballroom and Kiki scene are there to support them."—Tamara

Walking in a Kiki ball (photo by Jairo Alcantara).

Kiki houses can offer support to their house members that may not be available in mainstream houses, where a stronger emphasis is placed on competing in balls. In addition to a house parent, many young people also find a "gay parent" who takes on the role of mentor and provides support on a deeper personal level. In some cases, these networks of support may even offer physical housing or financial support for those young people who find themselves homeless.

"Someone who takes on a particularly proactive and influential role in your life can become what is known as a 'gay parent,' either a mother or a father. While this person does not necessarily need to be older than you are, they typically have more experience. While many people address me as a 'gay parent,' I personally refrain from using this term, as I am a straight trans woman. The role of mother involves supporting my children's best interests, encouraging them to strive for a healthier lifestyle by working, attending school, and making the right decisions. I also provide other forms of support, such as financial or spiritual support, and try to physically protect my kids. Over the course of time, bonds with your kids get tighter, and it goes from seeing their potential to seeing them progress into better people, which can make a gay parent just as proud as a biological parent. Unfortunately, in many cases, LGBT youth don't have good relationships with their biological parents or their parents aren't in their lives."—Jonovia

As exciting as it can be to battle, in some instances it can also be emotionally difficult. Some categories are based on talents and performing, and other categories are based on a certain aesthetic and the image that you are putting forth; yet realness is just a perspective—it's subjective.

"For my category I walk Realness. I'm being judged by my look. I'm being judged by how I pass in society or how I pass that night, and the way that I prepare is I have to say to myself that it's just for fun and it doesn't mean that I'm not a woman and this doesn't define who I am or that I'm inferior to my competition."—Evie

Balls can be a high-stress environment for many young people, even in the Kiki scene. Some youth start to use drugs or alcohol to calm their nerves before competitions or because they see other people around them using substances. Competition can be fierce, and many youth feel as if they have to dominate in order to gain recognition.

"I started out in the Ballroom scene at age 16. I was going through a trying time in an all-boys high school where I was not feeling comfortable with myself and looking for self-acceptance in all the wrong places. I began experimenting with drugs (marijuana). I got myself kicked out of school and began submerging myself more in the ballroom scene. Surprisingly, they weren't very accepting of my decision to transition. They felt like I came into the scene as a Butchqueen (boy) so that's how I should stay. I did many negative things that the scene taught me, such as escorting, walking the streets, and buying hormones off the street. I ended up leaving the scene. The only thing that kept me grounded through the whole thing was my mother. When she began to see that I was taking my transition seriously, she began supporting me in little ways that meant a lot. She got me multiple apartments so I wouldn't be out on the street or in a group home, and she eventually took me to rehab so I could get help for my drug problems. I was later approached by someone I admired about joining the new house they were opening. They finally saw me for my true self, so I joined. I began having fun again."—Tamara

As the older generation of youth who grew up in the Kiki scene is approaching the "age out" time, many youth struggle with how to move forward in the ballroom scene. There is no age cutoff for staying involved in Kiki, but most people say that by age 24 you should be moving on, as that is the age that you are no longer able to access services at the agencies. However, by this age, some youth are very attached to their houses, and they may stay on and help younger people to strategize for balls. Others may slowly make their way into the mainstream scene by auditioning or being recruited. Some may belong to both a Kiki house and a mainstream house for some time, and eventually leave Kiki behind them. Still others may move on from the ballroom scene altogether to focus on other aspects of their lives.

Bullies, Rumors, and Problems With Peers

Bullying takes many forms, from verbal and emotional harassment to physical intimidation and violent attacks. No matter what form it takes, bullying is never OK. Some people may tell us that bullying is just teasing or a normal part of growing up, but this is not true. Bullying is dangerous and has very real and lasting effects on our safety and self-esteem. Those of us who are bullied are more likely to experience depression and more likely to think about or attempt suicide. Bullying is incredibly serious and something that needs to be treated as such.

Even when we know that the bullying we experience is wrong, it can be easy to take the messages we hear from bullies personally. It is important to remember that what is happening is not our fault, and just because we hear these terrible messages does not mean that any of them are true. All students deserve to have a safe learning environment where we are not harassed, and our schools have an obligation to make sure that we have a safe place to learn.

Sometimes resolving the issues we are having at school can be as simple as a meeting with people in power. This is more likely to happen if we have a supportive administration

If we are being bullied, it is important to get as much support as we can. One way to make sure that we are heard is to write a document of everything that is happening at school—from the bullying and harassment to the response (or lack thereof) from teachers and administration. This document should include as much information as possible, including the dates, times, names of the people involved in the incident, our attempt to get help, and how the adult(s) responded. For example, "On Thursday, December 7, I was sitting in my homeroom class when Rob and Steve started calling me a fag. They did not stop when I asked them to stop. I then told the teacher, Ms. Wortham, what they said. She told me to be quiet and sit back down."

Teen (Elenore Toczynski).

and counselors at our school who are concerned about the safety of all students. We might try speaking with the assistant principal or the principal of the school. We can talk to them about the bullying we experience at school and the negative impact it has on our lives.

> *"At the beginning of 8th grade, my best friend and I came out together. We were given so much shit from our school, and one time when a staff member harassed me, I was the one who ended up getting in trouble. It was hell on earth."*

Unfortunately, sometimes teachers and administrators do not do anything about the bullying and harassment that we experience. When they do not do anything, it seems as if they are supporting what is going on. In some cases, adults in schools are directly harassing us. In other cases, they are indirectly participating in our harassment by failing to work with us to increase our safety at school or by being unwilling to accept that there is even a problem occurring. In these situations, we sometimes need to go to someone in a higher position, such as the school district superintendent or the school board.

If you are being bullied at school, it may be helpful to first create a plan to ensure your immediate safety. From there you can begin thinking about ways to improve the overall situation at your school. You can also identify an ally who will help you stand up against the discrimination you are experiencing. This could be a friend, counselor, social worker, teacher, parent, or guardian. This person should be willing to support you in what you are going through and to assist you in advocating for your safety with school administrators.

LGBTQ YOUTH PROGRAMS

LGBTQ youth programs, such as peer support groups and drop-in centers, can provide us with opportunities for survival and community that are lacking in our schools and other peer networks. These organizations provide safe spaces with affirming staff and volunteers and are populated with other youth who are grappling with similar problems and experiences.

LGBTQ-specific programming can be particularly important for those of us who are not getting emotional support from our families, teachers, or peers. Some of us feel extremely isolated in our homes, schools, and broader communities. We may feel like the people around us do not understand what we are going through. These spaces can become our surrogate families and homes, providing structure, safety, and a sense of belonging.

Youth programs also give us peer networks where our gender identity and expression are not considered a distraction or concerning, thus enabling us to have more typical adolescent connections. In addition to providing us with supportive and gender-affirming social interactions, LGBTQ youth programs can also be an important connection for those of us who are in need of social services, and counseling. Most LGBTQ youth centers and programs offer case management services that can help get us connected with other programs and agencies and possibly mental health providers. They also often provide a range of other life skills programs that can assist us with our self-esteem, HIV/STI prevention, and other aspects of health care specific to LGBTQ youth.

> *"For five years, I attended a trans youth support group weekly. This exposed me to lots of other trans people, some of whom I'm still in contact with. The trans youth group exposed me to racial, economic, and religious diversity I probably would not have otherwise ever seen. In particular, I doubt I would have otherwise gotten to know any prostitutes. Actually, I'm not sure I did get to know any in a true sense, but I got to hear about police harassment and so forth during weekly check-ins, and if I never developed a friendship with a person quite that different from me, I learned to be more comfortable with that diversity and the people who embody it. I also got a lot to think about in terms of how sex works. Because of the trans youth group, I've been to the Be-All, Forge Forward, and the Midwest Trans Youth Conference, which are all pretty different from each other."*

Many programs, particularly LGBTQ youth service programs, offer some amount of reduced cost or possibly free case management mental health services for at-risk LGBTQ

In 2011, a study by the Gay, Lesbian and Straight Education Network (GLSEN) on the experiences of trans youth in K–12 schools in the United States found that 87% of transgender students were harassed in school because of their gender expression and 89% because of their sexual orientation. Forty-four percent of all transgender students reported that they had been physically assaulted at some point at school in the past year. Sometimes teachers even made homophobic or sexist statements.

One of the best things we can do to arm ourselves is to learn about our rights. Contact local and national organizations such as the Transgender Law and Policy Institute, the Transgender Law Center, the Southern Poverty Law Center, the Sylvia Rivera Law Project, and the National Center for Lesbian Rights (not just for lesbians!). Memorize the laws that apply to you, and share the information with other trans people in the community.

Sometimes we feel like we have no support at school. If you are feeling this way, reach out to a national organization such as the Trevor Project (866-488-7386) or the GLBT National Help Center (800-246-7743). The Transgender Law Center also works with schools and families to advocate for our right to be safe in school.

Trans Bodies, Trans Selves New York City Forum (photo by Katia Ruiz).

youth. In most instances, services from these programs can be accessed without parental consent. These services allow us a degree of autonomy over our own mental health, giving us access to resources within a supportive environment. Sometimes there are time limits or age restrictions on these programs, effectively limiting the amount of time we can utilize the services. However, these services can be lifesavers for many of us.

Even for those of us who may not have a specific need for services like case management, LGBTQ youth programs can be a great way for us to increase our peer networks and to know about resources.

We may sometimes encounter other LGBTQ peers who ask inappropriate questions or do things that make us uncomfortable. They may not understand trans issues, or they may want to talk about and share experiences that we are not ready or interested in discussing with them. We might even be surprised to find that some of our trans peers may be just as insensitive as some of our LGB peers. Everyone has different levels of comfort when discussing their bodies, experiences, and identities. We might find ourselves having very heated discussions with others. Sometimes we learn a lot from these conversations. However, it is OK to set boundaries and ask for support from staff, volunteers, or mentors if we do not feel safe.

HOMELESSNESS

Homelessness among trans youth is extremely prevalent. Forty percent of homeless youth in the United States identify as LGBTQ. A study from the National Center for Transgender Equality showed that half of transgender people report having experienced homelessness in their lifetime (Grant et al., 2011). Most homeless youth are people of color.

Homelessness takes a variety of forms. Some of us may be living on the street, but others may be couch surfing after we have been kicked out of our homes, and we stay with friends for short periods of time. We might jump from one friend's place to another friend's place in order to have a place to stay. Whether we are staying on the streets or in other people's homes, our housing situation may be unstable.

For those of us who are homeless, accessing culturally competent homeless shelters is extremely important. Unfortunately, most mainstream shelter programs do not have staff, policies, or procedures that meet the needs of transgender youth. There have been reported cases of trans youth being refused services by homeless shelters solely because we are trans. This has happened in some religious-affiliated shelters. However, not all religious-affiliated institutions have harmful practices—there are many good ones as well.

Most homeless shelters that include youth-specific programs are gender segregated. Some places have policies that will allow us to be sheltered with others who have a similar gender identity as us only if we have had genital surgery. It is extremely unlikely that we will have been able to afford and access surgery, if we even wanted it in the first place.

Forty to None is an organization that works on helping to bring an end to LGBTQ youth homelessness. Check out their Web site to search for local organizations with housing programs.

The result is that these spaces are often unsafe and unwelcoming to those of us who are forced to make the decision between having a relatively safe, warm, and dry place to sleep and being respected for who we are. A possible compromise that we might make is to dress in more gender-neutral ways in order to survive the night. This is unfair, but it is better to feel disrespected and survive than to risk our safety being out on our own during the night. However, sometimes these institutions make life so unbearable for us that we feel no choice but to leave, as being on the streets is actually safer than the constant experience of harassment from the employees and other youth.

A lifesaving alternative for us can be LGBTQ youth–specific shelters, which are becoming more prevalent within major cities across the United States. These organizations are designed specifically to meet the needs of LGBTQ youth. Within these shelters, we are able to have our identity respected. For many of us, LGBTQ-specific shelters can help us access adult mentorship from within the community and enable us to connect with other resources that can assist in our journey toward stable housing.

Foster Care

The National Center for Lesbian Rights has created a document called "A Place of Respect" that instructs group care facilities on how to create a safe place for trans and gender nonconforming youth.

If we are under 18, or under 21 in a growing number of states, one option is to go into foster care. Some major cities like San Francisco, Los Angeles, and New York have group homes for gay and trans kids where we receive an allowance and are given help in applying for college. Each state has its own hotline to get into foster care. Search foster care hotlines and your state online in order to find what number to call to get into foster care. If you expect your stint to be shorter, and are under 23, call a Covenant House—if in a big city. In a smaller town, call the Trevor Hotline or the GLBT National Youth Talkline and find out what they suggest. Or get on the Internet and find the closest LGBTQ center. Call during open hours, tell them about being recently homeless, and ask them where to go.

As we age, it becomes more difficult to find foster care placements. In some places, we are put into group home settings as an alternative to foster homes. If they are not LGBTQ specific, these group homes are nearly always divided by assigned sex, leaving us in the difficult position of being housed in ways that do not affirm our gender identity.

The foster care system is not always well equipped to provide culturally competent service to us. A study by the Urban Justice League in New York and the New York City Administration for Children's Services (ACS) found that 70% or more of LGBTQ youth were removed or ran away from a foster care placement because they felt it was unwelcoming or hostile. However, there are some cities with specific LGBTQ foster care programs. In these places, many of the adults who volunteer to be foster parents are LGBTQ themselves.

DATING AND SAFER SEX

In addition to all of the typical pressures and concerns of teenage dating and sexuality, as trans youth, we navigate situations and issues that cis youth do not need to consider. Youth and trans people constitute two social groups that many adults believe should not be sexually active, as they often see our sexualities as somehow "inappropriate." This unrealistic standard sets us up for unhealthy relationships, higher risk sex, and fear of self-advocacy, but the truth is that we can have safe, healthy, and fun dating and sexual experiences.

Dating

As youth, we often transition within our existing community. However, even if the people we meet are familiar, they may have different levels of information about our trans identity. We may feel that our gender transition has been very public and assume that everyone has followed our changes along the way, but that is not always the case. As adolescents, we all have a lot going on, and we may not always be aware of what other people are going through.

If we are dating someone from our school and we are out, it is realistic to expect our partner is going to hear that we are trans, whether we tell them or not. They may even know already.

Trans man with 17-year-old trans woman at the "Southern Comfort" conference (copyright Mariette Pathy Allen).

If we are lucky enough to have access to a community of other trans youth, there is a pretty good chance we will have a crush on one of them at some point. After all, similarities seem to attract people more than differences. With all the complications that go with dating cis people, many of us find it more comfortable to date other trans people, who may be more familiar with the ways we think about our gender identity, presentation, or bodies.

As amazing as it can feel to date other trans youth, however, it is not exactly a get-out-of-jail free card. Many times, those of us who date other trans youth cross boundaries a cis partner would steer clear of. A shared trans identity is all too often mistaken for a license to ask inappropriate questions, cross boundaries without asking, or put unwanted meaning on a partner's body. We may not communicate about important issues because we assume that our trans partner will feel the same way that we do just because they are trans, too. The key to avoiding this pitfall is open communication—and lots of it. Just because two people are trans does not mean that they have the same ideas about gender, dating, sex—or anything really.

No matter whether our partner is cis or trans, dating requires open communication, respect of another's boundaries, and being open to understanding the other person's ideas.

Sexual Orientation

One of the first questions many of us are asked after coming out is what gender we are attracted to. Because everyone is presumed to be straight unless proven otherwise, most

Trans Bodies, Trans Selves New York City Forum (photo by Katia Ruiz).

straight youth do not have to come out as heterosexual. This is usually not the case for us. Disclosing a trans identity to a cis person will almost certainly leave them unsure about what our sexuality might be.

Because our gender identities tell us what gender we feel ourselves to be and not what gender(s) we are attracted to, most of us end up coming out twice: once as trans and once as gay, straight, pansexual, queer, heteroflexible, omnisexual, lesbian, asexual, questioning, or one of countless other sexual identity labels. The label we feel best matches our sexuality may change over time.

Disclosure of our sexual identity follows the same principle as does disclosure of our gender identity. We get to decide who we tell, when to tell, and how much we tell. When coming out to anyone as trans, we should get ready to have our sexual orientation questioned and have a plan for what we will say. If we are not sure what our sexual orientation is, it is OK to say, "I'm not sure but I am figuring it out." Most of us go through a period of questioning our sexual orientation. This is normal, healthy, and completely valid. We are not required to tell the world we are questioning if we do not want to. We can say that we are not willing to discuss the topic.

We are not the only ones whose sexuality may be in question. The people we date may experience a period of questioning, by themselves or others, about their own sexual identity when they date a trans person. Whether we identify as the gender our partner is typically attracted to or not, they may wonder if being attracted to us makes them any more or less gay or straight.

Many of us date people whose sexual orientation would not typically include genders like ours. That is OK. Sexual orientation is a fluid thing. If we identify as female and our partner identifies as a gay man, we are allowed to make up our own rules, stay together, and keep using the labels that we like for our own sexual identity.

Talking About Sex

As youth, we may find it harder to talk about what we do and do not want, because we have less experience. It is OK to say no or change our minds at any time. Just because we say yes to something one time does not mean that we are consenting to it at other times. And just because we say no to something most of the time, does not mean we cannot change our minds and try it later.

It is definitely OK to *not* want to do certain things. Some of us only want to make out, keep clothes on, cuddle, or give or receive massages. Others of us have oral sex only, or manual sex but not oral sex, and still others want to experience many different combinations of sexual behaviors. Lots of us do not want our genitals or chest area touched—or only sometimes, or only by certain people. Some of us have limits about certain parts of our bodies.

Trans Bodies, Trans Selves New York City Forum (photo by Katia Ruiz).

It is difficult for many people (trans or not) to talk about what we want physically. This is not a time to be shy. The best intimate experiences almost always evolve after a lot of communication before, during, and after.

The best way to get over the awkwardness of talking about physical intimacy and sex is to do it all the time. Really. Sex is a taboo topic in our culture. We are constantly bombarded with messages that we should not have sex until we are older and that our bodies are different as trans people. These combine to pack a pretty powerful punch. It follows that talking about physical intimacy and sex is often really awkward for us. For most people, it gets easier with practice. For more information about sex, see Chapter 17.

Good Consent Practices

Talking about sex is also what enables us to practice good consent. Consent is when someone clearly tells us about the things they want and do not want.

When we assume that our partner wants to be sexual when they have not said that they do, or try new things without confirming that our partner is interested, we are not using good consent practices. These bad behaviors are modeled for us all the time by adults.

Sure, the idea of sweeping in for a surprise kiss at the end of a first date can be romantic—but if it makes our date feel unsafe, or upsets them, that is no fun for anyone. What is even more romantic is knowing, without a doubt, that our date really wants that kiss, or (if we are on the receiving end) that our date cares enough about us to make sure we always feel safe and in control.

Try using open-ended questions such as "How would you like me to touch you?" "What would feel good for you?" or "What kinds of things have you liked doing in the past?" These kinds of questions give our partners an opportunity to tell us what they want, instead of feeling like they might have to say no. This is often called enthusiastic consent—and it can help build strong, sexy relationships between people.

Safer Sex Practices

Not all of us are having sex or even want to have sex. Some of us are saving sex until we are partnered with or marry someone. Many of us have limits as to how far we will go physically with someone. Regardless of if we are having sex or not, knowing about safer practices can increase our sexual health knowledge.

No sex is ever completely safe, but being proactive about our sexual health and safety can be empowering and set us on the road to positive sexual experiences. Contrary to popular belief, safer sex is not as simple as using a condom. If we are doing it right, having safer sex is a lifelong process of learning about our body, the risks associated with the types of sex we like to have, and the different kinds of protection available to us. Then, we need to make informed decisions about how we use protection, every single time we decide to have sex. See Chapter 17 for an in-depth discussion of safer sex techniques.

Survival Sex and Sex Work

Some of us may have engaged in sex work to support ourselves financially. "Survival sex" refers to the exchange of sex for food, shelter, or other basic survival needs. If we are engaging in sex work or survival sex, we have many more things to consider, when it comes to sex and our safety, than those of us who are not engaging in these behaviors. Remember that being a sex worker does not mean we are any less entitled to set clear and firm boundaries or that our clients are any less obligated to ask for consent. See Chapter 9 for more information about safer sex work.

MENTAL HEALTH CARE

Seeking out a therapist or counselor can be one of the best decisions we make. Having an adult to talk with who is not judging us may give us the freedom to explore our identities in new ways. As minors, we lack autonomy over our lives and many of our health care decisions. Because of this, it is extremely important for us to know our rights when

Not every relationship is perfect. Some relationships are downright bad. Unfortunately, many of us get into and stay in abusive relationships because it can be hard to recognize abuse when it is happening to us. Some types of abuse are easier to identify than others—hitting, verbal abuse, or penetrative rape—but these behaviors make up only a few of the many forms abuse can take. Some warning signs that we may be in an abusive relationship include that our partner is excessively jealous of the other people in our life, exercises poor consent or discourages our consent practices, or is manipulating or controlling of our gender. If you are in this kind of situation, open up to a close friend or adult mentor. There are also anonymous hotlines like the GLBT National Youth Talkline (1-800-246-7743).

Trans Bodies, Trans Selves New York City Forum (photo by Katia Ruiz).

Some of us are brought to therapy by our parents or guardians. We may end up having a very positive experience. However, there are some therapists who practice "conversion therapy," also known as "reparative therapy," where they try to change our gender identity or sexual orientation. If this happens to you, seek out an adult you trust, as this type of therapy can be damaging. States are beginning to pass laws to outlaw this type of therapy.

beginning to access therapy. From there, we can advocate for ourselves, ensure that our confidentiality is being respected, and make sure that we are receiving the highest possible quality of services.

Adults have the ability to control many aspects of our lives. This holds true for those of us who are attempting to access medical and mental health services. However, mental and sexual health are two areas in which some states offer provisions for confidential care. Confidentiality is key for many people seeking individual counseling or gender-related medical care. Confidentiality means that what we say to a provider is kept private. If we are minors (under 18), our parents often consent for our therapy and can have access to our confidential records. They may be able to talk to the therapist about what happens during sessions. That might limit what we talk to the therapist about, so it is a good idea to discuss with the therapist what they will and will not share with our parents.

There are things that our doctors and therapists are legally mandated to report. These things can be summed up as the "three hurts." A therapist must report (1) if we are in danger of hurting ourselves, (2) if someone else is hurting us, or (3) if we are hurting someone else. Therapists are also mandated to report if they suspect that child abuse is happening, even if it is not to us (e.g., if we talk about a sibling or friend who is being abused).

Even the most culturally conscious, LGBTQ-friendly provider is bound by legal mandates. Ultimately this is our appointment, and we get to determine what we feel comfortable disclosing within that space. If we have any questions about what will be reported, we can discuss them with our provider before disclosing.

Although being trans does not mean that we are required to go to therapy, if we find the right therapist for us, therapy can be a helpful and fulfilling experience.

> *"I began seeing a psychotherapist for my dysthymia (which could very well be related to my gender identity) and our sessions rapidly changed into discussion of sexuality and gender identity. I found my psychotherapist to be a great ally and resource, and she assisted me when I came out to my parents."*

Therapy may be a tool for personal discovery and acceptance as well as a tool for accessing gender-affirming medical interventions like hormones or surgery. Therapy can be a productive and empowering experience for us even if we do not feel as though we have specific trans-related issues to be dealing with. In addition, it can be a very effective tool for family members or friends who may be struggling with their own feelings about our transition.

MEDICAL CARE AND TRANSITION

As youth, whether or not we are trans, we have a lot to think about when it comes to medical care and physical well-being. Puberty comes with a lot of physical, mental, and emotional changes. For trans youth, these changes can trigger new needs in a health care setting. For example, as we begin to experience physical changes related to puberty, our doctors may ask us more questions about our bodies, our genitals, and our sexual relationships. We may not feel comfortable with the words our provider uses to describe our body or may want to ask questions that are not on their radar. But we still need to take care of our health. We only have one body, and even if we are not very comfortable in it at times, it is important to try to take care of it so that it will be there for us in the future.

Coming Out to a Provider

If we already have a provider we see regularly who does not know we are trans, it may be a good idea to come out to them, even if we do not have any intention of accessing hormones or medical interventions to transition. If your parent or guardian takes you to the medical provider, make a plan to ask the provider to speak privately during an upcoming visit. Most youth will speak privately with their health provider at some point, so this kind of private conversation is usually pretty commonplace. All the same, before sharing our identity with a provider, it is important to verify their stance on confidentiality—especially if we are not out to our family.

Because trans health care is not something many medical providers have a lot of knowledge about, we might want to help them learn about us. For example, we might want to teach them the language we use to talk about our body and gender identity. Educating our health care providers about transgender people can be stressful. Many people find that it is helpful to provide some educational material to their provider when they come out—that way we have some say in what information they receive. See Chapter 11 for materials you can provide to your doctor.

Puberty and Puberty Blockers

More and more of us are beginning medical transition as youth. Our options vary, depending on how far along we are in puberty. Puberty is a time where our testes and ovaries begin to produce large amounts of testosterone and estrogen and our body begins to grow rapidly. Everyone has both testosterone and estrogen in their bodies, just in differing amounts. Although people usually start puberty between age nine and thirteen, not everyone starts puberty at the same age, because everyone's body is different.

Puberty is divided into a series of stages, known as Tanner Stages. There are five stages, and before puberty children are in Tanner Stage One. During Tanner Stage Two, we grow soft, light pubic hair and develop breast buds or our testes begin to grow. Tanner Stage Two lasts a few months. Female-assigned people tend to start earlier than male-assigned people. Some female-assigned people may begin menstruating (though many others will not). In Tanner Stages Three through Five, our pubic hair will continue to become darker, thicker, curlier, and more prevalent. We will also get more hair under our armpits. The penis, testes, and scrotum will begin to grow. Some of us will experience spontaneous erections and ejaculation when sleeping or masturbating. By Stage Five, our genitals will be our adult size and shape, and we will have complete breast development.

Tanner Stage Two is the earliest stage that we are eligible to take puberty-blocking medication. Most Tanner Stage Two changes are reversible. If we have known that we were trans since we were very young and were fortunate enough to have our parents' support, we might be able to see a doctor who will prescribe us medicine to pause our puberty around this time. See Chapter 19 for a more in-depth discussion of how puberty blockers work.

Cross Sex Hormones

Hormones like testosterone and estrogen are often called cross sex hormones, even though everyone has both in their bodies in differing amounts. Those of us who would like to masculinize our bodies may take testosterone. Most will take it in the form of an injection every week or two, but others may use gels, creams, patches, or pellets. Those who would like to feminize our bodies may take a testosterone blocker, estrogen, and possibly progesterone. Most will take these in the form of pills, but others may prefer injections or patches.

Feminizing hormone treatment will cause breast growth, lower sex drive, decrease testicular size, decrease muscle mass, and increase body fat. If we begin hormones after going through male puberty, hormones will not change the pitch of our voice, our Adam's apple size, our height, or facial hair growth. Once those changes happen, hormones cannot reverse them. For those of us taking masculinizing hormones, testosterone will deepen our voice, make our clitoris bigger, make hair grow on our face and many other places (e.g., legs, arms, hands, stomach, back), stop our periods, and increase our muscle mass. See Chapter 12 for more information on hormones for transition.

THINKING ABOUT COLLEGE

The decision whether or not college is the right path for us is a difficult one. If we do decide to go to college, we face additional concerns, such as selecting a school that is going to be welcoming and supportive of our identities.

Trans-Friendly Colleges

When beginning the college application and selection process, we may think about what role our gender identity and expression will play in our decision. Are we looking for a college experience where faculty and fellow students may already be aware of transgender people and issues? A place where there is a strong LGBTQ presence on campus with active out trans students? A college where we can express our gender without disclosing our trans history to anyone?

In recent years, college ranking systems have begun to take notice of the particular needs of LGBTQ students. For example, the *Princeton Review* has added an LGBT-friendliness ranking. Additionally, there are LGBTQ-specific organizations that can be great resources to us when looking at colleges. Campus Pride, the largest national organization dedicated to LGBTQ students in college, publishes a yearly index ranking colleges on a variety of areas in terms of their cultural competency, friendliness, and safety for LGBTQ students. They also host LGBTQ college fairs in various cities across the country.

However, just because a school is "LGBT friendly" does not mean that they are necessarily friendly to trans students or even informed about us. If we are interested in going to a campus that will be welcoming of transgender students, or are curious about how our top choice schools rank, the Transgender Law and Policy Institute keeps tabs on which colleges and universities have policies on trans-inclusive nondiscrimination, gender-inclusive housing, name and gender change on campus records, as well as which schools cover transition-related medical expenses. This information can also be found on Campus Pride's Trans Policy Clearinghouse.

If our schools of interest are not on the list, there are some other ways to find out about them. Check the school's nondiscrimination policy to see whether it includes gender identity and expression. The policy should be easily accessible online. Find out if the school has an LGBTQ resource center or student group, which may be able to provide information about trans issues on campus or connect you with other trans students. We may also want to look into how the school handles specific issues that we are concerned about, such as housing policies, campus activism, or student health services.

There are many encouraging signs. As of May 2013, Campus Pride reported that more than 200 college campuses allow trans students to room with students of our affirmed gender. Almost 50 colleges have a process to change our name and gender in university records and almost 60 will cover hormone therapy. Most of these universities are in the Northeast. However, the University of Iowa was the first university to add a "transgender" box to its application.

Campus Housing

For many students, living in the dorms is an important part of the college experience. As trans students, we often face specific concerns about what this experience will look like. Traditionally, college dorms are segregated by gender. Roommates are typically assigned

Trans Bodies, Trans Selves New York City Forum (photo by Katia Ruiz).

The magazine *The Advocate* publishes a list of the top 10 transgender-friendly colleges and universities.

based on our legal gender. If we have not changed our legal documents, we will therefore be housed with a roommate who shares our birth-assigned gender.

Depending on where we live and where we are in a physical transition, altering our legal gender may not be an option. Thanks to organizing and activism by transgender students and allies, this is beginning to change. If we are already out as trans, we may be able to address this before we are assigned to a dorm.

While we may request to be housed with roommates of our affirmed gender, there are other solutions as well. Some possible compromises include being moved to a single room (and it is well within our right to advocate that we not incur any additional charges), moving to on-campus apartments, if the school has them, or arranging permission to move off campus, if we are at a school where students of a particular year are required to live on campus.

The TONI (Transgender On-Campus Non-Discrimination) Project has a searchable database of schools and their policies on transgender issues like housing, health insurance, and nondiscrimination policies.

Many universities have loopholes in their housing policies that allow students with medical conditions to live in single rooms or make other housing arrangements, and it is illegal for them to discriminate. A doctor's note advocating for a single room due to "gender dysphoria" may be a helpful tool for those of us who are willing to use it.

In response to advocacy by transgender, genderqueer, and ally students, many colleges and universities have also begun implementing gender-neutral housing options. At these schools, students who choose to apply have the option of living with other students regardless of their gender. Colleges usually designate a floor or building as a space for gender-neutral housing. For many transgender students this is an option that makes them feel the safest and most comfortable on campus.

If we come out in the middle of a school year, additional issues may arise if we are already living with a roommate in a gender-segregated dorm. Socially transitioning in the dorms involves different levels of coming out not only to friends but also to people like our roommate and residential advisor (RA). If we are coming out in this setting, having a support network of allies in place—friends, the LGBTQ resource center, or other campus groups—can make the process much easier.

College Athletics

Another site of potential struggle and opportunity for organizing within college campuses has been athletics. There are often very strict gender-segregated polices for competitive sports. These policies may be from the university itself or larger athletic bodies of governance for college sports.

According to the National Collegiate Athletic Association (NCAA), which governs college sports:

- Female-to-male student athletes who are not taking testosterone should be allowed to participate on either a men's or a women's team.
- Male-to-female student athletes who are not taking testosterone blockers and estrogen may only compete on a men's team.
- Female-to-male student athletes taking testosterone who want to play on men's teams must receive a medical exemption from the national governing body for their sport because testosterone is a banned substance in college athletics. Once they start testosterone, they are no longer permitted to play on women's teams.
- Male-to-female student athletes who have begun hormone treatment may play on men's teams at any point. However, they must have been on testosterone blockers and estrogen for at least one year before beginning to play on a women's team.

Women's Colleges

Historically, the conversation about trans students at women's colleges has revolved around trans men coming out on female-only campuses. However, as trans youth have gained visibility and more of us are coming out at younger ages, a number of young trans women have sought the opportunity to attend women-only colleges.

Some schools have stipulations regarding admission based solely on the basis of legal sex. For those of us who have not made changes to the gender markers on our official documents (e.g., ID, passport, or Social Security card), only those of us designated female at birth will be able to apply. Those designated male at birth, whether we identify as trans or genderqueer, may need to update our legal documents before applying to women's colleges. It is currently difficult to update many of these documents without extensive medical treatment, and as young people we may not have undergone the necessary treatments for doing so.

Policy questions are only one aspect of the issue. For the past several years there has been increased attention and concern around the issues created by transgender men attending women's colleges. Questions have been raised such as if trans men were right to apply to those schools in the first place and what is the most appropriate decision regarding students who come out as male who are already attending a women's school.

With support from allies, many trans men have made great strides in finding a place on these campuses. They have had some success in advocating for their rights to stay enrolled even while transitioning. The argument many of these men use is that they feel safe in women's spaces. This is usually because they see this as an important part of their pasts and believe that they should have the right to continue their studies within that environment.

However, other trans men decide to transfer out of women's colleges to other schools after they transition. Some reasons that they leave are that they do not feel comfortable in the environment, they have been asked to leave, or they are concerned that at some point they will wish to not disclose their trans status every time they tell someone what college they went to.

> "When I returned to Smith for my sophomore year, I returned using the name 'Mark.' No one was surprised, and Smith is home to a wide variety of gender-variant folks. I didn't have to explain myself over and over, most everyone was familiar with trans people. It allowed me to begin to socially transition in a very safe place. . . When I returned to Smith for my junior year, I wasn't there two weeks before I withdrew. The sense of not-belonging was overwhelming: Smith is an all women's school. I am not a woman, therefore I felt I really did not belong there."

Ollie Schwartz is a social justice advocate in the Pioneer Valley of Massachusetts trying to embrace a politics of joy and the process of learning.

Q&A (once known as "Queers and Allies" but now even more inclusive) has done important organizing around the exclusion of trans* women

Ollie Schwartz.

Smith first years.

from Smith. In the summer of 2012, Calliope Wong, a trans* woman and rising high school senior, received a letter stating that her application would not be reviewed because her Free Application for Federal Student Aid (FAFSA) form had a male gender marker. Wong started a Tumblr about her experience applying to Smith, sparking online controversy over the issue of trans* women at "women's colleges."

Q&A felt that there needed to be a student organization, working from within the Smith student body, to make Smith College a safe space for trans* women. Q&A helped to organize and host several events to educate the Smith community as well as the city of Northampton about trans* female identity. Additionally, Q&A held informational meetings and discussions for the student government and student body. A poster campaign dispelling common myths and misconceptions about trans* women and women's colleges was created to post around campus during the 2013–2014 school year.

Q&A, along with other on-campus student LGBTQ groups, met multiple times with Smith's "Diversity Working Group," as well as with the Head of Admissions and college Deans to negotiate demands and dispel fears that Smith would lose its status as a historically women's college. Q&A's research subcommittee provided legal information on how it is possible for women's colleges to accept trans* women without losing Title IX status.

Q&A started three large-scale online campaign initiatives as a way of indicating to the college how important it was that Smith change its admissions policy. The first campaign was an online photo/solidarity statement campaign in which anyone could submit a photo of themselves, or a statement they had written, to Q&A's Facebook or Tumblr page with the sentiment "Trans women belong at Smith." The second campaign was a petition signed by Smith College Alumni stating that they did not approve of discrimination against trans* women. The third initiative was an online trans-national petition with change.org. The petition was signed by almost 5,000 people and was formally delivered to the Dean of Admissions.

In a meeting with LGBTQ student organizations in April 2013, the college verbally agreed that Smith admissions will accept alternative documentation to confirm gender identity if there are inconsistent or non-female-gender markers on admissions materials, will no longer consider financial aid/FAFSA documents when evaluating an applicant's gender, and will allow Q&A to create a "best practices" protocol for admissions employees to use when interacting with or advising trans applicants.

Paying for School

The costs of attending college can be a barrier for many students. As trans youth, we may face particular challenges. Coming out may have complicated our relationship with parents or guardians, and we may no longer be able to count on their financial support. However, there are many ways that we can pay for education, including the following:

- *Loans*: Many students across the country take out loans to pay for their education.
- *Scholarships*: There are many scholarships available for LGBTQ youth for undergraduate and graduate school.
- *Financial independence*: To qualify for financial aid, the Free Application for Federal Student Aid (FAFSA) requires us to report how much money our parents make until we reach the age of 25. If we can demonstrate that we have been financially independent of our parents for two or more years, we can be considered independently from our parents and qualify for additional grants and loans.
- *Employment*: Many students, of all backgrounds, work their way through school with full-time or part-time jobs.

National Scholarships Available for LGBTQ Students:
- League Foundation
- Live Out Loud
- National Gay and Lesbian Taskforce
- Point Foundation

Remember that we are not alone in struggling with the costs of our education, and there are many excellent resources available online, and through career and college counseling services, that can provide us with additional information about how to pay for school. Being trans does not mean that we cannot afford to continue our education.

COMMUNITY BUILDING AND ACTIVISM

Young adults in the transgender community have a long and powerful history as activists, and, though often not credited, are responsible for much of the social change the LGBTQ community has seen. Transgender youth have often been at the forefront of activism and many of us continue to work tirelessly as activists and community organizers. We have been involved in a wide variety of social and political issues to improve the lives of transgender community members. Historically and today, many of us are standing up against abuse and mistreatment by police, politicians, and those in power. We are on the front lines of protests and in the backroom strategy sessions of political organizing.

History of Youth Activism

Historically speaking, transgender youth were some of the leading voices in what we now think of as early LGBTQ activism in the United States. The Compton's Cafeteria Riot took place in San Francisco in 1966, three years before Stonewall, a well-known moment in LGBTQ history. At Compton's, the trans community organized against police brutality, poverty, and social stigma that young, mostly gender nonconforming people were facing in that part of the city. They also produced a magazine spreading the word about these issues and the work that they were doing making communities safer for disenfranchised young people. Because of the ways in which language and our comprehension of gender have changed over time, the activists did not really consider themselves to be transgender. The majority of the youth were, however, violating gender norms daily, and many identified as drag queens. While assigning labels or identities to historical figures is complicated and should be done carefully, given contemporary definitions of the term *transgender*, in retrospect these youth organizers can be seen and understood as transgender or gender nonconforming activists.

Arguably the most well-known beginnings of what most consider the modern LGBTQ rights movement were the Stonewall riots in New York City. Although this event is one of the most significant events in US LGBTQ history, few are aware of the role that transgender youth played. Based on accounts from individuals who were in the Stonewall Bar, historians believe that the majority of active participants in the riot itself were young, homeless, and otherwise street-involved transgender youth.

When looking at the roles that transgender youth played in the beginning of the LGBTQ rights movement, it is not an exaggeration to say that they were instrumental in its foundation. Further, transgender youth have continued to follow this important activist role and fight for transgender inclusion in society and in the broader LGBTQ community each step of the way.

Youth Activism Today

As trans youth, we continue to remain instrumental in contemporary activism in schools and elsewhere. We have radicalized larger LGBTQ rights groups and have continued to push further toward inclusion.

"WHOSE STREETS? OUR STREETS!": QUEER AND TRANS YOUTH OF COLOR DEMAND OUR VOICE AND OUR SPACE

Ana Conner is a member of FIERCE, an organization working for the collective liberation of our people, and a student at New York University.

I wasn't living on the piers—a spot in the West Village where LGBTQ youth of color gathered—when they were fenced off for renovation in 2000. I wasn't even living in New York City—I was born and raised in a small town in the heart of Florida. But when I moved here and joined FIERCE—an organization by and for LGBTQ youth of color—I immediately began to understand what it meant to struggle with an identity often seen as *worthless* by West Village residents, *powerless* to those with decision-making power over the piers, and *lawless* to the NYPD's Sixth Precinct that polices the neighborhood.

From the Quality of Life policing tactics first launched in the West Village, to the so-called Clean Up Christopher Street campaign aimed at "ridding" Christopher Street of "dissidents," trans and queer youth of color have been incarcerated and displaced just for being ourselves. The effect of gentrification isn't something I could have imagined before being there. But it is a reality that other youth have shared: living there after being kicked out, with no other place to call home, and no other people to call family.

LGBTQ youth of color are shifting this reality from one where we are silenced to one where we're at the forefront of conversations, having our say in how our lives should be lived. Organizations like FIERCE demand that our lives are not worthless but actually beautiful, full of a deep history and importance. We are learning the history of the piers and the history of people's resistance to the homophobia, transphobia, sexism, racism, and ageism our people have faced for centuries.

FIERCE helps me understand how to navigate all spaces and create counternarratives that are powerful, even when the most oppressive institutions are against us. Through organizing we demand, "Whose streets are these? Who has the right to be here, to be safe? Whose safety is actually being taken away when there are more police on the streets?" This counternarrative developed by LGBTQ youth of color is deeper than the pier struggle—it is a way to understand the oppression people experience every day, and it shows us *we* have the say over our own lives, no matter how or where those lives are lived.

SCHOOLS

One of the key areas where we have made enormous progress as activists has been within school settings—both in K–12 education and within colleges. Transgender youth have played an important role in the advancement of "safe schools" and antibullying legislation in cities and states across the country in order to ensure that all students, regardless of identity or expression, have a safe learning environment. We have also often played important roles in the growing network of gay-straight alliances (GSAs) in middle schools and high schools across the country that enable LGBTQ students to gather in a supportive environment within their schools. Trans students have been a driving force toward inclusion on college campuses. We have made and continue to make headway on issues ranging from gender-neutral bathrooms and housing to our right to attend historically same-gender institutions such as women's colleges.

BATHROOM RIGHTS

Access to safe public restrooms is an issue that many transgender people face. This issue has also been a rallying point for a number of youth activists committed to increasing the safety and comfort of transgender people in public settings. One activist group that has since been discontinued was called PISSR or People in Search of Safe Restrooms. The group was initially based in San Francisco, but their work spread to other areas. They focused on the creation of gender-neutral bathroom facilities to increase safety of transgender individuals and the mapping of existing facilities so that transgender people could more easily access gender-neutral restrooms. The group also developed apps to locate the closest bathroom.

Transgender college students have been at the forefront of organizing for gender-neutral bathrooms on college campuses. If you are working to add gender-neutral bathrooms or locker rooms to your college campus, think about joining with other groups of students who want the same thing. Many students with disabilities want to advocate for single-stall, accessible restrooms. Students who have families may want to advocate for family restrooms or locker rooms. The more groups organized for the same cause, the better.

INTERGENERATIONAL ACTIVISM

As youth, we may focus our activism on issues specific to us, but many of us also work in partnership with adults. LGBTQ youth have taken on important roles within broader LGBTQ social and political organizing. For example, we have worked on issues like housing and employment nondiscrimination policies, as well as marriage equality.

In order to get involved with groups of activists, we must first find out about these groups. Most of them are easily accessed online. Some of them are focused on one political party, while others have more of a broad social justice focus. A great way to become an active member of these types of groups is to be dependable. Make it a priority to show up to meetings on time and to do what you say that you are going to do. If we sign up to volunteer somewhere, we need to do exactly that. If something comes up and you need help with transportation or you are not going to be able to make it, contact a group member as soon as possible and try to help find someone else to cover your shift. The more accountable we are, the more likely we are to become more active and involved in activist groups.

Within intergenerational activist settings, one issue that often comes up is ageism. Specifically, young transgender activists and organizers may not be taken seriously by adult activists. This is not specific to transgender youth—it is an issue faced by all youth organizers. Sometimes activist spaces provide a welcoming environment for us to feel part of a community. However, sometimes we can be used to do some of the most labor- and time-intensive work but might be removed from larger and more important conversations regarding strategy. Adults often talk over the perspectives or experiences of youth. At the same time, as youth we sometimes ignore the advice or suggestions of older people, which is another form of ageism. Something important for any organization is to ensure that they are incorporating the voices of youth activists in a way that is not tokenizing. Organizations can actively utilize the talent and energy that youth organizers bring to issues and recognize that we come into situations with particular backgrounds and experiences that might be different from theirs due to generational differences. Both perspectives need to be recognized and taken into account when doing this sort of work.

Activism takes a variety of forms. Within activist communities there are differing opinions about which types of activism are the most helpful or important. Some of us are more drawn to certain kinds of activism. For some of us, activism looks like working toward changing legislation. Others of us may feel that legislation will either take too long to pass or will be ineffective. Some people focus their work on community education or the creation of services. Others spend time working toward cultural competency within existing agencies. Some of us engage in direct actions (like the Stonewall riots),

Youth at Compton's Cafeteria riot anniversary, San Francisco, August 20, 2012 (photo by Liz Highleyman).

while others of us are opposed to direct action as an activist tool. There are as many kinds of activism and perspectives on activism as there are activists. For transgender youth activists there are a variety of outlets for our passion and activist energies—it is simply a matter of finding the right fit. See Chapter 24 for more information on getting involved in activism.

CONCLUSION

As trans youth, we face unique challenges that range anywhere from bullying in school to finding ourselves with nowhere to live. We may sometimes feel like we are alone, but there are networks of adults and other youth who care very much about us and our futures. We are growing up in a time when things are changing very rapidly—although it may not always feel like it. We can be part of this change. There are so many ways for us to make our individual marks.

ACKNOWLEDGMENTS

The authors would like to thank Gender Infinity Co-Founders Becca Keo-Meier, Robert McLaughlin, and Robbie Sharp for their help with this chapter.

REFERENCES AND FURTHER READING

Beam, C. (2007). *Transparent: Love, family, and living the t with transgender teenagers.* Orlando, FL: Harcourt Books.

Bergman, S. B. (2009). *The nearest exit may be behind you.* Vancouver, BC: Arsenal Pulp Press.

Berman, S. (2011). *Speaking out: LGBTQ youth stand up.* Valley Falls, NY: Bold Strokes Books.

Bornstein, K. (2006). *Hello cruel world: 101 alternatives to suicide for teens, freaks and other outlaws.* New York, NY: Seven Stories.

CaCart, M. (Ed.). (2009). *How beautiful the ordinary: Twelve stories of identity.* New York, NY: HarperCollins.

Cianciotto, J., & Cahill, S. (2012). *LGBT youth in america's schools.* Ann Arbor: University of Michigan Press.

Coyote, I. E. (2012). *One in every crowd.* Vancouver, BC: Arsenal Pulp Press.

Feinstein, R., Greenblatt, A., Hass, L., Kohn, S., & Rana, J. (2001). Justice for all? A report on lesbian, gay, bisexual and transgendered youth in the New York juvenile justice system. *Lesbian and Gay Youth Project of the Urban Justice Center.* Retrieved December 2013, from http://www.urbanjustice.org/pdf/publications/lesbianandgay/justiceforallreport.pdf

Gay, Lesbian & Straight Education Network. (2011). *The 2011 National School Climate Survey.* Retrieved December 2013, from http://glsen.org/sites/default/files/2011%20National%20 School%20Climate%20Survey%20Full%20Report.pdf

Grant, J. M., Mottet, L. A., Tanis, J., Harrison, J., Herman, J. L., & Keisling, M. (2011). *Injustice at every turn: A report of the national transgender discrimination survey.* Washington, DC: National Center for Transgender Equality and National Gay and Lesbian Task Force. Retrieved December 2013, from http://www.thetaskforce.org/reports_and_research/ntds

Krieger, I. (2011). *Helping your transgender teen: A guide for parents.* New Haven, CT: Genderwise Press.

Lowrey, S., & Burke, J. C. (2010). *Kicked out.* Ypsilanti, MI: Homofactus Press.

Pascoe, C. J. (2007). *Dude, you're a fag: Masculinity and sexuality in high school.* Berkeley: University of California Press.

Safe Schools Coalition. (n.d.). Homeless LGBT youth and LGBT youth in foster care. Retrieved December 2013, from http://www.safeschoolscoalition.org/rg-homeless.html

21

AGING

Joe Ippolito and Tarynn M. Witten

AGING IS A JOURNEY THAT WE ALL TAKE. It can be interesting, surprising, rewarding, and, at times, difficult. As transgender and gender nonconforming (TGNC) people, we face some of the same challenges as others, and we also have unique ways of experiencing the process of growing older. We have much to share with younger generations, and we carry with us the history of our communities.

WHO ARE TRANS AND GENDER NONCONFORMING ELDERS?

Those of us who are current trans elders came of age during a time when there were fewer options available for self-identity than there are today. We may not have learned about the concept of transsexuality until later in life, and when we did, may not have known where to turn for resources. The terms *transgender* and *genderqueer* did not exist when we were growing up.

> *"I am sixty, but... I am coming late to the party... I envy the younger trans people, and the more accepting generation that surrounds them. They do not know how lucky they are. When I was growing up no one had ever even heard of such things and crossdressers were thrown in jail. What a great thing the Internet has done for people like us!"*

Younger people may have the chance to transition in their teens or twenties, but for those of us who are elders, that may not have been an option. Some of us did transition at a young age. Others of us knew that we wanted to transition but could not do so given our circumstances. Many of us came to understand our transgender identity in mid-life or may be doing so now. It can be a very different experience to transition during our thirties or forties and live much of our lives as ourselves than to transition in our seventies. Later life transitions allow our decisions around the transition process to be made with the insights of maturity and lived experience. However, those of us who transition later in life often feel a degree of sadness over lost time and the compromises we had to make.

> *"Aging has been a gift for me—before I transitioned, I really had no hope, and no reason to go on. But since I have transitioned, I feel like I've been given another shot at an authentic and real life, and I feel younger now than I did before I transitioned."*

The term *elderly* is difficult to define. For some of us, we may start to identify as elderly when we reach a certain age. Organizations in the United States typically require a minimum age of 50 to 65 to qualify as a senior. As people live longer, the ages we consider elderly may be changing. In many ways, identifying as an elder or senior can be self-defined.

AGEISM

Ageism is discrimination against individuals as a consequence of their age. In many cultures, elders are pushed aside when we hit a certain age because we do not value aging or being old. This is due to the inaccurate belief that elders no longer make any significant contributions to society. Elders are seen as unproductive, overly dependent, and ugly. This mindset infuses the way we think about elders in our society, in both conscious and unconscious ways, perpetuates discrimination against elders, and keeps alive negative stereotypes of elderly people.

DOCUMENTARIES ABOUT TRANS ELDERS

Gen Silent (directed by Stu Maddux) includes trans woman KrysAnne as one of six LGBTQ seniors spotlighted. *Growing Old Gracefully: The Transgender Experience* (directed by Joe Ippolito) follows five trans elders.

SAGE Story is a national digital storytelling program for LGBTQ Elders, where we can share our stories and watch the stories of others online.

Trans Bodies, Trans Selves New York City Forum (photo by Katia Ruiz).

A common form of ageism is age discrimination in employment. Despite the United States' Age Discrimination in Employment Act (ADEA), which prohibits discrimination against those over 40 years old, many employers systematically hire younger workers for various reasons. Due to stereotypes about older people, they may feel that older people will have less energy, learn less quickly, and be resistant to changing the way they go about doing things. Older workers may have more experience, which in many contexts would be considered a good thing, but employers often do not want to pay salaries to older workers that match their experience; furthermore, employers might worry that because older workers may retire earlier, putting energy into training them is not "worth" the effort. Trans elders face additional barriers in employment due to our status as trans, making job searches and retaining jobs more difficult for us than for other groups as we age.

A pervasive stereotype about older people is that we are unattractive. This is extended to create assumptions about our sexuality. Many people assume that older people are not as interested in sex and do not have sexual needs. As trans people, we face these same stereotypes of being unattractive and having a sexuality that others may not respect. This can make it very difficult for us as older trans people to maintain a healthy self-image and find partners.

> *"I consider myself an older trans woman. I get older anyway. That's no problem. But I have the good fortune to get old as a woman."*

> *"I am considered an elder, and it's the best thing ever, I have outlived a generation that had suffered so much violence, hate, and HIV and AIDS. . ..I am blessed!"*

Ageism is a problem even within trans communities. Many younger trans people feel that trans elders have outdated views or that we are stuck in our ways. We can be made to feel invisible, as if our voices do not count. It is often assumed that older trans people are not aware of newer concepts such as genderqueer identity or pansexuality, despite many of us identifying in these ways. Younger people often view us as having rigid expectations of gender roles, when, in fact, many of us have had lifetimes to explore and think about gender and understand it in nuanced ways. There is potential for great intergenerational collaboration within trans communities. Those of us who are younger have much to learn from our trans elders, and vice versa.

It is important to remember that many of us, as trans elders, have been dealing with multiple forms of discrimination throughout our lives. There is often the assumption that older trans people are mostly white and middle class, perhaps because these are the demographics of many of the people we see represented at conferences or in community groups. As trans elders, we come from every racial and economic background, and have various sexual orientations. For many of us, experiencing discrimination is nothing new.

Despite discrimination and negative stereotypes about older people, there are many communities and contexts in which older people are treated with respect and our experiences are honored. One of the best things we can do to put ourselves in these situations is to think ahead about the aging process early in our lives.

> *"I do kind of like being considered an old woman. There is a certain respect that people naturally give to an older woman that I appreciate."*

> *"I keep getting better and better. I am more myself than I have ever been. I love being wise. Knowing so much. Having seen and experienced so much. Having been there 'when.' Wow, things are so much better for us now. There is so much more information, support, resources, options now than back then."*

WHY NOT?

Bertie Brouhard is a 67-year-old trans woman in San Francisco who is living a new life.

Engineers like me are educated and trained to solve problems. We ask "how" but never "why." This is helpful to know about me—a 67-year-old, retired, corporate sales engineer and trans woman.

While I have known since the age of five that my mind's gender and my body's characteristics did not match, I was raised in the Midwest during the fifties and sixties, when having a choice was not an option. My deepest, most precious secret was buried in my psyche for over 50 years so that I could get an education, have a career, get married, raise a family, and attempt a normal life of what was expected of me.

I sometimes wonder how different my life would have been if I had lived it as a female—but any senior living with deep regrets is a destructive and sad individual.

Find a therapist who has counseled others like you. If your family and friends will be supportive of your questioning, you are very fortunate. That may not be the case, so consider some of the following as to "when" is a good time for you: Where do you reside? How will you support yourself during your transition and after your gender change? You are about to heavily tax your reserves of the two commodities humans need most: love and work.

In terms of love, I am still puzzled over longtime friends' acceptance or rejection of the new me. I love and have become totally estranged from my former wife, my only sibling, my older son and his family, and numerous friends of many years. But I went to my church and my several volunteer organizations and gained their acceptance. It can be lonely in that new gender, and you need some love.

Life is expensive for those who do not transition. It can also be pricey for those of us who do. Add to the normal costs—bills, food, rent, etc.—the costs of changing your gender. Make a list of your priorities and assign to each a date for completion, a projected cost, and a source of funds. Engineers are forever doing cost-benefit analyses.

At any age and economic situation, you also need some daily activity that gives your life meaning. I was very fortunate to have retired from the corporate world at age 55 and have found psychological income in my several volunteer duties.

What and who do you see when you look in the mirror? When I'm applying makeup, I see a white-haired, older white woman whose smile comes from having aligned her appearance with her gender. I "pass" to the most important person I know—me. I can control how I feel, but not how others do. So to those whom I sense are confused and maybe uncomfortable, I say: "What don't you understand about me? Let's talk. What I have is not contagious, you know."

We engineers don't address "why," and only you can answer "why not" for yourself. The choices we make define us, and for me there was only one. I hope to grow very old as a peaceful woman.

THINKING AHEAD

We are never too young to think about growing old. Many of us do not start thinking about aging until we are around 40 years old, the age often considered to be the beginning of "middle age." While we may currently feel very energetic, socially active, and in good physical health, what will our energy levels, social life, and physical health look like in 15, 25, or 40 years?

As we begin to age, new social, financial, medical, and psychological challenges may emerge. Who will I spend time with when I am old? What does my financial future look like? Who will care for me when I get sick? Who will advocate for me if I cannot advocate for myself? How will my spiritual, faith, or religious needs be met? Will my family be there for me?

Starting in middle age, we may have age-related concerns that are specific to being TGNC people, including the following:

- Lack of reproductive or parenting options
- Remorse over not having lived in our preferred gender at a younger age
- Estrangement from our families and children, especially if we started transitioning later in life
- Separation from younger LGBTQ communities of which we were once a part
- Increased concerns about our transition-related or non-transition-related health
- Greater financial burdens
- Fears of the consequences of being "outed"
- Worries about whether we will be treated with care if we need to enter a nursing home or assisted living facility at some point

The psychological stressors we face as middle-aged trans and gender nonconforming people may lead us to feelings of depression, loneliness, anger, anxiety, frustration, and regret. These are all feelings experienced by many middle-aged people, regardless of their gender identity, but may be magnified because we are dealing with additional burdens. Attending local transgender support groups and connecting with others who embrace and accept us is key to getting through tough times, and it can help us to build social support networks that we can take with us as we age. Middle age is also a time when many of us seek out psychological support by meeting with therapists.

> "I am a more senior member of the trans* community, yes, and it's a strange position in which to be. On the one hand, I have a lot more life experience than many younger people who are transitioning, so I have a better under-standing of how to negotiate things like public services, networking, and employment. But on the other, all of this is as new to me as it is to trans* people half my age. Most of the people in my social circle are anywhere from 10 to 20 years younger than me, and that's actually something I really enjoy. I get a lot of energy and enthusiasm from these interactions that many people my age no longer have, and that helps me a great deal. My partner is 16 years younger than me, and it's comforting to know that ze and my younger friends will be with me as I grow older. I never had any children of my own, so aging has always been a subject fraught with uncertainty and trepidation for me. I'm a social person, so being alone and lonely was a concern. I don't think I'll end up that way now. I have too many people who care about me for that to happen. And I do feel a responsibility to them as well, to live the best life I can and to be an example of what a happy ending for a trans* person looks like."

In addition to psychological stressors, trans and gender nonconforming people are frequently at increased financial risk. For those of us who transition at a younger age, financial planning can be delayed due to lack of employment or the high cost of surgeries.

For those of us who transition during mid-life, our transition can significantly affect our finances as well as our relationships. Money we were once saving for retirement may now instead be needed for transition. If we are significant wage earners in our households, and lose our job as a result of discrimination, this can destabilize a relationship or family, leading to anger, resentment, frustration, depression, and isolation.

> "I turn 40 in a few months, and have spent half my life openly queer and gender bending. It is hard sometimes to really know how that has affected my life. I believe it's brought many positives. The negatives have been that I don't fit in people's boxes well, which I feel has made finding a life partner more difficult.

*The unpredictable effects of discrimination have also made planning my life, especially my financial life, more difficult."**

Spending time when we are younger thinking about how we want to age can be extremely helpful. It can allow us to identify the barriers we have ahead of us and to plan for exciting futures. Middle age can be a great time to connect with TGNC elders in our communities to learn about their lives and seek out their advice for growing older vibrantly and effectively.

HEALTH AND MEDICAL CARE

As TGNC elders, we are in many different situations regarding our transition-related and non-transition-related health. Some of us may have few health problems, and others of us may be burdened with health issues that interfere with our daily lives. Some of us have been taking hormones for many years and may be thinking about decreasing our hormone use as we age. Some of us began to transition later in life and are thinking about starting hormones now. Others of us are not interested in taking hormones. Some of us have had surgeries at a younger age, while others of us are considering doing so now, and still others of us are not interested in having surgeries. No matter what situation we are in, our health is an important part of our lives. Maintaining good health as we age improves our ability to remain independent and active.

Leading an Active Lifestyle and Minimizing Unhealthy Habits

Stereotypes about older people tell us that we will have less energy and be less active as we age. However, this is not true for many of us. There are a number of ways we can stay fit as we get older. Aerobic exercise, which increases our heart rate, and strength training, are both important. While some of us will continue to play sports or participate in running or bike races, many people begin to seek out activities considered low impact—those that put less strain on our bones—as we grow older. These include yoga, walking, swimming, and water aerobics. Many towns and cities have walking clubs for older people that meet outside in good weather and inside (often in shopping malls) in the winter. Water aerobics classes are typically geared toward older adults, and many gyms have other classes directed toward seniors. Some Medicare plans offer discounts at certain gyms. For those of us who feel more comfortable spending time with other LGBTQ people, many LGBTQ centers have groups for older adults, some of which include aerobic activity.

> *"I get older—and am still running Marathons."*

> *"I'm 58, and transgender for 40 years, though not really admitting it until the last seven. I guess I'm a senior member, though I know TG people in their 80's. I'm fighting age with as much energy as I can, staying fit by biking 20 miles a day and eating as healthily as I can."*

> *"I am 54 years old, but many people tell me I look 20 years younger. At the age of 51, I was dancing topless at a straight strip club beside 22 year old GGs. None of them had a clue that I was 51 or that I was transsexual until my friend told them. Then the strippers were like wow, she is incredible."*

In addition to maximizing our exercise, we may also spend time as we age thinking about what we put into our bodies. Eating balanced meals is important—while still allowing ourselves indulgences sometimes. Alcohol in small amounts can be part of a healthy lifestyle, although our bodies may not be able to process alcohol and other drugs and medications as quickly as when we were younger.

Tobacco is a significant problem in transgender communities, and it can be especially important for us as older trans people to minimize cigarette smoking. Hormones and

---

* Quotes in this chapter were taken from two sources. Those followed by an asterisk are taken from research done by the chapter author Tarynn Witten (2011). All others, like other quotes in the book, come from the *Trans Bodies, Trans Selves* online survey.

smoking can combine to increase our risks for blood thickening and blood clots that can lead to strokes. As we age, other factors also contribute to an increased risk of blood clots, so quitting smoking can be even more important as we age.

Preventive Health Care

As transgender older adults, we have many of the same health care needs as cisgender older people. Most preventive care—care that maintains our health rather than treating a disease—is the same regardless of gender. In order to stay healthy, it is important for us to be screened regularly for high blood pressure and high cholesterol, as these can contribute to heart disease and strokes—blood clots in the brain that can cause paralysis of body parts, as well as changes in our ability to think and talk. Providers usually also screen for diabetes, which is becoming more common. Despite the negative stereotypes about older people and sexuality, many of us are sexually active and will want to be tested for HIV and other sexually transmitted infections (STIs). Screening for some forms of cancer, such as colon cancer, is unaffected by our gender.

> "I am an older member of the transgender community, both because I have been involved longer than most who are still involved, and because I am pushing 60. Aging with a transgender identity has not been a problem for me so far. I believe that the education work that I have been doing since I started transition has paid off for me. I have a completely supportive medical system. I have been able to obtain proper care from all providers, from my primary care physician to the local hospital. I am also connected to the local elder service providers and have been working with them and the town Counsel on Aging to encourage acceptance for LGBT people."

The FORGE Transgender Aging Network email list offers a space for health care providers who work with trans elders to discuss issues and share advice.

BREAST AND REPRODUCTIVE CANCERS

The likelihood of developing cancers of the breast and reproductive organs (uterus, ovaries, prostate) is influenced by our hormone use as well as the hormones we were exposed to at a younger age that were produced by our own bodies. A general rule is that every part of the body deserves appropriate preventive care for as long as it is present. Those of us who have a cervix should receive Pap smears, and those of us with a prostate should have prostate exams. Screening for breast cancer is a good idea for everyone, as those of us who were assigned female at birth, even if we have had top surgery, may retain some breast tissue.

OSTEOPOROSIS

As we age, we are all at risk for osteoporosis, decreasing bone strength that can lead to fractures. Hormones can be protective against osteoporosis, so those of us born with ovaries or testes that have been removed may need to pay special attention to our bone health if we are off hormones. We may even consider taking small doses of hormones to help with bone strength. Our health care providers may recommend taking vitamin D and calcium as we get older.

SEXUAL HEALTH

Despite stereotypes that older people are less sexual than younger people, many older people are sexually active. For those of us who are, it is important that we continue to protect ourselves and our partners from STIs. Many of us believe our risk is low, but HIV rates are rising among older people in the United States. Sexuality is an important part of who we are throughout our lives, and many of us continue being sexual as we age, while keeping in mind the risks.

ORAL HEALTH

Oral health is often overlooked, but it can play a significant role in our health and social lives. Poor oral care can lead to cavities, pain, periodontitis (inflammation of the gums), and loss of teeth. Tooth loss can create problems eating and can also make us less likely to socialize because of embarrassment. Cigarette smoking can increase our risk for oral health problems. Daily brushing and flossing, as well as regular dental visits, can help protect us against oral health issues.

Medical Transition

As trans older adults, we vary in our use of hormones. Some of us are not interested in taking hormones, others have been on hormones for many years, and others of us are just beginning hormones. Wherever we are, it is important for us to think about how we want to approach hormone treatment.

TAKING HORMONES AT AN OLDER AGE

For those of us beginning to take hormones at an older age, it is very important to do so with the help of a health care provider, for a number of reasons. As we age, we are more likely to develop medical problems such as high blood pressure and high cholesterol that can increase our risk of heart disease and strokes. Combined with hormones, our risk may become even greater. While these medical conditions should not prevent us from taking hormones that affirm our identity, they are part of the picture when we make informed decisions about the amount and type of hormones to take. For example, if we smoke and have high blood pressure, our health care provider may suggest that we use an estrogen patch instead of taking estrogen pills and join a program to try to quit smoking, in order to decrease the likelihood of having a stroke. The provider may want to see us more frequently to make sure we are monitoring our blood pressure closely.

For those of us who are coming out as older adults, we may have a sense of "making up for lost time" and may be more likely to use hormones in an unsafe manner or neglect other aspects of our medical care. We may use more hormones than are prescribed to us or get hormones from people we know in the community rather than from a health care provider. It is important to know that taking higher doses of hormones does not speed up the process of physical changes, and it increases side effects as well as the risk for blood clots and strokes.

> "I don't feel my age. I actually feel younger and I believe that along with HRT my peace of mind has slowed down the aging process. I'm just going with my own harmonious flow."

> "I think the aspects of being female I felt uncomfortable about were connected to being young and sexy. I didn't like being a desirable object. I feel more comfortable with my curves as they get more saggy. I love my first couple of chin whiskers and I'm looking forward to more. Maybe I'll never need T."

SHOULD WE DECREASE OUR HORMONE USE AS WE AGE?

As we grow older, our bodies produce lower amounts of hormones. For cisgender women, this results in a period called menopause where fertility and menstrual periods end. Cisgender men also experience decreases in their hormone production and decreased fertility as they age.

Currently, there is very little research on whether TGNC people should stop or decrease our hormone use as we grow older. There are no recommendations by health care organizations for TGNC people to stop or decrease hormone use at a certain age. Some of us like the idea of decreasing our hormone use as we grow older. Others would like to continue standard doses. Either way, it is important for us to talk with our health care providers about our plans, as there are risks to taking hormones, especially if we have other medical conditions, and there are also risks to stopping them, especially if we have had our ovaries or testes removed so that our bodies are no longer producing hormones.

Surgery

Some of us who desire transition-related surgeries have had them early in life, while others of us have not. It may have taken us significant time to save enough money to have surgery, or we may not have come out until recently. For those of us who can afford surgery now and are interested in it, our options may be more limited than they were when we were younger.

Due to the robust tissue elasticity and health of young adults, most surgeries, including chest and genital surgeries, have the best results when performed early in adulthood. Nevertheless, many of us who are midlife or older experience psychological relief as well as an improved sense of self following gender-affirming surgeries. Older age, in and of itself, is not a contraindication for undergoing transition-related surgery as long as we are healthy enough to undergo the procedure. We may have to go through additional screening prior to surgery and our recovery time is often longer than that of younger people. Surgeons who perform transition-related surgeries can tell us more about the risks and benefits of undergoing surgery at an older age.

> *"I first began my transition at the age of 60 and will have my last surgery at the age of 63. Age is and has never been an issue for me but that is because of my health and looks. I am not on any type of medication based on my age and only take HRT medications. I feel very lucky in this regard because I have very good stamina, vigor, and mental ability."*

Some of us who cannot afford gender-affirming surgeries consider silicone injections. In the United States, these injections are frequently done by friends or acquaintances rather than licensed health care providers. Silicone injection can be extremely dangerous, and it can lead to serious disfiguring of our bodies and in some cases to clots in our lungs that cause our death. If we are aware of the risks and benefits of silicone injection, we can make informed decisions about its use. See Chapter 13 for more information on transition-related surgeries and silicone injection.

Mental Health

Mental health is an extremely important part of our overall health. Stress and depression can take a toll on our physical bodies and interfere with our relationships. As older TGNC people, many of us have experienced long periods of discrimination, violence, abuse, estrangement, and transphobia. These can lead to mental and emotional challenges such as anxiety, depression, posttraumatic stress disorder (PTSD), and even suicide.

Many of us grew up during a time when coming out or transitioning was not as common as it is today. We may have lived for years in a body and public gender identity that did not reflect how we felt inside, sometimes making us feel worthless and alone. We may have regrets about living so long without transitioning. Our families may have been less likely to understand us. For those of us who have taken hormones or had surgeries, if we started them later in life, we may not be as pleased with the results as we would have if we had transitioned medically when we were younger. All of these challenges of living as an older TGNC person affect our mental health.

Seeking out mental health care can be more difficult for TGNC people than cisgender people, and even more so for those of us who are older because there are fewer mental health care providers with experience working with TGNC elders. However, more providers are taking the time to learn about us and to be sources of support for us in transitioning and in living our daily lives. For more information on seeking out mental health care providers, see Chapter 14.

Substance Abuse

Drug and alcohol abuse in the elderly are well-known problems. As older adults, we are at high risk for substance abuse because many of us are losing social connections, grieving our partners and friends, being treated with disrespect due to stereotypes about the elderly, having financial difficulties, dealing with poor physical health, and facing our mortality. This is true of both transgender and cisgender elders.

Little is currently known about substance abuse in the elder trans population. We do know that compared to the general population, LGBTQ people are more likely to use alcohol and drugs, have a higher rate of substance abuse, are less likely to abstain from use, and are more likely to drink heavily in later life. For all of these reasons, it is important for us to pay attention to our use of alcohol and drugs and to look out for our friends and partners as we age. The most effective way to prevent substance abuse in our communities is to build strong social ties that give us a sense of purpose.

GENDER IDENTITY, SERVING IN THE MILITARY, AND RESPECT FOR ALL TRANS-GENDER VETERANS

Janice Josephine Carney facilitates a vet-to-vet peer transgender support group at the JP VA Hospital in Boston. Her book Purple Hearts and Silver Stars tells of her struggles as a Vietnam Veteran with PTSD as well as her transition.

In 1969, as butch lesbians, drag queens, and other gender-variant people at the Stonewall Inn exploded in outrage over years of mistreatment, I had to take a draft physical. All through high school I felt more female than male. I was blessed with living in the sixties, so I could have long hair, beads, frilly shirts, and leather pants. I graduated not sure what gender I really was, not sure of what my sexuality was. After a heated argument with my father over my hair, my clothes, and my sexuality, I had enlisted to get into the medical corps. I honestly believed that going to Vietnam would make a man out of me.

From the first day of basic training, I was up even before dawn to take my shower alone and then get in uniform before the rush to the showers. I survived my year in Vietnam with some damage. I served in Germany and survived rumors over my sexuality and rumors of doing drag shows with a threat of a "homosexual discharge" held over my head.

Of course, the Army could not redefine how I felt about my body, and neither could a long marriage. Depression, alcohol, and drugs could not hide me from myself, no matter how hard I tried. My last suicide attempt was after a day alone in my favorite summer dress, doing house cleaning.

In 1993, after a year of sobriety, I was sitting with my sponsor, and he asked me: What would it take for me not to feel the need to drink? In a moment of complete honesty, as I was looking at a woman in a colorful summer dress, I told him, a fellow Vietnam vet, that just wearing a nice sundress and being myself would do that. His advice was to go buy a dress.

Today I am a 100% service-connected, disabled veteran, and I am also one of the founders of the Transgender American Veterans Association. I facilitate a support group for fellow transgender veterans at the Boston VA. I hope to publish a memoir someday telling the story about how hard my struggle was, why I feel proud of my service, and why I am fighting for the rights of other transgender people to serve and to receive proper respect and treatment as veterans.

Abuse and Victimization

If you are an older trans person and you are being abused or threatened, contact the National Eldercare Locator (1-800-677-1116) to get connected with resources near you.

As older trans adults, many of us have experienced abuse and victimization as children, and sometimes throughout our lives. As we grow older, we become particularly vulnerable as we lose social connections and people who protect us, and as we become less physically able to prevent ourselves from being abused. Abuse of older people is often called "elder abuse." Abuse of older people can be physical or sexual but can also include verbal threats, manipulation, exploitation, or neglect. Abusers sometimes attempt to control our finances or property, or represent themselves to the outside world as caring for us while treating us with disrespect. All of these are forms of abuse, and there are resources to protect us and help us to stand up against abuse.

Working Within Health Care Systems

In the United States, health care coverage can be a convoluted web. Some of us have public insurance and others have private insurance. Some of us have no insurance coverage at all. As trans elders, we may run into various forms of discrimination in health care.

Even providers who have some familiarity with younger TGNC people may not expect us to identify as TGNC because of stereotypes about older people. The Affordable Care Act (ACA) is likely to improve the provision of health care in the United States and make more people, including older people, eligible for affordable health insurance plans.

Those of us over 65 who are US citizens are eligible for Medicare coverage. There are some instances where noncitizen residents are also eligible. Medicare part B covers routine preventive care regardless of sex or gender, including breast exams and mammograms, pelvic exams, and prostate exams. There are instances where TGNC people have had difficulty getting preventive care covered if our sex or gender on our Medicare information does not match our body parts. In this case, an appeal process may be necessary, but the care should be covered. Medicare Part D, which requires additional payments, covers prescription drugs such as estrogen, testosterone, and spironolactone. Hormones are covered when considered medically necessary. This is a good reason to develop a strong relationship with a health care provider who can advocate that our hormones are medically necessary for us. At the time of writing, Medicare does not currently cover transition-related surgeries, but there are numerous legal challenges to this policy.

Veterans of the US Military are entitled to health care through the Veteran's Health Administration (VHA). The VHA issued a directive in 2013 outlining the provision of care for transgender veterans. This document indicates that trans veterans be addressed by the correct gender and provided all necessary preventive care, hormone therapy, mental health services, preoperative evaluation, and postoperative care. The VHA does not provide for transition-related surgeries.

The Yahoo group TSVets connects transgender veterans.

STILL SERVING

Zander Keig, MSW, is a US Coast Guard veteran (1986–1988) and a social worker with the US Department of Veterans Affairs (VA), Veterans Health Administration (VHA) in Northern California, who coedited the 2011 Lambda Literary Finalist book Letters for My Brothers: Transitional Wisdom in Retrospect.

As a medically discharged veteran with a service-connected disability rating, I am afforded full medical care coverage at minimal cost through the Veteran's Health Administration (VHA). This includes medically necessary transition-related care, such as access to hormones. If I needed psychotherapy, I would have access to that as well. As a post-op transsexual man, I have no need for SRS-related surgeries, though I did learn recently about a California VA Medical Center that provided a trans male veteran with an erectile prosthesis and scheduled him for a urethral extension procedure.

I have had a variety of experiences with VHA employees, at VA hospitals and clinics across the country (California, Arizona, Florida, and Colorado). Usually, on visits for medical care, I primarily interact with registered nurses, nurse practitioners, and physicians who ask basic questions and are rarely aware of my transsexual status until I disclose and tell them what I may need. Mostly, I encounter surprise ("I never would have known!") and confusion ("What does that mean?"), but every once in a while I encounter a medical care provider who reacts very negatively. The most memorable negative experience occurred when a resident endocrinologist informed me that I would need to submit to a "genital inspection" before my hormone prescription would be refilled. I told her absolutely not; my genitalia have nothing to do with my hormone script.

My interactions with Veterans Benefits Administration (VBA) are usually not in person. Most of their business is conducted over the telephone, so they are less eventful. I am happy to report that my legal California marriage to my wife in 2005 is recognized by the VBA, which means they added my wife as a dependent and increased my disability compensation. I find comfort in knowing that if, and when, I encounter difficult people and/or processes at the VHA, I can rely on the information contained within the Veterans Health Administration Transgender Healthcare Directive, which was re-released in February 2013. In addition, the VA Office of Diversity & Inclusion for LGBT Programs has designated two individuals to be liaisons between the national office and local sites.

As a VA employee, I rarely disclose my transsexual medical history, yet I still find ways to advocate for trans* veterans, both locally and nationally, as a member of a VA educational workgroup. This workgroup has designed three online training modules focused on developing more capacity and competence for working with trans veterans who access health care at any VHA medical center, outpatient clinic, or community-based clinic. As a trans vet, I make every effort to promote the national and local efforts being accomplished by the VA so that my brothers and sisters will have a positive experience, or at least know how to advocate for themselves when they don't. *News and opinions presented here are solely those of the author and do not necessarily represent those of the Department of Veterans Affairs.*

For those of us without health insurance, there are a number of routes we may take to obtain preventive and transition-related care. Many public hospitals have programs to provide free or low-cost health care. This is also true of many LGBTQ health clinics. Some LGBTQ health clinics are even creating programs to specifically meet the needs of aging LGBTQ populations.

As we age, we face other barriers to good quality health care. We may begin to require assistance in our homes, spend time in hospitals, or need to move to nursing homes. Like the majority of older people, we fear the loss of control that often comes from aging but also have additional concerns about feeling safe and respected by people who enter our homes and in outside facilities. We should never be made to feel unsafe being open about our identities to caregivers, but we often do.

Our local LGBTQ centers often have connections to companies that provide nurses and home health aides, and they may be aware of which companies are LGBTQ friendly. Visiting nurse associations may also have information on how to find providers who are respectful of our identities. National organizations like Lambda Legal and SAGE (Services and Advocacy for GLBT Elders) often team up to work on legal issues related to LGBTQ older adults. They can be good resources for learning about state and local laws that protect us, as elders, against discrimination in nursing homes and retirement communities.

FAMILY

As older people, we have had lifetimes to experience our families of origin and also our self-created families. Many of us come from homes where our parents did not support or were not aware of our gender identities. Many of our parents are no longer living. For some of us, our siblings are loving and dependable, while for others, family connections are extremely strained. We may have learned over time to create our own families of LGBTQ people.

Many of us have adult children and even grandchildren. We may have come out before our children were born, during their childhoods, or once they were adults. They may still not know that we identify as transgender. Some of us are not open about ourselves because we are afraid our children will not allow us to see our grandchildren if we come out.

> "I have had some regrets about not transitioning earlier. When I've voiced these, trans and non-trans friends alike tell me that I could have wound up homeless on the streets, mistreated by the health care system, and I would have not met my partner, and we probably would never have created our daughter. It's the best of times to transition."

> "I have 3 children (one of whom is gay), and one grandchild with another on the way. When our family gets together, we have an interesting mix of two transsexuals, two gay men, along with my 2 straight daughters, straight son-in-law, and so far straight grandson."

It can be difficult to predict how someone will react to finding out about our gender identities. Many of us find that our families are, sometimes after some initial resistance, supportive of us and our identities, and we have many rewarding experiences with them as we age. However, for some of us, it is not possible to create an open and loving experience with our families of origin. Many aging trans and gender nonconforming people begin to construct new or alternative family systems consisting of friends, new dating partners, and even pets.

> "I just wish I'd been able to identify my true self earlier and transitioned earlier. But then, I probably wouldn't have had my wonderful daughter, who is the light of my life. Better late than never."

> "I hope that I live to a ripe old age and see my kids become successful as human beings (so far so good)."

RELATIONSHIPS

As transgender elders, many of us have been in long-term relationships during our lives, sometimes prior to coming out and other times once we have come out. For those of us who entered into relationships prior to transition, many of us work with our partners to stay together. However, some families can become separated over gender changes. In some cases, children and friends of the couple take the side of the cisgender partner, feeling as if that person was wronged. When this happens, we can lose the support of many people at the same time, and this can be a very lonely experience.

When we are older, finding dating partners who are open to the trans experience can be challenging and rewarding. While those of our generation may not have as much exposure to transgender people, there are also many open-minded, interesting people with nuanced views of gender developed over a lifetime.

> *"I consider myself to be a happy, well-adjusted, hanging onto middle age woman who has been blessed at sharing this path with another woman."*

> *"If it were not for my loving wife, I would not be able to survive this segment of my transition. She has allowed me to close my practice and just see a few patients a month who refuse to see another doctor."*

Despite stereotypes about older people being disinterested in sex, many of us would like to continue having fulfilling sexual relationships as we age. It is completely normal and healthy to have sexual needs and desires at all ages.

BUILDING COMMUNITIES

Studies of older people across the world demonstrate that strong social support networks are essential for our health and quality of life. As we grow older, we often begin to lose our social networks because friends move, pass away, or are unable to travel long distances to see each other due to physical constraints.

> *"I've struck up a quite close friendship with one of the other middle-aged trans women and we are like a couple of confidantes in many ways."*

There are a number of ways we can stay involved and make new friends that are supportive of us and our identities. Our local LGBTQ centers often have activities targeted at older adults. These may include social groups, exercise classes, book clubs, and movie viewings. Affirming religious institutions can also be a great place for us to meet friends,

The National Resource Center on LGBT Aging provides a map with lists of local resources for LGBTQ elders in each state.

The FORGE Transgender Aging Network hosts an email list for trans adults and our partners 50+.

GRIOT (Gay Reunion in Our Time) Circle is an organization of older LGBTQ people of color in New York City.

Trans Bodies, Trans Selves Seattle Forum (photo by Ish Ishmael).

if we are drawn to make spiritual connections. National LGBTQ aging groups like SAGE have local chapters. Some of us live far outside of cities or away from physical locations where we can go to receive support and make connections as trans elders. There are a number of email lists for trans elders and our partners.

> *"In the Pride Parade this coming Saturday, I am riding in the parade on the 'LGBT Aging Project' trolley/float. I am now 58.5 years old and definitely identify with my friends in the LGBT community who are reaching seniority and the many issues it poses."*

Many of us begin to feel distanced from our LGBTQ and trans communities as we age. As trans elders, we have the benefit of years of experience and we carry with us a living legacy of our communities. Some of us have been involved in activism, and many of us continue to do incredible work in our communities. There is a youth focus to many LGBTQ groups, and ageism leads to beliefs that older people are no longer on the cutting edge of activism. We have a tremendous amount to share with younger generations, and we can be great assets to activist communities.

> *"I am older than many, which does put me in the position of being looked up to, I think. I have some friends in their twenties who ask me a lot of questions, and that's ok with me."*

> *"I became involved with the Trans support group. I am around kids that are just coming to terms with who they are and it allows me to offer them advice that may make life less hellish for them than it was for me."*

> *"At age 62 I daresay I am senior. . . but I still don't know it. . . I run these youngsters ragged. . ."*

FINANCES

As trans elders, we often have lower incomes and fewer assets than other people our age. We may have had difficulties sustaining employment due to discrimination, or we may have needed to spend savings on surgeries. Many of us continue to work or to seek work as we age because we enjoy the connections we have through working, or because we need to make an income to support ourselves.

Employment

Finding employment can be difficult for us as transgender people no matter how old we are. Due to discrimination that often begins in childhood, we are less likely to finish high

2013 Rally for Transgender Equality (Ted Eytan, MD, Washington, D.C.).

LIFE STAGES

school and go to college. Even when we do build up credentials that make us good candidates, we still face discrimination in hiring for jobs. As older trans people, ageism adds another layer of difficulty to finding employment.

> *"I'm still married, that was one reason it took so long to transition. I was learning and so was my wife. It was a hard road and we made it, not unscathed. It took its toll. We have been married for 42 years now. I work at a different job, retired from my career and now I drive a school bus. I retired on my own, was not forced out."*

> *"Because I started transitioning later in life and I have a really good job that I'd like to keep post transition, I've been going really slow on the changes and letting people get used to one change before I start the next. My order started with hormones and weight loss, started hair removal, voice training, support groups, then when I came out at work I started changing the way I dressed, slowly. I stopped wearing ties the first thing and now I'm working on wearing more gender appropriate clothing."*

> *"I changed career fields a few years ago, to a field that respects age, rather than seeing it as a deficit."*

Retirement

Transitioning to retirement is a normal part of aging that most of us will face at some point in our lives. Retirement planning includes finding an acceptable retirement living environment, figuring out how we will support ourselves (often through Social Security or a pension), and obtaining medical care (often through Medicare), and deciding how we want to spend our days. Some of us are forced into retirement because of disability or illness, while others of us choose when to retire.

Some of us are fortunate enough to have savings, pensions, and reasonable Social Security benefits as we retire because we have had well-paying jobs. However, many of us do not have financial safety nets. We are less likely to have had long-term job stability or to be in relationships that are recognized by the federal government, from which we might gain benefits if our partners pass away.

> *"As a transsexual, my life didn't really begin until I was in my early 40s, so I haven't even begun my profession yet. I don't anticipate ever being able to retire."*

> *"Until we're fully accepted and integrated into society the trans community is always going to be at a disadvantage in economic terms and therefore at a disadvantage in providing a reasonable pension and health coverage for old age."* *

> *"My university was supportive of me, and I continued as a tenured member of the faculty. . . I retired from the university with emeritus status (and a scholarship named after me)."*

Some of us who have had jobs for many years in our birth-assigned genders are waiting to retire in order to transition.

> *"I am a late transitioner. I was in denial most of the years of my life. I did not seriously try to even begin to be full time until I retired."* *

Retirement planning ahead of time is essential. For some of us, retirement can be an exciting time when we think about who we are and what kinds of things we most enjoy doing. Even for those of us who cannot imagine being able to afford to retire, it can be a good idea to think about what we would do if we became disabled or otherwise unable to work.

HOUSING

Where we will live as we age is one of the most important decisions we make. Unfortunately, for many of us, this decision is not entirely ours, because of finances or because we live in prison or public housing systems. For those of us who do have choices about where we are going to live, we have a number of options depending on the level of care we need. Traditionally, our necessary level of care increases as we age, so that we may go from living in our homes alone to having assistance in our homes, or we may choose to live in a retirement community where we can start out in our own room or apartment, then receive care in our room or apartment, and then progress to more frequent nursing care.

Living at Home

Most people prefer to live in their own homes as they age. We become accustomed to caring for ourselves and having privacy when we want it. As we grow older, we may start to need help around the house or in dealing with our medical issues. Many of us have a few good friends, but they are often our own age and so cannot provide the physical help we need. If we have children or younger relatives, they can be good support systems. They may run into their own difficulties as caregivers and should be aware of the resources available to them as they care for us.

There are also programs where workers are sent to our houses to deliver meals or to check in on us. Our local LGBTQ centers can often provide us with more information on programs where the workers are aware of issues of gender and sexuality, and will be more likely to respect us for who we are.

Finding good quality medical help from respectful providers such as home health aides and nurses can be difficult and financially out of reach for many of us. As TGNC people, we may have taken hormones or had surgeries that make our bodies different from what providers are expecting, and this may create conflicts for them that they take out on us. There are many knowledgeable people in these positions. It may take some time to find them, but our local LGBTQ centers and national organizations on trans and LGBTQ aging can be helpful.

Retirement Communities

Because increasing visibility and acceptance of LGBTQ people has been relatively recent, there are few retirement communities specifically for us. This is beginning to change, and there are now a number of organizations working on creating senior housing projects for LGBTQ communities.

For most of us who enter retirement communities, they will not be LGBTQ specific but can be LGBTQ friendly. There are many ways to create a safe space for us to be open about our gender identities and feel respected in retirement communities. This may include creating brochures that include a diverse group of residents, updating application forms to include questions about gender identity and sexual orientation, hosting events or running groups that highlight LGBTQ issues, and offering gender-neutral restrooms.

"There should be LGBTIQ-friendly adult care facilities. I don't know of any." *

"It's crucial that mainstream (non-LGBT) nursing homes, assisted living facilities and retirement communities be trained in LGBT sensitivity and transgender sensitivity in particular so that LGBT people can live in these facilities as openly LGBT-identified people. We must also find a way to provide long-term care in a way that doesn't rely on exorbitantly expensive long-term care insurance or spending down in order to go on Medicaid for long-term care in nursing homes." *

Searching for a retirement community that will be accepting and respectful can be difficult but rewarding. In order to find out more about a particular retirement community, we

SAGECAP (SAGE Caring and Preparing) runs individual and group counseling and educational seminars for caregivers. Family Caregiver Alliance also offers a group for caregivers of LGBTQ elders.

Affordable LGBTQ Retirement Communities
55 Laguna, a project of Openhouse, will be a 110-apartment complex for low-income seniors in San Francisco.
John C. Anderson Apartments is a 56-apartment affordable housing project in Philadelphia's Gayborhood.
Triangle Square Hollywood is a retirement community in Los Angeles with more than 100 apartments for seniors who are 62 and older and earning 60% or less of the area's median income.
Spirit on Lakes Housing Co-op is a 46-unit project in Minneapolis for LGBT seniors earning less than half the area median income.

can talk with current residents, meet with staff, and look at application forms and group schedules.

Due to our income, many of us will live in public housing as we age. Public housing for older people has many of the same issues as private retirement communities, including lack of respect for our identities as transgender people. With the help of organizations such as Lambda Legal, this is changing. In 2012, the US Department of Housing and Urban Development (HUD) announced a new rule prohibiting discrimination based on sexual orientation and gender identity in federally funded housing. If we experience discrimination in obtaining housing or while we live in public housing, we can engage an LGBTQ legal organization to help us.

Nursing Homes and Assisted Living Facilities

The phrase "nursing home" can refer to a variety of different types of locations, but in general nursing homes provide medical care, while retirement communities sometimes do and sometimes do not. As trans people, many of us fear going into a nursing home more than a retirement community because it implies that we will need physical assistance or medical care, which could potentially reveal our transgender status to prejudiced health care providers. We may be worried that we will be mistreated by those who are supposed to care for us.

> "I'm angry about conditions for aging in general as well as specifically for GBLTQ people in nursing homes, hospitals, and assisted living facilities. They are nightmarish to begin with and worse when there's prejudice and harassment involved. It's very easy for staff to get away with extreme harassment in any medical institution and to so completely destroy a person's health and morale that they can never recover and escape the torture. That's my worst fear about aging."*

Some of us worry so much about what it could be like to be mistreated that we make a decision not to take medical steps to transition, or we keep our gender identities to ourselves. We may be out around certain people but always be prepared to "de-transition" if necessary. At times, we may ignore medical problems because we do not want to risk having to receive care from transphobic providers. Sometimes, and perhaps all too often, our fears drive some of us to suicide before we need higher levels of medical care.

> "I am kind of afraid of surgeries and seem to pass without any. At my age it might be hard to find a surgeon anyway, so I probably won't get any. Being able to de-transition upon need for serious medical care might be handy, too. Who knows."*

We should never be in a position where we feel the only answer is to end our lives. There are caring and compassionate people working for LGBTQ organizations across the country who can help us if we feel we have no other options. See Chapters 14 and 15 for more resources, including LGBTQ suicide hotlines.

There are many things that can be done to prepare nursing homes to provide good quality care to trans people. One of the most effective is to run educational seminars for employees. Many LGBTQ aging organizations will do this free of charge. Unfortunately, many elder care facilities are unwilling to participate, even in free trainings.

As potential residents of nursing homes, we can also do things to ensure we have the best experience possible. One of the most important things we can do is to bring an advocate with us—someone who can speak up about our identity and our wishes. If we can prepare ahead of time, we should be sure to choose someone we know to make health care decisions for us if we cannot make them, as well as outline who we would like to be able to visit us in medical facilities, and write down the types of care we would like to receive in different situations.

POSITIVE POLICY DEVELOPMENTS FOR TRANS ELDERS

Loree Cook-Daniels is policy and program director for FORGE, Inc.

Health care coverage. The implementation of the Affordable Care Act (ACA, often called "Obamacare") is lowering many barriers to health care, preventing "preexisting conditions" denials, lowering Medicare drug costs and copays, providing free preventive care, and expanding availability of care for those who are low income but not eligible for Medicare. The ACA also outlaws discrimination against trans people, and there are lawyers fighting to make it so that insurance companies can no longer deny coverage of hormones, surgeries, and other types of care that are available to non-trans people. At least four states have already ruled that insurance companies operating in their jurisdictions can no longer exclude such care.

Employment. Although job discrimination based on age and gender identity (or expression) is still rampant, some courts have held that Title VII of the Civil Rights Act covers gender identity and expression under its prohibition against discrimination based on sex. In 2011, the Equal Employment Opportunity Commission (EEOC) made enforcement of this provision one of its top priorities. The US Office of Personnel Management has also issued nondiscrimination provisions protecting trans federal workers and published guidelines that may help private employers adopt positive workplace transition practices.

Housing. In 2012, the US Department of Housing and Urban Development (HUD) issued an Equal Access to Housing rule prohibiting owners and operators of federally funded or federally insured housing, as well as lenders offering federally insured mortgages, from discriminating based on gender identity and sexual orientation. This rule includes elder housing and homeless shelters, and it also expands the definition of "family" to ensure that LGBT elders are allowed to live with partners and others who are not related by marriage or blood.

Veterans. Several studies have now shown that a higher proportion of trans elders are veterans, compared to both their non-trans and LGB age peers. That makes the issuance of two Veterans Administration (VA) Transgender Healthcare Directives particularly important. These documents, published in 2011 and in revised form in 2013, direct VA staff to provide care to trans patients "without discrimination," to keep personal information about transgender status and medical care confidential, and to provide all medically necessary health care to trans veterans, with the exception of gender-related surgeries.

Identification updates. Genital surgery as a requirement for identification changes is a barrier for all trans people but falls especially hard on late-life transitioners who may not be able to access such surgery due to preexisting health conditions. Major steps forward occurred in 2010 and 2011, when the US State Department revised its guidelines on how trans people can obtain passports in their correct gender. The new policy requires only a letter from a physician confirming that the person has had appropriate clinical treatment for gender transition.

Marriage. Benefits associated with marriage are often particularly important later in life, when access to Social Security benefits, tax-free inheritance, and pensions becomes critical. As laws forbidding same-sex marriage are struck down, more trans people and their partners will be able to marry, and marriages that existed before one partner transitioned will be in less legal peril.

Cultural competency. Numerous federal efforts are under way to increase the ability of many types of professionals to offer culturally competent services to trans people, including elders. Federally funded aging services providers have made available free, trans-inclusive cultural competency training and numerous trans-specific resources through the National Resource Center on LGBT Aging. Amendments in a pending reauthorization of the Older Americans Act would make this resource center permanent and designate LGBT elders as "underserved populations." The Centers for Medicare and Medicaid have been working on a trans-inclusive training video and guide for long-term care providers.

Access to federally funded services and protections. The Violence Against Women Act now forbids service providers from discriminating against LGBT victims of domestic violence, sexual assault, stalking, and dating violence. States have been informed that they can choose to protect same-sex partners under a Medicaid program that preserves a jointly owned house and income for the partner of a person who is using Medicaid to pay for their nursing home care. Hospitals are now required to prohibit discrimination based on gender identity or expression (regardless of local law), may not refuse care to trans patients, must recognize same-sex partners and honor their designation as surrogate decision makers, and must use a trans patient's preferred name. A 2010 Presidential Memorandum also guarantees trans hospital patients can be visited by same-sex spouses.

Taxes. A 2011 tax case, *O'Donnabhain v. Commissioner of Internal Revenue*, affirmed that it is legal for trans taxpayers to deduct their medical expenses for hormone therapy and gender-related surgeries.

Data. Many advocates have been working for years to develop gender identity and history questions that can be added to federal surveys, and working with federal agencies to implement those questions. In the meantime, we have also begun documenting how important this work is: The 2011 Institute of Medicine report, "The Health of Lesbian, Gay, Bisexual, and Transgender People: Building a Foundation for Better Understanding," includes a chapter on LGBT elders and will set us up for many more policy advancements.

LEGAL ISSUES

Even for those of us who have not been involved in many legal matters in the past, there are a number of important legal decisions to be made as we age that can affect us significantly. As transgender elders, it is especially important for us to be diligent about legal paperwork to ensure that we are treated the way we would like to be throughout our retirement, in any medical situations we may require, and when we pass away. There are a number of LGBTQ legal organizations that can help us to prepare our legal documents if we cannot afford to hire private attorneys.

ADVANCE DIRECTIVES AND LIVING WILLS

Advance directives, also known as living wills, are legal documents that allow us to specify ahead of time what kind of medical care we would want if we were too ill to make decisions. Some of us have strong feelings that in certain situations we would like to be kept alive by whatever means necessary, or in other situations, we would like to be kept comfortable, even if our lives are shortened somewhat. Advance directives allow us to make decisions about whether we would want an electrical shock to attempt to restart our heart if it stopped, a tube down our throat to provide breaths for us if we stopped breathing, feeding tubes if we could not eat on our own, or dialysis if our kidneys were failing. Advance directives can be especially important for those of us who do not have an obvious legal next of kin, such as a legal partner or child, who is aware of our wishes and would act on them as we desire.

POWER OF ATTORNEY AND HEALTH CARE PROXY

The phrase "power of attorney" refers to someone we choose to take over for us and make decisions on our behalf if we cannot make them ourselves. We can pick one person to be our power of attorney for legal decisions and another for medical decisions. The person we choose to make medical decisions for us if we cannot is called a health care agent, and we can specify who this person should be in a document called a health care proxy. As trans people, many of us have strained relationships with our families of origin. If we do not prepare ahead of time by designating someone we choose to be our health care agent, our children or other family members may attempt to make decisions about our health care for us that do not match our desires.

VISITATION IN MEDICAL FACILITIES

A hospital visitation directive is a legal document that provides a list of people who we want to be able to visit us in medical facilities. Many times, we are in relationships that are not recognized by the government due to discriminatory marriage laws or because we have made decisions not to become legally partnered. Hospital visitation directives can ensure that our partners and anyone else we want can visit us if we are ill.

PARTNER BENEFITS

For those of us in partnerships, we may be dependent on our partners for financial support. We may fear that when our partner retires, becomes disabled, or passes away, we will no longer have a steady income or a place to live. There are a number of discriminatory laws in place that prevent many of us from receiving Social Security benefits or pensions through our partners if they pass away. For those of us in partnerships that are not recognized by the federal government as marriages, we are not currently eligible to receive Social Security benefits through our partners. There are a number of legal challenges to these laws. National LGBTQ legal organizations can provide us with up-to-date information about their status.

WILLS AND ESTATE PLANNING

Many of us believe that we do not necessarily need to write wills if we do not have possessions we consider valuable such as cars, houses, or other expensive items. However,

The Web site for the National Resource Center on LGBT Aging has documents and videos that explain wills, Social Security benefits, and funeral directives.

writing a will is important for everyone. As trans elders, we are especially vulnerable to having our families of origin return to claim our property and to prevent those who we are close with from having access to important photos and other objects with great meaning to us.

In our wills, we can designate beneficiaries (people or organizations) to which we would like to leave our belongings, and an executor, who carries out the wishes we include in our wills. We can also express our wishes about how we would like our remains to be handled—whether we would like to be buried, cremated, or something else. For those of us with partners not recognized by the federal government as a spouse, it can be especially important to be clear about what is being left to that person. There have been cases where partners are left homeless when the other partner passes away because the family of origin claims the house and the state does not recognize the partnership.

BEING RESPECTFULLY LAID TO REST

Planning ahead for our deaths can ensure that our legacy is treated with respect. There are a number of potential challenges to creating funeral arrangements and a burial or cremation that is in line with our desires. There are cases in which trans individuals have had their gender identities disrespected in obituaries, at their funerals, and on their headstones. Families of origin may make these decisions, or funeral homes may refuse to bury trans individuals.

Things are beginning to change, such that even in more traditional settings such as the military, it is now often possible to be buried according to our own specifications. However, there are still environments, such as some religious communities, where we can be denied burial with family members due to a church's stance against transgender people.

Funeral directives are legal documents indicating our wishes about issues such as who is listed as our next of kin, what kind of clothing we would like to be wearing at our viewing or burial, what kind of service we would like to have, and what is written on our memorials or gravestones. If we do not put together funeral directives ahead of time, we run the risk of family members making decisions that would not line up with ours.

Many families choose to have an autopsy done in order to determine the cause of death and to assist in the progress of medical knowledge. Postmortem autopsy can present problems if the coroner's office insists on recording the death certificate in our assigned sex or if the autopsy reveals our trans identity to someone who did not previously know. This is among the many reasons we want to prepare ahead of time by having our wishes clearly laid out in writing. For help with funeral directives or any other legal issues, we can always seek out the advice of a national LGBTQ legal organization.

TRANS* DEATH

Sean E. Enloe, MD, is a pathologist in Southern California.

I am trained as a forensic pathologist—a physician who determines the cause and manner of death. Think of the doctor doing an autopsy in a movie or on TV.

I read an article back in the 1980s about the death of an individual who performed as a female impersonator. This individual, "X," died in a plane crash, and as X's estranged mother was the next of kin, the mother got control of X's body. The mother instructed the mortuary to cut her child's long hair to a short mannish style, to remove her child's breast implants, and to dress her child in a man's suit. While funerary rites are often said to be more for the living than for the deceased, it remains that acts like these can also function to erase or invalidate the true person who died.

In 2010, the office where I worked received a case of a woman who had died at home. Because this woman was transsexual and had not had gender reassignment surgery, some confusion arose. Her name reflected her preferred name (over her birth name) on both her driver's license and her Social Security card. Her sex was indicated as female on her driver's license. But because she retained male genitalia, when she arrived at the office, she was classified as "male." I asked the administrative arm of my office as to the guidelines for recording gender/sex on a death certificate. I was informed that there really are not any hard and fast rules, and that it is to the discretion of the office how to record such data.

In the United States, most jurisdictions fall into either a medical examiner system (an appointed physician) or a coroner system (an elected official, often affiliated with law enforcement). So the people who determine gender/sex on a death certificate are most commonly either a physician or a sheriff, neither of which may have explicit training/understanding of gender variance. The communities empowered to classify sex in death are those—in medicine and law enforcement—with whom many trans* individuals have unfortunately had much conflict. Death certificates are public records, so newspapers and others will continue to look upon the "sex" as labeled on the death certificate as authoritative, and an individual's identity can be erased by bureaucracy.

If the living do not speak for themselves, others may end up speaking for them. Even if one speaks loudly and clearly, there is no guarantee that any will hear. Unfortunately, the messages being communicated after a complicated life are often garbled and muted. Unless something changes, the trans* community will continue to be treated in death as poorly as it is often treated in life.

PREPARING PHYSICALLY AND EMOTIONALLY FOR DEATH

For many people there comes a point when we know that death is inevitable and soon. Leading up to this point, we may worry about being able to sufficiently voice our needs, feel close to our friends and families, and die with dignity. There are a number of ways to prepare ourselves for the reality of the physical and emotional changes that lead to death.

Palliative care is health care that focuses on providing comfort rather than prolonging life. It is often chosen by older adults facing terminal illness. The choice of palliative care can allow for our emotional, social, and physical needs to be met as we die. Often there is family education about the dying process, facilitation of grieving after death, and space is made for observances of individual practices such as prayer.

One important decision to consider is where we want to die. Most people would prefer to die in their homes, but unfortunately most end up dying elsewhere. If it is important to us that we die in our homes, we must make sure to be clear to our partners and family members, as well as in our legal paperwork, that this is our preference.

Some of us will find that when we are close to death we enter a state of confusion, in which we are not sure where we are, may not be able to pay attention to things, and may have experiences of seeing or hearing things that are not there. Delirium is caused by medical problems, and although it can occur in younger people it also occurs in many of us as we die. Our caregivers should be aware that delirium is a possibility and know that we are not ourselves when we are in this state.

The final days of life can be extremely complex, involving multiple individuals, organizations, and systems. The strengths that we have developed as transgender elders and the challenges that we have endured can affect medical, nursing, mental health, and caregiving relationships in our final stages of life. Death is a time to focus on our strengths gained over a lifetime. Spirituality can be a source of comfort, particularly if it supports us as worthy and valued.

During this period of time we face the last opportunities to define who we are and what our legacy will be. If we have not already done so, this is our last chance to create a personal legacy. Giving journals, photos, or treasured objects to valued friends or relatives can provide a sense of fulfillment and closure in the final stages of life.

CONCLUSION

Aging is a complex process that involves many challenges. As TGNC people, we face the aging process with additional stigma that can make our lives more difficult to navigate. There are ways we can plan for successful aging and a graceful exit. In the end, we are people in bodies that evolve and change over time. Yet these bodies are transient in the scheme of time and the changes are beyond our minimal ability to alleviate and control. Dignity can often be maintained while control cannot. What we leave behind—our history and our legacy—is what endures.

ACKNOWLEDGMENTS

The authors would like to thank their many colleagues, friends, clients, and the numerous study and survey participants for their respective participation, illuminating dialogues, and overall willingness to share their stories, thoughts, and concerns, without which we would have little to give back. A special thanks goes out to Hawk Stone, who initially helped put together our outline. Hawk, your insight and experience with transgender aging issues was extremely helpful in writing this chapter.

Tarynn Witten would like to thank Deirdre Condit, Brian de Vries, Brian Grossman, Mark Brennan, and Jamison Green for their many thoughtful and stimulating conversations. She would also like to thank the many survey respondents who, over the years, have provided the most important of all insights into transgender aging.

Joe Ippolito would like to thank Tarynn Witten for taking him under her wing in helping construct this chapter, as well as Jayden H. C. Sampson, Cody Poerio, Jess Kalup, Miss Major, and Jamison Green for their unique perspectives and thought-provoking discussions. He would also like to acknowledge the support of many other friends and family members, as well as the transgender clients he has worked with over the years who helped him understand the transition experience more fully, in particular those over 50 who helped him see the specific challenges transgender elders face.

REFERENCES AND FURTHER READING

Applebaum, J. S. (2008). Late adulthood and aging: Clinical approaches. In H. J. Makinodin, K. H. Mayer, J. Potter, & H. Goldhammer (Eds.), *Fenway guide to lesbian, gay, bisexual and transgender health* (pp. 135–157). Philadelphia, PA: American College of Physicians.

Belongia, L., & Witten, T. M. (2006). We don't have that kind of client here: Institutionalized bias against and resistance to transgender and intersex aging research and training in elder care facilities. *Gerontological Health Newsletter, Fall* 2006.

Cook-Daniels, L. (2006). Trans aging. In D. Kimmel, T. Rose, & S. David (Eds.), *Lesbian, gay, bisexual and transgender aging: Research and clinical perspectives* (pp. 290–235). New York, NY: Columbia University Press.

Fish, J. (2010). Conceptualizing social exclusion and lesbian, gay, bisexual and transgender people: The implications for promoting equity in nursing policy and practice. *Journal of Research in Nursing, 15,* 303–312.

Fredriksen-Goldsen, K. I., Kim, H-J., Emlet, C. A., Muraco, A., Erosheva, E. A., Hoy-Ellis, C. P....Petry, H. (2011). *The aging and health report: Disparities and resilience among lesbian, gay, bisexual and transgender older adults.* Retrieved January 2014, from http://www.lgbtagingcenter.org/resources/pdfs/LGBT%20Aging%20and%20Health%20Report_final.pdf

Fruhoff, G. A., & Mahoney, D. (Eds.). (2010). *Older GLBT family and community life.* New York, NY: Routledge Press.

Hunter, S. (2005). *Midlife and older LGBT.* Binghamton, NY: Haworth Press.

Kimmel, D., Rose, T., & David, S. (2006). *LGBT aging.* New York, NY: Columbia University Press.

Redman, D. (2011). *Fear, discrimination and abuse: Transgender elders and the perils of long-term care. Aging Today,* XXXII(2), 1–2.

SAGE (Services and Advocacy for GLBT Elders) & National Center for Transgender Equality (NCTE). (2012). *Improving the lives of transgender older adults: Recommendations for policy and practice.* Retrieved January 2014, from http://www.lgbtagingcenter.org/resources/pdfs/TransAgingPolicyReportFull.pdf

Weber, S. (2010). A stigma identification framework for family nurses working with parents who are lesbian, gay, bisexual, or transgendered and their families. *Journal of Family Nursing, 16*(4), 378–393.

Witten, T. M. (2003). Transgender aging: An emerging population and an emerging need. *Review Sexologies,* XII(4), 15–20.

Witten, T. M. (2004). Life course analysis: The courage to search for something more: Middle adulthood issues in the transgender and intersex community. *Journal of Human Behavior in a Social Environment, 8*(3–4), 189–224.

Witten, T. M. (2004). Life course analysis: The courage to search for something more: Middle adulthood issues in the transgender and intersex community. In M. L. Sullivan (Ed.), *Sexual minorities: Discrimination, challenges, and development in America* (pp. 189–224). New York, NY: The Haworth Social Work Practice Press.

Witten, T. M. (2004). Aging and gender diversity. *Social Work Today, 4*(4), 28–31.

Witten, T. M. (2007). Gender identity and the military: Transgender, transsexual, and intersex-identified individuals in the U.S. Armed Forces. *Palm Center.* Retrieved January 2014, from http://www.palmcenter.org/press/dadt/releases/palm_center_releases_study_on_gender_identity_in_u_s_military

Witten, T. M. (2009). Graceful exits: III. Intersections of aging, transgender identities and the family/Community. *Journal of GLBT Family Studies, 5,* 36–63.

Witten, T. M. (2010). Graceful exits: III. Intersections of aging, transgender identities and the family/Community. In C. Fruhauf & D. Mahoney (Eds.). *Older GLBT family and community life.* London, UK: Routledge.

Witten, T. M. (2013). It's not all darkness: resilience, robustness and successful aging in the trans-community. *LGBT Health, 1*(1), 24–33.

Witten, T. M. & Condit, D. (2013). Aging and the international trans-identified community: A social work imperative. *Journal of Gerontological Social Work*, submitted.

Witten, T. M., & Eyler, A. E. (2007). Transgender aging and care of the elderly transgendered patient. In R. Ettner, S. Monstry, & A. E. Eyler (Eds.), *Principles of transgender medicine and surgery* (pp. 285–310). Binghamton, NY: The Haworth Press.

Witten, T. M., & Eyler, A. E. (2012). *Gay, lesbian, bisexual, transgender & intersex aging: Challenges in research, practice & policy.* Baltimore, MD: Johns Hopkins University Press.

Witten, T. M., & Whittle, S. P. (2004). TransPanthers: The graying of transgender and the law. *The Deakin Law Review, 9*(2), 503–522.

SECTION 6
CLAIMING OUR POWER

US HISTORY
Genny Beemyn

22

GENDER NONCONFORMING INDIVIDUALS have been documented in many different cultures and eras. But can there be said to be a "transgender history," when "transgender" is a contemporary term and when individuals in past centuries who would perhaps appear to be transgender from our vantage point might not have conceptualized their lives in such a way? And what about individuals today who have the ability to describe themselves as transgender but choose not to for a variety of reasons, including the perception that it is a white, middle-class Western term or that it implies transitioning from one gender to another? Should they be left out of "transgender history" because they do not specifically identify as transgender?

These questions complicate any attempt to write a transgender history. While it would be inappropriate to limit transgender history to people who lived at a time and place when the concept of "transgender" was available and used by them, it would also be inappropriate to assume that people who are "transgender," as we currently understand the term, existed throughout history. For this reason, we should not claim that gender nonconforming individuals were "transgender" or "transsexual" if these categories were not yet named or yet to be embraced.

UNDERSTANDING GENDER NONCONFORMITY

Another difficulty in writing transgender history is that people in the past may have presented as a gender different from the one assigned to them at birth for reasons other than a sense of gender difference. For example, female-assigned individuals may have presented as men in order to escape restrictive gender roles, and both women and men may have lived cross-gender lives to pursue same-sex sexual relationships.

A scholar who has sought to address this issue is anthropologist Jason Cromwell (1999). He devised three questions for researchers to consider in trying to determine whether female-assigned individuals from the past who presented as male might have been what we would call "transsexual" today: If the individuals indicated that they were men, if they attempted to modify their bodies to look more traditionally male, and if they tried to live their lives as men, keeping the knowledge of their female bodies a secret, even if it meant dying rather than seeking necessary medical care.

Cromwell's approach can also be used for individuals assigned male at birth who presented as female. But his questions do not address the differences between transsexual people and individuals we now refer to as cross-dressers. To make this distinction, two other questions can be asked: If the individuals continued to cross-dress when it was publicly known that they cross-dressed or if they cross-dressed consistently but only in private, so that no one else knew, except perhaps their families. In either case, the important factor is that the people who cross-dressed did not receive any advantage or benefit from doing so, other than their own comfort and satisfaction.

NATIVE AMERICAN CULTURES

The European nations that colonized what is today the United States rejected and often punished perceived instances of gender nonconformity. But many Native American cultures at the time of European conquest welcomed and had recognized roles for individuals who assumed behaviors and identities different from those of the gender assigned to them at birth. These cultures enabled male-assigned individuals and, to a lesser extent,

Historians have often ignored or dismissed instances of non-normative gender expression, especially among individuals assigned female at birth, who were regarded as simply seeking male privilege if they lived as men. It was not until lesbian and gay historians in the 1970s and 1980s sought to identify and celebrate individuals from the past who had had same-sex relationships that gender nonconforming individuals began to receive more than cursory attention. However, in their attempts to normalize same-sex sexuality by showing that people attracted to others of the same sex existed across time and cultures, many of these historians assumed that anyone who cross-dressed or lived as a gender different from the one assigned to them at birth did so in order to pursue same-sex relationships. Many transgender people have begun to call attention to our own history, pointing to evidence that many of these individuals were not motivated primarily by same-sex attraction (Califia, 1997, p. 121).

501

One person cited by anthropologist Jason Cromwell who fits the criteria of a trans person in history is Billy Tipton, a jazz musician who lived as a man for more than 50 years and who was not discovered to have been assigned female until his death in 1989. Tipton apparently turned away from what could have been his big break in the music industry for fear that the exposure would "out" him. He also avoided doctors and died from a treatable medical condition, rather than risk disclosure.

female-assigned individuals to dress, work, and live, either partially or completely, as a different gender.

Spanish conquistador Cabeza de Vaca wrote one of the earliest known descriptions of gender nonconforming individuals in Native American society. In the 1530s, he described seeing, among a group of Coahuiltecan Indians in what is today Southern Texas, "effeminate, impotent men" who are married to other men and "go about covered-up like women and they do the work of women" (Lang, 1998, p. 67).

Like de Vaca, most of those who reported on gender diversity in Native American cultures were Europeans—conquistadors, explorers, missionaries, or traders—whose worldviews were shaped by Christian doctrines that espoused adherence to strict gender roles and condemned any expressions of sexuality outside of married male-female relationships. Consequently, they reacted to instances of nonbinary genders, in the words of gay scholar Will Roscoe (1998), "with amazement, dismay, disgust, and occasionally, when they weren't dependent on the natives' goodwill, with violence" (p. 4).

A less judgmental account was provided by Edwin T. Denig, a mid-19th-century fur trader in present-day Montana, who expressed astonishment at the Crow Indians' acceptance of a "neuter" gender. "Strange country this," he stated, "where males assume the dress and perform the duties of females, while women turn men and mate with their own sex!" (Roscoe, 1998, p. 3). Another matter-of-fact narrative was provided by Jacques Le Moyne de Morgues, an artist who accompanied a French expedition to Florida in 1564, who noted that what he referred to as "hermaphrodites" were "quite common" among the Timucua Indians (Katz, 1976, p. 287).

At the other extreme was the reaction of Spanish conquistador Vasco Núñez de Balboa. In his trek across the Isthmus of Panama in 1513, Balboa set his troop's dogs on 40 male-assigned Cueva Indians for being "sodomites," as they had assumed the roles of women. Another Spanish conquistador, Nuño de Guzmán, burned alive a male-assigned individual who presented as female—considering the person to be a male prostitute—while traveling through Mexico in the 1530s (Saslow, 1999).

As these different accounts indicate, Europeans did not agree on what to make of cultures that recognized nonbinary genders. Lacking comparable institutional roles in their

Zuni Two-Spirit person in photo titled, "We-Wa, a Zuni berdache, weaving" (John K. Hillers, 1843–1925, photographer, Smithsonian Institution. Bureau of American Ethnology, ca. 1871–ca. 1907).

own societies, they labeled the aspects that seemed familiar to them: Male-assigned individuals engaged in same-sex sexual behavior ("sodomites") or individuals that combined male and female elements ("hermaphrodites"). Anthropologists and historians in the 20th century would repeat the same mistake, interpreting these individuals as "homosexuals," "transvestites," or "berdaches" (a French adaptation of the Arabic word for a male prostitute or a young male slave used for sexual purposes) (Roscoe, 1987).

By failing to see beyond their own biases and prejudices, these observers mischaracterized the Native American societies that accepted gender diversity. Within most Native American cultures, male- and female-assigned individuals who assumed different genders were not considered to be women or men; rather, they constituted separate genders that combined female and male elements. This fact is reflected in the words that Native American groups developed to describe multiple genders. For example, the terms for male-assigned individuals who took on female roles used by the Cheyenne (*heemaneh*), the Ojibwa (*agokwa*), and the Yuki (*i-wa-musp*) translate as "half men, half women," or "men-women." Other Native American groups referred to male-assigned individuals who "dress as a woman," "act like a woman," or were a "would-be woman" (Lang, 1998). Similarly, the Zuni called a female-assigned individual who took on male roles a *katsotse*, or "boy-girl" (Lang, 1999).

Individuals who assumed different genders were apparently accepted in most of the Native American societies in which they have been known to exist, but their statuses and roles differed from group to group and over time. Some Native American cultures considered them to possess supernatural powers and afforded them special ceremonial roles; in other cultures, they were less revered and viewed more secularly (Lang, 1998). In these societies, the status of individuals who assumed different genders seems to have reflected their gender role, rather than a special gender status. If women predominated in particular occupations, such as being healers, shamans, and handcrafters, then male-assigned individuals who took on female roles engaged in the same professions. In a similar way, the female-assigned individuals who took on male roles became hunters and warriors (Lang, 1999).

Just as the cultural status of individuals who assumed different genders seems to have varied greatly, so too did the extent to which they took on these roles. Some adopted male or female roles completely, others only partly or part of the time. In some cases, dressing as a different gender was central to assuming the gender role; in others, it was not. Marrying or having relationships with other male-assigned or other female-assigned individuals was likewise common in some cultures but less so in others. "Gender variance is as diverse as Native American cultures themselves," writes Sabine Lang, (1999). "About the only common denominator is that in many Native American tribal cultures systems of multiple genders existed" (pp. 95–96).

GENDER DIFFERENCE IN EARLY AMERICA

Colonial Times

The cultural inclusion of individuals who assumed different genders in some Native American societies stands in contrast to the general lack of recognition within the white-dominated American colonies in the 17th and 18th centuries. To the extent that individuals who cross-dressed or who lived as a gender different from the one assigned to them at birth were acknowledged in the colonies, it was largely to condemn their behavior as unnatural and sinful. For example, when Mary Henly, a female-assigned individual in Middlesex County, Massachusetts, was arrested in 1692 for wearing "men's clothing," the charges stated that such behavior was "seeming to confound the course of nature" (Reis, 2007, p. 152).

One of the first recorded examples of a gender nonconforming individual in colonial America involved a Virginia servant who claimed to be both a man and a woman and, at different times, adopted the traditional roles and clothing of men and women and

While male-assigned individuals who assumed female roles often married other male-assigned individuals, their partners presented as masculine and the relationships were generally not viewed in Native American cultures as involving two people of the same gender. The same was true of female-assigned individuals who assumed male roles and married other female-assigned individuals. Because many Native American groups recognized genders beyond male and female, these relationships would better be categorized as what anthropologist Sabine Lang (1999, p. 98) calls "hetero-gender" relationships—not as "same-sex" relationships, as they were often described by European and Euro-American writers from the 17th through the late 20th centuries.

variously went by the names of Thomas and Thomasine Hall. Unable to establish Hall's "true" gender, despite repeated physical examinations, and unsure of whether to punish him or her for wearing men's or women's apparel, local citizens asked the court at Jamestown to resolve the issue.

Perhaps because it took Hall at his or her word that he or she was bigendered (what we would call intersex today), the court ordered Hall in 1629 to wear both a man's breeches and a woman's apron and cap. In a sense, this unique ruling affirmed Hall's dual nature and subverted traditional gender categories. But by fixing Hall's gender and denying him or her the freedom to switch between male and female identities, the decision punished Hall and reinforced gender boundaries (Brown, 1995; Reis, 2007; Rupp, 1999).

Relatively few instances of gender nonconformity are documented in the colonial and postcolonial periods. A number of the cases that became known involved female-assigned individuals who lived as men and whose birth gender was discovered only when their bodies were examined following an injury or death. Fewer examples of male-assigned individuals who lived as women are recorded, perhaps because they had less ability to present effectively as female due to their facial hair and physiques.

The 19th Century

The lack of a public presence for individuals who assumed different genders began to change in the mid-19th century, as a growing number of single people left their communities of origin to earn a living, gain greater freedom, or simply see the world. Able to take advantage of the anonymity afforded by new surroundings, these migrants had greater opportunities to fashion their own lives, which for some meant presenting as a gender different from the one assigned to them at birth.

Some headed out West, where, according to historian Peter Boag (2011), "crossdressers were not simply ubiquitous, but were very much a part of daily life on the frontier" (pp. 1–2). The industrialization of US cities led others to move from rural to urban areas, where individuals who lived different gendered lives created community spaces in which they could meet and socialize with others like themselves. The most popular of these gathering places were masquerade balls, or "drags" as they were commonly known. One of the earliest known drags took place in Washington, D.C., on New Year's Eve in 1885. The event was documented by the Washington *Evening Star* because a participant, "Miss Maud," was arrested while returning home the following morning. Dressed in "a pink dress trimmed with white lace, with stockings and undergarments to match," the 30-year-old male-assigned black participant was charged with vagrancy and sentenced to three months in jail, even though the judge, the newspaper reported, "admired his stylish appearance" (Roscoe, 1991, p. 240).

The growing visibility of male-assigned individuals who presented as female in the late 19th century was not limited to Washington. By the 1890s, female-presenting cross-dressers had also begun organizing drag events in New York City. These drags drew enormous numbers of black and white participants and spectators, especially during the late 1920s and early 1930s, when at least a half dozen events were staged each year in some of the city's largest venues, including Madison Square Garden (Chauncey, 1994). By 1930, public drag balls were also being held in Chicago, New Orleans, Baltimore, Philadelphia, and other US cities, bringing together hundreds of cross-dressing individuals and their escorts, and often an equal or greater number of curious onlookers (Anonymous, 1933; Drexel, 1997; Matthews, 1927). Organizers typically obtained a license from the police to prevent participants from being arrested for violating ordinances against cross-dressing.

The Sexologists

Another indication of the growing presence of individuals who assumed gender behaviors and identities different from the gender assigned to them at birth in the late 19th and early 20th centuries was the interest that US and European physicians began to show in their

While female-assigned individuals who presented as male did not hold drag balls in the late 19th and early 20th centuries, they were by no means invisible in society. Some performed as male impersonators to entertain audiences, while others cross-dressed both on and off stage. One of the most notable cross-dressers was Gladys Bentley, a black blues singer and pianist who became well known during the Harlem Renaissance of the 1920s. Bentley, an open lesbian, performed in a white tuxedo and top hat and regularly wore "men's" clothing out in public with her female partner (Garber, 1988).

experiences. Many of these sexologists, as they became known, did not make clear distinctions between gender nonconformity and same-sex attraction. Rather than treating same-sex sexuality as a separate category, they considered it only a sign of "gender inversion"—that is, having a gender inverted or opposite of the gender assigned to the person at birth. One of the leading advocates of this theory was Karl Heinrich Ulrichs, a German lawyer who wrote in the 1860s that his own interest in other men resulted from having "a female soul enclosed within a male body" (Meyerowitz, 2002; Rupp, 1999; Stryker, 2008, p. 37).

The sexologist who had the greatest influence on the Western medical profession's views toward sexual and gender difference in the late 19th century was Austro-German psychiatrist Richard von Krafft-Ebing. In his widely cited study, *Psychopathia Sexualis*, which was first published in 1886, Krafft-Ebing created a framework of increasing severity of cross-gender identification (and, in his view, increasing pathology). The range went from individuals who had a strong preference for clothing of the "other sex," to individuals whose feelings and inclinations were considered more appropriate for someone of the "other sex," to individuals who believed themselves to be the "other sex" and who claimed that the sex assigned to them at birth was wrong (Heidenreich, 1997, p. 270; Stryker, 2008; von Krafft-Ebing, 2006).

TRANS IN THE 20TH CENTURY

Magnus Hirschfeld

Not until the early 20th century did gender difference become considered a separate phenomenon from same-sex sexuality and start to be less pathologized by the medical profession. In his pioneering 1910 work *Transvestites*, German physician and sexologist Magnus Hirschfeld coined the word "transvestite"—from the Latin "trans" or "across" and "vestis" or "clothing"—to refer to individuals who are overcome with a "feeling of peace, security and exaltation, happiness and well-being...when in the clothing of the other sex" (p. 125).

Hirschfeld (1991 [1910]) saw cross-dressing as completely distinct from "homosexuality," a term that began to be commonly used in the medical literature in the early 20th century to categorize individuals who were attracted to others of the same sex. Through his research, Hirschfeld, who was homosexual himself, not only found that transvestites could be of any sexual orientation (including asexual) but also that most he met were heterosexual from the standpoint of their gender assigned at birth. In his study of 17 individuals who cross-dressed, he considered none to be homosexual and "at the most" one—the lone female-assigned person in his sample—to be bisexual.

It is significant that Hirschfeld included a female-assigned person in his study, as most researchers, before and after him, considered cross-dressing to be an exclusively male phenomenon. Also unlike other medical writers, especially psychoanalysts, Hirschfeld recognized that cross-dressers were not suffering from a form of psychopathology, nor were they masochists or fetishists. While some derived erotic pleasure from cross-dressing, not all did, and Hirschfeld was not convinced that it was a necessary part of transvestism.

While Hirschfeld was ahead of his time in many of the ways he conceptualized gender difference, he did not distinguish between individuals who cross-dressed but who identified as their birth gender and individuals who identified as a gender different from the one assigned to them at birth and who lived cross-gendered lives, which included cross-dressing. Among the 17 people in his study, four had lived part of their lives as a different gender, including the female-assigned participant, and would now likely be thought of as transsexual or transgender (Meyerowitz, 2002).

The Development of Gender-Affirming Surgeries and Hormones

Hirschfeld's Institute for Sexual Science, the world's first institute devoted to sexology, also performed the earliest recorded genital transformation surgeries. The first documented case was that of Dorchen Richter, a male-assigned individual from a poor German family who had desired to be female since early childhood, lived as a woman when she could, and hated her male anatomy. She underwent castration in 1922 and had her penis removed and a vagina constructed in 1931 (Meyerowitz, 2002, p. 19).

The institute's most well-known patient was Einar Wegener, a Dutch painter who began to present and identify as Lili Elbe in the 1920s. After being evaluated by Hirschfeld, Elbe underwent a series of male-to-female surgeries. In addition to castration and the construction of a vagina, she had ovaries inserted into her abdomen, which at a time before the synthesis of hormones, was the only way that doctors knew to try to change estrogen levels. In 1931, she proceeded with a final operation to create a uterus in an attempt to be a mother, but she died from complications from the surgery (Hoyer, 1953; Kennedy, 2007).

Before her death, Elbe requested that her friend Ernst Ludwig Hathorn Jacobson develop a book based on her diary entries, letters, and dictated material. Jacobson published the resulting work, *A Man Changes His Sex*, in Dutch and German in 1932 under the pseudonym Niels Hoyer. It was translated into English a year later as *Man into Woman: An Authentic Record of a Change of Sex* and is the first known book-length account of a gender transition (Meyerowitz, 2002).

Elbe was one of Hirschfeld's last patients. With the rise of Nazism, the ability for him to do his work became increasingly more difficult, and it became impossible after Adolph Hitler personally called Hirschfeld "the most dangerous Jew in Germany" (Stryker, 2008, p. 40). Fearing for his life, Hirschfeld left the country, and in his absence, the Nazis destroyed the Institute in 1933, holding a public bonfire of its contents. Hirschfeld died in exile in France 2 years later.

Although opportunities for surgical transition diminished with the destruction of Hirschfeld's Institute, two breakthroughs in hormonal research in the 1930s gave new hope to individuals who felt gender different. First, the discovery by endocrinologists that "male" hormones occurred naturally in women and that "female" hormones occurred naturally in men challenged the dominant scientific thinking that there were two separate and mutually exclusive biological sexes. The findings refuted the medical profession's assumption that only men could be given "male" hormones and women given "female" hormones, making cross-gender medical treatments possible (H. Rubin, 2006). At the same time, the development of synthetic testosterone and estrogen enabled hormone therapy to become more affordable and, over time, more widely available. In the 1930s and 1940s, few European and US physicians were willing to provide hormones to patients seeking to transition, but a small number of gender nonconforming individuals found ways to obtain them (Kennedy, 2007).

The first female-assigned individual known to have taken testosterone for the purpose of transforming his body was Michael Dillon, a doctor from an aristocratic British family, who had entered medicine in order to better understand his own masculine identity and how he could change his body to be like other men. He began taking hormones in 1939, had a double mastectomy three years later, and underwent more than a dozen operations to construct a penis beginning in 1946. His were the first recorded female-to-male genital surgeries performed on a nonintersex person (Kennedy, 2007; Shapiro, 2010).

The same year that Dillon began his phalloplasty, he also published a book on the treatment of gender nonconforming individuals, *Self: A Study in Ethics and Endocrinology*. The book focused on the need for society to understand people who, like Dillon, felt that their gender was different from the one assigned to them at birth. Dillon argued that such individuals were not mentally unbalanced but "would develop naturally enough if only [they] belonged to the other sex." He was especially critical of the psychologists who believed that they could change the sense of self of gender nonconforming individuals through therapy, when what their clients really needed was access to hormones and genital surgeries.

Making an argument that would become commonplace in the years that followed, Dillon reasoned that "where the mind cannot be made to fit the body, the body should be made to fit, approximately, at any rate to the mind, despite the prejudices of those who have not suffered these things" (p. 53). *Self*, though, was not widely circulated, and Dillon sought to avoid public attention, even taking the extraordinary step of going into exile in India in 1958, when the media discovered his past and ran stories about a transsexual being the heir to a British title.

The Rise of the Concept of Transsexuality

Instead of Dillon, Harry Benjamin, a German-born, US endocrinologist, became the leading advocate in the 1950s and 1960s for providing hormones and surgeries to gender nonconforming people. Benjamin (1966), like Dillon, saw attempts to "cure" such individuals by psychotherapy as "a useless undertaking" (p. 91), and he began prescribing hormones to them and suggesting surgeons abroad, as no physician in the United States at that time would openly perform gender-affirming operations.

Along with US physician David O. Cauldwell, Benjamin referred to those who desired to change their sex as "transsexuals" in order to distinguish them from "transvestites." The difference between the groups, according to Benjamin, was that "true transsexuals feel that they *belong* to the other sex, they want to *be* and *function* as members of the opposite sex, not only to appear as such" (1966, p. 13).

In 1949, Cauldwell (2006) was apparently the first medical professional to use the word "transsexual"—which he initially spelled "transexual"—in its contemporary sense. But in sharp contrast to Benjamin, Cauldwell believed that transsexuals were mentally ill and saw gender-affirming surgeries as mutilation and a criminal action. At the time, most physicians supported Cauldwell's position, assuming that biological sex was the defining aspect of someone's gender and was immutable, outside of cases of intersex individuals, where the "true" sex of the person may not be immediately known.

Increasingly, though, this belief was challenged by doctors and researchers like Benjamin who distinguished between biological sex and "psychological sex" or, as it came to be known, "gender identity." As more and more transsexual individuals were acknowledged and studied, these physicians and scientists developed the evidence to begin to gradually shift the dominant medical view to the contrary argument: that gender identity—not biological sex—was the critical, immutable element of someone's gender. Thus, transsexual individuals needed to be able to change the sex of their bodies to match their sense of self (Meyerowitz, 2002).

Christine Jorgensen: The Transsexual Phenomenon

Although Harry Benjamin was referring to the issue of transsexuality in general and not to Christine Jorgensen in particular with the title of his pioneering 1966 work *The Transsexual Phenomenon*, it would not be an exaggeration to characterize her as such. Through the publicity given to her transition, she brought the concept of "sex change" into everyday conversations in the United States, served as a role model for many other transsexual individuals to understand themselves and pursue medical treatment, and transformed the debate about the use of hormones and gender-affirming surgeries. Following the media frenzy over Jorgensen, much of the US public began to recognize that "sex change" was indeed possible.

Born in 1926 to Danish American parents in New York City, Jorgensen struggled with an intense feeling from a young age that she should have been born female. Among the childhood experiences that she recounts in her 1967 autobiography were preferring to play with girls, wishing that she had been sent to a girls' camp rather than one for boys, and having "a small piece of needlepoint" that she cherished taken away by an unsympathetic elementary school teacher. The teacher confronted Jorgensen's mother, asking, "Do you think that this is anything for a red-blooded boy to have in his desk as a keepsake?" (p. 18).

Although not mentioned in her autobiography, Jorgensen also apparently began wearing her sister's clothing in secret when she was young and, by her teens, had acquired her own small wardrobe of "women's" clothing. Many transsexual individuals dress as the gender with which they identify from a young age, but Jorgensen may have been concerned that readers would confuse her for a "transvestite" or a feminine "homosexual."

She did indicate being attracted to men in her autobiography, and she acknowledged years later to having had "a couple" of same-sex sexual encounters in her youth (Meyerowitz, 2002, p. 57). However, by her early twenties, Jorgensen gradually became aware that she was a heterosexual woman, rather than a cross-dresser or gay man, and began to look for all she could find about medical and surgical transition.

TRANSSEXUALITY IN 1950S TAIWAN

Howard Chiang is assistant professor of history at the University of Warwick and editor of Transgender China (2012).

In 1953, 4 years after Mao Zedong's political regime took over mainland China and the Nationalist government under Chiang Kai-shek was forced to relocate its base, news of the success of native doctors in converting a man into a woman made headlines in Taiwan. On August 14 that year, the *United Daily News (Lianhebao)* surprised the public by announcing the discovery of an intersex soldier, Xie Jianshun, in Tainan, Taiwan. Within a week, the paper adopted a radically different rhetoric, now with a headline claiming that "Christine Will Not Be America's Exclusive: Soldier Destined to Become a Lady." Xie was frequently dubbed the "Chinese Christine." This allusion to the contemporaneous American ex-G.I. celebrity Christine Jorgensen reflected the growing influence of American culture on the Republic of China at the peak of the Cold War.

Dripping with national and trans-Pacific significance, Xie's experience made *bianxingren* (transsexual) a household term in the 1950s. She served as a focal point for numerous new stories that broached the topics of changing sex and human intersexuality. People who wrote about her debated whether she qualified as a woman, whether medical technology could transform sex, and whether the "two Christines" were more similar or different. These questions led to persistent comparisons of Taiwan with the United States, but Xie never presented herself as a duplicate of Jorgensen. As Xie knew, her story highlighted issues that pervaded postwar Taiwanese society: the censorship of public culture by the state, the unique social status of men serving in the armed forces, the limit of individualism, the promise and pitfalls of science, the normative behaviors of men and women, and the boundaries of acceptable sexual expression.

Jorgensen read about the first studies to examine the effects of hormone treatments and about "various conversion experiments in Sweden," which led her to obtain commercially synthesized female hormones and to travel "first to Denmark, where [she] had relatives, and then to Stockholm, where [she] hoped [she] would find doctors who would be willing to handle [her] case" (pp. 81 and 94). While in Denmark, though, Jorgensen learned that doctors in that country could help her. She came under the care of leading endocrinologist Christian Hamburger, who treated her with increasingly higher doses of female hormones for 2 years, beginning in 1950, and arranged for her to have operations to remove her testicles and penis and to reshape her scrotum into labia.

While recovering from this latter operation in December 1952, Jorgensen went from being an unknown American abroad to "the most talked-about girl in the world." It seems astounding today to think that someone would become internationally famous simply for altering her appearance through electrolysis, hormones, and surgeries, but that was Jorgensen's experience when news of her gender transition reached the press (Serlin, 1995, p. 140; Stryker, 2000). A trade magazine for the publishing industry announced in 1954 that Jorgensen's story over the previous year "had received the largest worldwide coverage in the history of newspaper publishing." Looking back years later on the media's obsession, Jorgensen (1967) remained incredulous: "A tragic war was still raging in Korea, George VI died and Britain had a new queen, sophisticated guided missiles were going off in New Mexico, Jonas Salk was working on a vaccine for infantile paralysis.... [yet] Christine Jorgensen was on page one" (pp. 249 and 144).

Jorgensen was by no means the first person to undergo a gender transition, and some of these cases had been widely covered in the media. However, Jorgensen became a sensation, in part, because she had been a US serviceman, the epitome of masculinity in post–World War II America (though Jorgensen served in the United States and never saw combat), and had been reborn into a "blonde bombshell," the symbol of 1950s white feminine sexuality (Meyerowitz, 2002, p. 62).

The initial newspaper story, published in *The New York Daily News* on December 1, 1952, highlighted this dramatic transformation, with its headline, "Ex-GI Becomes

Blonde Beauty," and its accompanying "before" and "after" photographs. A grainy Army picture of a nerdish-looking, male-bodied Jorgensen in uniform is contrasted with a professionally taken profile picture of a feminine Jorgensen looking like Grace Kelly.

The tremendous attention that Jorgensen's transition received also reflected the public's fascination with the power of science in the mid-20th century. A tidal wave of remarkable inventions—from television and the transistor radio to the atomic bomb—had made scientists in the 1950s seem capable of anything, so why not the ability to turn a man into a woman? However, in the aftermath of the first use of nuclear weapons, Jorgensen's transformation was also pointed to as evidence that science had gone too far in its efforts to alter the natural environment. Jorgensen thus served as a symbol for both scientific progress and a fear that science was attempting to play God. By being at the center of postwar debates over technological advancement, she remained in the spotlight well after the initial reports of her transition and was able to have a successful stage career based on her celebrity status (Meyerowitz, 2002).

Anxieties over changing gender roles were another factor that contributed to Jorgensen's celebrity. At a time when millions of US women who had been recruited to work in factories during the war were being pushed back into the home in order to make way for returning servicemen, gender expectations for both women and men were in a state of flux. Suddenly, the assumed naturalness of what it meant to be male and female was being called into question. Not only could women do "men's" work, but men could also become women. As historian Susan Stryker writes, "Jorgensen's notoriety in the 1950s was undoubtedly fueled by the pervasive unease felt in some quarters that American manhood, already under siege, could quite literally be undone and refashioned into its seeming opposite through the power of modern science" (Stryker, 2000, p. viii).

MEDIA SPOTLIGHT: GENDER VARIANCE IN SPECULATIVE FICTION

Dallas Denny and Jamison Green

Gender-variant characters and themes are especially prevalent in science fiction and fantasy. One of the genre's superstars, Robert A. Heinlein, wrote several pieces that touch on this topic. His short story *All You Zombies*, written in 1958, is without a doubt the ultimate (and perhaps the only) example of time-travel gender-fuck fiction. The main (actually, only) character in the work is not only at various times male and female, and both the mother and father of their own offspring, but manages to set up the entire conundrum in the first place. Heinlein's 1970 novel *I Will Fear No Evil* features an ailing old man whose brain is transplanted into the body of a brain-dead young woman. His novel *Friday* (1982) resonates with many transgendered people because of its themes of discrimination and passing. Friday is an artificial person, laboratory born, and her social experiences closely reflect those of transsexual women.

Some science-fiction and fantasy authors have portrayed alien races with more or different genders that those on Earth. For example, Ursula LeGuin's 1969 *The Left Hand of Darkness* features aliens who are gendered only when reproducing, and who alternately take on male and female roles and characteristics. The aliens in Isaac Asimov's *The Gods Themselves* have not two, but three genders.

A number of science fiction authors (LeGuin included) have made feminist statements through the use of gender-variant characters in their speculative fiction. Science fiction critic Cheryl Morgan includes in this feminist category Angela Carter's *The Passion of New Eve* (1977). In this novel, a chauvinistic professor of English is surgically transformed into a woman and then experiences rape, enslavement, humiliation, and (almost) forced impregnation.

The Post-Christine Era

While many in 1950s America were deeply troubled by what Jorgensen's transition meant for traditional gender roles, many transsexual individuals, particularly transsexual women, experienced a tremendous sense of relief. They finally understood and had a name for the sense of gender difference that many had felt from early childhood and recognized that others shared their feelings.

> "Christine Jorgensen's return to the U.S. was a true lifesaving event for me.... The only thing that kept me from suicide at 12 was the publicity of Christine Jorgensen. It was the first time I found out that there were others like me— I was no longer alone."

*"When her surgery was on the front pages, I was giddy because for the first
time ever I realized it was possible."*

Many other transsexual individuals also saw themselves in Jorgensen and hoped to gain
access to hormones and surgical procedures. In the months following her return to the
United States, Jorgensen received "hundreds of tragic letters...from men and women who
also had experienced the deep frustrations of lives lived in sexual twilight." Her endocrinologist, Dr. Hamburger was likewise inundated with requests from individuals seeking to
transition; in the 10 and a half months following his treatment of Jorgensen, he received
more than 1,100 letters from transsexual people, many of whom sought to be his patients
(Jorgensen, 1967, pp. 149–150).

Deluged with requests from people around the world who wanted to travel to Denmark
for hormonal and surgical treatments in the wake of the media frenzy over Jorgensen,
the Danish government banned such procedures for noncitizens. In the United States,
many physicians simply dismissed the rapidly growing number of individuals seeking
gender-affirming surgeries as being mentally ill. Other, more sympathetic doctors were
reluctant to operate because of a fear that they would be either criminally prosecuted
under "mayhem" statutes for destroying healthy tissue or sued by patients who were
unsatisfied with the surgical outcomes. Thus, despite the tremendous demand, only a few
dozen, mostly secretive, genital surgeries were performed in the United States in the years
after Jorgensen first made headlines (Stryker, 2008).

Not until the mid-1960s did gender-affirming surgery become more available. The
constant mainstream media coverage of transsexual people in the decade following the
disclosure of Jorgensen's transition made it increasingly difficult for the medical establishment to characterize them as a few psychologically disordered individuals. At the same
time, the first published studies of the effects of gender-affirming surgery demonstrated
the benefits of medical intervention.

Harry Benjamin, who worked with more transsexual individuals than any other physician in the United States, found that among 51 of his trans women patients who underwent
surgery, 86% had "good" or "satisfactory" lives afterward. He concluded: "I have become
convinced from what I have seen that a miserable, unhappy male [assigned] transsexual can,
with the help of surgery and endocrinology, attain a happier future as a woman" (Benjamin,
1966, p. 135; Meyerowitz, 2002). The smaller number of trans men patients he saw likewise
felt better about themselves and were more psychologically well-adjusted following surgery.

Within months of the publication of Benjamin's *The Transsexual Phenomenon* in
1966, Johns Hopkins University opened the first gender identity clinic in the United States
to diagnose and treat transsexual individuals and to conduct research related to transsexuality. Similar programs were soon established at the University of Minnesota, Stanford
University, the University of Oregon, and Case Western University, and within 10 years,
more than 40 university-affiliated clinics existed throughout the United States (Bullough
& Bullough, 1998; Denny, 2006; Stryker, 2008).

The sudden proliferation of health care services for transsexual individuals reflected not
only the effect of Benjamin's work and the influence of a prestigious university like Hopkins
on other institutions but also the behind-the-scenes involvement of millionaire philanthropist
Reed Erickson. A transsexual man and a patient of Benjamin, Erickson created a foundation
that paid for Benjamin's research and helped fund the Hopkins program and other gender identity clinics. The agency also disseminated information related to transsexuality and served as
an indispensable resource for individuals who were coming out as transsexual (Stryker, 2008).

The establishment of gender identity clinics at leading universities called attention
to the health care needs of transsexual people and helped to legitimize gender-affirming
surgery. However, most clinics provided hormones and surgery only to individuals who fit
a very narrow definition of "transsexual"—someone who has felt themselves to be in the
"wrong" body from their earliest memories and who is attracted to individuals of the same
birth sex as a member of the "other" sex (i.e., a heterosexual trans person). As detailed by
trans writer Dallas Denny (2006):

To qualify for treatment, it was important that applicants report that their gender dysphorias manifested at an early age; that they have a history of playing with dolls as a child, if born male, or trucks and guns, if born female; that their sexual attractions were exclusively to the same biological sex; that they have a history of failure at endeavors undertaken while in the original gender role; and that they pass or had potential to pass successfully as a member of the desired sex. (p. 177)

Unable to meet these narrow and biased criteria, the vast majority of interested people were turned away from the gender identity clinics. In its first 2.5 years, Johns Hopkins received almost 2,000 requests for gender-affirming surgery but performed operations on only 24 individuals (Meyerowitz, 2002).

THE STORIES WE TELL: HISTORICAL NARRATIVES ABOUT TRANSGENDER IDENTITY

Jodi Kaufmann is an associate professor at Georgia State University.

Trans people spend a lot of time helping others to understand what it's like to be trans. There are three primary narratives trans people have turned to in order to share their stories.

The "hermaphroditic narrative" emerged in Germany with the story of Lili Elbe, one of the first transgender people to record her story. Elbe said she was a female "personality" born into a hermaphroditic (or what today would be called intersex) body, a body with both male and female reproductive organs. The hermaphroditic narrative—having a hermaphroditic body and a desire for men—allowed Elbe to receive a sex change operation in the West. Elbe's autobiography was translated into English in 1933, and her story spread in the United States.

The hermaphroditic narrative began to wane in the years following World War II, and the "sex-gender misalignment" narrative took hold. In 1949, psychiatrist David Cauldwell defined "trans-sexual" people as those who are physically of one sex and psychologically of the opposite sex. Harry Benjamin, an endocrinologist, helped spread this "born in the wrong body" narrative. In order to be diagnosed as trans-sexual by doctors like Benjamin, one had to use this narrative, and because only those with the diagnosis could access sex reassignment surgery, trans people felt pressure to use it.

The "queer narrative" began in the 1960s, when the assumed norms of binary gender and heterosexuality came under scrutiny. People started telling stories of who they were that did not align with the hetero-norm. The "queer narrative" hit academia when writer Sandy Stone called for posttranssexuality, or the acceptance of a wider range of expressions of sex and gender.

Over time, the ways in which we talk about transsexual identity and experience have changed. Each narrative has had personal and political significance, offering possibilities and limitations; for instance, the "sex-gender misalignment" narrative aided in gaining medical assistance for transitioning but also reinforced hetero-normative ways of thinking about sex and gender. There is no single narrative that fits every trans body and no narrative that remains free from political and personal limitations. It is critical to be aware of how we share and listen to experiences of sex and gender, because the narratives we use can have powerful consequences.

Transsexual men especially encountered difficulties convincing doctors to approve them for surgery. In the wake of the extraordinary publicity given to Jorgensen and the transsexual women who followed her in the spotlight in the 1950s and 1960s, transsexuality became seen as a primarily trans female phenomenon. The medical establishment gave little consideration to transsexual men, and some physicians questioned whether trans men should even be considered transsexuals (Meyerowitz, 2002).

Admittedly, many trans men did not recognize themselves as transsexual either. While they may have known about Jorgensen and other transsexual women, they did not know anyone who had transitioned from female to male or that such a transition was even possible. This sense of being "the only one" was especially common among the transsexual men who grew up in the 1950s and 1960s (Beemyn & Rankin, 2011).

Transsexual men who did transition often did not pursue surgery to construct a penis because the process was expensive, involved multiple surgeries, and produced imperfect results. Moreover, few doctors were skilled in performing phalloplasties. In the United States, the first "bottom surgeries" for trans men were apparently not undertaken until the early 1960s, and even when the gender identity clinics opened, the programs did only a handful of such operations (Meyerowitz, 2002). The vast majority of transsexual men had to be satisfied with hormone therapy and the removal of their breasts and internal reproductive organs, surgeries which were already commonly performed on women. However, since the effects of hormones (especially increased facial hair and lower voices) and "top surgery" enabled trans men to be seen more readily by others as men, these steps were considered more critical by most transsexual men.

The 1950s and 1960s: Early Organizing Efforts

In 1952, the year that Jorgensen became an international media phenomenon, a group of cross-dressers in the Los Angeles area led by Virginia Prince quietly created a mimeographed newsletter, *Transvestia: The Journal of the American Society for Equity in Dress*. Although its distribution was limited to a small number of cross-dressers on the group's mailing list and it lasted just two issues, *Transvestia* was apparently the first specifically transgender publication in the United States and served as a trial run for wider organizing among cross-dressers.

Prince relaunched *Transvestia* in 1960 as a bimonthly magazine with 25 subscribers. Sold through adult bookstores and by word of mouth, *Transvestia* grew to several hundred subscribers within two years and to more than 1,000 from across the country by the mid-1960s (Ekins & King, 2005; Prince, 1962; Prince & Bentler, 1972). Prince wrote regular columns for the magazine but relied on readers for much of the content, which included life stories, fiction, letters to the editor, personal photographs, and advice on cross-dressing. The involvement of its subscribers, many of whom came out publicly for the first time on the magazine's pages, had the effect of creating a loyal fan base and contributed to its longevity. Prince's commitment also sustained *Transvestia*; she served as its editor and publisher for 20 years, retiring after its hundredth issue in 1979 (Hill, 2007).

Through *Transvestia*, Prince was able to form a transgender organization that continues more than 50 years later. A year after starting the magazine, she invited several Los Angeles subscribers to a clandestine meeting in a local hotel room. The female-presenting cross-dressers were requested to bring stockings and high heels, but they were not told that the others would be there. When the meeting began, Prince had them don the female apparel, thus outing themselves to each other and forcing them to maintain their shared secret. Initially known as the Hose and Heels Club, the group was renamed the Foundation

Virginia Prince, pioneer (copyright Mariette Pathy Allen).

for Personality Expression (FPE or Phi Pi Epsilon) the following year by Prince, who envisioned it as the alpha chapter of a sorority-like organization that would have chapters throughout the country. By the mid-1960s, several other chapters had been chartered by Prince, who set strict membership requirements.

Only individuals who had subscribed to and read at least five issues of *Transvestia* could apply to join, and then they had to have their application personally approved by Prince and be interviewed by her or an area representative. Prince kept control over who could be a member through the mid-1970s, when FPE merged with a Southern California cross-dressing group, Mamselle, to become the Society for the Second Self or Tri-Ess, the name by which it is known today (Ekins & King, 2005; Stryker, 2008). Continuing the practice of FPE, Tri-Ess is modeled on the sorority system and currently has more than 25 chapters throughout the country.

CROSSDRESSING FOR SUCCESS

Angelika Van Ashley

At about the age of 5, I began to recognize myself as being different somehow from boys. I had no clue as to what was going on inside as a child growing up in the 1950s. I began to do research secretly in the mid-1960s, when I was in my early teens, to try to figure out what was going on, but what I found only said that my condition was an illness and curable. I finally discovered Masters and Johnson's research, which spoke of "transvestism" in a more humane and positive light. The term still felt clinical, but I saw myself reflected enough in the description to think "maybe that's what I am."

My now ex-partner was my support system for many years, and she learned about Tri-Ess on the Internet. There was a chapter, Sigma Rho Delta (SRD), near me in Raleigh, North Carolina. I wasn't looking for support or understanding, just simple camaraderie, and SRD provided that for me. It was fun.

The group began with a handful of members, but it soon grew exponentially as word got out via the street and the Internet. We went from three to 40 members. I served as vice president of membership and later as president. All persuasions and ages passed through our door. Twenty-somethings to people over 70 years young. Timid, garden-variety cross-dressers in hiding from years of accumulated fear. Bold and boisterous politicos. Fetish practitioners. The white glove and party manner set. Those in transition or considering it. Musical and artistic types. Truck drivers and doctors. Computer geeks and business owners. Individuals with disabilities or who were physically ailing.

We landed in restaurants, clubs, and at theatres. We played music together and laughed a lot at ourselves. We had picnics. Members who were so inclined bravely attended events of a political nature, such as lobby days at the state legislature, where we asked our elected officials their positions on the pending ENDA (Employment Non-Discrimination Act) and LGBT-inclusive hate crimes bill. We even crashed a high-dollar-per-plate Human Rights Campaign fundraiser that featured Representative Barney Frank and confronted him about his stance on transgender inclusion in the aforementioned legislation. We had a sense of strength within our own diversity.

Although membership declined and the group eventually disbanded, our lasting impressions and friendships have carried on past the decade of Sigma Rho Delta's existence. We still stay in touch and visit one another. We are proud of our unique heritage and the challenges that we met together and as individuals. We found pride in ourselves.

Transvestia and FPE/Tri-Ess reflected Prince's narrow beliefs about cross-dressing. In her view, the "true transvestite" is "exclusively heterosexual," "frequently...married and often fathers," and "values his male organs, enjoys using them and does not desire them removed" (Ekins & King, 2005, p. 9). She not only excluded admittedly gay and bisexual male cross-dressers and transsexual women but also was scornful of them; she openly expressed antigay sentiment and was a leading opponent of gender-affirming surgery. By making sharp distinctions between "real transvestites" and other groups, Prince addressed the two main fears of the wives and female partners of heterosexual male cross-dressers: that their husbands and boyfriends will leave them for men or become women. In addition, she sought to downplay the erotic and sexual aspects of cross-dressing for some people in order to lessen the stigma commonly associated with transvestism and to normalize the one way in which white, middle-class heterosexual male cross-dressers like herself were not privileged in society. In the mid-1960s, *Transvestia* was promoted as being "dedicated to the needs of the sexually (that's heterosexual) normal individual" (Ekins & King, 2005, p. 7; Stryker, 2008).

Prince further sought to dissociate transvestism from sexual activity by coining the term "femmiphile"—literally "lover of the feminine"—as a replacement for "transvestite" in the 1960s. "Femmiphile" did not catch on, but the word "cross-dresser" slowly replaced "transvestite" as the preferred term among most transgender people and supporters. As gay and bisexual men who presented as female increasingly referred to themselves as drag queens, "cross-dresser" began to be applied only to heterosexual men—achieving the separation that Prince desired.

Prince deserves a tremendous amount of credit for bringing a segment of formerly isolated cross-dressers together, helping them to recognize that they are not pathological or immoral, creating a national organization that has provided support to tens of thousands of members and their partners over the past 50 years, and increasing the visibility of heterosexual male cross-dressers. At the same time, by preventing gay and bisexual cross-dressers from joining her organizations, she helped ensure that they would identify more with the gay community than with the cross-dressing community and form their own groups; thus, Prince's prejudice and divisiveness foreclosed the possibility of a broad transgender or lesbian, gay, bisexual, transgender, and queer (LGBTQ) political coalition developing in the 1960s.

The largest and oldest continuing organization consisting primarily of gay male cross-dressers or drag queens, the Imperial Court System, was founded by José Sarria in San Francisco in 1965. Beginning with other chapters (known as "realms") in Portland, Oregon, and Los Angeles, the court system has grown today to more than 65 local groups in the United States, Canada, and Mexico; reflecting this expansion, its name is now the International Court System (Imperial Sovereign Rose Court, 2014). The primary mission of each chapter is to raise money for LGBTQ, HIV/AIDS, and other charities through annual costume balls and other fundraising events. Involvement often pays personal dividends as well. According to Steven Schacht (2002), a sociologist who has participated in the group, "courts also serve as an important conduit for gay and lesbian individuals to do drag and as a venue for formal affiliation and personal esteem (largely in the form of various drag titles; i.e. Empress, Emperor, Princess, and Prince) often unavailable to such individuals in the dominant culture" (p. 164).

BALL CULTURE DEVELOPS

By the late 1960s, black drag queens were organizing their own events. Growing out of the drag balls held in New York City earlier in the century, these gatherings began in Harlem and initially focused on extravagant feminine drag performances. As word spread about the balls, they attracted larger and larger audiences and the competitions became fiercer and more varied. The drag performers "walked" (competed) for trophies and prizes in a growing number of categories beyond most feminine (known as "femme realness") or most glamorous, including categories for "butch queens"—gay and sometimes trans men who look "real" as different class-based male archetypes, such as "business executive," "school boy," and "thug."

The many individuals seeking to participate in ball culture led to the establishment of "houses," groups of Black and Latin@ "children" who gathered around a "house mother" or less often a "house father," in the mid-1970s. These houses were often named after their leaders, such as Crystal LaBeija's House of LaBeija, Avis Pendavis's House of Pendavis, and Dorian Corey's House of Corey, or took their names from leading fashion designers like the House of Chanel or the House of St. Laurent. The children, consisting of less experienced performers, walked in the balls under their house name and sought to win trophies for the glory of the house and to achieve "legendary" status for themselves. Given that many of the competitors were poor African American and Latin@ youth who came from broken homes or had been thrown out of their homes for being gay or transgender, the houses provided a surrogate family and a space where they could be accepted and have a sense of belonging (Cunningham, 1995; Trebay, 2000).

The ball culture spread to other cities in the 1980s and 1990s and achieved mainstream visibility in 1990 through Jennie Livingston's documentary *Paris Is Burning* and Madonna's mega-hit song and video "Vogue." In recent years, many of the New York balls have moved out of Harlem. They continue to include local houses and groups from other cities competing in a wide array of categories. Reflecting changes in the wider Black and Latin@ cultures, hip-hop and R & B have become more prominent in the ball scene, and a growing number of performers are butch queens who imitate rap musicians (Cunningham, 1995; Trebay, 2000).

In the 1950s and 1960s, lesbian, gay, and bisexual cross-dressers also found a home in bars, restaurants, and other venues that catered to (or at least tolerated) such a clientele. Sarria, for example, performed in drag at San Francisco's Black Cat Bar in the 1950s and early 1960s and helped turn it into a social and cultural center for the city's gay community until harassment from law enforcement and local authorities forced the bar to close (Boyd, 2003). Lesbian, gay, and bisexual individuals—both those who did drag and those who did not—similarly carved out spaces in other US cities, despite regular police crackdowns against them.

Transsexual individuals also began to organize in the 1960s, though most of these efforts were small and short lived. In 1967, transgender people in San Francisco formed Conversion Our Goal, or COG, the first known transsexual support group in the United States. However, within a year, the organization had disintegrated into two competing groups, neither of which existed for very long. More successful was the National Transsexual Counseling Unit, a San Francisco–based social service agency established in 1968 with funding from Reed Erickson. That same year in New York City, Mario Martino, a transsexual man and registered nurse, and his wife founded Labyrinth, a counseling service for trans men. It was the first known organization in the United States to focus on the needs of transsexual men and worked with upwards of 100 transitioning individuals (Martino, 1977; Stryker, 2008).

Trans Power!

The 1969 Stonewall Riots in New York City have become legendary as the start of LGBTQ militancy and the birthplace of the LGBTQ liberation movement. However, Stonewall was not a unique event but the culmination of more than a decade of militant opposition by poor and working-class LGBTQ people to discriminatory treatment and police brutality. Much of this resistance took the form of spontaneous, everyday acts of defiance that were never documented or received little attention at the time, even in LGBTQ communities (Stryker, 2008).

For example, one night in May 1959, two Los Angeles police officers went into Cooper's Donuts—an all-night coffeehouse popular with drag queens and gay male hustlers, many of whom were Latin@ or African American—and began harassing and arresting the patrons in drag. The customers responded by fighting back, first by throwing doughnuts and ultimately by engaging in skirmishes with the officers that led the police to retreat and to call in backup. In the melee, the drag queens who had been arrested were able to escape (Faderman & Timmons, 2006; Stryker, 2008).

A similar incident occurred in San Francisco in 1966 at the Tenderloin location of Gene Compton's Cafeteria—a 24-hour restaurant that, like Cooper's, was frequented by drag queens and male hustlers, as well as the people looking to pick them up. As documented by historian Susan Stryker, the management called the police one August night, as it had done in the past, to get rid of a group of young drag queens who were seen as loitering. When a police officer tried to remove one of the queens forcibly, she threw a cup of coffee in his face and a riot ensued. Patrons pelted the officers with everything at their disposal, wrecking the cafeteria in the process. Vastly outnumbered, the police ran outside to call for reinforcements, only to have the drag queens chase after them, beating the officers with their purses and kicking them with their high heels. The incident served to empower the city's drag community and motivated many to begin to organize for their rights (Silverman & Stryker, 2005; Stryker, 2008).

Three years later, the much larger and more widely known Stonewall Riots—which started at the Stonewall Inn in the Greenwich Village neighborhood of New York City on June 28, 1969, and continued on and off for six days—inspired gender nonconforming people across the country and led to activism on an even greater scale. As with the earlier confrontations in Los Angeles and San Francisco, the immediate impetus for the Stonewall uprising was oppression by the local police, who regularly raided bars that were frequented by LGBTQ people to brutalize and arrest the patrons and to obtain payoffs from the bar owners in order to keep from being shut down. But the riots also reflected long-simmering anger. "Back then we were beat up by the police, by everybody.... You

The film *Screaming Queens: The Riots at Compton's Cafeteria* connects the events at San Francisco's Compton's Cafeteria to the historical movements of the 1960s.

Sylvia Rivera and many of the other Stonewall participants were active in the women's movement, the civil rights movement, and the anti–Vietnam War movement, and recognized that they would have to demand their rights as LGBTQ people, too. Rivera stated: "We had done so much for other movements. It was time.... I always believed that we would have [to] fight back. I just knew that we would fight back. I just didn't know it would be that night" (Feinberg, 1998, pp. 107, 109).

Felicia Elizondo and Dee Dee at Compton's Cafeteria riot anniversary, San Francisco, August 20, 2012 (photo by Liz Highleyman).

get tired of being just pushed around," recalls Sylvia Rivera, a Puerto Rican transgender woman who was a leader in the riots and the LGBTQ organizing that occurred afterward. "We were not taking any more of this shit" (Carter, 2004; Feinberg, 1998, p. 107).

On that June night, the police raided the Stonewall Inn and as usual began arresting the bar's workers, customers who did not have identification, and those who were cross-dressed. But unlike in the past, the other patrons did not scatter when they were allowed to leave. Instead, they congregated outside and, with other LGBTQ people from the neighborhood, taunted the police as they tried to place the arrestees into a patrol wagon.

Accounts from this point on differ as to what incited the onlookers to violence; it is likely that events happened so fast that there was not one single precipitating incident. As the crowd grew, so too did anger toward the police for their rough treatment of the drag queens and at least one butch lesbian whom they had arrested. People began to throw coins at the officers, and when this failed to halt the brutality or to alleviate years of pent-up anger, they hurled whatever they could find—cans, bottles, cobblestones, and bricks from a nearby construction site (Duberman, 1993).

Unaccustomed to LGBTQ people resisting police brutality and fearful for their safety, the eight police officers retreated and barricaded themselves into the bar. In a reversal of roles, the LGBTQ crowd then tried to break in after them, while at least one person attempted to set the bar on fire. The arrival of police reinforcements likely kept those inside the bar from firing on the protesters. However, even the additional officers, who were members of an elite riot-control unit, could not immediately quell the uprising. The police would scatter people by wading into the crowd swinging their billy clubs, but rather than flee the area, the demonstrators simply ran around the block and, regrouping behind the riot squad, continued to jeer and throw objects at them.

Sylvia Rivera, homeless, with Marlboro Man (copyright Mariette Pathy Allen).

At one point, the police turned around to a situation for which their training undoubtedly did not prepare them: a chorus line of drag queens, calling themselves the "Stonewall girls," kicked up their heels—à la the Rockettes—and sang mockingly at the officers. Eventually, the police succeeded in dispersing the crowd, but only for the night. The rioting was similarly violent the following evening—some witnesses say more so—and sporadic and less combative demonstrations continued for the next several days (Duberman, 1993).

The Roots of Radical Activism

The effects of the Stonewall Riots were immediate and far-reaching. Among the first to notice a change in the LGBTQ community was Deputy Inspector Seymour Pine, the police officer who led the raid on the bar that night. "For those of us in public morals, things were completely changed," Pine stated after the rebellion. "Suddenly [LGBTQ people] were not submissive anymore" (Duberman, 1993, p. 203).

The biggest impact may have been on LGBTQ youth. At the time of the Stonewall Riots, gay rights groups—often chapters of the Student Homophile League—existed at just six colleges in the United States, almost all of which were large universities in the Northeast. By 1971, groups had been formed at hundreds of colleges and universities throughout the country (Beemyn, 2003). Reflecting the sense of militancy that had fueled the uprising, many of the new groups referred to themselves as Gay Liberation Fronts, after the Gay Liberation Front (GLF) that was formed in New York City a month after the riots, and typically had a more radical political agenda than the earlier student organizations. Many of the GLFs were also initially more welcoming to cross-dressers, drag queens, and transsexuals than the pre-Stonewall groups, and a number of transgender people helped form Gay Liberation Fronts.

Transgender people also established their own organizations in the immediate aftermath of the Stonewall Riots. Sylvia Rivera and Marsha P. Johnson, an African American trans woman who had likewise been involved in the riots, founded Street Transvestite Action Revolutionaries (STAR) in New York City in 1970 to support and to fight for the rights of the many young trans people who were living on the city's streets. Rivera and Johnson hustled to open STAR House, a place where the youth could receive shelter, clothing, and food for free. The house remained open for two or three years and inspired similar efforts in Chicago, California, and England. Also in New York City in 1970, Lee Brewster and Bunny Eisenhower founded the Queens Liberation Front and led a campaign that decriminalized cross-dressing in New York. Brewster began *Drag*, one of the first politically oriented trans publications, in 1970 (Feinberg, 1998; Zagria, 2009). During this same time, trans man Jude Patton, along with Sister Mary Elizabeth Clark (formerly known as Joanna Clark), used funding from Reed Erickson to start disseminating information to trans people (Moonhawk River Stone, personal communication, May 12, 2013; Jamison Green, personal communication, June 6, 2013).

THE ANTITRANSGENDER BACKLASH

Discrimination from Lesbian and Gay Organizations

Despite the central role that trans people played in the Stonewall Riots and the political organizing that followed, much of the broader lesbian and gay movement soon abandoned them in an attempt to be more acceptable to the dominant society. Six months after the Stonewall riots, a group comprised mostly of white middle-class gay men, who were dissatisfied with the multiple issue politics and antiestablishment ethos of GLF, formed the Gay Activists Alliance (GAA) in New York City to work "completely and solely" for their own equal rights (Duberman, 1993, p. 232). The group did not consider the rights of trans people to be relevant to its mission; GAA would not provide a loan to pay the rent to keep STAR House open or support a dance to raise the funds. Transgender people also did not feel welcomed in the group. Johnson remembered that she and Rivera were stared at when they attended GAA meetings, being the only trans people and sometimes the only people of color there (Jay & Young, 1972). Similar gay groups that excluded trans people subsequently formed in other cities.

Transgender women also often faced rejection in the 1970s from members of lesbian organizations, who viewed them not as "real women" but as "male infiltrators." One of the most well-known victims of such prejudice was Beth Elliott, a transsexual lesbian activist and singer who joined the San Francisco chapter of the groundbreaking lesbian group the Daughters of Bilitis in 1971 and became its vice president and the editor of its newsletter. Although Elliott had been accepted for membership, she was forced out the following year as part of a campaign against her. She also faced opposition to her involvement in the 1973 West Coast Lesbian Feminist Conference. Elliott was on the conference's planning committee and a scheduled performer, but when she took the stage, some audience members attempted to shout her down, saying that she was a man. Others defended her. Elliott managed to get through her performance, but the controversy continued.

In a keynote speech, feminist Robin Morgan viciously attacked Elliott, whom she called a "male transvestite," who was "leeching off women who have spent entire lives *as women* in women's bodies." Morgan concluded her diatribe by declaring: "I charge him as an opportunist, an infiltrator, and a destroyer—with the mentality of a rapist" (Gallo, 2006; Stryker, 2008, pp. 104–105). Morgan called on the conference attendees to vote to eject Elliott. Although more than two-thirds reportedly chose to allow her to remain, Elliot was emotionally traumatized by the experience and decided to leave anyway.

The campaign against Elliott marked the start of the policing of "women's spaces" by some lesbian separatists to exclude transsexual women. Another target was Sandy Stone, a sound engineer who, as part of the all-women Olivia Records, helped create the genre of women's music in the mid-1970s. Stone had disclosed her transsexuality to the other women in the record collective and had their support, but when her gender history became widely known, Olivia was deluged with hate mail from lesbians—some threatening violence, others threatening a boycott if Stone was not fired. The collective initially defended her, but fearing that they would be put out of business, they reluctantly asked Stone to resign, which she did in 1979 (Califia, 1997; Devor & Matte, 2006).

Many lesbians had left activist organizations like GLF and GAA in the early and mid-1970s because of sexism among the predominantly gay male members, and there was not much that united the two groups, but one area of agreement was their rejection of trans people. In 1973, lesbian separatists and more conservative gay men in San Francisco organized an alternative Pride parade that banned trans people and individuals in drag; in subsequent years, this event became the city's main Pride celebration. At the New York City Pride rally in 1973, Jean O'Leary of Lesbian Feminist Liberation read a statement that denounced drag queens as an insult to women, which further marked the exclusion of trans people from the "lesbian and gay" rights movement (Clendinen & Nagourney, 1999; Stryker, 2008).

The Transsexual Empire

The most vitriolic and influential attack on trans people was Janice Raymond's *The Transsexual Empire: The Making of the She-Male*, published in 1979 and reissued in 1994. Raymond, a scholar in women's studies, was one of the leading voices against Sandy Stone and against all transsexual women in lesbian feminist communities. While Robin Morgan argued that Elliott had "the mentality of a rapist," Raymond went further, stating that transsexual women *are* rapists. In one of the most infamous passages, she claims: "All transsexuals rape women's bodies by reducing the real female form to an artifact, appropriating this body for themselves." She also contends that their supposedly secretive presence in lesbian feminist spaces constitutes an act of forced penetration that "violates women's sexuality and spirit" (p. 104).

For Raymond, transsexual women are not women but "castrated" and "deviant" men who were a creation of the medical and psychological specialties that arose in support of gender-affirming surgeries—"the transsexual empire" to which her title refers. Ignoring centuries of gender nonconformity in cultures around the world, she considers transsexuality to be a recent phenomenon stemming from the development of genital surgeries, which she erroneously traces to Nazi Germany (as stated earlier, the first known gender-affirming surgery was performed in Germany in 1931, two years before Hitler came to power). To resist being taken over by the evil "transsexual empire," Raymond advocates for a drastic reduction in the availability of gender-affirming surgery and recommends that transsexual individuals instead undergo "gender reorientation" (Stryker, 2008, p. 110).

Raymond's inflammatory rhetoric and false allegations could be readily dismissed if her arguments had not had such a significant effect. Influenced in part by Raymond's antitranssexual attacks, the gender identity clinics—which already served only a small number of trans individuals and were largely opposed by the medical establishment—performed even fewer surgeries and began to shut down altogether, starting with the Johns Hopkins program in 1979.

FEMINISM AND TRANS IDENTITY OVER TIME

Talia Bettcher is a philosophy professor at Cal State Los Angeles.

It may seem obvious that feminist and trans politics go together like peanut butter and jelly. In both feminist and trans politics, there is a concern with gender oppression, so there appears to be a common cause. Trans women not only experience transphobia but also sexism; many trans *men* have had firsthand experience with sexism prior to transition (and even after if they are transphobically viewed as "really women"). So it might be surprising to learn that some (non-trans) feminists have viewed trans people in hostile, transphobic ways.

In the 1970s and 1980s, influential "second-wave" (non-trans) feminists such as Robin Morgan, Mary Daly, and Janice Raymond represented trans women as rapists and boundary violators trying to invade women's space. Trans men were disregarded as mere tokens used to hide the patriarchal nature of the phenomenon of transsexuality. Raymond's *The Transsexual Empire: The Making of the She-Male* systemizes these hostile views, and in trans circles it is widely regarded as a "classic" of transphobic literature.

While there are still non-trans feminists with these types of views, they are now in the minority. Much of this has to do with the emergence of so-called third-wave feminism. Transgender people are now often thought of as "beyond the binary." One of the most important consequences of this development is that it became possible to view trans people as oppressed in a way that was not reduced to sexism. Perhaps the most important strand of third-wave feminism is the view that one cannot focus on only one kind of oppression (sexism) to the exclusion of others, such as racism (see Combahee River Collective, 1981). One important lesson of trans feminist Emi Koyama's work is that any form of trans/feminism which marginalizes other forms of oppression, such as racism, does so at its own peril.

Despite these positive developments, there remains an important challenge for "trans/feminism." Many trans people simply don't identify as "beyond the binary" at all—they identify as plain men and women. Obviously the "beyond the binary" idea doesn't provide much help to those trans people who, in this view, are regarded as "gender conservative." How do we understand trans oppression/resistance if *both* "beyond the binary" and "trapped in the wrong body" are found to be inadequate? We might need a completely new theory.

Bias in Health Care

Another factor in the closing of the Hopkins program and other gender identity clinics was a study published in 1979 by Jon Meyer, the director of the Hopkins clinic, and his secretary, Donna Reter, that purportedly showed "no objective improvement" among individuals who had undergone gender-affirming surgery at Hopkins, as compared to a group of transsexuals who had been turned down for surgery or had changed their minds (Denny, 2006, p. 176). Meyer and Reter's study has been widely criticized for the arbitrariness of how it measured "social adjustment," as well as for its value judgments: individuals who did not improve their socioeconomic standing, who continued to see a therapist, or who were unmarried or with a same-sex partner were deemed to be less well adjusted.

In addition, noticeably absent was any measure of the participants' satisfaction or happiness with their lives. Meyer and Reter did, however, admit that only one of the individuals who underwent gender-affirming surgery expressed any regrets at having done so (and in this person's case, because the surgery had been performed poorly). Other studies at the time, which considered the participants' feelings, found much more positive outcomes from surgery (Bullough & Bullough, 1998; Rudacille, 2005).

The apparent bias of Meyer and Reter's study was confirmed by a subsequent investigative report, which concluded that "the ending of surgery at the GIC [gender identity clinic] now appears to have been orchestrated by certain figures at Hopkins, who, for personal rather than scientific reasons, staunchly opposed any form of sex reassignment" (Denny, 2006, p. 176). One of these figures was the chair of the Psychiatry Department at Hopkins, Paul McHugh, who was responsible for closing the clinic. In an interview, he stated, "my personal feeling is that surgery is not a proper treatment for a psychiatric disorder, and it's clear to me that these patients have severe psychological problems that don't go away following surgery" (Zagria, 2010).

McHugh's position that transsexual people were mentally disordered was a widespread belief among psychiatrists in the 1970s, despite the decades-long history of physicians successfully treating transsexuality as a physical concern. In 1980, this illness model was codified into the third edition of the American Psychiatric Association's *Diagnostic and Statistical Manual of Mental Disorders* (*DSM*), which defined "transsexualism" as a "disorder" characterized by "a persistent sense of discomfort and inappropriateness about one's anatomic sex and a persistent wish to be rid of one's genitals and to live as a member of the other sex" (pp. 261–262).

Despite the efforts of some trans activists and allies to remove the diagnosis (just as "homosexuality" had been removed before the third edition), transsexuality continued to be listed as a psychological disorder in subsequent editions. The 1994 version of the *DSM* replaced the category "transsexualism" with "gender identity disorder," but the diagnostic criteria remained largely unchanged. "A strong and persistent cross-gender identification" was evidence of a psychopathology (p. 532).

The 2013 edition of the *DSM* makes significant progress in undoing the stigma associated with transsexuality by replacing "gender identity disorder" with "gender dysphoria," which is described as emotional distress resulting from "a marked incongruence between one's experienced/expressed gender and assigned gender." However, the latest version still defines gender nonconformity among children as pathological and includes a category of "transvestic disorder," which, according to trans medical policy writer Kelley Winters (2010, 2012), "labels gender expression not stereotypically associated with assigned birth sex as inherently pathological and sexually deviant."

TRANS ACTIVISM IN THE LATE TWENTIETH CENTURY

Growing Visibility

While the early 1970s to the early 1980s were a cultural low point for trans people, the period did have a few bright spots. Notably, the 1970s marked the beginning of a steady stream of nonsensational transsexual books, mostly by individuals who had been successful in society as men before transitioning to female. Except for Jorgensen's autobiography, the stories of transsexual women that were published in the 1960s and early 1970s were lurid exposés of female impersonators, strippers, and prostitutes with tabloid titles like *"I Changed My Sex!"* and *"I Want to Be a Woman!"* (Sherman, 1964; Star, 1963).

A new wave of transsexual autobiographies began with the 1974 publications of Jan Morris's *Conundrum* and Canary Conn's *Canary*. Morris, a renowned British author and travel writer who had accompanied the first known expedition to reach the summit of Mount Everest in 1953, describes how she sublimated her sense of herself as female for decades through constant travel before undergoing gender-affirming surgery in 1972. Conn, a rising teenage rock star, transitioned in her early twenties, which seems to have led to the end of her singing career, while Morris continued to be a successful writer. Another significant autobiography, *Mirror Image*, was written in 1978 by award-winning *Chicago Tribune* newspaper reporter Nancy Hunt.

The most well-known autobiography of the era was Renée Richards's *Second Serve*, published in 1983. Richards achieved international notoriety for successfully suing the Women's Tennis Association when it barred her from competing in the 1976 US Women's Open under a newly introduced "women-born women" policy. The court decision was groundbreaking and opened the door for other transsexual athletes. Surprisingly, though, Richards devotes relatively few pages of her autobiography to the case or her tennis career. Instead, she dedicates the majority of *Second Serve* to describing her struggle to accept herself as female, which came only after three failed attempts to go back to living as a man.

While the best-selling autobiographies by Jorgensen, Morris, and Richards, and to a lesser extent the works by Conn and Hunt, drew significant attention to the lives of transsexual women, the only full-length narrative by a trans man to be published in the United States prior to the 1990s was Mario Martino's 1977 book *Emergence: A Transsexual Autobiography* (Stryker, 2008). Just as Morris, Hunt, and Richards pursued traditionally male careers in order to conform to societal gender expectations and to try to convince themselves and others of their masculinity, Martino entered a convent school, hoping but failing to suppress his feelings and be more feminine. After transitioning, he began to provide support to other transsexual men.

Another high point for trans people in the 1970s and early 1980s was the expansion of organizing efforts by both heterosexual male and gay and bisexual cross-dressers, which transformed local groups into national organizations. Cross-dressers started Fantasia Fair (2011), a weeklong series of social, entertainment, and education events in Provincetown, Massachusetts. First held in 1975, "The Fair" has become the oldest continuing trans event in the United States. Transsexual women likewise established many more support groups in the 1970s and 1980s—sometimes inclusive of heterosexual male cross-dressers who chose not to affiliate with Tri-Ess, and other times inclusive of transsexual men. But few trans male individuals joined these groups, as they were dominated by transsexual women and, with meetings focused on topics such as female makeup and clothing tips, failed to address the needs of transsexual men.

A few trans male support groups were started in the 1970s and early 1980s, including groups in Los Angeles, New York City, and Toronto (Green, 2004). The first FTM-only educational and support organization in the United States, which was called simply "FTM," was begun in San Francisco in 1986 by Lou Sullivan, a gay transsexual man. The group published the quarterly *FTM Newsletter*, which became the leading source of information related to trans men and had hundreds of subscribers from around the world. In 1990, Sullivan also compiled the first guide for trans men, *Information for the Female-to-Male*

The story of Steve Dain, one of the first public trans men, was unfortunately eclipsed quickly from newspaper headlines by pieces about Renée Richards. Dain was a high school girls' physical education teacher who fought to retain his job after transitioning in 1976, appearing on talk shows across the country. Although he ultimately won the right to teach again, he could not find a school that would hire him, so became a chiropractor with his own business. He died in 2007 of metastatic breast cancer at age 68 (Jamison Green, personal communication, June 6, 2013).

Trans man Lou Sullivan helped mental health workers to understand the difference between sexual orientation and gender identity, and specifically pushed them to realize that trans people could be gay identified (Jamison Green, personal communication, June 6, 2013).

Crossdresser and Transsexual, and wrote the first book explicitly about a trans male individual—a biography of Jack Bee Garland, a female-assigned journalist and social worker who lived as a man for 40 years in San Francisco in the late 19th and early 20th centuries (Stryker, 2008). Sullivan died from complications from AIDS at the age of 39 in 1991.

Under the subsequent leadership of Jamison Green (2004), FTM, which changed its name to FTM International in 1994, became the largest trans male organization in the world. Green went on to become a more public figure than Sullivan had been, convening the first trans male conference in 1995 (thanks to a grant from Dallas Denny), educating police officers and lawmakers, and working to reform the World Professional Association for Transgender Health (WPATH) Standards of Care. Following in the footsteps of Stephen Whittle, Green was elected as the second trans President of WPATH.

THE FORERUNNERS: THE OUR TRANS BODIES OURSELVES COLLECTIVE

Yoseñio V. Lewis is a black/Latino FTM and long-term social justice activist and artist, and Rev. Moonhawk River Stone, MS, LMHC is an Interfaith minister, psychotherapist, consultant, educator, and writer.

Before transgender health care was a vibrant, multifaceted, comprehensive movement, there was the all-volunteer Eliminating Disparities Committee (informally known as the Transgender Health Care Committee) of the National Coalition for LGBT Health (NCLGBTH), active from 2003 to 2005. In 2004, we issued a report entitled "An Overview of U.S. Trans Health Priorities" and created the first of their kind fact sheets, one for trans men's health and one for trans women's health.

At that time, some of us had contact with the Boston Women's Health Collective, the producers of the ground-breaking feminist work, *Our Bodies, Ourselves (OBOS)*, and were offered the opportunity to review the groundbreaking inclusion of transgender issues and health concerns in the fifth edition of *OBOS*, which came out in May of 2005.

We began discussions about doing an analogous book for transgender people and calling ourselves the Our Trans Bodies Ourselves (OTBO) Collective. We created a closed yahoo group for communication (still a sort of new idea in 2006) and sought to invite as diverse a group of trans-identified individuals as we could. We had a formal consensus process for all decision making. It worked very well, and though it was time consuming, the results made the work we did authentic and powerful. Our archives contain those procedures and structures in great detail.

The OTBO Collective developed an elemental strategic plan for the book moving through 2009 to give our work form, structure, and guidance. We created subcommittees for the different areas of work and began the process of becoming our own nonprofit entity. We identified chapter areas and began some initial work on those chapters through what was then a brand new process: a wiki page (which is still up!).

Our OTBO Collective lived but a short 13 months. The practical difficulties all of us had (full-time work or school, full-time activist work, and/or caregiving for loved ones) proved our undoing. We also could not find funding beyond the Coalition's phone support to continue our work.

Yoseñio V. Lewis

Rev. Moonhawk River Stone

The OTBO Collective's most enduring sadness is that our book never came to be given to the transgender community. But we gave the transgender health care movement the shove and momentum it needed to blossom. Not bad at all for a "failed" Collective!

This volume, *Trans Bodies, Trans Selves*, is the next generation of our work—the blossom of the seeds we cast. Maybe it is just what we need to empower Our Many Selves forward into an increasingly welcoming and healthy world for all trans people.

The authors would like to thank the following people: Jessica Xavier, Donald Hitchcock, Susan Hollinshead, Mara Keisling, Emilia Lombardi, Samuel Lurie, Diego Sanchez, Ben Singer, Bobbi Williams, Becky Allison, Heather Stephenson, Judy Norsigian, and the late Hutson W. Inniss.

The 1990s: The Emergence of Trans Rights

A larger trans rights movement grew significantly in the 1990s, facilitated by the increasing use of the term "transgender" to encompass all individuals whose gender identity or expression differs from the gender assigned to them at birth. This wider application of "transgender" developed among writers and activists beginning in the mid-1980s and started to catch on more widely in the early 1990s.

Holly Boswell defined the term in a groundbreaking 1991 article "The Transgender Alternative," as "encompass[ing] the whole spectrum" of gender diversity and bringing together all gender nonconforming people (Stryker, 2008, p. 123). This understanding of "transgender" became most strongly associated with socialist writer and activist Leslie Feinberg, who called on all people who face discrimination for not conforming to gender norms to organize around their shared oppression in hir 1992 pamphlet *Transgender Liberation: A Movement Whose Time Has Come* and in hir subsequent books, *Transgender Warriors* and *Trans Liberation*. Writers such as Kate Bornstein and Martine Rothblatt also adopted the term, which helped make its usage commonplace by the late 1990s (Bornstein, 1994; Feinberg, 1992, 1996, 1998; Rothblatt, 1994).

The broad-based political movement that Feinberg envisioned came to fruition in response to continued acts of discrimination and violence against trans people. Reflecting the persistence of antitransgender bias among some lesbian feminists, trans women were banned from the National Lesbian Conference in 1991 and a postoperative transsexual woman, Nancy Jean Burkholder, was expelled that same year from the Michigan Womyn's Music Festival. The festival, an annual week-long women's outdoor music and cultural event, has been a pilgrimage for thousands of lesbians since it began in 1976. While the event had always been for "womyn only," Burkholder's removal was the first known exclusion of a transsexual woman; afterwards, festival organizers articulated a policy limiting attendance to "womyn-born womyn" (G. Rubin, 2006).

The growth of an out trans community over the course of little more than a decade is demonstrated by the different responses to the expulsions of Stone and Burkholder. While few spoke publicly in Stone's defense in 1979, the ouster of Burkholder in 1991 was widely denounced and led to protests at "Michigan" itself. Trans activists passed out thousands of "I might be transsexual" buttons to festivalgoers the next year, and following the removal of four more transsexual women in 1993, they created what became known as "Camp Trans" across from the entrance to the festival.

Camp Trans consisted of several dozen transsexual women and supporters who leafleted Michigan attendees and held workshops and readings that attracted hundreds of women from the other side of the road. The significance of this protest was noted by Riki Wilchins, one of the main organizers: "Camp Trans was the first time transpeople ever coordinated and pulled off a national event. Not only that, it was the first time that significant numbers of the hard-core lesbian-feminist community backed us" (Boyd, 2006; Califia, 1997, p. 227; Denny, 2006). The organizers of the Michigan Womyn's Music Festival, though, refused to change their policy, leading trans activists to re-establish Camp Trans in 1999. The festival leadership finally gave in to the pressure in the mid-2000s and no longer enforced their policy, while continuing to insist that only womyn-born womyn should attend. The situation is a version of "Don't Ask, Don't Tell": The festival organizers do not press the issue, and a number of trans women have attended the festival without calling significant attention to themselves. Camp Trans (2011) continues to be held to advocate, as their slogan states, for "room for all kinds of womyn."

It was not only lesbian feminists who discriminated against trans people in the early 1990s. When lesbian and gay leaders were planning to hold a March on Washington in 1993, transgender activists, with the support of bisexual allies, sought to have the word "transgender" added to the name of the event. Although some local organizing committees supported transgender inclusion, the march's national steering committee voted by a significant margin to use the name "March on Washington for Lesbian, Gay, and Bi Equal

Campers at Camp Trans (photo by Bex H.).

Rights and Liberation." The decision prompted many trans people to become more politically active and more organized.

Another major incident that mobilized a large number of trans people, especially many trans men, was the murder of 21-year-old Brandon Teena near Falls City, Nebraska, in the early hours of New Year's Day in 1994. Teena lived as a man, but he was outed as being assigned female at birth when the county sheriff's office reported his arrest on a misdemeanor to the local newspaper. Following the disclosure, two men whom Teena thought to be friends, John Lotter and Tom Nissen, beat and raped him, and a week after he reported the sexual assault to the sheriff, the two killed Teena and two others.

A view of Camp Trans (photo by Bex H.).

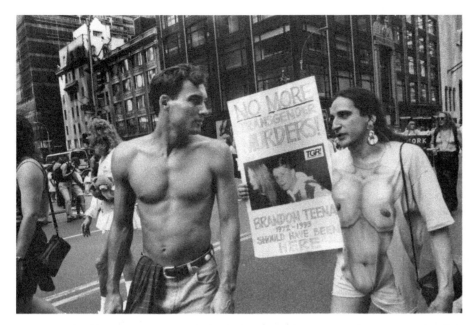

Brandon Teena should have been here, Gay Pride Parade, New York City (copyright Mariette Pathy Allen).

Teena's murder touched off a series of important protests by trans people and allies, who were incensed not only by the horrific murders and the bias of the police for failing to arrest Lotter and Nissen after the rape but also by the initial media coverage, in which Teena was often portrayed as a butch lesbian and referred to as "her" (Califia, 1997). In response to the particularly insensitive reporting of the *Village Voice*, members of Transexual Menace, a direct action group that Riki Wilchins and Denise Norris had just started in New York City, picketed outside of the newspaper's offices. The group and other trans activists also held a vigil outside of the Nebraska courthouse where Lotter was standing trial in 1995. Wilchins called the event "a turning point for trans activism," because it was the first highly visible national demonstration organized by trans people and helped draw unprecedented media attention to an antitransgender hate crime (Califia, 1997, p. 232).

Teena's life and death became the subject of many news stories, books, and movies, including Kimberly Peirce's 1999 film *Boys Don't Cry*, in which Hilary Swank played Teena and won an Academy Award for Best Actress. What also made this case different from most previous murders of trans people was that Teena's killers received significant sentences—Nissen was given life imprisonment without the possibility of parole and Lotter the death penalty.

THE START OF TRANS ACTIVISM, 1994–1995

Riki Wilchins, MA, has written three books on gender theory, founded GenderPAC and The Transexual Menace, and was selected by Time as one of "100 Civic Innovators for the 21st Century."

It started, as serious things often do, with a murder and a fight. The fight was the simple part. An attendee at the Michigan Womyn's Music Festival was stopped by two women from Security and asked if she was really a man. She refused to affirm or deny. So, asserting that they thought she was a man, Nancy Jean Burkholder was forcibly evicted from the event. Afterwards, the Festival quietly and retroactively announced a new policy it called "womyn-born-womyn"—a weird, supposedly feminist-y sounding neologism which everyone concerned understood to mean "no trannies allowed." Janis Walworth, a friend who had accompanied Nancy, reached out to several activists about coming to the next year's Festival to raise awareness—few people even knew what had happened or were aware of the policy.

Four of us showed up that year. We camped out across the road from the main gate in the National Forest. Not to miss a beat, Festival Security was soon talking with Park Rangers and asking them to throw us out, but fortunately there were no grounds for doing so. We planned several workshops, distributed a few fliers to surprised attendees driving and walking by, and sat back to see what would happen next. What happened was that hundreds of women walked miles out of the Festival to attend our workshops, hang out, and offer support. A few even came to stay. Our little campground became crowded every evening. It became obvious that this was something that could scale, and we began laying plans for a bigger, better presence the next year. Transgender people were pushing back.

In fact, the idea of transgender protest had been circulating in the community. Transgender Nation, modeled on (and some said a reaction to transphobia in) Queer Nation, had been launched by Anne Ogborn in San Francisco. It had some early successes, but hadn't really caught on. This was still at a time when many if not most of us still hoped to "pass." There were relatively few public trans-

Transexual menace logo (courtesy of Riki Wilchins).

gender activists. Susan Stryker had written a manifesto just a few years earlier in which she pointed to trans-visibility as a critical factor in launching transgender advocacy. But transgender people organizing politically and in public to confront cisgender bigotry (as opposed to coming together socially inside hotel conferences) was rare.

Some of us decided to print up a batch of "Transexual Menace" T-shirts, modeled on a combination of the Lavender Menace (who confronted NOW over its exclusion of lesbians) and the genderfuck of *Rocky Horror Picture Show*. We began handing them out any time we came together politically for events. They were visible, cheeky, and determinedly tongue-in-cheek, both outing ourselves but also mocking straights for their fear and loathing of transsexuals. . . and an instant hit. Being "out, loud, and proud" was new for trans people used to being very closeted.

I announced I was going to take a carload of T-shirts to the Southern Comfort conference in Atlanta with some of the NY Menace to see how they would play on a larger stage. This immediately launched widespread rumors that the Menace was coming to "disrupt" the conference and ruin the event. That was okay—the more hysteria the better. We could mock trans paranoia as well as cis paranoia. When I arrived, every one of the dozens of T-shirts was gone within 24 hours. Not just transsexuals, but academics, and even straight male cross-dressers (and their wives!) who had been closeted all their lives wore the black, blood-dripping red T-shirts. . . *over their dresses*. . . out of the hotel, all over Atlanta.

This was entirely new. Clearly, something was shifting in trans political consciousness. Pride was challenging, if not entirely replacing, passing. Within two years activists had started Menace chapters in 39 cities. Shifting, indeed.

Around this time, the *Village Voice* published a piece about the 1994 murder of FTM Brandon Teena, rubbing salt in the wound by positioning Brandon as a "hot butch," a lesbian dreamboat, and referring to him as "Teena" and "she" and "her" throughout. The Menace promptly picketed both the *Voice* and the piece's author. Many other gay and lesbian media outlets ignored the murder entirely because he wasn't (wait for it. . .) gay or lesbian.

The murder trial of Brandon's assailants, John Lotter and Tom Nissen, was set to start in Falls City, Nebraska. We decided there needed to be a visible, public response from the community. With Boston's Nancy Nangeroni and Tony Baretto-Neto, a transgender deputy sheriff from Florida (who provided security), we announced a Memorial Vigil outside the courthouse on the first day of the trial. We didn't know what would happen or if anyone would show. Forty-two people showed up, including Leslie Feinberg (author of *Stone Butch Blues*) and a quiet unknown filmmaker named Kimberly Pierce working on a script tentatively titled *Boys Don't Cry*.

Apparently, transsexuals in black Menace T-shirts was not a common sight in Falls City, Nebraska. By noon, the local neo-Nazis showed up, spitting at us out of the windows of their trucks and trying to run us off the sidewalks. Tony had liaised with the Sheriff's office beforehand and when a group of the skinheads advanced toward us on foot, a line of Deputy Sheriffs was all that stood between us and serious violence. It was chilling, knowing we were depending on the same Sheriff's office that had outed Brandon and led to his death, perhaps even some of the same officers. So after that, Tony founded Transgender Officers Protect & Serve (TOPS).

Back in Michigan, plans were forming for what was inevitably becoming known as "Camp Trans." That year, 30 of us showed up, again camping out across from the main gate. This time, instead of a few workshops, we had scheduled three solid days of workshops, musical events, and teach-ins, with a special speak-out by Leslie Feinberg. We drew almost a thousand attendees over three days, many of whom went back in wearing Menace T-shirts; even supportive members of Security wore them openly. Then, on the last day, a group of leather-clad Lesbian Avengers asked why we didn't just come inside. Kidding, I asked them why they didn't just send an escort. To my shock, they agreed instantly. That evening, four dozen of them showed up and escorted Leslie Feinberg, myself, and 10 other members of

Camp Trans into the Festival and to a presentation attended by hundreds of waiting fans and supporters. The trans-discrimination policy, while still official policy, was for all intents broken.

Alas, the train of trans murders was not. Brandon's death was a wake-up call. Once we started paying attention to and tracking transgender murders, it was shocking how many there. Deborah Forte, Channelle Pickett, Christian Paige, James Percy Rivers, Tarayon Corbitt, Quincy Taylor, Tyra Hunter—and that was just 1995.

This was not as immediately obvious as it seems. The Internet was new, there was no Google (that was three years in the future), many people still didn't have or use e-mail. Finding out about new victims meant calling activists in different cities or looking for local news that began with the vague and stigmatizing words: "The body of a man wearing women's clothing. . ."

Nancy, Tony, and I decided that whenever a transgender person was murdered, we would fly in to coordinate another memorial vigil. Transgender people from the local community always came out to support the events, and it created fresh media coverage and attention that had been absent.

Yet it quickly became apparent that we couldn't expect to wage a struggle against violence and discrimination from a psychiatric category. We could portray ourselves in media as patients suffering from a medical disorder, or as an oppressed minority demanding their political and civil rights, but it was very difficult to do both simultaneously. The American Psychiatric Association was conveniently holding their annual conference in New York that year. With signboards declaring "Keep Your Diagnoses OFF our Bodies!" and accusing them of "GenderPatho-Philia" (defined "as an unnatural need or desire to pathologize any kind of gender that makes you feel uncomfortable"), the NYC Menace picketed the APA. Our list of demands was brief: depathologize transsexuality, just as long ago they had depathologized homosexuality.

It soon became apparent that you couldn't stop the war from a M*A*S*H tent. Transpeople kept dying with regularity—one every few months. We needed to be on the front lines, or at least for transgender issues to be on the national agenda. All our actions had been local—one event, one city. I asked New York's Lynn Walker how we could start a more national movement and she answered (quite brilliantly, in retrospect), "start doing things at the national level." Out of that comment came two developments. First was GenderPAC, the first national organization devoted to political advocacy for the right to *gender identity and expression*. It was formalized at a meeting of the community held outside Philadelphia in 1995. The second was National Gender Lobby Day, with activist Jane Fee and Phyllis Frye (now Texas's first transgender judge).

One hundred four transgender activists and their partners showed up. The *New York Times* led their national news with us. Strangely titled "Shunning *He* and *She* They Fight for Respect," it was accompanied by the picture of a bearded Jamison Green sitting quietly in a suit on the D.C. Metro (which no doubt confused many readers). It was our first real print coverage of transgender political activism. Today you can't pick up the *Times, Washington Post, Time, Slate*, or any other major outlet without reading trans news. But that was the first big piece.

Street activism was all about being insubordinate and loud; it was serious theater, to compel media attention. Capitol Hill was a different game. This was being *professionally trans*, sitting in a business suit in Congressional offices and patiently explaining our community's needs. It was new and intimidating but also tremendously validating and exhilarating. We were no longer Kate Bornstein's *gender outlaws*; we were citizens, voters, taxpayers. We were legitimate. In spite of that, I frankly expected us all to get arrested on Capitol Hill when we inevitably had to use the women's rooms, especially the many male cross-dressers who had (bravely) shown up. But that didn't happen. And that morning, as the sun rose over the Capitol dome, all of us stood together nervously before a bank of microphones and media cameras, taking turns answering questions before marching off to our first Congressional appointments. It was a sight: 100 transgender people walking off together to meet their elected representatives. A doorway had opened. A community was on the move. Something new had begun.

Press conference in Washington, D.C. (copyright Mariette Pathy Allen).

In addition to Camp Trans and Transexual Menace, a number of other trans institutions and groups were established in the early and mid-1990s. Dallas Denny created the American Educational Gender Information Service (AEGIS) in Decatur, Georgia, in 1990 to disseminate information about trans people, which included publishing *Chrysalis Quarterly* and *The Transgender Treatment Bulletin* (AEGIS, 1999). One of the largest annual trans events, the Southern Comfort conference, began in Atlanta in 1991, and the

Blake, in costume. Blake Alford is one of the main organizers of the Southern Comfort Conference (copyright Mariette Pathy Allen).

International Conference on Transgender Law and Employment Policy, a yearly meeting to discuss strategies for creating transgender-supportive laws, was convened by attorney Phyllis Frye in Houston from 1992 to 1997 (Frye, 2001; Stryker, 2008). Also in 1992, Bet Power founded the East Coast FTM Group, the first FTM-only support group in the Eastern United States, in Northampton, Massachusetts. Today, it is the second-oldest continuing trans male organization in the world, after FTM International (B. Power, personal communication, June 15, 2011). In 1995, Wilchins began the Gender Public Advocacy Coalition (GenderPAC), a national organization whose accomplishments included producing some of the first reports on hate crimes against gender nonconforming people and holding an annual National Gender Lobby Day to urge members of Congress to address gender-based violence and discrimination.

The 1990s also saw the highly visible, direct-action tactics pioneered by radical groups like ACT-UP (AIDS Coalition to Unleash Power) and Queer Nation begin to infuse the transgender movement. The first trans organization to reflect this new queer activism was Transgender Nation, a subgroup of San Francisco's Queer Nation chapter, which was formed in 1992 by Anne Ogborn to fight antitrans prejudice within the chapter and within society (Stryker, 2008). Soon Transgender Nation chapters were established in several other cities, most notably in Washington, D.C., where the group helped lead the response to the death of Tyra Hunter, a transsexual woman who passed away in 1995 after a D.C. firefighter and an emergency room physician denied her proper medical treatment because she was transgender. Although Transgender Nation was short lived, it inspired the creation of two other chapter-based trans activist groups, Transexual Menace and It's Time America!, and led the trans movement to become more visible and more confrontational.

The Internet and Academia

The most significant factor in the development of a national trans movement may have been the rise of the Internet in the mid-1990s. As sociologist Eve Shapiro (2010) states, the

Internet revolutionized the movement by "allow[ing] transgender people to connect with one another more easily, especially those who live in geographically isolated places," and by "giv[ing] individuals ways to experiment with defining their gender" (p. 132). Shapiro shows how online activism mobilized large numbers of people and generated substantial media attention in the debate over the American Psychiatric Association's pathologizing of trans people in the *DSM*.

A 2006 national transgender study by Genny Beemyn and Sue Rankin also documented the importance of the Internet, especially for the participants under 50 years old, for whom the Web was their primary method of meeting others like themselves and accessing resources. The older participants less commonly socialized virtually, but many first recognized themselves as transgender and realized that they were not alone through exploring the Web. The study respondents in their forties or older often described feeling isolated or being in denial about their identities for decades—until they discovered online resources. Tina, an interviewee who had cross-dressed for 40 years, captured the sentiments of many participants: "I learned from reading, but I was *liberated* by the Internet!" (Beemyn & Rankin, 2011, pp. 57–58).

Like the growth of the Internet, the development of queer studies in the early 1990s helped create a space for trans people. Texts by queer theorists, such as Gloria Anzaldúa (1987), Diana Fuss (1989), Judith Butler (1990), Eve Kosofsky Sedgwick (1990), and Teresa de Lauretis (1991), laid the groundwork for transgender scholarship and greatly influenced how gender and sexuality were considered in academia. Transgender studies emerged as its own discipline in the late 1990s and early 2000s through conferences, academic email lists, special journal issues, and articles and books by the first generation of scholars whose primary area of research was transgender people. These scholars included Susan Stryker (1994), C. Jacob Hale (1996), Aaron Devor (1997), Judith Halberstam (1998), Jay Prosser (1998), Jason Cromwell (1999), Viviane Namaste (2000), and Stephen Whittle (2002).

The Internet helped to give voice to trans people of color. Monica Roberts, a black trans woman from Houston who transitioned in 1994, started the award-winning blog TransGriot, which has become one of the most well-known hubs for news and information about trans people of color (Roberts, n.d.).

LGB *and* T

The work of trans activists, writers, and scholars led a growing number of lesbian, gay, and bisexual individuals and groups to become supportive of the rights of trans people and to consider them a part of what became known as the LGBTQ community. While many lesbian feminists in the 1970s and 1980s were influenced by *The Transsexual Empire*, many young lesbians in the mid and late 1990s—some of whom had yet to be born when Raymond's book was published—had their attitude toward trans people shaped by Leslie Feinberg's *Stone Butch Blues* and Kate Bornstein's *Gender Outlaw*. Feinberg's semiautobiographical 1993 novel tells the moving story of Jess Goldberg, an individual who journeys from being a butch lesbian in the years before the Stonewall Riots, to passing as a man in order to survive the economic recession of the 1970s, to living outside of a gender binary in the 1980s. Bornstein's 1994 work combines memoir, performance, and commentary to offer insights into how society constructs gender. Many young queer women activists, as well as transgender individuals, considered these books necessary reading, and many instructors in LGBTQ and sexuality studies assigned them in courses in the 1990s.

Another point of connection between trans individuals and non-trans young queer women that resulted in increasing support of trans people was involvement in drag king culture. Individuals assigned female at birth have long experimented with gender and sought to blur gender lines by performing in "men's" clothing. The contemporary phenomenon of drag king performances emerged in the mid-1980s in London and San Francisco, and within a decade, drag king shows and competitions involving both transgender men and cisgender lesbians were regularly held in major cities in the United States, Canada, Europe, and Australia (Ashburn, 2010). "In the last fifteen years, drag king culture has created a rope bridge of intellectual dialogue between the lesbian and transgender communities," states Sile Singleton, an African American transgender person who organizes and performs as Luster/Lustivious de la Virgion in drag king shows. "Because drag kinging by its very nature invites self-exploration into gender, it has nurtured a noticeably less negative backlash toward transgendered bodies" (S. Singleton, personal communication, July 18, 2011). The first international event, the International Drag King Extravaganza, took place in Columbus, Ohio, in 1999. It brought together many drag king performers and troupes, as well as individuals who studied, filmed, and photographed drag kings, for the first time (Troka, 2003).

MALE, FEMALE, OR OTHERWISE

Sile P. Singleton is a scholar, philanthropist, parent, writer, social activist, and queer(ed) performance artist.

I was born in 1961, and grew up during the cresting height of several social movements (i.e., the civil rights movement, the women's liberation movement, the Black Panthers, the hippie movement, and anti-Vietnam war protests). Sitting at the dinner table, my formative years were filled with the background noise of Walter Cronkite's reports on social unrest and the demands for equality sweeping, not just the good old US of A, but the world. In every newspaper, there were headlines about people demanding to be seen and treated fairly.

However, the reality of my situation was not about personal freedom. My staunchly democratic and liberal mother was terrified by my "mannishness." Her usual reprogramming tactics included several verbal assaults referencing my walk and stance (like a peacock), my sweating and smell (like a football player), and my voice and laughter (like Barry White). I actually only pretended to be bothered by her attempts to "save me." Secretly, I was relieved that I was recognizable, as male, because somewhere I have always known, regardless of an anatomically correct appendage (or, in my case, lack thereof) on the heavenly chart, I am male. Now I won't say it is as simple as that, because for all the soul brother energy I ooze, I am most comfortable when packing in hot pants and 10-inch-high, matching lime pleather go-go boots. I couldn't feel more he than when the bangs of my circa 1971 magenta "Geraldine Jones"-styled wig begin to fall into my 3-inch-long "Patti Labelle"-styled eyelashes, with my chest bound tight into a 36-inch wall of pectoral bulk. What is most amazing about all of this is that I had little conscious knowledge of these facts, prior to my 1992 involvement with a little historical Midwestern phenom known as the H.I.S. KINGS Show.

H.I.S. KINGS, a female-to-male, cross-dressing, gender-bending, lip-synching, entertainment troupe, was one of the country's first drag king ensembles when it formed in Columbus, Ohio, in 1992. The troupe was the accidental brainchild of a couple of bored women's studies graduate students and three in-your-face rad-ass lesbians named Helen, Ivett, and Sue (hence, "H.I.S."). We had no idea that the wardrobe we decided to explore would be so critical to whom we see ourselves as now in terms of sex, sexuality, and gender identity.

The first show opened at a dyke bar named Summit Station in Columbus on September 13, 1992. That night five scared "kids," including a birthday girl, a brand new DJ, and three budding drag kings, took the stage with no real idea of what they were doing. However, when the light bulb lit and the opportunity arrived to share all of me as the show's premiere "Hostess with the Mostest," Lustivious Dela Virgion, I did not hesitate. We practiced for seven to twenty hours a week. I was surrounded by people with similar chemistry. It was an amazing experience to be able to hang out with folks who were open to and accepted "beings" who exhibited multiple genders. At its height, the experience was exhilarating. At its close, exasperating. All in all, it was a fantastic "coming of gender" trip. And now, 20 years later, I know I experienced utopia, as we dared to celebrate masculinity: male, female, and otherwise.

The efforts of trans activists and allies resulted in many national, state, and local organizations in the United States that had focused primarily on the rights of lesbians, gay men, and bisexuals to begin to address gender identity issues. The National Gay and Lesbian Task Force added trans people to its mission statement in 1997, and PFLAG (Parents, Families, and Friends of Lesbians and Gays) did so the following year. Other national organizations were initially more hesitant to include trans people in their work. The largest lesbian and gay rights group, the Human Rights Campaign (HRC), amended its mission statement in 2001 and GLAAD (formerly the Gay and Lesbian Alliance Against Defamation) only did so in 2013. On the state and local level, most of the organizations established since the mid-1990s have included trans people in their names and missions. Cases in point are the professionally staffed offices and centers that have been founded at US and Canadian colleges and universities to further sexual and gender diversity. Among the 26 offices and centers created before 1995, all but three had names that indicated that their constituencies were "gay and lesbian" or "gay, lesbian, and bisexual" individuals. Today there are more than 150 such centers and offices, and all are transgender inclusive in both their names and mission statements (Beemyn, 2002; Consortium of Higher Education LGBT Resource Professionals, 2011).

However, the proliferation of LGBTQ organizations has not always resulted in greater attention to the needs of trans people; in some cases, the "T" seems to stand for "token," rather than "transgender." The most infamous example of transgender inclusion being little more than rhetoric involved the Human Rights Campaign. In 1994, the organization drafted and had allies in Congress introduce the Employment Non-Discrimination Act (ENDA), a bill to protect workers based on their sexual orientation. Transgender leaders were incensed by the exclusion of "gender identity" and lobbied Congress and the public for it to be added to the legislation—only to have HRC work to thwart their efforts. Following the failure of the bill by one vote in the Senate, HRC continued to insist on shutting out trans people when the legislation was reintroduced the next year, fearing that a more inclusive bill would lose votes. In response, trans activists and allies picketed the organization's fundraising events, until HRC agreed to support an amendment to add "gender identity" as a protected class (Califia, 1997). Neither the amendment nor the original bill was approved by Congress, and the legislation was stalled for the next decade.

In 2006, ENDA was revived by openly gay Representative Barney Frank. However, after deciding that the transgender-inclusive bill would not readily pass, Frank put forward the legislation without protection for transgender people. Despite HRC's promise that it would support only transgender-inclusive legislation, the organization endorsed Frank's bill. HRC's about-face showed that some within the mostly older, more conservative lesbian and gay establishment continued to see transgender people as dispensable. In support of a trans-inclusive ENDA, nearly 400 LGBTQ groups—virtually every major LGBTQ organization other than HRC—formed a coalition called United ENDA (unitedenda.org) to advocate for the restoration of gender identity protection. Although the effort failed to change the bill (which passed the House of Representatives in 2007 but died in the Senate), it represented an unprecedented level of support for transgender rights, and the coalition succeeded in having gender identity language included in ENDA thereafter, demonstrating that much had changed since the movement first abandoned trans people in the 1970s.

Patrick Califia took on trans history and politics in his 1997 book *Sex Changes: The Politics of Transgenderism* (Berkeley, CA: Cleis Press).

POSTHUMAN BODIES, POSTHUMAN SELVES

Laura A. Jacobs, LCSW, is a psychotherapist and activist in the New York City area specializing in LGBTQ and sexual minority populations, a member of the board of directors of the Callen-Lorde Community Health Center, and the author of the upcoming book: Many Paths, The Choice of Gender.

"We know what we are, but know not what we may become."—
Hamlet, Act 4, Scene 5

Human identity has been intertwined with technology since the harnessing of fire. Transportation has changed how we move, electricity has restructured our days, agriculture has altered our diets, education has enhanced our thinking, and medicine has prolonged our lives. For trans and gender nonconforming people this is even more direct; hormones and surgeries reshape our bodies while telecommunications and psychotherapy fashion our selves. And this relationship will propel us into our futures.

The historical narrative of trans identity—"born in the wrong body"—was one of brokenness and victimization. Whether the error was attributed to biology, genetics, or a deity, such language positioned us as powerless, laboring to rectify a mistake outside our control. It reinforced "male" and "female" binaries of appearance and behavior. Trans people were thought to have been accidentally placed in the wrong category.

Drawing on Karl Ulrichs's notion from 1860 of gay men having "a woman's soul trapped in a man's body," early trans people adopted these narratives, offering them to providers who established diagnoses and treatments; the stories were repeated to others, who reiterated them once more, reinforcing the narratives further. Transition was understood as a means to remedy dysfunction, but it restricted identities to only those that fit within binary norms. No others were acceptable.

But many now consider themselves androgynous, Two-Spirited, genderqueer, or otherwise nonconforming. Through modern, client-centered treatment models, people can design for themselves bodies that may or may not be easily labeled, in innovative attempts to craft identity and to destabilize entrenched cultural constructions.

We can reinterpret trans identity as a call to explore through gender. Instead of insisting we *must* be one because we *cannot* be the opposite, or that we must be any particular gender because it represents a "true self," we can engage in open-ended investigation, without judgment or predetermined conclusion, remaking our genders in empowered choice and artistic self-creation. We need no longer justify our changes by victimization or feel compelled to live by preexisting norms. We can approach gender as an arena to examine questions of meaning within the human experience.

As technology further impacts the body, gender will be less associated with binaries or even a spectrum. Prosthetics are already available for many applications, in forms both naturalistic and unorthodox, unions of mechanization and living tissue restoring or enhancing abilities. And in the future, surgery and genetic modification will liberate us from the "two arms-two legs-genitals-torso-head" outline we have at present.

Simultaneously, cybernetics and virtual reality will enable us to exist in online worlds via direct links to the brain. Initially these arenas will be simplistic representations of external reality, but these environments will not be bound by material laws and the embodiments we assume will rapidly be more abstract. We may exist as pure intelligences, occupying nonfigurative bodies as desired for any given moment. Today's chatrooms and cartoonish avatars will be passé.

Ultimately we will abandon traditional gender expression and gender dimorphism. Genitalia and self will no longer be based on "penis/vagina," "masculine/feminine" ideals, and transition will not be a shift from one gender to another but from the original human figure to something entirely novel. There will be countless human manifestations; people will be multilimbed with alternate sensory organs, have numerous and interchangeable genitalia, and occupy genders that are context dependent and ever varying. Our identities will be unlike anything currently conceivable and gender itself may become infinite. Hopefully, this progress will be available to all.

Those of us who perceive our transitions as imaginative constructions of body, identity, and relationship to society can be at the forefront of this revolution. We can be among the first to evolve toward the posthuman.

CONCLUSION

We know less than we would like to about transgender history in the United States, especially about nonbinary genders in many Native American cultures before and following European conquest, the lives of gender nonconforming individuals in other communities of color, and the experiences of all people who transgressed gender norms prior to the 20th century. We do know that gender nonconforming individuals have been documented in communities and cultures in what would become the United States since the 16th century. The efforts of transgender people over the 20th century and into the 21st to achieve visibility and justice are adding rich, vibrant chapters to this history.

ACKNOWLEDGMENTS

My heartfelt thanks to Kylar Broadus, Laura A. Jacobs, Joanne Meyerowitz, Elizabeth Reis, Eve Shapiro, Susan Stryker, Eli Vitulli, Riki Wilchins, and Cristan Williams for their comments on this chapter.

REFERENCES AND FURTHER READING

American Educational Gender Information Service. (1999). *What is AEGIS?* Retrieved June 2011, from http://www.gender.org/aegis

American Psychiatric Association. (1980). *Diagnostic and statistical manual of mental disorders* (3rd ed.). Washington, DC: American Psychiatric Publishing.

American Psychiatric Association. (1994). *Diagnostic and statistical manual of mental disorders* (4th ed.). Washington, DC: American Psychiatric Publishing.

American Psychiatric Association. (2013). *Diagnostic and statistical manual of mental disorders* (5th ed.). Washington, DC: American Psychiatric Publishing.

Anonymous. (1933, April 8). Police keep crowd of 200 from third sex. *The Afro-American*, p. 9.

Anzaldúa, G. (1987). *Borderlands/la frontera: The new mestiza*. San Francisco, CA: Spinsters/ Aunt Lute.

Ashburn, E. (2010). Drag shows: Drag kings and male impersonators. In C. J. Summers (Ed.), *glbtq: An encyclopedia of gay, lesbian, bisexual, transgender, and queer culture*. Retrieved July 2011, from http://www.glbtq.com/arts/drag_kings.html

Beemyn, B. (2002). The development and administration of campus LGBTQ centers and offices. In R. Sanlo, S. Rankin, & R. Schoenberg (Eds.), *Our place on campus: Lesbian, gay, bisexual, transgender services and programs in higher education* (pp. 25–32). Westport, CT: Greenwood Press.

Beemyn, B. (2003). The silence is broken: A history of the first lesbian, gay, and bisexual college student groups. *Journal of the History of Sexuality, 12*, 205–223.

Beemyn, G., & Rankin, S. (2011). *The lives of transgender people*. New York, NY: Columbia University Press.

Benjamin, H. (1966). *The transsexual phenomenon*. New York, NY: Julian Press.

Boag, P. (2011). *Re-dressing America's frontier past*. Berkeley: University of California Press.

Bolin, A. (1988). *In search of Eve: Transsexual rites of passage*. New York, NY: Bergin & Garvey.

Bornstein, K. (1994). *Gender outlaw: On men, women and the rest of us*. New York, NY: Routledge.

Boswell, H. (1998). The transgender paradigm shift toward free expression. In D. Denny (Ed.), *Current concepts in transgender identity* (pp. 55–61). New York, NY: Garland.

Boyd, N. A. (2003). *Wide open town: A history of queer San Francisco to 1965*. Berkeley: University of California Press.

Boyd, N. A. (2006). Bodies in motion: Lesbian and transsexual histories. In S. Stryker & S. Whittle (Eds.), *The transgender studies reader* (pp. 420–433). New York, NY: Routledge.

Boylan, J. F. (2003). *She's not there: A life in two genders*. New York, NY: Broadway Books.

Brown, K. (1995). "Changed...into the fashion of man": The politics of sexual difference in a seventeenth-century Anglo-American settlement. *Journal of the History of Sexuality, 6*(21), 171–193.

Bullough, B., & Bullough, V. L. (1998). Transsexualism: Historical perspectives, 1952 to present. In D. Denny (Ed.), *Current concepts in transgender identity* (pp. 15–34). New York, NY: Garland.

Butler, J. (1990). *Gender trouble: Feminism and the subversion of identity*. New York, NY: Routledge.

Califia, P. (1997). *Sex changes: The politics of transgenderism*. San Francisco, CA: Cleis Press.

Camp Trans. (2011). *Camp Trans history: Trans inclusion in womyn's music and MMWF*. Retrieved January 2014, from http://camp-trans.org/about/history/

Carter, D. (2004). *Stonewall: The riots that sparked the gay revolution*. New York, NY: St. Martin's Press.

Cauldwell, D. O. (2006). Psychopathia transsexualis. In S. Stryker & S. Whittle (Eds.), *The transgender studies reader* (pp. 40–44). New York, NY: Routledge.

Chauncey, G. (1994). *Gay New York: Gender, urban culture, and the making of the gay male world, 1890-1940*. New York, NY: HarperCollins.

Clendinen, D., & Nagourney, A. (1999). *Out for good: The struggle to build a gay rights movement in America*. New York, NY: Simon and Schuster.

Combahee River Collective. (1981). Combahee River Collective Statement. Retrived March 2014, from http://circuitous.org/scraps/combahee.html

Conn, C. (1974). *Canary: The story of a transsexual*. Los Angeles, CA: Nash.

Consortium of Higher Education LGBT Resource Professionals. (2011). *Directory*. Retrieved January 2014, from http://www.lgbtcampus.org/find-a-lgbt-center

Cromwell, J. (1999). *Transmen and FTMs: Identities, bodies, genders, and sexualities*. Urbana: University of Illinois Press.

de Lauretis, T. (Ed.). (1991). Queer theory: Lesbian and gay sexualities. *differences: A Journal of Feminist Cultural Studies, 3*(2), iii–xviii.

Denny, D. (1997). Transgender: Some historical, cross-cultural, and contemporary models and methods of coping and treatment. In B. Bullough, V. L. Bullough, & J. Elias (Eds.), *Gender blending* (pp. 33–47). Amherst, NY: Prometheus Books.

Denny, D. (2006). Transgender communities of the United States in the late twentieth century. In P. Currah, R. M. Juang, & S. P. Minter (Eds.), *Transgender rights* (pp. 171–191). Minneapolis: University of Minnesota Press.

Devor, A. H., & Matte, N. (2006). ONE Inc. and Reed Erickson: The uneasy collaboration of gay and trans activism, 1964-2003. In S. Stryker & S. Whittle (Eds.), *The transgender studies reader* (pp. 387–406). New York, NY: Routledge.

Devor, H. (1997). *FTM: Female-to-male transsexuals in society.* Bloomington: Indiana University Press.

Dillon, M. (1946). *Self: A study in ethics and endocrinology.* London, UK: William Heinemann Medical Books.

Drexel, A. (1997). Before Paris burned: Race, class, and male homosexuality on the Chicago South Side, 1935-1960. In B. Beemyn (Ed.), *Creating a place for ourselves: Lesbian, gay, and bisexual community histories* (pp. 119–144). New York, NY: Routledge.

Duberman, M. (1993). *Stonewall.* New York, NY: Dutton.

Ekins, R., & King, D. (2005). Virginia Prince: Transgender pioneer. In R. Ekins & D. King (Eds.), *Virginia Prince: Pioneer of transgendering* (pp. 5–15). Binghamton, NY: Haworth Medical Press.

Faderman, L., & Timmons, S. (2006). *Gay L.A.: A history of sexual outlaws, power politics, and lipstick lesbians.* New York, NY: Basic Books.

Fantasia Fair. (2011). *History of Fantasia Fair.* Retrieved June 2011, from http://fantasiafair.org/History_of_Fantasia_Fair.aspx

Feinberg, L. (1992). *Transgender liberation: A movement whose time has come.* New York, NY: World View Forum.

Feinberg, L. (1993). *Stone butch blues.* Ithaca, NY: Firebrand.

Feinberg, L. (1996). *Transgender warriors: Making history from Joan of Arc to RuPaul.* Boston, MA: Beacon Press.

Feinberg, L. (1998). *Trans liberation: Beyond pink or blue.* Boston, MA: Beacon Press.

Frye, P. (2001). *History of the International Conference on Transgender Law and Employment Policy, Inc.* Retrieved June 2011, from http://www.transgenderlegal.com/ictlephis1.htm

Fuss, D. (1989). *Essentially speaking: Feminism, nature and difference.* New York, NY: Routledge.

Gallo, M. M. (2006). *Different daughters: A history of the Daughters of Bilitis and the rise of the lesbian rights movement.* New York, NY: Carroll and Graf.

Garber, E. (1988). Gladys Bentley: The bulldagger who sang the blues. *OUT/LOOK, 1,* 52–61.

Grant, J. M., Mottet, L. A., & Tanis, J. (2010). *Injustice at every turn: A report of the national transgender discrimination survey—executive summary.* Retrieved July 2011, from http://transequality.org/PDFs/Executive_Summary.pdf

Green, J. (2004). *Becoming a visible man.* Nashville, TN: Vanderbilt University Press.

Halberstam, J. (1998). *Female masculinity.* Durham, NC: Duke University Press.

Hale, C. J. (1996). Are lesbians women? *Hypatia.* 11(2), 94–121.

Heidenreich, L. (1997). A historical perspective on Christine Jorgensen and the development of an identity. In B. Bullough, V. L. Bullough, & J. Elias (Eds.), *Gender blending* (pp. 267–276). Amherst, MA: Prometheus Books.

Hill, R. S. (2007). *As a man I exist; as a woman I live: Heterosexual transvestism and the contours of gender and sexuality in postwar America.* Unpublished Ph.D. dissertation, University of Michigan, Ann Arbor.

Hirschfeld, M. (1991). *Transvestites: The erotic drive to cross dress* (M. A. Lombardi-Nash, Trans.). Buffalo, NY: Prometheus Books. (original work published 1910)

Hoyer, N. (Ed.). (1953). *Man into woman: An authentic record of a change of sex.* New York, NY: Popular Library.

Hunt, N. (1978). *Mirror image.* New York, NY: Holt, Rinehart and Winston.

Imperial Sovereign Rose Court (2014). "Over 45 Years of Noble Deeds." Retrieved January 2014, from https://www.facebook.com/ImperialSovereignRoseCourt/info

Jay, K., & Young, A. (1972). Rapping with a street transvestite revolutionary: An interview with Marcia Johnson. In K. Jay & A. Young (Eds.), *Out of the closets: Voices of gay liberation* (pp. 112–120). New York, NY: Douglas/Links.

Jorgensen, C. (1967). *Christine Jorgensen: A personal autobiography.* New York, NY: Paul S. Eriksson.

Kailey, M. (2005). *Just add hormones: An insider's guide to the transsexual experience.* Boston, MA: Beacon Press.

Katz, J. N. (1976). *Gay American history: Lesbians and gay men in the U.S.A.* New York, NY: T.Y. Crowell.

Kennedy, P. (2007). *The first man-made man: The story of two sex changes, one love affair, and a twentieth-century medical revolution.* New York, NY: Bloomsbury.

Koyama, E. (2003). The transfeminist manifesto. In R. Dicker & A. Piepmeier (Eds.), *Catching a wave: Reclaiming feminism for the 21st century* (pp. 244–259). Boston, MA: Northeastern University Press.

Krieger, N. (2011). *Nina here nor there: My journey beyond gender.* Boston, MA: Beacon Press.

Ladin, J. (2012). *Through the door of life: A Jewish journey between genders.* Madison: University of Wisconsin Press.

Lang, S. (1998). *Men as women, women as men: Changing gender in Native American cultures.* Austin: University of Texas Press.

Lang, S. (1999). Lesbians, men-women and two-spirits: Homosexuality and gender in Native American cultures. In E. Blackwood & S. E. Wieringa (Eds.), *Female desires: Same-sex relations and transgender practices across cultures* (pp. 91–116). New York, NY: Columbia University Press.

Martino, M., with Harriett. (1977). *Emergence: A transsexual autobiography.* New York, NY: Crown.

Matthews, R. (1927, March 19). Men dance with male "flappers" at artists' ball. *The Baltimore Afro-American*, p. 20.

Meyerowitz, J. (2002). *How sex changed: A history of transsexuality in the United States.* Cambridge, MA: Harvard University Press.

Minter, S. P. (2006). Do transsexuals dream of gay rights? Getting real about transgender inclusion. In P. Currah, R. M. Juang, & S. P. Minter (Eds.), *Transgender rights* (pp. 141–170). Minneapolis: University of Minnesota Press.

Morris, J. (1974). *Conundrum: From James to Jan—an extraordinary personal narrative of transsexualism.* New York, NY: Harcourt Brace Jovanovich.

Namaste, V. K. (2000). *Invisible lives: The erasure of transsexual and transgendered people.* Chicago, IL: University of Chicago Press.

National Gay and Lesbian Task Force. (2011). *Jurisdictions with explicitly transgender-inclusive nondiscrimination laws.* Retrieved March 2012, from http://www.thetaskforce.org/downloads/reports/fact_sheets/all_jurisdictions_w_pop_10_11.pdf

National Gay and Lesbian Task Force. (2012). *State nondiscrimination laws in the U.S.* Retrieved March 2012, from http://www.thetaskforce.org/downloads/reports/issue_maps/non_discrimination_1_12.pdf

Prince, C. V. (1962). 166 men in dresses. *Sexology, 3*, 520–525.

Prince, V., & Bentler, P. M. (1972). Survey of 504 cases of transvestism. *Psychological Reports, 31*(3), 903–917.

Prosser, J. (1998). *Second skins: The body narratives of transsexuality.* New York, NY: Columbia University Press.

Raymond, J. G. (1994). *The transsexual empire: The making of the she-male.* New York, NY: Teachers College Press.

Reis, E. (2007). Hermaphrodites and "same-sex" sex in early America. In T. A. Foster (Ed.), *Long before Stonewall: Histories of same-sex sexuality in early America* (pp. 144–163). New York, NY: New York University Press.

Richards, R., with Ames, J. (1983). *Second serve: The Renée Richards story.* New York, NY: Stein and Day.

Roberts, M. (n.d.). TransGriot: News, opinions, commentary, history and a little creative writing from a proud African-American transwoman about the world around her. Retrieved October 2013, from: http://transgriot.blogspot.com

Roscoe, W. (1991). *The Zuni man-woman.* Albuquerque: University of New Mexico Press.

Roscoe, W. (1987). Bibliography of berdache and alternative gender roles among North American Indians. *Journal of Homosexuality, 14*(3/4), 81–171.

Roscoe, W. (1998). *Changing ones: Third and fourth genders in Native North America.* New York, NY: St. Martin's Press.

Rothblatt, M. (1994). *The apartheid of sex: A manifesto on the freedom of gender.* New York, NY: Crown.

Rubin, G. (2006). Of catamites and kings: Reflections on butch, gender, and boundaries. In S. Stryker & S. Whittle (Eds.), *The transgender studies reader* (pp. 471–481). New York, NY: Routledge.

Rubin, H. (2006). The logic of treatment. In S. Stryker & S. Whittle (Eds.), *The transgender studies reader* (pp. 482–498). New York: Routledge.

Rudacille, D. (2005). *The riddle of gender: Science, activism, and transgender rights.* New York, NY: Pantheon Books.

Rupp, L. J. (1999). *A desired past: A short history of same-sex love in America.* Chicago, IL: University of Chicago Press.

Saslow, J. M. (1999). *Pictures and passions: A history of homosexuality in the visual arts.* New York, NY: Viking Press.

Schacht, S. P. (2002). Four renditions of doing female drag: Feminine appearing conceptual variations of a masculine theme. In P. Gagné & R. Tewksbury (Eds.), *Gendered sexualities* (pp. 157–180). Amsterdam, The Netherlands: JAI Press.

Sedgwick, E. K. (1990). *Epistemology of the closet.* Berkeley: University of California Press.

Serlin, D. H. (1995). Christine Jorgensen and the Cold War closet. *Radical History Review, 62,* 136–165.

Shapiro, E. (2010). *Gender circuits: Bodies and identities in a technological age.* New York, NY: Routledge.

Sherman, G. (1964). *"I want to be a woman!" The autobiography of female impersonator Gayle Sherman.* Chicago, IL: Novel Books.

Silverman, V., & Stryker, S. (Directors). (2005). *Screaming queens: The riots at Compton's Cafeteria* [Motion picture]. United States: Frameline.

Star, H. J. (1963). *"I changed my sex!" The autobiography of stripper Hedy Jo Star, formerly Carl Hammonds.* Chicago, IL: Novel Books.

Stryker, S. (1994). My words to Victor Frankenstein above the village of Chamounix: Performing transgender rage. *GLQ: A Journal of Lesbian and Gay Studies, 1*(3), 237–254.

Stryker, S. (2000). Introduction. In C. Jorgensen, *Christine Jorgensen: A personal autobiography* (pp. v-xiii). San Francisco, CA: Cleis Press.

Stryker, S. (2008). *Transgender history.* Berkeley, CA: Seal Press.

Sullivan, L. (1990). *From female to male: The life of Jack Bee Garland.* Boston, MA: Alyson.

Trans Respect Versus Transphobia Worldwide. (2012). *The TDOR 2012 update reveals a shocking total of 265 cases of reported killings of trans people in the last 12 months.* Retrieved March 2013, from http://www.transrespect-transphobia.org/en_US/tvt-project/tmm-results/tdor2012.htm

Troka, D. J. (2003). *The history of the first International Drag King Extravaganza.* Retrieved January 2014, from http://idke.org/about-2/history/

von Krafft-Ebing, R. (2006). Selections from *Psychopathia Sexualis with Special Reference to Contrary Sexual Instinct: A Medico-Legal Study.* In S. Stryker & S. Whittle (Eds.), *The transgender studies reader* (pp. 21–27). New York, NY: Routledge.

Whittle, S. (2002). *Respect and equality: Transsexual and transgender rights.* London, UK: Cavendish.

Winters, K. (2010). *Ten reasons why the Transvestic Disorder diagnosis in the DSM-5 has got to go.* Retrieved March 2013, from http://gidreform.wordpress.com/2010/10

Winters, K. (2012). *An update on gender diagnoses, as the DSM-5 goes to press.* Retrieved March 2013, from http://gidreform.wordpress.com/2012/12/05/an-update-on-gender-diagnoses-as-the-dsm-5-goes-to-press

Zagria. (2009). Lee Brewster. *A gender variance who's who.* Retrieved March 2013, from http://zagria.blogspot.com/2009/10/lee-brewster-1943-2000-retailer.html

Zagria. (2010). Johns Hopkins—part 2: 1966-1979. *A gender variance who's who.* Retrieved June 2011, from http://zagria.blogspot.com/2010/07/johns-hopkins-part-2-1966-1979.html

Lazlo Ilya Pearlman, Jae DK Szeszycki-Truesdell, and Kestryl Cael Lowrey

23

WE ARE EVERYWHERE. TODAY, VISIBLE TRANS PRESENCE across the art forms is growing faster than we can write about it. As trans and gender nonconforming people, we are making our marks in alternative and mainstream arenas in every genre. From filmmaking to performance art, photography to circus, burlesque, cabaret, theater, music of all kinds, writing, publishing, the visual arts, and in every other art form, we are there, telling our stories, carrying out our politics through our work, presenting our ideas, expressing our aesthetics, our talents, our passions, and our emotive worlds to diverse audiences through and throughout the arts.

We are behind the camera, and in front of it. We make trans-based art and not. We are present in the mainstream, working within the commercial artistic industries, and also doing it ourselves and in communities; making, performing, presenting, producing, and distributing our work in person and via print, cinema, and the Internet.

We are **Schmekel: 100% Trans Jews**, the polka-punk, klezmer, Queer Jewcore band; we are **Vaginal Davis**, African American intersex performance artist; we are 64-year-old **Genesis Breyer P-Orridge**, the 1970s founder of industrial music groups Throbbing Gristle and Psychic TV; and 19-year-old disabled video maker and pop/dance music performer **Pia Martell**. We are theater makers **Scott Turner Schofield**, **Mx Justin Vivian Bond**, and **Ignacio Rivera**. We are filmmakers **Lana Wachowski**, the director of *Bound* and the *Matrix* films; **Jules Roskam**, the director of *Against a Trans Narrative*; **Alexander L. Lee**, the maker of the genderqueer zombie short *A Night in the Woods*; **Gwen Haworth**, writer/director of *She's a Boy I Knew;* and **Buck Angel,** with his *Sexing the* Transman series. We are the FTM and drag king burlesque troupe **CHUBB**. We are writers and performers, poets and photographers, acrobats and storytellers, sculptors and hip-hop artists, actors and drag performers, dancers, cartoonists, publishers, and more.

Our work is seen and heard all over the globe. There are hundreds of films and videos by and about trans and gender nonconforming people in LGBTQ and mainstream festivals around the world, and more every year. The numbers of trans-specific film and performance festivals are increasing rapidly. We are touring live with bands like *The Cliks*, or solo like **Black Cracker**, in groups and troops like the **Tranny Road Show**, and with **Fresh Meat Productions**. Our writing is published by trans and genderqueer presses like **Homofactus** and **Topside**. The 2000s and 2010s are a hugely prolific time for us. The leaps and bounds of visibility of—as well as the art and craft of—trans and gender nonconforming work is exciting beyond belief.

It has not always been this way.

Gender variance and sex change have long been a theme across the arts, as illustrated by examples such as the second-century B.C.E. sculpture *Sleeping Hermaphroditus*, the cross-dressed characters of Shakespeare's sixteenth-century English comedies, and Virginia Woolf's 1928 novel *Orlando*, in which the title character changes sex over the course of the book. However, most of these occurrences of gender traversal and intersection in art and performance are framed as cross-dressing or symbolism, and not as a reflection or representation of transgender experience or identity.

Of course, there have always been gender nonconforming artists, but it is only within the 20th century that we began being open about our genders and daring to make work that specifically and explicitly documents our experience. Many early artists, such as

Coccinelle (French for "ladybug") was a glamorous showgirl at Chez Madame Arthur in Paris in the 1950s. In her later years she was an activist for trans rights and acceptance.

Black Cracker, producer/MC/writer (photo by Cyrille Choupas).

Billy Tipton, were not willing or able to be out about their gender history and pursued arts careers that did not foreground their genders. By the mid-20th century, roles for trans artists were growing within queer culture, with substantial overlap in the drag scene. This was particularly true of trans women involved in performance. San Francisco's **Cockettes**, as well as trans actresses involved with Warhol's New York City Factory, both altered late mid-century performance opportunities for trans artists. **Christine Jorgensen**, widely publicized as the first US citizen to receive gender-affirming surgery, went on to have a moderately successful career as an entertainer and actress. Other prominent trans women entertainers in the mid-20th century included **Bambi** and **Coccinelle** in France, **Carlotta** in Australia, and **Nanjo Masami** in Japan.

With increased public voice, trans people have become more visible as creators of art, rather than just as the subjects, characters, or figures explored by cisgender artists. The 1990s, 2000s, and 2010s have brought an explosion of trans arts, leading to a kaleidoscope of styles, forms, and genres.

The moment when trans and gender nonconforming people first made an impact on the modern mainstream arts can arguably be linked to the commercial success of two fiction films: *The Crying Game* (1992) and *Boys Don't Cry* (1999).

The fact that these two films made an impression on the mainstream is perhaps reflective of the changes in visibility happening around that time in LGB communities ("T" was not commonly added until the late 1990s, and "QIA" and other letters not until the mid-2000s). San Francisco gay newspapers deemed 1992 "The Year of the Queer," and "queer" visibility had begun to include visible trans people making work. **Kate Bornstein**, perhaps the most iconic modern trans artist, first performed her play *Hidden: A Gender* in 1989 in San Francisco, and her revolutionary first book, *Gender Outlaw* came out in 1995. The first published visual works by and for trans and gender nonconforming artists and subjects were **Loren Cameron's** *Body Alchemy* in 1996 and **Del La Grace Volcano's** *Drag King Book* in 1999. Dozens of other examples begin to proliferate in these years. Since emerging into the mainstream in the 1990s, we have seen trans and gender nonconforming participation and visibility in the arts grow exponentially.

The history and trajectory of trans and gender-variant people in the arts could be the subject of a book in and of itself. It would be impossible to include all of the trans artists working today. A short chapter cannot be exhaustive or complete but can offer a taste of our trajectory across some of the art forms.

TRANS PEOPLE'S SELF-REPRESENTATIONS IN MEDIA AND POPULAR CULTURE

Phoenix Freeman

Trans people are often depicted inaccurately in the Western world's media and popular culture. Current mainstream depictions of trans people are more affirming and positive, but we are still often portrayed as freaks, dangerous, mentally disordered, and immoral.

Members of minority groups often depict their population positively. However, it is essential that we do not believe that our population is "all good." I have witnessed some trans people treat others outrageously—make statements that are pejorative toward Asian trans people, toward cross-dressers, toward stealth trans people, or toward non-operative transgender people.

Unfortunately, there are people in all populations who mistreat others. Acknowledging this can be particularly difficult for people from a stigmatized minority group. Individuals may want to believe that their own minority "community" is a safe haven from problems found in the wider world. People can fear that acknowledging prejudice, discrimination, and violence in their own minority population might lead to them being called a bigot, or it might lead to the wider community further disliking the minority. Some also find it difficult to comprehend that someone who has experienced discrimination or abuse might also be willing to mistreat someone else.

Trans activists will most likely need to continue challenging negative stereotypes about trans people for many years. However, we should still seek to acknowledge and counter abuse and discrimination taking place in our own population. Doing so means that we are responsible and caring people.

FILM AND VIDEO

Artists are storytellers. Each of us represents our journey in different ways, with different kinds of storytelling, whether literal, symbolic or abstract, factual or fictional, through different media. For nearly 100 years, film has captured us as a way to tell stories. Early in our lives we begin our relationships with the big and small screens, being told stories, and most of us never stop watching.

As film and video artists, we know what it is to be stirred by these images, and we want to stir other people with them. We also know that our stories have been missing from the mainstream. However, until recently there were many barriers, including financial ones, to documenting our life stories with film.

Increasingly, with the advent of better and cheaper technologies, more practice, and more presentation opportunities, we can address these gaps and tell our own stories cinematically, whether via documentary or narrative fiction techniques.

Over the last 20 years, thousands of short and feature-length films and videos about trans and gender nonconforming lives, or that include or feature trans or gender nonconforming characters, have been produced, by all kinds of filmmakers of every gender, background, and experience—trans, gender nonconforming, and cisgender.

Documentary Film

Documentary filmmaking gives us the opportunity to present our perspectives on the facts of our lives. Because there are always many viewpoints and angles to any story, we can never say documentaries impart any fixed truth.

Trans and gender nonconforming documentaries are an important vehicle for presenting the voices and experiences of their subjects and their makers. As a medium for this representation, film is highly effective at reaching broad audiences. Films and videos can be seen in multiple venues at once and survive over time, leaving themselves as archives for future viewers. Furthermore, they can travel nearly anywhere at the speed of an Internet or cable connection.

Many of us feel that we have not yet found a documentary that portrays our experience.

> *"I have never seen a documentary that I really enjoyed. I can't quite put my finger on what they all seem to be missing. They each might have some good little point but for the most part they all seem to miss the mark for me. It might be that I have not found one that has been even remotely similar to me and my situation."*

For many of us, trans documentaries seem to be focused only on negative topics.

> *"I really liked TransGeneration, but that was the only positive documentary or film that I've seen. The others—Boys Don't Cry, Solider's Girl, etc.—are all depressing. Well-made, yes, but depressing and I don't think it's appropriate to say I ENJOYED them. Appreciated, yes."*

There are an increasing number of documentaries, and many filmmakers are trying to tell new, positive stories. There have been so many documentaries over the years that it is impossible to mention all of their significance in broader culture. Keep looking for documentaries that tell the stories you want to hear—there are many more than we could possibly include.

Two of the earliest documentaries about trans individuals focused on telling positive, uplifting stories about the triumph of becoming ourselves. Modern trans arts icon **Kate Bornstein** was the subject of a 1994 documentary, *Adventures in the Gender Trade*, by Susan Marenco and Jay Mason. In the film, intercut with shots of her performing the play *Hidden: A Gender*, Kate talks about her misfit childhood, her adult history, and her gender transition. In 1996, mainstream documentarian Bestor Cram made the pioneering *You Don't Know Dick: Courageous Hearts of Transsexual Men*. For the first time, trans men were filmed talking about their experiences, their early gender dysphoria, their transitions, and the positive and liberating effects on their lives of becoming themselves. The documentary won several awards and was shown on public television stations (PBS) in the United States, as well as on The Sundance Channel and Channel 4 in England.

Documentaries also help call attention to the violence and discrimination that many of us have faced. The story of the rape and murder of 21-year-old trans man Brandon Teena in 1993 in Humboldt, Nebraska, was first made as a documentary film in 1998 by cisgender lesbian filmmakers Susan Muska and Gréta Olafsdóttir. *The Brandon Teena Story*—released the year before its fictional counterpoint, *Boys Don't Cry*—played in LGBTQ film festivals all over North America, won multiple awards from those festivals, and received some mainstream attention, including an overall positive and basically understanding review by film critic Roger Ebert. The film includes a harrowing depiction of Brandon's experience of rape at the hands of locals upon realizing Brandon had been assigned female at birth, as well as Brandon's horrific treatment by the Humboldt sheriff as he interviewed Brandon about the rape, spouted transphobia, and refused to arrest Brandon's rapists, who finally murdered Brandon and two companions on December 31, 1993.

Highlighting a less visible form of violence, the 2001 documentary *Southern Comfort* told the story of trans man Robert Eads, living in the Black Hills of Georgia. Eads was diagnosed with ovarian cancer in 1996 and was refused treatment by more than two dozen clinics because he was trans. More than a year elapsed between the time of his diagnosis and finding a medical center that would treat him. *Southern Comfort* documents the last year of his life, after his cancer metastasized and he was not expected to survive. The movie does have its heartwarming and positive moments—Eads falls in love with a trans woman named Lola, reunites with his parents, and manages to attain his goal of attending the trans and gender nonconforming conference, Southern Comfort, one more time. Eads died in 1999 before the film was released.

For a period of time, it seemed to many of us that all we saw were tragic stories of discrimination and violence against trans and gender nonconforming people, but the same year as *Southern Comfort*, two more positive documentaries about genderqueer performance were released: *The Cockettes* and *Venus Boyz*. The first of these documented the history of San Francisco's famous and fabulous gender-bending performance troupe, **The Cockettes**, in the hippy heyday of the 1970s. The second, *Venus Boyz,* released 2 years after the publication of **Del LaGrace Volcano's** *The Drag King Book*, was the first feature film on Drag King performers and performance spaces in New York, London, and Zurich. Made by German cisgender filmmaker Gabriel Bauer, the film features cisgender drag king performers like Mo B. Dick (Mo Fischer), Dred (Mildred Gerestant), and Diane Torr, as well as pioneering trans and gender nonconforming identified artists Del LaGrace Volcano, **Bridge Markland**, and **Hans Scheirl**, with commentary by gender academic **Jack Halberstam**.

This visibility of trans and gender nonconforming documentaries by cisgender artists soon encouraged us to take the wheel and start making our own stories, addressing issues and politics that impacted our lives. In 2004, transgender artist and filmmaker **Tara Mateik** teamed up with the Sylvia Rivera Law project to create the video *Toilet Training*. The film focuses on the all-too-prevalent discrimination against gender nonconformity in public restrooms in schools, at work, and in the rest of the municipal world. Trans and gender nonconforming people share their experiences of verbal and physical harassment and violence often perpetrated both by transphobic users of the restrooms and by authorities such as management and police. Finishing with illustrations of possible policy change, *Toilet Training* is an educational video that, since its release, has been acquired by many libraries throughout the United States. The video is used to raise awareness, for diversity training purposes, and to fight discrimination against gender nonconforming people.

In 2006, **Gwen Haworth** released *She's a Boy I Knew*. For the first time, the trans subject of a film held her own camera. Gwen tells the story of her transition primarily through interviews with her family and friends, her parents and her lovers, asking them to recall her through the process. The film was her thesis project for her master's degree in filmmaking. Told with abundant gentle humor and compassion for the physical and emotional experience of everyone involved in her transition process (including herself), Haworth documents not only her own journey of becoming but the tandem journey of those important to her.

Many more of us have started to pick up the camera to ensure that our stories and our communities gain visibility and voice, and are empowered and celebrated. In response to the fact that most portrayals of trans and gender nonconforming people available to us have been focused on white subjects, 2008 saw the release of *Still Black: A Portrait of Black Trans Men*, written and directed by **Kortney Ryan Ziegler** and produced by Awilda Rodriguez Lora. *Still Black*, the first documentary to focus on African American trans men, gave us a glimpse of the lives and experiences of Kylar Broadus, Ethan Young, Jay Welch, Louis Mitchell, Nicholas Rashad, and Carl Madgett.

Other communities have stepped up to tell the story of their trans and gender nonconforming members as well. In 2008, Eliza Greenwood, a lesbian hearing sibling of a Deaf American, and Sel Staley, a Deaf American, released the film *Austin Unbound*, which explores the experiences of a Deaf trans man. *Austin Unbound* has been shown at LGBTQ, trans, and Deaf and disability film festivals all over the world.

Along with our breadth of representation, our visibility is growing exponentially. *Becoming Chaz*, in 2011, documented Chaz Bono's (child of Cher and Sonny Bono) gender transition. The film debuted at the Sundance Film Festival and was immediately picked up and broadcast by Oprah Winfrey's Network, in large part because of Chaz's famous parents and his own political and celebrity status. Chaz is a very visible trans

Sam Feder and Julie Hollar released the documentary *Boy I Am* in 2006. The film addressed the tensions in our communities as emerging trans identities changed the discussions around lesbian identities, feminism, and sexuality. In an interview for the public access television and online program *Gay USA* in 2006, Feder tells the interviewers that the choice to make the movie came from Sam's own questions about FTM trans-identified people, their acceptance (or lack thereof) in lesbian communities, and their reasons for "leaving" the lesbian identity. Through the stories of three young trans men in New York City, *Boy I Am* explores these questions and makes room for conversations between the lesbian communities and transmasculine communities.

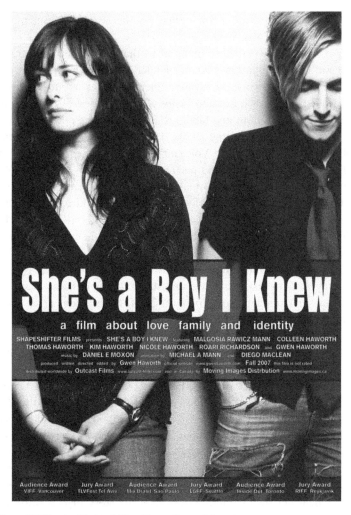

She's a Boy I Knew (Tif Flowers/Outcast Films/Gwen Haworth).

Still Black (Kortney Ryan Ziegler).

CLAIMING OUR POWER

man who has appeared on countless television talk shows and was a 2011 contestant on *Dancing With the Stars.*

As we move into the future, we are also starting to see documentaries where the trans or gender nonconforming identity of the subject is not the specific motor for the film. *The Ballad of Genesis and Lady Jaye* (2011) was directed by cisgender French filmmaker Marie Losier. It is the story of how **Genesis Breyer P-Orridge**, the 64-year-old founder of industrial music groups *Throbbing Gristle* and *Psychic TV,* and **Lady Jaye**, his partner of 15 years, bond with each other by creating their relationship as a third merged entity called a "Pandrogyne." Genesis moved physically toward his partner, undergoing a series of plastic surgeries. The film is a moving love story and also gives an illustration of a different experience of gender nonconformity—one that does not require the subject to align themselves with the narrative of being "in the wrong body" in order to choose to permanently modify their body's gender markers.

Today there are hundreds of short documentaries about trans experiences made by full-time filmmakers or by amateurs with a camera phone. One example is the explosion of transition videos appearing on Web sites like YouTube. We will continue to bring our stories to the screen into the future.

Trans Film Festivals include Gender Reel, Translations, TransScreen, and the Los Angeles, Netherlands, and San Francisco Transgender Film Festivals.

MEDIA SPOTLIGHT: OUR FAVORITE FILMS

Dallas Denny and Jamison Green

Dallas

In Billy Wilder's 1959 hit movie *Some Like It Hot,* down-and-out jazz musicians Joe (Tony Curtis, sax) and Jerry (Jack Lemmon, upright bass) witness the Saint Valentine's Day massacre and are spotted by gangster Spats Columbo (George Raft). Running for their lives, they disguise themselves as women and take jobs in an all-female band that is on its way to Miami. They are smitten by Sugar Kane (Marilyn Monroe), and, as Daphne (Lemmon) and Josephine (Curtis), they vie for her attention. On the train, Kane tells them she has sworn off male saxophone players and hopes to snare a millionaire in Miami.

In Miami, Joe disguises himself as a nerdy male millionaire; predictably, Kane pursues him. Meanwhile, Daphne is pursued by an actual millionaire, Osgood Fielding III (Joe E. Brown). At the film's conclusion Joe convinces Daphne she can't marry Osgood. Daphne makes up reasons (she smokes, she's infertile) to break up the marriage, but Osgood waves each one off. Finally, Daphne yanks off her wig and yells, "I'm a man!" Amazingly, Osgood responds, "Well, nobody's perfect."

I chose this film over my other faves (John Dexter's 1972 *I Want What I Want,* Alain Berliner's 1997 *Ma vie en Rose,* and Neil Jordan's 1992 *The Crying Game*) because it was absolutely remarkable for its time and because it has been seen by millions and millions of people all over the world. While Curtis hates his role as a woman, Lemmon is immersed, forgetting at times that he is, in fact, a man. Director Billy Wilder is at ease with the material and plays on homosexual tensions (Josephine kissing Kane, Osgood's love for Daphne) with sublime humor.

Jamison

My favorite film is *Little Big Man* (1970). Presented as a "Western" genre film (and even as "History," though it's very much fictionalized), this film was an incredible vehicle to display the acting talents of still-young Dustin Hoffman (then 33). It actually has a lot of gender exploration in it, from masculine women to feminine men—in particular, the character of Little Horse, a Cheyenne *heemaneh* (what might today be called a "Two-Spirit"), who provides a window into cultural acceptance of gender variance that many filmgoers in 1970 found surprising and challenging. Perhaps this script helped prepare Hoffman to take on his "cross-living" role in *Tootsie* (1982), in which Michael Dorsey's experience living as a woman, Dorothy Michaels, actually teaches Dorsey something about being a better man. It's not quite as clichéd as it sounds. It isn't really about a trans person, because Dorsey takes on the role of Dorothy as a challenge, and the cross-gender humor draws more from homophobia than transphobia, but underneath the slapstick elements that so often accompany gender crossing, there is hope for gender analysis. Even though that analysis is generally rooted more firmly in feminism than trans awareness, there's room for trans perspectives.

Fiction Films

Trans and gender nonconforming characters have always been a subject for cinematic narrative storytelling. In the mainstream we have historically shared the same fate as lesbian and gay characters, used primarily for comedy, horror, or exploitation. Early examples include films like *Glen or Glenda* (1953) and *Myra Breckenridge* (1970). *The Crying Game* (1992) similarly sensationalized transgender people, as a fiction thriller made famous by the surprise revelation that the main character's love interest was a trans woman who had not had bottom surgery.

In 1997, the highly emotional Belgian film *Ma Vie En Rose (My Life in Pink)* was the first feature film by cisgender director Alain Berliner. It tells the story of a 7-year-old gender nonconforming child, assigned male but who feels herself to be a girl. It was the first time we saw a fiction film dealing with a trans child, and the first fiction film to be completely on the side of the trans character.

Boys Don't Cry, a fictionalized portrayal of Brandon Teena's life and death, was released 1999, and it catapulted actress Hillary Swank, who portrayed Brandon, to fame when she won an Oscar for Best Actress. The film raised public awareness of hate crimes and gave the mainstream population the ability to conceptualize a trans male identity. Prior to that, for many in the mainstream, the term "transsexual" applied only to trans women.

There remains far less fiction film made by trans and gender nonconforming filmmakers than documentary. In 2001, the first narrative feature film made both by and about gender nonconforming people was released, and rather than being full of gender tragedy, it was a feel-good buddy picture! Steakhaus Productions and gender nonconforming writer/directors **Silas Howard** and **Harry Dodge** premiered *By Hook or By Crook* in the mainstream Sundance Film Festival that year.

In the mid-2000s, more cisgender narrative filmmakers found themselves drawn to our trans and gender nonconforming "true" stories. Narrative films both about us and featuring us—that were finally *not* using us just for comedy or exploitation—began to appear on the festival circuits.

In 2004, *Beautiful Boxer* was released. Directed by Ekachai Uekrongtham, it is based on the life and public gender transition of Muaythai boxer Parinya Charoenphol, now Nong Thoom, in Thailand. After a short time as a Buddhist monk, Nong Thoom became a kickboxing champion, discovering her transgender identity over the same period. Surprisingly, while one would expect the film to concentrate on the difficulties of coming out as a trans woman in a macho fighting world, the film is far more celebratory than it is tragic.

Also in 2004, France released the narrative film *Wild Side*, directed by cisgender filmmaker Sébastien Lifshitz, in which trans actress **Stéphanie Michelini** portrays the trans character Stéphanie, a sex worker who has to leave Paris and travel to a small town to care for her sick mother. She brings along her two flat mates, an Algerian hustler and an AWOL Russian soldier. The two fall in love with her and she negotiates a relationship with them both. The film also features gender nonconforming singer/songwriter **Antony Hegarty** of *Antony and the Johnsons*.

The number of trans and gender nonconforming narrative filmmakers is growing. These filmmakers, like **Gwen Haworth**, often produced their first major works as the culminations of their film school studies. In 2008, trans filmmaker **Elliot Montague** released the 50-minute narrative film *Mainstay*. Montague's film tells the story of Fischer, a trans man who returns home to Maine after hearing that an ex-lover has died.

In 2010, queer cisgender filmmaker Jake Yuzna released *OPEN*, a film that fictionalized characters from the earlier documentary, *The Ballad of Genesis and Lady Jaye*, and used them to tell another story. The plot centers on the young intersex character Cynthia, who meets Gen and Jay, a couple who are in the process of becoming a "pandrogyne," by surgically altering their faces to resemble the other and creating themselves as a merged third identity. Taken by the couple, Cynthia leaves her comfortable normative and suburban life to join them on an American road trip designed to embrace the destruction of her normativity.

2011 was the debut of *Tomboy*, a French update on *Ma Vie En Rose*, directed by cisgender filmmaker Celine Sciamma. Ten-year-old tomboy Laure moves to a new neighborhood where a local girl thinks Laure is a boy. Laure decides to become "Michael" and spends the summer presenting as male, even creating a phallus out of clay to insert into a swimsuit. Laure's younger sister finds out that Laure has been playing "Michael," but she keeps the secret from their parents and the other children.

In 2002, encouraged by the filmmaking of *By Hook or By Crook*, **Lazlo Ilya Pearlman** released his short film, *Unhung Heroes,* a short comic fiction about five trans guys who, after finding an Internet article announcing the first penis transplants are about to be performed, imagine a scheme to come up with over a million dollars in surgery money.

In *Romeos* (2011), written and directed by Sabine Bernardi, Lukas, a young trans man, meets and falls for a cisgender Fabio. The attraction is mutual but Lukas is still legally female, and the film turns on whether Lukas should tell Fabio he is transgender.

CLAIMING OUR POWER

It's relevant, cupcake.

Still from *Murder in Passing* (produced by John Greyson and Chase Joynt), a whodunit designed for Toronto's commuters, with episodes that appeared on subway platforms daily from January to March 2013.

While the majority of narrative films with trans and gender nonconforming protagonists have so far focused on our journeys of discovery, in large part because these journeys provide very strong and obvious character and story arcs that we all understand, we are slowly beginning to see more films in which being trans is simply one element of a character and the plot, rather than the defining one. Trans filmmaker **Rhys Ernst** premiered his short *The Secret of "The Thing"* at Sundance in 2012. The film follows a couple (a cisgender woman and a transgender man) traveling toward a mysterious roadside attraction called "The Thing." Rhys endeavored to write as if there were already many narrative trans films in the world, to skip ahead of the need to tell the story of becoming, and instead to tell a story in which transness is simply one of many story and character elements.

We are also starting to see established mainstream filmmakers stepping out from behind their cameras to reveal themselves as trans and gender nonconforming. **Lana Wachowski**, formerly known as half of the filmmaking team The Wachowski Brothers, is a Hollywood filmmaker best known for codirecting the lesbian thriller *Bound*, the *Matrix* movies, *V for Vendetta*, and *Cloud Atlas*.

Within the genres of both documentary and narrative filmmaking, we have seen growth in leaps and bounds. Artists have emerged and are emerging to tell our stories from within and without our community with more and more skill, nuance, balance, and depth. Established mainstream filmmakers are becoming visible as members of our community.

BALL CULTURE

Elizabeth Glaeser introduces the Ballroom scene.

For most, the history of Ball culture begins with the documentary *Paris Is Burning* filmed in the early 1990s or Madonna's hit "Vogue" from 1990. Ball culture in the 1980s and 1990s is often seen as a transient aspect of subculture on the brink of visibility. However, voguing dates back to the 19th century and is now seen as a revitalization by the "children" of the original culture—with many significant changes (Trebay, 2000). From the beginning, "ball culture was a space where gender, class, sexuality, and race coalesced and collided for one moment in time" as evidenced by the constant, yet underground history of the Ball culture and the burlesque nature of the performance (Monforte, 2010, p. 1).

The role-playing extravaganzas can be traced back to 1869 with female impersonation at the Hamilton Lodge Ball in Harlem (Chauncy quoted in Monforte, 2010, p. 28). According to a recent essay by Ivan Monforte, these first extravaganzas were similar to beauty pageants for male and female impersonators (2010). In the 1920s Harlem Cabaret scene, it was common for gay men who were female impersonators to entertain guests of the various social clubs in elaborate stage performances. These men used the ball space to feel at ease and express themselves (Phillips, Peterson, Binson, Hidalgo, & Magnus, 2011). In the early 1930s these events, referred to as "balls" or "faggot balls," took place at the Manhattan Casino, sponsored by Old Fellows, and attracted 200 black participants and 2,000–8,000 spectators of all races and sexual orientations (Monforte, 2010; Phillips et al., 2011).

Although tolerated in the larger community of New York, the disparity between spectator and participant created a level of disdain in the community (Monforte, 2010). Press enjoyed the events, but religious leaders and lawmakers enforcing prohibition eventually shut them down due to concerns about immorality. In other metropolitan areas like Chicago, according to *Wind City Times*, drag balls dated back to the turn of the century and were started as a way of extracting money from brothel owners by aldermen in their districts (quoted in Phillips et al., 2011, p. 4).

The structure of Ball culture as it is largely understood today came about in the 1970s. According to Frank Diamond's *The Queen*, ball participants' organization into "houses" came after the legend LeBeija lost to a white woman in a beauty pageant (Montforte, 2010, p. 28). The apparent racism in the judges' decision led supporters of LeBeija to create a "family-like" structure around her. These supporters then decided to create their own balls to combat the perceived racism of the "mainstream" pageant culture (Montforte, 2010).

A "house" became a group of people with a family structure, including a house mother and/or father and a collective of other members called the children (Philips et al., 2011, p. 517). Mothers and fathers were appointed by those who won awards or had standing in the community. Most were founding members of the houses in the early years. The trend gained popularity as the new houses hosted balls and other prominent members of the scene formed their own houses and family structures. The formation of groups also paralleled the increase in membership of gangs in New York in tandem with the roaring civil rights movement (Lawrence, 2012, p. 4). The sense of belonging and group identity within the houses was especially important for the younger members who often needed mentors like mothers and fathers when their own parents were intolerant of their lives as LGBTQ people (Lawrence, 2012).

Most houses were named for fashion houses like those in Paris and, as their popularity increased, so did the diversity of the ball performances. Many houses were known for a particular type of act or extreme dancing. In the early 1980s, as risk of HIV, substance abuse, poverty, and other hardships struck the community in inordinate proportions, houses sprung up in response (Montforte, 2010; Phillips et al., 2011).

The onset of HIV infection in the community created a paradigm shift in how the balls were conceptualized by those inside and outside of the community (Trumay, 2000). In 1989, Gay Men's Health Crisis (GMHC) started its own house and hosted balls in the name of educating and propagating safer sex practices. GMHC's House of Latex was named an official house in 1993. This source of community outreach (testing, referrals, support groups) encouraged and supported mentoring family members (mothers and fathers) in showcasing safe sex as well as substance reduction messages. With these messages integrated into the Ball culture, younger members came into the scene taking into account precautions, and balls had larger reign beyond escaping racism and heteronormative ideals. GMHC's annual ball attracts mainstream celebrities and media attention as well as acting as an "Academy Award" like venture for ball culture (Montforte, 2010; Trebay, 2000).

Balls today bear little resemblance to early pageantry and stage performances. Despite the performance differences between the balls of the past and today, aspects of parody and impersonation have remained static throughout the history of Ball culture. Balls are held a few times each month and contestants representing houses compete in different categories that have changed over the years, but they include dancing and impersonation. Judges, who are generally well-respected legends or other past contestants, give each contestant a number on a scale and decide on the winner in each category. DJs and MCs are responsible for crowd hype and keeping the show moving on schedule (Montforte, 2010; Phillips et al., 2011).

Ball competitions and surrounding houses create a safe, accepting space for participants to be part of a team and to belong somewhere (Trebay, 2000). The new "younger" Kiki culture grew out of the necessity to unite LGBTQ youth off the streets and out of survival sex work (Phillips et al., 2011). See Chapter 20 for more information about the Kiki Ball Scene. The new family system is supportive and comprehensive for youth who may find themselves otherwise homeless or without the support of loved ones. For the younger generations and those who have become legends and role models, performing continues to be the thread through this community, transcendent of race, gender, and sexuality.

REFERENCES

Lawrence, T. (2012). "'Listen, and you will hear all the houses that walked there before': A history of drag balls, houses and the culture of voguing." In Soul Jazz Records (Eds.), *Voguing and the House Ballroom Scene*. (Introduction). London: Soul Jazz Records.

Monforte, I. (2010). "House and Ball Culture Goes Wide." *The Gay and Lesbian Review Worldwide*, *17*(5), 28–30.

Phillips, G., Peterson, J., Binson, D., Hidalgo, D., & Magnus, M. (2011). House/ball culture and adolescent African American transgender persons and men who have sex with men: A synthesis of literature. *AIDS Care: Psychological and Social-medical Aspects of AIDS/HIV*, *23*(4), 515–520.

Trebay, G, (2000, January 11). "Legends of the Ball." *Village Voice*. Retrieved from http://www.villagevoice.com/2000-01-11/news/legends-of-the-ball/

MODELING

Trans and gender nonconforming models have been in demand and causing controversy since the 1960s. Fashion designers have often been drawn to our looks, but until recently, most models were not out as trans in their careers, and it was the discovery of their trans history that created the controversy. For some, that was the end of their careers, and for others, just the beginning.

English model **April Ashley** was among the earliest trans women to have a modeling career. In the early 1960s she appeared in fashion magazines like *Vogue* and in the Bing Crosby and Bob Hope film *The Road to Hong Kong*. Ms. Ashley was the first British citizen to have sex reassignment surgery. She is still a passionate trans rights advocate and, in December 2012, was made Member of the British Order (MBE), an honorific title given to those who are seen to have performed an outstanding service to Britain.

In 1971, **Tracy Africa Norman** started her modeling career in New York City, learning her first moves through the Ballroom scene, an urban LGBTQ performance community. Early on, she posed as a student and talked her way into fashion shows so she could study the models' techniques, then bluffed her way into her first interview after spotting and following a group of models she recognized, adding herself to the end of their group. She soon found herself standing in front of one of the top fashion photographers of the time, Irving Penn, who 2 days later offered her a shoot for Italian *Vogue*. The layout was successful, and Norman quickly gained popularity. She was outed as trans in the middle of a shoot for *Essence*, and the outing ended her New York modeling career. She and a

Today, top trans models are working throughout the fashion world—in print, on the runway, and in television and video. Big names include **Lea T, Isis King, Claudia Charriez, Sirapassorn Atthayakorn, Valentijn de Hingh, Jenny Hiloudaki**, and **Jenna Talackova**.

Up-and-coming gender non-conforming models include **Andrej Pajeic** of Serbia, **Stav Strashko** of Israel, **Casey Legler** (the first woman ever to be booked officially as a male model), Omahyra Mota (a cis female model who walks the runway in men's and women's fashion), and androgynous performance artist **boychild**.

Billy Tipton was a white American jazz pianist and saxophone player who had a successful minor career as a musician, bandleader, and later as a talent agent. He began living full time as male in 1940 and was only "revealed" as having been assigned female when he died in 1989.

Willmer "Little Axe" Broadnax, an African American gospel singer, was similarly successful in the same years. Broadnax was short statured and sang high tenor with a number of gospel groups. He was killed by his lover in 1992, and his autopsy subsequently revealed that he had been assigned female.

Bulent Ersoy, a Turkish trans woman, performed classical Turkish music in the 1970s, when she was regarded as an androgynous gay male artist. She transitioned in 1981, one year after a coup returned Turkey to a more oppressive state, and her performances were banned. She relocated to Germany, where she continued to act in Turkish films produced there. In 1988, after releasing an album of patriotic music, she was able to return to Turkey.

friend spent their last money on one-way tickets to Paris, where Norman became a showroom model for Balenciaga. Eventually she moved home to New Jersey and reconnected to the Ballroom scene, ultimately becoming the mother of the House of Africa. She was inducted into the Ballroom Hall of Fame in 2001.

Modeling in her native South Africa and Paris in the late 1970s, **Lauren Foster** got her biggest break in 1980 with a six-page editorial shoot for *Vogue Mexico*. When outed in a tabloid newspaper, transphobic press followed, and Foster gave interviews to try to maintain control over her story. For a long time, her career stalled and she booked work only in countries where she was not known, moving on whenever she was outed. After some years, she returned to New York, and then, out as trans, was asked to work with androgynous performing artist **Grace Jones**. This revitalized her career and encouraged her to remain out.

The first successful openly trans model was **Teri Toye**, who came to New York in the 1980s to study fashion at Parsons School of Design. After she transitioned, a chance meeting with designer Stephen Sprouse quickly had her on his runway, and more bookings followed. She walked for Gaultier, Comme des Garçons, Chanel, and Thierry Mugler, and was photographed by Steven Meisel and Nan Goldin, among others.

The late 1980s saw the first Brazilian trans woman model, Roberta Gambine Moreira, who modeled as **Roberta Close.** Close won the Miss Gay Brazil pageant in 1984, acted in Brazilian soap operas, and was photographed for print ads. She was the first trans woman to appear on the cover of *Brazilian Playboy* and also on the cover of the Brazilian men's magazine *Sexy*. She is the foremother of many other Brazilian trans models.

MUSIC

We all have a soundtrack associated with our lives. We begin listening early, influenced by our families and friends, our cultural environments, and our peer connections. Music exists for every occasion and every mood. It can be celebratory, melancholy, heartening, political, exuberant, yearning, thoughtful, exciting, sexy, and it can make us dance. In short, music truly *moves* us, physically and emotionally. As trans and gender nonconforming artists, we may be drawn early or later in our lives to pick up an instrument, a microphone, or a computer and make music to get audiences moving. Our trans and gender nonconforming experiences and identities may (or may not) be in the foreground of our lyrics, highlighted in our performances, and written in our biographies, interviews, and liner notes.

There are transgender musicians in every genre from bluegrass to rock, from hip-hop to classical music to klezmer and beyond. Some artists address trans experience and identity more than others. Many of us are moved by the past and current contribution of trans and gender nonconforming musicians to pick up an instrument ourselves.

Since the 1990s, visible and openly trans and gender nonconforming musicians have been appearing much more quickly across the gender and genre spectrums. Some are influenced by showgirl and rock and roll forbearers, and many others come more from political folk rock traditions, jazz, hip-hop, religious and ethnic music, classical, and even bubblegum pop traditions.

Solo Trans Musicians

Antony Hegarty is a UK-born composer, playwright, director, visual artist, singer, songwriter, pianist, and collaborator best known as the lead singer of the group *Antony and the Johnsons*. Hegarty identifies as transgender on the feminine spectrum and prefers male pronouns. He has an experimental theater and music background and his early work includes creating *The Blacklips Performance Cult*, an avant-garde drag theater troupe based in New York City, which he ran from 1992 to 1995. *Antony and the Johnsons* released their first album in 2000. In 2005 they won the prestigious Mercury music prize for their commercially successful album *I Am A Bird Now*. Hegarty has written a vast catalog of songs, several of which directly address transgender identity, including *For Today I Am a Boy* and *My Lady Story*.

Geo Wyeth is a singer, songwriter, performance artist, multiinstrumentalist, and piano prodigy. He grew up in the Hell's Kitchen neighborhood of New York City and attended Yale School of Music. Wyeth's first solo musical project was called *Novice Theory* in which he played accordion and piano and released two albums. Wyeth usually writes more metaphorically than literally, but his lyrics sometimes also directly address transgender identity, notably in *A Coming of Age Song* (2008) and *This is Not Coney Island* (2008). Wyeth is also the cofounder of PACK, an art collective and record label.

Currently in a class of her own is African American classical musician **Tona Brown**, the first openly trans woman to make a career as a violinist and vocalist—fields still dominated by normativity of all kinds and largely devoid of people of color. A child prodigy like Geo Wyeth, Brown began learning the violin at the age of 10, and won her first of many scholarships and competitions at 14. Besides her musical career she is a visible out presence on the lecture circuit and on the Internet, making an "It Gets Better" video and becoming a powerful advocate and role model for LGBTQ and people of color communities. In 2011, Brown sang the National Anthem at the LGBTQ Leadership Council Gala for President Obama, and in 2012, she released an EP *This Is Who I Am,* a collection of African American art songs and spirituals for voice and violin. Two other well-known classical trans musicians are **Wendy Carlos**, a composer, and **Sara Davis Buchner**, a pianist.

Lucas Silveira is the lead singer and guitarist of *The Cliks*. He became the first trans man on a major label when Tommy Boy Entertainment signed *The Cliks* and released their self-titled album in 2007. His lyrics do not often explicitly address transgender identity or issues, though occasionally they do, specifically the title song of *The Cliks* album, *Dirty King* (2009). Silveira's first solo album *Mockingbird* (2011) was also his first album post hormone replacement therapy.

Rae Spoon is a femme trans man country folk singer/songwriter. While the majority of his songs do not address transgender identity explicitly, he has written an anthem against transphobia, *Joan* (2010), featuring **Lucas Silviera** of *The Cliks*. Both Spoon's femme identity and presentation (he says he often passes as a woman) and his country genre make him a unique face and voice of transness.

Shawna Virago is a country rock, punk/feminist singer, songwriter, guitarist, activist, filmmaker, and author. She is the artistic director of the San Francisco Transgender Film Festival formerly known as TrannyFest. Many of her lyrics celebrate queer love and gender outlaws. Virago's partner is award-winning trans choreographer and dancer **Sean Dorsey**.

Veronika Klaus is a San Francisco–based trans woman jazz singer who has been performing in cabarets and clubs around the Bay Area and the United States and is currently recording her third album, *Something Cool.*

Laura Jane Grace, a Floridian punk musician, started the band *Against Me!* in 1997, releasing 5 studio albums, four EPs, one live album, two DVDs, 12 singles, four demos, and 10 music videos, and began her transition from male to female in 2012.

Trans man **Joshua Klipp** is a singer and dancer who has been making pop-dance music tracks and videos as well as dancing with his hip-hop troupe *Freeplay Dance Crew* since 2000. Most recently, his jazz project, *Joshua Klipp and The Klipptones*, was appearing in clubs around the San Francisco Bay Area.

Trans Musical Groups

The duo **Coyote Grace** (trans man **Joe Stevens** and cis woman Ingrid Elizabeth) started out in Seattle, Washington, as street performers, but they quickly gained national prominence. While both members of the group write songs, the bulk of the lyrics have been written by Stevens, and several of his songs directly address being a trans man, among them *Ghost Boy, Daughterson,* and *A Guy Named Joe/Joelvis.* Elizabeth's writing addresses the desire for queer masculinity in songs such as *Girls Like Me.* Coyote Grace opened for and played with the Indigo Girls for three tours in 2010. In 2011, Coyote Grace added an additional instrumentalist, Michael Connolly, and released their fifth album, *Now Take Flight.*

Jayne County is a Georgia native who moved to New York City in 1968 and took part in the legendary Stonewall Riots. County began playing gigs (as Wayne County) in the 1970s in and around the glam rock and punk movements. She officially began identifying as Jayne in 1979. County has released six albums and is still playing gigs at Max's and other venues.

Chris Pureka is a genderqueer-identified folk rock musician based in Northampton, Massachusetts. Pureka released her fourth CD, *How I Learned to See in the Dark* on Sad Rabbit Records in 2010.

"Katastrophe," aka rapper and trans man **Rocco Kayiatos**, began as a competitive slam poet in 1997 and started making beats in 2002. He was named Producer of the Year by Outmusic Awards for his debut album *Let's Fuck, Then Talk About My Problems* in 2004. His lyrics feature transness and gender identity as well as other contemporary cultural issues, both serious and playful.

With an electro-influenced sound, trans man **Black Cracker** has worked for years as a hip-hop producer. He released his first solo hip-hop/rap album *Tears of a Clown* in 2012 and published a book of poetry: *40oz Elephant, Poems by Celena Glenn & Black Cracker.* He is a two-time National Poetry Slam Champion and influential figure within Urban Word NYC, one of the nation's leading literary and performance organizations for youth.

Foxx Jazell is an Alabama native living and working in Los Angeles. Her party-rap tracks and videos like *Split Enz, Sex Thang, Hookup*, and *Sickening* are light hearted, confident, sexy, and infectious.

Heidi Barton Stink is a Caucasian genderqueer trans woman rapper. Her lyrics address gender and transgender issues; trans-, queer-, and homophobia; misogyny of all kinds; and wider social criticism particularly focused on capitalism and the US government.

"Indie" singer/songwriter **Angelica Love Ross** makes both acoustic and electronic neo classic soul and R&B tracks. She transitioned at age nineteen after six months in the military, and worked for several years under the radar as a model and actress. She now focuses on being an out and proud African American trans woman musician.

Storm Miguel Florez sings twangy guitar folk rock about growing up as an outsider in the United States. Tunes such as *Legend* recount the experience of coming of age in Albuquerque, New Mexico, as an assimilated Mexican American unable to speak Spanish fluently (copyright Portraits to the People).

Actor Slash Model was the duet music project of trans men **Simon Strikeback** and **Madsen Minax,** active between 2007 and 2012. Their music is a mixture of vaudeville and traditional bluegrass. Simon sings, plays ukulele, writes songs, and outside of Actor Slash Model is also an educator, an activist, and a lead organizer for Camp Trans. Simon and Madsen collaborate with other trans musicians in the band **The Homoticons** featuring **Jesse Alexander** (of Cobalt and the Hired Guns), **Elias Krell** (ex-opera singer/maverick accordionist), and **Colin Palombi** (of Velvetron). In 2009, Simon and Madsen also produced a documentary about transgender and gender-variant musicians called *Riot Acts: Flaunting Gender Deviance in Music Performance.*

SCHMEKEL: 100% TRANS JEWS

Starting in 2010 out of Brooklyn, New York, **Schmekel: 100% Trans Jews** are, as the title says, an all-trans, all-Jewish quartet making klezmer-inflected polka-punk tunes. Their hard-core polka-punk and religious ritual song *Mohel* is a spot-on comedic illustration of the intersection of their trans and Jewish identities. (*Schmekel* is Yiddish for "little penis," and a *Mohel*, pronounced "moyl," is a person trained to perform the ritual circumcision historically required of all observant Jewish males.)

Mohel
After my first shot of testosterone
Only two weeks and my schmekie had grown
Now I have a foreskin and I am a Jew

I called up my rabbi, said "What should I do?"
I don't need a fuckin' mohel!
The rabbi said, "Bubbe, you're not like us men,
you must follow the laws of the androgen,
you'll never be counted as one of the ten,
because you cannot produce any semen."
I don't need a fuckin' mohel!
Some of our forefathers had a foreskin
Adam and Noah are also our kin
Some folks eat goats and some folks say the sh'ma
So suck on my foreskin and sing Had Gadya!
My father doesn't know I have a foreskin
Had Gadyaaaaaa Had Gadya!

PHOTOGRAPHY

Photography has a long and strong history in LGBTQ arts. As long as there have been cameras, there have been photographers wanting to document and create art from our experiences, our perspectives, and in our communities. We want to be seen and to show what we see in a world that has largely not featured us. Often we specifically want to document our own and our community's processes of becoming.

Over the years many cisgender people have pointed their lenses in our directions. One of the most well-known examples may be Diane Arbus, working in the United States in the 1960s. Arbus is famous for her images of trans women as well as other culturally nonconforming subjects.

One early example of political self-representation on the gender nonconforming spectrum is French surrealist artist **Claude Cahun**, who, among many other artistic and political undertakings, took gender nonconforming photographs of herself beginning at the age of 18 in 1912, and continued through the 1940s.

Perhaps the first publication since Cahun of photographs of trans and gender nonconforming people by a member of our own community was **Loren Cameron**'s *Body Alchemy* in 1996. A self-taught photographer, author, and activist, Cameron is undoubtedly a pioneer in the portrayal of transgender people. Cameron began taking pictures to document his own transition. *Body Alchemy* was one of the first collections to capture trans bodies in an affirming instead of exploitative manner. In 2001, Cameron published the e-book *Man Tool: The Nuts and Bolts of Female-to-Male Surgery* with Zero eBooks. Cameron's most recent photo project emerged in 2006 from his personal experience becoming more and more attracted to masculine women, cisgender men, and trans men. The project, *Flex for Me: Sexing It Up with Gay and Bisexual FTMs*, candidly explores how queer trans men describe themselves and what they are looking for in a sexual partner, through the medium of online personal ads.

In 1999 **Del LaGrace Volcano** published *The Drag King Book*, the first body of work on gender nonconforming performers on the masculine side of the spectrum. The photographs gave the spotlight to visible Drag King artists and club nights in the United States and in Europe. The text was written by **Jack Halberstam**, whose landmark academic work *Female Masculinities* had been published in 1998 (with an intro by Volcano). Volcano is a self-identified intersex and gender-variant visual artist who continues to explore gender queering, queer femininities, trans bodies, and masculinities, and most recently is focusing on intersex activism and raising children in genderqueer families.

In 1997, **J. Jackie Baier**, already a professional photographer and filmmaker in Germany with nearly 15 years of experience, transitioned from male to female and her film and photography focus shifted as well. In 1999, and continuing for 10 years, Baier documented gender nonconforming nightlife, on the stage and the dance floor of the notorious Berlin night club House of Shame, hosted by trans woman Chantal. In 2009

XXBoys is a series of photographic portraits of trans men by **Kael T. Block**.

Mariette Pathy Allen is a cisgender photographer who has been taking inspiring portraits of trans communities since the 1970s. Her books include *Transformations: Crossdressers and Those Who Love Them*, *The Gender Frontier*, and *TransCuba*.

The Athens Boys Choir mixes spoken word with hip-hop, pop and jazz, and makes 1980s-inspired comedy music videos. While the "Choir" started as the spoken word duo of **Rocket** and **Katz**, trans man Katz is now the sole member. The Choir's first album, *Rhapsody in T*, was released in 2004, and included smart and succinct pop music–laced spoken word about transgender identity and the everyday experiences a trans man faces, such as choosing the bathroom of least resistance and the pros and cons of different sized packers.

In 2005, the major label Sony BMG decided to capitalize on two trends in Thailand: the phenomenal success of created all-female super groups like The Spice Girls; and the slightly taboo popularity of Kathoey ("Lady Boy") performers and culture. Putting these two ideas together, they created the first all trans women pop group, **Venus Flytrap.**

Harisu is a trans pop singer, model, and actress from South Korea. She is South Korea's first well-known transgender entertainer, and in 2002 became only the second person in Korea to legally change their gender.

Ai Haruna is a Japanese talk show host and singer who first made her fame by imitating popular cisgender singer Aya Matsuura. Haruna was named "Miss International Queen 2009" in a transgender beauty pageant in Thailand, becoming the first Japanese contestant to win the title.

In 2010, trans male singer **Paige Phoenix** was a contestant on the Australian version of X-Factor. During the interview he came out as trans, and that became a highlight of the episode.

In France, androgynous gender nonconforming rapper **Casey** produces hardcore political rap and performances from her experience of being black French Martinican in the racist and white ethnocentric French culture.

In Spain, 51-year-old **Manuela Trasobares Haro** is a classical mezzo-soprano singer, a painter who studied with Salvador Dali, and a politician who ran for Spanish Parliament in 2008.

In Germany, the first transgender teen pop singer has emerged: **Kim Petras**, who completed gender reassignment surgery at the age of 16 in 2008 (making her the youngest person to ever undergo such surgery), released her first electro-pop dance track the same year.

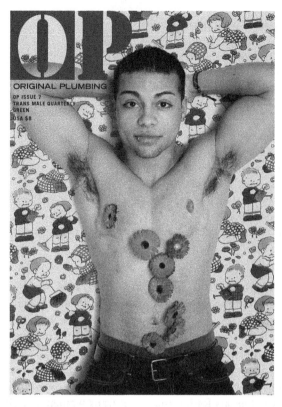

Cover of *Original Plumbing* Issue 7 (Green issue) (Damy Bee, photographed by Amos Mac).

she started *The Portrait Project* at the "T Lounge" club at Warehouse 9 in Copenhagen, Denmark. Baier created a photo studio in the warehouse and invited people from T lounge and other visiting artists and friends to sit for the camera. The photos were then mounted on the walls of the space, the subjects becoming the stars of their own exhibition in the Warehouse 9 gallery.

In 2009 in San Francisco, **Amos Mac** started *Original Plumbing.* The editor and photographer in chief of *Original Plumbing*, Mac is a trans man photographic artist who is

Zackary Drucker, as seen in *Translady Fanzine* (photo by Amos Mac).

dedicated to the visibility of trans male culture. *OP* is the first American magazine dedicated to trans male culture (**Jez Pez** began publishing Australia's first, *Dude: A Transmale Zine*, in 2011). Amos is also the editor, publisher, and chief photographer of *Translady Fanzine*, started in 2011, a fine art photographic periodical in which Amos focuses on a single woman of trans experience per issue and includes the model's experience in her own words.

In 2010, Israeli trans woman **Yishay Garbaz** published *Becoming: A Gender Flipbook*. The book is meant to be flipped through to create a simple animation of 2 years of Garbasz's gender transition. It is groundbreaking not only for the work itself but for the fact that it was released by mainstream publisher Random House.

In 2011, **Leon Mostovoy** created the photographic project *The Death of My Daughter*, which responds to Mostovoy's experience of being told by his mother after his transition that her daughter was gone. Mostovoy took two pictures of each of his subjects: in the first the subjects lie in coffins, eyes closed, still, dressed, and made up as "female," each representing the girl their parents saw them—or desired them—to be. They are artificial—the makeup is heavy, the hair is too perfect—they look like plastic prom queens and cheerleaders from another era, holding tennis rackets, flowers, and in one case, a book on how to become a doctor. They are their parents' fantasies. In the second portrait, they stand in front of the camera, dressed as the trans men they are today. They look confidently in the lens.

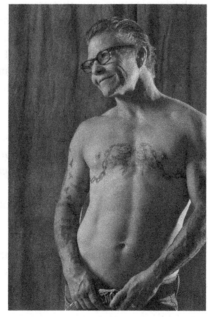

Leon Mostovoy: Diptych.

Individually and as a group, these photographers present a broad range of photographic possibilities. They have documented their own transition and processes, opening doors for other trans and gender nonconforming people, as well as reaching out to their birth and chosen families. They have revealed and celebrated hitherto hidden trans and gender nonconforming communities. They have been instrumental in creating and encouraging trans and gender nonconforming culture and cultural exchange. Some learned their craft out of their desire to communicate, and others brought their already honed craft into their lives. They have put their trans and gender nonconforming experiences to use, critically and emotionally examining other ideas and politics.

THEATRICAL ARTS

The live theatrical arts have a unique impact on us as audience members. Many arts researchers and scholars have said that when we see people live onstage (rather than in prerecorded screen-based performance), we do not watch and listen to them passively but instead experience and participate with them. This makes the live theatrical arts fertile ground for trans and gender nonconforming artists to make effective and affecting connections with their experiences, as writers, creator-performers, as actors, and as variety artists.

As in other art forms, there is little early visible history of trans and gender nonconforming theatrical artists, though there is substantial occurrence of gender crossing in theater and the variety arts. Shakespeare wrote many instances of cross-dressed characters into his comedic plays, and the early Japanese theater forms of Yaro Kabuki (all male), Onna Kabuki (all female), and the Chinese Peking Opera over the centuries saw both men and women performing in drag. The long and rich history of Drag Queening and that of the vibrant and more recent Drag Kinging has certainly influenced many of the trans and gender nonconforming theatrical performers working today.

Until recently, written theatrical works that included trans and gender nonconforming characters tended to use them in the same way as film did—for comic, tragic, or plot twisting effect, as in the 1976 play *Come Back to the Five and Dime, Jimmy Dean, Jimmy Dean.* These plays also tended to conflate gender and sexuality, presenting characters that were somewhat interchangeably identified as being, for instance a "woman in a man's body" and being gay, as in Mae West's infamous 1927 play *The Drag.*

Early Trans Theater

Since 1989, authentic trans and gender nonconforming characters have begun appearing more regularly onstage and in playwriting, mostly written and performed by trans and gender nonconforming identified creators. This was the year **Kate Bornstein** debuted her first theatrical show *Hidden: A Gender.* In 1994 trans man performer/writer **David Harrison** premiered his solo show *FTM,* in which he played himself going through his transition and experiencing the effects of testosterone, juxtaposing that with playing his own mother and her experience of using the testosterone prescribed to treat her breast cancer.

One of the first and few mainstream theater pieces to depict an authentic trans or gender nonconforming experience is the play *I Am My Own Wife* written by **Doug Wright** in 2003. Based on the true story of Charlotte von Mahlsdorf, a trans woman living in East Berlin during the second half of the 20th century, this Pulitzer Prize–winning play presents a compelling picture of one trans life. However, to date, the part of Von Mahlsdorf has always been played by a cisgender actor, cross-dressing for the role.

Solo Trans Performers

Solo performance is currently one of the most popular mediums for trans performers. The solo form gives trans artists the opportunity to offer authentic and nuanced narratives of trans lives and identities on stage, literally or symbolically. These performances are often multidisciplinary, blending monologue, movement work, comedy, music, and other performance modes. Though these performances are not always or necessarily autobiographical, many solo performers' work is heavily grounded in memoir. In its autobiographical form, trans solo performance is part of the long tradition of performers of marginalized identities taking to the stage to make ourselves known and tell our stories.

A trans actress who made (and continues to make) inroads in mainstream theater and television as well as on the solo stage is **Alexandra Billings**. Billings originally mounted her one-woman autobiographical show, *Before I Disappear*, in 1995. Told in vignettes and songs, *Before I Disappear* was a journey through Billings's life that shied away from nothing, presenting her difficult family history, her time as drag queen showgirl "Shante," her experiences as a gender nonconforming sex worker, her fight with drug addiction, her AIDS diagnosis, and her gender transition with passion and humor, using classic Broadway-style singing and character acting. In 2005, Billings had a supporting role in the made-for-TV movie *Romy and Michele: In the Beginning*, a prequel to the well-known film *Romy and Michele's High School Reunion*. It was one of the first times a trans actress played a trans character on television. Billings has also appeared on television shows such as *ER, Nurses*, and *Grey's Anatomy*.

Scott Turner Schofield creates full-length, theatrical solo performances first based on his experiences as a debutante in Georgia, and more recently on his experiences and encounters as a trans male touring performance artist. His shows include *Underground Transit* (2001), *Debutante Balls* (2004), and *How to Become a Man in 127 Easy Steps* (2007).

English gender nonconforming performer-creator and trans feminist **Joey Hateley** makes solo shows with his company Transaction Theater in Manchester, England. An accomplished physical performer, dancer, singer, and gender chameleon, Hatelely's solo shows, *A-Gender* (2004), *Engendered Species* (2007), and *The Gender Joker Show* (2010) take a close look, through the lens of parody and the absurd, at the societal requirements of gender and adherence to the gender binary.

A prolific and prizewinning novelist, composer, cookbook and theater manual author, and translator, Italian trans male playwright and performer **Davide Tolu** premiered his solo show *One New Man* in Milan, Italy, in 2004, touring it to many Italian cities to much acclaim. His other plays take on a variety of sociopolitical themes, including climate change, intergenerational and class conflict, and the critique of capitalism. As well as composing for musical theater and winning various awards, he also translated Leslie Feinberg's *Stone Butch Blues* into Italian in 2004.

Largely self-taught, **Sunny Drake** is an Australian trans male creator and performer who uses text, movement, puppetry, animation, ventriloquism, and sleight-of-hand magic in his theatrical one-person shows. Drake's work deals with gender and trans issues, sexuality, race and class privilege, and the search for love and intimacy. As well as his most recent show, *X* (2012), Drake has created two other successful solo theatrical performances, *Gender—Queer Seeking* (2008) and *Other-Wise* (2010).

D'Lo is a trans Tamil gender nonconforming playwright/performer/spoken word artist and stand-up comedian. D'Lo is a highly skilled performer adept at moving effortlessly between, for instance, himself, his mother, and Mahatma Ghandi. D'Lo has also written two multicharacter plays: *Ballin' With My Bois: Stories on Brotherhood, Basketball, Bisexuality, and the Butch Femme Phenomenon*, which premiered at WOW Café Theater in New York (2004), and *Boys That Pray* (2011).

Playwrights

Trans man playwright, journalist, and activist **Nick Mwaluko** was born in Tanzania and raised primarily in Kenya. He moved to New York in the mid-2000s and began publishing his journalism in the *Washington Times*, for the Reuters News Agency, and in the *Huffington Post*. He has written seven plays, the most well-known of which is *Waafrika*,

Imani Henry is a Caribbean trans man living in Brooklyn. He is an activist, writer, and performer. His highly acclaimed solo show, *B4T* (2002), explores the experiences of a variety of trans, butch, and otherwise masculine characters. *B4T* was the first explicitly trans performance to be produced at WOW Café Theater. WOW is historically a women's/lesbian performance space that began affirming trans participation in their mission statement in the early 2000s.

Candis Cayne has been acting in mainstream and alternative stage, television, and film for more than 15 years. In 2007 she became the first trans person to play a recurring trans character on primetime television when she won the role of Carmelita in *Dirty Sexy Money*.

Pangender actor, singer, and aerial artist **Em Grosland** has been seen in off-Broadway and regional theatres in Eve Ensler's *Emotional Creatures*, as the lead in *Peter Pan*, and as puppeteer and aerialist for the L.A. Opera's production of Wagner's *Ring Cycle*.

Actress, producer, and activist **Laverne Cox**, now known for her role on the Netflix series *Orange Is the New Black*, was the first African American trans woman to produce and star in her own television show, *Transform Me* on VH1, and also the first to appear on a reality program, *I Wanna Work for Diddy*.

With no prior experience, trans actress **Harmony Santana** was nominated in 2012 for the independent spirit award for her first acting job in the film *Gun Hill Road*, where she portrayed a young trans woman living in the Bronx, New York.

Calpernia Addams is an actress, director, and producer. She also coaches mainstream actors playing trans characters, and has worked with Jared Leto in Dallas Buyer's Club and Felicity Huffman in TransAmerica. She is well known for appearing in and producing a documentary on the all-trans-woman version of Eve Ensler's *Vagina Monologues*.

Pascale Ourbih is a French trans actress and activist. She played the lead character in the feature film *Thelma* (2001), by Pierre-Alain Meier, and is currently the director of the Paris LGBT film festival.

about an interracial relationship between two women in rural Kenya. Mwaluko also writes poetry and fiction that focuses on LGBTQ people of color.

Trans man **Deen The Playwright** is a first-generation South Asian American playwright and performer whose first full-length play, *Shut-Up!*, won him both the Dennis Johnston Playwriting Prize and the James Baldwin Award. His second play, *Where Children Play: The Story of Tank and Horse*, premiered at the Berkshire Fringe Festival and most recently his script, *Draw the Circle*, Premiered at InterAct Theater in Philadelphia in April of 2012.

Trans woman playwright **Jo Clifford** lives in Edinburgh, Scotland, where she runs Teatro Mundo. Since 1997, Jo has written more than 45 single-character and multicharacter plays on a variety of themes that have been produced all over Great Britain. Her 2008 solo show, *The Gospel According to Jesus, Queen of Heaven*, deftly injects trans characters into biblical stories in powerful and humanistic ways that infuriate the religious Right as much as they touch the rest of us.

PHYSICAL THEATER AND DANCE

Dance and physical theater are forms that offer performers and choreographers the opportunity to explore the creation of embodied meaning. So much of the trans and gender nonconforming experience is tied to our physical body and movement. We may move between, around, through, or away from genders; we may move through the physical effects of hormones or surgeries; we may move through a combination of these and other body-brain experiences. For some artists, dance and physical theater are ideal forms for presenting our stories of movement and change.

However, as for all dancers who do not fit the cultural norms, the focus on the body typical of many dance disciplines can make it difficult for trans performers to gain entrance into mainstream professional troupes. Rigid body standards and deeply ingrained gender norms in dance styles such as ballet have historically limited the opportunities available for nonnormative performers of all genders, including those of us who do not match the height, weight, ethnicity, and age expected of dancers. Perhaps because of this historic conservatism, more trans choreographers tend to work in dance theater, modern dance, and other contemporary and hybrid forms, often creating work that confronts the rigid requirements of more classical forms.

Sean Dorsey is the most well-known trans choreographer and dancer in North America. He is the founder of **Fresh Meat Productions**, an organization devoted to trans and queer dance and performance. Dorsey is particularly well known for creating *The Journal Project*, an award-winning piece based on the journals of Lou Sullivan. Sullivan was a gay trans man who was a key organizer of trans male communities in the 1980s and early 1990s. Sullivan died of AIDS in 1991, but he lives on in the work that he did to connect and mobilize trans men internationally. Dorsey's most recent project, *The Secret History of Love*, explores the ways that LGBTQ people survived and found community in the past.

A well-established and highly regarded trans choreographer and dancer who comes from the restrictive ballet tradition is **Jin Xing**. Based in Shanghai, China, Xing works with contemporary dance and dance theater as well as ballet. Highly trained in prestigious dance schools in New York and China, prior to transition, Jin Xing was a member of the Chinese military dance troupe, eventually attaining the rank of colonel. This background informs some of her dance, finding expression in movement styles and the music that she selects, and she jokingly credits her military training with her determination to constantly confront Chinese governmental bureaucracy and censorship of the arts.

French physical theater maker, dancer, and juggling artist **Phia Menard** created her Compagnie Non Nova in 1998, making multidisciplinary shows that blur the lines between dance, theater, circus, and performance art. In 2008, in collaboration with her company, she created the solo performance *P.P.P.* (Perilous Parallel Position) using ice as a medium to examine the themes of transformation and erosion, metaphorically and emotionally re-creating the experience of her then occurring transition from male

Sean Dorsey (photo by Lydia Daniller).

to female. The set was comprised primarily of 90 hanging blocks and spheres of ice that melted, softened, transformed, cracked, and eventually crashed onto the stage throughout the performance.

In addition to these established and mid-career trans creators, choreographers, and dancers, there are numerous young trans and gender nonconforming individuals emerging as the next generation to work in movement forms. Some of these artists include **Devynn Emory, Jai Arun Ravine, Niv Acosta, Iele Paloumpis, Jules Skloot, and Yve Laris Cohen**. Each of these choreographers has received increasing recognition in recent years, and it can be assumed that as their careers grow, the opportunities for future trans dancers and choreographers will expand as well.

Recent years have also seen dance troops that are not explicitly trans or gender nonconforming include trans dancers. The most well-known troupe is probably Vogue Evolution, which was at the center of some controversy after appearing on MTV's *America's Best Dance Crew*. MTV responded negatively to a trans dancer in the crew, **Leiomy Maldonado**, and almost did not allow her to participate in the competition. Following a strong response from trans and queer viewers, MTV apologized for their actions. Maldonado's story demonstrates that while trans dancers are starting to find opportunities in mainstream dance venues, there are still sometimes strong negative responses to their participation. However, the active mobilization of trans, queer, and ally audiences can help demonstrate that there is support for trans dancers.

DANCE ME TO THE END OF LOVE

Lazlo Ilya Pearlman is a performing artist and author with 30 years of experience making Queer and Trans theatre in the United States, the United Kingdom, and continental Europe, and is currently pursuing his PhD at the University of London Royal Central School of Speech and Drama.

Imagine we're in a dark club, and it's time for a performance. Music starts—a slow, trance-inducing track with a pulse-like rhythm—and the lights come up onstage. The performer sits on a chair, dressed in light-colored retro trousers, shirt, vest, and hat, holding a large bunch of flowers: red and yellow roses and multicolored mums. There is an empty coat rack on stage with him, tall and thin, in sandy-colored wood, with a hanger on it. The performer's movements are with the music, slow and romantic. Soon the sound shifts from the trance track into Leonard Cohen singing "Dance Me to the End of Love," and the performer rises to dance with the flowers, offering them to unseen partners.

Suddenly the music changes—it's the same song, but a 1960s swingy version. The performer drops the melancholia and grins as if to tell us, "This isn't serious," and snappily dances into the audience, handing flowers to everyone he encounters. He's peppy, upbeat now, and after he's given away all of the flowers he bounds back to the stage, taking off his vest as he goes. He puts the vest around the "shoulders" of the hanger on the hat rack and dances a stripping choreography in which all of his clothing ends up, piece by piece, on the stand. As the swingy track ends, he is naked, his body hidden behind his now fully clothed hat rack partner.

Then in the classic stripper's reveal, he steps out from behind the rack.

The audience is taken by surprise: This man has no penis; instead, he has a vagina! We are thrown out of the world we expected—our brains freeze and tilt. We feel multiple emotions at once: Among them are probably shock, delight, confusion, attraction, fear, and many others colliding into each other. Our worlds turn upside down.

But, unlike a classic striptease, this is not the end of the act. In a way, it's the beginning. Before our brains can begin the process of making "sense" of what just happened, the music changes back to the original trance track and the performer again steps down off the stage, back into the audience.

The now naked "stripper" chooses someone at random, stops in front of them and gazes directly into their eyes, without words, asking them to look back, and breathes quietly with them until their breaths are in sync and the contact changes them both. He moves on to another and repeats the experience, and another, changing the contact with each, and softening the energy in the room itself. The music swiftly changes again to a partner-dance version of the Leonard Cohen song, and the performer invites the person in front of him to dance—he is still naked, and the person is fully clothed. He takes the person in his arms for a few moments, then invites the person to continue dancing with another audience member. He chooses another person to dance with, and the process repeats until the entire audience is out of their seats and dancing in each other's arms.

After one last music change, to a disco version of the song, everyone continues dancing on their own and he dances among them, still naked, until he makes his way out of the playing space, never answering a single question, never offering an explanation, a biography, a gender lesson, or anything else about what they have seen. The audience dances on, left in the space of delight/surprise/confusion, having had an experience that perhaps no longer needs explanation.

This is my latest short performance, *Dance Me to the End of Love*, which I have shown about a dozen times as of this writing, to various kinds of audiences in various settings. The show illustrates one of the ways I work with my transsexuality onstage and why I do it. I want to use the surprise of my hybrid body as a tool to create emotional space in the audience, space without answers, without even formed questions, a space of new emotional vistas. This space is among the most important things we humans can access—a free space where everything we think we know about the world (at least the world of genders and sexualities) opens up to question. In this space lives opportunity: opportunity to let go of assumptions, of rules, requirements, and restrictions on the ways to be human.

This is just one of the ways that performers can use our transsexuality onstage, as well as tell our stories and call gender binaries into question with our texts.

Short Forms: Stand-up, Cabaret, Burlesque, and Variety

Many trans and gender nonconforming theatrical artists work in short-form performance, instead of (or in addition to) creating full-length and narrative shows. These include **Glenn Marla, Johnny Blazes, Ariel Speedwagon**, and **Gepetta**. Stand-up comedy, clowning, cabaret, vaudeville, burlesque, and drag are popular short-form performance styles. Often trans artists combine these genres when creating their work, crafting hybrid and innovative performance pieces that bridge the differences between styles. Creating variety performance acts can be a good option for emerging trans artists because they tend to be 10 minutes or less and do not require the same amount of resources as a full-length show. Some artists develop a repertoire of these short performances, which they later assemble into a longer piece. This approach allows artists to continuously develop and workshop new material in front of audiences in nightclub, cabaret, and bar settings, and later to present reworked, refined, and elongated versions to theatrical audiences as well.

One of the most well-known gender nonconforming cabaret artists (who now works primarily in full length cabaret shows) is **Mx Justin Vivian Bond**. Mx Bond (who prefers the pronoun V) has been making long and short form cabaret performances since 1989, when, as well as appearing in Kate Bornstein's *Hidden: A Gender*, Bond also began performing as Kiki DuRane, a drunken octogenarian lounge singer. Mx Bond was featured in the movie *Shortbus*; wrote an autobiography, *Tango: My Childhood Backwards and in High Heels*; and released two albums and an EP.

Visual Art/Performance Art

Visual and performance art is an exceptionally broad field of inquiry and techniques, including portraiture and painting, doll making, photography, video and new media, and sculpting with traditional materials like ceramics or found, recycled, or mundane objects such as needles, syringes, or bread. This breadth and malleability may make visual and performance arts particularly ripe for trans and gender nonconforming artists to express the complexity of our lived experience, theories, thoughts, and emotions.

Early trans and gender nonconforming artists are difficult to identify. Because visual art does not necessarily require the spotlight to be on the artist, the identities of many trans and gender nonconforming artists may be buried with them. One possible forebearer of today's trans and gender nonconforming visual artists is the painter Dora Carrington. Close to the literary Bloomsbury Group in the 1920s, Carrington seems gender nonconforming by today's standards. For a time she called herself only by her last name, "Carrington," dressed and cut her hair androgynously, had affairs with men and women, and her greatest love affair was with gay writer Lytton Strachey, who did much to support her painting career.

One trans variety artist who works entirely in short form is **Rose Wood**. Since 2006, Rose has been primarily performing at the infamous "Theater of Varieties" called The Box, with venues in New York and London. Rose's performances use heavy shock tactics, often including real and faked violence, bodily mess, and character reversals that work with the reveal of her gender nonconforming body.

The last few years have seen a large number of trans and gender nonconforming people working in traditional stand-up comedy. Perhaps the most well known of these is trans male comic **Ian Harvie**, who has toured with Margaret Cho. Harvie's routines work with his trans history and his experiences of LGBTQ and mainstream communities.

Morgan is a sixty-year-old trans woman comic (only six years into her career) whose writing focuses both on her transition and her recovery from addiction. One of her comedy routines in her show *Girl Junk*, "My 23,000 Dollar Hoo-Hoo," is a brilliant example of how a lighthearted look at gender and transgender identity can simultaneously reveal the trans subject as individual and universal, building bridges as the audience laughs at the absurdities of all human life.

Notable trans and gender nonconforming performers working in the unforgiving world of stand-up comedy include **Bethany Black, Christine Hecht, Clare Parker, Red Durkin, Al Stafford,** and **Jeffery Jay.**

Kathoey performers at a cabaret in Pattaya.

Canadian variety performer **Olive-or-Oliver** is a transgender burlesque performer who goes by the pronoun "they." Onstage, Olive-or-Oliver creates comic burlesque strips that often work with genderfuck drag, stripping from clown costume to bra and panties, to pasties and strap on, all the while spinning and doing tricks with their hoop.

Berlin gender nonconforming performer **Bridge Markland** has been making short and long performance works for more than 20 years and was featured in the 2005 documentary *Venus Boyz*. A striking physical performer, Markland often works with lip sync, strip/reverse strip, German masculine and feminine iconography, as well as clowning, puppetry, and abstract theater techniques.

French and German gender nonconforming performer **Ocean Leroy** has been living in Berlin and making work since 2002. Starting as a drag king, Leroy has created movement pieces such as a live singing half male drag/half female drag character dueting and dancing with himself, as well as political performance pieces on gender discrimination and community activism.

One of the most notable touring trans performance projects is the *Tranny Roadshow,* which ran from 2005 to 2012, and was organized by **Kelly Shortandqueer** and **Jamez Terry**. The Roadshow featured a wide range of trans and gender nonconforming performers, musicians, artists, and others, with some performers staying on the tour for multiple weeks and others jumping on just to perform in the tour stops near their homes.

In the 1970s, 20 years before her transition, **Misc. Pippa Garner,** in her male identity, Philip, began her career as a performance artist in California, creating objects and illustrations that satirized consumer culture. Over time, Garner shifted his gaze from looking at society and objects to looking at his own body and identity. Nearing her fiftieth birthday, from this exploration and desire came her decision to transition into herself and become Misc. Pippa Garner.

The 1980s saw the emergence of two out gender nonconforming artists whose work arose directly from their experiences of identity and gender, on arts scenes on opposite coasts of the United States: **Greer Lankton** and **Vaginal Davis.**

Born in 1958, **Greer Lankton** began making dolls out of found materials at age 10 that reflected her difficult childhood experiences of being a feminine boy. She transitioned at 21 and moved to New York City, where she continued to make dolls of all sizes and installations to house and display them. She was well known on the downtown New York art scene through the 1980s and 1990s and had a cult following. She died of a drug overdose in 1996 a month after her biggest show was mounted at The Mattress Factory Gallery in Pittsburgh, Pennsylvania. That show, *It's About Me, Not You*, is now on permanent display there.

Around the same time—in the late 1970s—in Los Angeles, intersex gender nonconforming artist **Vaginal Davis** began making artwork in many different fields, and she continues today. She published the zines *Fertile La Toyah Jackson, Shrimp,* and *Yes, Ms. Davis,* and ran an outsider art gallery called "Hag" out of her Los Angeles apartment from 1982 to 1989. She also led art bands with names like *Black Fag* and *The Afro Sisters* in the 1980s and most recently *Tenderloin,* based in Berlin, her current home. Davis has made films and videos, hosted weekly queer parties like the punk-based Sucker and the jazz and cabaret-oriented Bricktops in Los Angeles in the 1990s and 2000s, and currently hosts an early cinema series at Arsenal Film and Video Institute in Berlin.

Since the later 1990s, trans and gender nonconforming contributors to the field of performance and visual art have been emerging rapidly, contributing prolifically to complex conversations about gender and culture and many other sociopolitical areas, as well as about the visual and performance art forms themselves. One of these, **Dr. Jordy Jones**, began making work in the early 2000s. A trans man artist and academic, Jones is an independent scholar, curator, collector, creator, and author. Two noteworthy pieces by Dr. Jones were featured in *Self-Organizing Men*, a collection edited by Jay Sennet (2006). In *Letterman*, Jones puts together boxes of prescription testosterone in the shape of a T. In *T-Ball*, he utilizes injection needles, used for administering testosterone, to form a sphere by pointing the needle ends together in the center. Dr. Jones is also a published author in both academic and nonacademic contexts. His first scholarly publication was an analysis of the film *Hedwig and the Angry Inch* in *The Transgender Studies Reader*, a pivotal collection which won the Lambda Literary Award in 2006.

Born in 1960 in Great Britain, **Grayson Perry** won the prestigious Turner Prize in 2003. A gender nonconforming artist who works in ceramics and textiles, Perry publicly identifies as a transvestite. Perry's "feminine alter ego" (Claire) figures prominently in the work, and Perry often appears at openings and in interviews in Claire state. Perry's work uses the commonness and utility of the ceramic pot to render social commentary both accessible and ordinary to the viewer. Perry may be the only open transvestite artist working today. Not coming from a queer community or background, Perry offers a perspective on normative society generated from a heterosexual, cisgender, but still very much gender nonconforming, vantage point.

Tobaron Waxman is a visual artist and a vocalist. Tobaron traditionally trained as a cantor (singer of Jewish liturgical music). Since 1991 Tobaron has created award-winning performance works, installations, photography, videos, and films. Their work has been exhibited and screened in Hong Kong, Tokyo, Tel Aviv, and Ramallah, and throughout Europe and North America. Tobaron's wide-ranging projects include the recent biotech piece, *Prayer Shawl for Dina*. The piece, named after the biblical trans male figure, is a memorial for women harmed in the name of medical science. Tobaron combined samples of their own cells and HeLa cells (cells harvested without consent from African American

Livush (Enclothement). Wearable artworks (used testosterone syringes and packaging). (Artist: Tobaron Waxman, Textile designer: Atom Cianfarani).

Some ongoing performance opportunities for trans artists include the *Fresh Meat Festival* in San Francisco (started in 2002 and organized by **Sean Dorsey**), and *Trans/giving* in Los Angeles, a monthly performance event explicitly intended for trans performers, writers, and poets.

Stages: The Transgender Theatre Festival went on in 2003 at the 33-year-old WOW café theatre in New York City. In 2007, WOW staged the three-weekend-long festival *Trans Art*, which featured **Ignacio Rivera** remounting his acclaimed show *Dancer* for the run of the festival, as well as cabarets and parties featuring artists such as **Glenn Marla, Holiday Simmons, Switch N Play, Debanuj DasGupta,** and **Katie Tikkun.**

cancer patient Henrietta Lacks in 1951 and commonly used in tissue engineering) to engineer living tissue out of which to fabricate a miniature *tallit* (Jewish ritual prayer shawl). For their project, *Opshernish*, Tobaron was awarded the first-ever Audience Award of the Jewish Museum of New York. In *Opshernish*, Tobaron's waist-length hair hung from the ceiling while gallery visitors cut Tobaron's locks, then buzzed and shaved the artist's head, over the course of an eight-hour endurance/live art installation. Tobaron's published texts, curatorial projects, and lectures on performance, vocal technique, art, gender, and philosophy are considered significant contributions to the field of contemporary art. In 2013, Tobaron created the first Intergenerational LGBTQ artist residency in Canada. Tobaron's most recent written work is *Trans Women Artists: Interviews With Artists on the MTF Spectrum* with a foreword by Susan Stryker (forthcoming 2015). Tobaron continues to perform internationally, creating site-specific, live installations for the a cappella transsexual voice.

Nina Arsenault puts her physical transformations center stage in her solo performance *The Silicone Diaries*. On the surface, the performance documents Arsenault's bodily metamorphoses, which have involved over 60 surgeries, toward an inhuman ideal of beauty. Her most recent work *Whore of Babylon: An Apocalyptic Pin Up Calendar (2013)* deconstructs and queers the idea of the pinup.

Heather Cassils is a gender nonconforming performance artist, whose intertwining backgrounds as a personal trainer, athlete, feminist, and Fluxus-inspired visual artist, are the clear and powerful motors for her work. In her most recent project, *CUTS: A Traditional Sculpture*, she set out to create herself into a living classical statue while remaining outside of and confronting the gender binary. Cassils accomplished a major physical transformation through extreme bodybuilding, overfeeding, and a short course of steroids, adding 23 pounds of gym-based muscle to her body and exaggerating and hypermasculinizing it.

In London, **Jason Elvis Barker** and **Serge Rizzler** (with an enormous amount of help from the London and surrounding trans and queer communities) put on *The Transfabulous Festival of International Transgender Arts* in 2006, 2007, and 2008. It brought together local and international artists such as **Kate Bornstein, Ignacio Rivera, Joey Hateley,** and French gender nonconforming rap group **Queer MC: Kings Du Berry**. The festival ran workshops and panels on trans arts as well as politics, health and community, and culminated in a mega dance party.

In 2011, **Mandy Romero** and **Adrian Turrell-Watts** organized two immersive trans arts festivals in Cologne, Germany, and Liverpool, England. The larger of the two, *Tranny Hotel Liverpool*, saw the takeover of the iconic Adelphi Hotel, filling bedrooms, banquet rooms, hallways, elevators, and stages with international trans and gender nonconforming artists, including **Ane Lan** (Norway), **Reggina Fiz** (Madrid), **Rae Spoon** (Canada), **Jo Clifford** (Scotland), **Jonny Woo** (London), and **Thom Shaw** (London).

New Yorker **Morty Diamond** does not limit his art to performance, and he has edited two anthologies, as well as making three films. His performance art engages with mainstream assumptions about gender and transgender people, as well as confronting some of the more common tropes of trans experience. In the piece *Ask a Tranny*, Diamond sets up a small table or booth in which the general public is literally invited to ask him anything. His goal in this piece is to draw attention to the scrutiny trans people face, and the sensationalism around trans lives that is constructed by the mainstream media.

Also living and working in Los Angeles, trans artist **Zackary Drucker** uses a range of performance forms and devices to explore physical identities, her own and others. Perhaps her best known piece is *ONE FIST (You have one fist in my mouth and one fist up my ass and your arms are trapped inside me like a Chinese fingertrap)*. This live performance sees Drucker mummified on a rotating turntable while the soundtrack oscillates between academic discourse on gender and a voice that speaks about the artist's objectification.

Multidisciplinary artist, academic, and activist, **micha cárdenas** has created performance pieces that mix computer technology and video projection with durational body practices, and work intersectionally (looking at the interactions of multiple systems of oppression), engaging with (trans)gender, race, class, migration, borders, and limits. She has made several large-scale projects, including *Becoming Dragon*, a "mixed reality" performance that challenges the medical establishment's requirement that trans people live a one-year "real-life experience" before they can access hormones and surgery. She offers a replacement one-year "Second Life Experience" to lead to species reassignment surgery. cárdenas was also a lead researcher in the creation of the *Transborder Immigrant Tool*, a GPS device designed to map the areas nearest the US/Mexican border and locate and identify border patrols and "Homeland Security" operations as well as highlight food, water, and support communities near the border, in order to improve the odds of immigrant safety.

Gender nonconforming and mysterious **boychild** is an emerging performance and makeup artist whose work is almost undefinable. boychild makes performances that are drag and lip sync, both ungendered and full of gender, and that have elements of fashion show, dance, and Japanese Butoh, covered in florescent paint and foil, both heavily costumed and naked. boychild's body and work resist categorization, destroying distinctions of gender, sexuality, and race. boychild also models, and has done gallery shows and worked in music videos.

A trans male artist trained in the ceramic arts, **Kris Grey** works with his body and his trans identity both sculpturally and autobiographically. Like artist **Morty Diamond**, Grey also has an "ask a tranny" project, taking his sign with him whenever he travels and performing "ask a tranny" interventions. His live art gallery work *Untitled 2* sees his body as sculpture, painted white and standing naked behind a nude female body form, also white, which, at least in video documentation, plays with the illusion of being Grey's pretransition body. Over time Grey steps out from behind it to reveal his trans body, and the two sculptures stand side by side.

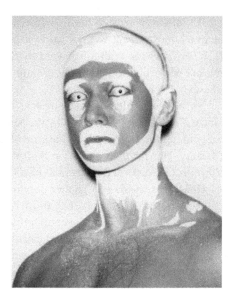

"boychild" (courtesy of boychild).

Wu Tsang. Still from *The Shape of a Right Statement*, 2008, HD video (NTSC) (courtesy of the artist and Clifton Benevento).

Minneapolis-based multidisciplinary artist **Andrea Jenkins** is a trans activist, a playwright, a visual, performance, and spoken word artist, and curator. In her visual work she uses collaging techniques to contrast popular consumerist imagery with graphics and texts of social justice. Her pieces draw attention to discrimination and injustice against African Americans, women, and trans and LGBTQ communities.

Wu Tsang is a Los Angeles–based gender nonconforming Chinese and Swedish American performance artist, filmmaker, and community activist. In 2012, Tsang released their first feature documentary film *Wildness*, about the experience of hosting a queer party and interacting with the traditional customers of the Silver Platter, a landmark bar in Los Angeles with Latina trans women clientele.

MEDIA SPOTLIGHT: GENDER VARIANCE IN MANGA AND ANIME

Dallas Denny and Jamison Green

Manga and anime are Japanese- originated media—comics and animations, respectively—that typically portray fantastical scenarios. In Japan, and increasingly in other countries, both males and females emulate characters from manga, anime, and related videogames; this is called *cosplay*. Many portrayals cross gender lines; when this happens, it's called *crossplay*. Cosplay has also become a staple of the visual kei movement in Japanese pop culture. Musically and sartorially, visual kei shares elements with Western glam, punk rock, and metal—often including androgynous self-presentation. Some visual kei artists, like Hizaki of the late band Versailles, perfect the appearance of female anime characters.

Teru, Kamijo, and Hizaki of the band Versailles, performing in Santiago, Chile, June 6, 2010.

Japanese comics frequently depict cross-dressing and sex changes. The main character in Shazuri Seino's *Girl Got Game* is a girl whose father forces her to live as a boy in order to play sports. Hisaya Nakago's *Hana-Kimi* has a similar theme. Emura's *W Juliet* is the story of a relationship between a tomboy and a feminine young man. Bisco Hatori's *Ouran High School Host Club* has a young woman dressing as a boy to get a job in order to pay for an expensive vase she has broken. *You and My Secret* features a masculine girl (tomboy) and a feminine boy switching bodies. There are dozens of other titles with trans characters.

The Hub Kids' Network's new show, the manga-influenced *SheZow*, features a 12-year-old boy who becomes a female superhero whenever he wears a magic ring. Although the show's producers deny the character is transgendered, right-wing organizations have protested it.

The anime series *Le Chevalier d'Eon* is loosely based upon the real-life exploits of the 19th-century French nobleperson le Chevalier d'Eon de Beaumont, whose sex was a subject of gossip and wagers throughout hir later years. In the anime, d'Eon is periodically possessed by the spirit of his dead sister and his physical form changes to female. Because d'Eon is drawn androgynously, the change is identifiable primarily by differences in clothing and hairstyle.

Rumiko Takahashi's *Ranma ½* features a young man who changes into a girl whenever he gets wet. The trans man who donated the *Ranma* comics to the National Transgender Library & Archive told Dallas that he found the title a powerful aid in his quest for identity.

WRITING/PUBLISHING

Transgender literary culture is as varied as the trans community. There are transgender novelists, transsexual memoirists, genderqueer poets, and others who defy labels altogether. Trans authors have contributed to a wide range of literary forms, including fiction, memoir, creative nonfiction, and poetry. Beyond this, there are innumerable trans characters written by cisgender authors, with varying levels of accuracy or cultural competency. Trans experiences and identities are increasingly present in mainstream literary cultures.

While there have always been trans and gender nonconforming writers, many of them remained unpublished and their work has been lost or buried. The emergence and growth of trans visibility in mainstream culture and the trans and gender nonconforming political movement has created more opportunities for trans writers to publish their work and attain a higher level of recognition for their art and craft. The former lack of publishing opportunities for trans writers meant that the only literary portrayals of trans and gender nonconforming subjects available in the culture were by cisgender authors. Not all of these portrayals are positive, and many of them are downright offensive.

It can be difficult to break trans writers out into specific genres, forms, and styles, as is normally done for describing a writer's work. Many trans writers incorporate poetry, memoir, and creative narrative into their work, crossing and blurring artistic boundaries to create new forms that speak specifically to their content.

Beyond blurring literary genres, trans writers often face the burden of representation in their work. It is often assumed that a trans author writing trans characters or experiences must be working from a memoir or autobiographical perspective, which can make it difficult for trans novelists and fiction authors to incorporate trans content into their work without it being assumed that they are representing their own experience. The burden of representation can also make it difficult for trans authors to write honest portrayals of trans experiences or include trans characters with flaws. There are already so many negative fictional portrayals of trans people that there is a lot of pressure to only portray trans lives and experiences in a positive light. Some trans authors complain that this expectation makes it difficult to write honestly about the communities that they live in and the people that inhabit them.

Not all trans writers include explicitly trans themes or characters in their work. There are a variety of reasons for this. Some authors do not want to deal with the expectation that they are speaking for the trans community, or want to be free from assumptions that their writing is primarily memoir. Others seek to reach mainstream audiences and are concerned that including explicitly trans content will make their stories less relevant or interesting to mass-market audiences. Still others find their writing inspiration outside of specifically trans and gender nonconforming themes.

Trans Authors

As with every other genre, it is impossible to profile every trans author ever published, but a sample can show us the diverse range of trans writers.

T Cooper deserves recognition as one the few out trans authors writing and publishing fictional novels today. Cooper's work includes *Some of the Parts, Lipschitz 6 or 2 Angry Blondes*, and *The Beaufort Diaries*. Though Cooper's books are not exclusively trans or queer, he does include transgender characters, and themes of gender, identity, family, and community thread through his work. Cooper has attained a level of mainstream success, having published in *The New Yorker* and *The New York Times*.

S. Bear Bergman writes memoir-based short stories and essays, which primarily focus on the day-to-day lived queer realities that Bergman experiences. He published a book prior to transitioning (*Butch Is a Noun*) that delved into his experiences as a masculine gender nonconforming person. His next book, *The Nearest Exit May Be Behind You*, includes stories of how his life changed after beginning transition, reflecting on the humor and frustrations that come with being read as male. Recently, Bergman has begun to publish children's books under the publishing banner Flamingo Rampant.

EliClare writes poetry that is packed with detail that brings his poems to life. His work is profoundly intersectional, balancing trans and crip experiences alongside antiracist activism and reflections on his childhood in rural Oregon.

Eli Shipley, a trans male poet based in New York City, writes layered and rich lyric poems. His work does not necessarily interface with trans themes, and he has joked that (as a college professor) he had a harder time finding a job because he was a poet than because he was trans.

Kit Yan and Kay Ulanday Barrett at the *Trans Bodies, Trans Selves* New York City Forum (photo by Katia Ruiz).

Leslie Feinberg may be the most well-known author within the trans community. S/he wrote *Stone Butch Blues*, chronicling a butch's coming of age and eventual decision to go on testosterone. *Stone Butch Blues* is published as a fiction novel, but it does have notable parallels to Feinberg's life. The book's portrayal of one character's journey through gender resonates strongly with many masculine gender nonconforming people, elevating the book to a canonical status within trans literature. Feinberg has gone on to publish other nonfiction and fiction books, including *Transgender Liberation, Transgender Warriors*, and *Drag King Dreams*. Feinberg is well known as an activist and leader within the trans community, and hir writing work is an extension of hir commitment to social change.

Ja'briel Walthour is a transgender advocate residing in Hinesville, Georgia—a small, military community located outside Savannah. She has contributed to the *Huffington Post* and has authored a children's book series loosely based on her experience growing up transgender in the South. Her books include *Apple of My Eye, Jacob's Journey, Fat Kids, Black Kids, Tomboys, and Cissies*, and *Where's My Rock?*

Publishing

The past decade has seen significant advances in publishing for trans and gender nonconforming people. There are now multiple publishing houses that are by and for trans people, as well as magazines and a vibrant zine community. These developments in trans publishing are making it easier for trans voices to be heard by broader audiences, as well as supporting the further development of authors and poets within the trans community.

One of the first publishing houses to focus specifically on trans and gender nonconforming authors and content is **Homofactus Press**. Homofactus was founded in 2006 in Michigan, first publishing the anthology *Self-Organizing Men*. Publisher **Jay Sennet** conceived of Homofactus Press with the mission of distributing literary works by and for trans people. This trans-owned independent publishing house went on to publish a book of **Eli Clare**'s poetry, **Scott Turner Schofield**'s collected plays, and several other nonfiction books that were specifically relevant to trans and gender nonconforming experience.

Kit Yan, an API (Asian Pacific Islander) poet and trans man, is a slam and performance poet. His sharp verse balances descriptions of conflict and discord within queer communities with graphic descriptions of joy, celebration, and possibility.

Trans pin@y (Philippine background) poet **Kay Ulanday Barrett** twists laughter and tears into his poetry, alternately admonishing, encouraging, and elevating the queer and trans communities that he heavily features in his work.

Ignacio Rivera performs slam poetry about his experiences as a genderqueer person of color, once again giving voice to the layers of intersectionality that mark much of contemporary trans poetic practice.

Ryka Aoki De La Cruz works in many mediums, including music and theater, as well as poetry. She has published multiple poetry chapbooks, and she regularly performs her poems across the United States. Her poetry is dense and lush, full of imagery and powerful metaphors.

J MASE III describes himself as a "Black/Trans/Queer/ Rowdy-as-Hell Poet with a capital [P] based in Philly." He is a "poet with a foul mouth and a good cause," who, in his piece *Neighbor*, tells us "every time a post-dyke transfag thrusts, a muthuhfucking fairy gets its wings!"

Another transgender publishing house, **Topside Press**, was founded in 2011 in Brooklyn, New York, by **Tom Leger** and **Riley MacLeod**. Tom Leger was inspired to found the press because he observed that, while trans voices were finding more outlets for memoir and creative nonfiction, there was a lack of transgender novelists and fiction authors. Topside Press seeks to foster the growth of transgender literary fiction authors, giving trans authors the opportunity to step out of memoir-based work if they so desire.

Zines

Zines are another dimension of transgender literature and publishing. Due to the limited publishing opportunities that have been available to trans and gender nonconforming people until recently, some trans writers have chosen to self-publish their work in handmade zines. There is a vibrant trans zine community, ranging from long-running serial zines to single-issue releases on special topics. Zines have been particularly popular with young trans people because they are an extremely accessible mode of publishing—all a writer needs is access to a photocopy machine. The self-published, small-run nature of zines makes them a highly ephemeral publication form. There are some zine libraries that have specifically focused on collecting queer and trans zines, but even these collections are very incomplete. Trans zines are an important part of trans literary culture because they offer a view of raw, unedited, young transgender writers.

The Queer Zine Archive Project (qzap.org) keeps a "living history" of past and present queer zines.

Trans zine titles include *Original Plumbing/Translady Fanzine* (New York/San Francisco), *Dude: Trans Male Fanzine* (Melbourne, Australia), *trans.zine* (Winnipeg, Manitoba), *Genderfailz Nos. 1 & 2* (Microcosm Publishing), *Gendercide*, and *Copper Rose* (Vancouver, British Colombia).

CONCLUSION

Trans and gender nonconforming artists are forging a vibrant trans arts culture, creating new space for ourselves and our work in the larger alternative arts, academic, and activist cultures, and making inroads into the mainstream arts. Today's artists will continue to grow and develop, and new artists will emerge, and are emerging, almost constantly. The visibility and impact of trans and gender nonconforming arts and artists cannot help but spread until we really will be found *everywhere*.

REFERENCES AND FURTHER READING

Fischer-Lichte, E. (2008). *The transformative power of performance: A new aesthetics.* New York, NY: Routledge.

Foster, S. L. (2010). *Choreographing empathy: Kinesthesia in performance.* New York, NY: Routledge.

Newman, T. (2013, October 2). Transgender people of color. *Huffington Post.* Retrieved January 2014, http://www.huffingtonpost.com/tag/transgender-people-of-color

Noble, K. A. (n.d.). *Changeling aspects.* Retrieved January 2014, from http://www.changelingaspects.com/index.htm

Ludwig, T., & Piechocki, R. (2007). *Trappings: Stories of women, power and clothing.* New Brunswick, NJ: Rutgers.

Lynn, S. (n.d.). *TG forum.* Retrieved January 2014, from http://www.tgforum.com/wordpress/

Roberts, M. (n.d.). *TransGriot: News, opinions, commentary, history and a little creative writing from a proud African-American transwoman about the world around her.* Retrieved January 2014, from: http://transgriot.blogspot.com

Transgender artists you should know: A roundup in honor of the Day of Remembrance. (2012, November 20). *Huffington Post.* Retrieved January 2014, from http://www.huffingtonpost.com/2012/11/20/transgender-artists-you-s_n_2160016.html

Trans-Genre Artists. (n.d.). *Trans Genre.* Retrieved January 2014, from http://trans-genre.net/artists/

ACTIVISM, POLITICS, AND ORGANIZING

24

Peter Cava

As transgender and gender nonconforming (TGNC) people, we share a vibrant history of coming together as activists and organizers. We have built community and claimed our power despite systems that limit our opportunities. We have worked to end oppression. This work has instilled hope and joy. Many of us consider ourselves activists; others of us do not. All of us make important contributions to social change. We can learn more about many of these contributions by reflecting on our activist histories, our political strategies, and our contemporary organizing.

IN MY BLOOD

Marisa Richmond, PhD, is the secretary of the National Center for Transgender Equality and the founder of the Tennessee Transgender Political Coalition.

Marisa Richmond with Diego Sanchez (MA) and Kylar Broadus (MO), Democratic National Convention, Charlotte, NC, Sept. 2012.

Politics have been in my blood prior to my first memories. Both of my parents stood up publicly against segregation even before I was born. When Stokely Carmichael, head of the Student Nonviolent Coordinating Committee, came to speak at several colleges in Nashville, we hosted a reception for him in our home. My first campaign occurred when my mother took me with her to distribute literature for John Kennedy for president. A few years later, she took me to see President Kennedy's motorcade through Nashville. As the open limo went by, barely 15 feet from me standing on the sidewalk, I swear he turned and looked right at me as he smiled and waved. I have been hooked on politics ever since.

Growing up, I did not see trans activism in my future. I thought being out as trans and being politically active were mutually exclusive. Was I ever wrong. I started thinking about being more active after the murder of Nashville native Christian Paige in Chicago in 1996. Contrary to press reports, we were not "best friends," but we were friendly. Her horrific murder, which remains unsolved to this day, touched many of us deeply who knew her.

During the 2004 Democratic National Convention in Boston, there was the first true Transgender Caucus, with seven delegates. Although I had participated in the delegate selection process in Tennessee, I was not an active candidate myself. I was thrilled to be selected as an at-large delegate from Tennessee in Denver in 2008. I knew I was the first from Tennessee, but a story in the *Washington Blade* revealed that I was the first African American trans delegate from anywhere. The significance of this historic achievement hit home on the first night of the convention. While I was sitting in the Tennessee section responding to a text message, a CNN camera pointed right in my face. When I checked my e-mail later in the evening, my inbox was full of comments. The ones that touched me the most were from other African American trans women who all said the same basic thing: "I saw someone who looked like me; I finally feel like I have a seat at the table."

COALITIONS AND CONFLICTS

Trans people have played pivotal roles in many social movements. At times, these movements have included and encouraged us; at other times, they have left us feeling alienated, even heartbroken. All of these instances can serve as lessons about how to build on the past.

The Feminist Movement

Feminism can be defined as a movement to end oppression based on sex or gender. Because of feminism, gender has become less hierarchical and less rigid. This social change has laid a foundation for contemporary TGNC activism. Today, many feminists and trans activists work together to challenge the continuing realities of sexism, misogyny, and restrictive gender roles.

Many feminists categorize developments in feminism into "waves." According to this model, the first wave took place in the 1800s and early 1900s and championed women's right to vote. The second wave emerged in the 1960s through the 1980s and has covered a broader range of issues, such as gender equality in the workplace and at home.

Second-wave feminism has included many perspectives. Some second-wave feminists have construed women as sharing a common experience of oppression and men as sharing a common experience of privilege. This analysis has helped these feminists to better understand, and organize around, their experiences. However, it does not account for the full diversity of our lives. Each of us has varied (and sometimes nonbinary) embodiments and expressions of gender that affect whether we have power or privilege in particular situations. Moreover, we have intersecting identities, such as race and class, that complicate the notion that all men have privilege over all women at all times.

Some second-wave feminists have separated women from men not only in theory but also in practice by creating women's spaces. These spaces have served as havens from a male-dominated public world. Attempting to make these spaces as safe as possible, some feminists have policed group members' identities. However well-intentioned, this practice has led to hurtful perceptions about, and practices toward, trans people. Some feminists have perceived transmasculine people as traitors—that is, as women who identify politically with men (Rubin, 2006, pp. 473, 476). When inclusive of trans men, these feminists have often gendered them as women. Conversely, these feminists have tended to perceive transfeminine people as infiltrators of womanhood and of women's space. Many commentators refer to feminists who think in these ways as "trans-exclusionary radical feminists" (TERFs).

> *"Many of the lesbian feminists I knew when I started my transition felt that I was betraying them by choosing to be a man. I knew that I would be betraying myself if I chose to keep living a lie."*

> *"The fetishistic (often infantalizing) embrace of trans men by lesbian communities is ungendering, othering, and transphobic."*

> *"All too often they try to include me as 'really a woman' or as a 'special decaf man-lite' while excluding those who should be welcome, like trans women and nonbinary people who were assigned male at birth."*

> *"Being rejected by feminists hurts so much because I value feminism dearly."*

Today, many trans people observe that feminism has become increasingly supportive and inclusive.

> *"The feminist movement has a shameful history of transphobia that is still going strong in many parts of the movement. Fortunately, many feminists are also speaking out on trans* issues, including trans* identities in feminist discussions, including trans* people in feminist spaces, and calling out feminists who exclude and bully.. . . I am deeply involved in feminism because I believe that feminism can be a safe, positive place for trans* people even if we're not there yet."*

> *"I have become involved in V-Day and The Vagina Monologues this year, whose purpose is to 'end violence against women and girls.' I have interpreted that to mean 'gendered violence.' I have felt very accepted within this group of mostly women. I was very worried about auditioning, because it asked for women performers only. I e-mailed the national V-Day organization, in addition to the organizers at my college. From both I received extremely supportive answers. They understood that trans voices were needed within the feminist community.*

When I changed my name and pronoun, they quickly changed as well, even asking me further questions to make me feel more accepted. By being a part of an activist community that is not exclusively queer and/or trans, I feel that my voice is louder and I am still making real change."

As feminism has grown and changed, new feminist perspectives have developed. Especially since the late 1970s and 1980s, sex-positive feminists have advocated for acceptance of a wider range of sexual practices, and women-of-color and poststructural feminists have pointed out that there is not just one experience of womanhood. According to many feminists, a third wave of feminism emerged in the 1990s. Third-wave feminists have emphasized the importance of welcoming difference, ambiguity, and even contradiction into feminism.

One of the newest feminist perspectives is **transfeminism** (alternatively written as *trans feminism*). In 2000, Diana Courvant and Emi Koyama created the Web site transfeminism.org, and Koyama wrote "The Transfeminist Manifesto" (2003). According to the manifesto, transfeminism "is primarily a movement by and for trans women who view their liberation to be intrinsically linked to the liberation of all women and beyond" (Koyama, 2003, p. 245). Since the manifesto, Koyama has elaborated that transfeminism also includes trans men and genderqueer people. More recently, transfeminists have published two anthologies (A. Enke, 2012; Scott-Dixon, 2006).

An ongoing feminist debate that impacts trans communities concerns whether feminine women are oppressed *by* their femininity or *for* their femininity. Many feminists believe that women are oppressed by feminine roles. These feminists may call for women to break free from femininity and may accuse transfeminine people of reinforcing gender stereotypes. However, trans feminist Julia Serano (2013) has emphasized that feminine people are oppressed *for* their femininity and that this oppression is a form of misogyny (pp. 49–53). Serano (2007) has therefore called for feminists to reclaim femininity, not to eschew it or to criticize transfeminine people (pp. 319–343).

Gay and LGBTQ Movements

The homophile movement was the mainstay of US gay political organizing in the 1940s and 1950s. (Prior to the advent of the word *gay*, many participants used the term *homophile* because it emphasizes *philia*, or "love.") Homophile activists lobbied, published, and led orderly demonstrations against discrimination. Transsexual man Reed Erickson funded an early homophile organization.

Fed up with injustice and inspired by other movements, gay activists became bolder in the 1960s. Both gay and trans activists participated in the 1969 Stonewall Riots, a series of violent uprisings against police who had been raiding gay bars in New York City. These uprisings served as catalysts in the formation of the gay liberation movement. Trans people, such as Sylvia Rivera, helped to create gay liberation organizations.

Soon thereafter, gay activists began to exclude trans people from the movement. Some of these activists felt that the movement should oppose the medical establishment because of its negative views about homosexuality. These activists worried that many trans people were becoming too dependent on the medical establishment for hormones and surgery (Stryker, 2008, pp. 95–98).

In the mid-1970s and 1980s, the pendulum of American culture swung in a socially conservative direction. Most gay people followed suit by leaving behind the gay liberation movement's countercultural clothing and haircuts in favor of a more conformist look. This new look became associated with the gay rights movement. Gay rights activists argued to conservative America that the only difference between gay and straight people is what they do in the privacy of their bedrooms. This argument marginalized trans people because gay rights activists thought of trans people's displays of difference as public rather than private (Valentine, 2007, pp. 29–65).

Julia Serano's book *Excluded: Making Feminist and Queer Movements More Inclusive* explores ways to infuse feminist and LGBTQ movements with broader goals.

"I have on occasion experienced discrimination from individuals within the greater LGB community. This discrimination generally takes the form that I as a trans person am highly visible as being different, which causes the straight community to have a negative view of the LGB community."

In the 1990s, the gay rights movement expanded into the LGBT rights movement. The acronym LGBT has signified greater inclusion. It has communicated that trans and LGB people have shared common struggles. For example, feminine boys and masculine girls have been bullied in schools across the country, simultaneously for their gender expression (which is thought of as a trans issue) and for their perceived sexual orientation (which is thought of as a gay issue). Therefore, everyone under the LGBT umbrella would benefit from greater social acceptance of diverse gender expressions.

Although the acronym LGBT has signified greater inclusion, it has led to some confusion. By separating LGBT identities into distinct letters, the acronym can imply that trans people are by definition not lesbian, gay, or bisexual, even though about half of us self-identify in these ways (Grant et al., 2011, p. 28). By grouping LGBT identities together, the acronym can perpetuate the misconception that trans identities are sexual orientations.

"There sure is a lot of ignorance on gender issues among gay and lesbian folks. Commonly, sexual orientation and gender are conflated in odd ways.... I often have to redirect the conversation to focus on gender, setting aside sexual orientation."

As LGBT communities have coalesced, many trans people have felt fully included in them.

"In the communities that I am involved in, I feel that my identity has been embraced. Actually, in most cases, the GLBT communities that I am involved in have become a replacement for the families I lost."

However, sometimes trans people still encounter exclusionary attitudes in spaces designated as LGBT.

"I marched in the NYC Pride parade and local Pride parade but TGs were a minority and oddity.... There was never anything said but we were definitely not embraced."

Some trans people find local LGBT communities supportive but have less faith that the national LGBT rights movement will stand up for us. Many of us were disappointed and outraged by the decision of the Human Rights Campaign (HRC) in 2007 to support a version of the national Employment Non-Discrimination Act (ENDA) bill that included sexual orientation but not gender identity or expression.

Urvashi Vaid's powerful book *Irresistible Revolution: Confronting Race, Class and the Assumptions of LGBT Politics* stresses the importance of intersecting identities in LGBTQ political work.

"Within my immediate community, I feel accepted by the LGB folk around me. They are supportive and accepting of my identity and other gender-variant and trans identities. Within the context of the larger community, I feel trans voices are marginalized and we are not embraced at all. Politically, we have been thrown under the bus so many times it has become depressing to count."

"My personal experience in the larger LGBT community has been fine, but watching the relationship on a larger scale in the press is often infuriating. I wish I could say that the debacle with the Human Rights Campaign and ENDA was an isolated case, but I don't think it is."

Many trans people critique the LGBT rights movement for its political priorities.

"The discrimination I deal with from the LGB community is in assigning resources. There is a large push on same-sex marriage and DADT ['Don't Ask, Don't Tell'] but very little on issues dealing with gender identity and expression. The reality is that trans people face much higher levels of discrimination. We are relegated to the sex trades because no one will hire us, and we are the

Left OUT Party, picketing annual fundraising dinner, July 26, 2008, San Francisco (photo by Cary Bass).

object of hate crimes at a much higher rate than the greater LGBT community. I feel that resources need to concentrate on ensuring that we can get a job and protect ourselves before we concentrate on areas where it would be nice to make gains but lives don't necessarily depend on it."

"When the term 'LGBT rights' is used, these days that seems to mean gay marriage, 'Don't Ask Don't Tell' abolishment, and fights that prioritize the needs of the most privileged LGBT people instead of those who are most marginalized— trans women of color, homeless gender-variant youth, undocumented LGBT folks, impoverished LGBT people who are HIV+."

"I've been told, flat out, that I should be okay with shelving my civil rights so that LGB people can get theirs. I was told that I should be okay with this because once LGB people 'get theirs' they have historically made things better for trans people, and trans-inclusion invariably follows. ... Being asked to surrender my civil rights in favor of someone else's, for a dubious ... lag in equality, because I'm seen as simultaneously a political ally and a political liability, is alienating."

A STARTING POINT

Mattilda Bernstein Sycamore, described as "startlingly bold and provocative" by Howard Zinn, "a cross between Tinkerbell and a honky Malcolm X with a queer agenda" by the Austin Chronicle, *and "a gender-fucking tower of pure pulsing purple fabulous" by* The Stranger, *is most recently the author of a memoir,* The End of San Francisco.

In 1993, at age 19, I attended the March on Washington for Lesbian, Gay, and Bisexual Rights ("transgender" was not yet part of the rhetoric). I went to protest with ACT UP (the AIDS Coalition to Unleash Power) for single-payer health care—we were hoping to gather hundreds of people for a civil disobedience action at the Capitol but ended up with only a few dozen arrests, and barely any media attention. Meanwhile, a million people attended the march: It felt like an endless stream of white gays in white T-shirts applying for Community Spirit credit cards while salivating over gays in the military.

Perhaps it seems naïve to think that universal health care could have become a central issue for the national gay struggle, but at the height of the AIDS crisis in the United States, when so many queers had lost friends, lovers, and entire social networks, there was more attention paid to accessing basic needs. The March on Washington stood for me as a watershed moment when the central issue for national gay politics became not the provision of health care for all, but the fight for the right to go abroad and kill people of color in unjust wars.

I was bashed just one day after a million gay people packed up their suitcases and fled our nation's capital (the place where I'd grown up), leaving no noticeable change except streets filled with garbage. That night two frat types spotted me making out with the person who would soon become my first boyfriend—they sprayed pepper spray directly into my eyes from a few inches away, sending me to the hospital where worried staff pumped saline into my eyes for an hour so I wouldn't risk losing my vision. This illuminated my politics in a way almost too palpable: The assimilationist gay version of "we're just like you" normalcy would never make visible queers safer.

This was nowhere more clear to me than in the campaign for same-sex marriage that soon eclipsed every other issue. Never mind that queers had struggled for decades to create transformative ways to love, live with, lust for, and take care of one another not based on state approval. Never mind that marriage was (and is) a central site of anti-woman, antiqueer, antitrans, and antichild violence. Forget about fighting for sexual liberation or self-determination—the gay establishment tells us that marriage will deliver "full equality." Even when the agenda shifts to fighting antiqueer violence, an issue that affects every queer person in some way, the focus remains on accessing fundamental systems of oppression, in this case by championing a law-and-order response centering around hate crime legislation. How far the gay movement has come from the original ideals of gay liberation, which centered around fighting against police control over queer lives.

The current "LGBT" movement prioritizes the desires of the most privileged while screwing over everyone else. It trumpets unquestioning patriotism, willful gentrification, and rabid consumerism in its never-ending quest for status in the status quo. But no one should be forced to get married or to join the military in order to obtain basic needs—housing, health care, food, a sex life that matters, and the right to stay in this country (or leave) should be resources available to all. Let's get back to a queer politic that demands gender, sexual, social, economic, and political self-determination for all. As a starting point.

During the 1990s, while the LGBT rights movement was picking up steam, a more countercultural movement—the queer movement—was hitting the scene. Since the 16th century, the word *queer* had referred to anything different from the norm ("Queer," 2013). By the early 20th century, *queer* had developed into pejorative slang for feminine gay men ("Queer," 2013). In the 1990s, members of HIV/AIDS and gay activist organizations, such as ACT-UP (AIDS Coalition to Unleash Power) and Queer Nation, reclaimed *queer* to communicate that they proudly differed from, and defied, the heterosexual norm.

Among trans people who feel excluded from the LGBT rights movement, many feel more at home in the queer movement.

> "I feel most at home with queer-identified people, and much less so with mainstream cis lesbian and gay people who are invested in getting access to privilege and want to disassociate [from] 'radicals' and 'weirdos,' which often means people like me."

> "I'm a radical queer. Friends and I follow the 'I'm not gay as in happy, but queer as in fuck you' mantra. I'm involved with such things as Bash Back!, Guerrilla Queer Bar, and other ways of creating space for queers and nontraditional lovers. These communities are beautiful—full of love and passion and consent and trust. I feel at home among these people. They've helped me to be who I am and to feel safe and strong when I walk down the street at night. My friends and comrades give me more strength than I ever thought was imaginable."

> "I quickly left the undergraduate GLBTA group in favor of the local 'fringe' queer community. Here I found queer master's and PhD students who completely embraced me, my sexuality, and my gender identity. I met the coordinators of our local drag shows—a couple of sweet lesbians who, to this day, remain two of the most tenacious trans advocates I know."

Some trans people feel less at home in the queer movement. Queer subculture celebrates sexualities and genders that are perceived as defying the norm. More particularly, because American culture associates defiance with masculinity, and because the male-female binary is the norm, queer subculture tends to celebrate genders that are masculine or non-binary, such as those of trans men and genderqueer people (Serano, 2007, pp. 346–348). Sometimes this celebration comes with a negative flipside: the devaluation of genders—such as feminine and binary ones—that are perceived as "not queer enough" (Serano, 2007, pp. 345–362).

IDENTITY POLITICS

Axil Cricchio is a PhD candidate and social science professor.

"Identity politics" describes how our identities shape the way we experience the world and navigate our position with others in social and cultural situations. Theorists have long been preoccupied with identity as either a biologically determined factor or as a socially constructed entity—or what is more commonly referred to as the *nature versus nurture debate*. Not all theorists have accepted the explanations for either category (nature or nurture) having more influence over the other when it comes to identity. Whether we self-actualize or someone names our identity for us, it is essentially agreed upon by many that identity is multifaceted.

Frank Browning suggests that the act of identifying is itself very limiting. He suggests that we have already begun to limit ourselves once we attempt to find an answer to the question, "Who am I?" He suggests that once we answer that question we have excluded all of the things that we are *not*. This brings up the notion of bi-oppositional categories, which are categories that can be considered opposite from one another, such as *female/male* or *heterosexual/homosexual*. These opposing categories bring up the possibility that identity is determined in relationship to other identities where one identity is considered the norm.

As we move toward the future, *transgender* is becoming more of a concept of boundary-fluid gender expression rather than the action of individuals changing their bodies and presentations of gender to match their identity. For some, it is becoming contextualized that gender is transformative, transgressive, and transcendent rather than a fixed, indisputable, biologically driven category. For others, the concept of transgender is completely embedded in the heteronormative, where transitioning one's gender can be seen much less as transcending gender roles, expressions, and presentations and, instead, as subscribing to a notion that one must change from one set of gender ideals to the *opposite* set of gender ideals. Given the complexities of identity theory, it may be that those who do not fit neatly into the rigidly constructed categories might be leading the way to rethinking how the categories were constructed in the first place, thus re-envisioning a politics of identity that encompasses all gender expressions.

Like the homophile, gay liberation, and gay rights movements before them, the LGBT rights and queer movements represent different strategies for social change. The LGBT rights movement seeks to extend the social structure's protections to LGBT people. Queer activists argue that this strategy cannot end oppression and that, instead, we need to change the social structure on a fundamental level.

Trans people have been involved in LGBTQ movements from the beginning. Unfortunately, we have found ourselves in a double bind: Many gay liberation and queer activists have thought of us as trying too hard to fit into society, whereas many gay rights and LGBT rights activists have thought of us as not trying hard enough. Nevertheless, we are building LGBTQ movements that encompass all of our needs.

PRIORITIZING THE LESS PRIVILEGED

Minister Louis J. Mitchell

As a child of the 1960s, I witnessed protest and prayer, flower power and uncombed hippie love, raised fists and black berets—all working to create new opportunities, options, and freedoms. While I had fears about my transition, I'd already survived addiction and suicide attempts. I knew how to make hard decisions.

More challenging than my transition from female to male has been my transition from woman to black man. The racism, in and out of the LGBTQ communities, has continued to shock, hurt, and dismay me. I understand why so many of my trans siblings choose not to be a part of these communities. What, if anything, do these communities have to offer?

I am frequently called upon to help groups and organizations with their "diversity." My challenge is almost always the same. It seems that rather than a consciousness of layered oppressions or issues, there is a notion of a continuum of oppression, that is, civil rights for women and blacks in the 1960s; civil rights for gay and lesbian folks in the 1990s; civil rights for transgender folks, now! This assumes a great many things, the most disturbing and egregious is that women, blacks, lesbians, and gay men have already overcome and really should just get behind "our" movements!

I often question the ways that "the movement" organizes—who has access, who has power, who prioritizes the issues? There also seems to be a pervasive idea that, unless one's work has been LGBTQ specific or unless you have academic achievement letters after your name or are titled by some organization, you have yet to arrive at a place where your voice, vision, knowledge, and experiences deserve to be broadly valued. This means that many longtime activists are underappreciated because their work has been on issues most pressing to their cultural communities. Unless and until some of these issues have been really explored and dealt with—and some amends made—I don't hold a lot of hope that the kind of diversity that is desired will be achieved.

I remain cautiously optimistic but choose to use the majority of my energy working in and with communities of color for our mutual support, not to the exclusion of other organizations, but being clear that I am privileging our work, our families, and our communities.

Morgan Bassichis, Alexander Lee, and Dean Spade (2011) have suggested ways to transform social systems rather than pushing for inclusion and equality within them. For example, a big problem that LGBTQ activists face is inadequate health care coverage. The "official" solution is to legalize marriage for same-sex couples so that more people will be able to share their health benefits with their spouses; in contrast, a transformative approach is to fight for universal health care (Bassichis, Lee, & Spade, 2011, p. 17).

The Philly Trans Health Conference works hard to make participation accessible. Attendance is free, the convention center is wheelchair accessible, the bathrooms are gender inclusive, large-print copies of the schedule are available, American Sign Language interpreters are present, and lunch (with nut-free, gluten-free, and vegetarian options) is served each day for a $1 suggested donation (no one is turned away due to lack of funds).

BUILDING MOVEMENTS THAT REPRESENT US

Having participated in the great social movements of the last century, trans people have learned valuable lessons. We have a chance to decide on our priorities and strategies as we move forward.

Intersectionality

Feminist and LGBTQ movements have not always accounted for the intersectionality of our identities. For trans people, our experiences are shaped not only by our trans status but also by how that status intersects with other aspects of who we are. We experience oppression and gain privilege simultaneously due to our race, class, physical ability, mental ability, sexual orientation, age, religion, nationality, immigration status, body size, and other identities. It also matters whether we are transfeminine or transmasculine, whether we live as trans part-time or full-time, whether we transition hormonally, whether we transition surgically, and whether we are read as members of our self-identified genders.

Ideally, all TGNC activists would use an intersectional approach. This practice would require us to ask difficult questions about how our organizations run and who benefits from them. For example, some of our groups do not have members who self-identify as disabled. We may want to ask ourselves why. Are the events accessible? Does the group create a space for people to be open about disabilities?

Organizations (trans or not) tend to attract like-minded people. We are most comfortable when those around us seem similar to us. We are not always aware that we are creating exclusionary environments. There are a number of factors to consider if we would like to build inclusive organizations. What words and photos are used on outreach materials? Where are events advertised? Are they easy to get to on public transportation? Do they require entrance fees? Are they held during hours when those with jobs can attend? Whose voices are prioritized? Are dissenting voices valued or tokenized? Who is in leadership positions? Whose contributions are compensated with money or benefits?

Our community is diverse. Our diversity includes a wide range of experiences, and our experiences lead us to distinct concerns. Activism based on intersectionality is, by definition, complicated. We may not be able to include all voices at all times. What is important is that we recognize our limitations and try to move beyond them.

Gender Categories

Trans activists employ various strategies to change exclusionary gender categories. Our strategies may depend on our theories of gender or on practical considerations.

- *Gender expansion.* This strategy expands the categories "woman" and "man" to include trans women and trans men, respectively. This expansion allows society to recognize trans women as women and trans men as men.
- *Gender multiplication.* This strategy multiplies gender categories beyond the man-woman binary, as they are in societies that recognize a third gender. This strategy is more inclusive of genderqueer people. However, if trans women and trans men are expected to self-identify as a third gender, then this strategy may communicate to trans women that they are not "really" women and to trans men that they are not "really" men (see Serano, 2007, pp. 29–30).
- *Gender abolition.* This strategy abolishes gender categories. For some of us, this outcome seems desirable but far off. For others of us, or in other circumstances, this outcome seems undesirable.

Rights versus Liberation

Many activists divide movements into those that pursue rights and those that pursue liberation. This distinction is also known as liberalism versus radicalism, or reform versus revolution. The goal of rights movements is to extend the social structure's protections to additional social groups, such as LGBTQ people. In contrast, the goal of liberation movements is to change the social structure on a fundamental level.

Activists disagree about whether to prioritize rights or liberation. Activists who prioritize rights in a particular situation may perceive rights as more attainable than liberation at that time. For example, some of us oppose militarism but perceive openly trans military service as more attainable than demilitarization. Some of us oppose marriage but perceive marriage reform as more attainable than marriage abolition. Alternatively, activists who take a rights-based approach may believe that the military and marriage strengthen their countries and families. In contrast, activists who prioritize liberation may perceive it as more urgent than rights or may believe that rights-based work reinforces oppressive social structures.

Judith Lorber and Lisa Jean Moore (2007) have explored how intersex and transgender activists may seek to assimilate into, separate from, or transform mainstream identity categories (pp. 155–156).

In 2013, Australia instituted three legal gender designations: "F," "M," and "X."

In 2013, Chelsea Manning was sentenced to almost 35 years in prison for leaking classified military documents, and she then came out publicly as a female who had been assigned male. These events served as a flashpoint for trans political debates because Manning's case relates to both trans military service and incarceration.

Crisilade Italian Trans March.

Trans politics may take the form of trans rights or trans liberation. When the social structure is not inclusive of trans people, trans rights can extend it. When the social structure inherently privileges some people over others, trans liberation can change it on a fundamental level. Knowledge of, and attention to, both trans rights and trans liberation are essential for organizing work.

CONTEMPORARY TRANS POLITICAL ISSUES

Current trans political issues are diverse and include public restroom access, health care, employment and poverty, housing and homelessness, incarceration, hate violence, and immigration.

Public Restroom Access

As TGNC people, we frequently face harassment, assault, and arrest in public restrooms. To avoid these experiences, many of us wait as long as possible to use the restroom. This practice can lead to serious health problems, such as bladder and kidney infections, cystitis, chronic dehydration, and urinary stones (Sylvia Rivera Law Project & Mateik, 2003).

Some socially conservative groups oppose gender-appropriate public restroom access for trans people. These groups claim that such access leads to harmful situations, such as predatory men entering women's restrooms. Like the stereotype that black men are rapists or that gay men are child molesters, this claim exploits sex panic to perpetuate oppression.

In the documentary film *Toilet Training* (Sylvia Rivera Law Project & Mateik, 2003), trans attorney Dean Spade responded to this claim: "The thinking that gender-segregated bathrooms keep people from engaging in sexual assault against women doesn't really comport with what we know about sexual assault. ... Sometimes [this thinking is] premised on the idea that if men [we]re in a bathroom with women, they wo[uld]n't be able to help themselves." To the contrary, men are responsible for their actions.

In 2013, GetEQUAL Texas and an activist coalition successfully advocated for the San Antonio City Council to pass legal protections against restroom discrimination based on gender identity.

San Francisco Trans March, 2012 (photo by Liz Highleyman).

CLAIMING OUR POWER

Spade continued with a second rebuttal: "When you mark a *W* or an *M* on a bathroom door, it does not function as a lock" (Sylvia Rivera Law Project & Mateik, 2003). Amber Hollibaugh of Queers for Economic Justice elaborated this observation: "If what we were most concerned about was making sure that no one was vulnerable to attack, then what we'd do is construct bathrooms where people had complete control over the space—meaning you could open a door and walk in and close the door and lock it, and you wouldn't share it with anybody else. It's always interesting to me how it gets displaced into a question of [gender] because it pits one group of people who are oppressed against another group of people who are oppressed. And frankly, to me, they look like they should be allies" (Sylvia Rivera Law Project & Mateik, 2003). Hollibaugh's observation serves as an invitation for cis and trans women to form coalitions to create safer spaces for everyone.

Health Care

Trans people face massive roadblocks to obtaining quality health care. Nineteen percent of us have been refused health care due to bias, 28% have been harassed in health care settings, and 50% have needed to educate our own providers about trans-competent care (Grant et al., 2011, p. 72).

Trans people face barriers not only to general care but also to medical transition. Some of us medically transition without professional supervision. This practice poses serious health risks. Often the primary barrier to this care is the prohibitive cost. Insurance companies rarely cover medical transition.

Trans activists address health care issues in many ways. In our communities, we may reach out to others about their health, or we may promote public health messages that encourage TGNC people to seek care or to participate in harm-reduction strategies. At work, we may ask our employers to change the health care policies that they purchase, or we may seek to extend health care coverage to domestic partners. At health care facilities, we may spend time teaching our providers. Along with our providers, we may fight with insurance companies to gain access to medication and procedures. On a broader scale, we may participate in activism for universal health care.

Regarding mental health, many trans activists feel concerned or conflicted about the psychiatric diagnosis of gender dysphoria (GD), formerly known as gender identity disorder (GID). GD is listed in the *Diagnostic and Statistical Manual of Mental Disorders*, fifth edition *(DSM-5)* (American Psychiatric Association, 2013,

Upon its release, the documentary film *Southern Comfort* (produced by Kate Davis, 2001) raised national awareness of barriers to health care. The film invites viewers to spend time with Robert Eads, a transsexual man with ovarian cancer. He requested help from dozens of doctors, but they turned him down due to bias. The film is not just about the tragedy of his death; it is also about the meaning of his life. It is about the support he offered to, and the relationships he forged with, other trans people.

The Human Rights Campaign (HRC) Foundation (2012) has developed a Corporate Equality Index that invites businesses to name the steps that they have taken for LGBTQ employees. The index covers whether companies offer trans-inclusive health care benefits. HRC's Healthcare Equality Index (Snowdon, 2013) surveys hospitals and clinics, covering similar topics.

Scenes from the 2008 San Francisco Trans March (photo by Jere Keys).

pp. 451–459). The *DSM* was created by the American Psychiatric Association (APA) to categorize mental illnesses so that psychiatrists can diagnose them accurately and treat them effectively.

Critics of the gender-related psychiatric diagnoses argue that they pathologize gender diversity. Many trans activists have lobbied the APA to remove these diagnoses from the *DSM*. Those of us who participate in this activism may belong to organizations such as GID Reform Advocates or campaigns such as Stop Trans Pathologization. We may employ various tactics: writing articles and blog entries, delivering lectures and presentations, holding rallies, protesting outside of APA meetings, or creating documentaries.

Some trans activists critique depathologization. For example, we may argue that having a diagnosis has allowed many trans people to access medical transition. From this perspective, depathologization may inhibit health care access. As another example, we may feel that the push for trans depathologization is motivated by, and reinforces, the stigma of having a mental illness or disability (Hill, 2012), and we may seek to remove that stigma (Gorton, 2013, pp. 646–647).

STORYTELLING AS ACTIVISM

Rebecca Kling is a transgender artist and educator who explores gender and identity through solo performances and educational workshops.

As a transgender child, there existed few depictions of people whose experiences mirrored my own. The vast majority of characters I viewed seemed happy with (or at least unaware of) themselves as gendered beings: on stage, on TV, in film, on the written page. The few who did identify as "trans" were sensationalized, dehumanized, ridiculed, or worse: on Jerry Springer, in *The Crying Game*, and through whispered locker room jokes about "chicks with dicks." As a transgender adult, I refuse to accept that the only possible depictions of trans people are offensive and belittling, told by and for a non-trans audience.

Storytelling is activism. From our first interactions with language, we want to hear tales of adventure and to tell the stories of our own life. As we grow older, we learn how our stories can impact the world around us: to shift emotions and change minds. As a performance artist, I share stories of my life as a trans woman; stories of failures and triumphs, of those who have supported me and those who have not, and I try to make sense of what it all means. In doing so, I combat the tales laid out in film and television of transgender characters labeled as "freaks" and "perverts." My art takes a stand that I exist. Others like me exist. By humanizing my transgender experience, I make it that much more difficult for others to dehumanize those like me—which, ultimately, is the core purpose of art, to call us to remember our common humanity.

TransJustice is a political group by and for trans and gender nonconforming people of color. It mobilizes its communities and allies into action to address the need for better jobs, housing, education, health care, and violence prevention.

Employment and Poverty

Almost all TGNC people face mistreatment when working or when seeking work. Ninety percent of us have been harassed or threatened with harassment at work, 26% of us have been fired due to bias, and we are nearly four times as likely as others to live in extreme poverty (Grant et al., 2011, p. 51).

When addressing employment issues, many trans activists emphasize an antidiscrimination strategy. This strategy's goal is to extend antidiscrimination laws and policies to include gender identity and expression. This inclusion communicates to trans people that we are valued, and it provides greater protection against employment discrimination. However, the degree of protection is limited. Discrimination is difficult to prove.

Some organizations emphasize an antipoverty strategy. These organizations promote structural changes that decrease poverty levels among all social groups. This strategy centers the experiences of people on public assistance and in street economies.

"Stop Attacks On Trans People," San Francisco Pride March, June 24, 2012 (photo by Liz Highleyman).

Many of us who organize to improve conditions related to unemployment and poverty are struggling under those same conditions. This struggle can make organizing harder.

> *"I have been involved in communities that have self-organized—either around things like health care, or in response to the more visible queer organizations failing trans people.... I find that often they have difficulty with instability. ... We're marginal and marginalized enough that it's hard to be politically active while at the same time eating regularly and keeping out of the rain."*

The Transgender Gender Variant Intersex Justice (TGI Justice) Project is a group of transgender people—inside and outside of prison—creating family and fighting against imprisonment. Its executive director is Miss Major, a black, formerly incarcerated, transgender elder.

TRANS POLITICAL LEADERS: ADELA HERNÁNDEZ

Jamie Roberts and Anneliese Singh

Adela Hernández, an electrocardiogram technician, became the first trans person elected to office in Cuba in November 2012. At 48 years old, she won her campaign for the Municipal Council of Caibarean, a coastal town in the province of Villa Clara. She came of age in a time of severe social and political persecution of sexual minorities in Cuba. She served 2 years in prison in the 1980s for a charge of "dangerousness" that was linked to her gender identity after her family disowned her and her father reported her to the authorities when she was 16. The Cuban government still does not recognize her female gender identity in its official records or on the ballot. Nonetheless, she won the respect of her neighbors (who know her as "Adela the Nurse") by participating in a neighborhood watch committee, known as the Committee for the Defense of the Revolution. Her election to her Municipal Council makes her eligible to be elected to the Cuban parliament.

Housing and Homelessness

Trans people may fall into homelessness because of family rejection, employment discrimination, poverty, or housing discrimination. Among those of us who have attempted to access shelters, 29% have been turned away altogether and 42% have been forced into gender-inappropriate facilities (Grant et al., 2011, p. 106). When we have gained access, 55% of us have been harassed, 25% have been physically assaulted, and 22% have been sexually assaulted (Grant et al., 2011, p. 106).

In the struggle to end homelessness, trans activists labor on many fronts. We may educate society about trans people. This education increases the likelihood that parents will accept their TGNC children rather than putting them out on the streets. Alternatively, we may combat employment discrimination and poverty so that we can pay our rent. With the help of legal organizations, we may battle discriminatory landlords or contest evictions. Within the shelter system, we may advocate for trans-inclusion policies, or we may start LGBTQ-specific shelters.

Incarceration

Impoverished and homeless, many trans people turn to street economies to get by. We may be incarcerated for living on the streets or for working them. People who engage in sex work are criminalized in general, and gender nonconforming people are made the targets of police more often due to our appearance.

Many prisons force us into gender-inappropriate facilities. In these facilities, we face routine, even systematic, abuse. We are harassed, physically assaulted, and sexually assaulted by staff and by other prisoners (Grant et al., 2011, pp. 166–168). Alternatively, we are placed in solitary confinement. This placement is supposedly to protect us from abuse, but it is a form of abuse in itself (Baus, Hunt, & Williams, 2006).

Trans prison organizations have different strategies for addressing incarceration. Some push for prison reform. This strategy involves establishing and implementing policies that render prisons more hospitable for trans people. Other groups advocate for prison abolition. This strategy's goal is to end the prison industrial complex, a network of connections between prisons and corporations. Prison abolitionists argue that prisons do not reduce oppression; rather, prisons serve as sites of oppression because the prison industrial complex grows and profits by targeting particular social groups for incarceration. Many organizations combine different types of strategies to fight the effects of incarceration on our communities.

Prison reform and abolition provide opportunities for trans prisoners to exercise agency. Many antiprison activist organizations have boards made up of currently and formerly incarcerated people so that their voices are heard during important decisions. In addition, some antiprison activists publish trans prisoners' writing.

Trans activists employ a wide range of tactics to improve prisoners' lives. Some activists visit trans prisoners or send letters of support. These visits and letters provide encouragement. In addition, they demonstrate to other prisoners and to staff that no one can take advantage of trans prisoners without the public finding out. Other tactics include fundraising for prisoners who do not have the income to buy necessary items, signing petitions to support the parole or transfer of prisoners, training probono lawyers to represent prisoners, lobbying for laws that change prisoners' treatment, providing cultural competency training for prison staff, and organizing conferences and rallies to raise awareness about prison reform and abolition.

The documentary film *Cruel and Unusual* (produced by Janet Baus, Dan Hunt, and Reid Williams in 2006) presents interviews with trans prisoners. Two of the interviewees, Linda and Ophelia, have filed lawsuits that have resulted in prison reform, improving the lives of other trans people behind bars.

Black & Pink is a support network for LGBTQ prisoners and "free world" allies. It works toward prison abolition and provides programs such as pen pal matching for prisoners and allies. Black & Pink's monthly newsletter shares writing and artwork by currently and formerly incarcerated people.

CONSTELLATING CONNECTIONS: TRANS JUSTICE, PRISON ABOLITION, AND THE HEARTS ON A WIRE COLLECTIVE

Pascal Emmer, Ceci, Anonymous @ SCI Dallas, and Adrian Lowe

Since 2007, the Hearts on a Wire Collective has been building a movement for gender self-determination, racial and economic justice, and an end to the policing and imprisoning of our trans and gender-variant communities. The title of our report, "This Is a Prison, Glitter Is Not Allowed," takes inspiration from an actual stamp used by a Pennsylvania state prison to return several glittery valentines that Hearts on a Wire had tried to send to our friends in lockup.

Attempts by prisons to prevent us from forming community across prison walls have only spurred our creativity and steadied our determination to spread the glitter further—to build a glimmering constellation of connections among those of us who are incarcerated and those of us on the outside.

The collective formed in response to the deep impact of mass imprisonment on transgender and gender-variant (T/GV) communities in Philadelphia. Centering the voices of T/GV people most affected by the prison industrial complex, we felt, was the only way to effectively organize for justice. The majority of T/GV people of color live in cities but are incarcerated in rural, white areas of the state. Physical distance and travel costs prohibit many prisoners from having visitors, as do punishments like solitary confinement.

Hearts on a Wire created a newsletter to facilitate the exchange of knowledge, resources, art, and poetry between T/GV people in 12 Pennsylvania prisons. A writer who goes by Anonymous @ SCI Dallas contributed an article to Issue 4, titled "Partner Violence: My Experience." Ceci, who was in another prison, wrote to the outside collective to express her gratitude to Anonymous for their article: *"That article saved me a lot of pain. It's so helpful to know that I'm not going through this by myself, and to know that there was someone there in the exact predicament I'm in and shared how they came through it. I cry of relief, and then I feel joy. I can't thank you enough."* The outside collective sent Ceci's letter to Anonymous, who was in solitary confinement. Anonymous wrote back with this response: *"I was at my wits end and got my bed sheet ready to hang up inside my cell. I asked God for a sign. It didn't take more than 10 minutes for Ceci's letter to arrive. I wasn't expecting it. I opened it and, still sobbing, I saw how profoundly I had helped her. Ceci saved my life at that very moment."* Anonymous alerted the outside collective that no one at SCI Dallas had received Issue 4 due to censorship by the prison. By receiving Ceci's letter, Anonymous learned that their article had been printed. When prison staff blocked the newsletter from reaching recipients, personal letters came through to deliver messages of hope and resilience.

Hearts on a Wire created a participatory action research study as another forum through which incarcerated T/GV people could connect. Incarcerated and recently released collective members offered their own knowledge of Pennsylvania's prison systems to inform the design, creation, delivery, and evaluation of the survey tool. Participants shared their experiences of prison, safety strategies, and ideas of transformative justice with one another and with the outside collective. Currently, the collective is working on a campaign for gender self-determination in the Department of Corrections' dress code. Members in prison continue to offer their critical insight as a compass to the collective's ongoing work of inside/outside organizing.

Hearts on a Wire banner (designed by Pascal Emmer).

Hearts on a Wire report (cover designed by Christian Morales).

Hate Violence

Hate violence refers to violence motivated by hatred for the victim's social group. Many TGNC people are targeted for violence based on gender identity or expression.

> *"At one point when I was about 20, I was beaten up pretty badly at a gay bar in Ohio by gay men who clocked me and felt I was trying to deceive them or make them straight in some way. I had several broken ribs."*

Trans activists respond to hate violence by memorializing trans victims and by working to prevent violence. The Transgender Day of Remembrance (TDoR) takes place annually on November 20 and memorializes trans murder victims. TDoR was started in 1998 by Gwendolyn Ann Smith to remember Rita Hester, a black trans woman murdered in Boston. Since then, TDoR has gained international recognition, with candlelight vigils taking place all over the world.

Some of the activists involved with TDoR have called for it to place greater emphasis on intersectionality. TDoR has tended to attribute the murders of trans people to transphobia (Lamble, 2008). However, intersecting identities affect our vulnerability (Lamble, 2008). For example, violence against trans women of color may be motivated by hatred for trans people, for women, for people of color, or for a combination of these identities.

Many LGBT rights organizations seek to include gender identity and expression in hate crimes legislation. This legislation expands law enforcement's power to police,

INCITE! Women of Color Against Violence is a national radical feminist organization. Its mission is to end violence against women of color, trans people of color, and their communities through organizing, dialogue, and direct action.

Survivor Project is a nonprofit organization that addresses the needs of intersex and trans survivors of domestic and sexual violence, providing support, education, resources, and opportunities for action.

prosecute, and punish hate violence. By doing so, this legislation sends a strong message that, as a society, we denounce hate.

Although this message is powerful, the result of hate crimes legislation may not be what we intend. This legislation mandates longer prison sentences for perpetrators, and prison abolitionists argue that longer sentences do not create a less violent or more just society. Moreover, law enforcement targets poor, brown, black, and trans people for mistreatment. For example, the police disrespect 47% of black trans people who interact with them, physically assault 15%, and sexually assault 7% (Grant et al., 2011, pp. 159–160). By expanding law enforcement's power, hate crimes legislation may increase classist, racist, and transphobic violence in our communities (Spade, 2011, p. 36).

Many antiviolence activists believe that the root causes of violence are structural classism, racism, transphobia, and other forms of bias—not bad individuals who need to be locked away (Spade, 2011, p. 211). These activists seek to dismantle structural oppression while supporting survivors, reforming perpetrators, and teaching nonviolent conflict resolution (see Spade, 2011, p. 211).

Immigration

Trans people face complicated barriers to immigration. These barriers particularly hinder those of us who have spouses of the same legal gender, those of us who have identity documents that do not match our lived genders, and those of us who are HIV positive.

Some trans people, known as refugees, flee our home countries because of persecution. We may petition other countries for asylum. The United Nations supports asylum in cases of persecution based on gender identity (UNHCR, 2010). In recent years, trans refugees have sought asylum in Australia, Canada, Denmark, and the United States (Chang-Muy, 2013).

Trans activists may host or mentor immigrants, donate money or time to nonprofit organizations that assist immigrants, or advance pro-immigrant legislation (Chang-Muy, 2013).

Those of us who are immigrants may face severe hardships—such as poverty, criminalization, and violence—not only in the countries that we emigrate from but also in those that we immigrate to (Aizura, 2012). To end these hardships everywhere, many trans activists envision, and aspire toward, nothing less than global justice.

ORGANIZING ON A PRACTICAL LEVEL

There are many ways to be an activist. Some of us engage in activism without calling it that. By living our daily lives as TGNC people, we can teach those around us. Others of us are involved in activist groups. In rural areas, the lack of LGBTQ visibility may make forming groups difficult. However, we may find ways to talk online or at conferences.

> "I am involved in a queer advocacy/potluck group. I was contacted by them because I had made a Facebook page to protest a women-only pharmacy that was denying access to trans women."

> "I am part of a 'Radical queer/genderqueer' group. We meet once a month for a picnic and just hang out and eat good food and talk about queerness. It's really just an excuse to catch up with friends and enjoy having a safe space to hang out in."

WRITING TRANS

Nick Krieger is the author of Nina Here Nor There: My Journey Beyond Gender.

Five years ago, when I first started writing about trans people, I had no idea what we were about, or that I was even trans, or where this writing could possibly take me. I wrote out of curiosity, confusion, and wonder—a desire to make sense of the trans-masculine people emerging from my lesbian community. In the beginning, I simply jotted down observations, questions, and overheard bits of dialogue on to note cards.

Driven by my own personal curiosity, I devoured everything written about trans lives and experiences: narrative nonfiction books, reportage, journalism, legal documents, health and medical studies, memoirs, diaries, and zines. It all functioned like a gigantic conversation by and about trans people. Rather than barging into the room, jumping up on a table, and blabbering away, I listened first.

I discovered that there was very little, especially in memoir, that covered trans identities outside the binary. I felt like my story, still very much unfolding, was missing from the existing literature, and that I had something valuable to add to the discussion. I wanted to create a new transgender paradigm that went beyond being "born in the wrong body." I wanted to show my experimentation and uncertainty, my quest to reinvent my body rather than fix a problem. I wanted to explore social issues like class, "male privilege," and misogyny.

Three years after first scribbling on my note cards, I wrote a book proposal using everything I'd learned about trans literature. During that time, through the process of writing, I had come to accept myself as trans. I understood myself as being neither man nor woman, but both. By framing my project to show the market void and timeliness of a memoir about the middle ground of gender, I was able to find an agent and a publisher.

For the next year and a half, my editor worked with me on my manuscript. While I didn't believe I had a responsibility to represent all, or even some, trans people, I considered it an honor to have the opportunity to tell my story. I tried to shape it in a way that progressed the ongoing conversation about trans lives.

I decided to cut the scene when I see my chest for the first time after top surgery. Despite the profound importance of this moment in my life, I felt that showing it would frame surgery as the be-all and end-all of identity, and that this has become a trans narrative cliché. I also made a late-breaking decision to change all mentions of "biological guy," the word used by my friends, to the more instructive term "cisgender guy." As a trans writer of any genre, you can reflect the world around you, or you can reshape the world to be one you want to live in.

Writing is power. Consider how you want to use yours. But please use your words and your voice. Your experience matters. Your pen and paper is an accessible tool to create understanding, enable social change, and inspire others.

Publish or self-publish your work. Read it at events. Post it to a blog. But do not miss the gift that this process offers: getting to know yourself. It is the most difficult paths that often yield the richest rewards on paper and in self-growth. That is my greatest lesson from my writing and trans journey thus far.

Defining Our Activist Groups

When joining or starting an activist group, we may ask ourselves which type will fit best. An unofficial group that gathers to talk? An official nonprofit organization? How will the group make decisions—based on majority vote, consensus, or another model? Will there be hierarchies? If so, how will we ensure that all members feel heard?

"I've been involved with the Transmasculine Advocacy Network (TMAN), a support/discussion group for people of color all along the transmasculine spectrum (butches, studs, bois, AGs, doms, trans men, etc.). . . . It has become pretty tight-knit and it's amazing to see so many trans- and transmasculine-identified people of color come together."

"I am the Executive Director and Founder of the Transgender Resource Center of New Mexico, a non-profit I have created to try to serve the TG community here in my state. We have a web site where we compile and list resources people need access to, like doctors, therapists, endocrinologists, support groups, even TG friendly local realtors and other vendors. . . . We are in the process of incorporating and acquiring our 501c3 so that we can raise funds to help subsidize treatments, legal fees and therapy for TG people, as well as providing micro-credit [to] the TG community to help start small businesses or go to school in order to improve employment opportunities."

Some of the Many Ways to Be an Activist

- Write about trans issues
- Mentor young people
- Participate in a protest
- Meet with a legislator
- Teach other people about trans issues
- Put a pin or sticker on your belongings
- Post comments on social media sites
- Become part of a lawsuit
- Host a book club
- Attend a conference
- Run for elected office
- Challenge ignorant statements in conversation
- Donate your time or money
- Live your daily life

Trans Bodies, Trans Selves New York City Forum (photo by Katia Ruiz).

Choosing Target Issues

Many larger organizations, such as HRC and the National Gay and Lesbian Task Force, have broad goals and take on many issues. Smaller groups tend to have narrower goals and focus on fewer issues. Our groups may define their goals through writing mission statements or performing needs assessments.

Needs assessments can be accomplished through various methods. Second-wave feminists have developed the method of consciousness raising. This consists of members talking with each other about their experiences. Through this conversation, members figure out how their experiences are shaped by systems of oppression and learn to better understand how to resist these systems and improve their lives.

The most elaborate method of needs assessment is a formal study conducted by trained researchers. Formal studies generate data that other people may consider more authoritative. However, these studies consume substantial resources and are not always necessary.

Developing Strategies and Tactics

Once we choose target issues, we may choose strategies and tactics. Strategies are overarching visions for how to approach an issue. For example, we may envision rights or liberation. Tactics are specific activities used to carry out strategies.

Direct action consists of acts that draw attention to problems with the current social system. These acts can be nonviolent (like rallies) or violent (like riots). Think twice—or three times—before engaging in violence. It increases risks of injury, arrest, and negative publicity.

Slogans are phrases that capture and communicate messages (Transgender Law Center [TLC], 2005, p. 23). They can be chanted during direct action or published on flyers, pins, bumper stickers, T-shirts, or Web sites. The purpose of activist slogans is to change public consciousness about political issues.

Political action consists of acts that bring about change in political spheres. Individuals may vote, sign petitions, work for political campaigns, run for office, or participate in legal cases. Organizations may support candidates, back or oppose laws, write amicus briefs, or bring legal cases forward.

Insider negotiations help with legislation and policymaking by allowing us to discuss our concerns with lawmakers and policymakers face-to-face (TLC, 2005, p. 23). Insider negotiations may be combined with other tactics. For example, ACT-UP negotiated with AIDS scientists while applying outside pressure through direct action.

Community service consists of helping our community members directly. We may offer LGBTQ people safe rides home at night, build new housing for our elders, take questions at a pride booth, or answer phone lines at a resource center. If we have specific skills, we may volunteer our services in finance, health care, legal work, or writing.

Education is a vital activist tactic. On an interpersonal level, we can educate others simply by talking about our experiences. Some trans organizations hold conferences so that members can share information and ideas. Many educators offer trans workshops or trainings. Workshops may explore various topics (such trans identities, trans issues, or trans etiquette) and may be specialized for particular audiences (such as teachers, health care providers, or businesses). At workshops, we may engage participants in dialogue or activities, and we may provide participants with resource guides. These guides may review key content or list contact information.

When facilitating trans workshops, we may want to take some time to think about our approach. Some suggestions include the following:

1. Avoid defining trans terms and concepts narrowly. Instead, emphasize the diversity of trans self-definitions (Hanssmann, 2012).
2. Avoid oversimplifying trans issues. Instead, emphasize the impact of race, class, and other intersecting identities on trans lives (Hanssmann, 2012).
3. Avoid representing trans people as passive victims. Instead, emphasize trans agency (see A. F. Enke, 2012, p. 69).
4. Avoid perpetuating the assumption that everyone is cis unless they come out as trans. Instead, emphasize the possibility that anyone we meet is trans (see A. F. Enke, 2012, p. 69).
5. Avoid drawing a clear line between cis and trans people. Instead, emphasize everyone's gender differences (see A. F. Enke, 2012, p. 69).
6. Avoid drawing a clear line between allies and oppressors. Instead, guide allies toward greater consciousness of their own transphobia and cis privilege (A. F. Enke, 2012, p. 69).

Trans activists have many tactics to choose from. We may gravitate toward particular tactics because of our individual strengths or styles. In addition, we may rethink and revise our tactics as we encounter new situations (TLC, 2005, p. 23).

MAKING A DIFFERENCE THROUGH ACTIVISM

Jessica Lina Stirba

Not everyone has the privilege to put their neck on the line in the service of a greater social good, but if you do, and if you want to make a difference, here are some suggestions.

Have a concrete goal. It's not enough to want to make the world a better place; everyone has a different idea of what a better world looks like, and you'll often find that it's the little differences that can cause the most tension between ideological allies. Instead, focus on a change over an ideal.

Work with your enemies. It can be incredibly frustrating when you see someone standing in the way of the path to a better world. It can be difficult to engage with these people—often gatekeepers who have privilege—on a productive level. But people respond poorly to invective and abuse, and the community of people with power is often a small one. It is important to engage with people whose beliefs run contrary to your own, and it's even more important to accept compromises when they land you closer to your goal. If you get too focused on the perfect way to succeed at a goal, you could miss an opportunity to settle the issue earlier, if less perfectly. That said, if an imperfect solution doesn't address the needs of everyone in your coalition, it's not a solution at all.

Don't get derailed. The same qualities that make your activism stronger can leave you open to being co-opted or derailed by your collaborators. There's not always malice associated with these situations. Often, more radical members of your coalition will feel that change is less legitimate if it's not done through their specific flavor of democracy or consensus, and often well-meaning opponents will offer splintering compromises through ignorance.

Plan to win. Sometimes it can be hard to believe that an issue is winnable. The only way you're going to be able to convince people that the change you want to see is a positive one is if you believe that it can be real in the future and grapple with what that means. Plan a strategy for what to do after you win and fully examine the potential repercussions of winning.

Have fun. In many ways this is the most important suggestion. Activism can be draining work. It's difficult to see a way the world can be a better place and have it seem to be so far away. This burns out many activists, and the only way to keep this from happening to you is to have some fun with it. Activism is a great chance to meet people, and you often get to know people whose perspectives come from a vastly different position than your own. Get as much as you can from the experience, and hopefully the balance will leave you feeling energized, not enervated.

SUGGESTED READING

Alinsky, S. D. (1989). *Rules for radicals: A pragmatic primer for realistic radicals.* New York, NY: Vintage Books.

Foucault, M. (1990). *The history of sexuality, volume I: An introduction.* New York, NY: Vintage Books.

hooks, b. (2000). *Feminism is for everybody: Passionate politics.* Cambridge, MA: South End Press.

INCITE! Women of Color Against Violence. (2009). *The revolution will not be funded: Beyond the non-profit industrial complex.* Cambridge, MA: South End Press.

Zinn, H. (2005). *A people's history of the United States.* New York, NY: HarperCollins.

Working With Media Outlets

Trans activists often work with media outlets, such as news organizations, radio and television programs, and social media. Sometimes we actively engage these outlets to increase trans visibility, to educate the public, or to spread news. At other times, media outlets discover us. In either case, we may want to prepare ourselves for media attention (TLC, 2005, p. 26).

When engaging in media campaigns, we may systematically reach out to media outlets. An initial step is to create a directory of target outlets. We may divide our targets by whether they are print, radio, television, or Web; whether they are regional or national; or whether they are general or specialized. An example of a specialized outlet is an LGBTQ newspaper.

Kye Allums is a graduate of the George Washington University, where he obtained his bachelor's degree in fine arts. While attending GW, Kye made history by becoming the first openly trans Division I athlete. Allums is now devoted to making a difference in the world by sharing his story, fighting ignorance about queer issues with education, and empowering everyone on the gender spectrum to speak out.

We may send out press releases. Press releases typically contain brief news items and contact information. Some organizations attach a resource guide with facts or quotations to the end of each press release.

Individual trans activists may volunteer to be interviewed or photographed. For example, Janet Mock, a writer and trans woman of color, has participated in many news interviews. Before talking with reporters, we may undergo media training or prepare talking points (TLC, 2005, p. 26). We may want to decide how we will respond if reporters make us uncomfortable. For example, reporters may ask inappropriate questions about our bodies, genders, sexualities, or life histories (Namaste, 2011, pp. 46–49). As another example, reporters may pressure us to pose for sensationalistic photographs (Serano, 2007, pp. 44–45).

WORKING WITH MEDIA

Pauline Park is the chair of the New York Association for Gender Rights Advocacy (NYAGRA) and president of the board of directors and acting executive director of Queens Pride House, an LGBT community center in the borough of Queens. She led the campaign for the transgender rights law enacted by the New York City Council in 2002 and has done transgender sensitivity trainings for a wide range of organizations.

Among the perennial questions that reporters ask transgender activists and advocacy organizations are these: How many transgender people are there? What makes people transgender? When did you become transgender? While some activists and organizations have attempted to throw out numbers concerning the transgender population in the United States, all such statistics are suspect because the US Census does not ask questions concerning gender identity or expression; even if the Census did, many transgender and gender-variant individuals most likely would not respond affirmatively to such questions. A simple response to this perennial question might be, "No one knows for sure because no government agency in the United States has ever done a comprehensive and reliable survey with a sufficient sample size."

If the objective of your organization or your campaign is to get a transgender rights law enacted at the state or local level, your media strategy must reflect that goal, and in interviews, your organizational representative should not be diverted into a discussion of the "origins" or "causes" of transgender identity, much less the question as to whether it is a "choice" or not. Simply make clear that you view that question as irrelevant and stick to your talking points, which you should have worked out in advance.

You should understand that you need not allow yourself to be drawn into a conversation about your own personal story; any personal details beyond your organizational title, your age, and your city of residence are entirely within your discretion to divulge or withhold. In speaking with the media, you have no obligation to divulge the name that was given to you at birth or on your government-issued identity documents if it differs from the name that you commonly use and that is consistent with your gender identity.

If the topic at hand is one of law or public policy, such as a transgender rights bill that is currently pending or a transgender health care initiative, reporters often ask for names of individuals who have been the victims of discrimination or violence in order to put together a "human interest" story. While the request is legitimate, you are under no obligation to provide names or contact information of such individuals; you are, however, under an obligation to check with those individuals first before you give their names or contact information to media outlets. If your organization or campaign has already successfully identified such individuals, you may want to provide them with media training so they know how to speak with media outlets about their personal stories of discrimination, violence, or denial of health care or social services. Ideally, an organization or campaign will identify several such individuals who reflect the full diversity—in terms of gender identity as well as demographic characteristics—of the local community.

Fundraising

Our groups may seek outside support through fundraising. This may include direct requests, such as phone calls, or events that raise money through entrance fees, raffles, or sales. Many fundraisers are now online, allowing potential donors to view videos or read materials and donate through a Web site.

For registered nonprofit organizations, personal donations are tax deductible and grants are available. Grants are usually larger. However, grants are time consuming and may have strings attached. Many organizations employ professional grant writers. Other

Funders for LGBTQ Issues provides an online directory of organizations that provide grants for LGBTQ work.

organizations send their members to grant-writing workshops. These are often offered at LGBTQ conferences.

It is important to thank donors and let them know how they have made a difference. Sometimes donors receive gifts. Donors often continue giving if they know that they are appreciated.

CONCLUSION

Trans activism has grown out of other social movements. As trans people, we have, at times, come to voice within these movements and, at other times, been silenced by them. Through these experiences, we have learned how to build our own movements. We recognize intersecting axes of oppression, develop new ways of doing (or not doing) gender, and advance rights and liberation. Today, trans activists participate in every kind of movement imaginable, all over the planet. Whichever movements we commit ourselves to, our goal is the same: to create a world where everyone can live free from oppression. Our activism, politics, and organizing may take many different forms throughout our lifetimes. Activism can be as simple as living our truths. When we do so, we have already begun to overcome oppression, here and now.

REFERENCES AND FURTHER READING

Aizura, A. (2012). Transnational transgender rights and immigration law. In A. Enke (Ed.), *Transfeminist perspectives in and beyond transgender and gender studies* (pp. 133–150). Philadelphia, PA: Temple University Press.

American Psychiatric Association. (2013). *Diagnostic and statistical manual of mental disorders* (5th ed.). Arlington, VA: American Psychiatric Publishing.

Bassichis, M., Lee, A., & Spade, D. (2011). Building an abolitionist trans and queer movement with everything we've got. In E. A. Stanley & N. Smith (Eds.), *Captive genders: Trans embodiment and the prison industrial complex* (pp. 15–40). Oakland, CA: AK Press.

Baus, J. (Producer & Director), Hunt, D. (Producer & Director), Williams, R. (Producer & Director). (2006). *Cruel and unusual* [DVD]. United States: Outcast.

Chang-Muy, F. (2013, April). *Human rights, refugees, and the rights of transgendered people.* Workshop conducted at the Second Annual Transecting Society Conference: Visualizing the Past, Present, and Future of Trans* Lives, Durham, NH.

Davis, K. (Producer & Director). (2003). *Southern comfort* [DVD]. United States: New Video.

Enke, A. (Ed.). (2012). *Transfeminist perspectives in and beyond transgender and gender studies.* Philadelphia, PA: Temple University Press.

Enke, A. F. (2012). The education of little cis: Cisgender and the discipline of opposing bodies. In A. Enke (Ed.), *Transfeminist perspectives in and beyond transgender and gender studies* (pp. 60–77). Philadelphia, PA: Temple University Press.

Gorton, R. N. (2013). Transgender as mental illness: Nosology, social justice, and the tarnished golden mean. In S. Stryker & A. Z. Aizura (Eds.), *The transgender studies reader 2* (pp. 644–652). New York, NY: Routledge.

Grant, J. M., Mottett, L. A., Tanis, J., Harrison, J., Herman, J. L., & Keisling, M. (2011). *Injustice at every turn: A report of the National Transgender Discrimination Survey.* Retrieved January 2014, from http://www.thetaskforce.org/downloads/reports/reports/ntds_full.pdf

Gwissues [Gwist]. (2013, April 12). *The transgender bathroom debate: Gwissues* [Video file]. Retrieved January 2014, from http://www.youtube.com/watch?v=JQHCwGQBzHM

Hanssmann, C. (2012). Training disservice: The productive potential and structural limitations of health as a terrain for trans activism. In A. Enke (Ed.), *Transfeminist perspectives in and beyond transgender and gender studies* (pp. 112–132). Philadelphia, PA: Temple University Press.

Hill, N. M. (2012, April). *Towards an alternative, collective liberationist stance on trans activism and DSM diagnoses.* Abstract from the Second Annual Transecting Society Conference: Visualizing the Past, Present, and Future of Trans* Lives, Durham, NH.

Human Rights Campaign Foundation. (2012). *Corporate equality index 2013: Rating American workplaces on lesbian, gay, bisexual and transgender equality.* Retrieved March 2014, from http://www.hrc.org/files/assets/resources/CorporateEqualityIndex_2013.pdf

Koyama, E. (2003). The transfeminist manifesto. In R. Dicker & A. Piepmeier (Eds.), *Catching a wave: Reclaiming feminism for the 21st century* (pp. 244–259). Boston, MA: Northeastern University Press.

Lamble, S. (2008). Retelling racialized violence, remaking white innocence: The politics of interlocking oppressions in Transgender Day of Remembrance. *Sexuality Research and Social Policy, 5*(1), 24–42.

Lorber, J., & Moore, L. J. (2007). *Gendered bodies: Feminist perspectives.* Los Angeles, CA: Roxbury.

Namaste, V. (2011). *Sex change, social change: Reflections on identity, institutions, and imperialism* (2nd ed.). Toronto, ON: Women's Press.

Queer, *adj¹*. (2013, June). *OED Online.* Retrieved from http://www.oed.com

Queers for Economic Justice. (2007, March 1). *Queers and immigration: A vision statement.* Retrieved January 2014, from http://sfonline.barnard.edu/immigration/QEJ-Immigration-Vision.pdf

Rubin, G. (2006). Of catamites and kings: Reflections on butch, gender, and boundaries. In S. Stryker & S. Whittle (Eds.), *The transgender studies reader* (pp. 471–481). New York, NY: Routledge.

Scott-Dixon, K. (Ed.). (2006). *Trans/forming feminisms: Transfeminist voices speak out.* Toronto, ON: Sumach Press.

Serano, J. (2007). *Whipping girl: A transsexual woman on sexism and the scapegoating of femininity.* Berkeley, CA: Seal Press.

Serano, J. (2013). *Excluded: Making feminist and queer movements more inclusive.* Berkeley, CA: Seal Press.

Snowdon, S. (2013). *Healthcare equality index 2013: Promoting equitable and inclusive care for lesbian, gay, bisexual and transgender patients and their families.* Retrieved January 2014, from http://www.hrc.org/files/assets/resources/HEI_2013_final.pdf

Spade, D. (2011). *Normal life: Administrative violence, critical trans politics, and the limits of law.* Brooklyn, NY: South End Press.

Stryker, S. (2008). *Transgender history.* Berkeley, CA: Seal Press.

Sylvia Rivera Law Project (Producer) & Mateik, T. (Director). (2003). *Toilet training: Law and order in the bathroom* [DVD]. United States: Silvia Rivera Law Project.

Transgender Law Center. (2005). *Peeing in peace: A resource guide for transgender activists and allies.* Retrieved January 2014, from http://transgenderlawcenter.org/issues/public-accomodations/peeing-in-peace

UNHCR. (2010, September). *The protection of lesbian, gay, bisexual, transgender and intersex asylum-seekers and refugees.* Retrieved January 2014, from http://www.refworld.org/pdfid/4cff9a8f2.pdf

Vaid, U. (2012). *Irresistible revolution: Confronting race, class and the assumptions of LGBT politics.* New York, NY: Magnus Books.

Valentine, D. (2007). *Imagining transgender: An ethnography of a category.* Durham, NC: Duke University Press.

AFTERWORD

A MESSAGE FROM THE FOUNDERS OF THE BOSTON WOMEN'S HEALTH BOOK COLLECTIVE

Authors of *Our Bodies, Ourselves*

"Passing the Torch" (Elenore Toczynski).

More than 40 years ago, in the early days of the second-wave feminist movement, a group of Boston-area women got together to talk about our experiences with health and sexuality. Most of us were in our twenties and thirties, and we set out to make a list of obstetricians/gynecologists whom we would recommend to others as doctors who respected us, listened to us, and gave us the information we needed. One by one, each of us realized we could not put our own doctor on the list. We saw that we needed to research necessary information ourselves, to trust our own experiences of our bodies, and to advocate for—among other things—medical training that would prepare physicians (predominantly male at the time) to partner with us in our health care decisions.

Meeting weekly, we learned to speak with increasing openness about our bodies—menstrual periods, sexuality, masturbation, and orgasm (imagine saying those two words aloud for the first time!). We helped one another discover that many difficulties for which we had been blaming ourselves—like postpartum depression or not enjoying sexual intercourse—were problems faced by many women, problems often rooted in lack of information and/or in the social arrangements of sexism. We created a course to share this new perspective with others, and when women asked for printed materials, we wrote up the topics. *Our Bodies, Ourselves* was born. Over the years, new editions of the book have grown with the women's health movement, expanding to include the voices of more and more women—lesbians, for example, and women of color, women with disabilities, older women, and, over the past decade, transgender and genderqueer people.

When Laura contacted our group a few years ago about the dream of *Trans Bodies, Trans Selves*, we were so excited. As with *OBOS*, a community of people who are the best experts on themselves has come together to create a resource of information, mutual support, and political advocacy that will strengthen many. Thanks to *Trans Bodies, Trans Selves* and all the transgender folks who have been writing and teaching over the past many years, we, a group of cisgender women, now know that we can no longer say "a woman's body" and mean only one thing. One person's body may have a penis and testicles, and be a woman's body. Another person's body may have breasts or a clitoris, and be a man's body. The revolutionary point is that we can name our gender identity for ourselves and rightfully expect respect and recognition. "Our bodies, ourselves" grows in meaning daily.

We welcome you as allies who will deepen and expand the work that has mattered so much to us. For example:

- We have, with the transgender community, a commitment to teaching medical personnel to treat their patients with informed respect. This is crucial for people of any gender who need gynecological and/or endocrine care. We will need to work together to promote the expansion of health and medical care training, accountability, and monitoring so as to include the whole range of competency requirements, encompassing every facet of any patient's identity.
- Let us continue to advocate for affordable and accessible health care, including hormonal and surgical treatments for trans people who choose them.
- We in OBOS and the women's health movement have long raised safety questions regarding the development and use of sex-related hormones like estrogen, progesterone, and testosterone, and advocated for more care in prescribing them. These hormones can be indispensable to transgender people who choose to use them. May we join in diligent advocacy to make these medications safer to use.
- We unite with you in wanting necessary health tests and screenings to be affordable, universally accessible, and sensitively done. The Pap test, for example, done to detect exposure to human papilloma virus (HPV), is recommended for people of any gender who have a cervix.
- The women's health movement understood many decades ago that violence is a health issue. May we work on this central health issue together!

Our Bodies, Ourselves has long affirmed the beauty of our bodies as they are, as we are. In the 2011 *OBOS* a trans woman named Danielle contributes to that conversation:

> All women are bombarded with media indicating why our bodies aren't perfect enough. But I'd say trans women (and trans men, to a lesser extent) are additionally laden with messages that our bodies can't be attractive. That my very existence is "naturally" repugnant and repulsive. Finding things to like about your body is incredibly important.

Cody, a genderqueer person, adds:

> Sometimes I just need to remind myself that I am hot and perfect and it's an act of bravery and defiance to think such things, in the face of this misogynist culture that wants me to hate myself. Then loving my body becomes political.

Chloe, a 23-year-old queer, trans woman, says this:

> Part of the reason having sex with other trans women was important to me early on was that it helped me come to love my own body, too. Seeing them and their body however it was—pre-op, non-op, post-op, whatever—as beautiful helped me see my own body as beautiful, too.

In the very first, newsprint edition of *OBOS* in 1971, we wrote about our initial efforts together: "We were excited and our excitement was powerful. We wanted to share both our excitement and what we were learning. We saw ourselves differently, and our lives began to change." Now, 43 years later, we honor the authors of *Trans Bodies, Trans Selves* for expanding this excitement, this learning, and this crucial work for social change. Huge congratulations from us to you on the book's publication. We look forward to reading it, to using it, and to sharing it with our loved ones.

By Wendy Sanford on behalf of OBOS founders Pamela Berger, Joan Ditzion, Vilunya Diskin, Paula Doress-Worters, Nancy Miriam Hawley, Elizabeth MacMahon-Herrera, Judy Norsigian, Jane Pincus, Wendy Sanford, Norma Swenson, and Sally Whelan, and in loving memory of OBOS founders Pamela Morgan and Esther Rome. With special thanks for help from Oliver Danni Green, Kody Hersh, Petra Doan, Ted Heck, and Norma Swenson.

Note: Short piece contributors have their bios listed with their short pieces. If you helped with the production of this book but do not see your name listed, we apologize for the mistake. We did our best to keep track of everyone involved. However, with a project this large we are bound to have left people out. Please inform us of any omissions and we will update them in the next edition.

Rahne Alexander (Advisor, Arts and Culture) is a multidisciplinary artist from Baltimore.

Rabbi Levi Alter (Advisor, Our Many Selves; Race, Ethnicity, and Culture; Religion and Spirituality; Aging; US History) is the spiritual leader of his congregation of Holocaust survivors, CEO of a health care corporation, president of FTM International, and a keynote speaker and organizer for major conferences and events.

Diane Anderson-Minshall (Advisor, Intimate Relationships) is the editor at large of *The Advocate* magazine and editor in chief of *HIV Plus* magazine as well as a journalist whose work has appeared in dozens of publications from the *New York Times* to *Glamour* magazine.

Jacob Anderson-Minshall (Advisor, Intimate Relationships) is a journalist and multimedia storyteller and the coauthor (with his wife, Diane) of *Blind Curves, Blind Faith, Blind Leap*, and the upcoming memoir, *Queerly Beloved.*

Michele Angello, PhD (Advisor, Coming Out, Mental Health Chapters) is a gender specialist working internationally with trans individuals and their families whose book *On the Couch With Dr. Angello* is a guide for parents who have gender-variant children, as well as for mental health and medical providers.

Joanne M. Arellano (Research Intern, Transgender Prison Issues) is a registered nurse.

Gabriel Arkles (Advisor, Immigration) is a collective member of the Sylvia Rivera Law Project and an associate academic specialist teaching at Northeastern University School of Law; he was also one of the founding board members of the Lorena Borjas Community Fund.

Kellan Baker, MPH, MA (Advisor, General, Sexual, and Reproductive Health) is the associate director of the LGBT Research and Communications Project at the Center for American Progress, a consultant on international transgender health with the Open Society Foundation, and an affiliated faculty member for LGBT health policy at the Center for Population Research in LGBT Health at the Fenway Institute.

Sadie Baker (Advisor, Activism, Politics, and Organizing) is an activist, an advocate for homeless and street-based LGBTQ youth currently working with Chicago's Broadway Youth Center, and a former core member of the D.C. Trans Coalition.

delfin bautista, MSW, MDiv (Author, Religion and Spirituality) is director of the LGBT Center at Ohio University, board member for Call To Action and the Alliance for GLBTQ Youth, and a member of DignityUSA's Young Adult and Transgender Caucuses.

Genny Beemyn, PhD (Author, US History) is the director of the Stonewall Center at the University of Massachusetts, Amherst, and the author of many works in LGBT Studies, including *The Lives of Transgender People* and *A Queer Capital: A History of LGBT Life in Washington, DC.*

Sarah E. Belawski (Author, Intimate Relationships) is an out and proud trans woman who works as a Senior Hearing Representative for the NYS Department of Labor. She has been the facilitator of the trans peer support group at the Capital Pride Center from 2010–2014 and has served on the Pride Center's advisory council. She has presented at the Philadelphia Trans Health Conference and engages in activist work in the Albany, NY area.

Jesse Benet, MA, LMHC (Seattle Forum Organizer) is cohost/cofounder of the Seattle-based podcast Gendercast and administers jail diversion reentry programs in a systems coordination role to push against the prison industrial complex that criminalizes individuals based on mental health/substance use conditions as well as race, class, and dis/ability.

Ady Ben-Israel, MA, LCSW (Editing Team; Advisor, Coming Out) is a New York City psychotherapist working with people across a range of mental health concerns, specializing in areas of gender identity and gender nonconformity, sex/sexuality, and dynamics of oppression and privilege. Ady is the co-producer of the training video BAD FIT: Challenging the Prevalence of Homophobia, Transphobia, and Heterosexism in Social Work Education.

Regina A. BlackWolf, MSW (Advisor, Coming Out, Mental Health Chapters) is a psychotherapist in the Seattle area specializing in working with LGBT people as well as supporting adults with other life changes and various mental health-related and substance abuse-related challenges.

Nayland Blake (Advisor, Arts and Culture) is an artist and educator living in Brooklyn New York. He is currently the chair of the ICP/Bard MFA program in advanced photographic studies.

Cooper Lee Bombardier (Advisor, Arts and Culture)

Marci Bowers, MD (Advisor, Surgical Transition) is a gynecologic surgeon, formerly of Trinidad, Colorado, now practicing in Burlingame, California. She has been providing surgical care for the transgender community since 1995, is a member of WPATH, and serves on the board of directors for GLAAD and the Transgender Law Center (TLC).

Avi Bowie, LMSW (Advisor, Parenting) works with LGBTQIA homeless and runaway youth as the associate director of Overnight, Drop-in, and Outreach at the Ali Forney Center. Avi is also the cofounder and a former facilitator of the Transgender and Genderqueer Parents and Prospective Parents group at the NYC LGBT Community Center.

Helen Boyd, MA (Advisor, Intimate Relationships) is the author of *My Husband Betty* and *She's Not the Man I Married*. She blogs at www.myhusbandbetty.com and teaches gender studies at Lawrence University.

Jennifer Finney Boylan (Author, Introduction), a professor of English at Colby College, is the author of 13 books, including *Stuck in the Middle With You: Parenthood in Three Genders* and *She's Not There: A Life in Two Genders*, and also serves on the board of directors of GLAAD and the board of trustees of the Kinsey Institute for Research on Sex, Gender, and Reproduction.

Cristin Brew, LMFT (Advisor, Our Many Selves) is a psychotherapist working with LGBTQ people in the Bay Area as well as an educator working to increase LGBTQ knowledge in the mental health field.

Kylar W. Broadus (Author, Legal Issues; Advisor, US History) is an associate professor at Lincoln University, a historically black college in Jefferson City, Missouri; division director of the Section for Individual Rights and Responsibilities in the American Bar Association; co-chair of the American Bar Association Committee for Sexual Orientation and Gender Identity; a board member of the National Black Justice Coalition; a 2010 Rockwood Institute LGBTQ Fellow; and a founder of the Transgender Law and Policy Institute and the Trans People of Color Coalition (TPOCC).

Diane Bruessow, PA-C, DFAAPA (Editing Team) has been practicing family medicine in New York and New Jersey for over 20 years; she has served as a consultant on trans health for federal health agencies, including HRSA and CDC; and she has contributed over a decade of national nonprofit leadership for the American Academy of Physician Assistants (AAPA) and GLMA: Health Professionals Advancing LGBT Equality.

Earline Budd (Advisor, Aging) is a transgender advocate and founding member and former executive director of Transgender Health Empowerment, Inc. She serves as a commissioner for the Office of Human Rights (OHR) and Mayor's Commission on HIV/AIDS in Washington, D.C.

Ronald Burton (Illustrator) is a Los Angeles–based artist and writer whose work plays in the fertile mud of mixed spaces—cultural, sexual, and political—where all the best life forms are invariably found.

Patrick Califia (Advisor, Sexuality)

Tamar Carmel, MD (Author, Mental Health Services and Mental Health Concerns; Editing Team; Board Member) is a community psychiatrist, family physician, and LGBTQ advocate/educator in Pittsburgh, Pennsylvania.

Peter Cava (Author, Activism, Politics, and Organizing) is a board member of the Palm Beach County Human Rights Council, the conference planning coordinator for Transecting Society, a PhD candidate in Florida Atlantic University's (FAU) Public Intellectuals Program, FAU's Lynn-Wold-Schmidt Peace Studies Fellow through its Peace Studies Program, and a writing consultant at FAU's Center for Excellence in Writing.

Sand Chang, PhD (Advisor, General, Sexual, and Reproductive Health) is a genderqueer Chinese American clinical psychologist with a private practice in the San Francisco Bay Area, member of the APA's Committee for LGBT Concerns (CLGBTC), and member of the APA Trans Practice Guidelines Task Force.

Christian, JD, BA (Intern, Legal Issues) is the President of Operations for a frozen yogurt franchise on the East Coast and a law school graduate with a concentration in Gender and Sexuality Studies, utilizing his legal training as a public speaker, community activist, and educator on trans issues.

Jules Chyten-Brennan (Author, Surgical Transition; Editing Team) is finishing his degree as an osteopathic medical student at the University of Medicine and Dentistry of New Jersey and starting a residency in Internal Medicine.

Eli Clare (Advisor, Disabilities and Deaf Culture) is white, disabled, and genderqueer, and happily lives in the Green Mountains of Vermont, where he writes and proudly claims a penchant for rabble-rousing.

Loree Cook-Daniels (Advisor, Aging) is policy and program director for FORGE, Inc.

Leah Cooperson (Advisor, Arts and Culture)

Axil Cricchio, MA, ABD (Advisor, Sex and Gender Development; Advisor, Global) is a community and social activist/advocate and adjunct faculty at California State University, Monterey Bay and the California Institute of Integral Studies in San Francisco, where he researches how the language of social systems and cultural constructs shape(s) the way we learn, embody, and perform gender presentation and gender roles as dominant aspects of our identity.

Paisley Currah, (Advisor, Legal Issues) is a professor of political science and gender studies at Brooklyn College and the Graduate Center of the City University of New York and is the co-editor of *TSQ: Transgender Studies Quarterly.*

Theo Czerevko (Advisor, General, Sexual, and Reproductive Health) is a social work student at Hunter College.

Annie Danger (Advisor, Arts and Culture)

Dallas Denny, MA, Licensed Psychological Examiner, TN (Ret.) (Author, Media Spotlights; Advisor, Sex and Gender Development) is a writer, activist, educator, former editor of *Chrysalis Quarterly* and *Transgender Tapestry*, former director of the Fantasia Fair, founding director of the American Educational Gender Information Service, Inc., and board member of Real Life Experiences.

Maddie Deutsch, MD (Author, Medical Transition) is an Assistant Clinical Professor in the Department of Family and Community Medicine and the Clinical Lead for the Center of Excellence for Transgender Health at UCSF, founder and director of the Transgender Health Program at the L.A. Gay and Lesbian Center, and sits on the editorial boards for the *International Journal of Transgenderism* and the *Journal of LGBT Health.*

Kylan Mattias de Vries (Advisor, Intimate Relationships) grew up in Vancouver, Canada, received his PhD in sociology from Southern Illinois University Carbondale, and is currently an assistant professor at Southern Oregon University, where he teaches sociology and gender, sexuality, and women's studies. Kylan's research interests include inequalities, intersectionality, queer theories, transgender studies, critical race studies, and social psychology.

Tara DeWitt, PhD (Advisor, Coming Out, Mental Health Chapters) is a psychologist who works with the LGBT community in the West Village area in New York City.

kd diamond (Illustrator) is an artist whose work has been featured in numerous books and anthologies, including *Gender Outlaws: The Next Generation*; Tristan Taormino's *Ultimate Guide to Kink*; S. Bear Bergman's *Backwards Day* and much more; she is also the founder of *Salacious* magazine.

Morty Diamond (Advisor, Arts and Culture) is a writer, artist, activist, editor of *Trans/Love: Radical Sex, Love and Relationships Beyond the Gender Binary* (Manic D Press) and *From the Inside: FTM and Beyond* (Manic D Press), working with and for the LGBT community for the past 12 years, focusing primarily on social justice issues concerning gender identity, and currently working on his masters of social work at San Francisco State University.

lore m. dickey, PhD (Author, Mental Health Services and Support, Mental Health Concerns) is a trans man, an assistant professor at Louisiana Tech University in Ruston, Louisiana, and an active member of the American Psychological Association.

Brooke Donatone, PhD (Editing Team; Advisor, Coming Out) is a senior clinician, LGBT liason, and leader of the Gender and Sexuality team at NYU Counseling and Wellness services.

Jack Drescher, MD (Advisor, Mental Health Chapters) is a distinguished fellow of the APA, emeritus editor of the *Journal of Gay and Lesbian Mental Health*, and a training and supervising analyst at the William A. White Psychoanalytic Institute.

L. Zachary DuBois, PhD (Advisor, Global) is a biocultural anthropologist whose Transitional Stress Study involved health measures and in-depth interviews with 65 trans men in New England about their transitional experiences. He currently conducts health disparities research as a postdoc at the University of Massachusetts Boston.

Ray Edwards, MA (Survey Intern) is a freelance research consultant and data analyst in social psychology working with transgender, genderqueer, and gender nonconforming communities in New York City and the San Francisco Bay Area, and is also currently in training to become an herbalist.

Randall D. Ehrbar, PsyD (Advisor, Coming Out, Mental Health Chapters) is a psychologist working at Whitman Walker Health Center in Washington, DC, and in private practice in Maryland with expertise in LGB and trans issues, serves on the editorial board of *International Journal of Transgenderism*, is a member of WPATH and the American Psychological Association (APA), is currently serving as a member of an APA task force writing guidelines for care of transgender clients, and served on the WPATH revision committee for the *Standards of Care* version 7.

Nancy S. Erickson, Esq, JD, LLM, MA in Forensic Psychology (Advisor, Our Many Selves, Legal Issues) is an attorney specializing in domestic violence and custody evaluations in cases involving child or intimate partner abuse.

Laura Erickson-Schroth, MD, MA (Lead Editor; Author, Sex and Gender Development; Founding Organizer; Board President) is a psychiatrist working with LGBTQ people in New York City, associate editor for the *Journal of Gay and Lesbian Mental Health*, and a board member of GLMA: Health Professionals Advancing LGBT Equality and the Association of Gay and Lesbian Psychiatrists (AGLP).

Shoshana Erlich (Advisor, Disabilities and Deaf Culture) is a hard of hearing, disabled, genderqueer activist, currently attending Ryerson University in the Child and Youth Care Program, who blogs for *Shameless* magazine about their experiences around intersectional feminism.

A. Evan Eyler, MD, MPH (Advisor, Mental Health Chapters, Aging) is associate professor of psychiatry at the University of Vermont College of Medicine/Fletcher Allen Health Care, and is coeditor of the books *Lesbian, Gay, Bisexual and Transgender Aging: Challenges in Research, Practice and Policy* and *Principles of Transgender Medicine and Surgery*.

Wesley Flash (Social Media and Fundraising) is a graduate of Hampshire College and NYU's Gallatin School of Individualized Study master's program. His research focused on LGBTQ YouTube-user trends and he was invited to present his work as a TEDx talk in New York City.

Riley Fitzgerald (Advisor, General, Sexual, and Reproductive Health)

Lila Freeman (Advisor, Intimate Relationships, Sexuality) is an artist and a public librarian in Brooklyn, New York.

Alex Gannon (Research Intern, HIV/AIDS)

Andrew Garland-Forshee, PhD, HS-BCP (Advisor, Coming Out) is a professor in the department of Early Education and Family Studies at Portland Community College (Portland, Oregon), and a contributing faculty member for the School of Social Work and Human Services at Walden University. He is a consulting editor for the *Electronic Journal of Human Sexuality* and a peer reviewer for the *International Journal of Childbirth Education.*

Pooja Gehi, JD, MA (Advisor, Immigration) is an activist, author, and attorney at the Sylvia Rivera Law Project in New York City, where she is director of immigrant justice and represents hundreds of low-income transgender and gender nonconforming clients in immigration proceedings, administrative proceedings, and civil rights litigation.

Cecilia Gentili (Author, Employment; Editing Team; Board Member) is a Trans-Latina originally from Argentina by way of Miami who is currently the Trans* Health Program Coordinator at APICHA community health center, and has worked at the Gender Identity Project at the LGBT Center in New York since 2011, as a volunteer, intern, and now consultant.

Miqqi Alicia Gilbert, PhD (a.k.a. Michael A. Gilbert) (Author, Sex and Gender Development; Advisor, Our Many Selves) is a professor of philosophy at York University in Toronto, Canada, director of Fantasia Fair, and the author of many articles on gender theory and argumentation theory as well as several books on the latter subject.

Vic Glazer (Advisor, Intimate Relationships, Sexuality) works in IT sales in New York City and volunteers with LGBT people in Brooklyn, New York.

Zil Garner Goldstein (Author, Social Transition and Employment; Editing Team; Advisor, Media; Board Member) is a nurse practitioner at Beth Israel Medical Group and the Peter Krueger Center in New York, where she practices primary care, focusing on transgender health, LGBT/queer health, and HIV primary care, and is involved with the Persist Health Project, which serves people in the sex trade.

Nick Gorton (Author, General, Sexual, and Reproductive Health) is a physician who provides health care to transgender patients at Lyon-Martin Health Services, while working closely with the Transgender Law Center.

Jamison Green, PhD, MFA (Author, Media Spotlights; Advisor, Legal Issues) is a writer, educator, and advocate residing in the San Francisco Bay Area, president of the World Professional Association for Transgender Health (WPATH), a director of the Transgender Law and Policy Institute, and author of *Becoming a Visible Man.*

Hilary Maia Grubb, MD (Author, General, Sexual, and Reproductive Health; Advisor, Sex and Gender Development; Mental Health Chapters) is a resident in General Adult Psychiatry at the University of California, San Francisco, and primary author of several new LGBT health curricula for the Columbia University College of Physicians and Surgeons, the Columbia University School of Nursing, and the New York-Presbyterian Hospital Family Medicine Residency Program.

Ali Harris (Transcriptionist, New York City Forum Group Facilitator) is a Brooklyn-based queer health advocate and organizer, presently pursuing his masters degree at the Mailman School of Public Health at Columbia University, with a career focus on improving research in transgender health care outcomes.

Evan R. Hempel (Survey Intern) is a transmasculine writer, activist, and dreamer from Boston, Massachusetts, as well as clinical research professional and data manager working out of Boston and Washington, DC, and a board member of Transgender Health Empowerment (THE) in Washington, DC.

Imani Keith Henry, MSW, MPA (Advisor, Our Many Selves; Race, Ethnicity, and Culture; Activism, Politics, and Organizing; Social Transition) is an activist, writer, and performer, and a staff organizer at the International Action Center (IAC), focusing on national organizing of communities of color and the lesbian, gay, bisexual, and transgender movement toward broader social justice and antiwar campaigns.

Lance Hicks (Author, Youth) is a mixed-race, transgender, queer Detroiter who does queer youth organizing, sex worker street outreach/support, and crisis intervention.

Tobi Hill-Meyer (Author, Sexuality, Sex Worker section of Employment chapter) is a multiracial trans activist and filmmaker who founded Handbasket Productions, where she created *Doing It Ourselves*, the first and currently only porn film made by and for trans women and their community.

Jack Hixson-Vulpe, BEd, MA (Publicity Intern; Advisor, Disabilities and Deaf Culture) is a PhD candidate in gender, feminist, and women's studies at York University in Toronto, Ontario, as well as a certified primary teacher and a social justice activist.

Ruben Hopwood, MDiv, PhD, (Author, Mental Health Services and Mental Health Concerns) is educated in psychology and theology, works at Fenway Health in Boston, MA, exclusively with the trans* community and health care providers, and is a member of WPATH, the American Psychological Association (APA), and APA Division 44: Society for the Psychological Study of Lesbian, Gay, Bisexual, and Transgender Issues.

Cassidy Anne Medicine Horse, MA (Advisor, US History) is a university instructor, invited lecturer, film director, LGBT political activist, transgender scholar, and researcher working in Bozeman, Montana, and member of the American Indigenous Research Association, American Association of University Women (AAUW), and the Montana State University LGBT Advisory Committee (AIRA).

Sel J. Hwahng, PhD (Advisor, Global) is a co-investigator at the Baron Edmond de Rothschild Chemical Dependency Institute, Beth Israel Medical Center, an adjunct professor at the Center for the Study of Ethnicity and Race, Columbia University, and has published over 20 articles and book chapters in peer-reviewed journals and edited volumes.

Suzanne Iasenza, PhD (Advisor, Mental Health Chapters) is on the faculties of the Institute for Contemporary Psychotherapy and Psychoanalysis (ICP) and the Derner Institute's Postgraduate Program in Psychoanalysis and Psychotherapy at Adelphi University. She is coeditor of the books *Lesbians and Psychoanalysis: Revolutions in Theory and Practice* (1995) and *Lesbians, Feminism and Psychoanalysis: The Second Wave* (2004) and maintains a private practice in psychotherapy and sex therapy in New York City.

Joe Ippolito, PsyD, LICSW (Author, Aging; Advisor, Coming Out and Mental Health Services) is a doctor of psychology, a behavioral health clinician with Allina Health Systems, a psychology professor at Metropolitan State University, the founder and chair of Gender Reel, the administrative director of *2 Queers and A Camera*, and the producer and director of *Growing Old Gracefully: The Transgender Experience*.

Christopher J. Irving (Advisor, Activism, Politics, and Organizing) is completing his MFA in creative fiction with a preference for postapocalyptic realism at Florida Atlantic University, where he works as a writing consultant at its University Center for Excellence in Writing. He has been teaching for 6 years.

Jay A. Irwin, PhD (Advisor, Mental Health Chapters) is a medical sociologist at the University of Nebraska at Omaha whose research focuses on LGBT physical and mental health, as well as transgender identity and advocacy.

Laura A. Jacobs, LCSW (Editing Team; Editor, US History; Board Member) is a psychotherapist, activist, and presenter in the New York City area focusing on LGBTQ and sexual/gender minority communities, on the board of directors for the Callen-Lorde Community Health Center, and is completing and pursuing publication of her own book, *Many Paths: The Choice of Gender*.

Andrea James, MA (Advisor, Social Transition) is a writer, director, producer, and activist focusing on LGBT media and transgender consumer issues, including *Transamerica*, the first all-transgender *Vagina Monologues*, and the Transsexual Road Map instructional site.

Aron Janssen, MD (Advisor, Children and Youth) is a child and adolescent psychiatrist specializing in gender and sexual development who has presented nationally and internationally on gender variance in childhood and adolescence, and directs the NYU Gender and Sexuality Service.

Kevin Johnson, MD (Author, Glossary; Editing Team; Mental Health and Surgery Editor; Board Member) is graduating from Weill Cornell Medical College in New York City, and pursuing a residency program in psychiatry. At Cornell he was cochair for *Q! LGBTQ Students in Medicine and Science at Weill Cornell*, promoting transgender medical education and advocacy.

Sean Johnson, MSW, MPH (2014) (Seattle Forum Organizer) is a student/researcher at the University of Washington, the cofounder/cohost of Gendercast, and a community activist passionate about building an intersectional movement that works toward liberation and equity for everyone.

Ami B. Kaplan, LCSW (Advisor, Aging) is a psychotherapist in New York City who works with transgender and queer individuals and family members and is a member of the Policy and Procedures Committee of the World Professional Association for Transgender Health.

Cael M. Keegan, PhD (Intern, Media) is visiting assistant professor of LGBT Studies at Hobart and William Smith Colleges, a member of the National Women's Studies Association's Transgender Caucus, and sits on the editorial board of the journal *Genders*.

Reese C. Kelly, PhD (Advisor, Sex and Gender Development) is assistant dean/LGBTQA advisor at Dartmouth College, a researcher and scholar of trans/queer theory, and a cochair of the Trans Caucus of the National Women's Studies Association.

Colt Keo-Meier, PhD (Author, Youth; Advisor, Children) is a clinical psychologist in Houston, Texas; cochair of the Committee for Transgender People and Gender Diversity of Division 44 of the American Psychological Association; cochair of the World Professional Association for Transgender Health Student Initiative; and cofounder of Gender Infinity, an annual Houston-based summer conference created for gender diverse and transgender children, youth, and their families.

Aidan Key (Author, Children; Advisor, Youth) educator and organizer, is the founder of the family education and support organization Gender Diversity, the director and founder of the Gender Odyssey conferences, cofounder of Gender Spectrum and Translations: Seattle's Transgender Film Festival, and speaks nationally on issues related to trans children, teens, and adults.

HeJin Kim (Advisor, Global) is a trans activist and blogger, who has worked on transgender, sex worker, and sexual health and reproductive rights issues in Europe, South Korea, and now in South Africa at Gender DynamiX.

Anna Kirey, MA (Intern, Global) is a researcher at the LGBT rights program of Human Rights Watch, founding member of the LGBT organization Labrys (Kyrgyzstan), advisory committee member of Urgent Action Fund, Global Fund for Women, and Mamacash Fund, and member of Post-Soviet Trans* Advocacy Network.

Jeremy Kirk (Advisor, Activism, Politics, and Organizing)

Kate Kourbatova (Author, Immigration; Advisor, Intimate Relationships) is a gender-fluid human from post-Soviet Eastern Europe who recently graduated from the University of Washington with a BA in anthropology and is now searching for the intersection between making a living and doing what they love.

SJ Langer, LCSW-R (Editing Team; Advisor, Mental Health Chapters) is a psychotherapist and writer in private practice in New York City, member of the Executive Committee for the

Institute for Contemporary Psychotherapies-Psychotherapy Center for Gender and Sexuality's Trans Symposium, and member of the organizing committees for the mental health programs for the Philadelphia Trans Health Conference.

Nichole Latimer (Social Media Intern Director) is an MA candidate in the Department of Social and Cultural Analysis at New York University, where her research focuses on the alternative political visions presented by digital communities of nonmetropolitan trans* youth.

Dana LaVanture, MD (Advisor, Surgical Transition) is a board-eligible general surgeon and a current fellow in Hand Surgery at the University of Connecticut.

Celeste LeCompte (Developmental Editor) is a writer and editor with more than a decade of experience working on environmental, public health, and social justice issues.

Jessie Lee (Advisor, General, Sexual, and Reproductive Health) is a hapa trans woman working in medical research and plans to pursue a biomedical PhD.

Arlene Istar Lev, LCSW-R, CASAC (Advisor, Coming Out and Mental Health Chapters) is a gender specialist and family therapist. She is a lecturer at the University of Albany and Smith College, and the author of *Transgender Emergence* and *The Complete Lesbian and Gay Parenting Book*, as well as one of many authors who revised the WPATH Standards of Care.

Rachel N. Levin, PhD (Advisor, Sex and Gender Development) is an associate professor in the Departments of Biology and Neuroscience at Pomona College and the principal investigator on a research project that examines biological influences on gender identity and sexuality that has over 1,000 participants.

Kestryl Cael Lowrey, MA (Author, Arts and Culture) is a Brooklyn-based scholar and performance artist, and is the creator of performances such as XY(T), 348, and RADCLYFFE: The Completely Honest and Mostly True Story of Victorian England's Second Most Notorious Invert.

Miss Major (Advisor, Activism, Politics, and Organizing) is 70 years old and lives in Oakland, California. She is affiliated with the Transgender, Gender Variant and Intersex Justice Project.

Zack Marshall (Author, Disabilities and Deaf Culture) is a trans guy with a disability and a passion for community-based participatory research, social justice, and supporting the development of more welcoming and accessible nonprofit organizations whose most recent disability-related work was with Griffin Centre's sprOUT, a collaborative community-based project developed in partnership with LGBTQ people labeled with intellectual disabilities.

Denise M. Maynard, MLAS, SAS/SDA (Editing Team) has spoken internationally on education, is the founder/director of Maynard's W.I.S.D.O.M. Inc., an educational consulting service, and has been an elementary educator since 1986, specializing in early childhood education.

Christopher A. McIntosh, MSc, MD, FRCPC (Advisor, Mental Health Chapters) is a psychiatrist and head of the Gender Identity Clinic at the Centre for Addiction and Mental Health, an assistant professor at the University of Toronto, and coeditor-in-chief of *The Journal of Gay and Lesbian Mental Health*.

Tey Meadow, JD, PhD (Advisor, Children and Youth) is a sociologist and the Fund for Reunion-Cotsen Fellow in LGBT Studies at the Princeton Society of Fellows; she is also on the board of directors of the International Gay and Lesbian Human Rights Commission (IGLHRC).

Dylan Thomas Mendenhall, BS (Advisor, Immigration) coordinates the forest monitoring program at EarthCorps and does restoration ecology research in partnership with the University of Washington.

Edgardo Menvielle, MD (Advisor, Children and Youth) is a child and adolescent psychiatrist specialized in problems related to the development of gender and sexual identity, Department of Psychiatry, Children's National Medical Center, in Washington, D.C.

Joanne Meyerowitz (Advisor, US History) is the Arthur Unobskey Professor of History and American Studies at Yale University and the author of *How Sex Changed: A History of Transsexuality in the United States* (Harvard University Press).

Shannon Price Minter (Author, Legal Issues) is the legal director of the National Center for Lesbian Rights, one of the nation's leading legal advocacy organizations for lesbian, gay, bisexual, and transgender people; and serves on the boards of Equality California, Faith in America, and the Transgender Law and Policy Institute.

Scott Loren Moore (Short Piece Editor; Editing Team; Advisor, Sex and Gender Development and Sexuality) is a teacher, a workshop facilitator, a writer, and an employee of the New York City Department of Education.

Zeraph Dylan Moore (Survey Intern) writes on queer and transgender topics for *The Alchemist's Closet, Wild Gender*, and *The Alchemical Postmodern Theorist*, a journal of queer possibility and off-the-map theory.

Chris Mosier (Advisor, Legal Issues and Social Transition; Volunteer) is an advocate, educator, athlete, and coach, and is the creator of transathlete.com.

Quince Mountain (Author, Religion and Spirituality) is an editor of *Killing the Buddha*, a literary magazine on religion.

Ronica Mukerjee FNP, LAc (Advisor, General, Sexual, and Reproductive Health) is a licensed family nurse practitioner and acupuncturist and director of Transgender Health at a community health center in New York City.

Deb Murphy (Advisor, Youth) is a youth services specialist working with LGBT youth in Houston, Texas.

Niyoka Nelson (Survey Intern)

Kate Nemeth (Fundraiser Videographer) is a writer and artist working with new media in New York City.

Leo Newball, Jr (Web Development and Design) started building Web sites in 1995, when domain names cost just $35 and everyone's favorite search engine was Yahoo! Fifteen years and a couple of executive position jobs later, he now uses his development, design, and data skills to create dynamic Web sites for a wide variety of clients in fields like film, nonprofits, and corporations.

Amanda Ocasio (Social Media Intern; Survey Intern) just finished her master's degree in History at Brooklyn College, where she focused on assorted issues related to gender. In Fall 2014, she will be joining the journalism program at Hofstra University as a graduate student.

Lisa O'Connor, MD (Editing Team; Advisor, Surgical Transition) a National Platform Speaker, is a board-certified family physician in solo practice dedicated to the transgender community; a board-certified cognitive behavioral therapist; a voting member of the World Professional Association for Transgender Health (WPATH); a member of The American Association of Sexuality Educators Counselors and Therapists (AASECT); a member of GLMA Health Professionals Advancing LGBT Equality; a member of The World Association for Sexual Health (WAS); a Kink Aware Provider (KAP) with the National Coalition for Sexual Freedom (NCSF); a retired US Army veteran; and a member of the Ad Hoc Committee for DADT Transgender Inclusion.

Johanna Olson, MD (Advisor, Children) is the medical director of the Center for Transyouth Health and Development at Children's Hospital Los Angeles. Her career is dedicated to clinical care and research promoting authentic living for all youth.

Asaf Orr (Advisor, Children, Youth, and US History) is a staff attorney at the National Center for Lesbian Rights and works on issues related to families and youth.

Heather Palmer (Publicity Intern)

Kristin Pape (Editing Team; Advisor, Disabilities and Deaf Culture, Coming Out, and Sexuality) teaches literary, film, and cultural studies at Pratt Institute in Brooklyn, New York, where she helped start and now advises the student group of women architects and the group for LGBTQ student architects.

Jude Patton LMHC, LMFT, PA-C (Advisor, Aging) is an out and proud trans* man who has provided medical and counseling services for LGBTI folks in southern California and in northwestern Washington State for the past 41 years, and one of the pioneers in advocacy and education regarding trans* health issues.

Pauline Park (Advisor, Activism, Politics, and Organizing), chair of the New York Association for Gender Rights Advocacy (NYAGRA) and president of the board of directors and acting executive director of Queens Pride House, led the campaign for the transgender rights law enacted by the New York City Council in 2002.

Lazlo Ilya Pearlman (Art Editor; Author, Arts and Culture) is a performing artist and author with 30 years of experience making Queer and Trans theatre in the United States, the United Kingdom, and continental Europe, and is currently pursuing his PhD at the University of London Royal Central School of Speech and Drama.

Kim Pearson (Advisor, Children) is Training Director and cofounder of TransYouth Family Allies (TYFA).

Karen Pittelman (Advisor, Immigration) is the author of *Classified: How to Stop Hiding Your Privilege and Use It for Social Change*, helps organize the Trans Justice Funding Project, and works as a writing coach in Brooklyn, New York.

Kel Polly (Author, Parenting) is a queer-identified gender activist with a passion for expanding social understanding of gender, promoting youth empowerment, and providing opportunities for children to explore gender expression, without fear of rejection. Kel lives with their partner of five years, and together they co-parent four children.

Ryan G. Polly, PhDc, MEd (Author, Parenting) is a queer-identified trans man, parent of four children, and PhD candidate at the California Institute of Integral Studies, researching the experiences of trans-identified parents.

Abigail Proffer, MD (Advisor, Parenting) is an obstetrician/gynecologist working in the Kansas City metropolitan area and is active in promoting women's health in the community.

MiKami Puchon, MSW (Advisor, Race, Ethnicity, and Culture) is a practicing social worker in Brooklyn, NY.

Jack Pula, MD (Advisor, Mental Health Chapters) is a psychiatrist and psychotherapist in New York City and an advocate for transgender mental health.

Anita Radix, MD, MPH, FACP (Editing Team; Advisor, General, Sexual, and Reproductive Health, Medical Transition, and Surgical Transition) is the Director of Research and Education and an internist/HIV specialist at the Callen-Lorde Community Health Center in New York City.

Naim Rasul, MA (Author, Race, Ethnicity, and Culture; Editing Team; Advisor, Our Many Selves; Board Member) is a case manager/health educator for trans and gender nonconforming youth within the Health Outreach to Teens (HOTT) Program at Callen-Lorde Community Health Center in New York City.

Katherine Rachlin, PhD (Kit) (Advisor, Coming Out, Mental Health Chapters) is a clinical psychologist and gender specialist in private practice in New York City, a past board member of the World Professional Association for Transgender Health and FTM International, and is an author/coauthor of a number of trans-positive published papers, book chapters, reports, and policy statements, including WPATH's Version 7 of the *Standards of Care for the Health of Transgender, Transsexual, and Gender Nonconforming People*.

Sara Rafferty (Advisor, Activism, Politics, and Organizing)

Lewis A. Raynor, PhD, MPH, MS (Advisor, Sex and Gender Development) is a genetic epidemiologist with a passion for social justice.

Elana Redfield (Author, Immigration) is an attorney with the Sylvia Rivera Law Project and a board member of the Lorena Borjas Community Fund, both based in New York City.

Elizabeth Reis, PhD (Advisor, US History) is the author of *Bodies in Doubt: An American History of Intersex*; the editor of *American Sexual Histories*; and Professor of Women's and Gender Studies at the University of Oregon.

Sari Reisner, ScD, MA (Advisor, Coming Out, Mental Health Chapters) is a research scientist at the Fenway Institute at Fenway Health and a postdoctoral research fellow in the Department of Epidemiology at Harvard School of Public Health who earned a doctor of science in social epidemiology with concentrations in quantitative methods, human development, and gender and health, and has coauthored more than 40 peer-reviewed journal articles and presented his research in transgender health nationally and internationally.

Bryce Renninger (Advisor, Global)

Heath Mackenzie Reynolds (Author, Social Transition; Author, Employment; Assisting Author, Religion and Spirituality) is a student at the Reconstructionist Rabbinical College of Philadelphia with over a decade of experience as a social services provider and community organizer in health centers, community organizations, libraries, and congregations. Heath has centered their work in trans, queer, and HIV-affected communities, Jewish communities, and with poor and working class people.

Mx. Ignacio G. Rivera, MA (Advisor, Sexuality), who prefers the gender-neutral pronoun "they," is an internationally known queer, Two-Spirit, Black-Boricua Taíno, lecturer, activist, sex educator, filmmaker, and performance artist whose body of work has focused on gender and sexuality, specifically on queer, trans, and sexual liberation issues within a race/class dynamic.

Ms. Jamie Roberts, JD (Author, Trans Political Leaders) practices law as a criminal defense attorney in middle Georgia and is recent co-chair of Georgia Equality, Georgia's statewide TLBG education and advocacy organization, as well as secretary of her County Committee of the Democratic Party of Georgia.

C. Rodriguez-Fucci (Advisor, Parenting) is a reluctant social work grad student and has a history of work in the queer and trans antiviolence movement. His long-term goal is to play more and work less. . . or, better yet, turn work into play! Cara is a proud parent and likes talking about the intersections, overlap, and complexities of our identities. . . particularly trans*, POC, queer, kinky, parent, survivor identities.

Amanda Rosenblum (Founding Organizer; Volunteer and Outreach Director; Editing Team; Board Vice President) is an educational programming manager at the Young Women's Leadership Network, a network of all-girls public schools in New York City, is currently enrolled in the Urban Education Masters Program at the CUNY Graduate Center, and has a special interest in prison advocacy and working with students.

Hershel Russell, MEd (Advisor, Aging) is a psychotherapist, educator, and activist working with LGBT communities and with families of gender nonconforming children in Toronto, Canada. He is lead mental health trainer for the Trans Health Connection program at Rainbow Health Ontario (RHO) and cochair of the Education Committee of the Canadian Professional Association for Transgender Health (CPATH).

Syd Salsman (Art Editing Intern) is a student at UC Davis and aspiring librarian.

Barbara Satin (Advisor, Aging) is an 80-year-old transgender advocate whose energies are focused on issues of LGBT aging and faith, currently serving as assistant faith work director for The National Gay and Lesbian Task Force. She is celebrating the opening of Spirit on Lake, a new, 46-unit affordable rental project for LGBT seniors in Minneapolis, a development in which she has been a major participant.

Dean Scarborough (Author, Sexuality, Sex Worker section of Employment chapter; Illustrator) hails from the Bay Area of California, where he is a feminist sex educator and a somatic therapist-in-training.

Toi Scott (Advisor, Race, Ethnicity, and Culture) is a visionary, community organizer, artivist, blogger, and author of *Notes from an Afro-Genderqueer*, as well as radical, brown, gender/

queer plays *Genderqueer Files:La Qolectiv@* and *Resistencia: Sangre*, who is an ordinary superhero working toward racial and gender justice and the eradication of oppression and disparities within the economic, food, and health systems.

Sem (Advisor, Coming Out, Mental Health Chapters) is a queer-identified mental health professional who specializes in working with college students and became aware of the power of gender identity and expression at a young age.

Judy Sennesh (Editing Team; Advisor, Youth) is a member of the board of directors of PFLAGNYC and is the founder and facilitator of the TransParent Project, PFLAGNYC's fastest growing support group.

Eve Shapiro, PhD (Advisor, US History) is a sociologist whose recent book *Gender Circuits: Bodies and Identities in a Technological Age* (Routledge, 2010) examines whether and how new technologies are changing the gendered lives of cisgender and transgender individuals.

Ilana Sherer, MD (Advisor, Our Many Selves, Children) is a pediatrician in the San Francisco Bay Area, founder and assistant medical director of the Child and Adolescent Gender Center at UCSF, and a charter member of the American Academy of Pediatrics section on LGBT youth.

Jonah A. Siegel, MSW (Central Organizer; Survey Director) is a doctoral student in social work and sociology at the University of Michigan, Ann Arbor, whose research focuses on deviance and punishment, the spatial distribution of crime, felon disenfranchisement, and poverty and social welfare policy.

Jake Silver (Social Media Intern) is a graduate student in the Department of Anthropology at Columbia University. His work, noted for its scholarship by the Association for Queer Anthropology, interrogates intimacy at varying levels—from the mundane to the sexual to the political—in order to understand the increasingly strategic uses of sexuality by modern nation-states.

Dena Simmons, MSEd (Research Intern Program Director; Advisor, Race, Ethnicity, and Culture; Board Member) is an educator and doctoral candidate in Health Education at Columbia University, Teachers College, whose research centers around teacher preparedness to address bullying. She is particularly interested in health disparities, the experiences of trans people of color in the health care system, the health risks associated with performing masculinity in the school setting, and the effects of educational policy on the health of the nation's children.

Holiday Simmons, MSW (Author, Our Many Selves) is Director of Community Education and Advocacy at Lambda Legal, a member of the Georgia Safe Schools Coalition, the Solutions Not Punishments Coalition, and the Trans People of Color Coalition, and a lover of nature, soccer, babies, and social justice.

Anneliese Singh, PhD, LPC (Author, Trans Political Leaders) is an associate professor at The University of Georgia, International Section Associate Editor for the *Journal of Counseling and Development*, and founding member of the Trans Resilience Project and the Georgia Safe Schools Coalition. Her research and advocacy focuses on the resilience of trans people of color and young people.

Michelle Skoor, (Volunteer) is a gender-queer papa person who is still figuring it all out.

Rev. Mykal O'Neal Slack (Advisor, Religion and Spirituality) is ordained clergy with Metropolitan Community Churches (MCC) and founder and lead organizer of 4Lyfe Ministries, a collective of activist theologians, ministers, vocalists, preachers, prayer partners, and teachers from all walks of faith and life, as well as the director of Spiritual Outreach for the Trans People of Color Coalition, the only national organization that seeks to promote the social and economic equality of all transgender and gender nonconforming people.

Oliver Slate-Greene (Video Producer) is equally passionate about sight, sound, motion and being transgender - I intend to be intentional in all aspects.

T. Evan Smith (Author, Sex and Gender Development) is associate professor of psychology and director of the women and gender studies program at Elizabethtown College. He is also a long-time volunteer with the Common Roads youth program of the LGBT Center of Central Pennsylvania.

Carey Jean Sojka, MA (Author, Intimate Relationships) is currently a doctoral candidate in sociology at the University at Albany, SUNY, and an adjunct instructor in gender, sexuality, and women's studies at Southern Oregon University.

Elizabeth Spergel (Survey intern) is a graduate of Wesleyan University, with a BA in feminist, gender, and sexuality studies.

Jeffrey Spiegel, MD, FACS (Advisor, Surgical Transition) is professor and chief of Facial Plastic Surgery at Boston University School of Medicine, director of Advanced Facial Aesthetics in Chestnut Hill, Massachusetts, is an internationally renowned surgeon with unique expertise in facial gender-confirming surgery.

Jessica Lina Stirba, JD, MS (Author, Employment; Editing Team; Advisor, Media; Board Member) is an activist and scholar living in Brooklyn with her loving partner and two cats.

Rev. Moonhawk River Stone, MS, LMHC (Advisor, Our Many Selves; Race, Ethnicity, and Culture; Aging; Religion and Spirituality; and United States History) is an Interfaith minister, psychotherapist, consultant, educator, writer, and keynote speaker in private practice in the Albany, New York area.

Chase Strangio, JD (Advisor, Immigration) is a staff attorney at the ACLU's LGBT and AIDS Project and is a founding board member of the Lorena Borjas Community Fund.

Rae Strozzo (Art Editing Team) is a transmasculine visual artist, writer, and educator (www. raestrozzo.com).

Susan Stryker, PhD (Advisor, US History) is associate professor of gender and women's studies and director of the Institute for LGBT Studies at the University of Arizona, coeditor of both volumes of *The Transgender Studies Reader*, and founding coeditor of *TSQ: Transgender Studies Quarterly*.

Melba J. Nicholson Sullivan, PhD (Editing Team; Advisor, Immigration and Mental Health Chapters) is the director of training and a senior staff psychologist with the Bellevue/NYU Program for Survivors of Torture.

Eli Szenes-Strauss (Editing Team)

Jae DK Szeszycki-Truesdell, MA, MPH (Author, Arts and Culture) is a transgender and gay activist with the privilege to have been educated at Purdue University and University of Illinois at Chicago. He lives in Oakland, CA with his husband, Marek, and dog, Zephyr.

Lana Thompson (Advisor, Activism, Politics, and Organizing)

Aubry Threlkeld (Advisor, Disabilities and Deaf Culture) is a doctoral candidate in Human Development and Education at Harvard Graduate School of Education whose research looks at how and when young people with dyslexia construct themselves as disabled and how that relates to cultural models of disability.

Elenore Toczynski (Illustrator) is a comic book artist and illustrator living in Philadelphia with a wiggly dog and lots of art supplies, and is working on an ongoing Web comic, a print comic series, and a graphic novel.

Onyinyechukwu Udegbe (Advisor, Disabilities and Deaf Culture).

Katya Ungerman (Art Editing Intern; Editing Team) is a playwright, filmmaker, and blogger who graduated from New York University's Tisch School of the Arts in May 2013.

Jeanne Vaccaro (Advisor, Sex and Gender Development, Intimate Relationships) received a PhD in performance studies at New York University, is an Andrew W. Mellon Fellow in Sexuality Studies at the University of Pennsylvania and writes about transgender performance and queer craft.

Reid Vanderburgh, MA, retired MFT (Author, Coming Out) is a retired therapist based in Portland, Oregon. He now focuses on teaching and writing about trans* issues. Reid began his transition process in 1995.

Jaimie Veale, PhD (Advisor, Sex and Gender Development) is a trans woman currently working on a postdoctoral research fellowship in trans people's health at the University of British Columbia.

Elias Vitulli (Advisor, US History) is a doctoral candidate in American Studies at the University of Minnesota whose work examines the history of the incarceration of gender nonconforming and trans people in the United States and has been published in *GLQ* and *Social Justice*.

Allison Vogt, LBSW (Advisor, Youth) advocates for LGBT victims and survivors of domestic violence, sexual assault, hate crimes, and human trafficking through direct services, advocacy, and education for the Montrose Center in Houston, Texas. Her blog, Ask Allie (www.askallie. org), is popular among teens requesting healthy relationship advice.

Sean Saifa M. Wall (Advisor, Sex and Gender Development) is an intersex activist and board president of Advocates for Informed Choice, an organization that advocates for the civil rights of children born with variations of reproductive or sexual anatomy. Saifa is currently living in Atlanta's West End.

Pau Crego Walters (Advisor, General, Sexual, and Reproductive Health; Mental Health Chapters; and Activism, Politics, and Organizing) is a social worker serving homeless youth in San Francisco, an independent activist/scholar within trans health politics, and member of the coordination team of the International Campaign Stop Trans Pathologization (STP).

Syrus Marcus Ware (Author, Disabilities and Deaf Culture) is a black, trans, and disabled visual artist, researcher, activist, and identical twin. His past projects include co-creating *Primed: The Backpocket Guide for Trans Guys and the Guys Who Dig 'Em* and coauthoring *How Disability Studies Stays White and What Kind of White It Stays*. Syrus is a PhD candidate at York University, focusing on disability arts practice.

Adrien A. Weibgen (Advisor, Social Transition; Volunteer) is a racial justice advocate, queer organizer, and 2014 graduate of Yale Law School who is pursuing a career working with and for communities of color in New York.

Linda Wesp, MSN, FNP-C, AAHIVS (Editing Team; Health and Wellness Editor) is a nurse practitioner providing primary care and research opportunities to LGBTQ and HIV-positive adolescents in the Bronx, and a local and national educator on transgender health.

Christopher White, PhD (Advisor, Sexuality) is a consultant in sexual health and sexuality education with over 20 years of experience and specializes in meeting the needs of the LGBT community.

Fresh! White, CPCC (Author, Our Many Selves) is a Mindfulness Coach and founder of Affirmative Acts Coaching, writer, LGBTQQI activist and conversation facilitator, Buddhist practitioner, supporter of trans* employment at the Transgender Economic Empowerment Initiative, inclusion enthusiast, and lover of life!

Riki Wilchins, MA (Advisor, US History and Activism, Politics, and Organizing) has written three books on gender theory, founded GenderPAC and The Transexual Menace, and been selected by TIME as one of "100 Civic Innovators for the 21st Century."

Willy Wilkinson, MPH (Advisor, Race, Ethnicity, and Culture) (www.willywilkinson.com) is an award-winning writer and public health consultant whose book, *Born on the Edge of Race and Gender*, is forthcoming.

Arthur Robin Williams, MD, MBE (Central Organizer; Board Vice President) is a psychiatry resident and documentary photographer. His work, *My Right Self*, a photo documentary exploring issues of identity, perception, and the body, was supported by an Open Society Institute Documentary Photography Project Grant.

Cristan Williams (Advisor, US History) is a pioneering trans activist and historian, the founder of the Houston Transgender Center and Archives, and the executive director of the Transgender Foundation of America.

Andre Wilson, MS (Advisor, General, Sexual, and Reproductive Health) is a health policy consultant specializing in transgender health and eliminating discriminatory "trans exclusions" in health benefits plans. Andre is senior associate at Jamison Green and Associates.

Kelley Winters, PhD (Advisor, Mental Health Chapters) is the founder of GID Reform Advocates, a writer and consultant on gender diversity issues in medical and public policy, and a member of the International Advisory Panel for the WPATH Standards of Care, Version 7.

Debby Wisnowski (Editing Team; Advisor, Children) is a mom to a transgender child and cofounder of Stepping Stones, a support group in New York City for gender nonconforming and transgender youth and their families.

Tarynn M. Witten, PhD, LCSW, FGSA (Author, Aging) is a fellow and recipient of the Inaugural Nathan W. and Margaret Shock New Investigator Research Award of the Gerontological Society of America; associate professor of Biological Complexity, Emergency Medicine, and Gerontology; an adjunct associate professor of Social Work and Women and Gender Studies at Virginia Commonwealth University; a member of the consulting consortium of the Healthy People 2010 Project; and founder and director of the Transgender Longitudinal Aging Research Study.

Kai Yohman (Advisor, Social Transition)

Kortney Ryan Ziegler (Author, Race, Ethnicity, and Culture) is an Oakland-based award-winning artist and writer, the director of the film *STILL BLACK: A Portrait of Black Transmen*, and the first person to hold a PhD in African American studies from Northwestern University.

Quito Ziegler (Advisor, Arts and Culture) is an artist, activist, curator, and producer who divides their time between Brooklyn and Vermont. They have produced exhibitions for the Open Society Foundations, taught at the International Center of Photography, curated shows with Visual AIDS and the MIX Festival, and organized a wide range of community-based art projects.

GLOSSARY

ADMIRER A person who is attracted to transgender or gender nonconforming people. Some (but not all) admirers may be considered "chasers." (*See* tranny chaser.)

AFFIRMED GENDER The gender to which someone has transitioned. This term is often used to replace terms like "new gender" or "chosen gender," which imply that the current gender was not always a person's gender or that the gender was chosen rather than simply in existence.

AFFIRMED MALE/AFFIRMED FEMALE A person who has transitioned, either socially or physically. An alternative to the terms *FTM/MTF* or *transgender man/transgender woman*.

AGENDER A person who does not identify with or conform to any gender.

AGGRESSIVE (AG) A term that describes someone assigned female at birth who is female identified and prefers to present as masculine—more commonly used in communities of color.

ALLY A person who helps to advocate for a particular group of people (i.e., transgender or LGBTQ people). Allies may help build more supportive climates and are knowledgeable about issues or concerns.

AMBIGUOUS GENITALIA Describes a condition in which an infant's external genitals do not appear to be clearly male or female. (*See* intersex.)

ANDROGEN BLOCKER Medication that blocks the effects of androgens such as testosterone and DHT. Also known as antiandrogen. The term *androgen blocker* is typically used to describe medications like spironolactone (nonselective androgen blocker), often taken by transgender women to block the effects of androgens. It is also sometimes used to describe medications like finasteride (DHT blocker) taken by people of all genders to combat hair loss.

ANDROGYNE Nonbinary gender identity. Those who identify as androgyne may see themselves as both masculine and feminine or neither. Some androgynes may undergo medical interventions (hormones or surgery) to appear more androgynous.

ANDROGYNOUS Having both male and female characteristics. Can be used to describe people's appearances or items of clothing. Not typically used as a self-description, though it can be.

ASEXUAL A term that describes a person who does not experience sexual attraction. This term is a self-identity.

ASSIGNED (FE)MALE (AT BIRTH) (AFAB/AMAB) A person who was assigned either a female or male gender at birth and may or may not identify as that gender.

ASSIGNED GENDER The gender that is given to an infant based on the infant's external genitals. This may or may not match the person's gender identity in adulthood.

ASSIGNED SEX The sex (male, female, intersex) that is assigned to an infant at birth.

BALLROOM COMMUNITY An LGBTQ subculture in which events (also known as "balls") are held during which people compete for prizes. Participants "vogue" (dance) and compete in various genres. Many people involved with ball culture belong to a house, which is led by a house mother and/or father.

BDSM A range of sexual practices involving dominance and submission.

BERDACHE An older term used by Europeans and European Americans to describe people in Native American traditions who were considered gay, transgender, or gender variant. This term has since fallen out of favor and may be considered offensive, as it comes from the French word for male prostitute. *Two-Spirit* is considered a more accepted term, and one with which many people today still identify.

BIGENDER A term that describes those who feel they have two genders. They may move between having a masculine and a feminine-based appearance or change their behavior depending on their feelings, location, or situation.

BINDING The process of using an elastic band, cloth, or commercially produced binder in order to flatten the chest.

BIO MAN/WOMAN/GIRL/BOY/GUY Short for biological. Commonly thought to be problematic terminology, since it implies biological illegitimacy for the identities of trans and gender nonconforming people. *Cisgender* is a preferred term by some people.

BIOLOGICAL SEX Sex determined by the physical characteristics of the body at birth, such as genetic markers, and internal and external genitalia. Biological sex may differ from gender identity. Like *bio man/woman*, this term is thought of by some people as problematic as it implies that there is no biological basis for trans identity.

BISEXUAL (bi) A self-identity used by some people who are sexually/erotically or emotionally attracted to men and women. Some people prefer the term *pansexual* because it opens the possibilities for attraction to more than two genders.

BODY IMAGE Refers to a person's feelings and opinions about their body. This can include one's size, sexual attractiveness, aesthetics, or strength.

BOI A self-identity used by various groups of (usually young) people, including some trans men, some gay men (often in "daddy boi" relationships), and some lesbians who identify as young, carefree, and sexually explorative.

BOTTOM SURGERY A term that refers to surgeries performed to alter the genitals or internal reproductive organs. These may include vaginoplasties, metoidioplasties, phalloplasties, or other procedures.

BRAIN ORGANIZATION THEORY Suggests that the same hormones that cause changes in internal sexual organs and external genitalia in the uterus may also cause changes in the brain that lead people to think in certain ways about their gender as adults.

BREAST AUGMENTATION A form of top surgery during which implants made of either silicone or saline are used to enhance the size of the breasts.

BUTCH A term that describes a person who appears and/or acts in a masculine manner—in accordance with that person's culture. Often used to describe lesbians. In the past, lesbian relationships were often set up as butch (masculine) and femme (feminine). Butch can be a self-identity, but it can also be used to speak about someone in an insulting way if this is not how the person identifies. (*See* femme.)

CARRY LETTER Document from a medical provider about a person's trans status that some people use to facilitate interactions with government employees while traveling or in day-to-day interactions where activities are gendered.

CHASER Someone with an attraction to trans or gender nonconforming people. (*See* admirer and tranny chaser.)

CISGENDER (cis) A person whose gender identity matches their gender assigned at birth. (non-transgender) Often preferred over terms such as "biological" or "natal" man or woman.

CISNORMATIVITY A term that describes the assumption that all people are cisgender or that those assigned male grow up to be men and those assigned female grow up to be women.

CISSEXISM A system of bias in favor of cisgender people, in which people whose gender identities do not match their assigned genders are considered inferior.

CLITEROPLASTY Surgical creation of a clitoris, typically performed as part of a vaginoplasty.

CLOCK/ED When a person is identified as trans while attempting to present as their affirmed gender (also known as being "read").

COMING OUT To take a risk by sharing one's identity, sometimes to one person in conversation, sometimes to a group or in a public setting. Coming out is a lifelong process—in each new situation a person must decide whether or not to risk coming out. Coming out and disclosure are similar but distinct concepts. Even if someone has come out, they may not be recognizable as transgender and may choose to disclose their identity as transgender in certain contexts.

CONVERSION THERAPY A controversial form of therapy that focuses on changing a person's sexuality to heterosexual or gender identity to cisgender. (Also known as reparative therapy).

CROSS-DRESS When someone wears the clothes typically worn by another gender, sometimes only in their own home, or as part of sexual play, and sometimes at public functions.

CROSS-DRESSER (CD) (dresser) Someone who cross-dresses. Can be a self-identity. Some cross-dressers consider themselves part of transgender communities and some do not.

CROSS-SEX HORMONE *See* hormone replacement therapy.

DEPATHOLOGIZATION *See* pathologization.

DESIGNATED (FE)MALE (AT BIRTH) (DFAB/DMAB) *See* assigned (fe)male (at birth).

DETRANSITION When one decides to stop or reverse transition. This can be done for a number of reasons, including difficulty with the physical or social transition process, frustrations with side effects from treatment, or a loss of desire to transition.

DHT BLOCKERS Medications that block the effect of DHT (dihydrotestosterone). Often used to treat scalp hair loss. DHT blockers include medications like finasteride and dutasteride.

DIAGNOSTIC AND STATISTICAL MANUAL (DSM) A diagnostic tool (book) created by the American Psychiatric Association (APA) that provides clinicians with a framework for understanding mental health issues and diagnoses. Current edition is the *DSM-5*. (*See* gender dysphoria, gender identity disorder, and pathologization.)

DIHYDROTESTOSTERONE (DHT) A type of androgen hormone. Testosterone is converted into DHT in specific areas of the body. Before birth, DHT promotes the development of male-appearing genitals. There is controversy over whether it can also be helpful (as a cream) in promoting phallic enlargement in adults. DHT also causes scalp hair loss (i.e., male pattern baldness).

DILATOR A piece of plastic or silicone that is used to maintain, lengthen, and stretch the size of the vagina after vaginoplasty. Dilators of increasing size are regularly inserted into the vagina at time intervals according to the surgeon's instructions. Dilation is required less frequently over time, but it is recommended indefinitely.

DISABILITY Socially constructed diagnosis that labels some people as different.

DISCLOSURE The act or process of revealing one's transgender or gender nonconforming identity to another person in a specific instance. Related to, but not the same as, coming out.

DISORDER OF SEX DEVELOPMENT (DSD) Medical conditions that affect the development of the genitalia and/or reproductive organs. Some people who have these conditions identify as *intersex*, a less clinical term.

DOUBLE-INCISION MASTECTOMY Top surgery to create a male-contoured chest. This technique is used on larger chests, and incisions are made under each breast in order to remove tissue.

DRAG The act of dressing in gendered clothing and adopting gendered behaviors as part of a performance. Some perform in drag for entertainment, and others as a political commentary, or for personal enjoyment.

DRAG KING Someone who dresses in masculine clothing as performance. Drag kings are typically assigned female at birth, but people of all assigned sexes and gender identities can perform as drag kings.

DRAG QUEEN Someone who dresses in feminine clothing as performance. Drag queens are typically assigned male at birth, but people of all assigned sexes and gender identities can perform as drag queens.

DRESSER Shortened form of the term *cross-dresser*, sometimes used as a self-identity.

DYKE A slang term used to describe lesbians. Often used in a derogatory manner, especially for masculine women, but some queer women and lesbians have reclaimed the word.

DYSPHORIA A generic term for discomfort or low mood. (*See* gender dysphoria).

ELECTROLYSIS The process of applying a tiny amount of electricity to hair follicles, which destroys their ability to grow new hair.

ENDOCRINOLOGIST A type of physician who specializes in conditions that involve hormones and affect the endocrine system. Many endocrinologists (in addition to primary care providers) prescribe hormones to transgender and gender nonconforming communities.

ESTRADIOL A form of estrogen.

ESTROGEN A hormone produced in the bodies of all people, though typically associated with women. Taken by those on the transfeminine spectrum to develop more feminine characteristics such as larger breasts, softer skin, and a more feminine fat distribution pattern.

FACIAL FEMINIZATION SURGERY A diverse set of plastic surgery techniques that are performed to alter the jaw, chin, cheeks, forehead, nose, ears, lips, or other parts of the face to create a more feminine facial appearance.

FAG A derogatory term used to describe gay men. Has been reclaimed by some people.

FE/MALE ASSIGNED AT BIRTH (FAAB)/(MAAB) *See* assigned female at birth (AFAB) or assigned male at birth (AMAB).

FEMALE/MALE IMPERSONATOR A person who uses clothing, makeup, and other materials to express a masculine or feminine gender expression for entertainment purposes. (*See* drag.)

FEMALE-TO-MALE (FTM, F2M) A term that describes someone who was assigned a female sex and gender at birth and currently has a male gender identity. May or may not have had surgery or taken hormones to physically alter their appearance.

FEMININE A term that describes behavior, dress, qualities, or attitudes that are associated with women. What is considered feminine differs based on culture, race, ethnicity, and environment.

FEMINISM A belief system and social movement supporting equality for women and men.

FEMINIZE The process of making someone or something more feminine. This may include, but is not limited to, putting on make up, dressing in women's clothes, or taking estrogen and/or androgen blockers.

FEMME Traditionally refers to the feminine partner in a butch–femme lesbian relationship. Now a self-identity used by some people who see themselves as feminine.

FINASTERIDE *See* DHT blockers.

GAFF A type of tight underwear that helps to keep the penis tucked between the legs. (*See* tucking.)

GATEKEEPER A medical or mental health provider who has the potential to restrict transgender and gender nonconforming people from obtaining hormones or accessing surgery to transition. Many clinics are moving from gatekeeper to informed consent models.

GATEKEEPING The act of restricting access. In trans communities, refers to a health provider and access to hormones or surgery.

GAY An identity term used by some people who identify as men and are attracted to men. Some women who are attracted to other women also identify as gay, although others prefer the term *lesbian.*

GENDER A set of social, psychological, and emotional traits, often influenced by societal expectations, that classify an individual as feminine or masculine.

GENDER-AFFIRMING SURGERY (GAS) Surgical procedures that help us adjust our bodies in a way that more closely matches our desired gender identity. Not every transgender person desires surgery.

GENDERBENDING Refers to the act of bending or playing around with gender expression or gender roles.

GENDER BINARY The concept that there are only two genders, male and female, and that everyone has to be either one or the other.

GENDER-CONFIRMING SURGERY (GCS) Another term for *gender-affirming surgery (GAS).*

GENDER DYSPHORIA (GD) A mental health diagnosis that is defined as a "marked incongruence between one's experienced/expressed gender and assigned gender." Replaces *gender identity disorder* in the *Diagnostic and Statistical Manual of Mental Disorders*, fifth edition (*DSM-5*).

GENDERED When something is divided based on gender. Clothes, activities, and spaces are often gendered.

GENDER EXPRESSION Refers to an individual's physical characteristics, behaviors, and presentation. This can include one's appearance, dress, mannerisms, speech patterns, and social interactions that are linked, traditionally, to masculinity or femininity.

GENDER FLUID Someone who embodies characteristics of multiple genders, or shifts in gender identity. (*See* genderqueer).

GENDERF*CKING *See* genderbending.

GENDER IDENTITY Our way of understanding our inner sense of being male, female, both, or neither. Sometimes clashes with the way other people view us physically.

GENDER IDENTITY DISORDER (GID) A previously used controversial diagnosis for transgender and gender nonconforming people. Was defined as having a "strong and persistent cross-gender identification," with "persistent discomfort with his/her sex or sense of inappropriateness in the gender role of that sex." Has since been replaced by the diagnosis of *gender dysphoria.*

GENDERLESS Not identifying with a particular gender.

GENDER MARKER A legal indicator of one's gender. This can include one's gender on a passport, birth certificate, driver's license, or insurance card.

GENDER NEUTRAL Not gendered. Can refer to language (including pronouns), spaces (like bathrooms), or identities (being *genderqueer*).

GENDER NONCONFORMING An umbrella term that describes those who do not fit into traditional gender expectations.

GENDER NORM Societal expectation about how people of different designated genders are supposed to act, live, and look.

GENDER POLICING Enforcing gender norms and attempting to impose gender-based behaviors on another person. This sometimes plays out for trans and gender-variant people in the assumption that someone is only "truly" transgender if they have gone through some form of medical and/or surgical transition, which earns their status as trans.

GENDER PRESENTATION The way that someone presents their gender, including their appearance and behaviors.

GENDERQUEER A term that is sometimes used to describe someone who defines their gender outside the constructs of male and female. This can include having no gender, being androgynous, or having elements of multiple genders.

GENDER ROLES Positions we take in social relationships based on our genders, such as men being the income earners or women taking responsibilities for housekeeping. The masculinity or femininity of specific roles in our societies differs based on our cultures and/or geographic location.

GENDER SCHEMA A psychological framework that helps us learn and understand the concept of gender as children.

GENDER SPECIALIST A type of mental health professional who specializes in transgender and gender nonconforming issues.

GENDER SPECTRUM The wide range of gender identities and expressions.

GENDER STEREOTYPE Assumption, expectation, or belief that a person will act or appear a certain way because of that person's gender or perceived gender.

GENDER-VARIANT A term that describes those who dress, behave, or express themselves in a way that does not conform with dominant gender norms. Used frequently to describe children and youth. Some people do not use this term because it can suggest these identities are abnormal. (*See* gender nonconforming.)

GENETIC GIRL (GG) (g-girl) Used by some people to refer to non-transgender women. Some people prefer the term *cisgender* because it does not make any assumptions about genetics or biology.

GENITAL RECONSTRUCTION Surgery that is directed at altering the physical appearance of one's external genitalia. This includes surgeries used to confirm one's gender identity. (*See* gender-affirming surgery.)

HERMAPHRODITE A historical term for *intersex* people that is considered offensive today.

HETERO Short for heterosexual.

HETEROFLEXIBLE A term sometimes used by those who do not identify as bisexual or homosexual but express curiosity or interest in same-sex attraction.

HETERO-GENDER A term that refers to relationships in many Native American traditions that involve two people with different gender identities—even though outside observers may assume they are same-sex relationships. For example, a relationship between someone who identifies as male and a male-bodied person who identifies as *Two-Spirit* may be considered a "same-sex relationship" by outsiders, but it involves two people with different gender identities.

HETERONORMATIVITY The worldview or assumption that heterosexuality is the norm.

HETEROSEXISM Attitudes, bias, and discrimination in favor of heterosexuality.

HETEROSEXUAL Describes a man who is attracted to women or a woman who is attracted to men.

HIR/ZIR Gender neutral pronouns than can be used in place of "him" or "her."

HOMO Short for homosexual. Often used as a slur against gay men.

HOMOPHOBIA The fear or hatred of people who are not heterosexual or do not appear heterosexual, which can lead to discrimination, rejection, and/or violence.

HOMOSEXUAL Describes a man who is attracted to men or a woman who is attracted to women.

HORMONE Chemical messenger that sends instructions to various tissues and organs in the body.

HORMONE REPLACEMENT THERAPY (HRT) Hormonal medications taken for gender transition. May also refer to hormones taken during menopause.

HOUSE In ball culture, refers to a group to which individuals belong. (*See* ballroom culture.)

HYSTERECTOMY AND SALPINGO-OOPHERECTOMY (HSO) A form of bottom surgery that involves removing the uterus, ovaries, and fallopian tubes. It may or may not include removing the cervix. This procedure is often done for cancer prevention, but it may also be done as a form of gender-affirming surgery.

INFORMED CONSENT Broadly refers to obtaining permission from a participant before making an intervention. Often used to refer to participants in a study. When discussing transgender health care, refers to a model adopted by many health clinics in which providers discuss the risks and benefits of hormones and/or surgery with a client and then allow the client to make their own choices. This deviates from the controversial "gatekeeper" model, which often requires health professionals to assess transgender people and decide whether hormones or surgery are appropriate.

INTERSECTIONALITY A sociological concept that describes the ways in which different forms of oppression such as transphobia, racism, homophobia, sexism, classism, ageism, and ableism interact with each other and are inseparable from each other.

INTERSEX A general term used for a variety of conditions in which a person is born with a reproductive or sexual anatomy that does not fit the typical definitions of female or male. Not everyone who has one of these conditions identifies as intersex. (*See* disorder of sex development.)

KEYHOLE (PERIAREOLAR) MASTECTOMY Top surgery to create a male-contoured chest. This technique is used on smaller chests and incisions are made along the areola, minimizing scarring.

KINKY Sexual practices that are outside the norm. Can imply a playful sexuality or BDSM.

LABIAPLASTY Surgery performed to create or enhance the labia. Often done at the same time as a vaginoplasty but may be an additional procedure.

LASER HAIR REMOVAL (or reduction) A process of hair removal that involves using a laser to destroy hair follicles.

LESBIAN An identity term used by some people who identify as female and are attracted to women.

LGBT/GLBT LGBT stands for lesbian, gay, bisexual, and transgender. Less commonly, GLBT reverses the order of the words *lesbian* and *gay*. More recently, the acronym has expanded and is more variable. As an example, LGBTQQIA stands for lesbian, gay, bisexual, transgender, queer, questioning, intersex, and allies.

MALE-TO-FEMALE (MTF, M2F) A term that describes someone who was assigned a male sex and gender at birth and currently has a female gender identity. May or may not have had surgery or taken hormones to physically alter their appearance.

MASCULINE A term that describes behavior, dress, qualities, or attitudes that are associated with men. What is considered masculine differs based on one's culture, race, ethnicity, and environment.

MASCULINE OF CENTER An evolving definition that recognizes the cultural breadth and depth of identity for lesbian/queer womyn and gender nonconforming/trans people who tilt toward the masculine side of the gender spectrum. This term can include a wide range of identities such as butch, stud, aggressive/AG, boys like us, trans masculine, and boi.

MASCULINIZE The process of making someone or something more masculine. This may include, but is not limited to, wearing masculine clothing, having a masculine hair style, growing facial hair, or taking testosterone.

MASTECTOMY A term that refers to the removal of breasts. Often used when describing cis women with breast cancer but also used by some trans men who have chest surgery. (*See* reconstructive chest surgery).

MEDICAL TRANSITION The process of taking hormones or undergoing surgical procedures in order to change one's body in a way that affirms one's gender identity. Surgical procedures are sometimes discussed separately as surgical transition.

METOIDIOPLASTY A form of bottom surgery that involves lengthening the clitoris/phallus of someone assigned female at birth. The procedure may include a "urethral hookup," which involves using tissue to extend the urethra and allow for standing urination.

MINORITY STRESS THEORY A psychological theory that suggests that those who belong to oppressed, marginalized, or minority communities (including trans and gender nonconforming communities) are at greater risk of mental health issues because of chronic stress, stigma, discrimination, violence, and prejudice.

MISC., Mre., Mx. Gender neutral titles similar to Mr. and Ms.

MISGENDER To make an incorrect judgment about someone's gender identity, intentionally or unintentionally.

MISOGYNY The hatred, dislike, or distrust of women, girls, and femininity.

MISPRONOUN To make an incorrect judgment about someone's pronoun preference, intentionally or unintentionally.

MIXTER (Mx) A gender neutral version of using Mr. or Miss.

MONAMOROUS Preferring one romantic partner at a time. (*See* polyamorous.)

MSM Acronym for men who sleep with men. Used frequently by health care providers and researchers working on ways to improve the health of this population. Allows for inclusion of men who sleep with men but do not identify as gay or bisexual.

NATAL SEX Refers to the sex assigned at birth, which is typically based on the appearance of the external genitals. Many people prefer the phrase "birth-assigned sex."

NEUTROIS The concept of having a neutral gender identity. Some people who identify as neutrois also desire to have gender neutral bodies. (*See* agender and nongendered.)

NONBINARY GENDER A gender that is neither strictly male nor strictly female. (*See* gender binary.)

NONGENDERED An identity term that describes not having a gender.

NON-OPERATIVE (non-op) A term for a transgender person who has not had surgery. The person may not be able to undergo surgery (often for financial reasons) or not desire to have surgery. Many people do not like the terms *non-op* and *post-op* because they can be used to divide people and to imply that some people are more or less trans than others.

OF TRANS EXPERIENCE (man or woman) A way of describing one's experience of having transitioned without necessarily identifying as transgender currently. Commonly used in African American trans communities.

OMNISEXUAL Attracted to people of all sexes and genders. (*See* pansexual.)

OPPOSITE SEX A phrase commonly used to refer to men when talking about women and vice versa. Many people avoid this phrase because it implies that men and women are so different from each other that they are "opposite."

ORCHIECTOMY A form of bottom surgery that involves removing the testicles. This operation may eliminate the need for testosterone blockers.

OUT Derives from the phrase "come out of the closet." Can be used as an adjective to describe someone who is open about their sexuality or gender identity (e.g. "She is out") or as a verb to describe the process of becoming more open or being forced by someone else to be open (e.g., "She came out," or "He outed her.")

PACKER A commercially available device worn under clothing in order to create the appearance of a penis and testicles. Most packers are soft, but hard packers also exist, which simulate the look and feel of an erect penis.

PACKING Putting things in the crotch of the pants to create the outward appearance of a penis and testicles.

PANGENDER A self-descriptor used by some people who identify as having many different genders.

PANSEXUAL An identity term for those who are attracted to people of many different genders.

PASS(ING) When a person can appear in public as their affirmed gender and not be identified as transgender. Also known as being read correctly. The term *pass* can be problematic because it suggests a level of secrecy and implies that trans people are responsible for dressing or behaving in certain ways so that other people will gender them correctly. Many people desire to pass in order to be treated as the gender with which they identify or to avoid discrimination or violence. The ability to pass can sometimes be used within trans communities to create artificial divisions between people. (*See* clock/ed, read, and stealth.)

PATHOLOGIZATION Refers to assigning medical or mental health diagnoses. The *gender dysphoria* diagnosis pathologizes the transgender experience. There are movements of transgender people, as well as health and service providers, to depathologize, or take away the diagnoses associated with, trans identity.

PENECTOMY A form of bottom surgery in which the penis is removed without the construction of a vagina. Penectomies are rarely performed in the United States.

PEOPLE OF COLOR (POC) A term designed to be an umbrella or catchall term for those who are not white or are not predominately of European descent. Includes a diverse group of people from multiple ethnicities, races, and backgrounds.

PERFORMANCE/PERFORMATIVITY The concept, developed by philosopher Judith Butler, that our genders are created through our behaviors rather than existing somewhere inside of us. According to this theory, the repetition of gendered behaviors stabilizes the categories of "man" and "woman."

PHALLOPLASTY A form of bottom surgery that involves the creation of a penis.

PHYSICAL TRANSITION The process of making physical changes to the body such as taking hormones, having surgery, or undergoing other procedures, as part of a gender transition.

POLYAMOROUS A self-identity used by some people who engage in multiple relationships at once.

POST-OPERATIVE (post-op) A term that means "after surgery." Can be used to talk about someone who has undergone gender-affirming surgeries. Some people avoid this term because they feel it serves to divide transgender communities.

PREFERRED (GENDER) PRONOUNS (PGP) Refers to the set of pronouns that a person prefers (e.g., he, she, him, her, ze, hir, they). It is polite to ask for a person's preferred gender pronouns when meeting for the first time.

PRE-OPERATIVE (pre-op) A term that means "before surgery." Can be used to talk about someone who has not undergone gender-affirming surgeries. Some people avoid this term because they feel it serves to divide transgender communities.

PRIVILEGE Refers to advantages conferred by society to certain groups. It may be difficult to see one's own privilege because these advantages are conferred by society and not seized by individuals.

PROGESTERONE A hormone that is sometimes taken by those on the transfeminine spectrum.

PRONOUN A word that can be used in place of a noun or a person's name. In English, pronouns used to describe people are gendered (e.g., he, she). Gender neutral pronouns are becoming more commonly used.

PSYCHIATRIST A medical doctor (MD or DO) who specializes in mental health and can prescribe medication.

PSYCHOLOGIST A doctor with a degree in psychology (PhD or PsyD) who can provide therapy. Most states do not permit psychologists to prescribe medications.

PUBERTY BLOCKERS Medications that delay puberty by blocking the effect of hormones. Can, in some cases, be used to delay puberty in transgender teenagers.

PUMPING A slang term for silicone injection, which entails the injection of silicone into certain parts of the body for cosmetic enhancement (i.e., lips, buttocks, hips). This procedure can be dangerous, especially if performed outside of a medical facility, but it is often used by those who cannot afford surgeries that would produce similar results.

QUEER A term that was historically used as a slur against LGBTQ communities. Has more recently been reclaimed by some people, although others are uncomfortable with its use. Can imply a transgressive stance toward sexuality and the gender binary.

QUEER THEORY An academic field in which scholars theorize about gender and sexuality and also think about the ways in which LGBTQ communities and LGBTQ people exist in history, art, and literature.

READ Used as a verb in a few different ways. Can describe being seen in your affirmed gender (i.e., "Dave is read as male") or, alternatively, being recognized as trans (i.e., "Karen was trying to pass but got read"). (*See* clock/ed and pass(ing)). Also sometimes used as slang for a verbal attack or taunting (i.e., "Wow, she told her off—that was a read!")

REAL LIFE EXPERIENCE (RLE) A period of time during which transgender individuals live full-time in their desired gender before starting hormone therapy or having gender-related surgery. In the past, most health providers required a real life experience before they were willing to prescribe hormones, but this is no longer standard practice.

RECONSTRUCTIVE CHEST SURGERY A form of top surgery that involves removing breast tissue and creating a male-contoured chest. (*See* mastectomy.)

REPARATIVE THERAPY *See* conversion therapy.

SAME-GENDER LOVING (SGL) A self-identity used by some people attracted to those of the same gender. More frequently used in communities of color.

SCROTOPLASTY The surgical construction of a scrotal sac. May include testicular implants.

SECONDARY SEX CHARACTERISTIC A gendered part or characteristic of the body that develops during puberty. Can include breast and hip development, facial and body hair, and voice deepening.

SEX Refers to biological, genetic, or physical characteristics that define males and females. These can include genitalia, hormone levels, genes, or secondary sex characteristics. Typically compared to gender, which is thought of as more social and less biological, though there is considerable overlap.

SEX CHANGE An older term for gender-affirming surgery. Some people do not like this term because it implies that a person's sex is changing, while many trans people feel they have always been who they are.

SEX REASSIGNMENT SURGERY (SRS) A term that can be used to refer to many different kinds of gender-related surgeries, though it is most typically used when talking about vaginoplasties. Some people prefer the terms *gender-affirming surgery, gender-confirming surgery*, or *genital reconstruction surgery*.

SEXISM Discrimination based on a person's perceived sex. Usually predicated by the belief that women are inferior to men.

SEXUAL ORIENTATION Refers to the kinds of people to which we are attracted. Typically used to describe the sexes or genders of those people.

SIGNIFICANT OTHERS, FRIENDS, FAMILY, AND ALLIES (SOFFA) Acronym used to refer to those who are close with transgender people. Can be used to find support groups or to indicate that an activity is open to not only trans people but also those close to them in their lives.

SILICONE INJECTION A potentially dangerous procedure that involves injection of silicone into certain parts of the body for cosmetic enhancement (i.e., lips, buttocks, hips). (*See* pumping).

SOCIAL CONSTRUCTION The idea that society has created or constructed (often not purposefully) certain concepts that may later appear to be biological. For example, many people believe that gender is a social construct that developed over time so that women and men would interact in certain ways, preserving male power.

SOCIAL TRANSITION Transitioning in the context of everyday life and social spaces, without necessarily taking steps to medically transition.

SPIRONOLACTONE (SPIRO) A medication that is often used to block the effects of testosterone in transgender women.

STANDARDS OF CARE (SOC) Guidelines developed by the World Professional Association for Transgender Health (WPATH) to assist health providers in caring for transgender people.

STEALTH A term used to describe transgender individuals who do not disclose their trans status in their public lives.

STRAIGHT Another term for heterosexual.

SURGICAL TRANSITION The process of undergoing surgical procedures in order to change one's body in a way that affirms one's gender identity.

TESTOSTERONE A hormone produced in the bodies of all people, though typically associated with men. Taken by those on the transmasculine spectrum to develop more masculine characteristics, such as increased facial and body hair and increased muscle mass.

TESTOSTERONE BLOCKER Medication that is often used by trans women to block the effects of testosterone.

T-GIRL A term some people use to describe transgender women, especially when comparing them to cisgender women (otherwise known as *g-girls* or *genetic girls*). Some people prefer the terms *transgender* and *cisgender* because they do not make any assumptions about genetics or biology.

TGNC Acronym that stands for trans and gender nonconforming. Often used when talking about groups of people with diverse gender identities.

THIRD GENDER/THIRD SEX A term that incorporates genders other than male or female, such as the Fa'afafine in Samoa, Kathoey or Ladyboys in Thailand, and Hijras in India and Pakistan. Some people in the United States, especially in communities of color, use the term *third gender* to self-identify.

TOP SURGERY Surgeries performed on the chest.

TRACHEAL SHAVE A procedure that minimizes the thyroid cartilage that makes up the Adam's apple. Also known as an Adam's apple reduction, thyroid cartilage reduction (TCR), or chondrolaryngoplasty.

TRANNY A derogatory term for transgender people, commonly for transgender women. Some trans people have reclaimed the term to describe themselves.

TRANNY CHASER A derogatory term that describes those who actively seek out transgender people for sexual or romantic purposes. Often used to describe self-identified straight men who seek out transgender women and fetishize them. Implies a negative motive on the part of the pursuer, or that desiring trans people is a negative thing, which makes this term controversial in trans communities.

TRANS A shortened form of the word *transgender*.

TRANS BOYS/GIRLS/GUYS Terms used by younger trans people to describe themselves.

TRANS FAG/TRANS DYKE Terms used by some trans people who also identify as gay or lesbian.

TRANS FRIENDLY Describes a person or group that is either an ally to transgender communities or is tolerant or accepting of those who are transgender.

TRANS MAN Transgender person who identifies as a man.

TRANS WOMAN Transgender person who identifies as a woman.

TRANS* An asterisk is sometimes added to the word *trans* to signify that trans communities are diverse and include many different identities. Can be read as "trans star."

TRANSAMOROUS A term that describes those who are attracted to transgender people. Preferred to the term *tranny chaser*.

TRANSFEMININE An identity term used by some trans people who see gender as a spectrum and themselves as falling toward the feminine side of the spectrum. Originates from communities of color.

TRANSFEMINISM An approach to feminism that is informed by trans politics.

TRANSGENDER An umbrella term that may be used to describe people whose gender expression does not conform to cultural norms and/or whose gender identity is different from their sex assigned at birth. Transgender is a self-identity, and some gender nonconforming people do not identify with this term.

TRANSGENDERED A controversial form of the word *transgender*, which some people use because it is an adjective rather than a noun and can imply movement and fluidity. Others avoid the term and consider it incorrect or offensive.

TRANSITION The process one goes through to discover and/or affirm their gender identity. This can, but does not always, include taking hormones, having surgeries, or going through therapy.

TRANSLATINA/O/@ An identity that combines one's experience being trans and being latina/o/@. The @ symbol allows the term to be used in a gender neutral way.

TRANSMASCULINE An identity term used by some trans people who see gender as a spectrum and themselves as falling toward the masculine side of the spectrum. Comes out of communities of color.

TRANS-MISOGYNY A term coined by trans activist Julia Serano, which describes a form of misogyny (hatred of women) specifically directed at trans women.

TRANSPHOBIA Fear, hatred, or discrimination toward transgender and gender nonconforming people.

TRANSSEXUAL A term often used to describe those who have undergone some form of gender-related surgery. Some people who identify as transsexual do not identify as transgender and vice versa.

TRANSVESTITE An older term for a person who cross-dresses. Has fallen out of favor and been replaced by the term *cross-dresser*, though some people continue to use it as a derogatory term for transgender people. This term still appears in some places, including some legal documents in the United States (i.e., Americans with Disabilities Act).

TUCKING The process of rearranging the penis and testicles in a way that avoids the appearance of a bulge.

TWO-SPIRIT A self-identity adopted by some indigenous North Americans who take on a multitude of gender roles, identities, and expressions. Those who identify as Two-Spirit often see themselves as embodying both masculine and feminine spirits and characteristics.

INDEX

Barker, J. E., 561
Barlow, J., 69
Barrett, K. U., 60–61, 267, 565
Barriers (condoms), 233–34, 372–73, 372f
Baso, S., 14
Bassichis, M., 574
Bathrooms
  activism, 473, 576–77
  allies, 150–51
  best practices, 149–51
  cultural, structural issues, 149
  resources, 150, 151
  safety in, 149
  schools, 205, 437–39
  workplace, 151, 162–63
Bauer, G., 541
Baus, J., 580
BDSM, 171, 387, 611
Beam, C., 448
Beautiful Boxer, 544
Becoming: A Gender Flipbook, 553
Becoming Chaz, 541–43
Becoming Dragon, 562
Beemyn, G., 529
Before I Disappear, 555
Behavioral issues in children, 426
Benestad, E., 404
Benjamin, H., 507, 510
Bentley, G., 504
Benton, M. (Emotions The P.O.E.T.),
  36–38
Berdache, 611.*see also* Two-Spirit
Berenbaum, S., 95
Bergman, S. B., 13, 564
Berliner, A., 416, 544
Bernardi, S., 544
Beth Simchat Torah, 68
Bettcher, T., 519–20
Beyer, G., 169
Biased-interaction theory, 99
Big Brothers Used Binder Program, 133
Bigender, 611
Billings, A., 555
Binding, 133–34, 611
Bio girl, 6
Biological sex, 611–12
Bio man/woman/boy/guy, 611
Biopsy, 255
Bipolar disorder, 322
Birl, T., 59
Birth-assigned gender, 15
Birth certificates, 179
Birthing process, 397–98
Bisexual, 612
Bitter herbs, 69
BKLYN Boihood, 30, 31
Black, B., 559
The Blacklips Performance Cult, 548
Black Trans men, 30
Black Trans women, 30
Blakemore, J. O., 95

Blanchard, R., 85
Blazes, J., 558
Block, C., 128
Block, K. T, 551
Bodies, labeling, 84–85, 266, 355–56
Bodies Like Ours, 90
Body Alchemy, 538
Body checking, 321
Body image, 612
Body image disorders, 321–22
Boenke, M., 399
Boi, 612
Bond, J. V., 537, 559
Bono, C., 541–43
Borderline personality disorder, 324
Bornstein, K., 8, 13, 72, 448, 523, 529, 538,
  540, 554, 559, 561
Boswell, H., 523
Bottom surgery
  cliteroplasty, 612
  costs, 278
  defined, 7, 278, 612, 615
  hysterosalpingo-oopherectomy, 236, 255,
    282–83, 615
  labiaplasty, 616
  metoidioplasty, 274, 280–81, 616
  orchiectomy, 222, 237, 263, 279, 361, 617
  penectomy, 279, 617
  phalloplasty, 274, 281–82, 364, 617
  scrotoplasty, 282, 618
  urethral hookup, 281
  vaginoplasty, 230–31, 263, 274, 279–80,
    280f, 286, 361, 364, 385
Boundaries (relationships), 344–45, 369–71
Boundaries (sexual), 464–65
The Box ("Theater of Varieties"), 559
Boychild, 547, 562
Boyd, H., 350–51
Boy I Am, 541
Boylan, J. F., 119
Boys Don't Cry, 525, 538, 540, 544
Boys like us, 11
Brain organization theory, 89–90, 612
The Brandon Teena Story, 540
Breast augmentation (nonsurgical), 133
Breast augmentation (surgical), 277–78, 612
Breast cancer, 229, 255, 263, 481
Breastfeeding, 398–99
Brennan, Farmer v., 208
Brewster, L., 518
Broadnax, W. "Little Axe," 548
Broadus, K., 34, 541
Brouhard, B., 478
Brown, S., 248
Brown, T., 549
Brown Boi Project, 27f
Browning, F., 573
BSTc, 89
B4T, 555
Buck Angel, 366
Buddhism, 70, 78

University of Michigan Comprehensive Gender Services Program, 222

University of Minnesota Program in Human Sexuality, 217, 222

Untitled 2, 562

Urethral hookup, 281

US Citizenship and Immigration Services (USCIS), 46, 49

Us Helping Us, 301

Uterine (endometrial) cancer, 230, 255, 481

Uterine development, 87–88

V

Vaginoplasty, 230–31, 263, 274, 279–80, 280f, 286, 361, 364, 385

Vaid, U., 570

Van Ashley, A., 513

Varenicline (Chantix), 224

Veale, J., 81, 99

Venus Boyz, 15, 541, 560

Venus Flytrap, 551

Vermont, 181, 182, 188, 193–94, 195, 205, 218, 219

Veterans, 484, 485, 492

Veterans Health Administration (VHA), 192, 219, 485

Viagra (sildenafil), 261

Vibrators, 376–77

Video. *see* film and video

Village Voice, 524, 526

Violent systems, dismantling, 187–88

Virago, S., 549

Virginia, Loving v., 196

Visual, performance art, 559–63

Vocal tract, 127

Vogue Evolution, 557

Voice, 127–28

Voicets, 127

Volcano, D. L. G., 15, 538, 541, 551

W

Waafrika (Mwaluko), 555–56

Wachowski, L., 537, 545

Wall, S. S. M., 90–91

Walters, P. C., 308–9

Walthour, J., 75–76, 565

Walworth, J., 525

Want, 56

Washington, 181, 188, 193–94, 195, 205

Waxman, T., 560–61

Wayne, 417–18

WBT scene, 547

Website resources. *see also* resources

  bathrooms, 150

  children, 423

  clothing, 130

  dating, 339

  disability, Deaf culture, 60

  employment, 160

  fundraising, 275

  genderqueer, 14

  groups, organizations, 143–46

  health care, 243, 254

  housing, homelessness, 462

  immigration, 40

  international communities, 14

  intimate relationships, 352

  mental health, support, 295, 423

  packing, 132

  parenting, child custody, 402, 423

  people of color (POC), 30, 31, 34, 528

  pornography, 366

  pronouns, 125

  religion, spirituality, 63, 67–69, 76, 79

  sex and gender, 83

  substance abuse, 320

  suicide, 315

  surgery, 275

  transgender generally, 7

  trans men, 6

  veterans, 485

  youth, 446

  zines, 566

Wegener, E. (Elbe, L.), 216, 399, 506, 511

We Happy Trans, 14

Welch, J., 541

Welfare Warriors, 246

Wes, 27–28

Whitman-Walker, 301

Whittle, S., 84

Whore of Babylon: An Apocalyptic Pin Up Calendar (2013), 561

Who Wants to Work for Diddy?, 26

Wicca/paganism, 70–72. *see also* religion, spirituality

Wilchins, R., 83, 525–28

Wildness, 563

Wild Side, 544

Wilkins, T. D., 31–32

Wilkinson, W., 29–30

Williams, R., 580

Williams, T. M., 457–59

Willingness, acceptance, 420–21

Wills, advance directives, 206, 493, 494

Windina, W. (Peter Drouyn), 148

Windsor, United States v., 196

W Juliet, 563

Wolfson-Seeley, C., 395

Women's college, 470–71

Women's Tennis Association, 521

Women Who Become Men: Albanian Sworn Virgins (Young), 85

Wong, C., 471

Wood, R., 559

Woolf, V., 537

Wordz, 36

WOW Café Theater, 555, 561

World Professional Association for Transgender Health (WPATH) Standards of Care, 177, 186, 220, 244, 274, 522

Wright, D., 554

Writing/publishing, 552–53, 560, 564–66

Wyeth, G., 549

SUGGESTIONS

Trans Bodies, Trans Selves would love to hear from you about your experience with this book so that we can make each edition better. Please send comments and suggestions to info@transbodies.com.